GREAT WAGNER CONDUCTORS

Also by Jonathan Brown

Parsifal on Record
Tristan und Isolde on Record

Great Wagner Conductors

A listener's companion

Jonathan Brown

Parrot Press
Canberra

First Published in 2012 by Parrot Press
P.O. Box 6077
O'Connor A.C.T. 2602
Australia
www.parrotpress.com.au

National Library of Australia Cataloguing-in-Publication entry

Author:	Brown, Jonathan, 1949-
Title:	Great Wagner conductors : a listener's companion / Jonathan Brown.
ISBN:	9780987155603 (hbk.)
Notes:	Includes bibliographical references and index.
Subjects:	Wagner, Richard, 1813-1883--Discography.
	Sound recordings--Catalogs.
	Conductors (Music)--Biography.

Dewey Number: 016.780266

Set in 10/12 pt Monotype Bembo
Printed in Singapore by Imago

To Camilla Webster
Zu ihr! Zu ihr!

The highest function of criticism is not mere judicial balancing of faults and merits, but consists in estimating whether a work of art and its interpretation are essentially good or essentially bad. If good, the critic's attitude towards it should be that of an advocate rather than a judge. Vulgar amusements take care of themselves, and are only too popular; but the highest art requires the most enthusiastic support it can get from those who are able to appreciate it, because enthusiasm is contagious, and only in this way can the indifferent and the unbelievers be induced to go to hear a great work of art repeatedly, and thus become converted and enthusiastic in turn.

– Henry Finck after hearing Anton Seidl's *Tristan und Isolde*, 1890

Contents

Part VI: America *felix*

Part VII: The German Heartland

Part VIII: Late Pickings

Part IX: Outsiders

Part X: Discographies

Acknowledgments

Many libraries and archives helped in the preparation of this book. The Library of Congress in Washington was especially helpful. The pride in, and care, the staff took of the materials I requested, and their willingness to share their knowledge of them, was remarkable. It set the standard for the other great public libraries I visited in the United States, in Chicago, New York, Boston, Philadelphia, Pittsburgh, San Francisco, and Los Angeles. Of American university libraries, those at Yale and Harvard were treasure troves, and their openness to an independent scholar from abroad was greatly appreciated. Visits to Columbia University, which holds archival material on Anton Seidl, and Northwestern University which holds Fritz Reiner's archives, were both rewarding. The Brooklyn Historical Society also held valuable archival material on Seidl. The microfilmed scrapbooks and photographic collections of the Metropolitan Opera and the Boston Symphony revealed many secrets. To all the taxpayers and benefactors that support these institutions, and to the staff who assisted me, I express my thanks.

In England, the British Library at St Pancras was the most comfortable port of call, though the primary sources on conductors were to be found in the grim Newspaper Reading Room in distant Colindale. There I was made to feel grateful, and I was grateful, for every ration of microfilm that was dispensed. The Westminster Music Library of the Victoria Library was much more accommodating, and had a vast collection of journals and secondary materials at the disposal of the public.

On the Continent, the newspaper collections at the Zentral- und Landesbibliothek Berlin and the Institut für Zeitungsforschung in Dortmund were the most accessible and comprehensive, though not complete. In Dortmund, when I asked for a Communist newspaper from the 1930s, the librarian declared after a brief search of the database, with studied neutrality, as if to gauge whether I understood her response, that no library in Germany any longer held a copy of the newspaper. In Milan, in a light-filled microfilm reading-room at the top of a spiral staircase rising from the dark and battered cloisters of the Biblioteca Nazionale Braidense, the staff went out of their way to produce every newspaper they could – Socialist, Fascist, Communist, even Catholic – that might have carried reviews of La Scala. At the Österreichische Nationalbibliothek in Vienna, the spiral staircase led downwards to the most subtly illuminated microfilm reading room of any library, yet it was largely deserted (most of Austria's historical newspapers are online). There the staff were very helpful: they dispensed with call slips and generously plied me with boxes of microfilm of newspapers I had not dreamed of requesting. In Munich, at the Bayerische Staatsbibliothek one had to read microfilm under the stairs where electricity had only been partially connected. Many a city archive revealed unexpected information – in Amsterdam, Bayreuth, Kassel, Leipzig, Munich, and Wuppertal – as well as the Generallandesarchiv Karlsruhe. The Richard Wagner Museum at Bayreuth was of course an essential call and its staff were very helpful. The theatre collections of the universities at Darmstadt, Hamburg and Cologne were extraordinarily rich and well-housed: Darmstadt in the re-built ruins of the old opera house, Cologne in an idyllic Schloss on the rural outskirts of the city. In Dresden the staff of both the Sächsische Staatsoper and the Sächsische Landesbibliothek - Staats- und Universitätsbibliothek (SLUB) were helpful in providing information. The nadir was reached at the Bibliothèque nationale de France in Paris. That scattered and grandiose institution, when not closed altogether, guarded its treasures like Fafner, and seemed bothered that a foreign visitor wanted to look at them.

I received help from the Hungarian National Library and the Hungarian Theatre Museum and Institute in Budapest, and the Music Library of Stellenbosch University in South Africa which opened up its Albert Coates Archive. In Argentina, the Biblioteca Nacional brought up many volumes of fragile newspapers for examination (there was no microfilm alternative); some were too frail to be produced at all.

In the case of individuals, I am indebted for answers to particular inquires to Therese Gassner, Staatsopernmuseum, Vienna; Brigitte Klein and Bernhard Wirth, Universitätsbibliothek Johann Christian Senckenberg, Frankfurt am Main; David W. Luz, Schwenkfelder Library & Heritage Center, Pennsburg, Pennsylvania; Jeffrey R. McGranahan, Historical Society of Montgomery County, Norristown, Pennsylvania; David Pilling, Royal Opera House Collections; Annett Rosendahl, Leipzig Opera; and Dr. Jürgen Schaarwächter and Stefan König, Max-Reger-Institut/Elsa Reger-Stifung, Karlsruhe. Tea Dietterich provided assistance with translations from the German, Spanish, and Italian, and Agnes Szabo from the Hungarian. Emma Jacobs, Annabel Grice, and Amy Webster provided invaluable gateways to information. Camilla Webster read the whole manuscript and made many valuable suggestions and corrections. Further acknowledgments are recorded in the introduction to the discographies.

The book was written well away from the action, in the libraries of the Australian National University and the Australian National Library in Canberra, and in a riverside cabin in the Snowy Mountains.

Preface

When the young Felix Weingartner heard *Tristan und Isolde* at the Royal Opera House in Berlin in 1882, he was horrified. He had just been to a glorious performance in Leipzig under Anton Seidl. This was quite a different affair. From the moment the overture began it was "an expressionless race through the music.... Disappointment followed disappointment." The orchestra was "much too loud, the *tempi* impossible!" He left early. When the young Wilhelm Furtwängler attended his first *Ring* cycle in Munich in 1912, under the famous Wagner conductor Franz Fischer, he had a similar experience. He had studied the piano-score enthusiastically beforehand, and was elated and aglow with love for Wagner's music. Yet the performances were profoundly disappointing. What he heard were "the most wonderful melodic curves trivialized." What he saw were "bland, overdone, empty theatrics." His love for Wagner seemed an illusion. It was shattered for years to come. In more modern times, Virgil Thomson went to a performance of the *Meistersinger* at the Metropolitan Opera in 1950. It was not one of his favourite operas, and he thought he should have stayed at home. But he wanted to hear Fritz Reiner conduct the piece, to hear it "done right." Yet afterwards he had little to say about it. Reiner had made everything sound harmonious. Still "no magic casement opened" for him. The beauties of Wagner's work had not been revealed.

Wagner's music is not the reason for these experiences. It is the performance that is to blame. A bad performance turns people off. It leaves them cold. A performance that is merely mediocre can leave people not knowing *what* to think. A great performance, on the other hand, comes like a bolt of lightning, like Donner with his hammer. And it is the conductor who is pre-eminently responsible for the standard of a Wagner performance. "If an audience is bored with Wagner," declared Richard Strauss, "it is the conductors who are to blame." There may be stars on the stage, but unless there is a great conductor in the pit, the full potential of Wagner's music will not be realized. The listener will not cross the rainbow bridge.

The conductors in this book all gave Wagner's music its due, and transported their audiences. They were great Wagner conductors essentially because of their personalities. And they all knew his music. They knew what he should sound like, and could impose their will on their orchestras to achieve it. This is not to suggest there was any uniformity in their approach. The great conductors differed markedly man from man. Who should be included in a pantheon like this, and who not, is of course a central question and people will have differing views. In this book it was less a personal choice than a naturally occurring result: when I weighed up the evidence of the accounts of those who heard the conductors in performance, and of recordings, the majors sorted themselves out from the minors. A glance at the table of contents may hold some surprises.

The way the greats emerged was threefold. Firstly, and this may surprise, I listened to recordings. I did not read about them or about historic performances not on record. Recorded music is afterall not only the primary source but also, with the passing of the conductors themselves, the most important remaining testament to their abilities. I sought out and listened to every fragment of Wagner's music on record that I could find (and many *are* mere fragments). The results are reflected in the discographies, so far as the conductors discussed in this book are concerned. Some historical recordings, which at first I listened to almost by accident, struck me as extraordinarily good in a way quite absent from many modern recordings. Some great performances struck like lightning. I had no doubt about this even though I am no performing musician. Weingartner once wrote that "performances of genius can only receive recognition either by another genius… or by that naïve instinct, often found among non-artists and the people." I must fall into the latter class, for I certainly do not belong to the former. In some cases I have commented upon recordings, especially "non-commercial" ones that have eluded or been ignored by industry reviews. In other cases I have given excerpts from contemporaneous reviews. Not all the recordings listed in the discographies have been commented upon. That may have been tedious and would have given disproportionate weight to the importance of recordings in the overall assessment of each conductor.

Secondly, I read many biographies and books about conductors. Curiously, the reading and the listening did not seem always to match up. On the one hand, some conductors seemed overlooked when on the evidence of their recordings they should not have been. On the other hand the contribution or status of some conductors seemed greatly exaggerated. Biographies are surprisingly thin and selective about their subject's performances. If a reader wants to know *how* a particular conductor conducted *Tristan*, often a biography will have little to say. The singular (and spectacular) exception is the fourth volume of Henry de La Grange's biography of Mahler, covering his final years in America. Not all biographers have such subjects, however, nor do they have such publishers. Often the mass of detail in biographies is on the non-musical aspects of a conductor's life. This is of course fascinating because many great conductors were also important cultural figures, and some were embroiled in political or personal controversy that makes for interesting reading. Too often the quality of their music-making is taken for granted or generalised. While biographers are bound to be selective in referring to performances, they are not bound to choose reviews which generally praise the feats of their subject, or ignore those which give a diametrically different view. There is, however, a tendency to do this. Apart from biographies, much general writing on conducting can be quite eloquent, even persuasive, but it is often unclear what music is being talked about. Whose music, what performance, what recording is lurking behind the generalisation? It has not been my object to reproduce well-worn biographical detail. Generally I have sought to confine detail to the Wagnerian highlights: to early experiences, to works conductors performed, and to what they wrote or said about Wagner as background to their performances. The biographical sources relied upon are given in the notes to each chapter.

Thirdly, I looked at reviews of performances. What I looked for were descriptions or opinions on what a performance was like: what did the conductors *sound* like? It is impossible to be absolutely sure, of course, but there is no better way than tapping someone on the shoulder who has just emerged from the opera house and asking them. Many published critics were eloquent about what they had seen and heard. The end of the nineteenth century and the first half of the twentieth century comprised a golden age in music criticism. In America there were James Huneker, W. J. Henderson, Henry Finck, Henry Krehbiel, and Richard Aldrich. These outstanding writers reported on the performances of Seidl, Mahler, Toscanini, Felix Mottl, and the young Artur Bodanzky. In England there were George Bernard Shaw, Alfred Kalisch, Herman Klein, Neville Cardus, and Ernest Newman. They covered the visits to London of Seidl, Hans Richter, Mahler, Strauss, Hermann Levi, Nikisch, Karl Muck and many others. Often these reviewers were not named in their newspapers. While it is possible in some cases to conjecture who the author was, I have not done this. Instead I have attributed a review simply to the newspaper in which it appeared, adding in parentheses in notes the name or initials of the author or *non de plume* if one appears in the original.

Most light is shed on a particular performance if, of course, several reviews are quoted. This way, by means of different perspectives, one gets a good idea of what the performance was like. Moreover, one can sometimes pick up a detail that other reviewers overlooked. For example, only one reviewer reported that a cat wandered about the stage during act three of Mahler's *Tristan* in London in 1892. And only one reported that an *organ* was added to the orchestration of Reiner's *Walküre* in San Francisco in 1936. Yet many reviewers attended these performances.

Of course not *every* performance of *every* Wagner work can be mentioned. I narrowed the field, firstly, by concentrating on Wagner's later masterworks where the skills of the conductor are most on show: *Tristan und Isolde*, *Die Meistersinger*, the *Ring*, and *Parsifal*. I made exceptions, where there was otherwise a dearth of material on the conductor. Secondly, I favoured performances by the conductors on their visits abroad: to England, France, Italy, Argentina, and the United States, as well as to Bayreuth festivals. Visits to foreign lands seemed to stimulate particularly fresh and illuminating comment from critics. Some German criticism has been included, of course, but music criticism in Germany and Austria between 1933 and 1945, when many great conductors were active, has been included sparingly, tainted as it was by extraneous matters of cultural correctness or nationalism. It was alarming to read, for example, this excerpt from the Vienna press of 1938: "we spit, if we may respectfully say so, on Toscanini and on his Jewish boosters and express our preference for Hans Knappertsbusch. Joyously do we renounce Toscanini's baton prima donna business and delight in the performance of a real German conductor." Not much objective music criticism can be expected from sources such as this.

There was another limitation I imposed on the book: conductors included here were all born in the nineteenth century. For them, Wagner's music was in their very blood. In the case of conductors born later, it is another story. There have certainly been some great performances from more modern conductors. Perhaps they deserve their own book *Great Wagner Performances*. But public taste has been clouded by the inordinate promotion of some over others by record companies and publicity machines. This will take time to wash out. Among the early conductors were some, it must be said, who are not included here, yet who conducted the occasional mesmerizing performance. Victor de Sabata's devastating *Tristan* and Wilhelm Mengelberg's gripping overtures and preludes are examples. Superb as these conductors were, Wagner did not make up enough of their repertoire for them to be in this company. They were simply great conductors who turned their attention to Wagner occasionally.

The picture that emerged was surprising. Not all "great" conductors appeared to be great *Wagner* conductors at all. Others, whose acquaintance I had initially made through the hiss of a historical record, had indeed been greatly admired for many extraordinary performances. Looking back at the biographies and finding many contemporaneous reviews absent, I thought there would be value in setting down the evidence to show how Wagner used to be conducted. The reports of early reviewers have languished too long in obscure newspapers. They deserve more than the dim light of a microfilm reader. The conductors they wrote about too deserve more than nebulous repute. They need to be brought a little more into the light of day, to be brought to life again.

The book had to start with Wagner. He was a revolutionary conductor. It was essential to know first of all what the composer-conductor did with his own music, and what he had to say about how it should be conducted. As with most things Wagnerian, his chapter occupies a larger space than any of those that follow him. He is of fathomless interest. The sections which follow are loosely arranged, more or less in chronological order. Some individuals might as easily have been included in one section as in another. Any idea of schools or common traditions of Wagnerian conducting is chimerical. Most of the conductors here claimed they were born conductors, not made. This was not hubris. They may have been impressed with one or other of their colleagues, and have spoken highly of them, but they were hardly influenced by them except in minor matters of technique. They may have drawn courage from them, but they certainly did not copy them. Their strong personalities were a guarantee of that. Only the weaker performers sought strength by association by claiming to have inherited secrets from on high. The last section deals with three conductors who do not, when the reports are in, really belong among those who have preceded them. This may disappoint and provoke some readers, but I can only point to the evidence. The book would have been incomplete if these erratic performers had been left out. Their inclusion, in any case, throws yet more glowing light on those who precede them.

This book has been written by someone who is neither a conductor, a musician, a musicologist, or a critic. However, it is not necessary for us to be musicians or to "know" about music to appreciate it, to read about it, or to write occasional responses to it. Nor is it necessary in the case of Wagner to "know" much about him or his ideas. What Wagner ultimately wanted was for his music to be played and listened to. "Altogether too much is talked and written about me," he once exclaimed privately. "A single stroke of the bow is of more significance than all this useless gabble. I need an audience of people who know nothing at all about my art-ideals, not those who make propaganda. The types of people that suit me best are the ones who do not even know that notes are written on a five-line staff."

Part I

Setting the Stage

1

The Case of Richard Wagner

Wagner was "not only the mightiest of all geniuses, but also the greatest conductor that ever lived." So wrote Wagner's arch-disciple Anton Seidl in 1895.[1] This is a view that has, more or less, prevailed in the hundred years since it was made.[2] Wagner had also written a seminal essay *On Conducting*, and had been intimately involved in the production of his own works. The task of an introductory chapter would seem, therefore, straight-forward: a brief account of Wagner's greatness as a conductor, a summary of *On Conducting*, and a few words on the composer's intentions. This would be a sensible backdrop to a consideration of the greatness of his conductors. In fact, it has turned out very differently. Wagner's conducting activities and his views have seemed to me ever more engrossing and enigmatic. The sources are scattered and the evidence is sometimes contradictory. The picture that has emerged throws less light on the subject than I ever imagined. And if the first chapter on Wagner takes up twice as much space as any on his conductors, such is the nature of Wagner.

In putting the picture together I have drawn on a wide range of sources, but have relied only sparingly on Wagner's own account in *My Life*.[3] His full-time conducting activities related there took place in his early years (1833-1849) and are often uncorroborated. His accounts are nevertheless charming and he rarely seems to inflate his achievements. Sometimes he is disarmingly honest about his failures. His story emerges, in modified form and with varying degrees of scrutiny, in many biographical

[1] Anton Seidl, "On Conducting," in *The Music of the Modern World*, vol. 1, (ed.) Seidl (New York: Appleton, 1895), p. 214; reprinted in Henry T. Finck, (ed.) *Anton Seidl: A Memorial By His Friends* (New York: Scribner's, 1899; Da Capo Press,1983)

[2] e.g., "a far better conductor than any of his conductors": Ernest Newman, *The life of Richard Wagner*, 4 vols (London: Cassell, 1933-1947), vol. 4, p. 471; "the greatest conductor of his day": Harold Schonberg, "Wagner, the Toscanini of His Day," *New York Times*, 22 January 1967, p. 93; "a great conductor, possibly the greatest ever": Michael Tanner, "All in the Timing," *Opera News*, vol. 68 no. 10 (April 2004), p. 36

[3] Richard Wagner, *My life*, (trans.) Andrew Gray, (ed.) Mary Whittall (Cambridge University Press, 1983). Ernest Newman wrote before embarking on his magisterial biography of Wagner: "One of these days, perhaps, an enterprising publisher will bring out an annotated edition of *My Life*, containing corrections of all Wagner's misstatements.... I say misstatements advisedly, not errors. Wagner practically never makes a mistake; what he does, I am sorry to say, is to tell fibs. He had too many documents in his hands to make many mistakes. ... In face of all this, the candid critic of him can put down the plentiful departures from the truth in the autobiography to nothing else but a deliberate intention to mislead." *New York Evening Post*, 18 October 1924, p. 7.

and other accounts.[4] One of his recurring themes on conducting, including his own conducting, is disgust – disgust at the standards prevailing in the theatres, at the repertoire, at the expectations of the public, at what could be achieved, and so on. One might take a particular view of this were it not for the fact that he *wholly* conceived of himself as a composer. Though he learned a lot from his youthful conducting, it was a tedious duty, a distraction from his main preoccupation. He threw himself into his theatre duties, and invariably emerged frustrated, disgusted and exhausted. It was not until he threw off the shackles of a conductor that he was able to devote himself to writing his great mature works.[5] When he finally did this, after the period in which he had composed the *Holländer*, *Tannhäuser*, and *Lohengrin*, we find ourselves, in view of what he went on to write, grateful that he did. We indulge his disgust.

What I am chiefly interested in here is, first, Wagner as conductor of *his own works*,[6] and second, Wagner the composer on *how his works should be performed*. Many biographical aspects of consuming interest are therefore not traversed. This may be frustrating for readers interested in Wagner's achievements as a conductor generally, as well as his proposals for the reform of orchestras and theatres. But these can be read about elsewhere.[7] In the volumes I did read, I found there is little coherent about Wagner. I was not surprised: he was after all a creative musician, and an especially mercurial one, not a philosopher or a teacher. Because my account draws on many sources, it is bound at times to seem a patchwork. But a true picture is more likely to emerge from many brush strokes than from a mere summary or from general statements. So first, let us see what happened when Wagner lifted the baton.

Wagner's early years as a conductor 1833-1842

The most important thing about this early period was, perhaps, that he learned how bad conditions were. His first engagement as a conductor was to rehearse a chorus in Würzburg for three months in 1833. His contract was not renewed. After a trial period of summer conducting at Bad Lauchstädt, he was appointed theatre director at Magdeburg. During the two years he held this post he acquired a thorough grounding in the opera repertoire of the day, most of which he did not like. He learned of the formidable difficulties of giving adequate performances with the

[4] For example Newman, *Life of Wagner*, and to a lesser extent William Ashton Ellis, *Life of Richard Wagner*, 6 vols (London: Paul, Trench, Trubner, 1900-1908) and Henry T. Finck, *Wagner and his Works*, 2 vols (New York: Scribner's, 1893, reprinted Greenwood Press, 1968).

[5] Ernest Newman wrote: "Wagner, as usual, did the artistically sensible if the morally shabby thing: he knew he would never become his full self if he went on living the life of a conductor, and he very wisely insisted on his friends keeping him in idleness": *New York Evening Post*, 10 November 1924, p. 12.

[6] Wagner conducted only five of his operas in complete form: *Das Liebesverbot* (Magdeburg, 1836), *Rienzi* (Dresden, 1842; Hamburg, 1844; Berlin, 1847), *Der fliegende Holländer* (Dresden, 1843; Berlin, 1844; Zurich, 1852; Munich, 1864), *Tannhäuser* (Dresden, 1845 and 1847; Zurich, 1855), and *Lohengrin* (Frankfurt, 1862; Vienna, 1876).

[7] For example, Norbert Heinel, *Richard Wagner als Dirigent* (Vienna: Praesens, 2006); William Braun, "Wagner's Development, Work, and Influence as a Conductor in the 19th Century," *The Opera Journal*, vol. 25 no. 3 (September 1992), 3-39; and Warren A. Bebbington, *The Orchestral Conducting Practice of Richard Wagner*, unpublished PhD thesis, City University of New York, 1984.

resources at his disposal. These he sought to improve. He also sought to perform his own works. *Die Feen* (1833-34) he never managed to get performed in his lifetime. He conducted his *Rule Britannia Overture* (1837) during a concert in the Magdeburg theatre. In one of the earliest reports of his conducting, and one that differs from his own description of himself as "a conductor full of fire and nuptial bliss,"[8] the *Neue Zeitschrift für Musik* wrote that he conducted "with imposing dignity, guarding against the fault... of conducting with both arms, *by keeping one perpetually a-kimbo*."[9] His *Liebesverbot* (1835-36) received but one performance, in Magdeburg on 29 March 1836. It was a disaster. At rehearsal Wagner only managed, by his own account, to keep everything together "by dint of continual prompting, loud singing along, and shouting drastic directions." On the night neither the orchestra nor singers knew their work properly. As the curtain was about to go up for the second performance, the singers broke out fighting, and the performance had to be cancelled. Wagner wrote: "That was the end of my career as conductor and composer of operas in Magdeburg."[10]

He went to Königsberg for a very short period in 1837 before being appointed music director at the German theatre in Riga. It had a small orchestra of 24 players. He did not like the repertory. He drove his singers hard, eventually alienating everyone, including the theatre director, Karl von Holtei, who dismissed him. In later life Holtei recalled that Wagner had "harassed the company with endless rehearsals, lasting for hours; nothing was right in his eyes, nothing was good enough for him, nothing shaded finely enough. This led to complaint after complaint; singers and orchestral players came to me with grievances against him. I had to admit to myself that Wagner was right; but I was not in a position to let him do as he pleased, for he would have killed my singers."[11] There was no love lost. He too was critical of himself, but for different reasons. He characterized this period in provincial theatres as an "abuse of my musical talent," a "thoughtless submission to frivolous theatrical tastes," and "an unthinking indulgence in a taste for trivial opera."[12] He fled to Paris.

For three years he did no conducting. But he did hear what a good conductor could do. François Habeneck rehearsed and conducted the Paris Conservatoire Orchestra in a revelatory performance of Beethoven's *Ninth Symphony*.[13] Wagner failed to get his *Rienzi* produced as he had wished. A performance of his *Columbus Overture* (1834-35) on 4 February 1841 was a "complete failure" as he himself admitted.[14] But his years of disappointment and suffering in Paris were not wasted. The first serious signs of his flare for music drama erupted in *A Faust Overture* (1839-40) and *Der fliegende Holländer* (1841).

8 an unsigned article by Wagner about musical life in Magdeburg in *Neue Zeitschrift für Musik*, 3 May 1836, quoted in Newman, *Life of Wagner*, vol. 1, p. 205

9 emphasis in the original (May 1837) quoted by Ellis, *Life of Wagner*, vol. 1, p. 22

10 Wagner, *My Life*, p. 119

11 quoted in Newman, *Life of Wagner*, vol. 1, p. 222

12 Wagner, *My Life*, pp. 89, 101, and 150

13 "Nowhere can you hear Beethoven's last and most difficult quartets treated more sympathetically, his *Ninth Symphony* played more perfectly, than in just that place. It was the sheerest artistic pleasure." Wagner's comment in Bayreuth, 29 August 1875, as recorded by Wagner's singing coach for the *Ring*, Julius Hey, in *Richard Wagner als Vortragsmeister, 1864-1876*, (ed.) Hans Hey, (Leipzig: Breitkopf und Härtel, 1911), p. 200

14 Newman, *Life of Wagner*, vol. 1, p. 274. Wagner was not the conductor.

Royal Kapellmeister in Dresden 1842-1849

He was drawn back to Germany for a number of reasons. Significantly it was to secure a performance in Dresden of *Rienzi* (1838-40). Its first performance was given on 20 October 1842. Wagner had been involved in rehearsals, and during the performance became increasingly alarmed at how long the opera was. He need not have feared. It was a "stupendous success."[15] He was surprised if not stunned at its reception. The conductor was Karl Gottlieb Reissiger (Wagner does not say so in *My Life*). Wagner took over from the sixth performance (on 20 November). Shortly after the first performance, two of the Dresden conductors died (not Reissiger). Propelled by *Rienzi's* success, Wagner was appointed Royal Kapellmeister for life. It was an appointment he said later he was very reluctant to take: "my contempt for the theatre was already total," and closer acquaintance with its management did nothing to change his views.[16] His efforts to improve and reform it over the years came to nought, though his ideas gained wide acceptance much later. He conducted the premiere of the *Holländer* on 2 January 1843. On his own admission, it was not a success.[17] It was given only four performances. In January 1844 he went to Berlin to conduct the last rehearsals and the first two performances (on 7 and 9 January) of the same work. He wrote that the audiences warmed to it after appearing at first to think "that I belonged in the category of bores," but by the end he was in no doubt that he had "scored a triumph."[18] The critics were almost all against the work, however, and after two more performances it was shelved for a quarter of a century. He was invited to Hamburg to conduct two performances of *Rienzi* on 21 and 24 March 1844. The first was a "spiritless performance"; the second more of a success. One critic noted that Wagner "was each time greeted with numerous salvos of applause."[19] Another wrote that the work "had never been performed [in Hamburg] in such a perfect manner and with such beautiful means."[20] Back in Dresden he conducted two performances of his *Faust Overture* on 22 July and 19 August 1844. It made little impression on the public, and Wagner seems to have lost interest in it for many years.[21]

He conducted the first performance of *Tannhäuser* on 19 October 1845. Perhaps because of the singing, it was a failure. The pianist Julius Dietz was present and later told Adolph Kohut[22] that he could see people asleep all round him. "Wagner himself was so depressed over this lukewarm reception of the work that at the conclusion of the performance he flung away his baton and hurried out of the orchestra."[23] At the second performance the house was "barely half-filled," but a spark caught in the third act so that by the fourth performance on 2 November, the theatre was "packed full."[24] Wagner admitted that the first performance had been "acknowledged generally to have been a failure," even by his friends, who thought it "poorly conceived and badly performed."[25] He did not record that he had conducted it. He gave *Tannhäuser* again

[15] *ibid*, vol. 1, p. 324
[16] Wagner, *My Life*, pp. 244-245
[17] *ibid*, p. 242
[18] *ibid*, pp. 263-264
[19] Ellis, *Life of Wagner*, vol. 2, pp. 60-61
[20] *Staats und Gelehrte Zeitung des Hamburgischen unpartheiischen Correspondendenten*, 23 March 1844, p. [6]
[21] *ibid*, vol. 2, pp. 72-73 and vol. 5, p. 20
[22] author of *Richard Wagner* (Berlin, 1905)
[23] quoted in Newman, *Life of Wagner*, vol. 1, p. 376n
[24] Ellis, *Life of Wagner*, vol. 2, p. 104
[25] Wagner, *My Life*, p. 312

in Dresden with a revised ending on 1 August 1847. There was a full house, but opinions were divided. He was invited to Berlin for a *Rienzi* which he conducted on 26 October 1847, as well as two further performances, but the press was against the music, although the musicians and the conductor were "handed the martyr's crown for their exhausting labours."[26] He returned to Dresden to newspaper reports of the failure in Berlin, but to the consoling news that two further performances had been given. He records that the conductor, Wilhelm Taubert, told him that these later performances were a success and that this "was attributable to himself [Taubert] and the extraordinarily judicious cuts he had made."[27] On 22 September 1848 Wagner conducted the finale to the first act of *Lohengrin*. It got, he said, "a rather lukewarm reception" from the Dresden public.[28] The Dresden theatre refused to stage the whole work.

Wagner looked back on his seven years as theatre conductor in Dresden with a mixture of regret and disgust: regret that he was so distracted from his artistic aims as a composer, and disgust with the routine and hopeless standards of the theatre, and the response he got to his proposals to improve them. When he tried radical ideas like appointing members to the orchestra on merit and was rebuffed, by both the orchestra and management, his interest in his daily duties understandably diminished. Newman concluded: "no man was ever less fitted by nature than Wagner to earn his living as a theatre conductor, for the simple reason that it was impossible to reconcile himself to the shifts, the compromises, the surrenders to which the most conscientious practising artist has to agree if he is to realise even half of his ideal. With Wagner it was all or nothing...."[29] During a visit to Dresden early in Wagner's tenure Berlioz had praised the "energy and precision" of Wagner's conducting in a letter to the *Journal des Débats*, a passage that Newman points out was deleted in his *Mémoires*.[30] But now, dejected and with his mind on bigger things, his work as a conductor became less important to him.

The most important conducting Wagner did in Dresden was probably outside the theatre, in his concert activities, notably Beethoven's *Ninth Symphony* on Palm Sunday 1846. The *Ninth* was also given in the opera house on 1 April 1849. Significantly for the history of orchestral conducting, the young Hans von Bülow was present. Within days the May revolution was in full swing. The opera house went up in flames on 6 May, and two days later Wagner, who had thrown his lot in with the revolutionaries, fled. This was the end of his full-time conducting career.

The Zurich years 1850-1858

After a short time in Paris, he went to Zurich. Although he had declined an offer of a position as opera conductor, he recommended another, Karl Ritter, who turned out to be so incompetent that Wagner felt obliged to step in to conduct the first opera of the 1850/51 season and several others thereafter. He had not conducted a work

26 *Königlich privilegirte Berlinische Zeitung*, 28 October 1847, p. [8]

27 Wagner, *My Life*, p. 356

28 *ibid*, p. 378

29 Newman, *Life of Wagner*, vol. 1, p. 351

30 *ibid*, vol. 1, p. 337; Ellis also records Berlioz's comment on the "unusual power and precision" of Wagner's conducting: *ibid*, vol. 2, p. 15

of his own for more than three years when he was dragged into a production of the *Holländer*, which he revised for the purpose, conducting four performances on 25, 28, 30 April and 2 May 1852, all to full houses. The *Eidgenössische Zeitung* of Zurich reported the success of all four performances. On 11 May it reprinted a review from the *Bund* of Berne: "To the success of *Der fliegende Holländer* its admirable execution, in the first place, contributed much. Under Wagner's control the orchestra becomes a single instrument, so to say, from which the master evokes the rich world of its tones with the finest of feeling and the freest of will."[31] By striking contrast, Wagner wrote to a friend in Paris on 2 May that the performances had been merely "passable."[32] He conducted no more opera until 1855.

He was active in the Music Society of Zurich between 1851 and 1855, conducting some twenty-two concerts, predominantly Beethoven. A rare appearance of his own work was the *Tannhäuser* overture at a concert on 16 March 1852. The public made a happy discovery: "Wagner was not only a distinguished conductor but also an eminent composer," proclaimed the *Eidgenössische Zeitung*. "His music to *Tannhäuser* is thoroughly original, individual, of plastic characterisation and indomitable force. Its success was extraordinary. The whole audience, assembled to a number never seen here before, was stirred to its deepest by this powerful romance, and finally gave vent to its feelings in a protracted storm of enthusiastic cheers."[33] Even Wagner had to admit the effect was terrific. He wrote to his friend Theodor Uhlig that "the women especially were 'turned inside out' and had to find relief for their emotion in 'sobs and weeping'."[34] Wagner was receiving recognition long denied him in Germany, but at the cost of physical exhaustion.

A year later he gave three concerts of his own works, on 18, 20 and 22 May, each of the same program. He had assembled an orchestra of seventy and a chorus of 110. The *Eidgenössische Zeitung* wrote (19 May 1853): "On a little raised platform in front of the orchestra stood the man whose magic wand all willingly obeyed... the whole house [was] spellbound by the wonders of this night."[35] Wagner too was unusually impressed. The performances to him were perfect. He had never experienced it before. He wrote to Liszt (30 May) that his chief object had been to hear something from *Lohengrin*, particularly the prelude: "Well, that has interested me above all else. The effect upon myself was uncommonly moving; I had to pull myself together by force, not to give way to it."[36] In spite of the rapturous reception and his own pleasure at what he had heard, he resisted calls to repeat the concerts the following week. He was exhausted.

It was not until March 1854 that he again conducted excerpts from his own works in concert – from *Rienzi* and *Tannhäuser* – then came his last appearances in concerts in Zurich on 23 January and 20 February 1855.[37] He conducted his *Faust Overture*, which he had revised for the occasion. He later recalled: "I... rehearsed our orchestra and performed it with success, or so I thought. Only to my wife did it seem that there was really not much in it, and she asked me, when I went to London later

[31] *ibid*, vol. 3, pp. 314-315, 499

[32] to Ernst Kietz, in John N. Burk, (ed.), *Letters of Richard Wagner: The Burrell Collection* (London: Victor Gollancz, 1951), p. 189

[33] quoted in Ellis, *Life of Wagner*, vol. 3, p. 294

[34] Newman, *Life of Wagner*, vol. 2, p. 171

[35] *ibid*, p. 109

[36] *ibid*, pp. 113-114

[37] Although he stayed in Zurich till 1858, this was his last public performance.

in the year, not to perform it there."[38] Intended no doubt to show, particularly to Cosima to whom he was dictating his memoirs, how little his first wife had understood him, it may nevertheless mean more than this. Minna loved Wagner and cared for his reputation. She had seen him conduct the *Overture* and said to him, "Don't do that in London" or words to that effect. Whether it was in response to this counsel or not, Wagner did not conduct the *Faust Overture* in London. On 23 February he conducted his last opera in Zurich, the third of six performances of *Tannhäuser* to which he had reluctantly agreed. Bernard Spyri reported in the *Eidgenössische Zeitung* (16 February) that the "rehearsals took place under the baton of the composer himself," and added enigmatically, "anyone who has ever attended a rehearsal of Wagner's will know what that means."[39] The enthusiasm of the Zurich public was again in evidence and, for the main, so was that of the press."[40]

The London visit of 1855

Wagner's visit to London in 1855 to conduct the Philharmonic Society is one of the most notorious, if not shameful, examples of how a public can be denied the delights of new music and music-making for decades by an ill-equipped, provincial and largely hostile body of critics. The episode has been exhaustively examined by Wagner's English biographers – Ellis devoted almost a whole volume to it – and need detain us but briefly here.[41] Apart from a selection from *Lohengrin* at the second concert, the *Tannhäuser* Overture at the fifth concert and its repeat by royal command at the seventh, the programs Wagner conducted were a miscellany of other works, anchored by Beethoven's symphonies, from the Third to the Ninth.[42] Some of the critical comment on the early concerts is eloquent testimony to the poetry and fire Wagner was able to inspire in the orchestra. The *Lohengrin* selections on 26 March "had a great effect, and a most favourable impression," according to the *Daily News* (27 March); Wagner's music "was found to have much breadth and clearness, flowing and rhythmical melody, and marvellous variety and richness of instrumentation."[43] The *Tannhäuser* overture on 14 May, which enjoyed the unusual number of three rehearsals, made perhaps a more powerful impression. It received from the critics either a stunned response or one of outright hostility: "We do not… feel able to pronounce an opinion of it" (*Daily News*, 16 May); "Some deemed it, though wild and eccentric, a work of originality and genius, while others condemned it *in toto*… we found… some beautiful and striking effects, mingled with much obscurity and confusion" (*Illustrated London News*, 19 May); "Destitute of melody, extremely bad

[38] Wagner, *My Life*, p. 512

[39] quoted in Chris Walton, *Richard Wagner's Zurich: The Muse of Place* (Rochester, NY: Camden House, 2007), p. 163

[40] Newman, *Life of Wagner*, vol. 2, p.182; Richard Wagner, *Prose Works* (trans.) William Ashton Ellis, 8 vols. (London: Kegan Paul, 1892-9), vol. 4, pp. 218-219; Wagner, *My Life*, p. 513

[41] Ellis, *Wagner's Prose Works*, vol. 5, *passim*; Newman, *Life of Wagner*, vol. 2, pp. 413-440; Wagner devoted but two pages to the concerts: *My Life*, pp. 517-518

[42] Facsimiles of the programs were reproduced in "Wagner in London (1)" by Stewart Spencer, *Wagner*, vol. 3 no. 4 (October 1982), pp. 110-113; they were also reproduced in Myles Birket Foster, *The History of the Philharmonic Society of London, 1813-1912* (London: John Lane, The Bodley Head, 1912), pp. 241-44.

[43] quoted in Ellis, *Life of Wagner*, vol. 5, pp. 203

in harmony, utterly incoherent in form, and inexpressive of any intelligible ideas whatever... a most contemptible performance" (*Morning Post*, 15 May); "A more inflated display of extravagance and noise has rarely been submitted to an audience" (*The Times*, 16 May), etc. etc.[44] Little is to be gleaned of the composer-conductor from ears and eyes such as these. From his own perspective, Wagner considered the overture had been "well played, [was] received by the public in a quite friendly manner, but [was] not yet properly understood."[45] For most of the time he was in London, Wagner was cold, sick, and distracted from his main goal – the scoring of the *Walküre*. He complained that the role of concert-conductor was "really repugnant and deeply humiliating."[46] Ellis estimates that a year was lost to Wagner's creative work from these London concerts, and twenty years or more to England's musical progress.[47]

Tannhäuser in Paris 1860

France was the next to receive and reject him. First, he gave three concerts of his own works in Paris on 25 January, 1 and 8 February 1860. They included orchestral and choral selections from the *Holländer*, *Tannhäuser*, *Lohengrin* and the new prelude from *Tristan und Isolde*.[48] Bülow had come to Paris to help with the chorus, as well as to give his own piano recitals. Wagner sent no free tickets to the press. This did not go down well with the critics, who nevertheless turned out in full force.[49] The early pieces were received with surprise and enthusiasm by the packed audience of the Théâtre Italien. But the *Tristan* prelude was problematic. Rehearsing it with the orchestra was a trial, Wagner wrote to Mathilde Wesendonck: "I had to guide my people through the piece note by note, as if to discover precious stones in a mine.... I succeeded in making this Prelude intelligible to the orchestra and audience, indeed – people assure me that it produced the deepest imaginable impression: but do not ask me *how* I brought it off!"[50] He repeated the program at two concerts in the Théâtre de la Monnaie in Brussels on 24 and 28 March.

Any idea of producing *Tristan* in Paris became impracticable. *Tannhäuser*, on the other hand, was demanded, yet the result was another shameful episode in the reception of new and great music. Fortunately, perhaps, Wagner was not on the podium on this occasion. He had assisted in many of the 164 rehearsals, coaching

[44] *ibid*, pp. 273-77

[45] letter (15 June 1855) to Wilhelm Fischer, in Richard Wagner, *Letters to his Dresden Friends*, (trans.) J.S. Shedlock (London: Grevel, 1890), p. 401

[46] undated letter from London to Wesendonck in A.J. Jaeger, "Wagner in London in 1855," in Robin Grey, *Studies in Music* (London: Simpkin, 1901, reprinted AMS Press, New York, 1976), p. 181

[47] Ellis, *Life of Wagner*, vol. 5, p. 370

[48] The order of the program was the *Holländer* overture; *Tannhäuser* march and chorus, introduction to act three, pilgrims' chorus, and overture; *Tristan* prelude; and *Lohengrin* introduction, procession to the minster, and introduction to act three (wedding march and bridal chamber scene): Auguste de Gasperini, *La nouvelle Allemagne musicale: Richard Wagner* (Paris: Heugel, 1866), p. 55.

[49] *ibid*, p. 57. The whole of artistic Paris was present, including Auber and Berlioz, according to *Le Ménestrel* (29 January 1860).

[50] letter (Paris, 28 January 1860) in Richard Wagner, *Selected Letters*, (ed. and trans.) Stewart Spencer and Barry Millington (London: Dent, 1987), p. 484

singers and orchestral players, but in the end to little avail. He had hoped as early as October 1860 to be able to do nothing more than "breathe the right spirit into a *technically* perfect thing."[51] Things did not quite turn out like this. The conductor in charge was one Pierre-Louis Dietsch whom Bülow described as a "pitiful creature... the most asinine, thickest-skinned, most unmusical of all

Fig. 1.1. Wagner conducting a concert of his own works in Paris.
Drawing by Charles Amédée de Noé ("Cham"),
Le Charivari, 27 February 1860

Kapellmeisters I ever came across in Germany."[52] Later he wrote that this "old man [he was 53] without intelligence, without memory, utterly unteachable... destitute of an ear... is to conduct... from a first violin part! Who never gives the orchestra a single

[51] letter to Wesendonck (20 October 1860), in Richard Wagner, *Letters to Wesendonck et al.*, (trans.) William Ashton Ellis (London: Grant Richards, 1899), p. 76

[52] letter to Raff (24 February 1861) quoted in Newman, *Life of Wagner*, vol. 3, p. 106

entry! Frightful!!"[53] Wagner did his best to help the incompetent Dietsch, but his efforts were pathetically ineffective.

In the countless rehearsals we had held, I had become accustomed to using this man like a machine; from my customary position on the stage, right in front of his desk, I had conducted the orchestra along with him, and in doing so had insisted on my tempi is such a way that I had no doubt they would be firmly maintained after I was no longer in the middle of things. Yet I now found that as soon as Dietsch was left to his own devices, everything began to waver, in that no tempo or nuance was strictly or consciously preserved.[6]

Wagner offered his own services as conductor, but this was rejected. Even the orchestra resisted the idea, he disarmingly recorded.[54] He thus had to resign himself to "a dull and spiritless rendering of my work."[55] The first performance was given on 13 March 1861. Disruptions and riots affected the second performance on 18 March, not wholly for musical reasons, and after the third performance on 24 March, which Wagner did not attend, he withdrew his approval for any further performances.

Itinerant conductor

In the years 1862 and 1863 Wagner was compelled for financial reasons to resume the distasteful role of a concert-giver. In Leipzig on 1 November 1862, to a virtually empty hall, he conducted the first performance of his *Meistersinger* prelude and the *Tannhäuser* Overture which, "safely led by his unerring baton of command, and animated by his fiery spirit, [was] imbued with a new, heightened magic."[56] In Vienna on 26 December 1862, 1 and 11 January 1863, he gave concerts of his own works, including excerpts from the first three parts of the *Ring* and the *Meistersinger* prelude. The conductor and composer, Wendelin Weissheimer, recalled the performance of the latter during which Wagner failed to give a cue to the brass at one point, and they remained silent. "With a strong tug, Wagner finally jolted the errant musicians into joining in. However, more than half a beat had passed between the correct and the late entrance, so that the consequences, even with this best orchestra in the world, were still incalculable at first... After the concert, Wagner admitted to me that this catastrophe terrified him no end at the time, but that the orchestra had found their way back in with admirable speed." Weissheimer also recalled a *Tannhäuser* Overture at a later concert which elicited cheers "beyond the wildest imagination," and a *Faust Overture* as "the most perfect case of conducting of any orchestra I have ever heard."[57]

Wagner also gave concerts during 1863 in Prague (8 February, 5 and 8 November), St Petersburg (19 and 26 February, 6 and 21 March, 2 and 5 April), Moscow (13, 15 and 17 March), Pesth (23 and 28 July), Karlsruhe (14 and 19 November), Löwenberg (2 December), Breslau (7 December), and Vienna (27 December).[58] In

[53] *ibid*, p. 107
[54] *ibid*, p. 632
[55] "*Tannhäuser* in Paris" (1861), Ellis, *Wagner's Prose Works*, vol. 3, p. 354; the first performance was on 13 March 1861.
[56] *Illustrierten Zeitung*, quoted in Wendelin Weissheimer, *Erlebnisse mit Richard Wagner, Franz Liszt und vielen anderen Zeitgenossen nebst deren Briefen* (Stuttgart: Deutsche Verlags-Anstalt, 1898), p. 196
[57] Weissheimer, *Erlebnisse mit Richard Wagner*, pp. 223-224, 226
[58] Stewart Spencer, *Wagner Remembered* (London: Faber and Faber, 2000), p. 112

1913 a Russian musician recalled a characteristic feature of his conducting during the visit to Moscow in 1863, namely a small variation in tempo. It "was limited to a light, barely noticeable variation, which did nothing to destroy the unity of the general tempo of the work. It was a kind of tempo rubato really... The variation in tempo was much more pronounced in the *Tannhäuser* overture."[59] Popular as he had been in some of these cities, the success did not materially remedy his financial situation. He fled to Munich from creditors in Austria in March 1864. He was saved shortly thereafter when, almost as soon as King Ludwig had ascended his throne, he summoned Wagner and assured him of future financial support.

Fig. 1.2 Wagner conducting in Vienna, 1863.
Drawing by Gustav Gaul

Der fliegende Holländer, Tristan und Isolde, and Die Meistersinger in Munich

The only one of his own works he conducted in Munich was the *Holländer* on 4 December 1864. It was the first production in the city, and reports were mixed. The performance was "generally a good one," according to the *Münchener Neueste Nachrichten*, though Wagner's direction was not wholly comprehensible.[60] The opera received "an exceptionally favourable and in parts even enthusiastic" reception, reported the *Bayerische Zeitung*, particularly the second and third acts, notwithstanding some difficulties in the chorus.[61] Wagner then conducted concerts of his own works in Munich's National Theatre on 11 December, and Residence Theatre on 1 February 1865. However, when it came to a performance of *Tannhäuser* (5 March 1865) and the

59 Spencer, *Wagner Remembered*, p. 147

60 *Münchener Neueste Nachrichten*, 6 December 1864, p. [2] and *Unterhaltungs-Blatt*, 11 December 1864, p. 1188

61 *Bayerische Zeitung*, 5 December 1864, p. [4]

first performances of *Tristan* (10 June 1865) and *Meistersinger* (21 June 1868), it was time to pass the baton.

Hans von Bülow's discovery of Wagner is a tale to be told later. For Wagner, it opened opportunities he could not have dreamed of, not least to have a young a musician of such consummate ability to prepare and champion his work. Whereas King Ludwig had saved him financially, Bülow saved him musically. When it came to the first *Tristan*, Wagner told the orchestral players at a rehearsal on 11 May that his health was in too poor a state to enable him to lead the orchestra himself. He assured them, however, of "his perfect confidence in his second self, Bülow."[62] The performances were everything he could have hoped for. Bülow also prepared the first *Meistersinger*, with Wagner always present and active, as the *Neue Freie Presse* reported:

> In a state of continuous excitement that makes one nervous, [Wagner] accompanies every note with a corresponding movement that the singers imitate as closely as they can; only someone who has seen the composer working and gesticulating in this way can have any idea of the multitude of nuances that he himself has thought up. Virtually every step, every shaking of the head, every hand movement, every opening of a door is "musically illustrated," and there is in *Die Meistersinger*, in particular, such a mass of music to go with the singers' dumb show that we should regard as a miracle if a production of the opera that was not rehearsed under the composer's direction managed to include all the gestures intended to accompany this music. Only when Fräulein Mallinger is singing does Wagner occasionally suspend his instructions and listen with visible pleasure, trotting to and fro, with one hand in his trouser pocket, or sitting on a chair next to the prompt box, nodding in satisfaction and smiling all over his face. But if there is something in the orchestra he does not like, as happens not infrequently, he leaps up as if bitten by a snake and claps his hands. Bülow breaks off and Wagner calls down to the orchestra: "*Piano*, gentlemen, piano! It must be quiet, quiet, quiet, as though it comes from another world!" And the orchestra begins again. "Even more *piano*!" Wagner calls out and makes the appropriate gesture with his hands. "So, so, so – good, good, good, – very nice.[63]

Wagner was learning of the many successes his earlier works were having in Germany, but there was nothing comparable to the first *Meistersinger* under Bülow on 21 June 1868. He reminisced three years later: "Only once, in Munich, did I arrive at rehearsing my work in full accord with my intentions, at least as regards its rhythmic architecture."[64] In *Actors and Singers* (1872) he wrote that he had never been as

[62] Newman, *Life of Wagner*, vol. 3, p. 358

[63] *Neue Freie Presse*, 21 June 1868, in Spencer, *Wagner Remembered*, pp. 186-187; also quoted in Herbert Barth, Dietrich Mack, Egon Voss (eds.), *Wagner: A Documentary Study* (London: Thames and Hudson, 1975), p. 214. It is interesting to compare Wagner's active participation in these rehearsals with one he attended for *Lohengrin* in Vienna on 11 May 1861 under Heinrich Esser. He sat on stage and it surpassed all his expectations: "I sat quite still the whole time, without moving; but one tear after another ran down my face": letter to Minna Wagner, Vienna, 13 May 1861, in Wagner, *Selected Letters*, p. 517; on the other hand, Angelo Neumann recalled that Wagner was "anything but pleased" with Esser's *Lohengrin*: *Personal Recollections of Wagner*, (trans.) Edith Livermore (London: Archibald Constable, 1909), p. 4.

[64] *Letter to an Italian Friend on the Production of* Lohengrin *at Bologna* (Lucerne, 7 November 1871), in Ellis, *Wagner's Prose Works*, vol. 5, p. 286; Wagner does not seem to mean that "my work" is a reference to *Lohengrin*; in his essay *On Conducting* (1869) he wrote: "I... don't know a soul whom I could safely trust to take a single tempo of my operas; [and then with perhaps a thought for Bülow he continues] at least no soul upon the general staff of our own time-beating army"; earlier in the essay he wrote of *Die Meistersinger* that "there lingers in my memory of a completely undocked [uncut], but at any rate completely correct performance in Munich": Ellis, *ibid*, vol 4, pp. 360, 359; alternatively, Edward Dannreuther's translation, 1887 (New York: Dover, 1989), p. 101

"heartily contented with an opera company" than at this first performance of the *Meistersinger*. By the time of the performance, "my singers and choristers... arrived at the mastery of a continuous *dialogue*, which came to them at last as easily and naturally as the commonest talk of everyday...."[65] After this performance he left Munich and retreated to Tribschen, his new house near Lucerne, where he wrote his tract *On Conducting* (1869).

Itinerant conductor again

His concert-giving at this period was minimal. A rare occasion was when he conducted an impromptu performance of his *Faust Overture* in Berlin on 30 April 1871. It was a second performance, conducted in appreciation of the musicians who had just performed it under Julius Stern. With Wagner standing before them the musicians were attracted to his baton "like a magnetic needle to the pole," wrote the *Berlinische Nachrichten*. "Only in moments when the masses [of musicians] were aflame with enthusiasm did he rise to full height, otherwise he simply provided small hints, soothing with both hands, effective with just a nod, often even having a profound effect by doing nothing at all. The orchestra realised who was standing in front of it. It played with the highest elasticity, with enthusiasm, in some instances even brilliantly, for example the brass section and the kettledrums."[66] The *Berlinische Zeitung* reported:

He picked up the baton, which he still knows how to handle masterfully, and began. A magical magnetic rapport seemed to develop between the orchestra and its conductor. Whether it was the careful and exact preliminary studies made by the musicians under Stern's direction, whether it was the rapt attention which drives even less practised souls to unexpected achievements, whether in the end it was the intellectual sharpness, the eloquent assuredness so visible in the baton guided by Wagner, we don't know – but this improvised performance was of a character that exceeded mere common relations between human beings, and will be remembered forever by anyone fortunate enough to have witnessed it.[67]

One such fortunate witness was an American music student, Amy Fay, who marvelled at Wagner's direction:

He didn't beat the time simply, as most conductors do, but he had all sorts of little ways to indicate what he wished. It was very difficult for them to follow him, and they had to "keep their little eye open," as B. used to say. He held them down during the first part, so as to give the uncertainty and speculativeness of Faust's character. Then, as Mephistopheles came in, he gradually let them loose with a tremendous crescendo, and made you feel as if hell suddenly gaped at your feet. Then, when Gretchen appeared, all was delicious melody and sweetness. And so it went on, like a succession of pictures. The effect was tremendous.... When he conducts he is almost beside himself with excitement. That is one reason why he is so great as a conductor, for the orchestra catches his frenzy, and each man plays under a sudden inspiration. He really seems to be improvising on his orchestra.[68]

65 Ellis, *ibid*, vol 5, p. 209. See the Bülow chapter below on *Tristan* and *Meistersinger* performances.

66 *Dritte Beilage zu den Berlinische Nachrichten von Staats- und gelehrten Sachen*, 2 May 1871, p. [1]

67 *Königlich privilegirten Berlinische Zeitung*, *Zweite Beilage*, 2 May 1871, p. 7

68 Amy Fay, *Music-Study in Germany* (London: Macmillan, 1886), p. 104

In Mannheim on 20 December 1871 he conducted the *Siegfried Idyll* at a Wagner Society concert with an orchestra of thirty-six, much larger than the small group assembled for its premiere for Cosima on Christmas morning in 1870. This time, as Newman pointed out for those who felt a pious duty towards to "the composer's intentions," there was a larger orchestra because Wagner had more room than a staircase and a lobby for his players to sit in, and more money to engage them.[69]

Fig. 1.3. Wagner conducting in Mannheim, 20 December 1871.
Ueber das Dirigiren (*On Conducting*) is written at the foot of the podium.
Drawing by Joseph Kühn

Around this time Anton Seidl, then Wagner's new assistant, first heard him conduct Beethoven and excerpts from his own works, and gave this account:

[69] Newman, *Life of Wagner*, vol. 4, p. 306; the performance appears to have been a rehearsal only which did not proceed to concert. Cosima's diary for 20 December mentions a rehearsal of the *Siegfried Idyll* in the morning – "great sorrow on my part to see it performed in front of so many strangers [and afterwards, over lunch] … R. animated, talks about the *Idyll*, and in the process hurts me very much": *Cosima Wagner's Diaries*, 2 vols, (trans.) Geoffrey Skelton (New York: Harcourt Brace Jovanovich, 1978-1980), vol. 1, p 441. The program for the concert in the evening consisted of the *Kaisermarsch*, the overture to *Zauberflöte*, Beethoven's Seventh Symphony, the preludes to *Lohengrin* and *Meistersinger*, and the prelude with concert ending from *Tristan* according to Richard Pohl, *Richard Wagner: Studien und Kritiken: Gesammelte Schriften über Musik und Musiker: Band 1* (Leipzig: Schlicke, 1883, pp. 186-205) and *Das Theatermuseum der Stadt Mannheim* (Mannheim, 1936), p. 60.

As a conductor, technically and intellectually, Wagner can surely be given the highest place. He ruled the musicians completely with his gestures – yes, even sometimes with his eyes alone. He lifted them up to the fairy realms of his imagination, and confided tasks to them which they had never before thought of.... In one of the rehearsals before the *Nibelungen* festival in Bayreuth, the oboe player declared that he could not conquer the technical difficulties offered by a passage in the first act of *Siegfried*, but a word of encouragement and explanation of the proper mode of delivering the phrase cleared away all difficulties to the complete satisfaction of the master..... He could charm as ravishing a *piano* out of the brass instruments as out of a violin; and to extract a *pianissimo* simultaneously from all the instruments of the orchestra was the most wonderful feature of his conducting. He was able to initiate the musicians in the melos of a composition without superfluous words; a sententious comparison, a witty remark would throw more light on Wagner's intentions than whole books which have been written about the controverted passages. In fact he was the enemy of many words; deeds were his demonstrations. His attitude before an orchestra was like that of a general, firm, sure, energetic; he did not shrink up [*sic*] to dwarf's size at a *piano*, nor jump up like a bird of prey at a *forte*, but seemed always a piece of majesty conducting, or rather composing the music.[70]

In January and February 1873 he gave concerts in Hamburg and Berlin to raise money for Bayreuth, but found the experience disheartening and exhausting. He declined an invitation from Hermann Levi, Court Kapellmeister at Munich since 1872, to conduct *Tristan*, saying it was beyond his physical capacity.[71] And in spite of his refusal to Levi to give a concert of his own works, he did so for Vienna on 1 March 1875, where he conducted the *Kaisermarsch* and *Götterdämmerung* excerpts, and received a rousing response.[72] Hans Richter was to have conducted the rehearsals but could not get leave from the Hungarian Opera to do so. Wagner went on to Pesth, where Richter had prepared the orchestra. On 10 March Wagner conducted excerpts from the *Walküre* and *Götterdämmerung*, and Liszt conducted his *Bells of Strassburg*. After the dress rehearsal, Richter remarked in his diary on "the insecure conducting of both conductors. However, Liszt conducted really better and more clearly than Wagner... The Master's unclear beat caused some hesitations."[73] Wagner then travelled to Berlin and gave concerts on 24 and 25 April along the lines of those in Vienna.

Lohengrin in Vienna 1876

On 2 March 1876 Wagner conducted for only the second time in his life a performance of *Lohengrin*. It was a benefit performance for the Vienna opera chorus. He had last conducted the work in Frankfurt on 12 September 1862, and there was some nervousness among the musicians. Richter recorded in his diary for 2 and 3 March that there were "a few moments of uncertainty, [but] the performance was excellent. To achieve a greater security the chorus master [Karl] Pfeffer and I conducted from the wings."[74] The young Felix Mottl was present and left a slightly

[70] interview in *New York Tribune*, 27 February 1887, p. 10 [71] Newman, *Life of Wagner*, vol. 4, p. 4

[72] *Neue Freie Presse*, 2 March 1875, p. 7. He gave a second concert on 10 March, and a third on 6 May.

[73] quoted in Christopher Fifield, *True artist and true friend: A Biography of Hans Richter* (Oxford: Clarendon Press, 1993), pp. 80–81; it should perhaps be noted that in the evening of this rehearsal Richter conducted *Der fliegende Holländer*, with cuts, in the presence of Wagner and Cosima. Richter wrote in his diary that some of his tempos and cuts annoyed Wagner very much, but they had been necessary to help a weak singer: *ibid*, p. 82. [74] *ibid*, p. 106

different account in his diary. Richter and Joseph Sucher positioned themselves in the orchestra, to the right and left of Wagner, in case something might happen because he had not conducted a theatre production for so long. "But they soon gave up their concerns when they saw how he – quite apart from the wonderful suggestive force of his personality – also directed the whole technically with the greatest perfection. It was a wonderful evening!"[75] Mottl noted the "very, very slow and infinitely broad" manner in which Wagner conducted the prelude,[76] as he was observed to have done too in Frankfurt.[77] Luigi Arditi recalled Wagner's manner of conducting at this performance as "sharp and hasty, and at times intensely nervous."[78] Another observer remembered: "Wagner in no way handled a baton like a professional conductor. In some places he would conduct extremely precisely and rhythmically, at others, when either tired or wrapped in his own thoughts, nonchalantly or not at all."[79]

Contemporary reports were more illuminating and expansive. Wagner's conducting deserved the highest praise according to the *Neue Freie Presse*: "it was hardly ever as arbitrary or nervous as some had feared, but was mostly full of concentrated energy; one could even say that so far as temperament is concerned this sixty-three-year-old composer put our thirty-six-year-old court conductor Mr Richter to shame."[80] Wagner's "magic baton had lost none of its power," according to *Die Presse*. "It is only during performances like these that one realises the kind of inspiring power a major composer's personality exerts when it is whole-heartedly engaged."[81] The *Wiener Sonn- und Montagszeitung* wrote of "the miraculous effect of the master's arm on the massed chorus and orchestra," notwithstanding that "Wagner's way of conducting singers who were not used to his methods threatened to embarrass them a few times." Nevertheless, it was a "sparkling performance" the likes of which had probably never been seen before.[82] The *Wiener Abendpost* considered it "a truly extraordinary performance" and gave what is perhaps the most detailed description of Wagner conducting one of his own works.

> [Wagner] guided the baton like an all-powerful magic wand. Great composers don't always make good conductors – Beethoven for instance wasn't, and Schumann even less so. Wagner, however, has always been famous for his conducting, from the very beginning, and deserves his fame.... We had seen Wagner conduct a concert on more than one occasion, but anyone

[75] diary entry for 2 March 1876: Willy Krienitz, "Felix Mottls Tagebuchaufzeichnungen aus den Jahren 1873-1876," *Neue Wagner-Forschungen* (Karlsruhe: Braun, 1943), 167-234, at p. 190

[76] Mottl transcribed much of what he observed at this performance, and at another of 15 December 1875 conducted by Richter and produced by Wagner, into his piano arrangement of *Lohengrin* published by Edition Peters. Notable jottings in his diary of this performance were the variety of dynamics and tempi achieved by Wagner, the serene pianissimo of the trumpets at the beginning of the Swan Chorus, the lively procession of the knights before the fight, the very fast tempo during the fight itself, an alarmingly long pause after Ortrud's mocking *Gott?* and before Friederick's horrified *Du wilde Seherin* ("You wild seer"), the lack of *portamenti* and recitative from the singers, their flowing dialogue, etc. Mottl's own performance of the prelude to *Lohengrin* seems to have echoed Wagner's in its breadth: see Timings.

[77] Weissheimer, *Erlebnisse mit Richard Wagner*, p. 158. Overall the performance was "very good," with the orchestra "all fire and full of life," according to the *Frankfurter Nachrichten – Extrabeilage zum Intelligenz-Blatt der freien Stadt Frankfurt*, 14 September 1862, p. 870

[78] Luigi Arditi, *My Reminiscences* (London: Sheffington, 1896), p. 185

[79] Joseph Sulzer, *Ernstes und Heiteres aus den Erinnerungen eines Wiener Philharmonikers* (Vienna: Eisenstein, 1910), quoted in Fifield, *True Artist*, p. 105

[80] *Neue Freie Presse*, 3 March 1876, pp. 5-6

[81] *Die Presse*, 3 March 1876, p. 10

[82] *Wiener Sonn- und Montagszeitung*, 5 March 1876, p. [3]

Fig. 1.4. Wagner conducting a rehearsal of his own works in Vienna, 27 February 1875. Drawing by Gustav Gaul

with the slightest experience in this area will know that there is a vast difference between the concert hall and the theatre. It truly was a great pleasure to watch Wagner. If one was ever able to say of an artist that he lived inside his works, and his works lived inside him, one can say this of Wagner. There are conductors whose conducting resembles some kind of pantomime dance, and others whose way of beating time is reminiscent of the turning of a coffee grinder. Wagner has nothing in common with either the caricature or the other phlegmatic type. His work animates him and determines all his movements – a glance, a slight raising of his hand, a softer or more energetic movement of his baton – during a *diminuendo*, his left hand is active, while his right hand keeps the beat, a softly soothing movement – now punctuated notes follow, the graceful waving motion of beating time replaced by a sharply accentuated one – a fiery, stormy movement, with the baton jerking upwards like a whirlwind of heavy weather – a short chord played by the whole orchestra, and his arm stops altogether for an instant, as if turned to stone. Allow us to highlight an example. Before Elsa and the women's chorus summon the saviour, the clarinet and bass clarinet introduce the moment with a deeply passionate melody.

Wagner then turned towards the respective musicians of the orchestra, and one could say that the movement of his hand expressed the strange recital of this part in an admirably faithful manner, note by note.

Earlier, we called his baton a magic wand – it really was as if he was conjuring up this music, these massive sounds right there and then by his magic powers. At times though, Wagner did not conduct at all, for instance during Lohengrin's *Nun sei gedankt, mein lieber Schwan*, so as to give free rein to the singer for his own interpretation. Wagner had his eyes and attention just about everywhere too. As the swan-boat approached, the choir was pushing towards centre stage too much, thus blocking the view. With a passionate, unmistakable movement of both hands, immediately understood by the choir, Wagner motioned them to separate to the left and right. To discuss the tempo taken by a great composer would be presumptuous, although at times one can have some strange experiences. For instance, we remember Spohr once truly rushing through his *Jessonda*. For Wagner, however, the opposite could be said: he showed a clear tendency to keep the movement broad and restrained. This gave the work some length, stretching the first act, for instance, across five quarters of an hour. Conducted in this way, a work which is already of such colossal size can have a slightly tiring effect.[83] The members of the chorus gave of their best: for them, it was a very special day.[84]

The Vienna *Lohengrin* was the last time Wagner conducted a complete opera of his own. But it was not the last time he had something to say about conducting his own works, either through his ever reluctant performance of excerpts, or during rehearsals for the *Ring* in Bayreuth in 1876.

Rehearsals for the Bayreuth Festival in 1876

Preliminary rehearsals for the *Ring* were held in Bayreuth in August 1875. There was one orchestral rehearsal per act per day, as Wagner sat at a little desk on stage. Gustav Adolph Kietz recalled: "Hans Richter was conducting. Wagner followed in the score, but was so excited that all the time he was moving not only his arms but his legs as well. Master Menzel managed to capture him in a crayon drawing in a very characteristic attitude, in spite of the darkness in the auditorium."[85]

During the period of rehearsals in 1876, it must be remembered that Wagner was constantly on the brink of nervous exhaustion, and sometimes became ill and had to withdraw from rehearsals because of the enormous strain involved in the momentous production. At times he triumphed over his frailty and indisposition, at others he can only have been manifesting them. Reading accounts of these rehearsals is engrossing, yet one comes away with little guidance except of the most general sort. Wagner had invited Heinrich Porges "to follow all my rehearsals very closely… and to note down everything I say, even the smallest details about the interpretation and performance of our work, so that a tradition goes down in writing."[86] A laudable

[83] Nikisch, who was a member of the orchestra during this performance, and Richter and Mottl, were probably influenced by Wagner in their interpretations of this work. They too were criticised for dragging the tempo. Mahler was said to have adopted Wagner's tempi exactly. See the respective chapters below.

[84] *Wiener Abendpost* (*Beilage zur Wiener Zeitung*), 3 March 1876, p. 2

[85] quoted in Barth, *Wagner: A Documentary Study*, p. 229

[86] letter to Porges dated 6 November 1872 in Heinrich Porges, *Wagner Rehearsing the "Ring"* (New York: Cambridge University Press, 1983), p. vii

Fig.1.5. Wagner at a *Ring* rehearsal in Bayreuth, 8 August 1875. Drawing by Adolf Menzel

objective, but it proved difficult to achieve. Another supporter who had the same idea was Richard Fricke· choreographer of the Bayreuth Festival, who proposed to write a production book, with Wagner's blessing. For this purpose he kept a diary of his Bayreuth work, which was only published in 1906.[87] The young Felix Mottl, who had been summoned to Bayreuth to assist, also kept a diary.[88] These three accounts, more than the discreet, protective diaries of Cosima, give us a valuable first-hand account of what Wagner was seeking.

To begin with Fricke's contemporaneous record: "Wagner speaks quietly,

[87] Richard Fricke, *Bayreuth vor dreissig Jahren* (Dresden: Verlag Richard Bertling, 1906), English translation "Bayreuth in 1876" by Stewart Spencer, in *Wagner* XI (1990), 93-109, 134-50 and XII (1991) 25-44. References will be to this English translation.

[88] Krienitz, "Felix Mottls Tagebuchaufzeichnungen," pp. 167-234; he described Fricke as "a funny, intelligent old gentleman who talks a bit much": *ibid*, p. 194

indistinctly, gesticulating a great deal with his hands and arms; the final words in any sentence give only an approximate idea of what he wants and you have to be fiendishly attentive."[89] On 10 May 1876 at a rehearsal of *Götterdämmerung* he wrote:

It is difficult working with Wagner since he never sticks to what he is doing. He leaps from one thing to another and cannot be pinned down to one question even though it could soon be sorted out. He wants to be his own producer but he lacks all the qualities necessary for this detailed work, since his mind, having the broader perspective forever in view, loses sight of all the details, so that by tomorrow he will have forgotten the moves that he worked out today. What's to be done?[90]

On 27 May Wagner was indisposed – "my nervous system is in a terrible state"[91] – but he was soon back, as Fricke recorded after a rehearsal with all the singers of *Rheingold* on 8 June:

they are getting discouraged since he wants it one way today and another way tomorrow. It's completely impossible to agree on a scene with all these changes. He keeps on interrupting and making altogether comical demands which the performers (who are not, after all, completely untried on stage) find thoroughly confusing.[92]

Fricke feared for Wagner's health. Indeed he did become ill, but it did not prevent him from returning to rehearsals. "Forgetting the pain he was in, he leaped up and down the high rocks, rearranging everything he possibly could and making a general mess of the whole thing." This was during a *Walküre* rehearsal on 17 June when, with his face swollen and bandaged in cotton wool and a thick towel, Wagner leapt around the rocks "like a young goat" to demonstrate the Hunding-Siegmund fight. At a further *Walküre* rehearsal on 20 June:

Wagner once again changed everything that he had blocked on the 19th. He went further and even altered the tempi in the orchestra; and for Brünnhilde's passage *Lebe, Weib, um der Liebe willen* (*Live, O maid, for the sake of love*), which he took very slowly yesterday, he now demanded a completely different tempo. He was terribly excitable, leaping everywhere and stamping his feet so that we went hot and cold all over.[93]

Fricke gave more accounts of Wagner changing everything from day to day, and by 26 June he had "given up the idea, at least for now, of keeping a proper production book."[94] He never completed one.

[89] Fricke, in *Wagner*, XI (1990), p. 98
[90] *ibid*, p. 97
[91] *ibid*, p. 140; in his diary for 29 May, Mottl records an incident which may show Wagner's nervous irritability at this period, or may merely be an example of what Wagner expected of his artists. During a rehearsal of *Das Rheingold* in Wahnfried with Max Strosser (Mime), at the point when Mime moans about how Alberich thanked him, rubs his back, and Wotan and Loge laugh (scene three, second part), Strosser may have asked Wagner what he wanted him to do. Mottl only records Wagner's response: "You know, dear friend, one cannot write down everything the way one imagines it. You can extend the stroking of your 'back' some, and can lustily stroke your a…! The oboes have such suspect little trills anyway." Mottl went on: "Mrs Wagner, attending the rehearsal in the background unnoticed by Wagner, silently disappeared when she heard this instruction!" (Krienitz, "Felix Mottls Tagebuchaufzeichnungen," p. 197). Cosima in her diary for 24-29 May merely notes: "Herr Schlosser also here, his demands are high." *Diaries*, vol. 1, p. 909
[92] Fricke, in *Wagner*, XI (1990), p. 148
[93] *ibid*, xii, p. 29
[94] *ibid*, p. 30; Fricke observed Wagner conducting his *Philadelphia March* in the Festspielhaus on 2 July 1876: "His conducting arm moves with such exquisite grace; his left hand mostly remains in his trouser pocket and is only raised when he wants *piano*, for *forte* he works with all fours. I – a non-musician – was

Fig. 1.6. Wagner at a *Ring* rehearsal, Bayreuth 1876, with Hans Richter in the pit

Among the singers Lilli Lehmann, who sang some minor roles at the first Festival, remembered Wagner's "goodness and consideration to his artists," especially to her. "He was troubled incessantly by others about little things [Fricke perhaps?], and, if he occasionally flew into a passion, it was not to be wondered at."[95] She paints a vivid picture of Wagner at an orchestral rehearsal:

> Wagner sat on the stage with his legs crossed and the score on his lap, if an orchestral piece was being given, or the orchestra rehearsed alone. He conducted for himself, while Hans Richter led the orchestra below. They, indeed, began together, but Wagner was so lost in his score that he did not follow the orchestra, that was often far ahead of him, and had long passed on to other

overcome by an indescribable feeling..." (*ibid*, p. 32).

95 Lilli Lehmann, *My path through life*, (trans.) Alice B. Seligman (New York: Putnam's, 1914), p. 208

tempi. When, at last he chanced to look up, he perceived, for the first time, that it was playing something quite different from what he heard with his spiritual ear."[96]

Hans Richter, who rehearsed the orchestra for hours in the mornings and the singers at the piano in the afternoons, made an interesting observation on what Wagner wanted from his music:

Wagner took no part in the [orchestral] rehearsals; his interest was exclusively in the staging of his works. A very curious trait in his character was that when it was a question of the music of other composers he took the greatest pains, going into the most minute details in order to arrive at absolutely perfect execution, whilst in connection with his own works he took little trouble and appeared satisfied so long as the music moved on. He only made a few observations and rarely asked for any repetition.[97]

Felix Mottl was astonished that Wagner made mistakes in recalling his work. In some cases he appears not to have known it at all. On 16 June Mottl noted in his diary: "The Master doesn't know his poem and always leaves it to us young people to prompt."[98] In other cases Wagner seemed not to know what to do about various scenes in the *Ring*: "One can easily write such crazy stuff, but to stage it is something else!!" he exclaimed.[99]

Against the background of these raw recollections, the full challenge facing Heinrich Porges may well be appreciated. To make something complete and coherent for posterity from the brilliant flashes, explosions, and dark patches that comprised the fireworks of rehearsals required a great deal of creative work. Reading Porges, it is difficult sometimes to know who is speaking: Wagner, or Porges, and if it is Wagner, is it Wagner at rehearsal or in his writings or sayings elsewhere? When he describes the way the orchestra is playing, it is not always clear whether this is the way Wagner wanted it, or whether it was simply the way Richter conducted it – and Porges is often overwhelmed by the music. Nevertheless, there are recurring points that emerge from his account of the rehearsals.

First, the orchestra should *never be excessively loud* when the drama is being sung. "This was a recurring problem during rehearsals.[100] Wagner declared that the orchestra should support the singer as the sea does a boat, rocking but never swamping – he employed that image over and over again."[101] He told the orchestra "to subordinate and adapt its accompaniment to the spontaneous expression of the singer" when Brünnhilde is with the Valkyries in act three of the *Walküre*.[102] On the other hand, when Wotan comes in, "the music should be played with the utmost energy."[103] The orchestra must be carried to "the extreme of loudness" in passages where the "symphonic art is sovereign," for example the descent into Nibelheim, and the return

96 *ibid*, p. 223

97 Edward Speyer, *My Life and Friends* (London: Cobden-Sanderson, 1937), p. 59; whether this was told by Richter to his friend Speyer, or Speyer is otherwise quoting Richter, is not clear.

98 Krienitz, "Felix Mottls Tagebuchaufzeichnungen," p. 199

99 *ibid*, p. 202

100 Julius Hey recorded Wagner saying at Bayreuth in 1875, harking back to his Würzburg days: "to have to listen in cold blood while an orchestra is heedlessly blowing and fiddling away *fortissimo* instead of a simple *mezzo forte*, and virtually playing the singers into the ground, *that* I call criminal": Hey, *Richard Wagner als Vortragsmeister*, p. 197.

101 Porges, *Wagner Rehearsing*, p. 12

102 *ibid*, p. 68

103 *ibid*, p. 70

Fig. 1.7. Richard Wagner at Tribschen, Lucerne, around the time of his essay *On Conducting* (1869). Photo by Jules Bonnet

Figs. 1.8-11. Wagner conducting in London, 1877.
Drawings by Henry Holiday

Fig. 1.12. Wagner conducting in London. Drawing by Leslie Ward ("Spy"), *Vanity Fair*, 19 May 1877

Fig. 1.13. Wagner in London, 1877.
Photo by Elliott & Fry

from Nibelheim, and when Alberich's leaves the stage after his curse in *Rheingold*; the beginning and end of act one, and the end of act two, in the *Walküre*; and the opening of act three of *Siegfried*, which Wagner described as "Wotan's last ride, ... yet another descent to the underworld."[104]

Second, and this is an illustration of the variety of Richter's tempi during rehearsal (he is never named in Porges' book): the *tempo should not be too fast*. For example, the pace should not be so fast as to prevent the singer articulating the words (the birdsong, and the Mime/Siegfried scene in *Siegfried*), or to prevent the singer expressing all the dynamic nuances indicated in the score (Wotan's narration in *Walküre*). If the dialogue is animated (Loge/Alberich in *Rheingold*) the tempo should be very rapid, otherwise it should essentially be the same as speech. And the *tempo should not be too slow*. For example, a noble melody charged with deep feeling, as when Brünnhilde approaches Sieglinde in act two of the *Walküre*, should not be prolonged: "the temptation to emphasize its lyrical aspect must be consciously resisted in order to preserve the dramatic character of the dialogue." [105] In fact Porges notes "how easily the emotional significance of a passage can tempt singers – and also instrumentalists – to linger; such lingering is really a form of self-indulgence, utterly unstylistic, the death of genuinely dramatic dialogue."[106] In the Mime and Siegfried scene in act one of *Siegfried*: "a slower tempo should never be so slow as to convey a feeling of actual calm";[107] and in *Götterdämmerung*: "Wagner was insistent that the performance of Waltraute's great narrative should at no point be dragged. An epic style must be preserved; nevertheless, at every moment one must feel more or less acutely Waltraute's fear and feverish haste...The calm closing bars must be as pianissimo as possible. But 'now', as Wagner puts it, 'comes the action again' and it is impassioned and violent." [108]

Porges records, and this is important in the light of Wagner's later comments on Richter's tempi, that he gave no special direction for the famous orchestral passages *Siegfried's Rhine Journey* and *Siegfried's Funeral Music*. In respect of the former, Porges recorded Wagner's mere non-verbal communication: "his facial expression and characteristically eloquent gestures and hand movements were sufficient to spur the conductor to achieve the desired combination of plasticity, eloquent precision and perpetually forward-driving energy. But never must there be any suggestion of hurry." [109]

Porges gives many examples of how particular passages should or should not be performed, slower or faster, louder or softer, but he also records other comments which tend to shift the sands beneath any belief that one is reading settled wisdom. Wagner wanted his artists to have "complete freedom of expression," which could only be achieved by complete immersion in the work, "thereby acquir[ing] that gift of self-abandonment."[110] It is not clear whether this formulation is taken from Wagner's writings or from his comments at rehearsal, but it does reflect Wagner's views.[111] Fricke quoted Wagner in plainer form: "The people up there

[104] *ibid*, p. 101

[105] *ibid*, p. 62 [106] *ibid*, p. 37 [107] *ibid*, p. 82 [108] *ibid*, pp. 125-6 [109] *ibid*, pp.119, 141 [110] *ibid*, p. 2

[111] In *The Performing of Tannhäuser* (1852), for example, he wrote: "the more creative [a singer] can become, through the fullest freedom of Feeling, the more will he pledge me to delighted thanks": in Ellis, *Wagner's Prose Works*, vol. 3, p. 175; Emil Heckel recalled this exchange during a rehearsal for Beethoven's Ninth Symphony at Bayreuth in 1872: "At the beginning of the quartet [Niemann said]: 'Master, if you

on the stage, the performers, have to set the tempo for every Kapellmeister, always assuming they are artists of genius."[112] Lilli Lehmann recalled how Wagner often used to advise the artists on how to deal with the "metronomic beat" in melodic phrases: "That is your affair; do with it as you will."[113] Yet there was one scene in particular in which he broke this rule and expressed an opinion: the scene with Siegmund and Sieglinde at the end of act two of the *Walküre*. "Here Wagner demanded accents of the utmost unrestrained vehemence... Wagner wanted an expression of the utmost passion, throbbing with joy and anguish. The singer must hold nothing back, must throw her whole soul into it."[114] Wagner no doubt remembered his favourite singer Wilhelmine Schröder-Devrient whose artistry deeply affected him. Porges concludes his account with the closing scene of *Götterdämmerung* where the orchestra too must hold nothing back. "The performance of the symphonic conclusion, 'saying everything', of this cosmic drama... demands of the conductor a grip of iron; like a Cyclopean wall the themes and melodies must pile themselves up before us."[115] Whether Richter had this "grip of iron" Porges does not say.

Wagner was not entirely happy with the *Ring* performances. So far as the orchestra was concerned, he had posted a notice in the pit saying "No preludizing! Piano, pianissimo, then all will be well."[116] He was reminding the orchestra it was not in the concert room and must not indulge in the glories of the music, but accompany the drama on stage. Richter had surely got this message by the time of the first cycle, but he may have tucked it away by the time of the second. James Davison of *The Times*, never an ardent Wagnerian, reported that the second cycle was a great improvement on the first. "The orchestra, playing louder is more effective... During the first series of performances... [the orchestra] played in a more subdued tone ...and, though their execution was faultless, it was not infrequently accompanied by a *quasi* sense of dullness...."[117] Wagner does not seem to have commented on this. For him, it was all in the tempo, and Richter, he says, had all the tempi wrong. Cosima, whose relations with Richter had never been good, recorded Wagner on 9 September 1876: "Richter not sure of a single tempo. ...everything must be done anew for the repeat performances. R. is very sad, says he wishes he could die!"[118] We shall return to Richter's tempi in due course. However, Richter no doubt tried to follow faithfully what he had been told at rehearsals (which may not have been much), at least for the first cycle. Wagner had nothing to say of his conducting of the crucial *Rhine Journey* and *Funeral Music*, so presumably he was satisfied their tempi were right. Wagner was

don't beat time for me here, I cannot sing'; Wagner answered: 'I shall not beat time – for it would make the rendering stiff. You must sing this passage with absolute freedom...'": Richard Wagner, *Letters to Emil Heckel*, trans. William Ashton Ellis (London: Grant Richards, 1899), pp. 35-36; also quoted in Spencer, *Wagner Remembered*, p. 217.

112 Fricke, *Wagner*, xi, p. 99

113 Lehmann, *My Path*, p. 223

114 Porges, *Wagner Rehearsing*, pp. 60-61

115 *ibid*, p. 145

116 quoted in Finck, *Wagner and his Works*, vol. 2, 294; he also quotes the famous direction to the singers: "Distinctness, the large notes come of themselves, the small notes and their text are the main things."

117 quoted in Robert Hartford, (ed.), *Bayreuth: The Early Years - An account of the Early Decades of the Wagner Festival as seen by the Celebrated Visitors and Participants* (Cambridge University Press, 1980), pp. 99, 101

118 *Diaries*, vol. 1, pp. 921-922; she also records Wagner saying "Never again! Never again!" (5 November 1876, p. 932), but he seems to have mellowed: he later said that the "production, as far as the conception was concerned, was on the whole extraordinary, wrong in only a few details" (29 June 1878, vol. 2, p. 159).

not in any case immune from changing his mind on questions of tempi, as Fricke noted, and there is nothing unusual about that. Such is the nature of tempi: it *can* vary from one day to another depending on a range of factors, including how things are going on stage. Perhaps the artists were freely expressing their roles, as Wagner had enjoined them, and Richter was faithfully following. In rehearsals for *Parsifal* in 1882 Wagner often called out from the stalls: "Faster! Faster! The people will be bored."[119] If boredom be the measure of a correct tempo, then we shall see just how bored people were with Richter's *Ring* tempi when we consider his conducting below.

The real reason for Wagner's dissatisfaction with the *Ring* was more profound: it was in the difference between his imagination and what could be achieved in practice. Albert Apponyi, a Hungarian enthusiast who attended all three cycles of the 1876 *Ring*, related the story of a friend, Mihálovich, who during an interval went to a part of the theatre reserved for the Wagner family.

> By chance he entered a room in which he found the Master sitting alone before a writing table and musing. Seeing someone he knew, Wagner rose and said, almost in a tone of discouragement: "No, that isn't what I imagined. It falls far short of what I intended." Mihálovich, thinking that the performance was responsible for his dissatisfaction, began to defend it. Wagner answered: "It's nothing to do with that. I know the people are doing their best; but what I have written is not what lived in my imagination."[120]

No one, ultimately, could please Wagner the dreamer and the idealist when he could not be satisfied with himself. Richter was faced with the art of the impossible, a theme we shall return to. It is no wonder Wagner referred to Richter in his *Retrospect of the Stage Festivals of 1876* (1878) as "my proved effector of impossibilities and pledge of all responsibilities."[121]

The London visit of 1877

The Bayreuth Festival had left a deficit, and Wagner felt compelled to help erase it. In these circumstances, he accepted an invitation to conduct a Festival of his own works in London. His return after 22 years has generally been presented as a triumph. His operas had only recently come to England – the *Holländer* in 1870 (in Italian) and 1876 (in English), *Lohengrin* twice in 1875 (at Covent Garden and Drury Lane), and *Tannhäuser* in 1876[122] – but now the composer-conductor had come, had conquered, and was widely accepted by the London critics and public alike. It was as if the shameful memories of 1855 had been erased. Francis Hueffer wrote in 1883 that Wagner "was received with universal enthusiasm."[123] Henry Finck in 1893 wrote that he had "made the artistic success of the undertaking the primary consideration,"[124] perhaps encouraging Herman Klein, music critic of *The Times* at the time of the

[119] Charles Villiers Stanford, *Pages from an unwritten Diary* (London: Edward Arnold, 1914), p. 171 reporting what Edward Dannreuther had told him; also quoted in Hartford, *Bayreuth: The Early Years*, p. 107

[120] Count Albert Apponyi, *The memoirs of Count Apponyi* (London: Heinemann, 1935), p. 93; Apponyi saw Wagner during his concert tour to Pesth in 1875, but did not comment on his conducting.

[121] Ellis, *Wagner's Prose Works*, vol. 6, pp.107-108

[122] Francis Hueffer, *Richard Wagner* (London: Sampson Low [1883]), pp. 20, 39

[123] Hueffer, *Wagner*, p. 106

[124] Finck, *Wagner and his Works*, vol. 2, p. 379

Festival, to recall in 1925 its "artistic success,"[125] an expression he had not used in his 1903 survey of musical life in London.[126] The phrase has since appeared and been elaborated upon by Wagner's biographers, including Newman and Westernhagen and other commentators.[127] The reality is somewhat different.

Assisted by Richter, he was to conduct six concerts exclusively of his own works, to which a further two were added mainly for financial reasons.[128] A large orchestra of 169 players had been drawn from London, the provinces, France, Belgium and Germany, and was headed by Wagner's favourite violinist and Bayreuth Festival Orchestra leader, August Wilhelmj. The orchestra had first been rehearsed in programs chosen by Wagner, by Eduard Dannreuther (an English pianist and strong supporter of Wagner in London), and then by Richter, who was fresh from conducting the *Ring* in Bayreuth. There were nineteen rehearsals in all.[129] Herman Klein attended the final rehearsal. He was dismayed to discover that Wagner appeared to have succumbed to "a severe attack of Albert Hall stage fright," not uncommon among artists who stepped upon the stage of that vast amphitheatre. After a few words to Wilhelmj and to Richter, "who was posted beside the conductor's desk," he raised his baton and led the orchestra through a superb performance of the "pompous and sonorous" *Kaisermarsch*. The young composer Hubert Parry was also at this rehearsal and was astonished at the effects Wagner wrought: "Wagner's conducting is quite marvellous – he seems to transform all he touches; he knows precisely what he wants and does it to a certainty. The *Kaisermarsch* became quite new. I was so wild with excitement after it that I did not recover all afternoon."[130] Then came the overture to the *Holländer*, and to Klein's disappointment and sorrow, there were three breakdowns: Dannreuther and the leader

[125] Herman Klein, *Musicians and mummers* (London: Cassell, 1925), p. 171; whether or not Klein was the author of the contemporary reviews of the Wagner Festival in *The Times*, they were not very informative about who conducted what at the Festival, or how; a reference to "indiscriminate applause" may have been a hint that not all conducting was of a uniform quality.

[126] Herman Klein, *Thirty years of musical life in London, 1870-1900* (London: Heinemann, 1903), pp. 72-78

[127] For example, Newman: "the artistic and social success of the undertaking was beyond question": *Life of Wagner*, vol. 4, p. 537; Curt von Westernhagen: "an immense artistic and social success": *Wagner: A Biography*, trans. Mary Whittall (Cambridge: Cambridge University Press, 1978), p. 517; Anne Dzamba Sessa: "general acceptance of Wagner's orchestral music... was... completed during Wagner's visit in 1877": *Richard Wagner and the English* (Rutherford: Fairleigh Dickinson University Press, 1979), p. 37; William Braun: "Wagner was given the complete acclaim that had been denied him [in 1855]: "Wagner's Development, Work, and Influence as a Conductor in the 19th Century," *The Opera Journal*, vol. 25 no. 3 (September 1992) p. 35; "Artistically, it was a great success, once again....": Michael Tanner, *Wagner* (London: Faber and Faber, 2010), p. 76; "Wagner's London concerts proved an artistic success with their audiences": Oliver Hilmes, *Cosima Wagner: The Lady of Bayreuth*, trans. Stewart Spencer (New Haven and London: Yale University Press, 2010), p. 141; by contrast W. J Henderson wrote in 1923: "The concerts were a failure"; while Henderson may have meant financially, he nowhere refers to them as a success, except remarking that it was "the beginning of Richter's great vogue as a conductor in London": *Richard Wagner, his life and his dramas* (reprinted New York: AMS Press, 1971), p. 144.

[128] The concerts were given on 7, 9, 13, 14, 16, 19, 28 and 29 May 1877, the last two being supplementary to the Festival itself. Assembling from contemporary sources what was actually performed, and by whom, is difficult. Changes were made to the printed programs of the third, fourth and sixth concerts, to the "sheer despair" of those present, because singers had become hoarse: *Morning Post*, 14 May 1877, p. 2; *ibid*, 21 May 1877, p. 2; *Athenaeum*, 19 May 1877, p. 651.

[129] Finck, *Wagner and his Works*, vol. 2, p. 379

[130] quoted in Charles L. Graves, *Hubert Parry, his life and works*, 2 vols. (London: Macmillan, 1926), vol. 1, p. 177

of the second violins tried to convey Wagner's wishes to the orchestra, but "it was of no avail. He utterly failed either to indicate or to obtain what he wanted, and at last, in sheer despair, he threw down his stick and requested Richter to do the work for him."

Fig. 1.14. Wagner conducting at the Albert Hall, 1877.
The Hornet, 9 May 1877

When Richter mounted the podium, the orchestra gave him a "thoughtless" round of applause, and he led them through the overture without any difficulty. "It was played as I had never heard it played before." [131]

[131] Klein, *Thirty years*, pp. 73-77, and his *Golden Age of Opera* (London: Routledge, 1933), p. 62; William Quirke also recalled how "the orchestra indulge[d] in unrestrained jubilation" as Richter led Wagner off after his attempts at rehearsal: *Recollections of a Violinist* (London: Dawson, 1914), pp. 12-13

Wagner opened the first concert with the rousing *Kaisermarsch* and excerpts from *Rienzi* and *Tannhäuser* – the March was taken "at a great pace" and "fairly took the house by storm"[132] – and everything met with "rapturous applause" and enthusiasm.[133] Then he began the *Rheingold*. After the orchestral prelude "the dull and dreary vocal parts produced weariness, and the audience began rapidly to leave the hall. Whether the composer was fatigued, or felt he no longer had the sympathy and support of his previously rapturous listeners, we cannot say, but after Loge, the cynical God of Walhalla, had his solo, the *bâton* was taken by Herr Richter."[134] Parry was present and noted in his diary: "many people found the *Rheingold* selection too hard for them."[135] Another observer noted that Wagner, whose "jerky and indecisive beat … had been getting more and more erratic the more tired he grew, retired from the conductor's chair, handing the bâton to Herr Richter, a most able conductor and musician …."[136]

It was not only when Richter held the baton that he was of assistance to Wagner. At the second concert, he "surreptitiously sub-conducted just in front of Herr Wagner,"[137] but whether this in fact helped is doubtful. It was an excerpt from the *Holländer*. "For the most part it was conducted by Wagner himself, and whether he felt dragged back to an artistic childhood, whether he was painfully conscious of a false position, or was personally 'out of sorts,' it is true that everything done under his *bâton* was dull and spiritless. The audience were quite conscious of this…. Wagner's *tempi*, with which, being his, we dare not quarrel, seemed unaccountably slow."[138] Richter expressed his concern about this concert privately in his diary: "great uncertainties: the musicians often did not understand the Master's beat… The impression made upon by the Master's conducting was of complete insecurity and – unbelievably – ignorance, or even more, total obliviousness of his own works. Thereafter the Master handed the baton over to me, as he became aware of the friction amongst the performers."[139] As Richter took the podium for his share of the next concert, the orchestra greeted him with "almost uproarious applause."[140] At the fourth concert, Wagner conducted scenes from *Lohengrin* with "cruel deliberation" according to one observer.[141] Wagner took the Prelude, according to Parry, "very slow and quite teased the band,"[142] just as Mottl had observed in Vienna the year before. Another observer wrote: "it is quite evident that the heart of the composer is not in his work as conductor of these concerts; he has grown more listless and apathetic apparently at each successive performance, and when Herr Richter takes the bâton a new

132 *Musical Standard*, 19 May 1877, p. 303

133 *Athenaeum*, 12 May 1877, p. 618; *Daily Telegraph*, 8 May 1877, p. 5

134 *Athenaeum*, 12 May 1877, p. 618; *Daily Telegraph*, 8 May 1877, p. 5: "there was an obvious falling off in warmth of the audience"

135 quoted in Graves, *Parry*, vol. 1, p. 178; Parry noted not only his enthusiasm and what he heard – applause and cheering – but also what he saw: many of the audience walking out at one concert, and one of his friends falling asleep once or twice at another.

136 *The Sunday Times*, 13 May 1877, p. 3

137 *Musical Standard*, 19 May 1877, p. 304; the historian of the Philharmonic Society was at the Festival "and well remembers the all-controlling power of Hans Richter, hidden behind Wagner's conducting desk, but really conducting everything": Foster, *The History of the Philharmonic Society*, p. 358n.

138 *Daily Telegraph*, 11 May 1877, p. 5

139 quoted in Fifield, *True artist*, p. 125

140 *Musical Standard*, 26 May 1877, pp. 321-22

141 *Daily Telegraph*, 16 May 1877, p. 5

142 Fifield, *True artist*, p. 124

spirit actuates the band, and the compositions obtain really animated interpretations."[143] After the final concert it was noticed that "the larger share of conducting [had] devolved on Herr Richter, whose skill in this respect appears to surpass that of Wagner himself."[144]

Fig. 1.15. Wagner on stage at the Albert Hall, 1877, as Hans Richter conducted his works. Drawing by Charles Lyall ("Egazz"), *Musical World*, 26 May 1877

[143] *Athenaeum*, 19 May 1877, p. 651

[144] *Illustrated London News*, 2 June 1877, p. 515

Here clearly lay the secret of success for the Festival. While the large orchestra was "by no means absolutely faultless," in the opinion of the critic Ebenezer Prout, it was "very far above mediocrity." He continued:

For this the credit is beyond a doubt chiefly due to Herr Richter, whom I have no hesitation in pronouncing the greatest conductor I have ever seen. His beat is remarkably clear and intelligible; while he possesses to an unusual extent that most precious faculty in a conductor of imparting his own feeling of the music to the performers, and of carrying his band along with him. The difference in the quality of the execution as soon as he took the bâton in hand was very striking; and it is not too much to say that but for him the selections from the *Ring der Nibelungen* must have been a failure. With Wagner as a conductor I must confess I was somewhat disappointed. His beat is most suggestive and expressive, and with players who are thoroughly acquainted with the music would no doubt tend to secure a most excellent performance; but it is altogether a different kind of beat from that to which our English orchestras are accustomed; and if any of the performers go wrong it gives them very little help in getting right again. It assumes, in fact, a more intimate knowledge of the music than the players really possessed. Herr Richter, on the other hand, never missed giving a cue to any member of the orchestra, and, although he mostly had a score before him while conducting, he very seldom had occasion to refer to it. To him more than anyone else the artistic success of the performances has been unquestionably due."[145]

If the triumph was in fact Richter's, the seeds of Wagner's shortcomings can be seen in the observations above. He loathed and felt humiliated at what he had to do (and could not do), was ill for much of the time he was doing it, and found little solace in half empty and emptying halls, despite the warm applause from those who remained. His friend Dannreuther said, "at the Albert Hall, Wagner did not do himself justice. His strength was already on the wane. The rehearsals fatigued him, and he was frequently faint in the evening. His memory played him tricks, and his beat was nervous."[146] While the venture had made a modest profit, it was only because Wagner himself had met additional concert expenses. Klein concluded a recollection of the festival: "I have more than a vague suspicion that he always looked back upon this eventful visit with mingled feelings of annoyance and regret."[147] And would he not have had a thought for Richter? This was the man who had saved the Wagner Festival from disaster, Klein reflected later, and created "for us a new orchestral standard, [gave] us fresh ideas on orchestral conducting, and generally speaking, [changed] the course of musical taste in this country."[148] So it was an artistic success after all.

[145] *The Academy*, 26 May 1877, pp. 472-473

[146] quoted in Klein, *Musical Life*, p. 78; George Bernard Shaw also reported Wagner's "nervous and abrupt beat" and thought his tempos were "capriciously hurried or retarded without any apparent reason": *The Wagner Festival*, 6 June 1877, in *Shaw's Music: The Complete Musical Criticism in Three Volumes*, (ed.) Dan H. Laurence (New York: Dodd, Mead, 1981), vol. 1, p. 126; other assessments are in accord with those above, for example *The Musical Times* concluded that Wagner was "unfitted" to conduct his own music: "The master, great as he is in other respects, is a poor conductor, equally lacking spirit and power of control": 1 June 1877, p. 276; the London musician Wilhelm Ganz wrote: "Unfortunately, he was no longer at his best and had lost something of his great skill as a conductor": Wilhelm Ganz, *Memories of a musician: reminiscences of seventy years of musical life* (London: John Murray, 1913), p. 171; Stanford recalled: "Wagner was too old and too tired to carry through a concert single-handed; and although the old force and fire showed itself in occasional flashes, such as the conducting of the *Kaisermarsch* at the opening of the Festival, the best results were obtained by his lieutenant, who possessed the patience and equanimity which the composer lacked": Stanford, *Pages from an unwritten Diary*, pp. 178-179.

[147] Klein, *Musical Life*, p. 78

[148] Klein, *Musicians and Mummers*, pp. 169-170

The final years

Wagner's remaining conducting activities shed little new light on his practices. He conducted two private performances of the *Parsifal* prelude at home at Wahnfried on Christmas day 1878 with members of the Meiningen Orchestra, one in the morning intended to awaken a slumbering Cosima, and another in the evening before an assembly of invited guests. He conducted it twice at a private performance for King Ludwig on 12 November 1880. Then there was his famous appearance during the final performance of *Parsifal* at Bayreuth in 1882. While Hermann Levi was conducting the Transformation music in the final act, Wagner came into the pit, took the baton from his hand, and conducted the performance to the end. Levi wrote to his father: "I remained at his side because I was afraid he might make a mistake, but my fears were quite groundless – he conducted with the assurance of one who had been nothing but a conductor all his life."[149] The applause that followed, he said, defied all description. The ever-devoted Levi put the most favourable light on this historic final appearance. The audience had been unaware Wagner was conducting. Wagner's friend Emil Heckel recalled that the plan had been known to only a few. Levi and Fischer had remained in the orchestra so that the players and singers might not miss their cues: "The Master was therefore able to devote himself exclusively to a thoroughly adequate rendering of rhythm and expression. It was marvellous, the profound feeling and mighty breadth conferred on the drawn-out phrases."[150] The power of the great scene with Amfortas, as he lay bleeding, longing for death, which Wagner took very slowly and restrainedly,[151] exceeded anything Heckel had ever witnessed.

Exhausted after the Festival and in poor health, the ageing Wagner repaired with his family to Venice. For what may be regarded as an old man's amusement, even folly, he decided on a private performance of his juvenile work, the *Symphony in C*, which he had never conducted. The Italian critic, Filippo Filippi, was in Venice at the time. He wrote that Wagner rehearsed "with the greatest ardour. He is sometimes nervous and irritable. Altogether he is well pleased with the orchestra at the Liceo, whose members applaud enthusiastically at the end of every division of the symphony."[152] After the performance on 24 December 1882 he laid aside the baton and exclaimed, "I have conducted for the last time."[153] True as this statement turned out to be, the reasons for it will forever remain ambiguous.

[149] letter dated 31 August 1882 in Barth, *Wagner*, p. 243

[150] Wagner, *Letters to Heckel*, p. 131

[151] Rüdiger Porges (ed.), *"Das Orchester muss wie die unsichtbare Seele sein." Richard Wagners Bemerkungen zum Parsifal aufgezeichnet während der Proben und Aufführungen 1882 von Heinrich Porges* (Berlin: Deutsche Richard-Wagner-Gesellschaft, 2002), pp. 70-71

[152] quoted in Finck, *Wagner and his Works*, vol. 2, p. 446; Finck was relying on Henriette Perl's, *Richard Wagner in Venedig* (Augsburg: Reichel, 1883) for his account of Wagner's Venice months. Cosima does not record the comment in her diary; she notes: "R. very content!": *Diaries*, vol. 2, p. 981.

[153] Finck, *Wagner and his Works*, vol. 2, p. 447; this was also related by the concertmaster to Anton Seidl, who wrote an account of preparations for the performance of the Symphony, which Wagner had wanted him to conduct, in a letter to the *New York Tribune* (17 September 1887), reproduced in H.E. Krehbiel, *Review of the New York Musical Season 1887-1888* (New York: Novello, 1888), pp. 117-121; according to another account, Wagner made the statement ("I will never conduct again") earlier, after the final rehearsal during which he had suffered an attack: Giuseppe Norlenghi, *Wagner a Venezia* (1884), p.196, as translated by John W. Barker, *Wagner and Venice* (Rochester, N.Y.: University of Rochester Press, 2008), p.158.

"Was Wagner a great conductor?"

This was the title Henry Finck gave to one of the chapters of his major study of *Wagner and His Works* (1893). He supposed – and it was a supposition – that he was "one of the greatest conductors of all time," despite the "indescribable tortures" he suffered from the practical work of conducting given the general inadequacy of means.[154] Ernest Newman wrote that Wagner was "a far better conductor than any of his conductors," and that this was the cause of the "perpetual disappointment where the performance of his own works was concerned."[155] Wagner's *bête noire*, Eduard Hanslick recognized Wagner as a "brilliant conductor" after a concert in Vienna in 1872.[156] Anton Seidl, we will recall, judged him as "not only the mightiest of all geniuses, but also the greatest conductor that ever lived."[157]

And so the consensus built. The difficulty with general assessments such as these, however, is: what music is being referred to? If it is Beethoven, there is little doubt that Wagner's conception of his music was profound and his execution of it, despite the imperfections, of decisive and historic importance. If it is Wagner conducting his own works, then the assessment cannot be the same. The evidence above does not show that he was consistently satisfactory, either to himself or to others. Success often eluded him, although success by itself is not a good measure of greatness, especially in the performance of Wagner's music in its day. Wagner was a reluctant conductor and hated presenting excerpts from his own works for a variety of reasons – inadequate resources at his disposal, fragments out of context, distractions from composing, ill health, etc – but one possibility is that his dissatisfaction was partly a recognition of his own abilities as a conductor. He was on sure ground with Beethoven, and he knew it, but with his own works he was less sure. He had vision, but he could not always communicate it to his orchestral players. Elliott Galkin concluded in his survey of conducting that generally "Wagner, like Beethoven, never achieved mastery in use of the baton. Nor, in spite of his extensive career, did he have sophisticated knowledge about pragmatic aspects of instrumental performance or rehearsal routine as did Mendelssohn and Berlioz; thus he depended greatly upon his concert-masters… [He] was more concerned with the emotional and aesthetic aspects of interpretation than with technical details of execution."[158] Ernestine Schumann-Heink, famous for her Waltraute at Bayreuth between 1896 and 1914, may have been reflecting a general view around Bayreuth at the time when she wrote in her memoirs: "[Wagner] was not a great conductor. He could not interpret his own work as an orchestra leader, strange as that may seem.

[154] *ibid*, vol. 1, pp. 420, 422

[155] Newman, *Life of Wagner*, vol. 4, p. 470, written not without a little irony; his views on Wagner's limitations as a theatre conductor are noted above.

[156] Eduard Hanslick, *Neue Freie Presse*, 14 May 1872, p. 2, in *Vienna's golden years of music: 1850-1900*, (trans. and ed.) Henry Pleasants (London: Gollancz, 1951), p. 105

[157] Seidl, "On Conducting," in *The Music of the Modern World*, vol. 1, p. 214; Seidl also wrote of Wagner in rehearsal generally: "at first things went topsy turvy at rehearsals, because of the impatience of the master, who wanted everything to be good at once; the strange, illustrative movements of his long baton startled and puzzled the musicians until they learned that the musical bars were not dominant, but the phrase, the melody, or the expression." *idem*

[158] Elliott W. Galkin, *A history of orchestral conducting: in theory and practice* (New York: Pendragon Press, 1988), p. 581

It was not his forte."[159] Wagner made an illuminating remark when reflecting on his triumphant performance of Beethoven's *Ninth* in Dresden on Palm Sunday in 1846: after it he had "the gratifying feeling that I had the capacity and power to accomplish just about whatever I wished if I seriously devoted myself to it. This led me to ponder why it was that I had not yet been able to perform my own compositions with equal success. ...every time my *Tannhäuser* went on the boards in Dresden, it taught me that the secret of its success was yet to be found...."[160] As a composer with limitations as a performing musician,[161] Wagner is in very good company. Just as there are great conductors whose talents as composers have eluded them, so too are there great composers whose talents with the baton have failed to do their own music full justice. For Wagner, his music in his own hands was a vision unfulfilled.

What Wagner wanted from his orchestra

For some who listen to Wagner, the orchestra is the key to everything about his music. In the *Ring* in particular, some of the most magnificent passages are orchestral, either purely orchestral or predominantly orchestral: for example, the transitional scenes in the *Rheingold*, the stormy opening of act one of the *Walküre*, the forest murmurs in *Siegfried*, and the Funeral Music in *Götterdämmerung*. Grieg's view from the first Bayreuth Festival was that *everything* was in the orchestra: "I think that the voice parts play only a secondary part in the *Ring* – the orchestra is all – and of primary importance."[162] Tchaikovsky was not an unqualified Wagnerian – he considered *Lohengrin* the best of Wagner's works – but he made some astute observations about his music. When he saw the *Walküre* in Vienna in December 1877, it confirmed his earlier judgment that "Wagner was really a symphonist by nature."[163] When he saw *Tristan* in Berlin in January 1883, he observed that "Wagner has transferred the centre of gravity from the stage to the orchestra."[164] Ernest Newman observed: "It is quite

[159] Mary Lawton, *Schumann-Heink, the last of the Titans* (New York: Macmillan, 1929), p. 175. She adored Cosima: "She was the greatest stage manager I ever knew... In my opinion, Wagner himself could never have done what Cosima did." pp. 179, 182, also p. 314

[160] Wagner, *My Life*, p. 333

[161] In other practical respects, Wagner was a flawed, though always ardent, musician. He took some violin lessons in his youth, but soon gave the instrument up. He could barely play the piano. He wrote in his *Autobiographical Sketch* (1843), when he had another 40 years to live: "In my whole life I have never learnt to play the piano properly": in Ellis, *Wagner's Prose Works*, vol. 1, p. 4. His friend August Roeckel wrote to Ferdinand Praeger in March 1843: "It seems strange, but his playing is ludicrously defective": quoted in Praeger, *Wagner as I knew him* (London: Longmans, 1892, p. 121). An admirer Judith Gautier (Mrs Mendes) recalled him singing and accompanying himself in *Siegfried* (in 1869): "He declared that, not being in any sense a pianist, this music of the future was too difficult for him." He kept playing. On another occasion they were playing an arrangement for four hands of the *Huldigungsmarsch*. "Let us play," said Wagner. "But I warn you I play very badly." On the third page he hesitated, then stopped, declaring the part too difficult: Gautier, *Wagner at home*, (trans.) Effie Dunreith Massie (London: Mills & Boon, 1910), pp.31, 56. As a singer, Wagner himself described his voice, when singing excerpts from *Tannhäuser* and *Tristan* with Bülow at the piano in Paris, as "the decomposed voice of a composer," enough to frighten any mastersinger except those of Nuremberg: Edmond Michotte, *Wagner's visit to Rossini*, trans. Herbert Weinstock (Chicago University Press, 1968), p. 15. His friend Ferdinand Praeger told Wagner his singing was "just like the barking of a big Newfoundland dog," yet added that "though his 'singing' was but howling, he sang with his whole heart": in Praeger, *Wagner as I knew him*, p. 237.

[162] report dated 13 August 1876 to the *Bergenposten* quoted in Hartford, *Bayreuth: The Early Years*, p. 66

[163] David Brown, *Tchaikovsky: a biographical and critical study*, 4 vols. (London: Gollancz, 1978), vol. 2, p. 247

[164] *ibid*, vol. 3, p. 210

clear, in many places, that the main thing Wagner had his eye upon was the orchestral tissue – the multiform and polychromatic play of motives telling their own story to the ear – and that the voice part has been made to fit in with this the best way it could, sometimes with success, sometimes not."[165] He considered in the case of the *Ring* and many parts of *Tristan* that the original conception was orchestral.[166]

Wagner may have begged to differ – or he may not. He was obviously aware of the power of his orchestral music, hence his desire to keep it down in the theatre lest it interfere with the sung drama. And he certainly recognized that his greatest art was the art of transition – from one extreme of temper to another, from one mood to another, from one situation to another – by means of a seamless musical tissue.[167] Whether it be a sustained powerful passage like the descent into Nibelheim in the *Rheingold* or a mere few bars, like the descent into hell before Amfortas' lament (*Wehvolles Erbe*) in *Parsifal*, his transitional music is supremely beautiful. What mattered most to Wagner, so he proclaimed, was what was happening on stage: the drama. Yet when Wagner is at his most inspired, it is the orchestra that is pre-eminent. In *Tristan*, the composer exclaimed, "You should hear nothing but the orchestra!"[168] Bruno Walter observed that the musician in Wagner often defied the dramatist: "in those scenes that are loaded with emotion or filled with poetry, music takes the lead to such an extent that the climaxes of opera resemble a mighty torrent of music on which float dramatic elements, rather than a drama that is being given expressive power by music."[169] A critic who heard Wagner conduct a concert of his own music in Vienna wrote: "You can never really call it 'accompaniment' with Wagner. The human singing voice is never the predominant focus. It fuses with the instrumental masses into an inseparable whole.... At times, for example in the scene between Siegfried and Brünnhilde, their singing seems to be a mere necessary evil in all the simultaneous richness of the orchestra.... [and in Brünnhilde's Immolation scene], sound became words, and words became sounds."[170] Certain passages of Wagner are so glorious that, in a performance of excerpts, conductors jettison the singers and give all to the orchestra.

Nevertheless, Wagner professed his keenness to keep the orchestra in its place, producing a subdued tone sympathetically subordinated to the singers so that every word of the drama, even of the Valkyries, might be heard. If the orchestra manages to follow and support the vocal part exactly, it will seem as if it almost disappears. "The sweet sign of the conductor's having completely solved his task in this respect would be the ultimate experience, at the production" he wrote in *The Performing of Tannhäuser* (1852), "that his active lead is scarcely noticeable."[171] In *Opera and Drama* (1851), he wrote of the need for the orchestra to adapt itself "*with the utmost closeness*" to the dramatic motive, in fact to guide our attention "*away from itself*, as a *means of expression*, and direct it to the *subject expressed*"; in a manner of speaking, it must put

[165] Newman, *Wagner* (London: John Lane, 1906), p. 143

[166] *ibid*, p. 151; he added: "This, indeed, is the one serious flaw in all the work of Wagner's prime."

[167] letter (Paris, 29 October 1859) to Mathilde Wesendonck in Wagner, *Letters to Wesendonck*, pp. 184–185

[168] letter to Nietzsche dated 25 June 1872, quoted in Joachim Köhler, *Richard Wagner: the last of the titans*, trans. Stewart Spencer (New Haven and London: Yale University Press, 2004), p. 538

[169] Bruno Walter, *Of music and music-making* (trans.) Paul Hamburger (London: Faber and Faber, 1961), pp. 149, 157

[170] *Wiener Abendpost (Beilage zur Wiener Zeitung)*, 2 March 1875, p. 6

[171] Ellis, *Wagner's Prose Works*, vol. 3, p. 175

Fig. 1.16. Wagner conducting in Vienna, 14 March 1875.
Silhouette by Otto Böhler

itself in the position "of *not being heard at all*" except as being one with the drama.[172] This extraordinary effect may have been precisely achieved at the first performances of *Tristan*, during act three. Wagner recalled: "the orchestra was wholly effaced by the singer, or – to put it more correctly – seemed part and parcel of its utterance."[173] At Bayreuth Wagner was able to heighten the illusion by making the orchestra and its conductor physically invisible, a device he had long planned in order to intensify its artistic effect.[174]

172 Ellis, *Wagner's Prose Works*, vol. 2, p. 371; emphasis in the original

173 *My recollections of Ludwig Schnorr of Carolsfeld* (1863), in Ellis, *Wagner's Prose Works*, vol. 4, p. 235

174 "I… should lay especial stress on the invisibility of the orchestra…" etc.: *Preface to the "Ring" Poem* (1863), in Ellis, *Wagner's Prose Works*, vol. 3, p. 276

Still, what *is* Wagner's orchestra, this instrument which Wagner sought to keep down and be for ever subordinate to the action? Nothing less than "the greatest artistic achievement of our age," he wrote, the "archetypal element" that embraces "all the action's motives in its mother-womb."[175] We recall Wagner's comments in rehearsal of the *Ring*, as given by Porges, of the orchestra as an ocean ("the great sea of Feeling itself"[176]), rocking but never swamping, the singer. In a rehearsal of Parsifal, Porges recorded, he said "the orchestra must be like an invisible soul."[177] In *Opera and Drama* (1851), where Wagner is in full poetic flight, the orchestra, "the conqueror of the endless floods of Harmony," is described "no longer as the ocean, but as a limpid mountain lake, lit by the sun-rays to its very bottom... [A] boat... is the verse-melody of the Dramatic Singer... borne upon the sounding surges of the Orchestra."[178] Without the orchestra, the singer is without life, of no use at all. It is "the Un-speakable" that the orchestra can express with greatest definition. "Just as Gesture reveals to the eye a thing which she alone can utter, so the Orchestra conveys to the ear a something exactly answering to that revelation....That which Poetry could not speak out... is imparted to the ear by precisely the language of the Orchestra."[179] And these are forebodings and remembrances – things that are fated to happen, and things that happened deep in the past. Henry Finck expressed the idea in simpler but still suggestive prose: "In Wagner's operas the function of the Greek chorus of commenting on the action is assigned to the orchestra, which, through the use of Leading Motives, has received the faculty of definite speech."[180]

What Wagner wanted from his conductors

So how were conductors to handle this Unspeakable, this ocean of sound? The obvious place to look, apart from the scores which we shall consider below, is Wagner's tract *On Conducting* (1869). An alternative title for this essay might have been *Against Conductors*, for he railed against the mere time-beaters, against those appointed without merit, against those who tolerated virtuosi and did not want reform of their orchestras, against those who lacked energy and force of character, against those who did not understand dramatic art, etc. For our present purpose it is important to note that most of Wagner's discussion was about the conducting of concerts;[181] he devoted only a few pages to the conducting of opera. No sooner had he begun on the latter than he postponed discussion of opera conductors to another day. "To properly denote their shameful dealings in this sphere, I should have to resort to a positive demonstration of the good and important work that could be done, and that might lead too far from the goal I have set before me; so I will defer that demonstration to

[175] *Prologue to a reading of the "Götterdämmerung" before a select audience in Berlin* (March 1873), in Ellis, *Wagner's Prose Works*, vol. 5, p. 306

[176] *The Art-Work of the Future* (1849), in Ellis, *Wagner's Prose Works*, vol. 1, p. 190

[177] Rüdiger Porges (ed.), *"Das Orchester muss wie die unsichtbare Seele sein." Richard Wagners Bemerkungen zum Parsifal aufgezeichnet während der Proben und Aufführungen 1882 von Heinrich Porges* (Berlin: Deutsche Richard-Wagner-Gesellschaft, 2002), p. 29

[178] in Ellis, *Wagner's Prose Works*, vol. 2, p. 314

[179] *ibid*, pp. 317, 319, 322; the orchestra must "plainly manifest to Feeling the Unspeakable of the Dramatic Situation": *ibid*, p. 370

[180] Finck, *Wagner and his Works*, vol. 1, p. 266

[181] *On Conducting* (1869), in Ellis, *Wagner's Prose Works*, vol. 4, pp. 299-350

another time."[182] He never resumed. Care needs to be taken therefore in inferring anything about the performance of his own works from his comments about concert conducting. He does include in his discussion of instrumental music, however, complaints about the tempo given in some performances of his preludes to *Tannhäuser*, *Lohengrin*, and the *Meistersinger*, and gives a detailed analysis of part of this last. He dispensed with metronome markings after his earliest operas, he says, and contented himself "with quite general indications for even the principal time measure, and devot[ed] all my forethought to its modifications, since our conductors know as good as nothing of the latter."[183] Here lies the key to what he has to say about his own works in this essay. "I need speak of nothing save the Tempo, which, contrary to all sense, is either rushed… or dragged… or rushed and dragged alike – but never treated with that intelligent Modification upon which I must reckon no less determinedly than on the playing of the proper notes…"[184]

The heart of Wagner's complaint seems not to be technical, or rather, cannot be resolved by attention to mere technical details. In his analysis of the prelude to the *Meistersinger*, for example, he wrote: "I believed I could safely leave the pace to the *conductor's common sense*, since the mere execution of such passages will of itself put more fire into the tempo if only one *yields to the natural feeling* of the bandsmen."[185] (my emphasis) In the case of the conductors he is unhappy about, those with an accurate ear, a quick eye, and who can read and play from the notes, he doubts whether they are "*true* musicians, as they betray not a spark of *musical feeling*."[186] This elusive quality, which radiates from the greatest conductors, requires among many other things temperament and self-confidence. Wagner said of singers: "even with the best-trained voice, singing alone is not enough for drama; it must be combined with temperament and a forceful inner drive."[187] Technique of itself is not enough. He wrote of a performance of Spohr's *Jessonda* at Leipzig that its conductor had shown "marked intelligence and reverential love: merely his Tempo was spoilt here and there by a touch of timidity, to be explained, again, by that lack of self-confidence which is innate in all German musicians. None trusts himself to say straight out: '*So is it.*'"[188] To Emil Heckel he wrote: "take the matter *by its spirit*: a thoroughly initiated, moreover a capable, energetic, and – above all – a *convinced* conductor, such a one is pledge to me of everything."[189] (my emphases)

Earlier in his essay Wagner makes the oft-quoted comment that "*a correct conception of the melos alone can give the proper tempo*"[190] (his emphasis), but he said this in a discussion of classical instrumental music. In his own works, he has claimed that melody is endless and everywhere, in every detail, revealing itself not only "to the connoisseur, but also to the most naïve layman" (though "hum it he cannot").[191]

182 *ibid*, p. 351; alternatively, Dover, p. 88 183 *ibid*, p. 305; Dover, p. 21 184 *ibid*, pp. 354; Dover, pp. 92

185 *ibid*, pp. 356-357; Dover, p. 96

186 *ibid*, p. 361; Dover, p. 102

187 Wagner (September 1875) as summarized by Hey in *Richard Wagner als Vortragsmeister*, p. 211

188 *Spohr's "Jesonda" at Leipzig* (1874), in Ellis, *Wagner's Prose Works*, vol. 6, p. 11

189 letter (Bayreuth, 28 April 1879) in Wagner, *Letters to Heckel*, p. 116 190 *ibid*, p. 303

191 *Music of the Future* (1860), in Ellis, *Wagner's Prose Works*, vol. 3, p. 338-340; though melody is important to Wagner, he is not clear when explaining what it means. For example, in *Opera and Drama* (1851) he describes it as "the most perfect expression of the inner being of Music," a simple proposition which he later expands: "Melody is the redemption of the poet's endlessly conditioned thought into a deep-felt

Melody does not give the proper tempo in his operas: *the drama* does. Wagner was never tired of saying that an insight into the drama gives the right tempo.[192]

My advice to friendly-disposed conductors of opera therefore might be summed up as follows: *If you are otherwise good musicians, in Opera pay heed to nothing but what is happening on the stage, be it the monologue of a singer or a general action; let it be your prime endeavour that this scene, so infinitely intensified and spiritualised by association with its music, shall acquire the "utmost distinctness": if you bring the distinctness about, rest assured that you at like time have found the proper tempo and correct expression for the orchestra.*[193] (the emphasis is Wagner's)

Approach the opera as *drama*, and the *music* will truly sound forth. Complete mastery by the orchestra of the music's technical difficulties is but the first duty of a conductor. "Once he has succeeded in this, the conductor has from then on to deal exclusively with the performers on stage, taking his instructions solely from what happens on stage, in whose spirit and movement the orchestra must accompany the drama."[194] A very good leader in Leipzig, Wagner observed, was capable of conducting and keeping an orchestra together, but was "entirely unable to penetrate a dramatic work which demands something far more than a good orchestra leader."[195]

To get the most out of the music, then, the conductor must attend to the drama and use musical imagination. Wagner conceived of his greatest music in dramatic terms. One might even say that if there was no dramatic element arising from his own intensely felt experience, then there was no good music.[196] Let us take the example of Wagner's non-operatic works. With one exception, they are not by Wagnerian standards inspired compositions, even the brash and showy overtures.[197] One can be forgiven for thinking that the composer of *Siegfried's Funeral Music* might have had something interesting to say in the *Weber Funeral Music* (1844), but not so: good mood music it may have been for a street procession for the re-interment of Weber's remains, but no more.[198] One might also have expected Wagner to have been inspired by gratitude in his homage march to King Ludwig, the *Huldigungsmarsch* (1864), but it is a surprisingly subdued work with only one good melody.[199]

consciousness of emotion's highest freedom: it is the willed and achieved Unwilful, the conscious and proclaimed Unconscious, the vindicated Necessity of an endless reaching Content, condensed from its farthest branchings into an utmost definite utterance of Feeling." *ibid*, vol. 2, pp. 104, 281

192 Wagner, *Letters to Heckel*, p. 140 (a reminiscence of Heckel); Ludwig Schemann remembered Wagner saying: "My baton will become the sceptre of the future. It will teach the tides which way to flow. In the end, tempo is everything. Rhythm, harmony, and beauty will then simply take care of themselves": *Hans von Bülow im Lichte der Wahrheit* (Regensburg: Gustav Bosse, 1935), p. 35

193 *The German Opera-stage of To-day* (1871), in Ellis, *Wagner's Prose Works*, vol. 5, p. 283

194 letter dated 6 October 1851 to Christian Stocks, Wagner, *Selected Letters*, p. 230

195 letter dated 3 September 1859 to Joseph Tichatschek about possible conductors for *Lohengrin* in Dresden (he was referring to Rietz), in Burk, *The Burrell Collection*, p. 159

196 One is reminded of Nietzsche's statement: "Wagner is one who has suffered deeply – that is his *distinction* above other musicians. I admire Wagner whenever he puts himself into music": *Gay Science*, p. 87; in *The Portable Nietzsche*, (ed. & trans.) Walter Kaufmann, as "Nietzsche contra Wagner" (Penguin Books, 1976), p. 664.

197 In addition to the ones mentioned above there is the *Polonia Overture* (1836), the *Rule Britannia Overture* (1837), and the once-popular *Kaisermarsch* (1871).

198 Wagner had been assured by witnesses who watched the event that "the impression of solemnity had been unspeakably sublime": *Weber's Re-interment (Report)* (1844), in Ellis, *Wagner's Prose Works*, vol 7, p. 232.

199 It receives its most sonorous and spacious rendering by the Musique des Gardiens de la Paix conducted by Désiré Dondeyne (Westminster WST-17014). The French excel here over all others, an irony Wagner

Fig. 1.17. Wagner conducting in Vienna, 1875.
Silhouette by Otto Böhler

The *Siegfried Idyll* (1870) draws on themes from *Siegfried* and a German cradle song and was inspired by Wagner's happy domestic situation, but it is perhaps limited by that, charming as it is. The *Grosser Festmarsch* (1876) written for the American centennial was simply a failure.[200] The one exception is the *Faust Overture* (1839-1840, revised 1855), the earliest manifestation of Wagner's genius. Tchaikovsky considered it "one of the most outstanding achievements of German symphonic music. I do not know a single lyrical artistic creation in which the tortures of the human spirit, doubting its own aims, hopes and beliefs, are expressed with such irresistible pathos."[201]

may have appreciated: "We Germans may pride ourselves on having the truest *understanding* of the works of Mozart and Beethoven, but the best *performances* of them are given by the French," he wrote from Paris to the Dresden *Abendzeitung* (6 April 1841): in Robert Jacobs and Geoffrey Skelton (ed. and trans.), *Wagner writes from Paris …* (New York: John Day, 1973), p. 126; the 1927 recording by Siegfried Wagner only goes to prove the point.

[200] Newman, *Wagner*, p. 175

[201] quoted in Brown, *Tchaikovsky*, vol. 1, p. 281

Wagner has written of the story that inspired the music,[202] but it is not necessary to know it to understand the music.This may be a heresy to some, but the fact is that a good conductor, with the "musical feeling" Wagner prized, does not need to know the story to give a convincing performance.[203] The essential point is: it was conceived of dramatically, and so it must be played.

Wagner's attitude to scores

So what is the good conductor to do with a score of Wagner's? In his early works in particular his scores are replete with directions. As if to illustrate the abundance, Henry Finck opened a page at random of Bülow's vocal score of *Tristan* (p. 188) and in seventeen bars found twenty-two changes in tempo and expression. "All these changes are on one page, requiring about half a minute in the performance!"[204] Nevertheless the scores may not always be the best guide to what must be done. On one occasion Wagner confesses that experience has shown him he was mistaken in a tempo marking in the *Holländer.*[205] During rehearsals for the *Ring* in Berlin under Anton Seidl in 1881, he said to the orchestra:"I *beg* of you not to take my *fortissimo* too seriously! Where you see *ff*, make an *fp* of it, and for *piano*, play *pianissimo*. Remember how many of you there are down there, against the one poor single human throat up here alone on the stage."[206] A literal reading of the score will not be enough. Wagner realised that in spite of "the most minute notation of the nuances of phrasing," the more talented conductor often has to explain to his orchestra the more important and "delicate shadings of expression; ...these communications, as a rule, are better understood and heeded, than the written signs."[207] And if these communications are to come from the "*true* musician," the conductor with "*musical feeling*," they are not likely to be written down.

Wagner's attitude to scores is well illustrated by the accounts he gave of his conducting of Beethoven's *Ninth Symphony* and Bach's motet *Singet dem Herren ein neues Lied* (BWV 225). It is well known that Wagner's revival of the *Ninth* in Dresden on Palm Sunday 1846 was one of his greatest contributions to the art of symphonic interpretation, one that had a decisive impact on the history of conducting, and one that may fairly be compared with Mendelssohn's revival of Bach's *St Matthew Passion* in 1829. The *Ninth* had been performed in recent years in Dresden, but ineffectually if not disastrously. Wagner's performance was a true revival, breathing life into a masterpiece that others thought comatose if not dead. Let us look at one aspect of his conducting: his handling of the final choral movement. He described his treatment of two parts of it. He wrote in *My Life* that he was not prevented by

[202] for example, in a letter (27 November 1852) to Theodor Uhlig: in *Letters to his Dresden Friends*, p. 300

[203] Newman made the point when he wrote: "The best tribute to the magic of Wagner's works is that they have survived the commentaries on them by Wagner and his friends. It is the music of *Lohengrin* that has kept it alive, and that will still keep it alive when the world has almost forgotten that its composer ever wrote prose": Newman, *Wagner* (1906), pp. 83-84.

[204] Finck, *Wagner and His Works*, vol. 2, p. 159

[205] *Remarks on Performing the Opera: "The Flying Dutchman"* (1852-53), in Ellis, *Wagner's Prose Works*, vol. 3, p. 215

[206] Neumann, *Personal Recollections*, p. 147

[207] *Proposal for a Music School for Munich* (1865), in Ellis, *Wagner's Prose Works*, vol. 3, p. 235

any "literalistic piety" from giving effect to what he perceived Beethoven's intended effect: "I treated the fugato ["in 6/8 time following the choral passage *Froh wie seine Sonnen fliegen* in that part of the finale marked alla marcia"] as literally a serious yet exuberant combat and took it in an *extremely fiery tempo* and with the greatest tension and force."[208] (my emphasis) In rehearsal with his singers,

> I tried in my own peculiar way to inspire them for their task; I succeeded in proving to the basses, for example, that the famous passage *Seid umschlungen, Millionen*, and especially the *Brüder, überm Sternenzelt muss ein lieber Vater wohnen*, could not possibly be sung in a normal way but had to be, as it were, proclaimed in highest ecstasy. I was so transported myself at this point that I think I really got everyone into quite a state, and I didn't stop until my own voice, which I had previously been able to hear through all the others, was no longer audible, and I could feel myself drowning in a warm sea of sound.[209]

(There is a recollection of this rehearsal by Gustav Adolph Kietz confirming Wagner's account, although it is written in terms so close to Wagner's own that one wonders whether Kietz had access to *Mein Leben* to refresh his memory.[210]) Another recollection, by Wilhelm Tappert, is of Wagner rehearsing the *Ninth* in Bayreuth on the occasion of the laying of the foundation stone in 1872: "The difficult *presto-intraden* of the last movement caused the master and his men much trouble. Wagner expressed his desire that all rhythm and accents should disappear here; a tone-flood should break in, sudden, wild irrepressible! It was difficult to carry out this idea, but after many attempts the interesting problem was solved. Then Betz got up and sang...."[211] Wagner was so carried away that "he gesticulated, stamped, and towards the close of the symphony he became so excited that his baton broke in two."[212]

In the case of Bach's motet *Singet dem Herren ein neues Lied* Wagner recalled with pride conducting a theatre-choir which had been schooled by Wilhelm Fischer, the chorus master in Dresden. It had been trained "to such a high pitch that, relying on the uncommonly correct and certain phrasing of the singers, I felt induced to take the first *allegro* – [formerly] interpreted as the most cautious *moderato*, for reasons of its hair-bristling difficulty – in its true *fiery tempo*, notoriously frightening all our critics

[208] Wagner, *My Life*, p. 331

[209] *ibid*, p. 332. Toscanini's comments in a rehearsal of the *Ninth* are evocative of Wagner: "I don't want to hear the notes any more, there must be no more notes. Only spirit here! ... Abandon yourselves to your hearts; it's not enough to interpret the signs you have on the paper in the front of your eyes. Look, I'm shuddering here. You must shudder too...": from a 1922 rehearsal according to Renato Simoni, quoted in Harvey Sachs, *Toscanini* (Philadelphia: Lippincott, 1978), p. 153.

[210] Spencer, *Wagner Remembered*, p. 51; there is confirmation of Wagner's account of the rehearsal of the cellos and basses by Marie Schmole (May 1895); she said they produced a hitherto unheard "evenness and tone volume giving the effect of human voices; the theme itself murmured like an ideal inspiration, surging and fading until at last it joined the full orchestra with violins and violas. Then all of them forgot to continue rehearsing and burst out into an enthusiastic cheer....," in Burk, *The Burrell Collection*, p. 129. At the performance itself, the *Neue Zeitschrift für Musik* (17 May 1846) noted "the basses were not completely synchronous at one stage during their recitative": quoted in Heinel, *Richard Wagner als Dirigent*, p. 84

[211] Wilhelm Tappert, *Musikalisches Wochenblatt*, nos. 23-26, 1872, quoted in Finck, *Wagner and his Works*, vol. 2, p. 267; Tappert also noted that Wagner made a few alterations to Beethoven's score to eliminate "certain minor imperfections in Beethoven's orchestration, which interrupted the melodic continuity and distinctness."

[212] *ibid*, p. 268

out of their lives."[213] (my emphasis). In both these cases I wonder whether we have ever heard them played at the *extremely fiery tempo* or the *fiery tempo* Wagner took them. Wagner was using those expressions against the practice of his day, but still, listening to what might be approximate examples from the many modern performances on record, I doubt it.[214] Maybe the critics had a point in being astonished at Wagner.[215] Whatever the case, these examples illustrate not only how freely Wagner conducted[216] but also how extreme, even fanatical, he was at seeking to get behind and beyond the score to what he perceived as the essence of the music.

The art of the impossible

Wagner believed it was impossible to realise adequate performances of his own works. He wrote a particularly fraught letter to his friend Ernst Kietz in 1852 after he had completed a guide to the performance of *Tannhäuser* for a forthcoming performance in Berlin: "*I cannot produce a real work of art with only artistic means at my disposal.* It would not help matters at all, if, for example, I were now in Berlin myself: the torture of the incompleteness and inadequacy of the practical experiment would be at least as great as the torture of abstaining from all experiments. I'm bound to go to pieces in this present-day world of ours."[217] (my emphasis) The agony of this self-knowledge is that *no matter what* the artistic means, his vision of his work *cannot* be realised: the score, the explanatory note, the staging, the singers, the conductor, even the composer's presence, can never in his mind do justice to the conception. A similar example of the impossible demands Wagner imposed – on himself no less than on his artists – is in a letter to Heinrich Esser in Vienna in 1859 about *Lohengrin* and *Tannhäuser*. "Much depends on the conductor, under certain circumstances everything," he wrote. "The singers are not to be allowed entire freedom in recitative, but all passages, even those without metrical accompaniment, must first be sung strictly in time, in order to *approximate exactly* my rhythmical declamation and accentuation. Only then, after having mastered them, may they be allowed to modulate with a certain dramatic liberty."[218] (my emphasis) On close analysis this instruction,

[213] *Homage to Ludwig Spohr and Wilhelm Fischer* (1860), Ellis, *Wagner's Prose Works*, vol. 3, p. 149

[214] A Beethoven *Ninth* conducted by Wilhelm Furtwängler on 19 April 1942 (the eve of Hitler's birthday; a recording first released in 2004: Archipel ARPCD 0270) has some moments of delirious exaltation, including in the choral sections, but not in the passages singled out by Wagner; the wild abandonment of Furtwängler's closing bars may be closer to Wagner's spirit, but they are orchestral. In the Bach motet Reinhard Kammler's conducting of the Kammerchor der Augsburger Domsingknaben in 1987 (Deutsche Harmonia Mundi DHM 77436-2) comes close to the spirit of Wagner's conducting, although I would not describe it as exactly fiery.

[215] The *Neue Zeitschrift für Musik* (17 May 1846) wrote of Beethoven's *Ninth* that "the tempo of the scherzo was almost too fiery, [yet] the finale's march would have benefited from somewhat faster movement"; it found the Bach *Motet* "much too fast, so that everything got jumbled up and you had to fear derailment at any time" (3 October 1848): quoted in Heinel, *Richard Wagner als Dirigent*, pp. 84 and 93.

[216] Berlioz heard Wagner's last London concert in 1855 and commented how Wagner "conducts in the free style, as Klindworth plays the piano": Newman, *Life of Wagner*, vol. 2, p. 440; Toscanini also noted that Wagner conducted Mozart's *Jupiter* Symphony "*a piacere*" (with freedom) in Ellis's account of the same London concerts, although he could not make out from the description what Wagner was actually doing, or where in the music he was doing it: B. H. Haggin, *Conversations with Toscanini* (New York: Doubleday, 1959), pp. 39-40.

[217] letter from Zurich dated 7 September 1852, in Burk, *The Burrell Collection*, p. 192

[218] letter from Paris dated 27 September 1859, *ibid*, p. 337

especially the phrase highlighted, hardly bears scrutiny. One knows what Wagner means – the utter devotion of the artists to his work; only then may they rise up and be, in effect, synapses of his artistic imagination – but reducing what he means to writing is a difficult and dangerous affair. For Wagner could not wholly convey what he meant or what he wanted, be it in prose or musical notation.

Consider how he approached the art of instrumentation. Anton Seidl described how first Wagner made "a complete sketch of the entire opera.... Next he made the orchestration – divided the music for several instruments. Sometimes he discovered that he had tones for which there was no instrument, and these he had to provide."[219] Music was wholly born in the fragrance of his imagination. "He rarely went to the piano while composing," Seidl added. The suggestive nature of his orchestration was described by Richard Strauss as an "al-fresco treatment of the orchestra" as distinct from the classical style of instrumentation. "The most obvious example of the fresco style is the treatment of the violins in the Magic Fire Music in the third act of *Walküre*. Executed by 16 to 32 violinists, this passage achieves a wonderful, exciting effect. A better musical description of the seething flames flickering in a thousand tints cannot be imagined."[220] No less an authority than the violinist Carl Flesch has proclaimed that these passages in the Magic Fire Music are "strictly speaking, unplayable."[221] Similarly the concertmaster of the Vienna Philharmonic, Willi Boskovsky, commented to Birgit Nilsson after a performance of *Götterdämmerung* that "it really *was* impossible to play all the notes that Wagner had set down."[222] Karl Goldmark was present at a concert rehearsal of the *Tannhäuser* overture in Vienna at which Wagner demanded the horns play with more *legato*. "After trying two or three times in vain, the first horn said: 'I pray, Master, this part cannot be played *legato* on the horn!' Wagner responded: 'Ah yes, my dear man, but what else are we artists for?' And the part was played *legato*."[223] Strauss relates a statement of Wagner's to the harpist during the first rehearsal of the end of *Rheingold* in Munich. When the harpist declared his part to be "absolutely unplayable," Wagner said to the artist, "You cannot expect me to be able to play the harp; you see what effects I want to achieve; now arrange your part as you like."[224] Strauss called this a "funny utterance," but I have no doubt Wagner was deadly serious. He wanted poetic effects; he did not want troubles of detail to impede his path. Richter has confirmed as much. George Bernard Shaw reported in 1885: "Herr Richter let slip the secret that the scores of Wagner were not to be taken too literally. 'How,' exclaimed the average violinist in anger and despair, 'is a man to be expected to play this reiterated motive, or this complicated figuration, in demisemiquavers at the rate of sixteen in a second? What can he do but go swishing up and down as best he can?' 'What indeed?' replied Herr Richter encouragingly. 'That is precisely what is intended by the composer.'"[225]

[219] F. B. Stanford, "With Seidl at Brighton," undated newspaper cutting (ca. August 1896) in the *Seidl Society Scrapbook (April 1896 – January 1897)*, pp. 55-57, at p. 56, Brooklyn Historical Society

[220] Berlioz, Hector, *Treatise on instrumentation*, enlarged and revised by Richard Strauss, including Berlioz' essay on conducting, translated by Theodore Front, rev. ed. (Kalmus, 1948), p. 43

[221] Carl Flesch, *The memoirs of Carl Flesch*, (trans. and ed.) Hans Keller (London: Rockliff, 1957), p. 75

[222] Birgit Nilsson, *La Nilsson: My Life In Opera* (Boston: Northeastern University Press, 2007), p. 68

[223] Karl Goldmark, *Erinnerungen aus meinem Leben* (Vienna: Rikola, 1922), p. 80

[224] Strauss in Berlioz, *Treatise on instrumentation*, p. 144

[225] *Dramatic Review*, 8 February 1885, quoted by Fifield in *True Artist*, p. 127

What Wagner could not do and what he could not explain falls ultimately to his artists. He wrote the music; he could not do everything. Much as he could explain and demonstrate, the heart of his advice often came down to musical common sense: take the score with confidence, find the spirit of the drama, play with conviction, play with energy, play with feeling, play with freedom, and so on. We have seen what Wagner could do. We have read to what he has had to say. Now we will turn to those who showed how it could be done: his great conductors.

Part II

Wagner's pupils

2

Hans von Bülow – His Master's Ideal

Hans von Bülow was the most astute of the early champions of Wagner. His awakening came early during a performance of *Rienzi* (1842), but the decisive moment was when he heard Franz Liszt conduct the premiere of *Lohengrin* in Weimar (1850). This turned him from the law to music. He became a Wagnerian, and sought out Wagner. As a brilliant young pianist, he also went to Liszt, whose daughter, Cosima, became his first wife and, famously, Wagner's second wife. He conducted the premieres of *Tristan und Isolde* (1864) and the *Meistersinger* (1868) in Munich, and then Cosima left him for the composer, and Bülow broke with Wagner. He never conducted Wagner's later works and showed some antipathy towards them. He is most remembered for his phenomenal achievements as a pianist. Yet through his writings, piano transcriptions, and conducting, Bülow promoted the music of Wagner, and weathered the storms of anti-Wagnerianism, with a determination, discipline and supreme artistry which is astonishing considering his personal circumstances. To the end he remained a steadfast champion of Wagner's ideals for the music drama, and served as a shining example to many younger conductors.

Early impressions and apprenticeship in Zurich

Born in Wagner's own town of Dresden in 1830, Bülow showed musical talent early on the piano, and began composing.[1] As a boy of twelve, he was overwhelmed at the first performance of *Rienzi* which, as we have seen, even stunned Wagner by its success (it was conducted by Reissiger). Many years later Bülow recalled: "It was a revelation to me; it filled my whole soul with enthusiasm and was the turning-point of my life."[2] Later told his daughter Daniella how he sat in the theatre, as she related, "in a state of feverish excitement; this work, this music opened up to him a whole new world. Then something happened to him, for the first and only time in his life. Dazed by sounds and emotions never yet experienced, for one whole act (the third?) he lost all sense of hearing, unable to grasp a note until the curtain fell and woke him

[1] see generally Wolf-Dieter Gewande, *Hans von Bülow: eine biographisch-dokumentarische Würdigung aus Anlass seines 175. Geburtstages* (Lilienthal: Eres, 2004); Alan Walker, *Hans von Bülow: A Life and Times* (Oxford University Press, 2010)

[2] "Von Bülow Interviewed," *Chicago Times*, 6 February 1876, p. 4

from his trance." He recognised the figure of Wagner bowing on stage: "gulping down his sobs, his little heart had but one wish, 'to throw himself at this man's feet.'"[3] The opportunity did not quite come yet. When he heard Wagner conducting Beethoven's *Ninth Symphony* on Palm Sunday 1846, he was even more determined to go to Wagner. And when he went with his mother to Weimar to hear Liszt conduct *Lohengrin* on 28 August 1850, he was decided.

It was not easy, however, for his parents wanted him to continue his legal studies. He went to see Wagner in Zurich and wrote to his mother informing her that the composer proposed he undertake practical studies with him the following winter, and conduct the opera in turns with another young enthusiast, the less talented Karl Ritter. He pleaded: to start conducting under Wagner's direction, what "would more spur a man on to activity and industry?"[4] His mother, herself an accomplished amateur pianist, was not inclined to approve, so Bülow solicited the support of his musical patrons. Liszt wrote encouragingly to Mrs Bülow: he "is evidently gifted with a musical organisation of the rarest kind," and Wagner assured her that his love of music was based upon "great, indeed uncommon, powers."[5] Without the actual approval of his parents, but with renewed encouragement from Wagner, he and Ritter walked for two days from Ötlishausen to Zurich. Wagner was most impressed: "the young Bülow evinced a great, even passionate emotion toward me. I at once... felt... a truly intimate sense of sympathy with such a highly wrought young person."[6] Bülow reported to his mother after his arrival that, "after another year and a half of semi-slumber at my legal studies, my life would have been broken, spoilt, unsouled."[7]

As it turned out, his apprenticeship to Wagner lasted only two months, but it was invaluable for his development. None of Wagner's operas were conducted while he was in Zurich, but there was thorough-going induction into the craft of preparation, rehearsal and performance. For example, he worked with Wagner for several days on a production of *Don Giovanni* and marvelled at Wagner's results: "such warm and living, such artistic and rational piety towards Mozart," he wrote to his father.[8] The operas that Bülow conducted himself may have been of no moment,[9] but as soon as he stepped up to conduct for the first time, Wagner noticed how he "wielded the baton with great surety and gusto. I felt immediately safe as far as he was concerned..."[10] The determination with which the dedicated young musician sought to raise standards was bound to rub badly against the experienced but habit-bound company. The battles came to their inevitable end. "Things and persons are too disgusting," he wrote to his father, "friction is never-ending. I can't go into the whole affair, but the main reason of our intending to give notice today is a quarrel with the husband of the prima donna, that lady having refused to sing any more to my conducting."[11] Nevertheless, "the two months here have not been wasted; I have learnt something that may be of the

[3] as told on a train trip from Dresden to Leipzig in 1884: Ellis, *Life of Wagner*, vol. 2, p. 136

[4] letter dated 16 September 1850 in Marie von Bülow (ed.), *The early correspondence of Hans von Bulow* (trans. by Constance Bache) (London: Fisher Unwin, 1896), p. 46

[5] *ibid*, pp. 50, 52 [6] Wagner, *My Life*, p. 456 [7] Ellis, *Life of Wagner*, vol. 3, p. 71

[8] letter dated 9 November 1850 in Ellis, *ibid*, p. 76

[9] see Newman, *Life of Wagner*, vol. 2, p. 172 [10] Wagner, *My Life*, p. 456

[11] letter of 2 December 1850 in Ellis, *ibid*, pp. 76-77

greatest service to me."[12] He assured his father: "I am now a follower – now a pupil – of Wagner's, and shall prove this by my actions."[13]

With Wagner's help, he was installed as theatre conductor in the nearby St. Gallen, with his friend Ritter as chorus director. His father visited him to hear him conducting

Fig. 2.1. Hans von Bülow in 1858. Drawing by Friedrich Preller

Der Freischütz and marvelled to his own father: "The house was full to overflowing, the applause tremendous, and the performance excellent. Hans conducted in every respect like a *Master, and without looking at the score.* The orchestra, some sixty in number, followed implicitly and with pleasure their twenty-years-old conductor."[14] However, conditions in St. Gallen were so bad – "abominable personnel, dreadful orchestra and shabby theatre," according to Wagner[15] – that he soon left and went to Weimar to study with Liszt.

[12] *ibid*, p. 77
[13] letter from Zurich dated 9 December 1850: Bülow, *The Early Correspondence*, p. 61
[14] letter dated 19 January 1851: *ibid*, p. 68 (Bülow was in fact twenty-one.)
[15] Wagner, *My Life*, p. 457

A Faust Overture

Wagner had impressed himself deeply on Bülow, and ignited in him a missionary zeal. "My having recognised the greatest artistic phenomenon of our century," Bülow wrote to his sister, "perhaps even of high importance in the history of the world – a recognition shared as yet by few – has woken an ambition in me, a sense of self, a thrill of life."[16] Soon he would make his debut as a man of letters, wielding his pen very much like a sword, in a series of brilliant, combative articles in the *Neue Zeitschrift für Musik* in defence of Wagner's music theories, and on the performances of his works in Weimar.[17]

In 1856, he wrote in two issues of that journal *On Richard Wagner's Faust Overture*, a guide for conductors, players and listeners, which in 1860 was reissued in a more complete form as a pamphlet.[18] The tract is an example of the extraordinary understanding and enthusiasm Bülow had for Wagner's work. Wagner himself wrote of his *Faust Overture* in 1852: "I consider it to be one of my best stand-alone musical compositions – and my friends [presumably Bülow among them] are of the same opinion. In the past, busy with opera – and as Dresden was lacking a proper concert hall – I never used to appreciate it, and almost completely forgot about it. Liszt has very successfully dragged it into the light of day. If I intended to get myself recognised by Germany's concert-going audience, to my mind I could not do this any more favourably than with this composition which I would still strongly rework for the purpose of releasing it."[19] This he did, and his concert performance of it in Zurich was not a success. Bülow was quick to appreciate its profundity. His elaborate and extensive exposition of it was in the true spirit of Wagner.[20] Bülow argued that it was not a mere reflection of scenes from Goethe's *Faust*, with themes for Faust, for Gretchen and for Mephistopheles.

> [Wagner's] work belongs to pure instrumental *lyrics*; wherefore let hearer and reader seek no dramatic truffles in its score... It is no *character* sketch, but a painting of *mood*; a peculiarity it shares with Schumann's *Manfred* Overture.... Wagner's *Faust Overture* is a *Stimmungsbild* [tone-poem], the artistically-rounded exposition of a state of soul, or of the motive which leads thereto. Its subject is no dramatic hero, nor that which stamps the character of such, a *deed*: its subject is *suffering*; no private suffering of a given Faust, but a suffering of universal-human scope. Not Goethe's Faust is its hero, then, but Humanity itself.[21]

[16] letter of January 1851 quoted by Ellis, *Life of Wagner*, vol. 3, p. 67

[17] Gewande, *Hans von Bülow*, p. 19

[18] *Neue Zeitschrift für Musik*, 1 and 8 August 1856, republished by C. F. Kahnt, Leipzig (31 pp.) in 1860. It is also to be found with a few corrections in Marie von Bülow (ed.), *Hans von Bülow: Ausgewählte Schriften*, 2nd ed. (Leipzig: Breitkopf & Härtel, 1911), part 1, pp. 203-231; a few pages are reproduced in an appendix to Egon Voss, *Richard Wagner. Eine Faust-Ouvertüre* (München: Fink, 1982); several passages in translation appear in Ellis, *Life of Wagner*, vol. 5, pp. 25-28.

[19] letter to Breitkopf und Härtel dated 28 October 1852 and quoted in Heinel, *Richard Wagner als Dirigent*, p. 71

[20] Wagner wrote: "Faust is the subject, and *woman* hovers before him only as an indefinite, shapeless object of his yearning; as such, intangible and unattainable. Hence his despair, his curse on all the torturing semblance of the beautiful, his headlong plunge into the mad smart of sorcery." letter dated 27 November 1852, Wagner, *Letters to his Dresden Friends*, p. 300

[21] translation in Ellis, *Life of Wagner*, vol. 5, pp. 24-25

Bülow gives the work his own generalized interpretation, in a way not dissimilar to the note Wagner wrote on the Prelude to *Tristan und Isolde* at the time of his 1860 Paris concerts.[22] Bülow stresses that his view – the impression the music makes on *him* – is not "any pretence to set up an authoritative programme" nor the only valid interpretation: it is *his* reading of the tone poem.[23] He also gives the work a detailed musical analysis, and comments on its form:

> It is not possible to compose with more perfect organic unity of form than Wagner has done in the *Faust Overture*. Place any "classical" overture with an "Introduction" by its side, and see if Wagner's tone poem does not throw it into the shade even formally.... not only tonal, but general emotional life courses through every vein of its form. Every note is written with a poet's blood.[24]

Henry Finck who quoted these lines in his 1893 study of Wagner commented: "what we marvel at, and what future generations will marvel at more and more, is that the professional critics and other 'experts' did not at once recognise the exquisite orchestral and harmonic novelties in the *Faust Overture*, and that its reception at first almost everywhere amounted to a fiasco."[25] Bülow was tireless in his promotion of this work. He wrote a piano transcription in 1855, and conducted the work for the first time in Berlin on 1 February 1856. It would become his most performed of all Wagner's works: he conducted it a further 35 times to 5 December 1892, the last occasion he conducted any Wagner.[26]

The Munich years

The eight years Bülow spent in Munich as director of the Royal Court Opera (1864-1872) constituted his single most important contribution to the performance of Wagner's works. In addition *Tristan und Isolde* (9) and the *Meistersinger* (9), which we will come to, he led performances of *Der fliegende Holländer* (5), *Lohengrin* (5),

[22] "...in one long breath he let that unslaked longing swell from first avowal of the gentlest tremor of attraction, though half-heaved sighs, through hopes and fears, laments and wishes, joy and torment, to the mightiest onset, most resolute attempt to find the breach unbarring to the heart a path into the sea of endless love's delight. In vain! Its power spent, the heart sinks back to pine of its desire – desire without attainment...": "*Prelude to Tristan und Isolde*" (1860), Ellis, *Wagner's Prose Works*, vol. 8, p. 387

[23] the interpretation is translated by Ellis, *Life of Wagner*, on pp. 25-27

[24] Finck, *Wagner and his Works*, vol. 2, p. 418

[25] *ibid*, p. 417. What present generations might well marvel at is the dearth of modern performances of the work, so the question of its reception hardly arises.

[26] The number of performances of other concert pieces by Wagner were: *Die Meistersinger* Prelude (19), *Der Fliegende Holländer* Overture (14), *Tannhäuser* Overture (11) and March (9), *Kaisermarsch* (6), *Huldigungsmarsch* (5), *Lohengrin* Prelude (4), *Tristan und Isolde* Prelude and Liebestod (4), Prelude with concert ending (3), *Rienzi* Overture (3), *Die Meistersinger* Act 3 Prelude (1), and *Die Walküre* Ride (1): Hans-Joachim Hinrichsen, *Musikalische Interpretationen – Hans von Bülow* (Stuttgart: Franz Seiner Verlag, 1999), p. 509, who also shows how the works of Beethoven and Brahms featured more regularly in his concerts: *Leonore Overture No. 3* (58), *Egmont Overture* (57), *Coriolan Overture* (50), *Variations on a Theme by Haydn* (33), *Academic Festival Overture* (15), etc.

Tannhäuser (1), and a revival of the early *Das Liebesmahl der Apostel*.[27] He also ventured to other cities to conduct Wagner pieces in his concerts. His manner of preparing for operatic productions was pioneering. He coached singers and instrumental players separately, then gradually brought them together in a unified performance. His method was observed during a *Lohengrin* production in 1867:

> Last week there were a million little rehearsals: (a) for first and second violins, violas, etc. alone, (b) for winds and horns alone, (c) for trumpets, trombones, and percussion alone; (d) for the off-stage band. Then there was a four-hour ensemble rehearsal for the strings, and now for each act there is a three-hour full orchestral rehearsal in the presence (though not with the participation of) the singers. All the stage rehearsals are for the present with piano, next week everything will be together. This new system, which is actually only tiring for the conductor, should prove very effective; Hans von Bülow spends ten hours a day in the theatre and probably spends the night there so that, by early morning, he is always first on the field of battle![28]

The military metaphor in the case of Bülow seems to have been appropriate. Another observer noticed (in a different context) that he had "a military martinet air… When he takes his place before the orchestra you expect to see him draw his sword, and every musician is ready to charge to the death. It is impossible not to feel the influence of his magnetic presence. He infuses new vitality into the most familiar compositions. His directions are animated with a knowledge that acts like inspiration. We are in the presence of a master spirit."[29] "Bülow is the Master of all conductors," wrote Hans Richter at the time of the 1867 *Lohengrin* rehearsals.[30]

And the masterful preparation proved itself in the performance. Peter Cornelius was rhapsodic: Bülow "played" *Lohengrin* "like one of Beethoven's great sonatas."[31] The *Bayerische Zeitung* called it "a model performance of the first rank. Everything was sheer atmosphere, richness, and beauty of tone. The precise ensemble playing led to the most nuanced, tasteful performance. One couldn't think of anything more perfect."[32] According to another who observed Bülow many years later with the Meiningen Orchestra, he achieved "minute regard for detail which is elaborated with the utmost diligence, but without detracting for a moment from the uniform conception of the whole; unerring precision combined with perfect rhythmic freedom; and, finally, a mastery in the art of phrasing which for its taste and charm need not fear comparison with the best efforts of Italian vocalisation…. such perfect orchestral playing has never hitherto been heard, which praise is due not only to the faultless purity and

[27] on 21 April 1869 according to Gewande, *Hans von Bülow*, though not included in the works listed by Hinrichsen, *Musikalische Interpretationen*, from which the other statistics come (pp. 514-15)

[28] *Die Signale*, 6 June 1867, quoted in Christopher Fifield, *True artist and true friend: a biography of Hans Richter* (Oxford: Clarendon Press, 1993), p. 18. A later description of Bülow rehearsing and conducting the Meiningen Orchestra is in Frederic Lamond, *Memoirs*, foreword by Ernest Newman (Glasgow: Maclellan, 1949), pp. 39-40.

[29] Ferdinand Hiller in the *Kölnische Zeitung*, quoted in *Hans von Bülow – A Biographical Sketch – His Visit to America* (New York: George F. Nesbitt, 1875), p.8

[30] letter to Alexander Reinhold dated 29 May 1867 quoted in Fifield, *True Artist*, p. 18

[31] "Der *Lohengrin* in München" (1867), in Cornelius, *Literarische Werkes*, vol. 3 (Leipzig: Breitkopf und Härtel, 1904-05), p. 113

[32] *Bayerische Zeitung, Morgenausgabe*, 19 June 1867, p. 1959, cited in Detta Petzet and Michael Petzet, *Die Richard Wagner-Bühne König Ludwigs II.* (München: Prestel-Verlag, 1970), p. 87

distinctness with which every detail in the score is executed, but also to the fulness and beauty of sound…."[33] With this indication of his working methods and achievements, we will turn to the historic first performances of *Tristan und Isolde* and *Meistersinger*.

The premiere of Tristan und Isolde

Tristan was the first Wagner opera Bülow conducted.[34] In September 1857 he and Cosima came to see Wagner in Zurich. "During that time," as Wagner would in due course dictate to Cosima, "I completed the text of *Tristan und Isolde* while Hans made me a fair copy of each act as soon as it was finished… Beyond this, we made a good deal of music." Hans would play piano arrangements from sketches of the *Ring* as Wagner "sang, as usual, all the parts…. Cosima listened with lowered head and said nothing; when pressed for her reaction, she began to cry."[35] The following year, Bülow had the privilege of being the first man to see the whole score when he started writing a piano arrangement in Venice. He wrote to a friend in astonishment: "What I know so far of this work is simply superb, remarkably poetic, much finer in details than *Lohengrin*, and everywhere new, bold, original. At the same time a thematic elaboration as lucid as it is logical, such as no opera heretofore has shown."[36]

Prague was, on 12 March 1859, the first city to have the privilege of hearing Bülow conduct the Prelude.[37] His private enthusiasm expressed to a friend in Leipzig in August 1859 found its way into the *Neue Zeitschrift für Musik*:

> No one expected such music from Wagner. This work joins on directly with the later works of Beethoven – no more analogy to Weber or Gluck. *Tristan und Isolde* stands related to *Lohengrin* as *Fidelio* to the *Entführung aus dem Serail* – as the C sharp minor Quartet to the 1st in F major, op. 18. I own to having fallen from one delighted surprise into another…. On every side, Wagner shows his pure, powerful musical knowledge. Of this Tone-Architecture, of this musical detail-work, you cannot form too exalted an idea. In Invention, *Tristan und Isolde* is W's most potent work – nothing is so sublime as for instance this second act. … He whom this opera does not convert has no music in him. Such rich polyphony does not exist in all the far too numerous earlier scores. You know me better than to think I have fallen into a fanatical enthusiasm: you know I never allow my heart to be carried away without first consulting the cooler judgement of my head. Well, my head has here granted unqualified permission. *T. and I.* can scarcely become popular: but every lover of music possessing to any extent poetical feeling must feel himself struck by the grandeur and power of the genius which reveals itself in this work….[38]

33 W. Langhams, "Hans von Bülow and the Meiningen Hof-Kapelle in Berlin," *Musical Times*, 1 February 1882, p. 83. No works of Wagner were performed at the concerts reviewed.

34 apart from a private performance of the *Holländer* for King Ludwig on 4 December 1864 (which is not included in the list of performances in Hinrichsen, *Musikalische Interpretationen*, p. 515)

35 Wagner, *My Life*, p. 553

36 letter dated September 1858 quoted by Finck, *Wagner and his Works*, vol. 2, p. 147

37 Hinrichsen, *Musikalische Interpretationen*, p. 156. Bülow performed it with his own concert ending. The concert included the *Faust Overture*.

38 translation in *Dwight's Journal of Music* (Boston), vol. 26, no. 2 (8 October 1859), p. 224; an excerpt from the letter is also in Barth, *Wagner: a documentary study*, p. 189. Bülow reiterated his view in a letter to Wagner from Munich on 8 April 1869: "Your *Tristan* stands in the same relation to *Lohengrin* as Beethoven's last quartets to his first": Richard Graf du Moulin-Eckart

"*Scarcely become popular*"? Wagner was the first to rebuke Bülow, ever so gently. "I deprecate as impractical your expression of doubt as to the likelihood of the opera's popularity. Such words are not spoken simply *among ourselves* but spread to those who do not understand us, or who are more or less permanently hostile, and this fact should always be considered in writing for publication."[39] It was nevertheless a minor indiscretion, and the reprimand did not dampen his enthusiasm.

In January 1860 he was in Paris to give piano recitals yet, as we will recall, found time to assist Wagner in giving his own concerts. "His active involvement was extraordinary in every respect," Wagner recalled.[40] In the summer of 1862 he and Cosima visited Wagner at Breibrich so Bülow could accompany Ludwig Schnorr on the piano in his trial for the role of Tristan. Wagner petitioned King Ludwig to appoint Bülow conductor of the Royal Court Opera to lead the first performance. Bülow was a man, Wagner wrote, "who is particularly close to me, and who is everywhere highly reputed as a consummate musician... a man of many parts who is also an artist of such extensive knowledge and especial aptitude for our present requirements."[41]

With the appointment secured, rehearsals could begin, but they were not easy (there were 27 rehearsals in all[42]), as the orchestra was not used to the revolutionary music of *Tristan*, and smarted under the demands of Bülow. Wagner recorded cryptically in his *Annals* for January 1865: "Hans difficult."[43] What he was difficult about is not clear, but Cosima Bülow's third child, Isolde (whose father was Wagner), was born on 10 April 1865, the first day of orchestral rehearsals. These began with act one; acts two and three were rehearsed on the following two days, and a general rehearsal was held on 2 May. At the beginning of the dress rehearsal on 11 May, Wagner addressed the audience and said of his conductor, "With him at my side, a second Ego, who knows by heart every minute detail of this score, which to many still appears as such a riddle, and who is familiar with my intentions in their most delicate nuances," he could have perfect confidence.[44] With some delay, because Isolde (Malvina Schnorr) had become hoarse, the historic first performance took place on 10 June.

(ed.), *Letters of Hans Von Bülow to Richard Wagner, Cosima Wagner, His Daughter Daniela, Luise Von Bülow, Karl Klindworth, Carl Bechstein* (trans. Hannah Waller) (New York: Alfred A Knopf, 1931, repr. New York: Vienna House, 1972), p. 210

39 quoted by Elliott Zuckerman, *The First Hundred Years of Wagner's Tristan* (New York: Columbia University Press, 1964), p. 55, fn

40 Wagner, *My Life*, p. 602

41 letter from Wagner to King Ludwig, 12 March 1865: Wagner, *Selected Letters*, pp. 637-8

42 *Neue Zeitschrift für Musik*, 14 July 1865, p. 250

43 *The diary of Richard Wagner, 1865-1882: the Brown Book*, ed. Joachim Bergfeld, trans. George Bird (London: Gollancz, 1980), p. 120. As Wagner's *My Life* ends in 1864 and Cosima's *Diaries* begin on 1 January 1869, we have no detailed account from these sources of what transpired during the period covering the first *Tristan* and *Meistersinger* performances. Wagner's brief and often ambiguous jottings in his *Brown Book* were intended as an *aide memoire* for further dictation of the autobiography which never took place.

44 Finck, *Wagner and his Works*, vol. 2, p. 135, who adds in a footnote: "In a private letter of this period Wagner speaks of Bülow as the only living conductor in whom he had full confidence." See also Newman, *Life of Wagner*, vol. 3, p. 358

During this time Bülow had to weather the storm caused by a comment he made when told that the necessary enlargement of the orchestra pit would involve the sacrifice of thirty stalls. "What does it matter," he shouted, "whether we have thirty *Schweinehunde* [pig-dogs] more or less in the place?"[45] The storm in the press hardly abated, despite Bülow's apology, and the press almost drove him and Wagner out of Munich. At the first performance, the gallery was cordoned off for fear of a demonstration which never eventuated.[46] There were three more performances, on 13 and 19 June and 1 July, and hostility towards them abated.

Although views were divided over the work itself, they were unanimous in their praise of the "incomparable performance" of the orchestra under Bülow.[47] The *Münchner Neueste Nachrichten* referred to the extraordinary demands made on it during rehearsals and proclaimed that "its playing met the most stringent demands of the critic, and that the spirit of the musical work found such an intelligent expression through Bülow that was well nigh impossible to find elsewhere."[48] Bülow was able to write to a friend: "Wagner's most difficult and eccentric opera has received the best performance and the richest success. And that in Munich!"[49] Bülow was elated, but within a month the Tristan, Ludwig Schnorr, was dead. In his eloquent tribute to this great artist, Wagner made an illuminating comment on the performance generally which sheds more light on Bülow's style than any other contemporary account:

> the orchestra disappeared completely vis-à-vis the singer, or, more correctly, seemed to be included in his performance… I attended the four performances we had of *Tristan*… And at the fourth performance after Tristan's love-curse, I felt constrained to declare determinedly to those around that "this was the last performance of *Tristan*; I would not allow another." – It may well be difficult clearly to convey the sense of my feeling over this.[50]

And he did not, and presumably could not. Years later, between rehearsals for the *Ring*, he would again recall "Bülow's superb direction" of the *Tristan* performances.[51] Ernest Newman wrote: "The performances as a whole gave Wagner the ecstatic sense of hearing a work of his for the first time virtually as he had conceived it."[52] With Schnorr dead, the prospect for more performances of *Tristan* was not bright, and within months, Wagner was driven from Munich for a combination of personal and political reasons.

45 Zuckerman, *The First Hundred Years*, pp. 55-56; Wagner mentions the affair ("May: 'Swinehounds' ") in his *Brown Book*, p. 120.

46 *Allgemeine Musikalische Zeitung* (Leipzig), 5 July 1865, pp. 437-8

47 Sebastian Röckl, *Ludwig II. und Richard Wagner 1864-1865* (München: C.H. Beck, 1903), p. 112; see also the press reports reproduced in Petzet, *Die Richard Wagner-Bühne*, pp. 51-54

48 *Münchner Neueste Nachrichten* (*Unterhaltungs-Blatt*), 22 June 1865, p. 598, cited in Petzet, *ibid*, p. 52

49 letter to Carl Bechstein dated 2 July 1865: Moulin-Eckart, *Letters of Hans Von Bülow*, p. 38

50 "Recollections of Ludwig Schnorr" (3 May 1868), in the *Brown Book*, p. 140; also in Barth, *Wagner: a documentary study*, p. 209

51 Julius Hey, *Richard Wagner als Vortragsmeister, 1864-1876*, (ed.) Hans Hey, (Leipzig: Breitkopf und Härtel, 1911), p. 199

52 Newman, *Life of Wagner*, vol. 3, p. 363

The premiere of Die Meistersinger von Nürnberg

As he had with Wagner's earlier works, Bülow was quick to spot and marvel at the new fruits of the Master. He first saw the orchestration of the overture to the *Meistersinger* in 1862, as it came from the pen of Wagner, and exclaimed to Karl Klindworth: "And what an overture! C major, in 4/4 time, bright and joyous, with a marvellous swing, fiendishly polyphonic, yet always clean and fertile, with an extraordinary, broadly treated combination at the close, of three (at one point, four) motifs!"[53] His second wife quotes another letter from 1866 written by Bülow while the score was almost complete: "[Wagner] is about to create his most classical (please forgive this trivial expression), most German, most mature and generally most accessible work of art. You cannot begin to imagine its absolute musical richness, the Cellini-like finely-detailed workings. This is my unshakeable belief: Wagner is the greatest composer, quite equal to a Beethoven, a Bach – and also far more…."[54]

By the time of the rehearsals in 1868, the Bülow-Wagner-Cosima triangle was more complicated, and imposed a great strain. Wagner noted in his *Brown Book*: "[May] Piano rehearsals: heavy, oppressive feeling from Hans' deep hostility and estrangement. Direction all restrained. Singers good… June: Orchestral rehearsals: serious troubles with H…. Apparent rebellion by orchestra. (Horn-player Strauss)… Dress rehearsal: again anger at – everything. No pleasure any more. (Final words to Company.)"[55] Again, all this is not clear – what were the anger and troubles about exactly? We know about the rebellious Franz Strauss, the accomplished horn player who was quite antipathetic to Wagner's later music. Maybe the rest of the orchestra feared Bülow's style in rehearsal:

> Bülow raps with his baton: "Gentlemen, if you please, let us begin," he calls in his thin, hoarse voice to the orchestra, which has been augmented by various brass players and numbers ninety. The music begins, Bülow uses his whole body to indicate the nuances he wants and puts such ferocious energy into each gesture that one begins to tremble for the violinists and the lamps within his reach.[56]

We know something of Wagner's final words to the company. So far as the orchestra was concerned, he simply said: "To you I have nothing further to say. We are German musicians; we understand each other without words"[57] – a far cry from the personal praise conferred on Bülow at the final rehearsal of *Tristan*.

The reaction to the first performance on 21 June 1868 was mixed. It was a huge popular success. The press agreed about the performance itself: its quality had reached a level hardly found anywhere in Germany, if at all.[58] Everyone gave "a most exquisite

[53] letter dated 5 August 1862 from Biebrich am Rhein, in Moulin-Eckart, *Letters of Hans Von Bülow*, pp. 3-4

[54] Marie von Bülow, *Hans von Bülow in Leben und Wort* (Stuttgart: J. Engelhorns Nachf., 1925), p. 217

[55] *Brown Book*, p. 167

[56] *Neue Freie Presse* (Vienna), 21 June 1868, p. 11, in Barth, *Wagner: a documentary study*, p. 214

[57] Finck, *Wagner and his Works*, vol. 2, p. 216

[58] Gewande, *Hans von Bülow*, p. 248; *Münchner Neueste Nachrichten*, 22 June 1868, p. [4]; *ibid, Unterhaltungs-Blatt*, 5 July 1868, p. 648; *Allgemeine Zeitung* (Augsburg), 22 June 1868, p. [4]; Petzet, *Die Richard Wagner-Bühne*, pp. 157-162 (press reports, though Bülow is not specifically mentioned)

Fig. 2.2. Bülow, around the time of his article on Wagner's *Faust Overture.*
Oil painting by Wilhelm Streckfuss, 1855

Figs. 2.3. and 2.4. Wagner and Bülow, with Wagner's dog Pohl.
Details of photographs taken by Joseph Albert in Munich on 17 May 1865 shortly before the premiere of *Tristan und Isolde*

Fig. 2.5. Bülow with baton

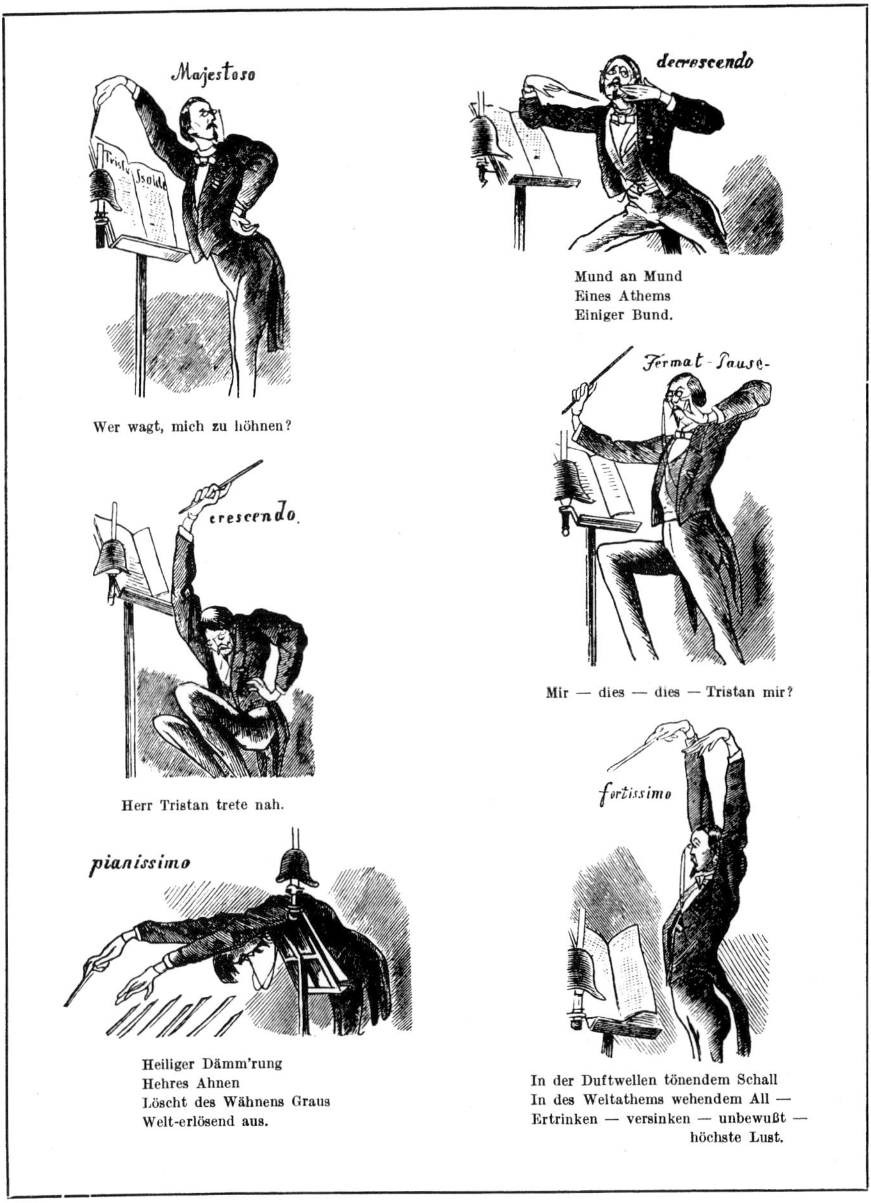

Fig. 2.6. Bülow conducting *Tristan und Isolde*.
Münchener Punsch, 2 July 1865

Fig. 2.7. Bülow in the 1860s

performance" under the "intelligent direction of Bülow," declared *Der Sammler.*[59] Yet the critical response at a deeper level was wanting. The leading Viennese critic[60] Eduard Hanslick considered the work "among the interesting cases of musical deviation or sickness," yet he made some astute observations about the performance:

> The chorus and orchestra of the Munich Opera emerged the victors from the musical battle of *Die Meistersinger*, it is a considerable achievement in itself that the unprecedentedly difficult ensembles do not fall apart. The chief credit for that, as for the accuracy of the whole performance, is due to Hans von Bülow, the conductor. Bülow's whole energy and agility, his astonishing memory and his enthusiastic devotion to Wagner are indispensable factors in the result.[61]

What Wagner himself thought of the production is not entirely clear. He jotted down in his *Brown Book* that he was "weary and exhausted" on the day of the first performance.[62] On 24 June he returned to Tribschen before the second performance and was unwell for ten days. He wrote to Bülow on 25 June calling for a further short rehearsal. He shared the view of visiting conductors that it had been an "incomparable" performance, though he wanted to iron out a few weaknesses, like some correct instrumental entries, probably caused by the novelty of the work and players' nerves. His main concern, however, was:

> still a lack of that indispensable discretion, that deliberate restraint in the level of sound (namely in the symphonic accompaniment of the musical dialogue on stage). Despite the need to retain the highest clarity of every character, in this case this involves the avoidance of any intense accentuation, and an adjustment of overall sound levels to the respective circumstances. While these would be advisable for all gentlemen as a whole, in this sense I would specifically recommend renewed rehearsal of the dialogue scenes between Sachs and Beckmesser in the second and third act: the scene between Walther and Sachs in the third act also suffered somehow due to a restless orchestra performance.[63]

During his illness he noted down: "Everything futile; complete failure of Munich attempts. Thought imperative never ever to return there.... Appalling reviews... must, on account of my needs, be glad to salvage *Meistersinger* as vulgar theatrical success."[64] Yet he writes to King Ludwig on 14 October 1868: "the evening of the first performance of *Die Meistersinger* was the high point of my career as man and artist... this performance of it... was the best that has even been given of any of my works."[65] The contradiction may readily be understood: there was no doubt the performance had been good and the popular success widespread, yet Wagner's deeper reaction to the critical reception, the *artistic* success of *Die Meistersinger*, remained bleak: Wagner was *still* not understood.

[59] 23 June 1868, p. 272

[60] "so far as musical critics can ever be said to lead anybody or lead to anything," as Ernest Newman interpolated in respect of a Dresden critic (*Life of Wagner*, vol. 1, p. 418), and which may also be apt for Hanslick

[61] *Neue Freie Presse* (Vienna), 26 June 1868, p. 2; in Barth, *Wagner: a documentary study*, p. 215. Hanslick went on to praise the work of Wagner himself, how "he brilliantly vindicates his reputation for genius in the field of *mis-en-scène*."

[62] There were a further eight performances in 1868.

[63] Wagner, *Briefe an Hans von Bülow [1847-1869]* (Jena: Eugen Diederich, 1916), pp. 266-7

[64] *Brown Book*, p. 167

[65] Wagner, *Selected Letters*, p. 731

After the ninth and final performance in 1868, Bülow reported to Wagner that it had gone "very well in parts. Richter took first horn [Bülow by this stage refused to have Franz Strauss in his orchestra] after he had played the organ [in the opening scene]... Orchestra excellent."[66] This was the last *Meistersinger* that Bülow would ever perform.

The Meistersinger Prelude

Occasionally in his concerts, however, he did conduct the prelude. At a farewell concert in New York on 2 May 1889, he confounded critics with the tempo he adopted. His performance was the "gem of the evening," according to the *Sun*, "which for variety of tonal color and accent and inspiriting influence much be cited as far excelling anything of the sort yet attempted on this side of the Atlantic."[67] The *Daily Tribune* agreed that nothing like it had ever been heard in New York, but was less impressed. "So far as the simple question of tempo is concerned..., it was sadly disturbing to all conceptions of the force which tradition ought to have. Neither Richter nor Seidl, both of whom are meant to be repositories of Wagnerian tradition (if a thing so modern as Wagner's music can be spoken of as a tradition) drawn from the fountain-head, plays this piece of music with anything approaching the speed that Dr. von Bülow adopted last night."[68] The *Musical Courier* was of a different view, and with reason:

> ... speaking about the performance of this masterpiece, strange as the rather quickened tempo of the stately opening phrases and the greatly accelerated episodes of the "guilds" themes in the woodwind may have seemed to many, it must be acknowledged that never before has New York heard a production of this prelude which even approximately equaled this one in clearness of bringing out the thematic material and its rich contrapuntal treatment, in the sharpness and decision of rhythm, in the gloriousness of its orchestral coloring and even in sonority.... The strictures passed upon the performance by some of the critics therefore seem to us unfounded, and, as a matter of fact, Bülow's reading was, with the above noted exception of the tempi, almost the identical one which the writer remembers to have heard under Richard Wagner's own baton at a memorable concert in Cologne in 1873.[69]

And extraordinarily, the performance was recorded.[70]

The end in Munich

The four years in Munich after the *Meistersinger* premiere in 1868 were difficult for Bülow, and 1868 was probably the worst of those. He wanted to get away from Munich, according to Cosima, because "one miserable journalist... denigrates everything that [he] does."[71] The King commanded a new production of *Tristan* which almost drove him to a nervous breakdown: Bülow demanded his own dismissal on the grounds of ill health a few days before the event. Eighty-four bars were cut out: ten from act one and seventy-four from act two.[72] However, the performance turned

[66] quoted in David Wooldridge, *Conductor's World* (London: Barrie & Rockliff, 1970), p. 64
[67] *Sun*, 3 May 1889, p. 2 [68] 3 May 1889, p. 6 [69] 8 May 1889, p. 367 (author not printed)
[70] see Discography, p. 625 [71] *Diaries*, vol. 1, 2 April 1869, p. 82
[72] letter to Carl Bechstein, 21 June 1869: Moulin-Eckart, *Letters of Hans Von Bülow*, p. 93

out well. Richter telegrammed Cosima: "Bülow came to life during the performance, afterward cheerful, calls of 'Bülow stay,' success tremendous."[73] Bülow himself reported to Wagner: "The orchestra was quite attentive and discreet in minor details. I for my part conducted far better and with more composure than before.... On the dramatic side I have nothing particularly bad to relate, simply because my eye and ear were too incessantly concentrated on a precise rendering of the music.... [It] was a better performance than any of your operas has ever had at any theatre. I would hardly except even the Dresden and Weimar ones of *Tannhäuser* and the Vienna *Lohengrin*. Yesterday's event is, therefore, and remains, one of great importance in the chronicles of music."[74] Yet his intensive work on *Tristan*, at a time of personal turmoil, literally finished him.[75] In August 1869 he took leave from Munich vowing never to return, and broke with Wagner.

The King of Bavaria was much affected by Wagner's operas, and by 1871 had made his desire known to Bülow that he wished another production of *Tristan*. Bülow agreed, writing to Cosima: "I keep this work jealously in my own hands."[76] In 1872 he gave four performances of it, together with three performances of the *Holländer*. The latter in particular created a great public response. The Wagners were not present – Cosima recorded their bitterness[77] – but many prominent European figures were, including Friedrich Nietzsche: "You have opened my eyes to the most exalted artistic impression of my life," he wrote to Bülow afterwards. "If I was unable to thank you immediately after those two performances, please attribute this to my total state of shock, which makes one unable to speak, to thank – only to hide."[78] At his official farewell concert on 24 August, Bülow conducted the *Faust Overture* and Beethoven's *Symphony No. 5* but, as often happens, it was not an actual farewell. King Ludwig requested *Tristan* again for 30 October 1872. Three years previously Bülow had hoped to end his time in Munich with this "gigantic but devastating production," as he had begun it. Now at last he was content.

Interludes in the British Isles

Among the countries Bülow travelled to as a virtuoso pianist and sometime conductor were England and Scotland. In England he shared the conducting with Eduard Dannreuther at Wagner Society Concerts in London on 9 May and 12 December 1873. At the first concert, he conducted the Prelude and Liebestod from *Tristan*, and the *Huldigungsmarsch*. The *Musical Standard* reported:

[73] *Diaries*, vol. 1, 16 June 1869, p. 108 and 21 June 1869, p. 111

[74] letter dated 21 June 1869 in Moulin-Eckart, *Letters of Hans Von Bülow*, p. 237; also quoted by William Ashbrook, "The First Singers of *Tristan und Isolde*," *Opera Quarterly*, vol. 3, no. 4 (Winter 1985/86), 21-2

[75] Zuckerman, *The First Hundred Years*, p. 60 gives the non-musical background: on 6 June 1869 Siegfried Wagner was born to Cosima and Wagner; on 15 June Cosima wrote to Bülow seeking a divorce; on 17 June he replied, in a letter that is a model of chivalry, agreeing; on 20 June he conducted *Tristan*. He gave a further private performance for the King on 22 June.

[76] letter from Rome, 22 October 1871 in Moulin-Eckart, *Letters of Hans Von Bülow*, p. 249

[77] see Cosima Wagner, *Diaries*, vol. 1, 25, 28 and 30 June 1872, pp. 503-4 and 506

[78] *Briefe und Schriften*, vol. 5, p. 551 quoted in Gewande, *Hans von Bülow*, p. 112

From the way in which he influenced his band, it was evident the musician was a born conductor; but we must protest against the way in which he suddenly stopped the performance, on account of one of the trumpet players playing a wrong note. The spectacle of a conductor stopping his band, and shouting out "A flat" to a delinquent, and then commencing again, is happily rare in England.[79]

Not rare in England at that time, however, was the hostile reaction to Wagner's music, an omen for Wagner's unhappy return visit four years later. "The extracts from *Tristan und Isolde*," the *Musical Standard* continued, "were most uninteresting; the music is vague, unmelodious, and excessively monotonous and confused." As for the *Huldigungsmarsch*, "the noise, or rather row, in it, is something terrific, and it is very deficient in definite melody."[80] Yet excerpts from *Rienzi* he conducted at the December concert created a better impression:

A glorious performance was this, both as regards the music and its artistical execution. To see Dr Von Bülow conduct (as he did the first part of the *soirée*) must have convinced the most sceptical and the most prejudiced of his critics that a great genius is present in our midst. Without any book, Dr Von Bülow kept his fine band together. He was in command of a good army. The doctor had no occasion, as once last spring, to correct a wrong accidental by calling out the right note....[81]

In Scotland he conducted in Edinburgh and Glasgow in 1875 and 1877-78 respectively, including some Wagner during his Glasgow season. More memorable than the music was Bülow's increasingly irritable and eccentric behaviour. "At one concert he got so excited because some piece he was performing went badly that he took up the music-stand and threw it into the audience, some of whom narrowly escaped being seriously hurt."[82] Bülow was probably as relieved as the public when the time came to leave.

Hanover years

In September 1877 Bülow accepted an appointment as director of the Royal Opera at Hanover. The following year he mounted a production of *Rienzi*, the first time he had heard it since 1842 ago in Dresden, and conducted it eight times. He opened the 1878 season with the *Holländer* (3 performances) and followed this with a triumphant new production of *Tannhäuser* (9). The opening night on 6 October had been the subject of keen anticipation.

There were many innovations. The overture was not begun as rapidly as usual. Everything increased in power and tempo very gradually up to the wildness in the Venusberg scene, Tannhäuser's song in Act 1 was also given a more sedate tempo. Several parts, which had been previously cut, were brought back so that Tannhäuser's actions, at least in the *Sängerkrieg*, appeared

79 17 May 1873, pp. 307-8; the *Athenaeum* in its review (17 May 1873, p. 639) did not mention the breakdown, only: "Dr Bülow conducted without the score before him, but he was amazingly quick in his anticipation of the ever-changing character of the instrumentation – his eye was all over the orchestra...".

80 17 May 1873, pp. 307-8

81 *Musical Standard*, 20 December 1873, p. 387

82 Frederic H. Cowen, *My art and my friends* (London: Edward Arnold, 1913), p. 114

more comprehensible. The prelude to act three, and Elisabeth's swansong often omitted, were restored. The whole opera was incomparably richer in its performance.... Bülow's conducting deserved a prize.... His influence in the musical sphere has become so powerful that the necessary balance to allow the drama to take its rightful place was missing.[83]

Bülow's uncompromisingly high artistic standards and extreme irritability reached a crisis during the second production of *Lohengrin* on 26 September 1879. He clashed with the tenor when he sang the Farewell to the Swan in act three out of tune. "You are not a Knight of the *Swan* but a Knight of the *Swine*," Bülow exploded. He refused to duel or to apologise, and had to resign.[84] Georg Fischer reported that parts of the production that had previously been cut were restored, resulting in a duration of four and a quarter hours.

As nothing at all has been reported about Bülow's conducting of *Lohengrin* around here Hanover]...his Munich performance might be considered, where it was reported: "one hardly ever mentions the singers, one only ever mentions his conducting, and they say there was no choir and orchestra ensemble like it for as long as people can remember...! What a long way he has come to reach this point, which we would arguably like to call his zenith."[85]

It was the last Wagner opera Bülow was ever to conduct. He was in Hamburg conducting and playing during the 1887/88 season, but he only included the occasional Wagner work in his concerts, such as the *Meistersinger* overture and *A Faust Overture*. People had been hoping he would conduct Wagner operas. There were more than forty Wagner performances during the season, all the operas except *Parsifal*, but he left these to Joseph Sucher and the young Felix Weingartner.[86]

Bülow on the later Wagner

In spite of his personal break with Wagner in 1869, Bülow never tired of, or wavered in, his belief in the composer's ideals. In 1872 he gave concerts in Munich in support of the Bayreuth project. "His concert for Bayreuth (sonatas) is said to have been brilliant," Cosima records in her diary.[87] He gave two further concerts for the Wagner cause in 1880, after the first Festival. As it was said, in effect he laid many of the bricks of the Bayreuth Festival Theatre: "He did not cease to do so, when the composer made his life desolate; for he knew and said that his work was being done for the work and not for the man...."[88] He demonstrated this in an interview

[83] Georg Fischer, *Hans von Bülow in Hannover* (Hannover und Leipzig: Hahn'sche Buchhandlung, 1902), p. 27

[84] Walter Damrosch, *My musical life* (New York: Scribner, 1926), p. 54. Georg Fischer gives a more detailed account of the clash: *Hans von Bülow in Hannover*, pp. 49-51.

[85] Fischer, *Hans von Bülow in Hannover*, p. 49

[86] Gewande, *Hans von Bülow*, pp. 185-6

[87] *Diaries*, vol. 1, 26 August 1872, p. 529

[88] Charles Villiers Stanford, *Pages from an unwritten Diary*, (London: Edward Arnold, 1914), pp. 267-268. Stanford gives another story illustrating the wit of Bülow. A woman asked to be introduced to Bülow at a reception at Dannreuther's house in London. "Oh, Mr. Bülow, you know Mr Wagner, don't you?" Bülow gave a long, low bow and answered without a sign of surprise, "But of course, madam, he is the husband of my wife." (p. 264)

during a concert tour of New York in 1875 when he echoed what he had written as a young man: "I consider [Wagner] the greatest musical genius that has existed since Beethoven....No one has laboured more earnestly and more faithfully to give the world a wider and truer estimation of the grandeur of Beethoven.... [Wagner's] aim is to wed music, words and everything connected with opera in such a manner that there will be perfect symmetry. The Bayreuth festival will be the carrying out of this idea to the fullest extent. The trilogy will be the accomplishment of a life-long purpose – the production of an opera symmetrical in all its details.... I will probably remain in America during the Centennial Exhibition. I shall not go to Bayreuth."[89] In another interview, this time in Chicago in 1876, he proclaimed:

I tell you why I worship Wagner as a composer, and Liszt, too, for that matter. Wagner has perpetuated in his epoch the drama of the Greeks in theirs. The drama, a unit to which all arts, music and every other one, must be subordinated. He seeks the creation of a symmetrical, and a noble model, to which they must all proportionately contribute. The Greeks wrote for Greece, Wagner being a German, writes for Germany, of course. But the revelation of the principle, and the perpetuation of this lofty ideal is for the whole world, and it will leaven the heart of the whole world. We shall see how this festival of Wagner's, this year, will turn out. It is my belief that it will be a crowning triumph for him.... I am not a violent partisan any more but I am a steadfast disciple."[90]

Bülow did not attend the Festival, but was happy it had come to fruition. Privately he had doubts whether the *Ring* achieved the ideals set for it. He greatly valued the score of the *Rheingold*, but only heard the entire *Ring* cycle for the first time in Munich in 1885, and on that occasion, *Siegfried* and *Götterdämmerung* for the first. After these performances he wrote: "Acts 1 and 2 of *Siegfried*, though unedifying, are certainly of high importance musically, compared with Act 3, which to me is a horror. *Götterdämmerung* on the other hand is a completely different picture: because this is finally dramatic instead of epic, it is in my view by far the cycle's most promising piece, which could only benefit if it was separated from it."[91] However, he was more dismissive to Albert Gutmann:

The *Meistersinger* and *Tristan*, those two master-works, will always be admired, but don't talk to me about the *Götter-Meschpoche* [clan or crew of gods]. Besides, the truth that Wagner aspires to he has not attained in the music-drama. Fundamentally the sung drama will always be a great lie. The recitative drama in combination with music, the task of the latter being to illustrate soul-states of the characters, – that is purer truth. The future belongs to melodrama.[92]

[89] "Bülow on Wagner," *New York Herald*, 1 November 1875, p. 7. (In this interview he also reiterated his infamous view that Verdi's *Requiem* was "trash... a series of common sensationalisms," a view he later apologised to Verdi for; Verdi suggested that Bülow's first thoughts might after all have been best: see Dyneley Hussey's summary of the affair in the *Spectator*, 3 June 1938, p. 1008 – a review of Toscanini's *Requiem*.)

[90] "Von Bülow Interviewed," *Chicago Times*, 6 February 1876, p. 4

[91] quoted in Werner Bollert, "Hans von Bülow als Dirigent," *Melos/NZ neue zeitschrift für Musik*, März-April, 2/1975, 88-95, at p. 89. The cycle took place on 8, 9, 11, and 13 September 1885. He expressed similar views to C.A. Barry, saying that after Siegfried "Wagner's music had so affected his nerves that he had had to spend two days in bed." Barry, "Some Personal Reminiscences of Hans von Bülow," *Musician* (London), 1 September 1897, p. 331.

[92] Albert Gutmann, *Aus dem Wiener Musikleben: Künstlererinnerungen 1873-1908* (Vienna: Gutmann, 1914), p. 16, quoted in Newman, *Life of Wagner*, vol. 4, p. 122n

So far as *Parsifal* was concerned, his first forays into act two on the piano became, as he said to his second wife, "more displeasing and headache-provoking" the further he went, adding he would attend one of the Bayreuth performances incognito.[93] He also wrote at the time: "*I don't want to belong to the Grail any more...* I can only keep a deprecating, let's say elusive, attitude towards the music of *Parsifal*, without wanting to pass any objective artistic judgement, which is something I would have to do, by the way, if I considered it becoming or opportune. Richard Wagner's highest manifestations of genius are (a) *Tristan*, (b) *Meistersinger*. All later works fill me with graduated antipathy. Aberrations – folly (looking at it from a musical point of view, and I *am* a musician....)."[94] He did not attend the first Bayreuth *Parsifal* in July 1882 – he stayed in Meiningen and was married; he also stayed away from Bayreuth when his daughter was married in Wahnfried in August – and he did not attend the first Bayreuth *Ring* cycle in 1876. When Wagner died in 1883, he did not go to Bayreuth for the burial, but he did go there for a performance of *Parsifal* in 1884.[95] When asked about his visit "he burst forth with a long and most eloquent eulogy of *Parsifal*, in which work he warmly argued that Wagner had successfully inaugurated a style of sacred music which was as new and original as it was perfectly beautiful."[96] Within hours of the eleventh anniversary of Wagner's own death, on 12 February 1894 Bülow died in Cairo.

Wagner and others on Bülow

For Wagner, Bülow was the supreme conductor. He had noticed it early in Zurich, and when Bülow was forced to move on from there to St Gallen, he won a warm response for his conducting in spite of the conditions. He wrote proudly to his father: "Wagner is right in saying that I have a great talent for conducting."[97] Julius Hey, one of Wagner's singing coaches for the 1875 *Ring* rehearsals, spent many hours with Wagner listening to his recollections and expostulations on German musical life. Wagner recalled, according to Hey:

> Bülow's brilliant performances at the Munich Hoftheater, when with virtuoso leadership, he occasionally obtained acceptance for shifts in tempo in some French and Italian operas, which resulted in the orchestra achieving astonishing virtuosity in its accompaniment to the singers.... Our German conductors have no sense at all for the Italian's *tempo rubato*, or they lack the courage to shape these indispensable shifts in tempo effectively. I remember quite well that this fact played no small part in Bülow's resolve to gain the respect of the Munich orchestra and audiences, who were strongly averse to this to start with, by performing like this.[98]

[93] Gewande, *Hans von Bülow*, p. 167. He did not go, however.

[94] letter to Eugen Spitzweg, August 1882, *Briefe und Schriften*, Vol. 7, p. 201, partly quoted in Marie von Bülow, *Hans von Bülow in Leben und Wort*, p. 218 and Gewande, *Hans von Bülow*, p. 167

[95] *Münchner Neueste Nachrichten*, 7 August 1884, p. 3

[96] C. A. Barry, "Some Personal Reminiscences of Hans von Bülow," *Musician*, 15 September 1897, p. 363

[97] letter dated 17 December 1850, Moulin-Eckart, *Letters of Hans Von Bülow*, p. 63

[98] Hey, in *Richard Wagner als Vortragsmeister*, pp. 141, 201

Hey concluded: "For Wagner, Bülow was and remained the incomparable master of the baton, the role model for conductors in the highest sense."[99] Introducing Bülow to Americans in 1871, a European correspondent wrote:

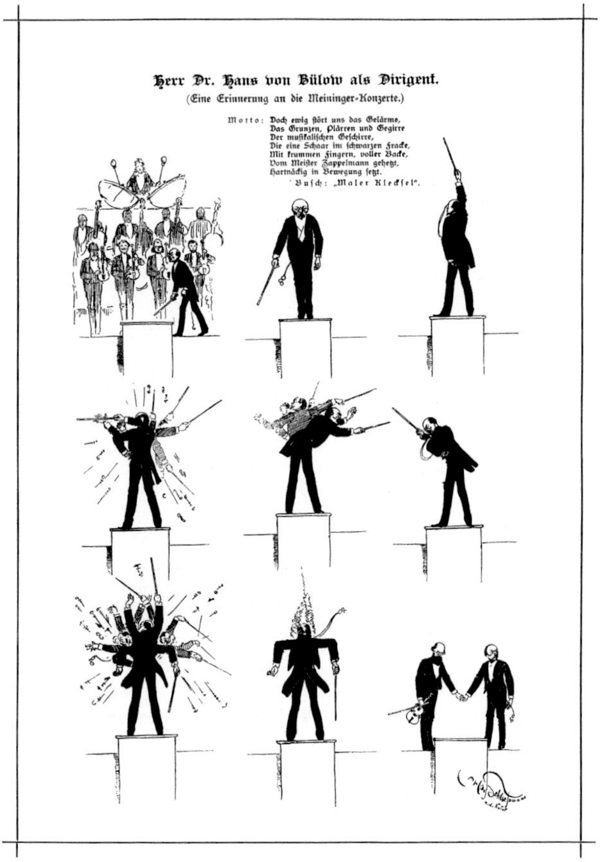

Fig. 2.8. Bülow conducting at a Meiningen concert.
Silhouettes by Hans Schliessmann

As Director of an orchestra Bülow is without a superior. He has a knack of inspiring his musicians with ambition, and a wonderful talent in discovering just where the weak parts are, besides a deep and thorough knowledge of the music even to the most insignificant note of the least important instrument. Sometimes when leading he seems possessed with some musical sprite or

[99] Hey, *ibid*, p. 141, also referred to by Newman, *Life of Wagner*, vol. 4, p. 425n, who added: "In later years Wagner thought most highly of Seidl." Charles Villiers Stanford wrote that "Wagner once stated that perfection in orchestral performances – probably of his own works – would be obtained at its best by rehearsals under Hans von Bülow and performances under Hans Richter:" *Interludes: records and reflections* (London: John Murray, 1922), p. 29. He does not give a source for this statement; his own view was that the position of these artists should have been reversed, and goes on to give a lengthy comparison between the two: pp. 29-38.

genius, and utterly to forget the audience. The superb rendering of Wagner's operas at Munich, during the past few years, is alone sufficient proof of his ability as director, and many others are not wanting.[100]

A final recollection is by Frederic Lamond, who studied piano and performed with Bülow: "...he was the greatest conductor who ever lived – not even Toscanini approaching him. I have seen and heard them all. No one, Nikisch, Richter, Mahler, Weingartner, could compare with him in true warmth of expression, which is the soul and substance of music and all art."[101]

Bülow on the younger generation

And what did Bülow think of the young musicians he heard on the podium? Who was close to him in spirit? In his heyday in Munich during the *Tristan* and *Meistersinger* years, he had the young Hans Richter working with him. He knew Bülow's practices well. We have seen how Richter admired his master. While Bülow was working on *Lohengrin* and *Tristan* in 1869, Richter was conducting the *Meistersinger*. Bülow reported to Wagner then on his "magnificent achievements."[102] He also said that "Richter may take over *Rheingold*,"[103] indicating possibly that Wagner may have expected or wished Bülow to conduct his *Ring* cycle, though this is unlikely;[104] King Ludwig certainly wanted Richter for the *Rheingold*. This was a measure of his confidence in the young conductor. Richter did take on responsibilities for the *Rheingold* productions, though he pulled out in protest at the mistreatment it was being given by management. When the time came for *Parsifal* at Bayreuth, Bülow thought Richter might not be suitable. He wrote to his daughter: "The beery complacency with which Herr Richter conducted the *Meistersinger* – though he was far better than his German colleagues of the baton – convinced me that the choice of Herr Levi for *Parsifal* would probably be better."[105] Long ago he had praised Levi's conducting to Wagner: "he is and has always been a Wagnerianer."[106] Bülow's recognition of Richter's talent for *Meistersinger* but not for *Parsifal*, and Levi's for *Parsifal*, was an astute judgement which, as we shall see, was borne out by history.

[100] "Hans Guido von Buelow. His Life and Works," *Dwight's Journal of Music*, Boston, 29 July 1871, p. [65] (signed "Sixela," Florence, 27 January 1870 [*sic*])

[101] Lamond, *Memoirs*, p. 43

[102] letter dated 21 June 1869, Moulin-Eckart, *Letters of Hans Von Bülow*, p. 237

[103] letter dated 3 June 1869, *ibid*, p. 234. Furthermore, "He can get it done better than I because he is unbroken, fresh, healthy, and ambitious." letter dated 23 June 1869 quoted in Fifield, *True Artist*, p. 30

[104] Ernest Newman gives some evidence that Bülow may have been invited to conduct in 1876: *Life of Wagner*, Vol. 4, p.473, but elsewhere says: "Wagner's instinct had probably warned him already in the 1860s that Bülow would never do for the *Ring*." (*ibid*, p. 122n). Egon Voss considers it likely Bülow was Wagner's preferred conductor for the first Festival, had it not been for the personal complications: *Die Dirigenten der Bayreuther Festspiele* (Regensburg: Gustav Bosse Verlag, 1976), p. 13

[105] letter to Daniella from London, 10 June 1881, Moulin-Eckart, *Letters of Hans Von Bülow*, p. 320

[106] letter from Munich, 8 April 1869, Moulin-Eckart, *Letters of Hans Von Bülow*, p. 231

Of other young conductors: whether or not he had heard Anton Seidl in practice, he once referred to him, possibly in the context of a forthcoming directorship of *Lohengrin*, as "the great Seidel [*sic*]," but noted he was in America.[107] Bülow had performed a Beethoven piano concerto under Felix Mottl's direction in 1884. After the concert they talked through the night and he got to know him well. Bülow wrote to a friend afterwards: "I enjoyed Mottl like no other Wagnerian. Great guy with a big future."[108] He was pleased about the choice of Mottl for the first *Tristan* at Bayreuth in 1886. He told his daughter: "My heart (which is in my ears) is so intensely, morbidly wrapped up in Tristan ('65 –'69 – '72), as also in Sachs, that I should have felt it oppressively as a profanation had Richter or, even more, that ... Seidl been going to conduct them."[109]

The younger generation on Bülow

Richard Strauss worked with Bülow for a short time in Meiningen, and was lavish in his praise of his master. He wrote after hearing a concert of the Berlin Philharmonic: "the *Tannhäuser* overture [was] simply the most fabulous thing, I still start to tremble when I think of what it sounded like! Bülow conducted like a god"[110] and "the orchestra played like an angel."[111] In his *Reminiscences of Hans von Bülow* (1910), Strauss wrote: "To anyone who ever heard him play Beethoven or conduct Wagner, or who ever attended his music lessons or listened to him during orchestral rehearsals, he was bound to be the example of all the shining virtues of the reproductive artist.... Whatever feeling for the art of interpretation I can call my own I owe, apart from my father... to Hans von Bülow"[112] Bülow thought highly of Strauss as an apprentice conductor,[113] supported his new music, and provided him with opportunities to conduct it, as well as conducting it himself.[114]

Gustav Mahler heard Bülow conduct two concerts of the Meiningen Orchestra in Hamburg in January 1884. These made a tremendous impression on him, and he wrote an impassioned, worshipful letter to Bülow begging to be taken on – "I give

[107] letter to Daniela from Düsseldorf, 9 November 1884, Moulin-Eckart, *Letters of Hans Von Bülow*, p. 368

[108] quoted in Frithjof Haas, *Der Magier am Dirigentenpult: Felix Mottl* (Karlsruhe: Info-Verlag, 2006), p. 101

[109] letter to Daniela from Lausanne, 8 June 1886, Moulin-Eckart, *Letters of Hans Von Bülow*, p. 373

[110] letter to Dora Wihan from Munich, 9 April 1889, Willi Schuh (ed.), *Richard Strauss: Recollections and Reflections*, trans. Mary Whittall (Cambridge University Press, 1982), p. 165

[111] letter to his father shortly after the concert, quoted in Gewande, *Hans von Bülow*, p. 318

[112] Schuh, *Strauss: Recollections and Reflections*, p. 118

[113] see also Strauss chapter, p. 520

[114] Tchaikovsky saw Bülow at a concert in Berlin in 1888 and wrote somewhat jadedly to his family: "In Berlin I heard works by Richard Strauss, the new German genius. Von Bülow fusses over him as he did over Brahms and others. In my opinion there has never yet been anyone of less talent and so full of pretension": letter from Magdeburg, 12-24 January 1888, Piotr Ilyich Tchaikovsky, *Letters to his family: an autobiography* (trans.) Galina von Meck (London: Dobson, 1981), p. 388.

myself to you completely" – but Bülow responded that he could not.[115] Seven years later Bülow heard Mahler conduct, and he wrote to his daughter: "Hamburg has now secured a really excellent opera conductor in Herr Gustav Mahler (a serious, energetic Jew from Budapest), who in my opinion equals the very best: Mottl, Richter, and so on. I heard him do *Siegfried* recently with Alvary (who again struck me as ideal in the title role). I was filled with honest admiration for him, for he made – no, forced

Fig. 2.9. Bülow conducting in Vienna.
Silhouette by Otto Böhler

– the orchestra to pipe to his measure, without having had a rehearsal."[116] In time, Bülow would have other opportunities to recognise Mahler's abilities, not least when he sprang into the breach to conduct a concert for an ill Bülow in Hamburg on 12 December 1892, a concert of Mendelssohn, Beethoven, and Wagner. There are, as we shall see, many similarities between Bülow and Mahler as musicians: their forceful approach at the podium, their insistence on exactness, the emotional intensity they brought to their music-making. In one respect Bülow's approach to opera was quite different from Mahler's, namely the relationship of the music to the drama.

[115] Henry-Louis de La Grange, *Mahler, Vol. 1* (London: Gollancz, 1974), pp. 112-113, where the full text of the letters can be found

[116] letter to Daniela, Hamburg, 24 April 1891, Moulin-Eckart, *Letters of Hans Von Bülow*, p. 426

Felix Weingartner, who worked with Bülow in Hamburg in 1887 and 1888 observed:

His conducting did not make things easy for the singers. He very properly demanded the utmost exactitude, and this he got, for he was always allotted the pick of the available talents for his performances. But the moment he sat down at the desk nothing but the orchestra seemed to exist for him; and he disregarded the stage, save for the correction of musical mistakes.... He conducted operas as if they were symphonic pieces to which voices had been added like so many instrumental parts.... Utterly wanting was that sympathy between stage and orchestra which forms a bond between the actual drama and the transcendental music....With Bülow everything remained on a purely musical footing, and he resented the stage-manager's interruptions, no matter how necessary they were.[117]

There may be an element of exaggeration in this – Weingartner also says surprisingly that Bülow "kept his eyes glued to the score," though he was by this time ageing – unless his observations stemmed only from rehearsals for Spohr's *Jessonda* which he was discussing. Nevertheless, this is a characteristic of Bülow we have seen displayed or suggested elsewhere: in his letter to Wagner on the 1869 *Tristan*, and in the observation about his Munich *Lohengrin*, and disastrously, in his intolerance of an imperfect tenor in his final *Lohengrin* in Hanover.

Bülow's historic service to Wagner can be seen to be continued, to some extent, in the work of these younger conductors, and it is to that beery chap, Hans Richter we shall first turn.

[117] Felix Weingartner, *Lebenserinnerungen* (Zurich, 1928-9), vol. 1, pp. 377-8 (this is part of a passage not included in the English version, *Buffets and Rewards*, 1937, translated in *Music & Letters*, vol. 18, no. 3 (July, 1937), p. 289; a different, shorter translation can be found in Newman, *Life of Wagner*, vol. 4, p. 122). After an interview with Weingartner in 1904 the *Musical Times* wrote: "[Bülow in Hamburg] only concerned himself with the orchestra, and left the singers to their own devices, while the action of the opera seemed to be felt by him as a downright hindrance to the performance. The three regular conductors – Sucher, Feld, and Weingartner himself – often had to take up positions in the wings to assist the bewildered singers with signs and cues, for, in spite of Bülow's marvellous memory, he would at opera performances simply bury his head in the score." "Felix Weingartner –A Biographical Sketch," *Musical Times*, 1 May 1904, p. 290. For Weingartner's impressions of a *Lohengrin* conducted by Bülow, see Weingartner chapter, p. 276.

3

Hans Richter – His Master's Musician

To judge the massive stature of Hans Richter and his unsurpassed number of Wagner performances in any way that does justice to his musicianship is a formidable task. Whereas Bülow conducted about fifty performances of Wagner operas in his lifetime, Richter conducted almost 900, including many at Bayreuth where he was a titan among his colleagues.[1] A supremely natural musician, calm in command of orchestral players who worshipped him, and self-effacing before audiences who adored him, he led the enlightenment to Wagner in Bayreuth, Budapest, Vienna and London. He became the yardstick against whom all Wagner conductors were measured, whether in the pit or on the platform. The welcome given him when he returned to England for one of his "Richter Concerts" in 1882 was typical:

> The modest, genial prince of orchestral conductors is in our midst once more... [these are] the abilities that make Herr Richter what he is. There are now few amateurs who cannot tell of the wondrous command and grasp he holds over his forces; the masterly influence that enables him to impart his own spirit and idea to each player; the extraordinary memory that permits him to dispense with the book from end to end of a programme; and last, but not least, the sympathetic nature, the artistic feeling, and the scholarly erudition that make his readings of almost every master so truthful and reverent.[2]

In view of the abundance of material on Richter's Wagner performances, I will pass over his concert performances in favour of the complete operas, particularly those of his landmark years at Drury Lane and Covent Garden in 1882, 1903-04, and in 1908-09 when he conducted Wagner in English. There will, of course, be glimpses of Vienna and Bayreuth, and a good look at his formative years with Wagner and his master's opinions of him. Rather than presenting and summarising the critical

[1] Richter's biographer, Christopher Fifield, has counted 899 performances of Wagner operas during a career spanning 1868 to 1912: *Lohengrin* (198), *Die Meistersinger* (141), *Die Walküre* (123), *Tannhäuser* (85), *Siegfried* (84), *Götterdämmerung* (78), *Das Rheingold* (63), *Tristan und Isolde* (57), *Der fliegende Holländer* (55), and *Rienzi* (15): *True artist and true friend: a biography of Hans Richter* (Oxford: Clarendon Press, 1993), p. 91 and Appendix I at p. 501. At Bayreuth, he only conducted the *Ring* and the *Meistersinger*: the *Ring* in 1876, 1896 (with Felix Mottl and Siegfried Wagner), 1897, 1901, 1902 (all three years with Siegfried Wagner), 1904 (with Franz Beidler), 1906 (with Siegfried Wagner), and 1908; and *Die Meistersinger* in 1888, 1889, 1892 (with Felix Mottl), 1899, 1911, and 1912.

[2] *Sunday Times*, 7 May 1882, p. 7. There was "no fuss or ostentation about him... he [was] simply worshipped by his band": T.R. Croger, *Notes on conductors and conducting* (London: Nonconformist Musical Journal Office, 1899), p. 21. Croger was conductor of the Nonconformist Choir Union Orchestra.

responses chronologically, I will group these under each of the major works. Finally, there will be some comparisons of Richter with other conductors to illuminate what for some who heard his performances was dazzlingly obvious: "there is only one great, one incomparable Wagnerian conductor in the world, and his name is Hans Richter."[3]

Early years with Wagner

Richter was born in Hungary, in the town of Raab (now called Györ) in about midway between Budapest and Vienna, on 4 April 1843. All his family were musicians: his father was a cathedral choirmaster who died when he was ten, and his mother an opera singer. He grew up in a musical atmosphere, sang in the cathedral choir and, at the age of seven, made his debut in an orchestra playing the drums. "The melody is in the flesh," he said recalling this juvenile experience, "but the rhythm is in the bones!"[4] Soon he joined what became known as the Vienna Boys Choir, and in 1860 joined the Vienna Conservatory to study various instruments, principally the horn. His varied abilities at the Conservatory earned him the nickname *Nothnagel* (Hope in Extremity) because he was often called upon to substitute for absentee players; on one occasion for the *Tannhäuser* Overture he played three instruments: the horn, cymbals, and triangle.[5] He also studied conducting. He went on to play in various orchestras in Vienna – a different instrument in each. "My wish always was to become a conductor," he said, "and to this end I was anxious to make myself practically acquainted with every instrument in the orchestra."[6] This practical facility would stand him in good stead with new orchestras: their players were amazed, impressed and inspired by his ability to demonstrate what was required in difficult passages.[7] After four years of orchestral work in Vienna, a momentous opportunity came his way.

Wagner had written to Heinrich Esser, one of Richter's teachers in Vienna, looking for someone who could copy out the score of the *Meistersinger* for the printer. Esser recommended Richter, and in October 1866, the twenty-three year old musician went off to live in Wagner's house, Tribschen, near Lucerne. Richter had seen Wagner before in Vienna: "I had seen him conducting, and had worshipped him, you know; but I had never spoken to him, though I had always longed to do so."[8] At Tribschen, Richter was far more than a copyist, a task at which he excelled. He was required to accompany Wagner on his long afternoon walks. He related:

> At that time I was still extremely shy and reserved, with little experience of the ways of society; but as these walks were to a certain extent part of my duty, I fancied that it was obligatory upon me to entertain the master who strode silently by my side. Goodness knows what tortures I underwent in my efforts to find subjects likely to interest him! I positively trembled as I started the dialogue on the spur of the moment. One day, shortly after my arrival – it was, I think, our

3 *Sunday Times*, 10 May 1903, p. 4 (Herman Klein, reviewing the *Ring*)

4 "Hans Richter," *Musical Times*, 1 July 1899, p. 442

5 Anna Brodsky, *Recollections of a Russian home: a musician's experiences* (Manchester: Sherratt & Hughes, 1904), p. 119

6 F. Klickman, "Moments with Modern Musicians: A Chat with Dr Hans Richter," *Windsor Magazine*, vol. 4 (July-November 1896), p. 339

7 as happened in London, for example: Croger, *Notes on conductors and conducting*, pp. 28-29

8 Klickman, "Moments with Modern Musicians," *Windsor Magazine*, p. 340

second or third walk – I thought I had hit upon a capital subject, and ventured to sound Wagner upon his own works. "Can you tell me, Herr Wagner, which opera you prefer, *Tannhäuser* or *Tristan*?" Wagner burst into a loud fit of laughter, and replied, "How can you ask such a silly question?" That was all his answer, and the conversation ended there! From that day I never ventured to break silence, unless Wagner gave me the lead, so that our walks became more silent than ever.[9]

Fig. 3.1. Hans Richter as a young conductor

[9] "Wagner and Richter," *Musical Times*, 1 April 1893, p. 208, a translation of an interview in *Le Guide Musical* (Brussels), 5 March 1893, pp. 115-16. Edward Speyer also told this story from what he claimed were notes he took at the time Richter told it to him, but his account bears a remarkable resemblance to the wording of the *Musical Times* translation: *My Life and Friends*, pp. 55-56. The word Speyer attributes to Wagner is "foolish," not "silly." Fifield, who also tells the story from an unattributed source uses "stupid" (*True Artist*, p. 16). (The word in French was *sotte*.) He later told the *Musical Times*: "These afternoon constitutionals were always of an absolutely silent nature. Not a word was spoken": 1 July 1899, p. 443.

Soon Richter was accepted into the family, becoming much more than Wagner's secretary. He would eat with the Wagners, play with their children who adored him, listen to Wagner reading aloud in the evenings, make music with Cosima, and accompany Wagner as he sang from his works. Judith Gautier, one of Wagner's friends (less so Cosima's), was a visitor on one of these occasions.

> The music of the *Meistersinger* is especially difficult to render at the piano and Wagner was not a very skilful performer – Richter knew that,[10] so he was very restless and followed the Master's playing, note by note, with the greatest anxiety. He knew it all, even the most uninteresting passages; he touched the notes that the hand of the Master was too small to include. From time to time he was carried out of himself, and struck the piano hurriedly saving an effect which was in danger of being lost, completing a harmony, or striking a chord between the Master's hesitating fingers. I am not sure that Wagner was not a little irritated by this infringement upon his territory.[11]

Nevertheless, the relationship continued, as Wagner became increasingly dependent on the prodigiously talented practical musician. By the time Richter left in 1871, to take up an appointment in Budapest, Cosima would write in her diary: "for us it will be difficult to let him go – we look on him, after all, as our eldest son!"[12]

Wagner's opinion of Richter as musician

In order to assess Richter as an interpreter of Wagner, it is necessary, as a first step, to know what Wagner himself thought of his abilities. There is no doubt Wagner was impressed by and depended upon Richter's practical musical skills. Richter was able to show, for example, that a difficult horn passage in the *Meistersinger* could be played just as Wagner had imagined it, and Wagner was delighted.[13] In June 1867 he went with Wagner to Munich to supervise Bülow's performance of *Lohengrin*. When the time came to prepare for the first *Meistersinger* in June 1868, Richter was talent-spotting singers, coaching them – "Nachbaur. (Richter's miracle)," Wagner jotted in his *Brown Book*[14] – and learning from Wagner, and no doubt from Bülow too, everything that was required to perform the music. When the prospect came for a *Meistersinger* in Dresden, Wagner put forward his young protégé:

> Being intimately acquainted with all my intentions, he succeeded in training both the Munich singers and the chorus to the most admirable accuracy in an astonishingly short space of time... he would [in Dresden] teach the right tempi down to the last shade, as well as the correct expression....[15]

[10] He told the unnamed author of "Richter and the First English *Ring*," *Musical Times*, June 1951, pp. 262-63, that he "never saw a man play the piano with such genius-like clumsiness as Wagner."

[11] Judith Gautier, *Wagner at home*, (trans.) Effie Dunreith Massie (London: Mills & Boon, 1910), p. 255. This probably happened in late July 1870 judging from Cosima's *Diaries*, vol. 1, pp. 248-249, 254-255

[12] 5 January 1871, *Diaries*, vol. 1, p. 318. Cosima recorded that Wagner bought Richter a dressing-gown on 21 October 1870 (*ibid.*, p. 286). Harold Bauer visited Vienna many years later and was received by Richter "in a loose dressing gown, so ragged and dirty that I was quite shocked." Richter told him it had been worn by Wagner. *Harold Bauer - His Book* (New York: W.W. Norton & Company, 1948), pp. 134-35.

[13] "Hans Richter," *Musical Times*, 1 July 1899, p. 443

[14] Joachim Bergfeld (ed.), *The diary of Richard Wagner, 1865-1882: the Brown Book*, (trans.) George Bird (London: Gollancz, 1980), p. 167. Nachbaur sang Walther in the first production.

[15] undated letter reproduced in the *Brown Book*, p. 150

He secretly rehearsed a group of players for the *Siegfried Idyll*, Wagner's gift to Cosima on Christmas Day 1870, which Wagner conducted while Richter played the trumpet.

Cosima's *Diaries*, begun more than two years after Richter had come to Tribschen, are replete with examples of congenial music-making, technical discussions about the horn, about the wretchedness of German conductors, and the occasional piece of instruction[16] – "In the evening all our musicians together; the *Idyll* is played; Richter distinguishes himself with his rapid grasp of *Götterdämmerung*." (28 December 1873) "Our musicians in the evening, R. goes through the second act of *Tristan* with R[ichter], unutterably moving… it is R[ichter] who pleases us most, with his primitiveness and his practical talent." (29 December 1873).[17] The word "primitiveness" in this context should not be considered derogatory. It recalls a perceptive comment made by the Hungarian violinist, Carl Flesch, who once played under Richter in Budapest:

> This disciple of the master belonged to the noble class of intellectually primitive, eminently natural musicians of genius whom the Austro-Hungarian monarchy had always produced in astonishing numbers.... a supremely competent conductor of the old, solid school.[18]

By his nature, Richter was never interested in theoretical matters. When asked by Siegfried Wagner what he thought of Wagner's voluminous writings, he said they were wonderful but he would have preferred another score from their author.[19] Many will have sympathy with this view, though some in Wagner's circle did not.[20]

The relationship between Richter and Wagner began to become distant after Richter left Tribschen in April 1871 to be with his mother in Vienna. He was appointed conductor in Budapest in August, and soon Cosima was writing, "he annoys [Wagner] because he has not been working for him and has not yet prepared the score of *Das Rheingold* for Schott."[21] In September it vexed Wagner that he was still not doing work for his old employer.[22] Richter visited from time to time, but Wagner was "still

[16] "Yesterday R. gave Richter a severe reprimand in connection with the *Jubelouvertüre* [Weber], which Richter had referred to in a dismissive attitude. R. demonstrated to him how solemn and festive, in a popular way, the Overture is… Richter was ashamed." *Diaries*, vol. 1, p. 344 (1 March 1871)

[17] *ibid.*, vol. 1, pp. 120 (conductors), 321 (horn), 715 (*Götterdämmerung*), 716 (*Tristan*)

[18] *The memoirs of Carl Flesch*, (trans. and ed.) Hans Keller (London: Rockliff, 1957), p. 152

[19] Siegfried Wagner, *Erinnerungen* (Stuttgart: J. Engelhorns, 1923), p. 141 quoted by Herbert J. Peyser, "Some fallacies of Modern Anti-Wagnerianism," *Musical Quarterly*, vol. 12 no. 2 (April 1926), p. 178. Fifield (*True Artist*, p. 338) claims that Richter had "certainly studied and assimilated" *On Conducting* (1869); as it was written while he was at Tribschen, this seems highly likely.

[20] One of them may have been a Norbert Dunkel who reported Wagner once saying: "'Richter is and remains a country bumpkin.' In Tribschen he would sit all day in the domestic quarters and tell them of Schopenhauer's writings without understanding a word of them himself. 'He's nothing more than a bungling artisan. As a man, he's always been a burden to me.'" Manfred Eger, *Hans Richter: Der Urdirigent der Bayreuther Festspiele* (Bayreuth: Druckhaus Bayreuth, 1995), p. 73. This book is a combination of two booklets: *Hans Richter – Des Meisters lieber Gesell* and *Hans Richter: Bayreuth, Wien, London und zurück*, both originally published in 1990 on the occasion of a Richter exhibition at Wahnfried. Eger gives no date or source for these comments, nor any information on who Dunkel was. Fifield (*True Artist*, p. 96) quotes the lines from Eger without mentioning Dunkel, thereby presenting the whole passage as Wagner's words. These bitter comments, if they were made at all, can only have been uttered, as Manfred Eger points out (*ibid*, p. 74), in one of Wagner's highly agitated states when he was prone to become abusive, and would make comments he was later to regret.

[21] Cosima Wagner, *Diaries*, vol. 1, p. 406 (29 August 1871) [22] *ibid*, p. 410 (8 September 1871)

weighed down by corrections – if only Richter were here!"[23] By March 1874 Wagner was "thoroughly depressed by the great difficulties of his task, and on top of that Richter, the only one who could help him, is now a theatre director! 'It's as if I wanted to become the minister of trade!' R. says."[24] Wagner was clearly reluctant to recognise that the young man's flourishing talents had led him elsewhere.

In June Richter visited the Wagners (the children were jubilant), and Wagner went through parts of the *Ring* with Richter. "In the evening the first act of *Siegfried*, very handsomely played by Richter."[25] "We know of no one in Germany," Cosima writes, "who could conduct even the minimal preliminary studies for the performances here."[26] (Richter was staying with them at the time, but was employed in Hungary.) He left them in July ("the children in mourning rags, tears and wailing, Rus [the dog] as the funeral horse!"[27]), and in August wrote "asking very touchingly that we not lose confidence in him!"[28] Whether Richter sensed that Wagner had begun to resent his growing independence, or whether he feared what was to come, is unclear. He soon sent news of his engagement and a photograph of his fiancée, and Cosima noted in her diary (having been told by someone else) that the fiancée was "of Jewish origin."[29]

After the marriage, they left Tribschen and Wagner made the obvious if not ominous comment to Cosima: "I have the definite feeling that Richter will now be pursuing other paths."[30]

They went to see him conduct the *Holländer* in Budapest, an abridged version sung in Hungarian and Italian, but it was a "Great disappointment!" Cosima recorded; "Nowhere else has so much been cut in the *Holländer* and Richter has also introduced cymbals etc. Astonishment over this Wagnerian *par excellence!*"[31] Soon Wagner was reflecting "very candidly about Richter and the strange way in which he has developed."[32] There was some cooling on Richter's part, reflected in correspondence, possibly influenced by adverse comments (or gossip) he had heard about Wagner.[33] Nevertheless, they remained on good terms and the Wagners visited Vienna, where Richter had been installed with Wagner's support, to hear a performance of *Tannhäuser*. The dress rehearsal was not impressive ("orchestra lifeless," etc.), but Wagner remained "admirably calm."[34] His faith or patience was well placed, for the performance turned out to be a "veritable triumph," Cosima wrote, "good beyond all expectations; nothing quite as R. intended it, but very full of life."[35] Richter had triumphed in a Wagner opera, though perhaps not in the manner envisaged by the composer.

Whatever Wagner may have wanted, Richter was the inevitable conductor for the first *Ring* in 1876. He was in Bayreuth for rehearsals in May, and after the first orchestral rehearsal of the *Rheingold* Wagner said, "it sounds wonderful."[36] The first rehearsal of act three of the *Walküre* was a "shattering experience," but then, at the

[23] *ibid*, p. 733 (17 February 1874). Seidl had arrived, as Wagner's assistant, in the autumn of 1872.
[24] *ibid*, p. 740 (9 March 1874)
[25] *ibid*, p. 766 (13 June 1874)
[26] *ibid*, p. 770 (2 July 1874)
[27] *ibid*, p. 777 (25 July 1874)
[28] *ibid*, p. 783 (26 August 1874)
[29] *ibid*, p. 821 (22 January 1875)
[30] *ibid*, p. 824 (7 February 1875)
[31] *ibid*, p. 831 (9 March 1875)
[32] *ibid*, p. 847 (17 May 1875)
[33] "a letter from Richter, so foolish and crude that one wonders how it is possible": *ibid*, p. 859 (24 August 1875)
[34] *ibid*, p. 876 (20 November 1875)
[35] *ibid*, p. 877 (22 November 1875) and note at p. 1135
[36] *ibid*, p. 910 (3 June 1876)

third *Walküre* rehearsal, there was "much vexation. Incorrect tempi in the orchestra," and two days later, after Wagner had supervised an orchestral rehearsal of *Siegfried* in the morning, "(Richter still knows little about tempi) – 'traces too many crotchets,' says R."[37] On the day Cosima recorded this, Wagner wrote to Richter (why he did not *speak* to him is a mystery – perhaps he was at rehearsals[38] – but the record is richer for his letter):

> My friend, it is essential that you attend the piano rehearsals, else you will not get to know my tempi. It would be very trying to have to make up for this in the orchestral rehearsals, where I do not like to discuss matters of tempo with you for the first time. Yesterday we hardly ever refrained from dragging, especially Betz [Wotan], whom I have allowed fiery tempos at the piano rehearsals, and also with Materna [Brünnhilde]. Even the Valkyrie were held back in some of the heated moments in the ensembles with Wotan. I really believe that throughout you are bound too much to beating crotchets, which always hinders a tempo, particularly as the long notes dominate when Wotan is angry. In my view one should beat quavers where one needs to be precise, but you cannot maintain the mood of a lively allegro by beating crotchets.... My dear Hans! The services you have rendered my orchestra are so great, and my recognition of your quite unique abilities and achievements is so meaningful that I fear we have given vent to our pleasure and left undiscussed – and with a certain timidity – the most important issues, as if to avoid giving the impression of disagreement or unhappiness.... I attribute the reasons for our differences simply to your being *on the whole* still too much unable to assist at the piano rehearsals....[39]

Thereafter a curtain of silence falls on the rehearsals as Cosima abandons her diary in the final frantic days of rehearsals and during the Festival itself,[40] during which time, as we have seen, Wagner's behaviour, or at least his instructions, became increasingly erratic or incapable of implementation.

After the Festival, Wagner reflected on the performances and what could be learned from them, and Cosima recorded the nub of his complaint: "Richter not sure of a single tempo – dismal experiences indeed!... in the concluding scene, after Siegfried's body had been removed, he saw that yet again Richter had not understood him."[41] Years later Wagner elaborated to King Ludwig, at whose side he had sat during the Festival performances, smarting at Richter's tempi:

> I do not know any conductor whom I could trust to perform my music in the right way, or any actor-singer of whom I could expect a proper realisation of my dramatic figures unless I myself had taught him everything bar by bar, phrase by phrase.... what horrified me was the discovery

[37] *ibid*, p. 912 (20 June 1876), p. 912-913 (21 June), p. 913 (23 June)

[38] Speyer quotes Richter's description of the two months' rehearsal schedule: "Every morning I rehearsed for four to five hours with the orchestra and all the afternoon at the pianoforte with the singers....": Speyer, *My Life and Friends*, p. 59.

[39] letter dated 23 June 1876 in Fifield, *True Artist*, pp. 108-109; also quoted in Egon Voss, *Die Dirigenten der Bayreuther Festspiele* (Regensburg: Gustav Bosse Verlag, 1976), p. 12, and the *Bayreuther Festspielbuch 1951*, p. 59

[40] She stopped writing her diary on 4 August 1876 (after she had received disturbing news about Bülow's health) and resumed after the Festival on 8 September, sketching the missing days from memory. Richter is not mentioned.

[41] *ibid*, p. 921 (9 September 1876); and later: "... the frustrations (Richter's tempi)": *ibid*, vol. 2, p. 131 (7 August 1878)

that my conductor [Richter] – whom nevertheless I regard as the best I know – often could not maintain the right tempo even when it had been achieved, simply because he was incapable of understanding why it should be thus and not otherwise.[42]

Years later Richter also reflected: "I remembered the Master's letter about beating 4/4. He was right! At the time there were many players from Meiningen in the orchestra who were inexperienced with opera, and [who were] not... used to seeing the *alla breve* style."[43] This suggests Richter had developed his style of conducting since 1876, and there is some evidence that he did so far as tempi were concerned.[44] Manfred Eger has written that for the conductor of the 1876 *Ring* to have lived up to Wagner's ideals, he would have had to be a stage director as well as a mind-reader.

It was probably Richter's one "mistake" to have conducted the score as a full-blooded musician. He did not take cues for tempos from the dramatic flow, but from the music. Given the kind of conductor Wagner envisaged, no one else could have lived up to his expectations either. Even during the last years of his life, he lamented that he knew of no artist capable of performing his works in the way he imagined them: "I don't leave a single person behind who knows my tempo!" He even denied that Hans von Bülow was competent enough independently to perform his works.[45]

Ernest Newman, who acknowledged that "Richter's great qualities were toweringly great," was never able to persuade himself that Richter was Wagner's ideal kind of conductor.

Wagner was all for the "singing" style, the modelling of beautiful and meaningful phrases as a great singer would model them, with all sorts of subtle variations of tone, accent and rhythm from note to note. Richter's manner was the opposite of this; for him the great thing was not the inner life of the line but the general breadth of the page; hence the four-square character that all music seemed to take on in his hands.[46]

[42] letter [dated 9 February 1879] quoted in Newman, *Life of Wagner*, vol. 4, p. 470, who described this as Wagner's tragedy: "He could never meet with executive artists of the same calibre as himself, a single actor or conductor or singer who could give his characters and his verbal and musical phrases the life with which his imagination had endowed them.... Wagner was a far better conductor than any of his conductors, a far better actor than any of his actors, a far better singer than any of his singers in everything but tone.... he was doomed to perpetual disappointment where the performance of his works was concerned; the best that his interpreters could give him was no more than an approximation to his ideal.... Richter never won Wagner's full commendation as a conductor: for one his rhythm was too four square": pp. 470-471, 475n.

[43] Richter's diary for 6 February 1897, quoted in Fifield, *True Artist*, pp. 110-111

[44] At Bayreuth in 1904, for example, a critic reported on the *Ring*: "Fortunately, Hans Richter does not share the current tendency to slow down. There are only a few things he handles heavily and broadly, but usually his tempo is lively, his interpretation intended to portray an easy flow....": Leopold Schmidt, *Berliner Tageblatt*, 1904, quoted in Susanna Großmann-Vendrey, *Bayreuth in der deutschen Presse*, Vol. 3,1 (1883-1906), (Regensburg: Bosse, 1983), p. 199.

[45] Eger, *Der Urdirigent*, p. 92. Richter's family seems to have shared this view: Eleonore Schacht-Richter, *Hans Richter: Leben und Schaffen des großen Dirigenten* (Bayreuth: Deutsche Richard-Wagner-Gesellschaft, 1995), p. 9. John Deathridge has written: "In Richter's defence it must be said that Wagner's standards were often utopian": "Bayreuth's National Front," *Times Literary Supplement*, 5 August 1977, p. 968 (a review of Voss, *Die Dirigenten der Bayreuther Festspiele*, 1976).

[46] "Wagner, Richter and the *Meistersinger*," *Sunday Times*, 26 October 1930, p. 5. Some of Newman's reviews of Richter's performances (which we will see below) belie his comment about its four-square character.

And so they drifted. Wagner was resigned to, and indeed sanctioned, cuts to his works conducted by Richter in Vienna: there was no practical alternative. The conductor is virtually absent from the last six years of Cosima's *Diaries*, which ended with Wagner's death. After attending a performance of *Parsifal* in Bayreuth in 1882, Richter returned immediately to Vienna. He never saw Wagner again. "Adieu! Good Hans! Greetings from the heart! Your good old Rich. Wagner," the master's last letter went.[47] His faithful conductor returned to Bayreuth on 18 February 1883, to carry Wagner's coffin to its grave.

Fig. 3.2. Richter, the busy Wagner conductor, 1891.
Drawing by Theo Zasche

Wagnerian highlights

While at Tribschen, we recall that Richter's duties with *Meistersinger* had made him eminently suited to work on the production in Munich in 1868. This he did, and shortly after its first performance, he was appointed a Court conductor and led his own performance on 27 July 1869, the first of some 141 occasions he would do so. He also prepared and conducted, to dress rehearsal stage, a production of the *Rheingold* in

[47] letter dated 28 January 1883 quoted in Fifield, *True Artist*, p. 198

1869 which the King wanted to see (Wagner had wanted it held back for a complete cycle), but resigned in protest at the stage management (Wagner was sympathetic with Richter) and left Munich, never to return till 1908. He conducted the premiere of *Lohengrin* in Brussels in March 1870 with "quite enormous" success,[48] displaying his prodigious memory by conducting without a score,[49] and then returned to Tribschen to copy out parts of the *Ring* for Wagner. He soon had prospects for Budapest. With Wagner's encouragement – "As both conductor and Kapellmeister you are in your element"[50] – he went there for four years (1871-1875). In 1875 he was engaged by the Vienna Court Opera and remained in the post for twenty-two years. His long association turned out to be "one of the milestones in the annals ofViennese music."[51] One of his most brilliant successes was the first performance of *Tristan* in 1883, despite its cuts, and in spite of the critics.[52] Richter had achieved what Wagner had failed to do in Vienna twenty-two years earlier when a long-rehearsed production of *Tristan* had had to be abandoned. Max Graf recalled Richter's Vienna years:

> I have often seen Hans Richter conduct at the Vienna Opera, and I dare say that, never again, as many great conductors as I have seen standing in his place there and elsewhere, have I seen a conductor so full of naturalness and simple strength. Nikisch, the pale salon gypsy with the romantic curls, was interesting; Gustav Mahler, a bundle of nerves with the highest kind of intelligence; Weingartner, elegant and formally impressive; Toscanini, a firebrand and a volcano. None of these was so imposing as Hans Richter, of whom Debussy wrote, after hearing him conduct in London: "He conducts as dear God would conduct if he had learned conducting from Hans Richter."[53]

It was from Vienna that he ventured to London as the valuable, if not indispensable, assistant to Wagner during his 1877 concert visit. "This was the man who was to save the Wagner Festival from disaster," wrote Herman Klein, "to create for us a new orchestral standard, to give us fresh ideas on orchestral conducting, and, generally speaking, to change the course of musical life in this country."[54] Klein said similar things about Richter's operatic debut in London in 1882, a season in which he conducted the Hamburg Opera company at Drury Lane in *Lohengrin* (three performances), *Holländer* (2), *Tannhäuser* (5), and the English premieres of *Meistersinger* (10) and *Tristan und Isolde* (2).[55] (If this were not historic enough, Anton Seidl was conducting the *Ring* almost

[48] as Cosima was happy to record in her *Diaries*, vol. 1, p. 202 (25 March 1870)

[49] Maurice Kufferath, *L'art de diriger l'orchestre: Richard Wagner & Hans Richter* (Paris: Libraraire Fischbacher, 1890), p. 100

[50] letter to Richter dated 29 July 1871 quoted in Fifield, *True Artist*, p. 50

[51] Marcel Prawy, *The Vienna Opera* (Vienna-Munich-Zurich: Verlag Fritz Molden, 1969), p. 41

[52] Speidel complained of "deadly boredom," and Hanslick wanted more than cuts: "a blue pencil is not enough, what is needed here is a sword": Prawy, *The Vienna Opera*, p. 53.

[53] Max Graf, *Legend of a musical city* (New York: Philosophical Library, 1945), p. 176 Debussy had recently attended performances of *Rheingold* and *Walküre* at Covent Garden and wrote: "It seems to me impossible to conceive of more perfect interpretations.... If Richter seems like a prophet when he conducts the orchestra, it is because he *is* Almighty God! ... (And you can be sure that God would not attempt to conduct an orchestra without first having consulted Richter!)," letter to Gils Blas, 30 April 1903, in François Lesure (ed.), *Debussy on Music*, (trans.) Richard Langham Smith (New York: Knopf, 1977), p. 189.

[54] Klein, *Musicians and mummers*, pp. 169-170

[55] "... a remarkable achievement. The rare excellence of these performances... has never been forgotten by any who witnessed them.": Herman Klein, *Thirty years of musical life in London*, p. 126. Statistics from Fifield, *True Artist*, p. 187

contemporaneously at Her Majesty's Theatre.[56]) We shall read reviews of some of these performances below. A further season of Wagnerian opera in London in 1884 was not a success, either financially or artistically, except for Richter.[57] He did not return to Covent Garden for nineteen years, for reasons never properly understood.[58]

We shall now consider some of the critical responses, mostly in England, to Richter's conducting of the major works of Wagner.

The early operas

The *Holländer* may not have been among Richter's favourite Wagner operas. Bruckner once asked Richter, as if to echo Richter's own "silly" question to Wagner, which was his favourite opera, *Tristan* or *Meistersinger*. "*Holländer*," he replied, "because I don't have to conduct it."[59] As for *Lohengrin*, he revived the opera in London in 1880 without cuts and sung in Italian. Nothing like it had been heard before in England.[60] "The orchestra… obeyed with that docile readiness which only a great conductor can command, and were simply perfect," wrote the *World*. "Richter takes some movements slower than is customary in this country; … this [must] be accepted, because better than anybody else does he know Wagner's intention."[61] In 1882 he conducted the first German *Lohengrin* in England at Drury Lane. In 1884 a performance at Covent Garden was described as an "exceptionally fine one" by the *Magazine of Music*.[62] There was, however, one disastrous aspect of the production: "a more ludicrous effect than that of the sunrise in the second act, which began in the upper part of the sky and gradually spread downward, we never seem to have seen."[63] A 1904 performance was described by the *Athenaeum* as "very strenuous…, [Richter's] *tempi* are always brisk, and we may presume him to know what Wagner wanted better than any person living. With Dr. Richter at the desk, for example, I should imagine it takes Ortrud about three minutes less to get into the palace with Elsa than under the guidance of any other conductor."[64] The *Star* considered:

> It was altogether a beautiful performance, and excellent in every detail. The guiding hand of Dr. Richter made its influence felt everywhere; and everything was spirited, brilliant, and strong. There was no sentimentality, no dragging, and no rough edges were to be seen, and we were transported into the romantic, poetical atmosphere which the poet-dramatist dreamed of, and which is so seldom realised. As was the case with *Tannhäuser*, Dr. Richter made one feel rather that *Lohengrin* leans on Weber than that it foreshadows the *Ring*.[65]

56 "Wagner's Music in England," *Musical Times*, 1 September 1906, pp. 589-94 (F. G. E.). As a measure of their differing drawing-powers, Richter was mentioned in advertisements for the Drury Lane performances, whereas Seidl was omitted altogether from the advertisements for Her Majesty's: *Morning Post*, 30 May 1882, p. 5.

57 *Illustrated Sporting and Dramatic News*, 19 July 1884, p. 479; *Magazine of Music*, August 1884, pp. 8-9: the German troupe was "of third-rate quality… *Tannhäuser* was wretchedly performed"; Richter in his diary agreed about *Tannhäuser*: "wretched performance": Fifield, *True Artist*, p. 206.

58 Harold Rosenthal, *Opera at Covent Garden: A Short History* (London: Victor Gollancz Ltd, 1967), p. 76

59 Fifield, *True Artist*, p. 259, citing "A. Göllerich and L. Auer, *Anton Bruckner* (Regensburg, 1936)" [n.p.]

60 *Athenaeum*, 5 June 1880, p. 735

61 2 June 1880, pp. 15-16

62 *Magazine of Music*, July 1884, p. 9

63 *Athenaeum*, 19 July 1884, p. 91

64 17 May 1904, p. 843 (Alfred Kalisch)

65 10 May 1904, p. 1 ("Crescendo"). "On the whole," the *Star* wrote of Richter's *Tannhäuser* a few days

In a *Tannhäuser* performance in 1904, Richter was also noted for his brisk tempi. "The March was played very rapidly," the *Star* reported; "but so beautifully was it phrased that the rapidity robbed it of none of its dignity, and gave it an unwonted brilliancy."[66] Indeed, "one has only to listen to [Richter] for half an hour to discover how absurd is the doctrine that dignity can only be obtained by dragging the time."[67]

Tristan und Isolde

The English premiere of *Tristan*, at Drury Lane on 20 June 1882, was "a triumph of the highest order," according to the *Sunday Times*.[68] Richter had been given twelve to fourteen orchestral rehearsals, and the orchestra was "very near perfection" – "the instruments might often have played what was *not* set down for them without much harm to the general result, [but] few would have known it," observed the *Daily Telegraph*[69] – and even those who had difficulties with the music acknowledged the masterly style and magnificence of Richter's conducting.[70] Anecdotes of him putting his hand on his heart and beseeching more passion from the strings are legion.[71] A 1904 performance was superb: "Over and over again it gave one a cold shiver down the back," wrote Alfred Kalisch in the *World*, "and the cold shiver is said by many to be the ultimate test of beauty in music. One would like to dwell in detail on Dr. Richter's *Tristan*, but I can only say generally that it is more massive and less sensuous than might have been expected, and altogether magnificent."[72] The lack of sensuousness was also commented on by the *Star* which compared the performance to those of other great conductors heard in London:

> There have been fine orchestral renderings of *Tristan* at Covent Garden under Mahler, Mottl, and Muck (the alliteration is accidental), but none was so complete and so completely rehearsed as last night's. It had its own distinguishing features, too, which gave it its own physiognomy. Mahler was perhaps more passionate, and Muck more subtly imaginative, and Mottl more highly colored, but last night everything was on a large scale: in the first act, and still more in the last act, it was overwhelming; in some of the love music a little more purely human weakness would have seemed almost welcome. But it was altogether superb in its mastery, its sense of proportion, and its finish of detail. As was the case on Monday with *Don Giovanni*, we heard numberless things which had been obscure before. Dr. Richter can make climaxes

earlier, "the chief characteristic of the rendering was that *Tannhäuser* was made to seem more like the successor of *Oberon* and *Euryanthe*, and less like a progenitor of *Tristan* and *Parsifal*." (7 May 1904, p. 2)

66 *Star*, 7 May 1904, p. 2 ("Crescendo"); also noted by *World*, 10 May 1904, p. 812 (Alfred Kalisch)

67 *Manchester Guardian*, 24 May 1905, p. 7 (unsigned, unlike a review of *Siegfried* on 5 May, p. 6 signed "E. N."). By 1907, Richter was being criticised for his "rigid adhesion to the orthodox slow tempi": *Sunday Times*, 26 May 1907, p. 4 (unsigned).

68 25 June 1882, p. 7; cf. *The Times*, 22 June 1882, p. 4: "the orchestra under Herr Richter materially contributed to general success of the performance." Hermann Winkelmann and Rosa Sucher sang the title roles.

69 21 June 1882, p. 3

70 *Illustrated Sporting and Dramatic News*, 24 June 1882, p. 351; *Athenaeum*, 24 June 1882, pp. 804-805

71 e.g. "Bravo, celli, quite correct, but you play like married people; a little more like the young lovers, please": "Hans Richter," *Musical Times*, 1 July 1899, p. 447; "Jouez avec âme": Kufferath, *L'art de diriger l'orchestre*, p. 101; "Play with soul": Finck, *Wagner and his Works*, vol. 2, pp. 289-290

72 10 May 1904, p. 812 (Alfred Kalisch). *The Times* wrote of a "whirl of dramatic motives in the first act… reproduced with rare force and distinction": 14 May 1904, p. 8.

Fig. 3.3. Richter in 1866, at the time he first worked for Wagner at Tribschen

Fig. 3.4. Richter with the Nibelung Chancery, Bayreuth, 1872

Fig. 3.5. Richter conducting the *Ring* in Bayreuth.
Drawing by Ludwig Bechstein.
Illustrated Sporting and Dramatic News, 26 August 1876

Fig. 3.6. Richter conducting the *Ring* in English in London.
Daily Graphic, 28 January 1908

Fig. 3.7. Richter conducting the *Tannhäuser* Overture in Vienna. Silhouettes by Otto Böhler

Fig. 3.8. Richter from his Vienna years, 1875-1897

Fig. 3.9. Richter on his seventieth birthday, 1913

such as no other conductor can, and he can graduate them with a nicety that seems impossible to anyone else.[73]

His last performance of *Tristan* for the season was "perhaps, his finest achievement," in the view of the *Daily News*. "Never has the impassioned music been played with such an intensity and glow of feeling. It was the culminating triumph of Dr. Richter's many triumphs this season. There was nothing of a perfunctory spirit in his direction of this work of genius."[74]

Die Meistersinger von Nürnberg

If there was but one of Wagner's operas that lay closest to Richter's heart, it was the *Meistersinger*. His affinity with the work may not be the only reason he was invited to conduct it at Bayreuth, and more frequently than any other work, nor may it stem only from his youthful work copying the score for Wagner and assisting Bülow at its first performance. It is the work that came closest to his nature. "There was a trace of Sachs' good humour, something of the utter honesty and simplicity of the German artistic conscience [that explained] why he was an ideal conductor of *Meistersinger*," wrote Hamburg critic, Ferdinand Pfohl.[75] "It is apparently the work which more than any other moves his inmost heart. It has, indeed, long been a favourite saying of his friends that he must be a direct descendant of Sachs, with whose artistic nature he has so much in common," wrote the *Star*.[76]

The English premiere at Drury Lane on 30 May 1882 was a "complete success," according to the press.[77] It came after Seidl had conducted the first English *Ring* at Her Majesty's Theatre earlier in the month. Louis Engel wrote in the *World*:

To the English public, the *Meistersinger* is a revelation.... Wagner provides the following incredible combination: a libretto without a horror, without a crime; music sometimes for forty minutes without brass – full of melody, chorus and concerted music – music not only learned and a most interesting study of counterpoint, handled with an ease delightful to behold, but music amusing to make you roar. The whole house burst out laughing at that mock serenade and at the competition of the singers: Wagner, who can be so noisy and so tedious, to be so *spiritual* and amusing![78]

73 4 May 1904, p. 1 ("Crescendo"). The *Observer* wrote: "Never, perhaps, has the orchestral portion of this wondrous work been more perfectly interpreted." (8 May 1904, p. 6).

74 20 June 1904, p. 4. In light of this and the other reviews quoted, Adrian Boult's reported comment in later life seems unduly dismissive: "the mood of *Tristan*... was nowhere near Richter. Nikisch was *the* man for *Tristan*, Richter was *the* man for *Meistersinger*." Fifield, *True Artist*, p. 464, citing the BBC's "Collectors' Corner," 8 April 1980, "and/or" a private conversation between Christopher Dyment and Sir Adrian Boult, 18 September 1972

75 quoted by Wooldridge, *Conductor's World*, p. 110 [from Ferdinand Pfohl's *Arthur Nikisch: Sein Leben, seine Kunst, sein Wirken* (Hamburg: Alster-Verlag, 1925), pp. 131-132]. Sir Adrian Boult also noticed "a kind of spiritual identification of Hans Sachs" in Richter: *My Own Trumpet* (London: H. Hamilton, 1973), p. 37.

76 21 May 1904, p. 1 (unsigned)

77 *Daily News*, 31 May 1882, p. 6; "brilliant success": *Daily Telegraph*, 31 May 1882, p. 3; "worthy of the highest praise": *The Times*, 31 May, 1882; p. 6; "thoughtful direction": *Morning Post*, 31 May 1882, p. 5; "a perfect triumph": *Academy*, 3 June 1882, p. 405; "perfection": *Illustrated Sporting and Dramatic News*, 3 June 1882, p. 279; "high praise to Herr Richter and his orchestra": *Sunday Times*, 4 June 1882, p. 7

78 7 June 1882, p. 10 (Louis Engel)

About the orchestral performance, he merely said it was led by Richter - "that suffices" - the work had found its "best interpretation." After the afflictions of the 1884 season, with a second-rate company,[79] the *Meistersinger* returned to London in 1904. E.A. Baughan was there:

It is over twenty years since Dr. Richter conducted *Die Meistersinger* in London, and as most authorities agree in considering his reading to be ideal, the performance last night was anticipated with great interest. In the main Dr. Richter differed from other conductors I have heard in the care with which he never allowed the orchestra to drown the voices. He seemed determined to make the comedy stand out on the stage, and to bring out all the delicate playfulness of the orchestral comment by precision of playing and clearness of rhythm. Besides these merits, which might be merely technical, I like the spirit of Dr. Richter's *Die Meistersinger*.... The orchestral music throughout the evening was saturated with the scent of lilac and of wallflowers after rain and with the peace of starlit summer evenings, so sympathetically did Richter bring out every beauty of the score.[80]

It was this *spirit* of the work that so impressed English listeners to Richter's interpretation, and that called for recourse to poetical descriptions and other gestures to convey its meaning. Another reviewer of a 1905 performance, wrote:

In a very special sense Dr. Richter creates *Die Meistersinger* anew. There is no English word which expresses fully the peculiar qualities which give his playing of the music its unequalled charm, but they are summed up in the German word *Innigkeit*. He makes every phrase like an expression of his own inmost soul. No one else makes the humor of the music so humorous or the romance so romantic or holds the scales so evenly between the two elements.[81]

There were more performances of *Meistersinger* in London, but it was not until 1909 that it was produced in English. Ernest Newman was pleased (and surprised) that the opera was "actually being sung, instead of being half-sung and half-declaimed, as it has been so often by German artists." Even the riot scene at the end of act two retained its musical quality. "The orchestral playing throughout was a feast of delight, especially in the woodwind accompaniment to Sachs' song in the second act, where every tone seemed to be chuckling and bubbling over with humour. Dr. Richter's whole reading of the score was an incomparable blend of fire and composure."[82]

[79] *Athenaeum*, 5 July 1884, p. 20

[80] *Daily News*, 21 May 1904, p. 8. The *Athenaeum* wrote that the "orchestral playing... was... the glory of the evening; the great conductor revealed all the beauty, freshness, and skill of the music": 28 May 1904, p. 697. The *Sunday Times* reported that there had been "an unfortunate collapse in the beautiful quintet at the end of the third act": 22 May 1904, p. 5.

[81] *Star*, 1 June 1905, p. 1 ("Crescendo"). German critics of Richter's performances at Bayreuth, at least those in Großmann-Vendrey's *Bayreuth in der deutschen Presse*, do not shed more light on Richter's secret than the English reviewers quoted. For example, one wrote that Richter portrayed "the meaty, healthy and particularly German nature of the *Meistersinger* music, with its pure line of transparent, high-altitude air" (Heinrich Chevalley, *Hamburger Fremdenblatt*, 25 July 1911, in Großmann-Vendrey, vol. 3,2, p. 74); in 1889 another wrote: "[Richter] has become... even more purposeful, more matter-of-fact and dry at the same time. At times, he conducted as if for an audience of Englishmen." (Paul Marsop, *Nord und Süd* (Breslau), April-May 1889, in *ibid.*, vol. 1, p. 84).

[82] *Birmingham Daily Post*, 26 January 1909, p. 6. The *Athenaeum* commented that "the singers must occasionally have found it hard at times to be heard over the orchestra": 30 January 1909, p. 142.

Fig. 3.10. Richter at Bayreuth in 1889 with a notice in his hat: "Please don't ask me for tickets to the dress rehearsal because I don't have any."

Der Ring des Nibelungen

Richter was famous as the conductor of the first *Ring* at Bayreuth in 1876, a work he was associated with for the rest of his life. We have already seen something of those initial performances from an inside perspective. As far as the public was concerned, the first production was greeted with an enthusiasm out of all proportion to Wagner's own critical comments, though there was also the hostility that had dogged Wagner's ambitious, revolutionary productions all his life. The music was so new that comments on how it was conducted were understandably few.[83] The English critics present were

[83] Tchaikovsky, I assume, was referring to the music not the performance when he wrote from Bayreuth: "Maybe the *Ring* is a great composition but I have never heard anything so boring and so drawn out as this": letter from 8-20 August 1876 in Tchaikovsky, *Letters to his family: an autobiography* (trans.) Galina von Meck (London: Dobson, 1981), p. 110.

not well disposed, but they all agreed that the orchestra was marvellous.[84] Joseph Bennett, critic for the *Daily Telegraph*, wrote: "Difficult though the music be, the tide of sound rolls on with unbroken smoothness reflecting lights and shades with infinite delicacy from its surface."[85] According to Francis Hueffer: "Hans Richter did wonders. Fire and precision appeared combined with the utmost delicacy…"[86] At the end there was a "seemingly minute-long, awed silence" before the "outburst of frantic enthusiasm" from the audience.[87] And it was to Richter, according to Lilli Lehmann, one of the Rhinemaidens, that the greatest credit was owed for the success of the Festival.[88] Twenty years were to pass before the *Ring* was next performed at Bayreuth.

At the second Festival in 1896, Richter conducted the first and last of the cycles. George Bernard Shaw considered the orchestra was not up to the standards he had expected of Bayreuth: the strings were poor, and "in the prelude [to *Das Rheingold*], the great booming pedal note – the mighty ground tone of the Rhine – was surreptitiously helped out, certainly with excellent effect, by the organ"; but at the appearance of Brünnhilde in the second act of *Die Walküre*, "the effect of the wind instruments was quite magically beautiful."[89] At the end, for "more than a quarter of an hour frantic applause and shouts, enough to bring the house down, were heard on every side, but … [Richter] remained obstinately invisible."[90]

His reappearance at Covent Garden in 1903 to conduct the *Ring* was, by all reports,[91] perhaps his crowning achievement in England. Richter had been allowed twenty-six rehearsals of a hand-picked orchestra of ninety-six, and his achievements were glorious, both in detail and in overall conception. The *World* wrote:

It is Dr Richter's wonderful architectonic power that lifts his conception and interpretation of the *Ring* so far above every other. He alone makes us feel the homogeneity of the colossal whole – for colossal it is with all its faults – while making a subtle difference between the calculated epic simplicity of *Das Rheingold*, the elemental passions and tragic conflicts of *Die Walküre*, the exuberant strength of *Siegfried*, and the relentless onrush of irresistible Fate in *Die Götterdämmerung*. He has the Olympian self-confidence which emboldens him to sacrifice immediate effect in certain places to the whole scheme. The splendid largeness of outline, the perfect proportions – not only within the four corners of each drama considered as a whole, but of each drama in relation to the other three – and the masterly clearness of every detail went to make the whole performance monumental. That epithet would seem to imply something of stiffness, of rigidity, or of square-toed pedantry, or music measured by a foot-rule; but nothing

84 *The Times*, 26 August 1876, p.4 [J.W. Davison], quoted in Robert Hartford (ed.), *Bayreuth: The Early Years - An account of the Early Decades of the Wagner Festival as seen by the Celebrated Visitors and Participants* (Cambridge University Press, 1980), p. 101; see also "Baireuth in 1876" in Charles Villiers Stanford, *Interludes: records and reflections* (London: John Murray, 1922), pp. 142-147

85 Joseph Bennett, *Letters from Bayreuth* (London: Novello, Ewer, 1877), p. 42, written 13 August 1876 after the *Rheingold*; after *Götterdämmerung* he wrote of "the matchless orchestra" (18 August, p. 78)

86 Francis Hueffer, *Half a century of music in England, 1837-1887: essays towards a history* (London: Chapman and Hall, 1889), p. 106 Hueffer wrote for the *Times* and succeeded J.W. Davison as music critic in 1879.

87 Sir George Henschel, *Musings & memories of a musician* (London: Macmillan, 1918), p. 136

88 Lehmann, *My path through life*, (trans.) Alice Benedict Seligman (New York: G.P. Putnam's Sons, 1914), p. 228

89 "Bassetto in Bayreuth," *The Star*, 22-25 July 1896, in *Shaw's music*, vol. 3, pp. 362-363, 371

90 Albert Lavignac, *The music dramas of Richard Wagner and his Festival Theatre in Bayreuth*, (trans.) Esther Singleton (New York: AMS Press 1970), p. 11

91 Many are quoted below but not all, for as the *Athenaeum* wrote in its own extensive reviews: "praise after a time becomes monotonous": 2, 9, 16 and 23 May 1903, pp. 570-571, 602, 634, 666.

could be further from the truth, for it is all instinct with energetic full-blooded life and flexible as Brünnhilde's own coat of mail.[92]

These views were echoed in the *Daily News*, but not without a hint of reservation. The orchestra in the *Rheingold* was "informed with a glowing, virile strength"; in the *Walküre* "the breadth, massiveness, precision and finish of the playing was so extraordinary that one hardly likes to urge that here and there certain points in the score might have been more emphasised; that the psychological value of the motives might have been insisted on with more emotional emphasis. It is, perhaps, a matter of opinion..."; in *Siegfried*, the orchestra was "the speaking voice, the narrator of the drama; the psychological interest had become abstract. And how wonderful is the invisible chorus, as Wagner called it!"[93] After the *Walküre* of the second cycle, the critic reflected:

There were moments last night (now that the glamour of almost faultless orchestral performances has lost some of its power of astonishing) – there were moments when I longed for a more acute and living emotion. This straightforward grasp and power and some want of extra insight into the romance and poetry of music have always been the strength and weakness of Dr. Richter's conducting. His unsuspected gift as an accompaniment of singers disarmed criticism at first, but now, great as his work is, I can imagine conducting which has more romance and more poetic understanding of the drama. Such a little more is required – just that quality which influences Ternina's Brünnhilde.[94]

The *Ring* returned in 1905, 1906 and 1907, with cascades of praise for Richter and his orchestra. In 1907 the end of the first act was conducted with "irresistible fervour," according to the *World*; "The curtain fell on a whirlwind of passion, and one asked oneself what had made Richter so young."[95] One discordant note, more personal than musical, was made by Ernest Newman after the start of the 1905 *Ring*: "tonight's performance [*Rheingold*] seems to me to have been on the whole cold and uninspired. But I must also make a further confession – that Wagner as an opera writer always appeals to me more forcibly in the study than on the stage."[96] As far as the orchestra was concerned, he thought it was "always beautiful and impressive" (*Rheingold*), "beauty itself" (*Walküre*), "it played exquisitely" (*Siegfried*); in all, it had been "a musical treat

92 *World*, 5 May 1903, p. 750

93 28 April 1903, p. 6, 30 April, p. 12, 1 May, p. 12 (E.A. Baughan)

94 7 May 1903, p. 12 (E.A. Baughan). As for Ternina, after the "triumphant conclusion" of *Götterdämmerung* the critic could only write – "well, it was one of those performances which makes the critic sensible of the impotence of praise." (11 May 1903, p. 12). The stage manager, Francis Neilson, recalled that: "Even Ternina, who was the severest critic of all – before the curtain and behind it – said the performances, taken as a whole, were finer than Bayreuth's or Munich's": *My Life In Two Worlds, Volume One, 1867-1915* (Appleton, Wisconsin: C.C. Nelson Publishing Company, 1952), p. 192. Francis Neilson also contributed to making this *Ring* an outstanding success: he was "a stage manager with true genius for his work," according to Herman Klein, reviewing the latter half of the second cycle in the *Sunday Times*, 10 May 1903, p. 4. The *Daily Telegraph* on the other hand, reviewing *Götterdämmerung*, considered the stage management a failure: 4 May 1903, p. 7. Neilson had been studying the *Ring* for many years and said Richter especially liked his *Rheingold*. When he told him that he had made "completely new prompt books," Richter "frowned and shook his head gravely... [and] said in sepulchral tones, 'Let the master rest.' And I said, 'Not by a damned sight!'": Neilson, *My Life In Two Worlds*, pp. 193-194. What happened to the prompt books in unclear. Neilson, for his part, considered Otto Lohse the finest Wagnerian conductor: "His fires were always ablaze. The verve, the energy, the exuberance, the magnetism of Otto Lohse as a conductor were never equalled." (p. 194).

95 7 May 1907, p. 811 (Alfred Kalisch)

96 *Manchester Guardian*, 2 May 1905, p. 6 (E.N.)

throughout the four evenings to hear the orchestral tissue handled with such absolute appreciation of its meaning, such beautiful phrasing, and so fine a sense of rhythm." (*Götterdämmerung*)[97] Such comments as these from Newman make one wonder at his later generalised description of Richter's music-making as all "four-square."[98]

The Ring in English

Ever true to his Master's ardent wish that his singers be heard and understood, Richter conceived of a *Ring* cycle sung in English, by English artists, and produced with the help of an English conductor, Percy Pitt. It was a "bold, if risky, experiment," but on the whole is was a success, according to the *Athenaeum*.[99] The key, of course, was whether the singers could be heard. Richter was less interested in the staging: it was the music that must reign supreme. "In the *Ring*," he wrote to Pitt, "the *aural* experience must not be disturbed by the *visual*."[100] Richter "followed the singers very sympathetically, and kept the orchestra down consistently," one critic observed after *Rhinegold*.[101] "As a whole," wrote Ernest Newman, "our tongue received fair treatment"; it was "as a rule, declaimed and sung clearly," with the orchestra "first-rate throughout."[102] Only in the first act of the *Valkyrie* would he "gladly have had a more tender nursing of some of the exquisite orchestral phrases; Dr. Richter's handling of them was just a trifle too sober and square cut."[103] After *Siegfried* another critic wrote, "It was possible to hear every word."[104]

By the time of the *Twilight of the Gods*, some of the singers were beginning to feel the strain: the Waltraute scene had to be omitted altogether because the singer had lost her voice. On an evening with weakened voices, a conductor can either restrain the orchestra further, or let the orchestra cover them in tone. Richter seems to have taken the latter course. "All through the evening the orchestra was rather too strong for the voices. Dr. Richter, in his enthusiasm for the score, as a rule does not spare the singers; but tonight he was sometimes merciless."[105] Things improved by the time of the second cycle: in the *Valkyrie*, the war-maidens' scene had never been given, according to one hearer, "with greater dramatic verve or sung with more precision or better tone. They were really warlike. The orchestra was again magnificent, and again Dr. Richter 'nursed' the singers with a tenderness such as he has rarely shown before."[106]

The English *Ring* was repeated in 1909. It was not the last *Ring* Richter conducted, but why cover them all? As Alfred Kalisch wrote in the *World*:

97 *ibid*, 4 May, p. 12; 5 May, p. 6; and 8 May, p. 8

98 *Sunday Times*, 26 October 1930, p. 5, quoted above

99 1 February 1908, pp. 137-38; and 8 February, p. 170

100 letter dated 7 January 1908 quoted in Fifield, *True Artist*, p. 401. A critic at the 1912 Bayreuth Festival lamented the fact that Richter (and Karl Muck) did not interest themselves in the scenic part of works, only the musical: Paul Bekker, *Frankfurter Zeitung*, 11 August 1912, in Großmann-Vendrey's *Bayreuth in der deutschen Presse*, vol. 3,2, p. 89.

101 *Star*, 28 January 1908, p. 1 ("Crescendo")

102 *Birmingham Daily Post*, 28 January 1908, p. 6 (E.N.)

103 *ibid*, 29 January 1908, p. 12

104 *Daily News*, 1 February 1908, p. 4 (E.A. Baughan)

105 *Birmingham Daily Post*, 3 February 1908, p. 8 (E.N.)

106 *Star*, 5 February 1908, p. 1 ("Crescendo")

What can be said that has not been said before? His interpretation of the *Ring* must always remain one of the monumental things in art, a great model and standard whereby all others must be judged, so heroic and yet so human, so massive yet so flexible does he make the music, so fine is the balance between all the conflicting elements in the drama. He is a wonderful study in the elimination of the superfluous: there is not an ounce too much pressure in the wildest climax and just the right number of ounces in each.[107]

Fig. 3.11. Richter in Vienna.
Silhouette by Hans Schliessmann

Parsifal

Richter never conducted *Parsifal.* For its premiere in 1882, Hermann Levi was the assigned conductor (if not Wagner's ideal choice because he was Jewish): Levi came with his orchestra from Munich provided by the King. Richter attended one of the 1882 performances, and recorded in his diary, somewhat ambiguously, "Great emotion."[108] In the division of responsibilities at subsequent Bayreuth festivals, Levi and others conducted the work. It is perhaps speculation more than justice to say of Richter, as Ferdinand Pfohl, did: "He was no ascetic, like Parsifal, no recluse lost in

[107] 26 January 1909, p. 136 (Alfred Kalisch)

[108] Fifield, *True Artist*, p. 196. Whether Hermann Levi or Franz Fischer conducted on this occasion (25 August) is not recorded by the Richard-Wagner-Museum in Bayreuth.

mystical rapture, but a man of the earth – and that is why he was no conductor of *Parsifal*."[109] George Bernard Shaw heard him conduct the prelude at a concert in 1885, and wrote how "it was very beautiful and very solemn – desperately solemn in fact."[110] On another occasion, however, in 1891, it was ill-rehearsed: either the orchestra should master the effect of "that wonderful throbbing, fluttering, winnowing cloud of sound which the violins make as the Grail descends," or let *Parsifal* alone, Shaw wrote.[111] Richter's performances were evidently variable because when Shaw heard *Parsifal* at Bayreuth in 1889, he reported that "perfection was not in the performance, which does not touch the excellence of the one which Richter conducted at the Albert Hall, but in the conditions of the performance."[112] The mystic abyss - the invisible orchestra - was not available in England.

Richter and other conductors

Bülow, it will be recalled, complained of Richter's "beery complacency" in conducting *Meistersinger*. He *was* a connoisseur of beer, and loved food, and there is a certain complacency in the Guild of the Masters. Perhaps it was this that Richter was so adept at reflecting. Whatever the case, Bülow maintained his misgivings in June 1881 when he wrote to his mother after a Richter concert in London (a Brahms symphony in particular): "He is still causing a great sensation here, but his casualness is finding for him his proper place amongst the ranks of the decreasing greats."[113] This was not a comment on Richter's Wagner. It is nevertheless partly a reflection of two different musical natures. The two conductors were very different spirits: Bülow with his intense concentration on the music, extracting every ounce of poetry, Richter with his calm confidence in the music, letting it flow, propelling it on its course. The English musician, Charles Stanford, had seen them both rehearse and perform, and made this general observation:

Richter was all for straightforwardness. He hated extravagance... his mastery of the orchestra was as great as von Bülow's, and he had authority and instrumental knowledge to back it. He took everything from the standpoint of common sense: for this reason, he was strongest in what he best knew – Beethoven, Weber, and the *Meistersinger*. He was not often electric, von Bülow was. He had magnetism, but not so much as von Bülow. He had an even temper, which von Bülow had not. His is the safer ground to follow, but also the less alluring.[114]

[109] Wooldridge, *Conductor's World*, p. 110 [from Pfohl's *Arthur Nikisch: Sein Leben, seine Kunst, sein Wirken*, 1925), p. 131]

[110] *Dramatic Review*, 2 May 1885, in *Shaw's music: the complete musical criticism in three volumes*, (ed.) Dan H. Laurence (New York: Dodd, Mead, 1981), vol. 1, p. 239

[111] "Wagner's birthday," *World*, 3 June 1891, in *ibid*, vol. 2, p. 359

[112] "Basseto at Bayreuth," *Star*, 1 August 1889, *ibid*, vol. 1, p. 715. The second performance was much better (p. 729), but his general view of the Festival was bleak: "Wagner is dead, ... the evil of deliberately making the Bayreuth Festival Playhouse a temple of dead traditions, instead of an arena for live impulses, has begun already....The life has not quite gone out of the thing yet." (p. 718). The *Musical Standard* commented on Richter's performance of the Good Friday Music that it "was somewhat mechanically played and one longed for more poignancy of expression": 17 June 1899, p. 379.

[113] quoted in Fifield, *True Artist*, p. 158

[114] Stanford, *Interludes*, p. 32; also quoted in Fifield, *True Artist*, p. 468

This, if anything, makes Richter sound a trifle dull. In light of what we have read of his performances, notably *Meistersinger* and *Götterdämmerung*, he was quite otherwise. An illuminating comparative comment was made by George Bernard Shaw:

[Richter] is a conductor of genius. To make an orchestra play the Prelude to *Parsifal* as Herr Levi makes them play it, is a question of taking as much pains and thought as he. To make them play the introduction to the third act of *Die Meistersinger* as they play it for Richter is a question of the gift of poetic creation in musical execution. The perfection attained by Herr Mottl is the perfection of photography. Richter's triumphs and imperfections are those of the artist's hands.[115]

Richter returned to Bayreuth in 1911 to retire, to a house provided by the town, which he called *Zur Tabulatur* in honour of the *Meistersinger*. "I read a lot; music – only Bach!" he wrote in the last year of his life.[116] He died on 5 December 1916. His last opera had been the *Meistersinger* at the 1912 Bayreuth Festival, a work he loved and which the public loved to hear him conduct. Wilhelm Furtwängler was at one of the performances. He recalled it as "undoubtedly the finest Wagner performance I ever heard":

The opera was performed in such a way that one did not have the feeling of being in an opera house at all. The impression was... of a conversation piece; all the verbal points were made as clearly as in a spoken play. One was not conscious of the fact that there was music going on, yet the performance took place in so musical an atmosphere that the total effect was tremendous. All that time ago. It was clear to me then what Wagner had in mind.[117]

Richter was Wagner's musician to the end. We will see something of his legacy in the other conductors that follow, though no two great musicians are ever alike. It is curious that for some his renown and contribution seem to have faded.[118] Yet he was a giant of his age. It is not surprising that his giant steps have left their mark.

[115] *English Illustrated Magazine*, October 1889, quoted in Hartford, *Bayreuth: The Early Years*, p. 146; also in *Shaw's Music*, vol. 1, p. 805

[116] letter to Michael Balling dated 13 January 1916 quoted in Fifield, *True Artist*, p. 452

[117] "Wilhelm Furtwängler Talking About Music"" (1950-51), trans. John Coombs, in the booklet accompanying the LP set *100 Jahre Berliner Philharmoniker*: DG 2740 260

[118] "To the present generation Hans Richter is little more than a name; and there is indeed a tendency to question his greatness. He would certainly not stand nowadays in the 'brilliant' class.... Orchestral playing is now on a higher level than in his day. The finely-shaded dynamics to which we are accustomed were scarcely known at that time. If I am rightly informed it was Gustav Mahler who introduced the modern school of orchestral playing.... However, within his sphere [Richter] was a great musician." unsigned article, "Richter and the First English *Ring*," *Musical Times*, June 1951, p. 263; see also Gunther Weiss, "Wer war Hans Richter?" *Neue Musikzeitung*, vol. 25 no. 3 (June-July 1976), 37-38.

4

Anton Seidl - His Master's Apostle

Anton Seidl died in New York in 1898 at the age of 47. His friend Henry Finck, music critic of the New York *Evening Post*, recalled the public's grief.

> Twenty thousand persons, it is said, attended the funeral of Beethoven. Wagner, Brahms and other modern masters had great honors paid them when they lay in their coffins; but it is doubtful if any musician who was not a creator of new works but simply an interpreter, ever was so imposingly honored in his death as was Anton Seidl. For nearly a week every Metropolitan journal devoted a column a day, and on Sunday following his death a whole page, to the great conductor and his sudden death. Nearly twelve thousand applications were made for tickets to the memorial services at the Metropolitan Opera House, though only four thousand had room in it; and while the services were in progress, and before, when one hundred and fifty members of the Musical Union played Chopin's funeral march outside, Broadway, for seven blocks was one surging mass of people blocking traffic. No statesman or general could have been more lamented, no poet or philanthropist more mourned than was Anton Seidl.[1]

And this, *for a Wagner conductor!* Finck had never seen so many people weep in public. Seidl's death was a calamity. In a mere twelve years in America, half of them at the Metropolitan Opera House, he had introduced all of Wagner's mature music dramas, given hundreds of concerts, and instilled a love of Wagner that in some quarters amounted to a frenzy.[2] Yet he was a placid, shy man. He led a quiet, outwardly happy, domestic life.[3] He was cool and controlled before an orchestra, and was adored by his orchestral musicians and singers. With his divine gifts as a conductor, he brought forth music that spoke directly to the hearts of the public who came to hear him in their thousands. Who was this man? Where did he come from? How did he do it? As we shall see, as a young man he grew up with Wagner; he became imbued with the spirit of Wagner's music; he became the apostle of Wagner; he was sent by Wagner to

[1] Henry T. Finck (ed.), *Anton Seidl: A Memorial By His Friends* (New York: Charles Scribner's Sons, 1899), p. 160-161; also reproduced by Finck in *My Adventures in the Golden Age of Music* (New York: Funk & Wagnalls Co., 1926), pp. 247-248

[2] The full story of this phenomenon is told in Joseph Horowitz's, *Wagner Nights: An American History* (Berkeley: California: University of California Press, 1994)

[3] There are many touching stories in Finck's *Memorial* about the Seidls' dogs. The couple had no children, but many dogs named after characters in Wagner operas. One day tragedy struck when Wotan (a St. Bernard) killed Mime (a dachshund).

America; and there, too soon, he died.[4] He left such a bountiful record of activity and impact, only a few gems are needed to show the true measure of the artist.

Early years with Wagner

He was born in Budapest on 6 May 1850. He quickly showed great ability as a pianist, but that never was his ambition. When he was a very young boy, he said he wanted to be a soldier, "naturally a field marshall at once – until later on, in my fourteenth year, when I decided to become the leader of an orchestra."[5] He conducted a boys' choir at school. He loved grand opera, and afterwards would try to play the melodies on the piano and imitate the gestures of the conductor. It was when he heard *Lohengrin* for the first time that he resolved to become a musician. His parents at first opposed his wishes – they wanted him to become a priest – but they relented.[6] He gave an account of his early years in an interview in 1887:

It was in my twentieth year that I resolved to adopt music as a profession. I had studied music from childhood, having a natural aptitude for it, and in the mere matter of pianoforte playing had made sufficient progress at twelve years of age to appear in public concerts. I had finished the usual high school and university studies when I made up my mind to earn a livelihood with music. I now went to Leipzig and entered the Conservatory, where for a year and a half I studied counterpoint and composition zealously.[7]

He described this time at Leipzig in more detail, and his subsequent apprenticeship with Richter, in an unpublished autobiographical note *Im Jahre 1872*:

In 1872, when Hans Richter was Director of the Royal Hungarian Opera House, I was still studying at the Leipzig Conservatorium, or at least pretending to do so. Frankly, once my theoretical studies were behind me, I actually learned more in the dark old concert hall in Leipzig than in the Conservatorium. I was always absorbed with the theatre and concerts. I attended all performances at the opera, the concert hall, and the Thomaskirche. I studied symphonies and operas at home. When I went to my teachers Wenzel, Coccius, Paul, Kretschmar or Papperitz with my piano assignments, they always said my intellectual understanding of compositions was miles ahead of my technical ability to play them. The one thing I wanted to do right from the start, to conduct, nobody could show me for reasons which of course are easily understood. Then I received news that my fellow countryman Richter was happy to accept me as an apprentice conductor. I did not hesitate for long, and travelled to Budapest with my scores and my dog. I learned more in one year with Richter than I would ever have in ten years elsewhere, that is, in a simple practical manner from a practical man, who is a real master of his art. No matter how sophisticated and clever others appear to be, there is only one artist

4 Seidl said: "Wagner often talked with me about America. He took much interest in this country, and he hoped for the success of his works here. He advised me to come here." F. B. Stanford, "With Seidl at Brighton," undated newspaper cutting (ca. August 1896) in the *Seidl Society Scrapbook April 1896 – January 1897*, pp. 55-57, at p. 56, Brooklyn Historical Society

5 *Daily Continent*, 26 April, 1891, p. 17.

6 Finck, *Memorial*, pp. 3-4

7 "Wagner's Traits and Work – Reminiscences by Herr Anton Seidl," *New York Tribune*, 27 February 1887, p. 10. The interview was probably with the music critic for the *Tribune*, Henry Krehbiel, who gave the literary polish to Seidl's English. In later years he declared to an American patron: "i have not the slightest desire to compose. I leave this wonderfull business to other gentlemen": letter dated 23 July 1892 to Mrs Langford, *Seidl Society Archive*, Brooklyn Historical Society, [1977.175 1892]

among conductors, and that is Hans Richter. I owe him an eternal debt of gratitude, not only for teaching me how to conduct, but also for recommending me to Wagner as a talent who one day would be beneficial for his cause. The fact that I was able to do just that, I owe above all else to my years of training with Richter, as well as to the next six intimate years in Bayreuth in the immediate vicinity of the tremendous Master.[8]

In the 1887 interview he said he studied the works of Wagner and Beethoven with Richter as well as taking lessons in the art of conducting. He recalled going with him to Bayreuth to attend the ceremony of the laying the cornerstone of the Wagner theatre in 1872.

The impressions made upon my mind on that occasion were so tremendous that I resolved at any cost to get near to Wagner.[9] The opportunity offered much quicker than I expected. At the cornerstone laying Wagner said to Richter:

"Send me a young musician who can carry out my intentions and aid in the musical work essential to the preparations for my *Nibelungen* representations."

Richter asked me whether I was minded to live and study a few years in Bayreuth. Of course I leaped for joy at the prospect, and after a few more months of study I went to Bayreuth in the autumn of 1872. The six years during which I lived in the house and near to Wagner will never be forgotten by me; they determined my whole future. My mode of thought, the manner in which thereforward I conceived everything; the vigor with which, thereafter, I attacked everything, all had their origin in that gracious and blessed house, where, with the utmost simplicity and naturalness, all strove continually for the loftiest and most ideal in life and art.[10]

When Seidl first presented himself at Wahnfried, so he told Herman Klein, he met Wagner sorting books in his library. He was struck dumb and could not utter a word of the speech he had prepared for the occasion. "At last Wagner dismissed him with the remark, 'If you work as well as you hold your tongue you will do.' And from that time forward his capacity for silence was a standing joke at Wahnfried."[11] He did not live at Wahnfried itself, but spent many hours there, playing the piano while Wagner sang, and playing with the children who affectionately called him "uncle."[12] Indeed, he appears to have fallen in love with Daniela, Cosima's daughter from Hans von Bülow, who seems to have reciprocated. Cosima became suspicious, and he rarely saw Daniela thereafter, feeling his presence in the house "was not looked upon with favor."[13]

[8] undated manuscript, 2 pages, *Anton Seidl Papers*, Columbia University [Box 3, folder 6]

[9] The highlight of the occasion was, of course, Beethoven's *Ninth Symphony* conducted by Wagner. When in later years Seidl was told what a deep impression his own performance of the *Ninth* had made, he "replied modestly…, 'Well, there you have Wagner's ideas on the subject.' What was specially striking was the elasticity of the tempi, making the music most spontaneous in its appeal….": Finck, *Memorial*, p. 120. James Huneker wrote: "I remember the 7th symphony – Wagner's 'Apotheosis of the Dance'; Seidl made the finale orgiastic – perhaps Wagner's idea, for the good Anton, I suspect was not an original conducting intellect – as was Levi, Richter, or as is Nikisch." letter to Henry Krehbiel dated 9 June 1918, *Letters of James Gibbons Huneker*, (ed.) Josephine Huneker (New York: Scribner's, 1922) p. 255

[10] *New York Tribune*, 27 February 1887, p. 10

[11] as told by Seidl to Herman Klein, *Thirty years of musical life in London, 1870-1900* (London: Heinemann, 1903), p. 410

[12] *Cosima Wagner's Diaries*, vol. 2, p. 68 (1 May 1878), p. 77 (27 May 1878), p. 89 (8 June 1878); her earliest reference to Seidl (12 February 1873) records him working daily with Wagner through his correspondence: *Diaries*, vol. 1 (1869-1877), p. 68.

[13] Francis Neilson, *My Life In Two Worlds*, vol. 1, (Appleton, Wisconsin: C.C. Nelson Publishing Company,

His formal work during the six years he was with Wagner mainly consisted of making copies of the scores of the *Ring* operas for the engravers. In this he may not, at least initially, have been faultless. Wagner had to summon Richter to Bayreuth in December 1872 to sort out an unspecified "fatal incident concerning the young Seidl," something which Richter did, yet played down in his diary as mere "unpleasantness with Seidl."[14] Of course, the incident may have had nothing to do with his work. Felix Mottl wrote in his diary during rehearsals for the *Ring* in 1876 that Seidl had organised a hashish party in the "Nibelungen Chancellery" which scandalised Wagner.[15]

Informally, the amount Seidl must have learned from Wagner during these years is immeasurable. Cosima describes evenings of Wagner's "studies with Seidl" – Seidl playing and Wagner singing – as "indescribable delight!"[16] and never hesitated to record Wagner correcting Seidl in a tempo[17] or occasionally "R's complete satisfaction" with his playing.[18] Gradually Seidl became more and more important to Wagner, as he himself came to realise. In 1875 he took Seidl with him to Berlin to assist in two concerts with the Bilse Orchestra. Franz Fridberg wrote in the *Berliner Tageblatt*: "In time he became Wagner's right hand; he was, in fact, the real conductor of our rehearsals. It was impossible to conceive all that this young man from Budapest heard and knew by heart. Before Wagner himself had noted errors in his own music, Seidl could be seen flying over chairs and desks to correct the blunder. The Master viewed the actions of his young famulus with paternal love, and repeatedly I heard him murmur, 'Ho, he! What would I do without my Seidl?'"[19] During the rehearsals for the first *Ring*, Seidl coached some of the principals and the men's chorus, pushed an on-stage contraption bearing one of the Rhinemaidens, and even conducted at some rehearsals. Julius Hey, the coach for Georg Unger the singer of Siegfried, described a 1875 rehearsal with Wagner present, singing along with Unger in a quiet voice, and Seidl at the piano:

> It is amazing how the young artist, with his admittedly moderate piano skills, is learning quite skillfully how to execute quite difficult orchestra effects intelligently on the piano, thanks to Wagner's direct instructions, and how this encourages the singer. The Master, positioned behind him, indicates every tempo (at the start, for instance, when there is a change), if necessary by beating on Seidl's shoulder and back with changing intensity.[20]

1952), p. 164. Neilson was a close friend of Seidl and accompanied him to Bayreuth in 1897. He says Seidl was in love with Daniela's sister, Eva, but the recollection may have been a lapse of memory: Eva was only 12 when Seidl left Bayreuth in 1878, whereas Daniela was 19. The love affair with Daniela is speculated upon by Arthur Farwell in "America's Gain from a Bayreuth Romance: The Mystery of Anton Seidl," *Musical Quarterly*, vol. 30, no. 4 (October 1944), pp. 448-457. See also Horowitz, *Wagner Nights*, p. 252.

[14] Wagner letter to Richter dated 16 December 1872 and Richter's diary for 7 January 1873 quoted in Christopher Fifield, *True artist and true friend: a biography of Hans Richter* (Oxford: Clarendon Press, 1993), p. 62

[15] diary entries for 7 and 8 June 1876: Krienitz, Willy, "Felix Mottls Tagebuchaufzeichnungen aus den Jahren 1873-1876," *Neue Wagner-Forschungen* (Karlsruhe: G. Braun, 1943), p. 198. The "Nibelungen Chancellery" was where Wagner's copyists (Seidl, Franz Fischer, Hermann Zumpe, Emmerich Kastner, and Mottl) did their work.

[16] 17 February 1878: *Diaries*, vol. 2, p. 29, also 22 February 1878 (p. 30)

[17] *ibid*, 13 March 1878 (p. 38), 21 March 1878 (p. 45), 11 July 1878 (p. 111), 13 July 1878 (p. 113)

[18] *ibid*, 25 August 1881 (p. 710): it was the "Entrance into the Temple of the Grail" from *Parsifal*.

[19] quoted (without a precise date) in Finck, *Memorial*, pp. 10-11 and in Nielson, *My Life In Two Worlds*, p. 195

[20] letter to his wife, Bayreuth 3 September 1875 in Julius Hey, *Richard Wagner als Vortragsmeister, 1864-1876*, (ed.) Hans Hey, (Leipzig: Breitkopf und Härtel, 1911), p. 211

The costume designer for the *Ring*, Carl Doepler, recalled one rehearsal in oppressive heat in June 1876: "There was a feeling of great ill-humour present. During the rehearsals of *Siegfried*, Wagner became extremely excited and forceful. He... made... angry remarks about his follower Seidl who could not produce immediately the *Tam-Tam* which was expected. The Master raged about the stage...."[21] We have already seen how erratic Wagner's behaviour was during these *Ring* rehearsals. Seidl, then as ever, was unflappable. He was silent, long-suffering, and devoted to his work. The New York music critic, James Huneker, painted this portrait many years later: "I saw much of Seidl. His profile was sculptural. So was his manner. But a volcano beneath. He was a taciturn man. He smoked to distraction. I've often seen him with Antonin Dvorak, the Bohemian composer, at the old Vienna Bakery Café.... The conductor and composer would sit for hours without speaking.... His Gothic head I've seen in mediæval tryptichs, as a donator at Bruges or Ghent or else among the portraits of Holbein. His shell was difficult to pierce, but once penetrated his friends found a very warm-hearted human."[22]

He left Bayreuth with Wagner's blessing. In his testimonial, Wagner wrote that during Seidl's five years "at my side helping me as an expert musician" in preparations for the *Ring*, he had "proved himself eminently capable at the rehearsals as well as at the performances, so that in case of necessity I should have considered it possible at any moment to put the directorship entirely in his hands, all the more because his leadership of concerts during several years has conclusively proven his qualifications as an energetic and careful conductor."[23] He later recommended him to Angelo Neumann who was planning a *Ring* in Leipzig: "Believe me when I tell you that no one (be he never so gifted and painstaking) who has not learned all these things thoroughly here under me in Bayreuth, can carry out my plans with absolute fidelity.... Take my advice and engage my young musical director Seidel [*sic*] for your rehearsals."[24] This Neumann did, and at the very first rehearsal "Seidl proved his extraordinary talents."[25] Wagner further urged Neumann to engage Seidl as music director: "None of the other conductors have such a clear understanding of my tempi, and the harmony between the music and the action. I have coached Seidel [*sic*] personally, and he will conduct your *Nibelungen* as no other can."[26]

Leipzig would not then engage him, however, and Wagner sent him instead with a recommendation to Vienna, where he was engaged as a singing coach,[27] thence, again with a recommendation from Wagner, to Leipzig as Kapellmeister at the Stadttheater. There he wanted to conduct *Tristan*, but Wagner objected; he wanted to "re-arrange"

[21] letter by Doepler dated 25 June 1876 quoted in Peter Cook (ed.), *A Memoir of Bayreuth 1876 - by Carl Emil Doepler* [1900], (trans.) Sabine Propach (London: The Author, 1979), p. 35

[22] James Huneker, *Steeplejack*, vol. 2 (New York: Scribner's Sons, 1921), p. 41

[23] the facsimile of the testimonial, dated 7 September 1877, is in Finck, *Memorial*, opp. p. 187; on 7 December 1877 Cosima recorded Wagner's unhappiness with the proofs of *Parsifal* which included bad copying by Seidl: *Diaries*, Vol. 1, p. 1002

[24] letter dated 21 June 1878 quoted in Angelo Neumann, *Personal Recollections of Wagner*, (trans.) Edith Livermore (London: Archibald Constable & Co, 1909), pp. 74-75. Wagner also spells the word "Seidel" in the testimonial of 7 September 1877.

[25] *ibid*, p. 77

[26] undated letter, ca. September 1878, *ibid*, p. 85

[27] from 1 November 1978 to 31 May 1879 according to Wilhelm Beetz, *Das Wiener Opernhaus 1869 bis 1945* (Zurich: Central European Times Publ. Co. Ltd, 1949), p. 113, who also spells his name "Seidel"

it, so it was postponed. He did conduct *Götterdämmerung*, however. Franz Fridberg of the *Berliner Tageblatt*, who had recently heard two performances of the work in Munich under Hermann Levi, was present. "Without wishing in the least to depreciate the merits of this great artist," he wrote, "I must say that, for me, Seidl's conception was the greater. There was in it more life, more movement, more poetry. In fact, I received the impression that night that of all the conductors I had got acquainted with, Seidl was the chosen interpreter of Wagner."[28]

Fig. 4.1. Anton Seidl as a young man

Seidl continued his story: "Thence I went to the Berlin Victoria Theatre, commissioned to direct the rehearsals and performances of the entire *Nibelungen* cycle. This was in 1881. Wagner came to Berlin with his entire family and attended the first and the fourth performances of the tetralogy; the enthusiasm and the triumph of the work were immense."[29] Wagner had in fact attended some of the rehearsals. Neumann recalled: "Wagner was absolutely and completely satisfied with Seidl, making only occasional and minor criticisms, and expressing the heartiest approval in warm and flattering terms."[30] Cosima noted their pleasure at these rehearsals: "the orchestra amazing.... [It] fills us with astonishment, and in our friend Seidl we are able to take genuine delight" (2 May 1881); "Seidl is greeted by R. as a pearl" (3 May 1881).[31]

[28] quoted in Finck, *Memorial*, p. 11

[29] letter from Seidl to the editor of the *Daily Tribune* ("Wagner's Symphony – How it was recovered," 17 September 1887, p. 10), also reproduced in Henry Krehbiel, *Review of the New York Musical Season 1887-88* (New York and London: Novello, Ewer & Co., 1888), pp. 119-120

[30] Neumann, *Personal Recollections*, p. 151

[31] *Diaries*, vol. 2, p. 662. Shortly after this Cosima made her last substantive entry about Seidl; it is the

After the performance of *Götterdämmerung*, Cosima wrote, "despite all the deficiencies in the acting, R. and I are very moved by it" (9 May 1881).[32] Wagner was certainly happier than he had been after the Bayreuth *Ring* under Richter.

The two conductors were nevertheless very alike. People who had heard them both perform Wagner "were always struck by the remarkable resemblance in the versions," according to Henry Finck, which is of course not surprising in light of their shared work under Wagner. "The main difference between [them] lay in this, that Seidl, the younger of the two, was more passionate, more emotional. He was, perhaps, the most emotional conductor that ever lived, especially in the dramatic sphere."[33]

The postponed *Tristan* was performed in Leipzig in January 1882. Its producer, Angelo Neumann, wrote to Wagner afterwards: "The splendid work brought [the artists'] enthusiasm to a white heat and pleased the public tremendously. Our capable Seidl did wonders with the orchestra, and the ensemble of the performance – though *I* should not be the one to praise it – was unanimously said to have been magnificent."[34] Wagner replied from Palermo on 16 January: "Of course I recognise in Seidl a born genius who needs only a little added warmth to astonish even me: and so I beg of you for the good of the *whole*, to give him a freer hand in the matter of the scenic arrangements than is usually given to the conductor, *for herein lies his speciality and what he has particularly learned of me!*"[35] Neumann did indeed engage Seidl for his Wagner Travelling Theatre, in 1882, and it was in the midst of this tour that Wagner died. Seidl was in France. He wept through the performance of the *Rheingold* that he was bound to conduct before he could travel to Bayreuth for the funeral. There, along with Hans Richter and Felix Mottl and others, he carried Wagner's coffin to its grave.

The Travelling Wagner Theatre goes to London, 1882

Angelo Neumann's Travelling Wagner Theatre introduced the cycle to many European countries, including Austria, Switzerland, Belgium, the Netherlands, Italy, England, as well as many German cities. Some 135 performances of the *Ring* operas were given, as well as 58 Wagner concerts, most of which Seidl conducted.[36] Looking at one of those cycles, in England, we get a glimpse of the young conductor through the unavoidable fog which still obscured the reception of Wagner's music in that country.

Seidl conducted four cycles of the *Ring* at Her Majesty's Theatre in London beginning on 5 May 1882. Richter was conducting a season of German opera at the

kind of enigmatic and slightly disparaging comment not uncommon in her *Diaries*: "Seidl's personality is discussed, and R. points out how he makes up for his lack of education with a silent manner." (29 August 1881), p. 711

[32] *Diaries*, vol. 2, p. 665; but after *Siegfried* on 28 May 1881, Cosima writes: "some of it good, much not, the enthusiasm still as great as ever. R. sad, says he is gradually being made to lose confidence in his work": *ibid*, p. 670

[33] Finck, *Memorial*, p. 168

[34] Neumann, *Personal Recollections*, p. 207. For Felix Weingartner's impressions of the performance, see Weingartner chapter, p. 272.

[35] *ibid*, p. 209. One of Wagner's last letters, to Angelo Neumann, contained the words "Seidl delights me greatly": Finck, *Memorial*, p. 16

[36] Finck, *Memorial*, p. 15; Ludwig Strecker, *Richard Wagner als Verlagsgefährte* (Mainz: B. Schotts Söhne, 1951), p. 265

Drury Lane Theatre on alternate nights from 18 May, including *Tannhäuser*, *Lohengrin*, *Meistersinger* and *Tristan*. London was, as the *World* put it, "not in an *embarras* but a *suffoqué de richesse* in matters musical."[37] Seidl's achievement in the circumstances was remarkable. "Like the Gustav Mahler of ten years later, he did marvels with a strange orchestra and proved that he had all the markings of an inspired leader," wrote Herman Klein.[38] The audiences were enthusiastic, from first to last, though in ever diminishing numbers, probably, the *Athenaeum* speculated, because of the "unusually high, not to say exorbitant, prices charged for admission."[39]

Seidl's orchestra was made up of sixty-six players, and the first row of the stalls in the theatre had to be sacrificed to accommodate them.[40] The conductor could be seen "standing in the centre of the orchestra instead of sitting – as usual – close to the stage."[41] He had arranged his orchestra "so that the strings were on one side of him and the 'wind' on the other; but the performers were not sunk in a pit as Bayreuth. This, we think, was a mistake," wrote the *Musical World*.[42] The tone of the orchestra surprised most reviewers who found it rough and sometimes brash. The *Illustrated Sporting and Dramatic News* thought the orchestra was inferior to the Bayreuth Festival in that it was "badly balanced": it had a "full complement of brass and wood wind, with only half the requisite number of strings" with the result that time and again "the strings were completely overpowered by the large body of wind instruments."[43] The *World* considered the orchestra "not superior to any of our English orchestras, and inferior in tone and ensemble to Richter's: the brass is rough and coarse sometimes, and not always in tune with the strings."[44] Some of the criticism of the orchestra may have shown a lack of familiarity with how a German orchestra was especially suited to playing Wagner's music: "the tone of the strings is what in technical jargon is known as 'woolly,' and, therefore, by no means pleasant to an ear accustomed to the crisp, bright quality of our English orchestras," observed *The Times*.[45] Similarly, another critic seems to have missed the point of beating the phrase: "Mr. Seidl, who knows his business thoroughly, has, to my thinking, too long a beat, to be so suddenly decisive, as is often necessary."[46]

Other ears were not displeased, however. At the "wonderfully perfect" performance of *Das Rheingold*, "the orchestra was in many respects splendid. It has a double complement of many of the wind instruments, and the trombones, which are much used, are in the hands of performers who manage to suppress the unpleasant braying with which we are only too familiar in English orchestras. We never remember to

37 10 May 1882, p. 11 (Louis Engel)

38 Klein, *Thirty years*, p. 101

39 20 May 1882, p. 645; "had the prices of admission been more moderate, the audiences would have been still larger": *The Academy*, 3 June 1882, p. 405

40 *World*, 3 May 1882, p. 12 (Louis Engel); *Monthly Musical Record*, 1 June 1882, p. 12 (Fr. Niecks). The orchestra may in fact have been slightly larger according to another report: "8 first and 8 second violins, 6 violas, 4 violoncellos, 4 double basses, 3 flutes, 4 clarinets, 2 oboes, 1 Cor Anglais, 4 bassoons, 8 trumpets, 8 horns, 8 sax-tubas, 4 trombones, 1 contra-bass tuba, drums and triangles.... The members of the orchestra are, we understand, from Hamburgh [*sic*] and other towns adjacent." *Musical World*, 27 May 1882, p. 326

41 *Daily News*, 6 May 1882, p. 3

42 13 May 1882, p. 283 (D.T.)

43 13 May 1882, p. 195; similar comments were also noted by the *Monthly Musical Record*, 1 June 1882, p. 12 (Fr. Niecks), the *Academy*, 13 May 1882, p. 349 (J. S. Shedlock), and the *Sunday Times*, 14 May 1882, p. 7

44 10 May 1882, p. 12

45 18 May 1882, p. 4

46 *World*, 10 May 1882, p. 11 (Louis Engel)

have heard any great work given with greater perfection...."[47] One of the features that struck the press was the ensemble, where great artists were seen to be "content to take a small part to-day and a big one to-morrow, so that every small part is given with a care, a conscientiousness, and a perfection of which a small artist is incapable."[48]

Most reviewers singled out the *Walküre* for special praise. After its first performance, the *Athenaeum* wrote, "it is almost impossible to speak too highly [of it]; in some respects, indeed, it surpassed the memorable rendering of the work at Bayreuth" (though in the journal's view the *Ring* was "an artistic mistake of a great genius... too severe a mental strain for those who look upon music merely as a relaxation.")[49] The *Walküre* was "simply perfection," wrote the *World*; only "the basses did not sufficiently come out in the orchestra."[50] After *Götterdämmerung* the *Manchester Guardian* judged that "Herr Seidl has such a complete mastery of the complicated score, that the English public has now a chance of forming a just opinion of Wagner's merits such as is not likely to occur again soon."[51] He was right: it would not be for another ten years that the chance would come again, under Mahler. In the meantime, although England had come a long way in the acceptance of Wagner's music between his first visit in 1855 and his second in 1877, it still had some way to go. The *Illustrated Sporting and Dramatic News* was sorry to learn that Angelo Neumann's travelling troupe had suffered a financial disaster from its season in London, but went on: "we cannot help rejoicing that English musicians and amateurs have manifested their disapproval of the work by 'staying away severely.'"[52]

Seidl on conducting

When the music and the style of its performance are new to reviewers, they tend not to say much about the conductor. Seidl's London venture is no exception. In America he received a warmer public and a more eloquent critical response. Before we look at some examples from this period, it is instructive to see what Seidl himself had to say about his art. His young friend in New York, Francis Neilson, frequently urged him to make notes for a book on Wagner, but he always responded: "No, it would not do. These things must not be told for a long time yet."[53]

[47] *Manchester Guardian*, 6 May 1882, p. 12

[48] *World*, 31 May 1882, p. 10 (Louis Engel); *Morning Post*, 8 May 1882, p. 2. Good ensemble in the *Rheingold* was singled out by the *Manchester Guardian*, 11 May 1882, p. 8

[49] 13 May 1882, pp. 612-614 [50] 10 May 1882, p. 12 (Louis Engel) [51] 11 May 1882, p. 8

[52] 3 June 1882, p. 279. The overall impression of failure given in Robert Hartford's "The first London *Ring*" (*Wagner*, vol. 4 no. 4 (October 1983), pp. 127-132) does not seem to be borne out by the general sense of the reviews above; Hartford drew on a limited range of sources, some different, and did not consider Seidl's contribution. To the extent that aspects of the production may have been wanting, Herman Klein recalled: "It was through no fault of Seidl's that the representations were at many points open to criticism; nor we may be equally sure, was he responsible for the number of extensive 'cuts' which disfigured the last two of the four music dramas." *Thirty Years*, p. 125

[53] Neilson, *My Life In Two Worlds*, vol. 1, p. 155; notable exceptions are Seidl's interview with the *New York Tribune* (27 February 1897) in which he describes Wagner's method of working and relaxing, and his letter to the same newspaper (17 September 1887) describing the background to Wagner's reconstruction of his *Symphony* (reproduced in Krehbiel, *The Musical Season 1887-1888*, pp. 117-121). What Neilson did do was prepare "prompt books" for the *Ring*, *Tristan*, and the *Meistersinger* based on what Seidl had told him of the Bayreuth *Ring* as well as Seidl's own productions at the Metropolitan which sought to do what Wagner

It was probably Seidl's other friends who prevailed upon him to write his seminal work *On Conducting*, a work not only on a par with Wagner's own tract on the subject, but more expansive on the performance of Wagner's music dramas than the composer's own treatment of them.[54] It is not bogged down by technical detail. Seidl was not given to questions of musical theory or music history. In fact, we are most fortunate to have his work on conducting at all, as can be gathered from his introductory remarks:

> The explanation of the fact that so little has been written about conducting is exceedingly simple and natural. Those who possess only a little of the gift can not write about it; and those who have it in abundance do not wish to write, for to them the talent seems so natural a thing that they can not see the need of discussing it. This is the kernel of the whole matter. If you have the divine gift within you, you can conduct; and if you have it not, you will never be able to acquire it. Those who have been endowed with the gift are conductors, the others are time beaters.[55]

Those who had the divine gift, in Seidl's view, included Bülow, Tausig, Richter, Sucher, Mottl, Weingartner, Strauss and Mahler. These men took the stand and conducted, without technical studies. Experience may have fortified them, but essentially, they had the gift. Seidl singled out just one technique he learned from another conductor. Once in Munich he saw Hermann Levi conduct recitatives "so admirably, with such remarkable precision, that I at once adopted his method of beating in similar passages."[56] For Seidl, *deference towards the artists* – the players and the singers – was paramount. He, like Wagner, wanted them to express themselves freely. The spirit of the artists was essential to the whole enterprise.

> The conductor stands in the stead of the composer. A gifted conductor brings it to pass through the medium of rehearsals that every participant, be he singer or player, feels that he too is leading and directing, though he is but following the baton. It is this unconscious reproduction, apparently from original impulse on the part of the performer, which is the secret agency whose influence the conductor must exert by the force of his personality. A true conductor will effect all this at the rehearsals, and keep himself as inconspicuous as possible at the performances; in this lies the difference between a time-beater and a conductor.[57]

This ability to surprise players with their own virtuosity was in evidence at Seidl's first rehearsal for *Parsifal* at Bayreuth in 1897. Heinrich Porges was there and wrote in the *Münchener Neueste Nachrichten*: "Anton Seidl is a conductor of the highest rank. That was made evident at once to the players whom he led with a firm hand; they applauded him already at the end of the first act, and after the second act, which he led with overwhelming passion, they broke out into a storm of applause."[58] Francis Neilson relates how Seidl made "strange noises" to singers during rehearsals, and how they always understood what he meant. "It was most amusing when Nellie Melba sang Brünnhilde in *Siegfried* at the Metropolitan. But she was never in doubt as to what

could not achieve at Bayreuth. He finished these in 1896, but what became of them is not known. (Neilson, *ibid*, pp. 146–47)

[54] Anton Seidl, "On Conducting," in *The Music of the Modern World*, vol. 1, Anton Seidl, Fannie Morris Smith, H. E. Krehbiel and W. S. Howard (eds.), at pp. 100-106 and pp. 201-214 (New York: D. Appleton and Company, 1895); reproduced in Finck, *Memorial*, pp. 215-240, with other writings by Seidl, predominantly about Wagner's music (pp. 205-214); the German manuscript is among the *Anton Seidl Papers* at Columbia University [Box 3, folder 1]

[55] Seidl, *On Conducting*, p. 100 [56] *ibid*, p. 106 [57] *ibid*, p. 203

[58] quoted in Finck, *Memorial*, p. 69

Seidl wanted."[59] To Lilli Lehmann, who sang Isolde and Kundry under his baton, he was the perfect leader: "He has always been to me the best of all Wagner conductors, who, beginning under Angelo Neumann, used the baton flexibly and unobtrusively, without seeking after sensational effects in conducting.... not the slightest discord ever arose between the artists up above and the conductor down below, who led his orchestra so gloriously."[60] The tenor Max Alvary was once reproached by another conductor for not having come in at "the first beat" at a certain place. He angrily retorted: "The first beat! I am an actor. I have no time to watch your beats. I was waiting for a huge wave of sound to plunge into with my voice; but the wave did not come." With Seidl, according to the reviewer who told this story after a performance of *Siegfried*, "these waves of sound, be they large or small, never fail to rise, and that is what puts the singers at their ease and makes him the ideal Wagner conductor."[61]

In the supremely important question of *tempo*, according to Seidl, the voices of the individual artists play a large part.

It is simple nonsense to speak of a fixed tempo of any particular vocal phrase. Each voice has its peculiarities. One singer has a soft, flexible voice, to which distinct enunciation is easy; another has a heavy, metallic voice, which sometimes requires a longer period for its full development, or is compelled to sing a phrase slower than the other, in order to achieve the same dramatic effect and distinctness. It was Wagner's habit to study and test the voices placed at his disposal, so as to discover the means which must be employed to make them reach the purpose designed. His tempo marks so far as they refer to the voice, are warnings against absolutely false conceptions – not rigid prescriptions – for time-beaters who follow them would be obliged to force the most varied organs into one unyielding mould.[62]

The size of the theatre or performing space is also important for tempo, as well of course for the orchestral dynamics. "The larger the room the broader must be the *tempi* to be understood in all parts of the house. The better the acoustics of the room the easier will be the conductor's task, the more pliant the orchestra."[63] He gave the example of a performance of *Tristan* in an auditorium in Chicago with forces from the Metropolitan Opera in New York. The acoustics were so good that the volume of the orchestra had to be reduced by almost a half. At rehearsal, the "orchestra sounded magical, and the performance revolutionized the ideas of all the artists.... in the evening [the orchestra] played with an insinuating delicacy, with such a nice adjustment of tone that to hear them was a marvel...."[64]

And *hearing* the singers is crucial to the music drama. We hear Seidl faithfully echoing Wagner's words:

the orchestra must never shriek and drown the voices of the singers, but support them. The orchestra ought always to bear in mind that on the stage above there is a man with something to say, which the sixty or eighty men below must support so that every tone and word shall be heard and understood. The composer did not write an orchestra part in order that it might drown the words sung on the stage. Wagner, even when conducting excerpts from his operas, was painfully anxious that every syllable of the singer should be heard. Frequently at the close of a vocal phrase he would arrest the sound of the orchestra for a moment, in order that the

59 Neilson, *My Life In Two Worlds*, vol. 1, p. 154. Melba's sole performance of this role, on 30 December 1896, almost ruined her voice.

60 Lehmann, *My Path Through Life*, pp. 343-344

61 *Evening Post*, 31 December 1896, p. 7

62 Seidl, *On Conducting*, pp. 103-104

63 *ibid*, p. 205

64 *ibid*, p. 206

final syllable should not be covered up. How often did he call out angrily, "*Kinder*, you are killing my poetry!"[65]

The question of *temperament* is vital to a proper understanding of the relationship of orchestra to singer. In the final act of *Tristan*, for example, the conductor:

must suffer with Tristan, feel his pains, follow him step for step through his delirious wanderings. That conductor is an offender who ruins the picture by blurring its outlines by playing too loudly, or destroys its pliancy by an unyielding beat. Think of the exciting task presented by the scene of Tristan on his deathbed! The conductor must be ever at his heels. Every measure, every cry must agree with the orchestra. If the singer one day sings a measure only a shade differently than usual, or begins or ends a rallentando or accelerando one measure earlier or later – an entirely natural thing to do – the conductor must be on hand with his orchestra, that the picture may not be distorted or blurred. He must have the brush of the composer and his colors always ready – in a word, he must live, suffer and die with the singer, else he is an offender against art.[66]

It is no wonder singers loved him. Jean de Reske once told Henry Finck: "In the third act of *Tristan* I have sometimes almost forgotten to sing on, so absorbed was I by Mr Seidl's wonderful orchestral eloquence."[67] Seidl himself was so absorbed that during the closing scene of *Tristan* he would "cry like a child, so that by the time the curtain had dropped he would be in a state of emotional collapse."[68] This absorption in the drama was not an accident of taste, but was essential to the whole Wagnerian project. A final point from Seidl:

When Wagner calls out to the conductor, "Recognise first of all the idea: the meaning of a phrase and the relation of the phrase or motive to the action, and the proper reading and the *tempo*, will disclose themselves of their own accord," he goes straight to the very root of the matter. Look again to *Tristan und Isolde* for an example. A large space of time in the first act is occupied by Isolde and Brangäne, who are alone in the tent. A few motives are continually developed, but with what a variety must they be treated – surging up now stormily, impetuously; sinking back sadly, exhausted, anon threatening; then timid, now in eager haste, now reassuring! For such a variety of expression the few indications, *ritardando*, *accelerando*, and *a tempo* do not suffice; it is necessary to live through the action of the drama in order to make it all plain. The composer says, "With variety" – a meagre injunction for the conductor. Therefore I add, "Feel with the characters, ponder with them, experience with them all the devious outbursts of passion, but remain distinct always!" That is the duty of the conductor.[69]

By most accounts Seidl fulfilled his duty to an astonishing degree, both in general accounts and in response to particular performances. Henry Finck wrote in the section "How Seidl conducted Wagner" in his *Memorial*:

When he had the best of material and plenty of preparation, he never failed to reveal the heart, pulse and the very soul of the great composer whose apostle he was. Then, not only did he

[65] *ibid*, p. 207 (*Kinder* means "children.") [66] *ibid*, pp. 210–11 [67] Finck, *Memorial*, p. 163

[68] *ibid*, p. 124 (Victor Herbert). Another orchestral player reports similarly at p. 119. It is no wonder Seidl hated social gatherings after his music-making. He wrote to a patron of his Seidl Society concerts: "You know, how I like this Sort of tiresome standing, handshaking, and empty phrasing of beautiful Summer trip and grand Success etc. But if you think it necessary, then I will go after the concert for half an hour in the adjoining Rooms." letter to Mrs Langford, 11 October 1897: *Seidl Society Archive*, Brooklyn Historical Society [1977.175 1897]; it is also no wonder Seidl did not believe the versatility of conductors was such that they could properly do Wagner one night and Lortzing the next: *On Conducting*, p. 204

[69] Seidl, *On Conducting*, p. 209

never drown the singers, but in the softest passages the orchestral tenderness was insinuating and caressing beyond comparison. The way he made his orchestra sing, sigh, whisper, exult, plead, threaten, storm, rage, was a marvel to every one who heard it. The dramatic surges of passionate sound in *Tristan* were irresistible.... In the later Wagner dramas he made the tempo vary endlessly and have as many little spurts and eddies and dashing falls, and trout pools full of speckled beauties, as a mountain brook. This phase of Mr Seidl's genius as a conductor was admirably described by W. F. Apthorp after a performance in Boston of *Tristan und Isolde*: "We must first speak of Seidl, for he was the heart and soul of it. It was he who made the fine performance of the others possible. His management of the orchestra was simply beyond praise; not once during the whole evening did the instruments unduly over-crow the voices on the stage. Then the orchestral performance, taken by itself, was a marvel of beauty; such delicacy of shading is exceedingly rare. It was not merely that succession of crass contrasts between fortissimo and pianissimo which sometimes parades under the name of 'shading,' but a hardly interrupted series of the more subtile [*sic*] and delicate nuances in dynamics and tempo. It reminded one of what Mr. Gericke once said of Wagner's conducting *Lohengrin* in Vienna: 'The most striking thing about it was the surpassing delicacy of all the effects; modifications of force and tempo were almost incessant, but were for the most part modifications by a hair's breadth only.'"[70]

Like Richter before him and Nikisch after him, Seidl came from Hungary, and what therefore particularly appealed to him, according to Finck, was "passion, impetuosity, lawless irregularity of tempo.... This same Hungarian instinct for change of pace, in accordance with the emotional character of the music, helped to make him the greatest of Wagnerian conductors, for modification of tempo is the soul of Wagnerian interpretation..... It might be said that he applied to the Wagner operas the spirit of Gypsy music, so far as emotional abandon and freedom from artificial metronomic fetters are concerned."[71]

The American highlights

Seidl made his debut at the Metropolitan Opera on 23 November 1885 with *Lohengrin*. This was followed by *Tannhäuser*, and soon thereafter the American premieres of the *Meistersinger* and *Tristan und Isolde*. In subsequent seasons he gave the American premieres of *Siegfried*, *Götterdämmerung*, and *Rheingold*. In all, he conducted 296 Wagner performances in New York and on tour during the six years he was at the Metropolitan Opera. Joseph Horowitz provides an interesting list of Seidl's personal ranking of Wagner's music dramas (the figures in parentheses are the number of Metropolitan Opera performances): *Parsifal*, *Tristan und Isolde* (32), *Siegfried* (42), *Götterdämmerung* (27), *Meistersinger* (41), *Walküre* (27), *Rheingold* (19), *Tannhäuser* (39), *Lohengrin* (47), *Holländer* (10), and *Rienzi* (12).[72] These figures include six complete *Ring* cycles. In the twelve years Seidl was in New York, there was a period (1892-1895) when he conducted no opera. In the 1891-1892 season there had been a wholesale change

[70] Finck, *Memorial*, pp. 67-68

[71] *ibid*, pp. 164, 166

[72] Horowitz, *Wagner Nights*, p. 184n (for the ranking; no source given); statistics from the Metropolitan Operas database (archives.metoperafamily.org); Hans Rudolf Vaget, "Anton Seidl – 'Conductor of the Future'," *Wagner*, vol. 19, no. 3 (September 1998), at p. 124 gives a total of 329 Wagner performances; it should be noted that Seidl also revered Bach, Beethoven, and Tchaikovsky, as they appealed strongly to his temperament. "Anyone who understands Wagner understands Beethoven or Bach also," he wrote in "A Defence of Wagner," *New York Morning Journal*, 10 May 1891, quoted in Elkhonon Yoffe, *Tchaikovsky in America: the composer's visit in 1891* (New York: Oxford University Press, 1986), p. 127

Fig. 4.2. Seidl, about 1880. Photo by Höffert

Fig. 4.3. Seidl in his American years, 1885-1897. Photo by Falk

Fig. 4.4. Seidl in New York, 1885. Photo by Wilhelm

Fig. 4.5. Seidl in New York, 1885. Photo by Wilhelm

to Italian opera when even Wagner's operas were sung in Italian, but under other conductors. During this time Seidl was active with the Philharmonic Society and Seidl Society concerts. We will look at a selection of reviews of these performances.

Lohengrin and Tannhäuser

First we must look at his debut, with *Lohengrin*, in 1885. New York had never seen such a conductor, the *Musical Courier* declared. Seidl could be seen to be conducting from memory, with his eyes forever on the stage. "He truly accompanied everyone, gave everyone his or her entrance sign, marked every rhythmic or dynamic change, and this for the large orchestra as well as for the singers. His manner of conducting is firm, bold and comprehensive. He makes you feel all the time that he knows what he wants and insists on it being done."[73] "He gave the orchestral language an eloquence that was new and thrilling," reported the *Daily Tribune*. He held all the forces together and "inspired them with so earnest a desire that even the short choruses of the first act… were sung musically and with precision."[74] The *Herald* stated: "To be a thorough musician is not at all sufficient for a correct rendering of Wagner's compositions. A dramatic temperament is not less essential, and Herr Seidl's nature combines both the musical and the dramatic requisites."[75] The *New York Times* was less certain. Although Seidl "often produced effects of great loveliness and power" and some "finely managed" crescendos, "the fortissimos being wrought up by well nigh imperceptible gradations," he was "not exactly a magnetic conductor, nor should we fancy he is gifted with much warmth." He was also far too energetic in front of the orchestra.[76] We shall read more of Seidl's interpretation of *Lohengrin* from his London performances in 1897.

He conducted his first *Tannhäuser* on 11 December 1885. As with *Lohengrin*, he gave it without many of the customary cuts. "Every point of the score was brought out with a significance, a vividness and a force that were simply startling," wrote the *Herald*. "The overture was given much more slowly and with infinitely more breadth and grandeur than people here have been accustomed to."[77] What was special according to the *Daily Tribune* was the "exceptionally virile, passionate and buoyant playing" of the orchestra, and "the effect of the confidence felt by the musicians in his firm and unerring beat and his masterly oversight" of everything on stage.[78] The *New York Times* acknowledged the "uncommonly smooth and symmetrical performance," superior to *Lohengrin*, and gave oblique recognition to Seidl for the achievement.[79]

Tristan und Isolde

The first American performance of *Tristan* on 1 December 1886 was a public and critical success of historic proportions. It was almost too glorious to talk of, as the *Evening Post* explained:

[73] 25 November 1885, p. 329. The opera's "poetic beauties and its thrilling climaxes" were brought out as never heard in New York. Finck, *Memorial*, p. 31; Henry Krehbiel also wrote of a performance that "was almost new" and that "disclosed many poetical beauties which had hitherto been overlooked": *Review of the New York Musical Season 1885-86*, p. 42

[74] 24 November 1885, p. 4

[75] 24 November 1885, p. 10

[76] 24 November 1885, p. 5

[77] 12 December 1885, p. 5

[78] 12 December 1885, p. 4

[79] 12 December 1885, p. 4

In speaking of last evening's performance one feels like a lover who sighs for something stronger than a superlative. In the opinion of the most capable judges, it was the grandest operatic performance ever given in this country; and those who heard *Tristan* in Bayreuth last summer apparently agree to a man that last evening's performance was on a whole superior to those given in the very centre of Wagnerism – notwithstanding the special advantages presented at Bayreuth by the smaller, ideally arranged, and darkened theatre.[80] And for this difference in our favor Herr Anton Seidl is chiefly responsible. There were as great singers at Bayreuth last summer as at the Metropolitan last night, but there was no conductor at Bayreuth to compare with Seidl. Previous to yesterday's performance one might have doubted who was the ablest living operatic conductor – Hans Richter or Anton Seidl. We have heard them both, scores of times, but after the impression produced on us last evening by Seidl's conducting of the second and third acts of *Tristan*, we do not hesitate a moment to pronounce him superior even to Richter. Such orchestral passion cannot be adequately compared to anything but a torrent of lava consuming every obstacle in its way. We cannot enter into details to-day; but if anyone doubts that an orchestra can speak the language of passion, and a hundred times more emphatically, and overpowering, let him go and hear the score of Wagner's masterwork as interpreted by his pupil.[81]

The press was unanimous in attributing the success of this first performance to Seidl. The *Musical Courier* wrote, for example:

Anton Seidl, who was the moving spirit of the whole performance, fairly outdid himself. He conducted almost entirely from memory and he did wonders with the orchestra, which followed his inspired guidance with more than their usual carefulness and earnestness. Their special efforts also told admirably in point of tone-production in the continuous dynamic changes which surge through the work and sometimes reach climatic [*sic*] fortissimos of immense power and sweep.[82]

The first performance was followed by many more on the same elevated plane.[83] Henry Finck recalled a Seidl performance of the Prelude and Liebestod at a Philharmonic concert which he said was "one of those exhibitions of interpretative genius with which, like Paderewski, he loves to amaze even his most enthusiastic admirers":

Tristan und Isolde is one of his specialities in which no living conductor equals him, but even he never conducted the Introduction and Finale as he did yesterday. What is the witchery which enables a great conductor to make 101 orchestral musicians play as if each were a consummate

80 Felix Mottl had conducted *Tristan* at Bayreuth in July 1886. Comparing the two, the *New York Times* gave thanks for the cuts and "Seidl's vigorous and impassioned tempos" and wrote: "The orchestra at the Metropolitan, if not as strong numerically as the Bayreuth band, was quite as proficient; the tone of the German musicians was somewhat richer and more homogeneous, thanks to the sunken orchestra in use at the theatre, something of muscularity and brilliancy, however, being possibly sacrificed by the innovation." (2 December 1886, p. 5)

81 *Evening Post*, 2 December 1886, p. [3], which was not alone in being unable to go into the details of the overwhelming performance in the time available: *Daily Tribune*, 2 December 1886, p. 4

82 8 December 1886, p. 357

83 for example: "Mr. Seidl, as usual, was the electric centre of the whole performance, infusing his spirit into everything and giving such an impassioned rendering of Wagner's masterwork as no other operatic conductor can." *Evening Post*, 3 November 1887, p. 6. "It was, of course, the night of nights for Herr Seidl. At the end of each act he was called before the curtain. At the beginning of the third act he was given a fanfare by the orchestra, and at the close of the opera was brought before the house seven times in all and presented with three laurel wreaths." *Herald*, 21 March 1891, p. 10.

> artist and a world-famous soloist? Whatever it may be – Mr Seidl has it, and he never revealed this gift more thrillingly than yesterday. There was a glow of passion, an uplifting of feeling, an ecstasy of emotion, a richness of color, a gradual approach to, and final consummation of, the climax that were simply overwhelming. For a person with heart disease it would be dangerous to hear such a performance.[84]

It is fitting that is was with a performance of *Tristan* on 27 November 1895 that Seidl ended his years of eclipse at the Metropolitan Opera.

Die Meistersinger von Nürnberg

Seidl's first *Meistersinger* for America on 4 January 1886 was another dazzling success. "The orchestra, under Herr Seidl's fine conducting," wrote the *Daily Tribune*, accomplished feats which its composition would have led one to think incredible, and

Fig. 4.6. Seidl in 1885. *Musical Courier,* 13 January 1886

again furnished cause for profound gratitude that so gifted and capable a musician has been brought into this country."[85] Seidl's last rehearsal, which had lasted eight hours, had revealed several weak points, according to the *Evening Post*.

> But it also revealed another thing – Herr Seidl's extraordinary genius as operatic conductor. Every weak point was "spotted" on this occasion – for he knows the whole score by heart – so that when it came to the public performance last evening, the smoothness and animation of the

[84] Finck, *Memorial*, p. 167

[85] 5 January 1886, p. 4

ensemble was little short of a miracle.... Although we have heard *Die Meistersinger* more than a dozen times abroad, and although in Vienna and Munich where the opera has been on the repertory for a number of years, some of the details are placed in a clearer light, yet for general animation we have never heard a performance superior, if equal, to last evening's; and this is in the first place due to Herr Seidl's thorough appreciation of Wagner's intentions. He put so much variety and "go" into his *tempi* that the performance never dragged for a moment....[86]

The orchestra's share in the success of the evening, "the lion's share," according to the *New York Times*, "was carried out in a flawless manner."[87] So superb was the orchestra in *Meistersinger*, Seidl may in fact have being going beyond Wagner's intentions, as he seems to have done on a later occasion when "his splendid orchestra really approached perfection. From beginning to end the admirable musical accompaniment was sung rather than played by the strings. Poetry, passion and lightness all found expression. We forgot the singers in the rapture of listening to the orchestration."[88] On a later occasion, he was required to conduct a dull, static production sung in Italian. Although he did so "with his customary skill," according to the *New York Times*, "he was forced to allow some of the singers to change some of the tempi remarkably."[89] The public's – or management's – fondness for German opera sung in Italian was not something Seidl had control over.

The Ring in America

London critics had greeted Seidl's *Ring* in 1882 with reserve. New York responded differently when he came to present the same works from 1886 onwards. The *Rheingold* he conducted on 4 January 1889 was the first in America. Music lovers had already acquainted themselves with the work or so they thought, wrote the *Press*.

But of what new power and beauty did its wondrous harmonies seem possessed under the magic of Seidl's wand! The orchestra, as if reflecting its leader's inspiration, played as it has not played before this season. In the first scene the shimmering accompaniment of the violins to the Rheingold motive given out by the horn was as delicate as dainty tracery; the ponderousness of the giant motive, in the second scene, as Fafner and Fasolt come to claim their reward from Wotan, was most effectively given, and the horns and the wood wind were heard to their best advantage in the motive of eternal youth during the struggle between the giants and Freia's brothers. Mr. Seidl's brasses were unusually rich and full, and rang out gloriously in the Walhalla motive at the close of the drama.[90]

Seidl's first *Walküre* in New York on 13 January 1886 "was the most beautiful that the work has ever received in this city," declared the *Daily Tribune*. "New life throbbed in the orchestra.... Changes in tempo enabled the artists to declaim with more fervor and greater dramatic truthfulness than has been the rule, while the orchestral part glowed with new eloquence and beauty – the climaxes especially being developed

[86] 5 January 1886, p. [2]: "the necessary cuts were not so extensive as those made in some German cities"

[87] 5 January 1896, p. 4

[88] *Herald*, 12 January 1889, p. 10. After this performance the *Evening Post* wrote: "Herr Seidl again demonstrated that as an interpreter of Wagner's music he is unapproached by any conductor the world over": 12 January 1889, p. 6

[89] 11 February 1896, p. 4

[90] 6 January 1889, p. 1

with tremendous effect."[91] Gustav Kobbé in the *Mail and Express* noted the "greater spirit of performance" compared to earlier ones under Walter Damrosch.

All the spirited scenes were given with more animation, the tempi being frequently accelerated where the quickening of the dramatic action demanded such nuances. As a result whole pages of the score seemed imbued with new life and impetuosity.... [T]he conductor interprets the work in the spirit in which it was composed. There were hundreds of such nuances in each act. Could even a casual listener fail to notice such self-evident improvements as the wonderful crescendo not long after the opening of the first act when the *Mitleid's* motif sweeps upward to a climax of pitying, loving grief; the sudden anger which seemed to agitate the orchestra with *Hunding's* growing excitement, the superb orchestral climax in the music depicting the hunted lovers in the second act, and the chorus of the Valkyrs...?[92]

Henry Finck in the *Evening Post* remarked on the "countless beauties" that were "so vividly and thrillingly brought out" from the score.

The secret of Herr Seidl's power lies in this, that he conducts *con amore* and at the same time with a fulness of knowledge that embraces the minutest details of the score. He knows everything by heart, so that instead of being obliged to peruse the score, he can face about every moment, and give the cue to some group of instrumentalists. It is a real pleasure to watch him in the conductor's chair. There is no grade of *forte* or *piano*, no *sforzando*, no *crescendo*, no *accelerando* for which he does not have an appropriate gesture. Now, it is well known that eloquent gestures, made under strong emotion, are contagious. Hence it is that all the members of Herr Seidl's orchestra are infected with his enthusiasm, and irresistibly follow him through every degree of dynamic expression and rhythmic shading. This is what is commonly called "magnetism" – the unconscious influence of one strong will on others.[93]

Seidl's *Siegfried* was also lively. He gave the American premiere on 9 November 1887. "Love, knowledge, devotion and enthusiasm were the mainsprings of Herr Seidl's efforts as conductor," wrote the *Daily Tribune*.[94] There had been only two weeks of rehearsals, the *Evening Post* reported, and the result was another "signal triumph." Its reviewer wrote that "perhaps no other conductor could have given such a finished and animated first performance as Herr Seidl, not only on account of his well-known enthusiasm for Wagner's art, but because he has doubtless conducted *Siegfried* more frequently than any other musician...."[95] In 1896 he directed the celebrated performance with Jean de Reske as Siegfried and Nellie Melba in her only appearance as Brünnhilde.

But no matter how fine the cast [wrote the *Herald*], no Wagnerian music drama can succeed without a conductor who is in his role as great an artist as the greatest of those behind the footlights. Mr. Seidl with his Beethoven-Liszt face had the performance completely under his control from the first tap on his desk to the last wave of his baton.

The nervous energy which he infuses into the orchestra, the subtle lights and shades, the numerous gradations in detail and the gradual development of all the parts toward the one grand climax at the end – these are characteristics of Mr. Seidl's leading, and give what we call realism to the most romantic art creations – make them rise up lifelike before us.[96]

[91] 14 January 1886, p. 4

[92] quoted in *Musical Courier*, 20 January 1886, p. 34, where several press reviews are excerpted, including the *New York Times* which considered the performance no different to those under Damrosch (14 January 1886, p. 4)

[93] quoted in *Musical Courier*, 20 January 1886, p. 34

[94] 10 November 1887, p. 5 [95] 10 November 1887, p. 5 [96] 31 December 1896, p. 10

Finally, enthusiasm greeted America's first performance of *Götterdämmerung* on 25 January 1888. Not enough praise could be bestowed on Seidl, according to the *Musical Courier.*

He brought out *Die Götterdämmerung* in the almost incredibly short time of nine days' rehearsing, a task for which in Europe they readily consume from three to four months, and yet with all this drawback of shortness of time for preparation it was the best performance, according to Mr. Seidl's assertion to the writer, of about eighty performances of this work that he had conducted in Europe. No wonder, therefore, that Seidl is almost hyper-enthusiastic in his praise of the orchestra, and no wonder also that the audience rose to Seidl and demanded his appearance on stage by prolonged applause, calls and cheers after each act, and that he bowed his acknowledgments thrice after the performance of the funeral march, when, with his usual and characteristic modesty, he pointed to the orchestra as being the ones to deserve and share in these ovations.[97]

Triumphant return to London, 1897

After the years securing Wagner's place in America, Seidl's final year of opera showed the public in London and Bayreuth just how far he had come, and perhaps what they had missed. In London he opened with a performance of *Lohengrin* at Covent Garden in which the much-loved tenor, Jean de Reske, was singing. Royalty was present, and "the huge house was crammed."[98] The opera was sung in German, unusual for London, though the chorus sang in Italian.[99] The critics had never heard anything like it. "With full remembrance of many commendable performances of the work in London, we do not think it has ever been more effectively given than on the present occasion," wrote the *Athenaeum*; "the orchestra, under Mr Seidl, cannot be overpraised. Every detail of Wagner's score – or such of it as remained, for the 'cuts' were as cruel as ever – was brought out in fullest relief, and the band was never permitted to overrule the voices."[100] The *Daily Chronicle* was struck by "the sheer barbaric strength of the first act, the terror and mysteriousness of the second, and the mystery and sadness of the last [which have] never before been so plainly expressed in the orchestra. And we would chiefly emphasise his wonderful breadth and vitality…."[101]

The subdued tone of the orchestra was one feature consistently praised. It was, for the *Daily News*, a pleasure to "to hear Wagner's music as directed by an intelligent German, who does not share the belief of his Italian and French colleagues that Wagner's music is inseparable from noise and who contrives to bring out the orchestral parts without drowning the voices on the stage."[102] The *Morning Post* echoed this point, and noted that in certain cases Seidl's "*tempi* differed from those usually adopted

[97] 1 February 1888, p. 93

[98] *Observer*, 23 May 1897, p. 6

[99] *Standard*, 24 May 1897, p. 5; *The Times*, 24 May 1897, p. 13

[100] 29 May 1897, p. 722. This review later reported an idea floated by Seidl that a series of *Ring* cycles be given at Covent Garden in 1898 with "only two acts on each evening, so as to permit commencement and termination at a reasonable hour, the acts to be played without any abominable cuts. How this is to be carried out is not very clear, but the proposal is certainly worthy of consideration": "Musical Gossip," *ibid*, 24 July 1897, p. 139; Seidl explained that he only made cuts with a "heavy heart," to meet the wishes of the public to have Wagner's operas reduced to four hours; to reduce them to three hours he said was impossible: Finck, *Memorial*, pp. 209-210

[101] 24 May 1897 (page number not recorded on the clipping in the *Anton Seidl Papers*, Columbia University [Box4])

[102] 24 May 1897, p. 3. The *Observer*, 23 May 1897, p. 6 made a similar point.

at Covent Garden, being generally more measured. For instance, in the middle section of the prelude to the third act a marked *rallentando* conduced to the general effect of the piece."[103] The *Standard* noted Seidl's distinguished lineage: "Berlioz first, and Herr Richter later, suggested to our English brass instrument players how to produce a pure, organ-like effect; and this was secured on Saturday evening, the band never drowning the singers."[104] Not only were the singers not drowned, but they "were allowed all due freedom in declamation, and no trace of confusion was felt."[105] The reviewer for the *Sunday Times* considered the performance of such "exceptional merit" that Bayreuth might have been proud to claim it for its own: "never have I in my wildest dreams hoped that the *Lohengrin* instrumentation would be executed with such exquisite delicacy and refinement. The pianissimos achieved by the brass, the velvety softness of the wood-wind, the beautiful cantabile-playing of the violins – these features constituted a new experience (at Covent Garden anyhow), and best of all they enabled the tones of the singers to penetrate with the utmost ease to the farthest corners of the house, aided thereto by the sounds of the orchestra, not overwhelmed and drowned on the way."[106] The *Musician* summed up:

> There are moments spoken of by Honoré de Balzac when interpretation almost reaches inspiration, when the artist and the creative genius seem to be one. If ever this point was neared in the Covent Garden Opera House, last Saturday night was the occasion. The magnetic current generated during Herr Anton Seidl's admirable conducting of the overture seemed to flow from the point of his magic wand, wielded with clean, decisive beat, and to animate every artist upon the stage. The familiar music seemed studded with novelties, the story acquired deeper meaning, the characters developed fresh distinction and greater significance. There were "diversities of gifts," but there was "the same spirit" throughout the whole of a splendid and noble performance.[107]

The other Wagner operas Seidl conducted at Covent Garden that season were the *Walküre*, *Tristan und Isolde*, and *Siegfried*. The *Walküre* performance too was "one of the finest ever given in London," according to the *Athenaeum*; "the Bayreuth master's orchestration was played in a way that he would have desired, for detail was brought out with all possible eloquence, and the glowing strains in the first and third acts have never been interpreted to more advantage, at any rate in London."[108] He was "an ideal Wagner conductor," declared the *Era*. "The richness and variety of the orchestra portions, so artistically interpreted, charmed every hearer. All the delicate ideas of the composer's score were brought out with the utmost refinement."[109]

103 24 May 1897, p. 3
104 24 May 1897, p. 5
105 *The Times*, 24 May 1897, p. 13

106 *Sunday Times*, 23 May 1897, p. 7 (H. K.), which also reported that, at the second performance, "Mr Seidl again conducted a magnificent performance": *ibid*, 30 May 1897, p. 8

107 26 May 1897, p. 44 (G.). The critic felt that a subsequent performance did not attain the "height of perfection" of the first night: "the chorus was not all that it should have been, several passages marked 'piano' being sung 'forte.' I hear, though, that Mr Seidl has recommended them always to sing loud, as whenever they sing soft, their intonation is incorrect": *ibid*, 2 June 1897, p. 64. Other journals to praise the performances included the *Daily Graphic*: Seidl's "masterly direction and control of the orchestra": 24 May 1897, p. 11; and the *Morning Post*: Seidl "preserved an admirable balance of tone throughout the performance": 18 June 1897, p. 6.

108 19 June 1897, p. 818; similarly *Observer*, 13 June 1897, p. 6; *Sunday Times*, 13 June 1897, p. 5; *The Times*, 14 June 1897, p. 10; *Daily News*, 14 June 1897, p. 3; *Morning Post*, 14 June 1897, p. 3; *World*, 16 June 1897, p. 37

109 19 June 1897, p. 7. Not every hearer was charmed, however. The *Musical Standard* recorded some dissenting views, not consistently, and not always clearly. It may have wanted more of what the Italian and French conductors brought, as referred to above.

The Times considered that his *Tristan* "must rank with the very best that have been given in London."[110] What struck the *Musician* was the "safe passion" of the "wonderful [orchestral] accompaniments."[111]

Siegfried was, as Seidl cabled home to his wife simply, his "greatest success and triumph."[112] The *New York Times* critic, W. J. Henderson, was present: "let us sing glory to Anton Seidl, for he is the presiding genius of this art-work. How his orchestra floats and lingers upon billowy waves of gorgeous tone! Without once drowning their voices, he succeeds in bringing to the surface every one of the lovely melodic fragments that are the drops in Wagner's ocean of beauty. His reading of the score is a complete and convincing exposition of his mastery of the inner meaning of Wagner's method of composition."[113] It was "a faultless performance," wrote *The Times*, which singled out for special mention "the magnificent performance of the introduction to the third act, and the instrumental description of Siegfried's ascent to the mountain."[114]

The season was a popular and financial success. The Wagnerian performances overshadowed everything else, partly because of the de Reske brothers who appeared in *Tristan*, *Siegfried* and *Meistersinger*, but also for other works in which they did not appear, such as *Walküre*.[115] A final word comes from the *Pall Mall Gazette* as the season was drawing to a close. It observed that Seidl was "anything but a showy conductor," that he had a "modest manner," yet:

> behind that manner are observed a rare power, an immense strength, and an intimately delicate comprehension. There are other great conductors who impress their genius upon you at once. You never hesitate or stand in doubt. Mottl, for example, provokes instant enthusiasm. He makes his point of view immediately apparent, and as his point of view is always that of a man of extreme talent, if not of actual genius, he stands at once revealed in his true light as a conductor of immense capability. Now, Herr Seidl is not so immediately impressive as this. His art grows upon you.

The writer referred to the "consistently beautiful playing" in Seidl's *Lohengrin*, how "the most careful attention was paid to the development of one instrumental part out of another," how in the second act, often considered dull by the critics, the orchestra became "the perfect interpreter of the drama." Then, in *Siegfried*, "Seidl's triumph was as great, though of a different order:"

> Here the drama is so various, so full of "points," of separate excellences, that the beautiful and dreamy consistency of *Lohengrin* is not, cannot be, an ambition to achieve on the part of the conductor. *Siegfried* is the drama of life's young passion, and like that passion changes and varies, blows hot and cold, is a tale told in many chapters. Now mark that Herr Seidl would clearly convey this idea to you if you did not know it before; knowing it, you are immensely impressed

[110] 15 June 1897, p. 7
[111] 23 June 1897, p. 124 (Robert Hichens)
[112] telegram from London dated 22 June 1897: *Anton Seidl Papers*, Columbia University [Box 2]
[113] *New York Times – Supplement*, 10 January 1897, p. 11
[114] 23 June 1897, p. 21; the second was an "incomparable performance" (*ibid*, 29 June 1897, p. 16), and at the third "there was an enormous and most enthusiastic audience" (*ibid*, 15 July 1897, p. 6); the "orchestral portion was magnificently rendered" according to the *Musical Times*, 1 July 1897, p. 462, "a very fine orchestral rendering of the music," according to the *Illustrated Sporting and Dramatic News*, 26 June 1897, p. 642; the *Musician* asked of the last performance: "who was responsible for the ruthless cut in the last act?": 14 July 1897, p. 187
[115] *Morning Post*, 26 July 1897, p. 6; *Athenaeum*, 31 July 1897, p 169

by the magisterial completeness with which he works out his idea. Last night again he was in almost perfect sympathy with the orchestra; it is really too bad that daily we recognize this master better when the season is now within a few days of its close.[116]

Parsifal at Bayreuth 1897

When the season did close, Seidl travelled to Bayreuth for the performances of *Parsifal*, the only time in his life that he conducted there. Because the work was restricted by Wagner's decree to performances at Bayreuth, he had of course never conducted the whole work, only concert excerpts in Brooklyn in 1890.[117] Before the performances and while the London season was still in progress, he had travelled to Bayreuth for rehearsals. After the first rehearsal he wrote to his wife from London:

I have just got back from Bayreuth. I can only say it was glorious.... Truly, Wagner's spirit had come over me; I heard everything distinctly from the beginning, which is very difficult in this lowered orchestral place. My wide experience in conducting in all sorts of places made it easy for me to surmount all difficulties. Everybody declared that no one had ever so quickly and unobtrusively adapted himself to the situation. Frau Cosima embraced me at least twenty times and wept; she said that the good old times seemed to have returned, that I had brought back the conception of the 1882 festival. My way of conducting as well as my face reminded her, she said, of her father. In a word, everybody congratulated me most cordially. The orchestral players declared they had never been conducted as on this occasion and wondered where I got all this.[118]

Seidl conducted the opening performance – Bayreuth's 100th – on 19 July 1897.[119] Henry Finck wrote that he had "met several American music-lovers who had attended nearly all the Bayreuth Festivals, and they declared that no one had ever penetrated so deeply into the spirit of *Parsifal* as Anton Seidl."[120] English music-lovers too were impressed. Herman Klein remembered "what a glorious treat it was to listen to the orchestra under him, immediately after the blurred and ponderous execution of the *Nibelungen* under Siegfried Wagner."[121] The *Musician* recorded Seidl's "masterly insight into the work" and "the profound impression made on the audience." It observed:

Seidl's *tempi* are decidedly fresher and livelier than Mottl's; but opinion must differ on such a subject and personal predilection must not allow itself to attempt to fix an absolute standard. But with all respect for difference in opinion, the *tempo* adopted in the Chorus of the Knights

[116] *Pall Mall Gazette*, 24 July 1897 (page number not recorded on the clipping in the *Anton Seidl Papers*, Columbia University [Box4])

[117] The *New York Tribune* wrote of this performance (13 March 1890) as "superlatively excellent, and the interpretation of the work by Mr. Anton Seidl an achievement which surpassed the brilliant work to which he has accustomed the people of New York at the representation of Wagner's dramas at the Metropolitan Opera House. It was evident in every measure of the music that he had undertaken the task with a zeal akin to religious devotion and that his knowledge was complete, his love perfect": quoted in an unidentified newspaper clipping dated 1 April 1890 in the *Seidl Society Scrapbook 1889-1891* [Vol. 4], Brooklyn Historical Society. Another unidentified clipping commented that the Flowermaidens' scene had been taken at such a "lively pace" that though the musicians could keep up, the singers hardly could.

[118] letter dated 9 July 1897, quoted in Finck, *Memorial*, pp. 69-70

[119] He conducted three further performances, and Mottl conducted four. Critics were divided over Mottl's tempi compared to Seidl's; the *Oberfränkische Zeitung* suggested they were slower (31 July 1897, p. 2).

[120] Finck, *Memorial*, p. 71

[121] Klein, *Thirty Years*, pp. 409-410; *Musical Times*: Seidl "once more gave the utmost proofs of his capacity for directing the most advanced works of the Bayreuth master."(1 September 1897, pp. 608-609)

in the third act, when carrying in Titurel's body, was too fast. It destroyed the solemnity of the scene, and did not admit of sufficient impressiveness, and precluded the *accelerando* which might increase as the knights become more passionate in their questions and appeals, and then may be allowed to quiet [*sic*] down as they lament that it is for the last time they are to see the grail uncovered. *Parsifal* is a solemn work in its first and third acts, and even if the Mottl *tempi* are too slow – as some think – yet the character of the work will bear the tendency in this direction with less loss to the whole, than in hurrying the *tempi*.[122]

The German correspondent for the *Musical Courier*, Otto Floersheim, told Henry Finck that he had not heard *Parsifal* performed at Bayreuth "more nobly, elevatingly and suggestively than under Anton Seidl's bâton."[123] Other German writers thought Seidl's conducting was "perfection" itself[124] and that he was a "worthy successor" to Levi.[125] Others, however, differed. Seidl "did not come anywhere near Levi," wrote the correspondent for the *Berliner Lokal-Anzeiger*. "I felt his tempos were not always correct – the introduction was far too slow."[126] The *Vossische Zeitung* considered that Seidl's first performance "did not quite seem to reach the heights of previous ones, for instance, those of 1882 and 1883" under Levi.[127] The principal reason seemed to be the tempos. The *Frankfurter Zeitung* wrote:

He conducted less in keeping with the tempos employed by Levi than those introduced by Mottl. His tempos had a tendency to be broad. As for his pauses in the Prelude, the audience's longing for the music was whipped up to a craving, like the need to breathe during a spell of breathlessness. Seidl took a somewhat midway point between Levi's and Mottl's interpretations. He showed a tendency to seek delicate variations in subtlety and tenderness which often suited the work extremely well. One example was the sensitively conceived music accompanying Kundry's approach to the spring in Act Three. However, in some other parts, we felt that an excess of tenderness spoiled things, for example, during the first part of the Grail Scene which was well nigh inaudible from the first diminuendo onwards.[128]

The *Bayreuther Tagblatt* reported that the Prelude was "a masterly feat": the audience followed "with reverent attention and breathless anticipation, and [it] left the greatest impression."[129] If Seidl's tempos had been "even broader than Mottl's,"[130] and his Transformation Scenes "sheer monumental greatness,"[131] this seems to have come from his artistic instincts. Although he was "piously following on from tradition," wrote the *Berliner Tagblatt*, he "also conveyed strong feelings of his own, and had the artistic energy and courage to give effect to the Master's intentions."[132] He gave "the fullest expression to the deeply fervent nature of *Parsifal*," wrote the *Münchener Neueste Nachrichten*, "with broad outpourings and the richest of feelings, making the music rise anew before us, as he deliberately emphasized its dramatic elements."[133]

[122] *Musician*, 28 July 1897, p. 223 (David Irvine). Mottl also conducted some performances of *Parsifal* at the 1897 Festival.

[123] quoted in Finck, *Memorial*, p. 41. In the same letter Floersheim said of Seidl's *Ring*, *Meistersinger* and *Tristan*: "they are still unequalled and surely have not been surpassed, although I have witnessed performances under Richter, Weingartner, Muck, Mottl, Schuch and many others."

[124] *Signale* (Leipzig), 3 August 1897, p. 519

[125] *Bayreuther Tagblatt*, 20 July 1897, p. [3]

[126] 21 July 1897, [p. 1]

[127] 21 July 1897 (*Abendblatt*), p. [2]

[128] 21 July 1897 (*Abendblatt*), [p. 1] (H.P.)

[129] 20 July 1897, p. [3]

[130] *Allgemeine Musikzeitung*, 30 July/6 August 1897, p. 458

[131] *Musikalisches Wochenblatt*, 29 July 1897, p. 415

[132] 21 July 1897 (*Abend-Ausgabe*), p. [1] (Martin Krause)

[133] 25 July 1897, p. [2] (Oscar Merz)

Seidl cabled home to his wife after performances the simple fact of their success: "my last parsifal immense success."[134] It was to be the last opera Seidl ever conducted. Offers flowed to him from opera houses and orchestras throughout Germany and in England, but it was to America he returned, exhausted and weakened, but to a promising future of opera and concerts.

Memories and Tributes

His sudden death on 28 March 1898 was at first attributed to food poisoning, but it was later found he had a number of chronic conditions, including of the liver. An attack of pneumonia in 1896 had brought him close to death, and had aged him ten years. One of his life-long passions had been cigars. He detested walking. He went for days without food when he was engrossed in his work. In these circumstances, it is less surprising that his body succumbed when his artistic powers were at their peak.[135]

One of the features of Seidl's conducting that lived long in the memory was his climaxes, as the *Musical Courier* recalled:

> No conductor that we have ever heard could build up such massive climaxes, such overpowering, such thrilling altitudes of tone. His breadth... was no less wonderful. With him there was the abiding sense of foundational security; his accelerandos were never feverish, a calm logic prevailed from the first bar to the last, yet he was a master of the whirlwind and rode it with a repose that was almost appalling.[136]

This was a view echoed by Henry Finck: "Seidl was the greatest *crescendo* maker this generation has heard... [He] had the passionate pulse, and he went down, down until the very bowels of the earth were reached.... As a master of climax, I have never met his equal.... The more furious the tempest of passion which he worked up, the more firmly did he hold his forces in rein until the moment arrived when they were to be loosed, so that all should be swept away in the *mêlée*."[137]

One of the principal characteristics mentioned by those who paid tribute to Seidl's life, and who tried to explain the secret of his power as an interpretative artist, was *temperament*. Despite his cool exterior, his modesty, his dislike of ostentation, and his calm ways at the podium, the way the music emanated from his personality, through his baton to the orchestra and to the audience beyond, was a revelation. How this happened was a mystery. It certainly was not a matter of mere technique. His long association with Wagner and the incomparable informal instruction it afforded were clearly crucial. "He was saturated with Wagner and it was his bible," wrote James Huneker. "He was an organism framed by nature and training for conducting. All else was subordinated to this unique purpose. The man was an incarnated bâton."[138] When a composition appealed to his temperament, and it was an essentially *dramatic* temperament, Seidl penetrated its heart, and his understanding was mirrored in the

[134] *Anton Seidl Papers*, Columbia University [Box 2]. The 1897 Festival was omitted altogether from Susanna Großmann-Vendrey's documentation in *Bayreuth in der deutschen Presse*, Vol. 3,1 (1883-1906) (Regensburg: Bosse, 1983)

[135] His widow, Auguste Seidl-Krauss, died in Kingston, New York, on 15 July 1939, aged 85.

[136] 30 March 1898, quoted in Horowitz, *Wagner Nights*, pp. 90-91

[137] Finck, *Memorial*, pp. 116, 135-36

[138] *ibid*, p. 115

music he brought forth. And the music came unalloyed. "He had no room in his convictions for mere refinement of nuance or precision of execution," wrote Henry Krehbiel, music critic of the *New York Tribune*. "Too much elaboration of detail he thought injurious to the general effect."[139] And the effect, when circumstances best permitted and sometimes even when they did not, was astounding. He understood what Wagner wanted, and he understood what lay behind the notes. This is what he divined and transmitted with his unique intensity and waywardness. "It was in his dominant freedom from the tyranny of musical notation that Seidl's greatness appeared most manifest," wrote Henry Finck. "He did not read from his scores as one would read from a book; but, like a great orator, he mastered their contents and then delivered them for the message that was there."[140] He was the medium through which the spirit of Wagner's music passed into the hearts of the public. He conquered those hearts. "All the lectures on Wagnerian subjects, all the explanatory programmes and the musical guides could not have brought about this result," wrote August Spanuth, music critic for the *New Yorker Staats-Zeitung*. Yet "Anton Seidl, with his keen and energetic beat and with tremendous temperament, did it."[141] The *New York Times* critic, W.J. Henderson, wrote:

> Jean de Reske voiced a general belief when he acclaimed Mr. Seidl as the greatest of Wagner conductors. The present writer is of the opinion that he excelled Richter. No living man knew the scores of the Wagner dramas better than Mr. Seidl. None comprehended their inner significance and the method of revealing it to the hearer so well. Calm, self-poised, conscious of his own mastery of these Titanic works of art, he entered with the fullness of a reflective and analytic intellect and a strong emotional nature into an exposition of their profoundest content.[142]

At his funeral service in the Metropolitan Opera House, he was honoured with words, but above all with music: "Anton Seidl is dead. Play the great funeral march. Envelop him in music. Let its wailing waves cover him. Let its wild and mournful winds sigh and moan above him. Give his face to its kisses and its tears.... That will express our sorrow – that will voice our love, our hope, and that will tell of the life, the triumph, the genius, the death of Anton Seidl."[143]

[139] Finck, *Memorial*, p. 135 [140] *ibid*, p. 96 [141] *ibid*, p. 156

[142] obituary notice in the *New York Times*, 3 April 1898, p. 7. The London *Times* wrote in its obituary: "No one, not even Dr. Richter himself, has played a more important part than Seidl in the diffusion of a practical knowledge of Wagner's music throughout the civilized world": 30 March 1898, p. 12.

[143] from the funeral service for Anton Seidl, in Finck, *Memorial*, p. 94.

Part III

Early Bayreuth Masters

5

Hermann Levi – Keeper of the Grail

Levi was the most spiritual of Wagner's conductors: austere, exact, and impassioned. He was the ideal, famous first conductor of *Parsifal*, and it was a miracle that he came to conduct it. Wagner's suggestion that he convert to Christianity before conducting the work was deftly rejected by the wily artist, and with great dignity and forbearance. In spite of the offence given, Levi remained convinced of the nobility and greatness of the composer. Like Bülow before him, he had to put up with much, but his artistic integrity left him in no doubt about the greatness of Wagner as musician. From 1882 to 1894, as long as his health permitted, he conducted *Parsifal* regularly at its only permissible venue, the Bayreuth Festival Theatre. The more he conducted it, the better his performances became. The peak of his achievement in that work became the standard others aspired to. In Wagner's other works he also penetrated differently from, and more deeply than, many of his colleagues.

The path to Parsifal

He was born on 7 November 1839 in Gießen, the son of a rabbi and a pianist.[1] He grew up surrounded by music. His brother Wilhelm, who changed his name to Lindeck, had a career in the early part of his life as an operatic bass.[2] Levi's studies at the Leipzig Conservatory from 1855 to 1858 included a course on conducting under Julius Rietz. Afterwards he enjoyed a number of conducting appointments at Saarbrücken (1859-61), Mannheim (1861-62), and Rotterdam (1862-64) where he first conducted a work of Wagner: a notable production of *Lohengrin*. He was appointed court conductor at Karlsruhe (1864-1872), and from there went to hear Bülow conduct the premiere of *Meistersinger* in Munich in 1868.

He corresponded with Wagner about a production of *Meistersinger* in Karlsruhe, but had private reservations about the work. He may at that time have been under the influence of the anti-Wagnerian, Vincenz Lachner, who had been his senior colleague at Mannheim, and who was mounting a severely cut version of *Meistersinger* at the

[1] see generally Peter Jost, "Hermann Levi," in *Die Musik in Geschichte und Gegenwart (MGG) – Personenteil*, Vol. 11 (2004), 33-34

[2] Levi was once rather tactlessly asked why he had a brother by the name of Lindeck. "Well, you see," he replied, "my name was originally Lindeck too, but I changed it to Levi." Sir George Henschel, *Musings & memories of a musician* (London: Macmillan, 1918), pp. 134-35

same time. The preparations caused a headache: "I've now had the score here for three days, and for three days I have been sleeping ever so dreadfully. Every night around the witching hour, the awful 570-page tome lies on my chest like a hundredweight to worry me for several hours."[3] The production appears to have gone well, however. He wrote afterwards: "All this *Meistersinger* has kept me well on the go this winter. Given our limited means, the performances were excellent. My own attitude towards it is quite strange, and should be left to oral reports only."[4] In later years he had nothing but admiration for the work.

His performance came to the attention of Wagner, and gradually he became drawn into his circle (a development Levi's friend Brahms deplored and which eventually led to a break between the two men). Levi was at Richter's *Rheingold* dress rehearsal in Munich in 1869, and was one of a number of conductors who declined to conduct the first performance after Richter refused to proceed. He soon met Wagner for the first time. He was appointed court conductor in Munich (1872-94, general music director 1894-96). It was from there that he travelled to Bayreuth for the first *Ring* rehearsals in 1875. The impression *Siegfried* and *Götterdämmerung* made on him then was "overwhelming," he wrote to his father; the invisible orchestra was "magically beautiful, never shrill, and yet clear and not indistinct; the singer is never covered by sound, and every word and every *piano* can be heard, although never such a large orchestra has been gathered together in a theatre."[5] He was engaged as a kind of musical assistant for the 1876 Festival, by which stage he had become a true follower of Wagner. The break with Brahms came around this time, as he related later to Edward Speyer: "A time came when I lost faith in him; it was when he began to compose symphonies. He paid me a visit in Munich in 1876, and as I saw him off at the station we both instinctively felt that we were parting for good!"[6] Levi conducted the *Ring* in Munich in 1878, and by 1880 he was attracting everyone to his Wagner operas; Wagner himself attended productions of the *Holländer*, *Tristan* and *Lohengrin* at the court opera.[7] Wagner was not too pleased with the tempi adopted for *Lohengrin* in Munich. Before long he was going through the opera with Levi at Wahnfried.[8]

The premiere of Parsifal

The ever curious and devoted King Ludwig commanded a private performance of the *Parsifal* prelude on 12 November 1880 which Wagner was to conduct. Levi was one of the few people present to hear it. The composer conducted it twice because, to Wagner's consternation, the King asked for a repeat. When he asked for the prelude

[3] letter to Vincenz Lachner dated 16 September 1868 quoted in Frithjof Haas, *Zwischen Brahms und Wagner – Der Dirigent Hermann Levi* (Zurich and Mainz: Atlantis Musikbuch-Verlag, 1995), p. 123

[4] letter to Brahms dated 22 February 1869, *ibid*, p. 127

[5] letter dated 30 August 1875 in "Hermann Levi an seinen Vater – unveröffentlichte Briefe aus Bayreuth von 1875-1889," *Bayreuther Festspiel 1959 "Parsifal" Programm* (Bayreuth: Festspielleitung Bayreuth, 1959), p. 6

[6] Edward Speyer, *My Life and Friends* (London: Cobden-Sanderson, 1937), p. 145. Brahms's *Symphony No. 1* was given its first performance in Karlsruhe in 1876, conducted by Otto Dessoff.

[7] Ernest Newman, *Life of Wagner*, (London: Cassell, 1933-1947), vol. 4, p. 604

[8] Martin Gregor-Dellin and Dietrich Mack (eds.), *Cosima Wagner's Diaries*, 2 vols. (trans.) Geoffrey Skelton (New York: Harcourt Brace Jovanovich, 1978-1980), vol. 2, pp. 557, 559 (10 and 17 November 1880)

to *Lohengrin* as well, to compare the two, Wagner handed the baton to Levi in disgust.[9] Ludwig Strecker was one of the friends present, and he recorded Wagner's timing, on both occasions, as fourteen and a half minutes.[10] On 19 January 1881 Cosima recorded Wagner's infamous announcement to Levi that he is to conduct *Parsifal*. "'Beforehand, we shall go through a ceremonial act with you. I hope I shall succeed in finding a formula which will make you completely one of us.' The veiled expression on our friend's face induces R. to change the subject."[11] Wagner had in fact not wanted Levi for *Parsifal*, preferring to nominate his own conductor, but had been told by the Munich Court Opera that he could not have the orchestra without its conductor. The King wrote of Wagner's absurd reluctance: there is "nothing so nauseous, so unedifying, as disputes of this sort: at bottom all men are brothers, whatever their confessional differences." Wagner thus had no choice. He wrote to the King on 19 September accepting "gratefully the heads [sic] of this musical organisation… without asking whether the man is a Jew, this other a Christian."[12] And so they set to work.

Wagner was in a very good mood when Levi went to Bayreuth in April 1881 to discuss the following year's production – "everything goes for the best," he wrote buoyantly to his father.[13] And Wagner too was resolute, if not happy: "You are my *Parsifal* conductor!"[14] Levi wrote to Wagner in December 1881 raising questions about *Parsifal*. Cosima records Wagner's response: "R says [Levi] no longer has the necessary keenness, somebody else should do it for him."[15] In March 1882 Levi raises difficulties over singers: "[Wagner] is not satisfied with our conductor's methods, he thinks of Richter's practical ways."[16] In a year Levi was defending Wagner – "he is the best, the most noble human being" – even defending his views on "Jewishness in Music" (1850, 1869).[17] From the exhilarating, exhausting rehearsals in July – nine hours a day for three weeks – he reported to his father how ecstatically beautiful the orchestra was, and how good Wagner had been to him.[18] We recall how dissatisfied Wagner was with Richter's *Ring* tempi six years earlier. So too was Levi to suffer, not only at rehearsal but also after the first performance on 26 July 1882. On 23 July Wagner was irritable about the way *Parsifal* was coming along, according to Cosima: "The tempi also dissatisfy him." At the dress rehearsal the next day, he "finds the tempi in the first act drawn out rather too long." He has lunch with Levi on 25 July and "once more goes through the tempi." At the 28 July performance the prelude is "drawn out," and as late as 14 August Wagner is seeking to discuss tempi again with Levi and others.[19] It is difficult to believe there was not some changeability in Wagner's views on the question of tempi.[20] Levi was no doubt sensitive and conscientious, and

9 Newman, *Life of Wagner*, vol. 4, pp. 604-605

10 Ludwig Strecker, *Richard Wagner als Verlagsgefährte* (Mainz: B. Schotts Söhne, 1951), p. 299. Knappertsbusch, at the 1951 Bayreuth Festival, came very close to this: 14' 13."

11 *Diaries*, vol. 2, p. 601

12 Newman, *Life of Wagner*, vol. 4, p. 612

13 "Hermann Levi an seinen Vater," p. 8 (14 April 1881)

14 letter to Levi dated 1 July 1881, Wagner, *Selected Letters*, (ed. and trans.) Stewart Spencer and Barry Millington (London: J. M. Dent & Sons, 1987), p. 915

15 *Diaries*, vol. 2, p. 759 (2 December 1881)

16 *ibid*, vol. 2, p. 826 (14 March 1882)

17 "Hermann Levi an seinen Vater," p. 9 (13 April 1882)

18 *ibid*, pp. 9-10 (July 1882)

19 *Diaries*, vol. 2, pp. 893-894, 899

20 It should be noted that on the two occasions Wagner himself conducted the *Parsifal* prelude, he did so with different timings: 13 minutes on 25 December 1878, and 14½ minutes (twice) on 12 November 1880.

had learned Wagner's instructions for the modification of tempi "off by heart" from the rehearsals. "The composer's artistic intentions, together with the written notes, were absolutely binding for him. He detested any randomness."[21] He was absolutely faithfully to his master.[22] At rehearsals Wagner often exhorted the orchestra not to drag (and occasionally not to play so fast), and it appears Levi heeded this advice. Heinrich Porges, who recorded Wagner's comments, noted that one rehearsal of act one had lasted two hours, whereas in performance "this act lasted about one hour and forty minutes."[23] After the first performances Wagner reported their "complete success" to the King, and could not "praise highly enough... the zeal of worthy Kapellmeister Levi."[24]

After the second performance, reported London's *Daily News*, there was deafening applause lasting about ten minutes, then the curtain opened to show Wagner surrounded by all his singers, chorus members, orchestral players, and all the workmen. "With agitated voice, he first thanked Herr Levi for his great zeal and devotion in executing his work, then expressed his gratitude to all others for their co-operation, and finally bade farewell to the audience.[25] He praised Levi in particular for "his never-ending persistence and his remarkable intellect" which he knew how to use to realise all his artistic intentions, and the "admirable perfection" he drew from the orchestral performance.[26] Levi was simply "brilliant," according to a Viennese journal.[27] He had "brilliantly preserved his reputation," wrote a Berlin newspaper, "as one of the most reliable, skilful, and tasteful of conductors."[28] Heinrich Porges recalled Levi's work with Wagner over this first *Parsifal*: "No-one who witnessed this artistic interaction will ever be able to forget Levi's gift of unbelievably quick comprehension, of the energetic urgency yet delicacy with which he managed to grasp all the directions emanating from the Master's spontaneous inspiration relating to the orchestra's performance during rehearsals, and how he had them executed."[29] Yet history has left an incomplete picture. At the performances he conducted, he was hidden in the depths of the covered orchestra, his name was absent from the programme, and his musical contribution was largely subsumed in responses to the work itself.[30]

21 Haas, *Hermann Levi*, p. 167

22 Ernst von Possart, *Hermann Levi – Erinnerungen* (München: C.H. Beck'sche, 1901), pp. 44-45

23 Rüdiger Porges (ed.), *"Das Orchester muss wie die unsichtbare Seele sein." Richard Wagners Bemerkungen zum Parsifal aufgezeichnet während der Proben und Aufführungen 1882 von Heinrich Porges* (Berlin: Deutsche Richard-Wagner-Gesellschaft, 2002), p. 78. Porges noted that under Wagner's own direction, when at the final performance he took over the baton in act three during the Transformation scene and conducted to the end, certain passages were taken more slowly and others more quickly than formerly: *ibid*, pp. 70-72.

24 letter dated 8 September 1882, in Herbert Barth, Dietrich Mack, Egon Voss (eds.), *Wagner: a documentary study* (London: Thames and Hudson, 1975), p. 242. For Levi's letter to his father on the last performance (pp. 243-34), see the Wagner chapter, p. 37.

25 2 August 1882, p. 3

26 *Münchner Neueste Nachrichten*, 1 August 1882, p. 1

27 *Deutsche Kunst- und Musik-Zeitung*, 2 August 1882, p. 287

28 *Vossische Zeitung, Erste Beilage*, 3 August 1882, p. [1]

29 obituary of Levi, *Münchner Neueste Nachrichten*, 15 May 1900, p. 2

30 The earliest survey of the 1882 performances included many press reviews, but Levi's name is absent: Wilhelm Tappert, *Für und Wider - Eine Blumenlese aus den Berichten über die Aufführungen des Bühnenweihfestspieles Parsifal* (Berlin: Barth, 1882).

Fig. 5.1. Hermann Levi, Munich, 1875

Fig. 5.2. The first *Parsifal*, 1882: conductor, Hermann Levi, set designer, Paul von Joukowsky, and technical director, Fritz Brandt

Fig. 5.3. The Bayreuth Festival conductors, 1889: Hermann Levi (*Parsifal*), Felix Mottl (*Tristan und Isolde*), and Hans Richter (*Die Meistersinger*)

Fig. 5.4. Levi rehearsing *Parsifal* in 1882, with Wagner directing through the trap-door.
Drawing by Josef Greif, a member of the orchestra

Fig. 5.5. Levi in 1898. Drawing by Franz von Lenbach

The later Parsifals

He conducted *Parsifal* at every subsequent festival until 1894, except when he was ill in 1888.[31] Every repetition enhanced his reputation. As early as 1883 the *Münchner Neueste Nachrichten* reported:

Above all, the person deserving our fullest and most unequivocal praise – no, the laurels – is the genius who is our Levi. He worked veritable wonders down there with his stalwart band of musicians. Matured through last year's experience, and privy to Wagner's most secret desires, Levi has made *Parsifal* wholly his own. In the tempos and shadings, no less than in its spiritual depth, last night once more provided brilliant proof of this highly gifted and seasoned gentleman's talents.[32]

In Levi's own estimation, as he wrote to his father, his performances improved more and more as time went on.[33] In 1889, for example, he was deeply moved by the performance. "It was the best that I have ever led, better even than 1882."[34] Afterwards he felt he could have begun again at the beginning, giving the whole work immediately. One critic reported that during the intervals people exclaimed: "*Parsifal* has never been so beautiful!"[35] However, George Bernard Shaw observed that "at Bayreuth… there is already a perceptible numbness – the symptom of paralysis." He was unshaken in his belief in "Richter's great superiority to Herr Levi as a Wagnerian conductor," at least as regards the prelude (Richter had not conducted the whole work). With adequate rehearsals and a competent conductor, London could have done better.[36] But Bayreuth had the monopoly on *Parsifal*, and Levi became its tradition, matters to which German critics attached particular importance, as this dispatch from the 1894 Festival illustrates:

He is the one with the true calling. He is most intimately familiar with the Master's intentions. And, the point that carries special weight in today's Bayreuth, he holds on to these traditions, and is therefore the chosen conductor for *Parsifal*. Under his direction, those mystical, solemn and rousing orchestral sounds found expression in consummate form, and the Knights of the Grail and the Flowermaidens were performed with graceful beauty and purity, and had a magical, sensual appeal.[37]

Shaw was also present at that Festival and reported candidly on the lamentable singing – "The more solemn Gurnemanz felt, the more he howled; the more fervent Parsifal became, the more he bawled" – and on the poor quality of the instruments and their "brute physical sound…." He judged the orchestra (he did not specifically mention its conductor) "a very carefully worked up second-rate one. The results of the careful working-up are admirable; the smoothness, the perfect *sostenuto*, the unbroken

[31] He conducted *Parsifal* in 1882, 1883, 1884, 1886, 1889, 1891, 1892, and 1894. In the first three of those years, he shared the conducting with Franz Fischer.

[32] 11 July 1883, p. 1

[33] "Hermann Levi an seinen Vater," pp. 14-23 (1883-1889)

[34] *ibid*, p. 22 (23 July 1889)

[35] Carl Vopel, *Die Gegenwart* (Berlin), quoted in Susanna Großmann-Vendrey, *Bayreuth in der deutschen Presse* (Regensburg: Bosse, 1977-1983), vol. 3,1, p. 95

[36] George Bernard Shaw, "Wagner in Bayreuth," *English Illustrated Magazine*, October 1889, in *Shaw's Music: the complete musical criticism in three volumes*, (ed.) Dan H. Laurence (New York: Dodd, Mead, 1981), vol. 1, pp. 789-96

[37] Alfred Holzbock, *Berliner Lokal-Anzeiger*, 22 July 1894, in Großmann-Vendrey's *Bayreuth in der deutschen Presse*, vol. 3,1, p. 121

flow of tone testify to an almost perfect orchestral execution in passages which lend themselves to such treatment."Yet the instruments left much to be desired: they had not been made by true artist craftsmen, "... and the worst of it is that no German seems to care."[38]

Tristan und Isolde and the Ring

Levi was also celebrated for his conducting of Wagner's other works. In the case of *Tristan*, he only gradually came to penetrate its music, according to Heinrich Porges, because "he showed much greater leanings towards the Apollonian than the Dionysian. It was anathema to his nature to proceed to the extreme boundaries of expression, to become caught up in the exuberance of ecstasy when one almost seems to lose touch with consciousness." Nevertheless, it was after Wagner had attended a performance of *Tristan* under Levi's direction in November 1881 that Levi became his chosen conductor of *Parsifal*.[39] A performance in 1887 earned Levi the "fervent gratitude" of the audience. He was "ceaselessly active, forward-striding, and forward-striving," and he and his "wonderful orchestra... played and accompanied with a fire, with a fullness yet a softness of tone, with a fervency and an understanding one will only ever hear in a German theatre."[40] By 1894 Levi was criticised by the Munich journal *Der Sammler* for showing signs of succumbing to "Bayreuth tendencies":

As far as tonal beauty of the entire instrumental part was concerned, under the direction of Herr Levi, both in the soft and the vigorous sections, it was perfect. With regard to rhythm, however, every now and again there were various instances of straining and distortion – as early as the Prelude, but even more in the Introduction to the third act – which seemed to originate not so much from Levi's natural and ingenious conception, but more from the understandable attempt to go along with some of the new Bayreuth tendencies. We can only oppose this with our urgent request that our excellent First Conductor not trouble himself with these, but follow his own intuition instead.[41]

For years people flocked to hear Levi's *Ring* at Munich's festivals. An English visitor in 1894, for example, reported to the *Musical Times* how his "masterly conductorship" had been "the chief cause of the musical success" of that year's cycle.[42] Among the many details "exquisitely executed," *Der Sammler* singled out, was the shimmering orchestral accompaniment to the glowing Rhinegold. "The whole performance of the work, regardless of a few small flaws, was of such significance, freshness and unity as we hadn't heard for a long time."[43]

The reason for his success as a Wagner conductor according to Heinrich Porges, was that "he grasped the spiritual substance of a composition with the most penetrating

[38] George Bernard Shaw, "Basseto at the Wagner Festival," *Star*, 21, 23-26 July 1894, and "Bayreuth's indifference to beauty," *World*, 1 August 1894, in *Shaw's Music*, vol. 3, pp. 277-281, 301-304

[39] obituary of Levi, *Münchner Neueste Nachrichten*, 15 May 1900, p. 1

[40] Oskar Merz, *Zur chronik der Münchener Oper* (München und Leipzig: G. Franz, J. Roth, 1888), Vol. 2, p. 45. Merz was a critic for the *Münchner Neueste Nachrichten*. Whether he had heard performances of *Tristan* by Seidl in New York, or by Richter in Vienna and London, is unknown, but they disprove his point about German theatres, as we shall see.

[41] 11 August 1894, p. 8

[42] 1 September 1894, p. 617

[43] 14 August 1894, p. 8. Franz Fischer usually conducted the *Ring* in Munich.

insight into its musical aspect, while never losing sight of the primacy, the magic, of the stage." His interpretations of the *Siegfried Idyll* and *Faust Overture* were also remarkable.[44]

The Paris and London concerts

Levi rarely travelled abroad, and on two occasions on which he did, to Paris in 1894 and London in 1895, we get close-up views of the conductor which had been denied us at Bayreuth, where he had been largely invisible.[45] It was Good Friday in 1894 in Paris and, of course, excerpts from *Parsifal* were on the programme. *L'art musical* wrote of Levi as "sober, energetic, and nervous":

> The conductor uses various gestures, at one time beating broadly, at another indicating only the initial tempo, sometimes not beating at all for a while. He hardly uses his left hand, contrary to the practice of Mr Mottl whose left hand is very expressive. To get a section of players to attack, Levi turns squarely in front of them, beats two or three measures, then turns back to face the orchestra as a whole.[46]

The same reviewer noted "an admirable blend of ensemble and precision of attack. In his polyphony there is absolute clarity and one hears everything. As for the nuances, the *pianos* abruptly follow the *fortes* with perfect sharpness, the *forte* cutting out cleanly instead of lingering during the first measure of the *piano*." In the prelude to *Parsifal*, "marvellously understood by Levi," he made the silences shorter than Paris audiences were used to under Colonne and Lamoureux. The Grail scene was "perfect, the tempi being those of the tradition set by Wagner, from whom Levi received them." The clarity and intensity of the Salvation theme (in the Prelude too) was "impeccable." Unfortunately there were no bells, so a piano in the wings had to be used to less effect. "The curious use of the horn in association with the cellos, which gave a fullness of tone and a velvety, keen flavour, was an effect Levi brought out wonderfully." The *Siegfried Idyll* was rendered with "exquisite expression."[47] *Le Ménestrel* described the performance as an "imposing and grand interpretation," and was "impressed by the power of the musical feeling."

> It does not seem to be possible to extend further the art of balancing tones, of making such supple rhythms, of softening the melodic lines, of preserving sections of instruments, now their mellowness, now their piercing tones, and of veiling the first appearance of a new sound so as never to disturb the balance of the orchestra as a whole. This playing conforms to the tradition of Wagner....[48]

The reviewer was impressed by the eloquence of religious sentiment: a calm, austere, and sumptuous expression of renunciation, of prayer, and of faith.

[44] obituary of Levi, *Münchner Neueste Nachrichten*, 15 May 1900, p. 1

[45] Uncommon too were his guest appearances in Germany outside Munich. Bülow considered him the best of his deputies (Richter, Levi, Mottl, Maszkowski) at the 1887/88 season: letter to Hermann Wolff dated 21 June 1888 referred to in Christopher Fifield, *True artist and true friend: a biography of Hans Richter* (Oxford: Clarendon Press, 1993), p. 264. He was given a stormy reception at a Berlin Philharmonic concert on 13 February 1893 when he conducted several Wagner pieces: Peter Muck, *Einhundert Jahre Berliner Philharmonisches Orchester*, 3 vols. (Tutzing: H. Schneider, 1982), vol. 1, p. 167.

[46] 29 March 1894, p. 100 [47] *ibid*, p. 100 [48] 1 April 1894, p. 101

At the concert in Queen's Hall in London on 25 April 1895, the prelude from *Parsifal* was performed, together with the *Huldigungsmarsch*, the *Siegfried Idyll*, and Elizabeth's greeting and the overture from *Tannhäuser*.[49] The reviewers were surprised and deeply impressed by Levi, including those who had heard him in Bayreuth and Munich. The *Musical Times* wrote:

> The *entente* between Conductor and orchestra could not have been more perfect had months been devoted to rehearsal. The orchestra, it is true, was an exceptionally fine one – and large to match; but the instantaneous – we had almost said electric – way in which it carried out the multitude of effects indicated by Herr Levi gave convincing proof of the man's compelling power.... [His] "readings"... approach, on the one side, those of Herr Richter in breadth of effect, dramatic insight, and dignity; and, on the other, those of Herr Mottl in clearness and particularisation of detail.[50]

Another journal drew more deeply on history: "The stooping, like Levi, in *piano* and rising in *forte* passages was a characteristic of Beethoven's conducting; and the much talked of occasional laying aside of the *bâton* was adopted by Liszt at Vienna in the forties, and later by Von Bülow."[51]

George Bernard Shaw, whose critical comments on the Bayreuth orchestra we have read, reported how good Levi considered English orchestras. The orchestra assembled for his Queen's Hall concert certainly responded quickly to him, with "verve and general animation," according to the *Athenaeum*.[52] It was fascinating to watch Levi himself. "The back of Herr Levi, when conducting, is full of passionate interest," wrote the *World*. "Volumes might be written upon it."[53] The *Illustrated Sporting and Dramatic News* painted a vivid portrait:

> Hermann Levi at the conductor's desk makes one think of Rubinstein at the piano; as the late master always played for himself and to himself, so does Hermann Levi conduct without the least concern about the audience. He listens to his own effects, smiles an approval to some single instrumentalist, nods gratefully to another, winks at a violin in the fourth or fifth row when a slip – immediately spotted – occurs, sways to and fro, bends in half to hush gradually an excess of sonority, marches suddenly forward as if to provoke some orchestral violence, lays his *bâton* aside at unexpected moments, and gives cues with a glance, an uplifted eyebrow, and altogether disports himself as if he were alone with his instrumentalists in front of him; his business being to animate the sum of individualists before him with the power of his personality, theirs to respond to the commands of his mind passively and implicitly. And what wonders does he achieve thus![54]

Of special importance for his Wagnerian conducting, as noted by the *Illustrated London News*, was the way he drew out the melody from the orchestra:

> With Herr Levi, all the effort consists in making a strong and effective point of the predominant melody. With a composer like Wagner, whose continuity of melody is handed on very subtly from instrument to instrument, this is a singularly difficult problem. It was triumphantly solved by Herr Levi. His attention to the "single note" is extraordinary; and the results he obtained were no less extraordinary. His interpretation of the *Tannhäuser* overture thus became unique in its delicacy and wiry strength....[55]

[49] 1 June 1895, p. 381. The soloist was Milka Ternina. Beethoven's *Symphony No. 7* was also performed.
[50] *idem*
[51] *Musical Opinion & Music Trade Review*, 1 June 1895, p. 559
[52] 4 May 1895, p. 580
[53] 1 May 1895, p. 26 (Robert Smythe Hichens)
[54] 4 May 1895, p. 291
[55] 4 May 1895, p. 562

George Bernard Shaw found the *Tannhäuser* overture a "revelation; the cadence to the song of Venus, and the final section of The Pilgrims' March, with the new reading for the drums, produced an effect never heard here before."[56] It was also a revelation for the *World*: "practically a new reading…, [with] extraordinary accuracy, intense care of every accent, and delicate variations of the time.… The Pilgrim's March was taken at an unusually slow pace until it reappeared at the close of the Overture, when Herr Levi gradually quicked [*sic*] it towards the final triumph of the violins, which, by the way, played with superb poignancy their streaming runs. The middle section of the Overture, which is so often a mere muddle, came to the ear with astonishing lucidity."[57] Herman Klein noticed that Levi's *Tannhäuser* overture "differed in twenty ways at least from Mottl's, which, as we know already, is completely unlike Richter's." He also commented on the "marvellously delicate and expressive rendering of the *Parsifal* prelude – a genuine reminiscence of Bayreuth"; and no less refined was the performance of the *Siegfried Idyll* "taken, of course, at Richter speed, and not at the absurdly slow tempo adopted by young Master Siegfried."[58] The *Huldigungsmarsch* was taken "a shade slower than usual, and gained much in impressiveness thereby," according to the *Morning Post*.[59] The *World* considered that in the overture to *Tannhäuser* and the *Siegfried Idyll* Levi "proved himself most conspicuously a great master in the art of conducting":

The level of pianissimo he obtained in the *Siegfried Idyll* was absolutely magical. His manner of imperatively calling upon the particular set of instruments which are concerned for the moment with the ruling melodic phrase is also remarkable. He makes a step forward on his little platform and, as it were, leads them out to the charge as if they were his troops. And this invariable armour of his with that which is, or ought to be, for the time the predominant partner in the orchestral concern, results in a pellucid clearness of the musical atmosphere. …he is the last man to leave the details – the waves on the surface of the stream, the currents in its depths – to take care of themselves. Every nuance is attended to. Every accent is observed. The utmost neatness prevails.… [The reading] is entirely different from Siegfried Wagner's. The latter, by his adoption of an extravagantly slow tempo, gives to it a sentimentality that, though not entirely ineffective, is disagreeable on the whole since it inclines to the sugary. This lovely music should not be made to mean too much. The effect it produces should be of a perfectly elevated, almost ethereal, simplicity. It is open-air music in its essence, and so Herr Levi understands it.[60]

London had now seen and heard all three of the great Bayreuth conductors. They were all different, all powerful in their own way. "If not the greatest conductor who has visited this country," wrote the *Observer* of Levi, "he has certainly but one rival: Richter."[61] The *Magazine of Music* attempted a more sophisticated comparison:

The different methods of Levi and Mottl point to a deep, essential difference between the men. Mottl plays out of his own personality, expresses the mood that is strongest in him at the moment; Levi plays what is in the score, and nothing but what is in the score. In all probability Mottl could not for the life of him tell you precisely what he is going to do.… This essential difference comes out in the quality of the playing. Mottl's is lyric, passionate, gorgeous with

[56] "Hermann Levi," unsigned sub-leader in the *Daily Chronicle*, 29 April 1895, in *Shaw's Music*, vol. 3, p. 348

[57] 1 May 1895, p. 26 (R.S.H.). *The Times* considered the *Tannhäuser* overture and the *Huldigungsmarsch* had been played with "almost absolute perfection… so splendidly as to quite disarm criticism." (26 April 1895, p. 10)

[58] *Sunday Times*, 28 April 1895, p. 6 (Herman Klein)

[59] 26 April 1895, p. 2. It was described merely as "noisy" in the *Daily News*, 26 April 1895, p. 7.

[60] 1 May 1895, p. 26 (R.S.H.). The *Daily News* (26 April 1895, p. 7) expressed similar views about the *Siegfried Idyll.*

[61] 28 April 1895, p. 7

colour, full of a wonderful virility. Levi's is rarely passionate, is certainly not virile, and the colour is never in excess of what the composer intended. One feels that he has not the magnificent breadth of Richter any more than he has the white-hot passion of Mottl. But he is wonderfully clear. I imagine he rarely misses fire, as both Mottl and Richter do very frequently. He takes, as it were, the main point of every bar, and devotes himself to fetching that out, and the details may go hang for anything he cares.... Levi's exactitude, his incisiveness, make him as great a conductor as his colleagues, only he is different from them. Some will like one conductor, and some another, until the end of the world....[62]

George Bernard Shaw concluded his review of the concert with this yet again slightly different characterisation:

Richter's bulk and grandeur, Mottl's concentrated force and finesse, and Siegfried Wagner's poetic charm were all fascinating, but they have not in any way forestalled the dry enthusiasm, the unerring artistic cunning, the wiry activity, the humorous sanity and tough, healthy, workmanlike delight in doing the thing with a sure hand as well as it can be done, of this amiably crafty old gentleman, who, after two rehearsals, plays with our rather stiff-necked London orchestra as a potter plays with his clay.[63]

Levi never returned to London, as many hoped he would. The following year he became too ill to work, and retired. He died in Munich on 13 May 1900.

Levi's legacy

Levi was modest about his own skills to the point of invisibility. "As a conductor, I don't have any dazzling qualities at all which I could use to impress an orchestra or audience on the spot. The only good I probably have most likely shows only after sustained activity."[64] The two rehearsals with his London orchestra hardly amounted to a sustained or prolonged relationship, yet he was able to make a powerful impression quickly. Two central qualities of his conducting have been identified by his biographers. Frithjof Haas singled out his ability to grasp music intellectually and analytically: he could see a whole work at once, and its thematic structure, clearly and vividly, and with compelling suggestive powers, he could pass on his own identification with the music, and his fervent emotion, to every participant and listener.[65] Another characteristic was noted by Ernst von Possart, one of great importance in Wagner opera: he understood how to shape the main moments of the drama. He was as much stage director in spirit as he was music director in fact. He understood the nature of acting, and could effortlessly adopt and express the character of another person through the orchestra. He made his orchestra an actor in the drama. He was able, in effect, to become the foundation of the music drama.[66]

[62] "The Munich Conductor," *Magazine of Music*, vol. xii (June 1895), p. 115. "There is no doubt he is one of the greatest we have," wrote the *Birmingham Daily Post*, 26 April 1895, p. 5.

[63] "Hermann Levi," unsigned sub-leader in the *Daily Chronicle*, 29 April 1895, in *Shaw's Music*, vol. 3, p. 348

[64] letter to Robert von Putkamer, dated 7 March 1887, quoted in Haas, *Hermann Levi*, p. 168

[65] Haas, *Hermann Levi*, p. 164, also citing Arthur Hahn, "Hermann Levi, ein Tonkünstlerporträt," *Nord und Süd* (Breslau, 1894), p. 195ff

[66] Possart, *Hermann Levi*, pp. 45-46

One of the most important appointments Levi made was the engagement of the young Felix Weingartner as his musical assistant at Bayreuth in 1886.[67] They had got to know one another's music and music-making well when Weingartner went to Munich for rehearsals of his opera *Malawika*. There he attended all of Levi's performances. He admired two elements of Levi's art in particular...:

> the wide range of his capacity which allowed him to master the style of *La Muette de Portici* with the same elegance as *Nibelungen* or *Don Giovanni*, and the spiritual nature of his interpretations. He shed everything material and reduced technique to a minimum. As a rule he only used slight, pregnant and most characteristic gestures. My own method of conducting owes much to him. Hans Richter was the strong, fair, Germanic type, Bülow the highly developed intellectual who would possibly have been capable of great things in any field in which he cultivated with his own unsurpassable energy. Felix Mottl was the full-blooded young go-ahead, very characteristically Austrian, while Hermann Levi was a man directly inspired by his art, outwardly uniting in himself the advantages of his colleagues, inwardly penetrating far deeper than they did.[68]

Although Weingartner manifested some of the conducting characteristics of Levi, he never followed him into the Grail Kingdom of Bayreuth. This was not because of any musical antipathy, but for reasons to do with its Titurel-tainted administration. Karl Muck was to become Levi's chief inheritor. Before we look at those two Knights of the Grail, let us turn to that "full-blooded young go-ahead," Felix Mottl, of whom we have already had several intimations.

[67] as he tells his father in a letter dated 30 June 1886: "Hermann Levi an seinen Vater," p. 17

[68] Weingartner, *Buffets and Rewards - A Musician's Reminiscences*, (trans.) Marguerite Wolff (London: Hutchinson & Co., 1937), pp. 135-136

6

Felix Mottl – "Death-devoted heart"

When Felix Mottl first went to London in 1894 to conduct a series of Wagner concerts, he gave an interview to the *Magazine of Music* and made a striking impression. "[He] is a tall, burly man fairly running over with energy. His voice is full, rich, and strong, whether in speaking, or singing (as he frequently does) to his orchestra at rehearsal. His smile is kindly, sympathetic; his laugh is hearty, even uproarious and contagious; and he is at once dignified and hail-fellow-well-met."[1] He showed he was a born leader of an orchestra; his music-making was infused with his good nature. The *Musical Times* summarised his concerts: "His 'readings' were marked by singular clearness, delicacy, and energy, great rhythmic freedom, and exceptionally strong contrasts of all kinds. Not a detail, not a point was lost, and altogether it was felt by those who made first acquaintance with the Carlsruhe conductor that his fame was well deserved."[2] He was a breath of fresh air in London. Some would have liked him to establish himself there as a stimulus to his greatest rival, Hans Richter.[3] Mottl had come flushed with success from Paris. There too he was seen as a new kind of conductor, a complete break from the serene old time-beater. "He belongs to a new generation of conductors," declared *Le Ménestrel*, "who begin by studying, by loving the works they conduct, by penetrating them so intimately that they appear to be interpreting their very thoughts, to be communing with the feelings and ideas of the composer, to be living his life."[4] This identification of Mottl with his music – his *abandonment* to the music – was also remarked upon by the conductor Nicolai Malko who saw him in St Petersburg in the last years of Mottl's life:

> Mottl belonged to those artists who, while conducting, identify themselves with the music, completely, sincerely, and because of an almost innate response to it. Of course it is not always possible to 'glow' perpetually, and not all of his performances were equally good, but the best ones achieved such tremendous climaxes! The crowning glory of these achievements was his *Tristan und Isolde* which, in my opinion, has never been surpassed.[5]

1 "Mr. Felix Mottl: An Interview," *Magazine of Music*, vol. 11 (June 1894), p. 124

2 1 May 1894, p. 315

3 George Bernard Shaw, "Herr Mottl's Insight," *World*, 25 April 1894, in *Shaw's music: the complete musical criticism in three volumes*, (ed.) Dan H. Laurence (New York: Dodd, Mead, 1981), vol. 3, pp. 191-92

4 *Le Ménestrel*, 25 March 1894, p. 93 (H. Barbedette)

5 Nicolai Malko, *A Certain Art* (New York: W. Morrow, 1966), p. 129. Dr. Alexander von Andreevsky was amongst those who witnessed the rehearsals for Mottl's gala production of *Tristan* in St. Petersburg on 10

As we shall see, Malko was not alone in this assessment of this great but variable Wagnerian.

Early life with Wagner

Mottl was born near Vienna on 24 August 1856 and, like Richter, was a boy soprano before going to the Vienna Conservatory. What he learned there (1870-1875) was probably of little relevance to his subsequent achievements. "Conductors are born, not made," he told the *Magazine of Music*. "Either a man can conduct, or he cannot. He certainly cannot be taught. If any college or academy proposes to teach conducting as an art, it is nonsense! ... He must be able to conduct the first time he tries. It isn't like the fiddle or piano, where a *technique* must be acquired first. The man must have the *technique* in him." Nor was there much to be learned from watching others conduct. "Of course one may get help from listening to the conceptions of other men; but the *technique* of conducting is so simple, and each man's is so different from every other man's, that to watch other people is not of so very much use."[6] Be that as it may, he did attend many Wagner operas, concerts, and rehearsals in Vienna between 1872 and 1875, and saw Wagner conducting concerts in May 1872 and March 1875, and Richter on many occasions. He himself conducted some of the concerts of the Wagner Society.

He first met Wagner with other members of the Society, "with throbbing hearts," at the Vienna railway station on 21 February 1875. Mottl was "overjoyed to see the magnificent Master!" and was soon received by Wagner and entrusted "to learn Hagen with Scaria" for the 1876 Bayreuth Festival.[7] He wrote at the head of his diary for 1876:

> The Bayreuth year! It is the most important in my artistic development and has left its mark on me for all time. I had the luck to be allowed to be in personal contact with Richard Wagner for three months, and to learn from him what an enthusiastic pupil of the great man can. Everything that I can do, I owe to this Bayreuth apprenticeship. I also begin from this period to look to art as the principal concern of my life. My strong sensual disposition, however, remains unchanged. In the end though, this is directly connected to any artistic activity anyway![8]

Wagner summoned Mottl to Bayreuth in May, and he worked in the so-called *Nibelungen Kanzlei*, assisted in rehearsals and made many interesting observations in his diary (see chapters on Wagner and Seidl). Wagner was no doubt impressed by the young Mottl, for he recommended him to Angelo Neumann at the Leipzig Opera as "remarkably capable. He is the last one of whom I can say the same; I know no

January 1910; they were overwhelmed and moved to tears: "Wagner-Rausch in Rußland," *Vossische Zeitung* (*Unterhaltungsblatt*), 9 February 1933. Andreevsky also told the story (as Malko did in a slightly different form) of how, towards the end of act one of a gala performance, the Tsar sent someone off to ask how long the act was going to take, which led to a disruption to the beginning of the sailors' chorus, for which Mottl of course was not responsible. On the Tsar and Wagner, see also the Coates chapter, pp. 222-3.

6 "Mr. Felix Mottl: An Interview," *Magazine of Music*, vol. 11 (June 1894), p. 124

7 Willy Krienitz, "Felix Mottls Tagebuchaufzeichnungen aus den Jahren 1873-1876," *Neue Wagner-Forschungen* (Karlsruhe: G. Braun, 1943), pp. 185-186. During this visit, Mottl and Arthur Nikisch and Emil Paur, as representatives of the Vienna Conservatory, presented Wagner with a silver cup.

8 Krienitz, "Felix Mottls Tagebuchaufzeichnungen," p. 189. It is not clear when Mottl added this passage to his diary.

others. His skill and versatility are extraordinary, as I have had ample opportunity of judging."[9] On this recommendation he was appointed as assistant conductor to Seidl and Nikisch, but very soon the opportunity came to work more independently at Karlsruhe. This must have come as a relief to him, as he had little regard for Seidl and Nikisch.[10] The Karlsruhe (1881-1903) and Munich (1903-1911) years were the heart of his professional life, and he transformed operatic life in both cities.[11] But it will be his performances elsewhere that we will look at: in Bayreuth, where he gave more than seventy performances between 1886 and 1906; [12] in London (1894, 1898, 1900); and in New York (1903-1904). Before looking at the later music-dramas, we will touch briefly on some of his performances of the early operas.

The early operas

Mottl introduced four Wagner operas to Bayreuth, including the early operas *Der fliegende Holländer* (1901), *Tannhäuser* (1891), and *Lohengrin* (1894). The opening performance of the *Holländer* on 22 July 1901 was of "almost ideal excellence" according to the *Musical Times*, Mottl conducting "with his usual ability and zeal."[13] With the covered orchestral pit, everything was clear, according to the *Berliner Tageblatt*. There was a greater richness of nuance than usual, and "a glowing polyphony as if illuminated by electricity."[14]

Reports of his performances of *Tannhäuser* are laced with criticisms of his slow tempi. The only benefit of slow tempi seemed to be that it served the purpose of clarity and accent. In 1891, when he introduced the work to Bayreuth with "somewhat more deliberate pace" than was customary, this enabled him to give "perfect attention to matters of accent and phrasing," in the view of the *Musical Times*,[15] or in Richard Strauss's words, to "succeed in bringing out... sharp contrasts with the clarity postulated by the action on the stage."[16] The risk of slow tempi, however, was that it let life drain away. In his London performances in 1900, when "again his *tempi* were open to criticism"[17] – one performance was the longest on record, according

[9] letter to Angelo Neumann dated 10 October 1879, in Neumann, *Personal Recollections of Wagner*, (trans.) Edith Livermore (London: Archibald Constable & Co, 1909), p. 99. Cosima also mentions in her *Diaries* (vol. 2, p. 378) that Wagner wrote to Neumann on this day. Mottl features very little in her diaries.

[10] He described Seidl after first meeting him in Bayreuth in 1876 as "not very pleasant" and "somewhat condescending" (Krienitz, "Felix Mottls Tagebuchaufzeichnungen," p. 194), and when Nicolai Malko once mentioned Nikisch to him in St Petersburg he "immediately said, 'Well, his technique is immense, but here,' and he indicated his heart, 'nothing.'" (Malko, *A Certain Art*, p. 133)

[11] on Mottl's life generally, see Frithjof Haas, *Der Magier am Dirigentenpult: Felix Mottl* (Karlsruhe: Info-Verlag, 2006)

[12] He started with *Tristan* (1886 premiere, 1889, 1891, 1892, 1906), thence *Parsifal* (1888, 1894, 1897, 1902), *Tannhäuser* (1891 premiere, 1892), *Meistersinger* (1892), *Lohengrin* (1894 premiere), *Ring* (1896), *Der fliegende Holländer* (1901 premiere, 1902).

[13] 1 September 1901, p. 619

[14] Friedrich Dernburg summarised from *Berliner Tageblatt*, 4 August 1901, in Großmann-Vendrey, *Bayreuth in der deutschen Presse*, (Regensburg: Bosse, 1977-1983), vol. 3,1, p. 174

[15] 1 September 1891, p. 537. Gustav Kobbe made an almost identical comment about a performance in New York in 1903: *Morning Telegraph*, 5 December 1903 (Metropolitan Opera Archives)

[16] Richard Strauss, *Bayreuther Blätter*, 1892, quoted in Robert Hartford, ed, *Bayreuth: The Early Years*, (Cambridge University Press, 1980), p. 159

[17] *Musical Times*, 1 July 1900, p. 478

to the *Sunday Times*[18] – it did not help him keep his forces together.[19] The *Star* wrote that the opening night had not been "an inspiriting performance…; till the third act he hardly seemed like the Mottl of old [he had first visited sixteen years before] – the incarnation of vigor and love of life and color and passion."[20] In a performance in New York in 1903, the *Evening Sun* wrote of a "rapture of andante throughout the evening" that was highly satisfactory.[21] The *Commercial Advertiser* characterised it more colourfully:

> Mottl conducted with a firm hand – in the overture with a tremendously firm hand. The pilgrims moved with slow and stately tread, and the music of the Venusberg gave signs of a reform administration. When, however, he got into the Bacchanale proper, he moved more swiftly. The music snapped and crackled with wicked intensity. No wonder it revolted the soul of Heinrich Tannhäuser![22]

Five years after introducing *Lohengrin* to Bayreuth in 1894, Mottl conducted the opera in London. Again, there was the problem of slow tempi, as the *Star* reported:

> We had heard much of the Bayreuth tempi in *Lohengrin*. Now we have heard them. Frankly they appear too slow. They may add dignity and breadth to some passages, but they take away life, color, and movement. And there is a risk that the setting up of such a norm will in time lead to a tradition as cramping, as paralysing, as those which Wagner set himself to demolish. And is it true that Wagner went so slow?[23] Is it true that with him a crescendo was necessarily also a *retenuto*, not to say *rallentando*? But granting the Bayreuth premises, the orchestral playing was very fine. There was abundant light and shade, and excellent phrasing, and, above all, unanimity.[24]

To the *Monthly Musical Record* this evening in 1899 was a "disgrace":

> The prelude was beautifully played, but when the curtain rose, disclosing the most ragged, pitiful, incompetent chorus ever seen even on the Covent Garden stage, Mottl appeared completely to lose his nerve… it helped to make [him] perverse. Perverse he was with a vengeance. When a passage ought to have gone very slow he took it as fast as the instruments could get in their notes; when one ought to have been taken quickly he obstinately held it back until one almost shouted for the next note to arrive.[25]

The reviewer for the *Daily Telegraph* was in sympathy, but was realistic and resigned. "In few places on earth do we look for absolute perfection, and certainly the interior of an opera house is not one of those places."[26]

[18] 3 June 1900, p. 6

[19] *Observer*, 20 May 1900, p. 6: "It is impossible to speak highly of Herr Mottl's conducting…."

[20] 16 May 1900, p. 1 ("Staccato"). George Bernard Shaw had reported for the *Star* from the 1894 Bayreuth Festival. He said the orchestra in *Lohengrin* "gave a first-rate exhibition of the Bayreuth specialty of producing a perfectly unbroken flow of tone. But the levelling process which this involves was overdone in the preludes: the climax of the first one missed fire somehow." He did not mention Mottl specifically. ("Bassetto at the Wagner Festival," *Star*, 21, 23-26 July 1894, in *Shaw's Music*, vol. 3, p. 287)

[21] 5 December 1903, p. 6

[22] 5 December 1903, p. 5

[23] For Wagner's view on the desirable length of *Lohengrin*, and Mottl's record, see "Timings" below.

[24] 9 May 1899, p. 1 ("Staccato"). The *Musical Standard* expressed similar views, and noted: "The slowness of tempi, too, affected those of the singers who are not used to it, though, of course, it suited Frau Mottl and Frau Schumann Heink." (13 May 1899, p. 297, "R. Peggio"). Others were favourably impressed: *Standard*, 9 May 1899, p. 5; *Morning Post*, 9 May 1899, p. 5; *Sunday Times*, 14 May 1899, p. 4; *Athenaeum*, 13 May 1899, p. 603.

[25] 1 June 1899, p. 129

[26] 9 May 1899, p. 9

Tristan und Isolde

Tristan was Mottl's first love. As a boy in Vienna he was besotted with it. At the age of seventeen he played the *Liebestod* in Liszt's arrangement to a Wagner Society evening. He spent evenings alone with the score: "Am mad about [*Tristan*]," he wrote in his diary; "Evening alone engrossed in my *Tristan*."[27] It would become for him the work of Wagner to which he was most devoted and for which he would be most famous. When he introduced the work to Karlsruhe in 1884, it was a " great festival day for art."[28] When he conducted its premiere at Bayreuth in 1886, it was to "almost unanimous admiration," according to the *Neue Zeitschrift für Musik* . He animated the players "in youthful fiery fashion... You could actually hear *fortes* and *pianos*, and the fine nuances applied to the accents had the most delightful effect."[29] So fiery, in fact, it was rushed to some ears: "The tempi were so fast, they completely blurred the characteristic tonal figures in the alto voices, and led to poor refinement of the orchestral fabric," wrote the *Kölnische Zeitung*.[30] *Le Temps* stated after Mottl's death that these Bayreuth performances of 1886 were simply unforgettable – "the torrent of force, of passion, of life, the intensity and depth of emotion, the prodigious fullness of the music and drama – these were the most beautiful representations of *Tristan* one had without doubt ever seen." In one fell swoop, Mottl had become one of the greats.[31] He conducted it there again at the 1889 festival. To the *Musical Times* it "amounted to a revelation even to those familiar with the work."[32] George Bernard Shaw wrote:

> Herr Mottl's strictness, refinement, and severe taste make the orchestra go with the precision and elegance of a chronometer. Discipline, rehearsal, scrupulous insistence on every *nuance* in a score which is crammed with minute indications of the gradations of tone to be produced by each player: these, and entire devotion to the composer's cause, could do no more. But they are qualities which appear everywhere, if not in everyone....[33]

Yet still, there were doubts about the tempi: "today all the tempos seemed doubly slow," recalled Leopold Auer, "the time taken for Isolde's confidences to Brangäne; the entry of Tristan into the tent, and their exchange of glances up to the moment when the latter drains the chalice, seemed endless to me."[34]

Ten years later he conducted the work in London where there were echoes of the comments made at Bayreuth. He appealed to the *Star* as in no other work, "although the orchestra was at times rough, and many beautiful details were slurred over. Mottl seemed to have been carried away by the music, or perhaps he had no fixed ideas concerning it, and was, therefore, less the Mottl who sometimes irritates us."[35]

27 Krienitz, "Felix Mottls Tagebuchaufzeichnungen," pp. 180, 183

28 *Karlsruhe Zeitung*, 5 December 1884, quoted in Haas, *Felix Mottl*, p. 67

29 *Neue Zeitschrift für Musik*, 6 August 1886 (Oskar Schwalm), quoted in Haas, *Felix Mottl*, p. 79

30 29 July 1886 (Otto Neitzel), quoted in Haas, *Felix Mottl*, p. 80, and more extensively in Großmann-Vendrey, *Bayreuth in der deutschen Presse*, Vol. 3,1, p. 57

31 4 July 1911, p. 4 (Pierre Lalo)

32 1 September 1889, p. 541

33 "Wagner in Bayreuth," *The English Illustrated Magazine*, October 1889, in Hartford, *Bayreuth: The Early Years*, p. 146, and *Shaw's music*, vol. 1, p. 805

34 Leopold Auer, *My Long Life In Music* (London: Duckworth & Co., 1924), p. 258

35 12 May 1899 (E. A. Baughan). "There was very little of the dragging which has often so irritated me in his conducting, and the whole went with a rough kind of spirit and glow which were tonic in their exhilarating effect. But beyond this rough spirit there was not much to admire": *Musical Standard*, 20 May

The *World* was carried away with Mottl:

He teaches [the orchestra] to understand and adore the spirit of life within it. He teaches it to reverence and to exalt in that glory of life, to be vital at every movement, not now and then, but at every single instant of an opera. How supreme, how amazing, is the vitality of Wagner's effort in the orchestral score of *Tristan*! It is a miracle. It demands almost miraculous energy – now still, now romantic, now serene, now excited, now terrible, but always the energy of intense life – from its interpreters. This superb, intelligent, and personally passionate energy Mottl and his men brought to it on Thursday.... Never before did I so acutely realise the greatness of Mottl. He knows what so many of us are fatally ignorant of. He knows what the word life means.[36]

In New York in 1904, he conducted three performances with the Metropolitan Opera (and three on tour), but he found it hard work getting the standard he was accustomed to. In rehearsals he complained to his diary "orchestra lacks zest," and a week later "orchestra satisfactory, but without any hint of ecstasy."[37] Of the singers: "[they] think they are only employed for the evening performances. Rehearsals are therefore considered a favour or a disgusting obligation!"[38] Nevertheless, his will seems to have prevailed, because the opening performance on 9 January stunned the critics. "Mr Mottl has been accused of being phlegmatic and Teutonic. Hear his *Tristan*, and you will find him as fiery and Hungarian as Anton Seidl himself," wrote the critic for the *Evening Post* who had heard him in Bayreuth in 1886 and considered this a grander performance. He had heard the opera at least fifty times, yet Mottl "revealed new beauties in the score – that inexhaustible mine of luscious melody and thrilling harmonies."[39] The orchestra responded to Mottl's baton with "fidelity," according to the *Mail and Express*; "the swelling out of long notes, the colorful proclamation of Wagner's noble outbursts, the poetic dwindling of the string and wood wind tones to mere threads of sound – these and a hundred other niceties of performance were attained as by the touch and regulation of a master."[40] To the *New York Times*, Mottl's reading deserved "to be enshrined among the few supreme memories of the Metropolitan Opera House."

The slips and flaws and insufficiencies – and there were plenty of them in the orchestra and on stage – could not dim the profound and compelling beauty of what he accomplished. The orchestra glowed and throbbed under his baton, pulsing with life, moving with never-ceasing propulsive energy. It was an interpretation full of an infinitude of details, of minute shading of color and dynamics, of subtle and incessant modifications of tempo expressive of every instant of emotional state, of every gust of passion, jubilation, ecstasy, and anguish that plays through the characters upon the stage, rising to magnificent climaxes, and to a splendid stress of passionate utterance, yet never, through it all, losing sight of the larger sweep, the higher sense of symmetry and proportion. Never before has Mr. Mottl disclosed a power and an insight so complete as in this performance: it left the impression of being absolutely right, of diving and seizing the very essence of Wagner's purpose through all the music.[41]

1899, p. 308 ("R. Peggio," who preferred Muck's performance the same month).

36 17 May 1899, p. 32 (Robert Smythe Hichens)

37 diary entries for 1/2 January (act three) and 8/9 January 1904 (acts one and two), in Haas, *Felix Mottl*, pp. 242-43

38 diary entry for 3/4/5 February 1904, *ibid*, p. 249

39 11 January 1904, p. 7

40 11 January 1904, p. 7

41 10 January 1904, p. 2. Ernst Krauss sang Tristan, and Marion Weed sang Isolde as a late substitute for Milka Ternina.

The *Sun* was in agreement at the magnificence of the reading: "Not since the days of the lamented Seidl have New Yorkers heard the glories of this drama brought out with such poetry, with such atmosphere, with such a picturesque perspective of nuance."[42]

From the second performance on 22 January the *Sun* gave some examples of Mottl's virtues, identifying the "hero theme" at the entrance of Tristan as the only shortcoming:

He makes tremendous tragedy of the crash with which Wagner sends the cup to Isolde's lips. He does marvellous things with the torrents of passion in the duet at the close of Act I, and still more wonders with the woodland music of Act II.... His accompaniment to *O sink' hernieder* is most beautiful. The manner in which he causes the orchestra to breathe the undulating chords is something indescribable. In the *Einsam Wachend*... the accompaniment was a dream. Performances of this kind leave little to be done in the way of detailed comment. The delight of such occasions causes the weary commentator to sink into a state of profoundly peaceful rest, murmuring, "The indescribable – here is it done."[43]

Such was the state of mind of the critic for the *Neue Zeitschrift für Musik* after a performance in Munich in 1909: "What Mottl's *Tristan* means can hardly be expressed in words. You have to experience it. You have to be personally gripped, shaken and elevated by the power of such spiritual vibrations to understand the indescribable emotions his interpretation elicits."[44] A performance in St Petersburg in 1910 made people tremble, as Nicolai Malko recalled: "the performance achieved such heights that those who were present cannot speak of it even today without agitation."[45] Mottl had burned his place into history with his *Tristan*.

Die Meistersinger von Nürnberg

He finished his 1900 season in London with a performance of *Meistersinger*, and was "in his best form, according to the *Athenaeum*."[46] In a "good and creditable performance," as the *World* summed it up, he had not obtained so much good work from the orchestra all season:

True, he could not always make up his mind to move things fast enough, but it was only seldom that his love of leaden-footed progression obtruded itself.... There was endless spirit and variety.... Herr Mottl treats the romantic music with a little more stolidity than a conductor of any other nationality could or would. His climaxes are not so passionate, so there is not so much a rush of exaltation about them – or, rather, what exaltation there is, is made to seem an affair of the head more than of the heart. The humorous music is not idealised by him at all. He makes no attempt to invest it with any spurious refinement by softening it down in any way. He is content to read it as a realistic embodiment of a *bourgeoisie* which had many excellent qualities, combined with many faults....[47]

[42] 10 January 1904, p. 7. The *New York Times* also made the point about Seidl: "Not since Seidl...; the orchestral part... was incandescent with the volcanic passion of the music:" 23 January 1904, p. 9

[43] 23 January 1904, p. 8

[44] 1 October 1909, p. 375 (E. von Binzer), quoted in Haas, *Felix Mottl*, p. 329

[45] Malko, *A Certain Art*, p. 130. Mottl was especially pleased with this production and the devotion and enthusiasm of the Russian artists: Haas, *Felix Mottl*, p. 330. He returned to St. Petersburg in January 1911. Too ill to conduct a second performance of *Tristan*, he gave a performance of *Lohengrin* instead: Malko, *ibid*, p. 134

[46] 7 July 1900, p. 34

[47] 11 July 1900, p. 29

The Times made the veiled comment, that there was a "slightly quicker pace than might have been expected, but here and there his besetting sin appeared."[48]

In the case of the prelude to the *Meistersinger* Mottl knew exactly what Wagner wanted. In Bayreuth on 26 May 1876, he recorded in his diary: "Wagner says that the *Meistersinger* prelude will without exception be taken too slowly. It should be a strong march tempo."[49] And that is how he presented it at his first appearance as a concert conductor at the Metropolitan Opera House in 1903. It "went in rapid tempo, with abundant spirit," wrote the *Mail and Express*.[50] His reading, according to the *New York Times*, was "sane, strong, vigorous, full of an al fresco freedom, yet also of infinite detail. His performance... had a splendid stress of vehement utterance, a deep breathed jubilation: it had no room for any approach to sentimentality."[51] It surprised those who had been expecting his slower tempi. He brought out "the stirring rhythmic pomp and made the contrapuntal interweaving of parts wonderfully clear. ... on the sentimental episodes he dwelt less than was to have been expected of one so addicted to lingering *tempi*."[52] His *Meistersinger* may not have reached the level of Richter, the pre-eminent interpreter of the day, but he did know something of its spirit.

Der Ring des Nibelungen

When Mottl visited London and New York to conduct the *Ring* or its individual operas, he found conditions less than ideal. Nevertheless, it is to these two cities we will go to get a sense of his accomplishments in the *Ring*. Anton Seidl was to have conducted three cycles of the *Ring* in London in 1898, but alas, he had died the previous year. Mottl was his "efficient substitute," judged the *Musical Times*.[53] The greatest obstacle he had to contend with was a poor English orchestra (though many of its players were foreigners). Although it had benefited, as the *Athenaeum* observed, from a "sunken arrangement,"[54] the *World* was critical of both its playing and its direction. "It has been said before now that English musicians will play a difficult score at sight better than any foreigners, but that they frequently never play it any better afterwards." It never improved throughout the three cycles, and Mottl was not strong on correcting its mistakes. "He has a wonderful sense of dynamic contrast, and a strength and force that inspire singers and players alike with confidence. But in 'spotting' wrong notes he is inferior to many of his colleagues."[55] Nevertheless, in the circumstances, he was often credited with being the driving spirit. Among his finest achievements were the transitional orchestral passages, such as the beginning of *Rheingold*,[56] the Descent to Nibelheim,[57] the final procession into Walhalla,[58] and Siegfried's Funeral March.[59] As

[48] 5 July 1900, p. 6
[49] Krienitz, "Felix Mottls Tagebuchaufzeichnungen," p. 196
[50] 30 November 1903, p. 5 [51] 30 November 1903 [52] *Evening Post*, 30 November 1903, p. 7
[53] "Music in 1898," *Musical Times*, 31 December 1898, p. 13
[54] 11 June 1898, p. 766 [55] 13 July 1898, pp. 30-31 (C.L.G.)
[56] "so suggestive of the surging depths of the Rhine": *Musical Times*, 1 July 1898, p. 462
[57] "showed Mr. Mottl at quite his best": *Daily Telegraph*, 7 June 1898, p. 8
[58] "a tremendous effect": *Star*, 7 June 1898, p. 1 ("Piccolo")
[59] "one of the most deeply impressive we have heard": *Daily News*, 13 June 1898, p. 9. "The magnificent rendering of the *Walküre*, and the energetic and impressive reading of the Funeral March in *Götterdämmerung*

to the overall spirit, there were some doubts, as expressed by the *Star*:

The *Rheingold* is a most difficult opera to conduct. There is so much darkness and half light in it. And anyhow Wagner does not (whether purposely or because he had not yet fully acquired the mastery over the orchestra and the leitmotive) make the themes stand out as he does in the rest of the *Ring*. And all this would make it more alien to Herr Mottl's characteristic bent, for he loves light, color, movement, passion. Therefore we hope that in *The Walkyrie* he will help to stir us still more deeply.[60]

And he did. "He made his orchestra play as no other Covent Garden orchestra has been heard to play for many a year," according to the *Illustrated London News*.[61] The *Star* considered Mottl had given the best *Walküre* yet heard in London:

From the first bar, poetry and passion flowed, as it were, from his bâton. The stormy prelude was splendidly played, and all through the first act the sensuous magic of the love music fell almost entrancingly on the ears. While every motive stood out with the firmest outline, there was no undue noise, and the singers could always be heard. And when it came to the drawing of the sword from the tree, we were carried on to the end of the act in a very whirlwind of passion, and all through it was the same.[62]

Still, the performance was marred by a very deliberate pace in act three as Brünnhilde announced Siegmund's death, and by poor violin-playing in the Magic Fire Music.

In *Siegfried* Mottl was "less intense and exciting."[63] A blemish was his "excessively slow rate of speed," especially in the Forging Song. Moreover, the orchestra did not know the work as well as the *Walküre*, according to the *Star*, which gave all the more credit to Mottl for getting the good performance he did.[64] *The Times* considered that of the two performances of *Siegfried* overall, there was "a feeling of tameness that was entirely absent under the late Anton Seidl's baton."[65]

The most disappointing part of the *Ring* was *Götterdämmerung*, but for reasons little to do with Mottl. When he came on for the second act, the audience gave him "one of those unprecedented and spontaneous tributes than an artist never forgets. Again and again were the cheers renewed," and some time had to elapse before he could take up his baton.[66] It was just as well the applause came at this point, for what followed on stage more or less destroyed any magical or majestic moments. "The last act was, to use a mild term, deplorable," wrote the *Illustrated London News*. "Workmen were to be found on the stage on the rising of the curtain, scenes automatically moved about without any reasonable motive, Wagner's directions were disregarded recklessly... Mottl alone saved the thing from fiasco."[67] The *Morning Post* singled

were the most striking features during the four evenings." *Monthly Musical* Record, 1 July 1898, p. 159

[60] 7 June 1898, p. 1 ("Piccolo") [61] 18 June 1898, p. 914 [62] *Star*, 9 June 1898, p. 1 ("Staccato")

[63] *Illustrated London News*, 18 June 1898, p. 914. He had to contend with the De Reske brothers who demanded cuts. This caused "a miniature tempest": *Daily Telegraph*, 15 June 1898, p. 10; "about twenty minutes were saved by cuts": *Star*, 10 June 1898, p. 1; including the Erda/Wanderer scene in act three – "This was unpardonable": *Athenaeum*, 18 June 1898, p. 798; "quite inexcusable": *Illustrated London News*, 18 June 1898, p. 916. There were no cuts in the second performance: *Sunday Times*, 26 June 1898, p. 6.

[64] 10 June 1898, p. 1 ("Staccato") [65] 25 June 1898, p. 11

[66] *Sunday Times*, 12 June 1898, p. 5 (Herman Klein, who also reported "not a single cut of any sort was made")

[67] 18 June 1898, p. 916

Fig. 6.1. Felix Mottl from his Karlsruhe years, 1881-1903

Fig. 6.2. Mottl in his youth

Fig. 6.3. Mottl at work during his Munich years, 1903–1911

Fig. 6.4. Mottl in Vienna. Silhouettes by Otto Böhler

Fig. 6.5. Mottl in Vienna, 1897. Silhouette by Hans Schliessmann

Fig. 6.6. Mottl in Munich, 1910

out some of the short-comings: "the burning pyre was a failure, the rising Rhine an absurdity, and from some parts of the house no sign could be perceived of any burning of Walhalla, no indication of any '*Götterdämmerung*'."[68] The *Musical Times* elaborated on the catastrophe:

> *Gutrune's* scream at the sight of the dead body of *Siegfried* was apparently mistaken for the whistle which signals the change of scenery, and literally brought down the house, causing the abode of *Hagen* to be lowered, as it should be at the close, to represent the rising of the Rhine. One of the prophetic ravens declined to fly off with its message, and when finally induced to do so, insisted on traversing space upside down. The stage mists were also badly worked. Wagner is partial to mists, but a mist that comes down at the rate of forty miles an hour and at once shuts out the scene possesses no mysticism.[69]

Mottl single-handedly salvaged the show, and the cycle. His share in its success was "simply incalculable," according to the *Star*.[70] The *Daily Telegraph* summed up: "Had it not been for his presence and co-operation, had it not been for an orchestra into whose ranks he infused a large measure of his own spirit, enthusiasm, and discretion, the artistic result of the cycle would have been infinitely less considerable."[71]

He was invited back to Covent Garden for two cycles in 1900. On this occasion there were fewer mishaps on stage ("in the *Walküre* the wind opened first one half of the door and disclosed a sunlit landscape; two minutes later the other half swung back tremulously and showed – moonlight"[72]), and there was an improvement in the orchestra, but with six rehearsals during the week and two other performances before the *Ring*, the players were tired.[73] "The wonder is," wrote Alfred Kalisch, "that the fiddlers had any arms and the brass had any lips left by [the end of *Götterdämmerung*]. To that, as much as to Herr Mottl's love for slow movements, I would ascribe the frequent impression of flagging and lagging which one experienced."[74] Mottl's "mania for dragging" was a common complaint in reviews.[75] Examples given were Loge's

[68] 13 June 1898, p. 4 [69] 1 July 1898, p. 463 [70] 13 June 1898, p. 1 ("Staccato")

[71] 13 June 1898, p. 10. The *Musical Standard*, which had uniquely found fault with Seidl's Wagner the year before, also did not admire Mottl's readings of Wagner: "I do not think he is a conductor of music-drama; so far as the singers are concerned he is excellent enough, but he has very little idea of dramatic rush and poignancy of expression; he allows motives to be played with scarcely any meaning, although we feel that they should reflect some of the dramatic tension of the drama; he views the whole musical texture as if it were a gigantic symphony and the motives under his bâton too often seem to be merely ingenious tricks with only a musical meaning. And then his tempo is nearly always too slow. For instance, his conducting of the Trauermarsch has been called most impressive, but to my mind it was much too slow, almost ludicrously slow. It was stretched on the rack to such an extent that it lost its vitality:" 18 June 1898, p. 387 (E.A.B.). Given the shortcomings of the orchestra, some of the singers, the stage-management, and even the critical reviews, it is no wonder Mottl identified the audience as the most remarkable feature of the twelve performances he conducted: letter to the editor dated 5 July: *Daily Telegraph*, 6 July 1898, p. 5

[72] *World*, 13 June 1900, p. 29

[73] The *Daily Telegraph* considered there could have been more rehearsals: the players "were not infrequently astray in the complexities of the score....there were but few rapid passages [for the strings] that came out quite cleanly." 11 June 1900, p. 9

[74] *World*, 13 June 1900, p. 29

[75] "Mottl spoilt many passages by his mania for dragging": *Observer*, 10 June 1900, p. 6; "Herr Mottl's pet weaknesses of excessive slowness and persistently disregarding the singers, were... not absent": *Star*, 7 June 1900, p. 1 ("Staccato"); "the band was made to go cruelly slow.... nor did it always have its reward in increased breadth or dignity thereby": *ibid*, 11 June, p. 1; "Mottl was certainly not in his best form, for, apart from the matter of tempi, there was frequently a want of grip....": *Athenaeum*, 16 June 1900, p. 760; "Mottl's dragging of the tempi was too marked... to allow the marvellous orchestral music to make its full effect...;

narrative and the finale in *Rheingold*, the prophecy to Siegmund and *Winterstürme* in *Walküre*, and "worst of all" the Waltraute scene in *Götterdämmerung*. "Herr Mottl's *tempi* may be right," wrote Alfred Kalisch, "but if they are, everybody else's, including Richter's, are wrong."[76] It was more than a question of tempi, however. Something had changed. After *Siegfried* the *Star* wrote:

Fig. 6.7. Mottl as drawn by F. Burkhard

The sensation of irresistible, irresponsible, volcanic youth which the work as a whole ought to give, was not there. Last night even some of the climaxes suffered from this curious change that has come over Herr Mottl. I call it curious because it is the very opposite of the virtues that were his greatness. Certainly no one could have accused him last night of a more pagan love for color and glow; and one listened in vain for the grandeur, coupled with polish, for which he used to be famous. Two years ago how different it was! I honestly think it is Mottl who has changed, not I.[77]

Overall the first cycle was welcomed, and Mottl given his due. The *Sunday Times* gave him credit: "though his habit of constantly gazing into the score would suggest the contrary, he displayed throughout a marvellous familiarity with the details of Wagner's stupendous work."[78] The *Musical Times* summed up: "Mottl cannot fairly

the climaxes… more than once lacked passion.": *Musical Times*, 1 July 1900, p. 478

76 *World*, 13 June 1900, p. 29

77 8 June 1900, p. 1 ("Staccato")

78 10 June 1900, p. 6; reviewing the second cycle the *Sunday Times* wrote that Mottl "may have curious ideas about Wagner's tempi, but I for one shall always 'take off my hat' to him as a great conductor" (1 July 1900, p. 6)

be said to have answered all expectations – expectations based, not on hearsay, but on previous achievement.... [However,] a conductor who is used to things as they are in Germany cannot but feel to some extent dispirited at having to cope with Covent Garden and its vagaries of stage management."[79] Whether or not he was dispirited, after the second cycle, which was better,[80] he never returned to London.

At the Metropolitan Opera in New York during the 1903/04 season he did not conduct a complete *Ring*, but made his debut with the *Walküre*, and followed it with a new production of *Siegfried*.[81] His debut was "a notable one," according to the *New York Times*.[82] Its chief music critic, Richard Aldrich, noted separately that some work had still to be done rehearsing the orchestra, but this would be remedied:

His reading of the score glowed with color and pulsed with life and vigor. From the subtlest pianissimo to the loudest crash of the full orchestra he commands and enforces an infinite variety of dynamic nuance. His tempos are elastic and full of expressive shades of variation. He builds up a climax with thrilling power, with seemingly endless reserves of tone. He succeeded, even at his first performance, in obtaining a beautifully clear elucidation of the thematic structure of the music, finished in detail, but of splendor and sonority in its larger proportions. It is clear that Mr. Mottl is above all a dramatic conductor: dramatic blood courses through his veins, and everything in his performance is made subsidiary and contributory to this one end, the elucidation of the dramatic significance of the music.[83]

Not all reviewers heard such a model performance as described by Mr Aldrich. The *Mail and Express*, for example, noticed how "Mr. Mottl dragged the tempi in the opening scenes [and elsewhere] in a manner scarcely tolerable to American Wagnerites....To make up, however, [he] took a new lease of life in the latter half of act one, and the scene between Siegmund and Sieglinde went with steady movement, reaching a rattling tempo" by curtain fall:

By thus exaggerating his slow and quick tempi, Mr Mottl lost, in the present writer's opinion, the chance to keep the orchestral part continuously interesting.There were moments when the music seemed about to come to a standstill from sheer lack of motive force. Climaxes were so long deferred that they seemed to bear little relation to one another of the intervening musical valleys. Only in the last act, when Wotan and his daughter finally meet for a farewell embrace, was the mighty emotion of a dramatic lifetime focused on one noble outburst – a climax superbly approached and magnificently inspiring. The dominating intellectuality and the too patient attitude toward details that had slowed Mr. Mottl's interpretation of the early parts down to an unimpressive dullness, were here swept away by a torrent of true emotional force.[84]

79 1 July 1900, p. 477

80 "The chief improvement was in the orchestra, which played with grip and fire; and there was variety and passion in it.The dragging of the times was very seldom noticeable, partly because Herr Mottl did really ordain quicker *tempi*, and partly because the slowness so often censured before was largely due to the lack of firmness and unanimity." *World*, 4 July 1900, p. 27 (Alfred Kalisch); also *Athenaeum*, 30 June 1900, p. 34

81 In all, he gave seven performances of the *Walküre* (including ones in Philadelphia, Chicago and Cincinnati), and six of *Siegfried* (including ones in Philadelphia, Chicago and Boston); three of each of these were parts of *Ring* cycles shared with Alfred Hertz.

82 26 November 1903, p. 4 (unsigned)

83 29 November 1903, p. 22

84 26 November 1903 (Metropolitan Opera Archives)

Another reviewer seemed to hear what both the *New York Times* and the *Mail and Express* alluded to:

Mr. Mottl is, of course, a believer in the present state of slow tempi in Germany, and consequently a good deal of *Die Walküre* was lingering sweetness long drawn out. But aside from that Mr. Mottl's conducting was admirable. It was full of color and *nuance*, of wide dynamic range and of eloquent touches, but it did not smother the voices. It was the conducting of a man who knows his Wagner, who has temperament as well as understanding, but is not carried off his feet by enthusiasm. Mr. Mottl is well poised. In fact there were times, as at the end of the first act, when a little more passion would have helped.[85]

The *Evening Post* noted that Mottl "possesses Anton Seidl's art of following the singers in every nuance..., and differs from him mainly in his greater addiction to broad, languid tempi and less inclination to whip up the band here and there, especially in the long monologues...."[86] The *Evening Sun* also recalled the Seidl days: "Not since the death of Mr. Seidl has any such wonder of conducting been vouchsafed to opera audiences. Not once were the singers over-burdened by the orchestra; always were they supported and surrounded in exactly the right degree."[87]

The rehearsals for Mottl's first *Siegfried* do not appear to have gone well, for he wrote in his diary at the beginning of December 1903: "Life here holds no interest at all. Theatre rehearsals are always the same. Nobody does anything more than fulfilling their damned duty and obligation. Nothing more than passable, at best, can come from that. And that's way too little in art!"[88] Of the performance on 18 January, the critics had mixed views. To the *Sun* it was "a source of delight. Like all conductors, [Mottl] failed to get the tremendous power that Seidl got in the forge scene, but in the more delicate parts of the score, such as the question scene, the *Waldweber* and the duet of Act III, he brought out the beauties of the music with exquisite finesse and a most poetic spirit."[89] The *Mail and Express* detected a "motivic force that Mr. Mottl's baton sent coursing through the orchestral performance":

Mr. Mottl's tempi were steadily inspiriting, his nuances secured constant variety and gave expression to significant factors in the design, without forcing themselves on one's notice: his balance of the several choirs of the orchestra was well maintained, and his climaxes were approached with psychologic [*sic*] judgement of the angle of ascent, and achieved with thrilling power. When the strings turned over a phrase to the wood winds, the latter took it up at just the proper degree of loudness, carried out its contour and provided exactly the color value that Wagner sought. ... He did not make the mistake of a too sustained tension: there was repose enough to keep the players and the audience on a comfortable and keenly interested basis. In the first act of *Siegfried*, for instance, there was a splendid effect produced by a climax of secondary power, accomplished when the Wanderer took his departure from Mime's cave. The long sustained tones fairly burned their way into the perception, and in no other way could the

[85] *Sun*, 26 November 1903, p. 7 [86] 27 November 1903, p. 7 [87] 26 November 1903, p. 2

[88] diary entry for 1/2 December 1903, in Haas, *Felix Mottl*, p. 238. Mottl nevertheless thought the first performance was good: "orchestra plays outstandingly, with warmth and devotion. Those poor people are worked to death. But if you take hold of them, they do give everything they have." (diary entry for 18 January 1904, in Haas, *ibid*, p. 244)

[89] 19 January 1904, p. 9. The *New York Times* too was impressed with Mottl's "complete identification with the spirit and intention of Wagner... [and] the elasticity and subtlety of his reading and the infinite wealth of detail...": 19 January 1904, p. 5.

> intensity of the dwarf's terror and foreboding have been secured. But this was utterly eclipsed at the end of the act, when, after an exciting version of the forging scene, there came a supreme burst of sound with the rending of the anvil by Siegfried's sword.[90]

Yet to the *Press*, Mottl's performance did not disclose "any new message" for New York. "We have heard *Siegfried* under much more satisfactory conditions in New York – from an orchestral viewpoint as well as in excellence of ensemble." Although the reviewer made allowance for the uncertainties of any first night, and for fewer rehearsals than the conductor may have been used to in Germany, he had shown with *Tristan* he could triumph over such obstacles. But "last night the ensemble was ragged; singers and orchestra were not always at one, and surprising to tell, Mr. Mottl's reading was wanting in delicacy and feeling. Can it be that Mr. Mottl, manly, vigorous and intense, lacks the gently poetic and sensuous characteristics which are also part of a conductor's equipment?"[91] Some, at least, of those "first night" uncertainties may have been overcome, for in a later performance the *Press* acknowledged that Mottl had "wrought such overpowering effects with the Metropolitan orchestra" that one wished he had been staying more than one season in New York. However, "it is a lamentable truth that conditions in the operatic life of New York are of a sort to make a stay of more than one season a disagreeable prospect for a man of Mr. Mottl's artistic calibre and reputation."[92] Disagreeable they had been, for he never returned.

Fig.6.8. Mottl as drawn by Enrico Caruso

[90] 19 January 1904, p. 7
[91] 19 January 1904, p. 7
[92] 10 March 1904, p. 5

Parsifal

Hermann Levi was ill in 1888 and could not conduct his customary *Parsifal* at Bayreuth. Mottl replaced him. It was his first *Parsifal* and it did not make the critics happy. The *Kölnische Zeitung* noted that the dragging of the tempi, whether under the influence of Cosima Wagner or otherwise, had created a painful impression of boredom.[93] *Nord und Süd* wrote that *Parsifal* suffered a considerable loss in quality under Mottl, for he was not mature enough yet for interpreting the work:

That Felix Mottl is one of the most gifted conductors of our time is in no doubt. He has temperament, imagination, and spirit in abundance. He makes all the psychological struggles within a character his own with the most delicate and fervent understanding. He has an expert eye for the charms of the colours of modern instrumentation and knows how to draw from them a fabulous glow. He certainly knows this himself, and produces a splendid intensity. But his talents are not yet balanced. He will have to become more steadfast in his striving, to deepen his experience, to sharpen his sense for grasping fine musical details. He has not yet mastered the technique of gradually introducing transitions. He is not completely at one with himself for the time being. At times he charges ahead a bit rashly. Then he jumps to the other extreme, to an almost pedantic deliberation at times. There is something nervous, unreliable, and feminine about him which he has not yet learned to control.... [His tempi were sometimes] too hurried, but for the most part were terribly dragged out so that the main scenes of the first and third acts lost almost all their dramatic characteristics....This drama, which leads through all the ups and downs of life, demands a conductor like the Munich Hofkapellmeister Hermann Levi. Mottl is no such artist yet, but can still become one.[94]

English and American visitors also remarked how Mottl's tempi were slower than Levi's, in particular the "persistent over-slowness" of the preludes to the first and third acts.[95] Overall this had led to a detrimental effect: the *Musical Times* did "not think the work gained in consequence."[96] Mottl had been inclined "to mistake the lack of spirit, and slowness, for majesty," according to an American visitor.[97] For Felix Weingartner, Mottl's performances were "great artistic crimes."[98]

Mottl certainly recognised Levi's greatness – "God, if all human beings could rise to the level of Levi," he wrote to Cosima, "that would be hardly bearable!"[99] – and

[93] 11, 18 November 1888 [Otto Lessmann?], quoted in Großmann-Vendrey, *Bayreuth in der deutschen Presse*, Vol. 3,1, p. 75

[94] *Nord und Süd* (Breslau), April-May 1889 (Paul Marsop), quoted in Haas, *Hermann Levi*, p. 537, *Felix Mottl*, pp. 83-84, and extensively in Großmann-Vendrey, *Bayreuth in der deutschen Presse*, Vol. 3,1, pp. 81-87.

[95] *The Meister*, vol. 1, no. 4 (22 November 1888), p. 146. Charles Villiers Stanford recalled how the "slow *tempi* of Mottl were positively disturbing. His prelude to *Parsifal* took half as long again as Levi's:" *Interludes*, p. 146. Whether this is an accurate recollection is doubtful, for he attributes it to his second visit to Bayreuth in 1883 when Mottl did not conduct *Parsifal*; his visit may in fact have been 1889, because he says he attended *Tristan*, *Parsifal* and *Meistersinger* which were given together that year; however, Mottl did not conduct *Parsifal* in 1889, only in 1888, 1894, 1897 and 1902.

[96] 1 September 1888, p. 539

[97] Louis Charles Elson, *European reminiscences: musical and otherwise: being the recollections of vacation tours in various countries* (Philadelphia: Theo. Presser, 1891), p. 80

[98] see also Weingartner chapter, p. 287.

[99] undated letter quoted in Haas, *Felix Mottl*, p. 139. Haas himself explains that Mottl "particularly emphasised the sacred pathos" of *Parsifal*; "but so far as universal spirituality and human poise are concerned, Levi was the superior one" (*ibid*, pp. 352, 139).

he was in awe of *Parsifal.* [100] Perhaps it was his deep awe, his utter devotion to the work, that led to his exaggeratedly slow tempi, at least occasionally, for he was not consistently slow, as his overall timings show. There may be an element of truth in the suggestion that Mottl was under the influence, if not the command, of Cosima Wagner in so far as his tempi were concerned,[101] but away from Bayreuth, did these influences have to persist? Or was his own musicianship, pure and simple, in evidence?

In London in 1897 he conducted the greater part of acts two and three with special dispensation from Bayreuth. The performances struck very different chords. In the case of the first concert, of act two, to the ears of the *Athenaeum* the orchestra played with "the dreamy tenderness" generally characteristic of Mottl.[102] The *Musician* found his conducting "a marvel of delicate sympathy and passionate force":

> Mottl is frankly a decadent. Face to face with the classics he is often puerile and ineffective, but in Wagner he is sublime. Not a detail of the score escapes him. He has an instinctive feeling for every curve of Wagner's melodic phrases, and yet throughout that bewildering maze of polyphony he never loses sight of the main lines of the mighty structure.[103]

Yet to the *Musical Standard*, quite a bit of the score seems to have escaped Mottl:

> Some parts went well under his direction; others badly. Let there be no mistake about this. There may have been a large number of "deputies" at this concert [i.e., substitute players not at the rehearsal]; but it was the reading, pure and simple, that did not strike us as a whole, as at all great.... There was much... that was heavy and wrong. He seemed to fear to "descend" into sensation; yet Wagner when he wrote the music at the end of the second act did go in for a bit of sensationalism. Our readers will remember the stage directions: "The Castle falls to ruins, the garden withers to a desert," etc. Herr Mottl made no point (surely easy enough to obtain!) with the music here; and as to the performance of the calm, reflective music that follows(such a stroke of genius), there must surely have been some misunderstanding. The latter portion of the act, indeed, could not have been more weakly or unclearly played. The closing music absolutely went for nothing! Some other expressive and beautiful parts in the work (that astound one as read by Herr Levi) were given, if the truth be told, a poor and unconvincing interpretation. It was not often one could say that the true feeling and accent of the music were represented. One felt, additionally, that the polyphonic detail of Wagner's music should have been represented with a greater degree of clearness. No, we could not call it a fine interpretation of the *Parsifal* music.[104]

When the third act was performed (the introduction and lines between Kundry and Gurnemanz were excluded[105]), these two critics came closer together in their responses. It was "a good performance on the whole," according to the *Musician*, but "lacked a good deal of the life and movement of [the second act], and it dragged

[100] "Art and love, the two great driving forces of our existence on earth... come into real, eternal life in *Parsifal*. They awaken and maintain all that's good, high-minded, beautiful and noble in us. Who could have experienced this without looking up to our Creator in faith and love, thanking Him with all our heart that He allowed us to witness this!": letter dated 27 August 1888 to Prince Max von Baden, quoted in Haas, *Felix Mottl*, p. 85

[101] for example, *Nord und Süd* (Breslau), April-May 1889 (Paul Marsop), quoted in Haas, *Felix Mottl*, p. 84

[102] 15 May 1897, p. 659 [103] 19 May 1897, p. 24 (R.A. Streatfeild [*sic*])

[104] 15 May 1897, p. 319. Frau Mottl sang Kundry ("very conscientiously") and Heinrich Vogl sang Parsifal ("his organ may not be what it was").

[105] *Athenaeum*, 22 May 1897, p. 690.

terribly in places."[106] The *Musical Standard* considered it a "stronger" performance than the second act, but "now and then one did wish for more precision, and clearness (and less deliberateness)... some of the music was rather unduly 'drawn out,' and... lost something of its power in consequence... but the strength and feeling of the music were generally at least adequately represented."[107] For this performance Mottl had had bells manufactured to his specification which were rung, not from within the orchestra, but from one side of the auditorium. They had a mixed effect – "the tone was certainly not bell-like"[108] – but they generally enhanced the Transformation music. The *Standard* wrote that it was "almost awe-inspiring,"[109] and the *Sunday Times* thought it "simply stupendous."[110] It was Mottl's last appearance that season in London. His interpretation had not appeared markedly different from Bayreuth. He was "the most variable of men," according to the *World* (at this concert "he was at his best"):

> His variability is the defect of his qualities, for he quaffs his inspiration from the mountain torrent of emotion and temperament – and this is a more exciting but less reliable source of supply than the deep and serene well-springs of the intellect, whither Richter so sedulously betakes himself. And so with Richter, there is no better and no worse, for all is best. Mottl's best, such as we had [with act three of *Parsifal*], is quite as good.[111]

He left London "in a blaze of triumph."

He was in New York at the time *Parsifal* was performed in its entirety in 1903 against the strenuous wishes of Bayreuth, but he had nothing to do with the production. He was of the inner circle of Bayreuth, and would have shared in their grief that *Parsifal* was to be given in a mere opera theatre. The conductor was Alfred Hertz. Mottl attended one of his orchestral rehearsals. "It is heart-breaking having to hear these sounds in a house of luxury and fashion. Hertz conducts as if in a rage, all rough-and-ready. In doing so, he does develop a zeal and seriousness which is touching enough.... I thank my Creator every day that not even the thinnest of threads connects me to this predatory establishment."[112] In response to reports that Mottl had been involved in some way with the production, Hertz affirmed this was not the case. In a letter to Mr. Sydney Loeb, published in the *Musical Times* after Mottl's death, he wrote: "It is an absolute fact that Mottl had *nothing whatever* to do with either the preparation or with the conducting of a performance of *Parsifal* at New York. ...the musical direction was *entirely* in my hands."[113] And it is to him that the ignominy and fame of those performances rightly belongs.

[106] 26 May 1897, p. 44

[107] 22 May 1897, p. 335 [108] *ibid*, p. 335 [109] 19 May 1897, p. 5

[110] 23 May 1897, p. 8 (Herman Klein) [111] 26 May 1897, p. 14 (Alfred Kalisch)

[112] diary entry of 16 December 1903, in Haas, *Felix Mottl*, p. 240. Mottl also heard some of Hertz's *Tannhäuser* and commented: "Hertz conducted with great brutality." (19 March 1904, *ibid*, p. 254). The Metropolitan Opera performance of *Parsifal* took place on 24 December 1903.

[113] *Musical Times*, 1 August 1911, p. 528 cf. *New Grove Dictionary of Music and Musicians*, 2nd edition: "he advised the conductor Alfred Hertz in the successful American première of *Parsifal* (1903) but could not conduct it himself owing to copyright disputes with Bayreuth" ("Felix Mottl," p. 231). Hertz's recordings of four excerpts from *Parsifal* (Berlin Philharmonic, September, 1913) can be heard on Naxos 8.110049-50 (1999).

The Welte-Mignon piano rolls

In 1907 Mottl recorded several Wagner pieces on piano rolls with a Welte-Mignon device, a process that was shrouded in secrecy and that remains mysterious.[114] Though lovingly restored by technicians, the ghostly results leave many questions unanswered as to the reliability of these rolls as a representation of the pianist's playing. At best, Mottl's pieces display a "dreamy tenderness" which, as we have read, a reviewer identified as a characteristic of his conducting. At worst, they are burdened by a heavy air of weariness or lethargy, the air of a funeral parlour. Wagner's music does not transpose easily to the piano. Stripped of the richness of its orchestral and vocal fabric, which are the heart and soul of Wagner's conceptions, the skeletal remains are pale reflections of the music they seek to imitate. The speed with which the rolls are fed through the reproducing machine of course determines the tempo of the music, and the pitch will remain constant even though this tempo is changed. Whether less enervating music would result if an artist rather than a technician fed the rolls through the machine is an open question. It is certainly difficult to imagine those in the music room at Wahnfried in June 1881 being "utterly transported," as they were when they heard Mottl play act three of *Tristan*, by playing such as on these piano rolls.[115]

The cup is drained

When Felix Weingartner paid tribute to Mottl after his death, he wrote of his style of conducting: "He did not absorb himself in small details but always looked to the large and simple lines. The characteristic of his conducting was a marked fondness for beating broad tempi. Even if one does not share his feeling, the personal note he achieved thereby worked in his favour."[116] Bruno Walter, who succeeded Mottl in Munich, considered him "most convincing in his interpretations of Wagner's musical dramas… because he was more richly gifted with electrifying spontaneity and improvising force than with the ability to consider minute details, and with the inclination to do educational work with the singers."[117] The Munich critic, Alexander Berrsche, identified two special characteristics of Mottl's conducting: "a beautiful, sensuous feeling for the great, broad melody, and an eminent sense of rhythm. In his interpretations, the orchestra sang as if with a human voice, and the rhythm strode along with an iron step. In this way he was able, not so much to transform the highest musical ardour of feeling into storm and stress, but rather into pathos."[118] The Hamburg critic and biographer of Nikisch, Ferdinand Pfohl, considered there were few conductors who could be mentioned in the same breath as Nikisch. "Hans von Bülow, Hans Richter – the Wagner disciples. Perhaps Felix Mottl as well – but then,

[114] A detailed examination of this process is to be found in Henry-Louis de La Grange, *Gustav Mahler, Vol. 4, A New Life Cut Short (1907-1911)* (Oxford University Press, 2008), Appendix 2B, pp. 1619-1635. For details of Mottl's recordings, see Discography.

[115] *Cosima Wagner's Diaries*, vol. 2, p. 678

[116] *Le Monde musical*, 15 July 1911, p. 203.

[117] Bruno Walter, *Theme and variations: an autobiography*, (trans.) James A. Galston (London: H. Hamilton, 1947), pp. 218-9

[118] Alexander Berrsche, *Trösterin Musika* (Munich, 1942), p. 610, quoted in Haas, *Felix Mottl*, p. 350

only perhaps. For in Felix Mottl there was still something of the old German school – especially in his technique – albeit imbued with a warm-blooded Austrian nature, a sense of style and a passionate musical intensity."[119]

Fig. 6.9. Mottl silhouette by Otto Böhler

From what we have read of Mottl's Wagner performances, Pfohl's "perhaps" is certainly fair: it can be no more than that. Whatever criticism there might be of his technique or his penchant for broad lines and broad tempi, it is interesting that these tended to become features of modern Wagner conducting, notably of Hans Knappertsbusch's. In his 1894 interview, Mottl said he thought conductors were taking everything much too fast. Pace depends, he said, especially in the concert room, on the size of the orchestra: with a large orchestra it must be slow and broad so the full mass of tone can have its effects, but with a small orchestra, it must be faster. He

[119] quoted by David Wooldridge, *Conductor's World* (London: Barrie & Rockliff, 1970), p. 110 [from Ferdinand Pfohl, *Arthur Nikisch: Sein Leben, seine Kunst, sein Wirken* (Hamburg: Alster-Verlag, 1925), pp. 131-32]

also said the *mood* of the conductor must be taken into account.[120] Clearly Mottl was a man of moods. As we have seen, sometimes his moods worked and sometimes they did not. In many cases they did not, or at least the mood Mottl was in did not resonate with reviewers. When he did achieve a great success, notably with *Tristan* and the *Walküre* (music of love and passion), it could only partly have been a matter of mood or inspiration. It may have been a stroke of luck. "When one knows that every success is only ever a coincidence," he confided to his diary after being complimented on a beautiful performance of *Tannhäuser* in New York, "one cannot suppress a feeling of deepest embarrassment and strong disgust!"[121] He was a true artist, an inspired conductor, and not without self-knowledge. Everything does not always turn out the way one might like.

When he was asked once what single work he would choose to conduct before he died, (Beethoven, Berlioz and Wagner were his favourite composers), he replied without any hesitation, "*Tristan und Isolde*."[122] Whether by choice or otherwise, that is what came to pass. He was conducting *Tristan* in Munich on 21 June 1911. The Isolde was Zdenka Fassbender with whom he was in love. (He had divorced his first wife, the singer Henriette Standthartner, the previous year.) As she sang her fateful words *Tod geweihtes Haupt, Tod geweihtes Herz* ("Death-devoted head! Death-devoted heart!"), Mottl became deathly pale, passed his baton to the first violin, struggled to his seat, and fainted. He was brought round and taken home, where he recovered, but only temporarily. He was strong enough to marry his Isolde on his deathbed, but a few days later, on 2 July, he died.

[120] "Mr. Felix Mottl: An Interview," *Magazine of Music*, vol. 11 (June 1894), p. 124
[121] diary entry of 4 December 1903, quoted in Haas, *Felix Mottl*, p. 238
[122] "Mr. Felix Mottl: An Interview," *Magazine of Music*, vol. 11 (June 1894), p. 124

7

Karl Muck – Knight of the Grail

Muck was a strict, ascetic musician. Poised and economical on the podium, he was utterly devoted to his work, and to the seriousness of his re-creative task. For him the composer's score was paramount. He used it always in performance. What he most brought to his music-making was an unerring yet flexible feel for tempo, secure rhythm and balance, and a vision of line and detail from which a whole work seemed to emerge. So carefully studied were his performances that they gave the impression they could not be otherwise. They were authoritative. They sounded pure, right and true. Selflessly, he thus discharged his duty. He was an ideal Knight of the Grail.

Yet his personal reserve, his self-effacing attitude towards music, inevitably led to less personal warmth than in some of the more instinctive, down-to-earth conductors. To *look* at Muck, one could see how serious, studious, even sardonic, the man was. Carl Flesch, who counted him among the great conductors of his time, wrote: "Rarely does one find such agreement between outward and inward qualities as with this excellent musician and conductor. His face was sharply profiled, his figure at once well shaped and spare, his mode of expression unsentimental, sarcastic: without and within, he was of a rugged, angular harmony."[1] This was the pre-eminent conductor of *Parsifal*.

Not surprisingly, Muck did not write about his work, or about the art of conducting. He refused to write memoirs. "I am a musician, not a writer," the *New York Times* reported him saying.[2] He even refused to write about Bayreuth where he was most famous. "I have always been a fighter as a reproductive artist," he wrote to one of Cosima's daughters, "but I have fought with the conductor's baton, not with the pen. I handle the baton as a skilled professional. I would handle the pen like a dilettante. And you may well know my dislike of any dilettantism. I always considered it my duty to disappear behind the music being performed, to work – but not to talk

[1] Carl Flesch, *Memoirs* (trans. and ed.) Hans Keller (London: Rockliff, 1957) p. 286. Similarly Albert Spalding: "… that aquiline profile, carved out of granite, over which was stretched a yellow and seamed parchment that had once, perhaps, been human skin. No warmth appeared to animate this head: only a kind of smouldering blaze in the half-closed eyes, the eyelids heavy with age. But fire there was, and a kind of sardonic humour that commanded the attention of every musician on the stage." *Rise to follow: an autobiography* (London: Frederick Muller, 1946), p. 7. See also Olin Downes, "Dr. Karl Muck," *New York Times*, 10 March 1940, p. 158

[2] "Music in Central Europe," *New York Times*, 22 December 1929, p. X9

about my work to the sweet vulgar crowd."[3] On one occasion he did talk about his work, to the *New York Times* in 1906:

There is only one thing for the conductor to do, that is to make beautiful music, true music. When he has done that he has done everything that is to be expected of him. In giving compositions he should not sound the personal note. His own personality has nothing whatever to do with it. To attempt to give an individual interpretation of the work of a composer is often to give exactly what the composer did not mean. The only way is to find the meaning of the composer and give his works as nearly as possible in the real and true style.[4]

To see how far he succeeded, we shall have a close look at the Wagner operas he conducted in London in 1899 – *Tannhäuser*, *Tristan*, *Walküre*, and *Meistersinger* – and to the fourteen Bayreuth Festivals between 1901 and 1930 where he was the chief conductor of *Parsifal*. We shall then give an ear to his recordings, which are among the first of the great Wagner recordings to have come down to us.

A life sketched

Muck (his name rhymes with *book*) was born in Darmstadt on 22 October 1859.[5] His father, Jakob Muck, was a lawyer and conductor, and gave his son his first music lessons.[6] The boy showed great promise as a pianist, studying at Würzburg and Leipzig and making his debut at the Gewandhaus in 1880, but his formal studies were in classical philology for which he earned his doctorate. His piano teacher, Rubinstein, expressed "intense disgust" when Muck declared his wish to follow a conducting career.[7] He had no formal training in conducting. Like others before him, he simply had the gift. How did he do it? "How can I say?" he replied to the *New York Times*. "It all lies in the gift of interpretation. If one has that he will know the truth when he has found it. That is all there is to it. I learn the truth according to my gift of interpretation and present it. That is all."[8]

His first engagement was at the Zurich Stadttheater (1880) as second conductor and chorus director. He then worked for a season at Salzburg (1881-1882), beside Hugo Wolf. His next appointment was to the newly-built Stadttheater at Brünn (Brno) (1882-1883), where his opening work was the first production of *Lohengrin* to use electric lighting. He also opened his years in Graz (1884-1886) with *Lohengrin*, on 14 April 1884, and made a powerful impression, breathing new spirit into the work and showing his mastery of everything on stage.[9] (He was invited back to Graz to conduct *Lohengrin* at the opening of the new opera house on 17 September 1899.) Among his other Wagnerian highlights in Graz was the city's first uncut Wagner opera, the *Meistersinger*, on 10 February 1885. He soon became the first conductor of the

[3] letter to Daniela Thode dated 10 October 1926 in Peter Muck, *Karl Muck: Ein Dirigentenleben in Briefen und Dokumenten* (Tutzing: Hans Schneider, 2003), p. 146

[4] 18 November 1906, p. X5

[5] Peter Muck, *Karl Muck*, p. 1; he was born in Würzburg according to the *Neue Deutsche Biographie*, Vol. 18 (Berlin: Duncker & Humblot, 1997).

[6] W. J. Liebenberg, "Generalmusikdirektor Muck," *unidentified journal*, 1949, p. 45, Graz Opera Archives

[7] as Muck told Olin Downes: "Virtuoso as Conductor," *New York Times*, 13 August 1933, p. X4

[8] "Dr. Muck Praises Boston Symphony Orchestra," *New York Times*, 18 November 1906, p. X5

[9] Liebenberg, "Generalmusikdirektor Muck," p. 45

German Theatre in Prague (1886-1892) in succession to Anton Seidl. From here he took the *Ring* to St. Petersburg and Moscow in 1889 and 1891, gave performances which "compared most favourably with Bayreuth itself" according to their producer, Angelo Neumann,[10] and created a storm in the press.[11] He not only conducted, but also lectured to the Russians on Wagner, not on all the leading motives and their role, but on the "epic narratives of the Scandinavian Edda, thus leading them to the very source and fountain head of Wagner's work."[12]

In 1892 he received the call to Bayreuth as a rehearsal conductor of *Meistersinger*, with a promise of two performances, a promise which was retracted by Cosima Wagner, apparently but implausibly, on the grounds that Richter objected.[13] He was appointed to the Imperial Court Opera in Berlin (1892-1912) and it was from there that he travelled to London in 1899 to conduct Wagner operas, which we will read about below, and to Bayreuth in 1901 to conduct *Parsifal* which he was to do almost to the end of his active life. A *Lohengrin* at Bayreuth in 1909 and a *Meistersinger* in 1925[14] were his only deviations from his devoted service to Wagner's last work. He spent two periods in the United States with the Boston Symphony Orchestra (1906-1908, and 1912-1918), where he included Wagner pieces in his concerts, but conducted no opera there. His last performance in the States was Beethoven's *Eroica Symphony* in the War Prison Barracks at Fort Oglethorpe, where he had been interned during the War with many excellent German musicians. It was apparently "one of his greatest achievements." He emerged from prison camp "gaunt and bronzed like an Indian brave (whom he resembled as much as he did Wagner)," [15] was deported, and never returned.

Back in Germany in 1919, the former Imperial Court Opera conductor found himself out of favour with the new republican authorities, and had to work as a guest conductor[16] before seeing out his days at the Hamburg Philharmonic and Staatsoper (1922-1933). His last Bayreuth Festival in 1930 was a bitter affair. Siegfried Wagner died that year, and his *bête noire* Toscanini, whom he had tried to keep out of Bayreuth, was performing and being given more rehearsal time than Muck was used to and expected.[17] He was also ageing, and it showed in his music-making. At the memorial service for Siegfried, Muck conducted Siegfried's Funeral Music which, according to

[10] Angelo Neumann, *Personal Recollections of Wagner*, (trans.) Edith Livermore (London: Archibald Constable & Co, 1909), p. 312

[11] Bärbel Hamacher (ed.), *Wagner in St. Petersburg* (catalogue of exhibition in the Neues Rathaus, Bayreuth, July-September 1993), pp. 24-25

[12] Herbert F. Peyser, "Karl Muck," *Disques*, August 1931, p. 249

[13] Christopher Fifield, *True artist and true friend: a biography of Hans Richter* (Oxford: Clarendon Press, 1993), p. 312

[14] Fritz Busch was scheduled to conduct but cancelled because of illness: *Signale für die musikalische Welt*, 19 August 1925, quoted in Peter Muck, *Karl Muck*, p. 139

[15] *New York Times*, 24 March 1940, p. 114. The story of Muck's internment, which was of doubtful legality (he was a Swiss citizen) is told by James J. Badal, "The strange case of Dr. Karl Muck, who was torpedoed by *The Star-Spangled Banner* during World War I," *High Fidelity*, October 1970, pp. 55-60.

[16] He approached Bruno Walter in Munich for work at a Wagner Festival in 1920. "I had not seen him for almost twenty years," Walter recalled, "and was moved by the contrast between the energetic, firm, and caustically sarcastic man in his forties whom I remembered, and the serious and obviously tired man of more than sixty now facing me.... [In his Wagner performances he] proved that he had lost none of his mastery. His clear interpretative style revealed simplicity, greatness, and strength." Walter, *Theme and variations: an autobiography*, (trans.) James A. Galston (London: H. Hamilton, 1947), pp. 261-2.

[17] Friedelind Wagner and Page Cooper, *The royal family of Bayreuth* (London: Eyre and Spottiswoode, 1948), p. 51; Peyser, "Karl Muck," p. 249

Alexander Kipnis, "was so old, like a piece of parchment, a piece of dusty old scenery" compared with the "unbelievably beautiful" *Siegfried Idyll* which Toscanini conducted at the same concert.[18] Muck too knew he was old. In his letter of resignation to Winifred Wagner he wrote, "… new forces must be put in control; and it must be upon young shoulders that the overwhelming burdens and responsibilities can be laid. For this sort of wheelwork I am no longer fit – I, whose artistic standpoint and convictions, so far as Bayreuth is concerned, stem from the preceding century."[19] One of his last public appearances was during the fiftieth anniversary commemorations of Wagner's death in February 1933. At a concert at the Leipzig Gewandhaus, "pitifully frail and shrunken and assisted on and off the podium by the help of two men, [he] conducted the *Parsifal* Prelude and the *Meistersinger* overture with a magnificence, breadth and a vitality which, at the close of the concert, stirred the overwrought gathering to a frenzy of enthusiasm."[20] In May, after a festival in honour of Brahms's centenary, he resigned after a disagreement with the Nazi authorities over the amalgamation of the Hamburg Philharmonic with the Staatsoper orchestra.[21] He retired to Stuttgart, to the care of an old friend from Boston days, where he died on 3 March 1940.

The 1899 London season – Tannhäuser

As a guest conductor from Berlin, he made his debut in London with *Tannhäuser*, only a few days after Mottl had made his debut with *Lohengrin*, and immediately made a distinctive impression.

> Dr. Muck is manifestly a German conductor of the first rank, and his reading of the orchestral portion of the opera was typical of the modern style of the Fatherland – that is, there was a tendency to exaggerate the tempo in slow and quick passages, but with excellent phrasing and accentuation, combined with great attention to detail. The opening of the overture was taken so slowly that the stately theme acquired a kind of wail, and the march in the second act moved so quickly that it lost much of its dignity. Otherwise, excepting some quite unnecessary cuts for which, maybe, Dr. Muck was not responsible, the orchestral playing possessed admirable features. The principal themes stood out clearly, the precision and attack were excellent, and the ensemble was always carefully balanced against the vocal tone.[22]

The *Musical Times* also commented that "like most German conductors of today, he was inclined to drag the slow portions."[23] To the *World*, the overture went with

[18] B.H. Haggin, *The Toscanini Musicians Knew* (New York: Horizon Press, 1967), p. 62. According to Haggin, Toscanini attended some of Muck's concerts in Boston and said "Muck was terrible! … Everything so slow! Muck was Beckmesser of conductors!" (*ibid*, p. 217)

[19] the full letter dated September 1930 is in Peter Muck, *Karl Muck*, p. 159, and is translated in Herbert Peyser, "Why Karl Muck left Baireuth," *New York Times*, 1 March 1931, p. X8

[20] Herbert Peyser, "Wagner in Germany," *New York Times*, 5 March 1933, p. X5; Hitler sat in the front row at the concert, and on his 80th birthday, Muck received the Order of the German Eagle from Hitler himself: *ibid*, 5 March 1940, p. 27

[21] Peter Muck, *Karl Muck*, pp. 168-169; *New York Times*, 5 March 1940, p. 27. Fred Prieberg reports that the Brahms Festival was disrupted by the Nazis because of a claim that Muck was of Jewish descent: *Trial of Strength: Wilhelm Furtwängler and the Third Reich*, (trans.) Christopher Dolan (London: Quartet Books, 1991), p. 42. As it turned out, Muck was sympathetic to the Nazis, which led the City of Hamburg to change the name of *Karl Muck Platz* in 1997 to *Johannes Brahms Platz*: "Carl Muck," in *Die Musik in Geschichte und Gegenwart (MGG) – Personenteil*, Vol. 12 (2004), 763

[22] *Standard*, 16 May 1899, p. 5

[23] 1 June 1899, p. 390 (the comment was applicable to *Die Walküre* too)

"oppressive sedateness, but the opera went well… Dr. Muck is wonderful in detail, but not so imperial as Mottl. The parts, under his care, seem paradoxically greater than the whole."[24] The overture seemed otherwise to the *Daily Telegraph*: "Mr. Mottl's successor has not quite the strong commanding beat by which the Carlsruhe conductor is known and appreciated. But he gave an excellent account of the famous overture, and, generally speaking did well for one in an unaccustomed place."[25] The *Athenaeum* agreed about the "exceedingly good" overture, but did not seem to share the view of his beat. Muck was seen to have "a firm beat and a comfortable, reassuring manner."[26] It was a new orchestra, however, and the conductor and players would need a little time to get accustomed to one another, and it was for this reason perhaps that the *Sunday Times* noticed a certain "restlessness of method" which could have accounted for "the indecision and lack of clearness" noticeable in many passages. However, the reviewer liked the "'sweet reasonableness' of his tempi and his decided capacity for bringing the singers and the orchestra into complete 'rapport' with each other."[27] The *Daily News* considered the orchestra might need a little time to become accustomed to his beat, and thought that in the Venusberg scene, the orchestra had "drowned the singers."[28] The *Illustrated Sporting and Dramatic News* commented on the "exquisite degrees of light and shade" in the orchestra, and considered that if he were equally successful in other operas of the German season "we shall have no reason to deplore the enforced absence of Herr Felix Mottl."[29]

Tristan und Isolde

This absence led to Muck making his second appearance with *Tristan*, which Mottl had conducted earlier in the week. It made for some interesting comparisons. The *World* considered "Dr. Muck conducted with less temperament than Mottl. He satisfied my intellect, but not always my heart. I thought Mottl's playing of *Tristan* was one of the truly magnificent achievements that has ever come under my notice."[30] However, to the reviewer of the *Musical Standard*, Muck's distinctive appeal was more satisfying: "I have at last found a Wagner conductor who realizes my ideal":

I heard Dr. Muck in *Tannhäuser* on Monday and I was then struck by his poetic grasp of the melody, but on Tuesday this quality was even more marked and, in addition, the complicated score of *Tristan* showed that the poetic grasp of the *Tannhäuser* melos was only a rough indication of the infinitely more subtle grasp shown in the conducting of *Tristan*. I am quite prepared to see it stated in quarters where Mottl is well-nigh worshipped that under Muck the music of this great drama lost something of the triumphant glow and persistent passion; but it did not really lose anything of the kind. When a climax is wanted, as in the Prelude, in the musicheralding the approach of Tristan to the trysting-place, and in the end of the love duet, Dr. Muck gave us wonderful force, wonderful because it was never mere physical energy but was always full of an acute nervous strength…. I would lay special stress on the fine dramatic appreciation he possesses of the significance of the motives and the particular form in which

24 24 May 1899, p.11 (R.S. Hichens) 25 16 May 1899, p. 10 26 20 May 1899, p. 635

27 21 May 1899, p. 6. *The Times*, on the other hand, considered Muck "might have exercised more control over his forces now and then, notably in the scene at the beginning of the Sängerkrieg, wherein the march and chorus were taken so rapidly as to quite nonplus the steady-going chorus": 20 May 1899, p. 10

28 16 May 1899, p. 9 29 20 May 1899, p. 448 (B.W.F.) 30 7 June 1899, p. 14 (R.S. Hichens)

they appear and re-appear. Apart from this Dr. Muck has a fine sense of phrasing, so that every instrumental solo is given its full singing value – in this he reminds me of Levi and of Nikisch.[31]

The reviewer also found that Muck gave the love duet "a spiritual tone which Wagner, if he meant anything at all by his poem, certainly intended." He also commented that the "elasticity of expression" which he obtained from his orchestra also marked his accompaniment of the singers. "It was delightful, too, to hear the orchestra kept down so that the dramatis personæ became the motive power of the drama."[32] The *Star* was struck too, especially by the way Muck reached into the "inner meaning" of the work:

He is not by any means an unemotional conductor, but he impresses one as a conductor who strives to be intellectual first and emotional afterwards. In other words his definition of art might well be "intellect tinged with emotion" rather than "emotion chastened by intellect." Thus it was not surprising that one of his great merits is the clearness with which he makes all the leading motives stand out, and that he made the most of the introspective parts of the music.

He has another quality which should insure his popularity here. He apparently cares more for beauty of tone in his orchestra than any German conductor I can call to mind, and to secure endless variety of tone-color and the creation of an "atmosphere," are his great aims, rather than extreme dynamic contrasts or an overwhelming body of sound.

He keeps the band down perfectly, and even in the most sonorous climaxes he is careful not to drown the singers. He caused the accompaniments to the love duet in particular to be played with real poetic beauty. He also did great things in the third act, divining the subtle changes of mood on the part of the singer. Altogether, Dr. Muck is an artist of the orchestra, not a mere kapellmeister – and there will, no doubt, be some controversy over the exact merit of his work.[33]

Different styles of conducting appeal to different temperaments, and as the *Star* itself points out below, one cannot say one is right and another wrong.

Die Walküre

Die Walküre was Muck's next opera. It "was accomplished in far more polished fashion," according to the *Sunday Times*; "the nuances were finer, there was no blurring of awkward passages for strings, and so well did Dr. Muck subdue the energy of his brass in the *Walkürenritt* that the battle between the voices and instrumentalists was for once not wholly one-sided."[34] He had "overcome the nervousness of his début," according to the *Daily News*, and gave "an excellent interpretation."[35] He kept "in quiet yet effective touch with the stage,"[36] and was "evidently not only saturated with Wagnerian traditions, but able to impart significance and vitality to the score."[37] The *Star* wanted to devote almost its whole column to Muck's conducting:

He obviously thinks it all out for himself, which is a great virtue. If I had to sum up in a phrase the essence of his reading of the *Valkyrie* I should say it was the intensest nervous energy. It is all very highly strung. There is nothing big or burly or blustering about it. He always exercises a

[31] *Musical Standard*, 20 May 1899, p. 308 ("R. Peggio")
[32] *ibid*, p. 309
[33] 17 May 1899, p. 1 ("Staccato")
[34] 21 May 1899, p. 6
[35] 20 May 1899, p. 5
[36] *Athenaeum*, 27 May 1899, p. 666
[37] *Standard*, 19 May 1899, p. 5

wise economy in working up climaxes, but they are always there when needed, and they leave him outwardly calm, for he is one of those conductors who appear to be directing his orchestra from an eminence outside and above, not one of those who seem to be one with it and swayed by the same impulses. Each class boasts great names, and one cannot say one is the right way, the other the wrong. I was particularly struck by the way he did the end of the first act. It is the fashion to take it all at high pressure from the spring song onwards, - he made it all a very gradual and subtly graduated crescendo of emotion to the end, which is admirable, except that the precise moment of the drawing of the sword from the tree loses a little in power. His handling of this is typical of his methods. It has become the fashion to drag the solemn warning of Brünnhilde to Siegmund so shockingly till the music seemed to stand still, and one wondered at each phrase whether Brünnhilde's breath could possibly last out. He imparted to it the right sense of movement, and secured the most touching expression. The whole of the last act was full of life and color, and interesting points of detail.[38]

Der fliegende Holländer

The next work was the *Holländer.* "[W]ith his magic wand [Muck] brought out all the significance of the music and showed us that in composing this opera Wagner had really begun his musico-dramatic style in earnest."[39] Muck conducted with "great intelligence,"[40] "exaggerating nothing, but allowing none of the smaller points to pass unnoticed,"[41] with a notable "attention to light and shade."[42] The orchestra was getting better each time. "He made them play last night quite admirably – with infinite variety of dramatic expression and unwonted finish in matters of detail. Once again he showed how all this is compatible with keeping them down."[43] There were, however, slips. "The orchestra and chorus were not invariably of one accord,"[44] and on stage various "stupidities were often destructive of impressiveness" (the Dutchman's ship refused to sail away or sink at the end, for example).[45] Sir Henry Wood attended one of these performances and said afterwards to the conductor: "What a bad performance! Full of mistakes both in the orchestra and on stage." Muck laughed "sneeringly," according to Wood, and replied: "Anything is good enough for England. Nobody understands." Wood was understandably furious, for he *did* understand, as indeed did some of the reviewers.[46]

Die Meistersinger von Nürnberg

The performance of the *Meistersinger* that followed "was one of the finest ever submitted to the judgement of a London audience," in the view of the *Observer.* "Seldom does any work receive such sympathetic and intelligent treatment.... To Dr. Muck... must be awarded the chief honours, for it was by the ensemble more than in the individual efforts that the triumph was achieved."[47] He and his players were "in a

38 *Star*, 19 May 1899, p. 1 ("Staccato")
39 *Musical Standard*, 27 May 1899, p. 322 ("R. Peggio")
40 *Sunday Times*, 28 May 1899, p. 4
41 *Daily Telegraph*, 24 May 1899, p. 10
42 *Standard*, 24 May 1899, p. 3
43 *Star*, 24 May 1899, p. 1 ("Staccato")
44 *Morning Post*, 24 May 1899, p. 2
45 *Standard*, 24 May 1899, p. 3; *Star*, 24 May 1899, p. 1
46 Sir Henry Wood, *My Life of Music* (London: Victor Gollancz, 1938), p. 66
47 *Observer*, 28 May 1899, p. 6. The *Daily News* agreed: "one of the finest we have heard in this country": 29 May 1899, p. 8.

Fig. 7.1. Karl Muck from his Graz years, 1884-1886

Fig. 7.2. Muck from his Berlin years, 1892-1912

Fig. 7.3. Muck with Hans Richter at Bayreuth, 1911

Fig. 7.4. Muck in London. Drawing by A. G. Witherby, *Vanity Fair*, 27 July 1899

Fig. 7.5. Muck in later years

most fortunate mood."[48] To the *Musical Standard*'s reviewer "he got more humour and geniality and brightness out of the music than I have yet heard. This splendid nervous vitality and the humorous, genial acting of the Eva, the Hans Sachs, the Magdalene, and the David accentuated the robust sanity of Wagner's music drama."[49] According to another, "two rare elements of strength" in the production were the Walther sung by Jean De Reske and the conducting of Muck.[50]

Dr. Muck was, perhaps, the real hero of the evening. He, too, proved himself a real and subtle humorist, and his way of doing the lighter pages is brilliantly clever, while his sympathy for the romance and the poetry with which the score is laden is of the keenest and deepest. And again he did some triumphant bits of generalship when disaster seemed impending. One cannot go into detail, but the playing of the orchestra in the scene where Beckmesser visits Sachs and the accompanying of *Wahn, Wahn* must be mentioned. The enormous audience was not unmindful of his efforts, and I was glad to see how warmly the men of the band cheered him – a thing not usual at Covent Garden.[51]

His style was not what audiences were used to in London. "We missed the force and fervour of a Richter or a Mottl," the *Athenaeum* noted.[52] Richter performed a number of Wagner pieces at a concert shortly after Muck's Covent Garden performance, including the prelude to act three of the *Meistersinger*. It seemed to the *Musical Standard* that Richter's interpretation "was not subtle enough, however fine it might have been from an absolute musical point of view. On the other hand, [Muck] conveyed just this sort of human content of which Wagner writes. But the Berlin conductor loses something of the glow of the vorspiel to *Die Meistersinger* which Richter so well conveys."[53] The *Morning Post* threw more cold water. Although it acknowledged the "entire success" of Muck's direction, it was not persuaded there was any "specific improvement" over the performances of another Covent Garden conductor, Signor Luigi Mancinelli.[54]

Parsifal at Bayreuth

Muck became almost an institution at Bayreuth with *Parsifal*, conducting the work at each of the fourteen festivals between 1901 and 1930. He sometimes shared the conducting with less distinguished conductors which only served to sharpen his profile. Whether he had ever heard Hermann Levi conduct it (1882-1894) is unclear, though it is highly likely he did, at least in 1892 when he was in Bayreuth as a rehearsal conductor. In 1931, after his retirement from Bayreuth, he robustly rejected accusations he had conducted with "insufferably protracted tempos" by appealing to the "long lists" of tempi recorded by the "alliance of tempo statisticians" which showed his tempi "agreed almost to the minute" with those of Levi in 1882.[55] In any case,

48 *Daily Telegraph* , 29 May 1899, p. 10 49 3 June 1899, p. 340 ("R. Peggio")

50 *Standard*, 29 May 1899, p. 3. This was Jean de Reske, described by another reviewer as "not at his best. He appeared languid, and had to nurse his voice with great care": *Star*, 29 May 1899, p. 1

51 *Star*, 29 May 1899, p. 1 52 3 June 1899, p. 697

53 *Musical Standard*, 17 June 1899, p. 379. *The Times* considered that "perhaps the overture was taken a little too fast, but after recent experiences this is surely a fault on the right side": 29 May 1899, p. 13.

54 *Morning Post*, 29 May 1899, p. 6

55 letter to Eva Chamberlain dated 13 April 1931, in Peter Muck, *Karl Muck*, p. 162. Levi and Muck each conducted many performances of *Parsifal*, and Muck's assertion is no doubt correct in respect of some of

after what the *Musical Times* described as a "very successful debut" in 1901,[56] the press began to identify his unique characteristics. The *Berliner Tageblatt* noted in 1904 how he kept the mystical and the romantic in the work apart with "great severity," without ever losing track of the theatrical effect. "That his absolute certainty, his intelligence – which does not tolerate any ambiguity, any incorrectness – was only beneficial to the performance goes without saying."[57] To the *Neue Zeitschrift für Musik* Muck's orchestra produced an "untarnished purity and the highest magic of sound."[58] The *Manchester Guardian* reported that his tempi were "considered too slow by some of the *habitués*, though his interpretation was admitted to be in all other respects above reproach."[59] In 1906, the *Signale für die musikalische Welt* commented on his "rhythmic resolution," something which arose more from an inner pulse than any exact measurement of time, and fitted well with the "substantial flexibility of his conducting," evident in "the most supple choreographic artistry in Klingsor's magic garden."[60] In 1906, the very pit for which Wagner had written *Parsifal* came under criticism: the *Vossische Zeitung* wanted more of the glorious detail of the orchestral fabric:

> [Muck] is a magician the way he invokes the greatness of the Prelude from the mystical abyss, melding the divine and the human. Never have I heard the armour-plated theme of faith sound more despairing. And the heartache and pained anguish of the love theme were struggling as if wrapped in fog. But the famous mystical abyss becomes a problem for me: the hidden orchestra requires correction! There have to be ways found to bring the individual sections of instruments to the fore, to a greater or lesser degree as required. Never is Wagner's palette of burning, deep-dark, and subtle, delicate colours richer than in *Parsifal*. But here they do not shine intensively enough. The concealed orchestra covers them up, mutes them too indiscriminately and uniformly. The finer detail of the music is lost. This is highly detrimental to the dramatic intentions of the work, and its ability to impress, which it mainly does through the orchestra.[61]

In 1912, he was described by the *Frankfurter Zeitung* as "seemingly predestined for [*Parsifal's*] ascetic acerbity and strictness, by virtue of his way of drawing sharp outlines, and his more linear than colouristic sensibility and creativity."[62] His last pre-War *Parsifal* was in 1914. When the audience came out after the first act, they learned that war had been declared. Many of the orchestral players, who were officers in the German and Austrian armies, left immediately to report to their barracks. "The few musicians that were left carried on somehow," related Ernestine Schumann-Heink, "and the performance was finished. Muck conducted."[63] What the orchestra sounded like with its diminished numbers she does not record.

his performances, but not all. Egon Voss gives a selection of timings in *Die Dirigenten der Bayreuther Festspiele*, pp. 99-100. Muck's tempi in 1901 *were* longer than Levi's in 1882. In 1902 the *Musical Times* noted that although Muck "did not drag it so much as one at least of his recent predecessors… he took it more slowly than Levi": 1 September 1902, p. 612. Voss has no timings for 1902.

[56] 1 September 1901, p. 619

[57] 6 August 1904 (Leopold Schmidt), in Großmann-Vendrey, *Bayreuth in der deutschen Presse*, Vol. 3,1, p. 197

[58] 3 August 1904 (Schering), in Peter Muck, *Karl Muck*, p. 74

[59] Arthur Johnstone, *Musical Criticisms* (Manchester University Press, 1905), p. 55

[60] August 1906, in Peter Muck, *Karl Muck*, p. 79

[61] 5 August 1908 (Georg Gräner), in Großmann-Vendrey, *Bayreuth in der deutschen Presse*, Vol. 3,2, p. 17

[62] 11 August 1912 (Paul Bekker), in Großmann-Vendrey, *ibid*, Vol. 3,2, p. 89

[63] Lawton, *Schumann-Heink*, p. 264. The performance in question was probably that of 23 July, the day on which Austria issued its ultimatum to Serbia, at 6 p.m., which would fit in with the account. War itself was not declared until 28 July, and there was no performance of *Parsifal* on that date. The only other performance that year was on 1 August. Schumann-Heink herself was singing in the *Ring* in 1914.

In his last five festivals, held between 1924 and 1930, he reached his "highest perfection" with *Parsifal*. Muck was now "the last great Wagnerian who not only keeps the Master's legacy as a tradition," according to the *Fränkische Kurier*, "but also carries it in his blood and in the nobility of his soul":

> His distinctive features are constructed from rhythm and dynamics. From these the motif extends like an archetype of classical greatness. He achieves a dignity in the building-up of tonal degrees of force, and a sanctity in extending a broadly-spread *piano* which does not admit of the slightest unevenness from any of the instruments. It is peculiar how under the invisible direction of this conductor the high tension emanating from the orchestra transmits itself to the listener. ... The majesty of its brass sounds, the basses digging down in passion and pain, the pastoral transfiguration of the woodwinds in the Good Friday magic, the rhythmic vehemence of the strings in the Kundry motif – all these are dramatic emotions of the highest intellectual intensity, carrying the sung word and the scene into the realm of the super-conceptual....[64]

The *New York Times* too had its music critic at the 1924 Festival. He agreed it was "an extremely impressive presentation.... The second act is given with more sumptuousness and movement at the Metropolitan; the performance, nevertheless, was dominated and poetized by the authority, will and imagination of Muck....."[65] *Musical America* considered it "a revelation. The indescribable, inspired, tender tone of the orchestra was heavenly; the ethereal, almost unreal sound of the Grail music was unequaled, and the tone and words of the singers were clear and distinct."[66] In 1925 Muck was trumpeted for his "doubtless authenticity and unshakable infallibility" by the *BZ am Mittag*; "he needs only begin and the monumentality and solemnity are instantly there."[67] "Objective yet full of warmth," wrote *Musik*; there was an "exceedingly clear relationship between the music and the drama, each carrying and strengthening each other."[68]

The young Lauritz Melchior sang Parsifal under Muck at Bayreuth in 1924 and 1925, and he must have been a difficult lion to tame. With Muck's tempi, he had to re-study his "breath distribution, dramatic timing, and the handling of words and phrases," according to his biographer who, probably reflecting Melchior's views, described the conductor as "a violent and harsh disciplinarian to the singers and the orchestra members alike." Melchior much preferred singing under the easy-going Michael Balling.[69] Frida Leider, on the other hand, who sang Kundry under Muck in 1928, found his way of conducting *Parsifal* "a great revelation." She had been somewhat apprehensive before the first orchestral rehearsal because he was known for his slow tempi. "Gradually the unearthly music took possession of me. In the second act, when I began my big scene with Parsifal, Muck's calmness and clarity enabled me to draw everything out of the role, as I had always tried to do. That *Parsifal* was one of my greatest artistic experiences."[70]

[64] *Bayreuther Festspiel-Zeitung* supplement to the *Fränkische Kurier*, 25 July 1924, in Peter Muck, Karl Muck, pp. 133-134

[65] 24 July 1924, p. 7 (Olin Downes). Artur Bodanzky was the conductor alluded to at the Metropolitan Opera.

[66] 23 August 1924, p. 4 (Maurice Halperson)

[67] 27 July 1925 (Adolf Weissmann), in Großmann-Vendrey, *Bayreuth in der deutschen Presse*, Vol. 3,2, p. 193

[68] *Musik*, quoted in Peter Muck, *Karl Muck*, p. 140

[69] Shirlee Emmons, *Tristanissimo* (New York: Shirmer Books, 1990), pp. 52, 86. Melchior sang Siegmund under Balling in 1924 and 1925. Emmons said that Muck had also displayed his "contempt for the human race" when conducting the Boston Symphony Orchestra.

[70] Frida Leider, *Playing my part*, (trans.) Charles Osborne (London: Calder and Boyars, 1966), p. 98; cf.

By 1927 Muck had become "one of the grand old men of German music – the only one of them at Bayreuth," according to the *Musical Times*.[71] His *Parsifal* was "a thing to remember" for the *New York Times*.

Muck takes the tempi – dares to take them – as slowly as the Bayreuth traditions exact, and never once does the musical line sag, or the opera lose its mood. The score, as he unfolds it, is indeed a monumental architecture. Each of the Wagner scores has its particular color and sonority. We doubt if any other conductor achieves in the same degree the peculiar clarity and luminousness of tone inherent in the *Parsifal* partition.[72]

The *Signale für die musikalische Welt* reached the peak of praise:

Dr. Muck, the best *Parsifal* conductor in the world, led its performance and gave us unutterable beauty, purity, sanctity and greatness. Such clarity of lines, such softness and suppleness of sound, such floating and flowing, such richness of nuances! Dr. Muck may use the slowest of tempos, because he fills them with beauty. This sweetness of the violins, this liberated sound of the woodwinds, this crimson fervency of the horns, this golden sheen of the trombones, this force of the double-basses: it is as if the sound had become detached from the instruments and had become spiritual and psychic.[73]

The reviewer demanded the conductor's baton only be handed to conductors of the very first order. After two more festivals, the baton for *Parsifal* would pass to Toscanini.

The 1927-1928 Parsifal recordings

One of the most cherished achievements in the history of the gramophone are Muck's excerpts from *Parsifal*. The three excerpts recorded at Bayreuth in 1927 – the Transformation music and Grail scene from act one, and the Flowermaidens' scene from act two – unfortunately have no solo singing. Perhaps it was too expensive to engage soloists. There were technical difficulties enough in managing the recording sessions, as one of the recording engineers recalled:

We recorded on the stage, which covered a huge area in the shape of an inverted "T". By using a semi-circular backcloth, we were able to reduce its effective size to something nearer our requirements. Arranging recording sessions was extremely difficult as we had to fit in with Festival performances and innumerable rehearsals, often called overnight, so, although we stayed for seven weeks, we managed to get only fifteen recording sessions.... We used only one microphone and had no tone controls of any kind.[74]

Emmons who claimed Leider was "challenged" by Muck's slow tempi, whereas Melchior had been "simply annoyed" (*Tristanissimo*, p. 86).

[71] 1 September 1927, p. 801. The other conductors that year were Karl Elmendorff (*Tristan*) and Franz von Hoeßlin (the *Ring*).

[72] 28 August 1927, p. X6 (Olin Downes). This critic later recalled that Muck's performances were the "ne plus ultra of interpretation" as regards *Parsifal*: *ibid*, 29 March 1929, p. 28.

[73] September 1927, in Peter Muck, *Karl Muck*, p. 150

[74] W.S. Barrell, "I was there – No. 4 – The Continent and Bayreuth: Bayreuth 1927 – Columbia recordings of *Tannhäuser* and *Tristan*," *Gramophone*, January 1959, p. 390. Christopher Dyment has pointed out that that there were fewer performance-free days in July and August 1927 than fifteen, and suggests Barrell may have been including some of the Bayreuth sessions of 1928: "The Recordings of Karl Muck – Some unresolved problems," *ARSC Journal*, Vol. IX, No. 1 (1977), pp. 66-67. *Tannhäuser* and *Tristan* under Elmendorf were recorded at Bayreuth in 1930 and 1928 respectively.

Fig. 7.6. Muck at his debut in Boston.
Hearst's Boston American, 14 October 1906

There were more than technical challenges: "the artists and instrumentalists were difficult to assemble. They had come to look upon the Festival as a holiday and resented the extra rehearsals and performances that robbed them of their spare time, even though the Columbia [Company] were paying good fees. The orchestral players were particularly difficult, and were always going on strike...."[75] In light of these difficulties and the technical problems that fatally afflicted other recordings made that year,[76] it is a miracle that Muck's work survived at all. In was added to by recordings at the Singakademie in Berlin of the prelude to act one in December 1927 and the greater part of act three in October 1928.

When the Bayreuth recordings were first released, *Gramophone* claimed that Columbia had "surpassed themselves... One of the chief merits of the series is that the *tempo* has nowhere been hurried to suit the convenience of the recording experts"; the Transformation scene was in particular "the most impressive of all."[77] It "defies better treatment," wrote the *New York Times*.[78] When the Berlin recordings came out,

[75] typewritten notes by Fred Gaisberg on Charles Gregory's career, in Jerrold Northrop Moore, *A Voice in Time: the Gramophone of Fred Gaisberg 1873-1951* (London: Hamish Hamilton Ltd., 1976), p. 180

[76] recordings made with Elmendorf and von Hoeßlin had to be rejected: Christopher Dyment, "Karl Muck at Bayreuth – Fifty years of recording in the Festspielhaus," *Gramophone*, August 1977, p. 290

[77] December 1927, p. 273 (Peter Latham). The *British Musician*, on the other hand, made no substantive comment on the recording in its review: December 1927, pp. 236-39.

[78] 27 March 1932, p. X9 (Compton Pakenham)

the response was more marked. Herman Klein had heard *Parsifal* twice under Muck and Bayreuth, and wrote that "the tempi and general interpretation of the music [was] in strict accord with the true Wagnerian traditions."[79] "Throughout poise is the watchword," wrote the *Phonograph Monthly Review*. "The performance is reserved: reverend [*sic*] rather than spirited... If one can enter wholly into its mood, such music and such a performance are deeply moving, even overwhelming."[80] *Disques* wrote words which still ring true decades later: "it may be said without fear of contradiction that this Muck set ranks with the greatest achievements of the gramophone."[81]

The recordings were first re-issued on CD in 1989, when many other *Parsifal* recordings by other interpreters had since appeared. It was an occasion to celebrate anew. "Karl Muck was undoubtedly one of the greatest Wagnerian conductors of all time," *Gramophone* exclaimed:

> Even under Knappertsbusch and Karajan, the Transformation and Grail scenes in Act 1 have not sounded so intense and searing, with a superb balance achieved between the orchestra's various sections. The rich yet never overbearing sonority, the swift yet contained tempos are evidence enough of Muck's long and fruitful experience in the work. This is grand, tragic music-making that would be hard to equal today.... [Act three] is even more valuable.... The results remain revelatory. What one marvels at here is the seamless movement, the unexaggerated but moving climaxes, the translucent sonority, the refinement of detail all leading to the inspired urgency of the choral pleadings in the second Grail scene.[82]

It is striking that whereas Muck's tempi were once seen as slow, now they are seen as "swift," a comment undoubtedly made against the background of contemporary performances. *Fanfare* observed that "Wagner's direction *Langsam und feierlich* (Slowly and ceremoniously) calls forth from Muck an easygoing Allegretto, while *Sehr massig* (Very moderately) produces something a bit faster."[83] Muck's robust defence of his tempi is thus no longer necessary. It is true that the timing of his act one prelude is almost one-and-a-half minutes longer than Wagner's own reported timing, but the seeds of its rightness lie in the profound musical judgement of its interpreter. Its very slowness and tautness make it the most serious, devotional, sacramental act – as holy and as still as a prayer. Wagner himself could not have demurred.

In spite of Muck's self-effacing view of the role of the conductor, his temperament shines throughout the excerpts. One feels the weight of inexorable tempo in the Transformation music – and one hears the original bells toll for the first and last time: they were destroyed in the War. The Grail scene, stripped as it is of all but the vigorous chorus, shining perhaps a little too brightly in the proximity of the microphone, is very effective: clean, astringent, and austere. There is a great lift in the Knight's spirit after the sacrament. In the third act, the prelude is deadly slow, soul-wrenchingly desolate and weary. The remaining part, from Parsifal's entry *Heil dir!*, is elevated. The tone is never warm, but austere, sometimes severely so – there are no soft, mystical

79 *Gramophone*, April 1929, pp. 478-79

80 March 1930, p. 208 81 March 1930, p. 24 82 April 1990, p. 1886 (Alan Blyth)

83 March/April 2000, p. 355 (William Youngren reviewing the Naxos re-issue). He makes a similar point in his review of the earlier OPAL set: *ibid*, January/February 1990, p. 344. See also John W. N. Francis's review in *ARSC Journal*, Vol. 21, No. 1 (Spring 1990), pp. 142-144. Robert Anderson wrote in the *Musical Times*, (January 1989, p. 31) that "sometimes Muck adopts a manner that Goodall might consider almost 'fast'."

edges – and there is a sense of inevitability, of correct tempi (of which there are many modifications), so that one has a sense of Muck's authoritativeness born out of a clear vision of the work. There is a classical shaping, the orchestra and voices making a seamless whole. At the end one feels chastened, rather than rapturous. Self-denying, strict, and unshakably devoted, Muck shows he is the perfect Knight of the Grail.

Fig. 7.7. Muck as concert conductor.
Drawing by G. Viafora,
Musical America, 12 September 1916

The other recordings

His other recorded Wagner excerpts all show the fruits of his stern discipline and ripe artistry. His earliest recording, the 1917 act three prelude to *Lohengrin*, is tightly controlled, and illuminates the delicate and lyrical passages in spite of the limitations of the acoustic recording process.[84] The discovery and publication in 1996 of a hitherto unpublished version from 1929 is obviously of fuller tone. The *Tannhäuser* overture is clear, correct and authoritative, like all Muck's recordings, only there is no abandonment when the music most calls for it. When he conducted the *Siegfried Idyll* at the Boston Symphony's opening concert in New York in 1906, the *New York Times* wrote that he "put a lot of patience into the *Siegfried Idyll*, whose

[84] A cautionary word from David Milsom: "we cannot speak from a position of certainty on any aspect of what we hear in these recordings," in his "Conditional Gifts: The Acoustic Orchestral Recordings of Edouard Colonne and Karl Muck and their Testament to Late Nineteenth-Century Performing Practices," *Early Music Performer*, Issue 16 (November 2005), p. 5; see also Christopher Dyment, "Karl Muck's Boston recordings," *International Classical Record Collector*, Autumn 1996, pp. 38-40.

charms, undeniable and delectable as they are, are mercilessly long."[85] His 1929 recording, "lighthearted and unemotional" as the *Phonograph Monthly Review* called it in 1931,[86] shows the same patience, and much intimacy and delicacy of playing, though an indulgent playfulness is not in Muck's repertoire. He also conducted the *Meistersinger* overture at the 1906 concert where he was observed to take the tempo "faster than most, with a loss of perhaps something of the most characteristic spirit of the work, though there is a splendidly propulsive energy gained by doing as he does."[87] The 1927 recording probably reflects this. It is spirited, just as Wagner wanted, but not as warm or thrilling as some other performances. His *Tristan* prelude too, steady as a rock, with its clear, dry lines, is not notably warm or indulgent. "The air is heavy, but the heaviness is not of lovesickness," wrote *Gramophone* at the time.[88] He is in his element with the demonic whistling and whirring of the Dutchman's ghostly themes in the *Holländer* overture, though this is not a version that ends with the bang of damnation or redemption. Finally, Siegfried's Funeral music from *Götterdämmerung* in 1927[89] is perfectly controlled and graduated. It is a dry-eyed, bitter funeral march.

The bitter end

Little is known of Muck's last years.[90] In 1936 he was reported to be "a sick and aged man living forgotten and half-bedridden in Stuttgart."[91] He was probably bitter. The scar of his humiliating and unjustified imprisonment in the United States may never have healed. Bayreuth which had brought him fame was inexorably moving into decline. To quote Carl Flesch again: "... he was a noble character endowed with all the gifts a good fairy can bestow, except benevolence and a love of humanity: he was a genuine misanthropist and had too few illusions about the world for his lack of imagination not to become noticeable in his art too."[92] This is a gloomy view, but one of a perspicacious musician. It is not wholly borne out by the reviews of his performances we have examined. The conductor probably had scant regard for his recorded legacy. Yet it is this that will ensure that his exacting and intense music-making will never be forgotten.

[85] 9 November 1906, p. 9

[86] April 1931, p. 211 (Robert H. S. Phillips); cf. *Disques*, April 1931, p. 72: "matchless thaumaturgy"

[87] *New York Times*, 9 November 1906, p. 9. At his opening concert in Boston, a similar point was made: "he took [the prelude] more rapidly than we are accustomed to hear it, and in this, too, brilliancy and precision of phrase and strong contrast of nuance were the dominating qualities, rather than the fire of eloquence or the glow of tenderness and passion": *ibid*, 13 October 1906, p. 9

[88] October 1931, Supplement, p. 2 (W. R. Anderson); the *Phonograph Monthly Review* (October 1930) found the recording completely satisfying: "There is none of... the exaggerated and emotionalized tension of so many concert performances. The tone-drama speaks with its own voice and not with an enforced ventriloquism."

[89] Herman Klein wrote in 1929: "nothing more grandiose or imposing, more gorgeous in tone or colour, has been heard from the gramophone": *Gramophone*, April 1929, p. 480. By comparison, the performance attributed to Muck from 1930 is quite messy and most unlikely to be his; see also Christopher Dyment's notes accompanying *Karl Muck*: Appian APR 5521 (1996).

[90] Peter Muck, *Karl Muck*, p. 171

[91] Olin Downes reporting from Bayreuth: *New York Times*, 4 February 1940, p. 125

[92] Flesch, *Memoirs*, p. 286

Part IV

A Touch of Russia

8

Arthur Nikisch – Apollo in Valhalla

There was something wild and fascinating about Nikisch. He thrilled and unsettled music-lovers. He belonged to no category, no school, and left no tradition. In some sense he was foreign, like a gipsy, his origin not quite clear. He was ruled by instinct and love. He wielded enormous power over orchestras, which followed him devotedly. Orchestral members played for him like individual artists, yet with the conductor's own unique insight and expression. He was deeply inspiring yet outwardly calm, and led people to believe he was a magician. The way he drew beauty out of an orchestra from the mere tip of his stick, and with the gaze of his eyes, was both a mystery and a miracle. He *looked* a man of genius. "His face suggested a brooding melancholy, physical lassitude in conflict with spiritual exaltation, profound suffering and disillusionment,"[1] and there was a "strange and weary melancholy" in his eyes.[2] He had a deep affinity with the demonic and the pathos of Wagner's music.[3] He brought these elements up from the depths, as it were, and like a god with a wand, transformed them into golden beauty. Not everyone was convinced that his was the right way, but all who heard him were dazzled by his brilliance.

Encounters with Wagner

He was born on 12 October 1855 in Lébény Szent Miklós – "but I really do not think that matters much," he said[4] – in a part of Hungary that, according to Carl Flesch, was "racially very mixed."[5] His father was of Russian origin, his mother Jewish.[6] Neither of his parent's families had "any marked predilection for music." However, his father was a keen amateur cellist, and Nikisch remembered as "red-letter

[1] Charles Frederick Kenyon, *Written in friendship; a book of reminiscences*, by Gerald Cumberland [pseud.] (London: Grant Richards, 1923), p. 230

[2] Carl Flesch, *Memoirs*, Hans Keller (trans. and ed.), (London: Rockliff, 1957), p. 148

[3] Ferdinand Pfohl, *Arthur Nikisch als Mensch und Künstler* (Leipzig: Hermann Seemann, 1900), p. 41; Adrian Boult, "Nikisch Remembered" (1950), in *Boult on music: words from a lifetime's communication* (London: Toccata Press, 1983), p. 95

[4] Nikisch in an interview in the *Daily Telegraph*, 9 April 1914

[5] Flesch, *Memoirs*, p. 148

[6] "Celebrities at Home: Herr Arthur Nikisch at Covent Garden," *World*, 29 April 1913, p. 605; and Gdal Saleski, *Famous Musicians of Jewish Origin* (New York: Bloch Publishing Company, 1949), p. 266

days" those occasions when Viennese musicians came to stay and made music.[7] By the age of seven, he was able to write down from memory piano arrangements of tunes he had heard on an "orchestrion," and in two years, after private lessons, he gave his first public recital in Butschowitz (Bučovice).[8] At the age of eleven, he entered the Vienna Conservatory where he studied for seven years, principally the violin under Josef Hellmesberger the elder, and theory under Otto Dessof, conductor of the Court Opera. He composed a little, and won a prize with one of his compositions, and made his student conducting debut with another, but never pursued that aspect of his artistry. Like Felix Mottl, he probably learned more outside the walls of the Vienna Conservatory than inside. While a student he deputized as a second violinist at the opera and in the philharmonic concerts, and heard and played under several real practitioners of the art of conducting.

In 1872, Wagner came to Vienna to give a concert in aid of the Bayreuth project. On the program were Beethoven's *Eroica Symphony*, the overture and bacchanale from the Paris version of *Tannhäuser*, and Wotan's farewell and the Magic Fire music from the *Walküre*. Nikisch and other students of the Conservatory were invited by Wagner to the two rehearsals for this concert, and afterwards a small delegation, including Mottl and Nikisch, presented Wagner with a silver cup, and Nikisch made a speech of thanks. "That moment, when I came face to face with the mighty master, will never leave my memory," Nikisch told the *Musical Times*.[9] Ten days later he was among the violinists in Beethoven's *Ninth Symphony* conducted by Wagner to mark the laying of the foundation stone for the Bayreuth Festival Theatre. There had been four rehearsals. "In those four rehearsals," he said, "I learnt more and received a deeper insight into the secrets of Beethoven's nature than I could possibly have gained in a year's study under normal conditions." Later he recalled:

> I can say that Wagner's *Eroica* in Vienna and then the *Ninth* at Bayreuth were an absolutely decisive influence, not only on my later grasp of Beethoven, but on my whole understanding of orchestral interpretation. To speak only of the obvious things: Wagner was certainly not what one might describe as a "routine conductor" – his very gestures were music in themselves. I have said before that the conductor's baton technique – if he is not just an uninspired time-beater – is a language whose mastery enables the listener to penetrate the feelings of the artist, and helps his understanding of the work being played. This was Wagner through and through.[10]

Hellmesberger the elder was, in Nikisch's view, the most significant musician in Vienna at the time. "The stimulation I received from this divinely-gifted artist was inexhaustible – one only had to have ears to hear, and a receptive sense for truth in art."[11] Of conductors, Nikisch said that, next to Wagner, Johann Herbeck, principal

[7] interview in the *Boston Daily Traveller*, 25 October 1890, p. 5

[8] "Arthur Nikisch: A Biographical Sketch," *Musical Times*, 1 February 1905, p. 89, reprinted as "The chosen of the chosen," *ibid*, June 1997, p. 23; *Boston Daily Traveller*, 25 October 1890, p. 5

[9] 1 February 1905, p. 90

[10] David Wooldridge, *Conductor's World* (London: Barrie & Rockliff, 1970), p. 102. Nikisch's "Erinnerungen aus meiner Wiener Jugendzeit" has been reproduced in a number of places, including Eugen Segnitz, *Arthur Nikisch* (Leipzig: Sally Rabinowitz, 1920), pp. 14-19; *Sang und Klang Almanach, 1920*, (ed.) Adolf Weissmann, (Berlin, 1921), pp. 37-41; Heinrich Chevalley (ed.), *Arthur Nikisch: Leben und Wirken* (Berlin: Ed. Bote & G. Bock, 1922), pp. 11-13; and Ferdinand Pfohl, *Arthur Nikisch: Sein Leben, seine Kunst, sein Wirken* (Hamburg: Alster-Verlag, 1925), pp. 19-23

[11] Segnitz, *Arthur Nikisch*, p. 19; Chevalley, *Arthur Nikisch*, p. 13

conductor of the Vienna Court Opera, and his beloved teacher Dessof, were those he sought to emulate.

After graduating with a prize in violin, he joined the Vienna Court Opera Orchestra (1874-1877) and played under Brahms, Bruckner, Herbeck, Liszt, Rubinstein, Verdi, and Wagner. He dreamed of being a conductor. The opportunity soon, and suddenly, came. Angelo Neumann had asked Dessof for help in finding someone to conduct the chorus at the Leipzig Opera. He recommended Nikisch. He was chosen, and had to leave Vienna in 48 hours. Once in Leipzig, he was asked to conduct an operetta to be given in a fortnight. He learned the work by heart – *Jean, Jeannette et Jeanneton* – and it was a great success. Neumann recognised his talent, and wanted him as one of his chief conductors in spite of his youth. Again, the opportunity soon came, for in the summer of 1878 he conducted *Tannhäuser* for the first time, in Vienna. It was in face of objections from the orchestra members who thought him too young for such an opera. After a rehearsal, however, they changed their mind decisively. The success of *Tannhäuser* launched him as one of the foremost conductors in Germany. It was followed by the *Ring*, which had been rehearsed by Nikisch's senior, Josef Sucher. When Sucher left in 1879, Nikisch was appointed principal conductor, a post he held for ten years.[12] In 1889 he was engaged by the Boston Symphony for a phenomenal sum, and remained for four years. He never conducted opera in the United States, though he received many offers.[13] He returned to direct the Budapest Royal Opera (1893-95), and then assumed two important concert posts – at the head of the Leipzig Gewandhaus and the Berlin Philharmonic – that he would hold for the rest of his life. This did not, of course, prevent many guest appearances, and of particular interest to us here will be his Wagner engagements at Covent Garden in 1907, 1913, and 1914. He had, however, begun his long association with the London Symphony Orchestra much earlier, in 1895, and it was his chosen orchestra for a tour to the United States in 1912.[14] Other appointments included Director of the Hamburg Philharmonic concerts, in succession to Bülow (1897), Director of the Leipzig Conservatory and leader of conducting classes (1902), and Director of the Leipzig Stadttheater (1905). He died in Leipzig on 23 January 1922, aged 67, of heart failure after a bout of influenza.

Nikisch on conducting

Nikisch wrote little about his work. He was an instinctive musician. As Carl Flesch said, in terms reminiscent of his comments on Richter, "he combined German musicality with Hungarian fire and Slavonic *morbidezza* (delicacy)... In intellectual respects one would say he was somewhat primitive. He read little or nothing, was fond

[12] *World*, 29 April 1913, p. 605; Angelo Neumann, *Personal Recollections of Wagner*, (trans.) Edith Livermore (London: Archibald Constable & Co, 1909), pp. 66-67

[13] *World*, 29 April 1913, p. 605. The American critic James Huneker had evidently heard Nikisch conduct opera in Europe, for he observed that Nikisch had "more power" than Toscanini and "more finesse" than Seidl. Huneker, "The Seven Arts," *Puck*, 16 January 1915, p. 8

[14] 21 days, 11,000 miles, 27 cities, 29 concerts: Percy A. Scholes, *The mirror of music, 1844-1944: a century of musical life in Britain as reflected in the pages of the Musical Times* (London: Novello & Co., Oxford University Press, 1947), p. 390

of cards, women, and company – the most perfect type of musician of genius from the former Austro-Hungarian monarchy."[15] Like Richter and Seidl, Nikisch had the gift. He believed the art of conducting could not be taught. In fact, he often expressed to the English conductor, Landon Ronald, "his utter disbelief" that conducting could be taught.[16] Nevertheless, there were certain things a conductor should be taught which did not fall within the normal scope of a musical education, and this is why he set up his conducting classes at the Leipzig Conservatory.[17]

He explained to the *Musical Times* how his students, who included established conductors, came to him from around the world. "These students – limited in number –attend all the rehearsals of the Gewandhaus concerts, following the music with scores in hand. They receive their practical lessons at the rehearsals of the Conservatory orchestra, where I criticise their actions and their methods and give all the help I can.... a young fellow [thus] comes on to the orchestra and handles his baton as if he were a fully-fledged Kapellmeister!"[18] As if it were so simple...! His final words in 1921 to another English conductor, Henry Wood, were: "*Let everything be a grand improvisation!*"[19] He thereby throws everything back onto the interpretative artist: there are no rules. Play it as you feel it! According to Otto Klemperer, Nikisch always said, "I can only conduct if I feel the music in my heart."[20] And so he would seek to transmit this to the orchestral players. Wood described how Nikisch, when rehearsing a melody, "invariably sang it to the orchestra with great emotional feeling – and then would say: 'Now play it as *you* feel it.'"[21] In this way, as if by magic, Nikisch's feelings would become the players' expression, and performances of great emotion and dramatic intensity would ensue. He explained his task at the time of a commemorative concert he gave in honour of Bülow:

The modern conductor must create anew, and therein lies the independent and creative nature of his art. That is why his individuality must play so significant a role today.... It is only since Hans von Bülow that there have been conductors who understood their task in this way. Berlioz understood – but he only conducted his own works. Once I have made a piece of music a part

[15] Flesch, *Memoirs*, p. 148. Nikisch was in fact "an inveterate, intrepid gambler" whose "ruling passion" made him penniless on many an occasion: Mark Hambourg, *From piano to forte: a thousand and one notes* (London: Cassell and Co., 1931), p. 125. In Leipzig the civic authorities had to pay his debts to prevent him fleeing his creditors; in return he had to conduct a *Ring* cycle at the Stadttheater; his estate was virtually bankrupt upon his death: Saleski, *Famous Musicians*, p. 269.

[16] Sir Landon Ronald, *Myself and others: written, lest I forget* (London: Sampson Low, Marston, 1931), p. 70

[17] *World*, 29 April 1913, p. 605

[18] 1 February 1905, p. 91; June 1997 reprint, p. 26. Albert Coates, a student of Nikisch's conducting course, said that his advice to his conducting students was "nearly always" on points of interpretation and performance, not baton technique: *World*, 5 May 1914, p. 741. Adrian Boult, who never had a lesson from Nikisch in his life, learned much from watching him conduct, particularly in Leipzig in 1912, and more than from anyone else: Alfred Kalisch, "Arthur Nikisch," *Musical Times*, 1 March 1922, p. 173; Boult, "Nikisch Remembered" (1950), in *Boult on music*, p. 94, and Boult, "Leipzig – September 1912," *Opera*, February 1975, pp. 121-125. Many others learned in this way, including Wilhelm Furtwängler, Erich Kleiber, and Fritz Reiner.

[19] Sir Henry Wood, *My Life of Music* (London: Victor Gollancz, 1938), p. 161

[20] Peter Heyworth (ed.), *Conversations with Klemperer*, revised edition (London: Faber and Faber, 1985), p. 115. See also Chevalley (ed.), *Arthur Nikisch*, p. 45. This may be one of the reasons he did not conduct much Schoenberg. "Schönberg!" he exclaimed in 1912, "If that is music then I do not know music. I cannot think of Schönberg as anything but a bluff....": *New York Times*, 8 April 1912, p. 11.

[21] Wood, *My Life of Music*, p. 160

of me, I can only build it up again from the beginning – but I must follow my own conviction, otherwise it will not be a reconstruction of integrity.[22]

In an interview with the *Daily Telegraph* in 1914, he explained the great difference between conducting opera and concerts. "The operatic orchestra must be extremely alert and 'electric.' Singers cannot always watch the conductor closely, so the latter is at times constrained to follow the soloist, and the instrumentalists, even when numbering more than a hundred, must be instantly appreciative of the slightest sign from their director, otherwise the effect might be disastrous. Concert work... is 'quite another routine.'" Although he was a brilliant conductor of Wagner, he did not believe in specialization. "He does not believe in the 'good Wagnerian conductor,' or the Beethoven or Brahms specialist. A musical director should have a wide knowledge, and do everything well." [23]

Nikisch in rehearsal

Nikisch's method as a conductor is well illustrated by a rehearsal of the *Tannhäuser* overture in London in 1904, to which the *Musical Times* was invited. The conductor was observed to be a model of courtesy towards the orchestra. Once the cellos had played their theme, after the opening bars by the wind, Nikisch said: "A little too academic; more feeling; a singing tone," and then sang the phrase to them with a beautiful voice. Further, at the first *un poco ritenuto* of the *Allegro* section for the cellos, he called for "More passion; do not forget to place more intensity in the *crescendos*." He made the horns "sing" their parts alone, and doubled the 1st and 2nd horn parts, for example, the 2nd horn in E, bar 46 of *Allegro*,[24] and the later portion of the Venusberg music.

He has a fine sense of the necessary working up to a climax. "Begin *mezza voce*, not too much of brilliance at first; then begin to broaden; you must *help* us to the great *crescendo*," and so on. A tremolo passage in the violins calls forth this remark: "Play as many notes as possible, so as to make a shiver in the back." At a full-toned passage he says: "It is marked by the composer *ff*, and you must keep it up." Such expressions as "immense crescendo," "more precision," "energy," all quietly and politely, but firmly spoken, are at once acted upon by his receptive colleagues of the orchestra.[25]

[22] quoted in Wooldridge, *Conductor's World*, p. 109 [from Pfohl, *Arthur Nikisch: Sein Leben, seine Kunst, sein Wirken*, pp. 70-71]

[23] 9 April 1914

[24] at p. 114 of Richard Wagner, *Overtures and Preludes in Full Score* (Mineola, N.Y.: Dover Publications, 1996). Nikisch doubled the horns, to eight, at a Berlin Philharmonic concert in 1895 to great effect, especially in the finale: "By doubling the horns, [he] succeeded in bringing out [the] underlying tenor voice, and the effect was so novel, beautiful and telling that the critics caught on to it, and it quickly became the subject of a most animated discussion." *Musical Courier*, 27 November 1895, p. 13 (Floerscheim, Berlin correspondent). He may have done the same thing at a Boston concert. "At the last return of [the Pilgrims'] theme, on the three trombones and three trumpets in unison, Mr. Nikisch introduced an effect which we had never heard before, and which, whether legitimate or not, was immensely impressive; he egged on the four horns to play in such an almost superhuman *fortissimo* that the middle parts stood out nearly as distinctly as the melody, and one heard this passage, for the first time, in *full harmony*." *Boston Evening Transcript*, 2 December 1889, p. 4

[25] *Musical Times*, 1 February 1905, p. 92; June 1997 reprint, p. 27

Not all rehearsals were as meticulous as this: often they would amount to a mediocre play through with a few comments at the end, yet an astonishingly inspired concert performance would follow on the night.

His re-working of the instrumentation in the *Tannhäuser* overture, one of his signature concert pieces, may have been effective to some, but did not please every listener. Debussy thought his virtuosity came at the expense of good taste: "he forces the trombones to a *portamento* [i.e., excessively] … [and] he stresses the horns at points where there is no particular reason for bringing them into prominence. These are effects without any appreciable causes and are amazing in a musician as Nikisch shows himself at all other times."[26] At an orchestral rehearsal of the *Liebestod* at Darmstadt in 1913, the young Erich Kleiber was present, and recalled in 1932:

> Our orchestra suddenly seemed transformed. We could none of us understand how Nikisch, with a single rehearsal, could draw from them such beauty of sound and such ecstatic depth of feeling. The score rang out as it rings in the silence of one's work-room after repeated sessions of intensive study. Absolutely uncanny were the mighty crescendos: where other conductors flail away with both arms, Nikisch just slowly raised his left hand till the orchestra roared about him like the sea. Yet the melodic parts were never obscured; it was an effect of art such as only he and Richard Strauss, as I was later to realise, could produce with the last pages of *Tristan*.27

Meticulous rehearsal on one occasion, and magic on another.

Nikisch on Wagner

In *talking* about Wagner, Nikisch had little to say. When asked whether he had any theories about the interpretation of the *Ring*, or of anything else, he merely smiled enigmatically, and said "a conductor should do his best to bring out all that is beautiful in a composition as clearly and as convincingly as possible."[28] That was not an idle comment, for beauty was one of the hallmarks of Nikisch's interpretations of Wagner. It comes up in descriptions of his performance more frequently than any other conductor, especially in comparison with Richter. The *Musical Times* summed it up:

> No one ever got from an orchestra more sensuous beauty of tone in all departments. His climaxes, if they had not always the monumental power of those of Richter, had an intensity of nervous energy that was irresistible. He had the secret of combining tremendous power with wonderful flexibility to an extent no one else has rivalled. A perfect example of this was in the Interlude in the *Rheingold* – at the point where the Nibelungs gather up their treasures in the caves below the earth – where he obtained an effect as new as it was legitimate. His *Meistersinger* performances were singularly lovely, but many preferred the Olympian repose and geniality of Richter. He represented Walter's view of life, the older man that of Hans Sachs. His *Tristan*

[26] Claude Debussy, *Monsieur Croche the Dilettante Hater* (1921), (trans.) B.N. Langdon Davies (London: Noel Douglas, 1927), reprinted in *Three Classics in the Aesthetic of Music* (New York: Dover Publications, 1962), p. 27. The Berlin Philharmonic was on tour to Paris.

[27] John Russell, *Erich Kleiber: A Memoir* (London: André Deutsch, 1957), p. 48; Klaus Geitel, *100 Jahre Berliner Philharmoniker: Grosse deutsche Dirigenten* (Berlin: Severin und Siedler, 1981), p. 54

[28] *World*, 29 April 1913, p. 605. The words quoted are a summary of Nikisch's response to the unnamed author of the article.

was a riot of brilliant colour and unbridled passion. The ideal performance of *Tristan* would be secured, it was said, if Richter conducted the first and third Acts and Nikisch the second.[29]

His climaxes seem to have been quite different from Richter's gradual, overwhelming crescendos: they would come suddenly, and just as quickly vanish. Tchaikovsky heard him conduct *Rheingold* and *Meistersinger* in Leipzig, and described how he could make "the orchestra now thunder like a thousand trumpets of Jericho, now coo like a dove, and now die away with breathtaking mystery."[30]

Of all conductors to have been shunned by Bayreuth, Nikisch's case is the most inexplicable – if one assumed decisions were based on aptitude. He told the *Boston Daily Traveller*: "In 1889 considerable talk was occasioned by my being unofficially approached on the subject of taking the leadership at Bayreuth during Herr Levi's illness. At the time Herr von Bülow presented me to a large party of musicians as the interpreter of Wagner's works."[31] What became of this approach he does not say. Perhaps he became a victim of the infamous Bayreuth anti-Semitism.

It is not known how many visits he made to Bayreuth to hear others conduct. Had he heard Richter conduct the *Ring* there? When he heard that Richter had been appointed to the Boston Symphony Orchestra in 1893, he reacted to the newspaper reporter who brought him the news: "Richter is the greatest conductor in the world. Everyone will say so of him. He is a great man.... I have known him for years, and can say he is superior to all conductors living."[32] Nikisch was in Bayreuth with his wife in 1906 to hear the *Ring* and *Parsifal* conducted by Muck,[33] but what he thought of either is unrecorded.

There is fortunately an abundance of testimony about Nikisch's Wagner performances in England which gives a fair measure of the conductor. In 1907 he conducted one performance of *Holländer* and two of *Tristan*. In 1913 he conducted three *Ring* cycles,[34] and, in 1914, two further cycles and two performances each of

[29] 1 March 1922, p. 173 (Alfred Kalisch). The only occasion Nikisch rose from his conductor's chair in the 1913 *Rheingold* was, according to Alfred Kalisch, at this "elemental climax": *World*, 29 April 1913, p. 617

[30] Alexandra Orlova, *Tchaikovsky: a self-portrait*, (trans.) R.M. Davison (Oxford and New York: Oxford University Press, 1990), p. 321. An abridged version of the words quoted is in Wooldridge, *Conductor's World*, p. 107. Tchaikovsky heard Nikisch conduct *Rheingold* in Leipzig on 23 December 1887 while on a concert tour. At his special request, Nikisch conducted *Meistersinger* on 29 January 1888, after which the composer wrote: "Very interesting": *Letters to his family: an autobiography* (trans.) Galina von Meck (London: Dobson, 1981), p. 392. Tchaikovsky praised Wagner's creative genius, but was not a Wagnerian: "wonderful symphonic episodes do not save the ugliness and artificiality of the vocal side of these musical horrors": letter of March 1889, *ibid*, p. 419.

[31] 25 October 1890, p. 5

[32] *Boston Journal*, 15 April 1893 (edition preserved in the Boston Symphony Orchestra Archives). Nikisch was reacting to a report that Richter was to take over the Boston Symphony. The report was accurate, but the appointment was never made because Richter could not secure his release from Vienna.

[33] Gerhardt, *Recital* (London: Methuen, 1953), pp. 41-42. The *Ring* that year was conducted by Hans Richter and Siegfried Wagner.

[34] with the exception of *Götterdämmerung* of the first cycle, when Nikisch was called back to Berlin and the "youthful and useful, if not inspired" Paul Drach conducted: *Musical Times*, 1 June 1913, p. 389. The only non-Wagner opera he conducted at Covent Garden was a single *Freischütz* on 16 January 1907.

Lohengrin and *Meistersinger*.[35] He also conducted excerpts from *Parsifal* at the Leeds Festival in 1913. In looking at these, we shall follow the earliest to the latest of the operas. His triumphant debut had been with *Tristan* on 15 January 1907.

Der fliegende Holländer

Richter's interpretation was still ringing in the ears of many reviewers in 1907, and Nikisch's distinctive approach did not quite persuade them. The *Daily Telegraph*, for example, remarked how the orchestra "played with peculiar fire and spirit," but it considered the performance as a whole did not come up to the level of the previous year's under Richter.[36] The *Daily News* remarked how "Nikisch made every possible dramatic point in the music, and his energy, if more nervous than and not so massive as Dr. Richter's, was full of life."[37] The orchestral playing was "a feature of the performance" for the *Morning Post*,[38] and seemed to play "with superb glow and tragic force" to the *Sunday Times*.[39] To the *World*, "one could not cease to wonder at the extraordinary beauty of the tone and the flexibility of the rhythm. But here and there a disrespectful questioning did obtrude itself whether he had not sacrificed some of the awe and mystery to the love of sensuous beauty."[40] This was a point taken by the *Star*, which nonetheless thought it "an excellent performance":

> Herr Nikisch's interpretation of the score is remarkably original and subtle. His truly pagan love of color asserts itself here, too, and he takes the whole out of the mystic half-light of legend in which most conductors dwell when dealing with this work, and brings us into broad sunshine. He does not make it as elemental or as deeply tragical as most conductors do (or at least try to do), but full of life and color and romance. His unique sense of flexible rhythm again helped to the production of some remarkably thrilling effects. His is not the view that will appeal to everyone. And there is not a little to be said in favor of the more usual interpretation, to which the almost Italian sweetness which Herr Nikisch gave us in some places is entirely foreign.[41]

No, Nikisch's view of the *Holländer* was not a view that appealed to everyone.

Lohengrin

Nikisch's two performances of *Lohengrin* in 1914 each came after a *Meistersinger* and a *Ring* cycle, and suffered as a consequence, partly because they were juxtaposed with more massive works, partly because the performers were tired. When the time came, there was simply a "lack of enthusiasm,"[42] or as the *Daily Telegraph* detected, "a sense of weariness over both stage and orchestra," at least at first, and ragged singing from the chorus; but gradually "the cloud began to lift and, once lifted, the sense of

[35] It is perhaps worth noting in light of the variety of reviews quoted that the views of Ernest Newman are not among them. He was music critic of the *Birmingham Evening Post* and was reviewing local musical events during Nikisch's appearances at Covent Garden (1907-1914), though he did attend Covent Garden's first performance of *Parsifal* in 1914 under Bodanzky.

[36] 18 January 1907, p. 11. The *Illustrated London News* also considered the *Holländer* "had been given in better fashion at Covent Garden": 26 January 1907, p. 136.

[37] 18 January 1907, p. 9 (E.A. Baughan) [38] 18 January 1907, p. 5 [39] 20 January 1907, p. 4

[40] 22 January 1907, p. 152 (Alfred Kalisch) [41] 18 January 1907, p. 1 ("Crescendo")

[42] *Athenaeum*, 9 May 1914, p. 666

Fig. 8.1. Arthur Nikisch early in his Leipzig years, 1879-1889

Fig. 8.2. Nikisch from his American years, 1889-1893

Fig. 8.3. Nikisch in the studio. Photo by Willinger

Fig. 8.4. Nikisch in the studio. Photo by Gerschel

Fig. 8.5. Nikisch in a silent film by Oskar Messter, 1919

Fig. 8.6. Nikisch from his Budapest years, 1893-1895

weariness went with it."[43] The performance was "somewhat unequal," according to the *Sunday Times*, but had "big moments, notably the imposing climax in the finale of the first act."[44] "The opening Prelude was charged with an atmosphere as rare as it was beautiful," wrote the *Standard*, "and the tone of the strings was clarity and purity itself."[45] Nikisch did "many wonderful things," according to the *Daily News and Leader* (without specifying them). "Not all of them will be unanimously approved of, but everything was extraordinarily interesting and full of imagination."[46] Only the *Westminster Gazette* expanded on the "beautiful playing" of the orchestra under Nikisch:

> Under his magic wand the whole score was suffused with a mellow radiance which seemed to paint the lily and gild even the refined gold of the music of *Lohengrin*. Very finely also Herr Nikisch realized the spirituality and exaltation of the music, as well as its tenderness and romance, and in general with the instrumentalists aiding and abetting him right worthily the performance was one of rare charm and interest.[47]

Nikisch, it will be recalled, played in the orchestra under Wagner in his sole performance of *Lohengrin* in Vienna in 1876 when he was criticized for dragging the tempo.[48] Interestingly, Nikisch too was criticized for dragging his tempi at Covent Garden. "Herr Nikisch's tempi do not err on the rapid side," wrote the *Standard*. "Some of the choruses dragged, but a stirring climax was secured at the end of the first act."[49] The *Daily Chronicle* reported that the principal soloists "seemed handicapped a little by the rather slow tempi which Herr Nikisch adopted in some places."[50] This was a criticism that Richter and Mottl, who also witnessed Wagner's *Lohengrin*, suffered at Covent Garden.

Tristan und Isolde

Nikisch was most renowned for his *Tristan* performances. For Ferdinand Pfohl, music critic in Hamburg where Nikisch conducted the work many times as a guest conductor, Nikisch was "**the** *Tristan* conductor.... he possessed the essence: the real *Tristan* poetry, the tragic romance of consecration of the night, yes, the actual *tragic expressivo*, the so painfully, yearningly, swelling melodics of the deep Wagnerian breath of life and suffering."[51] Put more simply by the genial English conductor, Sir Adrian Boult, *Tristan* "fitted Nikisch like a glove"[52] – it was "absolutely his cup of tea."[53] In England in 1907 Nikisch was particularly blessed to have the London Symphony Orchestra which he had first conducted in 1895 (and which played at Covent Garden). He declared "he had never previously conducted an orchestra which

[43] 2 May 1914, p. 7. The second performance was not reviewed.

[44] *Sunday Times*, 3 May 1914, p. 8 [45] 2 May 1914 p. 5

[46] 2 May 1914, p. 1. The second performance "was again an admirable affair," though the choral singing was poor and the fight between Telramund and Lohengrin was "a very tame affair": *ibid*, 14 May 1914, p. 5.

[47] 2 May 1914 (H. A. S.), p. 12

[48] see Wagner chapter, pp. 17-20 [49] 2 May 1914 p. 5 [50] 2 May 1914, p. 5

[51] Ferdinand Pfohl, "Mahler und Nikisch," in *Hundertjahrfeier des Hamburger Stadttheaters*, (ed.) Intendanz des Stadttheaters (Hamburg: Max Beck Verlag, 1927), p. 92 [52] Boult, *My Own Trumpet*, p. 37

[53] Robert Chesterman, *Conversations with Conductors* (London: Robson Books, 1976), p. 34

played *Tristan* with such finish and beauty of tone."[54] These characteristics of finish and tone struck the reviewers. "The character of the tone produced was particularly beautiful in every department," wrote the *Morning Post*, "and when accompanying the voice the much desired, but rarely heard full yet soft quality of sound, which gives the soloists full support without overwhelming them, was produced. The result of this tone was to bring to light fresh features in the score and to make the effect of those already familiar all the more potent."[55] The *Sunday Times* believed England had "never had a more magnificent interpretation of the work," and noticed how the London Symphony Orchestra "played with a sustained energy and fire, and withal with a wonderful lyrical grace and finish."[56] The *Observer* believed it was "one of the best we have seen in England," and observed how "the intensity of the music as a whole was maintained with remarkable vigour and, at the same time, splendid finish."[57] The *Daily Telegraph* was rhapsodic over the orchestra: "Now smouldering and fuming, now bursting into a blaze of sound, the music burnt its way with consuming energy. But yet one felt always that the fire had a restraining hand to guide and direct it, and that the passion of the tragedy would not be suffered to exceed its limits."[58] Three reviews were particularly expansive on Nikisch's style, and how it stood against what the reviewers were accustomed to. The *World* wrote:

To hear *Tristan* as conducted by Herr Nikisch is one of the most exciting experiences that can fall to the lot of a music-lover. His sense of beauty of tone, in which probably no conductor has ever rivalled him, finds the score its most congenial sphere. Emotions verging on the febrile, swiftly changing and fiercely raging, are his favourite topics. Nowhere in music is passion so highly strung as in *Tristan*; Herr Nikisch seems to give just another turn, and heightens the tension. It will be asked how is this consistent with unvarying beauty of tone and constant suavity of, sinuous melodic outline? That is his secret. ... [By contrast,] Dr Richter... astonishes us by showing how much that is elemental or superhuman there is in *Tristan*, how much underlying logic, and how much symphonic architecture.[59]

To the *Daily News*, Nikisch exceeded all expectations, which were already high. "His power of making his orchestra sing is familiar enough. He is a master of phrasing and has a grip of rhythm which enables him to squeeze the last drop of melody out of the music he conducts. In addition all his performances are inspired by a curious nervous vitality and by subtle and musical and poetic insight." He was known as a conductor in other contexts, yet...

How could we also know that he has true genius for stage work; that he is able to bring out all the beauty of the score as music pure and simple, and yet make it so plastic and expressive that every shade of emotion on the stage is reflected in the orchestra? As a matter of fact, there is little doubt that the inspiration of the conductor made itself felt on the stage, for singers well known to us did amazing things.[60] But the effect was that the singers dictated the spirit of the work, and that is the right effect, and one which Wagner himself desired.

54 *Illustrated Sporting and Dramatic News*, 26 January 1907, p. 937
55 16 January 1907, p. 8
56 20 January 1907, p. 4
57 20 January 1907, p. 4
58 17 January 1907, p. 11
59 22 January 1907, p. 152 (Alfred Kalisch)
60 Tristan was sung by Ernest van Dyck, Isolde by Félia Litvinne, and King Marke by Felix von Krauss. The *Daily News* noted that: "[Nikisch] accompanied the singers so well that they surpassed themselves.... The speech [of King Marke] is acknowledged to be a dramatic mistake, but so poignant was the singer's utterance that all theories were shattered for the moment." (16 January 1907, p. 8) The *World* agreed on Krauss's fine singing, but noted he had "a tendency to drag," one indication that Nikisch followed the singers (22 January 1907, p. 152).

Herr Nikisch's reading differed in some respects from the ordinary reading of *Tristan und Isolde*. He showed more reserve of force than is usual, so that he had plenty of climax in hand when it was required. The spirit of his conducting was not so physically energetic as Richter's, nor so mentally balanced as Dr. Muck's – the two interpretations of the music that stick in the mind. At the same time there was a terrific nervous energy, a plastic fire which at times glowed at white heat, and a beautiful and entrancing expressiveness. The love duet has never been sung by the orchestra with such tender and magical phrasing. Especially was this noticeable just before Brangäne's first song of warning to the lovers. Full of a strange beauty, too, was the opening of the third act, and Tristan's frenzy has seldom made such an effect on the orchestra. Above all, Herr Nikisch gives all possible significance to the motives without insisting on them by any hardness of emphasis. Their meaning was made clear by the character of the phrasing and by the subtle and long-drawn crescendi. In this respect the music played by the orchestra while Isolde awaits Tristan's obedience to her summons (in the first act) was a glowing example of what can be done by a great conductor with a fine orchestra.[61]

The *Star* was convinced Nikisch was the predestined conductor of *Tristan* – "there is a Tristanish touch in everything he does" – and its review must be quoted *in extenso*:

As one tries to sum up the total impression left by the performance, the first thing that comes to the mind is the beauty of it. Tone, color, melodic outline, all were replete with the subtle, sensuous, intoxicating charm which is the secret of his greatness. The real thing is the stimulating power of his climaxes: they are not things of weight and breadth, but of nervous tension. Last of all, one thinks of sundry purple patches of astonishingly clever detail here and there, and effects which are new.

Take, for instance, the curious sense of uneasiness and mystery at the point in the second act where Isolde is waiting for Tristan. Here we had all these things – a nerve-shattering climax, produced by growing power of sound less than by concentration; the most perfect beauty of tone; and new effects in the phrasing. The accompaniment here consists of triplets: with Richter each note is crystal clear: with Nikisch one had simply a sense of rushing notes. This small detail is mentioned just as an example of his method.

Extraordinarily effective, too, is his way of handling the end of the first act. It was perhaps not as heroic as it has been made by others – but it has never been so painfully human. And one wondered what had become of the dissonances for which one is accustomed to look. Noteworthy, too, was the way in which he delayed the climax, and made it all the more thrilling when it did come.

The whole of the second act was quite masterly. It was in a real sense a recreation of the score. The sultry hot-house atmosphere of it, the tempests of delirium, the alternating with nerveless languor, were almost painful in their reality. We have heard Tristan and Isolde represented almost as demi-gods struggling against fate, but have never before been made to realise them so keenly as ordinary mortals, with nerves strung up and goaded almost beyond human endurance. The other way is the saner, perhaps; but of the overpowering effect of this way there can be no doubt. The one is perhaps the more gently tragic, the other more deeply moving.

Magnificent too were the climaxes of the last act, and the Liebestod was a miracle of expression. Perhaps it was too sweet; but one could scarcely stop to criticise.[62]

[61] 16 January 1907, p. 8

[62] 16 January 1907, p. 1 ("Crescendo"). The only (and curious) point of criticism the *Athenaeum* could make was "an occasional tendency to exaggerate the pianissimos": 19 January 1907, p. 83. Yet the *Musical Times* singled out as memorable "the superb volume and balance of tone combined with fascinating delicacy and subtlety of phrasing and accentuation": 1 February 1907, p. 112

Reflecting on this 1907 performance, the *British Review* described it as "the most memorable evening in the Opera House in twenty-five years."[63] In 1882, the English premiere of *Tristan* had been conducted by Hans Richter.

Die Meistersinger von Nürnberg

By 1914, when Nikisch came to perform *Meistersinger* at Covent Garden, the press had the measure of Nikisch's greatness. It was "impossible to overpraise the orchestral playing, wrote the *Athenaeum*."[64] It was "quite a remarkable performance," according to the *Observer*, because the "wonderful orchestral moments were safe, of course, in [his] hands."[65] His reading "was superb in its deep poetic feeling and unfailing revelation of every beauty of the score," wrote the *Sunday Times*. "It was very noticeable how carefully he nursed his strings in places and what exquisite quality of singing tone he obtained from them. No doubt he occasionally slackened the pace to secure this, but it gave us some wonderful movements [*sic*]."[66] The *World* gave the context and some examples of these moments:

> It is impossible to imagine a *Meistersinger* in many ways more different from that of Richter, which must be regarded as the archetype of all that came after him and the standard by which they must all be judged. Yet, such is the magic of Nikisch's personality that I, for myself, know of no other except Richter whose conducting of the work has given me more intense pleasure. Nikisch's two ideals in all music which he takes in hand are flexibility and beauty; he invariably achieves them, and sometimes in doing so sacrifices something of significance and incisiveness. Thus one did miss in Nikisch's *Meistersinger* the peculiar note of humour, somewhat stolid and Teutonic if you will, but yet inimitable and a priceless asset of German culture. In exchange we had an amazing wealth of lyrical beauty and an irresistible glamour of romance. For instance, the close of the second act, after the brawl, was quite intoxicating in its loveliness. So were moments in the quintet and Sach's soliloquies. Sometimes in order to get these effects the tempo is unduly deliberate and there is perhaps a little too much rubato, but the total effect is almost unalloyed content. The way in which the brawl was made to grow in wildness from the beginning to the end was a great *tour de force*.[67]

It was "in some ways… as fine a piece of work as even he has ever done," concluded the *Daily News and Leader*.[68]

He conducted the prelude to the *Meistersinger* many times in concert, including at his first concert in Boston in 1889. "It was the most beautiful that I have ever been privileged to hear," wrote Henry Krehbiel.

> Herr Nikisch follows the composer's explicit directions, and departs as little and seldom as possible from the chief time of the composition. He brings out the first melody and the mastersingers' march in a broad style, solid and four-cornered, as beseems the representative melodies of Nuremberg's burgerdom. Even in the satirical middle part this solid ditty is not put off, but is used to intensify the effect of the unyielding pedantry of the singers' guild, but singing under and against it with a splendid stress of passionate utterance comes the melody in the strings

[63] vol. 2, no. 3 (June 1913), p. 452 (Home Gordon)
[64] 2 May 1914, p. 634
[65] 3 May 1914, p. 5
[66] 3 May 1914, p. 8
[67] 5 May 1914, p. 753 (Alfred Kalisch)
[68] 30 April 1914, p. 3 (A. K.). This is presumably Alfred Kalisch of the *World*. He added in the *Daily News*: "The constant stream of beautiful sounds which issued from the orchestra was almost intoxicating, and yet it was never sentimental or flabby."

which tells of the young knight's love and the young poet's protest against the formularies which are relied on to put him down. What is obviously the composer's intention is attained, not by a dislocation of the time, but by eloquence of expression. ... He never permits himself to fall into undue haste; he never obscures a figure or phrase, be it melodic or rhythmic, in order to reach a preconceived idea as to its proper tempo.... [B]y nice adjustment of parts, the voices of the composition are made to stand out brightly and self-reliantly... so carefully was the intrinsic character of each of its constituent melodies preserved that it glowed with warmth and feeling.[69]

Fig. 8.7. Nikisch at the Vienna Opera, 1912. Silhouette by Theo Zasche

Another observer at this concert was George L. Osgood of the *Boston Herald*: "I care little or nothing for the hair-splitting comparisons of the conductor's tempi, provided we get a musician with heart and head. My decided impression of Nikisch is that the heart speaks first and the strong brain controls the expression.... [The] freedom with which Nikisch manages his orchestra is not a mechanical one; it come from pure musical inspiration."[70]

[69] *New York Daily Tribune*, 14 October 1889, p. 6

[70] 13 October 1889, p. 6

Der Ring des Nibelungen

When Nikisch came to London in 1913 to conduct the *Ring*, the critics had again as their solid background the inspired and authoritative readings of Richter. They were dazzled by Nikisch's interpretation. It was so unlike Richter's that they were moved on the one hand to articulate differences of mood, and on the other to describe the details that most characterised Nikisch's approach. We look firstly at the general approach.

The *Daily News and Leader* observed after the *Rheingold*:

> The epic restraint of the elder man is absent from the work of the younger. Where the one is statuesque and architectonic, the other is picturesque and brilliantly mobile. Both have the gift of making climaxes which thrill. The one gets them by elemental strength, growing – as it seems – almost automatically; the other by a nervous intensity almost incredible. The one impresses by his almost austere restraint; the other carries us away on a stream of rare sensuous beauty.[71]

Characterized another way: "It might be said that whereas Richter seems to look on the score from the point of view of Wotan, Nikisch seems to speak to us with the voice of Loge – if it were not that this would seem to carry with it a suggestion of trickery and deceit."[72] After *Götterdämmerung*, the *Star* wrote, "They used to say that Richter conducting *Götterdämmerung* was like Jove wielding the thunderbolt; Nikisch was perhaps like Apollo or Hermes: but they were Olympians too";[73] and the *World* wrote, "In the one we get more the effect of tragedy marching slowly but surely to its end; in the other we are rather thrilled by swiftly moving workings of Fate."[74] The *Musical Times* may not have had Richter specifically in mind when it commented that "Nikisch's reading will not be loved by the patriotic Teuton; it has nothing of the storm and stress, the blaring brass and tearing string, with inaudible soloists and unintelligible action that a succession of German conductors have accustomed us to." Indeed, had Nikisch been around earlier he "would have won recognition sooner for the genius of Richard Wagner."[75]

There were several characteristics of Nikisch's approach mentioned in reviews, but in one way or another, they all commented on the rich tone of the orchestra: "the luscious quality of the strings and the rare purity of tone attained in the brass,"[76] "the liquid glowing mass,"[77] even in the softest passages, and how it never covered the voices.[78] Everything was clear and detailed. In fact, such was Nikisch's way that he could reduce the tone in the pianissimos "without its becoming cold, and therefore expressionless."[79] The *British Review* described him, not unfavourably, as "persistently

[71] 23 April 1913, p. 1 (A. K.) (after *Rheingold*). On the point of climaxes, the *Daily Telegraph* differed: "in every case the climaxes seemed to grow up naturally, inevitably, but sometimes with a force that was elemental in its strength:" 24 April 1913, p. 16 (after *Walküre*)

[72] *World*, 29 April 1913, p. 617 (Alfred Kalisch) (after *Rheingold*, *Walküre*, and *Siegfried*)

[73] 7 May 1913, p. 4 ("Crescendo") (after Nikisch's first *Götterdämmerung*, in the second cycle)

74 13 May 1913, p. 698 (Alfred Kalisch)

[75] June 1913, p. 389

[76] *Daily Telegraph*, 24 April 1913, p. 16 (after *Walküre*)

[77] *Musical Times*, 1 June 1913, p. 389 (after the first cycle)

[78] *Sunday Times*, 27 April 1913, p. 6 (after *Rheingold*, *Walküre*, and *Siegfried*); *Musical Times*, 1 June 1913, p. 389; *The Times*, 23 April 1913, p. 10 (after *Rheingold*)

[79] *Athenaeum*, 26 April 1913, p. 474 (after *Rheingold* and *Walküre*)

throttling down his orchestra."[80] Another distinguishing characteristic of Nikisch was the way he handled climaxes. As the *Times* summed up after his *Götterdämmerung* of the second cycle: "It is difficult to say how the great conductors of Wagner are able to lead the orchestra from climax to climax of massive sound without ever overwhelming the voices on the stage; but two or three of them – Dr. Richter and Herr Nikisch pre-eminently – possess the secret, and the rest do not."[81]

In the *Rheingold* there were several details that struck the *Daily News and Leader*:

> The opening was taken at a rapid pace, and the loveliness of the music when the sun first shines on the gold was ravishing. The first entry of the Walhall music was perhaps a little disappointing: but the vitality, the freakishness, and the beauty of the Loge music has rarely been brought home to us so cogently. The opening of Loge's great song in praise of Love was magical, and nothing was finer than the grotesque robustness and the relentless rhythm of the Giant music. The interludes describing the journeys of Wotan and Loge to and from Nibelheim were amazing in their grim dramatic power, and the climax after the ring was seized by Wotan was quite overwhelming, while the glitter and glow of the final scene were intoxicating.[82]

As for the "rapid pace" of the opening, it is interesting to note a different perspective from the *British Review*: "The curiously slow beat of the prelude to *Rheingold* gave an intensely suggestive conception of gently lapping water."[83] What surprised the *Star* was "the forcefulness of the fiercely dramatic moments."

> The scene of Alberich's curse, for example, and the big climax which comes just before it were wonderful. So were the interludes before and after the Nibelheim scene, which had all the strength of the blind forces of nature. The beauty of the Rhine Maidens' music was quite memorable – to go to the other end of the scale of moods.[84]

For the *Daily Telegraph*, throughout the score the "rhythmic impulse, flexibility, and clearness of detail, and sheer lyrical beauty, could scarcely have been surpassed."[85]

In the *Walküre*, the *Daily News and Leader* found that Nikisch emphasised "the purely human and emotional" more than any other conductor.[86] Of the details of special note were "the thrill of the climax when Siegmund calls on his unknown father for aid, the beautifully caressing rhythm of the Spring Song; and the wonderful way the Walhall theme first crept into the orchestra during Sieglinde's narration." Of the "purple patches" in the second act were "the climax of Wotan's monologue, *Nur eins noch will ich das Ende*, and the outburst at the point when Brünnhilde prevents Siegmund from killing Sieglinde," as well as the "superbly dramatic" end of the act.[87] One point on which this reviewer and that of the *Star* were in agreement was the deliberate pace of Wotan's second act monologue. As the *Star* expressed it, "there was possibly a little tendency to dwell on detail at the expense of the 'great line,' as the Germans call it, but it was all so finely done and the climaxes were so remarkable that it is easy to make too much of it."[88]

[80] Vol. 2, No. 3 (June 1913), p. 453 (Home Gordon)

[81] *The Times*, 7 May 1913, p. 10

[82] *Daily News and Leader*, 23 April 1913, p. 1 (A. K.)

[83] Vol. 2, No. 3 (June 1913), p. 454 (Home Gordon)

[84] *Star*, 23 April 1913, p. 4 ("Crescendo")

[85] 23 April 1913, p. 12. The *Observer* believed the orchestra may have had a little difficulty in adjusting to Nikisch's quite different conception of the *Ring*, judging from the "many moments of indecision" in its playing: 27 April 1913, p. 3.

[86] See following footnote. The *Daily Telegraph* observed that Nikisch's powers for working up a climax found fuller scope in the emotional music of the *Walküre*: 24 April 1913, p. 16.

[87] *Daily News and Leader*, 24 April 1913, p. 1 (A. K.)

[88] 24 April 1913, p. 4 ("Crescendo")

The interpretation of *Siegfried* was notable for its youthfulness, for here, "exuberance and impulsive orchestral freedom came with the youth and love of Siegfried."[89] It was "youthful, heroic, and dramatic" above all to the *Daily News and Leader*:

The massive power of the Wanderer's scene; the unbridled energy of the forging songs; the glorious loveliness of the forest murmurs – all were there. Herr Nikisch conducted with amazing mastery.... The first great effect he made was in the passage where the Wanderer leaves Mime in despair in the first act, and here – although the pace was a little deliberate – the total effect was overwhelming. The gradually growing strength and energy of the music in the forging songs was wonderful. Splendid, too, was the music of the fight with the dragon, and the sardonic humour of the scene where Mime tries to deceive Siegfried has rarely been made more incisive. The Erda scene and the finale were magnificent in the passionate and sensuous beauty.[90]

These scenes also impressed the *Star*, which added that "the balance between the stage and the orchestra was flawless." Nikisch's interpretation was "intensely emotional and mobile: possibly he sacrificed a little of the heroic element; but as a compensation he gives us a vast deal of sheer beauty which we hardly suspected to be there. The tremendous vivacity of his rhythms made the scenes in which the action moves most slowly seem full of incident. And though he occasionally was deliberate, the flow of the music never ceased."[91]

Nikisch was unable to be present for the *Götterdämmerung* of the first cycle, but was back for the second and it was a "thrilling experience," according to the *Star*:

It was very unlike any performance one had heard before; yet it in no way did violence to what we have been brought up to believe to be the true essence of the work. Again – as in the rest of the *Ring* – its chief features were its intense humanity and its supreme beauty; and yet the heroic elements were all there, and we felt the poignancy of the world-tragedy. There was a profusion of beautiful detail-work, but it did not obscure the main outlines, and it was splendidly consistent.[92]

Of moments in the work, the *Daily News and Leader* singled out (as did the *Star* in its own words[93]) the "splendid glitter and virility" of Siegfried's Rhine Journey, the "tremendously dramatic ending" of act one, the "barbaric force and the volcanic passions" of act two, the "fascinating beauty and delicacy" of the Rhine Maidens' scene, and the working up to "a glorious and impressive climax" in Siegfried's Funeral Music "which thrilled even hardened opera-goers."[94] Of this last scene, and Brünnhilde's Immolation, the *World* wrote of Nikisch's "extraordinary art in delaying a climax... but when the climaxes did come they were simply nerve-shattering; and the final peroration was a gorgeous mass of sound, and every thread in the orchestral fabric was unmistakably clear."[95] The *Star* commented on these scenes evocatively:

89 Vol. 2, No. 3 (June 1913), p. 455 (Home Gordon)

90 26 April 1913, p. 1 (A. K.). The *Athenaeum* considered "the forest music has never been given with greater delicacy": 3 May 1913, p. 502. So far as the forging songs were concerned, the *Observer* noted that the "ideas [of the singer of Siegfried, Peter Cornelius] of the movement of the music differed considerably to those of the conductor": 27 April 1913, p. 3.

91 26 April 1913, p. 4 ("Crescendo")

92 7 May 1913, p. 4 ("Crescendo")

93 for example, "the joy of life" in the Rhine Journey, "the magnificent savagery" of the vassals' chorus, "the fairy-like loveliness" of the Rhine Maidens scene, and "the tremendous power and noble rhythm" of the Funeral March: *Star*, 7 May 1913, p. 4 ("Crescendo")

94 7 May 1913, p. 1 (A. K.)

95 13 May 1913, p. 698 (Alfred Kalisch)

Fig. 8.8. Nikisch in concert. Silhouette by Otto Wiedemann

In his treatment of the last part of the act Nikisch reminded me of in a curious way of another of the great ones – Sarah Bernhardt. For minutes at a time he seemed to be doing nothing in particular, but still one felt that a personality was there: then, seemingly in obedience to a sudden impulse – but, in truth, cunningly prepared – came a climax of overwhelming force, all the more powerful because delayed for longer than any lesser person would dare to do.[96]

Nikisch returned to London for two more cycles in 1914, and the critical acclaim was in similar terms. Two comments, however, were new. One, by the *Daily News and Leader*, on the singing of Waltraute in *Götterdämmerung*, which it considered perhaps the finest singing of all four evenings: "It was of poignant dramatic significance too. Herr Nikisch took this particular scene a little slowly, but by way of compensation obtained an orchestral tone of ravishing beauty."[97] Beauty, it seems, was always Nikisch's

[96] 7 May 1913, p. 4 ("Crescendo")

[97] 28 April 1914, p. 5 (no author or initials) The singer of Waltraute was Kirkby Lunn.

most sublime strength, and his *Ring* was "astonishingly beautiful in parts." Yet was he entirely at home in *Götterdämmerung*? "It was a performance full of magnetism, though there are some moments when an ideal rendering demands a certain savagery and almost a determination to ignore beauty which some far lesser men can arrive at better than Nikisch," wrote the *World*. "Still, it was all intensely dramatic, the chorus of vassals sang very finely, and the closing scene was deeply moving."[98] After the second cycle, the *World* commented on Nikisch's "newer way" with the *Ring*, compared with Richter's:

> The newer way possibly results in more sheer beauty, more excitement, and possibly brings out more strongly the human elements; but we do not get from it quite the same feeling that the *Ring* is a world-drama, or the impression that a performance of it – particularly of the latter part of *Götterdämmerung* – is almost devotional. The new way is more secular, using that word without any suggestion of depreciation.
> It will be a question of temperament which one prefers; even the knowledge we have of Wagner's own feelings in the matter will influence different natures differently.[99]

Parsifal

Nikisch had a small window of opportunity to conduct *Parsifal* after its release from copyright in 1914 (he died in 1922), but he never did so.[100] He conducted the Prelude and Good Friday Music with the Boston Symphony in concert, and not unexpectedly, they sounded quite different from Bayreuth performances. The orchestra, for one, was too loud, as the *Boston Daily Advertiser* reported:

> It played louder than any band that Wagner, or Richter, or Levi, or Mottl ever led; the onslaught on *Parsifal* made the Bayreuthian fortissimi seem very puny indeed; the kettle drummer played as if he were thinking of Haydn's *Surprise Symphony*; the brasses thundered the *Glaubes-thema* in deafening fury, and the prelude was carried by assault. If the witlings of the paragraphic press are right, if Wagner is noise pure and simple, then this may be classed as the very best performance this prelude has ever received, but if one demands something of coherency, a degree of shading rather than wild extremes, a tride [*sic*] of accuracy in ensemble then the praise may turn to emphatic censure. It is wonderful that a man as musically-gifted as our conductor, who has heard the prelude performed in its best form, should have given such a hurly-burly of sound in its place....[101]

It had been played "with splendid warmth," wrote the *Boston Transcript*, "a warmth that was developed into a white heat at moments when some of the dreamy nature and reposefulness of the work seemed to be needlessly sacrificed."[102] It was "not all given as it should be," reported the *Beacon*, "its mystical, reflective moods... being broken up again and again by loud assertiveness and bustling sonority."[103] His performance of the Good Friday Music too left something to be desired according to the *Boston*

[98] 28 April 1914, p. 705, and 5 May 1914, p. 753 (Alfred Kalisch)

[99] 12 May 1914, p. 810 (Alfred Kalisch).

[100] Nikisch did include the prelude and excerpts in some of his concerts, in addition to those mentioned above, for example, at the Gewandhaus Leipzig on 9 March 1899, 13 February 1913, and 13 February 1919. The first *Parsifal* performances in Berlin in 1914 were conducted by Leo Blech and Eduard Mörike, and in Leipzig by Otto Lohse.

[101] 28 December 1891, p. 5 (Louis C. Elson)

[102] 28 December 1891, p. 5

[103] 2 January 1892, p. 5

Herald. Despite its excellences, there was a "lack of sentiment and feeling demanded in a perfect interpretation."[104] The "brasses were at least once a little too blatant," wrote the *Boston Daily Advertiser*, but this was "only temporary, and the good shading of the latter part of the number calls for recognition. Mr. Nikisch was especially successful in his accentuation of the figures with which this portion of the opera teem, so that the leitmotiven could all be followed by those who knew of their existence."[105]

In 1913 he conducted the Prelude and Grail Scene at the Leeds Festival, to good effect according to some reports, and with tempi that differed from Bayreuth,[106] but perhaps *Parsifal* was not "absolutely his cup of tea."

The Siegfried Idyll

It may be fitting to end with a recollection of Alfred Kalisch, whose perceptive and balanced reviews have done so much to bring Nikisch's Wagnerian music-making to life. The most beautiful things Kalisch remembered of Nikisch were, surprisingly, two performances he gave of the *Siegfried Idyll* in London. He had a small orchestra of seventeen players, and on each occasion rehearsed it for two hours. This was unusual, because he generally depended on his inspiration on the evening. The performances "were the very perfection of intimate charm and finish of detail. [Nikisch] himself confessed to me that he had been so moved that he could hardly keep going."[107] We may recall, this was just like Wagner himself, who was so moved conducting the prelude to *Lohengrin* in Zurich that he had to pull himself together by force, so as not to give way to his emotions. Even the gods are human.

[104] 11 October 1891, p. 12

[105] 12 October 1891, p. 4 (Louis C. Elson)

[106] "both interesting and impressive.... The orchestra played the solemn Prelude to the finest effect, and Mr. Nikisch drew out the last lingering notes to the uttermost." *Leeds Mercury*, 6 October 1913, p. 3 (F.T.) "Mr. Nikisch's tempi were generally on the slow side, yet he never loses his grip of the rhythm, and the *Faith* melody, though taken very slowly, did not drag.... under Mottl, Muck and particularly Fischer, the idea of the solemnity of the work has possessed them till the slow portions have been dragged out to an almost unbearable degree. Mr. Nikisch, however, never produced this impression upon his hearers, for his sense of rhythm is abnormally acute, and he is therefore able to give vitality to even the most sustained passages." *Yorkshire Post*, 6 October 1913, p. 7

[107] *Musical Times*, 1 March 1922, p. 173. Kalisch concluded: "At the second performance Richard Strauss was present, and said that he had seldom had such unalloyed pleasure. The only thing, he added, which marred it was a wild desire to get on to the platform and take the stick himself." This performance was probably the one given at the reception for Strauss at the Music Club in London (of which Kalisch was chairman) on 21 June 1914. Nikisch once conducted a "very good" performance with the Boston Symphony, notwithstanding "some startling liberties taken with the first phrases, a very bold and extended *ritenuto* being introduced." *Boston Daily Advertiser*, 13 March 1893, p. 5 (Louis C. Elson)

9

Albert Coates – Bacchus in Valhalla

Albert Coates was a big man with enormous energy. Everything about his music-making was on the grand scale. He was a natural musician, not given to writing or to exposition. He hardly talked about Wagner's music, yet he had an instinctive understanding of it. His performances often erupted with life, from deep within his volcanic musical temperament. Eruptions may be brilliant, but they can also be messy, and leave scars. Musical details were sometimes swept aside with Coates in the great, enthusiastic sweep of his vision. Musical colleagues and critics were singed at his forge. It was difficult for him to be accommodated, wherever he wandered. In Russia, the land of his birth, he was a foreigner. In Germany he was a Russian. In England he was never quite at home. In America he became a mere jester. A guest leaves but few, transitory traces. When Coates was invited into the opera house and the recording studio, there were some perfect moments. Yet viewed as a whole, from Valhalla as it were, his musical life was unperfected. But what he would have done with Valhalla…!

Russian beginnings

He was born in St. Petersburg on 23 April 1882. His mother was Russian-born, but both parents were of English nationality. His maternal grandmother, Mary Gibson (*née* Randall) was of Russian descent. She was quite different from Coates's English relatives. "Grandma Gibson was of a very different calibre altogether, her ancestors had evidently had Tartar blood in them, despite her Irish name of Randall, and she brought to our family an amazing virility and fearlessness which was the chief asset of all my Gibson uncles and aunts, including my own Mother."[1] Including, one might say, of Coates himself. His huge stature, his volcanic musical temperament, his love of Russian music – all showed he was an exceptional Englishman. His fellow students in Leipzig called him *Der Russe*, and not just because he was Russian-born. There were rumours he was of royal blood. They addressed him as *Gospoden Coatesky* [Lord Coates]."[2] When he was back in St. Petersburg as a conductor, audiences loved him

[1] Albert Coates, *Morning, High Noon and Evening*, typescript, carbon copy, 6 pages, no date, Box 9, *Albert Coates Papers*, University of Stellenbosch. Coates awaits his biographer. Information in this chapter has been drawn mainly from articles and reports based on interviews with him, and has to be viewed in that light.

[2] Dr. Felix Gross, "Albert Coates, *Spotlight* (Capetown), 17 October 1947, p. 41

for qualities they could recognise in themselves. "The general public were carried away by his *temperàment* – a word which in Russian conveys much more than the corresponding English term," recalled a fellow musician. "This *temperàment* swept all before it, yet revealed a superb finesse of interpretation. Until the revolution and for many years after it the name of Coates was one to conjure in Russia."[3] Coates's British nationality never prevailed over his mixed ancestry. His Russianness was to become a double-edged sword in England. On the one hand it gave him natural authority (as well as his real ability) in Russian music. On the other, it gave his enemies in the murky politics of musical life, and in the prevailing climate of suspicion about Soviet Russia, a reason to work against him.[4] Perhaps for this reason his family sought to obscure the connection.[5]

His father was a Yorkshireman who had gone to St. Petersburg as a boy, and had risen to become director of an English woollen mill. He was "immensely musical," and prominent musicians were often in their household. Among the many boys in the Coates family, one – "Jim (my Jonathan)" – was a very gifted amateur musician and taught his younger brother everything he knew. Evenings at home would often be spent playing music, improvising on piano and organ, and entertaining other musicians.[6] When Jim died suddenly in 1897, Coates was so devastated he turned away from music altogether, and went to study science at Liverpool University. On return to St. Petersburg he was set to work in the woollen mill, but could not suppress his musical ingenuity. When his father caught him writing music on an accounting ledger, he became resigned to the seriousness of his son's musical vocation. He was sent to Leipzig where he entered the Conservatory on 20 April 1900.[7]

[3] Sir Paul Dukes, *The Unending Quest* (London: Cassell & Co. Ltd., 1950), p. 42. Despite what Dukes says, Coates's name seems soon to have faded in the USSR: a report by Professor Eugene Broudo, "Musical Art in Soviet Russia," referred to him as "Kouts": *Musical Times*, 1 February 1929, p. 121. Dukes said he had been known to everybody in St. Petersburg as "Albert Carlovitch": *Unending Quest*, p. 45. In Elberfeld, the press referred to him as Coâtes. In Dresden, where records were destroyed in the War, his name seems to have survived through oral history, for a modern history spells it "Cohrts": Eberhard Steindorf and Dieter Uhrig (eds.), *Staatskapelle Dresden* (Berlin: Henschelverlag Kunst und Gesellschaft, 1973), p. 188. Elsewhere in continental Europe he was often called "Co-a-tes": press clipping from the 1914 season (undated, no source) in the Royal Opera House Collections.

[4] One of these "enemies" sought to prejudice a critic by telling him that Coates was "a Bolshevik and a menace to the peace of the peaceful musical profession." Charles Frederick Kenyon, *Written in friendship; a book of reminiscences*, by Gerald Cumberland [pseud.] (London: Grant Richards, 1923), p. 232. One influential critic, Ernest Newman, suggested in 1922, without giving any reasons or explanation, that his reputation in England was already fading: "Our Conductors II. - Albert Coates," *The Music Lovers' Portfolio*, ed. Landon Ronald (London: George Newnes, 1921-22), No. 11 [1922], pp. XLIX-L

[5] Coates's niece, who in 1934 was his secretary, said sharply during an interview: "Don't you dare call Uncle Albert Russian," she said. "He's not. He's Yorkshire." W.S. Meadmore, "Albert Coates discusses Russia," *Gramophone*, April 1934, p. 428. Coates's brother, Edwin, wrote to *The Times* in response to Albert's obituary: "There is no Russian blood in our veins." *The Times*, 31 December 1953, p. 8. Coates himself, of course, was the source of the many statements that his mother was Russian, a Russian lady, etc.

[6] Coates was the seventh boy. An eighth died in infancy. His father adored Johann Strauss in particular. Coates, *Morning, High Noon and Evening* (above)

[7] inscription form (ref. 7943), Königliches Conservatorium, now the Felix Mendelssohn Bartholdy Hochschule für Musik und Theater, Leipzig. His date of birth is recorded as 23 April *1881*. His graduation certificate (theory, piano, cello – conducting is not mentioned) is dated 30 May 1904.

The Pupil of Nikisch

As often happens in the case of prodigious talent, formal instruction counts for less than a happy accident. In Coates's case, his formal practical studies were in piano and cello, in which he excelled. The good fortune came in watching Nikisch at work, mostly at Gewandhaus concerts. So far as opera was concerned, Nikisch was only an occasional guest during Coates's time in Leipzig. About forty Wagner performances were staged each year at the Stadttheater, but Nikisch conducted only nine of them – all *Ring* operas or *Tristan* – and all in 1903.[8] Whether Coates attended any of these is unrecorded, though it is likely he did, at least the rehearsals.[9] He spent three months watching Nikisch, then did his first conducting at the Leipzig Opera.[10] We recall how Nikisch explained his teaching, mostly by giving his students the opportunity to watch him at work. Coates recalled his own experience in Nikisch's conducting class:

> I had never had a stick technique lesson in my life – Nikisch, my beloved master, didn't trouble about the stick – he took it for granted that we had all watched him closely during his rehearsals and concerts and could find out for ourselves. If we couldn't manage the stick part he just passed to the next pupil and the next and the next, and it generally fell to my lot to demonstrate a particularly natty bit like the trio in the 3rd of Beethoven which the others had just bungled. As there were about 30 of us in Nikisch's class, it sometimes became a real genesis and exodus for the class until the classroom sang with – "We want Coates, we want Coates" – I was anything but popular really, but they always were hoping I would bungle it with the rest, but that never happened. I suppose it was just in the blood and in my great love and affection for my master – for he seemed to lend me his wings when necessary.[11]

Coates's high standing in Nikisch's class has been vouched for by fellow students.[12] According to Coates, Nikisch too held him in high regard. "The conducting stick seems insufficient for your feeling, Coates; you'd better take a whip."[13] More pertinently, Nikisch once asked Coates to conduct a Mozart symphony. Afterwards he was overwhelmed with enthusiasm. "Why, you are a born conductor! You should not be a pianist. Where ever have you been before?"[14] Or as other accounts have it: "Born conductors are few, but you certainly are one."[15] Nikisch gave more and more attention to his star pupil. He allowed him – uniquely for a student – to play the cello

[8] The regular Wagner conductors were Richard Hagel and Bernard Porst. The records of the Leipzig Opera were destroyed during bombing on 3-4 December 1943; the Leipzig City Archive retains the opera playbills on microfilm, from which the above details were taken.

[9] Coates kept some programs of Nikisch's concerts, eg from 1900, 1906, 1909, all his life, but none of them were of Wagner operas: Box 3, *Albert Coates Papers*, Stellenbosch.

[10] sketch for an autobiography, 8 small notebook pages, no date: Box 9, *Albert Coates Papers*, Stellenbosch.

[11] "An Evening with two gifted friends in St. Petersburg," manuscript in Coates's hand, 2 pages, no date, Box 5, *Albert Coates Papers*, Stellenbosch

[12] Dr. Felix Gross, "Albert Coates," *Spotlight* (Capetown), 17 October 1947, p. 41; Aylmer Buesst, "Albert Coates: 1882-1953," *Music & Letters*, Vol. 35 (1954), p. 136.

[13] John F. Porte, "Gramophone Celebrities XX. – Albert Coates," *Gramophone*, December 1927, p. 270

[14] Frits Stegmann, "Ek Ontmoet Albert Coates," *Die Brandwag*, 24 January 1947, p. 17. Coates spoke highly of two other members of Nikisch's conducting class: Ossip Gabrilovich (1878-1936), conductor of the Detroit Symphony Orchestra (1916-1936), and Renzo Bossi (1883-1965), Italian opera conductor, composer, and teacher.

[15] *Cape Times*, 12 February 1947, p. 10

in the Gewandhaus orchestra. He conducted Coates in a Beethoven piano concerto at the Gewandhaus, in Berlin, and Hamburg.[16] He was an accomplished cellist and pianist when Nikisch appointed him a repetiteur at the opera.

Soon he was thrust into conducting. He made his debut with the *Tales of Hofmann*, when the other two conductors were ill and Nikisch had to leave town. It was a success and, in Coates's own words, he "never looked back."[17] Nikisch heard the second performance of *Tales* and advised him to abandon any plans of being a cello or piano virtuoso, and to devote himself to opera. He helped him secure a position of conductor in Elberfeld in 1906.[18] It is also likely that Nikisch was responsible for getting him to London in 1910 to conduct the London Symphony Orchestra, to Covent Garden in 1914 to conduct Wagner, and to Paris in 1914 to rehearse and conduct the first performance of *Tristan* in German ahead of Nikisch's own performance there.[19] Nikisch not only had a decisive effect on Coates's career, but most importantly inspired him in his music-making. "Each time I take up my baton," Coates wrote in 1934, "I see Nikisch before me. I hear his voice in my ears, and I would like to tell him I am trying to keep faith."[20]

German interlude

After two years in Elberfeld (1906-08), where he conducted some forty operas, including all of Wagner's works,[21] he went to Dresden as chief conductor (1908-09), and then to Mannheim (1909-10), before St. Petersburg exerted its pull. Of these German posts, Dresden was perhaps the most decisive in his flowering as a conductor of Wagner.

Everyone praised him as a rejuvenator of the Wagner operas. To rid performances, particularly that of the *Ring*, of those numerous slacknesses, incorrectnesses and lazinesses acquired by orchestras and veteran soloists through decades of routine proved to be difficult. Coates saw a chance to fulfil his ideals as Royal General Music Director at the Mannheim Opera. There his *Siegfried* became a sensation about which musicians and amateurs spoke for months. He had brought life again into the almost sterile conception of routine singers and players. Coates did away in music and acting with the silly histrionics of vain and overfed *Heldentenors* and the comfort-seeking laziness of 200-pound prima donnas. He restituted

16 Gross, "Albert Coates," *Spotlight*, 17 October 1947, p. 41

17 sketch for an autobiography, Box 9, *Albert Coates Papers*, Stellenbosch

18 Coates was likely responsible for Nikisch's guest appearance in Elberfeld in *Meistersinger* on 4 January 1908.

19 The oft-repeated statement that Coates shared a season, or shared the *Ring*, with Nikisch at Covent Garden in 1913 is incorrect. Nikisch was there, but Coates was not: see Harold Rosenthal, *Two centuries of opera at Covent Garden* (London: Putnam, 1958), pp. 758-60. Nikisch spoke warmly of his "friend and pupil Albert Coates" in an interview with the *Daily Telegraph* (9 April 1914), as he looked forward to hearing Coates open the season with *La Bohème* starring Nellie Melba.

20 Coates, (as told to R.H. Wollstein), "The Music of New Russia," *The Etude*, June 1934, p. 336

21 "Albert Henry Coates," *Musical Times*, 1 April 1914, p. 226. The Wagner works he conducted at Elberfeld and the dates of the first performances were: *Tannhäuser* (30 September 1906), *Lohengrin* (12 October 1906), *Walküre* (23 October 1906), *Tristan* (31 October 1906), *Meistersinger* (14 December 1906), *Holländer* (1 December 1907), *Parsifal*, Prelude, Flowermaidens' scene, Good Friday scene, Final chorus (11 February 1908), *Rienzi* (1 March 1908), and the *Ring* (3, 4, 11 and 14 April 1908): information from the Stadtarchiv Wuppertal.

the dramatic vehemence, the human factor and, at the same time, the lyrical poetry of the Wagnerian style.[22]

It is not surprising that the eruption of Coates onto the Dresden scene caused some friction with "the high and mighty Generalmusikdirektor, Ernst von Schuch... 'the first man in Dresden after the king – and not always after him.'"[23] The sensation with *Siegfried* led to Coates conducting eleven operas without knowing them.[24] It was during a performance of the *Walküre* that he was talent-spotted for the Imperial Opera in St. Petersburg. He resisted initially, in favour of Mannheim, after its director, Carl Hagemann, talent-spotted him during another Wagner performance:

> After my arrival at two o'clock in the afternoon, Schuch entrusted Coates with the direction of *Götterdämmerung* scheduled for that evening, without the latter ever having conducted the work before. Throughout the whole of the long performance, not even the slightest flaw occurred, and the young conductor displayed an elegant, yet assured manner of conducting – which had something of Nikisch in it – as well as a carefree way of playing – things which made the best of impressions on me, so that once the performance had finished, I said I was prepared to sign him.[25]

After a season in Mannheim, he was honoured by the king and that, he wrote, "did me in for Germany."[26]

Wagner in St. Petersburg

Coates was invited to conduct *Siegfried* at the Mariinsky Theatre in 1909. Such was its success that he was given a five-year contract from 1910, and asked to conduct Russian and Italian opera as well. This caused some resentment amongst the other staff conductors particularly as Coates became the favourite of the public and the Tsar alike. As the long-serving head of the opera, Eduard Nápravník (1839-1916), faded from the scene, Coates became the dominating force, the *de facto* musical director (protocol prevented the appointment of a foreigner) at a time Chaliapin dominated the stage.[27] He spent "four blissful working years" there – the Wagner years for which

[22] Gross, "Albert Coates," *Spotlight*, 17 October 1947, p. 54. In Mannheim where Bodanzky was first Kapellmeister he mostly conducted operetta and Weber: Ernst Leopold Stahl, *Das Mannheimer Nationaltheater* (Mannheim: Verlag J. Bensheimer, 1929), p. 262

[23] Buesst, "Albert Coates" *Music & Letters*, Vol. 35 (1954), pp. 137-8. Coates and Schuch would have been poles apart in their approach to Wagner. Felix Weingartner remembered how disappointed he was with Schuch's *Ring* which differed "from what I had heard under Richter, Levi, Seidl and Mottl. Everything was presented in a dainty, elegant, polished, man-of-the-world manner which was Schuch's own. There was nothing of the titanic primeval force which the music embodies.... The performance of *Siegfried* was technically perfect. Schuch had plenty of temperament and swing, but I felt in some way that they only affected externals. He would often glide quickly and brilliantly over passages of great depth." Weingartner, *Buffets and Rewards - A Musician's Reminiscences*, (trans.) Marguerite Wolff (London: Hutchinson & Co., 1937), pp. 151-2

[24] "What a nerve!" he wrote in his sketch for an autobiography: Box 9, *Albert Coates Papers*, Stellenbosch

[25] Hagemann, *Bühne und Welt* (Wiesbaden: Der Greif, 1948), p. 96. Coates had, in fact, conducted *Götterdämmerung* before, in Elberfeld on 14 April 1908, and to great acclaim: *Täglicher Anzeiger* (Elberfeld), 16 April 1908.

[26] sketch, *ibid.* The Dresden State Opera was unable to provide any information about Coates's activities in Dresden because everything was destroyed in the Second World War.

[27] Dukes, *Unending Quest*, pp.41-42. Dukes mentioned in a South African broadcast the private lunches

he was especially remembered[28] – until war came.[29] From 1907 the Mariinsky had offered subscriptions to the *Ring* in which different conductors directed different parts or whole cycles.[30] Coates made his mark in one of these, as its producer, Nikolai Bogolyubov, recalled:

The first subscription was conducted by Nápravník. This resembled a solemn, peaceful, soulful mass.... The second subscription was conducted by Coates.... While the music under Nápravník emitted the light from the altar of an invisible God, the same music sounded twice as fast under Coates, and reminded you of an orgy in honour of Bacchus. The orchestra literally burned, moaned, snarled, and submitted to the volcanic temperament of its conductor.[31]

The enthusiasm for Wagner grew to epidemic proportions, according to Nicolai Malko, who conducted at the Mariinsky from 1908 to 1918. "The new interest in German opera was probably due to the fact that the wife of the last emperor, Nicholas II, the Tsarina Alexandra, was German and had expressed a wish to hear more Wagner. ....about a quarter, if not more, of the two hundred operas presented during the year were by Wagner."[32] Coates ascribed the enthusiasm to the Tsar. In England in 1914 he let it be known that: "in St. Petersburg the Tsar never misses a performance of [*Tristan*], and frequently commands performances, always insisting that Mr. Coates shall conduct it."[33] Furthermore, he "invariably sits alone in his box."[34]

In 1911, the Mariinsky revived Wagner's early works, starting with the *Holländer* (presented as *The Homeless Sailor*). The opera only managed to remain in the repertoire for a single season, and was never performed again despite Coates's "brilliant work."[35] In 1914 he directed the first Russian performance of *Meistersinger*. The producer and designer had been sent to Germany to see how the opera was staged there, but their results do not appear to have met with success. The premiere on 20 March was received "with benevolence" by the audience and dismay by the critics.[36] Coates

the Tsar had with Coates to discuss musical matters. They were of surprising informality: "I have just shown His Imperial Majesty out of the room," the Tsar said to settle Coates; "you may now speak to Mr. Romanoff." typescript, 3 pp., 11 December 1953, *Albert Coates Papers*, Stellenbosch

28 Edwin Evans wrote in *Musical News and Herald* (27 May 1922, p. 658): "almost every Russian with whom I have spoken on the subject has told me that, in Petrograd musical circles... Coates [was] regarded as by no means a good Russian conductor, but an excellent Wagnerian."

29 sketch for an autobiography: Box 9, *Albert Coates Papers*, Stellenbosch

30 There were three cycles during 1909-10, for example, with four different conductors: *Rheingold* (Nicolai Malko), *Walküre* (Nápravník), *Siegfried* (Coates), and *Götterdämmerung* (Eduard Krushevsky): Rosamund Bartlett, *Wagner and Russia* (Cambridge University Press, 1995), p. 105.

31 Bärbel Hamacher (ed.), *Wagner in St. Petersburg* (Ausstellung der Bayreuther Festspiele und der Bayerischen Vereinsbank aus den Beständen des Staatlichen St. Petersburger Museums für die Kunst des Theaters und der Musik. 25. Juli bis 2. September 1993 im Neuen Rathaus, Bayreuth), pp. 32-33; partly quoted in Bartlett, *Wagner and Russia*, p. 105, citing Nikolai Bogolyubov, *Shest'desyat' let v opernom teatre* (Moscow, 1966), p. 157

32 Nicolai Malko, *A Certain Art* (New York: W. Morrow, 1966), pp. 123-124

33 *Star*, 12 February 1914, p. 4 ("Crescendo") Coates was correct. Tsar Nicholas II was known to have loved Wagner's operas, and was fond of singing Wolfram's *O du mein holder Abendstern* to his intimate circle: Dr. Alexander von Andreevsky, "Wagner-Rausch in Rußland," *Vossische Zeitung* (*Unterhaltungsblatt*), 9 February 1933.

34 "Celebrities at Home – Mr. Albert Coates in John Street, Adelphi," *World*, 5 May 1914, p. 5

35 Hamacher, *Wagner in St. Petersburg*, p. 34. The decor was created by Konstantin Korowin. Pavel Andrejew gave an "awesome performance" as the Dutchman.

36 I. Glebow (B. Assafjew) quoted in Hamacher, *ibid*, p. 36. Paul Dukes visited Coates at the Mariinsky

in later life acknowledged this production had ruffled traditionalists, though he was not sympathetic to them. "The great Russian scenic artists at one time created a *Meistersinger* that was quite unrecognisable." Décor was a means of rejuvenating an old opera, he believed, yet to break away from old traditions was inviting trouble.[37] Trouble indeed there was. Soon war broke out, German music was banned in Russia, and Coates never again conducted Wagner in St. Petersburg. He was a guest at Covent Garden in 1914 (before the outbreak of war), and although he remained in St. Petersburg for another four years or so, it almost destroyed him. After the Revolution, "Everything and everybody changed. A woeful experience. Ill and destitute." He got permission to leave temporarily, and fled across the seas. "England at last." [38]

Wagner in England

Central to our consideration of Coates as a Wagner conductor are the years he appeared at Covent Garden and elsewhere in London (1914-1938), and made his Wagner recordings (1921-1932). His performances in London were surprisingly few: *Parsifal* (18), *Tristan* (9), *Meistersinger* (8), *Tannhäuser* (6), *Rheingold* (3), *Walküre* (5), *Siegfried* (5), and *Götterdämmerung* (2).[39] He never conducted the *Holländer* or *Lohengrin.* The reasons he performed so little in England are matters outside the scope of this chapter. Suffice to say he was not free in England from the same lingering antipathy to "foreign" conductors that Wagner faced in 1855, and he never enjoyed a permanent appointment in an opera house. He did important concert work, especially with the London Symphony Orchestra, and was a strong advocate of Russian music. He dedicated much time to composing. He travelled more widely as a guest conductor than any other British conductor. He was, in fact, often not in England.

His later years in the United States (1939-1944) and South Africa (1946-1953) were bleak, if not barren, so far as Wagner opera was concerned, and the years in England in between held no promise.[40] The great possibilities with Coates were never realised. Many years before his departure to the United States he displayed unique insight into the power of film. "The future of the opera was with the film," he believed. "Imagine the possibilities! Opera on the stage had always been a compromise, on the

during this production and observed that he was "the only conductor who had a private room for his exclusive use. The other conductors, and there were several, when on duty used a cubby-hole just off the stage." He made no comment about the *Meistersinger* itself: *Unending Quest*, p. 44. This was the only "interesting" production of the season, according to Rosamund Bartlett, *Wagner and Russia*, p. 113.

[37] Coates, "Opera for South Africa," *The South African Music Teacher*, June 1947, p. 2. The producer was Nikolai Bogolyubov and the designer P. Lambin: Hamacher, *Wagner in St. Petersburg*, p. 36.

[38] sketch for an autobiography: Box 9, *Albert Coates Papers*, Stellenbosch. In Nicholas Pauw's thesis *Albert Coates* (Stellenbosch University, 1969), there is a facsimile of a list in Coates's hand of "operas conducted during the Tsarist regime 1910-1917 in the Imperial Opera House of St. Petersburg and during the Soviet regime both in St. Petersburg (Leningrad) and Moscow." (pp. 37-39) The 3-page list is undated, and concludes: "Dozens of other things which I simply can't remember." There is no Wagner on the list.

[39] information from the Royal Opera House Collections. Included are two performances each at His Majesty's Theatre and Streatham Hill Theatre, but not those he gave elsewhere in Britain.

[40] He conducted a number of performances of the *Walküre* in Capetown in 1948 with his wife Vera de Villiers (1891-1973) as Brünnhilde. Many of the singers had never sung in opera at all: *Cape Times*, 22, 26, 29 November 1948, p. 16 (on each date).

film it need not be. Why not Wagner on the film, with the great stars acting and seen and the great singers singing but unseen.... No one likes the *Rheingold* – no one understands it. But on the film!..."[41] Yet the films Coates was to became involved with were a far cry from this dream.[42] His concert engagements were minimal if not humiliating in these years.[43] Proposals for serious engagements did eventually come to him from Australia and England, but his health made acceptance of them impossible.[44] He died in Capetown on 11 December 1953.

Tannhäuser

To take Wagner's operas chronologically, so far as Coates conducted them, the earliest was *Tannhäuser* in English in 1920. Two characteristics were immediately evident. One was his "grip" on the orchestra, according to the *Times*: he "not only made the Venusberg music intensely vivid and vicious, but made us feel that even the platitudes of virtue, as Wagner has expressed them in the second act, mean something."[45] The other was his bright tempi. In fact, the chorus could not always keep up with the orchestra, "the rapid pace at which *Hail, bright abode* was taken eliminating all possibility of choral effect in the same way as it caused the contrapuntal accompaniment to be blurred," according to the *Morning Post*; "[Coates] did nothing to raise the performance from a somewhat uninspired level."[46] But he did try. The *Sunday Times* wrote that he "did well to encourage some of Monday's tired horses with the whip; if now and then he made them prance at a really indecorous speed – well, it was *Tannhäuser*, and better a *Tannhäuser* a hundred per cent too fast than a *Tannhäuser* ten per cent too slow."[47] The problem of over-worked, and under-rehearsed, orchestras often comes up in reviews of Coates's performances. The fact that "the last rehearsal is frequently the first as well" in England[48] was something he often lamented or deplored,[49] but it was a feature of musical life at the time which conductors and audiences had to live with.

[41] W.S. Meadmore, "Albert Coates discusses Russia," *Gramophone*, April 1934, p. 429. The vision was partly realized by Hans Jürgen Syberberg in his film of *Parsifal* (1982). Coates had been visiting the United States since 1920 for concert engagements.

[42] *Song of Russia* (1944, plays piano) and *Two Girls and a Sailor* (1944, conducts a *Concerto for Index Finger*)

[43] For example, he was engaged to conduct the Johannesburg Municipal Orchestra in conjunction with the S.A.B.C. Orchestra for a 26-week season in 1946, but on arrival found an under-sized group and a large measure of "incompetence, charlatanism, and ignorance." He became ill, and quickly moved to Capetown: Gross, "Albert Coates," *Spotlight*, 17 October 1947, p. 54; *Cape Argus*, 31 December 1946, p. 3.

[44] He was engaged to conduct concerts in Australia, and opera at Covent Garden, in 1950 (*Cape Times*, 1 October 1949, p. 16), and to appear in a televised BBC program "The Conductor Speaks" in 1953 with an orchestra of his choice, which was probably to be the London Symphony Orchestra (*Cape Times*, 16 January 1953, p. 9).

[45] 2 March 1920, p. 14 [46] 2 March 1920, p. 8 [47] 7 March 1920, p. 8 (Ernest Newman)

[48] Eva Mary Grew, "British Conductors III – Albert Coates," *British Musician and Musical News*, July 1929, p. 192

[49] Donald Brook, *Conductors' Gallery*, 2nd ed. (London: Rockliff, 1946), p. 42; *Die Brandwag*, 24 January 1947, p. 17. "Coates can whip up even a British orchestra to play like men possessed, and this leaves one wondering what he could do with more rehearsals in this country": Porte, "Albert Coates," *Gramophone*, December 1927, p. 269.

Tristan und Isolde

Tristan was Coates's favourite opera.[50] It was the first he conducted at Covent Garden in 1914, and the last Wagner opera he conducted there in his final season in 1938. He "immediately made his mark," according to the *Daily News and Leader*. "He has complete control of the orchestra and is an exceptionally sympathetic accompanist. His reading of the score is modelled, to a great extent, on that of Herr Nikisch, but is none the worse for that. The dominant factor of the whole was its youthfulness."[51] This same reviewer wrote again of the "ebullient youthfulness" of his reading. "It was perhaps the principal climaxes of the second act that showed Mr. Coates at his best, but the music of the third act was also very finely done."[52] In respect of climaxes, the *Observer* wrote of "an almost breathless climax [in the love duet] that appeared rather to take the singers by surprise, although they made a fine response."[53] The *Times* commented that his "*tempi* throughout the opera were like Richter's in being on the side of quickness, but he did not hurry or force the pace at all. The big climaxes as he took them were really exciting, but the level stretches, too, were always interesting because the details were attended to and were thoroughly alive."[54] The *Daily Telegraph* wrote how he showed "a sense of climax and 'grip.' This sense he shares with Nikisch, as also his delightful sympathy with the singers and his view of the humanness of the tale unfolded."[55] Coates showed again to the *Sunday Times* at a later performance that "consideration for the singers need not entail any loss either of sonority or colour, in the orchestration."[56] The *Westminster Gazette* wrote: "it is pleasant to be able to say at once that his success was undoubted. He may not be a Richter or a Nikisch... His reading was distinguished by smoothness and soundness rather than bigness or breadth. But on the whole he did exceedingly well."[57]

Coates went from Covent Garden to Paris to conduct the first performance in France of *Tristan* in German. The excursion is instructive in showing it was not only in England that Coates faced challenges in securing good performances. The venture was an Anglo-American production, with a cast drawn from disparate sources, and with a French orchestra.[58] It must have been hard work, and the results were mixed. *Le Monde Artiste* considered the production left something to be desired. Coates "did his best with an orchestra it appeared he did not know well."[59] The orchestra "lacked a little cohesion and unity," according to *Le Ménestrel*,[60] and appeared not to be well acquainted with the score. "Twice in the first act Mr. Coates had to snap his fingers to call the attention of some solo player who had completely missed a cue,"

[50] As reported by the *Star*, 12 February 1914, p. 4 ("Crescendo"), apparently based on publicity material, as there is similar wording in a report in the *World*, 21 April 1914, p. 665.

[51] 12 February 1914, p. 1 (Alfred Kalisch). Jacques Urlus sang Tristan, and Eva von der Osten sang Isolde.

[52] *World*, 17 February 1914, p. 265 (Alfred Kalisch)

[53] 15 February 1914, p. 6

[54] 20 February 1914, p. 8 (a review of the 3rd performance)

[55] 12 February 1914, p. 12

[56] 1 March 1914, p. 6

[57] *Westminster Gazette*, 12 February 1914. In the case of this press report, and others below without page numbers, they are from the Royal Opera House Collections where page numbers were not recorded.

[58] Peter Cornelius (Copenhagen) sang Tristan, Eva van der Osten (Dresden) Isolde, Johannes Fonss (Frankfurt) King Marke, etc., with the Boston Opera chorus, and the Orchestre du Théâtre de Champs Elysées. Coates conducted the first two performances, Nikisch the third. *Le Temps*, 20 May 1914, p. 5, and 12 June 1914, p. 5; Quaintance Eaton, *The Boston Opera Company* (New York: Appleton-Century, 1965), pp. 264-65

[59] 30 May 1914, p. 340

[60] 30 May 1914, p. 174

Fig. 9.1. Albert Coates, about 1922

Fig. 9.2. Coates and the London Symphony Orchestra, Columbia Studios, London SW1. Coates recorded for the Columbia Graphophone Company from 1919 to 1921, including the *Siegfried Idyll* on 11 March 1921

Fig. 9.3. Coates with the London Symphony Orchestra, Florence Austral and Frederick Collier, recording excerpts from *Götterdämmerung* for the Gramophone Company, Kingsway Hall, 75 Kingsway, London WC2, 18 October 1928

Fig. 9.4. Coates conducting the *Concerto for Index Finger* in the film *Two Girls and a Sailor* (1944)

Fig. 9.5. Coates in America

Fig. 9.6. Coates with José Iturbi in publicity for *Two Girls and a Sailor* (1944)

Musical Courier reported.[61] The reviews varied widely. *Comœdia* considered it a "triumphant evening" and in particular a "great personal success… for Albert Croates [*sic*]." His "particularly intelligent direction filled the musicians with wonder. The elegance and flexibility of his unobtrusive movements, the constant concern for the beautiful sound quality of the ensemble, the innumerable nuances subtly introduced, and the care he gave to hold back the overwhelming orchestra which so often drowns the singers in Wagnerian theatre, allowed us to enjoy to the fullest extent the tender and powerful work entrusted to his care."[62] *Le Monde Musicale* considered the production "ordinary enough." Coates "conducted the orchestra with care, with precision, sometimes a little softly. I would have preferred more force, more solemnity, at the entry of Tristan in the first act, a progression more marked in the Liebestod."[63] *Le Figaro* was quite negative. It considered under Coates's "indecisive" hand the orchestra "lacked precision, warmth and life. The tumultuous Wagnerian polyphony was too often blurred by hollow and confused tone."[64] *Le Temps* was unenthusiastic about the whole Wagnerian season.[65] "M. Coaty [*sic*] found the means to deprive *Tristan* of everything at one stroke: of movement, of grandeur, of force, of passion, of life, in fact everything which is contained in the music of Wagner, and which should be expressed by its interpretation."[66] *Öd' und leer das Meer!*

The Parisian example is salutary because it not only shows that reviewers heard or listened for different things in a performance, or that French orchestras may have been less skilled than English ones, but that Coates could only get imperfect results from a strange and under-rehearsed orchestra. With his peripatetic life, this became his lot. In St. Petersburg, the one place where he was permanently in authority, it had been difficult enough to discipline players "because of their overflowing temperamental gaiety."[67] Elsewhere, the conditions were hardly better, and certainly not conducive to high art. Coates's other performances of *Tristan* in England – in 1923, 1937, and 1938 – were all imperfect in some way, mainly because of inadequate means or hasty preparation or both. As in Paris, circumstances conspired against interpretation. Yet his sympathy for the work, and the vigour and energy of his execution, were always in evidence.[68]

61 10 June 1914, p. 42 (a review of the second performance, on 25 May)

62 22 May 1914, p. 1. "Warm ovations welcomed each of his returns to the podium, at the beginning of each act."

63 30 May 1914, p. 174 (G. C.)

64 22 May 1914, p. 4

65 It included the *Tristan* with Coates and Nikisch, and the *Meistersinger* and *Parsifal* by Weingartner.

66 *Le Temps*, 7 June 1914, p. 3 (Pierre Lalo). In fairness to the author, Coates is spelled correctly elsewhere in his article. He does not comment on Nikisch's performance, which the *Musical Courier* described as "almost ideal." Nikisch "in two rehearsals had brought the orchestra into a condition which they had not even remotely approached before, though it must not be forgotten, in justice to Albert Coates – himself a Nikisch pupil – that he had already laid the groundwork of preliminary rehearsals which enabled Nikisch to put his splendid finish on the orchestra in such a short time." Act three was apparently under-rehearsed: 1 July 1914, p. 10.

67 Grew, "Albert Coates," *British Musician and Musical News*, August 1929, p. 221

68 e.g., *The Times*, *Daily Telegraph*, and *Morning Post* of 26 June 1923; *Observer*, 16 October 1938, p.16 ("unhappy translation and an inexperienced orchestra"); *Daily Telegraph*, 13 October 1938, p. 14 (the "Corder version of the text" was used, and the "Junior London Philharmonic [had] not had time to absorb *Tristan* into its blood and marrow"); *The Times*, 2 December 1937, p. 12 (Coates "drove his team along with great energy, aiming at bold effects rather than at subtlety and finish – which was, in the circumstances, probably the wisest course."); *The Times*, 13 October 1938, p. 12 ("Coates drove his team with customary vigour, but the orchestra did not respond very well to his demands.")

Die Meistersinger von Nürnberg

This was the other work in his debut season at Covent Garden in 1914. "Mr. Albert Coates has very decidedly made his mark here, in spite of his English name," proclaimed the *Star*. His performance was "one of the very best in recent years":

> His reading of *Die Meistersinger* is vastly different from that which we had come to look on as the only one. One might say that whereas Dr. Richter used to look at it from the point of Hans Sachs, Mr. Coates sees more eye to eye with Walter – as a great many of the younger conductors not unnaturally do. That is a good point of view; in fact, the only one which would be really bad would be that of Beckmesser. Last night's performance was splendidly vigorous and impulsive, and yet well balanced. It had, moreover, a bracing atmosphere, in spite of an occasional tendency to over-sweetness.[69]

The *World* thought Coates had "won another great success":

> The whole performance was full of life and vigour, and if some might object that the romantic elements were perhaps accentuated at the expense of the rest, that was only a defect of the quality of the performance. At any rate it was a performance in which one could feel the presence of a strong personality from first to last. The ensembles all went smoothly, in the sense that the principal climaxes did not quite rise as high as they should have done. The same was the case with the quintet, which apparently had hardly greater intensity or volume at the close than at the beginning; though in every other respect it was extremely well done. We heard every note sung, which we rarely do."[70]

Not everyone was happy about the performance. To the *Westminster Gazette*, Coates's "reading of the music was rather humdrum."[71] The *Observer* considered he "conducted with ability, but, on the whole, the performance lacked distinction."[72] What is notable is how the performances improved as the season proceeded. After the third performance, the *Globe* wrote that Coates had gone "triumphantly from strength to strength. He remained sympathetic to the singers, but his respect for the score was shown in an added warmth of tone. His swinging rhythms were wonderfully alive, and he took the opera at a pace brisk enough to show, without the obscuring of any detail, that he realised the play Wagner has here given to the lighter side of his genius."[73] "Seasoned opera-goers unite in putting it down as one of the very best heard for a long time," wrote the *World*. "Mr. Albert Coates had got everything and everybody well in hand, and the smoothness of it was remarkable. There was a great improvement, as compared with the first performance, in the vitality of the ensembles, specially in the street brawl… There is little doubt that this last season marks a new epoch in Wagner performances."[74] By the fifth and final performance, even the *Observer* seemed to be impressed – almost: "The best moments in the production are to be attributed to Mr. Coates and his orchestra; the worst, to the moon and its invisible controllers."[75] Looking back over the season and the "truly magnificent" playing of the orchestra, the *Daily Telegraph* remarked on "the literally tremendous receptions accorded [Coates] on all occasions… receptions I have rarely seen equalled for warmth since the palmy days of Hans Richter."[76]

69 4 March 1914, p. 4 ("Crescendo")
70 24 February 1914, p. 305 (Alfred Kalisch)
71 23 February 1914
72 22 February 1914
73 4 March 1914
74 10 March 1914, p. 401 (Alfred Kalisch)
75 8 March 1914, p. 6
76 14 March 1914; the *Musical Times* of 1 April 1914, p. 227, reproduced excerpts from a further eight

Coates's next *Meistersinger* performances were with the British National Opera Company at Her Majesty's Theatre in 1924 and with the Metropolitan Opera Company[77] at Streatham Hill Theatre in 1933. He often included the *Meistersinger* overture in his concerts. On one occasion, there was an implied criticism from *The Times* that it "sounded like a quick march."[78] Yet that was exactly how Wagner wanted it, "a strong march tempo."[79]

The Ring of the Nibelungs

When Coates was given the *Ring* at Covent Garden in 1922, the first since 1914, it was a poisoned chalice. The orchestra was over-worked and under-rehearsed, according to Harold Rosenthal,[80] and the singers may not have been quite up to the task. "They have done their best," wrote the *Sunday Times*, "but they simply have not the vocal resources to do the thing adequately all round, and that is about all there is to be said about it."[81] In these circumstances, it was difficult for a conductor to leave his mark. The *Ring* in English had been pioneered in 1908. Now "in place of Hans Richter was Albert Coates, whose brain and vivid imagination and strong right hand were carrying on that wonderful Wagnerian tradition...."[82] The *Star* commented after the *Rhinegold* that Coates's "view of the work as a whole is lyric rather than epic. He makes each climax immensely effective, even impressive, but there is not quite the feeling of a homogeneous whole. Afterall, no one but Richter had the secret of that... ."[83] The *Star* also remarked on "thrilling" climaxes in the *Valkyrie*, even though Coates had "an inclination to hold back whenever an important motif comes to the front. The sensuous charm of the love music in the first act was beautifully brought out, and the outburst of fury at the end of the second act were magnificent. Sometimes – indeed often – Mr. Coates was very hard on the singers, particularly in the scene when Brünnhilde announces to Siegmund that he must die."[84] The *Morning Post* thought it a "fine performance," although Coates was "apt to sacrifice... spaciousness to emphasis and energy" and his attitude, it thought, apart from a thrilling Ride of the Valkyries, was generally "more orchestral than operatic."[85] In *Siegfried*, the opera most congenial to Coates's temperament, he had "lightness... at his fingertips"[86] and

reviews, not included above, but which fall within the parameters of the criticism quoted.

77 An English company formed to provide Wagner performances in English throughout Britain at affordable prices; the orchestra was 50 strong; the conductors were Robert Ainsworth, Aylmer Buesst, Albert Coates, and Charles Webber: *The Times*, 15 August 1933, p. 8, and 19 August 1933, p. 6.

78 *The Times*, 11 February 1930, p. 12.

79 Krienitz, Willy, "Felix Mottls Tagebuchaufzeichnungen," *Neue Wagner-Forschungen*, I, (1943), p. 196

80 Harold Rosenthal, *Opera at Covent Garden: A Short History* (London: Victor Gollancz Ltd, 1967), p. 105

81 4 June 1922, p. 8 (Ernest Newman, written after the first three operas of the second cycle, except for "an act or two"; he missed the first cycle; Coates only conducted the *Rhinegold* in the second cycle; the *Valkyrie* was conducted by Percy Pitt, *Siegfried* by Julius Harrison, and the *Twilight of the Gods* by Eugene Goossens; Newman described the last as nothing more than "a pedestrian plod with a few scattered moments of energy and ecstasy": 11 June 1922, p. 5). *The Times*, by contrast, concluded after the first cycle that the company had proved "that the most stupendous thing in all opera is not beyond their powers of interpretation": 23 May 1922, p. 12.

82 *Daily Telegraph*, 16 May 1922

83 16 May 1922, p. 3 ("Crescendo"). The *Morning Post*, by contrast, wrote that Coates's reading *was* homogeneous: 16 May 1922, p. 10

84 17 May 1922, p. 3 ("Crescendo")

85 *Morning Post*, 17 May 1922, p. 10

86 *Daily Telegraph*, 19 May 1922

was "splendidly rhythmic" in the forging songs,[87] though he was criticised for a rather too strident fortissimo in the brass.[88] The *Star* commented that there had been "some uncommonly brilliant playing and some thrilling climaxes, but Mr. Coates is still inclined to make the whole a little too restless – that, however, is a defect of his many fine qualities."[89] In the *Twilight of the Gods*, the orchestra was "the mainspring of the whole performance," in the words of the *Daily Chronicle*,[90] though this may have been another way of saying it was unduly prominent, as the *Star* thought.[91] "The accompaniment had none of the elfin lightness which the music longs for," wrote the *Morning Post*. "Mr. Coates's interpretation of the score had patches of eloquence and brilliance, but it was not as big as the music."[92] As for impressive moments, "the best orchestral playing" was in the Waltraute scene,[93] there was a "magnificent climax" in Siegfried's Funeral Music,[94] and he "led his forces through to a triumphant ending."[95] As the Rhine at the end overflowed its banks, so too did the orchestra flood Covent Garden. "Coates, magnificent in every other way, sometimes forgot that he had not the hidden orchestra prescribed by Wagner, and swamped the singers," wrote Percy Scholes in the *Observer*. "Is he just a little inclined to give us a brass *Ring*?"[96]

When the company repeated the *Ring* in 1923, there were fewer criticisms of singers being overwhelmed, but that may have been because the orchestra was not of full size.[97] The notable characteristics were Coates's feeling of climax, his vitality, and his rhythmic impulse and energy.[98] He returned for a single *Walküre* in 1929 and was greeted with "prolonged applause," reported the *Daily Telegraph*, as "a musician in whom the Wagner tradition is personified."[99] There was "splendid vitality in his reading," wrote the *Star*. "He revels in gorgeous orchestral colour and his climaxes are irresistible. ... he had a great ovation."[100] He revealed to *The Times* a different side from the conductor of the concert hall. "There he is usually an orchestral Jehu. Here in the theatre he drove well within the Wagnerian limits of speed and intensity, securing thereby a very beautifully lyrical first act, and striking a happy balance between orchestra and voices."[101] Two performances of *Siegfried* in 1935 met with varied reviews. To the *Daily Telegraph* he gave "a full sense of the size and massiveness of the music,"[102] yet to the *Manchester Guardian*, "he handled the score piece-meal," had "no large musical grasp," and his interpretation "did not tell of a deep and forceful

[87] *The Times*, 19 May 1922, p. 12

[88] *Morning Post*, 19 May 1922, p. 8

[89] *Star*, 19 May 1922, p. 3 ("Crescendo")

[90] *Daily Chronicle*, 23 May 1922

[91] 23 May 1922, p. 11 ("Crescendo")

[92] *Morning Post*, 23 May 1922, p. 10

[93] *Star*, 23 May 1922, p. 11 ("Crescendo") ("Miss Edna Thornton sang beautifully")

[94] *Sunday Times*, 28 May 1922, p. 7 ("Miss Beatrice Miranda sang Brünnhilde's catastrophic music superbly.")

[95] *The Times*, 23 May 1922, p. 12

[96] 28 May 1922, p. 10. By the end of *Siegfried*, Scholes remarked that "throughout the work we have heard the words quite unusually clearly": *ibid*, 21 May 1922, p. 10.

[97] *The Times*, 29 May 1923, p. 12. Arthur Hammond remembered a performance of the *Ring* with the British National Opera Company (he says in 1925): "The whole Company was as if transformed... all were inspired to give such performances as I have not heard surpassed in any other *Ring* cycle, even in Bayreuth": *Opera*, Vol. 5 No. 3 (March 1954), p. 160

[98] *Daily Telegraph*, 17, 18, 23, 29 May 1923; "... except for an occasional excess in the battering of the drums, the blaring of brass, and the forcing of *tempi*": *The Times*, 23 May 1923, p. 8

[99] 22 May 1929

[100] *Star*, 22 May 1929

[101] *The Times*, 22 May 1929, p. 14. "Jehu... driveth furiously": 2 Kings 9:20

[102] 25 September 1935

conception."[103] The work was "safe enough" in his hands, according to the *Sunday Times*;[104] the *Morning Post* considered he had "secured a clear rendering of the score,"[105] and to the *Observer* his direction was "a little slapdash, but full of spirit and supported by sound experience."[106] *The Times* came closest to discerning Coates's strength in *Siegfried* after a concert of excerpts in 1930: by his "temperamental congeniality [he] feels the fundamental impulse of Siegfried (and like Siegfried brushes on one side small details such as coarseness of tone)."[107]

Parsifal

1914 was the year of *Parsifal* in many opera houses, and Covent Garden was no exception. After Arthur Bodanzky had conducted the first fourteen performances, Coates conducted three.[108] The results were outstanding. "The mantel of Levi has fallen on Mr. Coates," declared the *Daily Telegraph*, for he adopted "precisely the same tempi of his illustrious predecessor of a generation ago."[109] His reading was "extremely picturesque and full-blooded."[110] His Grail scene was "one of intense solemnity,"[111] he began the second act with a "swinging tempo,"[112] although to the *Star* the Flowermaidens' scene and the Good Friday scene were made to hurry a little:

> The whole performance was full of power and energy. Mr. Coates emphasised and brought out all that there is of human passion in the music. The scene in Klingsor's Garden was very vividly played, there was much tenderness in the Flowery Mead scene, and the spirituality of the music was finely brought out. Mr. Coates manages ensembles with great skill, and the two Grail scenes were excellent in this regard. They were in all respects finely done, except that now and then the music was made to sound what, for want of a better word, we must call secular.[113]

There was a certain nervousness or restlessness detected in the first performance. The difference between the two was "enormous," according to the *World*.

> One could not help noticing one curious fact. We all know that Mr. Coates is the pupil of Nikisch, and in their nervous energy and their passion for beauty of tone they are closely akin; but there is one big difference between them – whereas the latter instinctively broadens out when a great climax comes, the former, almost subconsciously it seems, forces the pace. It may be a question of age, for it must not be forgotten that Mr. Coates is still almost an infant prodigy among conductors. In respect of hurrying, however, except in the Flower Maidens' Chorus, there was hardly any cause for adverse criticism on Saturday, and the intensity and elevation of the whole performance were most impressive.[114]

[103] 25 September 1935

[104] September 1935, p. 5 (Ernest Newman)

[105] 25 September 1935, p. 6 (S. G.)

[106] 9 September 1935, p. 16 (A. H. Fox Strangways)

[107] *The Times*, 11 February 1930, p. 12

[108] Egon Pollak conducted a further two. Coates had conducted excerpts at a Wagner commemorative concert in Elberfeld on 11 February 1908 when the text of *Parsifal* was read by Ernst von Possart.

[109] 16 May 1914

[110] *Daily News and Leader*, 24 April 1914, p. 2 (Alfred Kalisch). Of the second performance, the same reviewer wrote: "It is picturesque and vigorous and inspired by a love for beauty of tone beyond everything": *ibid*, 4 May 1914.

[111] *The Times*, 24 April 1914, p. 7

[112] *ibid*, 4 May 1914, p. 12

[113] 24 April 1914, p. 4

[114] *World*, 5 May 1914, p. 753 (Alfred Kalisch) (after the second performance on 2 May 1914). The *Star* was in agreement, although it thought the Flowermaidens' scene might have been taken more slowly: 4 May 1914, p. 4.

Coates returned to Covent Garden in 1919 to conduct *Parsifal* in English. Unfortunately the company "had been rehearsing practically up to the last moment, and was tired out before the curtain rose," so it could not, the *Daily News* concluded, be regarded as a "fair test" of what they could make of *Parsifal*.[115] Nevertheless, the *Sunday Times* considered "the orchestral playing approached – in spirit and in actual fact – very near the Wagnerian ideal. Mr. Coates's reading lacked nothing in dignity, balance, beauty or authority."[116] There were six performances, and by the time it returned in 1920, there had been a great improvement. With experience had come wisdom, according to the *Daily Telegraph*; "rarely, rarely has such exquisite orchestral playing been heard, even at Covent Garden."[117] It was "a thoroughly beautiful performance" to the *Daily Mail*, "the orchestra grandly throbbing and yearning in their pool of beautiful tone."[118] There was a "sense of dignity and solemnity, and... poetic atmosphere," and "majesty and mystery" in the Grail scenes, and "serenity" in the Good Friday scene that had been less conspicuous in 1919.[119] The atmosphere "was wonderfully right all through," wrote the *Star*. "If I was asked to say what was best, I should find it difficult to answer, but perhaps I should say it was the introduction to Act III and the beginning of the first Grail Scene, where the climax was thrilling. The whole Grail Scene was immensely impressive...."[120] It was a "masterly reading of the score," according to the *Sunday Times*.[121] The *Globe* declared that "no praise of Nikisch's illustrious pupil could verge on excess," noting his "delicate and subtle effects" and even some "rather slow" tempi.[122] The *Daily Mirror* considered it a "great performance, full of distinction and promise.... I doubt if Bayreuth... has had many better performances."[123] "There were moments when it reached an intensity which was altogether unusual," wrote the *Times*; "it compared very favourably with that seen at Bayreuth in 1914, a week before the outbreak of the war. Much of it was better sung, and the whole conception of the drama was more spontaneous and living."[124] Coates conducted two more performances of *Parsifal* with the British National Opera Company in 1922, and one in 1924. He was never invited to conduct at Bayreuth.

The Wagner recordings

Coates was a pioneer of Wagner recording. But pioneers, however intrepid, determined and well-intentioned they may be, will not always discover fertile ground or uncover seams of gold. The equipment available for his earliest expeditions in the studio was primitive: the acoustic method of recording; limited space and reduced orchestras; a few minutes only per disc; no singers for some selections; and peculiar orchestral arrangements for some endings. Coates was prolific as a recording artist. His range in Wagner was extraordinary, from a spectacularly dashing overture to *Die Feen* to the most thrillingly demonic *Faust Overture*, with vast slabs of the major works in between. In many cases his efforts have never been bettered. We will not examine *all*

[115] *Daily News*, 18 November 1919, p. 7 (Alfred Kalisch)
[116] 23 November 1919, p. 8 (H. B. Dickin)
[117] 25 February 1920, p. 11
[118] 25 February 1920
[119] *Daily News*, 25 February 1920, p. 2 (Alfred Kalisch)
[120] 25 February 1920, p. 3 ("Crescendo")
[121] 29 February 1920, p. 8 (no author cited, but Ernest Newman's arrival is announced)
[122] 25 February 1920
[123] 25 February 1920
[124] 25 February 1920, p. 19. Karl Muck conducted the performance referred to, on 23 July 1914.

his recordings but only the major selections, generally in their order of appearance. We will look too at how they were received, and how some of them sound today.

The most important of the early sets were the *Ring of the Nibelungs* and the *Mastersingers of Nuremberg* (1922-23), both sung in English. The impact these made at the time was immense. To *Gramophone* the first parts of the *Ring* represented "the high-water mark of recording achievement. I must have played them through already a dozen times and I think, after the various experiments with needles and soundboxes, that I can call them really flawless."[125] Today, they are mere shadows of what Coates succeeded in re-recording with the electrical process. They nevertheless bear some hallmarks of his strong style with the orchestra. In the *Rhinegold* the journey to Nibelheim is a storm of a descent, with growling orchestra, and banging anvils. Wotan makes a thunderous entry in act two of the *Valkyrie* as Brünnhilde flees, and Siegmund's defiance of death is a triumphant act of will, sweeping away any vestige of Brünnhilde's duty to let him die. The orchestra pumps away at the bellows in the forging song in *Siegfried*, and the ending, as Brünnhilde hails the radiant sun, is so ecstatic that the singers' words are even less comprehensible than usual. At the end of *Twilight of the Gods*, someone's voice can be heard singing Hagen's *Back from the Ring!*, and it may just have been Coates himself. There was no funeral music.

The *Mastersingers* was a very judicious selection from the opera, "an excellent example of… telescoping… where we get the gist of almost every scene on a very moderate number of records, wrote *Gramophone*."[126] So much of a Wagner opera – 28 sides – had never appeared before on record. The editor of *Gramophone* "played the records completely through four times, and a great many of them nine or ten times, with different instruments, needles, and soundboxes," and proclaimed them "the greatest operatic triumph that any recording company has hitherto achieved."[127] There was one qualification, however: "I could distinguish at most three complete phrases and about a dozen isolated words." So too is the listener's experience today. Nevertheless, there is again evidence of the vigorous conductor at work, in act one for example, in the playful spirit and orchestral flourishes in the meeting of Walther and Eva, and the steadfast melody flowing beneath the gathering of the Mastersingers for their roll call. In the Walther-Eva scene in act two, the orchestra is marvellous in the way it creates panic before their threatened flight, and how suddenly it subsides with tenderness as they stay. The end of the act was mercilessly compressed: no sooner has Beckmesser's song begun than a riot ensues, the Night Watchman arrives, and the act ends, yet throughout Coates maintains a steady beat and drive. The longest orchestral passage is in act three, accompanying Beckmesser's discovery of Sachs's note of Walther's song. It is vivid in its depiction of his eyes passing over the scraps of song, and of his shifting moods. In act three, there is real swing and joyousness in the dance

[125] April 1923, p. 18 ("Z" reviewing the *Rhinegold* and *Valkyrie* excerpts); *Siegfried* was reviewed in August 1923 (p. 57) when the reviewer was "thrilled by the clank of the anvil,… and by the superb confidence of Coates' conducting."

[126] September 1926, p. 136 (Peter Latham). Coates wrote an introduction to the notes accompanying the original 14 double-sided record set assuming "full responsibility for such arrangement and cutting of passages as was found necessary": *Gramophone*, December 1923, advertisements p. xviii. There was no Prelude in the 14-record set. Coates recorded it earlier (D 590). *Gramophone* referred to 15 double-sided records in its review of January 1924 (p. 156) but did not list the catalogue numbers.

[127] January 1924, p. 156.

of the apprentices on the meadow, and Walther's prize song, orchestrally, is a triumph: we cannot hear what Walther is singing but there is no doubt he is winning the singing competition. As *Gramophone* wrote: "the music of *The Mastersingers* is so lovely that one really does not mind about the words."

Coates's first set of *Parsifal* recordings, made in the earliest days of the new electrical process in 1925, were still fairly primitive. A true picture of the orchestral sound did not become apparent. *Gramophone* wrote: "The flutiness of the violins in their top register, the reediness of the string ensemble, and the queer acrid quality of the woodwind impart to much of the score a colouring that is not Wagner's and fill Klingsor's magic garden with a sulphurous, infernal light little likely to assist the schemes of the magician."[128] Others were more favourably impressed.[129] There remains cause for jubilation. Although all the words cannot be heard, the orchestra imparts full-blooded drama where necessary, especially when Gurnemanz reprimands Parsifal for killing the swan. When he leads him to the Grail Kingdom (the Transformation scene), the spirit of the music is optimistic. There is turmoil in Amfortas's Lament, but he is not weighed down by massive suffering: he is very much alive. The Grail scene is a deeply invigorating ritual, gradually becoming a celebration, an act of worship. Unfortunately, Klingsor's Magic Garden is an orchestral arrangement (Kundry is a trumpet, Parsifal a cello), as is the Good Friday Scene. To add to these excerpts, Coates recorded the Parsifal-Kundry scene in much better sound, and in German, in 1927-28. It is, whatever may have been thought by some at the time,[130] one of Coates's greatest recordings, a masterly display of sympathy for the singers and mirror of their moods. He caresses as Kundry tempts. When she is torn, he reflects her inner turmoil and horror; when she recollects, he reflects her tranquillity. At times her voice is like a cork in a boiling cauldron of orchestral sound. Coates *shows* us what we cannot hear in her words *nur schreien, wüten, toben, rasten* ("crying, raving, storming, raging"[131]): she is in a terrible, tortured, predicament. The scene is intensely dramatic, and unfortunately – unresolved. The Gramophone Company could not assemble everyone for the final two sides necessary to complete the act. Unfinished though it is, its greatness is not diminished.

Coates's *Tristan und Isolde* comes in five groups of recordings. The first two were acoustic sessions which have left little trace. Of these, in the act one excerpts from 1923, Coates made his small forces work hard. It is not possible to understand the words, but one feels the wind blast. The Love Duet from 1924 has more music in it than the superior recording from 1929, and in a way is even more fervent, but it is barely possible to hear what is being sung. Florence Austral, who sang Isolde as well as Brangäne, also twice recorded the Liebestod with Coates, but the recordings were

[128] September 1926, p. 135. An earlier review did not mention the conducting: *ibid*, November 1925, p. 289

[129] *The Times*, 10 November 1925, p. 12 (described the Grail scene as "one of enthralling beauty... of a tonal splendour unparalleled in the annals of recording"; *Sound Wave*, December 1925, pp. 908-909 ("Arpeggio"- a "momentous recording... a remarkable achievement")

[130] *Gramophone* regarded the recording of this scene "a failure," a "waste of time and energy.... On the stage, and notably at Bayreuth, it is an ineffable delight": October 1929, p. 203 (Herman Klein). *Disques* considered that the orchestral accompaniment, "a marvel of pure beauty and continuity of invention, [it was] superbly played by the London Symphony under Coates": March 1930, p. 24.

[131] Andrew Porter's translation in the English National Opera's and The Royal Opera's *Parsifal: Opera Guide 34* (London: John Calder, 1986), p. 114

never published.[132] The third recording, the Prelude, came in 1926 with the advent of the electrical process, and was recorded on two sides. Whether or not the performance was accelerated to achieve this end is unclear, but it has its own musical logic, and does not sound too fast. It is not conceived as an expansive concert performance, but eagerly looks forwards to the drama that follows. It is a performance of great passion, the orchestra growling at points, ravenous in its longing. The last few bars of deep strings are a masterpiece – "exquisite," *Gramophone* called them[133] – with their strong premonition of dire consequences. The fourth group of recordings made in 1927 was of parts of act three, which Coates made with other conductors.[134] It opens with the Prelude. Nikisch once played Coates a few bars from this on the piano and told him, "you are listening to the ocean singing its deep, everlasting song-story to a man wounded unto death but with hope ever rising in his heart. You must treat it as such."[135] Conducted by Coates, it is slow and deeply affecting, evoking a Tristan whose very vigour is a source of his wretchedness. The shepherd's piping is missing, as is most of Tristan's delirium. The orchestra, particularly the cellos, is decidedly dark and gloomy with Tristan, whereas with Kurwenal all is buoyant and hopeful; in Tristan's vision of Isolde the orchestra sings with ecstasy. The final *Tristan* recording was the famous Frida Leider-Lauritz Melchior Love Duet recorded in two cities with two orchestras in 1929, yet undisturbed in its intensity. It starts with a storm as Isolde extinguishes the torch – "use a soft needle," the *Musical Times* warned[136] – and hurtles to its final rapture, aided if anything by the cuts, as there is no warning from Brangäne for the lovers to heed. There are moments of sublime tranquillity from the orchestra. At others, Coates makes it swing and rock, always at one with the lovers, never overwhelming them. Indeed, some reviewers believed the orchestra was "far too much in the background"[137] and "too modest and subdued."[138] *Gramophone* wrote that it had a "final climax that makes you long for more."[139] But no more was there to be. The recording has often been re-issued, and its place is history now seems assured.[140]

[132] 29 July 1925 (Cc 6423, 2 takes) and 18 October 1928 (Cc 1375, four takes)

[133] August 1926, p. 121 (which continued: "The reading is strong, and just a little bit hurried, I feel. It may be this was to keep the music 'in the air,' but we want the sound to exhale rather than be extracted.") A later review stated: "how impressive is the massive weight of 'cellos and basses in that *pianissimo* passage right at the end!": *ibid*, January 1927, p. 325 (Peter Latham)

[134] Leo Blech and Lawrance Collingwood. *Gramophone* wished for all-German singers, and only remarked of the conductors that they deserved "the warmest praise": May 1928, pp. 503-4 (Herman Klein).

[135] Coates, "Afternoon in Nikisch's Luxury Flat in Leipzig," manuscript in Coates's hand, 4 pages, no date, Box 5, *Albert Coates Papers*, Stellenbosch

[136] April 1930, p. 204

[137] *Phonograph Monthly Review*, November 1930, p. 62 (R.H.S. Phillips) reviewing Victor 7273-74

[138] *Disques*, May 1930, p. 98, reviewing HMV D 1723-24

[139] December 1929, p. 312 (Herman Klein). There was no comment on the conducting; "the singing of the protagonists [was] magnificent."

[140] At the time, the records were soon eclipsed by more sizable but milder excerpts conducted by Karl Elmendorf at Bayreuth in 1928. Columbia falsely advertised these as "complete": *Gramophone*, December 1928, advertisements p. xviii, and January 1929, advertisements p. xiv. Frida Leider made no mention of her recording (or of Coates) in her memoirs: *Playing my part*, (trans.) Charles Osborne (London: Calder and Boyars, 1966); nor did Melchior's biographer, except in the discography: Shirlee Emmons, *Tristanissimo* (New York: Shirmer Books, 1990). A modern reviewer commented that "if one had not heard of Albert Coates, one could easily mistake his recordings for Toscanini": *Fanfare*, July/August 2003, p. 253 (Patrick Meanor).

The Gramophone Company's recording of extensive excerpts from the *Ring des Nibelungen* between 1927 and 1929 was the most ambitious undertaking in the history of recorded opera. It involved several conductors and orchestras in England, Germany and Austria, and came out in bits and pieces, some repeated, and none in sequential order. The first was the *Valkyrie*, conducted by Coates, Blech and Collingwood, which appeared in 1927. *Gramophone* immediately recognised that the earlier acoustic recordings were now "barely adequate." Moreover, "the contrast between Albert Coates's overwhelming fast *tempi* and those of Dr. Leo Blech is not as great as I had expected. Coates is not so appallingly energetic as he used to be and the records made under his baton are very fine."[141] To another reviewer, Coates was apt occasionally to go too fast: "words get lost, and the music loses much of its dignity." The best parts were considered to be those conducted by Blech: "as an Englishman, I hate to admit it, but the truth must be told. Blech may not be a finer conductor than Coates, but he has a thoroughly rehearsed orchestra (one that does not suffer from English conditions) and some of the finest singers in Europe. He scores immensely too because he refuses to be hurried."[142] Next came the *Götterdämmerung* selections, in 1929. They were "superlative," pronounced the *Phonograph Monthly Review*, "new heights, both in conducting and in recording, are reached."[143] *Gramophone* preferred the German orchestra and conductors to Coates, but only for their "sonority and slow, gradual approach to the climaxes."[144] The two orchestral passages *Siegfried's Rhine Journey* and *Siegfried's Funeral Music* were conducted by Karl Muck. Coates's own 1926 recordings of these were justly famous.[145] Lastly, in 1930 Coates's *Siegfried* selections were issued in Germany. (Another set of selections from *Siegfried* had been issued in England in 1929, with some of Coates's excerpts from *Rheingold*.) The new records were hailed by *Gramophone* as "the finest album of operatic records ever put before the public... The London Symphony Orchestra gives us some good playing, and Coates, whose readings of serener things are often marred by his ebullient Siegfriedish zest, is thoroughly at home, especially in the exultant finish to the first act."[146] The records were welcomed elsewhere. The *Phonograph Monthly Review* considered them an "overwhelming triumph" for their technical achievement, for the singing ("Melchior is the ideal Siegfried"), and for Coates: "my admiration for his Wagnerian readings continually increases.... The forging scene gives him an opportunity he is not slow in taking, and the music with the flames is whipped to white and thrilling heat. The other high spot is in the great scene where Siegfried breaks Wotan's spear and dashes up the fire-mountain."[147]

141 December 1927, p. 274 ("B.")

142 *Gramophone*, February 1928, p. 372 (Peter Latham)

143 August 1929, p. 390 (R.H.S.P[hillips].)

144 April 1929, p. 480 (Herman Klein)

145 In his survey of Wagner recordings in 1926, Peter Latham wrote: "If I were allowed only two Wagner records I fancy it would be these that I should choose": *Gramophone*, October 1926, p. 181; they were "properly famous when they first were issued": *Disques*, November 1931, p. 399; the *Rhine Journey* had been "a miracle six or seven years ago and made many a doubtful listener's hair stand on end": *Musical Record*, June 1933, pp. 27-28.

146 April 1930, p. 496 (H.L. Walters). Herman Klein agreed: "the acme of perfection appears to have been attained": *ibid*, May 1930, p. 548-549.

147 December 1930, p. 95 (R.H.S. Phillips) (a review of Victor set M-83, a 10-record set of *Siegfried* which included other excerpts issued earlier by HMV)

Fig. 9.7. Coates in America

There are moments when those witnessing historic events do not, and perhaps cannot, fully acknowledge the significance of what, in this case, they are listening to. None of those who first reviewed Coates's *Ring* recordings, except the last, approached a full realisation of the power of his conducting: the way he was able to make his orchestra comment on and reinforce the drama, and in orchestral passages *become* the drama, with an energy and conviction that remains unparalleled today. In the descent into Nibelheim in *Rheingold*, for example, the orchestra seems to vaporise, to *become* the sulphurous vapours rising and swirling as Wotan and Loge climb into the cleft. In *Walküre*, the orchestra is restrained, constantly lending Siegmund and Sieglinde support, punctuating their exclamations, never overwhelming them. Coates propels the drama forward until, as if he were saying to his orchestra "Now you can let go. This is *ours!*",[148] there is a controlled frenzy at the end which is wholly in keeping with the moment. In *Siegfried*, when the hero plunges the molten sword into a pail of water, the orchestra seems to transform itself into a cauldron, to *become* the steam hissing from the pail, until the steel cools. During Waltraute's narrative in *Götterdämmerung*, as she seeks to persuade Brünnhilde to return the ring to the Rhine, the sense of urgency in her mission is compelling, and so is her desperate, imploring call to Brünnhilde to end the agony of the gods. In the 1922 *Ring*, we will recall, this scene was described as one of Coates's best moments. So it is here. At no point should it be dragged, Wagner said.[149] Coates is absolutely in the spirit of Wagner. When Brünnhilde tells her to go back to the gods, to tell them she will never give up the ring, never give up love, and Valhalla can fall in ruins, Coates leaves us in no doubt about the catastrophic,

[148] as he used to say in a Wagner rehearsal: Bernard Shore, *The Orchestra Speaks* (London: Longmans, Green & Co., 1938), p. 81

[149] see Wagner chapter, p. 29

tragic consequences. These are supreme sound pictures. What is portrayed in the great scheme of the *Ring* may only be fragments, but like pieces of ancient sculpture, they can be unrivalled in their eloquence and effect.

What might have been

When Coates died in South Africa in 1953, there was a sense in England of lost opportunities.[150] It was certainly true. Coates's work was unfinished, his legacy fragmentary. In a way he was too big, too explosive, for ever-conservative England. "Many people think him to be too prone to stray from the traditions fixed by Richter," wrote a *Gramophone* reviewer in 1927 when Coates was near the height of his powers. "This may be because he was a pupil of Nikisch, who often differed from Richter's readings. Many gramophonists with whom I have discussed the matter express a preference for Bruno Walter's Wagnerian records, rating Coates as too unrestrained... it can at least be said that his readings are always full of interest and fire, even if not strictly authentic."[151] Already Tradition was raising its deadening hand. It is ironic that Coates's very vigour, enthusiasm and energy (his *perspiration* during a performance[152]) may have been a factor in turning the English against him. "Comparing him with, for example, the dignified Weingartner, the elegant Landon Ronald, or the unruffled Boult, people began to think that his methods were too theatrical to be true...."[153]

If there was no place for him in England, maybe it would have been different in continental Europe. There were reports that he had been offered the directorship of the Vienna Opera around the time Weingartner left (1911). The authorities in St. Petersburg, however, quickly made his situation too attractive for him to leave.[154] Maybe his English nationality would, in any case, have been a factor against any permanent position in Europe, as Harold Rosenthal suggested.[155] Maybe the cosmopolitan conductor never wanted it. Maybe his heart's desire was to conduct Russian music, and to compose. Whatever the case, the absence of a long-standing position in an opera house with an orchestra and singers he could cultivate over a long period must be one reason Coates's full potential as a Wagner conductor was never realised. For what he *has* left us, we must forever be grateful.

[150] e.g., "we allowed Coates to be shamefully under-employed": Robert Elkin, "Albert Coates – Some Reflections," *Musical Opinion*, March 1954, p. 349; "Coates, as he once was, would have made an excellent head at Covent Garden": *Music and Letters*, Vol. 35 (1954), p. 139 (Aylmer Buesst); "it is to England's lasting shame that men of far less value, and imported mediocrities, should have been chosen for a position which was rightfully his": *The Times*, 17 December 1953, p. 8 (letter from Mrs. Rose Morley)

[151] Porte, "Albert Coates," *Gramophone*, December 1927, pp. 271-72; cf. a later listener to Coates's Wagner recordings: "...quite possibly the greatest Wagner conductor of all time": Stephen M. Stroff, "Albert Coates," *Le Grand Baton*, No. 45, vol. 17 no. 1 (March 1980), p. 3; *Classic Wax*, No. 5 (November 1981), p. 6

[152] Coates's perspiration in performance was well known: Sir Henry Wood, *My Life of Music* (London: Victor Gollancz, 1938), p. 264.

[153] Elkin, "Albert Coates," *Musical Opinion*, March 1954, p. 347

[154] e.g., *Cape Times*, 12 December 1953, p. 8, and an unsourced newspaper article dated 5 July 1946 in the Clippings files – *Cape Times* and *Cape Argus* – Music and Biographies, South African National Library, Capetown

[155] Rosenthal, *Opera at Covent Garden: A Short History*, p. 99

Part V

Vienna Lights

10

Gustav Mahler – Fanatical idealist

That Mahler suffered agony in his music-making, and experienced ecstasy on those occasions he reached perfection, were inescapable facts to anyone who was engaged in his musical enterprise – orchestral players, singers, theatrical staff, and audiences. He pursued his goals tirelessly, intensely, and with an abiding faith in the possibilities of perfection. As a conductor he was "extremely analytical and exacting," in Richard Strauss's words. He pulled music apart in a search for clarity and perfection, celebrating his art "with great fanaticism," earning the enmity of his musicians as he went and casting a shadow over his great merit.[1] He had "blazing, indeed fanatical artistic zeal," wrote Bruno Walter, and displayed "incomparably passionate concentration while rehearsing and conducting."[2] Yet after a performance he would often come away in a mood of dissatisfaction, even self-loathing. He was "profoundly unhappy and depressed" after one of his *Ring* cycles in Vienna when he realized that the theatre – "that pigsty" – "excludes all perfection by its very nature."[3] In this, he was a man after Wagner's own heart. After Bach and Beethoven, Wagner was his hero.[4] His revolutionary *Tristan* in Vienna was justly famous. His performances in New York astounded, and confused, the critics. He discovered things in Wagner's scores that people had not heard before, including some things others would have preferred remain in the shadows. His path through Wagner's music was, as we shall see, one of agony and ecstasy.

Wagner in Mahler's life

He was born in Kaliště, a town in what is now the Czech Republic, on 7 July 1860. As a boy, he learned more about music from street bands, the local church, and the small opera theatre in Iglau than he did at home. The first Wagner music

1 diary entry quoted in Franz Grasberger, "Gustav Mahler und Richard Strauss," *Österreichische Musikzeitschrift*, 21 (1966), p. 283, in Henry-Louis de La Grange, *Gustav Mahler, Vol. 3, Vienna : triumph and disillusion (1904-1907)* (Oxford University Press, 1999), p. 391

2 Bruno Walter in *Der Merker* (March 1912), quoted in Norman Lebrecht, *Mahler Remembered* (London: Faber & Faber, 1987), p. 81

3 Natalie Bauer-Lechner, *Recollections of Gustav Mahler,* Dika Newlin (trans.), Peter Franklin (ed.) (Cambridge University Press, 1980), p. 100

4 J. B. Foerster, *Der Pilger* (Prague: Artia, 1955), quoted in Lebrecht, *Mahler Remembered*, p. 75

he is known to have heard is the *Festmarsch*, in Iglau 1873.[5] His earliest exposure to Wagner himself is a matter of some conjecture. Wagner was in Vienna shortly before Mahler enrolled at the Conservatory in September 1875, conducted three concerts of his own works from March to May 1875, and returned to supervise productions of *Tannhäuser* in November-December and *Lohengrin* in January 1876 conducted by Richter. Wagner himself conducted a performance on 2 March 1876. There appears to be no documentary evidence that Mahler attended any of these, though according to Ossip Gabrilowitsch, he *did* attend one of Wagner's concerts, and the effect of the music on him was "overpowering." He had no interest in "the personal element" – in Wagner the man, or the conductor – and left the hall promptly the music was over.[6]

He was at Vienna University (1877-80) when he joined the local Wagner Society,[7] and by 1880 was a member of a vegetarian group formed under the influence of Wagner's ideas. He was the only member of that group *not* to travel to Bayreuth in 1882 to hear the premiere of *Parsifal*.[8] He was in Olmütz (Olomouc) conducting when Wagner died in 1883. According to one of the singers at the local theatre, he was beside himself with grief. "I saw a man running demented, weeping loudly, through the streets. With some difficulty I recognized Mahler. ... 'The worst has happened. The master has died!' ... It was impossible to talk to Mahler for days afterwards. He came to rehearsals and performances, but remained inaccessible to everyone for a long time."[9] A few months later he went to Bayreuth for *Parsifal*: "It would be hard to describe what is going on in me," he wrote to a friend afterwards. "When I walked out of the Festspielhaus, incapable of uttering a word, I knew I had come to understand all that is greatest and most painful and that I would bear it within me, inviolate, for the rest of my life."[10] Whatever might be the full import of this enigmatic statement, for both Mahler the man and the composer, he was now on his way to becoming a total Wagnerian conductor.

[5] La Grange, *Mahler, Vol. 1* (London: Gollancz, 1974), p. 26. (Note: the revised Vol. 1 foreshadowed in the introduction to Vol. 4 (2008) was not available at the time of writing.)

[6] Clara Clemens, *My husband, Gabrilowitsch* (New York: Harper & Bros., 1938), p. 129, quoting from Gabrilowitsch's diary. Donald Mitchell assumes he must have been at some of these events: *Gustav Mahler: The Early Years*, (rev. & ed.) Paul Banks and David Matthews (London: Faber and Faber, 1980), pp. 52, 292. The *Kaisermarsch* and excerpts from *Götterdämmerung* and *Siegfried* were included in the concerts.

[7] founded in 1872 by Felix Mottl who left the Vienna Conservatory the year Mahler joined: La Grange, *Mahler, Vol. 1*, p. 33

[8] La Grange, *Mahler, Vol. 1*, p. 87. Mahler was at the Bayreuth Festival on five occasions: 1883 *Parsifal* (Levi and Fischer); 1889, *Parsifal* (Levi), *Tristan* (Mottl), *Meistersinger* (Richter); 1891, *Parsifal* (Levi), *Tannhäuser* (Mottl); 1894 *Parsifal* (Levi), *Tannhäuser* (Strauss), *Lohengrin* (Mottl); and 1896 *Ring* (Siegfried Wagner): Eduard Reeser, "Gustav Mahler and Cosima Wagner," in Herta Blaukopf (ed.), *Mahler's Unknown Letters* (London: Victor Gollancz, 1986), pp. 200-203. His reactions are largely unrecorded.

[9] letter from Jacques Manheit to the baritone Ludwig Karpath cited in Karpath's "Aus Gustav Mahlers Umfängen," *Wiener Journal*, 5 February 1930, in Lebrecht, *Mahler Remembered*, p. 31. According to La Grange, there is no known letter from Mahler mentioning Wagner's death: *Mahler, Vol. 1*, p. 92.

[10] letter to Friedrich Löhr, [22?] July 1883, in Knud Martner, (ed.) *Selected Letters of Gustav Mahler*, (trans.) Eithne Wilkins, Ernst Kaiser, and Bill Hopkins (London & Boston: Faber & Faber, 1979), p. 73. In 1883 *Parsifal* was conducted by Hermann Levi on 8, 10, 12, 16, 18, 22, 24, 28 and 30 July, and by Franz Fischer on 14, 20 and 26 July. Information provided by the Richard-Wagner-Museum, Bayreuth.

Early conducting

Poverty and practicality drove Mahler to seek his earliest conducting engagements. After a few weeks of operetta in Bad Hall near Linz in the summer of 1880, with a tiny orchestra, he conducted opera with similar forces at Laibach (Ljubljana) for the 1881/82 season. There was no Wagner. Nor was there any in 1883 in Olmütz: "I could not bear to massacre *Lohengrin*," he wrote to a friend.[11] Here his characteristic earnestness as a conductor was observed by Karl Muck: "He attempted to give first-class performances with an orchestra of thirty musicians, and naturally failed, to his eternal sorrow, because of the feeble means at his command. Because of this he put more strain on his nerves than anyone else would have done in his position. However, I do not remember his ever falling ill. He was indeed very thin, but he had a strong constitution and amazing energy."[12]

After a short season of Italian opera at the Carl-Theatre in Vienna in 1883, he went to Kassel. The most significant event there was the visit of Hans von Bülow and his Meiningen Orchestra in January 1884. Their concerts (which did not include any Wagner)[13] had a profound effect on the young conductor. "I beheld the fulfilment of my utmost intimations and hopes of beauty," he wrote to Bülow afterwards, begging to be taken on in any capacity; "let me become your *pupil*, even if I had to pay my tuition fees with my blood."[14] Bülow never took him on. In later years Bülow came to admire his conducting greatly, and indeed, recommended him as his successor.[15]

In late 1884, Mahler cast around for more substantive conducting duties. He was successful in securing posts in Prague and in Leipzig. Prague came first, and there the director, Angelo Neumann, and the senior conductor, Anton Seidl, were immediately struck by the young man's musicianship during a rehearsal for *Lohengrin*. They allowed him to conduct a performance of Cherubini's *Les Deux Journées*, and his energetic movements reminded them of Bülow.[16] He was assigned the serious operas he had sought. These included, during the single season he was in Prague, *Tannhäuser*, the *Meistersinger* (4 performances, uncut), *Rheingold* (5), *Walküre* (5), and the Transformation music and Grail Scene from act one of *Parsifal* on the third anniversary of Wagner's death.[17] Although he was feeling his way with these (Seidl left a month after Mahler's arrival), and received some negative press comments, he was clearly enjoying the work. He tried to get out of his obligations to Leipzig, but was unsuccessful.

[11] La Grange, *Mahler, Vol. 1*, p. 91

[12] *idem* (source not given)

[13] They were devoted to works of Beethoven (24 January) and Spohr, Brahms, and Weber (25 January): "Ein Blick zurück (1030) - Hans von Bülows Kasseler Konzerte," *Hessisch-Niedersächsische Allgemeine*, 21 January 1984

[14] letter in Kurt Blaukopf (ed.), *Mahler: a documentary study*, (trans.) Paul Baker (London: Thames & Hudson, 1976), p. 170.

[15] Donald Mitchell, *Gustav Mahler: the Wunderhorn Years: chronicles and commentaries* (London: Faber and Faber, 1975), p. 278

[16] Angelo Neumann, "Mahler in Prague," in *Gustav Mahler. Ein Bild seiner Persönlichkeit in Widmungen*, ed. Paul Stefan (Munich: R. Piper & Co., 1910), pp. 7-8, in Blaukopf, *Mahler: a documentary study*, p. 173. Mahler had said of Seidl's conducting during the *Lohengrin* rehearsal: "Good God, I should never have thought it possible to rehearse like that; it's wonderful!"

[17] La Grange, *Mahler, Vol. 1*, pp. 136-140. He performed the *Parsifal* excerpts on 13 and 21 February 1886, and later in Leipzig on 30 November 1887, and never again: La Grange, *Gustav Mahler, Vol. 4, A New Life Cut Short (1907-1911)* (Oxford University Press, 2008), p. 1611.

He debuted in Leipzig with *Lohengrin* on 3 August 1886, where his senior was Arthur Nikisch. One might have imagined that two such gifted young musicians in the same theatre might have liked and encouraged one another. The reality, however, was very different. Although Mahler admired Nikisch, he did not think he was in the same class as Bülow. "When I watch a performance by [Nikisch]," Mahler wrote to his sister, "I am as confident as if I were conducting it myself. He cannot penetrate the profound or the sublime, but how rarely can I myself express them! ... I have no personal contact with Nikisch. He is cold and distant to me – I don't know whether from pride or suspicion. Enough said! We pass each other in silence...."[18] Their repertoires were similar – Mahler conducted *Rienzi*, *Holländer*, *Tannhäuser*, *Rheingold*, *Walküre*, and *Siegfried* in his two years in Leipzig – yet their interpretations were obviously as different as their personalities. Mahler's individualistic approach to Wagner, including excessively rapid or lively tempi,[19] was inevitably viewed with reservation, even suspicion, by those who sought comfort in tradition. Cosima Wagner heard Mahler conduct *Tannhäuser* on 13 November 1887 and recalled in a letter to Hermann Levi: "the performance was worse than I would now have thought possible."[20] She never invited Mahler to conduct at Bayreuth.[21] On the other hand, Richard Strauss heard him conduct a performance of *Siegfried* in October 1887, and wrote to Bülow that he seemed "a highly intelligent musician and conductor; one of the few modern conductors who knows about tempo modification and he expressed splendid ideas generally, particularly about Wagner's tempi (opposed to the present accepted Wagner conductors)."[22] Inevitably, Mahler was soon complaining of being "a pale moon circling round the star of Nikisch."[23] When Nikisch was offered a whole *Ring* contrary to an earlier understanding, Mahler offered his resignation. In 1888 he took up the directorship of the Royal Hungarian Opera.

A Hungarian national opera

Mahler came into his own in Budapest. His artistic ambitions had free rein. He had complete control over artistic resources, and set out to present Wagner in Hungarian in a truly Hungarian national opera. He first presented *Rheingold* and *Walküre*, both of which benefited from extensive, and intensive, rehearsal. When *Rheingold* opened on 26 January 1889, auspiciously smoke, then flames, rose from the prompter's box. Fire-fighters were called, the blaze was extinguished, and the performance resumed. The result was a triumph. The reviews, the first to give a clear indication of his conducting, foreshadowed those of later years. One critic considered his orchestra "unsurpassable"

[18] letter written in October 1886 quoted in La Grange, *Mahler, Vol. 1*, p. 154

[19] La Grange, *Mahler, Vol. 1*, p. 150, citing press criticism of *Lohengrin*, *Rienzi* and *Tannhäuser*

[20] letter dated 19 June 1889 quoted in Reeser, "Gustav Mahler and Cosima Wagner," in Blaukopf, *Mahler's Unknown Letters*, p. 199

[21] There may be a non-musical reason Mahler was never invited to Bayreuth. Felix Mottl, who was a close associate of Cosima's in organising early Bayreuth Festivals, wrote to her on 9 July 1887: "Everyone tells me that he's very talented, but unfortunately he is Jewish!": letter quoted in Oliver Hilmes, *Cosima Wagner: The Lady of Bayreuth*, trans. Stewart Spencer (New Haven and London: Yale University Press, 2010), p. 167.

[22] letter dated 29 October 1887: Willi Schuh and Franz Trenner (eds.), *Hans von Bülow and Richard Strauss: correspondence*, (trans.) Anthony Gishford (London: Boosey & Hawkins, 1955), p. 61

[23] letter written in October 1886 in Blaukopf, *Mahler: a documentary study*, p. 177

with its "discreet accompaniment, its varied shadings, its dynamics excellently achieved in each instrumental group."[24] In the *Walküre* the same critic described how Mahler "saw to it that each phrase, each melodic line, each accent, had its meaning so that the words, music, and action all contributed to the dramatic effect." For once the brass was tamed. The conductor drew from the orchestra "sometimes powerful tutti that even at their height were never painful to the ear – sometimes eloquent, delicate murmurs, and sometimes electrifying crescendos. The clarity and precision of the rhythms had been unsurpassable, as had been the discretion of the accompaniments, thanks to which the singers had no difficulty in making themselves heard."[25] Buoyed by the success of these two productions, Mahler planned new ones of *Siegfried* and *Götterdämmerung*, but they never came to pass. The public began to react against too much German opera – the length of an uncut *Lohengrin* in September 1889, the first in Budapest, added to the malaise – and singers began to rebel against his harsh demands in the name of artistic excellence. Indeed, it was his "artistic fanaticism [that] brought him particularly violent opposition in Hungary."[26] The Hungarian Opera broke his contract in March 1891, and Mahler announced he was going to Hamburg.

Hamburg and London

Mahler's six years in Hamburg (1891-1897) constituted his heaviest load of Wagnerian opera. He conducted 220 performances: *Tannhäuser* (66), *Walküre* (33), *Meistersinger* (32), *Siegfried* (30), *Tristan* (19), *Götterdämmerung* (16), *Lohengrin* (8), *Holländer* (7), *Rheingold* (6), and *Rienzi* (3) – excluding those of his London season.[27] Added to these was a sprinkling of Wagnerian pieces in his concerts.[28] What stands out is the popularity of *Tannhäuser*, the opera with which he debuted in Hamburg without rehearsal and to great acclaim.[29] Tchaikovsky wrote from Hamburg in January 1892: "the conductor here isn't just some middling character: he's a positive *genius*... I heard him conduct *the most astounding* performance of *Tannhäuser*."[30] His *Siegfried* soon impressed Bülow, the conductor dearest to his musical heart: "Hamburg now has a new first-class opera conductor, Gustav Mahler (a serious, energetic Jew from Budapest), who, in my opinion, equals the greatest (Mottl, Richter, etc. ...). Recently I heard *Siegfried* conducted by him... and felt deep admiration for the way in which –

24 review of the dress rehearsal quoted in La Grange, *Mahler, Vol. 1*, p. 192

25 review quoted in La Grange, *Mahler, Vol. 1*, p. 193. His Wagnerian performances in his first season were *Rheingold* (9), *Walküre* (9), *Holländer* and *Lohengrin*.

26 La Grange, *Mahler, Vol. 1*, p. 226

27 Bernd Schabbing, *Gustav Mahler als Konzert- und Operndirigent in Hamburg* (Berlin: Verlag Ernst Kuhn, 2002), pp. 189-90. Details for London are given on the next page.

28 *Meistersinger* Prelude (2), *Siegfried Idyll* (2), *Faust Overture* (1), *Tristan* Prelude (1), *Kaisermarsch* (1), and *Tannhäuser* Overture (1): Schabbing, *ibid*, p. 75. La Grange does not include the last two pieces in his listing: *Mahler, Vol. 4*, pp. 1610-1613

29 "... a performance so perfect down to the smallest detail... a second Bülow...": *Hamburgisches Fremdenblatt*, 31 March 1891 (Carl Armbrust), quoted in La Grange, *Mahler, Vol. 1*, pp. 231-232. "How clearly, rhythmically defined, carefully nuanced and phrased everything seemed...": *Hamburgischer Correspondent*, 1 April 1891 (written after both *Tannhäuser* and *Siegfried*), in Blaukopf, *Mahler: a documentary study*, p. 192

30 Alexandra Orlova, *Tchaikovsky: a self-portrait*, (trans.) R.M. Davison (Oxford and New York: Oxford University Press, 1990), p. 390

without a single orchestral rehearsal! – he forced those rascals to dance to his tune."[31] Bülow's estimation was a help to Mahler's career in Hamburg. It was also a sign of their like approaches to music-making.

Mahler visited London for six weeks in 1892 mainly to conduct a number of Wagner operas: *Siegfried* (4), *Tristan* (4), *Rheingold* (2), *Walküre* (2), *Götterdämmerung* (2), and *Tannhäuser* (2).[32] Though the English-German orchestra was criticised at times for its roughness, a quality Mahler himself decried,[33] his performances were warmly praised. The English press had yet fully to warm to Wagner, however, and its reviews throw surprisingly little light on Mahler's interpretations.[34] After the opening performance of *Siegfried*, for example, the *Daily Chronicle* confessed: "the future of German opera is still problematical in this country."[35] The public, on the other hand, was learning from Mahler how powerful a great performance could be. The *Sportsman* reported after *Siegfried*: "Ladies who were divided between the desire to stay and the feeling that it was getting so late that they really must go, put on their cloaks to leave and then lingered about the doorways unable to tear themselves away from the charm of the enthralling music."[36] Mahler had his share of stage management horrors during the tour, including "a wretched cat which meandered about the castle grounds" in the last act of a *Tristan*,[37] and a failed scene-change during the Funeral music in *Götterdämmerung*, which caused him temporarily to leave the pit.[38] It was from a second and final *Götterdämmerung* that Bernard Shaw "fled in disorder" before Siegfried had died because, for him, "the limit of human endurance" had been reached.[39] Ever since 1877 Richter had been doing much in the concert hall to soften up the English public for its Wagnerian enlightenment. [40] Mahler's visit was a step along that path.

[31] letter to his daughter Daniela dated 24 April 1891, quoted in La Grange, *Mahler, Vol. 1*, p. 232

[32] Andrew Nicholson, "Mahler in London," in Donald Mitchell and Andrew Nicholson (eds.), *The Mahler companion* (Oxford University Press, 1999), p. 540. Mahler also conducted *Fidelio*.

[33] Mahler wrote to Alma (in English): "I found the circumstances of orchestra here bader than I thought and the cast better than hoped": quoted in Mosco Carner, "Gustav Mahler's Visit to London," *Musical Times*, May 1936, p. 408, and in Blaukopf, *Mahler: a documentary study*, p. 194.

[34] As noted by La Grange, *Mahler, Vol. 1*, p. 256. I have read some twenty newspapers and journals on Mahler's visit; there is nothing in them to compare with American reviews of 1908/11 from which we will read below. Andrew Nicholson (see note 32 above) presents a fair representation of the critical comment based on some eight journals. The reviews quoted here merely supplement his extensive account of Mahler's London visit.

[35] 9 June 1892, p. 5; it added there was no doubt Mahler was "a most capable Wagnerian conductor." Further illustrations of the attitude of the press, to Wagner more than Mahler, are evident in reviews of *Rheingold*: the *Pall Mall Gazette* complained that "the second act was rendered unutterably dull by the tameness of the singers and the slowness of the tempi" (23 June 1892, p. 2); after the second performance, which "failed to draw a very large audience," the *Musical Standard* commented: "the drama is very dull and often terribly tedious" (2 July 1892, p. 5). In contrast to the *Daily Chronicle*, the *Sportsman* noted after "a magnificent performance" of *Tristan*, that "German Opera is the only form of entertainment that can fill houses of the size of Covent Garden and Drury Lane": 16 June 1892, p. 4.

[36] 9 June 1892, p. 4, which wrote of Mahler's "masterly guidance" of the orchestra.

[37] *Daily News*, 16 June 1892, p. 5

[38] *Daily News*, 14 July 1892, p. 3; *Sunday Times*, 17 July 1892, p. 6. Mahler complained he had had "the most incredible difficulties" with *Götterdämmerung*: La Grange, *Mahler, Vol. 1*, p. 258

[39] *World*, 27 July 1892, in *Shaw's Music*, vol 2, (ed.) Dan H. Laurence (New York: Dodd, Mead, 1981), p. 680. The *Musical Standard* reported that "staunch Wagnerites were cruelly 'exercised' by the omission of the Norns scene": 23 July 1892, p. 61.

[40] J.S. Shedlock paid tribute to Richter after Mahler's "brilliant success" with *Siegfried*: *Academy*, 11 June

Glory in Vienna: 1897-1907

When Mahler arrived in Vienna in 1897, it was as if Siegfried were breaking Wotan's sword on the path to his glorious ascent. Richter had been the Wagner conductor *par excellence* for 20 years, and soon he would give way to a new hero. "Mahler burst over the Vienna Opera like an elemental catastrophe," recalled one of its orchestral players.[41] He was "young and energetic," as Egon Wellesz recalled, and "he changed everything. He was the sworn enemy of operatic routine. He dismissed singers and players who were either too old, or not up to his standard, and surrounded himself with a group of young singers, fanatically devoted to his ideas. They shared his aim of perfection and admired the man who carried them from success to success."[42] At the heart of these successes were complete series of all Wagner's operas (except *Parsifal*), revolutionary new productions with Alfred Roller of *Tristan* (1903), *Rheingold* (1905) and *Walküre* (1907), and Wagner operas without a single cut. Mahler himself conducted some 145 Wagner performances.[43] His debut with *Lohengrin* on 11 May 1897 after only one rehearsal attracted universal praise,[44] indeed was so successful that Karl Krauss shrewdly wrote: "intrigues are afoot against him already."[45] He conducted *Holländer* soon afterwards, and thereby completed his conquest of Vienna and was confirmed as permanent director of the Opera.[46]

It was probably his conducting of *Tristan* and its new production with Roller that were the pinnacle of his achievements in Vienna. Bruno Walter wrote after one performance of *Tristan*: "To hear this work conducted by Mahler is more than one can bear. I always have the feeling I might die in the middle of *Tristan* if I were to listen intently every second, and I sometimes wonder if that isn't what one *should* do."[47] With Roller he was able to achieve the total-work-of-art, where stage and music were at one. The *Tristan* production had "a mere suggestion of scenery, ... compensated for by

1892, p. 375. We may recall Richter's great difficulties in mounting complete Wagner operas in England: after his *Tristan* in 1884 it was a full 19 years before he would return to the theatre to conduct a Wagner opera. The *Monthly Musical Record* believed that Mahler's *Ring* had "taken a deeper hold than when performed at Her Majesty's Theatre ten years ago [under Seidl]": 1 July 1892, p. 184.

41 Franz Schmidt, "Autobiographical Sketch," quoted in Lebrecht, *Mahler Remembered*, p. 108

42 Egon Wellesz, "Reminiscences of Mahler," *The Score*, No. 28, January 1961, p. 52

43 *Tristan* (37) 1897-1907, *Rheingold* (20) 1897-1905, *Lohengrin* (19) 1897-1900, *Walküre* (16) 1897-1907, *Siegfried* (12) 1897-1901, *Holländer* (11) 1897-1900, *Götterdämmerung* (10) 1897-1901, *Meistersinger* (10) 1898-1901, *Tannhäuser* (8) 1897-1902, *Rienzi* (2) 1901: Franz Willnauer, *Gustav Mahler und die Wiener Oper* (Wien-München: Jugend und Volk, 1979), pp. 273-276. Mahler "conducted 649 performances [at the Vienna Opera], 62 of which he had rehearsed and prepared himself": La Grange, *Mahler, Vol. 3*, p. 739

44 La Grange, *Gustav Mahler, Vol. 2, Vienna: the years of challenge (1897-1904)* (London: Gollancz, & Oxford: Oxford University Press, 1995), pp.26-30. Some of the reviewers' comments are below.

45 *Breslauer Zeitung*, 16 May 1897, in Blaukopf, *Mahler: a documentary study*, p. 211

46 Heinrich Kralik, *The Vienna Opera House*, trans. Michael H. Law (Vienna: Brüder Rosenbaum, 1955), p. 41. It should be noted that Richter was not, and had never sought to be, director of the Vienna Opera, for he eschewed administrative work. When Mahler announced in 1900 that he wanted to take over all Wagner conducting, Richter left. Mahler did not, however, carry through with his intention: he engaged Bruno Walter and Franz Schalk as his assistants and assigned them most of the Wagner performances: Marcel Prawy in Sigrid Wiesmann (ed.), *Gustav Mahler in Vienna*, (trans.) Anne Shelley (London: Thames and Hudson, 1977), p. 83.

47 letter following the performance of 19 September 1901, quoted in La Grange, *Mahler, Vol. 2*, p. 379, together with another letter to his parents dated 29 September 1901: "It was an unattainable ideal, grandeur worthy of antiquity and quintessential simplicity (*Einfachheit im Wesen*)."

an intoxication of colour and light... everyone wrote about Roller's *Lichtmalerei* and Mahler's *Lichtmusik*...."[48] It marked a wholly new approach to opera. According to Henry-Louis de La Grange, "Mahler himself was aware that in *Tristan* he had realized his life's dream, a production as physically beautiful as it was rich in meaning and expression."[49] To maintain such heights in a constant stream of opera performances was, of course, impossible, as Mahler acknowledged. "I have become convinced that the idea of a permanent opera company directly contradicts modern principles of art," he said in an interview in 1906. "A modern opera director, even if he is a genius like Wagner, could never cope with such numbers if he wants to do justice to today's concept of artistic perfection."[50] And in 1907 he said: "of course I wanted to see all my performances on the same high level, that is, to attain an ideal which is simply unattainable."[51] Realizing the impossibility, he relinquished his post and turned his mind to composing, and to guest conducting.

Sunset in America: 1908-1911

Mahler debuted at the Metropolitan Opera on New Year's Day 1908 with an acclaimed performance of *Tristan*. While his musical interpretations won widespread support, the matter of cuts ate away at his popularity. After his second *Tristan*, the *Evening Mail* queried whether he would "gain the support of the American audience" if he attempted to cut the score as he did in that performance. "The audiences who attend Wagnerian productions know what they want and understand when they do not get it."[52] Mahler of course considered cuts "wholly unjustified" on artistic grounds, and in a German theatre an "utterly unforgivable mutilation of Wagner's works," but he felt compelled by conditions in New York to make them.[53] He was, in short, in an impossible situation. The arrival of Toscanini in November 1908 and his first excursion into Wagnerian opera with *Götterdämmerung* in December also diminished Mahler's unique standing in the German repertoire.[54] In all, Mahler conducted 21 Wagner performances with the Metropolitan Opera, *Tristan* (11), *Walküre* (5), and *Siegfried* (5)[55] before turning to conduct orchestral concerts, which occasionally included and sometimes wholly comprised Wagner excerpts.[56] His last Wagner opera was a glorious

48 Marcel Prawy in Wiesmann, *Gustav Mahler in Vienna*, p. 86

49 La Grange, *Mahler, Vol. 2*, p. 585. Mahler assigned Schalk to Roller's new production of *Lohengrin* (1904, Act 1, 1906, Acts 2 and 3). It was after Mahler's departure that Roller completed his other Wagnerian productions: *Siegfried* (1908), *Götterdämmerung* (1909), *Holländer* (1912), *Parsifal* (1914), etc.: La Grange, *Mahler, Vol. 3*, p. 951

50 *Musikalisches Wochenblatt*, August 1906, in Lebrecht, *Mahler Remembered*, p. 208

51 *Neues Wiener Tagblatt*, 5 June 1907, in Blaukopf, *Mahler: a documentary study*, p. 248

52 *Evening Mail*, 10 January 1908, p. 4

53 letter to Leo Slezak [undated, summer 1908] in Blaukopf, *Mahler's Unknown Letters*, p. 184

54 The Wagner operas Toscanini conducted while Mahler was in America were *Götterdämmerung* (6), *Tristan* (11), and *Meistersinger* (9). Mahler's standing with *Musical America* was not affected by Toscanini's first *Götterdämmerung*: "With Mahler fresh in memory, it did not seem a great performance." (19 December 1908, p. 3).

55 This includes performances on tour. Figures from the Metropolitan Opera Archives database: archives.metoperafamily.org/archives/frame.htm.

56 *Meistersinger* Prelude (19), *Tristan* Prelude and Liebestod (16), *Siegfried Idyll* (15), *Holländer* Overture (10), *Tannhäuser* Overture (8), *Lohengrin* Prelude (8), *Faust Overture* (7), *Götterdämmerung* Siegfried's Funeral Music (4), *Parsifal* Prelude (3) and Good Friday Music (2), *Rienzi* Overture (2), *Kaisermarsch* (2), *Tannhäuser*

Tristan on 12 March 1909. He said after it: "The stars were kind. I have never known a performance of *Tristan* to equal this."[57] He gave his last concerts in February 1911. He included the Act 3 Prelude and *Wahn* monologue from *Meistersinger*,[58] Hans Sachs's meditation on the madness and magic of the world. Weak and ill, he returned to Vienna, and died on 18 May 1911.

Mahler on Wagner

Mahler never wrote anything about Wagner. What he understood about him has to be gleaned from the way he performed his music. He did, however, make occasional comments to correspondents and colleagues, often ironic asides, sometimes contradictory, sometimes profound. Bruno Walter had many talks with him about Wagner as they worked together in Hamburg and Vienna. He was in no doubt "[Mahler] was a convinced Wagnerian, and remained one to his death." He vividly remembered Mahler's *Ring* and *Meistersinger* in Hamburg, and his *Tristan* in Vienna "both in its total effect and in many details," and how his *Lohengrin* "penetrated to the soul of the music, and directly to its dramatic essence."[59] Mahler once said to Walter during a discussion of Wagner's versatility as musician, poet and dramatist: "All being said, he remains to me most lovable as a musician."[60]

Mahler explained how he achieved a constant freshness in his performances: "I conduct for that young man in the balcony who has never heard *Lohengrin* and who must go home with an impression which will last all his life."[61] Natalie Bauer-Lechner recalls Mahler in 1893: "Whenever my spirits are low, I have only to think of Wagner and my mood improves. How amazing that a light like this ever penetrated the world! What a firebrand! What a revolutionary and a reformer of art such as had never existed before."[62] He wrote to her when he was working on a production of *Meistersinger* in Vienna in 1899: "I tell you, what a work this is! If German art were to disappear completely, one could reconstruct it from the *Meistersinger*. Everything else seems empty and superfluous by comparison."[63] Yet this was a work he soon dropped altogether from his repertoire.

Overture and Bacchanale (2), *Walküre*, Ride of the Valkyries and Magic Fire Music (2), *Siegfried*, Forest Murmurs (1): La Grange, *Mahler, Vol. 4*, pp. 1610-13, where dates, and several vocal excerpts, are also given.

57 Alma Mahler, *Gustav Mahler - Memories and Letters*, (ed.) Donald Mitchell, 3rd (ed.), (trans.) Basil Creighton (London: John Murray, 1973), p. 131. La Grange, *Mahler, Vol. 4*, p. 329. Tristan was sung by Carl Burrian, and Isolde by Olive Fremstad.

58 Sachs was sung by David Bispham at concerts on 7, 10 and 12 February 1911, and by Pasquale Amato on 13 January 1911, the only occasions Mahler programmed this piece. His last concert, on 21 February, was devoted to Italian music. Toscanini was present: La Grange, *Mahler, Vol. 4*, pp. 1179, 1611

59 Bruno Walter, *Gustav Mahler* (trans.) Lotte Walter Lindt (London: Quartet Books, 1990), pp. 23-24, 68

60 Bruno Walter, *Of music and music-making* (trans.) Paul Hamburger (London: Faber and Faber, 1961), p. 69. See also Mahler's comments to the young Bodanzky on Wagner in the Bodanzky chapter below.

61 comment to Josef Reitler, *Gustav Mahler*, p. 62, quoted in La Grange, *Mahler, Vol. 3*, p. 374

62 Bauer-Lechner, *Recollections*, p. 38. He described Wahnfried to Anna von Mildenburg, who was in Bayreuth to study Kundry, as once "the abode of one of the most glorious spirits in the history of mankind": letter of February 1897, Martner (ed.), *Selected Letters*, p. 210. Mahler had given Mildenburg as a Christmas present in 1895 a complete set of Wagner's literary works. They became lovers. La Grange, *Mahler, Vol. 1*, pp. 338, 340.

63 letter (no date) quoted in La Grange, *Mahler, Vol. 2*, p. 195

Devoted as he was to Wagner's works, it did not stop him fiddling with his scores. This may have produced some brilliant effects, but it brought him controversy and opposition. He once described the *Meistersinger* as "badly orchestrated" when his friend, the composer J.B. Foerster, wanted to study its polyphony and instrumentation.[64] According to Fritz Stiedry, who worked as a singing coach for Mahler in Vienna, *Meistersinger* was one of those works which "never quite suited him. He stylized, doctored, and distorted them. They seemed to be in disguise...."[65] Whether or not this was a comment on his interpretation, Mahler did leave a revised edition of the *Meistersinger* Prelude in Universal Edition Archive, Vienna.[66] His revisions to *Tannhäuser* caused much grief to Hans Richter who described them as "simply nonsense." Mahler was "either unaware of the characteristics of the instrumentation... or has not thought about them." Richter gave a detailed (and persuasive) example, and concluded: "Mahler's influence would be much more valuable if he would only drop his delusion of being able *to improve the great masters*, including Wagner, whose skill as an orchestrator was acknowledged by the most hidebound newspaper hacks...."[67] In the Prelude to *Tristan*, he added more double basses to enhance the overall effect.[68] He may have added "an extra piccolo or two to whistle in the masts" in the *Holländer* Overture to heighten its tempestuousness.[69] Richter also complained to Mahler of his use of the original score of the *Holländer* whose instrumentation Wagner had been at pains to tone down in later revisions. Mahler merely responded: "What I am doing would be all right with Wagner if he were alive today."[70]

Wagner's early works

The overture to *Rienzi* was the first Wagner that Mahler ever conducted.[71] He conducted the whole work occasionally in Leipzig and Hamburg, and then in Vienna in 1901 he threw himself into a revival, studied Wagner's shortened version, rejected it as "inadequate, ... contrary to musical sense," and prepared his own. The press was almost unanimously opposed. "If Wagner had attended [Mahler's] performance," Eduard Hanslick wrote, "how he would have rejoiced... no, how irritated he would have been, he who strove for thirty years to live down *Rienzi*."[72] He conducted one more performance, then never touched it again.

He conducted the *Faust Overture* eleven times in concerts, mostly in New York, and the force of his interpretation seems to have grown with experience. He

[64] La Grange, *Mahler, Vol. 1*, p. 382 (no date given, presumably late 1896). He preferred to send him *Carmen* in which, he said, "not a single superfluous note is to be found."

[65] Fritz Stiedry, "Mahler und Schuch," *Sang und Klang Almanach 1920* (Berlin, 1921), p. 20, quoted in La Grange, *Mahler, Vol. 3*, p. 390

[66] La Grange, *Mahler, Vol. 3*, p. 807

[67] *Neues Wiener Tagblatt*, 28 September 1902, in Blaukopf, *Mahler: a documentary study*, p. 222. Richter went on to say he nevertheless believed Mahler was the right person as Director of the Opera.

[68] La Grange, *Mahler, Vol. 3*, p. 387

[69] Henry T. Finck, *My Adventures in the Golden Age of Music* (New York: Funk & Wagnalls Co., 1926), p. 425

[70] *Neues Wiener Tagblatt*, 28 September 1902, quoted in Christopher Fifield, *True artist and true friend: a biography of Hans Richter* (Oxford: Clarendon Press, 1993)

[71] in Kassel on 23 June 1884: La Grange, *Mahler, Vol. 1*, p. 115

[72] La Grange, *Mahler, Vol. 2*, p. 321

Fig. 10.1. Gustav Mahler in 1884, the year he heard Hans von Bülow.
Photo by Eugen Kegel

Fig. 10.2. Mahler from his Hamburg years, 1891-1897.
Postcard inscribed to Bruno Walter

Fig. 10.3. Mahler conducting Beethoven's Ninth Symphony, Strasbourg, May 1905

Fig. 10.4. Mahler rehearsing his Eighth Symphony, Munich, September 1910

Fig. 10.5. Mahler conducting in Vienna, 1897. Silhouettes by Otto Böhler

Fig. 10.6. Mahler at the end of his Vienna years, 1897-1907.
Photo by Moriz Nähr

conducted it at a "dragging pace" at a Hamburg concert in 1894, without "expressing its significance clearly," and "breaking it up into episodes," according to local critics.[73] In Vienna he failed to convince at least one critic of the work's merits, though "he had done his best to lend interest to a work which had none, except for historical reasons."[74] In New York in 1908 he gave a "most thoughtful reading" according to another doubtful critic, which emphasized "intellectuality somewhat at the expense of what little of romantic feeling the work possesses."[75] To another his reading was "strikingly dramatic" – he wrought from every phrase "all they hold of pathos and tragedy."[76] He seems finally to have let loose in one of his last concerts in 1911: "not even Nikisch could have sent so many thrills down the spinal chords of last night's audience as Mr. Mahler did," wrote the *Evening Post*, "with his superbly virile, impassioned, throbbing proclamation of the glories of the *Faust Overture*...."[77]

Although not an early work, Mahler's performance of the *Siegfried Idyll* may well be considered briefly here.[78] In a performance in Vienna in 1898 he was considered by one critic to have "laid bare his heart" in a "noble and deeply felt interpretation," whereas to another it seemed he had "dissected" the piece and given an "anatomical plate" of the young Siegfried.[79] In New York his performances drew similarly divergent responses. The *New York Times* noted the "delicacy of the orchestral color" and the free and poetically conceived interpretation."[80] There was "a sense of haste" in parts of the *Idyll* at another concert according to the *Sun*; "one would have wished for a more loving presentation."[81] A few days later he seems to have responded, for according to the *Evening Post*, it "sounded ineffably lovely and superlatively tender."[82]

The *Holländer* featured a little more than *Rienzi* in his repertoire, but not greatly. After a performance in Hamburg in 1897, Bauer-Lechner told him how struck she was by the way "he had transformed soloists, chorus and orchestra almost without rehearsals, and set his personal seal upon them. 'That comes from personal involvement [*Furor*],' he replied, 'something which I cannot imagine a real conductor being without. It drives him to bring out what he feels in a work, to extort it from his performers, even from the most clumsy or incompetent amongst the orchestra, chorus and soloists.'"[83] After a performance in Vienna in 1901 conducted by his assistant, Franz Schalk, he was unhappy with the "restless tempos." In this opera the tempos should be infinitely smooth, "like the long waves of the ever rolling seas and the long shadows cast by this elemental work."[84] In New York he took to including the overture in his concerts because "he had fallen in love with it."[85] He seems to have given it all he had: "he knows no moderation," wrote the *New York Times*.[86] According

73 Krause and Sittard (no further information), La Grange, *Mahler, Vol. 1*, p. 41

74 Max Kalbeck in the *Neues Wiener Tagblatt*, as summarized in La Grange, *Mahler, Vol. 2*, p. 314

75 *World*, 14 December 1908, p. 7 (Reginald de Koven)

76 *New York Times*, 14 December 1908, p. 9

77 11 January 1911, p. 7

78 He performed it 21 times, second only to the *Meistersinger* prelude (36) in his programming of Wagner concert pieces: La Grange, *Mahler, Vol. 4*, pp. 1610–11.

79 Helm, and an anonymous critic in *Neue Zeitschfrift für Musik*, quoted in La Grange, *Mahler, Vol. 2*, p. 127

80 *New York Times*, 1 April 1909, p. 9. The same point was noted in a later concert: 18 February 1910, p. 7

81 14 February 1910, p. 5

82 18 February 1910, p. 9

83 Bauer-Lechner, *Recollections*, pp. 93-94

84 La Grange, *Mahler, Vol. 2*, p. 377

85 Alma Mahler, *Gustav Mahler - Memories and Letters*, p. 168. He conducted it ten times in 1910-1911.

86 11 January 1911, p. 7

to the *Globe*, the overture was "forced almost beyond belief. Violence of contrast and excess of accentuation persuaded one that Mr. Mahler wished this early Wagner music had been orchestrated by Richard Strauss and was doing his utmost to make up for the omission."[87]

Tannhäuser, as we have noted, occupied a pre-eminent place in Mahler's Wagner repertoire in Hamburg. This is curious. Perhaps it was in response to popular demand, for the critical reception was mixed, if not discouraging.[88] When he produced it in London in 1892, it was regarded as "one of the best performances... ever seen in this country" by the *London Illustrated News*; "it is rare indeed to see such perfection of ensemble or such a reverent interpretation of the letter as well as the spirit of Wagner's early work as the Hamburg artists gave us."[89] It was "not altogether *sans reproche*," according to the *Academy*, yet was nevertheless "one of the most serious and soul-searching performances" heard since Richter.[90] The *Observer* complained about "the absurd darkening of the theatre *à la Bayreuth*... To sell people 'books of words' and to deprive them of the light, so that the words become invisible, is hardly fair... Mr. Mahler – who was not called for – bowed his thanks for imaginary calls."[91] In Vienna in 1901 he revived the Dresden version. He was criticised by the *Abendpost* for performing the overture "bar by bar," by another critic for the "unbearable slowness" of the Hymn to Venus, and by yet another for "dragged out and distorted" tempos contrary to Wagner's indications and style. The *Arbeiter Zeitung* complained that "in the long run the numerous deliberate, calculated and contrived touches, the overall plan of the principal tempi, and the too-frequent, mannered deadening of the natural sound of the voices, became tiring."[92] He conducted it a few more times, and then dropped it from his repertoire. In America he included the overture in his concerts to great effect.[93]

Mahler's *Lohengrin*, according to some reports of his debut in Vienna, recalled Wagner's own performance. Theodor Helm wrote: "he knows *Lohengrin* inside out and takes the tempi exactly as (generally slower than one is used to here) Master Wagner himself took them when he personally conducted *Lohengrin* at the Vienna Court Opera on 2 March 1876.[94] A similar comment was made in an anonymous letter sent to Mahler the day after the performance:

> Your tempi, your nuances and accentuation – all these were "Wagnerian" in the fullest sense of the word. The Master himself conducted in this way..... you know how to modify the tempo with perfect fidelity to the Master's intentions. No detail is lost, yet nothing is out of proportion within the framework of the whole. A fine example was the almost imperceptible slowing-

[87] 11 January 1911, p. 5

[88] Carl Armbrust in the *Fremdenblatt*, 6 September 1894, was grateful for the opening of some cuts, and the retention of others: Schabbing, *Gustav Mahler*, p. 212

[89] 23 July 1892, p. 109. Max Alvary sang Tannhäuser; Theodor Reichmann, Wolfram; Katherina Senger-Bettaque, Venus; and Katharina Klafsky, Elizabeth. The performance was uncut. Mahler himself thought the two London performances were "brilliant": La Grange, *Mahler, Vol. 1*, p. 258

[90] 23 July 1892, p. 78 (J. S. Shedlock) – "in the overture the brass overpowered the strings"

[91] 17 July 1892, p. 7

[92] La Grange, *Mahler, Vol. 2*, pp. 354-6

[93] *ibid, Vol. 4*, pp. 387, 664, 699

[94] *Österreichische Musik- und Theaterzeitung*, 15 May 1897, p. 2, quoted in Sandra McColl, *Music Criticism in Vienna 1896-1897* (Oxford: Clarendon Press, 1996), p. 77

down in the opening chorus of the third act, in the passage *Rauschen des Festes seid nun entronnen* [Bridal Chorus].[95]

The *Neue Freie Presse* threw general light on Mahler's approach to Wagnerian opera:

Mahler is not only an extremely confident and spirited musician, he is an excellent dramatic conductor and has a sense of the theatre: his attention does not stop at the footlights – in fact,it really begins there. He gives correct rhythms to the chorus and the soloists, which is most essential to meaningful interpretation. It is already clear that he prefers the fluid tempos that Richard Wagner loved. He will not tolerate any dragging or distortion. From the orchestra he obtains great restraint in accompaniment, but also great power when it is required for dramatic effect.[96]

One critic summed it up. "Just as there is the total work of art [*Gesamtkunstwerk*], so is Mahler the total conductor [*Gesamt-Dirigent*]. With him there is no separation of concern for the orchestra from the direction of singers or chorus..."[97] After a couple of years, his interest in *Lohengrin* waned, or was supplanted by other work, for he never conducted it again after 1900.[98] He included the Prelude in his American concerts in 1910-11. There he made his celebrated comment to the orchestra *before* a rehearsal began: "Gentlemen, too loud!"[99] His performances drew mixed responses. The *New York Staats-Zeitung* recalled the "unforgettable effects" he achieved when "suddenly, with marvellous gestures, he brought in the winds. The very heavens seemed to open and, with a shudder, we glimpsed eternity."[100] Another critic of Mahler's first performance, on 2 March 1910, thought Mahler knew "too much" about the music.

[He] brings his whole intellectuality to bear so strongly upon realizing the utmost of tonal effectiveness that he too often has none left for a finer appreciation of the spirit of the music. He seems to be entirely devoid of reverence for the music which he conducts, and the result is a peculiar effect of musical and spiritual hollowness, despite the fact that the orchestra is doing its utmost....In the *Lohengrin* Prelude, such an electrical climax as Mr. Mahler's is rarely heard; but the marvelously exalted close, expressive of the benediction following upon the vision of the Grail, he tossed off in a handy way, as if he was glad to be rid of it....[101]

[95] Bauer-Lechner, *Recollections*, p. 91. The letter may have been written by an older member of the orchestra or, in La Grange's view, "almost certain[ly]" by Helm: *Mahler, Vol. 2*, p. 30. Mahler was criticised, it must be said, for an un-Wagnerian tempo on one occasion: "too rapid a tempo in the Prelude [to Act 3]." The critic, Gustav Schönaich, claimed that "Wagner himself had conducted it more slowly. Mahler replied that, in his opinion, the piece... was a reminiscence from Beethoven and that, when composers introduced such 'unconscious recollections' into their work, the 'copy' almost never altered the tempo of the 'original.'": La Grange, *Mahler, Vol. 2*, p. 118.

[96] Richard Heuberger, *Neue Freie Presse*, quoted in La Grange, *Mahler, Vol. 2*, p. 29

[97] Robert Hirschfeld, *Neue Freie Presse*, 16 May 1897, p. 5, quoted in McColl, *Music Criticism*, p. 78

[98] From 1900, the operas Mahler mainly conducted in Vienna were *Tristan*, *Marriage of Figaro*, *Magic Flute*, *Don Giovanni*, and *Fidelio*: Willnauer, *Gustav Mahler und die Wiener Oper*, pp. 273-278.

[99] Theodore Spiering, "Zwei Jahre mit Gustav Mahler in New York," *Vossische Zeitung*, 21 May 1911, quoted in La Grange, *Mahler, Vol. 4*, p. 683

[100] *New York Staats-Zeitung*, 21 May 1911 (Maurice Baumfeld), quoted in La Grange, *Mahler Vol. 4*, p. 1121, n. 64. Magnus Dawison recalled in 1933 how during a performance of the opera in Prague "Mahler made the wind instruments sound like a gigantic organ, which nevertheless accompanied the singers with great delicacy": La Grange, *Mahler, Vol. 2*, 173.

[101] Arthur Farwell, *Musical America*, 12 March 1910, p. 9. La Grange characterized this critic, who was reviewing a New York Philharmonic concert that included the Overture to the *Holländer*, the Preludes to *Lohengrin* and *Parsifal*, Siegfried's Funeral Music from *Götterdämmerung*, and vocal excerpts from *Walküre*

The comment by *Musical America* on Mahler's "intellectuality" was a theme that had emerged in reviews of his New York performances of *Tristan* in 1908-09, to which we will now turn.

Tristan und Isolde

The impact of Mahler's *Tristan* on audiences was so overwhelming, the reviews so abundant and rich, it is difficult to do full justice to his interpretation in any summary.[102] Bruno Walter was literally lost for words when interviewed for his 80th birthday.[103] Reviews of Mahler's debut in New York on New Year's Day 1908[104] describe the notable characteristics of his reading as clarity, liveliness, "extreme emotional concentration,"[105] and softness. "He subdued the accompaniments until they were but a shimmering background against which the voice stood forth without effort," wrote the *Herald*.[106] His tempos were somewhat more rapid than New York was accustomed to, as Richard Aldrich noted in the *New York Times*:

Mr. Mahler's tempi in *Tristan* are made for the enhancement of the dramatic effect, to keep the blood of life pulsing in the score; yet there was nothing subversive in them or destructive of the musical values. The skilful and elastic modification of tempo is one of the touchstones of fine dramatic conducting, and in this respect Mr. Mahler showed himself a master. There were innumerable instances of it through the score; take, for instance, the approach to the climax of the prelude. How often is this driven on with an obvious hurrying of beat! Mr. Mahler made an acceleration that was wellnigh imperceptible as it advanced, yet when he arrived at the climax the beat was materially increased.[107]

It followed from the poetic subtlety and refinement of Mr. Mahler's reading that the voices were given rights of which it is certain Wagner never intended them to be deprived. Chief of these is to be heard, and (if the singers' diction is of the true kind) understood. The orchestral part had all its beauty, all its dramatic power and effectiveness; it had all the contrast

and *Meistersinger*, as "determined to adopt a contrary position": *Mahler, Vol. 4*, pp. 684-5. The *New York Times* had no comment specifically on the *Lohengrin* Prelude, but noted Mahler's performance of the pieces "was intense in dramatic spirit," and had "climaxes in which Mr. Mahler summoned forth every possible sonority": 3 March 1910, p. 9.

[102] In the case of Mahler's New York debut, for example, La Grange draws from some 19 reviews in his extensive account: *Mahler, Vol. 4*, pp. 55-75. (Most of the reviews quoted here, but not all, may be found in his account where he generally quotes by reference to the names of the critics who are assumed to have written the unsigned reviews, rather than the newspapers in which the reviews appeared. Here I quote the sources, and make no assumptions about the authors of unsigned reviews.)

[103] "Mahler was a performing musician, the greatest which I ever met, without any exception... [his *Tristan*] "*was something unforgettable, indescribable...*": interview with Arnold Michaelis, 23 February 1956, Columbia BW 80 (LP); the words in italics were omitted from a reissue of the interview on Columbia KLC 2809/10 (1962), a commemorative issue of Walter's recording of Mahler's *Symphony No. 9*, and may not have been included in all subsequent reissues, of which there have been several.

[104] Alma Mahler considered this "one of the finest performances I have ever heard in my life. His triumph was immediate": *Gustav Mahler - Memories and Letters*, p. 129. There were cuts in the performance and this was the subject of criticism; Mahler's attitude to these has been touched upon.

[105] *Press*, 24 December 1908, p. 10

[106] 2 January 1908, p. 12

[107] Otto Klemperer heard Mahler conduct the prelude in Prague in 1908 and recalled: "I have never heard the climax of the *Tristan* prelude (which he naturally conducted without any increase in tempo) played with such emotional impact": *Minor Recollections*, (trans.) J. Maxwell Brownjohn (London: Dennis Dobson, 1964), pp. 17-18

and variation of power, of accent, of crescendo and climax. Yet it did not drown the voices, and here, too, was an added beauty brought into prominence that has not always been heard in Wagnerian performances, that of the blending of voices with the orchestral tone. How beautiful was the sound of Brangäne's warning song from the tower in the second act....

Mr. Mahler is a conductor after Wagner's own heart in his instinctively right feeling for the pervasive melody of the orchestral score. He seeks what Wagner called the "melos," and never lets it sink from its position of pre-eminence.[108]

The *Sun* compared Mahler favourably with Anton Seidl, as Aldrich and others did, and commented:

He was gentle with the brass. From the beginning of the vorspiel not a full forte of trumpets and trombones was heard till Isolde raised the cup to her lips and then it came with the crash of a catastrophe.... But best of all, the eloquent variety of Wagner's instrumentation was displayed by the simple process of bringing out clearly every solo phrase, while the harmonic and contrapuntal background was never slighted. Mr Mahler knows well how to hunt Wagner's melody...."[109]

The *Evening Post* considered it "difficult to say how Mahler's reading could have been improved. It brought out with microscopic clearness all the subtle melodic beauties of the score, gave the dissonances the proper degree of poignancy, left no orchestral flower to blush unseen. It was enchanting. Not since the days of Anton Seidl have we had a conductor who at every moment was at such close accord...."[110]

Judging from these reviews, it would be easy to conclude that Mahler's *Tristan* was perfect – the ideal *Tristan*. But this was not the case for some. The distinguished critic James Huneker hinted at what was missing when he emerged from Mahler's third performance: "What a performance! Mahler is a painter.... the Missus and I, we were forced to go home, our nerves taut, my mouth a dusty cavern and head humming with that marvellous music. Oh je! I cursed pictures and longed for a bath of tone."[111] He later expanded on his view:

This reading is the modern, not the tempest-tossed Wagner of other years. The analysts are busy with the masterwork, dissecting it, digging into it for new beauties. The torrential swing and profound poetry of Seidl are lacking. Mottl's massiveness seems a trifle slow and old-fashioned. Variety, tonal and rhythmic variety, and a potent musical intellect, are in Mahler's interpretation. Granting the validity of his dynamic scheme at the outset, his logic of tonal gradations is inescapable. From a pin-point pianissimo to a pin-point pianissimo the music surged through the three acts to adequate climaxes. It is a reading that laid bare the nerves of the music, and its tempi never relapsed into mere speed for speed's sake, or into swampy grandeur of the average conductor. One sighed for moments of more sultriness, more lightning and thunder. Mahler over-refines, the "scholar's fault." Tristan's entrance is not majestic, there are too much logic and too little sensuousness in parts of the second act; as for the final climax, Herr Mahler can quote Wagner at the dissidents; Wagner who said that the orchestra should serve merely as coloring material to beautify and emphasize the action.[112]

[108] 5 January 1908, p. X4. Heinrich Knote sang Tristan, and Olive Fremstad sang Isolde (her first performance of the role). [109] 2 January 1908, p. 7 [110] 2 January 1908, p. 7

[111] letter to Edward E. Ziegler dated 19 January 1908, in Huneker, *Letters* (ed.) Josephine Huneker (New York: Scribner's, 1922), pp. 79-80

[112] James Gibbons Huneker, "A new Isolde: Olive Fremstad," *Century Illustrated Monthly Magazine*, vol. 77 no. 1 (November 1908), p. 144, citing for the last sentence Finck's *Wagner*, vol. 2, p. 150. In Vienna, Mahler

Lawrence Gilman might be considered one of those dissidents, for he wrote in *Harper's Weekly*:

Mr. Mahler fails, in considerable measure, to lay bare the heart of this music. There is a greater and a deeper *Tristan* than that which he makes known. His fastidious taste, his admirable discretion, his respect for the voice parts, his horror of obvious effects leads him, in the end, astray. In this music is the mightiest, the most unconfined emotional declaration that the art of the world can show. This incomparable score – incomparable alike in its flaming passion and its superlative beauty – issued from the brain of Wagner at white heat: not to make evident and irresistible its very ecstasy, its unique ardors, is to be unfaithful not alone to its spirit, but to its letter: is, in other words, to be false to the genius of Wagner at its most precious and typical. It is not extravagant to say that so tame, so intellectual a performance of the last act of this music drama as that achieved by Mr. Mahler has not been heard in New York; the delirious longings of Tristan were scarcely recognisable as such; the exultant transports of Isolde's Liebestod were turned into a gently pathetic berceuse; the music was, to be frank, emasculated, shorn of almost all its glory and its strength....[113]

There were more colloquial expressions of disappointment in later performances. "Herr Mahler conducted as if he would like to make his omelet without breaking any eggs," wrote the *Bulletin*; "the muscular energy of Hertz gave way to a suavity of manner in Mahler...."[114] "One cannot call Mahler's *Tristan* warm-blooded," wrote the *Press*. "It is too sophisticated to fit such a description. But it is beautifully elaborated, extraordinarily clear in details and extremely intense."[115] It seems his performances did become more "warm-blooded" as the season went on, culminating in the last, glorious performance he declared he was so happy with. "Mr Mahler hurled all petty restraints to the four winds of heaven," wrote the *Sun*, "and turned loose such a torrent of vital sound as he never before let us hear.... the barbaric, beating flood of the tragedy he has not felt as he did last night... The advent of Tristan became genuinely heroic; the crash of the death motive when Isolde raised the cup to her lips was cataclysmal.... In short Mr. Mahler's reading last night had just those elements of power and passion which have been wanting in his previous interpretations."[116] It is possible that Mahler performed *Tristan* in a way very close to Bülow's, and hence to Wagner's ideal. *Tristan* is such a gigantic work, however, that in different hands and on different occasions it is capable of, and *appreciated* for, greater power and passion than Wagner, in his ideal

was described by Max Graf as conducting *Tristan* "with modern temperament, making vibrant, intense, hysterical climaxes of the period of Charcot and Freud": *Legend of a musical city* (New York: Philosophical library, 1945), p. 207; Erwin Stein recalled there had been "something feverish, even delirious, in Mahler's performance. Unrelieved yearning, white-hot passion and violent suffering were the central moods...": Harold Rosenthal (ed.), *The Opera bedside book* (London: Victor Gollancz Ltd, 1965), p. 301; Richard Specht used similar language: *Mahlers fiebernd-lechzender, übermenschlich schmerzvoller, versehrender, furchtbar aufwühlender Interpretation*: Specht, *Das Wiener Operntheater von Dingelstedt bis Schalk und Strauß: Erinnerung aus 50 Jahren* (Wien: Paul Knepler, 1919), p. 41; and Ernst Decsey wrote of "something ineffably tortured, torturing, unresolved": La Grange, *Mahler, Vol. 2*, p. 575.

[113] 25 January 1908, p. 30. Lest it be thought this sort of response was confined to a few New York critics, a French writer who heard a performance of the Prelude and Liebestod in Paris on 20 June 1900 considered Mahler too slick and too cold, that he was conducting Wagner as if he had never heard Richter: there was "a certain inexplicable and to be quite honest even rather unintelligent coldness here and there, alternating with superbly rendered passages." As for Mahler's evident clarity, the writer's response was: "why illuminate things that belong in the shadows?" Willy (*nom de plume*) summarised by La Grange, *Mahler, Vol. 2*, p. 265

[114] 29 January 1908 (Metropolitan Opera Archives)

[115] 24 December 1908, p. 10

[116] 13 March 1909, p. 5

world, may have wanted to admit. Mahler was faithful to this ideal but to the ears of some he suffered for his faith.

Fig. 10.7. Mahler in concert. Drawings by Otto Böhler.
Die Musik, 1910/1911, Heft 18

Die Meistersinger von Nürnberg

After a performance of *Tristan* in Vienna in 1900, the *Deutsches Volksblatt* wrote that "of all Wagner's works, *Tristan* was most suited to Mahler's 'non-German' temperament whereas the 'typically German' quality of *Die Meistersinger* and the *Ring* remained alien to him."[117] Fritz Stiedry too, as we have seen, had doubts about Mahler's suitability for *Meistersinger*, a work long associated with Richter in Vienna. It may indeed be a matter of temperament that explains why Mahler never wholly won acclaim for his performances. "For me, tempo is a matter of feeling," he once told a friend;[118] perhaps he did not feel entirely certain about *Meistersinger*. His tempos were often criticised, the prelude for being too fast,[119] and the rest for being too slow.[120] Yet in the case of the prelude, Wagner dreaded it being taken too slowly,[121] and in the case of the rest,

[117] as summarized by La Grange, *Mahler, Vol. 2*, p. 222. Max Graf considered "the middle register of [Mahler's] genius," which included Beethoven symphonies, *Meistersinger* and *Siegfried*, as "less striking" than his peak, *Tristan* and *Marriage of Figaro*: *Wagner-Probleme und andere Studien* (Vienna, 1900), in Blaukopf, *Mahler: a documentary study*, p. 215

[118] Josef Foerster, *Der Pilger. Erinnerungen eines Musikers* (Prague: Artia, 1955), p. 499, quoted in Schabbing, *Gustav Mahler*, p. 77, and La Grange, *Mahler, Vol. 1*, p. 313

[119] Vienna in 1899: "played too fast": *Neue Freie Press*, quoted in La Grange, *Mahler, Vol. 2*, p. 196; Paris in 1900: "slightly faster than usual": Gustave Robert, *La Musique à Paris 1898-1900* (Paris: Delgrave, 1901), p. 308, quoted in La Grange, *ibid*, p. 259, fn; and New York in 1908: "Its tempo was faster than that to which we have been accustomed, and to many the music doubtless lost something of its significance thereby": *New York Times*, 30 November 1908, p. 9

[120] in Hamburg in the 1891/92 and 1892/93 seasons: Schabbing, *Gustav Mahler*, p. 210

[121] Krienitz, "Felix Mottls Tagebuchaufzeichnungen," *Neue Wagner-Forschungen*, I, (1943), p. 196

Wagner's ends may also have been met: the slower tempi "brought out the strength and brilliance of the opera"[122] and forced the singers into "a sort of conversation," producing an effect of a "light, fast-flowing comedy."[123] The composer Wilhelm Kienzel heard one of the last of Mahler's performances in Vienna, and wrote in his diary: "I have never heard such polyphonic clarity in the Prelude, everything original yet never studied. The first act was wonderfully successful, the second very good too. On the other hand, in the third, where the wit, feeling, and substance of German humour are uppermost, Mahler failed in various ways. He just slowed everything down, which achieves nothing."[124] Audiences had been enthusiastic about his revival in 1897, but after ten performances over three seasons, he stopped conducting it. He kept the prelude in his concerts – it was his most chosen Wagner excerpt, particularly in the United States – and it often produced "a most stirring effect,"[125] though not the most fully satisfying. "He plays it with tremendous insistence from beginning to end," wrote the *Sun*, "… but the reflective spirit yearns for something of repose…. The prelude yesterday was one long torrent of sound and color, brilliant all the time and poetic almost never."[126]

Der Ring des Nibelungen

Reports of Mahler's *Rheingold* diverge. In London in 1892, the orchestra, as we have noted, suffered from a certain roughness. According to George Bernard Shaw:

> Its playing of the wonderful water music prelude suggested that the Rhine must be a river of treacle – and rather lumpy treacle at that; the gold music was arrant pinchbeck; Freia's return to heaven brought no magical waftings of joy to the audience; and the rainbow music, with its hosts of harps… might have been pleasant deck music during a steamboat excursion to Hampton Court, for all the success it attained in providing a splendid climax to the prologue of a mighty drama.[127]

This idiosyncratic response does not appear to have been shared by other reviewers. For example, the orchestra was, according to the *Daily Chronicle*, "splendidly conducted by Herr Mahler, who, standing in the midst of his band, anticipated every little feature of expression".[128] He conducted "with his usual intimate perception of all the beauties of the score," according to the *Daily Graphic*.[129] For the *Athenæum* "the atmosphere of crime and deception in which we are plunged is not pleasant to inhale… [but the] performance, on the whole, was of great excellence."[130] The *Rheingold* was the least popular part of a *Ring* in Vienna in 1898,[131] but with the new production with Roller in 1905 Mahler was able to achieve the "final subtle communion between stage and music," as Julius Korngold wrote. "It is [Mahler] who gives light to the orchestra. The element of tone-painting, which in *Rheingold* predominates over emotional

122 Albert Leitich in *Deutsche Zeitung*, August 1898, quoted in La Grange, *Mahler, Vol. 2*, p. 111
123 *Neue Freie Presse*, and Hirschfeld, quoted in La Grange, *Mahler, Vol. 2*, pp. 196-97
124 quoted in La Grange, *Mahler, Vol. 2*, p. 223
125 *New York Times*, 30 November 1908, p. 9
126 30 November 1908, p. 7
127 *World*, 29 June 1892, p. 24, in *Shaw's Music*, vol 2, pp. 659-60
128 23 June 1892, p. 6
129 23 June 1892, p. 7
130 25 June 1892, p. 832
131 La Grange, *Mahler, Vol. 2*, p. 112

expression, is completely fused with the paintings on the stage."[132] It was different from his earlier days in Vienna, according to Robert Hirschfeld, when "the gleams of torchlight flickered over the whole orchestra. [Now] the emphasis [had] changed to resignation, asceticism of sound, twilight, liquefaction."[133]

When Mahler conducted the *Walküre* as part of his first *Ring* in Vienna in 1897, it was against the background of a public used to the performances of Richter. Mahler's approach was livelier, lighter, and faster than the Bayreuth master's, and this had its cost. One critic observed that at the end "the notes but not the meaning of the music had been rendered."[134] This may have been Richter's point when he commented that the Magic Fire Music had been "brought out very well by Mahler. But that this end is a transfiguration (and he put his hand on his heart) and a painful resignation – of that Mahler has no idea!"[135] The following year a critic considered that Mahler's "nervous pace" had destroyed "the highly poetic atmosphere"; he would have done better "to follow Richter's example," in particular "his admirable broadening of the tempo in the closing phrases."[136] Another agreed: the Magic Fire Music "was far too hurried and completely lacked grandeur and solemnity."[137] As with *Rheingold*, it was with a new Roller production, in 1907, that Mahler came into his own, as Hirschfeld wrote:

> The performance as a whole was like an inspired improvisation that seemed born out of a moment of rapture. One noticed nothing of the hard work that had preceded it. There was freedom in every bar, the tempo often moved arbitrarily between an inordinate accelerando and ritardando. Mahler adapted the dynamics of the incredibly obedient orchestra to each passing weakness or strength of the singer. The nature of the performance – at times gliding along indulgently, and sometimes pushing on ahead in an energetic manner – derives entirely from Mahler's baton. It was primarily passionate, and in such an individual way that any other conductor would have changed the picture immediately... Never has the *Todesverkündigung* been more noble, more powerful, more tragic or more frightening. The whole of the last act possessed a hitherto unknown musical strength and purity.[138]

Some of these characteristics were noted in the productions in America from February to April 1907. The *New York Times* noticed how he infused the orchestral score "with a new and exquisite sort of beauty":

[132] *Neue Freie Presse*, 25 January 1905, in Blaukopf, *Mahler: a documentary study*, p. 239

[133] quoted in La Grange, *Mahler, Vol. 2*, p. 73

[134] Albert Leitich, *Deutsche Zeitung*, quoted in La Grange, *Mahler, Vol. 2*, p. 52

[135] Max Graf, *Legend of a musical city*, p. 210. Graf also relates how he had suggested to Mahler that his tempi might be a little too fast, at least against those of Richter adopted under Wagner at Bayreuth in 1876. Mahler replied: "Richter has no idea about tempi! Maybe he knew the right tempi then. Since then he has forgotten them."

[136] Theodor Helm, *Deutsche Zeitung*, quoted in La Grange, *Mahler, Vol. 2*, p. 113

[137] Theobold Kretschmann, quoted in La Grange, *Mahler, Vol. 2*, p. 348. It is interesting to note, by contrast, that in Hamburg Mahler's slow tempi were a point of continuous criticism: Schabbing, *Gustav Mahler*, p. 210.

[138] quoted in La Grange, *Mahler, Vol. 3*, p. 589 (source not given). Later recollections of this production include Erwin Stein (1953) who spoke of the "ravishing *pianissimo* of the heavy brass" in the *Todesverkündigung*, and of the orchestra generally playing "as delicately as chamber music" (Rosenthal, *Opera Bedside Book*, p. 298) and Otto Klemperer (1960): "The woodwind trills which usher in the third act were more piercing than I should have believed possible, and during the great C minor episode (*Nach dem Tann lenkt sie das taumelnde Ross*) the orchestra almost vanished into thin air. The conductor seemed to surpass himself at the close of the Magic Fire Music." (*Minor Recollections*, p. 15).

Like that of *Tristan*, as he conceives it, it was much subdued, reduced to a lower plane of dynamics. But on this plane, everything had perfection of outline and phrasing, clearness, and incisiveness of modelling, depth and richness of color, intensity of dramatic expression. The delicacy with which the orchestral part was played was such as to allow the voices always to prevail in the ensemble....Mr. Mahler's tempos are free and full of the subtlest variations; they are spurred to dramatic life and potency, yet how lovingly can he linger over certain passages charged with a special emotion and fill them with rich expressiveness![139]

The *Sun* considered he may have been inclined to subdue the orchestra "a little too much" in the first act, until it became clear that this was to represent "the repressed emotion of the scene"; in the second act, when there was no sleeping Hunding, "he let loose a torrent of glorious, vivifying tone."[140] "Certain of his tempos were extraordinary for their slowness" as in the *Todesverkündigung* according to the *Press*; "instruments were lifted into prominence which usually [had] been permitted to remain in the shadow."[141] Subduing the orchestra could, as in *Tristan*, leave some listeners unsatisfied. "He is curiously subdued, pacificatory and perhaps a little bit indifferent," wrote the *Telegraph*; "Wagner is surely capable of a little more emotion than Mahler elects to read into him. He was, after all, Wagner, and not Mozart."[142] Some subsequent performances, including on tour, seemed to improve. In Philadelphia, the *Norristown Daily Herald* reported that "every detail of light or shadow in orchestral coloring; every leitmotive enunciation, every accent of emotional import, and every curve of the varying, multitudinous rhythm and beat of tempo seemed to grow and blossom, like some wondrous, colossal plant of melodic flowers and harmonic fruit."[143] Back in New York, however, the constant stream of the ideal performances Mahler sought was elusive. "Sometimes there was a splendid moment," wrote the *Sun*, "as in the introduction to the second act, and again there would be a period of depression, as in the closing part of the first act. But perhaps conductors are not always inspired."[144]

Mahler's *Siegfried* in London in 1892 was "absolutely triumphant," according to the *Pall Mall Gazette*, one that "satisfied the most exigent Wagnerian."[145] One such demanding Wagnerian was George Bernard Shaw who described the performance as "vigorous, complete, earnest"; in his view Mahler's tempi had been set with "excellent judgment."[146] The delicacy of the orchestra was "altogether extraordinary," wrote the *Standard*. In New York too, in 1908, there were "exquisite nuances" noticed by the *New York Times*, in the Forest Murmurs scene, as well as "mighty climaxes" in the love music; Mahler "urged his men to huge crescendos."[147] The work's "emotional curve rose and subsided with the variety that comes from significance rather than accident or caprice," wrote the *Tribune*. "There were abundant contrasts, both of tempo and nuance, but with all of them the music never halted in its full and splendid flow."[148] But the balance was not always "just right" to the *Evening Post*:

139 8 February 1908, p. 7
140 8 February 1908, p. 8
141 8 February 1908, p. 10
142 8 February 1908 (Algernon St. John-Brenon)
143 14 February 1908, p. 2 (William Struthers). In Boston Philip Hale wrote of "a continuous flow of orchestral speech, ... varied, elastic, impressive, full of emotion": *Boston Herald*, 9 April 1908, p. 14
144 5 March 1908, p. 7
145 9 June 1892, p. 2. Max Alvary sang Siegfried, Katharina Klafsky sang Brünnhilde.
146 *World*, 15 June 1892, p. 26, in *Shaw's Music*, Vol. 2, p. 646
147 20 February 1908, p. 7
148 20 February 1908, p. 7

Compared with his *Walküre* and *Tristan*, it seemed less satisfactory than either of them. He gave the brasses more rein than in the other work. To name an instance, in the prelude to the third act, when the brasses are playing the Wanderer theme, and at the same time the violins and upper wood wind are playing the Rheingold motive (inverted in the next bar as the *Götterdämmerung* motive), while a third motive is played by the violas and 'cellos, basses and horns – the galloping Walküre figure; – in this passage Seidl used to have the brasses attack the chord sforzando, and then yield a little, so that the other themes could be heard. Mahler drove them at full force throughout the value of the chord, so the other parts were well nigh lost. This was a surprise, in view of the beautiful things he did in *Tristan* and *Die Walküre*.[149]

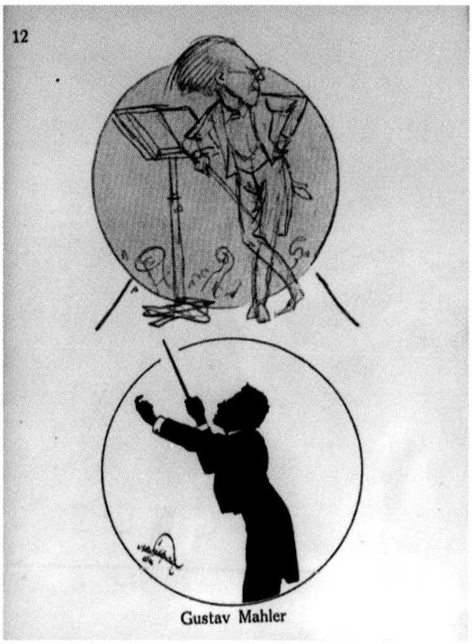

Fig. 10.8. Mahler in concert. Drawings by Hans Schliessmann

Another comparison with *Tristan* was made by the *Sun* which considered that the "intellectual and temperamental traits" in place in that work "failed to achieve a perfect exposition of the tremendous elemental force of the purely physical expression of *Siegfried*. Mr. Mahler was more scholarly than passionate in his reading. It was admirable, but it was not stirring, except in one or two episodes. It was immensely interesting; but it never overwhelmed."[150]

This last comment recalls one made about Mahler's *Götterdämmerung* in Vienna in 1897: it lacked "the elemental force of destiny."[151] The next year he was "criticized for a few moments of excessive haste, notably the Funeral March and the final scene."[152] Only the Funeral Music and the final scene were performed in New York, from which reports differ markedly. One found the "resonance and power" of the orchestra in the climax of the Funeral Music "extraordinary in their effect [;] the deeply poetic quality of the music was brought out with equal sureness."[153] Yet another could say: "so ineffective a performance, so cold, colorless and relentless an interpretation, we have

[149] 20 February 1908, p. 5 [150] 28 February 1908, p. 5
[151] Albert Leitich, *Deutsche Zeitung*, quoted in La Grange, *Mahler, Vol. 2*, p. 52.
[152] press comment summarized in La Grange, *Mahler, Vol. 2*, p. 115
[153] *New York Times*, 22 November 1909, p. 9

never heard? Why did Mahler adopt so hurried a tempo?...."[154] In a later performance "a brittleness of style" was observed, and in the handling of musical phrases, a lack of "reverent regard for their beauty." Yet in the final scene, "the conductor's reading of this music was of thrilling power and beauty."[155] This Immolation scene was the last he ever conducted from *Götterdämmerung*.

Parsifal

Mahler never had the opportunity to conduct the whole of *Parsifal*, and only conducted excerpts from it on six occasions. Whether he was temperamentally suited to the work is, in any case, doubtful. He once said that *Parsifal* "was not a work by Wagner but one by a Wagnerite."[156] A performance of the final scenes from acts one and three in Leipzig in 1887 received a bad review, though possibly not altogether for musical reasons.[157] In 1894 he rehearsed Willy Birrenkoven for Parsifal for that year's Bayreuth Festival, to the evident satisfaction of Cosima Wagner.[158] A performance of the prelude in New York in 1910 did not attract favourable reviews. The *New York Times* considered "the tempo of some of the sections were [*sic*] taken faster than they have been heard here generally, and the composition seemed to lose something in breadth and impressiveness thereby."[159] To *Musical America* the piece "suffered woefully from the lack of the conductor's self-submergence in the spirit of the work."[160]

"Poor Mahler!"

These last words are by Ernestine Schumann-Heink, the great Wagnerian singer who sang for Mahler in Hamburg. It was to him she attributed much of her success in Wagner.

> Gustav Mahler was a great conductor, but he was also one of the most hated conductors.... poor Mahler! He was thin and nervous and trembling to all music. It was always that he wanted and sought endlessly for perfection. He forgot that there is no perfection in this world. In his own mind and ideals, yes, but he forgot that when the orchestra was before him it was only eighty or a hundred men who were not geniuses like himself, but simply good workers. They often irritated him so terribly that he couldn't bear it; then he became a musical tyrant. And this people couldn't understand or forgive. They didn't see why he was so merciless, and so that he was misjudged wherever he went. It was a tragedy for him....[161]

He was the imperfect Wagnerite.

[154] *Press*, 22 November 1909, p. 10

[155] *Tribune*, 16 January 1911, p. 7. Brünnhilde was sung by Johanna Gadski.

[156] recollection of Ernst Decsey in *Die Musik*, 1911, quoted in Lebrecht, *Mahler Remembered*, p. 255

[157] The *Musikalisches Wochenblatt* criticized his "whole conception of the music," among other things: report summarized in La Grange, *Mahler, Vol. 1*, p. 171

[158] Reeser, "Gustav Mahler and Cosima Wagner," in Blaukopf, *Mahler's Unknown Letters*, p. 202

[159] *New York Times*, 3 March 1910, p. 9; at a later performance the piece was played "less well" than excerpts from *Tristan*: *ibid*, 28 January 1911, p. 11

[160] *Musical America*, 12 March 1910, p. 9 (Arthur Farwell)

[161] Mary Lawton, *Schumann-Heink, the last of the Titans* (New York, 1929), pp. 358-60

11

Felix Weingartner – Master of tempo

It was Felix Weingartner's good fortune, and ours, that he never conducted at Bayreuth. As a young musician, he was lucky to hear *Parsifal* in its early years. He was imbued with great Wagner performances by Seidl, Bülow, Levi, Richter, and Mottl. He was still young enough and musically sure of himself to rebel against the malign influence on Bayreuth of Cosima Wagner, "an educated dilettante" as he called her,[1] and the dragging tempos she encouraged. His polemical writings and performances kept Wagner alive when "tradition" threatened to stifle him. What most exercised Weingartner were questions of tempo, and his insistence that the tempo be aligned with the dramatic content of Wagner's works. This led to livelier tempos than audiences were generally accustomed to, especially devotees of Bayreuth. It was not a path followed by some of his colleagues. He would have viewed it as a battle not entirely won, another cause of bitterness among his long string of disagreements with theatre administrators and the like. At heart he wanted to be recognized as a composer, like Strauss, yet he was not, and the fact that he was a more talented conductor than Strauss was probably no consolation. He thought of himself as "an unrecognized genius."[2]

As a conductor, it was a different matter. He was renowned above all as a classical conductor, for "clear lines, formal balance, and a firm rhythmic foundation," as Carl Flesch remarked; "he rejected excess of any kind." At the heart of his art, Weingartner once said, "no rules exist." He could not explain the process whereby he could make an orchestra "live in my ideas."[3] He knew exactly what he wanted, and coolly, he could get it. He once explained his magic with orchestras: "At rehearsals we decorate the Christmas tree, and at the concert I light the candles."[4] This might well apply to his Wagner performances: they flickered, they brought light, they brought fire, and in proper time, they melted. We need not concern ourselves with his polemics against the later Bayreuth style. For as we will see, the proof of his arguments is in his performances, and in his recordings.

[1] Weingartner, *Bayreuth (1876-1896)*, 1897, edited translation of Lily Antrobus (1898) in Christopher Dyment, *Felix Weingartner: recollections & recordings* (Rickmansworth: Triad Press, 1976), Appendix, p. 99. A translation of the 2nd edition (1904) is in *Wagner* (edited by Stewart Spencer), vol. 14, no. 1 (January 1993), pp. 38-48 (Part 1) and no. 2 (May 1993), pp. 70-93 (Part 2). In this chapter the 1898 translation is used because it contains several interesting passages omitted from the 1904 edition.

[2] Carl Flesch, *The memoirs of Carl Flesch,* Hans Keller (trans. and ed.), (London: Rockliff, 1957), p. 150

[3] *New York Times*, 19 February 1905, p. SM7 [First Magazine Section]

[4] as told by his widow, Carmen Weingartner-Studer, in Dyment, *Felix Weingartner*, p. 21

Early experiences of Wagner

He was born on 2 June 1863 in Zara, on the Adriatic coast (now Zadar, Croatia), where his father was working as a Viennese civil servant.[5] His mother gave him early piano lessons, and his talents soon flourished.[6] He first heard of Wagner from a school friend, and when reports of the 1876 Bayreuth Festival were read out at home, his curiosity was aroused. His mother took him to a performance of *Tannhäuser*. He "had never heard anything to compare with the orchestral splendour" of the overture, he wrote; it was the "culminating point" of the whole performance.[7] In 1878 he attended the first performance of the *Meistersinger* in Graz. "Whether the performance was good or bad, it at any rate succeeded... in revealing to me the beauties of the masterpiece. It also opened my eyes with regard to Wagner's other works and induced me to study them and to read his writings. In a very short time I had become inoculated with the Wagner fever...."[8] He went to the Conservatory in Leipzig in 1881 to study piano and composition, but after some exercises in conducting, and a couple of concerts, he decided to become a conductor.

While at Leipzig he heard Seidl conduct a "magnificent" performance of *Walküre*, and in January 1882, a mesmerizing *Tristan*.

> From the moment when the doomed pair had drunk the fateful potion the action became more and more intense until the end of the act, so that the spellbound audience could hardly breathe. Anton Seidl was in his element; better than anyone else he knew how to lay a solid foundation and to build on this until a radiant temple emerged, the roof of which reached up to the very heavens. Nothing that I learnt in later life in regard to the finale of the first act of *Tristan* ever attained the heights reached by [Hedwig] Reicher-Kindermann and Seidl that night in Leipzig. The bond uniting these two gleamed through their performance, completely outshining everything else on stage.[9]

Indeed, the impression of this first act had been so great he felt let down by the last two, but he studied the score for the second performance and, from then on, he had no doubts about the beauties of the rest of the opera. When he heard another performance shortly afterwards in Berlin, but not under Seidl, he was "horrified" as soon as he heard the overture. "In comparison with Seidl's glorious reproduction, vibrating with expression, the performance seemed to me an expressionless race through the music, hacked off at the stops. Disappointment followed disappointment when the curtain had gone up; unsuitable scenery, Isolde with a powerful voice, but no actress, the orchestra much too loud, the *tempi* impossible."[10] Weingartner was learning more about Wagnerian art outside the Conservatory than within, and his thirst was unquenchable.[11]

As soon as the full piano arrangement of *Parsifal* was published, he bought a copy. "I wonder if the new generation can conceive of my feelings when I fetched the big

[5] "Felix Weingartner. A Biographical Sketch," *Musical Times*, 1 May 1904, p. 289, based on an interview

[6] Felix Weingartner, *Buffets and Rewards - A Musician's Reminiscences*, (trans.) Marguerite Wolff (London: Hutchinson & Co., 1937), p. 15

[7] *ibid*, pp. 36-37

[8] *ibid*, p. 43

[9] *ibid*, p. 64

[10] *ibid*, pp. 67-68

[11] He heard Bülow and the Meiningen Orchestra in Leipzig, though not in Wagner. He also met Nikisch and heard him in concert and opera, possibly in early Wagner, though not in the *Ring* or *Tristan*. He heard Mottl conduct an "excellent" performance of *Walküre* at a dress rehearsal in Karlsruhe in 1882.

blue volume from the music-shop and hurried away with it to [his friend] Bötcher's rooms. *A new work by Richard Wagner!*"[12] He pored over it, played it, and soon knew it by heart. He applied for a ticket to one of the inaugural performances at Bayreuth, and got one, indeed attended three performances. Of the first he recalled: "Darkness descended on the audience. Like a voice from another world the grandly conceived opening theme of the overture resounded. Incomparable!" He met Wagner briefly but did not speak to him – or rather, he was speechless when he *did* meet him: the composer put his hand on the young musician's throbbing chest, and said he must be thinking of the Flowermaidens.[13]

He returned to Bayreuth in 1883 and 1884, and as a musical assistant in 1886, when for the only time in his life he took the conductor's stand in the Festival Theatre. Levi and Mottl wanted to view the transformation scene in the last act at a rehearsal, and Weingartner offered to conduct. "I preserve these few minutes as a precious memory," he wrote. "Everything petty was forgotten – I was working in pure communion with the work of art and the spirit of the master in the temple he had dedicated to it."[14] What Weingartner learned at Bayreuth, both the good and the bad, will be touched upon when we look at his performances of the *Ring* and *Parsifal*.

To trace his conducting career briefly, he first applied to Bülow for a post as second conductor at Meiningen, but was rejected because he was considered too independent.[15] He was engaged at Königsberg (1884), Danzig (1885-87), and Hamburg (1887-89), but not in conditions that lent themselves to Wagner performances.[16] In Mannheim (1889-91) the second opera he conducted was the *Fliegende Holländer*, the first unabridged version heard in the city, and it "reaped universal praise," according to Weingartner. He also conducted a *Tristan*, and in Frankfurt a *Ring*.[17] He went to the Royal Opera in Berlin (1891-97) where his first performance of *Lohengrin* was "a tremendous success."[18] However, he felt "neglected in regard to Wagner's last works." He asked for a *Tristan*, but it was entrusted to the newly-arrived Karl Muck, as was a *Rheingold*.[19] Although he was eventually given a *Ring*, he felt slighted, resigned, and concentrated on concert work and guest appearances. For eleven years he held no opera post.

He was appointed to the Vienna Opera (1908-11) in succession to Mahler, where he became "the champion of the anti-Mahler clique." (His changes to the *Ring* are considered below.) He made enemies, resigned, and "left in his wake a strong tide of

[12] *ibid*, p. 65 [13] *ibid*, p. 81 [14] *ibid*, p. 148

[15] "I cannot make use of you," Bülow said to Weingartner: "you are too independent for me. I must have some one who will do absolutely what *I* wish. This you could not and would not do." "I fully agreed with him, of course," Weingartner wrote. Bülow engaged Strauss instead. See Weingartner, *On conducting* (1901) (trans.) Ernest Newman, in *Weingartner on music & conducting; three essays* (New York: Dover Publications, 1969), p. 18. On Weingartner's relationship with Bülow and Strauss, and his attendant bitterness, see David Wooldridge, *Conductor's World* (London: Barrie & Rockliff, 1970), pp. 73-76.

[16] Of Danzig and Hamburg he wrote: "Through both engagements I learned thoroughly the misery of small theatres.... Artistic conditions... were horrible. In Danzig four, or at most five, first violins, two contrabasses, singers of the third rank, and a wretched chorus. With it all there was no chance for proper rehearsals, since the directors would have such a large repertoire that nothing could be properly prepared....": letter to S. C. Williams quoted in *Boston Daily Advertizer*, 19 February 1912, p. 5.

[17] *Buffets and Rewards*, pp. 173, 175

[18] according to Weingartner; "the papers were enthusiastic in their praise. Only [one] held aloof.": *ibid*, p. 192

[19] *ibid*, pp. 202, 210

discontent."[20] While he had been an "elegant, amiable, smiling, worldly musician... a kind of antithesis of the demonic Mahler... he left no lasting traces behind him upon the opera."[21]

Vienna's loss was the world's gain, for the compass of his guest appearances ranged widely. While he subsequently held posts in Hamburg and Darmstadt, he made several journeys outside Germany and Austria to conduct Wagner: Rio de Janeiro (*Parsifal*, 1919), Montevideo (*Lohengrin*, 1919), Buenos Aires (*Parsifal*, 1920, 1922; *Ring*, 1922), Rome (*Tristan*, 1920), Naples (*Parsifal*, 1921), and Barcelona (*Walküre* and *Tristan*, 1924; *Ring* and *Meistersinger*, 1925). The focus of our attention will be on Boston (*Tristan*, *Meistersinger*, 1912-14), Paris (*Ring*, *Parsifal*, *Meistersinger*, 1911-14), and London (*Tannhäuser*, *Parsifal*, 1939). He returned to Vienna to the Volksoper (1919-24), where he opened with *Meistersinger* and closed with *Parsifal*, and to the State Opera for a 71st birthday *Götterdämmerung* in 1934, then for another term as director (1935-36), where he debuted with *Lohengrin*. He reintroduced guest conductors – Knappertsbusch conducted the *Ring*, Furtwängler *Tannhäuser*, for example – but soon resigned, officially "for reasons of health."[22] He returned to Switzerland, where he was a naturalized citizen,[23] and died on 7 May 1942 aged seventy-eight.

Wagner's early works

At a concert in New York in 1906 Weingartner conducted the *Faust Overture* and the *Siegfried Idyll*. The *New York Times* reported that "more exquisitely poetical a reading of the *Siegfried Idyll* could hardly be; it struck the note of reverie, of introspection, in a freedom of tempo that was like an improvisation."[24] The *Evening Post* was reminded of Seidl: it "was given with much elasticity of tempo, and at a general pace that approximated Mr. Seidl, while the coloring was less chameleonic."[25] The *Daily Tribune* also commented on the elasticity of tempo and the way Weingartner "quickened the pace of the remplissage in the middle of the piece, but with only partial success." The monotony of the work was inescapable. "Wagner's pretty tribute to his baby son" was not a composition of a solemn kind, and "Weingartner certainly did not conduct it as such. He played it lightly and cheerfully, and not at all as if he were obsessed by pious memories of the drama which contributed to its melodic material."[26] The *New York Times* considered the performance of the *Faust Overture* a "deeply felt, a dramatic interpretation... how vehemently declaimed and how pregnantly significant was the climax, and how subtly prepared, yet spontaneous in its effect?"

[20] Marcel Prawy, *The Vienna Opera* (Vienna-Munich-Zurich: Verlag Fritz Molden, 1969), p. 76, 85-87

[21] Max Graf, *Legend of a musical city* (New York: Philosophical Library, 1945), p. 214. It might be noted that Weingartner was "the first Director of the Vienna Opera to conduct with the entire orchestra *in front* of him": Henry-Louis de La Grange, *Gustav Mahler, Vol. 3, Vienna : triumph and disillusion (1904-1907)* (Oxford University Press, 1999), p. 181. He was also the first to put the name of the conductor on opera posters: he "liked seeing his name in print." Prawy, *The Vienna Opera*, p. 86.

[22] Prawy, *The Vienna Opera*, p. 150. Prawy noted that Weingartner was welcomed back warmly to Vienna "as Strauss's arch-enemy, Strauss having been Krauss's bosom friend." (*ibid*, p. 147).

[23] He was naturalized in 1931, according to the obituary in the *Musical Times*, June 1942, p. 192.

[24] 5 February 1906, p. 9 [25] 5 February 1906, p. 9 [26] 5 February 1906, p. 6 (H. E. K.)

Undoubtedly Mr Weingartner touched the heart of the mystery in all this music. He achieved the highest task of the interpreting artist in reproducing the very essence and spirit of the music, recreating it as it was embodied in the composer's thought, and making it live in the hearts of the listeners as it once lived in his. With this conductor pre-eminently the keenly analytical power goes hand in hand with a richly poetic imagination, an instinct of dramatic effect; the exquisite feeling for detail with the sense of the larger proportions.[27]

He performed the overture to *Tannhäuser* in his concerts. In Boston in 1912, where he "conquered the local public more speedily than any conductor since Nikisch" in the view of the *Boston Daily Advertiser*, his reading was "notable in the care with which he prepared his climax and so achieved the really massive effect many conductors miss through early warming up the artillery."[28] In Berlin in 1919, he is reported to have conducted it "with delicacy and verve. At the return of the chorus of the pilgrims, he put the horn section, which Nikisch had improperly emphasized, back into the middle voices where it belongs, and gave everything to the solemn brass."[29] He performed it at a "monster concert" in Vienna in 1926 with the combined forces of the Vienna Philharmonic and the Vienna Symphony orchestras, some 175 players, including 108 strings, and "the acoustic effect was overwhelming."[30]

In his twilight years, he conducted the complete *Tannhäuser* in London. It was a "dignified performance," according to the *Daily Telegraph and Morning Post*. His "finely equable style did not gloss over certain inconsistencies in the famous score, or carry any position by excited assault, but rendered all the rarest things with the utmost appreciation. It is unusual to hear this romantic opera treated so much like a classic; and the result was calculated rather to satisfy the faithful than to persuade unbelievers."[31] *The Times* remarked on "the singular beauty of the orchestral playing and the balanced judgment" the conductor showed throughout the score.

Dr Weingartner plays the whole with a careful consistency, never over-emphasizing the subsidiary points but often surprising the hearer by the beauty of sound where the orchestration is at its lightest, and at the same time with a readiness to build up a climax to a high pitch of excitation. The *stringendo* of the chorus of Tannhäuser's accusers which leads to the distant pilgrim's hymn at the end of the second act was an outstanding moment of histrionic effect, and the playing of the woodwind in the first scene of the last act gave a strange sense of calm expectancy as Elizabeth awaited the return of her lover.[32]

The performance "brought us not only the mellowness we now expect of this conductor in quiet episodes," wrote the *Observer*, "but a rather unexpected excursion now and then into the ardent."[33]

[27] 5 February 1906, p. 9. The *Daily Tribune* wrote of the "splendidly dramatic reading'" and the *Evening Post* of its "splendid climax." In Vienna in 1925 he performed it in a "masterly fashion," according to the *Musical Times*, 1 June 1925, p. 556.

[28] 19 February 1912, p. 5 (S. C. Williams)

[29] review from *Signale* [?], May 1919, quoted in Peter Muck, *Einhundert Jahre Berliner Philharmonisches Orchester*, Vol. 1 (Tutzing: H. Schneider, 1982), p. 473

[30] *Musical Times*, 1 April 1926, p. 365

[31] 5 May 1939, p. 10 (Richard Capell)

[32] 3 May 1939, p. 12

[33] 7 May 1939, p. 7 (Ernest Newman). One of the excursions into the ardent may have been in the Venusberg scene where one of the violinists recalled "he produced the most wonderful climax I had, or ever have heard. Venus exploded into millions of dropping fragments...." Andrew Brown, quoted in Dyment, *Felix Weingartner*, p. 36

Weingartner once attended a performance of *Lohengrin* conducted by Bülow in Eisenach. There were none of the "nervous caprices," he wrote, which Bülow displayed later in his career (in orchestral music, for he then rarely performed Wagner). "Bülow was great," he recalled, "... he led the marvellously disciplined orchestra which, though not of full capacity, emitted a surprising volume of sound, with a kind of simple grandeur."[34] Weingartner was evidently fond of *Lohengrin*, and understood it well. He believed Wagner constructed the prelude "with absolutely overwhelming logic, with expression, instrumentation, figuration, melody and polyphony building up, step by step, till the climax takes our very breath away."[35] He chose the opera for his first re-appearance at the Vienna Opera in 1935. The *New York Times* correspondent was there.

It was a *Lohengrin* in the grand manner, the kind of Wagner reading one used to get from men like Seidl, Mottl, Richter, Nikisch, Mahler, with never a phrase or a contour slighted, with every rhythm taut and tingling, with splendor and immensity in every climax; poetic, dynamic, vibrant with life, instinct with style. It was interesting to note once more how a conductor of this heroic old school can whip up the Wagnerian tempo without sacrificing a jot of the Wagnerian breadth – or, rather, how keenly such conductors divine that the true pace of works like *Lohengrin* and *Götterdämmerung* is not a sluggish and torpid but a fleet and animating one. And again one was amazed by the enormously energizing youth and the ardent temperament in this man of 71....[36]

Tristan und Isolde

Boston had been treated to a string of distinguished performances of *Tristan* when Weingartner took the podium in 1912. After only four rehearsals of an orchestra with no recent experience in Wagner, Weingartner was able to produce "a revealing, an engrossing, a truly thrilling performance," in the view of the *Boston Evening Transcript*. "The whole orchestra sounded balanced, euphonious, various of accent, yet unified into the music and the drama. From beginning to end, it was acting too. So had Mr. Weingartner given it fire, imagination, discrimination, new possibilities, new talents.[37] The *Boston Herald* considered Weingartner's interpretation "the great feature of the performance":

Mr. Mahler had an unusually fine sense of proportion; he respected the singers; he had a firm command of tonal gradations; but on the whole his reading was irreproachably academic. Mr. Toscanini's interpretation is still gratefully remembered. It was characterized by the qualities that made Mr. Mahler's conspicuous, but led by the Italian the music had a sensuous glow, a poetically romantic spirit....

[Weingartner's] reading of the score will not soon be forgotten. There was fineness in the working out of detail, but there was ever a continuous flow of musical thought, with its bursts and lulls of passion, with constantly varied expression. The orchestra sang a marvellous song. And this song was heard with the musical dialogue and monologue on the stage, not above them. The singers were supported and encouraged, not overwhelmed, not treated as though they were lifeless instruments in a tumultuous ensemble. There was the utmost sonority, but sound was

[34] Weingartner, *Buffets and Rewards*, p. 103 [35] *ibid*, p. 292
[36] Herbert Peyser, "Weingartner in Vienna," *New York Times*, 13 January 1935, p. X7
[37] 13 February 1912, p. 5. Jacques Urlus sang Tristan; Johanna Gadski, Isolde.

never noise. There was remarkable lucidity in ensemble, but each voice in the orchestra and on the stage was allowed its allotted say, to borrow the formula in *The Thousand Nights and a Night*. There was a control that was not tyrannical. All these results were brought about with apparent ease and simplicity, without spectacular gestures, and there was never the thought of a conductor standing between the composer and the audience. The composer spoke through him, and it was as though composer and interpreter were one.[38]

The *Boston Post* characterised the interpretation as "conspicuous for its continence as regarded quality of tone and the proportions of the climaxes. The voices were never covered. In the second act the quality of the orchestral tone was rich and deep like a soft carpet. The orchestra flamed up at certain moments with tremendous energy, moments the more effective by reason of the subtle scale of dynamics."[39] His performances did, however, cause the *Boston Evening Transcript* to raise some questions: "Did the conductor make too many cuts in *Tristan* to the destroying here and there of the contrast, the proportions, the culmination that Wagner designed? In his desire to make the music songful did he sometimes over-subdue its passionate accent?" Whatever the case may be, "Mr. Weingartner seemed such a conductor of individual genius… the large results of his work effaced all the secondary and intricate argument that it stimulated." [40]

He returned to the Boston Opera Company in 1913. According to the *Boston Post*, he seemed to find the orchestra "a finer body, more instantaneously responsive to his wishes than it was last winter, for he took his tempi always thoughtfully… ; in one instance, near the beginning of the second act, he indulged in an amount of storm and stress rather uncharacteristic of him. The players responded excellently. Mr. Weingartner, as it were, improvised on his instrument.[41] It seemed that whatever color or degree of force he desired, he could obtain it immediately at will."[42] The *Boston Evening Transcript* wrote:

Mr. Weingartner was in the vein as he has not been in any previous performance of Wagner's music-drama, seeming to imagine it more largely and to express it more puissantly than, in Boston, he ever has before. His orchestra was worthy of him…. In the fulness and sensibility of its tone, songful continuity, warmth of accent, sensuous beauty of phrase and expressive power in progression and climax it seemed not merely a transformed, but another, band….The outcome was a performance of *Tristan* such as in seven years this town has known only once – when Mr. Toscanini and the forces of the Metropolitan appeared in it three seasons ago.[43]

Die Meistersinger von Nürnberg

Weingartner heard Richter conduct the work at Bayreuth in 1888. It was a "great accomplishment," he recalled. "Richter directed the performance with a simple grandeur which was his very own." Unlike the *Parsifal* of that year, Richter had allowed

[38] 13 February 1912, p. 9 [39] 13 February 1912, p. 16 (Olin Downes) [40] 24 February 1912, Part 2, p. 5

[41] He "feels free to play on this instrument as he would sweep his hand across a harp," the journal wrote of a later performance: 11 February 1913, p. 3 (Olin Downes)

[42] 1 February 1913, p. 16 (Olin Downes) Carl Burrian sang Tristan, Olive Fremstad, Isolde.

[43] 1 February 1913, p. 8 (H. T. P.) Of an earlier performance this journal asked: "did not he and the orchestra with him stand a little outside its sensuous beauty? Often as the performance engrossed, it did not always transport." *ibid*, 1 February 1913, p. 8.

no one to interfere with his interpretation of the work.[44] *Meistersinger* was one of the first two Wagner operas Weingartner conducted. His Beckmesser was Rudolf Freny who had once performed before Wagner to the composer's satisfaction.[45] "Not so the conductor," Weingartner related, "to whom Wagner had said: 'Yours is an *andante* arm, that is not the way to conduct *Meistersinger*, it's a comedy'":

The typical *andante* of the average well-meaning conductor, characterized by Wagner with delicious irony as "German tempo," has at least the advantage of being a reproduction of the honest sedentary leisureliness of the beer-table. But the modern *rubato-andante* with its sheeps' eyes, its slimy wishy-washiness and its partly brutal impertinence, is a horribly degenerate form of that genuine quality, and smothers not only any swing or temperament, but also the noble impulses which make for broadness of outline. It is an unnatural distortion and should be discarded entirely.[46]

When he conducted the work in Boston on 6 March 1914, it was considered "a beautiful reading of the score" by the *Boston Daily Advertiser*, "a reading that was marked by the wonderful, constant rhythm, that is one of his chief glories, and a reading which brought out the full value of the many glowing pages of the great score."[47] It was the fifth performance Boston had enjoyed that year, and the first with his wife, Lucille Marcel, singing Eva. Earlier performances had been conducted by André Caplet. The *Boston Globe* reported that "passages that before [had been] boisterous were subdued, yet not to the loss of their vitality. It was a pleasure also to hear the music under a beat authoritative and incisive, yet elastic, and done with a sense of the tempi that considerably shortened the length of performance. Mr Weingartner is said to favor further cuts in the version now used…."[48] The *Boston Herald* considered there had been "no radical changes in the tempi already established in the opera house, but his control of the orchestra was marked, and there was the sharply defined rhythm and the poetic expression that characterise his leading and have given him his enviable reputation."[49] The *Boston Evening Transcript* wrote that "the conductor gave to the accompaniment the magical smoothness which he imparts to all his readings. And particularly there was to be noticed that quality which we can only call 'verve,' the quality of liveliness and sharpness without boisterous roughness. He did not have a distinguished cast, on the whole, and much of the time one preferred to listen solely to the orchestral comment on the action and forget about the characters."[50] The *Boston Post* paid tribute to the preparatory work of the conductor of previous performances, and commented:

Mr. Weingartner, of course, exerted his remarkable authority over his orchestra, his absolute knowledge of his score and all its traditions, and his deep sympathy for such music, to good effect. The breadth of certain climaxes, the long lines of his tonal structure and the

44 *Buffets and Rewards*, p. 43. He heard it again the following year, but it had "fallen off" – Richter had arrived late for rehearsals from London: Dyment, *Felix Weingartner*, p. 101. He adds that ten years later he heard it in London conducted by Luigi Mancinelli whose conducting "afforded me great surprise and pleasure; he had a profound understanding of the spirit of the work and produced it to perfection." Richter introduced *Meistersinger* to England in 1884; thereafter Mancinelli became its regular conductor at Covent Garden, from 1889 to 1898.

45 Freny sang Beckmesser at the first performance of *Meistersinger* in Hamburg on 9 April 1871.

46 *Buffets and Rewards*, pp. 163-4.

47 7 March 1914, p. 5

48 7 March 1914, p. 3

49 7 March 1914, p. 11 (Philip Hale)

50 7 March 1914, p. 4

Fig. 11.1. Felix Weingartner from his Mannheim years, 1889-1891

Fig. 11.2. Weingartner from his Berlin years, 1891-1898

Fig. 11.3. Weingartner in Berlin

Fig. 11.4. Weingartner in Vienna, 1935

Fig. 11.5. Weingartner conducting the Symphony Orchestra of Paris in the Overture to *Der Freischütz* (Weber), from a film made in the early 1930s

Fig. 11.6. Weingartner from his Vienna years, 1908-1911

eloquence of many a detail were noticeable. He has the score at his finger tips. The coolest of men in the conductor's chair, he nevertheless has an astonishing and instantaneous mastery of the situation.[51]

A few months later, at the Théâtre des Champs-Élysées, he gave Paris another "remarkable interpretation"[52] of *Meistersinger.* His direction was described as "intelligent, precise and lively" by *Le Figaro.*[53] *Comœdia* observed:

Weingartner gives to the work a very pronounced character of incisive clarity and lightness. His tempi are alert, his emphases precise. With his interpretation, there is no perceptible sense of tedium in the course of the four scenes so generously developed. No monotony: the orchestral colour is very skilfully distributed and the variety of the reflections is prodigious. he overture under his baton takes on a brilliance and firmness that is extraordinary; the scenes of the apprentices; the terrible riot of the second act; the arrival of the guilds are presented at the same time with a spirit the more subtle and the more charmingly familiar. The good-naturedness, the simplicity, the cordiality reign masterfully throughout this score. Softening carefully the too-violent tones, nuancing the accompaniment with delicious discoveries, Weingartner carries off everything in this interpretation with an ease and panache which amazed the musicians. His personal success was considerable.[54]

He opened his term as director of the Vienna Volksoper (1919-24) with a performance of the *Meistersinger*, which, in his own words, was "much appreciated."[55] He conducted it during his second term as Director of the Vienna State Opera. The *New York Times* reported after one performance: "What a *Meistersinger* this, which sprang to renewed and glorious life on the winged feet of Weingartner's blithe and exhilarating tempi!"[56] A few fragments recorded in 1934 and 1935 show the great variety in his tempo and characterization. The act one prelude bristles with life, the orchestra playing with energy, not effort, and submitting to subtle changes of tempo which make the whole of constant interest.

Der Ring des Nibelungen

In 1879 Weingartner went to Vienna and heard the complete *Ring* conducted by Richter.

I shall never forget what I felt when Hans Richter walked up to the desk and the low E flat of the overture to *Rheingold* floated out to us.... The tones of the orchestra rose majestically – this was the fulfilment of anticipatory dreams. True, I resented the "Nornen" scene and certain deficiencies which disturbed the picture my fancy had built up in advance, but the impression as a whole was overwhelming, and my boundless veneration for Wagner became more firmly fixed than ever.[57]

51 7 March 1914, p. 8

52 *Le Monde Artiste*, 30 May 1914, p. 340

53 29 May 1914, p. 5 (Henri Quittard)

54 29 May 1914, p. 1

55 *Buffets and Rewards*, p. 301

56 *New York Times*, 3 February 1935, p. X7 (Herbert Peyser). He also wrote of a *Holländer* performance: "What a *Dutchman* that smote one like a shock of primeval forces or the surge and sweep of the elements unbound!"

57 *Buffets and Rewards*, pp. 46-47. By contrast, Weingartner was disappointed with von Schuch's *Ring*: see the Coates chapter above, p. 222.

It was a new production of the *Ring* in Frankfurt that brought Weingartner his "first popular success as a conductor."[58] When he was given a *Ring* in Berlin in 1897, Lilli Lehmann was one of the singers: "It was an intense pleasure to see in the orchestra this idealist, who was then very young," she recalled. "The happiness of a self-chosen calling beamed in his face – the delight in work and in this co-ordination of like elements and qualities, with which he encouraged and inspired us artists."[59] His preoccupation with the work, and his understanding of it, can be gathered from an extended passage from his booklet *Bayreuth (1876-1896)* in which he expressed what he modestly described as "purely personal views" on the tempi:

> The first Act of *Walküre*, as well as that of *Siegfried*, presents a situation in which an elemental, uncontrollable power leads up to the central incident of the scene – in *Walküre* the powerful, all-consuming passion of Siegmund and Sieglinde; in *Siegfried* the holy, irresistible inspiration to complete the sword. The music expresses the innermost and most intimate soul of the situation, and its primordial power, never checked but ever increasing, should also be expressed in the tempi by a continuous *crescendo* that lasts during the whole incident. Naturally there are *decrescendi* and *ritenuti*, but I should like to set forth this problem, which is simply a matter of feeling and difficult to state fully in words, in the following way: "The conductor should draw over the whole scene an ever-rising, never-interrupted line of waves." … It is only the steady, irresistible crescendo to be found indicated in Wagner's directions as to time that can express the increasing tempo of the orchestral postlude, which rises almost to a frenzy; for when it has not been led up to, but erupts suddenly, it does more to check the receptive mood than it does to explain. Moreover, a motif sometimes appears, at first just on its own, either to introduce one of the characters or to prepare for some event, and then in the same form but as an accompaniment to the artist. In the last case, ought it not to be taken rather quicker – perhaps I should say less emphatically – than before? For instance, in the second scene of the *Rheingold*, if the whole conversation between Wotan and the giants were taken in the time of the first giant motif, then intelligent speaking and singing would be made impossible for the actors without their breaking up the words and the phrases. The same occurs in the third act of *Siegfried* at the words *Ein Vöglein schwatz wohl manches* and from then onwards. If the conductor does not make things move more quickly the artists do it for themselves out of a proper feeling for the expression of the phrases in question. The conductor must then do his best to make the orchestra keep up with them, and unpleasant vacillations are the result. As a witness of the scene once told me, at a rehearsal of *Rheingold* when it was being too pathetically treated, Wagner called out to the artists, "Be more light in hand, my children; this is a comedietta we are playing." The spirit, if not the words, of this remark should be taken to heart.[60]

In Vienna, Weingartner maintained Mahler's practice of giving four complete performances of the *Ring*, though his performance of the *Walküre* with cuts drew strong criticism. The cuts included one of the most important passages in the whole *Ring*, in act two of the *Walküre*, where Wotan cries out *eines will ich noch, das Ende – das Ende!* Weingartner claimed theatrical managers had complained to him about the length of Wagner performances, that uncut performances tired "a large proportion of the audience," and were a "positive danger" to fatigued singers. The cuts were, he

[58] *ibid*, p. 175

[59] Lilli Lehmann, *My path through life*, (trans.) Alice Benedict Seligman (New York: G.P. Putnam's Sons, 1914), p. 441. "Calmly, and with certainty and distinction, Muck conducted the third cycle…," she added.

[60] *Bayreuth (1876-1896)*, in Dyment, *Felix Weingartner*, Appendix,, p. 103

admitted, "interpreted as an act of hostility against my predecessor."[61] And so indeed they were. It was "a serious tactical error on Weingartner's part," in the view of Vienna Opera historian Marcel Prawy, "to break almost overnight (out of pure animosity towards Mahler) with what had become a tradition."[62] Weingartner responded to the protests and performed *Siegfried* and *Götterdämmerung* without cuts.

One writer remembered Weingartner's act one of *Siegfried* as the highlight of his three years in Vienna.

[It] unquestionably left the strongest impression. Every positive aspect of his character emerged – his crackling freshness, the healthy boyishness of his impetuosity, the spontaneous strength of his impulsive naturalness – and it had an inspirational effect. (It is worth noting that the natural mood of the second act and the wild, enthusiastic significance of the finale did not have the same immediacy.) Wherever the dramatic, elemental lines remained unbroken, the musician remained victorious, and his youthfulness made good what others had spoiled.[63]

After he had resigned from the Vienna Opera in 1911,[64] he was asked at short notice, when Felix Mottl became ill, to conduct the *Ring* in Paris. For those who had not heard it elsewhere, *Le Figaro* wrote, his performances were "a prodigious revelation," and were accomplished with only one rehearsal.[65] *Le Courier Lyrique* could not speak more highly of Weingartner:

What more can one praise: his clarity, his fluidity, his moderation, the balance of his execution, his sense of the changing value of themes, his art of the expressive colour of sounds, his care to subdue the orchestra, each time it is necessary, to allow the drama, the words, to come to the foreground, his poetic feeling for the picturesque, his ardour, his enthusiasm, in a word his lyricism, his power without heaviness. He carries the work within himself, and it seems by his magnetic baton he gives life to all those, singers and players, who must by their expressive means, make it throb for us. He was the soul of the first cycle, and if, in the course of these four evenings we have known sublime emotions, it is to him that we owe them.[66]

Le Monde Artiste considered the orchestral players had given of their best, realising the work in "conditions of beauty, force and harmony which could not be surpassed."[67] The musicians appeared to be "*listened* to," *Comœdia* observed, "which, alas, happens rarely in routine productions," and they responded by playing *feelingly*.[68] *Le Temps* published a *feuilleton* reviewing the two cycles, the second having been conducted by Nikisch. In view of the limited time for rehearsal, *Le Temps* considered Weingartner had not been able fully to leave his personal mark in *Rheingold* because everything had to be devoted to "beating time and maintaining order and precision." Nevertheless, the "general tempo had more continuity and firmness than ordinarily":

61 *Buffets and Rewards*, p. 268. Bruno Walter recalled in his memoirs that the protests were so vigorous "that he returned to the uncut version at subsequent performances:" *Theme and variations: an autobiography*, (trans.) James A. Galston (London: H. Hamilton, 1947), p. 156

62 Prawy, *The Vienna Opera*, p. 79

63 Richard Specht, *Das Wiener Operntheater* (Wien: Paul Knepler, 1919), p. 55

64 Bruno Walter conducted at the Vienna Opera during Weingartner's tenure and recalled: "His performances were distinguished by their neatness and smoothness, they had the élan and brilliance symptomatic of his concert work, but the dramatic element in the playing of music, so essential in operatic reproductions, was not sufficiently in evidence." *Theme and variations*, p. 195

65 18 June 1911, p. 5. Weingartner expressed himself very happy with the orchestra.

66 1 July 1911, p. 470 (Victor Debay)

67 17 June 1911, p. 372 ("Rameau")

68 16 June 1911, p. 1 (L. Borgex)

For the *Walküre*, everything was different... He conducted with an ardour and extreme will and was repaid by the results. Among the superb moments were the restrained eloquence of the Wotan-Brünnhilde scene in act two. In the third act, the performance of the Ride of the Valkyries was made truly extraordinary by the vigour of its tempo and its incisive rhythm; this was the cutting of the ice. And in the farewell scene, the magnificent lyricism of the singers and the intense energy of the conductor created an ensemble of admirable force and passion. The orchestral ending of the drama lacked a little expression and scale.

Siegfried appeared, of all parts of the *Ring*, to be the one most suited to the talents of Mr. Weingartner, in particular the first act with the lively or powerful rhythms of Nibelheim and the forge.... [although] the tempo was exceptionally fast... [which] led at times to some confusion. In the third act, the scene of the awakening of Brünnhilde was greatly hurried [and] the effect of the scene suffered a bit. The evening of *Götterdämmerung* was happier: the first act was one of imposing grandeur, the death of Siegfried had great pathos, and the funeral march had a vehemence and striking fierceness. With these few examples we can gauge the interpretation of Mr Weingartner. It is the more sober, the more just, the more firm, the more imperious... the passages of force and rhythmic momentum were executed admirably. In the passages of tenderness, of passion, or of exaltation, there was a little dryness or stiffness. If it is a question of precision, of tempo, or vigour – that was incomparable. If it needed a deep sensibility, or a fervent passion, or a grandiose emotion, the heart is not always there, or does not seem to be there. In summary, whatever be the value of these reservations or these deficiencies, the performances of Mr. Weingartner were very beautiful.

But those of Mr. Nikisch were of still greater beauty....[except that his Ride of the Valkyries] was a little too slow: the rhythm did not have the biting violence Mr. Weingartner imposed on it.[69]

In the 1920s he conducted complete cycles in Buenos Aires and Barcelona, and in Vienna again in 1935-36. Whether Weingartner's talents were most suited to *Siegfried*, as the French writer suggested, the conductor himself considered the *Walküre* the "jewel in the crown of the *Nibelungen*."[70] An English critic attended a performance of this opera during his second period at the Vienna Opera. "The great point" in the performance had been "the poetic insight of the musical interpretation":

The conductor... astonished me with his strong yet flexible control, his sensitive phrasing, his constant high-mindedness.... [He] concentrated on form and rhythm, and so finely did he attend to these matters that they seemed, as they should always seem, one and indivisible. I have never before heard *Die Walküre* sound so full and rounded in its teeming musical life; I have seldom before heard it sound so great as composition – that is, as organized and inspired music independent of the dramatic significance.[71]

In these years some fragments from Weingartner's *Götterdämmerung* performances were recorded, including an Immolation scene. What is notable in them is the surging, turbulent orchestra, and the enormous swelling of sound interleaving the vocal parts, which one hears more extensively on recordings of Albert Coates and Artur Bodanzky. The apocalyptic orchestral ending of *Götterdämmerung*, alas, was not recorded.

[69] *Le Temps*, 11 July 1911, p. 3

[70] *Buffets and Rewards*, p. 197

[71] Neville Cardus, *Cardus on music: a centenary collection* (ed.) Donald Wright (London: H. Hamilton, 1988), p. 79, reviewing a performance of September 1935. Weingartner conducted a complete *Ring* cycle on 4, 6, 9 and 12 September 1935.

Parsifal

Weingartner greatly admired Levi, as we have seen,[72] and was offended by the "faintly contemptuous" attitude of the Wagner family towards the great artist, "which they only imperfectly concealed behind the mask of friendship."[73] Crucially, Weingartner learned from Levi about tempi in *Parsifal*. He also learned about them from Mottl, who took over when Levi became ill, at the 1888 Festival.

If Richter can be called the musical custodian of *Die Meistersinger*, then Levi can with equal justice lay claim to the same title with reference to *Parsifal*. [But under Mottl] it was conducted in such a mutilated and dragging tempo that all feeling for melody and the natural continuity of the music was utterly lost. Almost every tempo that had been engraved on our consciousness and had been immovably fixed since 1882 was turned upside down.... The representations of *Parsifal* in 1888 were one of the greatest artistic crimes, the greatest of all perhaps, that Bayreuth has ever perpetuated.[74]

Weingartner conducted excerpts from *Parsifal* in London (1898),[75] and the whole opera after the expiry of its copyright in many cities, including Paris (1914), Rio de Janeiro (1919), Buenos Aires (1920, 1922), Naples (1921), Vienna (Volksoper, 1924; State Opera, 1935-36), and London (1939). We shall look at the Paris and London performances, and obliquely at Vienna.

Parsifal in Paris

In Paris, there were challenges in the way of his *Parsifal*. It was a Boston Opera Company production, the first performance sung in German, uncut, and with a relatively new orchestra – the Orchestra Monteux – playing opera for the first time. Weingartner nevertheless made his mark: "with comparatively few rehearsals he whipped the orchestra into shape in a most wonderful manner," reported the correspondent for *Musical Courier*, "and the few bits of raggedness were absolutely

[72] see the Levi chapter above, p. 149 [73] *Buffets and Rewards*, p. 146

[74] *Bayreuth (1876-1896)*, in Dyment, *Felix Weingartner*, Appendix, pp. 100-101. Weingartner recalls that the first act under Mottl lasted "about twenty minutes" longer than formerly [under Levi and Fischer], and the last act "at least a quarter of an hour longer" (p. 100). He appears to have attended a different performance from the one whose timings were recorded by Bayreuth: see *Timings* below. In *Buffets and Rewards* he refers to the "travesty" of this *Parsifal* of 1888, with its "dragging tempi which – incredible though it seemed – Mottl had been induced to adopt": p. 168

[75] The *Morning Post* reported: "The Prelude to *Parsifal*... was played with the close of the third act tacked on, a most ineffective arrangement which should never be repeated. The Prelude, so admirable in itself, is rendered far too lengthy thereby. Herr Weingartner's interpretation of this was excellent....": 18 May 1898, p. 5. "A great conductor at last," declared the *Daily News*. "He possesses much of the marvellous exactitude of Richter, with the life and fire of a Dr. von Bülow....The Prelude and closing scene from *Parsifal*... formed a wonderful illustration of the modern theory which insists upon the utmost clearness of every part – in point of fact a practical audition of the open score": 18 May 1898, p. 10. The *Musical Times* described him as "a poet among conductors. Weingartner is great, of that there can be no doubt after his superb performances on the 17th. ... Never have we heard more euphonious combinations of wondrous sounds than he conjured up in the awfully solemn Prelude and Finale to *Parsifal*:" 1 June 1898, p. 389. The *Musical Standard* wrote: "The *Parsifal* prelude with the close of Act III. tacked on (a vandalism, if ever there was one) was played with much solemnity, and the tempi as a whole were irreproachable, but one missed a certain poignancy of expression which surely was meant to be given...": 22 May 1898, pp. 321-322.

excusable" in the circumstances.[76] *Le Monde Artiste* considered he had conducted "brilliantly": he was "the great triumphant victor" of the evening."[77] *Comœdia* was more expansive:

A performance extraordinarily alive, sensitive and intelligent. A production without pedantry and without heaviness. A masterful tempo which drives the musical line without disturbance, but which does not allow him to be led astray by lingering without reason on inessential details. An interpretation moving and warm....

One would not know how to praise too much his musical interpretation of *Parsifal*. One knows that it is based on precise memories of a study done in the company of Wagner. It is intended to react against the conventional solemnity, the slowness and stodgy heaviness which an absurd tradition imposes too often on works written in the religious style. *Parsifal* is not a work of a purely contemplative spirit; *Parsifal* is about life, of human sensibility, of everyday emotion. By his restoring its true tempo, its easy pace, and sometimes its very vivaciousness, Weingartner has given the work all its profound philosophical meaning. The beautiful mystical pages retain all their ecstatic purity, but the impassioned dialogues, the scenes of remorse, of sensuous delight, of heartbreak, of gallantry, take on an unsuspected relief and accent.[78]

Le Figaro believed the work lost some of its "priestliness" under Weingartner's hands. Instead, he had emphasised "more the purely human side of the drama":

And a lively and profound emotion emanates from this subtle and flexible interpretation, more varied, more accentuated, more rapid than those to which we are accustomed. Perhaps the great religious and mystical scenes gain thereby in contrast with the familiarity and noble naturalness of the rest. In any case, they lose nothing by such interpretation, and the achievement of Mr. Weingartner does not compare with any other in purity, depth, and in elevation.[79]

The press did not all welcome Weingartner's interpretation. "*Eh bien non*," wrote *Le Ménestrel*, "let's be fair. Nothing has been revealed to us." A quarter of an hour may have been shaved off the first act, but Gurnemanz's "terrible sermon" to the two squires still seemed too long.[80] For another critic, the spirit of Bayreuth was missing. "I can assure you that in Weingartner's interpretation exists nothing, nothing, nothing of that spirit."[81] Weingartner would have been pleased.

Parsifal in Vienna

In 1935, Weingartner reacted to criticism of one of his *Parsifal* performances in Vienna which referred to "the conductor's youthful or aged haste."[82] He reminded the *New York Times* that he was the last among active conductors to have heard *Parsifal* in 1882:

[76] 24 June 1914, p. 16. Johannes Sembach sang Parsifal; Margarete Matzenauer, Kundry; Carel Van Hulst, Amfortas; and Wilhelm Fenten, Gurnemanz.

[77] 6 June 1914, p. 356

[78] 5 June 1914, p. 1

[79] 5 June 1914, p. 5 (Henri Quittard)

[80] 13 June 1914, p. 187 (Arthur Pougin) Weingartner's direction was described as "very firm, sometimes brilliant."

[81] *Liberté* (Gaston Carraud) quoted in Quaintance Eaton, *The Boston Opera Company* (New York: Appleton-Century, 1965), p. 266

[82] Herbert Peyser had reported in the *New York Times* (14 July 1935, p. X5): "Weingartner's *Ring* is indisputably great Wagner conducting and monumental on the classic lines of the Richter tradition, despite the speed of the Weingartner tempi (here let me add that the conductor's youthful or aged haste makes him a much less satisfying *Parsifal* interpreter, as at Eastertime we had occasion to see)."

While naturally a mathematically exact reproduction of that performance is not possible, and while a certain latitude must be allowed for the individuality of a conductor, there is one claim I can maintain with absolute certainty: *Dragging tempi in "Parsifal" are a lie.* In spite of its solemn contents, *Parsifal* is a dramatic work, and Richard Wagner – who thundered repeatedly against the German "andante arm" – was too great a dramatist to have endured heavy-footed tempi in dramatic happenings. Hermann Levi received with the utmost exactness the artistic intentions of the master and carried them out in unsurpassable fashion. And in the numerous performances which I heard under his direction after 1882 (and in some of which I assisted him), the image of *Parsifal* as Wagner wanted it fixed itself inextinguishably in my recollection. This is the picture I reproduce when I have the fortune to conduct this masterwork.

... For the fanfares of the 6/4 measures in the prelude Wagner gave the direction to hold the pauses between the individual fermata not mathematically but to a certain degree in a spiritual sense, so that the connection between the separate fanfares should not be wholly interrupted. Levi repeatedly called my attention to this....

Fig. 11.7. Weingartner in concert in Vienna. Drawing by Hans Böhler

Parsifal reveals broad passages like no other work of Wagner's – perhaps like no other stage work whatever. But also, on the other hand, many parts are of the greatest dramatic nobility. If one reads the directions accurately one clearly sees that dragging is wholly out of place in this as in every other musical art work. Dragging always smarts of dilettantism, and often one finds in *Parsifal* the direction "do not drag." It might be well if contemporary conductors concerned themselves with this question and listened to my interpretations, which are those of one who received *Parsifal* from the hands that first directed it.[83]

A recollection of a rehearsal in London in 1939 by a member of the orchestra supports one of the points propounded by Weingartner:

[83] letter to the music editor dated Vienna, 14 September 1935, *New York Times*, 6 October 1935, p. 161

At certain points in the work where there were particular chords in the wind and strings he said: "This is what the Master meant, this is the way he wanted it"; and he directed that these chords should overlap rather like the sustaining pedal on the piano, so that instead of being clear cut they tended to melt into each other. An obvious example where this treatment was appropriate occurs near the end of the Grail Scene in the first act, two bars after 121 [p. 216 of the full score, Peters Edition], where the strings come to rest on the Grail theme and the remainder of the orchestra then takes it up.[84]

The surviving recorded fragments of a performance in Vienna in 1936 show some of what Weingartner was insisting upon in his letter. What there is of the prelude flows, and radiates a sense of holiness and rapture. When Gurnemanz and the Knights step into the Grail Kingdom at the end of the Transformation scene, there is a mood of buoyancy or promise – they are about to renew themselves through ritual – and in the Grail scene itself, the tempo slows, and the mood is hushed and reverent: clearly the most important ritual is being performed. Once it is over, the pace picks up, the orchestra is light, the Knights are refreshed. The act two excerpts with Kundry are intensely dramatic, and crackle with life. The orchestra becomes an extension of Kundry's mind – troubled, awful, desperate, imploring. Her *lachte!* is like a whiplash, and there is a tremendous pause that follows. Together the fragments are enough to show the great variety of moods and action Weingartner drew from the drama. We are in earshot of a superb performance.[85] We shall consider his London performances in conclusion.

The commercial recordings

Weingartner is the first of our great conductors whose Wagner was preserved in any meaningful way. At first he was reluctant to commit his interpretations to record. He eventually came to recognise that "perhaps a younger generation of conductors and listeners might derive stimulus, even perhaps assistance, from such records."[86] His earliest recordings would have done much to feed his reluctance. The Liebestod and Magic Fire Music from 1914 used crude recording techniques. The latter required extra blasts from the wind, yet still there is a certain magic in the music. The non-commercial recordings of live performances in Vienna (1934-36) are mentioned above. Of the six Columbia recordings (1938-39), only one, the *Siegfried Idyll*, was made with the London Philharmonic. The tempos, and they vary considerably, lend themselves to

[84] Richard Temple Savage quoted in Dyment, *Felix Weingartner*, p. 45; also in Savage, *A Voice From The Pit: Reminiscences of an Orchestral Musician* (Newton Abbot: David & Charles, 1988), p. 62. He also said that Weingartner's "controlled approach distinguished the performances of *Parsifal*, which he never allowed to drag. Unlike some of the Wagner conductors of the period, such as Muck and Knappertsbusch, there was absolutely no feeling of lethargy in his handling of Wagner": Dyment, *Felix Weingartner*, p. 46.

[85] Weingartner has the distinction of conducting the first complete opera to be broadcast, namely, *Parsifal* at the Teatro Coliseo in Buenos Aires on 27 August 1920. "Supposedly some fifty people could hear the broadcast in the city, but there was news that it was heard by a radio operator in a ship harbored in Santos (Brazil)." César A. Dillon in notes to *Parsifal*, Fritz Busch, Teatro Colón, 22 September 1936, CD: Marston 53003-2 (2002). No recording survives. Catullo Maestri sang Parsifal; Sara César, Kundry; Giulio Cirino, Gurnemanz; Luigi Rossi Morelli, Amfortas; with an opera company from Rio de Janeiro.

[86] Dyment, *Felix Weingartner*, p. 21. Christopher Dyment reviewed Shinseido/EMI's 24-disc Felix Weingartner Edition, which included a disc devoted to Wagner, in *International Classic Record Collector*, Spring 2000, pp. 9-17.

a more exuberant interpretation than many others. It is rich, with a strong and sinuous bass line, but light and intimate. At times the music bounces with boyish joy. At others it could be even more swift and light-footed. It recalls the performance described by New York critics in 1906. It is also the closest of any conductor in its overall timing to Wagner's likely intentions.[87]

Fig. 11.8. Weingartner at the Vienna Opera. Silhouette by Theo Zasche

Of the recordings with the Orchestre de la Société des Concerts du Conservatoire de Paris, the act three prelude from *Tristan* has a delicate, chamber-like quality that is simply sublime. Yet it is indisputably a concert performance. The work stands alone. It is not played as if passion and shame had preceded it, and agony and desperation are to follow. *Gramophone* commented when it was first released: "if some conductors might draw more anguish from the music (or impose more upon it) Weingartner's sensibility frees it for its strange, heart-searing power."[88] It is very smooth, and very soothing.

The *Rienzi* overture was "one of the numerous victims offered up to the 'Bayreuth tempo,'" Weingartner considered. "This is a piece which bubbles over with youthful spirits, chivalrous, somewhat crude, but not trivial. Compare its want of effect when conducted by a true apostle of Wahnfried to the revolution that it can produce when for once it is played in the right manner."[89] One does indeed get a sense that the tempo is right in Weingartner's recording. It is played with such exuberance that the piece swings, and at places rocks. It is "full of verve and gusto," as the *Music Review* noted, "and with an *élan* that is really astonishing."[90]

[87] see Timings below, in particular the footnote to Richter's timing of the *Idyll*. Weingartner may have come even closer to Richter's timing at a concert in Buenos Aires in 1920: he conducted the *Idyll* "with exceptional poetry, clarity, nuance, flexibility and emotion…. [He] began the passage *Leicht bewegt* – lightly and swiftly – with lightness and fluidity. The tempo then increased slightly as the theme passed from woodwind to strings, varying between 120 and 126 crotchet beats. During the *crescendo* and vehement *forte*, which concluded the passage, it reached 132 crotchet beats. The *Lebhaft* – lively – passage began around this tempo, and even increased during the *crescendo* of the passage in triplets": *La Prensa*, 31 August 1920, p. 10.

[88] January 1940, p. 289 (W. R. Anderson)

[89] *Bayreuth (1876-1896)*, in Dyment, *Felix Weingartner*, Appendix, p. 101

[90] February 1940, p. 87. Knappertsbusch might be regarded a "true apostle of Wahnfried" in this context with his 1962 recording (13' 32"), compared to the "revolutionary" Weingartner (9' 56"), and the incendiary Coates (7' 58").

His interpretation of Siegfried's Rhine Journey is beautifully sculpted. At times it sounds like chamber music. Yet it is a tremendous journey: there is much energy and movement – Siegfried seems to *jump* into the Rhine – yet there are moments of reflection, of exploration. It is "the grandest of youthful high spirits," wrote *Gramophone*, adding in parentheses if not understatement, "Weingartner's speed is a bit faster than usual."[91] The interpretation of Siegfried's Funeral March is "less sharply etched and more mellow in sound" than the Rhine Journey, as the *American Music Lover* observed.[92] The first, famous crunching chord is subdued. The whole is less weighty, less grand, than in many other readings. Perhaps it was an example of Weingartner's aversion to excess.

Farewell to Parsifal

In the last years of his life Weingartner conducted three performances of *Parsifal* in London. The reviews were approving, but not exactly enthusiastic, for reasons a little out of the conductor's hands. *The Times* wrote:

> His long experience has taught him not only the art of sustaining a musical line of thought without over-insistence on climaxes, but exactly where the orchestra must understate in order that the essential features, words as well as music, of the vocal parts may be made clear. He gave considerable help to last night's capable though not particularly powerful cast of singers. Of almost every part the old Wagner-lover can say he has heard better... There were moments... which were dramatically disappointing, yet through the certainty of Dr. Weingartner's handling the wonderful web of the orchestral texture sustained the whole design and produced a performance of dignity and significance.[93]

"It was a performance lacking in gusts of passion or ecstatic climaxes," according to the *Daily Telegraph and Morning Post*, "but in compensation there was serenity and poise. The relation between the stage and orchestra was exact and the playing – particularly of the brass – was immaculate."[94] The performance was "uneven," in the view of the *Observer*. "The orchestra did its duty under Felix Weingartner, and earned our thanks in the overture and the accompaniment of Act III....[95] To the *Sunday Times* the performance was "in the main quietly moving rather than thrilling. There was hardly a big moment in it from the first to last, though in compensation we had long stretches of exquisite orchestral playing of the quieter kind."[96]

These reviews suggest a different Weingartner from Paris twenty-five years earlier. Serenity and poise were among the well-known characteristics of his conducting. But the dramatic fire seems to have faded. Now there is a mellowness. He was almost 76 years of age, and perhaps the lights on the Christmas tree were gradually going out.

[91] June 1941, p. 9 (W. R. Anderson)
[92] August 1942, p. 372 (P. H. R. [Peter Hugh Reed])
[93] 3 May 1939, p. 12. Torsten Ralf sang Parsifal; Germaine Lubin, Kundry; Herbert Janssen, Amfortas; and Ludwig Hofmann, Gurnemanz.
[94] 3 May 1939, p. 10 (J. A. Westrup)
[95] 7 May 1939, p. 12
[96] *Sunday Times*, 7 May 1939, p. 7 (Ernest Newman). Neville Cardus recalled Newman whispering to him during Weingartner's performance: "Before this 'Good Friday' is over it'll be Easter Monday." Cardus, *Sir Thomas Beecham: a memoir* (London: Collins, 1961), p. 88. Whether or not Cardus's recollection was accurate, Newman used this expression to describe a performance of the same scene by Karl Muck at Bayreuth: "I should not have been surprised to find that Good Friday had lasted until well into Easter Monday": *Sunday Times*, 10 August 1930, p. 5.

12

Bruno Walter – Singer in the pit

Bruno Walter was pre-eminently the singing conductor. He played for song, he played for singers, he played for drama. "Throughout my life there has been a singing within me," he wrote in his memoirs; "is not every production of music really connected with singing?"[1] His insight into song made him a great coach and accompanist. He conducted at a time when there were unusually good Wagner singers, and the extent to which he contributed to their great performances must remain a matter of some conjecture. Sometimes it was acknowledged by singers, mostly it was not. There were inevitably some singers with whom he could do little. Whatever his other considerable gifts, he was at home in the theatre. From the earliest days of his career he "felt amphibiously at home in both of [opera's] interpretative elements, the dramatic and the musical."[2] In this, Mahler was his master. Their work together in Hamburg and Vienna exercised a profound influence on the younger conductor. Walter became the torch-bearer for Mahler.[3] They were temperamentally different artists, yet shared many fundamental views towards music-making and opera, including an abiding love of Wagner's music.

Wagnerian strands

He was born in Berlin on 15 September 1876 as Bruno Schlesinger, and adopted Walter as a "stage name" in 1896, drawing on a number of Wagnerian characters, real and fictional: Walther von Stolzing, Walther von der Vogelweide, Frohwalt and Wehwalt.[4] As a boy he liked hearing the sound of Prussian military bands and the strains of the synagogue organ. He took piano lessons from his mother, sang beautifully, and displayed perfect pitch. "From the days of my childhood I have felt music to be the element for which I was born, in which I am at home, and which is the language

[1] Bruno Walter, *Theme and variations: an autobiography*, (trans.) James A. Galston (London: H. Hamilton, 1947), p. 11

[2] *ibid*, p. 13

[3] "In the opera house … he is Mahler's real successor, without the latter's sternness and contempt for the individual orchestral player": *The memoirs of Carl Flesch,* Hans Keller (trans. and ed.), (London: Rockliff, 1957), p. 344

[4] *Theme and variations*, p. 97. It became his legal name when he took out Austrian citizenship in 1911. He was unhappy about having to change his name, but had no choice: there were too many Schlesingers in Breslau and if he wanted an appointment there he had to adopt a different name: Erik Ryding and ReBecca Pechefsky, *Bruno Walter: A World Elsewhere* (New Haven and London: Yale University Press, 2001), pp. 21-22

I understand and am able to speak."[5] At the early age of nine he entered the Stern Conservatory where the name of Wagner was frowned upon. Around the age of thirteen, he attended *Tristan* for the first time at the Berlin Opera, conducted by Joseph Sucher:

From the first sound of the cellos my heart contracted spasmodically. The magic, like the terrible potion that the mortally ill Tristan curses in the third act, "burst raging forth from heart to brain." Never before had my soul been deluged with floods of sound and passion, never had my heart been consumed by such yearning and sublime bliss, never had I been transported from reality by such heavenly glory. I was no longer in this world. After the performance, I roamed the streets aimlessly. When I got home I didn't say anything and begged not to be questioned. My ecstasy kept singing within me through half the night, and when I awoke on the following morning I knew that my life had changed. A new epoch had begun: Wagner was my god, and I wanted to become his prophet.[6]

How he was going to do this, as a pianist, was not clear. Then, one day at a Berlin Philharmonic concert, he heard and saw, from a seat high up behind the drums, Hans von Bülow conduct a classic programme:

I saw in Bülow's face the glow of inspiration and the concentration of energy. I felt the compelling force of his gestures, noticed the attention and devotion of the players, and was conscious of the expressiveness and precision of their playing. It became at once clear to me that it was that one man who was producing the music, that he had transformed those hundred performers into his instrument, and that he was playing it as a pianist plays a piano. That evening decided my future. ... I had decided to become a conductor.[7]

He studied Wagner's essays *On Conducting* and on *Beethoven* – they left "profound and lasting impressions"[8] – and he studied and transcribed Wagner's scores. In 1891 or 1892 he won a free trip to Bayreuth where he "heard *Parsifal* and *Tristan* under Hermann Levi's direction, and, unless I am mistaken, *Fliegende Holländer* under Felix Mottl."[9] He returned more convinced than ever of his artistic mission.

His first professional engagement was at the Cologne Opera (1893-94) where he coached singers, for a *Meistersinger* performance among others, and during which time he heard a *Ring* conducted by Josef Grossmann.[10] He then went to the Hamburg Opera (1894-96), which was headed by Mahler, to work as coach and later conductor. Mahler's way of working deeply influenced him. "The object of Mahler's endeavours was to bring music and the many-styled drama into proper correlation... [His] piano rehearsals were unforgettably instructive to me because of his imperious and imaginative injunctions to the singers and his deep penetration into the works. At his orchestral rehearsals, his tyrannical personality forced the musicians by intimidation

5 *Theme and variations*, p. 11

6 *ibid*, p. 42; Martin Mayer, "Bruno Walter, The Working Musician of Beverly Hills," *Harper's Magazine*, February 1961, p. 75

7 *ibid*, p. 41. He spoke in general terms about Bülow's performances, and did not specify what his programmes were: pp. 49-50.

8 *ibid*, p. 44. "I did not choose [between Brahms and Wagner], I just loved both of them."

9 *ibid*, p. 57. He could not remember the precise year, and was mistaken about *Fliegende Holländer*, which was not introduced to Bayreuth till 1901, and *Tristan*: Levi never conducted *Tristan* at Bayreuth. In 1891 and 1892, there were performances of *Parsifal* (Levi), *Tristan* (Mottl) and *Tannhäuser* (Mottl), and in 1892, *Meistersinger* (Mottl and Richter).

10 "a young, gifted, and temperamental Viennese who... seemed lacking in seriousness and weight": *ibid*, p. 70.

and passionate stimulation into giving their utmost."[11] Walter's first opportunity to conduct Wagner was during a stage rehearsal of *Siegfried* when Mahler was delayed. "It was the stormy beginning of the third act, the awakening of Erda, whose mystical primordial strains I was privileged to conjure up. My luck lasted... until the passing through the fire..." Then Mahler arrived, but did not immediately relieve him.[12]

He had opportunities to conduct a wide range of repertory operas, including *Walküre* and *Tannhäuser*, before he went to Breslau (1896-97) on Mahler's recommendation. This was "the low point of my life," he recalled. "Operas came pouring in on me. They were repertoire performances, operas that needed no rehearsing."[13] After a season at Pressburg (1897-98) he went to Riga as chief conductor (1898-1900). There he conducted *Lohengrin*, *Meistersinger*, *Walküre*, *Tannhäuser*, and *Holländer*. In 1900 he went to the Royal Opera in Berlin (1900-01), where Strauss and Muck were the other two conductors. They were "active only in a strictly musical sense," he wrote, and did not involve themselves in stage production.[14] He was "strongly impressed by a *Götterdämmerung* under Muck, though it lacked the spontaneous dramatic impetuosity for which [he] longed."[15] The closest he appears to have got to conducting a Wagner work was Siegfried Wagner's *Der Bärenhäuter*. The performance pleased Cosima Wagner, Walter recalled. He told her afterwards he had been "impressed with the natural simplicity of the work." That was not enough for Cosima. She replied: "It has rather more than natural simplicity. My son succeeded, in his *Bärenhäuter*, in writing the finest non-tragic opera since the *Meistersinger*." Walter continued: "After that unbelievably daring, yes, blasphemous utterance of Richard Wagner's widow, there was nothing to do but change the subject." He mentioned Verdi, "in total disregard of a strict Bayreuth rule," and never met Cosima again.[16] And, of course, he was never invited to conduct in Bayreuth.

After only a year in Berlin, "under chaotic administrative arrangements,"[17] he went to Vienna (1901-12). There the "Court Opera glowed in the pure light shed by the genius of Mahler.... I consider *Tristan* at the beginning and *Iphigenia in Aulis* towards its end the culminating points of Mahler's activity as the head of the Opera."[18]

[11] *ibid*, p. 84. In this memoir (1947) Walter wrote: "I have retained no recollection of any individual performance under Mahler..." (p. 85); yet in his book on *Mahler* (1936), he wrote: "My most vivid impressions from his Hamburg period remain his *Ring* and *Meistersinger*; later, in Vienna, came a *Tristan*....": *Gustav Mahler* (trans.) Lotte Walter Lindt (London: Quartet Books, 1990), p. 23; in 1956 he said of Mahler's influence on him: "In Wagner! In Wagner... my first performance [of Mahler] in Vienna... in *Hamburg*... was *Götterdämmerung*... was *Tristan und Isolde* and this [or these] was an enormous impression for me, decisive for my whole life - *oh yes, it was something unforgettable, indescribable*": interview with Arnold Michaelis, 23 February 1956: Columbia BW 80 (LP); as noted in the Mahler chapter above, the words in *italics* were omitted from a subsequent reissue.

[12] *ibid*, p. 91

[13] *ibid*, pp. 105, 108

[14] *ibid*, p. 134

[15] *ibid*, p. 140. He was less impressed with a *Tristan* by Strauss (see Strauss chapter, p. 534). He had no recollection of concerts given by Strauss or Weingartner, only a number of "truly magnificent evenings" of Nikisch concerts: "I was warmed by his natural and fundamental musicianship."

[16] *ibid*, p. 139. He did go to Bayreuth, in 1901, as a guest of Ernst Krauss, and "heard several fine and carefully prepared performances conducted by Mottl" (*ibid*, p. 143). Mottl conducted only *Fliegende Holländer* that year.

[17] *ibid*, p. 142. The artistic leadership in Berlin may also have been a factor. When he was still in Riga he wrote to his uncle complaining that: "Berlin is perfectly satisfied with its Muckish mediocrity": Ryding and Pechefsky, *Bruno Walter*, p. 36

[18] *ibid*, pp. 150, 157. Mahler used Wagner's arrangement of *Iphigenia* and personally regarded it "the best

He heard a performance there of *Meistersinger* conducted by Richter "at which he displayed the full mastery of his leadership."[19] Walter fell quite under the spell of Mahler, as he admits, and was seen to imitate him both off the podium and on, as Richard Specht recalled:

> He went into contortions on the podium, he expressed and lived the music with his body, and his conducting was agitated, uneven, nervous, and impulsive. He made a cult of stormy vehemence, fervour, and passion, and tended to over-emphasize odd episodes and secondary passages. In time, however, he calmed down, his technique matured, and the real Walter, who was more easy-going and romantic, less harsh and eloquent than Mahler, finally came to the fore and asserted his innate sense of the drama, his zeal and enthusiasm, and his love of beautiful orchestral sound and ability to obtain it.[20]

Mahler assigned him *Walküre*, *Holländer*, and *Tannhäuser*. After a performance of *Tannhäuser* he was attacked in the press and declared "incapable of conducting even a military band," though Mahler assured him this was but an indirect attack on himself.[21] He opened the 1904 season with *Lohengrin*. Mahler departed in 1907. Walter was not impressed by his successor, Weingartner (1908-1911), due to "the fundamental differences of our natures."[22] After Weingartner's controversial cuts to *Walküre*, Walter conducted a performance with the cuts partially restored.[23] During this period he began travelling abroad. He made his concert debut in London in 1908 and, in 1910, his opera debut with *Tristan* at Covent Garden. When Weingartner left Vienna in 1911, he was succeeded by a non-conductor, so it was only a matter of time before Walter would seek another position.[24]

He performed *Ring* operas in Munich in 1912, dispensing with the movable lid over the sunken orchestral pit to ensure greater brilliance.[25] He duly became Royal Bavarian Music Director there (1913-22). His first opera in his new position was *Tristan*,[26] and during his tenure he conducted all of Wagner's operas, including *Rienzi*. In May 1914 Munich's first *Parsifal*, working closely with the stage director, Anton Fuchs, "religiously observing Wagner's stage directions."[27] These years were "the most

that Roller and I have achieved so far" (1907): Erwin Stein, "Mahler and the Vienna Opera," in Rosenthal, *The Opera bedside book*, pp. 313-15.

19 *Theme and variations*, p. 172

20 Richard Specht (no source cited) in Henry-Louis de La Grange, *Gustav Mahler, Vol. 2, Vienna: the years of challenge (1897-1904)* (London: Gollancz, & Oxford: Oxford University Press, 1995), p. 382. He concluded: "Whatever his faults may have been at the time, Mahler far preferred Walter's expressive intensity to Schalk's prosaic style." Specht made comments along the lines quoted by La Grange in his *Gustav Mahler* (Berlin: Schuster & Loeffler, 1913), pp. 123-5, and *Das Wiener Operntheater von Dingelstedt bis Schalk und Strauß: Erinnerung aus 50 Jahren* (Wien: Paul Knepler, 1919), pp. 77-8. A London musician recalled an occasion in rehearsal under Walter when, a split second before he brought down his baton, he "smilingly yelled at us: 'Too loud! Too loud!'" – an echo of Mahler's comment to a New York orchestra (see Mahler chapter, p. 261): Gerald Jackson, *First Flute* (London: Dent, 1968).

21 La Grange, *Mahler, Vol. 2*, p. 381; *Theme and variations*, p. 172; Ryding and Pechefsky, *Bruno Walter*, p. 44

22 *Theme and variations*, p. 196; see also Weingartner chapter, p. 285

23 Ryding and Pechefsky, *Bruno Walter*, p. 71

24 Hans Gregor, a stage director from the Komische Oper, Berlin was the new director: Ryding and Pechefsky, *Bruno Walter*, p. 85.

25 *ibid*, p. 98. A *Götterdämmerung* in Vienna had also been observed by the authorities from Munich, before sealing his appointment: *Theme and variations*, p. 210

26 Ryding and Pechefsky, *Bruno Walter*, pp. 104-5. Jacques Urlus sang Tristan, Zdenka Mottl-Fassbender Isolde.

27 *Theme and variations*, p. 220. His assistant conductors were Hugo Röhr, "a *routinier*," and Franz Fischer,

prolific period of my life," he recalled.[28] Yet like Mahler in Vienna, as the years drew to a close he felt had done all he could, and it was time to move on. Also like Mahler, he had become the victim of increasingly vitriolic attacks.[29]

Among his guest appearances in the years to follow were the German seasons at Covent Garden from 1924 to 1931, which included the *Meistersinger* (10), the *Ring* (8) plus five individual *Ring* operas, *Tristan* (7), and *Fliegende Holländer* (2).[30] He also conducted *Tristan* and *Walküre* at the Deutsches Opernhaus in Charlottenberg in 1924. He made his first Wagner recordings in this period. Apart from *A Faust Overture* in Berlin in 1923, they were with British orchestras made on his visits to England (1924-32). He was appointed head of the new Municipal Oper in Berlin (1925-29) where he opened with a performance of the *Meistersinger*. Political intrigues by Hans Tietjen, a "scheming and inordinately ambitious man," led to his departure, and he never conducted Wagner in Berlin again.

He conducted *Tristan* in Vienna in 1933, at two Salzburg Festivals (1933 and 1934), and on the inauguration of his term as artistic director at the Vienna State Opera (1936-38).[31] In Vienna in 1935 he recorded the *Siegfried Idyll* and parts of the *Walküre*. By the late 1930s Nazism was on the rise in Austria. One evening stink-bombs were thrown in the theatres and cinemas of Vienna. Walter was conducting *Tristan* at the State Opera. He was determined not to give the Nazis the satisfaction of having disrupted his performance. "I led the opera to its conclusion, but Isolde and Tristan – and especially the former – had become so hoarse through breathing in the vapours that the *Liebestod* was played by the orchestra without vocal accompaniment."[32] It was the last Wagner opera he mentioned in his memoirs. He was in Amsterdam when the Germans marched into Austria in March 1938. He did not return, and sailed for the United States from Genoa in October 1939.

The New World was not a land of promise for Walter so far as Wagner opera was concerned. The strands had broken. It was the beginning of a period, he wrote, in which he "would no longer be able to make full use of [his] powers."[33] Although he included Wagner excerpts in some of his concerts (1939-1957), and some of these survive on record, he never conducted Wagner at the Metropolitan Opera. He had unsuccessfully asked for a *Tristan* in 1942. When he was offered a *Parsifal* at short notice

"a simple, straightforward musician [who] confined himself at that time exclusively to conducting Wagner. The dyed-in-the-wool Wagnerites in the public – there were gradations – would whisper to one another that 'Fischerfranzl' was really much greater than Mottl. [Walter regarded this as a "heresy."] …I don't suppose that I witnessed more than a few of his performances, but I, too, sensed the greatness of his musicianship." (pp. 221-2).

28 *Theme and variations*, p. 226

29 By the end of 1922 the "dark powers of hell had already begun their work," Walter wrote, and swastikas were to be seen on the walls of Munich. Personal attacks on him were a factor in his departure, he wrote, but not decisive. *ibid*, pp. 227, 265-6.

30 Information from the Royal Opera House. At Covent Garden he was musical director "in everything but name": Harold Rosenthal, *Opera at Covent Garden: A Short History* (London: Victor Gollancz Ltd, 1967), p. 108.

31 A businessman, Erwin Kerber, was the director in succession to Weingartner (his second term as director). Between 1931 and 1937, *Tristan* was conducted by Strauss, Schalk, Knappertsbusch, Furtwängler, Walter, Karajan, and Böhm: Marcel Prawy, *The Vienna Opera*, (Vienna-Munich-Zurich: Verlag Fritz Molden, 1969), pp. 150-2.

32 *Theme and Variations*, pp. 352-3. The Isolde was Anny Konetzni: Prawy, *The Vienna Opera*, p. 153.

33 *Theme and Variations*, p. 269

in 1944, it was impossible for him to re-schedule his other engagements.[34] In 1959, he embarked on his Wagner recordings with the Columbia Symphony Orchestra. Although now an old man, music continued to have an "astonishingly rejuvenating influence" on him, as Dietrich Fischer-Dieskau witnessed. "Walter dragged himself to the podium where, as soon as the first notes sounded, he was transformed, infused with fire and dynamism."[35] And so in March 1961, aged 84, he mounted the podium and recorded his last Wagner, the Overture and Venusberg scene from *Tannhäuser*. He died at his home in Beverley Hills, California on 17 February 1962.

Walter as a Wagner conductor

In his later years, Walter tended to distance himself from his love of Wagner, characterising it as a youthful infatuation, a time when he was "enthusiastic for the great pathos and the big emotions."[36] The lessons he learned, however, stayed with him for his whole life. He acknowledged "the axiomatic significance" of Wagner's injunction in *On Conducting* that "proper *tempo*" was the true measure of whether or not a conductor understood a piece.[37] Walter clearly subscribed to this, but not as a rigid rule:

> I myself do not know why at one time I take a tempo faster, another time slower; why my expression may change from one performance to another; and so on. I do not approach music with reason. I never understood to rationalize what I did. My only way of making music is to come as near as possible to the intentions of the composer each time I perform his works, and the spontaneity which is an indispensable quality of each musical performance may very well account for differences.[38]

He also understood that "the *spirit of drama* must permeate [the conductor's] musical endeavours in the interpretation of an opera."[39] This is another Wagnerian dictum we shall see he followed in instruction and performance. Finally, he understood how the orchestra must *breathe* with the singers.

[34] Ryding and Pechefsky, *Bruno Walter*, pp. 283, 293-4. Walter conducted 119 opera performances with the Metropolitan Opera between 1941 and 1959.

[35] Dietrich Fischer-Dieskau, *Reverberations*, (trans.) Ruth Hein (New York: Fromm International Publishing Corporation, 1989), pp. 161-2

[36] interview with Arnold Michaelis, 23 February 1956: Columbia BW 80 (LP); in July 1958 he said that after hearing *Tristan*, Wagner "took possession of my soul and changed my life. That is not exaggerated, what I say. Well, and then it took some years, and then came Mozart into my life": interview with Albert Goldberg, Robert Chesterman (ed.), *Conversations with Conductors* (London: Robson Books, 1976), p. 23. His musical interests and talents soon embraced Mozart, Mahler and Bruckner.

[37] Walter, *Of music and music-making* (trans.) Paul Hamburger (London: Faber and Faber, 1961), p. 29

[38] letter to a Japanese student, 23 October 1953, quoted in Ryding and Pechefsky, *Bruno Walter*, p. 347. Yehudi Menuhin "marvelled to find such support, such adaptability" in Walter's accompaniment; he "knew in advance what degree of flexibility of tempo was required... He wasn't a man to defend a position brutally, he wasn't authoritarian; as with music, so with musicians (and I don't think he separated the one from the other), they were living, pulsing, feeling human beings upon whom the grid of dogma could not properly be dropped. His adaptability did not imply a lack of principle": Menuhin, *Unfinished journey* (London: Futura Publications, 1978), pp. 132-133. In August 1997 Menuhin wrote: "Unlike Toscanini, who imposed his concept upon both orchestra and soloist, Bruno Walter allowed each voice to speak or sing...": preface to Michele Selvini, *Bruno Walter - La porta dell'eternità 1876-1932* (Montagnola: Fondazione culturale della collina d'oro, 1999), p. [viii].

[39] Walter, *Of music and music-making*, p. 108 (emphasis added)

All music is singing. The ideal is to make the orchestra play like singers. Singing is the fundamental of making music.... My very first experience as a boy – I accompanied singers, lieder recitals. There you learn that you have to take breath – and breath-taking is the enemy of precision. This idea of precision in orchestral playing is very recent. It was a necessary reaction to a certain lackadaisical way of attacking tasks, and Toscanini in forwarding it did a wonderful service. But now precision has become an ideal, which is wrong.[40]

An understanding of the drama and a proper consideration of the singers were skills of Walter's which were appreciated by some of his most gifted Wagnerian singers. Lotte Lehmann extolled his "loving absorption in his work, and his exhaustive penetration of each part: he never gets lost in externals, but draws its spiritual content from the music and the words, as if from a magic well...."[41] When she first began working with him, "I started to *know* what I was doing instead of just feeling it."[42] Frida Leider wrote of his "great gifts," and of how he "was very good with the singers. He always kept the volume of orchestral sound... well under control."[43] Hans Hotter sang Wotan's Farewell for the first time in Amsterdam in 1936 under Walter:

I will never forget the radiance from an extraordinary artistic personality at the rehearsals in Amsterdam. ... He took the time for a one-on-one rehearsal and concentrated completely on [Wotan's Farewell]. With youthful élan and obvious enthusiasm this man in his sixties exerted his every effort to teaching me that Wotan in his paternal affection uninhibitedly gives vent to the full range of his human emotions. "Throughout these twenty minutes, you should be constantly close to tears – not in reality but in your artistic imagination. Otherwise you'll lose control. Try to imagine the face of your beloved daughter before you, and don't ever stop trying to express an abundance of emotion. It's not your own genuine sensation at the moment but rather the feeling you conjure up artistically that moves the audience."[44]

The profundity of Walter's advice is borne out by Hotter's performances, though only one was under Walter himself. Lauritz Melchior was more difficult to tame. His exuberant departure from printed rhythms and tempos was exasperating for more than one conductor, including Walter. "Melchior! My left hand is exclusively yours!" he once called up to him from the pit.[45] Melchior respected Walter, but preferred

[40] Martin Mayer, "Bruno Walter: The Working Musician of Beverly Hills," *Harper's Magazine*, February 1961, p. 76

[41] Lotte Lehmann, *Wings of song: an autobiography*, trans. Margaret Ludwig (London: Kegan Paul, Trench, Trubner, 1938), p. 230. A viola player in the Hallé Orchestra, Malcolm Tillis, commented how "orchestral playing under Bruno Walter [was] raised out of mundane routine on to a spiritual plane": *Chords and Discords: The Life of an Orchestral Musician* (London: Phoenix House, 1960), p. 136. Tillis played under Walter at a concert on 7 May 1954, which included the prelude from *Parsifal*, in aid of the Kathleen Ferrier Cancer Research Fund.

[42] "Bruno Walter, 1876-1962: Three Tributes" [Lotte Lehmann, Regina Resnik, John Parry], *Opera*, vol. 13 no. 4 (April 1962), p. 240

[43] Frida Leider, *Playing my part*, (trans.) Charles Osborne (London: Calder and Boyars, 1966), p. 88

[44] Hans Hotter, *Memoirs*, (trans. and ed.) Donald Arthur (Boston: Northeastern University Press, 2006), p. 18. He dated this as 1937, but it was on 15 March 1936 that he sang Wotan's Farewell at a Wagner Festival concert in Amsterdam under Walter. Part of the concert was broadcast and survives on record, though not the Farewell: see Discography.

[45] Robert Tuggle, *The Golden Age of Opera* (New York: Holt, Rinehart and Winston, 1983), p. 196. Walter showed his deft handling of Melchior, as well as his ability to follow singers, at the latter's debut in the *Walküre* of the second cycle in London in 1924. On the day of the performance (14 May) Melchior had still had no rehearsal and told Walter he "had never seen, nor heard, nor sung on any stage, the role I was supposed to sing that evening! [Walter] nearly had a stroke: but as it proved impossible to hunt up another

Leo Blech.[46] Walter, with his sense of the drama, of his singing orchestra, his feeling for the singers, summed up his role as opera conductor: "To tone down the orchestra without renouncing brilliance, weight and clarity – this was the squaring of the circle that occupied my whole life; and my only regret is that I cannot express the results of my endeavours in the form of practical advice."[47] We may not have his advice, but we do have evidence of his performances. At times they were greater than he modestly claimed; his 1926 *Rheingold*, for example, where, according to *Music & Letters*, he made "the music [play] the part of chorus, expositor and commentator in the wealth of the instrumentation, covering the whole play with a panoply of rich texture, the coloured robe of sound."[48] Wagner's early works (and *Parsifal*) do not appear frequently in Walter's repertoire.[49] He doubtless preferred to conduct the later works, and it is from these performances – of *Tristan*, *Meistersinger*, and the *Ring* – that his stature as a Wagner conductor can be gauged.

Tristan und Isolde

Walter firmly believed that "he who is a stranger to ecstasy cannot convincingly conduct Wagner's *Tristan und Isolde*."[50] This may be a necessary condition, but it is not a sufficient one. Walter's experience with *Tristan* did not always produce the effects of ecstasy he would have wished, as the responses to his London debut in 1910 show. He "began the overture a good deal slower and less passionately than some conductors

Siegmund, he was forced to bite the sour apple and let me sing the role without any rehearsal whatsoever…. The performance went quite well for me… only in the *Todesverkündigung* I made a mistake in the text and asked Brünnhilde [Frida Leider] the wrong question, and in the tension of the situation she jumped ahead in the music and answered it. This caused a minor confusion as the conductor had to skip to catch up with us, but it was so slight that only a very few were aware of it – even among the music critics": Ib Melchior, *Lauritz Melchior: The Golden Years of Bayreuth* (Fort Worth, Tex.: Baskerville Publishers, 2003), p. 34. *The Times* commented: "Herr Melchior's Siegmund was uneven; the story of his life was made rather unintelligible by hurry, the duet with Sieglinde was good singing, the pathetic scene with Brünnhilde he seemed not to be altogether sure of, and he conceived the wrong tempo for the sword song, though he was not allowed to adopt it. … Walter's conducting of the first act was irresistible….": 15 May 1924, p. 12. Melchior's biographer wrote: "Walter had not a word to say to Melchior" after this debut, and that he "was 'not helpful' to his singers….": Emmons, *Tristanissimo*, pp. 41, 72.

[46] "his touchstone of conductors": Emmons, *Tristanissimo*, p. 72. Melchior's view of Blech was shared by Frida Leider: "He was an ideal opera conductor, and knew, more than anyone else, how to lead his singers. … The years under Leo Blech will always be thought of as the golden age of the Berlin State Opera." *Playing My Part*, p. 94. Blech's years at the Berlin State Opera (or its predecessor) were 1906-23 and 1926-37. He was General Music Director from 1913. Erich Kleiber was also General Music Director from 1923 to 1934.

[47] Walter, *Of music and music-making*, p. 147

[48] vol. 7 no. 4 (October 1926), p. 373 (Halsey Ricardo)

[49] His repertoire, as given above, is drawn from Ryding and Pechefsky, *Bruno Walter*, *passim*. Ryding and Pechefsky discuss criticism of a 1899 Riga performance with two of his recordings of the overture at pp. 33-4. A 1924 *Fliegende Holländer* in London had mixed reviews. "The genuine Wagner prevailed, and we were made to feel the whitehot fervour of imagination…": *The Times*, 3 June 1925, p. 10; "an excellent [performance]": *Sunday Times*, 7 June 1925 (Ernest Newman); "too emphatic, too heavy. One missed the lyrical note… the pace of much of the music was too slow": *Daily Express*, 3 June 1925; it "did not convert the pleasant *Flying Dutchman* into grand opera with a big O": *Morning Post*, 3 June 1925.

[50] Walter, *Of music and music-making*, p. 106; interview with Arnold Michaelis, 23 February 1956: Columbia BW 80 (LP); interview with Albert Goldberg, July 1958, in Chesterman (ed.), *Conversations with Conductors*, p. 23

Fig. 12.1. Bruno Walter in rehearsal

Fig. 12.2. Walter from his Munich years, 1913-1922

Fig. 12.3. Walter recording in the Musikvereinsaal during his Vienna years where he recorded excerpts from *Die Walküre* in 1935

Fig. 12.4. Walter conducting the Berlin Philharmonic in the Overture to *Oberon* (Weber), from a 1931 film directed by Franz Schreker

Fig. 12.5. Walter conducting Pfitzner's *Das Herz*, Kroll Opera, 1931. Photo by Felix H. Man

Fig. 12.6. Walter at the Hollywood Bowl, from which Wagnerian excerpts survive on record from 1947 and 1953

do," wrote *The Times*.[51] The performance seems never to have picked up. It was "an accurate performance," according to the *Observer*, but "at times a certain depth of emotion seemed to be suppressed at the very moment of expression."[52] The *World* thought it a "very praiseworthy performance," but it "lacked glow and colour."[53] The *Sunday Times* characterized it as "thoroughly German in spirit, sound but unexciting."[54] There must have been some "temporary reason" for this, speculated the *Star*. Walter was known for his "crispness and spirit" in the concert hall, and in this case there had been a heavy performance and rehearsal schedule preceding the performance, and the orchestra showed it was tired. Nevertheless, the conductor "brought off some fine climaxes, especially in the last act; and on the whole he was more successful in the strenuous than in the gentler passages, when the modern German love of slow tempi was prominent."[55] It was not a great debut. A second performance was marred by a late substitute for Tristan,[56] though *The Times* considered Walter "conducted with real insight and skill, ... the beauty of the orchestral playing was among the most remarkable features of the performance."[57]

When he conducted it at Covent Garden again in 1924, he was at the height of his powers. To the *Manchester Guardian* he conducted with "absolute mastery."[58] The *Daily Telegraph* wrote:

> *Tristan* is said by some authorities to be the strongest card in Mr. Bruno Walter's Wagnerian pack, and certainly his reading of the wondrous score did not belie his reputation. Strong in its feelings for climax, clear in detail – and always authoritative, it was a reading that hardly ever failed to carry conviction and a sense of the music's inevitability.[59]

The *Star* considered it was a long time since a "finer orchestral performance" had been heard in London. "One might have wished for a little more sinuous charm in the love music in the second act, and less robustness, but granted the conductor's ideal, it could not have been better, and the number of real thrills was quite considerable. ... he regards each act as an organic whole; which is as it should be."[60] *The Times* was more reserved: it considered it had been "a very efficient performance in all respects, but it was lifted above the implication of that word mainly by Mme Frida Leider...."[61] The *Observer* considered "some of the conductor's tempi have been to British ears, very slow.... the love duet was dragged (though this may have been at the singers'

[51] 22 February 1910, p. 12. Jacques Urlus sang Tristan, Zdenka Mottl-Fassbender Isolde.

[52] 27 February 1910, p. 9 [53] 1 March 1910, p. 355 (Alfred Kalisch) [54] 27 February 1910, p. 4

[55] 22 February 1910, p. 2 ("Crescendo") "However," the review concluded, "he brought out all the points of the score well, and obviously has a thorough grasp of the music."

[56] Dr. Barnasch, from Elberfeld; Anna Bahr-Mildenburg sang Isolde. *Daily Telegraph*, 3 March 1910, p. 13; *Observer*, 6 March 1910, p. 9

[57] 3 March 1910, p. 13. Walter Legge wrote in his essay on Sir Thomas Beecham (1979): "According to T. B., audiences were only 'fairly good.' To other accounts, Walter's *Tristan* was a triumph; it must have been because an extra performance was added. This season made Beecham the musical hero of Britain": Elisabeth Schwarzkopf, *On and Off the Record: A Memoir of Walter Legge* (New York: Scribner, 1982), p. 152.

[58] 9 May 1924. Reviews from the 1924 season have been quoted from clippings in the Royal Opera House Collections, where page numbers were not recorded.

[59] 9 May 1924; "another triumph for Bruno Walter": *Daily News*, 9 May 1924

[60] 9 May 1924 ("Crescendo")

[61] 9 May 1924, p. 12. Tristan was sung by Jacques Urlus, not Lauritz Melchior as Frida Leider recalled in her memoirs: *Playing My Part*, p. 69. Later performances that season were sung by Gertrude Kappel and Fritz Soot. Leider sang with Melchior in the *Walküre* on 22 May 1924, conducted by Karl Alwin.

wish)...."[62] Walter "secured a fine rendering of the orchestral part," according to the *Yorkshire Post*. "His sense of dynamic values is evidently keen, also his perception of the exact moment when the force of a climax can be enhanced by slightly hastening the pace."[63] He conducted it again in 1925, the 100th performance at Covent Garden, as the *Morning Post* reported:

> We were given a fine and in some respects an unusually moving performance of *Tristan und Isolde* at Covent Garden last night. ... The [orchestra], under Mr. Bruno Walter, was again magnificent. A wonderful body of players wonderfully handled, strong but never overpowering the singers, and in the duet of the second act and the prelude of the third exquisitely tender. Mr. Walter was bold in his tempos, but he has an extraordinary flair for presenting us with the details of Wagner's orchestration. Thus nothing was slurred, nothing over-emphasised.[64]

The Times noted some "blemishes in the playing" of the orchestra. In future performances "he will no doubt have its tone sand-papered down to a perfect blend," the *Observer* noted. *The Times* continued:

> He allows no doubt about the places where the orchestra must come right into the foreground, the climax of the first act, of the love duet, and elsewhere. He is not afraid to allow the instruments to envelop the voices when they have more to say than the singers, yet his judgement is always alert, even in the moments of intensest excitement it is music, not a fury of sound, which he produces.[65]

A later *Tristan* was "rather unlucky in spite of Bruno Walter... The Tristan was a complete fiasco," according to the *Musical Times*. "As he was afterwards reported indisposed, and was seen no more, there is no need to name him."[66] Ernest Newman thought otherwise: it was Lorenz Hofer, he wrote, and as he "was tolerable neither to the eye nor to the ear ... I fled the theatre at the end of the second act...."[67]

The 1933 Salzburg Festival *Tristan* was a greater success. The Tristan was Hans Grahl, but it was Bruno Walter who towered above all else. It was "one of the four greatest *Tristans* of my experience," Herbert Peyser considered, "a reading in which every tempo was the last word of flawless rectitude and in which an incorruptible plan, a piercing vision and a lambent ecstasy lifting chanting to the stars each heart-shaking and imperishable measure."[68] At the 1934 Salzburg Festival Walter was again unlucky with his Tristan. *The Times* reported that one of the great disappointments of the festival was that the planned singers for the role of Tristan had "failed" the producers, and an aged Herr Starck sang. "However, Bruno Walter and the orchestra excelled themselves ... the final scene must rank as one of the season's triumphs."[69]

62 11 May 24: the review concluded: "But, when all is said, Walter is a great conductor."

63 9 May 1924. Several other newspapers reviewing the performance had no notable comments on the conducting, including the *Daily Express*, *Evening News*, *Daily Graphic*, and *Evening Standard*.

64 20 May 1925, p. 7.

65 20 May 1925, p. 14. Of a 1929 *Tristan* with Frida Leider and Erik Enderlein, *The Times* wrote that Walter "seemed to us to be a little lacking in suppleness and to overstate the extreme contrasts of quietude and fervour": 30 April 1929, p. 14.

66 1 July 1925, p. 638

67 *Sunday Times*, 24 May 1925, p. 7. To *The Times*, Hofer was "very much below the average, which has not been a high one": 20 May 1925, p. 14. Gertrud Kappel sang Isolde.

68 *New York Times*, 27 August 1933, p. X4 (Herbert Peyser). Gertrude Rünger sang Isolde.

69 4 September 1934, p. 10. The *New York Times* reported that Hans Grahl (who sang Tristan at the 1933 Festival) had been scheduled to sing Tristan, but was denied a visa. The "magic baton of Bruno Walter saved *Tristan und Isolde* from the disaster that German ill will tried to bring upon it and produced a thrilling representation": 1 August 1934, p. 2 (Frederick T. Birchall).

His Isolde was Anny Konetzni, the very singer who in the same scene in Vienna would soon be choked and breathless from the fumes of Nazi disruption, as Walter played on to the bitter end.

Die Meistersinger von Nürnberg

Mahler's influence on Walter in *Meistersinger* is apparent from a review of a performance Walter gave on Christmas Day, 1914. Notable were his "decided feeling for sonic beauty, his acute dissection of the score's subtle and complex architecture, his intoxication with analytical niceties, and his overall care in the handling of the orchestra," according to the *Münchner Neueste Nachrichten*, but missing were "*inner, tranquil strength*, composure, simplicity, and unaffected music-making, so different from the brilliant dissection and the conjuring, ecstatic display of energy with which Walter has attempted to reach this work, which is German, straightforward and indeed very great."[70] This was similar to the reservations expressed of Mahler's performances by those who were accustomed to Richter's.[71] Walter also resembled Mahler in the way he sought to co-ordinate the music with the action on stage.

At Covent Garden in 1925, one of the singers recalled how "he virtually produced the opera as well as conducting it – and what a fine producer he was! He took every one of the smaller masters through their roles, with a sense of characterization that was amazing. During one of the rehearsals I remember Friedrich Schorr saying, 'What an amazing actor' – and Schorr was no novice."[72] Unlike Mahler, however, Walter seems to have taken the prelude slowly. "The best," wrote *The Times*, "did not come at once."

Curiously enough the overture was rather heavily handled with the brass often so much in the foreground that we missed some of the charm of what was once described as Wagner's "vicious polyphony." ... [There was] a remarkably clear *ensemble* in the riot scene... [and] there was too much noisy playing and too little of the glamour of a midsummer night and morning in the tone. Nevertheless, there was much fine playing, which pointed out to us, as each performance of *Die Meistersinger* should, beauties which before had been unnoticed.[73]

The *Sunday Times* wrote that "in spite of a few rough moments," the "orchestra rose above itself under the masterly leading of Bruno Walter, who, with his vivid dramatic imagination, invariably heightens the effects of the singers when they are at their best, and as invariably, when they are below their best, still keeps us in the closest touch with the performer."[74] The *Morning Post* was "carried away by the magnificent playing of the orchestra. Mr. Bruno Walter was never in a hurry, and carried us along on the mighty stream of the music with splendid ease and mastery, and at the same time with never a detail slurred."[75]

[70] Alexander Dillmann, *Münchner Neueste Nachrichten*, 27 December 1914, quoted in Ryding and Pechefsky, *Bruno Walter*, pp. 117-8

[71] see Mahler chapter above, p. 265

[72] Parry Jones, who sang Augustin Moser, in "Bruno Walter, 1876-1962: Three Tributes," *Opera*, vol. 13 no. 4 (April 1962), p. 241

[73] 5 June 1925, p. 12; "it was a superb performance ... the orchestra and Bruno Walter (who began rather slowly) were clearly imbued with the magnificent spirit of the house": *Daily Telegraph*, 5 June 1925, p. 12.

[74] 7 June 1925, p. 7 (Ernest Newman)

[75] 5 June 1925, p. 8.

In 1929, judging from *The Times* report of that season, everything seems to have come together:

When Herr Bruno Walter conducts Wagner the orchestra at once becomes protagonist. Last night at Covent Garden for nearly five hours the story of *Die Meistersinger* was unfolded from the orchestra pit with not a detail missed nor a point of characterization unmade, with the utmost flexibility of rhythm and fluidity of tone, with the most delicate responsiveness to every hint from the singers and every shade of expression from the conductor's hand. Even the chorus in the last scene sang *Wach' auf* as though they, and not Beckmesser or Walther, were the competitors in this early competition festival; for suppleness in all the respects for which judges award marks this chorus would come out triumphant so far as Herr Walter conducted it.[76]

In his short history of Covent Garden, Harold Rosenthal wrote that these performances of *Tristan* and *Meistersinger* (1924-29) were "fondly remembered."[77] The 1924 season was indeed, as another recalled it, "a season which nobody concerned could ever forget – neither participants nor audience."[78]

Der Ring des Nibelungen

In 1924 "Wagner reconquered London," the *Musical Times* wrote in the bleak 1940s. "All the best singers of Mitteleuropa and Scandinavia then descended upon London. And there was Bruno Walter."[79] It was the season in which Walter made his strongest impression on London, notwithstanding a rear-view glance by the *Daily Telegraph*: "The two great conductors, Nikisch and Richter, who were wont to be the life and soul of the German seasons at Covent Garden, are gone and have not left their peer."[80] Ernest Newman wrote after the first *Tristan* and *Ring* cycle that "the one towering figure" of the season had been Bruno Walter:

His energy seems inexhaustible: after weeks of daily rehearsal he can still conduct the *Ring* and *Tristan* on five successive nights, with, apparently, perfect freshness and unbounded enthusiasm. I personally ask for no better Wagner conducting than this. Walter's understanding of the works is consummate. His range of expression is infinite, and he has the rare art of gradation, so there is always something more he can add, when it is wanted, to a climax that you would think is the biggest thing possible of its kind, and always something he can pare away from what you would say is the thinnest *piano* imaginable. With most conductors, the next stage after *piano* is *pianissimo*. With Bruno Walter, a composer's marking of *più piano* acquires a real meaning; and this *più piano* may have several shades before it fades away into pianissimo. Governing all this consummate technical skill is a poetic imagination of the first order: even those of us who thought we knew our Wagner by heart have caught our breath, time after time, at some new felicity of expression, some new emotional magic that Walter has revealed to us in the score.[81]

[76] 9 May 1929, p. 14

[77] Rosenthal, *Opera at Covent Garden*, p. 78. Indeed, he considered them so "exciting and musically satisfying" that it was "foolish and even harmful to opera" to dwell too much upon them.

[78] Vincent Sheean, *First and Last Love* (London: Victor Gollancz Ltd, 1957), p. 76. *Der Rosenkavalier* and *Ariadne auf Naxos* were also presented, the former for the first time outside Germany.

[79] "Wagner at Covent Garden," *Musical Times*, December 1948, p. 378 (R. C.). In the 1924 *Ring* the singers included Frida Leider, Lauritz Melchior, and Friedrich Schorr, and in an additional *Walküre*, Lotte Lehmann and Florence Austral. By comparison with Walter in 1924, the *Musical Times* wrote that in the 1948 Wagner season "the conductor [was] Karl Rankl, knowledgeable, ever-busy, ever-anxious. He makes his way through the bush and brier, hacking if need be."

[80] *Daily Telegraph*, 6 May 1924. Walter "conducted like an expert."

[81] 11 May 1924

Newman was not alone in his estimation of Walter's *Ring*. W. J. Turner wrote in the *New Statesman*:

The performance of the first cycle at Covent Garden this season is easily the best we have had in London since 1913.[82] This is due chiefly to the conductor, Herr Bruno Walter. He is the finest conductor of the *Ring* I have ever heard. He has the rare power of being able to maintain the rhythm alive in the smallest particular without ever breaking the design as a whole. The grand spaciousness of the *Ring*, which is perhaps its most remarkable quality, is spread before us by Herr Walter in a way I have heard no other conductor succeed in doing. Nothing is hurried or scamped, no detail is missed, but nevertheless everything falls into its proper place, and the sense of culmination, of inevitability slowly moving from climax to climax, is extraordinarily well achieved.[83]

Fig. 12.7. Walter about 1920. Drawing by Eugen Spiro

The *Rheingold* in this cycle got off to a rocky start. In the prelude, "the horns blurted and wobbled," the *Evening Standard* reported.[84] *The Times* continued: "the tone did not grow up into the overwhelming flood which it ought to be. There were later moments, too, where emphasis laid on detail seemed to check the flow. But such things were only incidental, and generally Herr Walter not only secured very fine playing, but brought out the significance of the orchestral music without overpowering the singers."[85] To the *Daily News* he managed to be "strong, picturesque, and, above all, … to build up massive crescendoes."[86] "The authority of his reading," wrote the *Manchester Guardian*, "and the plasticity with which he brings out every theme are beyond praise."[87] The *Saturday Review* commented on the *tempi*:

[82] Nikisch conducted in 1913. W. J. Turner (1889-1946), an Australian poet and music critic, arrived in London in 1907. Ernest Newman appears not to have heard Nikisch's *Ring* at Covent Garden in 1913 and 1914, for at the time he was reviewing local concerts for the *Birmingham Daily Post*.

[83] 17 May 1924

[84] 6 May 1924; "some crude and erratic brass tone": *Daily Graphic*, 7 May 1924 (Ernest Newman)

[85] 6 May 1924, p. 12

[86] 6 May 1924

[87] 6 May 1924

Walter takes the pace, as a rule, rather slower than we have been accustomed to of late. But this does not mean that the music drags; rather it enables the players and singers to give to the phrases their full sonority. He is able to do this, first because he has singers who can be relied on to hold their notes steadily for the requisite length of time, and secondly because he has the complete Wagnerian orchestra necessary to give the volume of sound.... So the music flowed on from the first deep E flat of the Prelude, growing always in weight, volume, and complexity. But, while there was this feeling of unity, the details are beautifully modelled. Phrases rise clear-cut out of the surface of the music and merge into it again, like goddesses of beauty born successively from the seething foam.[88]

The Times commented on the question of tempi in the *Walküre*.

In common with other great exponents of the *Ring*, Herr Walter gives plenty of time for everything. Indeed, his *tempi* were almost all, with one noticeable exception, on the slow side. That exception was the famous passage in which Brünnhilde prophesies the birth of Siegfried. Here the conductor swept along the singer (Mme Gertrud Kappel) at a pace which she seemed to find uncomfortably fast, but elsewhere he showed that energy does not depend on speed, and that tone depends on filling the notes full rather than on giving them initial accents.[89]

The *Scotsman* considered Walter had obtained some of the finest orchestral playing that has been heard in London since the days of Dr. Hans Richter."[90] The *Morning Post* explained Walter's special way of dealing with *leit motifs*. "There is not the underlining which was usual in the old traditional German versions – nothing of what Debussy called 'the visiting card' business in the leading themes; he makes it a homogeneous whole, one more harmonious and beautiful than has been heard for a very long time – if ever."[91]

In *Siegfried*, *The Times* noticed several "emphatic alterations of *tempo*."[92] The *Star* considered Walter "was even better than in the *Walküre*. His reading is big and broad, impressive without pretentiousness, and full of tenderness too – and of remarkable lucidity. The end of the first Act and the Fire Music were superb."[93] To the *Evening Standard*, it was "a matter of piling revelation after revelation.... [It] started by being fair and ended up by being superb."[94] Walter "gave us all the strength and the matchless poetry of the music," wrote the *Daily News*, "and it is long since we have heard a conductor with such a gift of making music grow gradually from a whisper to a fortissimo. His climaxes are great, but never noisy."[95]

The *Götterdämmerung* was "a really stupendous performance," according to the *Evening Standard*.[96] The *Daily News* wrote:

[88] Dyneley Hussey, "The Real Thing," *Saturday Review*, 10 May 1924, written after *Rheingold* and *Walküre*. He added: "I cannot see the conductor from my stall, but I fancy that he must have the same method as Weingartner, and that he is always accompanying the soloist, whether vocal or instrumental, with the rest of the orchestra. The result is, anyhow, that the important part of the moment is always audible."

[89] *The Times*, 7 May 1924, p. 12. Alma Mahler wrote that Walter "came very near to realizing Mahler's ideals" in the *Walküre*: *Gustav Mahler - Memories and Letters*, (ed.) Donald Mitchell, 3rd (ed.), (trans.) Basil Creighton (London: John Murray, 1973), p. 113. The slow *tempi* described by *The Times* bear little resemblance to those of Mahler: see Mahler chapter above, pp. 267-8

[90] 7 May 1924

[91] 7 May 1924

[92] 8 May 1924, p. 12. The *Daily Telegraph* (8 May 1924) did not agree with Walter's "innovation with regard to *tempi*," but did not say what it was.

[93] 8 May 1924 ("Crescendo")

[94] 8 May 1924

[95] 8 May 1924 (A. K.)

[96] 10 May 1924

Now that one can judge of Herr Walter's reading of the *Ring* as a whole, one can say without hesitation that it is the biggest and most heroic we have heard for years and years, and the most consistent. … Last night's performance had the right effect of going from strength to strength, and the contrast between the vehement human passions of the second act and the massive grandeur of the third was admirably brought out.[97]

There were mixed reports, perhaps of different moments in the opera, of relations between the orchestra and the singers. One praised the conductor for "never once drowning the voices, yet bringing out all the gorgeous colour of the music in a perfectly balanced whole."[98] Another had the impression "of [Walter] ignoring inevitable limitations of the human voice and overwhelming it with the magnificent tone of the orchestra, but he was only in this following the precedents of other Wagnerian conductors. The orchestra not only supplies the commentary, but often becomes itself the protagonist. There was also a rhythmic control of the ensemble music which deserves high praise."[99] The completion of the *Ring* left the reviewer of the *Manchester Guardian* in a state of elevation:

So admirable was the rendering of the colossal tetralogy that one was ready to accept it as one of the rare big experiences of one's musical life. …to hear the *Ring* as we Londoners have just done is to become convinced once again that, given such exceptional conditions, it will always retain its power and its glamour, and compel us to forget its ultra-pessimistic philosophy, its unsympathetic characters, and the constructive weakness of its endless arguments and tautological narrations of matters already seen in action. All these defects were gladly accepted as an excuse for a wealth of wonderful music. Mr. Bruno Walter, a Wagnerian conductor of exceptional genius, saw to it that the public realised its abiding greatness.[100]

London was more blessed than Bayreuth in 1924. *The Times* reported from the Green Hill on "the sense of proportion" found in Michael Balling's conducting.

With that, inevitably perhaps, goes a lack of adventurousness. I was never raised during this *Ring* to the pitch of excitement which Herr Bruno Walter produced at his performance in London. Who will ever forget the climax of the wedding-chorus in *Götterdämmerung*, with its every beat caught back a little more to pile up its terrific emphasis? Or his *Trauermarsch*, when the clash of cymbals was like the beating together of all the armour of the warriors in Valhalla to greet the greatest and newest-gathered of the heroes? There was nothing that reached that pitch here.[101]

Walter conducted eight *Ring* cycles in London between 1924 and 1931. There were special moments and defective details, but the mastery of his sweep was always present. At his last *Götterdämmerung*, there was a breakdown. As if he were doomed to suffer his master's travails, he was afflicted with the same staging mishap that frustrated

97 10 May 1924

98 *Sportsman*, 12 May 1924 (S. H. B.-S.)

99 *Daily Telegraph*, 10 May 1924. The *Morning Post* (10 May 1924) commented on the "great beauty of tone and sureness of rhythm." Comments here and above on Walter's sense of rhythm are of interest in light of Sir George Solti's general recollection: "I sometimes felt that Walter's rhythm was not incisive enough": *Solti on Solti: A Memoir* (London: Chatto & Windus, 1997), p. 115.

100 12 May 1924 (E. B.). In similar but more restrained vein *The Times* wrote: "[the performance] sent the audience away feeling that they had been witnesses of a great matter": 10 May 1924, p. 10.

101 2 August 1924, p. 8. Walter's *Ring* in 1927 was compared to the Wagner of another conductor that season, Robert Heger: Walter was "all vivaciousness and experimental energy, and [Heger] (entrusted with *Tristan* and *Parsifal*) a steady-goer, believing in long views and careful construction": *Musical Times*, 1 June 1927, p. 547

Mahler in London almost forty years earlier.[102] After a magnificent Funeral March, "there was a bad delay in the subsequent rise of the curtain. [He] had to stop the orchestra and the magical web of Wagner's musical design was broken, like the rope of the Norns."[103] It was Walter's last *Ring*.

Fig. 12.8. Walter at the opera, 1930s. Drawing by Hans Böhler

The Wagner recordings

Many of Walter's orchestral excerpts are from operas he did not often conduct: *Rienzi*, *Holländer*, *Tannhäuser*, *Lohengrin*, and *Parsifal*. For this reason they have some interest. On the other hand, his musical heart may not have been most enlivened by such works. In the case of the recordings from operas he *did* conduct, these do not, with one or two exceptions, rise to the level of his achievements in the theatre of which we have read. When he came to re-record Wagner pieces towards the end of his life, he kept away from dramatic excerpts, preferring preludes and orchestral arrangements.

Of his earliest recordings (1924-32) Walter himself had little to say. He suggested in later life that he was not pleased with the results. The earliest record-player, he said, was "a mechanical device emitting ugly imitative musical noises."[104] His performances had an intimacy and a delicacy that did not always record well. He did not have the force of an Albert Coates to break through technical barriers (though views on this varied).[105] Yet he could register mood. His unique acoustic recording, of *A Faust Overture* (1923), did triumph to a degree over its technical limitations. Although the

[102] see Mahler chapter above, p. 250 [103] *The Times*, 9 May 1931, p. 10

[104] Bruno Walter, "Some thoughts about The Musical Record," *American Record Guide*, January 1964, 374

[105] On *Siegfried's Funeral Music* (1931), for example, reviewers differed: "the recording is a good one, but we feel the phonograph is not yet quite equal to the demands of music of this intensity": *Music Supervisor's Journal*, May 1933, p. 64 (Paul J. Weaver); "the reproduction of that difficult instrument, the drum, is as true as the horns, harps and woodwind": *The Times*, 3 March 1932, p. 10; "There is a bite in the brass, a taste of fate's fangs...": *Gramophone*, January 1932, p. 332 (W. R. Anderson); "The preliminary kettle-drum beats, the sharp, cutting outbursts of the brass, the great upheaval that occurs on the second side – all is recorded with perfect balance, clarity and realism. Details missing or obscured by the none too refined recording in the Coates disc [1926] come out beautifully. It is an extraordinarily impressive achievement": *Disques*, May 1932, p. 123.

orchestra had to work furiously to make an impact on the wax, there is a poetry beneath the mist – a whistling of Hades (compared to hellfire from Coates). Although techniques became more sophisticated, his performance of this masterpiece continued to be ill-represented. The walls of the NBC studio in a 1939 performance were like blotting paper, and robbed the sound of the ruminative atmosphere of the earlier performance. As technology improved Walter said he found he learned from listening to his own performances. "I listen," he said, "and then I change it, the next time. This chance to listen again is a great contribution from the recording, and we owe it to the engineer."[106] He had this opportunity in abundance between 1957 and 1961 when he went into the studio to make stereo recordings for Columbia with a tailor-made orchestra. From almost one hundred recording sessions of various composers, seven Wagner excerpts emerged. They comprise a concert of ideal content and proportion. So happy was he with this new process that he confessed "he no longer got pleasure from hearing his old ones."[107] We might share his sentiments, except for what was recorded in Vienna in 1935.

The recordings he made from the *Walküre* with the Vienna Philharmonic in 1935 occupy a special place in the history of Wagner recording. The principal singers, Lauritz Melchior and Lotte Lehmann, had been his Siegmund and Sieglinde at Covent Garden in 1926, 1928, 1929, 1930, and 1931. They knew their work well, and more to the point, they knew one another well, and were outstanding artists.[108] The recording was made with their voices very much forward, which may have served the interests of clarity but, as the *Musical Times* noted, it "robs the orchestra not only of tone but of quality."[109] To make matters worse, when HMV transferred the recording to LP in 1962 the voices were "boosted up and the orchestral sound damped down" so that while "we get almost every inflection of Lehmann's warm, womanly glowing Sieglinde, we lose a lot of the very same qualities in Walter's interpretation."[110] One curious effect of this manipulation – and one must bear in mind Walter's words written at this time: "Recording is a great blessing, and the engineers have as great a responsibility to make it more and more real"[111] – is that the orchestra seems subdued, submerged, almost invisible – in fact, just as Wagner would have wished. This impressed contemporary reviewers:

The conducting of Bruno Walter exposes the brutality of the average Wagner conductor who invariably makes the composer noisy and rhetorical... He lends to *Die Walküre* the right

[106] Mayer, "Bruno Walter," *Harper's Magazine*, February 1961, p. 77

[107] John McClure [Walter's record producer], "The Making of a Legacy," *Gramophone*, April 1962, pp. 490-1; McClure wrote another version, "An Education and a Joy," *High Fidelity*, January 1964, pp. 41-43, 105, which was followed by a "selective and evaluative" discography by Robert C. Marsch, "The Heritage of Bruno Walter," *ibid*, pp. 44, 108-109 (Wagner recordings)

[108] For all the historic importance of these *Walküre* recordings, they are not discussed at all in Melchior's biography, *Tristanissimo*, or in Lotte Lehmann's autobiography, *Wings of song*. However, Melchior did recall his 1924 debut in *Walküre*, which Walter conducted (see above): "My Sieglinde was Lotte Lehmann. Her great amount of feeling, and the fact she was always entirely a woman, was of great inspiration to me. The way in which she threw herself into the part made me forget my nervousness": Lauritz Melchior, "Are Tenors Lousy Lovers?" *Stage Magazine*, January 1939.

[109] July 1936, p. 613

[110] *Opera*, February 1963, p. 117 (Harold Rosenthal). In its review of the same reissue, *The Times* wrote: "None of our outstanding conductors today, not since Kleiber, has conveyed so much of the truth and beauty in the act as Walter did:" 8 December 1962, p. 11.

[111] quoted in an editorial, "Some Notes on Bruno Walter," *American Music Lover*, September 1936, p. 176

lyrical impulse combined with the most scrupulous observance of Wagner's tempi instructions; Walter knows that rare secret of the conductor's art: how to keep time and, within the correctly directed line, obtain those nuances which mean the difference between living rhythm and dead time beating. At a hundred points Walter delights us by some imaginative stroke which lightens a whole page of the score – and how quickly, like a lovely mettlesome steed, does the Vienna Orchestra respond![112]

Walter's orchestra is intertwined with the singers to an extraordinarily subtle degree. Every detail is clear, yet subordinated to the whole. In the transitional music between scenes one and two, for example, Hunding's hunting horns are subdued and integrated into the tight orchestral fabric. The act grows in a constant, gradual arc to its impassioned ending. Not all of act two could be recorded by Walter because he was prevented from travelling to Berlin where the artists were based. His artistry was yet again a casualty of the Nazis.

"One great breath"

There was one piece that Walter loved to perform and to record above all others: the *Siegfried Idyll*. Its scale and its charm made it suitable for both concert hall and disc, but for Walter it was much more. Its sweetness and intimacy, its playfulness and doting innuendoes, had unique appeal to his poetic nature. "There is something almost feminine about his talent," Herbert Peyser wrote of Walter, "something inescapably sentimental and soft. It is graceful, tender, bewitchingly delicate this talent – a thing of rounded contours, of suave contacts and mellow lights."[113] He made six versions in the recording studio, and more than that number again were recorded from live performances. None of them is quite like another. The superb performance with a French orchestra in 1955, hushed and tender, contrasts sharply, for example, with the full and vigorous performance with the New York Philharmonic in 1957, a performance which suggests a strapping young Siegfried already in lederhosen. It is not surprising that in old age he chose not to re-record from Wagner the demonic and the ecstatic (*A Faust Overture*, *Tristan*), the appalling and earth-shattering (Siegfried's Funeral Music), but instead to caress again the cheeks of the young Siegfried. Preceding this last performance, a substantial rehearsal segment was recorded. Walter need not have felt anxious that he could give no "practical advice" on the art of conducting.[114] The rehearsal has an abundance of clear examples. Forever courteous, he explains Wagner's intentions (*più piano*),[115] calls to the musicians, singing sometimes to them: "flowing" – " one great breath" – "too loud, too loud" – "*sing*, celli" – "celli, *sing*" – "*everybody* sing." And so they play in the performance that follows, in a soft light and autumnal glow, until the music fades away, and Siegfried has breathed his last.

[112] Neville Cardus (4 May 1936), *Cardus on Music: a centenary collection* (ed.) Donald Wright (London: H. Hamilton, 1988), p. 81

[113] Herbert F. Peyser, "Bruno Walter," *Disques*, vol. 2, no. 12 (February 1932), p. 531. He adds: "Bruno Walter is not a conductor of what the Germans call large *Format*. I have never cared for his Wagner – not because it does not contain much that is enchanting, but because it lacks correct perspective and dimension." (p. 532). This was written before he heard Walter conduct *Tristan* at Salzburg (see above).

[114] *Of music and music-making*, p. 147, quoted above

[115] There is nothing in this 1959 rehearsal (see Discography) indicating what Solti called "his tendency, in rehearsal to talk to orchestras in literary terms, which seemed to me a fundamental mistake": *Solti on Solti*, p. 115.

Part VI

America *felix*

13

Arturo Toscanini – Maestro in control

Toscanini was a phenomenal force in music. Compared with German conductors, he more or less sprang from nowhere. He had a formidable memory. He held every note of a Wagnerian score in his head. He knew how it had to be played. Through agony and exasperation he imposed his will on his musicians. He presented music exactly as he saw it, exactly as it was written, and with a tempo that was for the large part infallible. Yet he was endlessly dissatisfied with himself. Like Mahler, he perceived an ideal and felt he rarely achieved it. The clarity, precision and intensity which he brought to his music-making had a piercing effect on the listener. He shone light where previously there had been none. People were amazed, and became fanatical admirers. In Wagner, however, there is a place for darkness and ambiguity that Toscanini's style of music-making did not always recognise. He never quite descended into Nibelheim. He was happier in the moonlight of Hunding's hut and the second act of *Tristan und Isolde* where his orchestra sang with the impassioned lovers. He was happier still, perhaps, in the *Liebestod* where, with Isolde discarded, he alone could reach for the stars. And for many years his star shone very brightly.

Wagner in Toscanini's life

He was born in Parma on 25 March 1867 of a modest family, and soon displayed spectacular musicality. He was sent to Parma Conservatory (1876-85) to study cello, piano and composition at the age of nine. He first heard Wagner's music when still a boy in 1878-79. It was the overture to *Tannhäuser*:

> – and I was bewildered. I remember a detail: my teacher brought a part for cello of this overture to school for me and made me study the various passages, which were very difficult for me at that time. In 1884 Parma was the first Italian city to perform *Lohengrin* after its success at Bologna and its fiasco at Milan. I was in the orchestra. I had then the first true, great, sublime revelation of Wagner's genius. At the first rehearsal and from the very beginning the prelude gave me magic supernatural impressions, with its divine harmonies which revealed to me an entire new world, a world that no one dreamed existed, before it was discovered by the supernatural mind of Wagner....[1]

[1] pencil notes written by Toscanini (no date), quoted in Alfredo Segre, "Toscanini – The First Forty Years, *Musical Quarterly*, vol. 33 no. 2 (April 1947), p. 162. The conductor was Vittorio Maria Lanzo (1862-1945). In 1938 Toscanini wrote to Ada Mainardi: "when Wagner set down this simple A major chord [the

In 1886, having finished his studies, he went on tour with an orchestra to Brazil where he was suddenly called upon to fill in for the conductor in *Aida*. He made such a success of it, conducting from memory, that his days as a cellist were immediately put behind him. In Turin in 1886 he coached singers for the *Holländer*, and in 1888 attended the first Italian performance of *Tristan* in Bologna. It made such an impression on him that he abandoned any ambition to become a composer.[2]

As he launched into his career as a conductor, Wagner's operas quickly assumed their place in his repertory. He first conducted *Holländer* in Palermo on 2 March 1893, and *Tannhäuser* in Genoa on 19 January 1895. The latter was a "colossal triumph," according to a Genoese newspaper, "the orchestra was marvellous in fusion, precision, color, chiaroscuri; full of power, of élan and spirituality, the orchestra mirrored at every moment the talent and soul of its conductor…."[3] He gave eight other performances, and conducted it in Treviso in June. He marked his appointment to the Teatro Reggio in Turin (1895-98) with a performance 22 December 1895 of *Götterdämmerung*, sung in Italian and with cuts. With only ten days of rehearsals, he had transformed the orchestra. There was "such fusion, such accuracy of interpretation, such a vital and youthful spirit" in it; he had been able to draw from the orchestra "every finesse of color and expression and magnificent pianissimi and crescendi," *La Stampa* reported.[4] Such was the work's popularity it was given twenty-two performances. It was an extraordinary feat.

It is quite possible he had not heard *Holländer*, *Tannhäuser*, or *Götterdämmerung* before he conducted them. He may have visited Germany in 1895, and whatever he heard there, he was not the sort of musician to be influenced by the interpretations of others, even those at Bayreuth.[5] His understanding and love of Wagner grew from

first chord of the prelude to *Lohengrin*] for the Violins and Woodwinds, I've always imagined that at a moment of great, sublime inspiration he disappeared from the earth, went up to heaven for a time, and came back down bringing that magical chord, of whose existence no one before him had dreamt. To me, you are that divine chord": letter dated 15 January 1938, in Harvey Sachs (ed. and trans.), *The Letters of Arturo Toscanini* (New York: Alfred A. Knopf, 2002), p. 322.

[2] The conductor was Giuseppe Martucci (1856-1909) whom Toscanini admired all his life: Harvey Sachs, *Toscanini* (Philadelphia and New York: J. B. Lippincott Company, 1978), p. 30

[3] unnamed newspaper dated 20 January 1895 quoted in Segre, "Toscanini," *ibid*, p. 162

[4] *La Stampa*, Turin (no date), quoted in Segre, "Toscanini," *ibid*, pp. 163-4

[5] He wrote to Ada Mainardi on 4 October 1937: "1895! The year of my first disappointment in those German-know-it-alls. That was when people in Italy were proclaiming that Wagner performances in the theatres of Munich and Bayreuth were perfect!" Sachs, *Letters*, p. 302. If this means he *did* travel to Germany in 1895, it is not recorded what he heard. As Sachs points out, there was no Bayreuth Festival in 1895. In Munich in 1895 the General Music Director was Hermann Levi, and the other conductors were Franz Fischer and Richard Strauss. In 1899 Toscanini went to Bayreuth with Giulio Gatti-Casazza and heard the *Ring* (Siegfried Wagner), *Meistersinger* (Richter), and *Parsifal* twice (Fischer): Gatti-Casazza, *Memories of the Opera* (New York: Scribners, 1941), p. 85. Gatti-Casazza did not record their impressions, but Toscanini wrote home: "I heard a good orchestral performance of *Meistersinger* but could only deplore the complete lack of good ensemble among orchestra, chorus and singers; the last, I can tell you between us, are dogs. These Bayreuth performances are a real hoax for people like me who are hoping to hear perfection": letter to the assistant conductor at La Scala, Pietro Sormani, dated 29 July 1899, in Sachs, *Letters*, p. 66. It appears Toscanini may also have been at the 1902 Bayreuth Festival. Among the *Toscanini Legacy Papers* in the New York Public Library is a letter to him from his wife Carla annotated in pencil "da Tai di Cadore Luglio 1902 a Bayreuth" (Correspondence 1902, Box 2, folder L21A). In Bayreuth in 1902, Mottl conducted *Holländer* and *Parsifal*, Muck *Parsifal*, and Richter the *Ring*. As for the influence of Richter on Toscanini, the New York *Press* wrote after a performance of Toscanini's *Meistersinger* that his reading diverged from other conductors:

his study of the scores. More than any other Wagnerian conductor, he was truly autochthonous. In his second season at Turin he gave the first complete performance of *Tristan*, on 14 February 1897, but it was marred by a battle to have the auditorium lights extinguished. He was only half-successful in this (they were dimmed) and he proceeded to conduct without any enthusiasm, and only gave it on five further occasions.[6] In his third season, he gave a rare performance of *Walküre* (which he conducted again in Milan in 1901 and Argentina in 1906, but apparently never again). He opened his term at La Scala, Milan (1898-1903) on 26 December 1898 with a largely uncut *Meistersinger* after a month of rehearsals, and produced "a performance of the highest order...," according to the *Gazetta musicale di Milano*. "The orchestra was stupendous, well balanced, [and] directed with admirable sureness...."[7] A "brilliant performance," according to the correspondent of the *Musical Times*. Toscanini "conducted with consummate ability."[8] Preceding this performance he had, in 1896, given several concerts which included the Norns scene from *Götterdämmerung* as a means of accustoming the public to Wagner.

During his time at La Scala, Milan, he presented *Siegfried* and *Lohengrin* (1899-1900), *Tristan* (1900-01),[9] *Walküre* (1901-02), concerts of Wagner excerpts including the Prelude and Good Friday Music from *Parsifal* on 13 April 1903,[10] and during his second term (1906-08) *Tristan* and *Götterdämmerung*. He also presented *Meistersinger* in Bologna (1904), and *Siegfried* in Turin (1905) as part of a planned complete *Ring* which never came to fruition,[11] and took Wagner operas to South America.[12] He conducted the second act of *Tristan* in Paris in June 1910.[13] His third term at La Scala (1920-29) included the *Meistersinger* (1923, 1928), *Tristan* (1923), and *Parsifal* (1928).

It is his appearances outside Italy, in Europe and North America, that we will look at in some detail below. With the Metropolitan Opera in New York (1908-15), he conducted *Götterdämmerung* (6 performances, first season only), *Meistersinger* (19), and *Tristan* (30). In Bayreuth in 1930 he conducted *Tannhäuser* (3) and *Tristan* (3), and in 1931 *Tannhäuser* (5) and *Parsifal* (5).[14] In Salzburg he conducted the *Meistersinger* in

"It may even diverge slightly from that of the great Hans Richter, though Toscanini himself asserts it is modelled on exactly the same lines": 13 March 1915, p. 7. The assertion was presumably made privately to the reviewer who, though unnamed, was probably Max Smith.

6 Sachs, *Toscanini*, p. 53

7 *Gazetta musicale di Milano*, 29 December 1898 (Giulio Ricordi), quoted in Sachs, *Toscanini*, p. 64. The *Corriere della Sera* considered it "far superior" to the one presented in Paris the year before: Segre, "Toscanini," pp.168-9. That performance had been conducted by Paul Taffanel (1844-1908).

8 1 February 1899, p. 120

9 Siegfried Wagner attended the performance of 12 January 1901: Sachs, *Toscanini*, p. 75.

10 "greeted with tolerant boredom by most of those present, including the majority of the critics": Sachs, *Toscanini*, p. 84

11 Toscanini never conducted a complete *Ring*, and never a *Rheingold* (Sachs, *Toscanini*, p. 90). This was made less clear by an earlier biographer who wrote of the 1924-25 season: "Toscanini conducted fourteen operas, some new and some old favourites. *Rheingold* and the *Walküre* were restaged; and in the subsequent year *Siegfried* and *Götterdämmerung*": Paul Stefan [Paul Stefan Grünfeldt], *Arturo Toscanini* (New York: Viking Press, 1936), p. 83.

12 1901: *Lohengrin*, *Tannhäuser* and *Tristan* in Argentina; 1902: *Meistersinger* in Argentina and Uruguay; 1904: *Lohengrin* in Argentina and Uruguay; 1906: *Tristan* and *Walküre* in Argentina, and *Tristan* in Uruguay.

13 *Le Figaro*, 20 June 1910, p. 4

14 Toscanini's Bayreuth performances were not broadcast. The first broadcast ever from Bayreuth was of *Tristan* on 18 August 1931 (Pistor, Larsén-Todsen, Furtwängler): *The Times*, 19 August 1931, p. 8. On the next day, Toscanini conducted his last performance at Bayreuth: *Parsifal* (19 August 1931).

1936 (4) and 1937 (3). That was the end of his Wagner operas. He was invited back to the Metropolitan Opera in 1950, but the invitation was never answered.[15]

He left a legacy of many recordings, mostly with the NBC Symphony Orchestra in New York (1938-54), some from the studio, some from the concert hall, some authorized and some not. However, his *Meistersinger* in Salzburg is the only complete Wagner opera to have survived on record. In his late 80s part of this was played to him and he was moved to tears. "This happened!" he exclaimed.[16] He died in New York on 16 January 1957.

Toscanini's approach to Wagner

As we have seen, Toscanini was very taken by Wagner's music in his youth. It was a lifelong veneration. He considered Wagner "the greatest composer of our time," according to his grandson, despite a reverence for Verdi.[17] Toscanini himself wrote, "Among operas, I value those of Verdi and Wagner above all," and "every time I glance at the score of *Parsifal*, I say to myself: This is the sublime one."[18] The *Meistersinger* was, according to an early biographer, his "favourite among Wagner's works, and the one he has most freshly enlivened for us."[19] In a conversation about Verdi and Wagner Toscanini once described *Meistersinger* as "a masterpiece," as "good, very good, but it is heavy, heavy, so heavy. *Falstaff* is light, it is quick*silver*." As he was preparing it for Salzburg he sighed, "*sempre* C Major... Beautiful, yes... but too much C Major."[20] At a rehearsal of act two of *Tristan* under Bruno Walter at Salzburg in the 1930s, he said to a companion: "If they were Italians, they would already have seven children; but they're Germans, so they're still talking."[21]

These throw-away lines about Wagner's works do not give the full measure of Toscanini's understanding of or love for Wagner's operas. He did not set down his views about them in writing. He was not the literary or intellectual type. He was "basically naïve in the best sense of the word," as Otto Klemperer said.[22] He read as

[15] Sir Rudolf Bing, *5,000 nights at the opera* (London: Hamilton, 1972), p. 156

[16] Hugo Burghauser, in B. H. Haggin, *The Toscanini Musicians Knew*, 2nd ed. (New York: Horizon Press, 1980), p. 170. Burghauser, who played in the orchestra, implies it was the second act from the 1936 performance (with Lotte Lehmann and Charles Kullman) that was played to Toscanini, for he tells it after he has recounted his visit backstage in 1936 when Toscanini exclaimed: "*Com' un sogno*. Like a dream. It is a heavenly dream." However, it was likely to have been the act two from the 1937 performance (Maria Reining and Henk Noort) that was played to him, as no recording of act two from 1936 has survived.

[17] John Freeman and Walfredo Toscanini, *Toscanini* (New York: Treves Publishing Company, 1987), p. 8

[18] answer to a newspaper questionnaire (1932), in Sachs, *Letters*, p. 136. He appears to have performed *Parsifal*, as a whole, only in Milan in 1928 and Bayreuth in 1931. Shortly before he died he told an acquaintance it was "unnecessary to go to *Parsifal* to hear extraordinary harmonies: one could hear them in Frescobaldi": Sachs, *Toscanini*, p. 318.

[19] Stefan, *Toscanini*, p. 51

[20] Samuel Chotzinoff, *Toscanini: An Intimate Portrait* (New York: Knopf, 1956), pp. 20, 56

[21] Margarethe Wallmann, *Les Balcons du Ciel* (Paris: Laffont, 1976), p. 71, quoted in Sachs, *Letters*, p. 216

[22] in conversation in 1969, in Peter Heyworth (ed.), *Conversations with Klemperer*, rev. ed. (London: Faber and Faber, 1985), p. 115-6, where Klemperer also described Toscanini as a "splendid conductor with a phenomenal sense of sound and memory... his Wagner was very good. I heard him conduct *Die Meistersinger* in Milan. Excellent, excellent." Of this 1923 performance he had earlier said, "I have never again heard such a consummate musical rendering of this work anywhere else in the world": *Das Tagebuch* (Berlin), 25 May 1929, in Martin Anderson (ed.), *Klemperer on music: shavings from a musician's workbench* (London: Toccata Press, 1986), p. 198.

much as he could about Wagner's works and what the composer had to say about them, in early life at least.[23] He already knew his scores by heart. He also appreciated Wagner's aims in the theatre. The music and drama had to be one. Preferably, he had to control both. A glimpse of him at work in Milan in 1922 during a stage rehearsal of act three of the *Meistersinger* is reminiscent of Wagner during rehearsals for the *Ring*: he was "literally running and jumping all over the stage, first to this group, then to that one, demonstrating positioning, gestures, clapping his hands to keep the piano and the massive forces together, shouting and singing."[24] And then there was the orchestra. In a rehearsal of act two of *Tristan* in 1926:

> Toscanini talked, shouted, shrieked and implored his musicians. He struggled and wrestled for the sake of his realisation of his conception of the music, and he did not end his struggle before this wonderful instrument gave itself up to him, wholly subjugated, ready to follow the maestro's vision which, pitiless and unsparing, towards himself and his musicians, he had to realise.[25]

This illuminating passage, which is not uncommon in descriptions of Toscanini at work, illustrates his driving need to impose his will, his way of performing the music, on all the artists involved.

Follow the leader

Toscanini's approach had its advantages but also affected the nature of his Wagner performances in the theatre in a way that was not strictly Wagnerian. Essentially, it affected the degree of freedom given to other artists. He generally had an unerring sense of tempo, although even he would disagree with himself on occasions,[26] and it had to be followed by the whole ensemble. In preparing for the *Meistersinger* at Salzburg he pointed out that the "Wagner recitative, which vocalists treated with freedom permissible only in cadenzas, was meant… to be sung in strict time, and he pointed to Wagner's own words to prove it…."[27] One of his most devoted champions, Lotte Lehmann, who sang for him at the 1936 *Meistersinger*, recalled how he demanded "absolute precision and at the same time the most complete spiritual surrender to the music, an ideal that must remain an unattainable ideal for those who do not happen to be gods."[28] She wrote further:

[23] for example, in Salzburg: Chotzinoff, *Toscanini*, p. 55; cf. his later life: "I have not known him, in years of acquaintance, countless conversations, and many hours of collaboration, to evidence interest in a book…": Charles O'Connell, *The other side of the record* (New York: Alfred A. Knopf, 1947), p. 105

[24] journalist Giulio Ciampelli cited in Sachs, *Toscanini*, p. 153

[25] Elisabeth Ohms, "Reminiscences of Arturo Toscanini," *Gramophone*, November 1953, pp. 177-8. The performances were cancelled because Toscanini was not well.

[26] B. H. Haggin quoted Toscanini in 1942: "In 1936 I make *Rhine Journey* with Philharmonic. … In Carnegie Hall is right tempo; when I hear record, is wrong tempo. Last year … I listen [to it again on the radio] … in 1936 is wrong tempo; now is right tempo! *Ah Dio santo!*": *Conversations with Toscanini* (New York: Doubleday, 1959), pp. 18-19.

[27] Chotzinoff, *Toscanini*, p. 56. Wagner's words along these lines are quoted in the Wagner chapter above.

[28] Lotte Lehmann, *Wings of song: an autobiography*, (trans.) Margaret Ludwig (London: Kegan Paul, Trench, Trubner, 1938), p. 227. Frances Alda, who sang Italian opera under Toscanini at the Metropolitan Opera, wrote: "He is one of those who are obsessed all their lives by an insatiable passion of perfection. His devotion to art was so ardent, so whole-souled, that he could not – it was simply that he *would* not – agree without vehement protest to any presentation that was less than the best that could be achieved": Frances Alda, *Men, women, and tenors*, (1937, repr., New York: AMS Press, 1971), p. 207

But I must say one thing: the great fear which every singer feels before him – and I don't know one who would say that he had no fear of him – often keeps one from being really free… his glowing fanaticism, made doubly expressive through his tempestuous Latin temperament, demands the utmost of every one to such an extent that, expecting thunder every moment, you are confused and consequently often unable to give what you are really capable of giving.[29]

Lauritz Melchior, his Tristan and Parsifal at Bayreuth, wrote: "Everyone was afraid of him, and his will prevailed in all ways. He didn't budge an inch from the concept he had as far as TEMPO was concerned, and he did not follow a singer who took liberties."[30] But provided the tempo, and the rhythm, were right, he did not interfere. Alexander Kipnis, his King Marke at Bayreuth, surprised Toscanini with some of his accents at rehearsal. He "looked up, but he didn't say anything. He insisted on the *rhythm* being the way he wanted it; but he never told me anything about phrasing, and he never said anything about the phrasing or accents which represented my feeling."[31]

Toscanini's attitude towards the Wagnerian sung drama – towards the singers who *sing* the music drama – was not different from his attitude towards other artists he accompanied. Yehudi Menuhin recalled:

Toscanini was not the perfect accompanist after the fashion of Bruno Walter. Indeed it would be hard to find conductors more antithetical – Walter the wayside stroller who admires every flower, Toscanini the purposeful traveler with his eye fixed on the goal. He, I am sure, separated music and musician, subordinating the second to the overriding importance of the first with an integrity that could seem ruthless in its refusal to tolerate the least self indulgence of ornament or exaggeration.[32]

Adolf Busch, who also played under Toscanini, wrote that "in order to play with him… you *have* to be in agreement with him. For that reason he cannot abide soloists in the usual sense. He told me himself: 'I cannot *accompany*, I can only make music.'"[33]

The effect of his approach on singers is abundantly evident in performances of the *Meistersinger*. At his first performance at the Metropolitan Opera on 26 March 1910, he "seemed so immersed in the wondrous song of the orchestra that he seemed unconscious of the value of the dialogue, and the singers sang to his beat with a

[29] Lotte Lehmann, *My many lives*, (trans.) Frances Holden (New York: Boosey & Hawkes, 1948), p. 93 She also wrote: "I became really free in singing with him": p. 94.

[30] Ib Melchior, *Lauritz Melchior: The Golden Years of Bayreuth* (Fort Worth, Tex.: Baskerville Publishers, 2003), p. 178. Nor did he always help them when they got lost. In one of the 1930 Bayreuth performances of *Tristan*, as Birgit Nilsson related, Melchior and Larsén-Todsen got lost in the delirium of their meeting in act two. "Todsen rushed forward with outstretched arms to get help from the conductor but Toscanini tore his hair and cried from confusion. Because he conducted from memory, he was unable to rescue the singers. The duet, as the story goes, ended in musical chaos": Birgit Nilsson, *La Nilsson: My Life in Opera* (Boston: Northeastern University Press, 2007), p. 154. Ernest Newman was very unhappy with Melchior and Larsen-Todsen in his review of the 1930 *Tristan*: *Sunday Times*, 10 August 1930, p. 5. The *New York Sun* reported after a performance of *Götterdämmerung* in 1909: "It is indisputable that his direction throws not a little responsibility on the singers, for he indicates their entrances infrequently. His attention seems to be centred on the playing of the orchestra": 25 February 1909.

[31] Haggin, *The Toscanini Musicians Knew*, p. 63

[32] Yehudi Menuhin, *Unfinished journey* (London: Futura Publications, 1978), pp. 169-170. Toscanini told Menuhin that Walter was "A sentimental fool!": p. 172. Elsewhere he wrote: "[Walter] always seems to me a *weeping willow*…": letter to Ada Mainardi, 19 January 1935, in Sachs, *Letters*, p. 182.

[33] letter to Rudolf Serkin, 29 November 1931, in Irene Busch Serkin, *Adolf Busch: Letters – Pictures – Memories*, (trans.) Russell Stockman, vol. 2, (Walpole, New Haven: Arts & Letters Press, 1991), p. 275

nervous anxiety which worked serious injury to the play and obviously contravened the intentions of the composer."[34] The *Evening Post* reported that in the quintet "he did not allow [the singers] sufficient time to breathe and to prolong the luscious chords as they should be, especially at the end."[35] *Musical America* wrote that Beckmesser "did not always succeed in keeping company with the conductor."[36] In 1914 the *Daily Tribune* observed: "the people of the play sang and acted as if under nervous constraint. There was no opportunity for them to declaim their lines effectively or to indulge in effective action. They had to adjust everything to Signor Toscanini and his orchestra."[37] In 1915 the *Evening Post* went to the heart of the matter:

> With all the merits of the cast, the performance fell short of being a great one, for the reason that Mr. Toscanini did not allow the singers sufficient scope to manifest their individualities. Like the late lamented Gustav Mahler, he harbors the mistaken notion that the singers on the stage are simply parts of the orchestra, like the clarinets, flutes and trombones. That was not at all Wagner's idea. To him (read his essays on *Tannhäuser* and Schnorr) the conductor was simply an accompanist, whose duty it is at every moment to follow the singers, watching their every breath for a necessary pause or two. It is difficult to sing Wagner under this Italian's bâton, because he thus believes in the opera czar instead of the opera star.[38]

The comments quoted above were made, it must be noted, by people who acknowledged the overwhelming beauty and power of his readings. They were merely explaining one effect of his approach. The supreme beauty of Toscanini's performances came from the orchestra.[39] We shall now look at what he achieved in the Wagner operas he most frequently conducted, from *Tannhäuser* to *Parsifal*.

Tannhäuser

When Toscanini inaugurated the Bayreuth Festival in 1930 with *Tannhäuser*, he had not conducted it for many years. The New York *Sun* reported he was "the cynosure of all eyes and his name was on the tip of every tongue. Even Wagner seemed to be forgotten."[40] Yet when it came to the music, it was otherwise. On display was the "ardent imagination of the young Wagner of 1845," according to Ernest Newman. Toscanini had achieved this "not by any factitious pumping into an old score of something exciting to us but alien to it, but by the simple process of playing it just as it is, plus some inner impulse, indefinable and unseizable in itself, that derives its extraordinary power from the fact that it puts in the forefront of our consciousness

[34] *Daily Tribune*, 27 March 1910, p. 7

[35] 28 March 1910, p. 11

[36] 2 April 1910, p. 32. "During the first act there were numerous instances of disagreement in tempo between the conductor and several of the singers, but thereafter such drawbacks were less in evidence."

[37] 16 January 1914, p. 7 (Henry Krehbiel)

[38] 13 March 1915, p. 2. *The New York Times* considered his reading was "occasionally lacking in dramatic plasticity, in the elasticity that gives the actors an opportunity to make the most of the situations, to develop the potentialities of the comedy.... Some of his tempos seemed unduly deliberate, as those in which scenes of excitement are developed": 13 March 1915, p. 13.

[39] Sometimes indeed it was too much, as in a 1914 *Meistersinger*: "there were times when the instrumental part was too loud. It is a pity that Mr. Toscanini cannot go back a dozen rows behind himself when he is conducting and hear some of his *Meistersinger*. He would certainly use the soft pedal oftener if he did this": *Sun*, 16 January 1914, p. 7.

[40] 7 November 1930 (Karl K. Kitchen) (Metropolitan Opera Archives)

not the conductor but the composer."[41] To the *New York Times*, Toscanini had raised "an unequal opera… into a work of high dramatic purpose and an almost consistent musical style."[42] To German critics, the most striking feature was clarity, as Alfred Einstein wrote in the *Berliner Tageblatt*:

With Toscanini, everything is of an ultimate clarity and precision, of an ultimate certainty of rhythm. Let us simply admit that we have never seen a piece of the original *Tannhäuser* – the entry of the guests – endowed with such freshness and festiveness. Nor have we seen the Parisian Venusberg music provided with such rousing verve and orchestral elaboration. I recall only one single "Italian" moment: at the end of the first act, when the six male voices sing at Tannhäuser: a sextet à la *Lucia*….[43]

Bernhard Diebold wrote in the *Frankfurter Zeitung*:

What we have to thank him for is clarity. His incredible skill is "drawing." He draws lines like a classicist. He does not paint with broad colours. One can hear the second and third voices under the principal line. One can inspect the innards of the score. Crystal clear. A musical X-ray. Thus, hardly romantic, in spite of the dramatic, highly-driven introduction to the third act….[44]

It was orchestrally splendid, with concert-like displays of virtuosity.

He conducted *Tannhäuser* again at the 1931 Bayreuth Festival when again his "beauty of sound," as *Musical America* reported, "was nothing less than a tonal re-birth" for many episodes in the score, and when transitional passages glowed with "golden lyricism." But an "excessive refinement" combined with the restraining Bayreuth acoustic "softened, and in a sense tamed," the work: there was "a movement less propulsive than we have come to expect of this genius of the baton. There are those who are convinced that Toscanini has gone back to Wagner himself for the slow tempo at which he takes Tannhäuser's *Hymn to Venus*. The German opera tradition may be wrong…"[45] After the 1931 Festival, Toscanini conducted only orchestral excerpts from the work, including the Bacchanale in his final concert on 4 April 1954 in which he momentarily lost his way.[46]

[41] *Sunday Times*, 29 May 1938 [*sic*], p. 7. In his review of the second performance in 1930, Newman's comment was brief: "Toscanini drew the utmost beauty of tone and phrasing from the orchestra, and, as usual, communicated his own magnetism to the singers": *Sunday Times*, 10 August 1930, p. 5. The singer of Tannhäuser, Sigismund Pilinszky, had been unwell and was not in good voice at the first performance, but had improved by the second. He sang Tannhäuser in Columbia's recordings made that year at Bayreuth. These were conducted by Karl Elmendorff. According to Edward Sackville-West and Desmond Shawe-Taylor, who were at Bayreuth in 1930, "the impress of [Toscanini's] work is strongly felt in them": *The Record Guide* (London, Collins, 1951), p. 648.

[42] *New York Times*, 31 August 1931, p. X6 (H. C. Colles): "almost consistent" because it was the revised Paris version that was performed

[43] Alfred Einstein, *Berliner Tageblatt*, 24 July 1930, in Susanna Großmann-Vendrey, *Bayreuth in der deutschen Presse*, Vol. 3,2 (Regensburg: Bosse, 1983), p. 213. Alexander Kipnis, who sang the Landgraf, recalled another Italian touch: "I remember one thing he insisted on: in Bayreuth the melodic turns in *Tannhäuser* were done in the German way, as part of the rhythm of the measure; but Toscanini insisted on the more graceful Italian way, in which they were delayed and sung as a quick introduction to the next beat": Haggin, *The Toscanini Musicians Knew*, p. 63.

[44] Bernhard Diebold, *Frankfurter Zeitung*, 24-25 July 1930, in Großmann-Vendrey, *ibid*, p. 216

[45] August 1931, p. 5 (Oscar Thompson)

[46] Freeman and Toscanini, *Toscanini*, p. 68

Tristan und Isolde

Toscanini's *Tristan* was greeted with euphoria – and surprise – wherever he conducted it. An *Italian* conductor was conducting a German opera as no German could ever conduct an Italian opera! A sober and succinct account of Toscanini's style is from the *New York Tribune* in 1913, by which stage he had given more than twenty performances with the Metropolitan Opera:

His reading of the score is one in which he strives always for beauty of line, for form, for grace of contour, and yet, in spite of all, he never sacrifices strength of passion or the sense of impending doom. His is a universal rather than a Latin *Tristan*; for *Tristan* is, afterall, a work for which the Rhine is no true boundary, and in the love music in particular Teutonic force is only sublimated by being restrained by a fine Italian hand. Such a hand is Arturo Toscanini's.[47]

The *Press* described a characteristically "overpowering" performance of 1912: "Exquisitely chiseled in detail, beautifully measured, wonderfully balanced and symmetrical in design, clear, limpid and mellifluous from beginning to end, it was a perfect exposition of the musical substance of the score."[48] Ernest Newman found many revelations in Toscanini's Bayreuth *Tristan* of 1930, yet "all, or practically all, that he had done was to play the notes just as Wagner directs them to be played."[49] A German critic made a similar observation:

[It was] a *Tristan* where no "conception" was any longer noticeable. One was unable to distinguish the nationality of the conductor: he transformed the notes directly into sound and spirit. Nowhere was there any "surprise." It was always just the way it was supposed to be, the way one envisages it in one's dreams.... The tempi were never sluggish..... The rhythms were razor-sharp.... One could feel the bar lines as with Haydn.... The usual "uncontrollable" ecstasy [at the end of act one] was rendered totally precise... Spiritual romanticism turned to musical classicism. Form was completely at one with expressive delirium. That is the highest art. It applies to Wagner. And to Toscanini too.[50]

To return to New York, and to the *Press* again, its reviewer commented on Toscanini's first performance in 1909: "From a purely technical point of view it was a marvel of detailed perfection – as minutely elaborated, as finely worked out, as

[47] 25 December 1913, p. 7 [48] 31 December 1912 (Metropolitan Opera Archives)

[49] "Genius and the Classics," (1 March 1931), Ernest Newman, *More essays from the world of music: essays from "The Sunday Times,"* selected by Felix Aprahamian (London: John Calder, 1958), p. 23. Newman's report on the 6 August 1930 performance said nothing substantive about the conducting: *Sunday Times*, 10 August 1930, p. 5.

[50] Bernhard Diebold, *Frankfurter Zeitung*, 24-25 July 1930, in Großmann-Vendrey, *Bayreuth in der deutschen Presse*, Vol. 3,2, p. 217. On the point of "nationality," it is recorded that Alexander Kipnis, who sang King Marke, and Serge Koussevitzky who was present at the 1930 performances, considered *Tristan* was performed "like an Italian opera," as did some other singers and critics, according to Kipnis: Haggin, *The Toscanini Musicians Knew*, pp. 63-64. Also, Alma Mahler wrote: "However polished Toscanini's conducting of *Tristan* might be, we always felt that his Wagner suffered from a surfeit of Italian nuances": *Gustav Mahler - Memories and Letters*, (ed.) Donald Mitchell, 3rd (ed.), (trans.) Basil Creighton (London: John Murray, 1973), p. 163. For another account, Mahler told Bruno Walter: "He conducts it in a manner entirely different from ours, but his way is magnificent": Walter, *Theme and Variations: an autobiography*, (trans.) James A. Galston (London: H. Hamilton, 1947), p. 306. Reginald Goodall heard Toscanini's rehearsals for his London concerts in the 1930s (which included Wagner), and said: "he had great clarity, but he was too Italian for me; I like my music to come up from the bowels of the earth": John Lucas, *Reggie: The Life of Reginald Goodall* (London: Julia MacRae Books, 1993), p. 43.

unflagging in vitality as if it had been, say, a symphonic poem."[51] This point about technical perfection, which precedes a long eulogy on the poetry of Toscanini's reading, explains both his approach and the tremendous impact it had on some listeners. To Ernest Newman Toscanini's orchestra came as a revelation, "like a dagger stroke."[52] Yet daggers can be damaging. The reading was "a cruel one for the voices," the *New York Times* observed:

> His climaxes were often… overpowering; but it was sometimes difficult to tell by the ear alone whether or not there was a singer singing behind the orchestra. We have heard from Mr. Mahler how the orchestra in *Tristan* and others of Wagner's later music dramas can give eloquent utterance, and can build up climaxes and can express the sum of all he attributes to it, and yet hide the tone and even the enunciation of no singer's voice. It is the logic and the necessity of the aesthetic theory of Wagner's music dramas that this must be the right proportion. There is evidence enough and to spare that this was what Wagner wished – and found that he seldom obtained.[53]

The *Evening Post* noticed that on many occasions, especially in the last act, Toscanini "permitted his men to play so boisterously that the huge voices of Gadski, Homer, and Burrian were almost inaudible. He should ponder the words of Anton Seidl… [on Wagner's wish not to drown the singers.]"[54] The *World* wrote that: "at climactic moments… one seemed to be listening to an orchestral recitation, with a more or less audible vocal obligato."[55] At a later performance the *Philadelphia Record* was so impressed by the orchestral performance that it commented: "it would have been sufficient to hear Toscanini play the opera without any vocalization."[56] That may be the way Toscanini wanted it. "He looks on the score as a glorious symphony, which it certainly is," wrote the *Evening Post*, "but the vocal parts are more important still, and the orchestra should follow, not lead."[57] He was not always like this. On some occasions he was in "perfect sympathy with the singers,"[58] when "every syllable uttered by [them] could be understood with ease by the most distant listeners."[59] So – at moments he was carried away, at others he was hushed. "Vesuvian in grandeur are the lava streams of passion which he hurls out," wrote the *Evening Post*, "[yet] how infinitely tender are his orchestral whisperings at quiet moments."[60]

For some, Mahler's interpretation had been swept away by Toscanini's. "Mr. Mahler's was striking in several ways," wrote the *Boston Herald*, "as in exquisite sense

[51] 28 November 1909, p. 10 [52] Newman, *More essays*, p. 23 [53] 28 November 1909, p. 11.

[54] 29 November 1909, p. 9. The reviewer quoted a passage from Seidl's "On Conducting" reproduced in the Seidl chapter above., pp. 114-5 [55] 28 November 1909 (Reginald de Koven)

[56] 7 January 1914, p. 2. Toscanini's many studio recordings of the *Liebestod* never included a voice.

[57] 16 January 1914, p. 7. *Musical America* wrote after Salzburg, 1936: "For him *Meistersinger* is a wonderful symphony, for the completion of which the drama, or if you like, the comedy, takes place": September 1936, p.23.

[58] *Sun*, 5 January 1911, p. 5, yet of a later performance: "there are still occasions when Mr. Toscanini is not considerate of the singers": 31 December 1912, p. 5

[59] *Musical America*, 14 January 1911, p. 33, which added: "Could Wagner but have lived to know Toscanini!"

[60] 5 January 1911, p. 9. Likewise in Philadelphia: "his lambent spirit was abroad not only in the orchestra, but among the singers on the stage. His reading of the score is one which strives for clarity of utterance, for beauty of line, for grace and delicacy of shading without sacrificing force or robbing the passionate climaxes of their due emphasis. Realizing that mere noisiness is not expressive, he restrains his musicians with a firm but tactful hand, preferring to carry the singers along in the sweep of his sane enthusiasm rather than engulf them in a din of instrumentation…": *Philadelphia Evening Bulletin*, 7 January 1914, p. 6

of proportion; in the respect paid to the singers; in fine gradations of tone; but on the whole it was academic. It lacked the sensuous glow, the lulls of passion; the romantic spirit, and the imaginative sweep of Mr. Toscanini's reading."[61] Others, however, missed Mahler's interpretation. Ossip Gabrilovich reported in a letter to Bruno Walter of his disappointment after hearing Toscanini conduct *Tristan* in 1914. However *technically* great he might have been, he was "not to be compared with Mahler or Walter himself. Essentially an orchestral conductor, he didn't have as 'spontaneous and compelling' an effect on the singers as Walter had."[62] James Huneker was a great admirer of both Mahler and Toscanini, yet he longed for something more:

> [Toscanini] belongs to the Brahmin conductors; to the company of Richter, Levi, Seidl, Mottl, Mahler. A more poetically intense *Tristan* than his reading with the lovely Olive Fremstad as the impassioned Isolde, I have seldom heard. Toscanini is a superman. In that frail frame of his there is enough dynamic energy with which to capture Gehenna. He is all spirit. He does not always achieve the ultimate heights as did Seidl, as does Arthur Nikisch. While his interpretation of *Tristan* is a wonderfully worked-out musical picture, yet the elemental ground-swell, which Anton Seidl summoned from the vasty deep, is missing. But what ravishing tone-colors Toscanini mixed on his orchestral palette![63]

Anton Seidl's ghost still hovered above his great successors at the Metropolitan Opera.

Die Meistersinger von Nürnberg

Toscanini demanded plenty of rehearsal time for his first *Meistersinger* in New York in 1910. It was "worth waiting for," the *New York Times* wrote. "It was in almost every respect a profoundly beautiful and poetical performance of the work. Upon the musical side especially it reached a pitch of perfection, of ravishing, intoxicating loveliness, of pure beauty of sound, of instrumental color, that was perhaps unique of its kind." There was a reservation, however, and it has already been adverted to: "it seemed at times as if Mr. Toscanini were so intent upon the musical continuity of the orchestral score that he failed to make due allowance for the declamatory points [in the first act] and for which the singers must be given their opportunities."[64] The *Sun* wrote of "moments of lofty beauty.... his technical treatment of the orchestral part of the work was perfect in its elegance, its exquisite balance and clearness, its precision and its continence. It was a flawless exposition of his conception of the composition." This is how it seemed:

> That part of the music which sang the passions of Walther and Eva and the aspirations of the youthful poet, Mr Toscanini read with insight and sympathy, with conviction and exquisite

[61] 11 January 1910, p. 14 (Philip Hale). The pianist, Samuel Chotzinoff, later a music critic, recalled how in his youth: "Toscanini had overpowered my senses and my judgment. He had made me *forget* Mahler, a conductor whom only a few months earlier I had looked upon as the greatest in the world": Chotzinoff, *Day's at the Morn* (London: Hamish Hamilton, 1965), pp. 134-135.

[62] quoted in Erik Ryding and ReBecca Pechefsky, *Bruno Walter: A World Elsewhere* (New Haven and London: Yale University Press, 2001), p. 118.

[63] Huneker, *Steeplejack*, vol. 2 (New York: Scribner's Sons, 1921), pp. 40-41. For Huneker's views on Mahler's *Tristan*, see above at p. 263

[64] 27 March 1910, p. 11. The principal singers were Walter Soomer, Sachs; Robert Blass, Pogner; Leo Slezak, Walther; Albert Reiss, David; Johanna Gadski, Eva; Florence Wickham, Magdalene.

musical finish. No one could hope to hear this music treated with greater delicacy of touch, with more artistic refinement, with more fastidious consideration for the relation between voices and orchestra.

But the comedy passages suffered from the manifest inability of the conductor to saturate himself in the spirit of the scene and from his failure to follow every nuance of the dialogue. To enter briefly into more careful account, the first act was all clarity and delicacy. Pogner's address was improved by the slightly quickened tempo at which it was taken. The dance of the apprentices was heavy, tame and angular. The first appearance of the knighthood theme of Walther was entirely wanting in musical importance. The finale was rigorously analytical and wooden. All through the act the tempi were rigid and the dialogue was always, to use a musical expression, *a battuta.*

In the second act the apprentice dance was again heavy and inelastic. The scene between Sachs and Eva was fairly light but lacked orchestral color. The scene between Eva and Magdalena was wooden. The famous monologue of Sachs was beautifully accompanied. The finale of the act was musically wonderful in its clarity, yet it lacked something of the temper of a riotous outbreak such as the scene presents to the eye. The parts for the women's voices were never so well brought out, but the women themselves might as well have been graven images. The moonlight music at the very end was excellently done, but we have heard it read with more imagination.

Sachs's *Wahn, Wahn* was admirably treated and the prize song went as a matter of course. The farcical scene of Beckmesser was somewhat leaden footed but not bad. The quintet was taken at a broad but not unreasonable tempo. Here Mr. Toscanini was better than his singers. The gathering of the guilds was deficient in spirit and the entrance of the masters quite tame. But the chorale was admirably treated.[65]

There was other press comment on how striking Toscanini's skills were, what an impact they had, yet how unfulfilling the whole could be. The *New York American* considered that in some respects Toscanini's reading was preferable to that of Alfred Hertz, in others less so. There was a disconcerting tendency "to give prominence to the brass and celli at the expense of the violins" in the prelude; there were noticeable changes in the rhythms, phrasing and tempi in the first act; "on the whole, it cannot, without straining the truth, be said that Toscanini's version of the first episode in *Die Meistersinger* fulfilled the hopes raised by the maestro's wonderful interpretation of *Götterdämmerung* and *Tristan und Isolde*.... The third act – the great test – did not realize the promises of the second. Of the depth, richness and earnestness which Wagner put into his orchestration, something seemed missing."[66] In other performances with the Metropolitan Opera - there were 19 between 1910 and 1915 – there continued to be praise, even amazement, at the orchestral splendour of Toscanini's reading, yet reserve, even disappointment, that all the possibilities of the work had not been realized.[67]

[65] 27 March 1910, p. 7

[66] 28 March 1910 (Charles Meltzer) (Metropolitan Opera Archives)

[67] To give further examples: "his handling of the orchestra was such as to make plain the full and intricate beauty of the music. And while the performance as a whole was not one of supremely imaginative eloquence, it nevertheless never fell below adequacy": *Evening Journal*, 7 March 1912 (Irving Weil); "With all the beauty of certain kinds that belonged to Mr. Toscanini's reading, it was not one that will take a rank among his most successful achievements... The audience was unusually apathetic and found little to rouse it to enthusiasm": *New York Times*, 16 January 1914, p. 10; cf. the *Press*: "[the audience] sat trembling with excitement from the first vigorous strains of the prelude to the sublime choral ending": 16 January 1914; "The performance last night did not provide unalloyed pleasure... *Die Meistersinger* is to [Toscanini] a great orchestral song, full of splendor, rich with a multitude of orchestral voices... but it is something vastly

Fig. 13.1. Arturo Toscanini from his Metropolitan Opera years, 1908-1915

Fig. 13.2. Toscanini at Bayreuth, 1930

Fig. 13.3. Toscanini at Tribschen, 1938. Photo by Jean Schneider

Fig. 13.4. Toscanini in rehearsal, New York, 1940s

Fig. 13.5. Toscanini on tour with La Scala, 1929

Fig. 13.6. Toscanini on tour with the NBC Symphony, 1950

In the case of the Salzburg *Meistersinger*, the opening performance on 8 August 1936 was, by most reports, magnificent. Toscanini himself called it "a moving performance. I don't think I've ever obtained a better performance."[68] However, Herbert Peyser, who had heard Toscanini conduct the work in New York twenty-five years earlier, still had the impression that "despite its marvelous clarity, its sculpted workmanship and its exquisite plasticity of thematic molding, the first act is a shade over-precise and unyielding."[69] To Neville Cardus the performance would "remain in the mind for a lifetime, because of its beauty and dignity of proportion," yet this took time to emerge:

Toscanini gave to the first act a certain rigidity; the mastersingers were made to toe a strict line, and David in his explanations to Walther was allowed no time for boyish appreciation of his own momentary authority over the knight and the scene. For a while I chafed under Toscanini's Latin clarity; I wanted the humour that expands and releases, not the wit that contracts and braces up. Probably the interpretation never did find the girth of a Richter humour, that large mildness of laughter which has no use for the crack of the whip of an epigram.[70]

This act one, more or less complete, can be heard on disc, and Cardus's comments are borne out. Toscanini is indeed rhythmically secure to the point of rigidity. During the gathering of the mastersingers, for example, where it is possible for the rhythm to come from the waves of glorious, growing, underlying melody, expanding in accord with the occasion, it seems to march on to the beat of a military roll call. Reviews of this Toscanini performance differ, however, as they do in some other cases, even to the point of contradiction.[71] To illustrate, *The Times* considered that in this very same *Meistersinger* the "great moments" grew under Toscanini's hand "out of the very texture of the music with an inevitability that made them seem all the greater."

The pace was often quick, and it is, perhaps, worth recording that the first act was played in 77 minutes – exactly the time taken by von Bülow at the first performance in Munich and several minutes less than the average German performance. What is more important is that, while the tempi gave an unusual vitality to the performance, the singers always had ample space for what

more.... Last night, as on other occasions when Signor Toscanini conducted, the people of the play sang and acted as if under nervous constraint": *Daily Tribune*, 16 January 1914, p. 7 (Henry Krehbiel); "Mr. Toscanini revels in the orchestral score, wreaks himself upon it. His performance is a marvel of rich and changing color, of exquisitely wrought detail.... But Mr. Toscanini has considerably less interest in what goes on upon the stage...": *New York Times*, 13 March 1915, p. 13.

68 letter to Ada Mainardi, 9 August 1936, in Sachs, *Letters*, p. 210

69 *New York Times*, 23 August 1936, p. X5. Sachs's second act monologue lacked "a certain Germanic quality. Lightness, indeed airiness, is a hallmark of this reading... for the rest, [it] is by turns all wit, all lyric song, all filtered sunlight and luminous transfiguration."

70 review dated 28 August 1936 in *Cardus on music: a centenary collection* (ed.) Donald Wright (London: H. Hamilton, 1988), p.120. Toscanini conducted the work on 8, 14, 18, and 22 August 1936. The review in the *Sunday Times* by a "special correspondent" does not comment on act one: 23 August 1936, p. 5.

71 The comment of his biographer – "reviews of Toscanini's performances in the first half of his career are as much a hindrance as a help in any attempt to imagine his music-making as it then sounded": Sachs, *Toscanini*, p. 165 – is perhaps a little too pessimistic. While Toscanini reviewers do indeed comment on the same performance differently (regardless of whether or not they liked it), their observations can give a good idea of what was going on. For example, the *Evening Post* expressed disappointment at the way the last fourteen bars of the prelude to act three of the *Meistersinger* had been played: "Wagner's directions are *sehr breit, ausdrucksvoll*; then for the last four bars, *zögernd*, and, finally, *molto rallentando*. Even without these directions, a conductor ought to feel the imperative need here of a great slowing up; without it, the sublime becomes commonplace. But Toscanini played it without any *rallentando* at all; he did not feel the heavenly beauty in those last two bars": 13 March 1915, p. 2. One can hear this on the 1937 Salzburg recording.

they had to do. There was never anything of that sense of strain which is often evident when other conductors with less understanding of the singers' problems attempt to cover the ground at an impossible pace.... Fast or slow, under Signor Toscanini's direction, the rhythm is always taut, yet never inflexible.[72]

In later years Cardus recalled how he had not wanted to hear Toscanini's *Meistersinger* a second time: "his approach to the music seemed uncongenial. Mind you, this was in Toscanini's later years, when his musical arteries were beginning to harden."[73]

The question of congeniality was not, however, new. It arose for *Musical America* after a 1915 performance when it had written of the "comparative inadequacy" of Toscanini's *Meistersinger*: "the stubborn fact remains that it is not as congenial to him as most operas on which he expends his energies. The fact is, after all, legitimate enough. If a singer is temperamentally ill-suited to a certain rôle why should not a conductor show to less advantage in some operas than others?"[74] That Toscanini loved the work is not in doubt. In fact his enthusiasm was more than New Yorkers could bear. He gave the work with practically no cuts, and with little thanks. "After four hours," the *Evening Post* reported after one performance, "the hearers began to steal away silently, regretfully, and the last scene was sung and played to little more than half an audience." He had made the opera last nearly an hour longer than the "Wagnerian high priest," Anton Seidl, who was able to make many little cuts. Toscanini had committed "an unpardonable æsthetic crime."[75]

Der Ring des Nibelungen

Toscanini never conducted the *Rheingold*.[76] He conducted the *Walküre* only rarely. It was the only opera from which he chose any sizeable vocal excerpt to perform in concert, the love-awakening of Siegmund and Sieglinde in act one. The two recordings – in 1941 with Lauritz Melchior and Helen Traubel, and in 1947 with Set Svanholm and Rose Bampton – show some of the characteristics of Toscanini's conducting noted above. The performances are very directed, and to the extent this creates tension – a sense of love about to break forth – it is very effective, and there

[72] *The Times*, 22 August 1936, p. 8 ("Our Special Correspondent"). "The quality which distinguished it from any other one has heard is, in one word, the sheer musicality of every bar... every note of it was tingling with life." The 1937 performance differed little from that of 1936: *ibid*, 17 August 1937, p. 8 ("Our Special Correspondent").

[73] Robin Daniels, *Conversations with Cardus* (London: Gollancz, 1976), p. 144-5

[74] 20 March 1915, p. 40, which listed "the cardinal failings of Mr. Toscanini's reading – the want of elasticity, the lack of dramatic *rubato*, the failure to allow for those indefinably subtle modifications of pace which Wagner's comedy imperatively demands of its singers. Curiously enough, there was also a lack of warmth in some of the most poetic episodes" [and proceeds to give examples]. *Musical America* concurred: "he does not seem to conduct *Die Meistersinger* with the same understanding that he does *Tristan*": 17 March 1915, p. 27. The *Sun* observed that Toscanini's reading had "always been peculiarly inconsistent, and it continues to be so. Slowness of tempo and extreme rigidity mar some episodes...": 13 March 1915, p. 5.

[75] 21 January 1911, p. 6. "We implore him to restore the Seidl cuts, in the interest of the singers, of the audiences, of Wagner himself."

[76] Sachs, *Toscanini*, p. 90. In a review of *Götterdämmerung* in New York, the *Evening Post* reported he had conducted *Rheingold* at La Scala "twenty times in one brief session... a feat never accomplished in any German city": 11 December 1908 (Metropolitan Opera Archives). Presumably this was a reference to *Götterdämmerung* which he conducted twenty-two times in the 1895-96 season in Turin: Sachs, *ibid*, p. 50.

are occasional surges of orchestral song beneath the singers. In the earlier performance Melchior seems more constrained, perhaps because he was trying hard to please the conductor – "Toscanini implored him to just *keep* the tempo, to just sing it *correctly*," his biographer wrote[77] – and there is a certain tightness, a woodenness that makes an interesting comparison with the free-flowing spirit of the Bruno Walter recording. The final passage in the 1947 performance is much more free-flowing and naturally passionate. Irving Kolodin noted after the concert how the singers had been "slightly overwhelmed by the torrents of spring-sounding music," and how "on the whole his pace is slower than that favored by most conductors," but he was forgiven.[78]

Fig. 13.7. Toscanini in New York. *Musical America*, 9 September 1916

Siegfried was another *Ring* opera Toscanini rarely performed. In a 1899 production in Milan there was, according to the *Perseveranza*, an "orchestral performance… perfectly clear, never exuberant or inclined to overwhelm the vocal part. Every thought, every theme, was executed with clarity. The right sonority, never loud and at the same time always vibrating; *élan*, passion, life, were characteristic of this stupendous interpretation."[79] After this, *La Sera* did not hesitate to call him "the best of our conductors."[80]

Götterdämmerung was his first Wagner work at the Metropolitan Opera in 1908. He made a tremendous personal impression. "With such a phenomenal Wagner leader at the Metropolitan," wrote the *Musical Courier*, "men like Hertz and Mahler lag

77 Shirlee Emmons, *Tristanissimo* (New York: Shirmer Books, 1990), p. 100

78 *Sun*, 7 April 1947, p. 15. The *Herald Tribune* wrote that the performance "was marked by a pervasive expressive intensity and eloquence": 7 April 1947, p. 12 (F.D.P.).

79 *Perseveranza* (Milan), 27 December 1899, quoted in Segre, "Toscanini," p. 169

80 *La Sera* (Milan), 27 December 1899, quoted in Segre, *ibid*, p. 169

superfluous in that institution, for they are merely routiniers, while the Italian is a truly inspired artist with temperament, imagination and vital musical feeling. Toscanini is today the leading operatic attraction of New York."[81] The *Press* too marked him out as "the real 'star' of the performance":

Perhaps the word "intense" describes the most characteristic trait of Toscanini's reading. The same electrifying current of magnetism throbbed through Wagner's score.... There was an undercurrent of poetic feeling, beautifully reserved and delicate at times, and again rising to the surface with torrential force. There was passion, now suppressed, now leaping into flame, but always controlled by a great will and mind. There was profound understanding of the musical and literary significance of the drama; there was extraordinary mastery of detail and an all-compelling grasp of the broad dramatic outlines.

... The Rhine Journey music... he whipped up to an extraordinary speed; the Funeral March he expanded to a remarkable breadth[82].... there was no admixture of sugar.... His reading was rugged, rather than sentimental.[83]

The *Sun* wrote that it was to Toscanini that "went the cometlike glory of the night. He was the nucleus; *Götterdämmerung* was the tail":

Mr. Toscanini naturally feels above all the sensuous quality of Wagner's melody, and it is in this in all its ebb and flow that he seeks and exposes. Whenever the sensuous beauty of the melody is such as to tempt a conductor to dwell unduly on the phrase, to exaggerate the rhetorical pause, to smooth out all the rugged edges of the instrumental declamation, Mr. Toscanini yields to it with avidity and spreads the syrup out on the bread as thin as possible.

The results of such treatment are easily noted. In most of the first act they took shape in elongation of tempi till the scenes at times lost their innate strength. Hercules was transformed into Apollo with an accentuation of the effeminacy always noted in statues of the latter god. But there was another side to the picture. Whenever the sensuous beauty of the pure melody was to be exposed only by deepening its lines by adhering to the firmly dramatic nature of its contours, Mr. Toscanini rose to the occasion. This was, for example, notably the case in the splendid choral passage of the second act, which went with admirable verve.[84]

Musical America was likewise struck by the way Toscanini "laid great emphasis on the melodic side" of the work, and how "in the sensuous passages [he] was inclined to drag out the tempos until much of their virility was lost." However, "whenever sensuous beauty" was called for, he was quite "equal to his task." But this was not enough. "With Mahler fresh in memory it did not seem a great performance."[85] It was also not "a new revelation" to the *New York Times*, but it was "a performance of remarkable energy and dramatic power, as well as one of great musical beauty." There were passages in which Toscanini was "carried away by the sweep of the music," and which led to "a degree of tone against which the voices struggled in vain."[86] The *Telegraph* was more poetic: "Its overwhelming eloquence glows into the ear in a strong current, unvexed by fault or impediment of utterance."[87] Toscanini's appreciation of

[81] 16 December 1908, p. 28

[82] The *Evening World* reported that a few people started to leave during the Funeral March, and they were hissed: 11 December 1908, p. 15 (Sylvester Rawling). The *Evening Sun* wrote that "the ultimate death dirge did not produce... popular effect": 11 December 1908.

[83] *Press*, 11 December 1908, p. 10

[84] *Sun*, 11 December 1908, p. 7

[85] 19 December 1908, p. 4

[86] 11 December 1908, p. 8

[87] 11 December 1908 (Algernon St. John-Brenon)

the score, according to the *Daily Tribune*, was "fine in its knowledge of its splendid melos, and this was brought out in the orchestral music as it has seldom been – not only in its melos, but its sonorous euphony and its fascinating elasticity."[88] He gave five performances in New York and one in Chicago in the 1908-09 season, and never performed it again. Despite the critical acclaim of the first performance, it was not popular with the public, at least not with the "social element" who paid for boxes and were conspicuous by their absence,[89] and it was too long even with the Waltraute scene omitted. Again, people left; there were few remaining by the night's end.[90] After a sixth performance, in Chicago in April 1909, Toscanini never conducted the work again.

Parsifal

Parsifal was another of Wagner's operas Toscanini conducted only on rare occasions – in Milan in 1928 and Bayreuth in 1931 – and this seems odd considering his professed love of the work. He approached the task in Bayreuth with utter devotion. His reading of the music had a "fervor of consecration," according to Herbert Peyser:

It is the most intimate and unsparingly searching revelation of Toscanini's soul that any music has ever made. It is a kind of intensely personal rite, a confession of faith so embracing in its scope, so consuming in its expression that one kneels in adoration before it even while one may emphatically disagree with this or that of its premises. When you have heard this *Parsifal* you are suddenly aware that you stand in a new relation to Arturo Toscanini – that, in effect, it is *Parsifal* which has newly disclosed Toscanini to you, rather than the reverse. Taken by and large it is an uneven interpretation, one filled with the defects of its qualities. For me its greatness is divided between the first and third acts. I cared far less for the second, some of which seems curiously remote from the imaginative sympathies of the great conductor. I missed something of the characteristic seriousness of the music in the garden scene and some of the sense of the psychologically piercing and cumulative. I felt little of the demonic in the treatment of the Klingsor scene, in consequence of which that entire episode appeared to me dull. But in the first act and again in the third I had the impression that Toscanini might have taken as his device some such sentiment as that with which Beethoven prefaced the *Missa Solemnis* – "from the heart may it go to the heart."[91]

Musical America, which wrote of "the most silken texture" given the score, "glowing with a peculiarly remote warmth, rather than shot through with the fire and iron of Muck," also had reservations about the second act:

In the Klingsor scene, the Toscanini performance was frankly disappointing. It lacked the bite, the edge, the malice, the evil of Muck's. Nor were the temptations of the flower-maidens the most sensuous of our experience. The second act, in its entirety, seemed to us over-sensitized, over-refined. The first and last were almost beyond compare....[92]

Most notable was the pace of the performance and its overall length – the longest on record – and the effect this had on its quality. It appears to have hovered between "a hieratic solemnity"[93] and a life-sapping dullness. "Many are of the opinion that

[88] 11 December 1908, p. 7
[89] *Sun*, 19 December 1908 (Metropolitan Opera Archives)
[90] *Evening Post*, 25 February 1909, p. 7
[91] *New York Times*, 16 August 1931, p. 100
[92] August 1931, p. 5 (Oscar Thompson)
[93] Stefan, *Toscanini*, p. 103

everything Toscanini touches turns to gold," wrote Lauritz Melchior, who sang Parsifal in Toscanini's Bayreuth performances, "but I want to say that I don't quite agree. As much as I loved to sing *Tristan* and *Tannhäuser* under his baton, I found his *Parsifal* too slow and dull – but I suppose he couldn't care less what my opinion is...."[94] That supposition was certainly correct, for "Toscanini appeared to be performing the ritual of *Parsifal* for himself alone and, immersed in infinitudes, was scarcely conscious of the presence of an audience."[95] One member of the audience, English pianist Harriet Cohen, acknowledged it was "a performance of consummate perfection, but this didn't prevent me from being bored by much of it."[96] Others fell asleep. "Every now and then," the *Frankfurter Zeitung* reported, "one can see the victims of his implacability around you, who have gone from Orpheus to Morpheus, falling through the *caesuras*, sometimes unfortunately not without emitting accompanying noises."[97] The *New York Times* correspondent commented on this "almost abnormal slowness of pace," even compared to Muck:

> Irrespective of the spiritual and emotional basis underlying these tempi, I do not believe that, in the last analysis, such a gait is favourable to the best interests of *Parsifal*. What under Muck was a magnificent and architecturally justifiable breadth of movement became under Toscanini something that verged now and then on perilous elongations of phrase, actually threatening here and there the integrity of the design.

Nevertheless:

> The glory of sheer flowing sound, the infinity of hair-breadth nuance, the cherishing solicitude for myriad detail which distinguished the prelude, the Gurnemanz music in the first act, the mystical ceremonials of the temple scene, the marvelous introduction to the third act and the Good Friday Spell – these things of course, were no more than is expected by those who know the ways of Toscanini. To hear his treatment of the first act narrative of Gurnemanz is something like observing a strange and wonderful undersea flora through immeasurable depths of translucent water. The transformation music, the agony of Amfortas, the funeral march of Titurel have a breadth, a poignant accent, and a plangency that wring the tears from the listener's eyes, without possessing, however, all of the edge and the iron that Muck has brought to these and other pages.[98]

Toscanini was not altogether happy with Bayreuth, which he described as "an ordinary theatre" not a "temple."[99] It appeared unlikely he would be back for the next festival, in 1933, under the direction of Wilhelm Furtwängler and Heinz Tietjen. He never conducted *Parsifal* again.

[94] Ib Melchior, *Lauritz Melchior*, p. 178
[95] *New York Times*, 16 August 1931, p. 100
[96] Harriet Cohen, *A bundle of time: the memoirs of Harriet Cohen* (London: Faber, 1969), p. 191
[97] Heinrich Simon, *Frankfurter Zeitung*, 28, 29, 31 July 1931, in Großmann-Vendrey, *Bayreuth in der deutschen Presse*, Vol. 3,2, p. 225
[98] *New York Times*, 16 August 1931, p. 100. For the length of Toscanini's performance compared with others, see Timings below.
[99] Sachs, *Toscanini*, p. 217. "The disaster here is that one can never have a whole ensemble for the rehearsals": letter dated 5 July 1931 to his wife: Sachs, *Letters*, p. 131. In its report above, the *New York Times* said the orchestra was vastly better than in 1930, having been assembled by Furtwängler, who conducted *Tristan* at the 1931 festival.

Fig. 13.8. Toscanini in Copenhagen. *Politiken*, 22 August 1936

The Wagner recordings

The chief disappointment about Toscanini's Wagner recordings is that he did not make more of them. He had an ambivalent attitude towards the recording process and the industry, but became an assiduous user of it. In the case of Wagner he never marshalled the forces to record a complete work, and only rarely sizeable chunks.[100] Why he did not perform and record with some of the great Wagnerian singers available, like Kirsten Flagstad, must remain a matter of some speculation,[101] for he did record a number of Verdi operas.[102] What he did record – and what has come down to us in broadcast and television recordings – comprises the largest collection of Wagner *concert* pieces by any conductor. There is every overture and prelude, in one version or another, with and without Wagner's concert endings, the *Faust Overture*, the *Siegfried Idyll*, the well-known orchestral passages, and even arrangements and selections of questionable taste, such as the concert ending to the Rhine Journey and a *Parsifal*

[100] The 1941 performance of the Dawn music, Duet, Siegfried's Rhine Journey from *Götterdämmerung* is the only *sung* version, but it has the same strange arrangement by Toscanini at the ending that appears on his other recordings.

[101] In Flagstad's case, "the explanation from people who knew them both rather well was that Toscanini would not share top billing with any other artists, which would have been obligatory with a singer of Kirsten Flagstad's stature": Howard Vogt, *Flagstad: Singer of the Century* (London: Secker and Warburg, 1987), p. 162. There is but one recording of Toscanini conducting a *sung Liebestod*, the fragment with Elsa Alsen in 1932. They were unequal partners. Desmond Shaw-Taylor wrote that Toscanini "was prepared to throw out the glorious Friedrich Schorr from his *Meistersinger* cast of 1936, replacing him with the reliable but decidedly inferior Hans Hermann Nissen." He grew more and more content to work with singers who were "docile and obedient": "The Gramophone and the Voice," *Gramophone*, October 1957, p. 171.

[102] Spike Hughes wrote: "perhaps it was Toscanini's Verdi which proved the greatest revelation of all": "Toscanini and Opera," *Gramophone*, February 1957, p. 321.

"Synthesis".[103] The notable exceptions are the prelude to act three of *Tristan* and the transformation music from *Parsifal*. This may not have been accidental. The latter is such a dense tableau of changing moods, of a "psychologically piercing" character, where time and line shift uncertainly, that the passage may not have suited Toscanini's temperament or special musical skills. The former has a long passage for a soloist, the *cor anglais*. He performed the Ride of the Valkyries many times.

Toscanini was very particular about approving his recordings before release. When listening to playbacks, according to a member of his NBC orchestra, he "never made any comment about the beauty or texture of the sound in the recording; his attention was always focused on the tempo, drive, and orchestral balance."[104] The sound of his recordings is often very poor, not least in the dry acoustic of NBC Studio 8-H where, ironically, Toscanini could better achieve, or hear, the clarity and musical line of his performances. Notwithstanding the limitations of repertoire and sound quality, the *approved* recordings are definitely superior to any of the others. With most conductors there is a special quality, a spark of spontaneity or of occasion, in their live recordings. In the case of Toscanini is it different. Toscanini's interpretations were not searching but always the same. The recordings he approved were those where he was able to get precisely what he wanted from his interpretation, where he was able to *control* the outcome. One of his most brilliant recordings is the 1946 *Faust Overture* – "I've approved the *Faust Overture*," he wrote after some months of reflection[105] – where the degree of control is absolute. It is as if he were holding down a high-tensile spring, which when released explodes with demonic force, keeping its perfectly determined trajectory. His live performances of this work do not quite come up to the same level. In 1935 with the BBC Symphony Orchestra, for example, he can he heard singing, *trying* to get his desired effects, instead of getting them. Wagner's music is not all suited to the tightly held treatment he gives to the *Faust Overture*. The intensity he obtains from the orchestra can exclude other qualities, such as "mystery and resignation,"[106] and can be antithetical to some situations in the music-drama. In the riot scene at the end of act two of the 1937 *Meistersinger*, for example, there is incredible clenched-fist control: the effect is of a well-coordinated punch-up, not the riot it should be.

Toscanini was in his 70s when most of his recordings were made. It is arguable whether they are a reliable guide to his earlier performances of whole works.[107] In

[103] Fritz Busch attended a Toscanini Wagner concert in London in 1937: it "had incredible things in it, and I learned a lot; the program was hideous, and I heard a number of notes in that concert that I had never heard in Wagner heretofore, as he didn't write them. For Siegfried's Rhine Journey he used an arrangement (his own?) that was, let us say, highly unusual, and the same can be said of the Ride of the Valkyries. I also like to avoid in concert the Prelude to the 3rd Act of *Lohengrin*, with its ending after the C-minor etc., which was hideous": letter to Adolf Busch dated 27 July 1937, in Irene Busch Serkin, *Adolf Busch: Letters – Pictures – Memories*, vol. 2, p. 370. In this context,

[104] Samuel Antek, *This was Toscanini* (New York: Vanguard Press, 1963), p. 116

[105] letter dated 1 May 1947 to Elsa Kurzbauer, New York, in Sachs, *Letters*, p. 416

[106] Denis Matthews, *Arturo Toscanini* (Tunbridge Wells: Midas Books; New York: Hippocrene Books, 1982), p. 105. The words followed a comment by an unnamed conductor friend on a Brahms symphony recording of Toscanini: "Where I wanted rhythm I found it, where I wanted clarity I found it, where I wanted expression I found it – but it was all too intense, inhuman in fact."

[107] Harvey Sachs wrote that his recordings "do not and cannot represent him adequately." He described his first records (1920–21), as "about fifty minutes of nearly worthless commercial material": *Toscanini*, p. 322. The recordings were all re-issued in 1996 on Symposium 1189; there was no Wagner among them.

some works – *A Faust Overture*, the *Siegfried Idyll*, the prelude to *Lohengrin* – he was able to concentrate great energy with brilliant results. In other cases he has been severely criticised.[108] The 1936 recordings with the New York Philharmonic are the closest to natural music-making, though Toscanini himself described them as "shameful."[109] He was always dissatisfied with his work.[110] The recordings from Salzburg in 1936 and 1937, despite their technical limitations, are the closest we can get to Toscanini as a true Wagner conductor. We have read something of those, and of his other performances of the *Meistersinger*.

Last train to Valhalla

There are many ways of proceeding along the Wagnerian path. One can amble along, admiring the flowers and the birds, strolling to high vantage points, wading through deep streams, abandoning oneself to reverie. One can go by boat, floating down the river, moving with its currents, subject to it eddies. One can take an ocean liner, rolling over surging seas. One can make one's own way by car, setting one's own pace, accelerating, breaking, changing lanes, honking the horn, flashing the lights. Or one can take the train. If conductors ever had a totem, Toscanini's would be the train. It is a great way to travel. One is borne along, protected from the elements, secure in direction and destination. The iron tracks ensure the train rolls without deviation. It travels from the beginning to the end of its route in perfect time, without any surprise of speed or direction. One cannot see the sky above or the ground below, but the steady line of landscape is forever in view out of the window. If one is watching from the platform, thrilling gusts of wind blow as the train rushes by. But as the train vanishes from sight, the ambler, the seafarer, and the driver might be content to think that it is but one way to go. Toscanini's way was unique.

David Wooldridge wrote that his recordings were "largely shallow and of no enduring worth… [made by a man] who seemed bent on the very destruction of music in his insistence that it serve his will, and be compelled to sing instead of being allowed to sing": *Conductor's World* (London: Barrie & Rockliff, 1970), p. 318; Joseph Horowitz wrote: "Taken as a whole Toscanini's octogenarian recordings [which include most of his Wagner]… document final rites of simplification": *Understanding Toscanini: how he became an American culture-god and helped create a new audience for old music* (New York: A.A. Knopf, 1987), p. 343. Horowitz has many illuminating comments on individual recordings. The NBC broadcasts and recordings are thoroughly documented and commented upon in Frank, *The NBC Years*.

108 For example, the 1952 Prelude and Liebestod (LM-6020) which Robert Marsh described as "over-refined, the antiseptic souvenir of passion rather than its full-blooded actuality… they have had all the life played out of them": *Toscanini and the Art of Orchestral Performance* (New York: Collier Books, 1956), p. 173. In a review of the 1949 Prelude and Good Friday Music from *Parsifal* (DB 21270-2), Alec Robertson wrote: "The brass are shrill and bodiless, the timpani sound like tea trays, and flute, oboe and clarinet – as one hears only too clearly in the *Good Friday Music* – lack the individual character to which we are accustomed, and are either acid or toneless": *Gramophone*, July 1951, p. 31; "splendidly played but abominably recorded": Edward Sackville-West, *Gramophone*, November 1951, p. 123.

109 see Discography below

110 For example, in 1937: "I feel very much inferior to what I would like to be… Because I feel that I can never reach the point that I ought to reach, that ought to be reached… That's the cause of my suffering! … In short, I'm like a *woman giving birth*!": letter dated Salzburg, 25 August 1937, in Sachs, *Letters*, p. 279

14

Artur Bodanzky – Mahler's disciple

Bodanzky made a strong impression when he arrived at the Metropolitan Opera in 1915. The doyen of New York critics, James Huneker, saw and heard his first performances:

> In the twilight atmosphere of the orchestra at the Metropolitan Opera House, an atmosphere of smothered fire and gloom, stood a tall, thin figure, thin to meagreness, whose long, delicate hands played upon an invisible instrument which sang and thundered; a river which became a cataract of jewelled sounds at the relentless call of those outstretched fingers of the left hand and the electric wand in the right. It was Artur Bodanzky conducting a Wagner music-drama.... Alert, vivacious are his movements, and his orchestral army responds to every gesture. The simile of the river is not a fanciful one; a stream of tones, caressing, liquid and euphonious, flows beneath this magician from Vienna. ... He may look like a pessimist, but he is the reverse. He is as fiery as a Hungarian and as elastic in his moods as a Viennese. He is as gay as a boy at times. ... Bodanzky differs from his predecessors, Hertz and Toscanini; nevertheless in the chiefest matter he is on the side of the angels. He is a versatile, brilliant and subtle conductor, and it is a bold dissenter who takes exception to his broad musical conception, tho one may demur here and there as to details.[1]

When he died suddenly twenty-four years later, the impressions seemed different. He had been so long "a relentless machine of work," wrote Irving Kolodin in his history of the Metropolitan Opera, "that few thought of him in terms of failing health, or of health at all."[2] In obituaries he was acknowledged as a great or notable Wagner interpreter, whose name would forever be linked to the era of Kirsten Flagstad and Lauritz Melchior. And to cuts to Wagner's operas. The quality of his performances varied greatly over his long career. He was always subject to the constraints of New York. He was also a man of moods, and swung from great highs to wretched lows. He was in many ways a true pupil of Mahler: idealistic, dictatorial, occasionally shattering, and at other times imperfect. Mahler was the greater idealist. Bodanzky learned to compromise. Both died young, but Bodanzky lived an extra eleven years. We should be grateful, for it is from these years that his Wagner recordings come, a fragmentary but invaluable legacy of an intensely dramatic conductor.

1 James Huneker, "A Don Quixote of the Baton," *Independent*, 7 February 1916, pp. 196, 198

2 Irving Kolodin, *The Metropolitan Opera, 1883-1950: A Candid History* (New York: A. A. Knopf, 1953), p. 490

Wagnerian beginnings

Bodanzky was born in Vienna on 16 December 1877, the son of a Hungarian paper manufacturer. His father loved opera, but not Wagnerian opera, and gave his son a toy xylophone when he was four. He hoped his son would become a doctor, but the toy sparked his interest in music.[3] When he heard *Der Freischütz* for the first time at the age of six, he turned to music forever.[4] He had to slip away secretly to see his first Wagner opera, as he related: "It was *The Flying Dutchman*. What an impression that was! 'These people of mine are just crazy,' I thought, excited by the originality and beauty of the work which I had always heard derided. Next I saw *Lohengrin* and was up in the air with delight."[5] He remembered Wagner's first impact on him:

> If there comes a moment in the opera when you are involuntarily thrilled, as though an electric shock had traveled up and down your spine, then that is a good opera. That is what Wagner did to me when I first heard his music. I was a boy in Vienna and I did not understand him at all, but I knew there was something there worth trying to understand.[6]

He was sent for studies to the Academie Gymnasium and the Vienna Conservatory where he specialised in the violin. A fellow student remembered him as "about an inch wide and a mile high," aggressive in everything he did and always either "wild with excitement, joyous, or else so low in spirits that nothing could arouse him."[7] These mood swings would be reflected in his music-making all his life. He attended every Wagner opera he could. After he graduated in violin and composition in 1896, he went to the Vienna Opera as a first violinist. Mahler became director in 1897. Bodanzky's years playing under Mahler, and the informal contacts he had with him and his circle in coffee houses, seem to have been more important than the Conservatory. "There the real things came out, things that could not be taught in all the classrooms of the world... always they discussed the arts. And every night I learned something that was to be of use to me later."[8] He first heard Mahler conduct in 1897. It was *Lohengrin*:

> I thought I knew *Lohengrin* by heart, but I found I was hearing it for the first time. All the other times, I now knew, it had been stale; the point had not been brought out. I suddenly realized what being a conductor meant: from that moment I changed my whole plan of life and decided to become a conductor.[9]

3 "The New Metropolitan Conductor," *Musical Advance*, vol. 3, no. 4 (December 1915), pp. 1-2; "The Metropolitan's New Wagner Conductor," *New York Times*, 10 October 1915, p. 61

4 Bodanzky, "Has America no time for Music?" (written from an interview), *The Craftsman*, vol. 29 (October 1915 – March 1916), p. 231

5 Bodanzky, "For uncut Wagner," *New York Times*, 9 February 1930, p. X8

6 "The Wagner Observances," *New York Times*, 5 February 1933, p. X6

7 Samuel Thewman, later a stage manager at the Metropolitan Opera, quoted in the *Herald Tribune*, 24 November 1939, p. 18

8 *Evening Post*, 21 December 1925 (Metropolitan Opera Archives). He says he "was not more than sixteen." In the *Musical Advance* article (above) it is reported he was *fourteen* when he was playing the violin under Mahler. However, at these times (ca. 1894 and 1892 respectively) Mahler was still in Hamburg; he arrived in Vienna as Director in 1897. Bodanzky's playing may have been *ad hoc*; he is not listed among members of the orchestra in Wilhelm Beetz, *Das Wiener Opernhaus 1869 bis 1945* (Zurich: Panorama, 1949), pp. 86-94.

9 Bodanzky, "For uncut Wagner," *New York Times*, 9 February 1930, p. X8. His friends told a different story. During a ballet the old-timers in the orchestra tricked him into playing into what should have been a pause: he was so disgusted with himself that he determined then and there to become a conductor: S. J. Woolf, "A Conductor Looks Over the Audience," *New York Times Magazine*, 18 January 1931, p. 11.

The first Wagner opera he played in was the *Holländer* conducted by Mahler in 1898. His first visit to Bayreuth was in 1899. He was very poor and could only afford one ticket. He chose *Parsifal*, and did not eat the whole day he was in Bayreuth:

> Muck conducted. He lifted his baton for the *Vorspiel* and the orchestra breathed the sacrament motif. I was enthralled. The curtain parted. Eagerly I watched and listened, enraptured, caught up to another world. Before my eyes passed the long train of knights in stately procession, the ominous moment of the uncovering of the Grail; then the long stately march again. The splendid monotony lulled my senses, my excited mind no longer ruled my weary body – and I fell asleep! All through the second act I slept; slept while Parsifal sported with the Flower Maidens, slept through the seductions of Kundry, slept when Klingsor hurled the sacred Spear – until, with a crash of the orchestra, castle and garden crumbled to ruins, and I awoke. I was so enraged that I burst into tears – fierce, hot tears.[10]

For the next seven years his musical activities revolved around operetta – first with a tiny orchestra in Budweis (1900), then in Vienna at the Karlstheater (1900/02), St. Petersburg (1902/03), Paris (1904), Vienna again at the Theater an der Wien (1904/05), and Berlin at the Lortzing Theatre (1905/06). He hated it.[11] The only serious opera work was a seven-month period assisting Mahler at the Vienna Opera as coach (1903/04).[12] His appointment to Angelo Neumann's German Theatre in Prague (1906/09) was the first important step along the Wagnerian path. There he conducted his first Wagner opera, *Tannhäuser*, in 1907, and followed it up with *Meistersinger*, *Rheingold* and *Walküre*. All the rest he did in Mannheim (1909/15),[13] and *Parsifal* in London in 1914.

On his way to Mannheim in 1909 he visited Bayreuth. Compared with what he had known from Mahler, he was disappointed in the *Ring* (conducted by Michael Balling), though he enjoyed *Lohengrin* and *Parsifal* (both conducted that year by Karl Muck and Siegfried Wagner). He let his views be known, and when they were reported in the press, a fifteen-year coolness developed between him and Siegfried Wagner.[14] When Bodanzky produced a radical *Tannhäuser* in Mannheim in which the Bacchanale was played out behind red veils, the coolness became a freeze. "The deviation from Wagner's own superb directions for the performance led to disaster," he recalled.[15] Siegfried Wagner attacked him for the innovation in an open letter.[16] Bodanzky became another in the long list of talented conductors never to be invited to conduct in Bayreuth.

After his *Parsifal* debut in London, Giulio Gatti-Casazza sent for him to succeed Alfred Hertz at the Metropolitan Opera (1915-39). He left the Opera briefly in 1929

[10] Bodanzky, with Donald Marshall, "Fourteen Years at the Metropolitan Opera House," *Saturday Evening Post*, 29 October 1929, p. 89

[11] R. H. Wollstein, "Artur Bodanzky," *Musical Observer*, vol. 28 no. 5 (May 1929), p. 8

[12] from 15 November 1903 to 30 June 1904: Beetz, *Das Wiener Opernhaus*, p. 113

[13] Carl Hagemann, head of the Mannheim Opera in 1906-10 and 1915-20, wrote that Bodanzky was "a big hit in Mannheim like no one before or since." He was struck by his "fervour, impulsiveness and deliberateness," as well as his talent for music-drama: *Bühne und Welt* (Wiesbaden: Der Greif, 1948), p. 95.

[14] *Saturday Evening Post*, 29 October 1929, p. 90. Siegfried Wagner and his wife attended a *Lohengrin* conducted by Bodanzky on 8 February 1924, the first Wagner opera Siegfried had heard at the Metropolitan Opera: *New York Times*, 9 February 1924, p. 16.

[15] Bodanzky, "Wagner and the Box Office," *The Etude*, April 1938, p. 266

[16] Bodanzky, "For uncut Wagner," *New York Times*, 9 February 1930, p. X8

to conduct orchestral concerts, but a combination of the stock market crash and the failure of his successor Joseph Rosenstock at the Metropolitan, found him back as a "guest conductor" for several years, which effectively was the rest of his life. He travelled to Europe regularly during summers, but rarely conducted Wagner there. He made his few commercial Wagner recordings in Berlin in 1927/28, conducted three performances of the *Walküre* in Amsterdam in 1928, and a *Ring* in San Francisco in 1935. Otherwise, he gave his life to New York. In his 24 years at the Metropolitan Opera he conducted 584 Wagner performances: *Tristan* (141), *Walküre* (119), *Lohengrin* (91), *Meistersinger* (88), *Tannhäuser* (70), *Parsifal* (61), *Siegfried* (59), *Götterdämmerung* (53), *Rheingold* (26), *Fliegende Holländer* (16), including ten uncut *Ring* cycles (1930-39).[17] After a quiet summer in Vermont in 1939, he became ill with severe arthritis in his conducting arm, and died of a heart attack on 23 November 1939, a few days before the opening of the 1939/40 season.[18]

Bodanzky on Wagner

Bodanzky was pre-eminently a practical musician, and wrote little about music.[19] He did, however, give a number of illuminating interviews. In 1916 he surprised one reporter by declaring that *Lohengrin* was one of the two best operas ever written (the other was Verdi's *Trovatore*): "the composers gave of their very best in these products. Wagner and Verdi, in my judgment, turned out nothing in their late periods, notwithstanding their increased resources, that is more valuable to the world than what they did in the freshness and enthusiasm of their early periods." In company with *Lohengrin* he placed *Tristan* and *Meistersinger*.[20] In this same interview he gave some valuable insights to his approach to performing Wagner. One was on the question of dynamics:

> I was surprised to find when I came to the United States that the mention of Wagner conveyed the idea of forte and fortissimo. For Wagner's orchestration implies piano as well as forte. In general his instruments and his voices, as I think of them, ought to have equal rights; but because his scores are symphonic in character, many conductors are led to give the orchestra too much prominence. It is the same way with Weber and German Opera as a whole.

[17] statistics from the Metropolitan Opera database, and they include operas conducted on tour. The *Rheingold* of the tenth uncut *Ring* (1939) was conducted by Erich Leinsdorf.

[18] He was survived by his widow, Ada Bodanzky, who destroyed all his papers, and died on 19 April 1961. His son had pre-deceased him in a car accident. He was also survived by a married daughter, Elizabeth.

[19] "He loves to read; Dickens is his favorite author, and when so minded, he will quote entire pages of his works, by heart": R. H. Wollstein, "Artur Bodanzky," *Musical Observer*, vol. 28 no. 5 (May 1929), p. 8. Frequently when he had no performance to conduct he and his wife would go to the movies "where they remain long enough for him to smoke a whole cigar. He never knows who is playing nor what the action relates to. Then home again and several hours with a book. He reads no magazines and no newspapers, except occasionally the stock market reports...." He loved playing bridge. "The greatest pleasure that Mr. Bodanzky experiences outside of conducting a Mozart opera is to hold a four-spade hand.... He plays well and always yells at his partners": Allene Talmey, "Volcanic Bodanzky," *Evening World*, 15 December 1928, p. 5.

[20] *Christian Science Monitor*, 15 April 1916, p. 16. Asked what was "the finest melody Wagner wrote," Bodanzky *sang* the melody from act two of *Lohengrin*, after the Elsa-Ortrud duet, as the music proceeds in G Major. In later life he reiterated his view that *Lohengrin*, *Tristan* and *Meistersinger* were Wagner's "three greatest achievements": *Christian Science Monitor*, 28 February 1931, p. 7.

To find the proper points at which the orchestra or the singers should predominate is a matter of taste with the man conducting. These points often are not indicated in the score. Passages of course are marked loud and soft, but the times when forte should be less strong and when piano should be strengthened, that a theme may be clearly heard, are for the conductor to judge.[21]

He did not seek a "personal reading" from Wagner's scores:

I go exactly according to what Wagner writes. I think that a conductor who puts forward his own ideas in place of the composer's is the worst kind possible. I regard him as the ideal one who has his players follow conscientiously what is written on the page of music before them. For after that is done, there is ample scope for everybody concerned to put in his own touch of interpretation.[22]

This ideal of strict adherence combined with freedom to interpret is strikingly close to Wagner's heart.[23] And if it seems a little dry, that was not Bodanzky's approach:

I find it is necessary to live through the whole production emotionally, I find that I must not only know the music, the methods of the singer, the reason for the scenery, the stage management, the full adjustment and development of my orchestra, but that at the same time I must live heart and soul in the tragedy that I am conducting. I must be Tristan when Tristan sings, heartbroken through love, dying because love was greater than life.... I must be the poet who sees into the future and the philosopher who weighs the present impersonally.[24]

He had some doubts about the *Ring*, at least in his youth. One day, he related, he summoned up the courage to tell Mahler about "the flaws I thought I had found to the music dramas and of artistic mistakes I thought Wagner had made." Mahler listened patiently, and then compared Wagner to an air-borne Zeppelin. "That," he said, "is the way to see a Zeppelin; it is very fine. But do not go too close to it. You will see the seams, and it will not be so fine. Wagner is like a Zeppelin; do not examine him too minutely." That convinced Bodanzky. It was the music, not the ideas.[25]

Bodanzky cuts his cloth

"The good conductor must have vision and will; he must know exactly what he wants, and then be a tyrant to obtain it."[26] This is what Bodanzky said and this is

[21] *Christian Science Monitor*, 15 April 1916, p. 16. He expressed similar views in his article in *The Craftsman*, vol. 29 (October 1915 – March 1916), p. 199.

[22] *Christian Science Monitor*, 15 April 1916, p. 16. He extended this view to the staging of Wagner's operas. "To my mind, Wagner stands beside Sophocles and Shakespeare as the third great foundation pillar of drama." Wagner's stage directions were so rich and precise in their detail "that to deviate from even the slightest of Wagner's own indications is enough to ruin a performance.... Wagner's imaginative powers were so sure and so intense that he was able to set down, once and for all time, the only way in which his works should be mounted, to insure their proper effect": Bodanzky, "Wagner and the Box Office," *The Etude*, April 1938, pp. 265-266. He seems to have moved away from the more imaginative approaches he adopted in *Tannhäuser*. In 1924 he spoke of his wish to do a guest performance in Europe of a *Tristan* in which there would be "no suggestion of any time or place, just the music, the lovers' impassioned addresses." His ideal was to put the singers in the orchestra, and to have a company of actors – an 18-year-old Irish princess and a 24-year-old Tristan – play out the action on stage "with all the power of youth.... But these things, he admitted, were not for New York, where a finished and standard product is demanded at any price": *New York Times*, 26 October 1924, p. X7.

[23] see Wagner chapter above, p. 48

[24] *The Craftsman*, vol. 29 (October 1915 – March 1916), p. 199

[25] *Musical Courier*, 17 April 1919, p. 21

[26] Bodanzky, with Donald Marshall, "Making Music," *Saturday Evening Post*, 9 November 1929, p. 22

what he did. Or this is what he *endeavoured* to do. Many performers responded well to his high artistic demands, including great singers. Indeed, the *singers* often had an inspirational effect on his conducting.[27] The pleasure he drew from such collaboration was the knowledge that Wagner was becoming better appreciated by the public.[28] He could not always get from the orchestra, however, the quality of performance any great conductor would have wished. For many years there was insufficient time for rehearsal, inadequacies amongst the players, and no money to do anything to improve what was described at one time by Irving Kolodin as a "persistently disgraceful" situation.[29]

To satisfy the people who made opera possible in New York, he had to make cuts to Wagner's operas. He had never presented abridged Wagner performances in Mannheim, but in New York circumstances were different.[30] His purpose was above all "not to weary the public. I want every performance, if possible, to end by eleven or else shortly afterward. To give an audience too much music is criminally mistaken kindness and real irreverence to the composer."[31] In this he was responding to the practicalities of opera life at the time. "I feel that in America the opera must be somewhat adjusted to the lives of the people, of all the people, not only the aristocracy but the hard working people, who seem to be very sincere music lovers here.... The tired man who would enjoy two hours' music, or three, the woman who is entertaining at dinner and who is attending a reception at midnight, children who have long days of study, all feel exhausted after four hours of concentrated attention, even though the effort brings them unlimited joy."[32] For all his considerateness of audiences, it was not repaid by their greater attention. After a decade, he could barely disguise his contempt. "The social code at the Metropolitan is to come late and leave at will."[33] He devised ironical "golden rules" for the audience which included: all performances to commence *before* people took their seats, doors to be left open to admit street noises,

[27] For example, the *New York Times* wrote after Frida Leider's debut as Isolde "one interpretation set off the other; the whole performance took fire, and gained a rare cohesion, vitality and atmosphere": 17 January 1933, p. 23; after Kirsten Flagstad's debut as Sieglinde: "Mr. Bodanzky, inspired, no doubt, as a hard-working conductor well may be, by a new dramatic current on the stage, was effective and convincing in his conducting": 3 February 1935, p. N4; after Flagstad's debut as Isolde: "we do not remember any *Tristan* of his which took on such intensity and glowing color and tonal splendour": 7 February 1935, p. 22; and after a Lotte Lehmann Sieglinde: "Mr. Bodanzky appeared to draw fresh power from the collaboration of Mme. Lehmann": 17 January 1937, p. 45 (all comments by Olin Downes).

[28] no more so than through the interpretations of Flagstad: *Etude*, April 1938, pp. 219, 266

[29] Irving Kolodin, *The Metropolitan opera, 1883-1935* (New York: Oxford University Press, 1936), p. 340, describing the situation in 1925/26. Bodanzky expressed his view: "This ideal of unlimited rehearsal – the only way to produce a flawless performance – lies very near my heart.... It is not the practice at the Metropolitan, and cannot be without a large annual deficit": *Saturday Evening Post*, 9 November 1929, p. 65. In Bodanzky's day "standards of orchestral performance at the opera were not nearly so high as they have since become. This was in no way the fault of Mr. Bodanzky but rather the shortcoming of a management which, genuinely interested in beautiful vocal color, had much less concern with the sonorities coming out of the pit": Robert Lawrence, *The World of Opera* (New York: Thomas Nelson & Sons, 1956), p. 137.

[30] Franz Schalk conducted three uncut *Ring* cycles in 1899, and Emil Paur three cycles in 1900, after which the practice was abandoned until Bodanzky revived it in 1930; thereafter he conducted one uncut cycle each year until his death.

[31] "Bodansky to 'cut' long operas," *Musical America*, 16 October 1915, p. 10. He had also announced on the day of his arrival, on 8 October 1915: "If the length of a Wagner music drama bores the public, it should be cut, and I intend to see to it that such cuts will be made in the works under my direction." He perpetuated the cuts made by Seidl, Mahler, Toscanini and others: Kolodin, *The Metropolitan opera, 1883-1935*, p. 220.

[32] *The Craftsman*, vol. 29 (Oct. 1915 – March 1916), p. 197

[33] *New York Times*, 19 April 1925, p. X7

all patrons to be required to buy librettos not to read but to rustle, and that they be able to talk freely – "this is the opera, not a golf links."[34] By the end of his career, the "outrage" of latecomers disturbing the music was "beginning to decrease," but had not stopped entirely: the doors were not yet closed at the beginning of a performance.[35] His cuts, encouraged by some critics and criticised by devout Wagnerians, were not enough for these audiences. It was not until the special matinee performances of the uncut *Ring* in 1930 that the devout were satisfied, and the audiences were attentive. There were other reasons for the cuts, to accommodate lazy or weak singers,[36] and above all financial: to limit overtime. In this, Bodanzky bent to management. He was cooperative. "He never got mixed up in anything," Metropolitan Opera Director Gatti-Casazza recalled, "never caused trouble...."[37] As an artist, Bodanzky of course favoured uncut Wagner – "no musician would want to cut the tiniest bit from any of Wagner's work."[38] But as long as the public remained divided, he had to compromise. If art suffered as a consequence, it was not the fault of Bodanzky, but of New York.

With almost 600 Wagner performances at the Metropolitan alone, the quality of Bodanzky's performances was bound to vary. He suffered from the usual vagaries of artistic resources, both in his often over-worked and only gradually rejuvenated orchestra, and in singers of variable strengths.[39] Above all, he was a man of moods. Ecstasy and tedium were both observed in his performances. What is drawn on here is a selection from hundreds of reviews, especially first performances, of the late works only. It will show the great characteristics of his conducting, without ignoring the flaws.[40]

[34] "Bodanzky chides opera patrons here," *New York Times*, 22 December 1930, p. 20

[35] *The Etude*, April 1938, p. 266

[36] Lauritz Melchior, the Metropolitan Opera's star Tristan between 1929 and 1950, was a strong advocate as well as a beneficiary of cuts: "Wagner is too long for the average operagoer... I have no patience with those esthetes who shout 'Let us not touch a single note,' and consider the scores sacred.... A four or five hour opera is a strain on singer and listener": "Melchior Urges Cuts in Wagner," *New York Times*, 23 January 1934, p. 22. Erich Leinsdorf, who followed Bodanzky at the Metropolitan, could never persuade Melchior to sing Tristan uncut, even though Melchior had done so in Bayreuth in 1930 under Toscanini, and 1931 under Furtwängler: "To Cut or Not to Cut?" *Opera Quarterly*, vol. 10 no. 1 (Autumn 1993), p. 9. Leinsdorf also wrote: "The Met, during the time when I was a regular conductor there (1937/38 to 1942/43), had cuts in all evening performances of Wagner, but not in matinees of the *Ring* cycle. The reasons for the difference were financial, as was to be expected at a time of economic depression. Overtime for all hands in the pit and backstage cost a fortune – and still does": *ibid*, p. 6.

[37] Giulio Gatti-Casazza, *Memories of the Opera* (New York: Scribners, 1941), p. 225

[38] Bodanzky, "For uncut Wagner," *New York Times*, 9 February 1930, p. X8. He excepted *Rienzi*.

[39] Sometimes this could be depressing. In a *Tristan* from 1929: "Mr. Bodanzky waved the baton. There was no infectious life in the proceedings generally and the conductor looked as if he could not help matters. The audience was apparently interested in the performance": *Sun*, 13 February 1929 (W. J. Henderson). Rudolf Laubenthal sang Tristan, and Gertrude Kappel Isolde. Bodanzky could adjust his orchestra when one singer was strong and the other not. In a *Tristan* from 1934 he allowed the orchestra "to swirl and blaze and mount to molten climaxes" for Melchior, yet modulated the tone for the weaker Isolde, Kappel: *New York Times*, 7 January 1934, p. N3 (Olin Downes).

[40] Many reviews, particularly in later years, had little comment on Bodanzky's conducting, presumably because they had said it all before; this was the subject of some complaint, e.g. letter to the editor, *New York Times*, 4 March 1928, p. 123.

Tristan und Isolde

Bodanzky's first *Tristan* in New York on 1 December 1915 immediately marked him apart from his predecessor. Alfred Hertz had always shouted at the orchestra "*Mehr! Mehr!*" to get ever more volume from them.[41] Bodanzky restrained his orchestra, and let the singer's every word be heard. The orchestra "occupied its true place in the dramatic ensemble," the *New York Times* wrote. Yet its "playing was of potent and surging dramatic significance, of never-failing dramatic euphony, beautifully modeled plasticity of phrase, and subtle dramatic nuance."[42] He showed he belonged to the "front rank of *Tristan* interpreters," according to the *Evening Post*. "He is too young to have learned from the master himself, but he has imbibed from the master's disciples, principally Mahler, the true feeling for the "infinite melody. His performance... was surcharged with dramatic feeling and regard for beauty of color in this marvelous web of tone."[43] Mahler's style is evoked by the *Tribune* which wrote of Bodanzky's "suave, polished and beautifully articulated" performance; while other performances had "throbbed with a more heightened passion..., it was in the more delicate shadings and on the intellectual side that his reading excelled."[44] He stood comparison with Nikisch, in the view of the *Press*, with his "forceful, convincing and eloquent" interpretation.[45] The *Herald* reported that:

in the lobbies groups of "tempo fiends" compared him with Toscanini, Hertz – and those who walked with canes – brought up the immortal shade of Seidl. But when they all got through riding their hobbies they agreed that Mr. Bodanzky was conducting not only a brilliant but a great performance. The first act at times lacked the great, temperamental throb, but the second act was a whirlwind of emotion in its tense moments and a lyric masterpiece in the manner in which this young master of the baton led the accompaniments to the love music.[46]

James Huneker admired the interpretation "because of its fine blending of imagination and emotion. The orchestra moved like a richly-wrought, richly-colored tapestry. The climaxes were stirring, the mystic ecstasy present, and the love episodes intense."[47] The *Sun* wrote:

Mr. Bodanzky's reading of the score was very full-blooded. He lost none of the stormy passion which Wagner put into the orchestral waves. The voices rocked and swayed above the tempest, but they were never submerged. The balance between singers and players was well kept, and at the same time the intensity of the more subdued parts of the orchestration was never lost any more than was the outpour of emotions in the louder passages.

There were masterly touches in the details of tempo, as for example in the immense breadth given to the music announcing the entrance of Tristan into Isolde's cabin. There were fine subtle shadings in such passages as the repetition of the glance motive after the potion had sent *Tristan's Ehre* to the land of dreams. There was a wealth of luscious tenderness in the duet of the second act... Mr. Bodanzky's conducting had imagination and vigorous expression of it. That is the sum of the matter.[48]

[41] Howard Taubman, *Opera Front and Back* (New York: Charles Scribner's Sons, 1938), p. 155
[42] 2 December 1915, p. 11. Jacques Urlus sang Tristan, Melanie Kurt Isolde.
[43] 2 December 1915, p. 15 [44] 2 December 1915, p. 9 [45] 2 December 1915, p. 6
[46] 2 December 1915, p. 12 [47] *Independent*, 7 February 1916, p. 198 [48] 2 December 1915, p. 9

To *Musical America* this first performance was "immeasurably finer" than his performances of *Götterdämmerung*, *Parsifal* (both of which we will consider below) and *Lohengrin*, though it felt something was missing because of his "repressive measures" with the orchestra.[49] It was this characteristic perhaps which made the *Evening Post* the following year feel "like shouting to him to put on more steam – much more steam."[50] In this later performance the *World* commented on the absence of "the wealth of poetic beauty which Mr. Toscanini extracted from the score." Bodanzky displayed fine musicianship but his "contrasts in tonal light and shade… never throbbed as when Mr. Toscanini and Mr. Mahler presided at the conductor's stand."[51]

This was an opera Bodanzky grew into with the years. After the War, when it was re-introduced in English in 1920, he achieved great heights:

> Mr. Bodanzky did things of wondrous potency and beauty with his band yesterday. Lifting his hearers to mountain heights of feeling and plunging them into awful depths, but he was never more eloquent than when he subdued the instrumental voices so that the song of the singers might be heard, and occasionally understood. The same intensity of emotional utterance might have been attained had he set the pegs of his orchestra a degree or two down in the dynamic scale. We say this in the full glow of appreciation for his fine interpretation of the score. It was often transporting. But his fortissimo climaxes frequently shattered the equally if not more important climaxes of the singers.[52]

Repression was giving way to passion, careful husbandry to inspiration. In 1926 the *New York Times* was dumb-founded:

> He conducted as never before in personal experience of his performances. He conducted the opera with which another Arthur – Arturo Toscanini – made history at the Metropolitan. Was there a rival and a shade back of Mr. Bodanzky's chair? Or was he merely in a fortuitous frenzy of inspiration? At any rate, things happened.... Mr. Bodanzky let loose. He summoned a degree of fire, of freedom, of elasticity, a sweep of passion, a power of climax that he may have intimated, but on no occasion we remember achieved, in the past. The orchestra rose to him. The singers were borne along on the flood of tone. This does not imply they were inconsiderately treated. On the contrary, there was as a rule excellent balances, poetic atmosphere, occasions when the orchestra was, as it were, inaudibly present, while the voices of the lovers soared through the night....[53]

The *Herald Tribune* was also surprised in this performance at his "fervour and absorption which tempted one to the suspicion that he had fallen in love all over again with the music of *Tristan*." One thing especially impressed: "he does not yield to the temptation to hold back his orchestra just before the climactic chord of the *Liebestod* –

[49] 11 December 1915, p. 2

[50] 16 November 1916, p. 9

[51] *New York World*, 16 November 1916 (Metropolitan Opera Archives)

[52] *Tribune*, 21 November 1920, pt. 1, p. 17 (H. E. Krehbiel). Tristan was sung by Johannes Sembach, Isolde by Margarete Matzenauer. The *New York Times* commented how "floods of orchestral tone surged with a sweeping eloquence under Mr. Bodanzky's hand": 21 November 1920, p. 21 (Richard Aldrich). When *Tristan* was restored in German in 1922, the *New York Times* described the performance with almost identical wording: 29 November 1921, p. 15.

[53] 17 January 1926, p. 28 (Olin Downes). Tristan was sung by Rudolf Laubenthal, Isolde by Nanny Larsén-Todsen. In later years Downes wrote: "*Tristan* has seldom been his opera. We say seldom, because on certain occasions he has appeared to be much more moved by the music than on others. There is a romantic sweep and glow to the score, there are colors of purple and gold in the instrumentation that he appears to ignore." *ibid*, 7 November 1930, p. 33.

a cheap atrocity which we have heard some very great conductors perpetrate."[54] The same newspaper commented on a *Liebestod* in 1930 "which he took at a felicitous tempo, one almost as grave as Muck's, and which he phrased with noble breadth and elegiac beauty." Sometimes, however, he "chose a pace disturbingly precipitate, as in the First Act love duet, which obscured the texture of the score by its headlong scramble and made the music almost incoherent. Perhaps he was thinking too seriously of Richter's adjuration to his players while rehearsing the score of *Tristan*: 'Gentlemen, forget that you are married men!'"[55] The critic for the *Post* felt that after Tristan and Isolde had drunk from the cup, "though one knew dimly the true nature of the draught, what a delicious shock ran up one's spine when Mr. Bodanzky's trembling violins announced that the pain was, for the present, in for love, not death!"[56] Not all his performances stirred the critics like this, but "when Bodanzky is in the mood and has a responsive cast," wrote the *New York American*, "he is the equal of any conductor in ability to draw effulgence and flame from the score of *Tristan*."[57]

Die Meistersinger von Nürnberg

The *Meistersinger*, Bodanzky once wrote, was "my favourite of all Wagner's works."[58] The *New York Times* wrote of his "profound awareness" of the work after a 1938 performance.[59] Almost without exception, it was observed to be the Wagner opera in which he was most at home.[60] His first performance at the Metropolitan on 7 January 1916 marked a departure from Toscanini's, as the *New York Times* explained:

When Mr. Toscanini took it in hand there were other beauties of a remarkable kind revealed, but it was observed then that it was hardly the true *Meistersinger* that Mr. Toscanini knew.

[54] *Herald Tribune*, 18 January 1926, p. 13 (Lawrence Gilman)

[55] *ibid*, 12 January 1930, Sect. 1, p. 12 (Lawrence Gilman). This same newspaper wrote of *Tristan* on 20 November 1931: "Bodanzky was possessed by one of his extraordinary moods, resulting in a performance of the first act (uncut) faster by eighteen minutes than the usual one of Fritz Busch, in Dresden": quoted in Kolodin, *The Metropolitan opera, 1883-1935*, p. 413. It is interesting to note that Bodanzky in 1935 and Busch in 1946 *both* took 77 minutes to conduct act one: see Timings below. The closest to an eighteen-minute disparity is between Toscanini's 90 minutes (1930) and Böhm's 73 minutes (1973).

[56] 30 November 1937, p. 10 (Samuel Chotzinoff) [57] 19 January 1935, Final Ed., p. 10 (Leonard Liebling)

[58] Bodanzky, "Wagner and the Box Office," *The Etude*, April 1938, p. 266

[59] 10 March 1938, p. 18 (Howard Taubman)

[60] For example, "Bodanzky had conducted no other work with 'quite the insight' he showed in *Die Meistersinger*": Henderson on the 9 November 1923 performance, quoted by Kolodin, *The Metropolitan Opera, 1883-1950: A Candid History*, p. 371; Olin Downes: "*Meistersinger* appears to be much more his opera than *Tristan*": *New York Times*, 16 January 1925, p. 5; "his best 'role,' his best impersonation, through his orchestra and singers, of Wagner": *ibid*, 29 November 1925, p. 29; "surely one of his finest achievements": *ibid*, 15 March 1935, p. 24; cf. *Mail*, 10 November 1924: "It is probably not one of Wagner's operas with which Mr. Bodanzky is the most sympathetic. Something of its busy humor, its robust breadth, the pomp and richness of its civic stride are discouraged and even desiccated under the watchful precision of Mr. Bodanzky's pedagogical baton, but he is infinitely painstaking and his orchestra is finely groomed"; yet Henry Finck wrote of this same performance: "The biggest and pleasantest surprise was Artur Bodanzky. He has so often conducted the Wagner operas in slovenly, uninterested fashion that I had given up all hope. Last night he was somewhat listless in the first act; but after that, carried away by a glorious flood of surging music, he rose to the situation magnificently. Toscanini or Mörike could hardly have done it better – or Hertz either. The abundant orchestral melodies, the lovely and infinitely varied orchestral colors, the thrilling sonorities, and stupendous climaxes, all were revealed in stunning fashion. So he can do it after all! Why not try and do it often?" *Post*, 10 November 1924 (Metropolitan Opera Archives).

Die Meistersinger for him apparently meant the orchestral score first and foremost, and to this he devoted much of his marvelous power in producing a performance of splendid euphony and brilliance and eloquence of orchestral tone. What went on upon the stage was in effect, though, of course, not in intention, subordinated to the wonderful orchestral beauty upon which he wreaked himself. The spirit of this comedy of medieval burgess life in Germany was necessarily foreign to the great Italian conductor, and it was unquestionably cramped in the frame to which Mr. Toscanini confined it.

Mr. Bodanzky's reading is one that takes in the world in all its various elements. It is concerned primarily in the spirit of Wagner's fundamental principle that the play is the thing, and all the musical investiture of the work is intended and calculated to interpret, to illuminate, to enhance its effect. There is first of all a pulsing life and a dramatic vitality in the whole course of the performance. Many of his tempos are faster than have recently been heard here. Even more notable is the extraordinary flexibility of his tempos, the plasticity of his phrasing, of which the primary purpose is to accompany the action upon the stage, to give it the freest play; never to limit it or hem it in by the necessity of conforming to a purely musical conception of the orchestral part. In nothing else is this so essential as in comedy, where the action is drawn on less broad lines than in the elemental tragedies.[61]

The *Sun* also made a comparison with Toscanini. "If [Bodanzky's] reading of the romantic pages lacked something of the alternating sensuous languor and passionate poignancy of Mr. Toscanini's, it was more in accord with German tradition. It had a certain exuberance of feeling that was not found in the mellifluous interpretation of his predecessor." This was particularly evident with the apprentices whom Bodanzky "stirred up a little since last season, when their pranks seemed not to appeal to Mr. Toscanini's delicate sense of beauty."[62]

As in the other operas, Bodanzky's variable mood was evident in later performances. On one occasion, in the second act, "the last pages had not the boisterous humor that Wagner unquestionably intended," according to the *New York Times*. "A spirited performance of the last scenes should cause the listener and beholder to split his sides with laughter…," but it did not.[63] On another occasion, he conducted "a performance of skylarking spirits suggesting Summer holidays in Nuremberg and points east."[64] Indeed, he set sail for Europe a few days later. Sometimes his tempi were considered

[61] *New York Times*, 8 January 1916, p. 7. It also commented that Bodanzky "kept the orchestra in its proper place as to dynamics," and the singers could be heard. Eva was sung by Frieda Hempel, Magdalene by Marie Mattfeld, Walther by Johannes Sembach, Hans Sachs by Hermann Weil, and David by Albert Reiss. Frieda Hempel, who sang Eva under both Toscanini and Bodanzky (1915-17), considered Bodanzky "was always in too much of a hurry. He rushed his tempos to such a degree that when I sang with him I could hardly get my words out": Hempel, *My Golden Age of Singing* (Portland, Oregon: Amadeus Press, 1998), p. 132. In view of her comment, it is interesting to note the *New York World*'s observation of this performance: "At no time did Mr Bodanzky insist that an artist hurry along in order to have the sung phrases go in 'strict time.' He moulded his music into periods that were smooth and flowing": (8 January 1916) (Metropolitan Opera Archives)

[62] 8 January 1916, p. 7. In light of these observations, it is interesting to recall Toscanini's reported comment after hearing Bodanzky at the Metropolitan Opera in 1921: "a good musician, precise and cold; 'no blood'": Howard Taubman, *Toscanini* (London: Odhams Press, 1951), p. 310. Bodanzky is said to have commented on Toscanini: "He is simply the conductor's conductor": Harvey Sachs, *Toscanini* (Philadelphia and New York: J. B. Lippincott Company, 1978), p. 146 (no source cited).

[63] *New York Times*, 13 November 1928, p. 43

[64] *New York Times*, 9 April 1931, p. 35

too fast, even rigid,[65] and at others too slow, sometimes in the same performance. To the reviewer of the *Sun*, Bodanzky "has always taken the prelude to the scene in Sachs's workshop too slowly, with the result that the latter part of it has a tendency to disintegrate; and there are moments in the first act where the contrary is true and a broader curve of phrase is desirable."[66]

In his last years he presided over a rejuvenated production. "Mr. Bodanzky, never in his long career here, has given us a *Meistersinger* which so completely realized Wagner's intentions," wrote the *Herald Tribune*. It was "a veritably magical tonal web of unceasing loveliness."[67] It was the "most exhilarating and satisfactory" performance for many a year, according to the *New York Times*. The "unawaited glory of sound, as well as the rhythmic impulsion that set every page of the great prelude atingle with life, was unabatingly maintained in all that followed."[68]

Der Ring des Nibelungen

Bodanzky once said that the *Rheingold* was "the best of Wagner's scores, perhaps, to look at, but the poorest to sound":

> I have never known a conductor who did not confess he had difficulties with it. You see, Wagner here was breaking away from his early style and was marking out a course for his later music-drama. He wrote beautifully as the eye sees, but he missed reaching the ear. He produced only scattering pages that said what he was aiming to express. And strangely enough, he wrote in a way to overpower the singers, though that was precisely what he tried not to do. The scores of *Walküre* and *Siegfried*, while they give you a fuller and more varied sonority, allow the voices to be much better heard.[69]

At his first *Rheingold* at the Metropolitan on 3 February 1916, he seems to have succeeded in not drowning the singers, in spite of what the *New York Times* described as the "abundant vigor and dramatic accent" of the reading and "powerful and impressive climaxes."[70] The work was "peculiarly suited to [Bodanzky's] temperament and his musicianship," the *Herald* considered.[71] He read the score with "musical intelligence, skill and refinement," according to the *Press*:

> Under his guidance the playing of the orchestra, if not entirely faultless, was delicate, transparent and rhythmically alive. It never put a wall of adamantine sound between the listener and singer. It permitted almost every well enunciated word of the text to carry an intelligible message to the ear – an important consideration in *Rheingold*.

[65] "There is a beat that is precise, energetic, but a little regimental, a little Prussian. For this reason some of the warm lyricism, some of the beauty and ecstasy of the Summer night, which permeates Wagner's score, were lacking": *New York Times*, 4 November 1926, p. 24 (Olin Downes); Lawrence Gilman reviewed this same performance fresh from a visit to Munich, where Hans Knappertsbusch, "a brutal and disaffecting conductor," had performed the work: "he is not to be named in the same breath with Bodanzky, who conducted last night's performance with unusual sensitiveness and consideration": *Herald Tribune*, 4 November 1926, p. 25; of another *Meistersinger* the *New York Times* wrote: "The pace was too fast. The effect was hurried": 13 November 1931, p. 26 (Olin Downes). Max Lorenz debuted as Walther.

[66] 15 January 1938, p. 28 (Oscar Thompson)

[67] 15 January 1938, p. 7 (Jerome Bohm)

[68] 15 January 1938, p. 18. Eva was sung by Elisabeth Rethberg, Magdalene by Kerstin Thorborg, Walther by René Maison, Hans Sachs by Friederich Schorr, and David by Karl Laufkoetter.

[69] *Christian Science Monitor*, 28 February 1931, p. 7

[70] 4 February 1916, p. 7

[71] 4 February 1916, p. 9

Yet more than once – as for instance at the entrance of the Giants – did one miss yesterday the massive sonority and weight sought by the composer. Evidently Bodanzky tries to make up in intensity and electric incisiveness (true disciple of Mahler that he is) for what the instrumental performance lacked in ballast. But Wagner knew very well what he had in mind when he evolved the score of *Rheingold*....[72]

The *Evening Post* shared the first but not the second part of this perspective. "Even Mr. Hertz never let loose a greater volume of orchestral din than did Mr. Bodanzky when the dwarfs had given up their gold; but, on the other hand, practically every word the singers uttered was comprehensible, even at the back of the house, for the orchestra is the accompanist, as Wagner wished it to be, when Bodanzky conducts."[73]

The *Rheingold* was never cut at the Metropolitan. However, there was a pause sometimes placed at the end of scene two.[74] This was described by the *New York Times* in 1917 as "an interruption appreciated by the audience and even by many on stage."[75] While this may still have been the case in 1935 when Bodanzky led a *Ring* cycle in San Francisco, it was criticised by the *San Francisco News* as "nothing short of crime, artistically speaking," yet had been requested "so that the first night audience might promenade."[76]

The *Walküre* was one of the two Wagner operas Bodanzky performed at Covent Garden in 1914. The *Sunday Times* considered he had conducted "with care and discretion," but that there could have been "a greater breadth of outline and a bigger emotional sweep."[77] It was perhaps this aspect that Alfred Kalisch had in mind after the second performance:

It is obvious that a new school of Wagner conducting is growing up in Germany, of which [Bodanzky] is a good exponent. Its chief characteristic may be briefly summed up by saying that its aim seems to be pictorial, whereas one might say that the ideal of the older school was statuesque. In one sense of the word the moderns attend more to detail, and in another sense they heed it less. They devote more attention to color, but, on the other hand, they do not give so much importance to the prominence of individual themes and motifs. They do not allow the rest of the orchestra and voices to accompany a leitmotif announced by a single instrument as much as the older men used to.[78]

A lack of breadth was also commented upon across the Atlantic. In 1928 the *Herald Tribune* wrote that "things went as they have gone before with this score, a rough and shallow tone, a hurrying, impatient tempo, lacking breadth and nobility."[79] In 1930

72 *Press*, 4 February 1916, p. 8

73 4 February 1916, p. 9. The *Sun* commented likewise: 4 February 1916, p. 7. *Musical America* considered Bodanzky's "prelude lacked its larger significance – the forces of elemental life awakening to action... The cyclonic outbursts as the Nibelungs leer into the captive Alberich's face, the slaying of Fasolt and the entrance of the gods into Walhalla left little to be desired in point of sonority": 12 February 1916, p. 4. The *Herald* believed Bodanzky "hastened some of his tempi," but "on the other hand, he took some incidents, such as the finale, with such majesty of breadth that it sounded more impressive than ever before": 4 February 1916, p. 12.

74 except in the uncut cycles from 1930 onwards: *New York Times*, 22 February 1930, p. 18 (Olin Downes)

75 5 January 1917, p. 4

76 2 November 1935, p. 4 (Marjory Fisher)

77 22 February 1914, p. 6. The *Observer* thought the orchestral performance was "somewhat lethargic... there was seldom any actual coming to grips with the fine thematic material," but noted that Bodanzky was pre-occupied trying to co-ordinate his orchestra with what was happening on stage: 22 February 1914, p. 6.

78 *World*, 3 March 1914, p. 353 (Alfred Kalisch)

79 2 March 1928, p. 14 (M. W.). Bodanzky's first *Walküre* at the Metropolitan Opera on 16 December

Fig. 14.1. Artur Bodanzky, Mannheim, 1909

Fig. 14.2. Bodanzky rehearsing the Metropolitan Opera Orchestra
New York Tribune, 4 March 1917

Fig. 14.3. and 14.4. Bodanzky rehearsing *Tristan und Isolde* at the Metropolitan Opera

Fig. 14.5. Bodanzky rehearsing, ca. 1935

Fig. 14.6. Bodanzky from his Metropolitan Opera years, 1915–1939

the *Brooklyn Eagle* commented: "Almost always his tempi were judicious; indeed, only in the first pages of the *Todesverkündigung* did we feel a lack of breadth and wish for a greater gravity."[80] As often, Bodanzky's mood could change everything, and it did in a later 1930 performance which, according to the *Evening Post*, "reached and maintained such a high level of excellence and eloquence as to seem to us little short of a revelation."[81] The *New York Times* wrote of this performance:

> The whole interpretation, finely integrated, unified in spirit and detail had that loving care and warmth of expression which a great performance cannot be without. The conductor was in full command of the situation and no performer was outside his mood and influence. His conception, very clear, finely organized, poetical, brought all the individual parts into harmonious relation with its scheme. ... Also: The singers did not have to shout, for Mr. Bodanzky's accompaniment, save at the moments when the music must swell and flood and inundate everything with its splendor, was a model of finesse.[82]

By 1937 there was virtually a new orchestra, and in one performance, which survives on record, even veteran opera-goers could not recall a parallel. Bodanzky "was completely and magnificently in the vein," wrote the *Herald Tribune*."[83] The *New York Times* agreed: Bodanzky was "thoroughly in vein... imperious in insisting upon the utmost significance of interpretation on the stage and in the orchestra pit. Once his baton rapped in a way that made the listener think of the crack of the whip!"[84]

Bodanzky's first *Siegfried* at the Metropolitan on 15 January 1916 tempted the *New York Times* "to indulge in superlatives."[85] The *Tribune* was less sure. There was "at times a lack of temperament and a certain want of elemental power.... his *Siegfried* did not quite reach the heights of greatness."[86] He had re-arranged the brass to bring them all together at one end of the pit. "The unanimity of the brass was improved," wrote the *Sun*. "More important, however were the excellences in respect of tempi, lucidity and elasticity."[87] He was showing more feeling for climax than he had before, according to the *Evening Post*. "There were several thrilling climaxes – the majestic harmonies accompanying the awakening of Brünnhilde were splendidly brought out, and the wild beauty of the first scene of the third act – that wonderful primeval world music – was *echt-Wagnerisch*."[88] *Musical America* was surprised by the performance:

1915 was not widely commented upon in the press. He made some judicious restorations: "Mr. Bodanzky's cuts are much the same as Mr. Hertz's. He made two restorations, both in the part of Wotan – *Als junger Lieber Lust mir verblich* – which is hardly ever sung. In the third act he also restored some portions cut by Hertz, but not by Seidl": *Evening Post*, 17 December 1915, p. 11.

[80] 28 February 1930, p. 20 (Edward Cushing)

[81] 30 October 1930, p. 13 (Oscar Thompson): "For us it was a better *Walküre* in its entirety than any of four we heard abroad last summer – in Bayreuth [Elmendorf], Berlin, Dresden and Munich – though we should have preferred it without the four cuts the conductor made." Walter Kirchhoff sang Siegmund, Maria Müller Sieglinde, Friederich Schorr Wotan, Karin Branzell Fricka, and Gertrude Kappel Brünnhilde.

[82] 30 October 1930, p. 36 (Olin Downes). By contrast, a 1934 *Walküre* was "one of the sleepiest... the writer has heard in this city, and prevailingly mediocre in tone, Mr. Bodanzky's tempi, at least for two long acts, had the effect of extreme deliberation... the vital spark, most of the time, was missing": *New York Times*, 27 December 1934, p. 24 (Olin Downes).

[83] 19 December 1937, Sect. 1, p. 28 (Lawrence Gilman)

[84] 19 December 1937, p. 45 (Olin Downes); it was "a performance of superior energy and impact": *Sun*, 20 December 1930 (Irving Kolodin) (Metropolitan Opera Archives).

[85] 16 January 1916, p. 14

[86] 16 January 1916, p. 11

[87] 16 January 1916, p. 11

[88] *Evening Post*, 17 January 1916, p. 9

We make free to confess that we anticipated no such exhibition of virility, no such rugged power or grandiose sweep of line as Mr. Bodanzky gave us in the first scene of the third act, no such heroic sonorities in his climax building as we found wherever dynamic liberty was needed. Only once – in the slaying of Fafner – did he miss fire. For one of Mr. Bodanzky's habitual tendencies the first and third acts were truly admirable in exultant force and dramatic quality. And the forest voice enchanted by their poetic delicacy. It is strange, this phenomenon of Mr. Bodanzky. Demonstrably capable of letting himself out, why will he not drop his reserve oftener?[89]

Why, indeed. In 1926 he could bring animation, joyousness, and exuberance. "For once, the first act had sparkle, laughter, vivacity and the pulse of nature."[90] Yet in 1932 a performance was considered "heavy and dull. It dragged its slow length along in a soporific manner... there was little life in any scene."[91] In 1937 his orchestra became "a saga of forest and heroic legend."[92] And in 1939, he presented "the very essence of the score" in "a performance which in accent, color and sense of form established the mood and significance of the occasion."[93]

Bodanzky made a triumphant debut at the Metropolitan Opera with *Götterdämmerung* on 18 November 1915.[94] To the *Evening World* he "suggested the late lamented Gustav Mahler... a dynamo of energy, with long, supple arms, hands that seemed to talk, and a comprehensive eye scarcely less significant than Mr. Toscanini's. The orchestra, apparently, had taken to him unreservedly. Together they brought out new beauties in the lyric passages, observed the daintiest of nuances, and thundered in the crescendoes."[95] The *Herald*, too, was struck by the similarities with Mahler – "when that leader was young and vigorous." Bodanzky read poetry into the score, demonstrated "sentiment but not sentimentality," respected the singers by "subduing the orchestra so that the voice is always given the chance to soar above the accompaniment," and brought out "submerged themes" without ever sacrificing them for the general dramatic effect.[96] The *New York Times* considered him to be "a conductor of exceptional and highly interesting qualities":

His reading of the score was filled with the red blood of dramatic power, free and flexible in tempo, pulsing with the ebb and flow of passion. The playing of the orchestra was noble and beautiful in tone and tonal balance.

Mr. Bodanzky is evidently one who is possessed of Wagner's idea of bringing out always the unceasing surge of significant *melos* in the orchestra. He kept his orchestral forces within the limits that are necessary to allow the voices to prevail and to be clearly heard.

Within these limits he secured a marvelous flexibility and range of dynamics and the full potency of dramatic expression intrusted to the orchestral voice without heavy footedness or an over-bearing dominance that forces the singers to shout.[97]

[89] 22 January 1916, p. 52

[90] *New York Times*, 11 March 1926, p. 18 (Olin Downes). Melchior sang Siegfried.

[91] *Sun*, 16 January 1932, p. 11 (W. J. Henderson). Max Lorenz debuted as Siegfried.

[92] *New York Times*, 23 February 1937, p. 24 (Olin Downes)

[93] *New York Times*, 23 February 1939, p. 24 (Olin Downes)

[94] Jacques Urlus sang Siegfried, Melanie Kurt Brünnhilde, and Margarete Matzenauer Waltraute.

[95] *Evening World*, 19 November 1915 (Sylvester Rawling) (Metropolitan Opera Archives). The *World* wrote: "The turgid qualities which invariably obtained in this masterpiece when Bodanzky's predecessor, Alfred Hertz, conducted were happily absent last evening": 19 November 1915, p. 11

[96] 19 November 1915, p. 12

[97] 19 November 1915, p. 11

The *Evening Post* was struck by the slowness of some of his tempi which suggested the influence of Bayreuth,[98] but the conductor did know "how to whip the players into a frenzy and how to build a true Wagnerian climax":

In two respects Mr. Bodanzky is likely to improve on both Mr. Hertz and Mr. Toscanini: he follows out Wagner's idea that the singers are more important than the orchestra, and he is willing to make cuts – a point on which his predecessors were foolishly obstinate. The way in which he kept the orchestra subdued last night, except at the places calling for power, was most praiseworthy, and how rich and mellow the soft passages sounded![99]

Fig. 14.7. Bodanzky conducts. *Musical America*, 15 January 1916

"Musically the performance was the most finished at the Metropolitan since a memorable one conducted by Signor Toscanini," wrote Henry Krehbiel in the *Tribune*. "A leaden hand which weighed tons upon Wagner's music [Hertz] has been replaced by one which respects the composer's nuances and the euphonious flow of his interwoven melodies."[100]

[98] The *Press* took a different view. "One could not quarrel with any of his tempi. They were correct because they seemed to grow out of the emotional essence of the music": *Press*, 19 November 1915, p. 7 (Max Smith).

[99] 19 November 1915, p. 9. The cuts were enumerated, and included the Norns scene and the scene with Alberich. The Waltraute scene was retained. "Mr. Bodanzky follows the example of Hans Richter."

[100] 19 November 1915, p. 9. *Musical America* may have missed Hertz because its reviewer took time to warm to Bodanzky's interpretation, yet it praised his consideration of the singers, as Mahler had shown: 27 November 1915 p. 2; the *Sun* too was impressed by the relation of the orchestra to the singers: "Mr. Bodanzky seemed to have in mind Wagner's own injunction to conductors to seek to bring about the utmost distinctness in what was going on upon the stage. And behind all there was a profound musical enthusiasm and imagination": 19 November 1915, p. 7.

In the years that followed we see the same pattern of variability. In 1930, for example, Bodanzky was described as "workmanlike and weariless" by the *Herald Tribune*. "There was roughness aplenty in the performance, and the orchestra was its familiarly delinquent self."[101] Yet in 1932 the *Sun* crowned him the "hero" of the evening. "Certainly concentration and integrity are elemental requirements in a conductor, yet on this occasion, against impromptu singing, a struggling orchestra and clumsy staging, they towered impressively."[102]

Parsifal

Many good conductors throughout the musical world tackled *Parsifal* for the first time in 1914. Not all were instantly successful, including Bodanzky, as reviews of his debut at Covent Garden on 2 February 1914 show. He had to contend with an orchestra strange to the work, imperfect stage management,[103] and critics used to the unique acoustic of Bayreuth who complained of a lack of atmosphere. He was able to demonstrate to the *Glasgow Herald* that he knew his work well: "if his reading is not equal in expressiveness to that of the great Hermann Levi, it is in any case sound and workmanlike in the best sense."[104] Some critics were concerned about tempi, including the *Daily News and Leader*: he was "inclined to be deliberate in some of the narrative portions when Gurnemanz speaks, but once or twice in the Grail scene the pace was rapid. The most severe criticism that can be made is that there was some lack of atmosphere and imagination; but that is so much a matter of individual sentiment that it hardly amounts to much...."[105] The most severe criticism came from Ernest Newman writing in the *Birmingham Daily Post*:

> Candour compels one to say that *Parsifal* has made a rather unfortunate beginning in England.... The musical part of the performance, notwithstanding all its conscientiousness, hardly ever reached any real height. The conductor, Artur Bodanzky, of Manchester,[106] seems to have almost every good quality except imagination. He was apparently bent on getting as many and as perfect pianissimos as possible. In this he certainly succeeded; but he has little sense of contrast, and his tempi are maddeningly slow; and of all operas, *Parsifal* simply will not bear being dragged. ... The chorus of Flower Maidens went very well musically, in spite of Mr. Bodanzky's slowness of tempo making it almost as sad as the average tango.[107]

Subsequent performances improved in detail as well as general atmosphere, and there developed more "awe and mystery."[108] By the fourteenth and final performance according to the *Star*, "a perfection of ensemble and a smoothness were achieved as one rarely gets anywhere."[109]

[101] 18 January 1930, p. 10 (Lawrence Gilman)

[102] 18 March 1932 (Irving Kolodin) (Metropolitan Opera Archives)

[103] The transformation scenery failed in the third act and Bodanzky, after some minutes' silence, omitted the scene and went straight to the Grail Kingdom: *Star*, 3 February 1914, p. 4 ("Crescendo"); Bodanzky, *Saturday Evening Post*, 9 November, 1929, p. 23.

[104] 3 February 1914, p. 9. Along similar lines, the *Musical Times* wrote that Bodanzky "showed he is an industrious and competent conductor, if he did not betray genius": 1 March 1914, p. 187.

[105] 3 February 1914, p. 1 (Alfred Kalisch); "and it must not be forgotten that a London début is an ordeal."

[106] *sic*, not Mannheim, presumably a printer's error, possibly mischievous

[107] 3 February 1914, p. 6. It concluded: "A performance as the one we have had tonight is not calculated, I am afraid, to make *Parsifal* popular."

[108] *World*, 10 February 1914, p. 217 (Alfred Kalisch)

[109] 11 March 1914, p. 3 ("Crescendo")

At his first performance in New York on 25 November 1915, his reading had become "authoritative and full of comprehension" according to the *New York Times*; he seems to have given it "the right atmosphere."[110] It was a "wonderfully poetic" interpretation, wrote the *Herald*.[111] According to the *Tribune*, "the work took on a new significance and a heightened beauty. The mysticism of the music, its recondite meanings, its intellectual brooding, was what inspired the conductor, and the result was a performance of rare beauty, charm and imaginative power."[112] It was the most impressive performance ever given at the Metropolitan, in the view of the *Evening Post*. "The orchestral tones melted into one another, there was no coarseness from the brass, there was the utmost refinement from the strings, the rhythm was elastic and at the same time firm, the orchestra 'bore the singer as the sea bears a boat, without sinking it' (the words are Wagner's); in short, all that is meant by Wagner's word *melos* was exemplified in yesterday's performance."[113] To the *Press*, Bodanzky's performance inspired not only the audience:

> That the Austrian leader was largely responsible for the exquisitely euphonious, transparent and finely finished playing of the orchestra no one would be likely to deny. But the sphere of his art extended much further. Why, for example, did Johannes Sembach sing and act the title role as he had never sung and acted it here before if not because of Artur Bodanzky's influence? Why did Melanie Kurt's superb portrayal of Kundry surpass her previous achievements if not because of the support and the inspiration she received from Artur Bodanzky? Why did Carl Braun deliver the words and music of Gurnemanz in tones of almost *bel canto* character if not because Artur Bodanzky never permitted the orchestra to force the voices of the singers? ...
>
> Among the various readings of *Parsifal* heard by the writer for the *Press* in Bayreuth and other places abroad more than one was inferior to his, few superior and none quite as thrilling as the second act. A man who can accomplish what Bodanzky did on this occasion under conditions somewhat trying is not only a great conductor, but an artist to the core.[114]

Over the next 23 years, he seems often to have struck a deep chord with the work, though not to everyone.[115] He conducted a performance in 1927 with "dignity, intensity and mastery," according to the *Post*, "and was largely responsible

[110] 26 November 1915, p. 13

[111] 26 November 1915, p. 12. The *Sun* too commented on the "poetic mood of the more reposeful parts of the score": 26 November 1915, p. 9.

[112] 26 November 1915, p. 9

[113] 26 November 1915, p. 9. *Musical America* again seemed to be missing Hertz: "Delicacy is not always a suitable substitute for red blood.... Withal, Mr. Bodanzky rarely causes his orchestra to seethe and to glow...": 4 December 1915, p. 4. By contrast, James Huneker detected blood. He wrote that it had "lost something of that droning, psalm-singing quality which makes this sacrosanct religious festival play such a bore to genuine musical people. It was conducted as if it had red blood in it, which, in spots, it has, and the second act was as exotic and sensuous as it should be": *Independent*, 7 February 1916, p. 198. There is a "droning, psalm-singing quality" about the Grail scene recorded by Gramophone in 1913 with the Chorus and Orchestra of the Königliches Hofoper conducted by Bruno Seidler-Winkler (not on LP or CD: for details, see the author's *Parsifal on Record* (Westport: Greenwood Press, 1992), pp. 46-47.

[114] *Press*, 26 November 1915, p. 6 (Max Smith)

[115] For example, Irving Kolodin quotes two reviews of Henderson where the performance "moved heavily on leaden feet... intellectual and scrupulously careful [but] it seldom attains heights of emotion" (1920), "apathetic and resolutely industrious by turns" (1928): *The Metropolitan Opera, 1883-1950: A Candid History*, pp. 331, 401; "his baton marks neither affection nor respect for this vast and noble and incomparable master-work": *Herald Tribune*, 30 March 1929, p. 10 (M.W.).

for the atmosphere created by the whole performance."[116] His reading of act three in a 1928 performance, in the view of the *Herald Tribune*, "was penetrated with the essential moods of the music: its poignancy, its elevation, its ineffable tenderness."[117] In 1933 the same newspaper considered he had "never given us a more sensitively tempered reading" of the score. "The broader tempi which he has adopted, the fine expressiveness of his phrasing, the profundity of feeling that he disclosed – these were deeply influential yesterday upon a performance that was often worthy of the incomparable music...."[118] In 1936 he made a "deeply affecting impression" upon the *New York Times*. "Every slightest detail in nuance and dynamics was meticulously considered in a reading which forcefully established each and all of many conflicting moods of the masterpiece."[119] The *Sun* commented on an evocative performance in 1938. "His tempi were broad, if not as slow as Muck's or Toscanini's at Bayreuth" but he "withstood the test of inevitable comparisons."[120] Finally, of a 1939 performance the *Herald Tribune* wrote:

> Artur Bodanzky conducted in his most inspired vein. It was possible to differ with him here and there in his pacing of the incomparable score, but the exaltation, the profound tenderness and the intensity of his conception contributed largely to this enthralling presentation of Wagner's crowning creation.[121]

Fig. 14.8. Bodanzky in 1919

[116] 16 April 1927 (Olga Samaroff) (Metropolitan Opera Archives). She concluded: "The audience dispersed in silent reverence."
[117] 7 April 1928, p. 8 (Lawrence Gilman)
[118] *ibid*, 10 March 1933, p. 9 (Lawrence Gilman)
[119] 11 April 1936, p. 18
[120] 19 March 1938, p. 30 (Oscar Thompson)
[121] 9 March 1939, p. 13 (Jerome Bohm)

The Wagner recordings

It is a matter of regret, and of mystery, that Bodanzky did not make more studio recordings. When his first records came out, they made a very promising impression. The *British Musician* wrote of his Parlophone records:

He shows himself both a master of orchestral performance and a musician of very bold individuality. His success with the *Lohengrin* Prelude is exceptional. This piece of sustained writing, which for a while is almost motionless, does not always cohere even with good conductors; and when this happens it becomes dull. Bodanzky, without loss of its ethereal qualities, holds it together as compactly as if the piece were a passage from Beethoven. He makes the music sweeter, nobler, more essentially serene, and more fluid than do most conductors. His climax is majestic. ...[122]

Other reviews too showed he had potential,[123] but in the world of commercial recording, it did not develop.

In the case of his live performances, which we know varied in quality, it is plain that the broadcasts caught on record in the last years of his life may not reflect all he was capable of, especially in his early years. Like Toscanini, his stature cannot depend on his recorded legacy alone, although unlike Toscanini, it is a more reliable guide because it consists of more live performances of whole works. What we do have is formidable. His conducting struck many as having resemblances to Mahler. More than Bruno Walter, he may in fact be the true pupil of Mahler.[124] His recordings might even be regarded as the closest we can get to "hearing" what Mahler's Wagner was actually like.

The recordings have never been "popular" in the market place. Their sound is always poor, sometimes so bad it is difficult to know what one is hearing. Listening becomes an acquired skill. Established magazines have generally been circumspect about publicising and reviewing non-commercial material emanating from radio broadcasts. None of this has made the reception of Bodanzky easy. There are many

[122] vol. 3 no. 10 (February 1928), p. 311. It continued: "His nature and technique have full scope in the *Mastersingers* Prelude, where the middle scherzo of the apprentices is converted by him into a genuine scherzo, – the instruments seem to become the boys and the young men of this scene. Bodanzky's lovers in the prelude are no doubt a trifle mercurial, but the music wants this ready-wittedness...." A briefer review in *Music & Letters*, vol 9, no. 2 (1928) by "S. G." uses similar language and may have been by the same author, e.g., an "aspect of Bodanzky's genius is displayed here, in the passage of the apprentices, which in his hands becomes a true scherzo": pp. 193-4.

[123] A review in *The Times* was particularly impressed by the "technical side" of the recordings: 27 December 1927, p. 7. *Gramophone* doubted "if the *Meistersinger* recording is to be beaten by anything we have from other companies," but missed in the *Lohengrin* prelude "the ethereal quality Wagner wanted at the start": January 1928, p. 332 (K. K.). Compton Pakenham in the *New York Times* considered that "for sheer weight and sonority" the performance of the *Meistersinger* prelude "outclasses" von Schillings, noting that the Muck version was "generally regarded as the standard for the gramophone:" 29 May 1931, p. X10.

[124] Herbert Peyser wrote: "It is a paradox of long standing that the most representative Mahler pupils inherited the mannerisms and the superficialities of their teacher rather than this or that aspect of his greatness. He seems to have diffused something hard and sullen, which communicated itself to the conductorial talents he helped to mold and robbed their musical approach of an essential resiliency, candor and grace. For this reason I have always felt Artur Bodanzky to be a much more typical Mahler pupil than Bruno Walter": "Bruno Walter," *Disques*, vol. 2, no. 12 (February 1932), p. 531. Ferruccio Busoni too regarded Bodanzky as one of Mahler's "real pupils" (1912) as well as "one of the finest conductors" (1919): *Letters to his wife*, (trans.) Rosamond Ley (London: Edward Arnold, 1938), pp. 148, 297

striking features and unique moments in the recordings, some of which strike a chord with what we have read of his performances. The recordings are, in a word, extraordinary.

The *Tristan* excerpts from 1933 and 1934 suffer from particularly bad sound. What can be said is that, beneath the overpowering surface noise, there is a performance teeming with life. Moments like the ferocious curse from Isolde, the scorching delirium of Tristan, and the sweeping, broad-armed, phrases of comfort from Kurwenal, indicate that an intense drama is underway. In 1935 Bodanzky can be heard in better sound, energetic and decisive, always with an ear to the drama. After Tristan and Isolde drink the potion, there is quite simply pandemonium, the "headlong scramble" that alarmed one reviewer in 1930, yet which is wholly in keeping with the spirit of the occasion. The pace set at the beginning of act two is quite fast, befitting the impatience of Isolde and leading inexorably to a joyous reunion. Most notable about this act are the deep rhythmic waves from the orchestra underlying Brangäne's warning, Tristan's reply to King Marke, and his blissful vision *Wie sie selig* in act three. As in 1935, the 1937 performance opens with a broad prelude, and rises to tempestuous levels when Isolde calls forth violent storms. As frustration and fury run through her, Bodanzky is ever there with his orchestra. There is a tremendous lead-up to the extinguishment of the torch, and an overwhelming reunion which almost bursts with ecstasy. The dramatic points he makes with the orchestra, such as in the transitional passage after the lovers are exposed (*Rette dich, Tristan*), and the contrast between the wretched Tristan who longs to die and the exuberant Kurwenal who rejoices that Tristan still lives, are masterly.[125]

The *Meistersinger* from 1936 shows Bodanzky in shifting moods. It opens with a prelude that thrills and soars. The variety of pace and mood is extraordinary: it sings, it longs, it dances, it swings, and it triumphs. In the opening scene the love interest is played out clearly against the background of congregational singing, as the orchestra fairly brims with flirtatiousness. In the next scene David rollicks through the singing rules. And in the third scene, the whole moves along like an unceasing conversation. Pogner's reflections in act two bring a corresponding change to the orchestra, which is subdued and itself seems thoughtful. Yet it rises again for the riot, which seems a *real* punch-up, ending with a climax of rioters tumbling over one another before they disappear into the night. The spirit of the first act is not entirely held throughout the third. This suggests Bodanzky may have been tiring (one even wonders whether the recording of act three belongs to the same performance), but it is nevertheless a very spirited, joyous performance.

In the *Rheingold* recording, the stealing of the ring and Alberich's curse are clearly at the heart of Bodanzky's interpretation. This scene is the pivot of the orchestral drama. He creates tension before the theft by setting a smart pace that aptly reinforces Loge's smart deception of Alberich. When the ring is wrenched from the finger of Alberich, he gives a wonderful, dreadful, cry before Bodanzky gives him a rousing send-off back down the sulphur cleft to Nibelheim.

[125] Further comments are in the author's *Tristan und Isolde on Record* (Westport: Greenwood Press, 2000), pp. 1-4, in sharp contrast to David Hamilton's view: "Good provincial conducting": "*Tristan* in the Thirties, Part II," *Musical Newsletter*, vol. 7 no. 2 (Spring 1977), p. 16.

Notable moments in the parts of the *Walküre* performances that have survived are the sense of catastrophe Bodanzky creates as Wotan ponders his despair (1934), and of threat to the terrified Valkyries as Wotan approaches and Brünnhilde panics (1934, 1937). In this act Bodanzky manages to maintain Wotan's rage, make the orchestra blow fate and fire as Brünnhilde embraces her fate, and conjure sumptuous playing from the orchestra in Wotan's farewell (1937).

The *Siegfried* recording shows great variety of pace, some of it quite fast, but always attuned to the drama. For example, he hurtles through the Mime/Siegfried scene to demonstrate their mutual irritation, and sets a pace for Alberich/Mime scene perfectly suited to their squabbling. The slaying of the dragon is spirited, not cumbersome; the forest murmurs not at all rushed. There are wonderful legato stretches after Siegfried has penetrated the fire and advances toward Brünnhilde. Then, when he draws his sword and cuts away her coat of mail, there is a dramatic change of mood: she is not a man.

The *Götterdämmerung* recording is intensely dramatic. There is a tremendous orchestral build up to Brünnhilde's *Zu neuen Taten*, and Bodanzky gallops through as Brünnhilde and Siegfried sing of her horse Grane – he *makes* Grane gallop. There is a buoyant journey down the Rhine for Siegfried, and a violent change of mood after he has drunk Gutrune's welcoming draught. In her admonition to Brünnhilde, Waltraute has moments of stagnant despair alternating with frantic warning. The orchestra brilliantly acts out many moods in act two: there are flashes of realisation and fury from Brünnhilde; Alberich, Hagen and his men are glitteringly evil; and there is an ever-pressing urgency in the evolving conspiracy against Siegfried. When his murder comes, it is explosive. And as he is carried away, a slow, deep rhythm pervades the funeral march. Brünnhilde's farewell (*Starke Scheite*) is the shortest by far of any performance of this passage. It has enormous variety of mood and tempo, and overall is affirmative and optimistic. Brünnhilde is passionate in her love for Siegfried, furious at her betrayal, resigned, and ultimately destructive: she *hurls* the firebrand into the pyre, and gallops to her death. This is all told by the orchestra. The final few minutes of orchestral playing are a veritable flood, destroying all in its wake. There is no wallowing in the waters of the Rhine in Bodanzky's interpretation. It is a triumphant, cataclysmic ending.

The remarkable features of the 1938 *Parsifal* recording – he was only strong enough to conduct acts one and three – are the changes of pace, and of mood, in accordance with the drama. He achieves this to a degree not heard in any other recording. For a conductor often associated with fast tempi, this may be a surprise. His prelude is very broad, intensely solemn. Then, as Gurnemanz calls the knights to prayer, there is quite a change of pace. The day has broken. Kundry arrives, and the tempo brightens again, until Amfortas appears on his bier and the orchestra pulls right back. When Parsifal sings of the men on the edge of the forest who laughed and galloped away (*sie lachten und jagten davon*) the whole passage is taken at a gallop until suddenly… Parsifal faints, and the orchestra and tempo subside dramatically. After the swan has been shot and Parsifal arrives there is turmoil from the orchestra, and a ferocity in the calls for retribution (*Strafe den Frevler!*). In Amfortas's prayer, there is turbulence in his suffering, as well as prayerful pleading; agony, as well as anger. As the ritual of the

Grail scene gets underway, there is deep rhythm in the slow passages – a return to the solemnity of the prelude – and afterwards, a real spring in the step of the knights. They are clearly refreshed. The whole Grail scene has the effect of a profound release. The entire first act has extraordinary variety, even stark contrasts. In act three, it is a relief to have Bodanzky back with his variety of shadings and tempi. He moves Gurnemanz and Parsifal along, and his final Grail scene is very affirmative, even full-blooded. He had come a long way since London.

History lesson

The golden years of Wagnerian singing in New York in the 1930s are rarely associated with Bodanzky. Without him, however, it is unlikely the principal singers would have achieved their great performances. He and his orchestra were their indispensable allies. The important ones paid him tribute. Lauritz Melchior, whom he had trained and advised in his early years, became a good friend: "[Bodanzky] was, inside his coarse outer shell, a warm-hearted human being who went through fire and water for his musicians and artists on stage. To him the best was only just good enough."[126] Frida Leider, who made her debut at the Metropolitan in 1933 as Isolde was convinced of "his outstanding artistry" from her very first rehearsals.[127] Lotte Lehmann wrote how "Bodanzky conducted an inspired performance" at her debut as Sieglinde in 1934. "I got on splendidly with him straight away."[128] And Kirsten Flagstad, whom Bodanzky had "discovered" for the Metropolitan, spoke with more warmth about him than any other conductor she had worked with.[129] Theirs had been a "magnificent collaboration" according to her friend and conductor, Edwin McArthur. "She not only admired his genius; she loved him as a daughter would a father."[130] Other writers have been more sparing.[131] History has dealt a grim hand to Bodanzky. But he is not dead. Not only was he "one of the few 'living' conductors" as James Huneker wrote,[132] but scratch the surface of any of his recordings and he will spring quickly to life.

[126] Emmons, *Tristanissimo* (New York: Shirmer Books, 1990), p. 117

[127] Frida Leider, *Playing my part*, (trans.) Charles Osborne (London: Calder and Boyars, 1966), p. 152

[128] Lotte Lehmann, *Wings of song: an autobiography*, (trans.) Margaret Ludwig (London: Kegan Paul, Trench, Trubner, 1938), p. 221

[129] Louis Biancolli, *The Flagstad manuscript* (London: William Heinemann Ltd., 1953). p. 74

[130] Edwin McArthur, *Flagstad: A Personal Memoir* (New York: Alfred A. Knopf, 1965), pp. 103-104. He mentions later in his book that Wilhelm Furtwängler was "her favorite of all": p. 290.

[131] He is barely referred to by Harold C. Schonberg in *The Great Conductors* (New York: Simon and Schuster, 1967) or by David Wooldridge in *Conductor's World* (London: Barrie & Rockliff, 1970); Irving Kolodin's histories of the Metropolitan (cited above) do not fully acknowledge his artistic contribution, in fact are critical of it: e.g., *The Metropolitan opera, 1883-1935*, p. 389; Martin Mayer wrote: "cutting, cutting, cutting… Until he lost interest, however, his was a powerful personality in the pit." *The Met: One Hundred Years of Grand Opera* (New York: Simon & Schuster, 1983), p. 135; cf. C. J. Luten: "There has been no one like him and his team in any repertory theater since": "The Bodanzky Record," *Opera News*, Vol. 36 No. 8 (15 January 1972), pp. 28-29.

[132] quoted in the *New York Times*, 24 November 1939, p. 1 (obituary)

Part VII

The German Heartland

15

Wilhelm Furtwängler – Wagner's symphonist

Few who remained in Germany during its years of terror could have done more for German music, or for Wagner, than Wilhelm Furtwängler. No one could have survived the regime unscathed: musicians forced into exile suffered, but so did those who remained. German music as a whole was profoundly disrupted. Furtwängler's noble and naïve attempt to hold the torch of German art high was misused, thwarted, and almost snuffed out. The political circumstances in which some of his great Wagnerian performances of 1933-1944 were given, and of which recorded excerpts survive, hardly bear contemplation. Before that era, except for a short youthful period, opera had never been his central musical activity. His heart was set on composing, yet he was a master symphonic conductor. When he did conduct opera, as he increasingly did from 1932, he brought some of his mastery from the concert room. He was pre-eminently suited to Wagner. His untainted pre-war Wagner recordings are few and valuable. His post-war recordings are more prolific, but are patchy. Sometimes they show a tired, lost man, as if his mood or centre of gravity had deserted him. Occasionally he was up there with the stars, as with the *Ring* at La Scala in 1950. Slowly, he re-entered the recording studio. He left some gems, some of historic proportions, and some less precious stones. Above all, he left us with a sense of the illuminating power of the symphonist, of what Wagner can sound like when a great orchestral conductor steps into the pit.

Wagnerian awakening

He was born in Berlin on 26 January 1886 into a highly intellectual, middle-class family. He received his musical training and education privately. As a young man he was keener on composing than working in any theatre or concert hall. He did not become a conductor after any practical experience in an orchestra. In fact the German critic, Alfred Einstein, wrote that he was not a "born conductor" at all, not as his seniors Felix Mottl and Arthur Nikisch were.[1] It was from these two musicians that Furtwängler learned most about his art. Nikisch was of fundamental importance to him. He told a musician friend in 1912 that he was "the only one from whom I

[1] Einstein, "Wilhelm Furtwängler," *Monthly Musical Record*, January 1934, in Catherine Dower, *Alfred Einstein on Music: Selected Music Criticisms* (New York: Greenwood Press, 1991), p. 155

can learn, even if I will do it differently."[2] He did indeed do it differently, in a way that befuddled many observers and some practitioners. He also must have learned something about his craft from the two years he spent under Mottl at the Munich Court Opera where he was a repetiteur (1907/09), though he does not seem to have acknowledged this.[3] He possibly also learned from Hans Richter whose *Meistersinger* so impressed him.[4] In any case, his early years of conducting – Zurich (1906/07), Munich (1907/09), Strasbourg (1909/11), and Lübeck (1911/15) – contained little of Wagnerian interest. He conducted mainly operetta or concerts, although these did include the occasional Wagner piece. Then in 1912 he had a bad experience:

My father gave me tickets for four performances of the *Ring of the Nibelungen* in the then Munich Hoftheater. These performances, conducted by the famous Wagner conductor Franz Fischer with the best singers of the Munich stage, were certainly no better or worse than many others. And yet they thoroughly destroyed my illusion and love of Wagner for years afterwards.... The most wonderful melodic curves were trivialized, made banal by the movements of the singers and their style of singing... Theatre, nothing but theatre... Only later, in fact only after I began to conduct the works myself, did I understand the entire range of their greatness....[5]

He had his first opportunity with the *Meistersinger* on 20 November 1913, the only Wagner work he conducted in his four years as a concert conductor in Lübeck. According to his friend Lilli Dieckmann, he inspired the singers and the chorus to rise above themselves.

Of course, the pure orchestral parts were the best, what with this band of most devoted servants, formed and trained by his spirit and his will. The prelude, the end of the second act, the beginning of the third – all of indescribable beauty: poetry, deepest empathy, and new creation. The first chord of the prelude was utterly precise so that, to paraphrase Hans von Bülow's words, one could gladly anticipate the entire work's success.[6]

This sense of knowing how a work conducted by Furtwängler would end as soon as it had begun – an immediate sense of an over-arching conception – was a characteristic of his conducting throughout his life.

When Bodanzky was called to the Metropolitan Opera from Mannheim in 1915, a search committee was established, and Furtwängler applied for the post. He auditioned with *Fidelio*. The performance did not go all that well, particularly in the chorus, but Bodanzky said to him afterwards, "You have done wonders with the orchestra... in Mannheim you will have a much better choir at your disposal."[7] He

[2] letter from Lilli Dieckmann to her mother, February 1912, in Karla Höcker (ed.), *Wilhelm Furtwängler: Dokumente – Berichte und Bilder – Aufzeichnungen* (Berlin: Rembrandt, 1968), p. 42; see also Elisabeth Furtwängler, *About Wilhelm Furtwängler*, (trans.) Hanni Raillard (Woodside, California: Wilhelm Furtwängler Society of America, 1993), p. 28

[3] Hans-Hubert Schönzeler, *Furtwängler* (London: Duckworth, 1990), p. 15

[4] see Richter chapter above, p. 103

[5] "Wagner as Musician" (1936), in Wilhelm Furtwängler, *Notebooks 1924-1954*, (ed.) Michael Tanner, (trans.) Shaun Whiteside (Quartet Books: London, 1989), p. 81; he wrote in similar terms in an essay on Wagner and Nietzsche: "What remained seemed to me bland, overdone, empty theatrics; and the few obviously beautiful orchestral passages in no way could make up for the overall impression of dishonesty from within. I was cured of Wagner for a long time": quoted in Elisabeth Furtwängler, *About Wilhelm Furtwängler*, p. 70.

[6] letter from Lilli Dieckmann to her mother, December 1913, in Höcker, *Wilhelm Furtwängler*, p. 43-45

[7] Schönzeler, *Furtwängler*, p. 28. Bruno Walter, General Music Director in Munich, also recommended

got the job. His five years in Mannheim (1915/20) were the only period of his life in which his musical activities were exclusively devoted to opera. They also built the foundation of his work as a Wagnerian conductor. He conducted all the Wagner operas except *Lohengrin*: *Holländer* (14), *Walküre* (14), *Tristan* (10), *Siegfried* (9), *Parsifal* (7), *Rheingold* (6), *Götterdämmerung* (5), *Tannhäuser* (3), and *Meistersinger* (3).[8] At heart, however, he was a concert conductor, and that is chiefly where his musical interests led him. In the opera house at Mannheim he had not really been in his element. Carl Hagemann, head of the Mannheim Opera during Furtwängler's years there, thought that "Furtwängler is not a man of the theatre, neither in general as an organiser, nor in detail as an artist. He does have a sense of the theatre, but the theatre is not in his blood." He lacked the ability to make quick decisions necessary in the theatre, and to improvise when things went wrong. "Nothing was ever correct or good enough for him… and he kept changing his mind, which drove his superiors, peers, and employees to despair."[9]

At the head of an orchestra alone, he was less distracting and distracted. In 1920 he succeeded Richard Strauss as conductor of the Preussische Staatskapelle in Berlin. In 1922 following Nikisch's death he became head of the Berlin Philharmonic and the Leipzig Gewandhaus. He toured the United States (1925/27), though never to conduct opera,[10] and from 1928 visited Britain regularly. By 1927 he was the leading conductor in Vienna. He was appointed head of the Städtische Oper in Berlin in 1928, artistic director of the Bayreuth Festival in 1931, and director of the Staatsoper Berlin in 1932. These years as one of his biographers wrote "must have been among the happiest of Furtwängler's life."[11]

Furtwängler for the post as "one of the most inspired of the up-and-coming young conductors, even though still lacking experience in the operatic field." (p. 27)

[8] These and other performance statistics are chiefly gathered from the listings in John Hunt's *The Furtwängler Sound*, 6th edition (London: John Hunt, 1999).

[9] Hagemann, *Bühne und Welt* (Wiesbaden: Der Greif, 1948), p. 99, partly quoted in Schönzeler, *Furtwängler*, p. 32. Hagemann considered Klemperer "the greatest theatre conductor" amongst those he had worked with: *Bühne und Welt*, p. 101. According to Mrs Furtwängler, her husband was producer as well as conductor on only one occasion, a *Tristan* in Vienna in 1943: "something didn't go quite right in the first act on stage. After that, he decided never again to be his own producer: "Frau Furtwängler remembers," interview with Alan Blyth, *The Times*, 22 March 1973, p. 13.

[10] He did, of course, include Wagner items in his concerts, and on one occasion gave an all-Wagner program which cannot be described as a success. The *Herald Tribune* wrote: "It was depressing, for example, to hear him play the Finale to *Die Walküre* last night with so defective a sense of its continuity and integrity of line – to hear him chop the noble cantilena into small, spasmodic segments, rhythmically disjointed and insignificant. It was disheartening to hear the *Tristan* Prelude, that singing and pyramidal flame, drained of its passion and its intensity, truncated and diminished. We should not have supposed that it could sound so casual, so soft, so gelatinous. Mr. Furtwängler was happier in the opening pages of the *Liebestod*, where he found a persuasiveness of pace and tone and dynamics that reached to the heart of the music and laid it bare. Yet when he came to that soaring crescendo that should scale the dawn, the ascent was but pedestrian – Isolde's soul remained among the mists and bracken of the world, earthbound and sorely shackled." (2 March 1927, p. 18, Lawrence Gilman). The *New York Times* gave no details of the conducting; it suggested the applause given Furtwängler was more for the general esteem in which he was held than for his performance of the evening. (2 March 1927, p. 29, Olin Downes). The *Sun* too gave no details; it considered that Ernestine Schumann-Heink "was the brilliant star of the occasion, both in the applause given her and in her performance." (2 March 1927, p. 23)

[11] Schönzeler, *Furtwängler*, p. 37. He conducted relatively few Wagner operas in this period: 1920 (3), 1921 (1), 1922 (1), 1923 (0), 1924 (4), 1925-27 (0), 1928 (4), 1929 (12) 1930 (2), 1931 (3), 1932 (17).

In 1933, he stood side-by-side with the older Richard Strauss as the head of musical life in Germany. Yet as Alfred Einstein wrote at the time, it was "a truly lonely position, full of inward and outward dangers."

> In order to make him the supreme head of musical life, to entrust him with the musical executive, as it were, the new State has been obliged to get rid of all, or almost all, of the musicians whose stature was comparable to his. Bruno Walter, who possesses a far deeper and more universal comprehension of opera than Furtwängler, has been condemned to a life of travel. So has Otto Klemperer. Furtwängler, it is true, has tried hard to keep him as the conductor of the best Berlin Choral Society. But Klemperer also belongs to opera. At the Berlin State Opera, except for unimportant people, only Leo Blech has remained....[12]

The years from 1933 to 1944 were Furtwängler's most intense period of Wagner conducting.[13] Although he soon fell out with the authorities because of his support for Hindemith, and for the integrity and independence of art more generally, he was used occasionally for propaganda purposes, and in some cases in Wagnerian performances of great acclaim.[14] His music-making was not unaffected, however, by the brutality of the political circumstances. As early as 1937, the *New York Times* correspondent in Vienna observed, "I cannot rid myself of the disquieting feeling that his experiences in recent years have taken a spiritual toll of Furtwängler which is irremediable."[15] For many complex reasons, he remained in Germany till the end, or at least until very near the end, when he was in imminent danger. He went to Switzerland in February 1945.[16]

He marked his first post-war appearance at the Berlin Staatsoper with a performance of *Tristan* on 3 October 1947, but after two more performances conducted no more

[12] "Wilhelm Furtwängler," *Monthly Musical Record*, January 1934, in Dower, *Alfred Einstein on Music*, p. 156

[13] The number of his Wagner operas in Berlin, London, Paris, Vienna, Salzburg, Zurich and Stockholm was: 1933 (22), 1934 (25), 1935 (15), 1936 (22), 1937 (34), 1938 (22), 1939 (5), 1940 (5), 1941 (2), 1942 (7), 1943 (11), 1944 (9).

[14] For example, *Meistersinger* at the Staatsoper Berlin on 21 March 1933 on the inauguration of the new Reichstag ("Potsdam day"); *Meistersinger* on the eve of Nazi Party meetings in Nuremberg on 8 September 1935 and 5 September 1938; *Tristan* at the Munich Festival on 10 June 1935; *Lohengrin* at the opening of the Bayreuth Festival on 19 July 1936; and *Parsifal* at the opening of the Bayreuth Festival on 23 July 1937. Hitler was present on all these occasions. Excerpts from the 1938 Nuremberg and 1936 Bayreuth performances were recorded, as well as a 1943 Bayreuth Festival *Meistersinger*. For the cameras, he performed the *Meistersinger* prelude in a swastika-bedecked factory in Berlin on 26 February 1942. "One thing I had to accept, of course, and let wash over me: National Socialist propaganda. I was exposed to this propaganda more than others...." Furtwängler in 1945, *Notebooks*, p. 160. For more on propaganda involving Furtwängler see Michael H. Kater, *The twisted muse: musicians and their music in the Third Reich* (New York: Oxford University Press, 1997), pp. 200-201.

[15] Herbert F. Peyser, "Opera in Vienna," *New York Times*, 18 April 1937, p. 17

[16] Friedelind Wagner met Furtwängler in Paris in 1938 when he was conducting *Siegfried*. "'Tell me,' he asked over and over again, 'how did you get out? How did you manage to make such a decision? What can I do? How can I get out of Germany?' Every time I answered, 'You are outside of Germany now. Throw away your return ticket.' But I knew he would never do it." Friedelind Wagner and Page Cooper, *The royal family of Bayreuth* (London: Eyre and Spottiswoode, 1948), p. 193. In his own words (1945): "I was able to do more for true Germany and, as a result, for peace and the arts of the world here than anywhere else.... In individual cases I have consistently worked against National Socialist terror and racial politics, and what I was able to achieve here justifies, in my eyes, my having remained in Germany." *Notebooks*, pp. 159-160; for a discussion on Furtwängler's decision to stay in Germany and documentary evidence of the people at risk he helped (at least eighty), see Fred K. Prieberg, *Trial of Strength: Wilhelm Furtwängler and the Third Reich*, (trans.) Christopher Dolan (London: Quartet Books, 1991), pp. 269, 330-331, 344 n45.

Wagner until 1950 when there were three cycles of the *Ring* at La Scala. These, and the act-by-act radio performances of the *Ring* in Rome in 1953, were among the few notable Wagner activities that remained. At La Scala he also conducted *Parsifal* in 1951 and *Meistersinger* in 1952, but recordings of these do not appear to have come down to us. He made his historic studio recording of *Tristan* in London in June 1952, but did not conduct opera again at Covent Garden, nor at Bayreuth. A proposal that he do so at the Metropolitan Opera in 1952 was rejected by the board.[17] The War and its aftermath had taken its toll on Furtwängler, and he died in Germany on 30 November 1954, aged 68.

Furtwängler's approach to Wagner

"I can't stand Wagner – and *Tristan* in particular," the fifteen-year-old boy wrote to his close friend Bertel von Hildebrand. And to his aunt: "I also heard the *Meistersinger*. Unfortunately they have not made the slightest impression on me." Two years later he wrote "very negatively" to Bertel about *Parsifal*, and its "fretful searching after moods."[18] Slowly he changed his mind. As always, he thought most searchingly and seriously about the music he was to conduct, and "only after I began to conduct the works myself did I understand the entire range of their greatness...."[19] After he had prepared his first *Ring* for 1916-17 he wrote in an illuminating way about the role of the conductor:

> More so than any other work by Wagner, the *Ring of the Nibelungen* can be distorted in its effect by an inadequate performance. Guidelines to perform such a work, however, only the music can give. This is linked to its function within the total artwork. The music is, also in the *Ring*, the final and most differentiated tool of the poet: the one through which he expresses himself most distinctly. It is actually creating the style of the work. Hence, from it, each gesture, each scene, must go out; to it again, return. Therefore, the musician is the real executor of the poetic will.[20]

The primacy of the conductor was thereby asserted. And in this task, "the final and highest goal which a conductor can attain," he told students in a discussion about Wagner, "is to conduct a *legato* melody, that is to say conduct a melody in such a way that it is really received as *legato*, something living and breathing which really flows."[21] These are clues to the way Furtwängler approached Wagner's scores. It has often been described as symphonic.[22] Alfred Einstein wrote:

[17] Sir Rudolf Bing, *5,000 nights at the opera* (London: Hamilton, 1972), p. 118

[18] letters quoted in Elisabeth Furtwängler, *About Wilhelm Furtwängler*, p. 65

[19] "Wagner as musician" (1936), in *Notebooks*, p. 81. He continued: "I am no Wagnerian, in so far as I see Wagner as a genius who provides us with norms and a sense of direction. He is and remains an exceptional case as a musician. But he is one of the most productive geniuses that the world has ever seen, a creator of almost colossal dimensions, for whom any standard is inadequate. He must be taken as he is."

[20] *Mannheim Theater News*, quoted in Elisabeth Furtwängler, *About Wilhelm Furtwängler*, p. 68

[21] remarks at the Berlin Hochschule für Musik (1950, 1951), trans. John Coombs, in booklet (p. [13]) accompanying *100 Jahre Berliner Philharmoniker – Wilhelm Furtwängler*: DG 2740 260 (6 LPs) (1982); also quoted in John Ardoin, *The Furtwängler Record* (Portland, Oregan: Amadeus Press, 1994), p. 194

[22] In reviews of *Lohengrin* at Bayreuth, 1936: "Furtwängler also remains the symphonic theatre conductor here," Hans Heinz Stuckenschmidt, *Deutsche Zeitung Bohemia* (Prague), 23 July 1936, in Susanna Großmann-Vendrey, *Bayreuth in der deutschen Presse*, Vol. 3,2 (Regensburg: Bosse, 1983), p. 265; "The reading had a quality of symphonic architecture.... Certain phrases lacked the operatic saliency and bite: they appeared to

Furtwängler's conducting is based on his extraordinary feeling for tone, on his capacity to grasp long symphonic passages. He belongs to a generation in whose youth the enormous influence of Wagner was still at its height. As an opera conductor, therefore, he is decidedly a Wagner conductor; hence everything written under the influence of Wagner, in the widest sense (the works of Strauss and Pfitzner for example) finds in him a perfect interpreter. He also builds up an opera on the symphonic plan, on the basis of the orchestra; the voices are but organic parts of the symphonic construction, which have to fit in and submit. *Tristan* under Furtwängler is more perfect than even *Meistersinger*.[23]

"His is the great symphonic *Tristan* of the age," wrote the *New York Times* correspondent, Herbert Peyser, who had heard Furtwängler's *Tristan* at Berlin, Vienna, and Bayreuth.[24] Otto Klemperer alluded to this approach when he recalled a *Meistersinger* conducted by Furtwängler fifty years earlier: "When there was a symphonic piece for the orchestra alone, it was very good. But when there were singers, it was not so good. He was no opera conductor."[25] There is some anecdotal evidence from singers in support of this view. Lauritz Melchior considered him "a somewhat erratic conductor. He let his own emotions run away with him and conducted the orchestra with little or no consideration for what was happening onstage. Consequently his tempo was different for every performance, which made him difficult to follow."[26] Frida Leider also sang under Furtwängler and recalled how he "insisted upon extensive rehearsals.[27]

be conceived as symphonic themes rather than as heightening and vitalizing dramatic commentary." Olin Downes, *New York Times*, 20 July 1936, p. 10 and 9 August 1936, p. X5; "When all's said, he is primarily a symphonic rather than an operatic conductor": Herbert F. Peyser, "Trend Among Conductors in Vienna," *ibid*, 2 January 1938, p. 130; "Furtwängler has been accused of approaching all operas symphonically. This is true only of Beethoven and Wagner." Schönzeler, *Furtwängler*, p. 32.

23 "Wilhelm Furtwängler," *Monthly Musical Record*, January 1934, in Dower, *Alfred Einstein on Music*, pp. 156-7

24 *New York Times*, 14 July 1935, p. X5, reporting from Vienna, where he noted there was a "criminal omission" in act two of Furtwängler's performance. His views on the Bayreuth performance are below.

25 Peter Heyworth (ed.), *Conversations with Klemperer*, rev. ed. (London: Faber and Faber, 1985), p. 119. Sir George Solti agreed with Klemperer's view of Furtwängler: "He was a superb musician and he thought profoundly about music, but he didn't really 'breathe' with singers. When he was in the orchestra pit, I always had the strange impression that he didn't quite belong there": *Solti on Solti: A Memoir* (London: Chatto & Windus, 1997), p. 76. Furtwängler himself made a revealing comment to a member of the Berlin Philharmonic: "Fundamentally, Toscanini is an opera conductor... We here are engaged in a different profession": Gregor Piatigorsky, *Cellist* (New York: Doubleday, 1965), p. 109.

26 Ib Melchior, *Lauritz Melchior: The Golden Years of Bayreuth* (Fort Worth, Tex.: Baskerville Publishers, 2003), p. 235. Melchior, who also sang under Furtwängler in *Tristan* and the *Ring* at Covent Garden considered him "a better symphony conductor than opera conductor." An orchestra member recalled: "Furtwängler considered the *Ring* purely orchestrally, it seemed to me. He took no notice of the stage; the curtain got stuck and would not go up for the third act of *Die Walküre* so the Valkyries were singing away behind it, but when the stage manager came to apologize afterwards the maestro had not even noticed. This encouraged the great tenor, Lauritz Melchior, to have a little fun by holding his high notes for far too long because he knew that Furtwängler would just go on conducting, regardless." Richard Temple Savage, *A Voice From The Pit: Reminiscences of an Orchestral Musician* (Newton Abbot: David & Charles, 1988), p. 54. This last point may have some corroboration in an observation Ernest Newman made of a *Tristan* with Melchior at Covent Garden in 1935: "Furtwängler was more deliberate in the first act than in the other two.... Unfortunately... some of the singers took advantage of this orchestral concession to spin their phrases out still further on their own account, with the dual result that the vocal and orchestral lines did not always coincide and there was sometimes an effect of dragging." *Sunday Times*, 26 May 1935, p. 7, and in a *Ring* in 1938 which "at times even dragged too slowly – Lauritz Melchior, accustomed to a quicker tempo for Siegfried's sword-songs, seemed to find the slower pace of them difficult...": *Spectator*, 10 June 1938, p. 1056 (Dyneley Hussey)

27 This comment must be understood chiefly in the context of opera. In the case of concerts it was

The great concert conductor was always anxious about his reputation in opera. There were often minor disputes between us at rehearsal because, in his concentration upon the music, he was apt to forget the singers."[28] This could have almost catastrophic consequences, as during a *Ring* at Bayreuth in 1936. "The lack of cooperation between the stage and the conductor led to mishaps some of which had to be heard to be believed," Walter Legge reported to the *Manchester Guardian*. "There were two such major accidents in *Götterdämmerung*; one when Siegfried parted from both Brünnhilde and the orchestra, the other when the Rhine Maidens and Dr. Furtwängler lost touch for several bars and both parties tried almost every expedient but that of a complete stoppage to get into stride again."[29] In some cases Furtwängler had no opportunity for rehearsal at all, like a *Siegfried* in Paris, when he told Hans Hotter as he turned up a mere hour before the performance: "Don't look down at me too often. I'll keep up with you." According to Hotter, it was "a thrilling, electrifying performance."[30]

Furtwängler's advice to singers was not to interrupt the melodic line which, in effect, he was determining. "Sing without much deliberation. Let the music flow

different. "He is no believer in an excessive amount of orchestral practice": Herbert F. Peyser, "Wilhelm Furtwängler," *Disques*, January 1931, p. 443; Furtwängler himself wrote: "... in my view the value of rehearsals is generally overestimated" (1937): Ronald Taylor (ed.), *Furtwängler on Music: Essays and Addresses* (London: Gower Press, 1991), p. 20; "Conducting means free creation. Everything else must be preparation." (1927) *Notebooks*, p. 9; "The most important and the best thing, namely that imperceptible variability of tempo and colour, can in no way be achieved mechanically by means of rehearsals." (1929), *ibid*, p. 35; he opposed too many rehearsals because "it cannot do justice to *living masterpieces*. The great masterpieces are subject to the law of improvisation to a far higher degree than is commonly realised." Furtwängler, *Concerning Music* (trans.) L.J. Lawrence (London: Boosey & Hawkes, 1953), p. 47. In any case, rehearsals appear not to have been his *forte*: "his rehearsals were boring. He never had the indisputable technical command that so much impresses the orchestra.... [Yet] I remember an extraordinary one of Wagner's Good Friday Music from *Parsifal*... with the Santa Cecilia Orchestra, when he obtained the utmost in beautiful sonorities from his players." Massimo Freccia (Italian-American conductor and associate of Toscanini), *The sounds of memory* (Salisbury: Michael Russell, 1990), p. 142.

[28] Frida Leider, *Playing my part*, (trans.) Charles Osborne (London: Calder and Boyars, 1966), p. 135. She added: "But he was so conscientious a musician that a little discussion solved all problems, and the harmony of our work together was never seriously disturbed." Lotte Lehmann, who sang Eva and Sieglinde under Furtwängler, wrote: "We got on magnificently together." *Wings of song: an autobiography*, (trans.) Margaret Ludwig (London: Kegan Paul, 1938), p. 217. As for Kirsten Flagstad, Furtwängler was "her favorite of all" according to Edwin McArthur, *Flagstad: A Personal Memoir* (New York: Alfred A. Knopf, 1965), p. 290; it was Martha Mödl who "lived up to his highest ideal" according to Elisabeth Furtwängler, *About Wilhelm Furtwängler*, p. 73, and the respect was reciprocal: Martha Mödl, *So war mein Weg: Gespräche mit Thomas Voigt* (Berlin: Parthas, 1998), p. 107. Rudolf Bockelmann wrote extensively on Furtwängler's conducting in his diary for 1937, as quoted by Berndt W. Wessling, *Furtwängler: eine kritische Biographie* (Stuttgart: Deutsche Verlags-Anstalt, 1985), pp. 158-160.

[29] *Manchester Guardian*, 15 August 1936, in Alan Sanders (ed.), *Walter Legge: Words and Music* (London: Duckworth, 1998), p. 38

[30] Hotter, *Memoirs*, (trans. and ed.) Donald Arthur (Boston: Northeastern University Press, 2006), p. 62. If his memory served him correctly: he said the performance (the Wanderer), his first under Furtwängler, took place "a few years before the war," and that Siegfried had been sung by one of his favourite colleagues, Max Lorenz. The performance in fact took place on 27 December 1938, and the Siegfried was Joachim Sattler. Hotter attributed his good memory to his mother, and to his wife who had "carefully saved my reviews throughout the sixty-plus years of our marriage." (p. 246). Clearly she had not been in Paris on this occasion for the reviews of Hotter were glowing. *Le Temps* saw a "superb Wagnerian future opening before him": 29 December 1938, p. 5 (C.T.). The performance was broadcast on Radio-Paris.

naturally!" he said often to Dietrich Fischer-Dieskau and other singers.[31] Hotter explained how Furtwängler would encourage singers to make music in a continuous stream: "Don't let yourselves be tempted to interrupt the music at the bar line. Bar lines are there to remind you of the rhythm, the beat. If you've got rhythm in your blood, just imagine the bar lines are just written in pencil; you can erase them any time you want them, when you don't need them any more."[32] And so the music flowed. In a *Siegfried* in London *The Times* observed: "Dr. Furtwängler's unhurrying but strongly flowing reading makes for clarity, and all the singers, including Mime and Alberich, who so often bark their words without making them clearly audible, could and did sing them distinctly. On the surface of the stream waves blew up now and then, but always relatively to the situation and not for point-making."[33] As we shall see, although for Furtwängler the musical heart of the performance lay in the orchestra, he was often exceedingly restrained in order to allow the singers to make their own music.

Furtwängler wrote extensively about conducting, mostly in fragmentary form in his *Notebooks*, including on Wagner. His statements and aphorisms always bear pondering – the seriousness with which they are made *compels* the closest attention – but one must be wary about drawing rules for his approach. What he described in a good performance (for example, Richter's *Meistersinger*) and what he prescribed or applauded in good conducting does not necessarily mean he achieved these in his own performances. What may have appealed to him intellectually, like the theories of the musicologist Heinrich Schenker, may not have been accurately mirrored in his music-making.[34] All his work had the freedom and creativity of profound personal struggle. "He was a German musician," Edwin Fischer wrote, "… in the Faustian sense, that of eternal struggler and seeker."[35] He would abandon himself to a work to understand it, yet the end was always elusive. "Art cannot be understood," he wrote, "but only *experienced*."[36] And finally, "the ultimate end of art is still its practical performance; the meaning of music still lies in the playing."[37] How then did he play the music dramas of Wagner?

Furtwängler conducted more than 300 Wagner operas in his lifetime, though Wagner's early operas appear to have had little attraction for him.[38] *Tristan* (68) and *Meistersinger* (65) were his favoured operas, and although he conducted individual *Ring* operas many times, he conducted only sixteen complete cycles. *Parsifal* he conducted surprisingly little: at Mannheim (7 performances 1916-20) when it would have been a natural part of his repertory duties, at Bayreuth (10 performances 1936-37) when there was little alternative (Muck had retired, Toscanini refused to conduct), and at La Scala (5 performances 1951). We shall look at how some of his performances of the late operas were received.

[31] Dietrich Fischer-Dieskau, *Reverberations*, (trans.) Ruth Hein (New York: Fromm International Publishing Corporation, 1989), p. 127

[32] *Memoirs*, p. 64

[33] 20 May 1937, p. 14. Erich Zimmermann sang Mime, and Eugen Fuchs Alberich.

[34] "I am a man of experience," Furtwängler proclaimed in his *Notebooks* in 1939. "If experience tells me that this is the case, I would not only admit it but also act accordingly. In this most vexed of questions, theories have no meaning." (p. 101)

[35] Daniel Gillis (ed.), *Furtwängler Recalled* (Zurich: Atlantis, 1965), p. 37

[36] 1941, *Notebooks*, p. 134

[37] 1939, *Notebooks*, p. 118

[38] He conducted *Lohengrin* on only twelve occasions (1929-30 and 1936, Bayreuth), the *Holländer* fourteen times (1915-20), and *Tannhäuser* sixteen times (1916-38). By contrast, he conducted the Overture to *Meistersinger* 145 times – his fifth most frequently performed concert piece: Hunt, *The Furtwängler Sound*, 6th ed., p. 188.

Tristan und Isolde

The Bayreuth Festival of 1931 was the only occasion Furtwängler and Toscanini appeared together. Toscanini had conducted *Tristan* at the 1930 Festival, and now that Furtwängler was conducting, comparisons were inevitable. Hebert Peyser reported for the *New York Times*:

One may concede at once that the Furtwängler orchestra does not boast the fabulous sound of Toscanini's. But, for that matter, what living conductor's does? The Toscanini orchestra is a singing unit – a virtuoso bel cantist, if you will. Furtwängler's is a virtuoso orchestra that attains for the most part an extraordinary degree of finish and tonal beauty – but, first and last, an orchestra in an instrumental rather than in a vocal sense. The *Tristan* prelude is a seizing experience at the hands of the German conductor. It illustrates marvelously – as does so much else in the score – Furtwängler's intuitive feeling for a graduated and controlled but ineluctable crescendo. But it does not, like Toscanini's, distil in the opening phrase the whole unassuageable yearning of the human heart for the non-existent and unachievable. The first act has breadth, bite, ruggedness, austerity, and the entrance theme of Tristan was stupendous and crushing. I do not deny that I approached the second with something like dread, for such music as that of the garden scene is of Toscanini's kingdom. But if Furtwängler's first act was great, and if his third act was greater, it was even more by his second that this performance enscrolled itself on Bayreuth's records in characters of flame. I recall no presentation of this act – neither Hertz's nor Mahler's nor Toscanini's nor Muck's – which has excelled the present one in soaring ecstasy of lyric mood, in majesty of far-flung line and in the progressive luxuriance of its unfoldment. The heart of the love duet – the pages following the *Sink hernieder* and Brangäne's tower song – were of almost intolerable beauty, thanks not only to the magical suggestiveness of Mr. Furtwängler's scheme of light and shade, but also to the exquisite playing of the orchestra and a proficiency of individual instrumentalists that lent the orchestral texture something of the delicate transparence of chamber music. But never was there in it all anything tenuous or diminutive. In the utmost trait of subtlety was always implicit the vast, imperative sweep of Wagner's architecture, and an unfailing rectitude in the relation of the part to the whole.[39]

The *Frankfurter Zeitung* considered the first act had been a little affected by inhibition, as if Furtwängler was entering the festival theatre "with its almost stifling traditions, a little hesitantly and probingly," and was missing direct contact with the audience which the sunken pit entailed. Nevertheless, the second act was "almost unsurpassable," though it should have enjoyed freedom from its enclosed space. "The third act kept to the heights scaled by the second. It was drenched in the abysmal dejection of waiting in vain, up until the very moment when the joyous certainty of reunion dawned. Even the always somewhat irritating fighting scene… was also symphonically arranged by virtue of its energetic progression. Then this fantastic work entered the blessed cove of death with beautiful restraint and detachment."[40]

Tristan was the work Furtwängler made his debut with at Covent Garden on 20 May 1935. According to *The Times*, it was a performance "remarkable for its intelligibility."

[39] 23 August 1931, p. X6. Furtwängler's debut with *Tristan* was on 23 July. Lauritz Melchior sang Tristan, and Nanny Larsén-Todsen Isolde. Peyser's report is dated Bayreuth, 1 August 1931. Furtwängler conducted two further performances on 3 and 18 August. The latter was broadcast, and parts of it were recorded by Danish Radio: see discography.

[40] Heinrich Simon, *Frankfurter Zeitung*, 28, 29, 31 July 1931, in Großmann-Vendrey, *Bayreuth in der deutschen Presse*, Vol. 3,2, p. 226

No doubt he would have been glad to have had another rehearsal or two with the orchestra, who seemed not quite prepared for the slow measure of the prelude and certain later passages, and who from time to time had to be repressed by the rapid nervous movements of his left hand. But there were none of those cataclysmic climaxes which obliterate the most powerful voice; even the greeting of Tristan and Isolde in the second act was perfectly audible, ecstatic without becoming incoherent, and almost all the time Mme. Leider and Herr Melchior seemed to be singing well within their range of vocal power.[41]

Even Ernest Newman, who had been troubled by Furtwängler's "besetting sin" in the concert room of making "effects for effect's sake," was impressed: "As a whole his reading was one of great dignity, beautifully modelled and finely proportioned. If it lacked the intensity of some performances we have had at Covent Garden, it had poetic qualities of its own."[42] To the *Daily Telegraph* it lingered upon "the contemplative and pathetic aspects."[43] "Furtwängler feels the sadness of it all reflectively," wrote Neville Cardus; "he strikes a graver note; he touches everything with the 'pathos of distance.' His *Tristan und Isolde* belongs to romance and the night...."

In Furtwängler's conception the orchestra is an eloquent commentary, or Greek chorus, a miraculous and beautiful part in a larger whole. He never permits the singing to be overwhelmed by instrumental tone; the stage action and the instrumental playing are in his control sensitively and subtly related. He has a genius for mingled quietness, roundness, and intensity. With Furtwängler tragedy is an internal idea, a spiritual experience, not a disturbance or upheaval of physical forces. Pulsation and not emphasis is the mark of his art; I have never heard the scene of the meeting of the lovers in Act 2 done with Furtwängler's proportionate power; we could hear every note and cry of the singers, yet the urge of the orchestral crescendo was grand and reckless, giving us a glorious sense of the primrose path to the everlasting bonfire. The effect was achieved by passionate rhythmical stress and concentration – not by noise.[44]

His way with *Tristan* in these 1931 and 1935 performances can be found again in his historic 1952 recording which we will look at below.

Die Meistersinger von Nürnberg

We have read how, with his very first *Meistersinger*, Furtwängler made the orchestral passages stand out. In Paris twenty years later, it was again the orchestra which stood out. With the chorus and mastersingers singing in French, and the German artists singing in German, the orchestra would have indeed have seemed a natural, unifying force. There were mixed reports of these 1934 performances. The reviewer for *Candide* wrote: "In my soul and conscience, before the court of opinion, I am compelled

[41] *The Times*, 21 May 1935, p. 14

[42] *Sunday Times*, 26 May 1935, p. 7. Newman wrote that Furtwängler "now and then indulged in a pianissimo or a rallentando that went rather beyond the limits of what was really required, but never to the point at which the effect became a blemish on the score." These points were appreciated by others. The *Morning Post* was pleased with "the real pianissimo before the second climax of the duet in the second act.... [although] one missed the fire, the lyrical intensity, of the previous performance [under Beecham]": 21 May 1935, p. 14 (F.T.). The *Daily Telegraph* was impressed by "the arresting rallentando and pianissimo, made more pronounced than one had ever known it before, just before the *sehr drägend* of the last section of the great duet": 21 May 1935, p. 10 (Richard Capell).

[43] *ibid*, 21 May 1935, p. 10 (Richard Capell)

[44] "Furtwängler at Covent Garden – *Tristan and Isolde*" (22 May 1935), in Neville Cardus, *Cardus on music: a centenary collection* (ed.) Donald Wright (London: Hamilton, 1988), pp. 106-107

Fig. 15.1. Wilhelm Furtwängler from his Mannheim years, 1915-1920.
Photo by G. Tillmann-Matter

Fig. 15.2. and 15.3. Furtwängler in 1931.
Drawings by N. van Kempen, *Der Deutsche Rundfunk*, August 1931

Fig. 15.4. Furtwängler recording in the Musikvereinsaal, Vienna,
where he recorded Wagner in 1949 and 1954. Photo by Elfriede Hanak

Fig. 15.5. Furtwängler conducting *Don Giovanni*, Salzburg, 1954, from a film. Photography directed by S. D. Onions.

Fig. 15.6. Furtwängler in the postwar years. Photo by Roger Hauert

to declare that Wilhelm Furtwängler has just given a very bad performance of *Meistersinger*. Everywhere there were hesitations, bad attacks, discrepancies, and breaks in the ensemble."[45] By contrast, *Le Monde Musical* wrote: "We have re-discovered the Furtwängler of better days, attentive to the slightest detail, obtaining from the marvellous opera chorus and orchestra a depth of execution which contributed, for the large part, to the perfection of the ensemble, the solo parts having been entrusted to worthy German artists."[46] *Le Temps* was more expansive:

> Mr. Furtwängler did not appear to have the penetrating touch he did in *Tristan und Isolde*. He is visibly less familiar with the scores of the *Walküre* and *Meistersinger*. He conducted the first act of *Meistersinger* with a kind of hurried neutrality, a care-free rapidity detached from its object. We only found his rare and elevated style again from the middle of the second act. His searching spirit was perceptible, however, in the last part of the satirical drama which was seen, so to speak, through a filter. Never, perhaps, have we heard a deeper, more sculpted orchestral interpretation, done with such variety, such probing, subtlety and calm. Like all the great conductors, Mr. Furtwängler at no time gave the impression of conducting with rapidity. Each of his sinuous gestures was thoughtfully determined.[47]

He returned for two more performances in 1936, but again the reviews were mixed. *Le Ménestrel* mentioned that the chorus still "lacked precision, bite, and strength."[48] To *Candide* it was a performance "extremely simple and persuasive."

> He does not weigh down the text with exaggerated pathos. He does not seek to draw from each phrase a deep philosophy. He does not aim for the sublime. He has the intelligence to keep to all of the score its atmosphere of a "musical comedy," which still does not prevent him from obtaining absolutely irresistible effects of poetry and nobility when the situation demands it. All seems to have been admirably understood by Furtwängler in his interpretation, one so clear, so cordial, so light, and so right. There is all the *gemüt* of life and of the town of Nuremberg and that, I believe, is precisely the right tone for this masterpiece.[49]

Furtwängler returned to Bayreuth in 1943 and 1944 to conduct the *Meistersinger*. We have an almost complete recording of one of those performances, and parts of others in Vienna, and shall consider these below. He conducted six performances at La Scala in 1952. The *Corriere della Sera* wrote of the first: "The orchestra truly sparkled with the power of its sound, the astonishing clarity of its counterpoint, and the beauty of its wonderful, iridescent, harmonious, multicoloured palette of instruments."[50]

[45] Emile Vuillermoz in *Candide* (no date) as quoted in René Trémine, *Furtwängler et la France* (Paris: Société Wilhelm Furtwängler, 1987), p. 39.

[46] 30 June 1934, p. 196 (Arthur Dandelot)

[47] 13 June 1934, p. 3 (Henry Malherbe). Furtwängler had conducted *Tristan* in Paris on 29 and 31 May, and *Meistersinger* on 5 and 7 June. Toscanini was in Paris at the time to give concerts. He attended the opening performance of the *Meistersinger*, but walked out. "The Overture began, it was ill-rehearsed and inexact, he began to curse to himself; the curtain rose, the chorus was singing the chorale in French and a quarter tone off-key. At this moment Toscanini rose and announced, 'We go.' ... The next morning Furtwängler phoned and said that he had come from Berlin and had not had sufficient time to prepare the performance." George R. Marek, *Toscanini* (New York: Atheneum, 1975), p. 100. Furtwängler had rehearsals on five days according to the archives of the Paris Opéra: Trémine, *Furtwängler et la France*, p. 39.

[48] 22 May 1936, p. 172 (Paul Bertrand)

[49] 28 May 1936 (Emile Vuillermoz) as quoted in Trémine, *Furtwängler et la France*, p. 41

[50] 1 March 1952, p. 2 (f.a.); see also Angelo Scottini, *Furtwängler in Italie* (Paris: Société Wilhelm Furtwängler, 1990), p. 29. The performance of 9 March 1952 was broadcast and tape-recorded for re-broadcast, in two parts, on 22 and 24 March, but no trace of the recording was found by Scottini in the Italian Radio archives.

To the *Corriere Lombardo*, on the other hand, Furtwängler "seemed less dynamic than usual, almost depleted, inclined to some sluggishness and heaviness."[51] Whether this was the production Neville Cardus saw or not, it is clear he had heard him in the work, for in his appreciation of Furtwängler he wrote that while his ability to penetrate "into the brain centre of *Tristan* and *Parsifal* was absolute and consummate... lack of geniality kept him outside the warmest spaces of *Meistersinger*."[52] Just as a conductor's temperament can make a congenial work glow, so too can it inhibit the full realization of quite a different work. Cardus said: "I have heard *Tristan* conducted under Toscanini sound as much lacking in nervous tension and tragic shadow as I have heard *Meistersinger* under Furtwängler lacking in steadiness of pulse and geniality of diction."[53] Later he said: "Even a great conductor can't be a medium for all music. For example, I would go anywhere to hear Furtwängler conduct *Tristan*, but I wouldn't want to hear him conduct *Meistersinger*."[54]

Der Ring des Nibelungen

Furtwängler's conception of the *Ring* seems to have surprised and disappointed some English critics. The 1937 *Ring* in London was not what they were used to. *The Times* wrote after the first *Rheingold*: "Those who declare that in Wagner it is the music which matters most and that the orchestra is the best part of the music may have been dissatisfied by his restraint, but the method gave a performance of remarkable clarity."[55] During the second cycle *The Times* gave its opinion that Furtwängler's interpretation was "not lyrical or dramatic but essentially epic – a saga to be narrated, and in such a narration clarity is the first of virtues since vividness, force, feeling, and all the others are then added to it."[56] To achieve this clarity – a stated ideal of Wagner – the orchestra was subdued. In *Rheingold*, for example, the benefit was that "every particle of the texture was clearly revealed, and the mood not only of the opera as a whole, but of the various parts, was realised with extraordinary sensitiveness."[57] But at what cost? Ernest Newman wrote that in spite of "the consistently beautiful playing from the orchestra... the performance struck me as one of the most lifeless I have ever heard."[58] A week later he went into some detail: "the score sounded like exquisite chamber music. The trouble was that the *Rheingold* is not chamber music," a point on which Alban Berg would have agreed: "I wasn't at all convinced by [Furtwängler's] *Rheingold* performance," he wrote to Schoenberg in 1928, "with its attempt to interpret Wagner as chamber music."[59] Newman considered Furtwängler was "perfectly correct, so far as the letter goes, in the subdued tone he drew from everyone," but that he made a "cardinal error" in taking a "merely literal or abstract interpretation of the markings

[51] 1-2 March 1952, p. 4 (Teodoro Celli)

[52] *Manchester Guardian*, 2 December 1954, in Gillis, *Furtwängler Recalled*, p. 32

[53] Cardus, *Talking of music* (London: Collins, 1957), p. 15

[54] Robin Daniels, *Conversations with Cardus* (London: Gollancz, 1976), p. 147.

[55] 14 May 1937, p. 10

[56] 25 May 1937, p. 14

[57] *Observer*, 16 May 1937, p. 10

[58] *Sunday Times*, 16 May 1937, p. 5

[59] letter dated 7 December 1928, in Juliane Brand, Christopher Hailey, Donald Harris (eds.), *The Berg-Schoenberg correspondence: selected letters* (Basingstoke: Macmillan, 1987), p. 380. Reviewing Furtwängler's debut at the Vienna State Opera with *Rheingold* on 17 October 1928, Julius Korngold did not mention any chamber-music-like quality in his review in the *Neue Freie Presse*, 19 October 1928, pp. 1-3.

p and *pp*" instead of determining the scale of intensity from the *fortissimi* downwards, that is, from the "peak moments of the action: ...in the Rhine Maidens' cry of delight when the gold begins to glow, and when Alberich forswears love and seizes the gold." Furtwängler seems not to have reached these peaks.

On the whole, it has been a very undistinguished *Ring*: in many places it has been under-voiced and consequently under-vitalised. Furtwängler's contribution to the proceedings has been musical rather than dramatic: he and the orchestra have given us some exquisitely polished playing, but neither have the greatest imaginative heights of the score been scaled nor the profoundest depths been plumbed.[60]

Interestingly, these views echo those of a British visitor to Furtwängler's *Ring* at Bayreuth in 1936. Walter Legge reported to the *Manchester Guardian* of the "magnificent orchestra, an instrument of ravishing tone, marvellous precision... almost inhuman in its infallibility."

Yet, for all the excellence of the playing the performance of the *Ring* was, as a whole, under-vitalised. Rarely was there a real *fortissimo*. *Pianissimi* there were in plenty, and several grades of tone further down the scale into the regions of the inaudible. And rhythmically as well as tonally the cycle was lifeless.

Only at rare moments, as in the scene between Siegmund and Brünnhilde in the second act of the *Walküre* and the second act of *Götterdämmerung* was the music given its full stature. One felt that Dr. Furtwängler was a tired man, able to muster the requisite tension of nervous vitality only under the stimulus of the heroic singing that Frida Leider occasionally gave him.[61]

Fig. 15.7. Furtwängler at Bayreuth, 1936.
Drawing by N. van Kempen, *Bayerische Ostmark*, Bayreuth, 19 August 1936

Other observers of the London *Ring* revealed disappointment at certain aspects, not always wholly attributable to the conductor. The *Spectator* wrote after the *Walküre*: "It was good to hear this music deployed under Dr. Furtwängler's direction in all its

[60] *Sunday Times*, 23 May 1937, p. 7

[61] 15 August 1936, in Sanders, *Walter Legge*, p. 38

leisurely grandeur, with the orchestra really supporting the voices and the singers always given time to get out their words. Yet it was a curiously unheroic performance.... The first act... was curiously unexciting."[62] The *Daily Telegraph* considered that *Siegfried* had been "on the whole rather sombre."[63] The *Observer* wrote after *Siegfried* that "Furtwängler's *Ring* may disappoint some Wagnerians because it does not force home the self-conscious pressure and size of the thing: yet how rich, complete, earnest, and sensitive it is, and how wonderfully everything on the stage comes into its own!" ... The last part of the *Ring* cycle was not the success that the earlier ones were."[64]

When Furtwängler returned to London in 1938 for two further *Ring* cycles, there were some similar misgivings, which at least showed a deliberate consistency in Furtwängler's interpretation. *The Times* wrote after *Rheingold*:

> Dr. Furtwängler's reading of the score is admired for its clear punctuation. The shape of the music is delineated in relation to each episode of the drama. He is determined that his audience shall perceive what it is all about, and in order to do so he is considerate of the singers to the point sometimes of reducing the tone beyond what such clearness requires. An example was the scene of the giants where the voices of Herr Weber and Mr. Norman Allin were in no danger of being lost.[65]

Ernest Newman again commented on the "mainly under-toned, and consequently under-vitalised, but beautifully proportioned" orchestral playing in *Rheingold*[66] and, after *Siegfried*, on Furtwängler's "habit of flood-lighting the peaks and keeping the plains almost continuously in a subdued half-light... this method, though highly favourable to the climaxes, deprives the body of the work of much of its varied dramatic life."[67] But what Furtwängler took away with the one hand he seems to have given with the other. "Furtwängler has the great conductor's ability," wrote the *Spectator*, "to see the end afar off, and never allowed subsidiary details or minor climaxes to intervene between the hearer and the main form of this vast musical structure."[68] Furtwängler's chief merit, *The Times* wrote after *Götterdämmerung*, was his "sense of proportion":

> The Norns' scene in the *Vorspiel*, that first recapitulation in this part of the vast symphonic drama in which the Norns take us through the main points of the story, was unusually subdued, a tranquil recollection of things past. It was as if the music, like the Norns themselves, were perceived through a thin veil, and it was only at the entry of Brünnhilde's new theme that the orchestral sound was allowed to develop a passionate intensity. And as the first act was carried through to its terrible climax of Siegfried's theft of the ring, so the whole was made to lead

62 4 June 1937, p. 1052 (Dyneley Hussey)

63 20 May 1937, p. 14 (Richard Capell). It was Max Lorenz's debut as Siegfried in London: "There has not been a more finely accomplished Siegfried in our time."

64 23 May 1937, p. 14

65 *The Times*, 19 May 1938, p. 14. In the second *Walküre*, according to the *Observer*, "Furtwängler seemed less anxious than usual to protect the singers from an overwhelming accompaniment. Mr. Melchior, of course, needed little protection...": 5 June 1938, p. 10

66 *Sunday Times*, 22 May 1938, p. 7. Neville Cardus commented after *Siegfried* how "The conducting of Dr. Furtwängler smooths the course perhaps fastidiously.... Yet we have a price to pay: [his] sense of detail and balance of periods lessen the rhythmical drive of the orchestra. As a consequence we feel, more than we ought to feel, the mechanism of Wagner's sequential bridge-passages." *Cardus on Music*, p. 85

67 *Sunday Times*, 29 May 1938, p. 7. He did not go to *Götterdämmerung*, but instead to a performance of Verdi's *Requiem* conducted by Toscanini.

68 10 June 1938, p. 1056 (Dyneley Hussey, who heard only a broadcast of one scene of *Rheingold*, the second *Walküre* and *Siegfried*, and the first *Götterdämmerung*)

up to the final cataclysm and its succeeding peace. At this performance of *Götterdämmerung* it seemed unusually appropriate that the orchestra should have the last word, and that that word should be no mere perfunctory cadence, but this grand peroration.[69]

Parsifal

Why Furtwängler conducted *Parsifal* so rarely is a mystery considering his apparent affinity with the work. Of the foreign visitors to Bayreuth for his 1936 performances, Walter Legge considered that "the attenuated orchestral tone" of which he had been critical in the *Ring* "was better suited to *Parsifal*"; it was refreshing "to hear a performance more worthy of the Bayreuth tradition."[70] He did not go into detail, nor did *The Times*,[71] though Olin Downes of the *New York Times* agreed on one point: the first performance on 20 July "was nearer to the traditional standards of the Festspielhaus, though it must be admitted that it was inferior, orchestrally speaking, to the interpretations given in other seasons by Karl Muck and Toscanini."[72] *Le Temps* cast some doubt over Furtwängler's interpretation, which was "dictated by the nature of his temperament," but again did not go into details.[73] Perhaps it was the matter of temperament that explains the *Herald Tribune*'s comment that Furtwängler's achievement, when compared with those of Muck, Toscanini and Strauss, was "perhaps the most personal of all."

His broad tempi for the prelude and solemn intensity in the Good Friday Spell, and the dolorous accents of his interpretation of the sorrows of Amfortas were in contrast with the readings of Strauss, who tried to conquer the huge dimensions of the score by speeding up the tempi. Furtwängler builds broad, slow forms. His brilliant dynamics and magnificent phrasing triumphs over all possible length.[74]

The German press echoed and elaborated these views. On the matter of tempo firstly, Furtwängler was observed by the *Deutsche Allgemeine Zeitung* to have maintained a balance between "the sacred breadth" of Muck and Toscanini and "the more operatic, invigorating" interpretation of Strauss.[75] "If Furtwängler managed to leave his own mark on the performance," wrote the *Deutsche Zeitung Bohemia*, "this was due to the structure of his tempos. He takes them more broadly than Strauss, the prelude to act one even more broadly than Toscanini, who conducted the 'longest' *Parsifal* in living memory. But this breadth is filled with such intensity, is phrased so brilliantly, that it is never felt to be dragging."[76] He set tempos "without any exaggeration one way or another," according to the *Berliner Lokal-Anzeiger*, and "put them on solid,

69 28 May 1938, p. 12. Siegfried was sung by Lauritz Melchior, Brünnhilde by Anny Konetzni.

70 *Manchester Guardian*, 15 August 1936, in Sanders, *Walter Legge*, p. 38. Helga Roswaenge sang Parsifal; Marta Fuchs, Kundry; Ivar Andrésen, Gurnemanz; Herbert Janssen, Amfortas; Robert Burg, Klingsor.

71 "a very high standard": 13 August 1936, p. 8

72 16 August 1936, p. X5

73 6 August 1936 (Gustave Samazeuilh). This and the reviews that follow on Furtwängler's 1936 *Parsifal* are from the Richard Wagner Museum in Bayreuth, unless otherwise stated.

74 2 August 1936 (H. H. Stueckenschmidt)

75 22 July 1936 (Robert Oboussier)

76 Hans Heinz Stuckenschmidt, *Deutsche Zeitung Bohemia* (Prague), 23 July 1936, in Großmann-Vendrey, *Bayreuth in der deutschen Presse*, Vol. 3,2, p. 266. Furtwängler approved of the closed orchestra at Bayreuth, but only for *Parsifal*: "it sounds really fabulous": remark to the Berlin Hochschule für Musik, in booklet accompanying *100 Jahre Berliner Philharmoniker – Wilhelm Furtwängler*: DG 2740 260

broad ground, and developed their movement in a wonderfully organic way."[77] A second notable feature of Furtwängler's style was his skill at transitions. "[He] is a master of transitions," declared the *Münchener Neueste Nachrichten*. He "never loses the thread" and presents the varying scenes in the drama "with a great uniform cohesion, reproduced seamlessly. Nothing is rendered too long or too short, too strong or too weak; balance rules the whole in an equalizing manner." The transition in the third act from the arrival of Parsifal to the Good Friday scene was "the climax of the whole performance."[78] It was a scene in which, according to the *Deutsche Allgemeine Zeitung*, Furtwängler "guided the orchestra into transfiguringly soothing sounds. He deliberately eschewed over-emphasizing the inner musical climax, being more concerned with the overall sweep of the act."[79] The *Hamburger Zeitung* noted "no sharp edges anywhere: the transitions between the numerous colour changes were superbly balanced, particularly – breathtakingly so – in the great Transformation Music."[80] Fourthly, there was the magic of the Furtwängler sound. He had "the deep, solemn attitude the musical world [of *Parsifal*] requires," wrote the *Berliner Lokal-Anzeiger*, "and this provided him with ample opportunity to indulge his marked, most finely-tuned feel for sound to his heart's content.... He sensualized the spiritual and spiritualized the sensual."[81] Likewise, the *Deutsche Allgemeine Zeitung* commented how in act one "the sorrowful, darkening mellowness of the strings in the Amfortas scene at the forest lake, and the austere greatness of the enthralling, soaring Transformation Music became sensual experiences which still, somehow, managed to appear wonderfully de-sensualized;" in act two "the elevation of sound to a spiritual sphere was most poignantly felt."[82] The *Hamburger Fremdenblatt* wrote of the "wonderful" preludes, "every single one a masterpiece of orchestral interpretation... those shimmering, song-like melodies and the vividness of the middle voices so often blurred by others."[83] The *Westfälische Neueste Nachrichten* reported "impressions of the most solemn dignity, of an almost ethereal melting, of a complete de-materialisation of orchestral sound," of "the dramatically demonic mood" of the Klingsor scene, and of "the charm of blossoms intoxicating the senses" in the Flowermaidens scene. "Furtwängler endows *Parsifal* with the grand lines of a dramatic symphony, the individual movements of which one could observe in the almost classical manner in which he adheres to form."[84] His interest in the "symphonic structure" of *Parsifal* made it seem more of a "symbolic drama" to one observer,[85] and to another "Furtwängler made *Parsifal* into a sequel to *Lohengrin*. He gave to the whole something movingly lyrical. The way he kept this up was admirable. However, there is hardly any doubt that the work's overall dramatic character lost some of its forcefulness through this approach."[86]

Many of these characteristics were noticed in his *Parsifal* at La Scala, Milan in 1951. It was the first time the work had been sung in Italy in German and in its

[77] 21 July 1936 (Walter Abendroth)

[78] 22 July 1936 (Oscar von Pander). A further comment – "He spreads out the score with superior calm and assuredness. His spiritual sense of sound breathes intimacy, bridging the gap between the subjective and the objective. In his hands, the Good Friday magic becomes an indescribable wonder of tonal culture." – comes from the Nazi newspaper *Völkischer Beobachter*, 22 July 1936 (*Norddeutsche Ausgabe*), p. 9, and was written by its editor, Alfred Rosenberg, who was later hung as a war criminal.

[79] 22 July 1936

[80] 21 July 1936 (Walter Hapke)

[81] 21 July 1936

[82] 22 July 1936

[83] 21 July 1936 (Karl Schönewolf)

[84] 24 July 1936 (Otto Daube)

[85] *Deutsche Allgemeine Zeitung*, 22 July 1936

[86] *Hamburger Zeitung*, 21 July 1936

entirety. The *Corriere della Sera* remarked how Furtwängler "smoothed and softened the enveloping instrumental polyphonies to the great advantage of the singing... [and] gave wonderfully proportioned prominence to the monumental palette of timbres and colours in the score, rendering it flowing and fluid, composed, elegant, serving the ends of acoustic balance"; it was "religiously expressive, almost perfect."[87] *Avanti!* too considered it "an almost perfect spectacle," noting how Furtwängler restrained the orchestra from "sonorous excess."[88] He made it a "truly exemplary" performance, according to *Milano-sera*, with "clear, homogeneous direction"; rarely had the orchestra of La Scala shown such "symphonic cohesion."[89] His tempos, however, seemed to have quickened, as Elisabeth Furtwängler related:

During the premiere of *Parsifal* in Milan, Dr. Otto Erhardt, the director, came, excited – as he easily was – running into my loge and shouted, "He has beaten Richard Strauss!" – "How so?" – "Yes, Richard Strauss conducted in Bayreuth the famous fastest *Parsifal*, and your husband used even less time for it." (The first act lasted with Toscanini over 120 minutes, with R. Strauss 110, with Furtwängler 103.)[90] Later, Furtwängler joined us; a discussion occurred. He explained that he would play the great, significant, and important passages absolutely with gravity, not to shorten their beauty. However, he would move on and accelerate and sum up things – as, for example, in the first act, the Gurnemanz *Erzählung* – and thereby the final time might generally be shorter. "Nevertheless: there, where I deem deliberate tempos appropriate, there I use them." This, presumably, was one reason why one did not get bored during his *Parsifal*.[91]

One critic did seem to be bored, however. Without its customary cuts, he remarked on "the insufferable slowness of the enigmatic Wagnerian recitatives."[92] Nevertheless, the performances were generally well-received. They were seen as Furtwängler's definitive consecration as a conductor of Wagnerian opera.[93] Three weeks later he performed the Good Friday Music with the Berlin Philharmonic in Cairo. The live recording of this concert piece is as close as we shall come to the Milan *Parsifal*.

The Wagner recordings

Furtwängler was a reluctant recording artist. He disliked the four-minute stretches of the early days of recording because they broke the flow of his music-making. Only when it became possible to record long stretches on tape did he realise it was possible to get a better representation of an actual performance. By then, however, he was not really interested in going into the studio. The most important ingredient was still missing: "the collective experience" of making music before an audience. "He was convinced that for a total success of a concert an audience is needed in addition to the conductor and orchestra.... This falls away with a gramophone record."[94] The "true" Furtwängler is to be found better in live performances when he rose (though not

87 25 March 1951, p. 2 (f.a.). Hans Beirer sang Parsifal; Martha Mödl, Kundry; Joseph Greindl, Gurnemanz; Otto Edelmann, Amfortas; Alois Pernerstorfer, Klingsor.

88 25 March 1951, p. 4 (R. I.)

89 26-27 March 1951, p. 2 (b. d. f.)

90 These figures are at slight variance with Bayreuth records, and a contemporary report: see *Timings*.

91 Elisabeth Furtwängler, *About Wilhelm Furtwängler*, pp. 75-76

92 *Quotidien La Patria*, March 1951, as quoted in Scottini, *Furtwängler in Italie*, p. 25

93 Scottini, *ibid*, p. 25. See the discography under 1951 for a note on a rumoured recording from this season.

94 Elisabeth Furtwängler, *About Wilhelm Furtwängler*, p. 95

always) to the occasion. The post-war studio recordings are generally a disappointment. Why he agreed to make some of them, like the overture to the *Fliegende Holländer* (1949) – he had not conducted the opera since 1920 – is a mystery. Perhaps he could not say no.[95] All his live recordings are worth listening to, though some of them are in very bad sound. HMV's "test" recordings of the 1937 Covent Garden *Ring*, for example, clearly failed their test, technically. Not all recordings are commented on here,[96] merely a choice from the most remarkable.

Pre-eminent among the early recordings are the *Lohengrin* Prelude and *Tristan* Prelude and Liebestod from 1930. These are the only substantive recordings Furtwängler made before 1933, when his music-making was disrupted by the political situation. *Disques* remarked of them in 1931 "Furtwängler has never done more completely satisfying and thrilling phonograph work."[97] Herbert Peyser marvelled in particular at the contrivance of the dynamic scale:

> He is a past master of what the Germans call *Steigerung* – a word that our "enhancement" and "intensification" render only imperfectly – of the crescendo and the tapering dynamic decrease. These qualities make his *Lohengrin* Prelude, His *Tristan* Vorspiel and Liebestod and his *Eroica* funeral march unforgettable experiences. And yet they are never obtained at the expense of line or clarity or the correct adjustments of detail to a carefully elaborated architectural plan.[98]

English reviewers reflected some reservations about his live Wagner performances. *Gramophone* wrote of the *Tristan* Prelude recording that it "leans rather heavily on the time, so the passion seems to lose some of its fire."[99] *Music and Letters* considered it "a perfectly faithful, restrained interpretation."[100] A much later view has considered the 1930 Prelude and Liebestod "almost too neat and dapper, but marvellous and symphonic – the young Furtwängler," compared to the "more intense, rugged readings" of 1938, where there is still "the same utter quietness in the opening of the Prelude."[101] He also recorded a soft, undulating, and sublime *Parsifal* Prelude in 1938, the only occasion on which he did so. The brass is subdued so as not to disturb the whole structure of the piece, giving it a unified symphonic sweep. The Good Friday Music, an awkward excerpt without its voices, is made into an elongated, very effective concert piece. It begins uncleanly, a classic example of Furtwängler's *sfumato* style, not neat and precise, but vague and suggestive, more like Rembrandt than Dürer.[102]

The excerpts from the two live *Meistersinger* from Vienna (1937) and Nuremberg (1938) both have one virtue, the inclusion of the Quintet – "the key to his

[95] Elisabeth Furtwängler said in a discussion of Furtwängler's recordings and his indifference towards commercialism: "Furtwängler, fundamentally, could not say 'No'." *About Wilhelm Furtwängler*, p. 97

[96] They are all considered in some detail, with discographies by John Hunt, in John Ardoin, *The Furtwängler Record* (Portland, Oregan: Amadeus Press, 1994), pp. 193-220, and to a lesser extent, but equally perceptively, in Peter Pirie, *Furtwängler and the Art of Conducting* (London: Duckworth, 1980), *passim*.

[97] September 1931, p. 305

[98] *Disques*, January 1931, p. 443

[99] review of the prelude: *Gramophone*, April 1932, p. 468 (W. R. Anderson); a similar view was expressed of an earlier issue of the Prelude and Liebestod: *ibid*, July 1931, p. 49

[100] review of the Prelude and Liebestod: *Music and Letters*, October 1931, p. 429 (Sc. G.)

[101] Pirie, *Furtwängler*, p. 96

[102] stylistic elements noted generally in Elisabeth Furtwängler, *About Wilhelm Furtwängler*, p. 32, and Furtwängler, *Notebooks*, p. 161

interpretation of the *Meistersinger*," as it was heard in Milan[103] – which is sorely missed from the otherwise all-but-complete Bayreuth recording (1943). There is more music, and in better sound, from Nuremberg. What it shows is how much Furtwängler excels in the scenes of contemplation and love, like Sach's *Fliedermonolog* and the first part of the Eva-Sachs scene. It is remarkable how he *responds* to passionate singing by women, whether in quiet, rapt moments – Eva in the Quintet – or in impassioned outbursts – as when Eva declares her love and gratitude to Sachs. He also seems to create a world of his own, a world of symphony and melody which discreetly presses

Fig. 15.8. Furtwängler in 1938.
Drawing by Fritz Meisel, *Berliner Lokal-Anzeiger*, 13 January 1938

at the singers. At Bayreuth in 1943 this world is more abundant: the orchestra is a sturdy, seamless underpinning of what happens on stage, lending colour to the action. There are moments of great orchestral beauty. The way the melody rises as Pogner, Beckmesser and Walter arrive in act one, rising almost imperceptibly to a crescendo of great occasion, not volume, is marvellous. After Walther has sung for Sachs for the first time (*Am stillen Herd*) and Sachs is appreciative (*Ein guter Meister!*), the orchestra glows with warmth and sympathy, in effect, in agreement. Again, in the *Fliedermonolog* Furtwängler succeeds in the contemplative, suggesting there is something behind, something not yet quite clear in, Sach's rumination. As Sachs realises what might-have-been with Eva, there is such a tone of tenderness, of adoring tenderness, that it displaces any suggestion of lingering longing. As Eva and Walther conspire to elope, the orchestra exerts such pressure that they almost burst forth from their hiding place. Then Beckmesser sings and the crowd is aroused. Furtwängler provides rock-solid support throughout the rowdy scene that follows, lending stability to the chaos, as well as egging on the rioters, until a magnificent orchestral climax arrives as Sachs stretches out and stops the elopement. Act three opens with a profoundly meditative prelude, and the mood extends into Sach's *Wahnmonolog*. The orchestra pulls at him as he "digs into his own flesh" before a magical transition to serenity (*Ein Kobold half wohl da!* –

[103] *Milano-sera*, 2 March 1952, p. 3 (b. d. f.)

"a goblin must have helped"). The orchestra seems to take deep breaths of glorious morning air before Walther sings his *Morgenlich leuchtend.* It breaks into glory when Eva spots Walter dressed in his glittering apparel. And at the end of his demonstration song (*Huldreichistes Bild*) the orchestra swells in glory, spelling the end of any illusion that anyone but Walther is destined to be Eva's husband. Act three ends in a sacred *Wach auf!* and monologue from Sachs. Everyone is clearly engaged in a holy activity – honouring art. Walther's final song is glorious, without being triumphant, and finds its apotheosis in Sach's final *Verachtet mir die Meister nicht.* The orchestra is warm and ever-present. It is like a universe in which everything else takes part. The ending is both a celebration and an affirmation. In this great, moving war-time performance, Furtwängler gives everyone of his best. Or to paraphrase Nietzsche, he gives them art lest they perish of the truth.

The live performances of *Tristan* – excerpts from 1931, 1941, 1943, and 1947 – are more interesting in some respects than the famous complete studio version. They are more lively, a benefit of the "communal experience" Furtwängler so valued. The first notable feature is their subdued mood and smooth edges. There are huge orchestral waves, with deep swells that never break, and dark, violent rumblings from volcanoes that never erupt. The effect is quite other-worldly. A second feature is that, for Furtwängler, the heart of the opera clearly lay in the love duet in act two, including Brangäne's warning. This scene is made the heart of the work by the pressure of beauty he draws from the orchestra. The singers and the orchestra are equal partners in Furtwängler's conception. This can make it difficult for the singers sometimes because the orchestra is large. One result of the smoothness is that some dramatic points are under-stated. The extinguishment of the torch in act two is accompanied by a great gust of wind from the nether world, not a hurricane of impetuosity, anger or cataclysm. The whole of the transitional passage that follows, leading to the thrilling encounter of the lovers, is in the nature of gathering waves: they rise with great force, as if they were cosmic waves, then subside for the love scene. They rise again in a gradual crescendo leading to the lovers' exposure: broad phrases, rising slowly with force and with a sense of inevitability. In act three of the 1943 Vienna performance (there are stretches of lucidity and horror in both Tristan's singing and the sound of the recording), Furtwängler keeps the orchestra steady on its inexorable path; he maintains sanity while Max Lorenz goes mad. He gives the impression of very large forces at work, even in moments of delirium, forces that are much larger than mere mortal singers. There is a sense that we are observing more a display of metaphysics than of drama. Hagemann's observation that Furtwängler was "no man of the theatre" need not be considered derogatory. Furtwängler occupied quite a different realm.

These characteristics are evident in the much-discussed studio recording of 1952, a production that has dominated the market-place and public taste for many years. Furtwängler himself was pleased with it, indeed surprised,[104] though it is not clear

[104] After listening to the records he said: "I have to admit, now they have reached the point where one can make records.... I was, above all, astonished by the effect of Wagner's work ... the record is still but an imperfect substitute for the collective experience....": Elisabeth Furtwängler, *About Wilhelm Furtwängler*, p. 99. Ludwig Suthaus, who sang Tristan, said that "Furtwängler dreamed of making a recording which would give the listener the impression of a performance in the opera house, and so we singers had to sing out over the large Wagner orchestra exactly as in a live performance": Gillis, *Furtwängler Recalled*, p. 171

whether a recording of a carefully rehearsed public performance would not have been better than three weeks spent recording in long stretches in a studio. The product is not perfect, and the process may have contributed to its defects.[105] Furtwängler may have been given too much time. One perceptive contemporary reviewer, who had also heard Mahler, was Erwin Stein. He had concerns about the tempi, and "certain *ritardandi* which grow dead before their final point of rest, [and] instances of a few slow bars within an otherwise fast tempo, which, drawn out, relax the dramatic tension instead of increasing it." He gave a number of examples and concluded: "Compared with Mahler's, Furtwängler's recorded performance dwells in a cooler climate."[106] For a younger generation, on the other hand, it came "as an inspired and exalting revelation of a work which [was] relatively unfamiliar."[107] One of the orchestral players recalled how Furtwängler "seemed to conduct almost as if in a dream."[108] The music does indeed proceed like a seamless dream, one phrase melting into another, with huge gradual swells from a deep ocean. A feeling of calm pervades the whole work. Events unfold gradually. The love scene smoulders rather than blazes. The wind occasionally blows at the coals, but generally it is a warm glow, a distant rapture. Tristan's wound is deep and gently throbbing, not searing. He is borne upon cool, deep waves of sound, not crashing waves. He is not in a scorching fever, nor in unbearable pain. There is indeed a coolness, a smoothness in the performance. There is not the ecstasy, the "extreme emotional concentration," of a Mahler performance. Nor is it a Bülow performance of the kind that caused Wagner to cry "No more!" It is a gentle, tender, *loving* interpretation, beautifully recorded. One can safely return to it time and time again. And people do.

If Furtwängler had heard the recordings of his *Ring* at La Scala in 1950, he may have eschewed the studio for *Tristan*. Here, in spite of its short-comings, was the thrill of a great collective experience. Here, too, is Kirsten Flagstad. It is no wonder he asked for her for the *Tristan* recording. The way he responds to her as Brünnhilde is

[105] The long stretches of recording do not disguise, indeed they contribute to, the disparity between different sections. For example, in HMV ALP 1030-35 there is a noticeable change of temperature in scene 3 of act two. It is clearly not a continuous take with the love scene that precedes it – the grief and anguish are not as intense. This may not be apparent in later issues not heard by Furtwängler and not approved by its producer, Walter Legge. As *Gramophone* put it, the recording "has been further clarified by recent tape-transfers since its original issue": July 1961, p. 61 (Desmond Shawe-Taylor). See also the note to the recording in the discography.

[106] *Opera*, Vol. 4 No. 6 (June 1953), p. 363. Another who had heard both Mahler and Furtwängler was Richard Specht: "Furtwängler is not as elemental as Mahler was – or to be more precise: the elemental in him is subject to a constant corrective through spiritual insight": *Wilhelm Furtwängler* (Wien: Wiener Literarische Anstalt, 1922), p. 12. Whether Specht had heard Furtwängler in Wagner – he had only performed Wagner in Lübeck, Mannheim, and Baden-Baden by that stage (1913-21) – is not clear. Hans Keller reported that Mahler's and Furtwängler's "approach to their job was strikingly similar, according to those who played under them." He mentioned Arnold Rosé, Frederich Buxbaum, and Franz Schmidt: *Criticism*, (ed.) Julian Hogg (London: Faber & Faber, 1987), p. 24. Peter Pirie was presumably being rhetorical when he wrote: "Furtwängler was the greatest Wagner conductor since Mahler and Wagner himself; this is not now disputed": *Furtwängler*, p. 91.

[107] *Music Review*, Vol. 14 (1953), p. 167 (D. M.). The reviewer for *Gramophone* declared: "I have no hesitation in putting this set alongside the Decca *Parsifal* [conducted by Knappertsbusch] as yet another of the superlative achievements of recorded music: March 1953, pp. 245-6 (Alec Robertson)

[108] Peter Beavan, *Philharmonia days: a few brief memories of my early days with the Philharmonia Orchestra* (London: The Cook Robin Press, 1976), p. 3

distinctly more exciting than his accompaniment of her as Isolde. From the moment of her arrival in act two of *Walküre*, when she gives an immense, rock-leaping whoop! with *Hojotoho!*, it is as if he is transfixed by her. He is characteristically splendid with the gloomy Wotan, yet almost more so with Brünnhilde when she sadly gathers herself up to carry out his will that Siegmund should die. When Siegmund sings of his love for Sieglinde, the orchestra is compellingly rhapsodic: Brünnhilde's change of mind, to let him live, is wholly credible. When she explains to Wotan in act three why she defied his will, she is positively bathed in orchestral glory. Act two of *Siegfried*, which does not quite have the constant, lively interest of act one, comes alive in the orchestra when the woodbird sings that it will lead Siegfried to Brünnhilde. Needless to say, their love scene in act three receives the most ardent accompaniment. In *Götterdämmerung* Furtwängler responds to her fury and determination (*Heilige Waffe!*) with wild sympathy, as indeed he did with her at Covent Garden in 1937 with an inferior orchestra, and with Frida Leider also in 1938. It is a great collaboration. For all the care that was given to later studio or broadcast studio performances, there is not the zest of La Scala's "collective experience," nor the consistency of mood and the inexorable sweep through the music.

All about love

"I am no Wagnerian," Furtwängler protested in his *Notebooks* in 1936. He was not in his own estimation the complete "Wagnerian." Nor was he the complete Wagnerian conductor. He was in his zenith in the love scene in *Tristan*. In the *Meistersinger* where there was love interest, his orchestra was at its most effulgent. In his *Ring* the most emphatic and gloriously played moments are those in which he seems to be telling us what matters most. In *Rheingold* the heart of his conception is that the gold is evil. After a tremendous symphonic descent into Nibelheim to get the gold, the slowly-growing crescendo as Alberich's terrified slaves pile up the loot is given a frightening, poisonous glow. *Walküre* is all about love: Siegmund's and Sieglinde's, Wotan's and Brünnhilde's. Furtwängler's cellos growl darkly for Wotan – his gloom at what must transpire is fundamental to the whole *Ring* – yet his magnificent farewell to Brünnhilde puts love at the very forefront of the drama. So too in *Siegfried*, it is love that predominates, not the heroics or antics of Siegfried. The whole, triumphant build up to the forging of the sword in act one seems less a presage of the killing of the dragon than of Siegfried's finding his way to Brünnhilde. In *Götterdämmerung* everything leads to and is overshadowed by the final Immolation scene, a rapturous affirmation of love from which all trickery, evil, and treachery are swept away. The world is, so to speak, redeemed through love. On different occasions Furtwängler tells us all this with varying degrees of success, depending on his artists, his mood, and his health.[109] It is not a view of the *Ring* everyone will share. But it is a mark of his greatness as a Wagnerian conductor that he can convey with such compelling force what his interpretation of the work is. It is all about love.

[109] There may be a more prosaic explanation of what Furtwängler was doing in the *Ring*. According to his wife, "he used to hurry through passages that he didn't care for so much, such as the Mime-Siegfried scenes. When he was a bit bored himself, he went faster. Then for the beautiful passages he slowed down": "Frau Furtwängler remembers," *The Times*, 22 March 1973, p. 13 (Alan Blyth).

16

Fritz Busch – Wagnerian cast adrift

In the 1932 film of Fritz Busch conducting the overture to *Tannhäuser* in Dresden, it is frustrating to see several shots of him with his head partly cut off. For many years this seemed attributable to incompetently produced copies of the original footage. Then the film was lovingly restored, and behold! the cuts were still present. There is a reason for this, and it is emblematic. The cameraman's focus was on the baton, not the face – on the conducting, not the conductor. Busch surely agreed to this camerawork. For him the music and his orchestra were everything. He was not interested in the cult of the conductor. He was a "profoundly musical, frank and honest" man, in the words of Carl Flesch, "an enemy of all pose, straightforward, uncomplicated and unsentimental, a typical German conductor in the best sense of the word."[1] Throughout his career he was not particularly known as a virtuoso or a celebrity. He was not the sort of musician who would become a star in the United States. There the public would "applaud him politely for his musicianship and integrity," but did not "demonstrate enthusiasm," according to one observer.[2]

The United States was not in any case his home. He belonged to Germany. Yet his compatriots had expelled him. The Nazis literally ejected him from the Dresden opera house in March 1933. And of his orchestra members – the very musicians we see in the film made only a few months earlier – only two walked out with him. He had to leave Dresden. His natural development as a conductor was broken. He was condemned to the life of a visiting and festival conductor. What we will look at here will be his sole appearance at the Bayreuth Festival – in 1924 with the *Meistersinger* – and the scattered Wagner performances he gave outside Germany, notably in Argentina from 1933 when he was at the height of his powers, and some of the recordings that

[1] *The memoirs of Carl Flesch*, trans. and ed. Hans Keller (London: Rockliff, 1957), p. 324; cf. Antal Dorati: "He was – or so it seemed to me – the least German of German conductors.... [He] was a refreshing, mercurial man, a splendid musician, an excellent conductor, a fine, upright person...": Dorati, *Notes of seven decades* (London: Hodder and Stoughton, 1979), p. 80

[2] David Ewen, *Dictators of the Baton*, 2nd ed. (Chicago: Ziff-Davis, 1948), p. 222. Ewen had seen Busch's Wagner performances at the Metropolitan Opera. Rudolf Bing, sometime head of that opera company, recalled: "Fritz Busch was not only a great conductor and a courageous man, ... he was also a warmhearted, straightforward, kind, and helpful human being": *5,000 nights at the opera* (London: Hamilton, 1972), pp. 32-33. An orchestral player recalled: "I found him scholarly, benign and always helpful. He had a great sense of humour and can be said to have secured his aims by sheer goodwill": Gerald Jackson, *First Flute* (London: Dent, 1968), p. 127. Jackson played under Busch at Glyndebourne in 1951.

have survived of these performances. These will be enough to get the measure of his music-making, and to show what Dresden and Germany lost.

The ruptured life

He was born on 13 March 1890 in Siegen, Westphalia, the son of an violin maker. His father made him and his brother Adolf miniature violins, and at a very early age they were making music together. "I could read music before I could read words," he said fifty years later.[3] By the age of eight he wanted to be a conductor, and put up a picture in his room of his idol, Felix Weingartner. His brother excelled at the violin, so Fritz turned to the piano, and proceeded to the Cologne Conservatory (1906/09), taking up in addition, for pleasure, the viola, brass and timpani. At sixteen he had his first opportunity to conduct – the orchestra of the conservatory. He attended Fritz Steinbach's conducting classes. "I had never seen or heard a good conductor until the moment when Fritz Steinbach crossed my path," he wrote in his memoirs; "… in Steinbach, I felt the value of a conductor's personality."[4] He had a personality of his own too, however, and eventually fell out with his teacher: he refused to imitate his style. When Nikisch visited Cologne in 1908 to conduct the *Meistersinger*, Busch played the timpani. He was amazed to discover how, under Nikisch, the orchestra sounded better than with other conductors: "even indifferent musicians were carried away with enthusiasm," he wrote:

> Nikisch was not good at training orchestras; he was lacking in industry and patience. He was the born guest conductor, an improvisor of genius who had hardly his equal for the apparent ease and pleasing way in which he attained the greatest effects, of course simply through his complete mastery of the subject. It cannot be disputed that he was one of the greatest conductors, from whom we young people could learn an infinite deal.[5]

Outside the conservatory he also heard Mottl, Richter, and Weingartner, and attended their rehearsals whenever he could.

His own first appointment was to Riga as a junior conductor (1909/10). From there he went as conductor of a spa orchestra at Bad Pyrmont (1910/12); to Gotha as chorus director (1911/12); and to Aachen (Aix-la-Chapelle) (1912/18) as the municipal music director. There he amazed people by his sudden leap into *Tristan*. "It was astonishing how he approached the work, especially as he had never conducted a grand opera before. Although he was mainly preoccupied with the orchestra, the devoted singers went along with his idiosyncratic tempi, which were determined as if the work were a symphony."[6] Thereafter, his first significant appointment was to

[3] Lilian E. Foerster, "Fritz Busch mounts the podium," *Opera News*, 26 November 1945, p. 8

[4] Fritz Busch, *Pages from a musician's life*, (trans.) Marjorie Strachey (London: Hogarth Press, 1953), pp. 50-51. Knappertsbusch was the only other promising student in Steinbach's conducting class. "Conducting is the art which it is least possible to teach," Busch wrote, "and the expression 'a born conductor' is certainly justifiable": p. 56

[5] *ibid*, p. 60. Elsewhere he referred to "the straightforwardness of Richter; the insinuating charm of Nikisch, [and] the demonical power of Toscanini which goes to the most daring extreme of aggression in every way": p. 58.

[6] Otto Erhardt, *Fritz Busch Portrait*, Brüder Busch Archiv (M 3, S. 3), quoted in Bernhard Dopheide, *Fritz Busch* (Tutzing: Hans Schneider, 1970), p. 57

the Stuttgart Opera (1918/22) in succession to Max von Schillings. He debuted with *Tristan* and added forty-five works to his repertory, including a new production of the *Ring* in the midst of the November 1918 revolution. It was itself a revolutionary production in its use of projected light in a way unprecedented in Wagner's works.[7]

During his time in Stuttgart he gave a guest performance of the *Meistersinger* in Dresden. However, it was his invitation to conduct symphonic concerts that was decisive for his move to Dresden. No sooner was the first rehearsal over than the orchestra wanted him appointed their leader (to the chagrin of another Dresden conductor, Fritz Reiner, who promptly resigned).[8] He was duly appointed General Music Director of the Dresden Opera. The eleven years he spent in Dresden (1922/33) were, in a way, the most fruitful of his career. He conducted some 80 operas, and 800 opera performances,[9] including 162 Wagner performances. *Meistersinger* was the second opera he conducted at Dresden after his debut with *Fidelio*, and it was the work of Wagner's he most loved to conduct. He conducted it fifty times in Dresden (his second most frequently performed Wagner work was *Tristan* – twenty-five times), and it was the one work he conducted at Bayreuth in 1924.[10] He opened eight of his eleven seasons at Dresden with a work of Wagner. Yet in his writings and interviews, he was curiously silent about the composer and his works. For all the activity in Dresden, it is not clear Busch viewed it as the high point in his career. "It was a period of learning, of maturing and sometimes of success," he wrote when declining the invitation to return for the 400th anniversary of the Dresden State Orchestra in 1948.[11] What he aimed at were "such performances as corresponded with what Wagner demanded for a complete operatic work of art"; these were not possible in "the clumsy organisation of a German theatre. Seasonal work, which he later got at the Teatro Colón, provided artistic conditions closer to his ideal, away from the daily and unbroken routine of the theatre.[12]

Bayreuth 1924

If Busch had hoped to find improved artistic conditions at the Bayreuth Festival in 1924, he was to be sorely disappointed. Siegfried Wagner was in charge, and he had very particular and inflexible ideas about the singers, and they were not good – neither the ideas nor the singers. Busch sought improvements, but his efforts were rebuffed as merely "the whim of a congenial but over-zealous fellow." He held "about a hundred rehearsals of the individual singers" because the musical assistants available to him "were not of much use." He tried to make up for what the singers lacked "in beauty of tone and vigour" with the "greatest exactitude." The orchestra was excellent and the chorus splendid. The *Meistersinger* was a popular success. "There were moments in which the spirit of Richard Wagner… could be felt lingering among us," he wrote.[13]

[7] Dopheide, *Fritz Busch*, p. 63; *Pages from a musician's life*, pp. 120-21

[8] Gottfried Schmiedel, "Fritz Busch and the Dresden Opera," *Opera*, vol. 11, no. 3 (March 1960), p. 175 (reprinted without illustrations in Harold Rosenthal, ed., *The Opera bedside book*, 1965)

[9] *Die Musik in Geschichte und Gegenwart (MGG) – Personenteil*, Vol. 3 (2000), p. 1344 (Bernard Dopheide)

[10] Dopheide, *Fritz Busch*, pp. 124-125

[11] Schmiedel, "Fritz Busch," p. 181

[12] *Pages from a Musician's Life*, pp. 186, 189

[13] *ibid*, pp. 168, 161, 165

Hitler was present at the opening performance.[14] Such was the jubilation at the end of the work that the audience broke into *Deutschland über Alles*. Busch was alarmed at the growing nationalism. Siegfried Wagner issued a statement the following day expressing surprise that the close of the performance should have been "interpreted politically" and regretting that "such a commonplace melody" should have been sung at the conclusion of such a great work.[15] Busch was asked to return in 1925, but declined. He urged Siegfried to engage Toscanini, but was told: "A foreigner is not really suitable for Bayreuth."[16] With the coming to power of the Nazis in 1933, Busch was not really suitable for Dresden either. He was an outspoken pacifist and democrat, and reports that he might go to the Berlin State Opera had been attacked in the press.[17] At the beginning of a performance of *Rigoletto* on 7 March, he was prevented from continuing by Nazi intruders. As he left the pit, a mere two violinists in the orchestra walked out with him. ***Aus*** he scrawled across his appointments diary.[18] He never returned to Dresden.

South America

Busch was asked to replace Toscanini at the 1933 Bayreuth Festival, but refused. He sailed for Argentina, to "a new, free world," on 15 June 1933 to lead a season of German opera at the Teatro Colón.[19] He returned regularly, conducting all of Wagner's major works over the years.[20] These appearances were perhaps, and quite unexpectedly, the highlight of his life as a Wagnerian conductor. The conditions amazed him, as he wrote to his brother:

> The orchestra is absolutely first-rate; many Italians trained by Toscanini and others. Very sensitive, brilliant first violins and cellos; second violins and violas better in Dresden. As a whole, however, by no means inferior to Dresden, and with greater verve. No mere time-servers.... Many Casals pupils among the cellists. I conduct *Meisters.* by heart in rehearsals, at night with the score open on my stand, as the German singers not reliable enough at this working pace. But lovely voices.... Not making any cuts in Wagner, so the 3rd act of *Meisters.* takes a full hour and a half. I'll be curious to see how the audience reacts.[21]

[14] Busch recalled in 1945: "My life was really in danger [in Dresden in 1933], and after *Rigoletto* I was kicked out of my job, but Hitler, as I was told later, sent a telegram to the S.S. men that I was not to be touched. Perhaps he remembered my performances in Berlin and Bayreuth, which I know he had attended": Foerster, "Fritz Busch," p. 9. "Or perhaps," as Foerster commented, "since the Führer was dismissing all conductors of Jewish blood, it was important to retain one who was not a Jew. In a violent conversation with Goering, Busch refused ever to conduct for the Nazis."

[15] *New York Times*, 24 July 1924, p. 7

[16] *Pages from a Musician's Life*, p. 186

[17] Fred K. Prieberg, *Trial of Strength: Wilhelm Furtwängler and the Third Reich*, (trans.) Christopher Dolan (London: Quartet Books, 1991), pp. 39-41

[18] tamely, if not misleadingly, translated as "all over" in the booklet accompanying *Fritz Busch – Edition Staatskapelle Dresden, Vol. 30*: Profil PH07032 (3 CDs, 1 DVD) (2008). A facsimile of the relevant page of his diary is included in the lavishly-illustrated booklet. The notes, by Eberhard Steindorf, give extensive detail and documentation on Busch and Dresden.

[19] *Pages from a Musician's Life*, p. 217

[20] *Holländer* (1934, 1936), *Tannhäuser* (1935, 1942), *Lohengrin* (1936, 1942), *Tristan* (1933, 1934, 1943), *Meistersinger* (1933), *Walküre* (1934), the *Ring* (1935), *Parsifal* (1933, 1936, 1942). He also toured from Argentina, for example, to Uruguay in 1936 for a *Walküre*.

[21] letter to Adolf Busch dated 3 August 1933, in Irene Busch Serkin, *Adolf Busch: Letters – Pictures –*

Cuts did in fact become necessary. "Somehow Toscanini did *Die Meistersinger* in 1908 without any," he wrote to his brother. "But since operas don't begin until 9 o'clock at night, the entire audience was asleep in the 3rd act."[22] Busch performed *Parsifal* on 4 August with cuts, and then *Tristan*:

> Musically I am experiencing the best performances of my career. The singers first rate, the best today's German stage has to offer. Orchestra a joy! Full of dedication and feeling, with an uncommon tonal finesse. The thinner French woodwinds and brass take away all of the density from the Wagner sound. Since above all they are extraordinarily responsive dynamically, I can achieve utter transparency. You can understand every word from the stage. All performances sold out, despite the crisis. Reviewers absolutely unanimous in their total admiration for my work.[23]

He was invited to return in 1934, again to an exhausting schedule: "... a performance of the *Walküre*, with cuts, thank God, but still lasting 4 hours, and in the evening the dress rehearsal of *The Bartered Bride*! This is roughly what the work is like every day."[24] And what an impact his work had on the public! "They are going wild over *Walküre*, and the performances are jammed... the orchestra is the moist virtuosic one you can imagine. 'At night' there are almost never mistakes, despite the horrendous work the people have. An *incredibly* gifted race."[25] Soon he was rehearsing the *Holländer* alternately with the *St. Matthew Passion*, then *Siegfried* with performances of *Tannhäuser* (from 9.30 pm to 1.00 am), and *Rheingold* without any breaks. It was exhausting, exhilarating, and – for us – fruitful. From his years in South America we have live recordings of his *Lohengrin*, *Parsifal*, *Walküre*, *Holländer*, and *Tristan*.

The next, and final, stage of his Wagnerian work was at the Metropolitan Opera in New York. In the years 1945 to 1949 he conducted *Tristan* (19), *Lohengrin* (13), *Tannhäuser* (13), and *Meistersinger* (6). Recordings of broadcasts of *Lohengrin* and *Tristan* survive.[26] He also made some commercial recordings of Wagner excerpts with Torsten Ralf and Helen Traubel. If the achievements of these years do not match the fervour of his South American years, it may partly be explained by his health. In the last five years of his life he was not well, and this was partly attributed to the corrosive effects of his rupture with Germany.[27] He returned to his home country only in 1951 for a few radio concerts and recordings. His last appearance was at the Edinburgh Festival on 8 September 1951, in *Don Giovanni*. He died of a heart attack in London on 14 September, aged 61.

Memories, trans. Russell Stockman (Walpole, New Haven: Arts & Letters Press, 1991), Vol. 2, p. 291

22 letter to Adolf Busch dated 4 July 1933, in Busch Serkin, *ibid*, p. 286

23 letter to Adolf Busch dated 15 August 1933, in Busch Serkin, *ibid*, p. 292. In a further letter he wrote: "The only thing that spoils my delight in my triumph is the thought that Kleiber enjoyed a similar one years ago, though a number of people, in order to comfort me, insist that mine is more genuine. Even so, decent musicians like Toscanini, Weingartner, Nikisch, and a number of good Italians have also conducted here": letter to Adolf Busch, 7 September 1933, p. 294.

24 letter to Adolf Busch, 4 July 1934, in Busch Serkin, *ibid*, p. 309

25 letter to his family, 4 August 1934, in Busch Serkin, *ibid*, p. 311

26 The statistics are from the Metropolitan Opera database; they include performances on tour. He also conducted *Tristan* in Los Angeles on 19 April 1948. During his years with the Metropolitan Opera (1945-50), he conducted some 121 performances, 51 of which were the Wagner operas listed above, starting with *Lohengrin* on 26 November 1945 and ending with *Tristan* on 23 February 1949.

27 Sir George Solti wrote: "I believe this departure from his home and country [in 1933], which he loved so much, may have contributed to his premature death at the age of sixty-one, only a few years after the war": *Solti on Solti: A Memoir* (London: Chatto & Windus, 1997), p. 42

Busch the Wagnerian conductor

When Busch arrived for a season of opera in New York in 1945, he had a reputation as a Mozart conductor from Glyndebourne and a Wagner conductor from Bayreuth. He did not wish to be known as such. "Mr. Busch denies specialization, declaring firmly that he wants to be 'an all-round conductor,'" it was reported after an interview.[28] He did not write or speak about Wagner, unlike some other great conductors. He did, however, conduct many of Wagner's works. To gauge what sort of conductor he was of Wagner's music, we will look at reviews of the late operas he conducted at Bayreuth (*Meistersinger*), at the Teatro Colón (*Tristan*, *Meistersinger*, the *Ring*, *Parsifal*), and at the Metropolitan Opera (*Tristan*, *Meistersinger*). We shall then consider his few commercial recordings, and those live from South America (*Holländer*, *Lohengrin*, *Tristan*, *Walküre*, and *Parsifal*), and from the Metropolitan Opera (*Lohengrin* and *Tristan*).

Tristan und Isolde

Tristan was a work into which he threw his heart and soul in Dresden.[29] In his first season in Buenos Aires in 1933, it was the second Wagnerian opera he conducted. The performance was considered to be "on the same high level" as the *Meistersinger* that had preceded it, in the view of the *Buenos Aires Herald*, indeed as "the most complete" ever heard in the city.[30] "With a perfect sense of truth and a magnificence of expression," wrote *La Nación*, "Busch directed the piece in all its passion, poetry and pain, with all the intensity of feeling that moves its characters. It would be difficult to imagine a more eloquent interpretation of the intimate details of this work, of the internal force that makes it unique in lyrical theatre."[31] It was the centrality and importance of the orchestra that impressed *La Razón*. "Balance and cohesion went hand in hand and the accent and sentiment were just right. The poetic, musical life-force of the orchestra surged to the fore, adding ever more intensity to the anxieties of Tristan and Isolde, to their aspirations, ecstasies and hopelessness, cut through with an eternal and revitalised passion."[32] The conductor displayed the full measure of his temperament with *Tristan*, according to *La Prensa*:

> Busch has the gift of unravelling each note and chord to reflect a character's internal life without needing to resort to excessive sonority (so often assumed to be associated with a spirited temperament), excessive sparkle, obsession with originality, or being disrespectful. This has once again proven to be one of the most profoundly emotional and painful interpretations of this work, more faithful and personal than any great Wagnerian drama that we have ever heard.
>
> The intense passion of the Prelude brought out Busch's rare expressivity. His suggestive and flexible baton extracts from the orchestra its sound and the extent of its emotion, as if giving life at the beginning of the second act to the poetic pantheism of nature and in the big love scene that follows, to the almost subhuman passion unleashed by Tristan and Isolde, with a sensuality

[28] Foerster, "Fritz Busch," p. 8

[29] see the Strauss chapter, p. 535, where Strauss's 1933 performance of *Tristan* was compared to Busch's

[30] *Buenos Aires Herald*, 12 August 1933, p. 6 (W. E. G.); *La Nación*, 12 August 1933, p. 8. Lauritz Melchior sang Tristan; Anny Konetzni, Isolde; Kerstin Thorborg, Brangäne; Walter Grossmann, Kurwenal; Michael Bohnen, King Marke; and Stefano Ballarini, Melot.

[31] 12 August 1933, p. 8

[32] 12 August 1933, p. 18

that is not overcome by music. The painful finale also found a sensitive reader in Busch, a director who knows how to move the listener magnificently, and without overstatement.[33]

The *Buenos Aires Herald* considered Busch could have given more in the finale. Overall his performance was:

rich in detail, perfectly balanced, and full of shading. He misses nothing in the score, his reading is colourful and varied, yet one could have wished, in a work like *Tristan*, that more of the sweep of passion had shaken the orchestra. This was especially the case in the great death scene in the last act, where Herr Busch seemed anxious to keep Iseult's voice above the orchestra. Technically, perhaps, correct; but in this culminating scene the voice becomes one more instrument and blends with the rest. The overture and preludes, however, were particularly fine, the prelude to the third act being exceptional for its musical beauty.[34]

For the *Deutsche La Plata Zeitung* Busch seemed to penetrate the depths of *Tristan* less through "intellectual insight" than through the "sure instinct" of a sensitive musician:

One is reminded of the greatness of a Mottl, of the consuming flame of a Nikisch. The orchestra plays with muted passion, supporting the singer, remaining clear at all costs, yet managing to carry us away into all states of ecstasy, into all the shimmering beauties of sound. The first act is played with steely defiance, with every word clearly heard from the stage; the second act… is a lyrical work painted in all the variations of a melancholic, dark blaze of colour; the third act fades from the highest flames of ecstasy into the faint shimmer of the hereafter with its *Liebestod*. Incredible is his gift for great surges, incredible also is the length and greatness of breadth Busch offers us with his interpretation. …a true service in memory of Wagner, of sublime and gripping expression![35]

This was, the newspaper declared, a performance that would "stay alive in the memory and the musical world of Argentina." He conducted further performances in Buenos Aires in 1934 and 1943, and by all reports lost none of his power in the work.[36]

At the Metropolitan Opera, Busch's *Tristan* performances between 1946 and 1949 received measured praise from New York critics.[37] The *New York Times* admired his "authoritative treatment of the score without agreeing with many of its details." Without enumerating these details, the review continued:

The reading is straightforward, full-blooded, musicianly and sincere. The romantic ebb and flux of the music, its sensuous coloring and nuance, of a sort that Wagner attempts in no other

[33] *La Prensa*, 12 August 1933, p. 15
[34] 12 August 1933, p. 6 (W. E. G.)

[35] 12 August 1933, p. 8 (Fr.). Busch conducted an all-Wagner commemorative concert on 3 August 1933. "The aura of a great conductor's personality was probably never so evident in Buenos Aires as on this occasion…. One got the impression that the sounds [from the orchestra] never flowed from deliberation, but from a highly developed artistic instinct." *ibid*, 8 August 1933, p. 10 (Fr.)

[36] For example, in 1934: "the best that we have ever heard. His personal interpretation prevailed as it so beautifully balanced the work's romantic breadth with the powerful undercurrent of passion that feeds it. Emotional and clear, nuanced and clean, the orchestra interpreted the dense polyphony of themes with authority and care to capture perfectly the spirit of this formidable score": *La Nación*, 22 August 1934, p. 9; in 1943: "Busch, one of the greatest directors of this work, once again poured all his passionate strength and dramatic potency into this score last night. He developed and exalted in this throughout the course of the three acts, culminating in the heart-rending notes of the finale": *La Prensa*, 24 July 1943, p. 12.

[37] Of the 19 he conducted, three were broadcast: his first performance on 30 November 1946 (on disc), 3 January 1948, and 11 December 1948. His final *Tristan*, on 23 February 1949, was the last Wagner opera he conducted.

work, are only partially achieved. The opera was conceived somewhat like a symphony. It is a flamingly romantic and passionate tone-poem. A Tristan of more sensibility, intensity and glamour is our ideal.[38]

The fourth performance – the first in the following season – was viewed by another reviewer of the *New York Times* as "a sensuously-textured, admirably adjusted account of the orchestral score." Busch's reading of the prelude was "wholeheartedly commended for its transparency, sensitivity and effectiveness as all that ensued in the orchestra pit."[39] Busch conducted "with a sure and experienced hand," according to the *Brooklyn Eagle*. It was an "admirable" performance. "He was in sympathy with the singers and they with him."[40]

The broadcast performance of 3 January 1948 was Busch's first performance for the 1948/49 season, illness having kept him away from earlier work. The *Herald Tribune* wrote:

To his discourse of the orchestral score Mr. Busch brought out [not] only the essential incandescent touch in its seethingly climactic pages, but the poetic sensibility and inwardness demanded elsewhere; and even in the most impassioned outbursts he never forgot that even such voluminous voices as those which participated in this memorable performance have their limitations, and that Wagner's symphonic scoring must be tempered if they are to be heard above it.[41]

The *Journal-American* noted that Busch "brought not only first-class musical direction but the necessary incentive for the singers to do their best."[42] He made "the most in shading, flow and pace," according to the *Sun*.[43] "Under his baton matters of pace and balance were admirably established and maintained," wrote *PM*. "The music surged and receded, glowed with an inner light or burst into flame, as one had always hoped it would."[44] He made good use of his "fine ingredients," wrote the *Post*, "and out of them fashioned a performance that will not be soon forgotten by those who heard it."[45]

Die Meistersinger von Nürnberg

The re-opening of the Bayreuth Festival in 1924, at which Busch conducted the *Meistersinger*, was marred by Siegfried Wagner's stubborn insistence on his choice of singers. The three conductors, Busch, Muck and Michael Balling, and the chorus master, Hugo Rüdel, had built up from scratch an entirely new orchestra. It was a "unit of highest precision and uniform tonal effect," according to the *Berliner Tageblatt*. But Siegfried would only allow the conductors "the most minute of influences over the casting of the performances they were conducting, and there were hard-fought battles over this during rehearsals." But Siegfried was "simply incapable of making

[38] 3 February 1946, p. 38 (Olin Downes). "Tristan" is not in inverted commas in the original, as it is elsewhere in the review. Lauritz Melchior sang Tristan; Helen Traubel, Isolde; Alexander Kipnis, King Marke; Joel Berglund, Kurwenal; Kerstin Thorborg, Brangäne.

[39] 21 November 1946, p. 50 (Noel Straus). Set Svanholm had replaced Melchior as Tristan.

[40] 1 December 1946, p. 33 (John Ball Jr.)

[41] 4 January 1948, Sect. 1, p. 41 (Jerome D. Bohm). Melchior sang Tristan; Traubel, Isolde.

[42] 5 January 1948, p. 9 (Miles Kastendieck)

[43] 5 January 1948, p. 9 (Irving Kolodin)

[44] 7 January 1948, p. 16

[45] 5 January 1948, p. 24 (John Briggs)

the right choice of soloist."[46] Nevertheless, within these confines, Busch conducted the opening *Meistersinger* according to the *Frankfurter Zeitung* "with a fresh approach, exuberant in its delicate details and almost Italianate *melos*."[47] The *Allgemeine Musik-Zeitung* wrote:

His distinctive rhythms, his sharply defined yet very subtle expansion of the tempi imparted a noble, formal unity to the work. The orgy of sound at the close of the first act, the brutality of the riot scene, the freshness of the meadow scene, had immense impact, and was like monumental sculpture.... At the same time, Busch allowed the blossoming romance to unfold with an unending, flowing *melos*...."[48]

The *Berliner Börsen-Courier* was struck by "the way Busch filled the second act with a transparent magic, the way he juxtaposed the intensity and pain of Sachs in his workshop with the revelation of rapturous happiness, and the way he made transitions melt and contrasts stand out against one another." The "intoxicating climaxes" came when orchestra and chorus joined forces: in the riot scene and the *Wach auf!* chorus.[49] *Musical America* was at the festival and counted Busch "among the outstanding conductors of today. Steeped in the Hans Richter tradition yet full of his own individuality, his performance was excellent despite the fact that the orchestra, disadvantageously concealed, could not do justice to the spirited splendor of the score." The rousing response of the audience, which sang *Deutschland über Alles*, was quite understandable: "We Americans, in the same situation, would not have acted differently."[50]

The *Meistersinger* was the first Wagner opera Busch conducted in Argentina in 1933. At the performance Busch displayed what *La Prensa* described as his most characteristic qualities: "a personality that is vigorous, sensitive, expressive and communicative, [a conductor who has] a real ability to inspire his subordinates. This was particularly evident in last night's introduction, which was directed with absolute clarity, strength and delicacy. Perfectly balanced sound was demonstrated with the riot in the second act, intense poetry at the end of the second act, profound and majestic emotion in the prelude to act three, and of course, the extraordinary energy of the grandiose finale."[51] The *Buenos Aires Herald* described Busch as "a master of shading and delicacy," but felt he could at times have displayed more energy. "For instance, in the overture, as well as shortly before the close of the piece, the drums are suddenly heard on four repeated notes, in an ironical, crashing outburst of electrical effect. But in neither case did the conductor quite achieve this effect. He took the passages a little too smoothly."[52] Perhaps this is what *Deutsche La Plata Zeitung* referred to when it said

[46] *Berliner Tageblatt*, 1 August 1924 (Adolf Aber), in Susanna Großmann-Vendrey, *Bayreuth in der deutschen Presse*, Vol. 3,2 (Regensburg: Bosse, 1983), p. 181. The singers included Hermann Weil, Sachs; Karl Clewing, Walther; Lilly Hafgren, Eva; Hanns Beer, David; and Heinrich Schultz, Beckmesser.

[47] 3 August 1924 (Karl Holl), in Großmann-Vendrey, *ibid*, Vol. 3,2, p. 186. The *New York Times* music critic, Olin Downes, was at the Festival, but his report (24 July 1924, p. 7) did not mention Busch; an Associated Press report did mention the conductor, but said nothing about the performance other than the nationalistic demonstration at the end: *ibid*, 23 July 1924, p. 15.

[48] *Allgemeine Musik-Zeitung* 51 (1924), S. 611, quoted in Dopheide, *Fritz Busch*, p. 97

[49] *Berliner Börsen-Courier*, late July 1924 (clipping in the Richard Wagner Museum, Bayreuth)

[50] 16 August 1924, pp. 1, 3, 18 (Maurice Halperson, who had attended the first Bayreuth Festival as well as six others)

[51] 9 August 1933, p. 17

[52] 9 August 1933, p. 9 (W. E. G.). August Seider sang Walther; Edith Fleischer, Eva; Walter Grossmann,

that with Busch one hears and feels "none of the extremes," yet "[e]very individual voice is heard. Every word sung can be understood – a subtle subordination of the orchestra to the stage, with the most radiant happiness of sound. Sparkling merriment and darkest grief at a moment's notice. Any dragging-out of over-long tempos and monotony of expression is avoided." What was particularly striking were the "agogic finesses":

> i.e. those small and minute changes in tempo which in keeping with dynamic shadings continuously redesign the expression of a phrase, and provide it with highlights full of nuances.... Busch... generally applies those principles which [Hugo] Riemann called "agogic accumulation": the deliberate delaying of driving and surging sections, which make the eventual surge so much more powerful. For example, the arrangement of the "riot" fugue at the end of the second act, and the extraordinary design of Sachs's speech on the festival meadow.... From the chamber music of the first act, which Busch renders as a comic-baroque show, to the character of the second act, which is as lyrically soulful as it is theatrically merry, the great transition occurs. It is beautifully crowned by the melodic stream of the Quintet and the festival meadow's jubilation.[53]

La Razón was struck by the restraint Busch showed with the orchestra:

> Busch clearly understood that the libretto had as much a right as the music to reach the ears of his listeners and ensured that the orchestra did not drown out the voices. This same orchestra was clear and balanced and either subtly supported the singers or gently enveloped them, creating the sweetest sound. They also lifted their sound at the appropriate moments, to be incisive and majestic for example in the magnificent prelude, or to accentuate Sach's deep but simple goodness, his manners and generosity. In this way, they also created the fantastic poetry of St. John's night, and perfected the "ecstasy of happiness" that represents the very beauty and soul of the glorious Quintet.[54]

The next *Meistersinger* performances Busch gave were with the Metropolitan Opera in 1947/48. His first, on 1 February 1947, was a charity performance, and in accordance with tradition, critical comment in the press was limited. The *Sun* considered the performance "somewhat unsettled, and lacking in mood." One result of subordinating the orchestra to the singers was the loss of "a certain sweetness and warmth" in the score. But one moment of "undoubted magnificence" was the *Wach auf!* chorus. "The whole episode was beautifully prepared, sung with a breadth and eloquence altogether uncommon. More of this freedom, a less metric beat elsewhere would have given the performance a lift it lacked."[55]

The second performance, on 17 February 1947, "started splendidly with an inspired reading" of the Prelude, according to the *Musical Courier*; "Mr. Busch conceives [it] as a real overture to a comic opera. It fell short of expectations later in the evening when a certain nervousness at times seemed to seize the performers. However, in spite of this, Wagner's work triumphed again...."[56] The *New York Times* reported: "The affection,

Sachs, (a last-minute substitute for Michael Bohnen); Hermann Wiedemann, Beckmesser; Kerstin Thorborg, Magdalena; Karl Laufkoetter, David; and Helmut Schweebs, Pogner.

53 9 August 1933, p. 7 (Fr.)

54 9 August 1933, p. 14

55 3 February 1947, p. 10 (Irving Kolodin). Herbert Janssen sang Sachs; Astrid Varnay, Eva; Set Svanholm, Walther; Margaret Harshaw, Magdalene; John Garris, David; Gerhard Pechner, Beckmesser; Deszö Ernster, Pogner.

56 1 March 1947, p. 25 (Dr. Henry W. Levinger). Torsten Ralf sang Walther; Martha Lipton, Magdalene; otherwise the cast was as for 1 February 1947.

Fig. 16.1. Fritz Busch from his Dresden years, 1922-1933

Fig. 16.2. Busch in the pit at Dresden

Fig. 16.3. Busch in the pit at the Metropolitan Opera

Fig. 16.4. Busch conducting the Dresden Staatskapelle in the *Tannhäuser* Overture, from a 1932 film directed by Franz Schreker

Fig. 16.5. Busch in rehearsal

flexibility and insight of Mr. Busch's leadership made for an integrated and warmly human performance... that won the hearts and applause of the capacity audience."[57]

Der Ring des Nibelungen

Busch led an historic *Ring* cycle in Buenos Aires in 1935. He had given audiences a taste of the gods with a *Walküre* in 1934. The 1935 cycle was the only one he gave in Argentina. Decades later it was recalled as "an unforgettable performance."[58]

The *Rheingold* was described as "simply stupendous" by the *La Nación*. By Buenos Aires standards, the audience was unusually punctual and engrossed. The orchestra, "magnificent in its vigour, colour, poetry and transparency," joined with those on stage in a way that everything "was achieved with such consistency and artistry that we doubt it could be surpassed on the most respected stages in Europe."[59] The *Buenos Aires Herald* was also impressed by the ensemble. Busch "gave a sinuous version of the score," it wrote; "all the artists sang and acted well, and each was practically as good as the rest."[60] It was "a lively and expressive" reading, according to *La Prensa*, which "with the utmost respect was sped up slightly to suit our modern tastes."[61] *Deutsche La Plata Zeitung* wrote how Busch's orchestra:

...increasingly plays to perfection. Particularly in the deep brass, and even in the tubas, his Wagner orchestra sounds smooth and elegant, supple yet majestic, but above all exact. The singer is never drowned. Words retain their penetrating power, and the orchestra emits a colour requiring the highest discipline and culture which has been achieved in only a very few weeks. The score acquires a grand line, but also illustrates detail. The vividness of the whiplashes, the irony of Loge, the graphic power of the giant motive, as well as the flowing, beautiful nature themes themselves, all have their own wonderful profile and exceptional warmth and beauty.[62]

At the end of the opera there were "deafening and prolonged rounds of applause."[63]

The brilliance of Busch's *Walküre* in 1934 was tinged with sadness, according to *Deutsche La Plata Zeitung*, because audiences could "only enjoy the great streams of Wagner's *Ring* one drop at a time," especially as they now had someone who had demonstrated his powers to do the whole cycle.[64] When that came to pass in the following season, the newspaper proclaimed: "the critics had better remain silent – or else rejoice." It could but list the virtues of the performance:

The introduction of thunderstorm and isolated showers, the accomplished chamber music-style solution of the whole first half of the first act, where brass and strings sprout like the most tender, soulful shoots and then melt away; the uncanny tempo of the finale to the first act, with its sharp rhythm, and the magnificently surging violence, the overpowering explosion of

[57] *New York Times*, 18 February 1947, p. 30 (Howard Taubman). Of a later performance, Olin Downes noted merely that Busch "led orchestra and ensemble with an experienced hand": *ibid*, 9 March 1948, p. 26.

[58] letter from Eduardo Arnosi, *Opera*, May 1993, p. 513

[59] 17 August 1935, p. 13. Jaro Prohaska sang Wotan; René Maison, Loge; Eduard Habich, Alberich; Hans Fleischer, Mime; Karin Branzell, Fricka; Alida Vane, Freia; Max Lorenz, Froh; Alexander Kipnis, Fasolt; Helmut Schweebs, Fafner; Paula Weber, Erda; and Editha Fleischer, Leonor Boerner, and Camilla Kallab, Rhinemaidens.

[60] 17 August 1935, p. 4 (W. E. G.)

[61] 17 August 1935, p. 16; see also note in *Timings* below.

[62] 17 August 1935, p. 10 (Fr.)

[63] *Buenos Aires Herald*, 17 August 1935, p. 4

[64] 1 August 1934, p. 8 (Fr.). Gotthelf Pistor sang Siegmund; Margarete Teschemacher, Sieglinde; Walter Grossmann, Wotan; Edith Fleischer, Brünnhilde; Alexander Kipnis, Hunding; and Karin Branzell, Fricka.

white-hot passion! The magnificent illustration of the scenes with Fricka, or with Brünnhilde and Wotan; the solemn beauty of the brass accompanying the announcement of death where, as in the first act, all of Wagner's instructions regarding correct performance are strictly adhered to, such as those very weak, medium-strength, half-strength and strong nuances, so that one's ear absorbs a constant stream of beautiful impulses of the most individual character. And what majesty, what self-abandonment and detached melancholy is expressed in Wotan's farewell![65]

La Razón observed that the orchestra sounded "fundamentally changed" under its visiting music director: "individual faults notwithstanding, [it] experienced the mysterious power that characterises directors of the calibre of Fritz Busch... and managed to be meticulous and incisive, serious and exalting, as required." As for Busch's style: "he creates the necessary equilibrium between voice and orchestra, where the orchestra has a clear concept of its role and significance. Discreet or dazzling, restrained or effusive, the orchestra's tones remain distinct without ever losing their quality in full flow."[66] It was "a reading of exceptional quality" so far as *La Nación* was concerned, one "characterised by a deep sense of poetry, an ardent impulse, a magnificent sense of rhythm, not forgetting luminous clarity amid the most complex of polyphonic themes.... Let us agree: not since the far off days of Arturo Toscanini have we heard an interpretation of this calibre in a theatre of Buenos Aires."[67]

Siegfried was given "a brisk reading of the score with various cuts," which the press supported, given "modern sensibilities."[68] The performance was as "superb" as other parts of the tetralogy.[69] "Busch was firm and imperious, as always, and led with the authority of a great artist who is also an extremely skilled intermediary," wrote *La Razón*, "hence there was a clear, precise and fluid orchestra which knew how to be both discreet and booming, lively and poetic, tender and majestic, as required."[70] He showed "a fine sense of balance and regard for the subtleties of the score," observed the *Buenos Aires Herald*. "His version was delicate and very expressive, and he put a lot of vigour and sound into the climaxes."[71] More expansive was *Deutsche La Plata Zeitung*. Busch belonged to "those few intuitive conductors of genius" who did not need to do much probing to understand Wagner's intentions; he was a conductor who was able to "trace Wagner's hand in its entirety, yet remain subordinate to the singer":

The forging rhythm in the introductory scene never gets so loud that it claims a right to independence. Rather it is tamed motion, power, and verve, providing Siegfried's youthful exuberance with a captivating sense of vitality. The contemplative medieval forest poetry resounds in all its unsentimental, magical beauty, and is rather more alluring and demonic than the bourgeois Ludwig-Richter way [*sic*]. Wagner's illustrative tonal gestures – the serpent in the tubas, the words of Alberich, the mocking of Mime – ring out as sharp as a razor and full of character, but are never over-emphasized.... A closer analysis should be written about the magnificent conception of the final act. It is simply compelling. Sheer musical passion suffuses

[65] 24 August 1935, p. 8 (Fr.). Max Lorenz sang Siegmund; Alida Vane, Sieglinde; Jaro Prohaska, Wotan; Anny Helm Sbisá, Brünnhilde; Helmut Schweebs, Hunding; and Karin Branzell, Fricka.

[66] 24 August 1935, sect. 2, p. 4. *La Prensa* observed that "the orchestra, although a little tired, responded to the directions of maestro Busch with discipline, and achieved rich and melodious sounds that spoke volumes of their abilities": 24 August 1935, p. 15.

[67] 24 August 1935, p. 10

[68] *La Prensa*, 31 August 1935, p. 16. Max Lorenz sang Siegfried; Hans Fleischer, Mime; Eduard Habich, the Wanderer; Anny Helm Sbisá, Brünnhilde; Helmut Schweebs, Fafner; and Camilla Kallab, Erda.

[69] *La Nación*, 31 August 1935, p. 10

[70] 31 August 1935, sect. 2, p. 4

[71] 31 August 1935, p. 4 (W. E. G.)

the polyphonic texture woven by the horns and brass, making this an unforgettable feast for one's ear and heart. One of the greatest conductors of our time transforms Richard Wagner's gigantic art into an uplifting experience in the appropriate *al fresco* style.... Busch conducted a performance of truly festival dimensions.[72]

Götterdämmerung was abridged, indeed was much shorter than previous versions, again "to suit modern sensibilities, and if this detracted from the solemn splendour of the work," wrote *La Prensa*, "it was sublimely worthy of the gods on stage. In doing so, [Busch] put the work within the reach of those who fear Wagner, and above all Wagner as he is in this cycle, with its immense proportions and a prevailing tone that is gloomy and essentially Germanic." It was in fact "striking in its vivacity."[73] To *La Razón*, "Busch and the performers demonstrated the same level of conviction and authority so notable and admired in previous evenings. Busch demanded and received from his orchestra sounds that were intense as well as light, that were moving and heroic, as appropriate. At the same time he managed to ensure the balance and necessary proportion of sound was maintained between orchestra and stage."[74] *Deutsche La Plata Zeitung* again gave us the larger picture, describing it as a performance "of actual highlights, with broad shapes and tremendous passion":

Busch adds some characteristics of his own to what we come to demand of a *Götterdämmerung* conductor: the austere severity of sound in the orchestra which, except for the unending line of singing strings with their silky-smooth sound, is well-rounded and noble in tone, even in the brass, and therefore powerfully phrased. The masterful solo horn player also deserves mention. Yet all would remain patchwork if not for the synthesizing power of the conductor. He takes the work apart painfully, mercilessly during rehearsals and then welds it together into new dramatic life of the highest intensity at the moment of re-creation. The climaxes end up anything but forced or nervous. There is no external flame dramatically shooting upwards. But instead, breathtaking, contrasting effects between tremendous pauses make for a bold, *al fresco*, dramatic conception. The building-up of the men's scene – what a wonderful male chorus! – ; the bloodcurdling oath scene; the no less powerful trio of revenge with wedding music breaking into it; the glistening beauty of the orchestra at Siegfried's hour of death; the sublime contour of the funeral music – all of first-class dimensions, beyond all trifling details, yet always with the greatest of accuracy and elasticity of sound remaining focused on the dramatic mission of the score.[75]

Although Busch conducted the *Walküre* again in Buenos Aires in 1940, the complete cycle of 1935 was the last he would ever conduct.

Parsifal

He conducted *Parsifal* in Buenos Aires during his first season in 1933, and again in 1936 and 1942. The first performance was "one of the most perfect versions of *Parsifal* ever produced," according to *La Nación*. Busch's personality was well-suited to the work. "His execution will without doubt be remembered as exemplary: the transparent clarity and perfect equilibrium, the unwavering precision throughout the

[72] *Deutsche La Plata Zeitung*, 31 August 1935, p. 8 (Fr.)

[73] 7 September 1935, p. 14. Max Lorenz sang Siegfried; Jaro Prohaska, Gunther; Alexander Kipnis, Hagen; Anny Helm Sbisá, Brünnhilde; Alida Vane, Gutrune; Karin Branzell, Waltraute; Eduard Habich, Alberich; Camilla Kallab, Edith Fleischer, and Leonore Boerner, the Norns.

[74] 7 September 1935, sect. 2, p. 3

[75] 7 September 1935, p. 10 (Fr.)

movements, and the sombre sense of emotion."[76] His first performance crowned all others given in Buenos Aires, according to *Deutsche La Plata Zeitung*. "His tempos are never too broad, despite the broadening of his phrases. His gifts of dramatic intensification and magical creation of moods combine to form the perfect sound-picture of the score." The main impression he left was "the perfect independence and clarity of the orchestra, combined with its compelling submission to the stage. Never once is a singer drowned." The whole range of sounds "remained of the noblest beauty, particularly with regard to the deep brass, which... played with such assuredness as never witnessed before in the history of the Teatro Colón. Busch shaped the Prelude to the third act, a moving portrait of aimless spiritual wandering, magnificently, and the choruses blended wonderfully into the great gamut of changing moods."[77] The *Buenos Aires Herald* was struck with how "remarkably smooth" the performance was. Busch "brought out all the shading and detail possible from the intricate score, and withal gave a poetic if not too sonorous rendering of the great work. Here and there, perhaps, one might have wished for a little more loudness in the fortissimo passages, but Busch is evidently afraid of losing the 'musical line,' and never allows his orchestra [to] act wildly."[78]

This smoothness and balance in execution were also noticed by *La Razón*, which added that the orchestra "demonstrated discretion, fluidity and extraordinary transparency, along with the intense sensitivity and profoundly reflective air demanded by Wagner...."[79] For *La Prensa*, Busch's performance reached the same heights as the other Wagner works he had conducted that season:

> The most intimate intentions of Wagner, the different emotions that prevail in the three acts, the high mysticism of the Prelude, the noble and expressive Good Friday Spell, and the perfect union between orchestra and stage – all these elements were brilliantly and faithfully interpreted by the great German director. On very few occasions, if ever, has the Christian sentiment of the score been recreated with such magnificence or solemnity. The success achieved by the maestro last night was one of the most deserving ever seen in our theatre.[80]

He conducted the work again in 1936 and although the first performance of that season was not considered on the same high level as 1933,[81] the final performance was broadcast and survives on record.

The Wagner recordings

Busch made very few commercial recordings, and they are of little value. The only Wagner he recorded with the Dresden Staatskapelle (apart from the film of the *Tannhäuser* overture) was an incomplete prelude to act three of the *Meistersinger*.

[76] 31 August 1933, p. 13. Lauritz Melchior sang Parsifal; Anny Konetzni, Kundry; Walter Grossmann, Amfortas; Helmut Schweebs (replacing an indisposed Michael Bohnen), Gurnemanz; Hermann Wiedermann, Klingsor.

[77] 31 August 1933, p.9 (Fr.)

[78] 31 August 1933, p. 2

[79] 31 August 1933, p. 16

[80] 31 August 1933, p. 17

[81] *La Prensa*, 5 September 1936, p. 16: "The score needed more rehearsal to give it the polish, detail and expression of the [1933] version, one of the best ever heard in Buenos Aires"; *La Razón*, 5 September 1936, p. 4: "...overall, it was perfectly respectable"; cf. *La Nación*, 5 September 1936, p. 12: "We are already familiar with Busch's precise reading of the work, full of poetry and nobility. It is almost certainly one of the most perfect interpretations that has been heard here."

Whether it was intended as a "filler" for the *Nutcracker Suite* Overture on the other side of the record is unknown, but it is a matter for regret that both sides were not devoted to the *Meistersinger* prelude, for what we do have is an exquisitely studied performance. The whole act three prelude does exist from a 1946 concert. It is a powerful though not particularly introspective performance. Its effect is marred, moreover, by proceeding immediately into the sprightly, gay dance of the apprentices and a rather empty entry of mastersingers who have no crowds to welcome them. Busch had a sunny, optimistic disposition, so it is odd that he did not record the act one prelude. The 1946 excerpts with Torsten Ralf singing various Wagner roles are of no interest at all orchestrally. They were evidently made to promote the singer. The performances are more a recording of the notes than the making of music. The orchestra is subdued, and may indeed have been a reduced Metropolitan Opera Orchestra. The one excerpt when it might have swollen with glorious sound was *Morgenlich leuchtend* from *Meistersinger*, but the opportunity was not taken. The Love Duet from *Tristan* recorded the following year is a further disappointment. Nevertheless, the *New York Times* considered that "thanks to Mr. Busch's incandescent conducting, this performance takes precedence over the Flagstad-Melchior-McArthur combination of some seasons ago."[82] Whilst this is in part true (McArthur's conducting is particularly drab, however fond Flagstad was of him), the reviewer for *Gramophone* came closer to the truth:

> This recording is so bad that I played it several times to make sure that, in some strange way, my ears were not deceiving me. The distorted mushy opening, the indistinct and blurred orchestral playing throughout, the coarse tone, the spasmodic climaxes... should alone have caused the recording to be considered unworthy of issue in this country.... Altogether a lamentable affair.[83]

Whatever Busch may have thought of studio recording, on the evidence he left us it is likely he was quite detached from the process, even uninterested in it: it was literally an exercise of setting down the notes, not an engagement in serious music-making. For that we must go to his live recordings.

His 1936 *Holländer* performance has great vivacity and bite. It swings from the ardent to the apocalyptic, and is everything one could want from the conducting of this youthful work. It is heard through a sea-mist of surface noise, and is complete in three acts. It is the fastest on record. A strong south wind blows it along, as Busch creates stormy effects in wind and sea through ship-rocking rhythms, tempestuous timpani, and fluttering flutes. In more tranquil moments, the orchestra *sings* the melody, as in the accompaniment to the Dutchman and Daland in their act one duet, and to the Dutchman and Senta in the first of their act three duets. The choral accompaniment is thrilling. When the girls learn their sailor boys are coming home, the orchestra whips them into a frenzy of excitement. In act three, a rollicking pace is set for the sailors' chorus, and when they are joined by their women, it fairly rocks. Their call to the Dutchman's crew *Wacht doch auf!* is enough to wake the dead – which it does. There is one arresting moment in Daland's aria *Mögst du, mein Kind, den fremden Mann.* As Daland sympathises with the plight of the wandering Dutchman, a surge of longing comes from the orchestra at *aus seinem Vaterland verwiesen* ("exiled from his homeland") as if Busch knew exactly what the Dutchman felt.

[82] 14 December 1947, p. X7 (Howard Taubman)

[83] December 1949, p. 126 (Alec Robertson)

The performances of *Lohengrin* that survive on record, such as they are – from 1936, 1946 and 1947 – do not permit observations of the kind reviewers were able to make of the performances themselves because of the poor, sometimes appalling, quality of the recorded sound.[84] What is detectable, or notable, however, is the "youthful drive" remarked on by one critic at the 1945 performance.[85] Vigour characterises the whole first act, including the prelude. Busch's resolute, emphatic conducting puts as much life as possible into the first, scene-setting part of the work. The orchestra has the right sort of energy and assertiveness for the pumped-up men of Brabant, for their charge and counter-charge, their swearing, pronouncing, and proclaiming as they set the scene for the duel. Busch creates a musical mood in which truth and justice are indeed to be decided by the sword.[86] In 1947 the build-up from the barren, orchestra-less quartet of men – their paean to Might is Right – to the orchestra-buoyed chorus

Fig. 16.6. Busch at Bayreuth for *Die Meistersinger*, 1924

[84] For example, of Busch's debut at the Metropolitan Opera on 26 November 1945, the *New York Times* wrote that not for many years had the work had "so engrossing an interpretation": 27 November 1945, p. 17 (Noel Strauss). Olin Downes wrote of a later performance: "Mr. Busch's reading of the score was exemplary": *ibid*, 31 March 1946, p. 53. *Fanfare* noted that the sound on the Archipel CDs (2004) is "far superior" to that of the Melodram LPs (1985), and further commented: "From the marvelously sustained, quiet, and powerful performance of the Prelude to the last page of the score, Busch's mastery is evident – though there are many brief cuts…": May/June 2005, p. 233 (William Youngren).

[85] *Musical Courier*, 1 December 1945, p. 7 (Dr. Henry W. Levinger)

[86] In this first post-war production of *Lohengrin*, the nationalistic, rabble-rousing lines of the German king – "Let all who are German be prepared to fight that none will ever again affront German soil!" – were omitted.

before the duel is superbly effective. The great, slow crescendo in the chorus at the end of act two as Lohengrin and Elsa enter the Minster creates an intense, heightened sense of holiness. Busch is attuned to the superb under-currents of melody in the orchestral accompaniment to the Elsa-Ortrud duet in act two where the two quite different women sing at cross-purposes, united through one of Wagner's most lovely melodic passages, and repeated after they have left the stage. In the 1936 performance Busch uses portamento to achieve a beautiful cantabile effect in this passage (more intense, more complicit, than in 1947).[87] Having Marjorie Lawrence as Ortrud may also have inspired him. The introductory orchestral bars before her invocation of the gods (*Entweichte Götter!*) have more than mere fury: they signal a subterranean shift of mood, a descent into new realms of wickedness.

The two recordings of Busch's *Tristan*, from Buenos Aires in 1943 and New York in 1946, provide ample evidence of his mastery in this work. There is considerable, undesirable atmosphere from the quality of the recordings themselves – suspicious tape edits, tiny repeats, pitch changes, a tape change in the midst of Isolde's curse (1943), and a shepherd piping through a thicket of coughs (1946) – but these cannot diminish the force of the performances. In 1943 Busch attacks with vigour. In the prelude there are dramatic changes of mood and pace, of contrasting psychological states, which signal the torrent of emotion to come. Towards the end of act one, as Tristan and Isolde's ship approaches land, he rouses the orchestra to a swinging rhythm as the sailors call anchor ahoy. After Tristan and Isolde have drunk the love potion, the orchestra is unleashed. Brangäne can be *seen* running around in a panic. The delirium of the lovers is laced with danger. The opening of act two almost bursts with Isolde's barely pent-up expectations, her longed-for and forbidden meeting. She extinguishes the torch with glorious abandon, and when Tristan arrives there are cascades of sound from the orchestra as the lovers are momentarily extinguished by glorious tone. Busch is better in these moments of heightened excitement than in painting the night sounds of the love duet. He is more attuned to drama. When King Marke arrives with his men, Busch's vigorous accompaniment propels them onto the stage, and makes the King burn with pain at what he encounters. The torrent of pain becomes Tristan's in the opening of act three, and rises to a feverish excitement during his first vision of Isolde. From what one can hear, it appears that Melchior was not in his best voice, and may have been conserving himself. If he was flagging, Busch was not. The large part of Tristan's agony is taken up and expressed by the orchestra. As Isolde's ship approaches, there is such intense excitement that it is a wonder the ship is not dashed upon the rocks. When it does arrives, the frenzy of Tristan's bandage-ripping is wholly told by the orchestra. The passion of this scene is matched by a blazing Liebestod at the end. The performance as a whole leaves one exhausted.

The 1946 performance shares some of these characteristics, and highlights some different ones. Busch is noticeably attentive to the stage, particularly to Isolde. He rises with her in perfect accord for her curse. When the lovers drink the potion, the orchestra consumes it with a gulp. Thereafter the ship hurtles to shore: to beach, if not to dock. In act two Busch produces some very effective orchestral touches, like the lovely transition from hunting horns to trickling stream (*nicht Hörnerschall*). His love

[87] The 1947 performance is distinguished by the Lohengrin of Melchior: none of his major "numbers" was cut.

scene quivers with life, then subsides, then grows to an explosive conclusion: the lovers are exposed as if by a phosphorous bomb. The act three prelude is laced with pain and longing. Busch seems wholly to understand the pain of Tristan's frenzied expectation, providing him with a soft bed of tone to sooth his torture one moment, and rising with him in another of searing pain, as bandages dangle from his open wounds. The scene of Isolde's approaching boat has unequalled power. There are waves of sound battering and threatening and hastening her ship, and pounding at Tristan's heart. *Everyone* is involved: Tristan, Kurwenal, the shepherd, even the prompter – *hinab!* (*get up!*) he cries to Tristan – the scene burns with intensity. When King Marke arrives, the orchestra is suitably combative, until all is revealed. At the end, Busch holds back and then, at the climax of Isolde's Liebestod, catapults her to the stars.

Uruguay had apparently never heard the *Walküre* before Busch arrived in 1936. Judging from the fragments that have survived, it may never have heard such a performance since. Busch conducts with the utmost energy, creating gusts of wind, rushes of sound (*Hojotoho!*, as Brünnhilde enters), and explosive moments (*Wälse!*, as Siegmund draws the sword from the tree). There is great variety of expression in the orchestra. With ever-shifting tempo and dynamics Busch creates surges and swoops, moments of suspicion, of reflection, and others of defiance, as Siegmund and Sieglinde grow in self-recognition. The compact and highly pressurised ending is like a hot wind blowing on budding flowers: they *burst* into life. In the second act, Busch makes it seem the whole world shifts under Wotan as he realises his predicament (*O heilige Schmach!*). In the third act, he makes the Valkyries wild and free – then panic-stricken. These are but few of the audible moments in the surviving material which, all in all, is broken, incomplete, and in very poor sound. As Wotan sings his magnificent farewell, there are sea-sickening fluctuations of speed which make it impossible to go on. But one does go on, for this is all we have of Busch's *Ring*.

With *Parsifal* we are more fortunate. There is a complete recording (of an abridged performance in Buenos Aires) from 1936 and it has been restored to better sound, though not so good that the hushed Grail Scene can be fully appreciated. The most remarkable feature of the conducting is again the dramatic changes of tempo and dynamics. Kundry arrives on the scene with a gallop, sweeping all aside her, then the pace slows down, and then further slows down as Amfortas embarks on his first monologue of suffering. There is a dramatic change when the Knights spot the wounded swan: the music tumbles with the bird as it falls to the ground. Gurnemanz and Parsifal step off to the Grail Kingdom to the accompaniment of grand, hopeful transformation music. Busch puts a whip in Klingsor's hands in act two, and stirs up a strong breeze for the Flowermaidens as they flutter and swing, and pester Parsifal with their chatter. Kundry has moods of tenderness and ferocity, and after their kiss, there is an eruption of revelation and resolve in the orchestra. After Kundry spits out her devastating *lachte!*, in the appalled silence that follows, distant dance music can be heard faintly from another radio frequency. Variety again is the hallmark of the orchestral playing in act three, especially when Gurnemanz rouses Kundry from her slumbers. In the last scene, Busch puts a stirring kick in the Knights' plea to Amfortas to get on with his ritual duty (*Enthüllet den Gral!*). And the heavily cut performance moves to a swift conclusion.

Late recognition

The early live recordings of Busch were largely overlooked by reviewers as doubtful products of fly-by-night companies aimed merely at the specialist collector. The 2002 release of the *Parsifal* recording, unveiling possibly the final discovery and restoration of one of his Wagner performances, surprised and pleased several reviewers. The reviewer for *Opera Quarterly* wrote: "We associate Busch indelibly with Mozart, forgetting his stature as one of his generation's most celebrated interpreters of Verdi, Wagner and Strauss. The majesty in both the opening prelude and the conclusion of act 1 is something to cherish, likewise the lyrical flow of the entire Good Friday Spell, with the orchestra responding to Busch's typically elegant approach."[88] *Opera News* remarked how Busch "brings Mozartean clarity and momentum to Wagner's most static score. Tempos are brisk compared with the languors favored by later generations of conductors, but the ultimate result is no less profound and often more convincing – notably in the exquisite singing lines of the Good Friday music and the intensity achieved in the two Grail scenes."[89] Recognition of Busch as a Wagnerian conductor had come late. This was his lot.

When he arrived in Bayreuth in 1924 to conduct *Meistersinger*, he was not known and was at first unrecognised. Lauritz Melchior passed on the story to his son:

> As he walked toward the Festspielhaus early in the morning he heard singing coming from a wooden building. It was obviously a choral passage from *Die Meistersinger*, the opera he was to conduct, and he realized that the chorusmaster, Hugo Rüdel, whom he had never met, must be holding a rehearsal. He decided to attend.
>
> As he walked up to Rüdel and began to introduce himself, the chorusmaster interrupted him brusquely. "You're late!" he barked. "The second tenors are over there! He was pointing. "Go take your place."
>
> Meekly Busch did as he was told; he was handed a sheet of music – and lustily sang along with the others.
>
> But Rüdel was far from satisfied. In fact, he singled out the second tenors as being particularly inadequate, an opinion Busch secretly shared with him.
>
> "You will have to shape up," Rüdel complained bitterly. "How can I present a chorus like this to the Herr Musikdirektor Fritz Busch, when he arrives here to conduct for the first time?" And he pointed an accusing finger at the second tenors. "Tenors alone!" he ordered – and Busch sang along until a break was called.
>
> Then he introduced himself to Rüdel.[90]

The embarrassment and amusement can be imagined. But he was known at last.

[88] vol. 19 no. 4 (Autumn 2003), p. 814 (Roger Pines): an extensive review, excellent in its detail. The recording was also reviewed by William Youngren in *Fanfare* where he made the perceptive observation that Busch repeats several bars before the entry of the Flowermaidens, probably to give stagehands time to change the scene from Klingsor's castle to the magic garden: vol. 26 no. 5 (May/June 2003), p. 190.

[89] vol. 67 (April 2003), p. 78 (Robert Croan). See also *ARSC Journal*, vol. 34 no. 1 (Spring 2003), p. 109 (Gary A. Galo). The sound restoration of the sixteen original discs was undertaken by Ward Marston and Jon Samuels.

[90] Ib Melchior, *Lauritz Melchior: The Golden Years of Bayreuth* (Fort Worth, Tex.: Baskerville Publishers, 2003), pp. 74-75

17

Erich Kleiber – Universal conductor

Kleiber embraced a wider and more radical spectrum of opera than any other conductor of his day. His renown rests on his pioneering twentieth century productions. Yet he also embraced the works of Wagner, and infused them with a driving spirit and keen theatricality. He was the total musician. "He was completely and absolutely devoted to his music; it was a great, ruthless, selfless love," wrote an opera impresario, "it was his religion."[1] Little else mattered. He was not gregarious. He did not like attending other conductors' performances. "I don't think I could sit through more than one act of *Tristan* if I weren't conducting," he once said.[2] He rarely gave interviews. He read little serious literature, preferring detective stories. He was independent-minded in the opera house, with explosive results for the management. He was a musician's musician. Like Mahler, he could not tolerate sloth.[3] He worked his singers hard, sometimes till they were hoarse (and he became hysterical),[4] but he understood them as few conductors did. He could sing to them. He knew their voices, "when to press for the greatest intensity, when to let [them] coast for a few moments."[5] And he took great pains to teach his orchestras what he wanted. For this they gave him their undying support.[6] He was an ideal opera conductor. In his hands, a Wagner opera could not fail to be great.

The life sketched

He was born in Vienna on 5 August 1890. His mother was a "pioneer Wagnerian" who, Kleiber remembered, played piano transcriptions of *Lohengrin* and *Tristan* at home though she died when he was only six.[7] His father died the year before.

[1] David Webster, "Kleiber: An Appreciation," *Tempo*, New Ser., No. 39 (Spring 1956), p. 5

[2] John Russell, *Erich Kleiber: A Memoir* (London: André Deutsch, 1957), pp. 155-58; also Richard Temple Savage, "Erich Kleiber 1890-1956," *Opera*, April 1954, pp. 221-22

[3] Blaukopf, Kurt, *Great conductors*, (trans.) Miriam Blaukopf (London: Arco, 1955), p. 97

[4] Frida Leider, *Playing my part*, (trans.) Charles Osborne (London: Calder and Boyars, 1966), pp. 71, 74

[5] Russell, *Erich Kleiber*, p. 153; "Kleiber was pre-eminently a teacher, and the first thing he set out to teach was that idleness and slovenliness have no place at all in the life of an artist." (p. 155)

[6] Thomas A. Russell, "Erich Kleiber: from an Orchestral Player's Point of View," *Musical Opinion*, February, 1938, pp. 404-5; Richard Temple Savage, *A Voice From The Pit: Reminiscences of an Orchestral Musician* (Newton Abbot: David & Charles, 1988), pp. 58, 128, 140, 170; Malcolm Tillis, *Chords and Discords: The Life of an Orchestral Musician* (London: Phoenix House, 1960), p. 136

[7] Russell, *Erich Kleiber*, p. 21

The little boy went off to live with his grandfather in Prague for a few years, then returned to Vienna in 1900 to live with an aunt in a house near the Volksoper. It was a poor family. There was no piano at home. Kleiber took violin lessons, and played chamber music, but his real musical education was in the opera house. There were "three supreme revelations" in his musical life, he used to say, "Moments when I said to myself '*Now* I could die, and regret nothing.'" One of these was his first hearing of the prelude to act one of *Lohengrin*.[8] It is doubtful that it was conducted by Mahler, who was director at the Vienna Opera at the time, for he had given up conducting the work after the 1899/1900 season.[9] Mahler was nevertheless a decisive influence on the young Kleiber. It was hearing Mahler conduct his *Sixth Symphony* in Vienna on 4 January 1907 that made him want to become a conductor.[10] However, it was only near the end of Mahler's time at the Vienna Opera (1907) that Kleiber regularly bought standing-room tickets to hear him conduct opera. What Mahler conducted during his last two seasons was mostly Mozart (*Magic Flute*, *Marriage of Figaro*, *Don Giovanni*, *Così fan tutte*, *Abduction from the Seraglio*), *Fidelio* and *Iphigenie in Aulis*. The only Wagner operas he led were *Walküre* and *Tristan*. By 1907 Kleiber was in his "*Tristan* period" – as he described it: "the immeasurable, untakeable *Tristan*, which makes one feel like the thousandth part of an atom."[11]

In July 1908 he left Vienna and, "for all practical purposes, he never returned there."[12] He did do so on a few occasions. In 1928 he conducted the Vienna Philharmonic's first performance of Mahler's *Fourth Symphony*. The *Musical Times* reported: "He represents the modern type of 'nervous,' analytical conductor that Mahler inaugurated... He is a conductor laden with energy and concentration, a great leader gifted with a magnetism that extends to orchestra and hearers alike, and brought the home-comer a tremendous success."[13] The only opera he conducted in Vienna was *Rosenkavalier*, in 1951. He was not at heart a Viennese. He once said, "People ask me why I never conduct in Vienna. The answer's quite simple: because I come from there."[14]

In Prague (1908/12) he studied art and history at university and took some conducting lessons at the conservatory. These amused him, but he did not really value them.[15] His real education was again in the theatre, watching productions and rehearsals. In only a few months he had heard *Meistersinger*, *Lohengrin* and *Siegfried* at Angelo Neumann's German Theatre. The first rehearsal he attended was of *Rheingold*: "as he watched the conductor, he noted that his beat was not quite precise, that he never helped or corrected the singers, and that there was an air of making-do about

[8] *ibid*, p. 26. The others were the overture to Lortzing's, *Waffenschmied* and the last-act trio in Strauss's *Rosenkavalier*. Mahler conducted four performances only of *Waffenschmied*, in 1903/04. Kleiber had left Vienna before the premiere of *Rosenkavalier* there on 8 April 1911 under the direction of Franz Schalk. (Mahler never conducted it; he died on 18 May 1911.)

[9] Franz Willnauer, *Gustav Mahler und die Wiener Oper* (Wien-München: Jugend und Volk, 1979), p. 273

[10] Russell says this was "towards the end of 1906" (p. 28). However, Mahler only conducted it once in Vienna, on the date above.

[11] Russell, *ibid*, p. 29

[12] *ibid*, p. 29. During the currency crisis in Germany in 1923, he returned to conduct some concerts with the Vienna Philharmonic: *Musical Times*, 1 November 1923, p. 802.

[13] 1 February 1928, p. 173 (Paul Bechert)

[14] quoted in Mark Audus, "Erich Kleiber (1890-1956) Free Radical," *Gramophone*, August 2002, p. 36

[15] Georg Freund, *Erich Kleiber, artista luchador* (Montevideo: The Author, 1940) (an "authorised" biographical study), p. 12

the whole proceedings. 'Well,' he said to himself, 'I could certainly do better than that.'"[16] Thereafter he attended rehearsals regularly. One day Neumann spotted him and asked him to help out with the final scene of *Götterdämmerung*. By 1911 he was assisting in chorus rehearsals, coaching singers in minor roles, accompanying them, spending his meagre savings on scores of *Lohengrin* and *Tristan*, and quietly establishing a reputation. He was invited to conduct in Darmstadt in October 1911. On the strength of his performance, he was offered a three-year contract as third conductor. He accepted, and stayed till 1919. One of the first things he did was to send for a photograph of Mahler, "that dazzling example, most – most – *most* venerated Mahler, to remind me of wonderful evenings in the Vienna *Stehplätze*."[17]

One of his most striking experiences was the visit of Nikisch in 1913 to conduct *Tristan* at the Darmstadt Spring Festival.[18] In addition to Mahler and Nikisch, Kleiber greatly admired Toscanini, and Hans von Bülow whom he had never heard, but whose visiting card, autographed for Kleiber by Bülow's widow, he carried about in his wallet as a lucky charm.[19] During Kleiber's seven years at Darmstadt Felix Weingartner was the General Music Director. One of Kleiber's tours was to take the Darmstadt Opera company to Bucharest for a performance of *Lohengrin*. In 1919 he was appointed first conductor at Barmen-Elberfeld (1919/21). Nikisch wrote to congratulate him: "What shall *I* do in Darmstadt without Kleiber?"[20] Thereafter he went to Düsseldorf (1921/22), to Mannheim (1922/23) where he gave a particularly triumphant *Meistersinger*,[21] and then to Berlin (1923/35).

Kleiber's Berlin years were his most renowned. His appointment had at first attracted hostility in the press – Bruno Walter and Otto Klemperer had been "overlooked" – but the public liked him. He made his debut with *Fidelio* as a trial for appointment as General Music Director. Frida Leider was among the singers, and recalled:

> Early on in rehearsals a great deal of controversy sprang up among the singers, for Kleiber's way of conducting was all his own, and not everyone could follow him. For my part I found the rehearsals most interesting; Kleiber was a musician of strong temperament and great vitality. The production, which he prepared with great care, was a huge success and he was engaged. His greatest talent, however, lay in the field of modern opera.[22]

In his first five weeks he conducted eight major productions, including *Lohengrin*, *Meistersinger*, *Rheingold* and *Siegfried*. He wrote home: "… when I conduct, I leave it to my heart, and my feelings, and my respect for what the composer wrote, to tell me what to do. Everything else comes second for me – if it comes at all!"[23] Kleiber had replaced Leo Blech, but Blech returned in 1926 and the two "generals" worked happily together, according to one of Blech's assistants,[24] until Kleiber left in 1935. While the lion's share of Wagner fell to Blech, Kleiber ventured into new works.

[16] Russell, *Erich Kleiber*, p. 36. This story was also told by Freund, who wrote that when Kleiber first caught sight of Wotan in shirt-sleeves and not costume, his youthful illusions were "shattered:" *Kleiber*, p. 12

[17] Russell, *Erich Kleiber*, p. 47

[18] see Nikisch chapter, p. 200

[19] Freund, *Erich Kleiber*, pp. 30-31

[20] Russell, *Erich Kleiber*, p. 58

[21] Freund, *Erich Kleiber*, pp. 15-16

[22] Leider, *Playing my part*, p. 67. She considered Leo Blech the ideal opera conductor: see Walter chapter, p. 300. Adolf Weissmann noted in 1927 that Kleiber was "known for giving particular care to modern works that appeal to his vitality:" *Musical Times*, 1 April 1927, p. 367

[23] Russell, *Erich Kleiber*, p. 66

[24] Curt Prerauer, "People xiii: Erich Kleiber," *Opera*, January 1952, pp. 38-39

He conducted several historic first performances and other striking new works.[25] He did maintain Wagner in his vast repertoire. He conducted the *Meistersinger* on 1 January 1924 to inaugurate the affiliation of the Kroll Opera to the State Opera. He participated in the outdoor summer festivals at Zoppot – the Bayreuth of the north. During one of his *Walküre* performances there he recalled how "a forest bird had kept pitch and time with the singer," and less pleasantly how "an enormous unidentified worm had crawled slowly up one of the legs of his rostrum until at last the first violin said, '*Psst, Maestro! Fafner kommt!*'"[26] Back at Berlin he conducted performances of *Tristan*, *Siegfried*, *Parsifal* and a triumphant *Ring* cycle to mark the re-building of the State Opera in 1929.[27] He began travelling abroad for concerts (not opera), notably to Buenos Aires (1926, 1927), Moscow (1927), and New York (1930-31, 1931/32).[28] He conducted *Parsifal* in Berlin in 1931 and 1933. In keeping with his radical disposition, he produced a performance of Wagner's youthful and forgotten *Das Liebesverbot* as part of the fiftieth anniversary commemoration of Wagner's death in 1933.[29] His last two performances at the State Opera were of *Tannhäuser* on 1 and 3 January 1935. These were not public performances, but for senior Nazi officials and their guests. It was an odious task. He deplored the cultural policies of the Nazis. He refused to lead a team to Buenos Aires for a season of German opera in 1933 after Fritz Busch's initial refusal. He cancelled a concert on 5 December 1934 as a gesture of solidarity with Furtwängler who had been forced to resign over his support for Hindemith.[30] He was threatened in the event he did not appear for *Tannhäuser*. But he had the last trick. Knowing the Gestapo would conduct a weapons search of the entire building before the performance, he locked an alarm clock in his desk drawer. They detected the noise, and forced open the desk to defuse what they thought was a bomb.[31] Kleiber resigned a few days later.[32]

Then began a world of wandering, a path that passed through Amsterdam, London, Buenos Aires, Montevideo, Havana, New York, and Rome. South America took a special liking to him. He wrote to his wife after a packed out concert in Buenos Aires in 1939, which included the Grail Scene from *Parsifal*, that "the people seemed to take to it, and to me, wholeheartedly. There was tremendous applause, although

[25] These included Janáček's *Jenůfa* (1924), Krenek's *Die Zwingburg* (1924), Berg's *Wozzeck* (1925), Schreker's *Der singende Teufel* (1928), and Milhaud's *Christophe Colombe* (1930).

[26] Russell, *Erich Kleiber*, p. 66

[27] *ibid*, p. 117; Leider, *Playing my part*, p. 110: it was "a real triumph, and the Berlin press was unanimous in its praise for my part in the proceedings."

[28] Toscanini attended one of his concerts in 1930. "Not bad at all," he wrote in a letter. This was "high praise indeed from Arturo Toscanini," according to Harvey Sachs, *The Letters of Arturo Toscanini* (New York: Alfred A. Knopf, 2002), p. 120

[29] In the cycle of 12 operas from 4 May to 18 June 1933, he also conducted *Holländer*, *Lohengrin* and *Parsifal*. The other conductors were Blech (*Rienzi*, *Tannhäuser*, *Walküre*, *Götterdämmerung*), Furtwängler (*Tristan*, *Meistersinger*), and Elmendorff (*Rheingold*, *Siegfried*).

[30] Fred K. Prieberg, *Trial of Strength: Wilhelm Furtwängler and the Third Reich*, (trans.) Christopher Dolan (London: Quartet Books, 1991), pp. 77, 158; Alexander Werner, *Carlos Kleiber: eine Biografie* (Mainz: Schott, 2008), pp. 20-23

[31] Friedelind Wagner and Page Cooper, *The royal family of Bayreuth* (London: Eyre and Spottiswoode, 1948), p. 106

[32] with effect on 1 February 1935: Prieberg, *Trial of Strength*, p. 158; Erik Levi, *Music in the Third Reich* (New York: St. Martin's Press, 1994), p. 104

every piece ended *p* or *pp* and I try not to take a bow after something like Act 1 of *Parsifal*."[33] Shortly afterwards he was in Montevideo. "If you had been here last night you would have seen what *real* excitement is like! After the *Tannhäuser* overture they got up and roared – people told me it is only at a bull fight that you expect such a noise."[34] The significant Wagnerian highlights in this period were the operas he conducted at the Teatro Colón in Buenos Aires between 1937 and 1949. He led some 66 Wagner performances: *Meistersinger* (17), *Walküre* (10), *Götterdämmerung* (9), *Tristan* (9), *Tannhäuser* (5), *Parsifal* (5), *Siegfried* (4), *Holländer* (3), *Rheingold* (3), and *Lohengrin* (1).[35] The late operas among these, and a *Holländer* (1938) and *Tristan* (1952) at Covent Garden, and a *Lohengrin* in Copenhagen (1953), will form the basis for our consideration of Kleiber the Wagner conductor.

When Kleiber returned to Germany in 1951 to the old Berlin Staatsoper, now in East Berlin, his few appearances were fraught: he resigned before officially taking up his appointment. He would brook no interference from any quarter, of whatever political shade. His dreams of a musically reunited Berlin became a casualty of yet another War. In those Cold War days, his work in the Communist East may have eliminated any prospect of a career in the United States.[36] He had an irascible, stubborn, and sometimes rude manner.[37] When he arrived at Covent Garden after the War, he told the management, who hoped for a trouble-free visit: "When there is no trouble in a theatre, I make it!"[38] He became virtually *persona non grata* in West Germany. He had problems too in Vienna. He lived in Switzerland. There, while preparing for a performance of *Parsifal* at La Scala at Easter, he died of a heart attack on 27 January 1956, aged 65.

Kleiber on recording

Kleiber was not very impressed with the early recording process, though he was amused by it. "Imagine!" he exclaimed to his sister, "you'll be able to hear me even when I'm not there."[39] In a 1929 interview he said that "we had to play in front of a big horn, with a small orchestra, five or six first violins in all. It took great pains to put on wax any work! How much effort and rehearsals to get a good record!"[40] One such record, his only acoustic Wagner record, was the *Meistersinger* Prelude made in 1926.

[33] letter dated 26 October 1939, quoted in Russell, *Erich Kleiber*, p. 181. The other Wagner pieces included in the concert were the prelude to *Lohengrin*, and Siegfried's Rhine Journey and Funeral March.

[34] letter dated 15 November 1939, quoted in Russell, *Erich Kleiber*, p. 182

[35] Roberto Caamaño, *La historia del Teatro Colón, 1908-1968* (Buenos Aires: Editorial Cinetea, 1969); Duilio A. Dobrin, *Erich Kleiber: The Argentine Experience (1926-1949)*, Doctor of Arts Dissertation, Ball State University, Indiana, 1981, pp. 87-124

[36] Sir Rudolf Bing, *5,000 nights at the opera* (London: Hamilton, 1972), p. 51. He conducted some concerts with the NBC Symphony Orchestra in 1947/48.

[37] He was "sometimes violently and decisively rude:" Russell, *Erich Kleiber*, p. 154. He was "ill-mannered, excitable and thoroughly splendid:" Antal Dorati, *Notes of seven decades* (London: Hodder and Stoughton, 1979), p. 74

[38] George Harewood, *The tongs and the bones: the memoirs of Lord Harewood* (London: Weidenfeld and Nicholson, 1981), p. 168

[39] Russell, *Erich Kleiber*, p. 71

[40] "A talk with Erich Kleiber about recordings," *La Prensa*, 6 October 1929, trans. Maria M. Dillon de Suarez, in Dillon, *Erich Kleiber*, p. 129

With the advent of electrical recording, things were different. Now "we make a record as we wish, with the full orchestra, as in a concert and the microphone picks up the sound." But he did not like the process from an artistic point of view:

It's interesting, but still very imperfect. Slow tempi and pauses do not come out well. For example at the beginning of the *Tristan* prelude [which he never recorded], after the first sigh of the cellos, there's a silence written by Wagner. It is not possible to do it on records. Instead of silence you hear the needle noise....The bad thing about a record is that it fixes forever a certain performance, a unique emotional moment, when really never two musical performances are the same. One day I feel the music in a way, the next day it's otherwise. Which is the true one that should remain on the record? It's a matter of state of mind. Blood doesn't flow every day at the same speed. A record fixes that which is versatile, the living thing.... [Making records] is no more than a simple entertainment. On records one misses the rapport between the public and the artist, that understanding, that spiritual communication which creates an emotional atmosphere, an "astral atmosphere," as a theosophist would say.[41]

A record is "canned music," he said further. "A man who only listens to records in a phonograph and does not go to concerts is like one who only eats canned meals... it's good for people to eat fresh food." However, he did see some value in records, as "an authentic document" of the way certain composers performed their own music, and in the educational use that could be made of them, for example by singers. And he believed that with technical developments it would be possible to record long stretches of music. "In Germany we are recording a lot, specially with English engineers. They're the best experts in this field...."[42]

The commercial Wagner recordings

Despite his reservations, Kleiber apparently liked his early Vox records.[43] The few, rare, Wagner recordings among them do have some interesting features. The earliest, the prelude to the *Meistersinger* from 1926, was his only acoustic recording. The performance has some suggestion of lightness in its texture, but this may be merely the reduced forces in the studio. The pace is somewhat heavy-going at the beginning and towards the end, and nowhere as sprightly and incisive as his electrical recording from 1931 which is very much in the spirit of the "strong march tempo" that Wagner wanted. Unfortunately several bars were excised. In both the *Holländer* and *Tannhäuser* overtures, Kleiber employs dramatic modifications of tempo and dynamics, slowing the music right down in places and reducing the volume to nought.[44] The effect heightens the expressiveness of the music, creating an intense sense of expectation. Another characteristic of Kleiber's style is a lighter orchestral texture. Siegfried's Funeral Music, for example, does not have the weight of fate or seem to be the end of humanity. It is funereally slow and measured. It has the rhythm of a death march. It seems to be at the one time a concert piece – a reflection on tragedy – as well as a part of a drama. It is music bound to the hero who has just died.

[41] Dillon, *ibid*, p. 130 [42] *ibid*, p. 130 [43] *ibid*, p. 12

[44] The effect in the *Tannhäuser* overture is not as apparent in the recording with the NBC Symphony Orchestra from 1946, where the timing is the closest to Wagner's own of any of the conductors considered in this book. I have only heard the first of the two records from 1926 containing the *Holländer* overture.

In the last decade of his life, he made many important recordings for the Decca company. There was no Wagner among them.[45] Shortly before his death he wrote a preface for the *Decca Book of Opera* in which he again expressed his reservations. "Opera is the most complicated of all forms of music," he wrote. "So heterogeneous are the forces involved that hardly ever can a performance be called quite satisfactory." As for opera recordings in the studio: "No recording can convey the nuances of stage action – and many of our best singers are also distinguished actors. Nor can it convey those intimate vibrations, those gusts and counter-gusts of sympathy and excitement, which colour every performance in the theatre and make it significantly different from those given on other occasions by the same performers."[46] Although he would have been appalled at the "needle noise" of the surviving records of his performances from Argentina, he would have been pleased they were of live performances, where the wind gusts and astral flights are much in evidence.

We shall look at some of these live recordings, but first, there were two early works he conducted which were not preserved on disc.

Das Liebesverbot

It was true to Kleiber's revolutionary character that he should have chosen to conduct *Das Liebesverbot* as his share of the fiftieth commemoration of Wagner's death in 1933. It was also yet another first performance for Kleiber at the Berlin State Opera. In a program note,[47] he wrote of Wagner's genius in *Die Feen* and *Das Liebesverbot*, and of their parallels with *Tristan* and the *Meistersinger*, and of how the rousing overture of *Liebesverbot* foreshadowed the Venusberg music of *Tannhäuser*. But the whole work was too long, he considered, and would have tried the patience of the audiences. There were too many repeats. They impeded the action. So it was cut, though he did try to keep the melodic flow intact. He also "lightened up" the often dark instrumental texture. The critic for *Die Musik* could neither approve nor disapprove of Kleiber's re-touching, because he did not know the work well enough. But he would have liked to have been able to form his own opinion on what the music of the young Wagner was all about. He found the performance, though carefully prepared by Kleiber and conducted with sensitivity and virtuosity, "sound, but not exactly ravishing."[48] The same critic reported along similar lines to the *Musical Times*: "As few people are likely to hear *Das Liebesverbot* again, it is a pity that Kleiber did not perform the whole work."[49] The correspondent for the *New York Times* applauded the exhumation of *Die Feen* and *Das Liebesverbot* – *Die Hochzeit* was also performed in concert – which "showed them, once and for all, to be fresh and living products of incipient genius rather than still-born museum pieces. Indeed, *Das Liebesverbot* seems to be thriving

[45] "Kleiber was no friend of the gramophone, and it is paradoxical that the most enduring achievement of his last years should be his recordings for Decca." Russell, *Erich Kleiber*, p. 230

[46] *The Decca Book of Opera* (London: Werner Laurie, 1956), pp. 15-16

[47] "Die Berliner Einrichtung des Werkes," in Julius Kapp, *Das Liebesverbot von Richard Wagner* (Berlin-Schöneberg: Max Hesses Verlag, 1933), pp. 14-16; also published in Dutch as "De Jonge Wagner – *Das Liebesverbot* en *Die Feen*," *De Muziek* (Amsterdam), February 1933, 206-209

[48] vol. 25 no. 5 (February 1933), p. 372 (Hugo Leichtentritt).

[49] April 1933, p. 367 (Hugo Leichtentritt); Kleiber conducted "with his usual skill and vivacity."

at the Berlin Staatsoper and, for aught one knows, may develop into a box-office feature."[50] But this was 1933 and Kleiber did not have much more time in Berlin.

Der fliegende Holländer

In the weeks before Furtwängler's two *Ring* cycles at Covent Garden in 1938, Kleiber conducted two performances of the *Holländer*. It was his first appearance as director of an opera in London. The musicians in the Covent Garden orchestra at that time "were physically at much less than our best," according to one of them. "But then Kleiber appeared for the first stage rehearsal. He began with the prelude to Act III of *The Flying Dutchman*. With the first downbeat our tiredness dropped away, and something like a wave of ozone swept through the house. Everything came to life again, and we said, 'That's something worth shaving for.'"[51] *The Times* wrote that "his success was assured from the vivid playing of the overture onward through a well-controlled performance."[52] The *Daily Telegraph and Morning Post* considered that throughout the performance "a powerful and knowledgeable hand was felt, and the orchestra responded with brilliancy."[53] Kleiber seemed to the *Observer* to show "a master's hand, controlling singers and orchestra with equal intensity...."[54] He had also conducted *Der Rosenkavalier*, and the *Sunday Times* remarked that in both he "proved himself an opera conductor of the first water, with not only a sensitive feeling for musical detail but the surest sense of dramatic gradation."[55] He had a mixed bag of singers – Margarete Kubatzki sang Senta out of tune according to *The Times*, whereas Herbert Janssen's Dutchman was judged by the *Observer* as "one of the finest in the opera of our generation." Kleiber did not return to Covent Garden with Wagner until 1952.

Tristan und Isolde

"If you are going to conduct *Tristan*," Kleiber once said to an orchestral player, "you need a very cool head and a very warm heart, and the head must be in control of the performance – otherwise it will get out of control."[56] A disciplined control is indeed a feature of Kleiber's interpretations, and can be detected from reports and recordings of several of his performances (1938, 1948, 1952), but it is never at the expense of feeling. In Buenos Aires in 1938, he showed a full understanding of the Wagnerian orchestra, as *Deutsche La Plata Zeitung* recorded:

"The orchestra is an ocean, the singer is a ship, the conductor must ensure the ship floats, that it reaches its destination in these unbelievable surges of sound." These are the words Erich Kleiber used to describe... the *Tristan* orchestra. He steered this enormous accumulation of glowing passion, defiant anger, surging desire just as audaciously and assuredly as he forced the dark tragedy of "blissful malice, doomed happiness" into expressions of poignantly authentic emotions. He is a dramatist, lyricist and enthusiast....We have a *Tristan* conductor who not only

[50] *New York Times*, 5 March 1933, p. X5 (Herbert F. Peyser).
[51] Russell, *Erich Kleiber*, p. 166
[52] 3 May 1938, p. 12
[53] 4 May 1938, p. 12 (Richard Capell)
[54] 8 May 1938, p. 16
[55] 8 May 1938, p. 7 (Ernest Newman)
[56] Richard Temple Savage, who played under Kleiber at Covent Garden and elsewhere, quoted in Christopher Dyment, *Felix Weingartner: recollections & recordings* (Rickmansworth: Triad Press, 1976), p. 46

experiences the fever of passion and enables us to experience it with him, but who also leaves the work's structure untouched, letting it speak for itself, with all the genius Wagner endowed upon it. The dramatic climaxes of the first act were beautifully accentuated. The orchestra remained a shimmering, translucent ocean of sound at all times. The magical structure of the second act found expression in the love duet, with the lyrical wistfulness of the music's magical beauty, and lush saturation of tone in Brangäne's call after the initial flames of passion had been unleashed. The fevered dreams of the final act, the expressive, soaring turns of Tristan's vision, the transcendental sacredness of the *Liebestod*, reached new heights. Yet still, every word of the singers remained clear, while no orchestral counterpart, no contrapuntal association, no nuance of sound was lost.... [The] orchestral direction was exceptional.[57]

To *La Nación* Kleiber's interpretation "reached heights rarely attained" at the Colón:

The lively conductor Erich Kleiber is intimately versed in the Wagnerian spirit and it is difficult to find fault with the manner in which he presented this score. Perhaps, for example, and this applies to the second act in particular, we could have seen a more concentrated sense of emotion or inner depth of poetry. But this is a question of personal temperament which in no way affects the general manner in which this great conductor has interpreted Wagner's intentions. His orchestra was clear, perfectly balanced and demonstrated magnificent rhythm, and perfectly matched the spirit of the work overall.[58]

The "musical life-force" of the performance was undoubtedly Kleiber in the view of *La Razón*. "His execution was meticulously detailed yet incisive, an intelligent and sensitive interpretation of this work. It was rich in precision and nuance and successfully achieved the necessary balance of sound. Erich Kleiber's orchestra supported and inspired those on stage...."[59] *La Prensa* noted how Kleiber's interpretation of the prelude and finale was "very expressive but with an excessively slow movement."[60]

One can hear this in the recording made a few days after this performance (and in the 1952 Munich recording). It is striking how, as with his *Lohengrin* interpretation, the orchestra is often subdued, respectful and even protective of the singers: everything points to the stage. Yet in the pit he wields a subtle but powerful control that heightens tension and, curiously, highlights the drama. The most impassioned moments come like a torrent. His prelude is very slow, and deadly serious. It is reflective of tragedy on a vast scale. The Liebestod is on the same expansive scale. In between, there is great drama. The orchestra is lively, but does not show off. His interpretation of act one suggests that Isolde's instruction to Brangäne to prepare the death potion is the heart of the act, not her curse or the drinking of the potion. Kleiber slows the orchestra right down to a deadly pace to make this point. Act two is rapture and intense lyricism, whatever the pace. He slows right down again for the love duet, providing a soft bed of voluptuous sound. Brangäne's warning is also slow and rapturous so as not to disturb the lovers. He then works them up into a reckless frenzy of passion until... they are caught: King Marke's men leap onto the stage with tremendous energy and pace.

57 14 September 1938, p. 6 (Fr.) The cast was the same as for 18 September 1938: see Discography.

58 14 September 1938, p. 13

59 14 September 1938, p. 11

60 14 September 1938, p. 18 "Nevertheless, the score's humanity and passion found a faithful and communicative conductor in Kleiber, and was particularly outstanding in the second act." *Deutsche La Plata Zeitung* noted (14 September 1938, p. 6): "He strictly adheres to the 6/8 beat of the Prelude, with no increases in tempo." The reviewer was reminded of the "ebb and flow" expression Strauss gave of the Prelude, which he had learned from von Bülow: see Strauss chapter, p. 537.

Fig. 17.1. Erich Kleiber in his Darmstadt years, 1912-1919

Fig. 17.2. Kleiber around the time of his Telefunken recording of *Siegfried's Funeral March*, 1931

Fig. 17.3. Kleiber in the 1930s

Fig. 17.4. Kleiber at the Berlin Staatsoper, 1950s.
Photo by Abraham Pisarek

Fig. 17.5. Kleiber conducting the Berlin Staatskapelle in Telemann's *Tafelmusik*, from a 1934 newsreel

Fig. 17.6. Kleiber in the 1950s

The strings create a sort of "hollow" impression in their accompaniment to the King, as if the world has dropped from beneath him. After he is done with his monologue, Tristan and Isolde sing their lines very slowly as if to suggest they are in quite a different world. In act three there is delirium from the orchestra in Tristan's first vision (*Isolde kommt! … Kurwenal, siehst du es nicht!*) and when Isolde's ship *does* come, heaven and earth move, as the orchestra throws up the most turbulent and perilous waves. In this 1938 performance Max Lorenz is utterly beside himself (when he can be heard beneath the thicket of surface noise), completely abandoned in his excitement. He acts with the utmost conviction; singing is secondary. In this scene, we are a long way from the prelude, until the Liebestod arrives, and the slow, cosmic pace returns. In the 1938 Liebestod, Isolde's voice is but cosmic dust above an overwhelming flood of orchestral sound and hiss of surface noise.[61]

In the 1952 Munich performance, Kleiber is more subdued with his Isolde. Ever respectful of his singers, this was an instance where he needed to be. His accompaniment in the Liebestod is powerful, but it is more an undertow that carries the listener away than a tidal wave. When the records of the Munich performance were first released, *Opera Quarterly* wrote:

> This is in fact a great *Tristan*, and it should certainly be in the collection of anyone who loves the work or who has had the slightest interest in Wagner. For Kleiber offers a model of Wagner conducting. Always rhythmically alert yet never driven, very free and flexible yet never eccentric or distracting, he shapes the orchestral part as effectively as any conductor I have ever heard.[62]

Reviewers of the 1952 Covent Garden *Tristan*, performed only weeks before the Munich performance, were singularly impressed by the orchestra. "Kleiber elicited incomparably lovely orchestral playing in a reading that was richly lyrical, unhurried, and free from mannerisms and a too personal interpretation," wrote the *Scotsman*.[63] The "great things" in the performance according to the *Sunday Times* "were the sensitive playing under Erich Kleiber and the firm yet flexible shaping of the drama where the orchestra was concerned. On the stage things did not go so well."[64] The production, by Heinz Tietjen, was "stiff and static," according to *Stage*, and the singing of Set Svanholm and Helena Braun as Tristan and Isolde was lacking.[65] Kleiber's subdued way of proceeding through the drama did not appeal to everyone. "He obtained orchestral playing of extreme delicacy," wrote the *News Chronicle*, "which lent the Love music of Act II great and unusual supremacy, though the prelude and sterner stuff of the first act lacked 'bite.'"[66] The reviewer for the *Kensington News* wrote, "I have not heard

[61] "As far as one can hear, the orchestra gives its collective all," wrote Alan Blyth in *Gramophone* (April 2004, p. 91); Kleiber conducted "a blazing yet inward interpretation that outclasses both Bodanzky and Leinsdorf."

[62] vol. 1 no. 3 (Autumn 1983), p. 294 (William Youngren). Whereas the 1938 recording has some very bad surface noise (after Isolde extinguishes the torch), the loss of a few bars (after they drink the love potion), and wavering speeds (the prelude to Act Three), the technical "enhancements" of the 1952 recording are, if anything, worse: an "average recording level" is applied throughout which eliminates any distinction between *ff* and *pp*. Not only are climaxes suppressed, but quiet passages are ruined: in the magical transition from distant hunting horns to burbling brook (*nicht Hörnerschall*) the valves of the woodwind are disturbingly audible, and during the shepherd's piping every bronchial affliction in the audience is painfully clear.

[63] 14 May 1952. This and other press reports of this performance are drawn from the Royal Opera House Collections.

[64] 18 May 1952

[65] 15 May 1952. It commented that Kleiber "kept the pace flexible and had a loving care for beauty of detail."

[66] *News Chronicle*, 13 May 1952 (G. D.)

the orchestra play so well for a long time, but I do not agree with Kleiber's almost funereal pace, which persists from the opening of the Prelude to the closing bars of the Liebestod. I prefer Karl Rankl's interpretation...."[67] *The Times* thought otherwise:

It is a great performance not so much for singing that would in itself call for superlatives, but because under Mr. Erich Kleiber it is a supremely lyrical performance, in which declamation is never offered as a substitute for singing and, dissolved in the flood of music that pours from the orchestra and from the stage, there is an unusually satisfying dramatic conception being realized on a plan of singular beauty and grandeur. ... There was much more quiet singing from everyone last night than is usual in Wagner, and it was made possible by the extreme delicacy of the orchestral playing... the playing of the orchestra bound all voices together in a completely integrated interpretation.[68]

Die Meistersinger von Nürnberg

The *Meistersinger* was the Wagner work Kleiber most conducted at the Teatro Colón. It was a work in which his bright spirit reigned. His first performance there in 1937 "was brilliant, expressive and considerate of the beautiful score," according to *La Prensa*. "From start to finish, Kleiber managed to reveal the minute detail of the orchestral effects without ever losing sight of the work's great Wagnerian ideals."[69] For *La Razón* it was "a singularly happy evening.... Other versions have expressed more violence of tone or intensity of expression, but none has been richer in nuance nor spontaneity of inspiration, nor more perfect in form. This stupendous interpretation captured the spirit of a race and the atmosphere of a historical period."[70] It was more comedy than festival according to the *Deutsche La Plata Zeitung*. Particularly striking were:

the comedy-like tempos, the miniature artworks painted by the orchestra in the church and "Tabulatur" scenes, the atmosphere heavy with emotion throughout the summer night of act two, the wonderful gamut of oboe sounds, the buoyant double-basses, and the beautiful phrasing and soulfulness of even the smallest detail. The mastersingers marched too quickly in the prelude, but in the third act the comedy widened, became broader. Hans Sachs's heavy-scented melancholy led to profundity. The character sketch of Beckmesser in the cobbler's workshop rose up sharply and precisely from the orchestra pit with uncanny psychology. And on the festive meadow, with bright C major brilliance, the grandeur and broad nature of the hymn celebrating the immortality of German art were palpable. This final scene grew, from the technical accomplishment of individual artists, and from the gift of knowing just how to provide virtuoso accompaniment to the singers, into a remarkable musical highlight of the year.[71]

[67] 6 June 1952 (Denby Richards)

[68] 13 May 1952, p. 2. Kleiber's biographer wrote that this *Tristan* was "in the opinion of one of our finest judges, more beautiful, as far as the orchestra was concerned, than any – Furtwängler and Toscanini not excepted – that he had ever heard." Russell, *Erich Kleiber*, pp. 209-210. No source is given for this opinion, and none in precisely those words is among the thirteen press clippings collected by the Royal Opera House Collections. Reviews for this period were unfortunately very brief, e.g. "Best all-round performance – that of the orchestra under Erich Kleiber:" *Evening Standard* (Charles Reid). Some reviewers did not comment on the conducting at all, e.g., *Daily Telegraph*, *Daily Herald*, and *Daily Mail* (Richard Capell).

[69] 6 October 1937, p. 18

[70] 6 October 1937, p. 11

[71] 6 October 1937, p.12 (Fr.). Jaro Prohaska sang Sachs; Max Lorenz, Walther; Cecilia Reich, Eva; Karl Neumann, Beckmesser; Karl Laufkötter, David; Lydia Kindermann, Magdalene; and Ivar Andrésen, Pogner.

This same newspaper remarked similarly after a 1941 performance on Kleiber's emphasis on the comical rather than the reflective nature of the work: "he loves fast tempos" and "stark contrasts" more than fluid transitions; "his orchestra plays masterfully, flashing and sparkling with great clarity," though it lacked a certain "inner warmth and calm."[72] The *Argentinisches Tageblatt* commented on the expressive nature of Kleiber's interpretation, "rich in contrasts, grand and logical in its structure and line," and it praised the "clarity and transparency" of the orchestra, the precision of the ensembles, and the "ideal balance" between the orchestra and singers.[73]

After a 1946 performance the *Buenos Aires Herald* wrote:

> Mr. Kleiber's musical direction – by which I do not refer to his standing in the pit and conducting the opera – was magnificent. More than any other opera, this is the true touchstone for a conductor. He must have conducted this opera innumerable times in his career, but at no moment on Tuesday night did his reading smack of routine. The security of singers – soloists and ensembles –, the wonderful quality of tone emerging from the orchestra are all his work. How admirably subdued he held the orchestra throughout the evening, not once covering the singers. Not a single bar lost its significance, and everything was read with a rightness of tempo and nuance that showed an intimate understanding of Wagner's art.[74]

To the last, in 1949, he conducted this work in Buenos Aires "in the great Wagnerian tradition."[75] His performance this season was "a brilliant version, full of life and strength," according to *La Prensa*.[76] "[He] drew from the orchestra a sense of precision and transparency in both form and sentiment," reported *La Razón*: "it was strong yet discreet, lyrical yet magnificent, and always respectful of the performers on stage."[77]

Der Ring des Nibelungen

Kleiber performed one complete *Ring* cycle at the Teatro Colón in 1947, as well as some of the individual operas on other occasions: *Walküre* (1940), *Siegfried* (1938), and *Götterdämmerung* (1948). Reviews and, to a limited degree, surviving recordings, give some indication of his approach. The 1947 *Rheingold* was well received by critics and audiences alike according to *La Prensa*, Kleiber having "produced a version that was carefully arranged, just right in its movements and authentic and communicative in its expression."[78] *La Nación* described his version as "vigorous and expressive in the Wagnerian tradition," one that "facilitated the performances of the singers on stage."[79] *La Razón* proclaimed Kleiber "one of the greatest conductors of our time. As always, he brought into play an extreme sense of knowledge and passion, achieving a sublimely transparent and balanced performance, full of nuance and life."[80] In the recording of the second performance in the 1947 season, the microphone was placed close to

[72] *Deutsche La Plata Zeitung*, 31 August 1941, p. 7 (Fr.)
[73] 30 August 1941, p. 6 (J. M. [John Montés])
[74] 29 August 1946, p. 14 (F. M.). The reviewer decried Kleiber's extension of the customary cuts: half of Sachs's concluding address (sung by Herbert Janssen) was also cut. Torsten Ralf sang Walther; Rose Bampton, Eva; Lydia Kindermann, Magdalena; Roberto Maggiolo, David; Federico Lechner, Beckmesser; and Emanuel List, Pogner.
[75] *La Nación*, 3 September 1949, p. 7
[76] 3 September 1949, p. 9
[77] 3 September 1949, p. 6
[78] 6 August 1947, p. 18. For cast details, see Discography.
[79] 6 August 1947, p. 12
[80] 6 August 1947, p. 13

the orchestra, which tilts the balance in favour of the orchestra. Though it can be heard with great clarity and distinctness, especially the woodwind, it is at the expense of the general atmosphere. Kleiber's approach is lively and light. "He keeps things moving and does not linger unduly over narratives and subordinate details," wrote the *American Record Guide*, "... and delivers a thrilling and well-shaped performance."[81] Of all the gods, his sympathy shows most particularly for Loge.

Fig. 17.7. Kleiber at the time of his first Wagner recordings in 1926-1927

In the *Walküre* of 1940, *La Nación* saw "further proof, if needed," of Kleiber's position as "one of the most respected and sensitive conductors of Richard Wagner's scores. His interpretation of this well-known work was one of the best audiences have seen here. Vigorous and expressive, brilliant and sonorous, his orchestra achieved this without fuss or resort to distasteful effects."[82] It was "a very personal version," according to *La Prensa*: "the movements, in general, were faster than is generally considered in keeping with Wagnerian tradition. While this lightened some passages, it robbed others of their solemnity of emotion. The orchestral interpretation was expressive and clear and in perfect concordance with the performances on stage, earning Kleiber warm applause from the audience."[83] One of these points was echoed by *Deutsche La Plata Zeitung*:

Kleiber succeeds in just about anything where detailed phrasing, variety, dynamics and rhythm are concerned. But to find that tragic line and to render it tangible for its listeners – particularly

[81] November/December 2002, p. 261 (John P. McKelvey)
[82] 24 August 1940, p. 13. For cast details, see Discography.
[83] 24 August 1940, p. 16

with regard to the heroic world of the *Todesverkündigung*, which is always the most difficult problem for any conductor in the *Walküre* – to render vividly and majestically those slow but organic developments, the monumentality, the whole solemnity and perfect tonal beauty of the scenes drenched with deepest despair – can he succeed there? The technical solution is so difficult because the Teatro Colón's wind instruments are not well balanced across all of their groups – an old deficiency which again became apparent yesterday. The heroic itself, the mythical uniqueness, the symbolic power, endowing universal human aspects in tonal pictures of solemn greatness – all this requires visionary interpretation. But with merely musical and virtuoso talents, which make for captivating sounds in individual details, the great over-arching tensions are lost, and the alpine climaxes are simply not endowed with all their fantastic power. Some parts are taken too fast, some too broadly, creating deliberate accentuations.[84]

Others saw that what was missing from Kleiber's interpretation was in fact a virtue. Kleiber "frees Wagner's music from its solemn heaviness," wrote the *Argentinisches Tageblatt*, "something other conductors consider the chief characteristic of the composer's inspiration. Kleiber's generally quite fast, flowing tempos, always musically motivated, bring the work back to intense life, making it more palatable, especially for the modern listener."[85]

The surviving recording of this 1940 performance suffers from very bad surface noise, and at time fluctuating speeds. The orchestra is recorded so far forward that the Valkyries, for example, can hardly be heard in their Ride, which is nevertheless a tremendous riot, with a spirit of flight throughout. Wotan can hardly be heard at all at the beginning of his Farewell (*Leb wohl*): either the orchestra is overwhelming him, or the recording is unbalanced, or Herbert Janssen has almost lost his voice, which may be the case, because he sings with great emotion in the quieter passages. Despite these inhibitions, one can admire the very clean, strong strings in the orchestra and the way, alert and vigorous, it flows through the first act like a strong storm. The second act, despite its cuts, and possibly because of them, is quite gripping. And in the third, the orchestra has some glorious moments, as in Sieglinde's final plea and Wotan's stormy arrival which throws the Valkyries into a wild panic. Kleiber is a master of the transition, as he shows in the shift to tranquillity after Wotan's final angry words to the Valkyries. "This is a thrilling, exciting, fast-moving, and overwhelming performance," the *American Record Guide* declared, "well sung and superbly played and conducted."[86] *Fanfare* found the sound "absolutely awful," and advised its readers to await publication of other recordings of the work, which was broadcast five times that season.[87]

Kleiber's 1938 *Siegfried* at the Colón was "one of the best that has ever been seen on this stage," declared *La Nación*. "From the pit there was clarity, precision, rhythm and magnificent power..."[88] To *La Prensa* it seemed a version that was "expressive, very personal in its movements, considerate in detail, and perfectly fitting overall."[89] Kleiber displayed to the *Argentinisches Tageblatt* "much temperament and a sense for vivid contrasting effects":

[84] *Deutsche La Plata Zeitung*, 24 August 1940, p. 6 (Fr.)
[85] 24 August 1940, p. 3 (J. M.)
[86] July/August 2001, p. 271 (John P. McKelvey). The reviewer acknowledged the big problem of the sound quality and suggested it was better to go to Karl Böhm's 1967 Bayreuth Festival performance for "the same thrilling level of tension and excitement."
[87] July/August 2001, pp. 252-253 (William Youngren)
[88] 5 October 1938, p. 16. For cast details, see Discography.
[89] 5 October 1938, p. 20

As always with Kleiber, the polyphonic fabric of the work was carefully delineated, and the ideal tonal balance between stage and the orchestra – shimmering in all its colours – was again striking. Under his direction, the forest murmurs were recreated in a tender and atmospheric manner, and the final scene was fully expressive, tonally sonorous, with an intelligent climax.[90]

Fig. 17.8. Poster by Hans Jürgen Kallmann. Kleiber opened this 1933 cycle with *Das Liebesverbot* and closed with *Parsifal*; he also conducted *Holländer* and *Lohengrin*; Leo Blech conducted *Rienzi*, *Tannhäuser*, *Walküre*, and *Götterdämmerung*; Wilhelm Furtwängler conducted *Tristan* and *Meistersinger*; and Karl Elmendorff conducted *Rheingold* and *Siegfried*.

Deutsche La Plata Zeitung admired Kleiber's adherence to "strict conductor virtues":

Clean lines, logical emotional phrasing, sharp thematic characteristics, a lyrical sound-world, enchanting pianissimos, and dramatic accents of inescapable effect. He demands that those incredible parts of the work, which were composed in Triebschen after a twelve-year break, be the climax of all expression. The C major chords of the greeting to the world are illumi-

[90] 5 October 1938, p. 6 (J. M.)

nated by shimmering light. The E major duet with the horn theme and the peace melody all have contrapuntal clarity, high sacredness, and beauty of orchestral colour. Everything comes together on this occasion: production and execution, instrumental direction and vocal artistry. Stage life, the symbolic play on the anvil, the scenes in the forest and on the Valkyrie rock, all delight. The audience, which was genuinely enthusiastic, greeted the performance with thunderous applause.[91]

The appearance after seventy years of parts of this performance was an exciting occasion for anyone with an ear to the discovery of historical recordings. The excerpts were issued in honour of Max Lorenz, the singer of Siegfried, but it is equally to the honour of Kleiber, as the spirits of the two seemed intertwined. The performance is on an unprecedented level of exaltation. Kleiber's conducting is incisive, energetic, and rhythmically secure. He creates spring in Siegfried's step. The build up and insistence upon his heartfelt question: *Wer ist mir Vater und Mutter?* is one wonderful orchestral effect. He makes gusts of panic swirl around Mime when Siegfried threatens him. And when Mime sings of his evil intention to poison the young hero, the strings shimmer as if Siegfried were slipping into unconsciousness. The scene of the killing of the dragon is unusually spirited, from the moment Siegfried decides to rouse the dragon with his own horn (and what an excellent horn it is) to the moment of triumph when he withdraws his sword from the dying dragon's heart (*Nothung trägst du im Herzen!*). The pace is electrifying. Kleiber is truly in the company of Coates and Bodanzky. Apart from the cuts, some listeners may also regret the loss of the clarity in the words: they cannot always be understood even when they are heard. Lorenz is an enthusiastic, wayward singing-actor at the best of times, and in this performance he gets carried away, as the listener is carried along, somewhat breathlessly, trying to keep up with him. The pace is wholly in keeping with the spirit of the music, and the orchestra tells us everything we cannot hear from the singers.

In the *Götterdämmerung* at the Colón in 1947, *La Prensa* wrote again of "the very personal interpretation" Kleiber gave to some parts. He "directed a version of the score that was vigorous, brilliant and filled with emotion. The final act, in particular, reached the pinnacle of grandeur and human expression."[92] *La Razón* described the orchestral performance as "extremely faithful [which] in no way precluded a sense of mystery, poetry or vigor."[93] The recording of this performance is unfortunately in very poor sound, indeed on a par with the *Rheingold* from the same season: the orchestra is recorded too closely for comfort, at times sounding scrawny and under-strength, depriving it of any sense of weight.[94] This is only an aural defect, however, for the zestful spirit is still in evidence. The final, uncut, act has remarkable moments. The funeral march has the raw power of a warrior fallen (with quick "bam bams"), and less grand nobility than in some other interpretations. Brünnhilde's Immolation scene is a tremendous show, and the final orchestral part quite incendiary.

91 *Deutsche La Plata Zeitung*, 5 October 1938, p.6 (Fr.)

92 3 September 1947, p. 22. For cast details, see Discography.

93 23 August 1947, p. 10. The German and English newspapers of Buenos Aires, quoted elsewhere in this chapter, were either no longer published or had ceased reviewing opera by 1947.

94 *Opera Quarterly* noted in an extended review of this recording: "if one can listen beyond the imperfect playing of the orchestra and ignore the occasional sonic distortions – for some this is a big 'if' – one will discover a great conductor at work:" vol. 20 no. 1 (Winter 2004), p. 145 (Robert Baxter).

Parsifal

Kleiber conducted five performances of *Parsifal* at the Teatro Colón in 1940, and a further five in 1946. His first performance in 1940 was considered by *La Nación* as "one of the best we have ever seen." He "perfectly captured the Wagnerian spirit and this was supported on stage with rare efficiency."[95] "His transparent and sensitive orchestra kept within the boundaries prescribed by the composer, and was in perfect balance with the voices on stage," wrote *La Razón*. "The arrangement and harmony, in line with the tone and emotion demanded by the drama and music, resulted in a version that was lucid, intense and impressive."[96] Kleiber had opened a number of cuts, "an error" in the opinion of *La Prensa*, "as modern sensibilities struggle with acts of such excessive proportions. This includes Wagner's work, with its slow movements and mystical and poetry-driven atmosphere. However, this version earned a warm welcome from the audience."[97]

It was a performance that "showed complete balance in all details, was lovingly polished, and carefully expressed with regard to its polyphonic structure," according to the *Argentinisches Tageblatt*. "With Kleiber, the basic mood of the work, whether mirrored in the religious sacredness of the Grail pictures or in the naïve faith of the Gurnemanz scenes, finds a solemnly-restrained, smooth interpreter, while the demonic aspects of Kundry and Klingsor are arranged in a dramatically gripping fashion bound to impress."[98] From *Deutsche La Plata Zeitung* came a note of equivocation, similar to its response to Kleiber's *Walküre* performance. It acknowledged that Kleiber interprets "the mystical nature of the Grail scenes as nobly as the voices of nature in the Good Friday scene," and that the Parsifal-Kundry scene was conducted "in a particularly beautiful and moving fashion." In the first act Kleiber adopted very broad tempos. "He may well be lacking in power and tension as far as the pivotal dramatic aspects are concerned, but with that excellent orchestra of his, he not only manages to produce beautiful sounds, but also to play them most passionately and powerfully."[99]

In 1946 Kleiber was said by *La Nación* to have "achieved a most lively performance from the orchestra in the great Wagnerian tradition."[100] The version was, to *La Prensa*, one that was "considerate, sensitive and faithful, although some movements were slightly too slow."[101] "Once again," wrote the *Argentinisches Tageblatt*, Kleiber "managed to give a performance that was brilliantly balanced, carefully detailed in its polyphonic structure, and in which all details were lovingly and carefully finished. Thanks to his intelligent immersion in the spirit of the different worlds, he knew how to express the disparity between them credibly."[102] Although fragments from one of these performances from 1946 are on record, we must await a more reliable recording from this season (if one exists) before being able to tell how Kleiber conducted the work. The studio recording of the Prelude and Good Friday Music from the same year suffers from the acoustic of the NBC radio studio, yet it is a vigorous rendering, with its share of reverent, hushed passages.

95 21 September 1940, p. 12
96 21 September 1940, p. 13
97 21 September 1940, p. 16
98 21 September 1940, p. 3
99 21 September 1940, p. 6 (Fr.)
100 18 September 1946, p. 10
101 18 September 1946, p. 16
102 17 September 1946, p. 4

Swan song

In 1953 Kleiber conducted a complete *Ring* cycle in Rome. It was broadcast but appears to have been "irretrievably lost."[103] A *Lohengrin* from Copenhagen in the same year is a different affair. Excerpts came into the public domain only in 2005, and quite unexpectedly.[104] They come from a superb performance – all the important passages in the opera are intact – and show Kleiber to be the perfect accompanist and creator of atmosphere. The prelude grows from exquisitely shimmering strings to a tightly controlled, explosive climax, disturbed only by the sound of people walking about, possibly behind the curtain, possibly latecomers. Kleiber creates a hushed, magical atmosphere as Elsa enters. Indeed, the way he restrains the orchestra throughout makes it a delicate, floating, ethereal presence throughout the drama. The atmosphere can be powerful. When Lohengrin first approaches, the orchestra, subdued but spacious, suggests both excitement and relief. The hushed opening of act two creates a presentiment of evil. It is as if the orchestra is spellbound by Ortrud: even at her ferocious invocation it does not overwhelm her. Act three is complete and opens with hushed choruses. At the beginning of scene three it rises to rousing pageantry, reaching its height as the heralds trumpet the arrival of the king, but not so brashly as to puncture the whole conception of other-worldliness. The orchestra is so eloquent in this performance, in the most subtle and delicate ways, that it almost disproves Wagner's dictum that the words must be heard and be understood. They can certainly be heard, but unless the listener understands Danish, it falls to the orchestra to tell the tale. And what a wonderful tale it is under the baton of Kleiber! It makes one yearn for further manna of this kind. Assuredly, somewhere, it exists.

103 César A. Dillon, *Erich Kleiber: A Discography* (Buenos Aires: Ediciones Tres Tiempos, 1990), p. 61

104 The *Lohengrin* is not included among the unpublished recordings listed by Dillon, but there is mention of a (still) unpublished *Meistersinger* from the Teatro Colón in 1949.

Part VIII

Late Pickings

18

Hans Knappertsbusch - Heavy-weight of Bayreuth

There was "something of the breaths of Olympian air" surrounding Hans Knappertsbusch, one of his great singers, Hans Hotter, recalled.[1] The conductor was physically huge and severe. He conducted with the force of his personality, not through careful cultivation. One moment he would listlessly glide through the bar lines. At another he would deftly turn "a *pianissimo* into a *fortissimo* simply by lifting his cuff link." At yet another he would stand up and the orchestra would almost blow the roof off.[2] He was immensely popular in Munich, Vienna and Bayreuth. He was a people's conductor. He eschewed the intellectual life: he loved good food and wine, a game of cards, a quip, and a crude joke. He was unsparing in his comments on his colleagues.[3] He was fiercely independent, and paid a price for it, but eventually accommodated himself to the politics of 1933-45. After the war, he rose to become the champion of Bayreuth from 1951 to his death in 1964. Yet there were mists that hung over his musicianship. Not everyone liked his heavy-going style. His qualities belonged more to Valhalla than to Olympus. He was a chosen hero for the Green Hill. There he told of the fate of the gods in *Götterdämmerung* with dark force. And there he performed the solemn ritual of *Parsifal* with holy rapture. His name, above all, will forever be associated with these works.

[1] Hans Hotter, "Hans Knappertsbusch 1888-1965 In Memoriam," *Opera*, vol. 17 no. 1 (January 1966), p. 20

[2] "listlessly glide": Günther von Noé, "Erinnerungen an Hans Knappertsbusch," *Das Orchester*, vol. 37 (October, 1989), p. 978; "lifting his cuff link": Erich Kleiber quoted in Rudolf Betz and Walter Panofsky, *Knappertsbusch* (Ingolstadt: Verlag Donau Kurier, [1958]), p. 41; attributed to "the commentator Erich Deiber" in David Patmore, "'Kna': Giant, general and gentleman," *International Classical Record Collector*, vol. 4 (Autumn 1998), p. 19; "blow the roof off": Richard Temple Savage, *A Voice From The Pit: Reminiscences of an Orchestral Musician* (Newton Abbot: David & Charles, 1988), p. 53

[3] His record producer, John Culshaw, once asked what he thought of Richard Strauss as a man. "I played cards with him every day for years," said Knappertsbusch, "and he was a pig": Culshaw, "Kna Remembered" [1965], reprinted *Gramophone*, August 1993, p. 13. For his even less flattering, and crude, view of Herbert von Karajan, see Wolfgang Wagner, *Acts: the autobiography of Wolfgang Wagner*, trans. John Brownjohn (London: Weidenfeld & Nicholson, 1994), p. 118. For another example of his crude sense of humour, see Birgit Nilsson, *La Nilsson: My Life in Opera* (Boston: Northeastern University Press, 2007), p. 67.

Rough road to the Green Hill

He was born on 12 March 1888 into a family of factory owners in Elberfeld (now Wuppertal). His parents followed his musical progress proudly, but without encouragement. After his first venture into conducting in a casino at the age of twelve, his future in music studies seemed assured.[4] He went to Bonn University to study musicology and philosophy. His dissertation on the nature of Kundry, now lost,[5] is the earliest indication of his fascination with *Parsifal.* While at Bonn he also took piano lessons at the Cologne Conservatory, and attended the conducting class of Fritz Steinbach (Fritz Busch was a fellow student). Steinbach soon dismissed Knappertsbusch as his "most untalented pupil."[6] Knappertsbusch also learned something from Otto Lohse, director of the Cologne Opera.[7] Most importantly, he learned from Hans Richter and Siegfried Wagner at the Bayreuth Festivals in 1909 and 1911.[8] He may, indeed, have formally assisted them, as some reports state, although his name is not listed in the official records for those years.[9] He recalled in an interview in 1922: "In Bayreuth I was surrounded by almost all the great artists, and took away for the rest of my life the most unforgettable impression of Haus Wahnfried. The departure of Hans Richter after the memorable 1912 production of *Meistersinger* remains especially memorable to me. Really, this brilliant man – Muck too – has had a very strong influence on my artistic development."[10] He showed his respect for the Old Master after one of his *Götterdämmerung* performances at Bayreuth in 1957 when he said to Walter Panofsky, who had never seen him so happy, "I think Hans Richter would have been pleased with me."[11]

His first engagement was as a conductor of a military band in the theatre at Mülheim an der Ruhr. He then went to Bochum (1911/12). His lucky break came with *Parsifal* at his home town of Elberfeld. During its first performance on 11 January 1914 the conductor, Ernst Koch, became ill after the first act. The director asked Knappertsbusch whether he would dare finish the performance. He did dare, and he brought the second and third acts "without any preparation to such a level of artistic perfection that he was offered employment that very evening."[12] He conducted

[4] Betz, *Knappertsbusch*, p. 8. It is highly likely the 18 to 20-year-old Knappertsbusch attended some of Albert Coates's performances during the Coates's tenure in Elberfeld (1906-08). Indeed, it may have been admiration and gratitude that accounted for Knappertsbusch's introduction of Coates's *Samuel Pepys* to Munich in 1929.

[5] Maximilian Kojetinsky, *Hans Knappertsbusch: Bayreuther Festspieldirigent 1951-1964*, Ausstellung der Bayerischen Vereinsbank (München, 1977), p. 6

[6] Kurt Blaukopf, *Great conductors*, (trans.) Miriam Blaukopf (London: Arco, 1955), p. 114

[7] Wilhelm Zentner, "Knappertsbusch," *Neue Deutsche Biographie*, Vol. 12 (1980), p. 157

[8] At Bayreuth in 1909 Michael Balling conducted the *Ring*, and Karl Muck and Siegfried Wagner both conducted *Lohengrin* and *Parsifal*; in 1911 Siegfried and Balling conducted the *Ring*, Muck and Balling *Parsifal*, and Richter *Meistersinger*. Richter's last *Meistersinger* was in 1912; his last *Ring* had been in 1908.

[9] Egon Voss, *Die Dirigenten der Bayreuther Festspiele* (Regensburg: Gustav Bosse Verlag, 1976), p. 58

[10] *Münchner Neueste Nachrichten*, 21 May 1922, quoted in Hans Rudolf Vaget: "Musik in München. Kontext und Vorgeschichte des *Protests der Richard-Wagner-Stadt München* gegen Thomas Mann," *Thomas Mann Jahrbuch*, Band 7 (1994), p. 61. Furtwängler also heard Richter's *Meistersinger* in 1912: see Richter chapter, p. 103, for his impressions.

[11] Betz, *Knappertsbusch*, p. 6

[12] W. G. Knappertsbusch, *Die Knappertsbusch und ihre Vorfahren* (Elberfeld, 1943), pp. 209-210. The author (Knappertsbusch's brother) incorrectly gave the date as 1913. Knappertsbusch conducted the work 25 times in 1914/15: Alfred Mayerhofer, "Hans Knappertsbusch," *Wuppertaler Biographien*, 6. Folge (Wuppertal: Born-

another *Parsifal* on 1 February,[13] and repeatedly thereafter throughout the season. In his five years in Elberfeld he conducted almost all of Wagner's works.[14] He also toured Holland with his Elberfeld forces before the First War.[15]

In 1919 he went to Leipzig as first conductor, where Lohse was now head of the Opera. Lohse was not quite at ease with the talents of the younger conductor, so it was but a short stop for Knappertsbusch on the way to Dessau (1919/22). There, in 1920, he became the youngest General Music Director in Germany.[16] He learned how to run a large opera house, and became known for his Wagner interpretations. However, in January 1922 the opera house burned down and his duties came to an end.[17] In the summer of that year he conducted *Siegfried* at the Zoppot Waldoper, the Bayreuth of the North, the only occasion he conducted at this outdoor Wagner festival.

The Munich Years 1922-1935

A new opportunity happily presented itself. In Munich, where Bruno Walter presided over the opera, the "dark powers of hell had already begun their work," and Walter decided to relinquish his post.[18] Knappertsbusch was his candidate to succeed him, so it was reported, and he debuted on 5 October 1922 with a performance of *Tristan und Isolde*.[19] Shortly after taking up his duties, he broadened into concert work in Vienna, sharing with Clemens Krauss, Bruno Walter, and Leopold Reichwein the duties formerly held by Furtwängler. One report from Vienna in 1924 held that Knappertsbusch had "fallen short of expectations."[20]

Reports of his Wagner performances at Munich were mixed, but generally not good. *The Times* correspondent wrote from the 1925 Festival, at which Knappertsbusch

Verlag, 1966), p. 99; Joachim Dorfmüller, *Wuppertaler Musikgeschichte* (Wuppertal: Born Verlag, 1995), p. 54.

13 A facsimile of the poster for the 1 February 1914 performance, with "*Kapellmeister* Hans Knappertsbusch," is in Betz, *Knappertsbusch*, opposite p. 44. Knappertsbusch has been incorrectly credited with becoming the first German outside Bayreuth to conduct *Parsifal*: *Die Musik in Geschichte und Gegenwart (MGG) – Personenteil*, Vol. 10 (2003), p. 330. Klemperer conducted it at nearby Barmen on 4 January 1914.

14 The works of Wagner he conducted in Elberfeld and the dates of the first performances were: *Parsifal* (1 February 1914), *Meistersinger* (3 February 1914), *Tannhäuser* (20 March 1914), *Lohengrin* (13 October 1914), *Rheingold* (19 January 1915), *Walküre* (4 February 1915), *Siegfried* (3 March 1915), *Götterdämmerung* (11 March 1915), *Tristan* (2 November 1915), and *Holländer* (3 October 1915): information from the Stadtarchiv Wuppertal. The Elberfeld Theatre was destroyed by bombs on 25 June 1943.

15 *Parsifal* in Rotterdam in May 1914, and *Siegfried* and *Tristan* in Amsterdam in June and July 1914: Joachim Dorfmüller, "*Was er für Bayreuth bedeutet hat, ist längst Geschichte* – Zum Werk des Elberfelder Dirigenten Hans Knappertsbusch," *Bergischer Almanach 1989*, p.122

16 Arnd Richter, "Sein Leben war Dienst an der Musik," *Oper 1988* (Jahrbuch der Zeitschrift *Opernwelt*), p. 54

17 *ibid*, p. 54

18 Walter, *Theme and Variations*, p. 227. "On October 4 the racially unobjectionable Hans Knappertsbusch took over as Walter's successor": Erik Ryding and Rebecca Pechefsky, *Bruno Walter: A World Elsewhere* (New Haven and London: Yale University Press, 2001), p. 148.

19 *New York Times*, 19 November 1922, p. 95. Before his formal appointment, he conducted *Meistersinger*, *Zauberflöte*, and *Walküre* in May 1922.

20 "Musical Notes from Abroad – Vienna," *Musical Times*, 1 May 1924, p. 461. *The Times* reported from the Munich that year: *Meistersinger*: "conducted with plenty of vitality… all his lively rhythms were much too jerky in the prelude": 5 May, p. 8; *Rheingold*: "The orchestra under Herr Knappertsbusch played well without generating that intense excitement which ought to mark the climacteric moments": 8 August, p. 10; *Walküre*: "the last act seemed excessively slow": 8 August, p. 10; *Götterdämmerung*: "a good many flaws in the playing, and the horns became very unruly during the dawn scene in Act II": 18 August, p. 8.

conducted the *Ring* and *Tristan*: "His Wagner has suffered from the lack of a fully-developed rhythmic sense, which causes him to pass too quickly over the longer notes in a phrase, and sometimes to give undue importance to the shorter. In *Tristan* he made the time-honoured error of confusing haste with passion."[21] Lawrence Gilman heard him conduct a *Meistersinger* in 1926 and reported to the *Herald Tribune*: "he is a brutal and disaffecting conductor, and has no more business to be chief conductor of the Munich Opera than we have. He is not to be named in the same breath with Mr. Bodanzky...."[22] In the same year, the Munich critic Alfred Einstein wrote: "The misfortune for Knappertsbusch is that, while within his limits he is a splendid second conductor, he stands in the position of a first. [...] And so the Munich Opera no longer stands in the first rank."[23] In 1927 Olin Downes of the *New York Times* heard Muck conduct *Parsifal* at the Bayreuth Festival and then proceeded to the Munich Festival to hear it conducted by Knappertsbusch. "The Bayreuth *Parsifal* was this season the crown of its festival. Mr. Knappertsbusch is far from Dr. Karl Muck when it comes to the reading of the score. In the light of his performance, the Muck tempi justify themselves more than ever, with perhaps the single exception of the scene of the Flower Maidens, where the Bayreuth tempi seem a little ponderous.... [However,] even with a lack of a first-rank conductor, the Wagner performances here have notable vitality and distinction."[24] At the 1928 Munich Festival, Knappertsbusch conducted *Meistersinger*. Einstein reported to the *New York Times*: "[He] conducts with a fine wrist; aside from a few raw spots his work is less nationalistically German than formerly. The first half of the second act, until Beckmesser appears, is ideal, interpreted with the finest tone-feeling and without that over-emphasis on sentiment which makes one want to run away."[25] From the 1930 Munich Festival, where he conducted seven Wagner operas, Herbert Peyser reported to the *New York Times*: "the devastation wrought by Herr Knappertsbusch's incorrigible conducting is sometimes a little less than spectacular.... He has developed with the years a mania for appallingly slow tempi – on the theory, perhaps, that slowness and breadth amount to the same thing."[26] The 1931 festival was devoted to Wagner operas exclusively, with the exception of *Idomeneo*, and was no better in his view: "It can scarcely be otherwise so long as a mediocrity like Hans Knappertsbusch continues to prevail at the conductor's desk."[27] Yet *The Times* of London was impressed by the *Meistersinger* which opened the Festival:

[21] 21 August 1925, p. 8

[22] 4 November 1926, p. 25

[23] *Frankfurter Zeitung* [?], 8 March 1926, quoted in Vaget, "Musik in München," p. 63

[24] 4 September 1927, p. X6. Knappertsbusch's *Don Giovanni* was also "a disappointment.... There was little delicacy and not always the precision of attack in the playing."

[25] 23 September 1928, p. X6. In *Così fan tutte* Knappertsbusch was found "not only stiff, unmusical and wilful, but entirely lacking in feeling for the work." Einstein also heard *Lohengrin* conducted by Leo Blech ("a lively and fine balance between a reverential pose and dramatic effectiveness") and *Tristan* conducted by Karl Elmendorf ("much more variety" than Knappertsbusch). Adrian Boult heard Knappertsbusch conduct act one of *Tristan* in Munich on 1 August 1928: "even those who remember the two monumental performances under Nikisch at Covent Garden in 1907 could hardly claim that a more terrific climax was then achieved than by Knappertsbusch at the end of the first act": *The Times*, 15 September 1928, p. 8.

[26] 21 September 1930, p. X7. Peyser added that Knappertsbusch "made an excursion into Austria during August to conduct a concert of the Vienna Philharmonic and came back somewhat the worse for the slings and arrows of Austrian criticism."

[27] *New York Times*, 6 September 1930, p. 90. He conducted *Idomeneo* "with a hand of lead and in an unimaginably crude and undistinguished fashion."

From the first chord of the overture there was precision and assurance, and one had the feeling that the orchestra was being directed by a master hand. The impression of control and fine musicianship was steadily strengthened as the opera proceeded, and before it had concluded Wagner-lovers of long experience were agreeing that Professor Knappertsbusch (who has directed no less than 200 performances of *Die Meistersinger*) was giving them one of the finest interpretations which they had ever listened to.[28]

Götterdämmerung in Munich

These reports indicate that not everything was going well for the General Music Director. The performances at the Munich Festival had been "steadily going downhill ever since Bruno Walter was deposed," according to Peyser, and the performances of 1932, which were exclusively Wagner, had "unquestionably been the most listless and disheartening in a decade." Of the *Ring* he wrote:

The first of the two customary *Ring* cycles culminated in what was perhaps the most distressing performance of *Götterdämmerung* I have ever witnessed on either side of the Western ocean. The first grave-digger was unquestionably Herr Knappertsbusch, who dragged the music to the point of refined torture and who seemed, especially in the first act, to be conducting in a kind of somnambulistic trance. At any rate, he took more than two hours and fifteen minutes to reach the end of this act, which normally requires slightly less than two. In the process certain passages became virtually unrecognizable. Herr Knappertsbusch further indulged to the full a habit he has of mercilessly accentuating and distending bits of figuration and inner parts of no thematic significance. The whole reading was a shocking exhibition of insensitiveness and vulgarity.[29]

A *Walküre* the following year, "shepherded by Herr Knappertsbusch as by one wandering aimlessly through the byways of a heavy dream, was quite the most abysmal I have ever endured."[30] It is not surprising that Knappertsbusch's conducting began to cause concern in high places. Was he up to the job?

Unfortunately he believed that, even with no ear, he could, with his temperament, still produce good music. To attend the opera when he was conducting was a real penance; the orchestra played too loud, the violins were blanketed by the brass, and the voices of the singers were stifled. Instead of melody one was treated to a series of intermittent shrieks, and the wretched soloists looked just like a lot of tadpoles; the conductor himself indulged in such an extravaganza of gesture that it was better to avoid looking at him at all.[31]

These were the words of Hitler. Knappertsbusch was pensioned off, and forbidden further work in Bavaria.[32]

To portray Knappertsbusch as a political victim would be to over-simplify his demise. For years he had neglected the opera and its orchestra, had mishandled artists'

[28] 25 July 1931, p. 10

[29] *New York Times*, 28 August 1932, p. X4. Peyser also heard Knappertsbusch conduct *Götterdämmerung* in Vienna in 1937, and "spent a full five hours fuming and raging at the perverse and vulgar distortions which [he] practiced on Wagner's score and deafened by the almost ceaseless orchestral racket he unloosed." *ibid*, 4 July 1937, p. 101.

[30] *New York Times*, 27 August 1933, p. X4

[31] Hitler speaking at dinner at Berghof, 30 April 1942, in *Hitler's secret conversations, 1941-1944,* trans. by Norman Cameron and R. H. Stevens (New York: New American Library, 1953), p. 364

[32] Michael H. Kater, *The twisted muse: musicians and their music in the Third Reich* (New York: Oxford University Press, 1997), pp. 44-45

contracts, and had authorised opulent productions when there were inadequate funds.[33] True, there were reports that he had offended the Nazis. He supported Furtwängler protest over the Nazis's treatment of Hindemith; he staged contemporary and "foreign" operas; he reportedly dropped one of Hitler's favourite singers; he refused to join the Party; and he refused to hang a portrait of the *Führer* in his office, saying, "a Lenbach was good enough" for him.[34] On the other hand, he had shown what those in authority would have regarded as "leadership" by instigating the "asinine and vicious manifesto" attacking Thomas Mann for his great essay *Sorrows and Grandeur of Richard Wagner* in 1933.[35] But Hitler had a view of the future of the Munich Opera, and it did not include Knappertsbusch. He was "not a suitable conductor for the Munich Opera. He was more fit for concerts," Hitler was heard to say. He rejected entreaties that Knappertsbusch be allowed to stay: "That military bandleader must go!"[36] And go he did – to Vienna.

In Vienna, despite "his rigid, unpoetic brand of Wagner" shown in Munich,[37] he was very popular, as Herbert Peyser reported to the *New York Times*. He pondered Knappertsbusch's "intense dislike for rehearsing, filing, polishing, carefully preparing performances, his habit of trusting to luck and to a singer's or an orchestra's experience."[38] Peyser observed of Knappertsbusch's popularity in Vienna that he was sometimes "more frenziedly acclaimed before he has conducted a note than after he has concluded an act or a symphony."[39] This phenomenon was observed in another report from Knappertsbusch's first public appearance in Munich after the War, in 1947.[40] This suggests his popularity did not rest wholly on musical premises,

[33] Kater, *Twisted muse*, p. 44

[34] *New York Times*, 3 February 1935, p. X7 (Herbert Peyser) and 26 February 1936, p. 17. For example, he was criticized for putting on the "foreign" opera *Lucedia* by the American Vittorio Giannini on 20 October 1934. Nazi demonstrators disrupted a Knappertsbusch performance of *Siegfried* on 16 December 1934; he had to surrender his baton to another conductor: Hans Hotter, *Memoirs*, (trans. and ed.) Donald Arthur (Boston: Northeastern University Press, 2006), p. 85. Hotter was not singing on that occasion. The Lenbach referred to may have been the portrait of the earlier Munich General Music Director, Hermann Levi.

[35] Erich Heller in his introduction to Thomas Mann, *Pro and Contra Wagner*, trans. Allan Blunden (London: Faber and Faber, 1985), p. 12. The manifesto, published in the *Münchner Neueste Nachrichten* on 16/17 April 1933, is reproduced on pp. 149–151 of Mann's book, together with the signatories, who included Siegmund von Hausegger, Hans Knappertsbusch, Hans Pfitzner, and Richard Strauss. Knappertsbusch's letter instigating the "protest" is reproduced in Vaget, "Musik in München," p. 48. Knappertsbusch threatened elsewhere: "Whoever dares publicly to belittle the man [Wagner] who like few others has represented the power of the German *Geist* to the world will have something coming to him": quoted in Michael Kennedy, *Richard Strauss: Man, Musician, Enigma* (Cambridge University Press, 1999), pp. 278–9 (source not given).

[36] Kater, *Twisted muse*, p. 45. Clemens Krauss replaced Knappertsbusch in 1936.

[37] *New York Times*, 14 July 1935, p. X5 (Herbert Peyser)

[38] 24 January 1937, p. 155. He had conducted a *Ring*, *Tannhäuser*, *Lohengrin*, and *Meistersinger* in 1936; excerpts from some survive on record: see Discography.

[39] *New York Times*, 18 April 1937, p. 17. "The one thing I like unreservedly about him is his apparent contempt for applause and his habit of cutting it off and beginning the music while the public tumult is still at its height. [This can be heard at the beginning of acts one and two of the 1955 Munich *Meistersinger* recording.] But there are people, I understand, who are beginning to take umbrage at this. From the musical standpoint I feel about Knappertsbusch's conducting today exactly what I have felt about it for fifteen years – its absolute want of musical sensitiveness, its consistent lack of feeling for grace, for proportion, for structure, for beauty of orchestral sound, and often seemingly irresponsible choice of tempi and a coarseness sometimes amounting to brutality."

[40] Sir George Solti, *Solti on Solti: A Memoir* (London: Chatto & Windus, 1997), p. 90, quoting a U.S. Government official's report. Solti gave his own view of Knappertsbusch: "In a way, he was a German

even – or especially – with the critics. "One thing must be said openly," declared the Vienna press in 1938, "we spit, if we may respectfully say so, on Toscanini and on his Jewish boosters and express our preference for Hans Knappertsbusch. Joyously do we renounce Toscanini's baton prima donna business and delight in the performance of a real German conductor."[41]

His years in Vienna (1936/44) were not altogether happy. He was deeply affected by the death of his only child, 19-year old Anita, in June 1938.[42] He made many visits home to Germany and abroad. An invitation to Covent Garden in 1936 to conduct *Parsifal* and *Rosenkavalier* was blocked by the German authorities.[43] He appeared regularly at Salzburg (1937, 1938, 1939, 1940, 1941). He conducted *Ring* cycles in Vienna (1937), Berlin (1940 twice), Wuppertal (1942, 1943), and Budapest (1942). Some of his Wagner performances were recorded,[44] and others were given on notable occasions, such as *Tristan* on 12 March 1938 when German troops arrived in Vienna,[45] *Siegfried* at the Berlin State Opera on Hitler's birthday in 1940, and *Götterdämmerung* at the Vienna State Opera on 30 June 1944, the final performance before the Opera was closed down for "total" war. It was bombed on 12 March 1945. Why Knappertsbusch stayed in the "Greater Germany" after his forced retirement in 1936 is a matter for some speculation. He was very loyal. After several other conductors had left for political reasons, he reportedly said he would "rather toil in a quarry than leave Germany."[46]

version of Sir Thomas Beecham, with a personality so strong that it swept everything before it. He had tremendous control over an orchestra – his crescendos, for instance, were so powerful that they nearly knocked the house down – but I don't think he ever thoroughly mastered a score's details. He was notorious for not wanting to rehearse": p. 91. Knappertsbusch's first concert in April 1947 was Brahms.

41 unidentified Viennese newspaper quoted in the *New York Times*, 8 May 1938, p. 161

42 She died in Munich on 2 June 1938. Astrid Varnay wrote that Knappertsbusch "was so distraught by her death that he was unable to conduct for one whole year": Varnay, *Fifty-five years in five acts: my life in opera* (Boston: Northeastern University Press, 2000), p. 199. Hunt's concert register shows he resumed concert appearances on 15 July 1938. Recordings survive of his *Walküre* and *Götterdämmerung* in Vienna in September 1938: see Discography.

43 Harold Rosenthal, *Opera at Covent Garden: A Short History* (London: Victor Gollancz Ltd, 1967), p. 129. After diplomatic intervention, he was allowed to travel for three performances of *Salome* in 1937.

44 The excerpts on the *Edition Wiener Staatsoper Live* series (see Discography) were made mostly to record the singers, and for this are generally of great interest. The most extensive and impressive orchestral excerpts are from the *Siegfried* on 18 April 1936.

45 Marcel Prawy, *The Vienna Opera* (Vienna-Munich-Zurich: Verlag Fritz Molden, 1969), p. 153. On 13 March the Anschluss law was proclaimed. On 14 March Knappertsbusch conducted *Tiefland* with Hitler present. Knappertsbusch reportedly bowed and gave the Nazi salute: Richard Newman, with Karen Kirtley, *Alma Rosé: Vienna to Auschwitz* (Portland, Oregon: Amadeus Press, 2000), p. 94. This private performance is not listed in Hunt's *Kna*.

46 Kater, *Twisted Muse*, p. 40. On 18 April 1943 and 19 April 1944 he performed for Hitler's birthday celebrations, probably to the chagrin of the *Führer* who would have preferred Furtwängler (he had performed on 19 April 1942); there is newsreel film of these concerts on *Great Conductors*, and *Great Conductors – The Golden Era of Germany and Austria*: Dreamlife DLVC 8092 and 8094. "All over the German Reich, and later in the occupied countries as well, Knappertsbusch was a frequent guest performer, and he led the very best orchestras, including the Berlin Philharmonic.... A few months before the regime's collapse, the security service of the SS judged Knappertsbusch to be 'a decent man, in personal as well as political respects. Though not exactly an active National Socialist, he has always shown true German conviction' [5 February 1945]": Kater, *Twisted Muse*, pp. 45-46; Fred K. Prieberg, *Trial of Strength: Wilhelm Furtwängler and the Third Reich*, (trans.) Christopher Dolan (London: Quartet Books, 1991), pp. 291, 301. The SS were presumably unaware of the incident during an interrupted rehearsal in Vienna when "with an unprintable oath he sent an ash-tray flying against a loudspeaker from which one of Hitler's speeches was being broadcast": Prawy, *The Vienna Opera*, p. 154.

When the exiled Emanuel Feuermann met him on a train bound for Vienna, he asked him why.... "It was pathetic. He did not attempt to justify his present status. He merely shrugged his shoulders to implicate his human frailties."[47]

A new dawn on the hill

After the War he was reappointed General Music Director of the Munich Opera, but was soon removed.[48] After a year on the blacklist, he was permitted to resume work, though not as head of the Munich Opera. He marked his return to Wagner in Vienna (Theater an der Wien) on 20 April 1947, and in Munich on 11 April 1948, with *Walküre*. He began making some Wagner records for the Decca company in 1947. Bayreuth then called.

The Bayreuth years were the crowning achievement of his life. First, he was chosen to conduct a Wagner concert on the occasion of the re-opening of the Festival House on 22 May 1949. Then he was the "almost unanimous choice" to direct the re-opening of the Festival in 1951. He appeared at every festival but one between 1951 and 1964. He withdrew from the 1953 Festival because of disagreements over the modernity of Wieland Wagner's productions. "As soon as the spirit of Richard Wagner moves back into the Festspielhaus, I shall be the first to return," he telegrammed Wieland.[49] But after the success and sudden death of his replacement, Clemens Krauss, he returned for each festival for the rest of his life. He mostly conducted *Parsifal* (1951-52, 1954-64), but also the *Ring* (1951, 1956-58), *Meistersinger* (1951-52, 1960) and *Holländer* (1955).

Although he lived and conducted in Munich, where he was much loved, he travelled widely in continental Europe as a guest. Among his appearances in Wagner were Stockholm (*Ring*, 1950), Naples (*Rheingold* and *Walküre* 1952; *Ring*, 1953), Paris (*Ring*, 1955, 1957; *Siegfried* and *Götterdämmerung*, 1958; *Tristan*, 1956 and 1958; *Holländer*, 1960), and Milan (*Tristan*, 1957; *Holländer*, 1959). He kept away from England

[47] Seymour W. Itzkoff, *Emanuel Feuermann, Virtuoso* (Alabama: University of Alabama Press, 1979), p. 180

[48] The notes to *Hans Knappertsbusch In Memoriam*: Tahra TAH 606-609 (2007), p. 23 (unsigned, but evidently prepared in co-operation with Knappertsbusch's family) state he was reappointed General Music Director in August 1945, only later to be banned by the American occupying authorities. Hunt's concert register lists a number of Munich concerts (no opera) that he conducted at the Prinzregentheater between 17 August and 16 September 1945. In November 1945 the U.S. Army Headquarters in Frankfurt announced he was blacklisted because "he participated in Nazi-sponsored musical activities, although he was never a member of the Nazi Party": *New York Times*, 11 November 1945, p. 40. Knappertsbusch told a different story as Marcel Prawy related: "One evening immediately after the war there was a performance of *Die Meistersinger* in Munich with Knappertsbusch conducting. The proceedings started with an American officer coming on the stage and making an interminable speech. What follows is best described in Knappertsbusch's own words: 'I was just standing there, and I suppose my right hand must have twitched – anyway, there was a sudden terrific C major chord from the whole orchestra.' Next day he was banned": *The Vienna Opera*, p. 171. There is no *Meistersinger* listed in Hunt's *Kna*. Knappertsbusch's reappointment as General Music Director (1945) and the appointment of his successor, Georg Solti (1946-52), are listed in Ulrike Hessler, *The Munich National Theatre: from royal court theatre to the Bavarian State Opera* (München: Bruckmann, 1991), p. 95. Knappertsbusch resumed conducting in January 1947.

[49] Telegram dated 13 April 1953, sent after taking Wieland's *Ring* to Naples. He had also written to Wieland on 30 August 1951 declining to participate in further festivals, but Wieland got him to change his mind. There were other occasions he indicated he wanted nothing more to do with the festivals. He was wooed back "prompted in the main by his extreme veneration for Richard Wagner's synthesis of the arts," according to Wolfgang Wagner: *Acts*, pp. 117, 120-123; *New York Times*, 24 July 1953, p. 10 (Henry Pleasants).

and the United States. When the Metropolitan Opera made overtures to him, he was not "available."[50] In his lifetime he conducted over 2000 opera performances, mostly in Dessau (102), Munich (1335), Vienna (325), and Bayreuth (95).[51] Of Wagner, the works he most conducted were *Meistersinger* and *Parsifal*, the latter receiving 55 performances at Bayreuth alone under his baton.[52] His last appearance was in the pit at Bayreuth in *Parsifal* on 13 August 1964. He died in Munich on 25 October 1964, aged seventy-seven.

Knappertsbusch's way with Wagner

Knappertsbusch was not an intellectual, and did not write about how or why he performed Wagner the way he did. He nevertheless made no secret of the fact that he owed Wagner "the greatest and profoundest" debt. His life was immersed in Wagner. Knappertsbusch "only ever sought and found his real musical fulfilment in Wagner's world," wrote Walter Panofsky. "No matter how reserved he pretends to be, he completely loses himself in Wagner's world."[53] There are two aspects of his practice that must be considered before turning to the operas themselves, because they affected everything he did: rehearsals, and tempi.

The curse of rehearsals

Knappertsbusch was averse to rehearsals. He appears to have favoured the spontaneity of the moment over the hard work of careful preparation. "He hated rehearsals," the former head of the Vienna Philharmonic recalled, "improvising was closer to his heart, and he handled this with virtuosity."[54] Hans Hotter recalled the first time he appeared under him: "shortly before the performance [his] dressing room door opened and a gruff voice snarled, 'Do you know the piece?' That was pure Kna! 'Well, ... I ...,' I stammered, 'I think so.' 'So do I,' he replied, and disappeared."[55] Amusing as accounts like this are, and there are many, they signal a risky if not reckless approach. If Knappertsbusch himself was not lazy, his approach was bound to play into the hands of lazy musicians, and to discourage others who simply needed guidance. Singers generally spoke fondly of him,[56] but performances sometimes showed evidence of

[50] Sir Rudolf Bing, *5,000 nights at the opera* (London: Hamilton, 1972), p. 133

[51] notes to *Hans Knappertsbusch In Memoriam*: Tahra TAH 606-609 (2007), pp. 26-27

[52] His Bayreuth appearances are listed in Franz Braun, *Hans Knappertsbusch zur Erinnerung* (München: Hans Knappertsbusch-Gesellschaft, 1988), pp. 71-74; Hunt lists an additional *Meistersinger* (26 August 1952); however, the Richard-Wagner-Museum in Bayreuth has informed the author there was no Festival performance of the work on that date. Hunt notes that Knappertsbusch conducted *Parsifal* almost 200 times in his lifetime: *Kna*, p. 6.

[53] Betz, *Knappertsbusch*, p. 7

[54] Otto Stresser, quoted in Richter, "Sein Leben," p. 59

[55] Hotter, *Memoirs*, p. 130. Hotter also said: "I remember him so often saying, 'Don't look at me; I can follow you'": *New York Times*, 19 May 1991, p. H25.

[56] Frida Leider was warned before a Munich *Ring* in the 1930s: "You'll need another pair of lungs for Knappertsbusch," but she said, "musically I got on very well with him": Frida Leider, *Playing my part*, (trans.) Charles Osborne (London: Calder and Boyars, 1966), p. 151. Astrid Varnay said his broad tempi made clear diction possible; however, Günther Treptow had advised her "to take very deep breaths, because you never know how wide he would spread those endless arms of his"; she said, "I often had tender thoracic muscles after a Knappertsbusch performance": Varnay, *Fifty-five years*, pp. 170-171. Martha Mödl

neglect.[57] His record producer lamented his practice: "Knappertsbusch preferred not to rehearse at all, unless he was forced to do so; he liked to take the chance that he could bring off a performance on the spur of the moment. When it happened, which was more often than not, it was magnificent; when it didn't, it was little short of catastrophic."[58] This is what once happened at Salzburg:

> It is astonishing how badly the Vienna Philharmonic can play under a conductor like Mr. Knappertsbusch after performing like archangels for Mr. Toscanini twenty-four hours earlier. The audience visibly winced under the excruciating things done to the beautiful closing bars of the first act [of *Der Rosenkavalier*], and the list of misdemeanors could be depressingly extended. But Mr. Knappertsbusch is known to be no friend of rehearsals, and the results last night showed it.[59]

Thus neglect, if not recklessness, had its cost. But in Knappertsbusch's world, who really cares? His attitude was one of the qualities which made him so popular. He was "blond and Aryan looking," Herbert Peyser reported in 1938, "and has the qualities which the Germans call *Draufgängertum*."[60] The imperfections in his performances, which can be heard in the numerous recordings of his live performances, were not mere occasional accidents, but the fruits of his manner of working. They represent his attitude towards art.

Time or eternity?

The other notable feature of Knappertsbusch's way was his slow tempi. He was asked about his choice of tempi during the 1951 Bayreuth Festival. He referred to his time with Hans Richter at the turn of the century, and said "his aim was to come as close as he could to the interpretation of his master."[61] Whilst this may have been his aim, it was very imperfectly realised. To take the example of the *Siegfried Idyll*, which appears to have been very close to Knappertsbusch's heart:[62] the comparison of a Richter performance in London in 1880 (14' 30") with the longest of Knappertsbusch's many versions in 1949 (20' 36") more or less speaks for itself. Hermann Levi performed it in London in 1895, and it was reported to have been "taken, of course, at Richter speed, and not at the absurdly slow tempo adopted by young Master

was circumspect when asked about his broad *tempi*: Mödl, *So war mein Weg: Gespräche mit Thomas Voigt* (Berlin: Parthas, 1998), p. 52. Birgit Nilsson too did not directly speak of their effect on her singing when discussing Knappertsbusch, "Wagner conductor number one," in *My Memoirs in Pictures*, trans. Thomas Teal (New York: Doubleday, 1981), p. 70. See also recollections of Paul Kuen and Marianne Schech in Braun, *Hans Knappertsbusch*, pp. 7, 90, and Régine Crespin, *On Stage, Off Stage*, (trans.) G.S. Bourdain (Boston: Northeastern University Press, 1997), p. 67.

57 At the 1951 Bayreuth Festival: "One had the impression that occasionally the singers, even well-trained, healthy young singers, did not have the strength to hold on to a sustained note as long as the conductor required in certain passages. One felt that some scenes were interminable": *New York Times*, 12 August 1951, p. 86 (Howard Taubman)

58 John Culshaw, *Putting the Record Straight: The Autobiography of John Culshaw* (London: Secker & Warburg, 1981), p. 108

59 *New York Times*, 29 July 1937, p. 15 (Herbert Peyser)

60 *New York Times*, 2 January 1938, p. 130. *Draufgängertum* can mean both adventurousness and recklessness.

61 *New York Times*, 12 August 1951, p. 86 (Howard Taubman)

62 Arnd Richter, "Dokumente eines großen Erbes," *Neue Zeitschrift für Musik*, 149 (July-August 1988), p. 82

Fig. 18.1. Hans Knappertsbusch from his Dessau years, 1919-1922

Fig. 18.2. Knappertsbusch from his Munich years, 1922-1935

Fig. 18.3. Knappertsbusch rehearsing *Tannhäuser* at Salzburg, 1938

Fig. 18.4. Knappertsbusch rehearsing at the Paris Opera, late 1950s

Fig. 18.5. Knappertsbusch conducting the Transformation music from *Parsifal* at Bayreuth, from a film

Fig. 18.6. Knappertsbusch in the pit at Bayreuth

Fig. 18.7. Knappertsbusch at Bayreuth. Photo by Rudolf Betz

Siegfried."[63] Knappertsbusch's approach was not authentic, strictly speaking. The *Idyll* was conceived by Wagner as a small chamber piece to be played in the lobby and staircase of Tribschen to awaken Cosima on the morning of her birthday in 1870. With Knappertsbusch's heavy, symphonic approach, she may have been tempted to return to her bed. But perhaps not. There is enough in his interpretations to wake any sleeping mother. His way may not be as intimate, fleet-footed, and playful as the readings of some other conductors: in their place Knappertsbusch evokes images of a dawdling, over-fed young boy, aimlessly day-dreaming, and of a very elderly, doddery, doting parent. This is no less affecting a rendition than others, much as it may surprise us to find it so.

An instructive parallel can be drawn from a performance by Siegfried Wagner of the *Meistersinger* overture in London, Siegfried was another conductor not noted for his liveliness. "His conducting was too depressing to be describable as maddening," wrote George Bernard Shaw, "but it made us all feel as if we were at a garden party in a cathedral town being welcomed by a highly connected curate who failed to find any tea for us." After Wotan's Farewell and Magic Fire Music, the critics got up and left, "for the man seemed hopeless." Shaw was no longer a music critic, and he stayed:

> Then an incredible thing happened. The last item in the program was the overture to *Die Meistersinger*. The last, and, as it at once promised, the worst. Its slowness, its genteelness, made me doubt whether I was not dreaming. I felt that the overture would certainly peter out and stop from sheer inertia if he did not speed up the final section. Instead, to my amazement, he achieved the apparently impossible feat of slowing it down. And the effect was magical. The music broadened out with an effect that is beyond description. It was immense, magnificent. At the end the audience, which ten minutes before would have murdered him but for the police, was frantically recalling him to the platform again and again and again and yet again.[64]

This is not to suggest that Knappertsbusch was more in the tradition of Siegfried Wagner than Hans Richter, but to show how effective a slow performance can be even when it strays from the ways of authenticity. Wagner wanted a "a strong march tempo" for his *Meistersinger* overture,[65] yet his son gave a performance that was emphatically otherwise, and it was a triumph. Knappertsbusch's last performance of the overture, in 1963, his slowest by a mile, was likewise not in the spirit of the composer.

There are some other notable instances of Knappertsbusch defiance of Wagner. One was the Waltraute-Brünnhilde scene in *Götterdämmerung* in which Waltraute pleads with her sister to return the ring to the Rhine, lest the world of the gods come to an end. It is a long scene, and Wagner was insistent in 1876 that it not drag: "at every moment one must feel more or less acutely Waltraute's fear and feverish haste."[66] Knappertsbusch's timings of this scene give a fair idea that he does not share this sense of urgency.[67] One reviewer of his 1951 *Götterdämmerung* asked:

> Is there really any compelling reason to slow down Waltraute's narrative to such an extent that the singer has to break up her phrases to get breath? Wagner's own intentions are hardly open to

63 *Sunday Times*, 28 April 1895, p. 6 (Herman Klein)

64 a "Postscript" (1937) to "Siegfried's Tod," *Pall Mall Budget*, 15 November 1894, in *Shaw's music*, ed. Dan H. Laurence (New York: Dodd, Mead, 1981), Vol. 3, p. 338

65 Willy Krienitz, "Felix Mottls Tagebuchaufzeichnungen aus den Jahren 1873-1876," *Neue Wagner-Forschungen* (Karlsruhe: G. Braun, 1943), p. 196

66 see Wagner chapter, p. 29

67 see Timings

misunderstanding. He says *Mässig, doch immer wechselvoll* (moderato, ma sempre tempo rubato) and later *Etwas breit, doch nicht schleppen* (poco largamente, ma senza slentare). That ought to help any conductor to find the right speed for this section.[68]

The paradoxical point is that Knappertsbusch's pace is effective. But only just. Waltraute's opening words *Höre mit Sinn, was ich dir sage!* (listen carefully to what I have to say to you) are so slow and clear they verge on the impertinent, to Brünnhilde and the audience. But she listens. And so do we. Waltraute leads us into a narrative that is more visionary than urgent. Brünnhilde is stubborn, so Waltraute must sing on. At the pace Knappertsbusch sets it seems as if Brünnhilde is spellbound by what she sees, paralysed with indecision. The whole scene is like an act within an act. And it is quite mesmerizing.

Another example where his turgid pace is very effective is in the opening scene in *Rheingold* which opens *in* the Rhine. "Water is a heavy medium," one perceptive commentator put it, "and Knappertsbusch always suggests that the Rhinemaidens move in water, conveying the languid, resisting feel of water through his weightier phrasing of Wagner's string figures, his broader tempo and denser sound. He also allows the Rhinemaidens to sing the music with a lovely, lazy lilt."[69] Alberich's chasing of the Rhinemaidens in this restrained, watery environment is a nightmare. His limbs are held back. He cannot catch up, however much he tries. The orchestral sound is suffused with heavy-footed slipperiness. He simply cannot get his hands on what matters. It is an agonizing pace, but wholly appropriate to the drama.

Whatever the wonderful sound-worlds Knappertsbusch creates with his slow *tempi*, he is sometimes trapped by the uniformity of his approach. What works in one scene, or in one drama, will not work in another. In act one of his *Walküre*, the warm spring air wafts in slowly as the doors to Hunding's hut fly open; Knappertsbusch does not convey the ardour. In the 1957 recording, Siegmund gets quite carried away, as he should, at *Siegmund heiss' ich*, and has to wait for Knappertsbusch to catch up (and it is probably the latter's voice we can hear on the recording pulling him back). His Valkyries are laden with heavy armour that does not permit any rush of panic or easy flight. It is moments like these that make one wonder whether there is any dramatic blood coursing through Knappertsbusch's veins. He has his mind set on *his* way, and this sometimes does not serve the demands of the drama.

Where Knappertsbusch succeeds is in the creation of atmosphere and mood, pre-eminently in the dark caverns of *Götterdämmerung* and in the Grail Kingdom rituals of *Parsifal*. In these worlds, defects of detail and questions of tempo seem unimportant. The musical worlds created, or allowed to unfold, are, despite their rough spots, so enticing, luxuriant, and entrancing, that one sometimes wishes they would go on for ever. And sometimes it seems as if they do. For Knappertsbusch seems to conduct "not time but eternity."[70]

[68] Adolf Aber, "Tradition and Revolution at Bayreuth," *Musical Times*, October 1951, p. 455. Aber also referred to Wagner's letter to Richter during the 1876 rehearsals, printed in the *Festpielbuch* (quoted in Richter chapter above), and wrote "I hope Herr Knappertsbusch will read the letter carefully."

[69] Paul Dawson-Bowling, "Knappertsbusch: the recorded legacy," *Opera*, vol. 39 (March 1988), p. 292

[70] Ernest Newman quoted in Harold Lawrence, "Maestros and their disk timings," *New York Times*, 4 April 1954, p. X10; this was perhaps a reference to Newman's comments on Knappertsbusch after the 1951 Bayreuth *Ring*: "He seems to be racked every now and then by a spasm of placidity during which, for a

The commercial recordings

Before turning to the important live recordings, it is necessary to touch on his products from the studio, and on the reception they received. Early recording sessions did not serve Knappertsbusch well, and his attitude to recording did little to help matters. The earliest records from 1928 "give little or no indication of the great Wagner conductor he was to become," wrote Harold Rosenthal. "The sound is so poor that even as an historical curiosity" the recordings had little to commend them.[71] When the *Meistersinger* overture was released in England in 1932, it was described by *Gramophone* as having "a hearty body, if a rather sluggish spirit.... I should call this performance pedestrian: it wants passion and humour both. For once we have time-beating, not interpretation."[72] A 1947 recording of this same piece with the Orchestra of the Suisse Romande was called a "porridge of a record" by the *Music Review*.[73] The balance between the voices and the orchestra in the 1949 *Meistersinger* duet *Gut'n Abend Meister* was so poor in *Gramophone's* view that "those who do not know the score well will miss much of the exquisite orchestral detail."[74] A *Rienzi* overture from 1947 was regarded as "disappointing" for its deliberateness and lack of brilliance; and *Siegfried's* Forest Murmurs from 1950 wanted clarity of articulation: "though it may be realistic to make the 'murmurs' sound so confused, it is not what Wagner intended. The notes sound as if they were stuck together and were trying to tear themselves apart."[75]

The most substantial studio recordings Knappertsbusch made in this period were the complete *Meistersinger* (1950-51), and act one of *Walküre* (1957) as a first part of a possible and later abandoned *Ring*. The *Meistersinger* was generally regarded as unsatisfactory in its day, mainly for technical reasons. "The balance between voices and orchestra is at times absurd," wrote the *Musical Times* after the appearance of act two in 1950. "The recording engineer seems to have forgotten that in Wagner's 'unending melody' the voices are only so many strands of sound in one highly organized texture..."[76] *Gramophone* commented that "the relative remoteness of the orchestra quite defeats Wagner's intentions, and the music, instead of being carried forward on a golden flood of tone, is reduced to a series of loud ejaculations with an indistinct cushion somewhere in the background."[77] This "hopelessly unrealistic" balance was somewhat rectified in the recording of later acts in 1951, but these suffered from an odd "ultra-sentimental *ritardando*," according to *Opera*.[78] Knappertsbusch's tempi caused some surprise. "There are places where one wishes he would get along with the show a little more rapidly," wrote the *New York Times*, "but on the whole it is a

minute or two, I have the feeling that I have passed beyond time into eternity": *Sunday Times*, 12 August 1951, p. 2.

71 *Opera*, vol. 18, no. 9 (September 1967), p. 764. He was reviewing Deutsche Grammophon LPEM 19601 which included all the 1928 recordings except *Lohengrin* and *Holländer*.

72 April 1932, p. 468 (W. R. Anderson); reviewed again in 1940: "rather dull on the whole": *ibid*, August 1940, pp. 61-2

73 vol. 10 (1949), p. 327 (Hans Keller)

74 *Gramophone*, April 1950, p. 204 (W. R. Anderson)

75 *ibid*, April 1951, pp. 253-4 (W. R. Anderson)

76 March 1951 (Basil Douglas), a review of act two: "A pity, as the performance is an extraordinarily good one, finely controlled, eager, and spacious."

77 January 1951, p. 168 (Desmond Shawe-Taylor)

78 vol. 2 no. 5 (April 1951), pp. 243-4 and vol. 3 no. 3 (March 1952), pp. 173-4 (George Harewood)

thoughtful, well-planned reading."[79] "Knappertsbusch is an immensely experienced Wagner conductor, " *Gramophone* acknowledged, but "addicted to slow tempi, as in the opening Chorale, where he disregards Wagner's marking and slackens the tempo from that of the Prelude (they should be the same)."[80] The faintness of the orchestra was a matter of regret: "the conductor seems to present the work, at times, with the intimacy of chamber opera.... [He] takes every opportunity to indulge in delicate orchestral tracery, but as a result of his continual restraint many points are lost... The recording must be blamed for patches of dullness."[81] One of these is the absence of any chorus at essential moments: there is no clatter of physical activity during the dance of the apprentices, and the entry of the mastersingers happens in a vacuum, without any cheering or clapping from the crowd. The apprentices's call for silence *Silentium!* is thereby rendered meaningless. The whole recording is an argument in favour of live recordings.[82]

The 1957 *Walküre* recording signalled the end of serious efforts to record Knappertsbusch in the studio. After the first session, the recording producer asked him into the control room to listen to what had just been recorded. "Listen to it? But I have just heard it." From this remark it was clear their working methods were incompatible. Knappertsbusch withdrew.[83] The "routine of the recording studio confused him," the producer later recalled.[84] The results were not altogether encouraging. He conducts "in his usual staid fashion," wrote the *Musical Times*.[85] It was a "rather measured" reading, wrote *Opera*, "one misses the lyricism, though the climax of the act is wonderfully built up and realised."[86] The *American Record Guide* noted the "tempi were on the slow side," and speculated that "it may be he holds back in deference to the singers."[87] *Gramophone* was impressed at the way "Knappertsbusch dwells lovingly, but not unduly, on the lyrical passages of the exquisite score and infuses plenty of vigour into it where needed, achieving an exciting climax in the last pages." The review concluded: "What now is going to be done about Act 2?"[88] Nothing, was to be the answer. For "Knappertsbusch took very badly to recording conditions," his producer

79 17 February 1952, p. 98 (Howard Taubman)

80 July 1952, p. 29 (Desmond Shawe-Taylor)

81 *Gramophone*, February 1952, p. 209 (Alec Robertson) – a review of acts one and three

82 It should be acknowledged that the recording was well received by the *American Record Guide* when it was first issued: "everything is sweet and harmonious": January 1951, p. 180 (C. J. Luten); but not on reissue: "the conductor, though his credentials are well-known, is slack, lackadaisical, insensitive, and in general well below his usual form": September/October 2006, pp. 291-2 (John P. McKelvey, who first bought the recording "54 years ago").

83 as told by Sir George Solti in *Solti on Solti*, p. 109; also told by Gordon Parry, a Decca recording engineer, in *International Classical Record Collector*, vol. 3 no. 11 (Winter 1997), p. 37

84 John Culshaw, "Kna remembered" [1965], reprinted *Gramophone*, August 1993, p. 13

85 October 1959, p. 532 (Dyneley Hussey). As to the accompanying excerpts from *Götterdämmerung*, Siegfried's Rhine Journey and Funeral Music (1956), they were "played with stodgy deliberation and without an ounce of poetry."

86 vol. 10 no. 8, August 1959, p. 535 (Harold Rosenthal). As to the *Götterdämmerung* excerpts, they were "not the best examples of Knappertsbusch's Wagner – at least that is what one felt immediately after hearing Toscanini's accounts of those passages."

87 March 1959, p. 468 (Philip L. Miller)

88 June 1959, p. 24. "I cannot write with equal enthusiasm of Knappertsbusch's playing of Siegfried's *Journey to the Rhine* or the *Funeral March*, both of which, and the latter especially, are rather sluggish rhythmically.... The deliberate playing of the horn call theme in the scherzo-like section of the *Journey* suggest Siegfried going very gingerly down the mountain side and has no spring in it. All this is regrettable...." Another *Gramophone* reviewer had commented on the lack of intensity in these excerpts: January 1958, p. 332 (M. M.).

wrote, "and no matter what we did, the genius which he so certainly revealed in the theatre refused to come alive in studio conditions.... In the theatre I believe that he was a Wagner conductor of supreme ability. But on records he was a total failure."[89]

Fig. 18.8. Knappertsbusch at the head of the Elberfeld school band, ca. 1906

The live recordings

As can be expected in live performances, there are often moments of spontaneity, inspiration, routine, and imperfection. There is also audience noise and the prompter's intrusion. This was certainly the case with Knappertsbusch's performances. When there are so many live recordings, and the evidence of imperfections accumulates, it is difficult not to conclude that a care-free attitude was an essential attribute of his style, or a necessary consequence of his attitude towards rehearsal and his trusting to the inspiration of the moment. When Henry Fogel reviewed some seventeen live recordings for the *ARSC Journal* in 1982, including some Wagner, he concluded that generally "one glorious moment [was] followed by a lapse." He formed what he believed was "a valid picture of Knappertsbusch's art as his audiences heard it":

> On the whole, I'm afraid it was too inconsistent, too wayward. There are certainly individual performances here that show blazing insight and a firm grip on the whole. But there are too many that lack those qualities, and in the end Knappertsbusch seems a highly talented, gifted musician brushed with genius, but lacking in the discipline to apply that genius to his art in the most consistently productive way.[90]

The most important, and certainly most pleasurable, live performances are those that were edited from a number of recorded performances, namely *Parsifal* from 1951 and 1962, and *Götterdämmerung* from 1951. These are synthesized recordings representing

[89] John Culshaw, *Ring Resounding* (London: Secker & Warburg, 1967), pp. 78-79. Culshaw was at that time, it must be borne in mind, promoting another of his Wagner recording artists, Georg Solti. The reviews quoted above appear to have been disregarded in a 1998 survey in *International Classical Record Collector* which stated: "the reviews of his records for Decca throughout the late 1940s and 1950s were always enthusiastic": David Patmore, "'Kna': Giant, general and gentleman," vol. 4 (Autumn 1998), p. 23.

[90] "Kna Live," vol. 14, no. 2, p. 67. John Deathridge has found "most of Knappertsbusch's Wagner performances on record... dead on arrival": notes to Reginald Goodall's live *Parsifal* recording, Royal Opera House, London, 8 May 1971: ROHSO12 (2008), p. 10.

the best moments in Knappertsbusch's performances. They bring us glorious Wagner by Knappertsbusch, but not as audiences heard him. We shall look at some of his performances of Wagner's late operas, chiefly based on these live recordings.

Tristan und Isolde

The interesting aspect of Knappertsbusch's 1950 Munich *Tristan* recording, his sole complete recording of the work, is that the cast is very similar to that available to Kleiber in 1952, yet the performances could not be more different. Whereas Kleiber subdued his orchestra for the sake of his singers, Knappertsbusch did not, with the result that his Isolde had to shriek. (By 1952, the act two duet with the same singers had to be cut.) The performance as a whole is not particularly notable. There is something of Knappertsbusch's ruggedness. The curse in act one is a long, heavy-handed affair – a sledge-hammer of a curse, in fact. The love duet is long too, so long in fact that one begins to long for King Marke's men to arrive. When they do there is a mighty surge from the orchestra, but the men's boots are leaden and the men cannot leap onto the stage with any alacrity. There are moments in Tristan's delirium in act three that make one wish for Tristan's death-wish to be granted. A massively powerful Liebestod ends the show. The recording was described in 1998 as having "extended spells of sloppiness and flaccidity unimaginable in any other Wagner conductor of equal reputation,"[91] and in 1979 as "one of the great performances. No other 'live' version achieves the powerful narrative drive that impels this from first page to last; something that the studio cannot hope to emulate."[92] Many other live performances have appeared on disc since 1979.

Knappertsbusch's studio excerpts from *Tristan* in 1959 were "nothing very special," according to their producer,[93] and the singer of the Isolde, Birgit Nilsson, did not seem very impressed: he "put his heart and soul into our recording… [but] was not the ideal conductor for recordings. He preferred the ocean waves of the opera performance to the dry swimming of the studio."[94] The prelude in these excerpts was "not warm enough – not impassioned enough – for my Wagner," wrote the reviewer for the *Music Review*, but by the time the Liebestod is reached "the orchestra is really with her in a beautiful performance."[95] Beautiful as she may be, "Knappertsbusch's lethargic conducting does not help her…," wrote *Gramophone*.[96] He does not show from these examples that *Tristan* is particularly close to his heart.

[91] *Fanfare*, July/August 1998, p. 266 (William Youngren). In an earlier review he wrote: "I still feel that Knappertsbusch drags his feet somewhat through acts I and II, coming alive only in Act III, which is really quite wonderful": *ibid*, March/April 1995, p. 334.

[92] Robin Holloway in Alan Blyth, ed., *Opera on Record* [(London: Hutchinson & Co, 1979), p. 364] quoted by Blyth in his review of the Gala reissue in *Opera*, vol. 45 no. 12 (December 1994), p. 1387. The only other live recordings available to Holloway at the time were De Sabata (1951), Karajan (1952), and Böhm (1966). All of these are great in their own way. Knappertsbusch's *Tristan* at La Scala Milan in 1957 struck critics as "an entirely German rendering," a "devoted" interpretation: *Corriere della Sera*, 29 March 1957, p. 6; one in which "we could not have wished for a more poetic atmosphere": *Corriere Lombardo*, 29-30 March 1957, p. 3; and, although he was "unconcerned with detail,… he contrived to draw great arches of orchestral architecture, enthralling and fascinating to the extreme": *La Notte*, 29-30 March 1957, p. 11.

[93] Culshaw, *Putting the Record Straight*, p. 220

[94] Birgit Nilsson, *La Nilsson*, p. 225

[95] vol. 21 (1960), p. 356 (J. B.)

[96] October 1960, p. 207 (Desmond Shawe-Taylor)

Die Meistersinger von Nürnberg

It is with some relief that one can leave the stale air of the studio *Meistersinger* (1950-51) and descend into the lively, relaxed atmosphere of the Bayreuth pit (1952). Contemporary reports suggest the performance in 1952 benefited from the replacement of Herbert von Karajan.[97] Knappertsbusch brought a "leisurely dignity coupled with sustained concentration and an apparent determination to make every note tell," according to the *Music Review*. "Sachs's famous ejaculation was shown, with an inevitable fitness, to be the psychological lynchpin of *Meistersinger*."[98] The *Musical Times* wrote that Knappertsbusch's treatment "had a continual regard for detail, and a pace which, though slow, was always moulded to the architecture of the score."[99] The slow pace does suit some scenes, such as the Pogner/Beckmesser scene in act one: they stroll leisurely, arm-in-arm, to the roll call of the mastersingers accompanied by beautifully caressing sounds from the orchestra. One does not have the sense that time is dragging at all. There is variety in the tempo, and in Sachs's *Fliedermonolog*, this variety is quite magical, befitting the object of Sachs's contemplation. The gentle pace aids the seductiveness of the Sachs/Eva scene, and generally the sun seems to shine through the performance. This does not seem so, however, to all ears. The *American Record Guide* regarded it as "a routine performance, professional enough to put the opera across, but scarcely worth preserving. The conductor is unpredictable, sometimes falling into lethargy...."[100]

At Munich in 1955 there was not quite the pressure of occasion of Bayreuth, and certainly not its powerful choruses in the congregation and among the apprentices. The orchestra is generally subdued – it has "an almost chamber-like transparency," wrote the *American Record Guide*[101] – and suffered from a lack of weight and volume on occasion, as in the confusion at the end of act one, when there was no need to take care not to drown the singers, and during the riot scene in act two. Knappertsbusch is good throughout the lively, swinging, trade union picnic, with wonderful crowd noises leading up to the arrival of the mastersingers. But then the orchestra does not give the occasion its due. Likewise at the end, there is not quite the avalanche of affirmation that should attend that triumphant scene. One has the feeling the conductor was not inspired throughout that evening.

The editor of *Opera* was present at Bayreuth in 1960 and heard the *Meistersinger*. He reported: "Hans Knappertsbusch's broad and steady tempi were impressive enough in the great choral scenes; but often the action was slowed down, and there was certainly a lack of poetry and tenderness in his reading."[102] The performance of 23 July 1960 on record is quite the worst in Knappertsbusch's Wagner discography. Although it is one of the longest performances on record, many crucial parts are taken at a literally breathtaking speed. The prelude to act three is taken at such a reckless pace that one wonders whether Knappertsbusch had received bad news in the interval.

97 *New York Times*, 24 August 1952, p. X7 (Henry Pleasants)

98 vol. 13 (1952), p. 304 (Geoffrey Sharp) (performance of 30 July 1952)

99 October 1952, p. 463 (Richard RePass). The comment was applicable to *Parsifal* as well.

100 July/August 1998, pp. 278-279 (Ralph V. Locarno)

101 January/February 1997, p. 242 (Kurt Moses) (also reviewing the 1952 recording)

102 *Opera*, Special Number, Autumn 1960, p. 45 (Harold Rosenthal)

The quintet is rushed, the arrival of the mastersingers is too brisk, even in the *Preislied* Walther is pushed. The performance as a whole is lacklustre, erratic, and waywardly driven without any consideration for the drama. At the end one is not uplifted, but let down. "Sadly," one commentator noted, "the great man was not on form."[103] *Fanfare* considered the performance "just about hopeless… Kna was, notoriously, a conductor who got bored easily, and when he was bored he let everyone know it by allowing his attention to stray from the task at hand."[104] Yet still, others have heard this performance differently.[105]

Der Ring des Nibelungen

Knappertsbusch's performances of the *Ring*, as we have them on record, were gigantic. The massiveness of his orchestral soundscapes marked him out for the world of gods. Like a giant, he lumbers, and sometimes stumbles, through the vast score. Buried in the sulphurous, burning pit of Bayreuth, his orchestra rumbles, occasionally erupts, and at moments creates waves of quiet sublimity and ecstasy. Everything is on a huge scale. The strides across the rainbow bridge into Valhalla are enormous. The bellows that Siegfried pumps are vast. Brünnhilde's sleep is deep and profound. And the crashing, vengeful waters of the Rhine obliterate everything. There are moments in the *Ring* in which Knappertsbusch conducts with unparalleled force: when the Nibelungs pile up the gold in *Rheingold*, when Hunding's hunting horns blare in the night in *Walküre*, and when Hagen's horn calls brazenly, brutally in *Götterdämmerung*. Indeed, it is in this last work that Knappertsbusch pulls no punches. The evil doings, the sense of impending catastrophe, the drug-taking, hatred, envy, deception, conspiracy, betrayal, murder, outrage, humiliation, shame… Knappertsbusch seems to understand them all profoundly. The scenes of Alberich driving his Nibelungs, of Siegfried and Gunther swearing blood-brotherhood, and of Hagen's men gathering, are frightening in their ferocity. Knappertsbusch creates a universe, and free-wheels through it with a weight of inevitability.

None of the three *Ring* recordings is wholly satisfactory. The blemishes are not all Knappertsbusch's doing. He objected to innovations in the "New Bayreuth," and if these included replacing the anvils with an electronic gadget to simulate them in *Rheingold* in 1956 and 1957, then he was wholly justified. The effect is quite ruinous in the great orchestral passages. In 1958 he seems to have been given but a single anvil. There is an excess of steam in act two of *Siegfried*, obscuring the music. In 1958 too the pernicious "average recording level" was inflicted on the opening of *Rheingold* with the bizarre result that, while the opening chord sounds loud and strong, thereafter the volume seems to diminish as the orchestral sound swells. In 1957 the prompter had a hefty task, even with Hans Hotter in his act two monologue in *Walküre*. Miraculously Hotter maintained the illusion: as the prompter handed the words up to him, he sang

[103] Dawson-Bowling, "Knappertsbusch: the recorded legacy," *Opera*, vol. 39 (March 1988), p. 292

[104] *Fanfare*, July/August 1998, p. 266 (William Youngren)

[105] "The wit and often hidden humor behind Knappertsbusch's craggy face and almost forbidding stature shine in fresh tempi, bright conversational exchanges, and festive pageantry. Nature, philosophy, and human warmth are illuminated abundantly, and a more deeply satisfying *Meistersinger* can hardly be imagined." *Opera Quarterly*, vol. 1 no. 3 (Autumn 1993), p. 274 (Robert Baustian)

them as if they were branded on his heart. The synthesised *Götterdämmerung* from 1951 was rehearsed by Karajan[106] and has fewer defects, and both these factors may have helped its reception.[107]

Reviews of both the performances and the recordings from these years vary, reflecting in part the consequences of Knappertsbusch trusting to the luck of the moment. *Opera* found in 1956 that Knappertsbusch's "leisurely tempo was a sore disappointment" in several places, though in general his tempos had "such inner vitality that they keep the music constantly moving, while allowing him to make effects of heart-warming tenderness and dignity."[108] In 1957 *Opera* found his reading "sonorous and firmly paced, but eschewed beauty of detail; it was really a little dull."[109] In 1958 it was "an overwhelming performance which we can only hope will be preserved on records."[110] That was a hope fulfilled.[111]

Parsifal

Knappertsbusch's radiant performance of *Parsifal* at the re-opening of the Bayreuth Festival in 1951 was a celebration and a consecration. Ernest Newman reported to the *Sunday Times*:

> About the musical part of the performance I can hardly bring myself to speak, so ravishingly, heart-breakingly beautiful was it. This was not only the best *Parsifal* I have ever seen and heard but one of the three or four most moving spiritual experiences of my life. The exquisiteness of the orchestral playing was beyond the power of words to describe. Hans Knappertsbusch conducted, and in a style that calls for the highest praise, but I understand that the rehearsals (extending over several weeks) have been taken by the greatly gifted Karajan.... No one who heard this performance will ever forget it.[112]

[106] Wolfgang Wagner recalled that at the 1951 Bayreuth Festival word went round that "the best performances were obtained when Karajan rehearsed and Knappertsbusch conducted in the evening." *Acts*, p. 118. See also Ernest Newman's comment on the 1951 *Parsifal* below.

[107] The recording is extensively reviewed in the *ARSC Journal*, vol. 31 no. 1 (Spring 2000), pp. 150-152 (Gary A. Galo): "a performance clearly on a plane with the conductor's *Parsifal*, and one which confirms his reputation as one of the supreme Wagner conductors on record": p. 151; "this performance is a splendid and unique achievement; it deserves to stand very high among all the *Götterdämmerungs* recorded since": *Fanfare*, June/July 2004, p. 224 (William H. Youngren); "the set catches the depth of the Bayreuth acoustics and, more important, the sense of a great occasion caught on the wing": *Opera*, vol. 50 no. 10 (October 1999), p. 1243 (Alan Blyth) – this is somewhat of an illusion: see note to the recording in Discography

[108] vol. 7 no. 10 (October 1956), p. 595 (David Cairns)

[109] vol. 8 no. 10 (October 1957), p. 623 (William Mann)

[110] vol. 9 no. 11 (November 1958), p. 718 (Ralf Steyer)

[111] The 1956 recording, and Knappertsbusch's other *Ring* recordings, were reviewed extensively by Gary A. Galo in the *ARSC Journal*, vol. 29 no. 2 (Fall, 1998), pp. 233-7; by Henry Fogel in *Fanfare*, March/April 1998, pp. 261-3: although "a maddeningly uneven conductor... this is the finest of his surviving Bayreuth *Ring* Cycles"; and by Alan Blyth in Opera, vol. 49 no. 6 (June 1998), pp. 659-660. The 1958 recording was reviewed by John P. McKelvey, who was at Bayreuth for the 1958 performance, in the *American Record Guide*, vol. 65 no. 3 (May/June 2002), pp. 224-5: "Despite his apparent sloppiness and disarray, it is Knappertsbusch who has mastered the larger issues and the subtleties that dwell beyond the written texts. The present issue... gives us one of the greatest *Rings*, perhaps *the* greatest, on records."

[112] *Sunday Times*, 5 August 1951, p. 2; *Bayreuther Tagblatt*, 11 August 1951, p. 11. Part of the performance was preserved on a record which is amongst the rarest in Knappertsbusch's discography: see Discography. Newman listened to Knappertsbusch's 1951 *Parsifal* recording on his death bed: Vera Newman, *Ernest Newman: a memoir by his wife* (London: Putnam, 1963), pp. 268-269.

So, while Knappertsbusch reigned, another governed. He was saved as on other occasions from the consequences of his aversion to rehearsals by the industry of another.[113] His extraordinarily slow tempos drew some comment. The *New York Times* considered the opening performance "had a steady, life-giving pulse. His pace was broad, but not excessively slow."[114] In the final scene on 10 August he "appeared to lose all sense of time and spun the texture out well beyond its normal length," according to the *Music Review*. "As a result the spell was broken and the scene failed to make the effect it should; an error of direction rather than execution."[115] The reviewer for *Opera* observed: "His tempi are on the slow side, but only once, in the *Herzeleide* scene, did I feel a drag."[116] Adolf Aber wrote in the *Musical Times*:

> As to *Parsifal*, Hans Knappertsbusch has found his own style, one that is deeply rooted in genuine piety, recently made more transcendent still by sad happenings in his life. In fact his approach to both works [the *Ring* and *Parsifal*] is that of a priest celebrating a high mass. There is no concession to those "in a hurry," no employment of cheap effects, but an almost blinding clarity in the development of the texture and musical framework, not one detail getting lost.
>
> I find it very difficult to argue with an artist of this stature, but I cannot help expressing some doubt about the correctness of some of his tempi.... The prelude to *Parsifal* starts in 4-4 *Sehr langsam* (*molto lento*); when the 6-4 section begins, three crotchets should be equal to two in the first section. ...[117]

Sometimes concerns over one detail or another, like this, qualified reviews which otherwise praised Decca's synthesis of recorded performances. Among the more interesting comments were those of Hans Keller who was in Vienna during Knappertsbusch's first two years there (Keller was forced to leave in 1938). Of his performances in those days Keller gives some account:

> Knappertsbusch has enormously developed during the past 15 years or so. Among many other virtues, he is now one of the two or three conductors alive who can manage a *subito piano* convincingly, nor can I think of more than one who would realize the character and tempo of the 2nd act's opening (*heftig, doch nie übereilt*) with equal understanding and success. All the more painful, however, is one's surprise at such sporadic blemishes as the violins' and violas' syncopations over the quaver movement of the celli in the introduction to the 3rd act: they sound as if played by an amateur band which "counts" the beats of the bar by accentuating them. The recording may of course have magnified what in reality was a smaller flaw.[118]

Generally this *Parsifal* was welcomed in its day as a theatrical recording without peer, "a triumph of modern phonographic work," as the *American Record Guide* declared.[119] It was indeed – there was no comparison – and then Knappertsbusch surpassed

[113] In 1955 Knappertsbusch agreed to conduct the *Holländer* on the condition that Joseph Keilberth undertook all the musical rehearsals, except the dress rehearsal: Wolfgang Wagner, *Acts*, p. 122.

[114] *New York Times*, 31 July 1951, p. 16 (Howard Taubman) [115] vol. 12 (1951), p. 324 (Geoffrey Sharp)

[116] vol. 2 no. 11 (October 1951), p. 557 (David Harris)

[117] Adolf Aber, "Tradition and Revolution at Bayreuth," *Musical Times*, October 1951, p. 455. It is possible the "sad happenings in his life" refers to the death of his daughter in 1938. Both his wives outlived him: Ellen (m. 1918, div. 1925) in 1987, and Marion (m. 1926) in 1984.

[118] *Opera*, vol. 3 no. 8 (August 1952), pp. 499-500

[119] March 1952, pp. 201-202 (Peter Hugh Reed): "I find his handling of the Transformation Scene in Act 1 rather deliberate in pace and not as dynamic as others make it"; cf. "I found it almost unbearably moving": *Gramophone* on the same scene: March 1952, p. 224 (Alec Robertson).

Fig. 18.9. Knappertsbusch as drawn by R. P. Bauer

himself with yet another recording, this time by Philips, from his 1962 Bayreuth Festival performances. Superbly recorded, in gorgeous sound, the performance is more alert, vigorous and propulsive than any of his other performances. The texture of the orchestra is like silk, and at moments like cashmere. So soft and supple, it furnishes the singers with a cushion of sound. Jess Thomas, who sang Parsifal, recalled how Knappertsbusch "always cued slowly, with a kind of inner peace. There was a soft orchestral attack, with a cloud of sound rising up, and one's voice sat easily on top of it."[120] For once Knappertsbusch was engaged in the drama. Throughout Gurnemanz's long monologue in act one, he makes the scene interesting and charged with expectation through constant changes of tempo and dynamic. As Gurnemanz and Parsifal step off to the Grail Kingdom, the orchestra gives a spring to their feet: there is immediately a sense of refreshment. The orchestra becomes the drama in the Grail scene. Huge arcs of sound prop up the ailing Amfortas, magnificently sung by George London, as in 1951.[121] Even his lacerations are luxuriant. The famous slow tempi have

[120] *New York Times*, 7 April 1974, p. 131

[121] He expressed more of a storm of suffering in Amfortas's lament in 1951 than in 1962. He wrote in his 1951 diaries: "I am physically and mentally in rare form. I managed to get a set of dumb-bells and am simply bulging with muscles." (13 July) "My second and third Amfortases were even better than the premiere. One [viewpoint] says I am the best protagonist of this role in the history of Bayreuth – if I can believe such a lavish compliment. In any case, it comes from the Wagners themselves." (12 August): Henry Pleasants, "From London to Vienna with Love," *Opera Quarterly*, vol. 9 no. 3 (Spring 1993), pp. 76-77. Wieland Wagner said to London's wife after a rehearsal of *Parsifal*: "Grandfather could not have visualized anyone greater than George": Nora London, *Aria for George* (New York: Dutton, 1987), p. 126.

an unexpected effect in the struggle between Parsifal and Kundry: it is heavy, they pull this way and that, but they are trapped by their fate. Knappertsbusch's transformation music has magnificent grandeur: an inexorable movement of tectonic plates of sound, powerful, inevitable, earth-shattering. The blessedness of the Good Friday scene provides the crown. The superb blending of orchestra and choral voices at the end leaves one breathless. "Anyone who has difficulties understanding the music and poetry of this final Wagner work," wrote Hans Hotter, the unsurpassable Gurnemanz, "has never heard it in Knappertsbusch's interpretation."[122] One can hardly hope for a better performance or recording than from 1962.

Wandering in the Grail Kingdom

For the brave and dedicated listener, and for the utterly devoted, there are ten complete live performances of Knappertsbusch's *Parsifal* on record. These are in *addition* to the two perfected commercial versions. And more will doubtless come. Each of the unexpurgated versions has its moments – and they are often great moments – but there are also wearying lapses or doubts that seem to have bedevilled all his performances.[123] At times in act three, the mood of sterility and of stagnation as Gurnemanz and his men wait for Parsifal, for salvation, is so slow, so deadly, that one wonders… might Knappertsbusch have lost his way? Or as the men trudge off to the Grail Kingdom, persistent and unrewarded penitents, to the accompaniment of the magnificent grind of the transformation music, might Knappertsbusch have actually lost his way with the knights of the Grail – not another damn unveiling of the Grail? Collectors and reviewers have their favourites, though critics seem more or less to have given up reviewing the recordings as they trickle out. Knappertsbusch has become an institution. People know what to expect. He is taken for granted. Hans Keller reported from Bayreuth in 1956: "Knappertsbusch's *Parsifal* was the one outstanding interpretation in Bayreuth's first week, but I have not heard or seen anybody draw attention to it."[124] What more could they say except perhaps: "His *Götterdämmerung* and *Parsifal* abide no question?"[125]

[122] Hotter, *Memoirs*, pp. 208-209

[123] For example, in 1958: "his *Parsifal* afforded one of the most profound musical experiences I have known" (20 August); in 1961: "on the night I heard him he did not cast his accustomed spell…." (5 September): *Opera*, vol. 9 no. 10 (October 1958), p. 633, and Festival Number, Autumn 1961, p. 57 (both Andrew Porter)

[124] *Musical Times*, September 1956, p. 489

[125] Andrew Porter in *Opera*, vol. 9 no. 10 (October 1958), p. 633

19

Clemens Krauss – Fleet-footed Wagnerian

Light, cheerful, and cultivated, Clemens Krauss embraced all music with consummate skill. He had a magic touch. There was ample room under his famous cape, with its red silk lining, for the biggest of Wagner's great works. Though he is most remembered for his collaboration with Richard Strauss, and for his musically profitable connections in Nazi Germany, by a happy accident we also have a record of his Wagner achievements. The turbulent Vienna years (1929-34), the unhappy Berlin years (1935-36), and the celebrated Munich years (1937-44) have yet to be fully documented. Krauss still awaits a scholarly biography. The Wagnerian highlights we will concentrate on here are several new productions he conducted in Vienna: *Meistersinger* (1929), *Walküre* (1930), *Siegfried* (1931), *Götterdämmerung* (1931), and *Parsifal* (1933); and in Munich: *Tristan* (1937), and a Munich Opera *Ring* on tour to Italy in 1938. After the war, he emerged to conduct, among other things, *Tristan* (1951) and *Meistersinger* (1953) at Covent Garden. There he became known for his fondness for Charles Dickens and the adventures of Sherlock Holmes. Even more important for some, he showed, like Wagner and Anton Seidl, that he had a profound affinity with dogs: they adored him wherever he went.[1] Ever quick to take up an opportunity to conduct, he happily filled in for the rebellious Knappertsbusch at the Bayreuth Festival in 1953 where he conducted the *Ring* and *Parsifal*. On the strength of these appearances, the last of which survive on record, we will see he takes his place with ease among the great Wagnerian conductors.

Opportunities along the path to the Green Hill

He was born in Vienna on Good Friday, 31 March 1893. His mother, Clementine Krauss, was 15 years old at the time. His father, Hector Baltazzi, aged 41, was a cavalier – "a daring steeplechaser and jumper" – whom Krauss never met.[2] He was brought up in his mother's family which had many connections, some distinguished, with the theatre and opera. The first display of his musical gifts was in song: he had a beautiful

[1] Ida Cook, "Clemens Krauss," *Opera*, vol. 5, no. 2 (February 1954), p. 86

[2] Clemens Krauss, "*Autobiographie à la minute*" [ca. 1953] in Erik Maschat, "Clemens Krauss," trans. Peter Hutchison, *Recorded Sound*, no. 42-43 (April-July 1971), p. 741 According to Krauss, his mother "was barely seventeen" and his father "was forty-four" when he was born. Oscar von Pander, *Clemens Krauss in München* (München: C.H. Bock, 1955) gives the following biographical details on p. 9: Clementine Krauss (25.4.1877 – 18.4.1938), Hector Baltazzi (21.9.1851 – 2.1.1916).

treble voice. He was given lessons and, like Hans Richter before him, he was engaged as a chorister in what became known as the Vienna Boys Choir. There he learned the essentials of music. At the age of twelve, through his acquaintance with the masses of Haydn and Mozart, Beethoven's piano sonatas, and Schubert's songs which he sang himself, he decided to become a musician. He went to the Vienna Conservatory and studied music theory, composition and piano. He explained the influence of Vienna in a biographical sketch written towards the end of his life:

To the question, which teacher influenced my musical progress, I can only say it must have been the carriers of the Viennese tradition who laid the foundations of my musical life. I have no idea today when it was that I first heard such works as *Die Zauberflöte* and *Fidelio*, but I am aware of being influenced even now by the tempi that I heard in those days, long before the gramophone became a household object. An irresistible urge makes me cling still to those traditional – and to me seemingly innate – *tempi*.[3]

Hans Richter had left Vienna in 1900, and Mahler in 1907 when Krauss was fourteen. He had sung in the Vienna Boys Choir under Mahler at the Vienna première of his *Third Symphony* on 14 December 1904.[4] In his autobiographical sketch he does not say he heard Mahler conduct:

It was Franz Schalk who handed on Hans Richter's interpretations of Wagner's music dramas to me, and thus conveyed the intentions of Wagner with regard to the performance of the *Ring* tetralogy and *Die Meistersinger*. Richard Strauss instructed me in Hans von Bülow's analysis of the *Tristan* score – for Bülow, as conductor of the world première, was presumably in possession of all Wagner's wishes.[5]

Krauss's first professional engagement was as chorus director at Brünn (Brno) in 1913. There he conducted his first opera, *Zar und Zimmermann*, on 13 January when the scheduled conductor suddenly fell ill. Thereafter he went to the German Opera in Riga (1914), to Nuremberg (1915) where he included *Lohengrin* in his repertoire, and thence to Stettin (Szczecin) (1916-21) where he introduced further Wagner works to his repertoire: the *Ring*, *Parsifal*, and *Tristan*. This was an important period in his development because he was able to travel to hear Nikisch in Leipzig and Berlin:

If I must... dwell on the development of my interpretative personality and the subjective intentions which I follow when conducting, I must think above all of one man who had a profound and decisive influence on me. Arthur Nikisch is my real master in conducting. I was staff conductor in the Stettin theatre for five years, and during this time I had opportunities to hear his Berlin Philharmonic concerts and to attend numerous rehearsals under him. I studied this unrivalled conductor's art, and let his fascinating yet wholly natural personality impress itself upon me. His presence taught me that one may refer to a conductor as an "artist" only when what he has learned becomes part of his nature, so that he is able to make complicated art sound simple – not the reverse (which is the practice of many conductors who would have the world believe that directing an orchestra is akin to black magic).[6]

He became director of the Graz Opera (1921-22) and from there was talent-spotted for the Vienna Opera. He was invited to conduct *Rheingold* and *Walküre*

[3] "*Autobiographie à la minute*," p. 742

[4] Kenneth Birkin in *Music & Letters*, vol. 70 no. 3 (August, 1989), p. 435; Henry-Louis de La Grange, *Gustav Mahler, Vol. 2* (Oxford University Press, 1995), p. 347n

[5] "*Autobiographie à la minute*," p. 742

[6] *idem*

in Vienna on 22 and 24 February 1922 respectively, and *Rosenkavalier* on 3 March. He had not finished when Richard Strauss engaged him as a conductor.[7] He also gave conducting classes at the Vienna Academy of Music and Dramatic Art, but it was a short sojourn, for he was soon appointed director of the Frankfurt Opera (1924-29). He said goodbye to Vienna, for the time being, with a performance of *Götterdämmerung* on 29 June 1924. As Krauss entered for the beginning of the third act, a storm of applause broke out that Vienna had rarely seen, his earliest biographer recalled. "As Siegfried's horn rang out, one could recognise Krauss himself in the call, his innermost being was revealed. One understood the reason for his departure. One had a presentiment – one suddenly knew the conditions for his return."[8] He returned as head of the Opera in 1929.

But first in Frankfurt, he began to gain an international reputation. His "noble – if at times all too controlled – conducting" had won him many admirers in Vienna, reported the *Musical Times*.[9] He travelled to the Soviet Union, Spain, and the United States for concerts. In New York he included the *Meistersinger* overture in one of his programs. It was played "with contagious enthusiasm," according to the *New York Times*. "The music was warmly lyrical in essence and, for all its movement, properly expository. When the orchestra, at the moment of Wagner's veritable explosion of genius, enunciated four themes at the same time, Mr. Krauss contrived that all four, and not merely two, were heard. He did this without over-elaboration. He brought the well-known overture to a stirring climax."[10]

On 1 September 1929 he took up duties as director of the Vienna State Opera (1929-34) in succession to Franz Schalk. Although the position had first been offered to Furtwängler, who would not accept it,[11] Krauss was, of all those who had ever been offered the post, "perhaps the one with the best qualifications."[12] He also taught at the Academy of Music again. He worked very hard at the Opera, conducting most operas himself. With the exception of Richard Strauss, "star conductors" were not welcome.[13]

His first new production, the *Meistersinger* on 30 September 1929, was an "outstanding success.... This was the first time a Viennese audience heard Krauss's quick *tempi*. Accustomed to the traditional leisurely *Meistersinger* handed down by Richter and Franz Schalk, people were taken completely by surprise. From the very first bars of the Overture there was much catching of breath."[14] Among his new productions were *Walküre* (20 April 1930), *Siegfried* (21 May 1931), *Götterdämmerung* (11 October 1931), *Parsifal* (13 February 1933), *Rienzi* (25 March 1933), and *Holländer* (9 May 1934 – a revival). *Rheingold* had been given its new production by Furtwängler in Schalk's day. The remaining *Ring* operas under Krauss, however, were quite different. "The new *Ring* made many friends, but many enemies too," wrote Marcel Prawy. "Looking back, one must admit it was admirably conducted by Krauss, but there was

[7] Clemens Krauss-Archiv Wien, ed., *Der Prinzipal: Clemens Krauss: Fakten, Vergleiche, Rückschlüsse* (text, Signe Scanzoni; research, Götz Klaus Kende) (Tutzing: H. Schneider, 1988), and review by Kenneth Birkin in *Music & Letters*, vol. 70 no. 3 (August, 1989), p. 435

[8] Anton Berger, *Clemens Krauss*, 3rd ed. (Graz: Leuschner & Lubensky, 1929), p. 3

[9] 1 February 1925, p. 172 (Paul Bechert)

[10] 20 March 1929, p. 25 (Olin Downes)

[11] *New York Times*, 20 December 1928, p. 32

[12] Marcel Prawy, *The Vienna Opera* (Vienna-Munich-Zurich: Verlag Fritz Molden, 1969), p. 132

[13] Prawy, *ibid*, pp. 134-35. The other in-house conductors were Robert Heger, Hugo Reichenberger, and Karl Alwin.

[14] *ibid*, p. 136

not perhaps the uniformity of style that one would have expected of a production of this calibre...."[15] One of the most important contributions Krauss made to the Vienna Opera during these years was to build up the ensemble, to strengthen the tradition exemplified by Mahler. He abolished the claques, brought in new blood, and built up a faithful team of singers. There is a window into these years through the *Edition Wiener Staatsoper Live* recordings (1933-34), though it is a frosty window, with much obscured. Most audible are the voices, though some lively orchestral direction can be discerned. One of the most remarkable fragments is from the *Rheingold* of 28 February 1933. The Rhinemaidens sing so well together – an ensemble in perfect unison – that they sound like so many chords of an organ, though the sound is so poor this may be an acoustic illusion.[16]

With the political developments in Berlin unfolding, new opportunities presented themselves. As the Nazis expelled, forced from office, retired, or otherwise made musical life impossible for Fritz Busch, Erich Kleiber, Wilhelm Furtwängler, and later Hans Knappertsbusch, Krauss always seemed there, ready and willing to step up to the podium. While many other musicians took advantage of the political turmoil to further their own careers, opprobrium fell more heavily on Krauss because he was a great musician. People had expected him to act differently. Within days of Furtwängler's demise at the Berlin State Opera, Krauss was in Berlin signing a contract to replace him.[17] On his return to Vienna he was booed for having dealt so quickly and profitably with a regime hostile to Austria.[18] He was released from his contract immediately, and went to Berlin. There he straight away set about leaving his mark, as the *New York Times* reported:

> First of all, he exploded a bomb by informing certain singers that their claims to the exclusive proprietorship of certain rôles were once and for all at an end. Next, he set about restudying *Die Meistersinger*, ostensibly for the purpose of celebrating the Saar victory, in reality, as many insist, to do away with the last vestige of the Furtwängler production – which less than two years ago had the Berlin press and public by the ears. Even the orchestral parts used by Furtwängler are said to have been thrown out and new ones ordered.[19]

Nevertheless, this *Meistersinger* and a later *Ring* cycle were "enthusiastically received,"[20] not least because he had persuaded several of Vienna's outstanding

[15] *ibid*, p. 136. The highlights, according to Prawy, were Maria Jeritza as Brünnhilde and Lotte Lehmann as Sieglinde.

[16] Vol. 14 of the *Edition Wiener Staatsoper Live* is devoted to Krauss's Wagner performances.

[17] Furtwängler's forced resignation took place on 5 December 1934. On 9 December Krauss travelled up from Vienna. On 10 December he agreed to a ten-year contract: Fred K. Prieberg, *Trial of Strength: Wilhelm Furtwängler and the Third Reich*, (trans.) Christopher Dolan (London: Quartet Books, 1991), pp. 143, 170.

[18] On 11 December he conducted *Falstaff*. "As he made his way to the rostrum he was greeted with a chorus of boos and catcalls and I still have no regrets at having joined in, though nowadays I am disposed to view Krauss's blatant opportunism more leniently than I did at the time": Prawy, *ibid*, p. 145. "There was tremendous booing at his last performance, in which I participated": George Hall, "Marcel Prawy: the last interview," *Opera*, vol. 54 no. 7 (July 2003), p. 794. Prawy was 91 years old, and died on 23 February 2003, one week after the interview. See also Heinrich Kralik, *The Vienna Opera House*, trans. Michael H. Law (Vienna: Brüder Rosenbaum, 1955), pp. 74-76 on Krauss's diminishing popularity in Vienna.

[19] 3 February 1935, p. X7 (Herbert Peyser)

[20] Kenneth Birkin, reviewing *Der Prinzipal: Clemens Krauss*, in *Music & Letters*, vol. 70 no. 3 (August, 1989), p. 436. "This period was distinguished by a magnificent *Ring*....": Cook, "Clemens Krauss," p. 85.

singers to follow him to Berlin.[21] Within months of his arrival, however, rumours were circulating about a possible move to Munich. He had been "something of a square peg in a round hole" at the Berlin Staatsoper, according to the *New York Times*. "The Berliners have declined to warm up to him, and the singers he brought with him from Vienna are resented by the 'old reliables' of Unter den Linden as a 'Viennese clique.' To be sure, Krauss has a long-term contract. But even Wotan winked at a contract with giants when it served his purpose to do so."[22]

After further political manoeuvring, not least by the scheming opera czar Heinz Tietjen,[23] he went to Munich where he debuted in January 1937. He had many important tasks to perform to make Munich into the opera capital of the Reich, and he set about doing so with the same energy he had shown in Berlin. The Munich Opera was to have, in Willi Schuh's words, "a transfusion of blood such as it has not known for a very long time."[24] A singer who had once been a defender of Knappertsbusch recalled that under Krauss it was not long before "the glitter of the productions could hardly be surpassed."[25] He presented 43 new productions during his eight years in Munich, including the *Holländer* (12 June 1937), *Tristan* (16 July 1937), *Lohengrin* (9 July 1938), *Tannhäuser* (15 July 1939), *Rheingold* (29 October 1939), *Walküre* (28 January 1940), *Siegfried* (28 December 1940), *Götterdämmerung* (29 June 1941), and *Meistersinger* (27 June 1943). Other notable Wagnerian events in those years were a *Ring* cycle he took to La Scala, Milan in 1938 (29 March-3 April), and a *Meistersinger* in 1943, the 75th anniversary year of its première.[26] In October 1943 the opera house in Munich, and Krauss's own house, were destroyed by bombs. In March 1944 he conducted a performance of the *Holländer* for German radio, which is now a famous recording of the work.[27] In June 1944 he settled in Salzburg.

After the war he was banned from conducting in Germany and Austria for two years. In December 1946 the Austrian Commission held that "it had been proved that he was not a Nazi party member nor a party candidate, [and] had never held any type of political or semi-political position."[28] He gave his first concert with the Vienna Philharmonic in May 1947. His association with Hitler's grand plans for opera in the

[21] In addition to his wife, Viorica Ursuleac, they included Gertrude Rünger, Josef von Manowarda, Franz Völker, and Erich Zimmermann: *New York Times*, 3 February 1935, p. X7; Michael H. Kater, *The twisted muse: musicians and their music in the Third Reich* (New York: Oxford University Press, 1997), p. 48

[22] report from Vienna, 20 July 1935, *New York Times*, 4 August 1935, p. X4 (Herbert Peyser)

[23] Jealous of Krauss's prominence, he more or less blackmailed him into moving to Munich: Friedelind Wagner and Page Cooper, *The royal family of Bayreuth* (London: Eyre and Spottiswoode, 1948), pp. 121-2; Hans Hotter, *Memoirs*, (trans. and ed.) Donald Arthur (Boston: Northeastern University Press, 2006), p. 202.

[24] quoted by Kenneth Birkin in his review of *Der Prinzipal: Clemens Krauss*, *Music & Letters*, vol. 70 no. 3 (August, 1989), p. 437

[25] Hildegard Ranczak, quoted in Kater, *The Twisted Muse*, p. 50

[26] Pander, *Clemens Krauss in München*, pp. 12-18. His concerts in those years included no Wagner.

[27] *American Record Guide*: "poor sound... but one still gets the feeling that a first-class conductor is at work": September 1983, p. 68 (Kurt Moses); *Opera*: "an unsurpassed reading as regards tension and attack. It is adorned by Hans Hotter's similarly unsurpassed Dutchman... Unfortunately the distortion of the voices remains intrusive...": January 1996, p. 24 (Alan Blyth); *Fanfare*: "still the best... it boasts the flawless conducting of Clemens Krauss and Hotter in his prime in one of his greatest roles...": January/February 2003, p. 212 (William Youngren).

[28] *New York Times*, 11 May 1947, p. 54. Like Furtwängler, he gave help and protection to Jewish artists. Kater also concluded: "there is not a shred of hard evidence that Krauss was ever a nominal let alone a confirmed Nazi, before or after 1935": *The Twisted Muse*, p. 52

Third Reich nevertheless exacted their toll. He was never again to have a permanent post. He travelled widely as a guest conductor in his final years: to Central and South America, Egypt, England, Greece, Holland, Yugoslavia, Portugal, Italy and Spain. He never returned to New York. When an agent proposed him to the Metropolitan Opera, Rudolf Bing replied: "I would not wish to have [him] *near* my house. It is typical of the Viennese to accept him back with all honours."[29] Although he did conduct again in Vienna, including "a fine *Meistersinger*" in 1952 according to one English visitor,[30] he was thwarted in his endeavours to be re-appointed director of the Vienna State Opera. Those in power had not forgotten 1934.

The important Wagner performances he conducted during this period included a *Tristan* (1951) and *Meistersinger* (1953) at Covent Garden, and *Parsifal* and the *Ring* at the 1953 Bayreuth Festival. There Wieland Wagner had deemed him a "worthy replacement" for Knappertsbusch.[31] He was engaged for the following year, and for concerts as far away as Berlin, Brazil and Australia,[32] when he died during a concert tour in Mexico City on 16 May 1954, aged 61. He was buried at his home in Ehrwald in the Tyrol on 12 July 1954.

Krauss as Wagner conductor

Krauss was a universal conductor. He was "a master of his craft in all its many facets," wrote Hans Hotter, in musical and artistic matters, in his guidance to singers, in theatre administration, and in teaching.[33] He was "constitutionally unable to be a specialist," according to one close observer, Erik Maschat.[34] If it was good music, he would play it. His interests were as broad as Erich Kleiber's and Fritz Busch's. Like them, when Wagner operas came his way, he would embrace them with all his musicality. When discussing *Tristan* in 1943, "he explained that although he could grasp the origins of the work – the fearful closeness of love and the death-wish – through his knowledge of life and of Wagner, for him the work was above all 'a piece of glorious music.'"[35] What he sought to do was to present the music as it was, as it was intended by the composer – nothing more:

> To interpret the improvisations which the great masters set on paper must be the aim of every responsible performer of their works. Knowledge of the original and authentic intentions of the composer is therefore a well from which the interpreter must always be ready to draw.... It is not the task of the conductor to make visible demonstrations of feelings engendered in him by the music so as to transmit his own private reactions to his listeners. Rather it must be his aim

[29] Sir Rudolf Bing, *5,000 nights at the opera* (London: Hamilton, 1972), p. 133. Bing himself was born in Vienna. He became a British citizen in 1946.

[30] George Harewood, *The tongs and the bones: the memoirs of Lord Harewood* (London: Weidenfeld and Nicholson, 1981), p. 116

[31] Wolfgang Wagner, *Acts: the autobiography of Wolfgang Wagner*, trans. John Brownjohn (London: Weidenfeld & Nicholson, 1994), 120

[32] Pander, *Clemens Krauss in München*, p. 11. Wolfgang Wagner reflected that "It was... abundantly clear from Krauss's behaviour in 1953 that his Karajanesque claims to omnipotence would have made his collaboration with my brother an awkward one": *Acts*, p. 120.

[33] Hotter, *Memoirs*, pp. 88-90. Among his conducting pupils in Salzburg were Herbert von Karajan and Otmar Suitner.

[34] Maschat, "Clemens Krauss" [n. 2 above], p. 740. Maschat was onetime head of the Sound Archives of Bavarian Radio, Munich.

[35] Pander, *Clemens Krauss in München*, p. 51

to translate into sound the vision of the work with which his imagination supplies him – so to speak, to shape music out of tonal material.[36]

His approach was quite different from the great German romantics. Furtwängler described him (or defamed him) in a letter to Strauss in 1936: "He possesses a certain cold elegance and a technique that is not without its interest to experts, but beyond that he has nothing, not even the slightest, to offer, and he lacks even a trace of force and warmth.... It is simply impossible to describe Krauss as an essentially German artist."[37] Otto Klemperer echoed this view in 1969: Krauss was "a gifted conductor, but unimportant; quite unimportant."[38] These comments were made against a background of personal bitterness: Krauss twice replaced Furtwängler, in Vienna and Berlin, and Krauss flourished in the musical life of a Germany which had excluded Klemperer. They do, nevertheless, indicate that Krauss had a different approach to music-making from his colleagues. Nowhere is the difference more evident than at Bayreuth in 1953 when Krauss replaced Knappertsbusch. But let us not describe the difference. "It is a waste of time and effort," Krauss wrote, "to try to do justice to one's musicality in mere words. One may try to feed the unconscious into the retort of the mind in order to obtain clarity, but even this cannot reveal the mystery of the gift of musical understanding."[39] Let us turn instead to examples of Krauss's music-making in the late works of Wagner.

Tristan und Isolde

One of Krauss's celebrated performances in Munich was a new production of *Tristan* on 16 July 1937 – "the Day of German Art" – in front of Hitler, members of the diplomatic corps, the political and military elite, and leading personalities from throughout the Reich. Julius Pölzer sang Tristan, and Gertrud Rünger sang Isolde.[40] Krauss interpreted the beautiful score "in a masterly fashion," according to the *Münchener Neueste Nachrichten*:

His fine sense for a spacious structure, for soft nuances in the transitions and for a perfect tonal balance were brought out to wonderful effect in this richly emotional music with all its different contrasts. The natural flow of the unending melody was never interrupted, not even slightly disturbed. The conductor took the tempos in the prelude and in some slow parts of the second act very broadly, and in doing so achieved intense climaxes of unbelievable power. So much livelier was the way the passionate parts of Isolde's narration and the nocturnal dialogue flowed by. We would also like to mention that at the much talked-about point in the second act, where Tristan says *im Tod sie ließ an das Licht gelangen* ("in death she let go into the light"),[41] contrary to some previous performances three years ago, an E flat minor chord could be heard again, just the way the Master wanted it. The orchestra played with perfect tonal beauty and precision.[42]

[36] Krauss, "*Autobiographie à la minute*," p. 741

[37] letter dated 9 May 1936 quoted in Kater, *The Twisted Muse*, p. 48

[38] Peter Heyworth (ed.), *Conversations with Klemperer*, revised edition (London: Faber and Faber, 1985), p. 48

[39] Krauss, "*Autobiographie à la minute*," p. 742

[40] Other singers included Ludwig Weber, King Marke; Hans Hermann Nissen, Kurwenal; and Luise Willer, Brangäne. The producer was Oskar Walleck, and the set designer, Benno von Arent, both leading Nazis.

[41] p. 450 of the C.F. Peters, Leipzig/Dover score

[42] *Münchener Neueste Nachrichten*, 18 July 1937, p. 4 (Oscar von Pander). Knappertsbusch conducted

Some of these characteristics can be heard in one of Krauss's rare studio recordings of Wagner: the Prelude and Liebestod recorded in London in 1949. Conditions in the studio were not good, but Krauss's interpretations were viewed by the *Music Review* as "imaginative, sensuous and dynamic. He obtains opulently languid atmosphere in the Prelude, backed by clean *ensemble* and scrupulously yet poetic observation of Wagner's nuances. The controlled drive behind the work-up to the climax from the *belebend* section, and the tense handling of the runs on upper strings, are especially notable. The performance of the *Liebestod* is not so steady...."[43] After this session, he never returned to the studio to record any more Wagner.

He did return to London, however, to conduct a performance of *Tristan* at Covent Garden in 1951.[44] Conditions in the orchestra were only gradually improving, and this showed in the opening prelude, according to the *Spectator*, "though during the rest of the performance the playing was well above average."[45] One orchestral player recalled Krauss's appearance: "To the orchestra he was invariably calm and courteous; his baton was very long and his beat very small. We had a minimum of rehearsals for his *Tristan*.... I have never again felt the hairs on the back of my neck tingle as they did in the 'Death Motif' in Krauss's *Tristan*."[46] He "imposed shape and no little beauty on the various stages of passion," according to *Music Survey*.[47] The performance was in "the hand of a master," wrote the *Manchester Guardian*; it was an interpretation:

> ... less exciting than some we can recall (Beecham's, to name one) but which had now almost forgotten virtues. The quality of the sound and the dynamic relationships were most beautifully managed; instead of being driven the singers were, in the truest sense, accompanied, one result being that the words were all clear and there was no shouting. Another result was that the emotional exhaustion which often sets in before the end of the second act was never experienced. Certainly the first act (in which in any case Mme Flagstad was something below her best) became in this rendering comparatively cool, but in the second act at the great broadening out at the words *Es werde Nacht, dass hell sie dorten leuchte* the sudden intensity was all the more thrilling, and the great singer was once more producing that stream of golden tone which makes her Isolde, if not the most dramatic of her time, at least the most purely beautiful.
>
> Mr. Krauss's handling of the last act, too, showed how moving Set Svanholm could make Tristan's last delirium.[48]

The Times was impressed that Krauss did not pack too much into the opening prelude, that he did not make it a concert piece:

> The Prelude was only the Prelude; it was not lashed into a passion; and the whole of the first act was pitched on the low emotional plane of an exposition. This is not to say there was no

Tristan in Munich on 14 July and 6 August 1934.

[43] vol. 12 (1951), p. 344 (William Mann). *Gramophone* commented: "A ripe, humane, and sometimes noble recording, which perhaps misses only the richest warmth of the brass. I like the broad generosity of the style...": December 1950, p. 142 (W. R. Anderson).

[44] Set Svanholm sang Tristan; Kirsten Flagstad, Isolde; Norman Walker, King Marke; Constance Shacklock, Brangäne; Sigurd Bjorling, Kurwenal; and Geraint Evans, Melot. Conditions in the English press at the time appear not to have permitted much space for music criticism. No reviews were found in the *Daily Telegraph*, the *Observer*, or the *Sunday Times*.

[45] 1 June 1951, p. 717 (Martin Cooper)

[46] Richard Temple Savage, *A Voice From The Pit: Reminiscences of an Orchestral Musician* (Newton Abbot: David & Charles, 1988), pp. 131-2

[47] vol. 4 no. 1 (October 1951), p. 363 (A.E.F.D.)

[48] 31 May 1951, p. 5 (Philip Hope-Wallace)

Fig.19.1. Clemens Krauss from his Brno years, 1912-1913

Fig. 19.2. Krauss in Vienna, 1943

Fig. 19.3. Krauss in Bayreuth, 1953. Photo by Siegfried Lauterwasser

Fig.19.4. Krauss in Vienna

Fig. 19.5. Krauss toasts

eloquence or no beauty, only that it was quieter and the preparation for a lyrical rather than a heroic performance.

No flame shot into the air until Isolde extinguished the torch in Act II, when the temperature was changed in an instant. But still the great love-duet was quietly played and sung. Here, as in the *Liebestod*, the rapture was lyrical, the tone saturated instead of strenuous, so that there was rarely need for a *fortissimo*, but when it did come it was the more telling.[49]

Die Meistersinger von Nürnberg

Krauss's first new production in Vienna was, as mentioned, the *Meistersinger* on 30 September 1929. It was a performance notable for its clear, light and youthful character. It was "a most scrupulous cleansing of orchestral and singing parts," according to the *Neue Freie Presse*:

Clemens Krauss does not look for a particular *leitmotif* as the basis for his interpretation, for example, "musical comedy." Rather, he approaches the work from a fresh and clear perspective.... Essentially, everything that is beautiful and characteristic in this wonderful work comes out distinctly – distinctly in the orchestra, distinctly in the singing, and most of all in the cohesion of orchestra and stage.... First and foremost was the respect for the singers' rights in the dialogue. There was also rich and varied nuances of timbres and tempos, overall power and wholesomeness of the line, and a constant flow of tone. In this regard, there were some particularly comedy-like accelerations at the beginning and the end of the well-balanced overture, which were not at all out of place, and which boldly proclaimed the *Meistersinger* theme to be its motto. The finale of the singing-school scene was confidently structured. The rhythm in the brawling scene was unshakable, suggesting a certain fate for Nuremberg and its poor town clerk. Magnificent too was the accentuation of the dialogue in that so blissfully relaxed scene between Sachs and Walter before the creation of the *Preislied*. Strangely enough, the Quintet came off the least successful. Eva seemed to be irritated from her very first cue. Are we mistaken to see the reason for this in the conductor's tendency to accentuate voices that are not usually made prominent? This certainly had a surprising effect on some occasions. Voices that arise from the darkness do not always blend with one another, and they simply did not blend in the Quintet. It is possible something similar happened in the prelude to the third act. Under Schalk, it sounded richer, warmer, and more solemn.... Overall, there was so much of the beautiful and laudable to be heard that we did not think twice about joining in with the applause surging around the young conductor at the desk.[50]

The *Wiener Zeitung* was struck how Krauss gave an element of comedy, of cheerfulness to the work:

This resulted in faster tempos than usual. Only the lyric parts, and the waltz on the festival meadow, were taken more slowly than usual. With ingenious economy, the orchestra was muted to accommodate the requirements of the stage, so that the voices could move freely, without orchestral tone putting them in chains. At times, this muting was insufficient. At other times, the strings in particular were pushed too far to the back. The cheerfulness was animated, youthful, yet at the same time it lacked the pathos and grandeur which the complicated polyphony of this score alone demands. But youth has spirit, a certain tendency to live in the moment, so that it was only natural that the climaxes especially grew with verve and youthful power.[51]

[49] 30 May 1951, p. 8

[50] 2 October 1929, pp. 2-3 (Julius Korngold). Among the cast were Josef Kalenberg, Walther; Wilhelm Rode, Sachs; and Lotte Lehmann, Eva. A recording of the Quintet survives from 1934: see Discography.

[51] 2 October 1929, p. 4

When he returned to London in 1953, the Covent Garden orchestra was still improving. "The orchestral playing under Clemens Krauss was less distinguished than the best of the singing," wrote the *Daily Telegraph*, "which it sometimes obscured."[52] The orchestra seemed to the *Sunday Times* "curiously low-powered and lacklustre at times, but it had its shining moments."[53] It was "oddly inert and occasionally ragged" until well into the second act, according to the *Evening Standard*.[54] As for the interpretation itself, the pace and texture seemed to surprise the reviewers. "Was the overture played faster than usual and did it sound rather superficial?" asked *The Times*. "It did; but it was intentional on the part of Mr. Clemens Krauss... [The performance had] a lighter gait than usual."[55] The *Scotsman* commented that:

> his conception of the work, as is usual with him, is an overall one. When he begins the overture, he sees the end of the opera as his goal. There is no time to dally unduly on details; everything reasonably in its place and then let's get a move on. We missed the sensual beauty and sheer magic that Sir Thomas Beecham conjured up, but had to admit that the opera, uncut, passed very quickly.[56]

To the *Manchester Guardian*, Krauss seemed a "classical interpreter,... a conductor of Wagner who puts singing parts first, gives the singers time to breathe, and sees that we hear every word." Under him, "*Die Meistersinger* is a German comedy emotionally measured for us so that we are not knocked out in round one but warmed steadily and slowly as by an autumn sun until the streaming beauty of the third act warms us through and through. All before has seemed surprisingly light and rapid...."[57] "In sum," concluded *The Times*, "this was a singularly homogeneous performance, not vocally outstanding, but conveying the lighter side of Wagner's protean genius with very pleasing effect."[58] The Covent Garden performance seemed characteristic of his approach: his *Meistersinger* is a comedy, nowhere is it "stifled by false pathos," wrote Kurt Blaukopf. "Throughout, we are under the impression that it is the action that determines and exudes the musical flow and not *vice versa*.[59]

Der Ring des Nibelungen

The new production of the *Ring* in Vienna in the 1920s and 1930s was staggered, and the *Rheingold*, as mentioned, had been conducted by Furtwängler, in 1928.

[52] 4 July 1953. The reviews quoted above of this *Meistersinger* performance are from the Royal Opera Collections. Hans Hopf sang Walther; Paul Schoeffler, Sachs; Benuo Kushe, Beckmesser; Friedrich Dalberg, Pogner; Murray Dickie, David; Elisabeth Schwarzkopf, Eva; and Constance Shacklock, Magdalene.

[53] 5 July 1953 (Ernest Newman). Richard Temple Savage, who played in the orchestra in act three only, wrote that "the practice in those days (introduced by Rankl) [was] to change the principals of woodwind and horns" for the third act in view of its length: *A Voice from the Pit*, p. 131. At Knappertsbusch's Munich Festival *Meistersinger* in 1931, there had been a *complete* change of orchestras for the third act: *The Times*, 25 July 1931, p. 10.

[54] 4 July 1953 (Charles Reid) [55] 4 July 1953 [56] 6 July 1953

[57] 6 July 1953 (Philip Hope-Wallace)

[58] *The Times*, 4 July 1953, p. 8. Of the 6 July performance, which was broadcast, *The Times* wrote that Krauss "only threw away one moment of magic though it was, alas, the midsummer's eve music at the end of the second act. Had the brawl been bigger immediately beforehand, the contrast might have been more breathtaking": 7 July 1953, p. 2.

[59] Kurt Blaukopf, *Great conductors*, (trans.) Miriam Blaukopf (London: Arco, 1955), p. 120

Krauss's *Walküre* opened on 20 April 1930. He appeared to be very much in the vein of Mahler, and for this he was praised and criticised. The reason lay principally in his intense concentration on detail. At times he took too great care over the score, in the view of the *Wiener Zeitung*. "The line of the great whole sometimes threatened to get lost in details – and sometimes trivial details at that, which are pushed into the foreground. His temperament is more outward than inward. This often resulted in whipped-up ecstasies, with the brass swirling above the rest of the orchestra and breaking over the voices in a devastating manner."[60] To the *Neue Freie Presse*, this was "an important new production by a very talented conductor":

Fig. 19.6. Krauss in 1932. Drawing by Elisabeth von Steiger

Mahler emphasised the wildly-troubled, dark, sinister side of this work, and brought out the strongest tragic accents from the very first scene with Wotan and Brünnhilde onwards, spreading an eerie grandeur over the adagio of the *Todesverkündigung*. Krauss's assured musical sense takes a similar direction, boldly striving to do anything but de-emotionalize Wagnerian expression, but rather emphasizing it down to the very last detail in a Wagnerian-romantic manner. He traces with particular empathy all that which is mysterious, tenderly-emotional, softly touching the soul. He immerses himself – at times perhaps lingering too lovingly – in all that soulful pantomime music. A magnificent impetuosity rushes forward through the Valkyrie scene, and Wotan's farewell overflows with moving warmth. Fascinated and fascinatingly, the beautiful orchestra responds.[61]

The same journal found Krauss "young, fresh, and also unruly" in the new production of *Siegfried* on 21 May 1931. He "played Siegfried from the desk":

He emphasised the forward-striving of the Siegfried rhythm in a refreshing and fetching manner, impetuously shaping the symphonic intensifications, and the fearful music, in the lead-up to the

[60] 23 April 1930, p. 7 ("rb")

[61] 23 April 1930, pp. 2-3 (Julius Korngold). Maria Jeritza debuted as Brünnhilde.

smithy scene. Phrases retain their dramatic, picturesque or emotional feeling, and once again, the passionate and soulful elements, such as those in the forest murmurs, have been traced with loving concentration. Sometimes it feels as if Krauss is hunting down those *Meistersinger* elements which are so attractively inherent in the *Siegfried* score. His and the orchestra's strongest achievement occurred in the final scene: Brünnhilde's awakening and becoming one with Siegfried. It overflowed with an ecstatic pulsing of true Wagnerian-romantic life, headily played and sung.[62]

If Mahler could be heard in Krauss's *Walküre*, it was Richter that resounded in his *Götterdämmerung*. With the new production on 11 October 1931, the emphasis was on the music, wrote the *Wiener Zeitung*:

No new production can deny that. It was very gratifying to see that Krauss did not simply want to achieve a new production at all cost. For the most part he held it to the old Hans Richter tradition, or let the tradition hold him back, something that is likewise of no little merit. Sometimes the tone of the strings and the warmth of the winds sounded so sensuous and melodious that one could believe one was hearing a reproduction of the orchestral sound under Richter. Some elements, however, were pushed to the back (the orchestral preludes), then at other times into an almost blazing tempo, and sometimes into an occasional dance-like, lively, hopping rhythm. Yet the broad, strangely singing sound of our orchestra, the old Viennese Wagner style, remained predominant.[63]

To the *Neue Freie Presse* it seemed as if the tragic spirit of the work had awakened his own. In performances to date, Krauss had been observed to take "a healthy, accurate, musical approach" to *Götterdämmerung*, one of "youthful verve and fire, sometimes even a bit of nervous impatience":

This time, however, he not only stood above the gigantic material with superior calm, never once flagging in the whole five hours, but he also assiduously urged the drama towards greatness. It seemed as if every occasion for dramatic compression and intensification had been perceived from the inside, and not merely externalised for contrived effect. The same way the *Meistersinger* reveals the tonal secret of the horn, so does *Götterdämmerung* for the trombone. The way Krauss provided all brass displays with warm and even nuances! Siegfried's Rhine journey was alive, sparkled, cheered, was razor-sharp despite all its accelerated tempos. This Rhine music was still the music of a beautiful, energetic German-ness of the past, unshaken in spirit and mind. The male chorus rushed forward, broadening the way they like, and the dramatic altercations after Brünnhilde's entry sparked with elemental force. A most intense build-up in the Funeral March. Rarely has this magnificent orchestra sounded so harrowing.[64]

In 1938 Krauss took the Munich Opera to La Scala, Milan to present a *Ring* cycle as part of an excerise to strengthen relations between the two countries. The Italian responses give an interesting glimpse of the conductor's style that was to emerge at Bayreuth in 1953. Krauss was one of the "paramount factors" in the performance of the *Rheingold*, according to *Il Popolo d'Italia*. He was "poised, yet authoritative, always lively, and magnificent in his tireless vigour."[65] His "typical style and special sensitivity" were evident right from the prelude, according to *Il Secolo La Sera*; he achieved a rare homogeneity in the orchestra and an excellent ensemble on stage.[66] His "exceptional

[62] 23 May 1931, p. 2 (Julius Korngold). Josef Kalenberg sang Siegfried; Maria Nemeth, Brünnhilde; Emil Schipper, the Wanderer.

[63] *Wiener Zeitung*, 13 October 1931, p. 4 ("rb")

[64] 13 October 1931, p. 3 (Julius Korngold)

[65] 30 March 1938, p. 5

[66] 30 March 1938, p. 3

skill" was remarked upon by the *Corriere della Sera*: "he interpreted the [work] so that the voices of the singers on the stage took precedence; the movements were kept light and swift; the tempo agile and flowing; the germinal ideas – in themselves highly dramatic – understated. All the while, the lovely, pliant, sonorous orchestral ensemble was kept firmly in hand by the calm gestures of the conductor."[67] In the *Walküre* the orchestra left a different impression on *Il Secolo La Sera*: it was "lifted from its former subordinate role to one that is on a par with that of the stage, although without the overpowering liveliness that characterised the interpretation of Victor de Sabata, and one that favoured above all heroic accents."[68] He was particularly effective, according to *Il Popolo d'Italia*, "in passages of markedly emphatic rhythm, vigour and solemnity."[69] To him was largely owed the huge success of the performance, according to the *Corriere della Sera*:

> with its fresh, almost new, impact (especially in the first and third acts), which lifted the not inconsiderable weight of the score, obtaining a balance of sound, and a rendering of sober and measured effects – legitimate in Wagner – on which the evocative musical power of the drama still depends. The orchestra was even more disciplined and integrated than on the first night, and never left Krauss's control, allowing the symphonic highlights to emerge best from the "mystic depths." The singers... were held constantly at the forefront of the entire performance, a device that greatly enhanced the symphonic drama.[70]

By the time of *Siegfried*, Krauss had left his mark. He "conducted with customary zeal and powerful self-assurance," according to *Il Popolo d'Italia*, "and was particularly appreciated when he was able to display the rhythmic vigour and driving force of his dramatic fire."[71] *Il Secolo La Sera* had little to add. Krauss had again "done his utmost to meet the high expectations of La Scala, where opera aims at standards of perfection which the Germans expect from their concerts."[72] To the *Corriere della Sera* the performance "seemed totally impeccable":

> Krauss's conducting and preparation – clearly evident in the orchestra and on the stage – demonstrated once again his admirable intention to adhere to the movements, rather than, perhaps, to the intensity of expression and colour desired by the composer. This uncut version, therefore, seemed slightly more restrained than the productions staged at La Scala in earlier years (except for that conducted by Siegfried Wagner in 1930). On previous occasions, using abridged versions, the tempo, accents, rhythms and contrasts were obliquely emphasised or reduced, resulting in a more rapid succession of effect."[73]

Götterdämmerung was attended by a phalanx of Nazi and ministry officials to emphasize the propaganda purpose of the visit. Whether for this or other reasons, the press appears to have refrained from reviewing it.[74] One writer has claimed that the strongest impression left on the Italian audience had been Hagen's men in act two who sang with "Teutonic wildness."[75] One can well imagine.

[67] 30 March 1938, p. 2
[68] 31 March 1938, p. 3
[69] 31 March 1938, p. 5
[70] 31 March 1938, p. 5
[71] 2 April 1938, p. 6
[72] 2 April 1938, p. 3
[73] 2 April 1938, p. 2
[74] A report in *Il Secolo La Sera* merely wrote: "There was much applause for the conductor, Krauss, who had given his all to this exacting Milanese presentation." (4 April 1938, p. 3)
[75] Pander, *Clemens Krauss in München*, p. 107

One great fortune that arose from Knappertsbusch's intemperate withdrawal from the 1953 Bayreuth Festival is that it gave us a record of Krauss's Wagner performances that otherwise would have been lost. His abilities as a Wagner conductor would forever have been obscured by the respect he was shown by his odious admirers.[76] Krauss threw light on Wagner as Knappertsbusch rested in the shade. Hans Hotter recalled:

> We, the members of the cast, all sensed the way that, especially in his 1953 Bayreuth *Ring*, his commanding style revealed the full scope of Wagner's music drama, guiding us through the performances with an impressive tranquillity, yet generously allowing us all the freedom we needed to delineate our roles as we felt them – almost as if he had some premonition that this would be his swansong at Bayreuth.[77]

Not all artists, perhaps, felt the same freedom that Hotter did in the face of Krauss's dramatic urge. His pace at the beginning of act three of *Walküre* was particularly fast, as Astrid Varnay recalled: "Krauss wanted to use a quick tempo to illustrate Brünnhilde's worried haste, trying to bring Sieglinde to safety before Wotan catches up with them. He urged the orchestra to a frenzy, which in turn had me delivering that scene breathlessly."[78] However much Varnay may have protested, Krauss was astute in his dramatic judgment, as reviews of the recording have shown.

In calling the 1953 *Ring* "a flawless achievement," *Opera Quarterly* considered Krauss's *tempi* "neither courageous nor complacent, merely correct. His sense of balance is perfect and his dynamic flexibility exquisite. For example, *Walküre* act 3 begins at a hectic, exhilarating pace, the bustling atmosphere giving way to a poignant farewell scene and a grandiose finale – this is the most gradual and emotionally satisfying extended *ritardando* ever conceived."[79] *Fanfare* described the conducting as "blinding brilliance and rich lyricism in perfect balance."[80] *Opera* described it as having "an inspiriting, fiery feeling that in its way is just as valid as Kna's epic interpretation."[81] Alan Blyth wrote in *Gramophone* that "many, including myself, consider [the Krauss *Ring*] to be the most compelling and best-cast cycle." He was reviewing a reissue in 2004, in better sound:

> Since reviewing its incarnation almost 16 years ago, I have never lost faith in its values: a truthful, admirably paced, deeply-felt traversal, performed by a real ensemble of singers working in dedicated fashion over a short span of time....
>
> Over all presides Krauss with a judicious blend of the dramatic and the spiritual, and the rare gift of maintaining line and musical argument through even the slowest passages. Where physical

[76] "For the Nazis, Krauss was a god." etc. Sir George Solti, *Solti on Solti: A Memoir* (London: Chatto & Windus, 1997), p. 75

[77] Hotter, *Memoirs*, p. 207. He added: "fortunately, there is a universally lauded CD recording of that 1953 *Ring*, a challenge to all subsequent Bayreuth recordings." Hotter described Krauss as "both midwife and godparent" at his first Wotan in *Walküre* in Munich in 1940, and gave several examples of his advice, including "to interpret his roles, especially the dramatic ones, strictly in Italian *bel canto* style" as Wagner had instructed his singers: p. 37.

[78] Astrid Varnay, with Donald Arthur, *Fifty-five years in five acts: my life in opera* (Boston: Northeastern University Press, 2000), p. 181. Varnay sang Brünnhilde in the first cycle conducted by Krauss; Martha Mödl sang the role in second cycle conducted by Joseph Keilberth.

[79] vol. 6 no. 4 (Summer 1989), p. 126 (Christopher J. Thomas): a review of the "double duration discs" by Rodolphe Productions: RPC 32503-9 (7 CDs)

[80] vol. 21 no. 4 (March/April 1998), p. 262 (Henry Fogel)

[81] vol. 49 no. 6 (June 1998), p. 659 (Alan Blyth)

energy or incandescence are of the essence, Krauss inspires his orchestra to provide them.... Krauss's reading is one of the quickest in the Bayreuth annals, but that very pace gives the piece a direct vigour and dramatic consistency not always heard in [Knappertsbusch's] deeply considered, reverential reading. Krauss imparts a wonderful feeling for the particular texture and tempo needed for each scene, culminating in the cleansing, sustained ecstasy of the work's close.[82]

The *New York Times*, in 1993, considered it "the best on records," easily surpassing all other *Rings* for "consistency" and "overall excellence" in its casting:

But what lifts this *Ring* to preeminence is the conducting of Clemens Krauss. Best remembered today as a master of the music of anyone named Strauss (especially Johann Jr. and Richard) and the librettist of Richard Strauss's valedictory opera *Capriccio*, Krauss here proved himself a supreme Wagnerian; his sudden death at 61 in May 1954 robbed the world of many more great Wagner performances.

In this *Ring*, his conducting combines the sweep and intensity of the Toscanini-Böhm modernist Wagner style with the Germanic brooding of Furtwängler in an utterly convincing blend of those seeming opposites. Tempos move forward purposefully, on the whole, but without slighting the music's mystery and tragedy. And the intensely dramatic and ecstatic moments, those great outbursts to which Wagner rises with satisfying frequency, are delivered with blinding passion.[83]

Fig. 19.7. Krauss as drawn by Hugo von Bouvard

In *Rheingold* there are several moments where he particularly distinguishes himself from Knappertsbusch. The deep rumblings of the opening prelude grow into swirling waters until, the pressure being so great, the Rhinemaidens burst into song. Krauss keeps them moving, ever dancing, never swimming, in the Rhine. Unlike Knappertsbusch's 1956-58 *Rheingolds*, Krauss had a full complement of anvils for his descent into Nibelheim. But generally, his *Ring* is not one in which the orchestral passages stand out. The transitional passages seamlessly grow out of, and subside into, the drama they are linking. The focus is always on the stage; the orchestra underpins

[82] June 2004, p. 90: a review of Archipel ARPCD 0250-13. Blyth was referring to Knappertsbusch's 1951 *Götterdämmerung*.

[83] 16 April 1993, p. C27 (John Rockwell)

the drama. At the intensely dramatic moments, however, the orchestra will rise like a serpent. It sweeps Freia up in a panic, for instance, when the giants approach to take her away.

Krauss is a singer's conductor. It is no wonder Hans Hotter loved him. In his act two monologue in *Walküre*, Krauss sets a mood of great gravity as Wotan begins to whisper his lines. Of this "dauntingly difficult scene," Hotter wrote how Krauss taught him to give it "a diversified interpretation," for it is a scene which, Krauss observed wryly, "as measured by the many things that happen in it, is actually too short."[84] As Hotter sings, Krauss weaves the orchestra around his words, making it grow out of the scenes he describes and subside into the drama that follows, like incoming and outgoing waves. Even in Wotan's greatest anger, Krauss's orchestra does not overwhelm him. Throughout, the singers hold centre stage. At the end of *Götterdämmerung*, after the shrieks of Hagen and others at the sight of the raised fist of the dead Siegfried, Brünnhilde (Varnay) floats in on a cloud of sound, and sets the immolation scene alight with her singing – the flames can be *heard* in the latter part of the scene – and after she has ridden into the flames, Krauss washes everything away with torrents of gorgeous sound. In place of devastation, there is bliss.

Parsifal

The new production of *Parsifal* in Vienna on 13 February 1933 to commemorate Wagner's death 50 years earlier was a "festive evening for the orchestra," according to the *Wiener Zeitung*. The highlight was the first act "in its very forceful, solemn mood, despite the broadened tempo. This was one of Krauss's best, most uniform performances. From the second act onwards, the effect faded, not least because there was a lack of melodic feeling, of emotion in the climaxes on stage, the Flowermaidens scene and the Good Friday magic. Yet careful, thorough work showed through everywhere."[85] To the *Neue Freie Presse*, Krauss had demonstrated he was "a proper *Parsifal* conductor," one who, "floating on an ocean of solemnity and dignity," had been able through careful rehearsal to "create various nuances, with the effect of changing an open orchestra into a concealed one."

He has made the most beautiful artistic work of it. He has achieved a sublime, transfigured, pure, almost metaphysical performance, both in the orchestra and on stage. Nothing of that mystical sound, the sacred sounds of faith, purification, rapture, and holiness was lost. How noble the Philharmonic, how noble the Opera Chorus! For all this, Krauss's Mass did not forget that which must not be forgotten: that it is to be celebrated in the theatre.[86]

Krauss's *Parsifal* at the 1953 Bayreuth Festival did not meet with everyone's approval. "Krauss was a rather disappointing conductor," reported *Opera*:

It is hard to define just why [his] direction was unsatisfactory. It was partly because of a lack of warmth and glow in the orchestral tone, partly because of a lucid and expository approach which seemed reluctant to allow any lingering (the performance was, in fact about half-an-hour

[84] Hotter, *Memoirs*, p. 137

[85] 15 February 1933, p. 6 ("rb"). Max Lorenz sang Parsifal; Gertrude Rünger, Kundry; Richard Mayr, Gurnemanz; Emil Schipper, Amfortas. Excerpts from Krauss's 13 April 1933 *Parsifal* were recorded: see Discography.

[86] *Neue Freie Presse*, 15 February 1933, p. 2 (Julius Korngold)

shorter than is Knappertsbusch's). Krauss sounded too detached, not emotionally committed to the score. But when all this has been said, one must still record the conviction that this Bayreuth *Parsifal* was one of the most memorable operatic performances that the world today can provide. Individual flaws counted for far less than the inherent seriousness which marked every detail of its performance.[87]

The *Music Review* attended a performance on 2 August (not the one above, which is on record) and found it "a great disappointment":

Certainly *Parsifal* under Krauss was a new experience, but not of the kind that one would willingly repeat. He concentrated his energies and enthusiasm on the second act which was played with commendable fire and precision, to the detriment of the much more important first and last acts whose atmosphere was never fully generated – as it must be if *Parsifal* is to mean anything at all. For long stretches I was bored as Krauss sounded...[88]

When the recording was issued in the 1980s, reviewers in *Fanfare* were surprised. Previous recorded performances had ranged from Knappertsbusch's to Boulez's. "[Krauss's] performance is a relatively fast one... yet it never seems rushed or slapdash, but always natural and easy. Yet it's a curiously unassertive and somehow finally unimpressive performance from an orchestral and directorial point of view. Nothing is wrong with it, but changes are missed...."[89] *Gramophone* found many similarities with Krauss's *Ring*:

It is wonderfully direct and consistent in tempos and their relationship, pellucid in texture, and he is not unaware of the work's spiritual content. Nobody achieves the tensions and the world-weariness of the transformation and the Amfortas music so acutely as Krauss, nobody is quite so evilly energetic in the Prelude to Act 2, and few manage the sustained, cleaning ecstasy of the finale, from *Nur eine Waffe*, so tellingly. Yet I cannot welcome it with quite the enthusiasm with which I greeted his *Ring*, simply because the later, 1962, Knappertsbusch version on Philips has very many of Krauss's virtues, to which he adds a deeper understanding of the work's inner meaning. Knappertsbusch also enjoys the benefits of a greatly superior recording.[90]

The superiority of the Philips sound was also acknowledged by *Opera Quarterly*. It suggested Krauss's performance was rooted more in the theatre ("greasepaint") than in a chapel ("incense"):

Krauss's approach, vivid and flesh-and-blood rather than ruminative and angelic, is superbly suited to the dramatic confrontation between Kundry and Parsifal in act 2. The prelude boils and seethes. The air of Klingsor's magic garden is full of electricity as it is of the perfume of flowers. Kundry's attempt at seduction crackles with tension and drive.

Reverential sobriety and spiritual profundity, though perhaps not so plentiful and all-pervasive as with Knappertsbusch, are by no means lacking in Krauss's interpretation. The transformations have plenty of magisterial weight. The orchestral texture, especially that in the music accompanying the Flower Maidens' gossamer warbling and Kundry's enticing dialogue with Parsifal in act 2, is bewitchingly transparent. And the opera's cathartic finale is suitably radiant.[91]

[87] vol. 4 no. 9 (September 1953), pp. 538-539 (Andrew Porter)

[88] vol. 14 (1953), p. 306 (G. N. S.)

[89] vol. 7 no. 1 (September/October 1983), p. 286 (William Youngren on the Melodram LPs; Paul Turok had reviewed the Rodolphe LPs in vol. 6 no. 1: "My reaction, like his, was mixed," Youngren wrote.)

[90] September 1988, p. 483 (Alan Blyth, reviewing the Laudis CDs)

[91] vol. 7 no. 2 (Summer 1990), pp. 163-164 (William Albright, reviewing a further Rodolphe CD reissue)

The virtue of Krauss reading is indeed in the drama. It is a reading that moves more than meditates. From its very first bars there is a sense of hope and refreshment. Then there is real excitement when Kundry arrives. Unusually, there is spirit in Gurnemanz's monologues: he is not a bore but quite alert and alive. His exchanges with Parsifal are lively (though marred by an over-conscientious prompter).[92] The transformation scene is bright and adventurous, giving a sense of moving into a new world. The Grail scene is life-affirming. Whereas George London wallowed and luxuriated in his lament under Knappertsbusch, he is kept more on the surface by Krauss, and seems to be writhing in pain. The second act, as the commentators above reveal, is where Krauss is outstanding. From Klingsor's vaporous summons of Kundry, to the whiplash he puts in Klingsor's hand, to the extraordinarily pressed, agitated Flowermaidens worried their beloveds may have been killed, the orchestra is thrilling. In the first part of the Parsifal-Kundry scene, the orchestra is like a watchful lion. After the kiss, it pounces. Wagner's directions for Kundry – "very passionately," "in wild ecstasy," "breaking out in fury," etc. – are wholly reflected in Krauss's churning orchestra. In the third act the singers seem quite at ease, even stimulated, by the pace he sets, and by the encouragement he gives them, for example, as the orchestra swells richly before *Du salbtest mir die Füsse* and glows before *Mein erstes Amt*. Weight is there, in the massive, moving Transformation music, and luxury too, as the sensuous, soothing strings prop up the ailing, pleading Amfortas. It is a refreshing, up-lifting, and redeeming performance.

Beyond Bayreuth

At the end of the 1953 Festival, Wieland Wagner was deeply impressed with Krauss. He said to Hans Hotter, "That man, I'm sure, is going to play an important role in Bayreuth's future."[93] That was, alas, not to be. He pursued a tireless timetable after the Bayreuth Festival with concerts with the Bamberg Symphony throughout Germany, other concerts in Hannover and Stuttgart, *Fidelio* in London, a *Salome* recording in Vienna, a Richard Strauss concert with the Vienna Philharmonic to mark the composer's 90th birthday, and thence to Mexico. It was an exhausting schedule. A few hours after a concert in Mexico City, he died. There was speculation that the high altitude may have made him more susceptible to the fatal heart attack. Others suspected he had suffered from a broken heart after the aborted appointment to the Vienna State Opera. "Clemens Krauss had everything," wrote the Vienna Opera historian Marcel Prawy. "As a musician he was gifted with a touch of genius... But first and last he was, as we have seen, a careerist and an opportunist.... it was his feckless opportunism that toppled him in the end."[94] Whatever the cause, he died in the Valley of the Damned. He was buried in another valley, deep in the Tyrol, very close to Germany, at the foot of the Zugspitz.

92 It is disconcerting to hear Parsifal having to be prompted *Das weiss ich nicht* to questions put to him in act one; and Parsifal's question to Gurnemanz, *Wer ist gut?*, is answered by the prompter: surely Ludwig Weber knew the answer.

93 Hotter, *Memoirs*, p. 208

94 Prawy, *The Vienna Opera*, p. 146

20

Karl Böhm – Light at the end

Karl Böhm emerged from Germany's dark years slowly. He had taken an early opportunity to lead one of the country's most distinguished orchestras, in Dresden, where he got a solid grounding in a wide range of music, including Wagner's. He had to wait until the last decade of a long active life, after the heavy clouds of Knappertsbusch had lifted from the Green Hill, to be invited to the Bayreuth Festival. There he left a permanent mark. The way he illuminated and enlivened Wagner's music-dramas, often selflessly, propelled him to celebrity status. These were his glory years, especially in *Tristan*, and we shall devote most of our attention to them. In the 1930s he took his Dresden company to London for *Tristan*, and made an historic first recording of act three of *Meistersinger*. These will be our early markers. They will show that his Bayreuth years were but a late display of his greatness in Wagner, not a late blossoming. He was always a true Wagnerian.

Wagnerian strands in his life

He was born in Graz, Austria on 28 August 1894. His father was a cabinetmaker, an amateur singer, a Wagner enthusiast, and a frequent pilgrim to Bayreuth, where he made friends with Hans Richter and many of the singers.[1] His mother was also "incredibly musical," Böhm wrote in his memoirs.[2] Most of his musical instruction was informal: listening to bands as a child, sitting in the gallery of the Vienna Opera as a young man ("Sadly, I never heard Mahler."[3]); or private, mainly on the piano. Apart from a couple of semesters at the Graz Conservatory, his formal studies were in law. This was only a "safety net" in the event that a musical vocation did not present itself.[4] Good fortune came in the First War when, in 1917, he was kicked by a horse and had to spend the rest the war in the opera house in Graz, first as a singing coach and later as a conductor.[5]

[1] Franz Eugen Dostal, *Karl Böhm, Begegnung mit Richard Strauss* (Wien: Doblinger, 1964), p. 9; Robert Breuer, "Böhm Remembers," *Opera News*, August 1974, p. 12

[2] Böhm, *A life remembered: memoirs,* trans. John Kehoe (London: Marion Boyars, 1992), p. 40

[3] *ibid*, pp. 26, 56

[4] Thomas Heinitz, "Eighty years on – Karl Böhm talks to Thomas Heinitz on the occasion of his eightieth birthday," *Records & Recording*, September 1974, p. 24

[5] Helena Matheopoulos, *Maestro, encounters with conductors of today* (London: Hutchinson, 1982), p. 107

His father, who had helped his son onto this first rung of the ladder, once asked Richter, "How does one become a conductor?" Richter replied: "You get up on the podium – and either you can do it, or else you'll never learn."[6] And that is what the young Böhm did. He was never taught conducting, and never had much to say about the art.[7] He learned by watching and listening. Felix Weingartner made a "great impression" on him in concerts.[8] After four years in Graz (1917-21), Bruno Walter engaged him for Munich. He taught the young conductor much about Mozart. "I was a bigoted Wagnerian for a long time... I owe my discovery of Mozart to Bruno Walter."[9] Böhm also paid tribute to Richard Strauss as an influence on his Mozart interpretations.[10] For his instruction in Wagner, he owed everything to Karl Muck.

Muck had returned to Graz, which was his wife's home town, after internment in the United States during the First World War. He attended Böhm's first performance of *Lohengrin*. He said to the young conductor that the Bridal March (*Treulich geführt*) had been conducted "like a polka," and invited him to call on him for "a few authentic Bayreuth tips on Wagner":

> Twice that week I went to him with my scores, and Muck went through them with me, page by page. ...his hints were indeed invaluable. He played a major role in my life – through his wisdom and profound knowledge of Wagner, which he had obtained from Cosima. ... [He] talked to me about the acoustic conditions in Bayreuth, and said to me, even then, "You ought never to lose yourself in the 'mystic abyss.' You can never be too loud with the orchestra in relation to the stage. You can turn it right up, but you'll never cover even a singer with a weak voice: that is the miracle of Bayreuth."[11]

Muck was "the first and greatest influence on me," he said,[12] although it turned out the two were very different conductors. It was on Muck's recommendation to Walter that he was called to Munich, where he stayed for six years (1921-27). Unfortunately Walter was to remain in charge for only one further year. "After him came Knappertsbusch, with whom I had to come to terms, since both externally and inwardly his way of making music was the exact opposite of Bruno Walter's."[13] As we can judge from Knappertsbusch's time in Munich,[14] Böhm's task must have been a heavy one. He may have been speaking ironically when he said some fifty years later: "From both I learned all I needed to know."[15]

In Munich he conducted his first *Tristan* and *Ring*, and in his six years there, some 528 performances of 73 operas.[16] Thereafter he went to Darmstadt as General Music Director (1927-31), making his debut with *Meistersinger*. His new productions there included *Götterdämmerung* (1927), *Lohengrin* (1928), *Meistersinger* (1928), *Holländer* (1929) and *Tannhäuser* (1930). It was in a performance of *Meistersinger* in 1930 that he

[6] Böhm, *A life remembered*, p. 156

[7] He gave some practical advice to Kurt Klippstatter, "A Conversation with Karl Böhm," *Instrumentalist*, vol. 38, no. 8 (March 1979), p. 18

[8] Böhm, *A life remembered*, p. 26

[9] Felix Schmidt, "Karl Böhm: the last interview," *Fanfare*, May/June 1982, p. 76

[10] Joseph Wechsberg, "Karl Böhm," *Opera*, vol. 28, no. 12 (December 1977), p. 1124; Böhm, *A life remembered*, p. 69

[11] *ibid*, pp. 97-8

[12] "Karl Böhm talks to Alan Blyth," *Gramophone*, December 1972, p. 1107; Matheopoulos, *Maestro*, p. 109

[13] Böhm, *A life remembered*, p. 41

[14] see Knappertsbusch chapter, pp. 447-50.

[15] "Karl Böhm talks to Alan Blyth," *Gramophone*, December 1972, p. 1107

[16] "Böhm Remembers," *Opera News*, August 1974, p. 13

was talent-spotted for a position in Hamburg (1931-34).[17] While in Hamburg he made guest appearances with *Tristan* in both Vienna and Dresden, and was offered positions in both cities. He refused the Vienna offer, because it had been made behind the back of Clemens Krauss, but accepted the Dresden position, after what he described as "the ugly departure of Fritz Busch." He gave his first official performance there on 7 January 1934, once again with *Meistersinger.*[18]

The Third Reich was to present many opportunities for Böhm.[19] The years in Dresden (1934-43) were particularly fruitful artistically. He conducted some 689 opera performances, personally preparing all the Wagner productions, both scenically and musically.[20] He took the company to London in 1936 for a performance of *Tristan*, which we will look at below, and made many recordings for the Electrola company as it re-recorded many works with non-Jewish artists.[21] These included some Wagner excerpts and the first ever complete act three of *Meistersinger.* When the latter set was released in the United States and Britain shortly before the outbreak of the War, it was warmly received, and with some irony. "If *all* our statesmen in all countries would listen to the voice of Hans Sachs," Neville Cardus wrote, "listen to it with faith, understanding and tolerance, a way could be found out, surely, from our present blindnesses. I commend the idea especially to Herr Hitler, who regards Wagner as his favourite composer."[22] Hitler evidently did not heed the words, though

17 Böhm recalled a six-year period in Darmstadt in his recollection "*Lauter junge, moderne und fleißige Leute* am Darmstädter Theater 1927," in Hermann Kaiser, *300 Jahre Darmstädter Theater in Berrichten von Augenzeugen* (Darmstadt: Eduard Roether Verlag, 1972), p. 142

18 Böhm, *A life remembered*, pp. 57-58. Although it was nine months after Busch's expulsion when Böhm first appeared in Dresden, his appointment was announced a mere two months later: *New York Times*, 5 May 1933, p. 9. He served a short period as guest before taking up his appointment on 1 January 1934: Gottfried Schmiedel, "Karl Böhm and the Dresden Opera," *Opera*, May 1960, p. 324, reprinted in Harold Rosenthal, *The Opera Bedside Book* (London: Gollancz, 1965), p. 289.

19 His acceptance of the Dresden post has been characterized as showing "not only a lack of tact and compassion but also extreme careerist opportunism at the expense of personal morality": Michael Kater, *The twisted muse: musicians and their music in the Third Reich* (New York: Oxford University Press, 1997), p. 65. Böhm was never a Nazi, but as Kater points out, he did perform at politically-charged events, like conducting *Meistersinger* at the opening of Nazi Party rallies at Nuremberg, and participating in Hitler's birthday festivities in 1944: p. 65. He made public declarations in support of Hitler and the Nazis, for example on the occasion of the plebiscite in 1938 to ratify the annexation of Austria: "Anybody who does not say a big YES to our Führer's action and give it their one-hundred-per-cent support does not deserve to be called a German!" quoted in Fred K. Prieberg, *Trial of Strength: Wilhelm Furtwängler and the Third Reich*, (trans.) Christopher Dolan (London: Quartet Books, 1991), p. 231. In his last interview, he said: "I've carried on a lot in my day; I've been a sinner, you might say. I've lied and done a lot of things which wouldn't help my reputation any. But I've always been honest with music, always correct": Felix Schmidt, "Karl Böhm: the last interview," *Fanfare*, May/June 1982, p. 74.

20 Böhm, *A life remembered*, pp. 59, 61

21 David Hamilton wrote in his review of *Böhm in Dresden* (four volumes of EMI/ Electrola LPs): "my guess is that many of these recordings were made principally as replacements in the Electrola catalogue for non-Aryan versions of the same standard works, no longer marketable in the Third Reich": *ARSC Journal*, vol. 14 no. 1 (1982), p. 66. A reviewer wrote of the *Lohengrin* Bridal Chorus (DA 4456): "If there is any special merit attached to this performance I have failed to notice it; to me it is just a sound, competent rendering, well recorded, which might have been improved by a more artistic 'fading out'": *Gramophone*, August 1939, p. 110 (H. F.V. L.).

22 review dated 8 May 1939 reprinted in *Cardus on Music: a centenary collection* (ed.) Donald Wright (London: H. Hamilton, 1988), p. 122. Alec Robertson wrote in *Gramophone*: "The emotional state I find myself in as I start to write this review is perhaps the best tribute that could be paid to the reality of the recording": May 1939, p. 521. Peter Reed wrote in the *American Music Lover*: "All in all I would say this

doubtless he heard the recording. After Böhm's faithful service, Hitler secured him the directorship of the Vienna Opera (1943-45) – Knappertsbusch was now his junior – and granted him the Martial Order of Merit on 30 January 1943.[23] It is difficult to estimate what his music-making was like during these years. Contemporary reviews "as have survived from those years," wrote Vienna Opera historian Marcel Prawy, "are virtually valueless."[24] There are recorded excerpts from several of his *Meistersinger* performances from 1943-44, and these provide some continuity in our view of his performances of that work recorded between 1935 and 1979.

With the bombing of the Vienna Opera House on 12 March 1945 and the defeat of the Nazis, Böhm faced a two-year ban on performance and teaching.

Then his six "years of wandering," as he called them, began. Of his Wagner performances, a *Tannhäuser* in Naples was "pretty much a sensational success," he recalled, "and brought me a *Meistersinger*, a *Tristan* and a *Parsifal* in Italy. Later in San Carlo I did *Die Walküre*."[25] He went to Buenos Aires in 1950 to conduct the German season, began with a *Walküre*, and stayed four years. Then came the call to return to Vienna. It was a call he was very reluctant to accept.[26] At the gala re-opening of the opera house on 5 November 1955, he conducted the *Meistersinger* overture and the *Blue Danube* waltz (and *Fidelio* in the evening). But it was to be a short stay. He toured a good deal, and people resented his absences. When questioned about this on his return from a tour in the United States in February 1956, he responded to the press: "I've no intention of sacrificing my career to the Vienna Opera." The locals took this very much amiss, and he was booed when he next appeared in the house. He resigned the directorship the next day.[27]

For the rest of his life he appeared as a guest conductor in many countries. From the recordings we have from these years, we can be grateful he did *not* sacrifice his career to Vienna. The notable Wagnerian appearances, some of which we will consider below, included at the Metropolitan Opera in New York *Meistersinger* (1959), *Tristan* (1959-60), *Walküre* (1960), *Parsifal* (1961), *Holländer* (1963, 1965, 1966, 1970) and *Lohengrin* (1966-67), and at the Bayreuth Festival *Tristan* (1962, 1963, 1964, 1966, 1968, 1969, 1970), *Meistersinger* (1964, 1968), the *Ring* (1965, 1966, 1967), and *Holländer* (1971). A final *Tristan* was filmed at the Orange Festival in France in 1973. He continued touring in his final years, notably to Japan where there is film of him conducting the

recording is one to write home about, one to enjoy again and again, one to rejoice in and perhaps even to shed tears over; one for which we can be most grateful": December 1939, p. 290.

[23] Levi, *Twisted Muse*, p. 65

[24] "The Vienna Opera in the Third Reich 1938-1945," in Prawy, *The Vienna Opera* (Vienna-Munich-Zurich: Verlag Fritz Molden, 1969), p. 154

[25] Böhm, *A life remembered*, p. 117

[26] "I didn't even want that job – I knew the Viennese and their world championships in intrigues. They succeeded in driving even such famous musicians as Gustav Mahler and Herbert von Karajan from their opera directorships. I took that job only because of the begging and pleading of the Vienna Theatre Management": Felix Schmidt, "Karl Böhm: the last interview," *Fanfare*, May/June 1982, p. 77

[27] Prawy, *The Vienna Opera*, p. 182. He did go on to conduct a number of new productions as guest, including *Holländer* (6 May 1959), *Lohengrin* (16 May 1965), and *Tristan* (17 December 1967). Of Wagner's works at the Vienna Opera, he conducted 15 *Meistersinger* (1943-1960), 11 *Tristan* (1933-1971), 6 *Lohengrin* (1965), 4 *Tannhäuser* (1939 and 1949), and 3 *Holländer* (1959): Franz Hadamowsky, ed., *Die Wiener Hoftheater (Staatstheater), II. Teil 1811-1974* (Wien: Brüder Hollinek, 1975) and Harald Hoyer, *Karl Böhm an der Wiener Staatsoper (1933-1981): eine Dokumentation* (Wien: österreichischer Bundestheaterverband, 1981), *passim*. The authorities eventually appointed him "Austrian General Music Director" on his 70th birthday, in 1974.

Meistersinger overture. He also continued to make recordings, including some Wagner excerpts (1978-80), though perhaps he should not have done so, for by that stage his powers were fading.[28] He died in Salzburg on 14 August 1981, aged 86.

Böhm on Wagner

Wagner was second only to Mozart in Böhm's pantheon.[29] Indeed, it was Wagner who was the brightest star until Walter opened Böhm's eyes to Mozart in Munich in 1921. In his memoirs he recalled that although he "was always conducting Wagner," in Munich he "felt somewhat distanced from him. That may have something to do with the fact that the Nazis made so much of him, and that one reacted defensively against that – for it was well known that Hitler was a great admirer of Wagner.... After the war I found my way back to Wagner."[30] As a natural, born conductor, he wrote or spoke little about what he was trying to do in conducting Wagner. The centre of his creative powers was not his brain, but his heart.[31] He watched other conductors, and made some astute observations about them, for example about Muck and Walter:

> I heard *Die Walküre* from both of them. Bruno Walter conducted the Sword motif with gentle gestures, the resultant sound was less dramatic than with Muck, who conducted it with dagger thrusts – but on the other hand the lyrical passages of *Die Meistersinger* or *Tristan* suited Bruno Walter better, and he radiated far greater warmth than Muck.[32]

Böhm admired some of the older conductors, and even said he would like to conduct like some of them – "Oh, yes. Bruno Walter, Karl Muck, von Schalk, Weingartner, Nikisch, Toscanini, Bernstein, Klemperer..."[33] – but he seems to have had little to say about his contemporaries or their way with Wagner.[34] Böhm was his own man, "absolutely self-taught," as he described himself.[35] He fashioned Wagner in his own forge. When he tackled the *Ring* for Bayreuth in 1965 in his seventies,

[28] The recordings were "slack, shapeless and ill-balanced – and should never have been released," according to David Hamilton, "Böhm in Dresden," *ARSC Journal*, vol. 14 no. 1 (1982), p. 69.

[29] Heinitz, "Eighty years on," *Records & Recording*, September 1974, p. 25

[30] Böhm, *A life remembered*, p. 95. In his 1965 diary he wrote that "[I] had somewhat distanced myself from [Wagner] due to my love of Mozart": Franz Endler, *Karl Böhm: ein Dirigentenleben* (Hamburg: Hoffmann und Campe, 1981), p. 161.

[31] Dostal, *Böhm*, p. 23

[32] Böhm, *A life remembered*, p. 98

[33] Robert T. Jones, "Karl Böhm Chafes Over Music Trend," *New York Times*, 4 March 1969, p. 32. He always carried a ring of Nikisch in his pocket when on the podium; the ring had been given to him by Nikisch's eldest son after he had heard him conduct a performance of *Tristan* at Bayreuth: Barbara Fischer-Williams, "A Question of Spirit: Karl Böhm: Conductor and Communicator," *After Dark*, April 1971, p. 37.

[34] Böhm had known Wilhelm Furtwängler well but had little regard for his ego, according to Howard Klein in the *New York Times* who quoted Böhm: "Furtwängler once told me the world was missing a great composer because he was too busy conducting. But Strauss found time to write *Salome* and *Elektra* in the days when he conducted about 120 performances a year for the Dresden Court Opera [Strauss was a conductor in Berlin at the time he composed these two works]": 14 February 1965, p. X9 Böhm admired Carlos Kleiber: "A genius of a man, like his father [Erich Kleiber] – a difficult man whose game-playing is hard on all around him. I've often told him what a maniac he is – sweet but crazy... I hold [Leonard Bernstein] in very high esteem as a conductor. He's a magnificent musician, wonderfully creative": Felix Schmidt, "Karl Böhm: the last interview," *Fanfare*, May/June 1982, p. 77.

[35] "I did a couple of semesters in Vienna, but never had any real conductor-training. I just copied everything from the [Graz and Vienna] conductors. I'm absolutely self-taught (autodidact)": Schmidt, "The last interview," *Fanfare*, May/June 1982, p. 75.

he wondered in his diary whether at that age he should have got involved at all with a work "cut out for titans." But he had begun his musical life with Wagner, and so he would end it, but differently. "I had found a new, modern Wagner style, refined by Mozart… I managed to convince everyone!" [36] He explained in his memoirs:

So I conducted the *Ring* and took care, as did Wieland Wagner, to reduce the whole cycle to a human dimension, free from all over-Romantic ballast, in which I appear to have succeeded for a famous Munich critic asked me in an interview how I managed to find an entirely new style in *Rheingold*, a style that was no longer boring for a modern audience. I replied that I could only suppose that, having long been distanced from Wagner and the *Ring* and through my intensive preoccupation with Mozart and Bach, I had found something like a Wagner style refined through Mozart and Bach.[37]

Likewise he said in 1972: "in the old days I conducted Wagner before I knew Mozart and Bach; now I conduct his works, that is Wagner's, purified by the other composers. That's my opinion."[38] Whether he "purified" his approach to Wagner because he had emerged from a long love affair with Mozart, or had recovered from an alleged distaste of the Nazis' fondness for Wagner, is an open question. In any case, it was his way and it made its impression, as Birgit Nilsson, his Brünnhilde of 1965, recalled: "Böhm, who was known primarily as a Strauss and Mozart interpreter, surprised many with his sure grasp of Wagner. It was no Knappertsbusch *Ring* with long, sustained phrasing and crescendos reaching bombastic fortissimos. Böhm's tempi were more flowing, and compared to Kna, his orchestral sound was transparent in its brightness and clarity."[39] His style also suited his producer, Wieland Wagner.[40] The absence of earlier recordings of the *Ring* make it impossible to measure whether there was in fact the change that Böhm said had come over him. In the case of *Meistersinger*, on which he had virtually nothing to say in spite of the fact that it appears to have been his most frequently-performed Wagner opera,[41] there is a range of recordings: they range from the 1935 newsreel of a performance before Goebbels at the opening of the new Deutsche Oper in Berlin, to the Bayreuth performances of 1964 and 1968, and beyond in the case of the overture. A "purification" of style over the years is not abundantly evident in his performance of this work. One observer who attended Böhm's Bayreuth performances wrote that the quality of "unforced lyricism and dramatic pulse" evident in the live performances was also a notable feature of the 1938 recording of act three, as well as "his acute ear for detail."[42]

[36] Endler, *Böhm*, p. 161

[37] Böhm, *A life remembered*, pp. 99-100. Further, "the many long years during which I have occupied myself with Mozart had prepared me – partly consciously, partly unconsciously – for a purification of Wagner style": p. 144.

[38] "Karl Böhm talks to Alan Blyth," *Gramophone*, December 1972, p. 1107

[39] Birgit Nilsson, *La Nilsson: My Life in Opera* (Boston: Northeastern University Press, 2007), p. 168

[40] He said in conversation: "The goal of Wagner interpretation today should be less pedal, less pathos, less shouting, a reduction of the subtle blend of tones. This works particularly well with Latin conductors. I might also count Karl Böhm among this group of conductors. They brighten up the dark works of Wagner with Mediterranean clarity of spirit": Antoine Goléa, *Gespräche mit Wieland Wagner* (Salzburg: Salzburger Nachrichten Verlag, 1968), p. 11

[41] "Though exact figures are hard to obtain it seems likely that he directed the work more often than any other 20th Century conductor": John P. McKelvey in *American Record Guide*, March/April 2006, p. 251.

[42] *Opera*, December 1994, p. 1386 (Alan Blyth). The reviewer referred to Böhm's "1968 and 1969

What Böhm did do was keep very closely to the score, and to his singers. He was not one who consciously sought to impose his own "vision." This was the secret of his success, according to Leonie Rysanek, one of his Wagner singers: "he serves the composer with all authenticity. He never puts on a show to tell the audience, look, this is *my* special interpretation. And he loves music and voices; he cannot live without music."[43] His natural deference to his singers is illustrated by a comment made by Birgit Nilsson on her first rehearsal with him in Rome in the 1950s:

> He was obdurately grim and disagreeable. I was either too fast or too slow in my tempo. No matter how I tried to change, he was not satisfied. I was singing then for the first time with Böhm and really tried to follow him like a shadow. That was a mistake: when one tried to subordinate oneself, he would become nervous and choppy in his tempi. If one simply took one's own tempo, that which was most natural, then he followed impeccably.[44]

This is not to say he was easy-going. His fidelity to the score and devotion to hard work to get the music right led to stormy scenes. Astrid Varnay recalled "violent scenes" at rehearsal. "Böhm had no patience whatsoever with people who had not prepared their work as assiduously as he."[45] He acknowledged this. "Everyone who knows me as a musician is aware of how much value I place upon detailed study and the greatest possible perfection in rehearsal."[46] There are ways and means of achieving this, and by modern standards, he probably went too far. "Böhm had the unfortunate habit," Birgit Nilsson recalled, "of singling out someone performing a smaller role to be the 'whipping boy' on whom he could vent all his irritation. I think Böhm was the last of his generation of conductors allowed this freedom."[47]

His approach never led to rigidity, or frigidity, in performance, and this is nowhere better in evidence than in his treatment of *Tristan*. The earliest significant Wagner event he experienced was a *Tristan* he heard as a boy, "with Karl Burrian and Anna Bahr-Mildenburg, a heldentenor and Wagner soprano such as can no longer be found today."[48] He first conducted the work in Graz, as he told the *New York Times*:

> "You know, when you conduct your first *Tristan* you are dissolved." At the end of the first act he was wringing wet and Muck came backstage to visit. Muck himself had the reputation of being able to conduct an entire opera without needing to change his collar. He approached young Böhm wordlessly, pinched the tab of his dripping collar, and growled one word: "Beginner!"[49]

Meistersingers at Bayreuth," whereas in fact Böhm conducted it in 1964 and 1968. Berislav Klobucar conducted the work in 1969, and took over the final two performances in 1968 after Böhm had been taken ill "with feverish influenza": *Opera*, Festival Issue, Autumn 1968, p. 81.

[43] "The Böhm Balance," *Opera News*, August 1974, p. 16. Rysanek sang Elisabeth, Senta, and Sieglinde under Böhm.

[44] *La Nilsson*, p. 196. She sang Venus, Isolde, and Brünnhilde under Böhm.

[45] Astrid Varnay, with Donald Arthur, *Fifty-five years in five acts: my life in opera* (Boston: Northeastern University Press, 2000), p. 202. She sang Isolde with Böhm in 1963 (sharing with Birgit Nilsson), but is not on record in Wagner with the conductor. Nor is Hans Hotter, who sang his first Kurwenal under Böhm in Munich in 1937, and had admired Böhm from his student days: *Memoirs*, (trans. and ed.) Donald Arthur (Boston: Northeastern University Press, 2006), p. 125.

[46] Böhm, *A life remembered*, pp. 103-104. He also demanded many rehearsals with orchestra, full cast, and chorus, which made him a very expensive conductor: Sir Rudolf Bing, *5,000 nights at the opera* (London: Hamilton, 1972), p. 139.

[47] *La Nilsson*, p. 130

[48] Breuer, "Böhm Remembers," *Opera News*, August 1974, p. 14

[49] Edward Downes, "Ardent Mozartean," *New York Times*, 13 October 1957, p. 129

His ardour never diminished. "His interpretation of *Tristan* was a declaration of love from beginning to end," recalled Nilsson, his most illustrious Isolde.[50] He first performed the work at Bayreuth in 1962 – "my ordeal by fire"[51] – and was truly carried away:

I can remember a performance as if it were today; the second *Tristan* that I conducted in Bayreuth in which Nilsson and Windgassen were singing so indescribably beautifully that the flood of sound took hold of both the orchestra and me so strongly that I suddenly had the feeling that if I wasn't careful, I would have been washed away![52]

He pulled himself together. He reminded himself that "conducting does not only consist of losing oneself in the music, …but also of keeping a firm grip on the orchestra and stage. There must always be this compromise, this balance between letting oneself go completely and maintaining control."[53] In *Tristan* above all, however, he surrendered to the music. While "clarity of the text should… be the first law of opera," in *Tristan* the word had to give way to the spirit. To be able to hear the words and understand the philosophy in the love duet was neither possible nor desirable. "Wagner himself said that it was not absolutely necessary in such an unequivocal situation as is represented by this love duet, for the verses, although lovely in themselves, to be more than just a means by which this most beautiful of all love scenes may be expressed in music."[54] In examining some of Böhm's performances of the later works of Wagner, *Tristan* not surprisingly features prominently.

Tristan und Isolde

He made a mark early in his career with *Tristan*. At a performance in Darmstadt on 8 May 1927, before he had formally taken up his appointment as general music director, he showed "extraordinary determination, generous creative powers, superior mastery of the subject matter, temperament, musicality and absolute authority," according to the *Darmstädter Tagblatt*.[55] When he took the Dresden State Opera Company to London in 1936 for performances of *Der Rosenkavalier* and *Tristan*, he left many impressions. What stood out was the unity of music and stage, though the quality of some of the leading singers left something to be desired. Ernest Newman wrote in the *Sunday Times*:

Karl Böhm… is obviously an opera conductor of outstanding intelligence [and] seemed to aim throughout at a general level of tone that was below what we are accustomed to have in opera. Whether this is a matter of general artistic bias or simply dictated by the necessity of not

[50] Birgit Nilsson, *My Memoirs in Pictures*, trans. Thomas Teal (New York: Doubleday, 1981), p. 24

[51] Breuer, "Böhm Remembers," *Opera News*, August 1974, 14

[52] *A life remembered*, p. 147. The second performance was on 4 August 1962. One reviewer remembered the "often breathtaking intensity" of Böhm's 1962 performances, and how they "conjured up memories of Toscanini": *Deutsche Wochenzeitung*, 22 September 1962 (Alfred Pellegrini).

[53] Matheopoulos, *Maestro*, p. 103. Böhm told Matheopoulos in the interview (1979) that the experience happened "at either the second or third performance [14 August 1962]… Nilsson and … Windgassen … had sensed that something out of the ordinary had happened." Neither performance is on record, only the first on 24 July 1962.

[54] *A life remembered*, p. 148

[55] quoted in Hubert Unverricht and Kurt Oehl, eds, *Musik in Darmstadt zwischen den beiden Weltkriegen* (Mainz: Schott, 1980), p. 22

Fig. 20.1. Karl Böhm from his Darmstadt years, 1927-1931

Fig. 20.2. Böhm from his Dresden years, 1934-1944

Fig. 20.3. Böhm at the time of his early Wagner recordings, 1935-1940

Fig. 20.4. Böhm rehearsing *Die Walküre* at Bayreuth, from a film

Fig. 20.5. Böhm at the Metropolitan Opera, 1972. Photo by Ilse Bing

Fig. 20.6. Böhm in later years

drowning voices that are almost all on the small side, I cannot say. But Böhm's method certainly justifies itself in the main. It allows us to hear every word of the singers, which is a consideration of prime importance in Wagner and in Strauss, for it gives the drama its full rights.... For the rest the orchestral playing, like most other things in art, is an affair of gradation and proportion rather than of actual volume. Gradation and proportion in these performances under Böhm have been exquisitely calculated; and one result of it has been that when the whole strength of the orchestra has been let loose on a climax the effect has been stupendous.[56]

This last point was also observed by Walter Legge:

His sense of tone gradation is uncanny, and his restraint in the employment of the full intensity of orchestral tone enables him to give the necessary climaxes almost unbearable effect. The power and life of sound at the crucial moments – Isolde's curse, the entries of Tristan in the first and second acts, and just before Tristan's death – had to be heard to be believed. The soft playing was no less impressive.[57]

The *Observer* commented on the beautiful playing of the orchestra. "Those magically tender bars that follow Brangäne's warning in the love-duet, Tristan's entries in the second and third acts, were great and not merely delirious moments. In them one felt of Dr. Böhm, as Bernard Shaw once wrote of Mottl, that excitement completed rather than destroyed his self-possession."[58]

If there was one criticism of the orchestra's playing, it was in the matter of rhythm. Böhm "secured from the orchestra playing that was always beautifully clear and unhurried," wrote *The Times*, "yet just wanting in the strong undercurrent of rhythm that would have changed admiration into rapture."[59] The *Spectator* considered Böhm, in both the Strauss and the Wagner performances, "thoroughly efficient.... His defect, which is a lack of feeling for the underlying urge of the rhythms, was more obvious in *Tristan*. But he gets the orchestra, whose strings are excellent – there are some weak places in the wind – to play well all the time and really to accompany the singers."[60] Yet without really good singers, justice could not be done to Wagner. While the "Isolde sang all around her notes and rarely on them,"[61] the singer of Tristan "would have been ideal in the part – had he known in the least how to sing."[62] Justice would come twenty-three years later, in New York.

The triumph of Böhm's *Tristan* with Birgit Nilsson at the Metropolitan Opera in 1959 was to mark the beginning of a fourteen-year partnership. Although her appearance dominated press coverage on this occasion, the other impressive feature of the production was Böhm's conducting. He gave "equal solicitude to every phrase and every chord, and yet always had a firm concept of the whole," wrote the *Herald Tribune*; "upon my word, he threads the parts, one by one, weaving them into the ordained

[56] 8 November 1936, p. 7

[57] review for the *Manchester Guardian* reprinted in Alan Sanders, (ed.), *Walter Legge: Words and Music* (London: Duckworth, 1998), p. 43

[58] 8 November 1936, p. 16

[59] 4 November 1936, p. 12

[60] 6 November 1936, p. 809 (Dyneley Hussey)

[61] *idem*. Anny Konetzni sang Isolde.

[62] *Observer*, 8 November 1936, p. 16. Julius Pölzer sang Tristan. Other reviewers were also critical of the singers: Pölzer was the "least satisfactory": *Morning Post*, 4 November 1936, p. 14 (S. G.); Pölzer was "disappointing" and Konetzni "somewhat prosaic": *Daily Telegraph*, 4 November 1936, p. 12 (Richard Capell); cf. Ernest Newman: "The great feature of the performance was the Tristan of Julius Pölzer": *Sunday Times*, 8 November 1936, p. 7. The honours generally went to Paul Schöffler (Kurwenal) and Sven Nilsson (King Marke).

pattern. His sane, healthy, experienced, and imaginative musicianship was evident from the first notes of the prelude. How magnificently the Met's orchestra can play under such leadership!"[63] The *New York Times* agreed:

His is a vigorous, dramatic conception. He is painstaking in his regard for instrumental textures and balances. One can hear subtleties in the pit often obscured in routine readings. And how the Met orchestra played! Rhythms are incisive. Some conductors favor more leisurely tempos, but Mr. Böhm's choice of a vivid pulse has its merits.

One's only reservation is that he holds the orchestra back just a shade at the climaxes. With an Isolde like Miss Nilsson he can let the thrilling Wagnerian waves of sound flood the theatre. This soprano will ride them triumphantly.[64]

Nilsson was not the only Isolde Böhm had at the seven Bayreuth Festivals at which he conducted the work. At the second performance in 1963, for example, it was Astrid Varnay. Under Böhm, *Opera* reported, the orchestra "swelled and raged as though at any moment it might rise out of the pit, and this turbulence was matched on the stage. But it was a superbly controlled turbulence … for all the occasional faults of ensemble inherent in a really impassioned performance, this *Tristan* was a triumph – for producer, conductor and singers, and especially Varnay's self-unsparing Isolde."[65]

The Tristan recordings

When Böhm was asked to record *Tristan*, he agreed only on condition that it was done "live" in Bayreuth.[66] In fact, the set of records that was to eventuate was recorded one act at a time over successive days during rehearsals in 1966. An audience of around 1,000 was invited to aid the acoustics. After a two-day break from recording came the premiere, and this and the following two performances were recorded. "It was interesting," Böhm recalled, "that when we compared them with the recordings made during the public 'rehearsals' we had to make very few corrections." There had been a breakdown in act two; "we had to stop, and you can tell in the course of the rehearsal/performance how difficult it was to crank it up again and re-establish the atmosphere." Continuity of performance was very important to him. "This work must have a single *Steigerung* (intensification) from the opening notes to the end of the *Liebestod*," he said, "a quality that is almost impossible to get in a recording studio."[67] This *Tristan* recording was among the small number of his records that gave him greatest satisfaction.[68]

[63] "Met Has a New 'Isolde' – And She's a True Princess," *New York Herald Tribune*, 19 December 1959, p. 8 (Paul Henry Lang). Tristan was sung by Karl Liebl.

[64] "Birgit Nilsson as Isolde Flashes Like a New Star in 'Met' Heavens," *New York Times*, 19 December 1959, p. 1 (Howard Taubman). She made her Metropolitan Opera *broadcast* debut with *Tristan* on 9 January 1960. The microphones were unprepared for her explosive entry. They were also too close to the singers in the love duet. Ramon Vinay was completely worn out by act three: the illusion of the dying Tristan is disturbed, as one listens to the recording, by apprehension of actual pain. On 28 December 1959 Nilsson had three Tristans: Vinay (Act 1), Karl Liebl (Act 2), and Albert DaCosta (Act 3).

[65] *Opera*, Festival Number, Autumn 1963, p. 73 (Jeremy Noble) [66] *A Life Remembered*, p. 102-3

[67] Robert S. Clark, "Stereo Review talks to Karl Böhm," *Stereo Review*, December 1970, p. 67. He also said in a discussion of this recording: "In the studio, you can of course correct everything, but you sometimes lose the line of a performance, or at least it's very hard to retain it": "Karl Böhm talks to Alan Blyth," *Gramophone*, December 1972, p. 1107.

[68] Heinitz, "Eighty years on," *Records & Recording*, September 1974, p. 25. Another was Haydn's *Seasons*.

Its critical reception was extraordinary. Harold Rosenthal, who had heard Böhm's *Tristan* in London in 1936, wrote in *Opera*:

I rank this with the now almost historic De Sabata-Callas-Gobbi *Tosca* as one of the most exciting and satisfying complete operatic recordings ever recorded. The live quality of the performance, the superb conducting of Karl Böhm, and the singing of the principals could scarcely be bettered.... I doubt whether [Böhm] has ever given so impassioned yet at the same time so poetic a performance as he does here. The orchestral playing is outstanding and the Bayreuth acoustic is admirably captured; but over and above this is the magic of the truly great performance – that mysterious something I have written about in the past, that only occasionally happens when stage, pit, and audience are linked together in a unique experience.[69]

The recording presented "the opera orchestra of one's dreams" to the *Saturday Review*. "There are no gimmicks, no echo chambers only *Tristan*. And that, despite some defects in the singing, is already something. The sound of the Bayreuth orchestra, under the baton of a great conductor, lifts the album into a special class."[70] The *New York Times* wrote of Böhm's "taut control, virile passion yet clear-headed objectivity" that brought "a tensile continuity to the music." It noted the fast tempos. "Certainly there can be greater excitement at faster speeds. But it is more. The shaping of the phrases is such that one hears them as units in a continuum."[71] The *American Record Guide* noted:

not only that the smallest indications [in the score] are observed scrupulously but also that all this is done without the slightest loss of spontaneity or sense of line. The tonal palette Böhm favors is lighter in prevailing density than one generally encounters in orchestral performances of this opera. (In this respect one is reminded of the Wagnerian conducting of Artur Bodanzky at the Metropolitan in the late thirties.) Moreover, this lightness is obtained with no loss in power when power is required.... This recording is inimitable and for the ages.[72]

And so it has kept its age. A reviewer for *Gramophone* in 2000 recalled how the recording "struck the planet like a meteor. Other Wagnerians – Mahler, Toscanini, Clemens Krauss, de Sabata, the young Karajan – had gone some way to 'purifying' the Wagner style but none quite as radically as Böhm does here. '*The* recording of *Tristan* for those who dislike *Tristan*.'"[73]

There are several non-commercial, live recordings of Böhm conducting *Tristan* at Bayreuth. They are even more electrifying than the composite, commercial recording. In this, he differed from Knappertsbusch. There are of course the usual technical deficiencies – radio static, *ad hoc* adjustments to the radio frequency, bumps to the tape recorder, sonic instability, inexplicable, momentary silences, etc. – as well as performance faults,[74] but overall these are of no moment. The recordings, made from broadcasts

[69] vol. 18 no. 2 (February 1967), pp. 158-9

[70] 28 January 1967, p. 63 (Robert Lawrence)

[71] *New York Times*, 1 January 1967, p. 73 (Howard Klein). The review concluded: "there is no question that this is the finest complete *Tristan* in stereo, and the best since the Flagstad-Furtwängler set."

[72] December 1966, p. 288 (C. J. Luten). In a survey of Böhm's recordings in 1974, this same reviewer wrote: "This was like no *Tristan* before – spare, de-romanticized, everything extraneous pared away to expose the nerve ends of drama and music. Wieland's concept had a strong effect on Böhm's pacing and shaping of the score – lean and transparent, taut of line, propulsive yet without strain or breathlessness": *Opera News*, August 1974, p. 22.

[73] Richard Osborne, "Lightning Conductor: Karl Böhm," *Gramophone*, July 2000, p. 41. Osborne was quoting "my friend Mr Westbrook."

[74] Neidlinger is quite miscast as Kurwenal in the 1970 performance: exhilaration is not in his repertoire.

between 1962 and 1970, all feature Wolfgang Windgassen and Birgit Nilsson. With Böhm, they became a powerful force. There are moments in the performances which are so passionate and overwhelming, there is almost the breakdown Böhm feared. He recorded in his diary after the opening performance of 1964: "a great moment of art. The performance was so brilliant, so thrilling, that at the conductor's desk I sometimes had to be careful not to be swept away. An awesome success – everything, even on the radio – you could sense the extraordinary."[75] Sometimes he does appear to have been swept away.[76] Listening to the live performances, one can see how Böhm almost tilted into chaos. No one depicts so incisively and dangerously the thin line between bliss and agony, between fervour and abandonment. The heat and power he generates beneath the singers is staggering. Windgassen seems sometimes to sing as if a branding-iron had been pressed into his side. Böhm's act three from 1968 is, without doubt, one of *the* great interpretations on record, not least because Gerd Feldhoff's Kurwenal is the most fitting and tragic counterpoint to Windgassen's Tristan. For her part, Nilsson rages and coos above a whirlpool of sound. When the lovers meet in act two there is a firestorm of frenzy. These are intensely dramatic performances. When Wagner forbade further performances of *Tristan* after the initial four in 1865,[77] there could have been no greater testament to the power of the performers. In similar vein, one can say that Böhm's live performances are so overwhelming, so shattering, that one can hardly bear to listen to them again.

Böhm's last *Tristan* was filmed at the Orange Festival in 1973, with the same distinguished principal soloists. One can hear the fire of the orchestra still, and this time one can see the wind blowing against Isolde's dress. "The unforgettable conducting of Karl Böhm," wrote *Opera*, "helped the immense crowd on its hard stone steps, with a chilly breeze blowing down its neck, almost physically to experience the superhuman passion of the two lovers and the agony of the man who so magically expressed it."[78] By 1977 he was uncertain whether he would ever be able to conduct another *Tristan* again "because he gets so carried away."[79] He never did. It now remains to us to get carried away listening to those of his performances that survive on record.

Die Meistersinger von Nürnberg

There is too little of the filmed performance of 1935 to get a sense of Böhm's interpretation of the *Meistersinger*. The *Berliner Morgenpost* reported that he "set a tone of hearty, musical freshness, adopting from the Prelude onwards a very lively, comedy-style tempo, and kept to it throughout the evening. His fine sense for sound ensured there was no flashiness, and that nothing of the precious orchestral fabric or of the

[75] facsimile of diary entry for 18 July 1964 reproduced in Endler, *Karl Böhm*, p. 157. This performance is not, at the time of writing, on disc.

[76] In act three of the 1970 performance, for example, the brass seem to have completely lost their place after Tristan's final *Zu ihr! Zu ihr!*: this may have been a moment when Böhm actually *did* lose control in the excitement.

[77] "Recollections of Ludwig Schnorr" (1868), in Herbert Barth, Dietrich Mack, Egon Voss (eds.), *Wagner: A Documentary Study* (London: Thames and Hudson, 1975), p. 209

[78] *Opera*, Festival Issue, Autumn 1973, pp. 68–9 (Tony Mayer)

[79] Wechsberg, "Karl Böhm," *Opera*, vol. 28, no. 12 (December 1977), p. 1122

singing was lost."[80] Of the historic recording of act three of *Meistersinger* from 1938, it was "unpleasant" to make, Böhm recalled, "if only because one had to keep on 'reheating' the atmosphere. This recording created a furore, especially in America...."[81]

Fig. 20.7. Böhm in 1921

Indeed, it was regarded "all around [as] one of the best opera jobs done on records to date," according to the *American Music Lover*. "Böhm never allows the music to lag, nor is he guilty of lingering hungrily over the many passages of tenderness and beauty in which the act abounds. The spirit of the conductor is definitely felt throughout the entire performance, and it is a spirit that knows and appreciates the true spirit of Wagner."[82] In England the records were also well received by *Gramophone*, with some misgivings about the singers:

[80] 17 November 1935, p. [37] (Josef Rufer). Artur Rother conducted the second performance on 17 November: Detlef Meyer zu Heringdorf, *Das Charlottenburger Opernhaus von 1912 bis 1961* (Berlin: Deutsche Oper, 1988), vol. 2, p. 370. [81] *A life remembered*, p. 101

[82] December 1939, p. 290 (Peter Hugh Reed)

But conductor and orchestra, intimate with every note, give a really splendid, and magnificently recorded, rendering of their part, which is so large a part of the whole. The precision of attack, the moulding of phrases, the ascent to the climaxes – all of thrilling effect – the generally rich tone of the strings, mellowness of the woodwinds, the perfectly steady and fine-toned horns, the vivid trumpets of the crowd scene, here is a catalogue of virtues.[83]

The recording has stood its ground with the passing of time. One reviewer in 1995 who had heard the original records almost fifty years earlier still considered them "unsurpassed by any other recording." He recalled when he first heard the set:

It was permeated by warmth and humanity, Austrian rather than Prussian, its timeless plot discerned through a golden haze. Once begun, it seemed to find its own way, and to live its own life, without any apparent shaping from the conductor. Indeed, it appeared as though it *needed* no conductor, that it flowered spontaneously, traversing an inevitable course to a splendid finale, a Wagnerian paean to German *Kultur*.[84]

The suggestion that the conductor is invisible, as Bruno Walter in a way appears with his 1935 *Walküre* recording, is a paean to the conductor. It is discernible again in the excerpts from Vienna in 1943 and 1944. While it is true that there is "splendidly flexible and always interesting conducting,"[85] the focus throughout is on the singers, on the sung drama on the stage, in such a way that the orchestra seems unobtrusive – yet it informs and enlivens the whole performance. In slow passages like the *Flieder* and *Wahn* monologues, there is some beautiful orchestral playing underpinning the reflective singing of Sachs.

Böhm conducted five performances of *Meistersinger* at the Metropolitan Opera in 1959. It had not been performed for a season, and its resuscitation was far from routine. His first performance (which was broadcast and released on disc in 2010) "was filled with vitality," according to the *New York Times*; even after a heavy schedule the orchestra could still "summon so much freshness and crispness. Under Mr. Böhm's guidance, the pit, which is a prime ingredient in Wagner, was alive."[86] The beginning was "especially good," the *Journal American* reported. "Not only did the first act move with purpose, but the music acquired an unusual amount of transparency," though there was a "tendency to let the orchestra play too loud" from time to time.[87] It was "a beautifully integrated performance," wrote the *Musical Courier*, "notable for its continuity and development from beginning to end. The orchestra under his direction was in top form, taking and yielding precedence as the situation demanded."[88] The *New York Post* was impressed by the liveliness of the production. "There was a prevailing winged transparency throughout, yet the robustness of the strong lines in a Dürer drawing, were ever present. The rhythmic momentum moved to and from its accentual

[83] May 1939, p. 521 (Alec Robertson)

[84] *American Record Guide*, January/February 1995, p. 257 (John P. McKelvey) reviewing Pearl 9121; cf. another reviewer of Profil 5038: "As for conductors, Karajan, Kempe, and Kubelik have left us accounts of the score that are as convincing and well thought-out as Böhm's. So with all due respect to him, it's time to move on!": *ibid*, May/June 2006, p. 229 (Kurt Moses).

[85] *Fanfare*, July/August 1995, p. 394 (William Youngren)

[86] *New York Times*, 23 January 1959, p. 18 (Howard Taubman). Otto Edelmann sang Sachs; Lisa Della Casa, Eva; Sebastian Feiersinger, Walther; Regina Resnik, Magdalene; Paul Franke, David; Karl Dönch, Beckmesser; and Giorgio Tozzi, Pogner.

[87] 23 January 1959, p. 15 (Miles Kastendieck)

[88] March 1959, pp. 12-13 (Carl Gutekunst): review of 22 January performance

propulsion with an exciting vigor."[89] To the *World Telegram and Sun*, the performance was both "polished and vital," and had "unusual freshness and lightness, despite the complexities of fabric. Mr. Böhm has a way of keeping things within a controlled and intimate frame. Both chorus and orchestra sounded bright and vibrant," and were evidently in the hands of "a true Wagnerite."[90] He was perceived as "authoritative and lucid" by the *New Yorker*.[91] Paul Henry Lang wrote in the *Herald Tribune*:

> As I have observed before, the eminent Viennese conductor does things in their context. What he does in the first act has a bearing on events in the second – he does not just proceed from scene to scene. *Die Meistersinger* is a warmly human opera full of song and whimsical comedy, something many conductors used to the torrid chromaticism of *Tristan* tend to forget. Last night we heard songs and singing; the conductor never permitted the truly operatic atmosphere to be sacrificed.
>
> This does not mean that the orchestra did not get its due. On the contrary, it has seldom sounded so luminous and flexible. The prelude, taken at a lively tempo and with bounding élan, caused the public to break into applause when the curtain rose. The well-indoctrinated Wagnerian does not do such a thing unless carried away. Even more remarkable than the pure instrumental pieces was the consistently precise, warm and delightfully light accompaniment. But the conductor watched the stage and made sure that the singing dominated.[92]

The *Saturday Review* noted the performance had "sonority, understanding, and even a degree of fervour," and suggested Böhm's pacing may have been influenced by an understanding that "time was of the essence": that he had to complete the performance within four and a half hours to avoid overtime costs that would accrue after midnight.[93]

The Bavarian Radio broadcasts of Böhm's *Meistersinger* from Bayreuth in 1964 and 1968 are further vindication of the live recorded performance favoured by Böhm. The earlier is in poorer sound, though it is the more striking performance.[94] The way the orchestra is made to be an instrument in the drama is evident from the start. At the end of the church scene it is almost possible to *see* eddies in the congregation as flowing dresses are swept up and the people rapidly depart. In the transition to the second scene, Böhm creates gusts to sweep away the first. Then the sap rises and a warm spring breeze blows, and rushes to consummate itself in the finale, as if to burst into bloom. Böhm does not linger over this act. It has incredible momentum, and lasts exactly as long as the first performance under Bülow in 1868. The arrival of Walther in act two for his secret night tryst with Eva has such excitement that it approaches the delirium of the meeting of Tristan and Isolde. Böhm presses the lovers so intensely that they almost do elope from beneath the noses of Sachs and the others. When the crowd scene comes, it is an ordered cacophony of shouting and movement like a Bruegel painting, until Böhm sweeps them away with a burst of orchestral sound as the nightwatchman approaches. In the long act three, everything is directed to the scene on the meadow, and the glorious finale, a triumph of love and art.

89 23 January 1959, p. 47 (Harriett Johnson)

90 23 January 1959, p. 19 (Louis Biancolli)

91 31 January 1959, p. 88 (Winthrop Sergeant)

92 23 January 1959, p. 8

93 *Saturday Review*, 7 February 1959, p. 26 (Irving Kolodin)

94 Commenting on a reissue of the 1968 performance, the *International Record Review* wrote: "The orchestral playing is as sumptuous as you might expect. Karl Böhm's conducting impresses when sampled a little at a time. Taken in whole acts, it proves somewhat exhausting in sheer energy…": December 2008, p. 85 (Roger Pines).

Der Ring des Nibelungen

When Böhm first conducted the *Ring* at Bayreuth in 1965, it was a breath of fresh air. The *Music Review* praised the "superlative conducting":

> Böhm made everyone happy (including the singers) by lightening up the texture and dynamics of the orchestra, which is apt to be on the heavy side. At the proper climactic moments, however, he allowed the splendid Festival orchestra to speak out, even to rage, most eloquently, and these climaxes were the more effective for the carefully-controlled dynamic differentiation that characterized the performances. Thanks to Böhm's sense of form, the huge four-day work unfolded with extraordinary naturalness and inevitability. Every detail was an integrated part of the musical whole.[95]

Recordings of further performances of the *Ring* in 1966 and 1967 were released commercially, and they too breathed new life into the drama. C. J. Luten wrote:

> Here is a swift, intense and compact *Ring*. The shades of Furtwängler and Knappertsbusch have been exorcised. What is left is a supercharged drama, cleansed of pan-Germanic connotations and sentimentality. The *Ring*'s message comes through loud and clear: power corrupts. According to Wieland, the *Ring*'s only heroes are Siegmund and Sieglinde, who dare everything for love alone. In this performance there are a few routine vocalists, and not all the hazards of taping live events are overcome. What it does have is spontaneity, and individual voice and a consistent point of view. Best of all, it has a burning intensity unique among recordings of the *Ring*, and its sonics evoke the Festspielhaus acoustics.[96]

Intensity the recording certainly has. The most inspired, dramatic conducting is in *Götterdämmerung*, scene four, act two, when the orchestra lurches from accusation to revelation, furious at treachery, determined on vengeance. Birgit Nilsson as Brünnhilde is possessed, lashing out with her weapon, piercing everyone within earshot. Unfortunately, it seems the engineers may have imposed their own sense of sound balance, most notably in *Rheingold* and *Walküre*, for the orchestra is generally given too much prominence. Whether this was to cover a weaker generation of singers (Nilsson excepted) is not clear. But sometimes there appears to be too much noise – not the "Bayreuth Sound" at all – as if the orchestra were being lifted onto the stage and the singers had to strain to be heard. Lost is the "lightening up" of texture and dynamics noted at the 1965 performances.[97] Rather, there is a certain relentlessness as features of the drama are covered with a uniformity of sound. There is not the naturalness of the Krauss radio recording. Nor is there the restraint we read of in Böhm's earliest performances. What is intact is his pacing, which is urgent and dramatic. But even this may have been partly intended to protect the singers (except Nilsson). Publication of the original Bavarian Radio tapes in due course may shed a truer light on these Bayreuth performances.

[95] vol. 26 no. 4 (November 1965), p. 346 (Everett Helm)

[96] C. J. Luten, "Playback: a survey of Karl Böhm's opera recordings," *Opera News*, August 1974, p. 22

[97] *Gramophone* observed from the recording that Böhm was, "on the whole, a Wagnerian with a light hand. There have been occasions when he has scarcely seemed to possess the steadiness and gravity for Wagner; and there are places in this recording where he can suddenly be at a loss": September 1973, p. 536 (John Warrack). A later reviewer observed that Böhm's interpretation was "on the whole on the fast side. That, for me, comes as a welcome change from the predominantly slow readings we have admired in London recently from Goodall, Colin Davis and Mackerras": July 1976, p. 211 (Alan Blyth); "Böhm makes the ear move forward with the music": October 1994, p. 207 (Alan Blyth).

Fig. 20.8. Böhm in the pit at Bayreuth in 1963

Parsifal

Wagner's last work was not one Böhm frequently performed. He did not conduct it at all in Vienna or Bayreuth. In twenty years of appearances at the Metropolitan Opera, in more than 200 opera performances, he only conducted it three times. On the first occasion in 1961, the orchestral sounds he evoked "were the most consistent reminder that here was enacted one of the most magnificent tonal dramas in the repertory," wrote *Musical America*. "The mystic power of the play moved inexorably without dragging – intense but not ponderous."[98] The *New York Times* commented:

> Whatever excitement that the evening provided came from the podium, where Mr. Böhm conducted an unusually supple performance. There was no feeling of haste, but somehow the music moved faster, and with more assurance, than it normally does. In the great second act, Mr. Böhm brought the music of the first scene to a resounding, beautifully controlled climax. All of the foreboding, intense quality was there, just as in the next scene the sinuous melodies of the flower maidens were allowed to sing out without any feeling of constriction. There was not a moment where the guiding hand of Mr. Böhm was not felt. He was not merely beating time; he also controlled the score and his singers.[99]

The "real stars" of the performance, according to the *Herald Tribune*, were the orchestra, "beautifully paced" by Böhm, and the choruses.[100] "As the perfect Wagnerite that he is," wrote the *World Telegram and Sun*, "Mr. Böhm seemed in complete command of all the external and internal forces at work in the monumental score. The timing and dynamics were impeccable."[101] His late, sole recorded excerpt from the work, the

[98] May 1961, p. 33 (Jack Diether). Jerome Hines as Gurnemanz was especially praised; he became unwell and some of his lines in act three were cut.

[99] 23 March 1961, p. 29 (Harold C. Schonberg)

[100] 23 March 1961, p. 13 (Ronald Eyer)

[101] 23 March 1961, Sect 2, p. 24 (Louis Biancolli). By contrast, the *New York Post* considered the performance a "listless rendition... [that] did nobody a service, certainly not the composer": 23 March

Prelude with Wagner's concert ending, does move faster than any other conductor. But it is superb in the circumstances. It is a brighter, more optimistic, "healthy" reading than, say, Knappertsbusch's which is heavy with the languor and perfume of suffering.

The end of the line

When Böhm last went to Bayreuth in 1976, to conduct the overture and final scene of *Meistersinger* on the 100th anniversary of the Festival, he was then regarded, as the *New York Times* reported, as "the grand old man of German conducting." He was "to this generation what Wilhelm Furtwängler and Hans Knappertsbusch were before the war. Unlike most old conductors, Mr. Böhm has become more lively. His tempos get faster and faster, and there is a wonderful alertness to his work. He may be somewhat feeble physically, but an ardent spirit burns within."[102] He continued to record, including some Wagner overtures and preludes in the studio, but the lights were going out. In his last decade he almost became a "star," as the *Spectator* noted. "The reason why the dreaded word 'star' should ultimately be withheld is that it was characteristic of his work that he never came between a composer and his listeners, never forced an interpretation on the notes, but had that indefinable genius for allowing them to be heard to their best advantage."[103] It is for this reason that he sometimes seemed, in the best possible sense, invisible in his music-making. What he gave us was glorious music, not merely music imprinted with his personality. When he died in 1981, it was more than just the loss of another great conductor. "To many people," wrote the *New York Times*, "he stood as the last representative figure in the German-Viennese tradition of music-making that included such legendary figures as Wilhelm Furtwängler, Clemens Krauss, Erich Kleiber, Karl Muck and Bruno Walter."[104] He was in some ways the last. But in his selfless way, when he thought of the future of his art, he considered the singers first, especially for the continued vitality of Wagner's music dramas. "After Nilsson there is no one," he said in 1969. "I do not know what will happen to Wagner when she is gone."[105] That, with his own passing, is something to ponder.

1961, p. 53 (Harriett Johnson).

[102] 24 July 1976, p. 12 (Harold C. Schonberg)

[103] 22 August 1981, p. 24 (Rodney Milnes)

[104] 15 August 1981, p. 1 (Peter G. Davis)

[105] Jones, "Karl Böhm Chafes Over Music Trend," *New York Times*, 4 March 1969, p. 32

Part IX

Outsiders

21

Richard Strauss – "enjoying himself"

There was something disappointing about Strauss as a Wagner conductor. Wagner's music occupied an important place in Strauss's musical universe. "At work and in private conversation," Hans Hotter recalled, "he never tired of pointing out that, as far as he was concerned, Richard Wagner was the only composer besides Mozart who could be taken seriously."[1] In opera houses, where he conducted his fair share of Wagner operas, he seemed proud of his achievements. "I am generally regarded as a very good Mozartian and Wagnerian conductor," he wrote to Hugo von Hofmannsthal, setting out what he was prepared to do as director of the Vienna Opera.[2] "Above all he loved *Lohengrin* with its brilliant A major," recalled Karl Böhm, "and *Tristan*."[3] After that came *Parsifal*, though he was never able to get used to the pathos of the *Ring*.[4]

Strauss had an impassive and minimalist manner on the podium. This is plain to see in any of the film footage of him conducting. He does not seem to be fully engaged or to care what his musicians are doing. Sometimes he said as much in rehearsal. "I don't want to restrict you, gentlemen," he told the Cologne Festival Orchestra in 1905, "just play *Tristan* the way you are used to playing it."[5] This suggests it did not matter to him how it went, and indeed this is how it sometimes seemed to audiences. "Strauss again slept through the whole performance," they used to say in Vienna.[6] Although this appearance might have been deceptive, the results of his performances

[1] Hans Hotter, *Memoirs*, (trans. and ed.) Donald Arthur (Boston: Northeastern University Press, 2006), p. 96. Richard Specht characterized Strauss's preferences: "Beethoven is his church, Mozart his love, Wagner his *credo*": Specht, "Dirigenten. II. Richard Strauss," *Musikblätter des Anbruch* (Wien), vol. 2 no. 5 (March, 1920), p. 187.

[2] letter dated 5 August 1918 in Hanns Hammelmann and Ewald Osers (trans.), *The Correspondence between Richard Strauss and Hugo von Hofmannsthal* (London: Collins, 1961), p. 310

[3] Karl Böhm, *A life remembered: memoirs,* trans John Kehoe (London: M. Boyars, 1992), p. 92

[4] Ernst Krause, "Richard Strauss," in Klaus Geitel and others, *100 Jahre Berliner Philharmoniker: Grosse deutsche Dirigenten* (Berlin: Severin und Siedler, 1981), p. 72; Michael Kennedy, *Richard Strauss: Man, Musician, Enigma* (Cambridge University Press, 1999), p. 67

[5] Paul Redl, former chorus director of the Vienna Opera, in a letter to Strauss in May 1947 reminding him of the Cologne rehearsals, quoted in Willi Schuh, "*Tristan und Isolde* im Leben und Wirken Richard Strauss," *Bayreuther Festpielbuch 1952* (Bayreuth: Niehrenheim, 1952), p. 81

[6] B.H. Haggin, "Vienna's Great Conductors," *Encounter*, July 1977, p. 22. Haggin had interviewed Hugo Burghauser, a bassoonist in the Vienna Philharmonic for many years, on the conductors he had worked under. Burghauser described Strauss as "an extraordinary, not sufficiently recognized, grandiose conductor, one of the greatest, but so self-effacing in appearance that in spite of the greatest effect people were not aware how great a conductor he was.... [He] conducted a perfect Wagner": Haggin, *The Toscanini Musicians Knew*, 2nd ed. (New York: Horizon Press, 1980), pp. 154, 160.

were often disappointing. Sometimes he was bored, and the music sounded dull. At other times, things got out of control. When he was really enjoying himself, Wagner's music sounded Straussian, especially *Tristan*. His friend Max Graf observed how "Strauss conducted the music of the second act – Strauss-like – as an ecstatic hymn, as he did the love music of *Heros Life*....as if it were a relative of *Elektra*."[7] Not all of Wagner's music, however, is amenable to a display of Straussian temperament.

He conducted much Wagner throughout his long career. By one count it amounted to 619 performances: *Meistersinger* (86), *Tristan* (74), *Tannhäuser* (59), *Holländer* (52), *Lohengrin* (50), *Rienzi* (21), *Parsifal* (12), the *Ring* (12) , and separate performances of *Rheingold* (4), *Walküre* (14), *Siegfried* (6), and *Götterdämmerung* (3).[8] Among these were triumphs and disasters. Commentators and biographers have generally ignored Strauss's achievements as a Wagner conductor. Some have preferred the broad generalization with little or nothing to back it up.[9] Perhaps this reflects unease at Strauss's declining powers as a conductor early in a long life, as his renown as a composer grew. Since his death, his music has become even more popular. One writer has suggested Strauss "peaked" as a conductor toward the close of the nineteenth century.[10] Another has suggested "he would have done better not to [have] take[n]" his two conducting appointments in Munich (1886-89 and 1894-98) and Vienna (1919-24).[11] One Strauss scholar has concluded that "his place would have been simpler to determine" if he had died before the end of the first war.[12] Though this comment was made about Strauss as composer, it might equally apply to his other musical activities in the remaining thirty-five years of his life. Finding the peaks is difficult.

In order to see what Strauss was like as a Wagner conductor, we shall look closely at: his debut in Bayreuth with *Tannhäuser* (1894); a Wagner concert in London (1897); his performances of the *Meistersinger* from his Munich and Berlin years; his debut in Vienna with *Lohengrin* (1920); an overview of his *Tristan* performances from Weimar (1890) to Munich (1935); his re-appearance in Bayreuth for *Parsifal* (1933); and the 1928 recordings. He conducted only a few *Ring* cycles: they were routine, repertory productions which seem to have attracted little comment.[13] The performance figures above indicate where Strauss's real interests in Wagner lay.

[7] Graf, *Legend of a musical city* (New York: Philosophical Library, 1945), pp. 207, 251

[8] numbers gathered from Franz Trenner, *Richard Strauss: Chronik zu Leben und Werk* (Wien: Dr. Richard Strauss GmbH, 2003) which lists Strauss's activities day-by-day. As will be seen, the chronicle may not always be the complete picture.

[9] There is no comment on Wagner, for example, in Jan C. Manifarges, *Richard Strauss als dirigent* (Amsterdam: Maas & van Suchtelen, 1907), or Paul Bekker, "Richard Strauss als Dirigent" *Allgemeine Musikzeitung*, 39 (1912), pp. 1050-51. David Wooldridge wrote in *Conductor's World* (London: Barrie & Rockliff, 1970) that Strauss's *Tristan* and *Meistersinger* were "among his greatest performances" (no elaboration), and made the claim that from 1892 "the thirty-two-year-old Strauss had no peers on the German operatic conductor's podium": pp. 86, 92.

[10] Karl Krueger, *The way of the conductor: his origins, purpose and procedures* (New York: Scribner, 1958), p. 147

[11] Kurt Wilhelm, *Richard Strauss: An Intimate Portrait*, trans. Mary Whittall (New York: Thames & Hudson, 2000), p. 292

[12] Norman Del Mar, *Richard Strauss: a critical commentary on his life and works* (London: Barrie and Rockcliff, 1965-1972), vol. 3, p. 472

[13] According to Trenner, *Strauss: Chronik* he conducted ten cycles in Berlin: 1899, 1900, 1901, 1902 (2), 1905, 1906, and 1907 (3), and two in Vienna: 1920 and 1921. I have seen no reviews (despite some searching), nor any accounts of them in secondary sources, except for the occasional anecdote, for example, Max Graf's observation: "Strauss's Wagner style was the Wagner style of a new era. He preferred faster tempi, great climaxes, and sometimes – as at the end of *Walkyrie* – real Strauss strettas": *Legend of a musical*, p. 251.

From Munich to Munich

He was born in Munich on 11 June 1864. His father, Franz Strauss, was a renowned horn player in the Munich Court Opera whose skills were admired by Wagner, but who did not reciprocate the admiration. The older Strauss "approved" of *Tannhäuser* according to his son, but *Lohengrin* was "too sweet for his liking and he was incapable of appreciating the later Wagner."[14] The father "stoutly refused to become a Wagnerian,"[15] and his attitude temporarily retarded the awakening of the young Richard. When he was four years old, he took his first music lessons from his mother, and later took piano, violin and counterpoint lessons. His father kept him "very strictly to the old masters," he recalled. "You cannot appreciate Wagner and the moderns unless you pass through this grounding in the classics."[16]

When he went to see *Siegfried* at the age of fourteen, he was "bored stiff," as he wrote to a friend, "so horribly that I cannot even tell you…," though it must be said he later repudiated these "airy, empty-headed, impudent opinions" about Wagner, and regretted they had ever been published.[17] When he first heard *Tristan* a year later, he did not "understand" it at all.[18] Then he secretly began studying the score against his father's orders:

> I can well remember how, at the age of seventeen, I positively wolfed the score of *Tristan* as if in a trance, and how intoxicated I was with enthusiasm, which was only cooled when I attempted once again to find in the live performance a heightening of the impressions which I had gained through eye and spiritual ear in reading the score. New disappointments and new doubts, new recourse to the score – until I realised at last that it was the discrepancy between a mediocre performance and the intentions of the great master, which I had correctly divined from the score, which prevented the work from sounding in the performance as I had already heard it with the ear of the mind. Having realised this I became … "a fully fledged Wagnerian."[19]

He went to the University of Munich in 1882 and 1883, but soon dropped out, preferring the informal instruction of the opera house and the concert hall to any studies at a conservatory. He was in Bayreuth for the premiere of *Parsifal* in 1882, and saw Wagner at a dress rehearsal, but the work made little impression on him at that time (or at the 1886 Festival).[20]

14 "Reminiscences of My Father," in Willi Schuh (ed.), *Richard Strauss: Recollections and Reflections*, (trans.) L.J. Lawrence (London: Boosey & Hawkes Limited, 1953), p. 127

15 "Richard Strauss," *Musical Times*, 1 January 1903, p. 9 (an unsigned article written after an interview)

16 *Musical Times*, 1 January 1903, p. 10

17 Kennedy, *Strauss*, pp. 16, 22. The full text of Strauss's comments on Wagner in the letter, with sketched illustrations from the score, is in Wilhelm, *Strauss*, pp. 24-26; also in Bryan Gilliam (ed.), *Richard Strauss and his world* (Princeton University Press, 1992), pp. 207-209.

18 "On the Munich Opera" (1928), in *Recollections*, p. 81. According to Kurt Wilhelm, Strauss also took no notice of Wagner who was present at a *Tristan* he attended on 9 November 1880: *Strauss*, p. 26; Cosima does not record any *Tristan* on this date: Martin Gregor-Dellin and Dietrich Mack (eds.), *Cosima Wagner's Diaries*, (trans.) Geoffrey Skelton (New York: Harcourt Brace Jovanovich, 1978-1980), vol. 2, p. 556.

19 "Reminiscences of My Father," in *Recollections*, p. 132; also in Kennedy, *Strauss*, p. 26

20 Matthew Boyden, *Richard Strauss* (London: Weidenfeld & Nicholson, 1999), p. 15; Willi Schuh, *Richard Strauss: a chronicle of the early years, 1864-1898*, (trans.) Mary Whittall (Cambridge University Press, 1982), p. 53; "I cannot work up much sympathy for *Parsifal*," he wrote to Bülow on return from Bayreuth on 11 August 1886: Willi Schuh and Franz Trenner (eds.), *Hans von Bülow and Richard Strauss: correspondence*, (trans.) Anthony Gishford (London: Boosey & Hawkins, 1955), pp. 37-38

His father treated him to a visit to Berlin in 1883 where he heard *Tristan*[21] and, crucially, introduced him to Hans von Bülow who began taking an interest in the young musician. Bülow asked him to compose a suite for wind instruments. He then made him conduct it in Munich without any rehearsal. After this debut, he was engaged by Bülow as an assistant conductor in Meiningen.[22] Bülow found Strauss's conducting "positively breathtaking. If he wants to he can step into my shoes tomorrow…," he wrote.[23] Strauss, too, was deeply impressed with Bülow whose daily rehearsals he attended. "In particular, I found the way in which he brought out the poetic content of Beethoven's and Wagner's works absolutely convincing. There was no trace anywhere of arbitrariness. Everything was of compelling necessity, born of the form and content of the work itself…."[24] Bülow was at this stage no longer conducting Wagner operas, only the occasional concert piece.[25] The impact of Bülow's conducting on the younger musician was profound.[26] Another decisive, if not greater, influence was the acquaintance with Alexander Ritter, a violinist in the Meiningen Orchestra, who introduced Strauss to Wagner's writings, and those of Schopenhauer.[27]

After a few months as a junior conductor in Weimar (1885-86), Strauss went to a similar post in Munich (1886-89) where Hermann Levi and Franz Fischer were his seniors. With those two senior Wagnerian conductors present, Strauss did not have the opportunity to conduct Wagner operas. At one point, however, he was asked to take over a new production of *Die Feen* when Levi suddenly fell ill in 1888. "[I] put untold energy into preparing the work really well," he wrote to Bülow, and then it was taken away and given to Fischer to conduct. Strauss was deeply disenchanted.[28] He loathed Fischer: "one of the most untalented musicians I have ever met and a real criminal on the rostrum."[29] He was also not impressed by Levi, at least not in Beethoven.[30] He was more impressed with Felix Mottl, whose *Tristan* he heard at Bayreuth in 1886, though it "suffered too much," he wrote at the time, "from hurried tempi (in my opinion) to be quite perfect, and from a certain carelessness in the treatment of

[21] "Recollections of My Youth and Years of Apprenticeship," in *Recollections*, p. 135

[22] *Musical Times*, 1 January 1903, pp. 10-11. "Bülow did not even listen from the hall, but nevertheless pronounced his début first class, and Strauss a born conductor": Wilhelm, *Strauss*, p. 33

[23] letter to Spitzberg quoted in Kennedy, *Strauss*, p. 40

[24] "Reminiscences of Hans von Bülow" (1910), in *Recollections*, p. 120

[25] Hans-Joachim Hinrichsen, *Musikalische Interpretationen – Hans von Bülow* (Stuttgart: Franz Seiner Verlag, 1999), pp. 509, 514-15

[26] see Bülow chapter, p. 76. According to the information in Trenner, *Strauss: Chronik*, he was present to hear Bülow conduct Wagner on three occasions, all in Berlin: 23 January 1888, *Meistersinger* Prelude; 4 March 1889, *Tannhäuser* Overture; and 30 January 1890 *Lohengrin* Prelude (rehearsal and concert).

[27] "Recollections of My Youth and Years of Apprenticeship," in *Recollections*, p. 138. Although Strauss was in Meiningen for six months (1 October 1885 to 1 April 1886), his apprenticeship with Bülow lasted only a matter of weeks, for Bülow resigned in November 1885 after a quarrel over Brahms; Strauss was then in sole command of the orchestra, though he spent many hours at Bülow's home: *ibid*, pp. 136-137.

[28] letters to Bülow dated 25 March and 17 June 1888 in Schuh and Trenner, *Bülow and Strauss Correspondence*, pp. 66, 74-76

[29] "Reminiscences of My Father," in *Recollections*, p. 131

[30] He wrote to Bülow on 26 December 1887 after Levi had conducted a performance of Beethoven's *Ninth Symphony*: "[it] was the lowest, most atrocious reproduction of a musical work of art that I have ever experienced… I could have knocked Levi down… I thought painfully of you": Schuh and Trenner, *Bülow and Strauss Correspondence*, p. 62; Strauss may have been reflecting anti-Semitism in this comment: Kennedy, *Strauss*, p. 49.

the orchestra."[31] He heard Nikisch conduct *Rheingold* in Leipzig in 1887: "a splendid conductor, orchestral tone splendid, the utmost precision, very capable singers...."[32] He returned to Bayreuth in 1888 to hear *Meistersinger* under Richter and *Parsifal* under Mottl.

His first substantial Wagner conducting came with a move back to Weimar into another junior position (1889-94). In Weimar he founded a branch of the Wagner Society, and began to give lectures on Wagner while he played on the piano.[33] Strauss had received some instruction from Cosima Wagner on *Lohengrin* and *Tannhäuser* in Bayreuth in 1889, where he was a musical assistant.[34] He was happy with his first performance of *Lohengrin* on 6 October 1889, though half the singers set their own pace, disregarding what Strauss had told them at rehearsal. Cosima was very impressed with a later performance, and he was invited back to Bayreuth as musical assistant in 1891 and offered some conducting – *Meistersinger* and possibly *Tristan* – which illness prevented him taking up.[35] During his illness he dreamed of *Tristan*, and on recovery produced his first performance of it on 17 January 1892 after intensive rehearsals. "It was the most wonderful day of my life!" he wrote to Cosima, claiming that under his hand the score "acquired something intimate like chamber music."[36] According to one newspaper, "many aspects of the performance revealed an astonishing increase in artistic capabilities" thanks to "the invigorating, inspiring influence of our brilliant conductor... who was really the soul of this excellent performance."[37] Among the 199 performances he conducted in his five seasons in Weimar were 48 performances of Wagner works: *Tannhäuser* (19), *Lohengrin* (17), *Tristan* (9), *Rienzi* (5), and *Meistersinger* (1). Other Wagner operas were not assigned to him.[38]

Tannhäuser in Bayreuth

Strauss had been present for the introduction of *Tannhäuser* into Bayreuth in 1891. Mottl conducted, and Strauss was enthusiastic about the production[39] When he took

[31] letter to Bülow dated 11 August 1886, in Schuh and Trenner, *Bülow and Strauss Correspondence*, p. 38; he also found Mottl's tempi too fast in 1899, as he explained to his father: "Mottl conducted *Tristan* very beautifully except for some excessively fast tempos, which, extraordinarily enough, were the wish of Frau Wagner": letter dated 12 July 1889, quoted in Schuh, *Strauss: a chronicle of the early years*, p. 229.

[32] letter to Bülow dated 24 January 1887, in Schuh and Trenner, *ibid*, p. 48

[33] Wilhelm, *Strauss*, p. 44

[34] Kennedy, *Strauss*, p. 55

[35] letter to Bülow dated 8 October 1889, in Schuh and Trenner, *ibid*, p. 85; Kennedy, *Strauss*, p. 46

[36] letter quoted in Kennedy, *Strauss*, p. 67; the correspondence between Strauss and Cosima Wagner on this performance is quoted extensively in Schuh, *Strauss: a chronicle of the early years*, p. 229-232

[37] *Musikalisches Wochenblatt*, 28 January 1892, quoted in Schuh, *Strauss: a chronicle of the early years*, pp. 234-5

[38] statistics drawn from Raymond Holden, *Richard Strauss* (New Haven and London: Yale University Press, 2011), pp. 167-71. Strauss also recalled having conducted *Holländer* in Weimar: "Recollections of My Youth and Years of Apprenticeship," in *Recollections*, p. 142. He appears to have been mistaken. There is no Weimar performance of *Holländer* listed by Holden or Trenner. Wilhelm wrote that Strauss had been "allowed" to conduct "all the German operas in the Weimar repertory except *Fidelio*, *Fliegende Holländer*, *Meistersinger* and the *Ring*": *Strauss*, p. 43. Strauss conducted his sole *Meistersinger* on 28 February 1894 without rehearsal in place of a planned *Tristan*: Trenner, *ibid*, p.114.

[39] Schuh, *Strauss: a chronicle of the early years*, p. 228. His essay "On the Production of *Tannhäuser* at Bayreuth" (*Bayreuther Blätter*, 1892), is reproduced in Robert Hartford (ed.), *Bayreuth: The Early Years - An account of the Early Decades of the Wagner Festival as seen by the Celebrated Visitors and Participants* (Cambridge University Press, 1980), pp. 156-160.

the baton himself to conduct it at the Bayreuth Festival in 1894, he had performed the work nineteen times in Weimar.[40] This experience did not tell in Bayreuth. Although there were some good short reviews and happy impressions,[41] the predominant view was that the performance was a failure. The *Allgemeine Musikzeitung* considered it "a bitter disappointment." Strauss conducted "in a somewhat awkward and dry manner, so that the weak applause after the first and second acts was unfortunately somehow justified."[42] The *Berliner Lokal-Anzeiger*, which described Strauss's conducting as "assured, if a bit prosaic at times," also noted the lack of applause after the first two acts, which "did not really succeed in generating that special *Festspiel* mood. Only the last act, when the chorus, orchestra and atmospheric production came together, was wholly worthy of Bayreuth."[43] The *Vossische Zeitung* was annoyed at some details:

Horns and trumpets on stage were frequently off-key – which may have been due to the great heat – but not everything was crystal-clear in the chorus either. Strauss took the Entry of the Guests in the second act at quite a lively pace, which is probably good and correct: it provides the whole scene with a joyful, festive character, instead of that veneer of deadly serious solemnity with which it is often endowed. Yet the chorus did not always follow as quickly as the orchestra was moving forward, resulting in small differences between the two.[44]

The *Musical Times* reported that there was "an uneasy suspicion that Mr. Strauss is scarcely as yet up to the Bayreuth standard. Certainly the orchestra under his bâton played in a somewhat tame and perfunctory fashion."[45] The correspondent for the *New York Times* reported that the orchestra under Strauss had not seemed to be the same body of men that had played in the previous two performances: Levi conducted *Parsifal* and Mottl *Lohengrin* that year. "Despite his Weimar reputation, the young composer and conductor is not equal to the responsible task of leading such an orchestra. He lacks the requisite authority over the players. The tempi to-day [22 July] were dragged to an irritating degree, and in consequence the whole performance suffered."[46] George Bernard Shaw reported to the *Star*:

The overture was smooth but pointless, not to be compared with dozens of London performances.... Strauss, the new conductor, seemed a hopeless failure; he kept the band as smooth, but also as inane, as a linen collar; and his *tempi*, except for an occasional gallop in the

[40] His first *Tannhäuser* did not turn out harmoniously in all respects, for he was given to using "utterly passionate accents"; in the overture "the Venusberg accents should never sound so obtrusive to our ears; [they were] sporadically flaring fires instead of a passionate smouldering...The Pilgrims' Chorus suffered from changes and distensions in tempo for the sake of contrast – something Wagner would not have wanted": *Weimarische Zeitung*, 7 May 1890, quoted in Kenneth Birkin, "Richard Strauss in Weimar. Part 2: The Opera House," *Richard Strauss-Blätter*, New Series, no. 34 (December 1995), 15-16

[41] "The ensemble was of a great and overwhelming beauty in all its component parts... the prelude was performed most movingly": *Bayreuther Tagblatt*, 23 July 1894, p. [4] (B. J. Zimmermann). "The orchestral part came off beautifully, something that must be attributed to the new conductor, to whom the vigorous character of the performance must also be ascribed": *Musikalisches Wochenblatt* (Leipzig), 16 August 1894, p. 397 (Martin Krause). "The chorus and orchestra under Strauss's directorship were excellent": *Tägliche Rundschau*, 24 July 1894, p. [7]. It was "a most brilliant début": Gustave Samazeuilh in his introduction to Rollo Myers (ed.), *Richard Strauss and Romain Rolland - Correspondence* (London: Caldar and Boyars, 1968), p. 2; Samazeuilh did not mention the Bayreuth *Tannhäuser* in his "Richard Strauss as I Knew Him" (trans. Robert L. Henderson), *Tempo*, New Ser., no. 69 (Summer 1964), pp. 14-17.

[42] 3/10 August 1894, p. 418 (Otto Lessmann)

[43] 24 July 1894, [p. 5] (A. H-ck.)

[44] 26 July 1894, [p. 3] (E. K.)

[45] 1 September 1894, p. 608

[46] "Tannhaeuser Not Satisfactory," *New York Times*, 23 July 1894, p. 5 (W. Von Sachs)

wrong place, were for the most part insufferably slow. After Mottl's handling of *Lohengrin* this sort of thing would not bite on us at all; and we all sat wishing we had not come, and that Strauss had never been born. ... During the interval [between acts two and three] I met with no apologist for the performance.[47]

It light of these reports, it is curious that one modern writer, without any reference to contemporaneous reviews (their absence from the standard German sources is also curious[48]) could have written that with this Bayreuth debut Strauss had "placed himself in the same league as Levi and Mottl as one of the great Wagner conductors."[49] Most writers on Strauss have deftly stepped over this first appearance. He was passed over for the 1896 Festival. His achievements in 1894 may have been part of the reason. He quarrelled with Siegfried Wagner in January 1896, went to the Festival that year, found it a "pigsty to beat all pigsties,"[50] and did not return to conduct until 1933, after Siegfried's and Cosima's deaths.

Back in Munich

Meanwhile, he had received a call to return to Munich (1894-98) as Levi's health was declining. His first opera was *Tristan* on 29 June 1894. The musical structure of the work "came to light with surprising clarity," the *Münchener Neueste Nachrichten* wrote after the performance. "On the one hand, the *tempi* swelled with soulful naturalness, adagios and largos were filled with lively expression of deep and poignant effect."[51] He soon followed with *Meistersinger*, and the same journal "praised the compelling clarity and definition with which he was able to express his artistic will through his baton, particularly in the fight scene which otherwise always gives an impression of chaos."[52] He conducted around 127 Wagner performances during his four seasons in Munich, including the summer seasons: *Tannhäuser* (44), *Tristan* (40), *Meistersinger* (22), *Rienzi* (19), and *Holländer* (2).[53] It is notable he did not conduct the *Ring*, which was Fischer's

[47] "Bassetto at the Wagner Festival," *Star*, 21, 23-26 July 1894, in *Shaw's music: the complete musical criticism in three volumes*, ed. Dan H. Laurence (New York: Dodd, Mead, 1981), vol. 3, pp. 288-9; Shaw reported to the *Pall Mall Gazette* along similar lines: *ibid*, p. 307.

[48] The selection of press articles on the 1894 Festival in Susanna Großmann-Vendrey, *Bayreuth in der deutschen Presse*, vol. 3,1 (Regensburg: Bosse, 1983) includes nothing on Strauss's conducting of *Tannhäuser*. The *Neue Zeitschrift für Musik* only reviewed Mottl's *Lohengrin* and Levi's *Parsifal*. The Richard Wagner Museum in Bayreuth holds no reviews.

[49] Roswitha Schlötterer-Traimer, "Richard Strauss als Dirigent," in *Richard Strauss: Autographen, Porträts, Bühnenbilder: Ausstellung zum 50. Todestag*, ed. Harmut Schaefer (München: Bayerische Staatsbibliothek, 1999), p. 53. "The musical world hardly noticed the successes scored by both Strauss and Pauline ...," according to Kurt Wilhelm, *Strauss*, p. 69. His wife Pauline de Ahna sang Elisabeth in *Tannhäuser* and a Flowermaiden in *Parsifal* in 1894.

[50] He wrote in his diary for 11 January 1896: "Momentous conversation with Siegfried Wagner, unspoken but nonetheless irrevocable separation from Wahnfried-Bayreuth. Only indirectly my fault": quoted in Schuh, *Strauss: a chronicle of the early years*, p. 414; "pigsty..." letter to his wife: p. 416.

[51] 1 July 1894, quoted in Schlötterer-Traimer, "Richard Strauss als Dirigent," pp. 53-54

[52] *Münchener Neueste Nachrichten*, 21 August 1894, as summarised by Schlötterer-Traimer, *ibid*, p. 54

[53] statistics are drawn from Holden, *Virtuoso Conductors* (New Haven and London: Yale University Press, 2005) who, after researches into Strauss's diaries, identified many more performances than previous scholars: Holden, "Richard Strauss in London," *Richard Strauss-Blätter*, no. 37 (June 1997), p. 44, n. 7. Schuh counted 46 Wagner performances: *Strauss: a chronicle of the early years*, p. 389. Trenner listed 79: *Tannhäuser* (26), *Tristan* (25), *Meistersinger* (18), *Rienzi* (10). Holden gave a somewhat different listing in his *Richard Strauss* (2011).

preserve, nor of course *Parsifal*, which was Bayreuth's preserve. Most important to him were *Tristan* and *Meistersinger* in which, he recalled, "I… perfected my technique."[54] We shall look further at his interpretation of these works below. By contrast, he included only one Wagner piece in his Munich concerts, the *Faust Overture* on 22 March 1895.[55] The experience of these years did not make him a suitable successor for Levi, however, whose illness forced his retirement in 1896. Strauss "must be ruled out for our current crisis," wrote *Der Sammler*, and he was.[56] That year he began to extend his activities internationally, conducting in Belgium, Russia, Holland, Spain, France, and London.

The 1897 London Wagner concert

When Strauss made his debut at Queen's Hall in London on 7 December 1897, English audiences had heard "conflicting reports" from Germany as to his ability as a conductor.[57] Although it was billed as a "Wagner Concert," Strauss included two of his own works on the program, one of Mozart's, and the preludes to *Tristan*, *Meistersinger*, *Tannhäuser*, and the Good Friday Music from *Parsifal*.[58] The varying reports from London do little to resolve the conflicting reports from Germany. The *Musical Times* considered "Strauss proved himself a somewhat unequal conductor" in the Wagner selections.[59] The *Daily News* reported that he exhibited "a good deal of fussiness and redundancy of gesture." He showed London a Wagner it was not accustomed to. He was "apparently content with a smooth and technically correct performance, varied at times by a force which nearly approached mere noise, and boasting little of that exquisite attention to light and shade, and clearness of the inner parts, which render memorable a performance under Hans Richter."[60] The *Glasgow Herald* made a similar observation: he was "rather a fidgety conductor, and seems to strive at noise rather than at any nicety of expression. He was doubtless nervous, and will probably be heard to greater advantage later on. But he certainly does not seem to be the equal of Richter,

[54] "Recollections of My Youth and Years of Apprenticeship," in *Recollections*, p. 143. Strauss's *Tristan* was the one Wagner work Gustave Samazeuilh singled out as making "a great impression" in Munich: "Richard Strauss as I Knew Him," *Tempo*, New Ser., no. 69 (Summer 1964), p. 14.

[55] Schlötterer-Traimer, "Richard Strauss als Dirigent," pp. 66-68. He also conducted it with the Berlin Philharmonic on 2 November 1896; the *Allgemeine Musik-Zeitung* found it "satisfactory, but not excellent": quoted in Peter Muck, *Einhundert Jahre Berliner Philharmonisches Orchester* (Tutzing: H. Schneider, 1982), vol. 1, p. 240. Schlötterer-Traimer lists Strauss's other Munich concerts, including on tour from Munich, which included: *Meistersinger* overture (20 August 1899, Augsburg), *Tristan* prelude and Liebestod (23 May 1904), *Rienzi* overture, *Lohengrin* prelude and *Kaisermarsch* (all 23 September 1914), and *Tristan* prelude (3 June 1931, Innsbruck, and 14 August 1936, Munich): *ibid*, pp. 66-68.

[56] 10 October 1896, p. 7. "Our musical life has been lacking inspirational power ever since Levi first fell ill [earlier in 1896]…. What such a gifted musician as Richard Strauss can achieve in a leading role will hopefully become apparent in the future, but he must be ruled out for our current crisis. In fact, we are still lacking an actual 'First Conductor.'" Weingartner and Mottl were mentioned as suitable successors. Strauss was offered a reduced salary and left: Franz Trenner, "Richard Strauss at the Conductor's Desk of the Munich Opera House," *Richard Strauss-Blätter*, New Series, no. 25 (June 1991), 23. Hermann Zumpe was appointed Levi's successor (General Music Director) in 1901.

[57] *Daily News*, 9 December 1897, p. 8

[58] The other works were *Tod und Verklärung*, *Till Eulenspiegels lustige Streiche*, and *Eine kleine Nachtmusik*. Most of the reviews were devoted to a discussion of Strauss's works. Some did not comment on the Wagner excerpts at all, eg, *The Times*, *Musical Opinion & Music Trade Review*, *Graphic*.

[59] 1 January 1898, p. 25

[60] 9 December 1897, p. 8

Mottl or Levi."[61] His readings of certain passages were characterised as "eccentricity" by the *Musical Standard*, "but it is not worth quarrelling with him because he plays the virtuoso a little too much."[62]

The *Tristan* prelude and the *Meistersinger* overture were pieces over which reviewers expressed different opinions. One thought the *Tristan* prelude "lagged, despite Herr Strauss's vigorous endeavours,"[63] while another felt it "left something to be desired."[64] The *Musical Standard* considered Strauss had not exhibited "absolute control" over the orchestra as Richter, Lamoureux and Nikisch were able to do, but Strauss was nevertheless able to obtain the effects he desired, "although it may be somewhat roughly. His interpretations were surcharged with a distinguished poetic feeling. He did not realise the passion of the *Tristan and Isolde* vorspiel (any ordinary conductor can do that), but, instead, he brought out what I may call the poetic-philosophy of the love and death of Tristan and Isolde."[65] The *World* thought the *Meistersinger* overture "horrid; niggling, undignified, without any splendour of noble cheerfulness, rather – dry and rattling."[66] The *Daily Telegraph* considered that "Strauss [had] made but a moderate impression" as a conductor and had "revealed no new beauties" in the Wagner pieces:

> There were many weak places when it came to Wagner's turn. The *Tristan* Prelude went only passably; the *Meistersinger* overture, which began well, was marred by a most ineffective trifling of the tempo at the climax of the piece. Much of the deep poetic feeling of the *Charfreitagszauber* was missed because Mr. Strauss chose to hurry the time. In short, Wagner went to the wall for once, and had to put up with renderings that were scarcely second-rate. The Munich conductor has no remarkable faculty for controlling an orchestra....[67]

Others heard differently. The *Athenaeum* thought "by his astonishing energy [Strauss] imparted new life" to [the Wagner] selections which might well be termed hackneyed."[68] Another considered "he approached perfection" in the *Meistersinger, Parsifal* and *Tannhäuser* selections.[69] The *Morning Post* considered that although Strauss was "somewhat inclined to let his feelings get the better of him," he conducted the *Meistersinger* overture with "splendid vigour."[70] The *Musical Standard* too was impressed:

> The *Meistersinger* overture was full of colour and fire, but the best thing achieved by the young composer was the performance of the *Tannhäuser* overture. To make so hackneyed a work interesting is a wonderful achievement in itself; but Strauss did more than that; for he put before us all the spirituality of the drama, the eternal fight between good and evil, the eternal battle between the flesh and the spirit.[71]

The Wagner selections "were given with a measure of *verve*, grip in accent, and passion," according to the *Standard*; this "proved" Strauss was "a born conductor."[72] The *Sunday Times* wrote: "the body of sound that came forth in the culminating

[61] 8 December 1897, p. 7
[62] 11 December 1897, p. 109 (R. Peggio)
[63] *Pall Mall Gazette*, 8 December 1897, p. 11
[64] *Illustrated Sporting and Dramatic News*, 11 December 1897, p. 606 (B.W. F.)
[65] 11 December 1897, p. 109 (R. Peggio)
[66] 15 December 1897, p. 32 (Robert Smythe Hichens)
[67] 9 December 1897, p. 10
[68] 11 December 1897, p. 830
[69] *Illustrated Sporting and Dramatic News*, 11 December 1897, p. 606 (B.W. F.)
[70] 9 December 1897, p. 5
[71] 11 December 1897, p. 109 (R. Peggio)
[72] 8 December 1897, p. 5

climax of the *Tristan* prelude, and the coda of the *Meistersinger* overture, has never been exceeded in a London performance of these pieces." But the predominant view was one of disappointment. The *Sunday Times* continued: "Herr Richard Strauss may not be a great conductor in the sense of having the power to instantly impress his individuality upon an orchestra or to obtain readings that shall shed new light or throw fresh rays of colour into works already familiar. But this, be it remembered, was his first appearance in our midst…."[73] Would he return to conduct Wagner in London again? "'As the passing of leaves is, so is the passing of men,' especially conductors," wrote the reviewer for the *World*. "At present I do not feel an intense anxiety to stay the passing of Richard Strauss, as conductor."[74] He never conducted Wagner in England again.[75]

Die Meistersinger in Berlin

In 1898 Strauss was appointed Kapellmeister at the Royal Opera in Berlin, the "blue ribbon of musical appointments in Germany."[76] He was made General Music Director in 1908 (with Karl Muck), but in 1911 it was agreed he would relinquish this post and henceforth be a guest conductor.[77] He remained throughout the first War, and in 1918 was made Intendant of the renamed Berlin State Opera. His first opera in Berlin was *Tristan*, and in the twenty years there, he conducted many Wagner operas.[78] Pre-eminent among these was the *Meistersinger*. He had conducted some 22 performances in Munich, but little is known about them other than that they were praiseworthy.[79] The same might be said of the performances in Berlin, even of the new

[73] 12 December 1897, p. 4 (Herman Klein)

[74] 15 December 1897, p. 32 (R. S. H.). By contrast, another considered Strauss had "made a very favourable impression as a conductor, and in that capacity we shall ever be pleased to welcome him, with this proviso, that he generously forbear including his own works into the programme, and I am neither a bigot nor a pedant": *Illustrated Sporting and Dramatic News*, 11 December 1897, p. 606.

[75] Strauss's Wagner conducting was not commented on by Raymond Holden in his "Richard Strauss in London," *Richard Strauss-Blätter*, no. 37 (June 1997), pp. 18–53. In his *Virtuoso Conductors* (2005) he described Strauss as "an outstanding conductor who commanded the respect of musicians, audiences and critics alike": p. 119. Lest it be thought that it was only English critics who criticised Strauss's Wagner, he did not strike a happy chord either at a Paris concert in 1908: "With the prelude and Liebestod from *Tristan*," Pierre Lalo wrote in *Le Temps*, "we were plunged into worry and doubt. The prelude was more feverish than called for, hurried, brusque, lacking breadth in its development, lacking power in its suffering. The Liebestod too lacked in ecstasy and mystical peace. Then came the Good Friday Music driven with a vehemence at which one cannot refrain from expressing surprise, and which does not appear to be the essential quality of this episode of *Parsifal*." It was hardly like the performance, Lalo recalled, of the same piece recently performed by Vincent d'Indy "and inspired by the example and memory of Hermann Levi": *Feuilleton du Temps*, 28 April 1908.

[76] *Musical Times*, 1 January 1903, p. 12

[77] Wilhelm, *Strauss*, p. 134. Leo Blech had been appointed to the Royal Opera in Berlin in 1906 and was made General Music Director in 1913. Frida Leider recalled: "He was an ideal opera conductor, and knew, more than anyone else, how to lead his singers. … The years under Leo Blech will always be thought of as the golden age of the Berlin State Opera": *Playing My Part*, p. 94. Blech's years were 1906–23 and 1926–37.

[78] 253 Wagner performances up to 1939, including as guest conductor, according to Julius Kapp, *Richard Strauss und die Berliner Oper* (Berlin, 1939), p. 39, as quoted in Holden, *Virtuoso Conductors*, p. 132. Trenner in *Strauss: Chronik* lists 225 for 1898–1919: *Meistersinger* (65), *Holländer* (41), *Lohengrin* (20), *Tristan* (16), *Ring* (10) – as well as separately *Walküre* (12), *Siegfried* (6), *Rheingold* (4), *Götterdämmerung* (3) – *Tannhäuser* (7), *Rienzi* (4), *Parsifal* (4), and three other performances: *Tristan* (1894, 1928) and *Lohengrin* (1926)

[79] as noted by Helga Schmidt-Neusatz, "Richard Strauss als Kapellmeister der Münchner Hofoper (2)," *Richard Strauss-Blätter*, New Series, no. 50 (December 2003), 106. Of his first performance in 1894, *Der*

Fig. 21.1. Richard Strauss from his Berlin years, 1898-1919

Fig. 21.2. Strauss in Weimar, about 1890.
Postcards inscribed for Engelbert Humperdinck

Fig. 21.3. Strauss rehearsing *Till Eulenspiegel*, from a film of the 1930s

Fig. 21.4. Strauss in Berlin

Fig. 21.5. Strauss in Paris, conducting *Salome*, September 1935

production he gave on 3 October 1903.[80] Particularly illuminating, however, were reviews of a *Meistersinger* Prelude Strauss conducted with the Berlin Philharmonic on a visit to Vienna in 1895. It was played with much virtuosity, but "like a battle symphony," quite against its spirit, according to *Die Presse*. "One was cast down, not up-lifted. Poetry was abandoned, emotion driven out – an ultra-modern conception."[81] The *Wiener Abendpost* acknowledged that Strauss was a master of tempo rubato, but considered such an approach in the *Meistersinger* prelude no advantage at all:

> Strauss rushed the grand final movement of the prelude, where the three motives meet, with a nervous accelerando, the way that is common with Italian conductors at the end of an overture or a finale. This served to drown out completely the solemnity and grand emotion of this orchestral hymn. He also took liberties during the course of the remainder of the prelude which were quite un-Wagnerian. The Master actually wanted the beautiful E-major episode, in which the violins first play the *Preislied* motive with sweet, honeyed tone, to be played with the tempo considerably slowed-down. Richter takes the tempo of this episode in this way. Strauss, however, rushes along this passage, which has an inherent character of rapturous calm, in a nervous allegro, and takes away the whole of its true nature. It becomes hasty, rushed, particularly the sextolets and thirty-second notes in the build-up to the climax which remain simply incomprehensible.[82]

In his Vienna years, Strauss never conducted a performance of the complete *Meistersinger*.[83]

So far as the Berlin years are concerned, there were occasional reports of a "remarkable" *Meistersinger* and an "excellent" *Tristan*,[84] but the general account seems to be variable. "Let's not even talk about his *Tristan und Isolde* or his *Meistersinger von Nürnberg*," Richard Wanderer wrote in the *Neue Zeitschrift für Musik* in 1905. "If he isn't in the right mood, we don't get much out of them." Like singers, the conductor had his off days. "However, if you find Strauss in a good mood, then it is sensational."[85]

Sammler noticed "a certain restlessness" in the first act, several debatable ritardandi and accelerandi, and "a certain measure of free, individual interpretation," but overall it was "nicely structured, subtle and full of spirit"; the orchestra was "too strong, particularly in the first act… [but] was much more discreet in the second, and the beautiful prelude to the third was of extraordinary tenderness": 21 August 1894, p. 8; the *Münchener Neueste Nachrichten* referred to "the forceful clarity and assertiveness" Strauss employed "to express his will with regard to tempos and powerful sounds"; the riot scene at the end of the second act was presented "with a vividness and transparency of structure, an assuredness and sharpness, which was astounding": 21 August 1894, p. 4.

80 "too large for any praise": *Vossische Zeitung*, 4 October 1903 (L. P.); "Strauss exuded an all-vitalising aura… the riot scene was very well executed musically": *Berliner Tageblatt*, 4 October 1903 (L. S.)

81 3 April 1895, p. 11

82 3 April 1895, p. [1]. The *Neue Freie Presse* had no substantive comment on the prelude in its review.

83 Götz Klaus Kende, "Was Richard Strauss in Wien dirigierte," *Richard Strauss-Blätter*, New Series, no. 19 (June 1988), 29-41. He only conducted the prelude on one other occasion in Vienna, at a university concert with the Vienna Philharmonic on 9 March 1922. Presumably this was the occasion when afterwards, as Max Graf related: "he rushed up to me, red and excited, and cried out, radiant with joy: 'Everything improvised! All without rehearsal!'": *Legend of a Musical City*, p. 202. Strauss wrote on aspects of the performance of the *Meistersinger* in "On Conducting Classical Masterpieces," an undated manuscript published after his death in Schuh, *Recollections*, pp. 52-55.

84 Sir Dan Godfrey, *Memories and music: thirty-five years of conducting* (London: Hutchinson, 1924), p. 96 (*Meistersinger*); "The Wagner Festival at Munich," *Musical Times*, 1 November 1911, p. 728 (*Tristan*); Otto Klemperer recalled in 1969: "about 1905 I heard his *Tristan*. Very good. And his *Meistersinger*. Excellent": Peter Heyworth (ed.), *Conversations with Klemperer*, rev. ed. (London: Faber and Faber, 1985), p. 47

85 Richard Wanderer, "Richard Strauss als Dirigent," *Neue Zeitschrift für Musik*, 72 (27 September 1905),

The New York critic, James Huneker, interviewed Strauss in 1903, before his first visit to the United States in 1904, and wrote: "As a conductor he ranks among the great ones. He is particularly sympathetic in his readings of modern works...."[86] He did not mention his Wagner, although he had heard Strauss conduct *Tristan* in Berlin "masterfully."[87] After the interview with Strauss, Huneker confided to a friend: "This *entre nous* – he is bored to death with life."[88]

Lohengrin in Vienna

At the Vienna State Opera (1919-24), where he was co-director with Franz Schalk, Strauss conducted most of Wagner's works – not *Rienzi*, *Meistersinger* or *Parsifal* – in total some 41 Wagner performances, compared to 71 of his own.[89] He debuted, as Mahler had before him, with *Lohengrin* on 1 January 1920,[90] a work with which he had impressed audiences in Berlin.[91] The choice of *Lohengrin* for his debut suggested to the *Wiener Abendpost* Strauss's "predilection for the earlier Wagner" which was quite understandable in the composer of *Die Frau ohne Schatten*. It was a newly-rehearsed production in which Strauss's influence was mostly directed to operatic effects, to the movements of the ensemble and the great climaxes of the finales:

> He lavished special care on the preludes to the first and third acts, giving them a clear, sharp shape. He took special care with the sensitive *melos* of the first prelude not to show any sentimental clouding. He was careful to preserve a pure picture of the transparent, crystal-clear A-major music. On the other hand, the middle part of the prelude to the third act provided room for sounds of tender sentimentality – between the passionate beginning and the ending a poetic, fairytale mood wove and floated.[92]

The *Neue Freie Presse* considered Strauss had maintained the lyrical-romantic character of *Lohengrin*. He "made music" of the opera, "true and passionate, as it is written in every note." He seemed to live inside everyone's feelings simultaneously.

p. 752. Sir Thomas Beecham echoed this view: "It is not known in this country that the most accomplished conductor since Nikisch was Richard Strauss – when he was in the right mood": Harold Atkins and Archie Newman (eds.), *Beecham stories: anecdotes, sayings, and impressions of Sir Thomas Beecham* (London: Futura Publications, 1979), p. 60. The *Berliner Tageblatt* acknowledged Strauss's variability: "One cannot demand – nor is it likely – that Richard Strauss's performances will always be of the same quality as yesterday's *Tristan* performance, but he will always produce something unique": 6 November 1898, p. [2].

86 James Huneker, *Overtones: A Book of Temperaments* (New York: Charles Scribner's Sons, 1906), p. 24

87 letter to Henry T. Finck, 8 March 1904, in *Letters* (ed.) Josephine Huneker (New York: Scribner's, 1922), p. 33

88 letter to Edward E. Ziegler, Berlin, 17 June 1912, *ibid*, p. 130 (misdated; in fact *1903* according to Arnold T. Schwab, *James Gibbons Huneker: Critic of the Seven Arts* (Stanford University Press, 1963), p. 331, n. 52)

89 Holden, *Virtuoso Conductor*, p. 133. Trenner in *Strauss: Chronik* lists 36 performances: *Lohengrin* (10), *Tristan* (9), *Holländer* (9), *Ring* (2), as well as separately *Walküre* (2), and *Tannhäuser* (2). The new or newly studied productions were *Lohengrin* (1920), *Holländer* (1922) and *Tannhäuser* (1923). After his resignation he returned on occasion to conduct *Lohengrin* (3) and *Tristan* (4).

90 His first opera appearance in Vienna had been a guest performance on 22 May 1919 in *Tristan*, with scenery from Mahler's time: Trenner, *Strauss Chronik*, p. 407.

91 "The focus for our senses moved to the orchestra" as the work "flowed by at a lively pace in an unobstructed stream": *Berliner Tageblatt*, 1 February 1915, p. [3] (A. W.); Strauss had created "something delicious, so wonderfully alive, that it resulted in unmitigated joy" despite the odd "tempo or bad dynamic that went against the grain": *Vossische Zeitung*, 1 February 1915, p. [2] (M. M.).

92 2 January 1920, p. 4

"Tempo, phrasing, accentuation and dynamics were brilliantly self-evident." Intensely dramatic moments were invested with "a gripping energy and punch." And "the perils of the endless four-four beat – of the 'German andante' of the opera – were overcome thanks to the impetus of a fine internal rhythm."[93]

In this period, as in his later Berlin years, his interest in conducting was diminishing. Artur Schnabel recalled:

> He did not always make the same efforts in his conducting. From time to time he did the wonders of which he was capable, but more often, particularly in operas, he was just enjoying himself. I heard operatic performances during which he behaved as if he were quite alone. He would enjoy certain parts and caress them but would just pass over other less challenging or moving ones.[94]

The same attitude was observed at rehearsals, as Leo Wurmser recalled: "he could not be bothered to repeat difficult passages several times at rehearsals. He would explain what he wanted and try it out once or twice; if it went all right, well and good, if it did not, he would shrug his shoulders and leave it at that."[95] Strauss was opposed to new productions in Vienna, and this made it a difficult period for the Opera. After a quarrel with Schalk, he left and never held a permanent position again. It is not a period of Strauss's life that history has smiled kindly upon.[96]

Fig. 21.6. Strauss conducting at the Vienna Opera, 1920. Drawing by Theo Zasche

[93] 3 January 1920, p. 2 (Julius Korngold)

[94] Artur Schnabel, *My life and music & Reflections on music* (London: Longmans, 1961), p. 59

[95] Leo Wurmser, "Richard Strauss as an Opera Conductor," *Music & Letters*, vol. 45 (1964), p. 14; Wilhelm: "He did not rehearse very much, or for very long": *Strauss*, p. 202

[96] Del Mar, *Strauss*, vol. 2, pp. 218-23, vol. 3, pp. 474-75. Wilhelm wrote: "the failure of the dual directorship lay in the difficulties of the time": *Strauss*, p. 172.

Tristan und Isolde

Tristan was a singularly important work to Strauss both as composer and conductor.[97] Its "feverish longing and passion was felt by him with unbelievable force," remarked Richard Specht, "and was expressed as such."[98] Yet on the podium, he was remarkably cool. Max Graf related how, after a particularly thrilling first act of *Tristan*, he said: "'Feel me here!', and placed my hand on his armpit. 'Absolutely dry! I can't stand conductors who perspire!'"[99] He made an immediate impression with the work in Weimar and in Munich, his performances often being described as brilliant, with only the odd surprise or reservation.[100] In Berlin, Bruno Walter recalled how a performance seemed "subjectively fiery, but musically super-*rubato*, in contrast to a powerful performance under Mahler that I had heard in Vienna several weeks before."[101] He was indeed different from Mahler, as the *Neue Freie Presse* indicated after his first performance in Vienna in 1919:

Strauss is by no means a modern-nervous *Tristan* conductor. In fact, he is anything but. How pleasant his grand line, his calm breadth, the healthy, natural tracing of the *melos*, the sound allowed to flow in an unbroken stream! When the dramatic plot requires it, however, all the impetus of Strauss's temperament appears. His dynamic accents are not to be trifled with. Fiery waves flood the music.[102]

The *Wiener Abendpost* noticed how, even after only little more than an hour's rehearsal, the work seemed suffused with a completely new spirit:

He conducts in an exceedingly elastic manner and is lavish with subtle tempo variations. A highly sensitive speed sensor, he is obedient to the slightest of musical expressions. Thus, during the prelude, almost every bar, sometimes even every part of a bar, had its own tempo, so that the expression was a continuously escalating one – lifted by driving ahead, rushing; lifted by subsiding, yielding. Thus at decisive points, barely measurable moments were inserted, where emotional vibrations created huge waves. Or bars appeared so closely together, literally pressed into each other, that they made our hearts beat in feverish excitement. Then again, Strauss would let things take their usual course for many a page, only intervening here and there to create a bit of order, to provide encouragement. In this regard, he completely confined himself to the role of *Kapellmeister*, taking care of technical things with masterly skill. Still, all your nerves remained in a state of continual excitement, just waiting for the moment when a typical slight tensing of the conductor's elbow muscles would immediately influence the course of the music. Like a coiled spring, leaping at the slightest pressure, engaging the wheels of the orchestra.[103]

97 see generally Schuh, *Bayreuther Festpielbuch 1952*, pp. 70-90

98 Specht, "Dirigenten. II. Richard Strauss," p. 188

99 *Legend of a musical city*, p. 201

100 The brilliance of his conducting was noted after his first performance in Weimar "despite some naysayers": *Weimarische Zeitung*, 20 January 1890, quoted in Birkin, "Strauss in Weimar," p. 22; also in Munich in 1894, where "two reductions in tempo [not specified where, and] the simplified recitation of the sailor's song" were singled out as particularly touching: *Münchener Neueste Nachrichten*, 23 August 1894, quoted in Schmidt-Neusatz, "Strauss als Kapellmeister," p. 102; by contrast, *Der Sammler* criticised "a tendency to breadth which was not always beneficial, for instance, after Tristan's first declamation in act three, which was excessively drawn-out, and the whole opera took some fifteen minutes longer than usual!": 23 August 1894, p. 8; after an 1896 performances he was described as "a brilliant interpreter of the *Tristan* score": Oscar Merz quoted in Schmidt-Neusatz, *ibid*, p. 117; and proved himself "a truly brilliant artist and conductor with this opera like hardly any other": *Der Sammler*, 19 June 1896, p. 8; in 1898 he was described as "one of the gifted *Tristan* conductors of the day": *Münchener Neueste Nachrichten*, quoted in Schmidt-Neusatz, *ibid*, p. 120.

101 Bruno Walter, *Theme and variations: an autobiography*, (trans.) James A. Galston (London: H. Hamilton, 1947), p. 140. Mahler last conducted *Tristan* in Vienna in 1907.

102 23 May 1919, p. 11

103 23 May 1919, p. 3 (Kr.)

Of another performance in Vienna in the 1920s a reviewer for *Wiener Journal* noticed how Strauss:

restrains or accelerates the tempo very freely, sometimes just for only a beat, to allow a certain instrumental effect to emerge in all its glory.... [He] also takes the great love duet at a relatively fast pace. The lovers are thirsty for life, not tired of it. This he crystallizes from the musical storm, in spite of the melancholic, yearning lamentations of the poem.... The whole performance was unsentimental, perhaps even a little austere. It was without any embellishment or ornamentation of feeling, and had an extremely agreeable truthfulness.[104]

Reviews of the last occasions on which Strauss conducted *Tristan* – in Dresden on 13 February 1933 for the 50th anniversary of Wagner's death, and in Munich on 13 November 1935 – are particularly illuminating because they compare him with other notable conductors. The 1933 performance was broadcast, but unfortunately not recorded.[105] The *Dresdner Neueste Nachrichten* compared him with Toscanini at Bayreuth (using nationalistic language inevitable for the day). Both were devoted to the work. Both kept passion under complete control:

Yet Strauss is different from Toscanini. He is more German, softer in his emotions, and even more detached. Toscanini is like an iron-fisted general, Strauss like a "trustee." He is somewhat the opposite of Fritz Busch, to name the third great conductor here. Busch gets intoxicated by sound when listening. He enthusiastically wallows in enthusiasm. He gives himself over to passion more easily. When Busch conducts *Tristan*, it is glowing. With Strauss, it becomes a shining crystal. The orchid-like beauty of a tonal greenhouse, which has intoxicated us for a century, flowers in that ecstasy which Busch the musician experiences and shares with his audience. The conducting composer Strauss builds the overwhelming architecture of a work of art, the shape of which is largely owing to himself. With the Italian Toscanini, his innate sense of form is fused with the primary instincts inherent in people of southern European origin. And strangely enough, Strauss's tempos are much tighter, much more compressed than Toscanini's, who was trying to exceed even the "Bayreuth breadth."[106]

[104] Else Bienenfeld, *Wiener Journal* [no date], quoted in Schuh, *Bayreuther Festpielbuch 1952*, p. 81. The English writer and critic, Neville Cardus, talked of reports of Strauss's *Tristan*: "Every time I went to Vienna, Hofmannsthal and Berg, and famous orchestral players such as Arnold Rosé, used to assure me that Strauss's conducting of *Tristan* was one of the most unforgettable experiences in music.... everyone who remembers Strauss's performance of *Tristan* says it was very intense and equalled in our time only by Furtwängler": Robin Daniels, *Conversations with Cardus* (London: Gollancz, 1976), p. 84.

[105] A listener in Berlin was not impressed by the radio transmission: "the unity of the performance, its intensity and range, and its orchestral sophistication could only be very vaguely guessed at... the violins sounded dull, and there were no clear colours in the orchestra, which often seemed to be submerged in a mechanical monotony into which the kettledrums exploded like cannon fire": *Vossische Zeitung*, 13 February 1933. There were other shortcomings: "an appalling muddle" in the orchestra at the beginning of the third scene in act two (*sehr schnell*), "with some of the orchestra playing twice as fast as the others" – Strauss had changed his beat; eventually the orchestra managed to come together again: Wurmser, "Richard Strauss as an opera conductor," p. 13. Herbert Peyser reported to the *New York Times*: "I must admit that his first act seemed to me this time somewhat lackadaisical. But from the second act on his reading increased steadily in passion, poignancy and splendor. In the third, he bestrode the summits": 5 March 1933, p. X5.

[106] 15 February 1933, p. 2. It is possible Busch, who was General Music Director in Dresden, was present at this performance. He recalled how Strauss's conducting in these years showed "a strange mixture, peculiar to him, of apathy and masterly directness which is not without an element of suggestion. This style of conducting practically never appears exciting but it *can* arouse excitement in the hearer. Then there seems to be direct contact with genius": Busch, *Pages from a musician's life*, (trans.) Marjorie Strachey (London: Hogarth Press, 1953), p. 22A; "my impressions are only of his later years," Busch added. He was expelled by the Nazis on 7 March 1933, and did not return to Germany in Strauss's lifetime.

The *Dresdner Anzeiger* described how the performance began with a prelude with no particular tonal charm, with scenes broadly spun out, and with great technical control. There were moments of "the real, Straussian temperament": short, sharp accents, a broad climax with Isolde's first scream, a second act that floated transcendentally, and a third act with unbelievably exciting climaxes. It made some comparisons:

With Toscanini, from first note to last, Tristan appeared to be the ideal of noble boundlessness – of boundless nobility. Everything was covered in Roman conformity (*Formkultur*). Furtwängler achieved a strangely spiritual performance of the third act. Tristan's last words were full of pure ecstasy. This effectively was the real *Liebestod*. This was the climax of the drama. With Strauss, Tristan dies to sounds just as spiritual. Yet this "death" (*Tod*) remains a transition to "transfiguration" (*Verklärung*). It is almost as if he were projecting his own creation onto the Wagnerian. He plays a hero's life (*Heldenleben*) in music, wonderfully Straussian, achieving something so extraordinary in the last beats of Isolde's *Liebestod*, that every word falls silent before such a brilliant revelation. Those who die this way have everlasting life.[107]

Strauss had hoped to end his conducting of Wagner with this *Tristan* performance. He was invited to conduct it in Vienna, but declined.[108] He did conduct it again, however, in Munich in 1935. It was a passionate performance, as Oskar von Pander reported, with wild movements in the dialogue, nothing at all symphonic, nothing prolonged:

There was unbelievable tension in the performance. Tempos were generally tighter than usual. There were no reflective, long drawn-out passages of uniform pedantry, but everywhere escalations of unbelievable passion and vital power. There was more rubato and elasticity than one usually hears in Wagner, particularly striking in the prelude. In general, there was much freedom of tempo and phrasing, so that the re-creation by such a great master was given exceptional appeal. One felt a highly expressive personality at work here, one who knew both in detail and in general what this demonic work is about.[109]

This time, as Strauss noted in his diary, it really was the last *Tristan*.[110]

The Tristan prelude

Strauss's performance of the *Tristan* prelude has been given much attention. Sidney Bloch, an occasional conductor in Berlin during Strauss's time, recalled how he had never heard anyone else make such an impression with the piece. "Strauss reached peaks of tension like no other, it was like a new work."[111] Herbert Peyser wrote after the complete work in Dresden in 1933: "I recall performances of the Prelude under

[107] 14 February 1933, pp. 2-3

[108] "The day before yesterday I conducted, in Dresden, for the last time in this life, *Tristan*, in honor of the death of the great master, and with it I definitely finished my activity as a conductor of Wagnerian wonder works," he wrote to Max Graf. "Such a renunciation is painful, but sometime one has to say good-bye": *Legend of a musical city*, p. 256.

[109] quoted in Schmidt-Neusatz, "Strauss als Kapellmeister," pp. 120-121

[110] Schmidt-Neusatz, *ibid*, p. 121

[111] Sidney S. Bloch, "Richard Strauss als Dirigent," in Otto Zoff, *Die grossen Komponisten gesehen von ihren Zeitgenossen* (Bern: Alfred Scherz, 1952), p. 323; the title of Bloch's piece became "The Greatest Conductor of his Time" in Phoebe Rogoff Cave's translation of the book: Otto Zoff, *Great Composers through the Eyes of their Contemporaries* (New York: E.P. Dutton, 1951), p. 422. This is the sole comment Bloch made on Strauss's Wagner conducting.

him in years gone by that were almost too much for human nerves to bear."[112] Leo Wurmser was also at the Dresden performance and asked Strauss "about his very free interpretation" of the prelude; "he told me that he had it from Bülow, who conducted the first performances. It ought, therefore, to be authentic, although it does not conform with tradition."[113] Strauss himself wrote in one of his notebooks: "My performance of the *Tristan* prelude (ebb and flow) is yet another thing that I owe to the teaching given me by Bülow by word of mouth."[114] Strauss did not actually hear Bülow conduct it. Nor did he prepare it under Bülow's direction.[115] How much he got from a discussion must be a matter of some conjecture. He conducted a performance in Weimar on 26 January 1891, before his first performance of the complete work, which Hermann Levi heard: "Your *Tristan* prelude gave me great joy yesterday. I have not heard it so beautifully played since 1871 (under Wagner), for extraordinarily enough this is the one piece that Mottl has never been really successful in."[116] Willi Schuh, Strauss's biographer, has explained how the two interpretations differed:"Mottl's tempo markings – 'Do not hurry!' 'Never hurry! If anything, broader!' 'Remain a tempo!' 'Slow down very gradually' – are completely incompatible with the Bülow-Strauss conception of 'ebb and flow,' embodied in a powerful surge in the tempo and a flowing re-establishment of the pace (which is to be associated with the Wagner's marking 'gradually holding back slightly in pace')."[117] Schuh then quotes from a 1936 review:

Strauss conducted the *Tristan* prelude in the grand manner of one drawing in and letting out a single breath, which is said to go back to Hans von Bülow.... There is a marking in Wagner's score... *belebend* ["getting livelier'] half a bar before the onset of A major, or more precisely, the exact point at which it ceases to apply. All conductors except Strauss (but including Mottl and Fischer) have always slowed the tempo again as early as the middle of the first bar in A major. But according to Wagner's marking the music should not begin to slow until the beginning of the second bar. Strauss is the only one to observe that exactly and the effect is stupefying, downright revolutionary. Correctly played, the one and a half bars are revealed as belonging to a totally different expressive type from the one to which we are accustomed, as describing exactly the same shape in miniature that Strauss's interpretation does over the whole piece.[118]

112 "Wagner in Germany," *New York Times*, 5 March 1933, p. X5

113 Wurmser, "Richard Strauss as conductor," p. 107. In a performance in Switzerland in 1903 Strauss applied great freedom: he "achieved an effect which far exceeded anything experienced till now... a brilliant interpretation": Ernst Mohr, "Richard Strauss als Dirigent in der Schweiz," in *Schweizerische Musikzeitung*, vol. 84 no. 6 (1 June 1944), 237.

114 previously unpublished notebook entry quoted (without a date) in Schuh, *Strauss: a chronicle of the early years*, p. 233

115 "I do not know [Bülow's] conducting of the *Tristan* prelude, and unfortunately I do not at present foresee an opportunity to hear it," he wrote to Cosima Wagner on 14 March 1892. No opportunity would come, for Bülow had conducted it for the last time in Berlin on 7 December 1891: letter to Cosima quoted in Schuh, *ibid*, p. 233, and Hinrichsen, *Hans von Bülow*, p. 509.

116 letter dated 18 February 1891 quoted in Schuh, *ibid*, p. 233. Another writer gives 18 February 1898 as the date of Levi's letter, the day after Strauss had conducted a complete performance of *Tristan* in Munich: Schmidt-Neusatz, "Richard Strauss als Kapellmeister der Münchner Hofoper (2)," p.120.

117 Schuh, *ibid*, pp. 233-234. Wurmser too explained: "He did not, on the whole, follow Mottl's markings in the Peters score [reprinted by Dover Publications], although these were supposed to be based on Wagner's own remarks when he was supervising rehearsals in Vienna": Wurmser, "Richard Strauss as an opera conductor," p. 11.

118 Alexander Berrsche,. *Trösterin Musica* (Munich: Hermann Rinn, 1949), p. 246, quoted in Schuh, *ibid*, p. 234

Wurmser also recalled Strauss telling him that "he regarded the opening cello phrase as the masculine, Tristan element and the oboe phrase as the feminine, Isolde; so he usually took the first phrase slightly pressing forward, and the second one slightly hesitating.... His basic tempo was, on the whole a flowing one.... He took the whole prelude *quasi rubato*."[119] We will consider his recording of the prelude below.

Parsifal in Bayreuth

Strauss went to Bayreuth in July 1933 in controversial circumstances. Toscanini had declined an invitation to work there, and Strauss promptly offered to conduct *Parsifal*. Whatever his reasons for doing so, it is unlikely they were musical. Although he was a leading German musician of his day, he was hardly the most qualified candidate to conduct *Parsifal*. He had only conducted four performances of the work before, in Berlin in 1917. At Bayreuth he showed little enthusiasm. One seasoned festival visitor, Herbert Peyser, wrote that Strauss's interpretation "[did] not stand comparison on any count with those of either Muck or Toscanini. It was largely casual and featureless and even slovenly tonight [22 July], particularly the first act being pedestrian and dull, though blame for this rested on some of the leading singers hardly less than on Strauss. Thanks to the vividly dramatic singing of Frida Leider as Kundry, the second act picked up somewhat."[120] Ernest Newman reported to the *Sunday Times*:

> Strauss gave few signs that he is particularly interested in *Parsifal*. I am told that he got through the performance in about the shortest time on record, and I can well believe it. Unfortunately, however, *Parsifal* is not a work that is improved by acceleration: the very essence of it is a certain timelessness, in the metaphysical sense of the word; room must be given to the marvellous score to develop its lovelinesses and subtleties at their ease.... while we never feel at Bayreuth this year that the performance is in the hands of an orchestral master who has taken the music and the drama up into his own being and given them out again transformed, the orchestral players, of their own accord, again and again gave us moments of the rarest beauty.[121]

He concluded that Strauss had "proved himself to be a very poor substitute indeed for Toscanini."[122] The young Walter Legge wrote in his review of the performance:

> Strauss's first act was, with certain exceptions, dull. The music of Gurnemanz, Parsifal, of the Grail, of the Good Friday Spell seemed to mean nothing to him.
>
> With Kundry's entrance he found music after his own heart, he knew just how to make the most of the wild phrases, but the rest of the first act inhabits a spiritual world foreign to Strauss's own. The second act is more in his line; he understands the Klingsor-Kundry scene, he gave to the music of the Flowermaidens' scene sensuality.... Later in the act his sympathies were obviously with Kundry; but his fast tempo ruined that usually overwhelming dramatic passage in which Kundry tells Parsifal how she mocked Christ.[123]

Strauss's "great days as a conductor are over," Legge concluded.

[119] Wurmser, "Richard Strauss as an opera conductor," p. 12

[120] *New York Times*, 23 July 1933, p. N2. Fritz Wolff sang Parsifal; Ivar Andrésen, Gurnemanz; Heinrich Schlusnus, Amfortas; and Gotthold Ditter, Klingsor.

[121] 30 July 1933, p. 5 [122] 6 August 1933, p. 5

[123] Elisabeth Schwarzkopf, *On and Off the Record: A Memoir of Walter Legge* (New York: Scribner, 1982), pp. 24–5

What particularly struck audiences, according to Friedelind Wagner, was the "flabbergasting speed" of his *tempi* which caused word to sweep through Bayreuth: "Strauss's *Parsifal* is wonderful. It's like a waltz all the way through. You actually stay awake."[124] He had told players during rehearsal: "The Master has already composed *Parsifal* to be very slow, so one doesn't need to add to this by also conducting it slowly."[125] Although much shorter than Toscanini's in 1931, his overall timing did not

Fig. 21.7. Strauss rehearsing *Parsifal* in Bayreuth.
In the foreground from left, Hugo Rüdel, Daniela Thode, Luise Reuß-Belce, and Heinrich Schlusnus (Amfortas). *Hamburger Nachrichten*, 24 July 1933

[124] Friedelind Wagner and Page Cooper, *The royal family of Bayreuth* (London: Eyre and Spottiswoode, 1948), pp. 92-3

[125] reported by Paul Pretzsch, Bayreuth, 24 July 1933: unidentified newspaper clipping in Richard Wagner Museum, Bayreuth

differ markedly from other performances. As the French critic, Gustave Samazeuilh, recalled, the difference was in the way he conducted the recitatives: "he astounded old Bayreuthians and the theatre's artistic staff by his increased tempi in the recitatives, considerably shortening the accustomed length, but managed with such artistry that all the opera's great scenes retained their spaciousness and majesty."[126] Strauss himself wrote a decade later about the performance of *Parsifal*. He was clearly keen that an audience not be bored, and that if that happened, it was the conductor who was to blame. The conductor must keep "the wider view of the dramatic line of a Wagner act" and sustain it "until the curtain drops":

> When conducting *Parsifal* one should distinguish between three clearly defined groups of expression, whose style and content must determine the tempo:
>
> The liturgy… to be sung without sentimental ritardandi with sistine "objectivity": the purely ecclesiastical element.
>
> The narrative group: personified in Gurnemanz who, as a kind of "evangelist," should be maintained throughout in an objective, instructive manner. In his part we find the words which are otherwise very unusual in Wagner: "Do not drag." It demands much tact and dramatic intuition on the part of the conductor not to impede the steady flow of music in this part.
>
> The immediate experience (Amfortas, Kundry, Parsifal): This allows free play to a purely emotional presentation to achieve the most immediate effect, provided always that the greatest rhythmic exactitude of declamation is not impaired.[127]

He acknowledged that conducting was a "difficult business," and it appears his good sense did not translate into a good performance on this occasion, not at least in the view of English and American critics.

German critics were different, and appear to have been swept up by the intense nationalism that infected the 1933 festival. Heinrich Chevally, for example, considered Strauss "the greatest living musician in the world today, and an earthy German to boot… he simply belongs to Bayreuth."[128] Strauss's approach immediately marked it out from "the pathos of Furtwängler's devotion, and the fanatical commitment embodied in the such different ways of Muck and Toscanini," according to the *Deutsche Allgemeine Zeitung*. The "tightening of the tempos in the first act took away some of the internal weight from individual phrases, as well as some external gravity and interconnected symbolism." But in the second and third acts there was "an escalation of unheard-of intensity."[129] Oskar von Pander, writing for the *Münchner Neueste Nachrichten*, considered that Strauss had conducted *Parsifal* better than he did Mozart or any of his own works:

> With Strauss, the tempo is much livelier than is usually adopted for this sacred play. Yet it loses nothing of its pious and heartfelt mood either, something which of course must always be retained. And the theatrical piece that is *Parsifal* also received immense drive so far as purely dramatic effect is concerned. Totally new aspects, tensions and triggers which one would

[126] Gustave Samazeuilh, "Richard Strauss as I Knew Him," *Tempo*, New Ser., no. 69 (Summer 1964), pp. 16-17. In his contemporaneous review, Samazeuilh had merely written: "Certain passages were perhaps more free-flowing than is customary in the great Grail scenes": *Le Temps*, 1 September 1933.

[127] "On Conducting Classical Masterpieces," *in Recollections*, p. 55

[128] *Hamburger Fremdenblatt*, 24 July 1933, p. 1

[129] 24 July 1933, p. 3 (Oboussier)

hardly ever have expected are suddenly illuminated. Those long drawn-out movements, further extended by slow tempos (for instance in the case of Gurnemanz in the first act) become more comprehensible thanks to tighter tempos... Of course, Strauss is no mystic – but he is a musician of such great calibre that he managed to convince with this *Parsifal* performance, despite its veering away from all those well-worn paths, and left everyone deeply moved.[130]

Alfred Einstein wrote:

In no way did he interfere with the character of the work, not even in the second act, where most conductors introduce a *furioso* as a contrast to the breadth and solemnity of the two contiguous acts. Nor as a conductor has Strauss ever given us anything greater, more concentrated, or more comprehensive than this act. The first was also allowed unimpeded flow in all its spontaneity and amplitude, without once breaking the thread. Only in the last act did the tension seem to give a little, yet without losing any of the full, sonorous glamour.[131]

Einstein was a distinguished Jewish critic of the day, and one cannot exclude the possibility that he was constrained from writing more frankly about Strauss. Hitler was present in force at Strauss's performance, had personally thanked the conductor, and was soon to appoint him President of the Reichsmusikkammer (1933-35). Immediately Einstein had dispatched his final report from Bayreuth, he fled the country.[132]

Strauss returned to Bayreuth in 1934 and conducted three performances of *Parsifal*. Later, in Munich, he conducted a *Tristan* (1935), *Lohengrin* (1936) and *Holländer* (1937). He said goodbye to Wagner's "wondrous works" in Salzburg on 12 August 1939, with a performance of the prelude and closing scene from *Meistersinger*.[133] He died in Garmisch on 8 September 1949, aged 85.

The 1928 recordings

Strauss made only two Wagner recordings, the overture to *Holländer* and the prelude to *Tristan*, in 1928. Whether they reflect the conductor at his best is doubtful. They were made when he was losing interest in conducting. Harold Schonberg discussed Strauss's non-Wagner recordings in his *Great Conductors*: "The only thing that explains such conducting is the suggestion that Strauss considered those sessions merely as a paying assignment, to be finished as soon as possible. Karl Böhm insists that Strauss in the concert hall was nothing like Strauss on records. But the records leave a bad impression. They are disgraceful, and certainly no testimony to Strauss's probity."[134]

[130] 24 July 1933, p. 2

[131] "Bayreuth Festival, 1933," *Christian Science Monitor*, 18 September 1933, p. 10, reprinted in Catherine Dower, *Alfred Einstein on Music: Selected Music Criticisms* (New York: Greenwood Press, 1991), p. 149. Einstein was writing of the 22 July performance, as the American article is adapted from reviews in the *Berliner Tageblatt*, 24, 26, 27 July 1933, reproduced in Susanna Großmann-Vendrey, *Bayreuth in der deutschen Presse*, vol. 2 (Regensburg: Bosse, 1983), p. 247.

[132] on 28 July 1933, as recorded in his diary, when he went to England: *Alfred Einstein memorabilia, 1912-1952* (Box 1, Folder 3), Jean Gray Hargrove Music Library, University of California, Berkeley; see also the "Brief Biography" of Einstein in Catherine Dower, *Alfred Einstein on Music: Selected Music Criticisms* (New York: Greenwood Press, 1991), p. 9.

[133] Trenner, *Strauss: Chronik*, p. 598. A 1944 recording of a *Meistersinger* prelude purportedly conducted by Strauss is not authentic: see Discography.

[134] Harold C. Schonberg, *The Great Conductors* (New York: Simon and Schuster, 1967), p. 241. Ernst

George Szell, who prepared orchestras for Strauss in the recording studio, has lent support to this view.[135]

The Holländer overture

Strauss first conducted the *Holländer* overture in Meiningen at the request of the family of his patron, the Duke of Saxe-Meiningen. He wrote to Hermann Levi: "With unexampled impudence, never having set eyes on the score before, I conducted a brisk and breezy performance of it at sight. It went very well."[136] Hans Hotter, who sang the Dutchman under Strauss in 1937, was very struck by these "brisk tempi."[137] These are indeed in evidence in the recording made more than forty years after his first attempt. Leo Wurmser recalled Strauss's interpretation from Vienna days: "a combination of following the composer's instructions with a certain amount of rubato where the dramatic or poetic content of the music seemed to require it." In an article written some 40 years after the event, he proceeded to go into great detail to explain this.[138] Separately he said that "unless my memory is at fault – Strauss's basic tempo was definitely slower than it is on the record,"[139] but Strauss may have changed his mind over the years, as Wurmser himself notes.[140] His memory may not in fact have been at fault, for a reviewer of the new production Strauss conducted in Vienna in 1922 remarked on "the slowing-down of some of the tempos" which may have been intended to achieve clarity. "In order to achieve such clarity of line," the *Neue Freie Presse* noted, "it is understandable that the romantic semi-darkness has to take something of a back seat."[141] The impression Strauss creates on the record, through a certain detachment and lightness of touch, is of the stormy surface of a shallow sea, of pleasure yachts scudding across the choppy surface, not of any deeper menace in the storm.

Krause sought to refute Schonberg in "Richard Strauss the Conductor," *Richard Strauss-Blätter*, Old Series, no. 9 (June 1977), 14-19.

135 In a filmed interview in 1969 he said: "There were two Strauss's as a conductor: one who was interested, and one who was not interested; and, very often, you had the feeling that he was just serving time or earning his fee and waiting for the card game that came after the performance, so sometimes it would be like this: he would be terribly bored, and in the finale of *Fidelio* (Beethoven) with his [Szell mimics Strauss conducting and taking out his watch from his pocket] looking at the watch [then Szell speeds up his conducting]": *The Art of Conducting: Legendary Conductors of a Golden Era*: Teldec 42668-2, which has scenes of Strauss conducting from *Till Eulenspiegels lustige Streiche*.

136 letter quoted in Kennedy, *Strauss*, pp. 41-42

137 Hotter, *Memoirs*, p. 96

138 Wurmser, "Richard Strauss as an Opera Conductor," p. 5. Norman Del Mar commented: "Wurmser was devoted to Strauss and in his eulogies writes disparagingly of other world-famous conductors besides Fritz Busch": *Strauss*, vol. 2, p. 346, n. 36.

139 Wurmser, "Richard Strauss as Conductor," *Recorded Sound*, no. 24, 1966, p. 108 – an article based on a broadcast talk on the BBC on 19 December 1964

140 "Richard Strauss as an Opera Conductor," p. 5

141 *Neue Freie Presse*, 21 February 1922, p. 7 (Julius Korngold). The performance sounded to the reviewer as if Strauss may have been using the original 1843 version (as Strauss later advised Klemperer to do in Berlin in 1929).

The Tristan prelude

As noted above, Leo Wurmser went into some detail regarding Strauss's performance of the prelude to *Tristan*. In a commentary on the 1928 recording he said:

If you listen to the opening you will find that the basic tempo is quicker than is usual in present-day [1964] performances, and you will notice some big rubati – those that Wagner indicated – and some smaller, quasi improvised ones. I remember that Strauss wanted the last quaver of the first full bar played in tempo, as opposed to the customary exaggerated espressivo, which made it sound like a 4/8 bar. But in the recording this has not quite come off.[142]

This is an instructive comment in several respects, not least because it reveals the recording is not exactly what Strauss wanted, or had achieved in performance. His reading on record is neither an expansive or romantic one, nor is it particularly intense. While it is hardly "stupefying," it is very interesting. The orchestra has a light, evanescent texture, and its volume is restrained. There is a freedom, almost an improvisation, of tempo.

The bell tolls

Strauss loved some of the works of Wagner. "In the face of him," he wrote in the commemorative year in 1933, "only awed silence or the propaganda of deeds is appropriate."[143] He admired some of Wagner's great interpreters, Bülow, Richter and Mottl in particular. Others he did not admire, like Nikisch and Weingartner.[144] Mahler he liked, as a conductor.[145] Love and admiration are not enough by themselves, however, to make a conductor a great interpreter. Nor are the occasional good performances. The sum of reports of the conductors dealt with earlier in this book plainly differs from that left by Strauss. He had a unique way, detached and easy-going. He does not belong in their company. Even his attitude towards conducting generally, in particular his light-hearted "Ten Golden Rules for the Album of a Young Conductor" (ca. 1922),[146] have been characterized as cynical.[147] Harold Schonberg concluded more broadly in *The Great Conductors*: "it seems doubtful if Strauss ever had the big vision: the passion, the fervent belief, the sheer dedication to art – the one-sidedness if you will – that is the mark of the great interpreter."[148] Strauss's heart lay elsewhere.

142 Wurmser, "Richard Strauss as conductor," p. 108

143 "Strauss über Wagner," *Dresdner Anzeiger* (*Sonderbeilage*), 12 February 1933, p. 3

144 Romain Rolland in his diary (1900), in Myers, *Strauss and Rolland Correspondence*, p. 133

145 "Strauss did not consider Mahler a composer at all – 'simply a very great conductor'": Busch, *Pages from a musician's life*, p. 172. See also Mahler chapter, p. 248.

146 in Schuh, *Recollections*, p. 38. Strauss made one amendment to these in 1948.

147 Del Mar, *Strauss*, vol. 2, p. 221; Schonberg, *The Great Conductors*, pp. 238-39

148 Schonberg, *ibid*, p. 242

22

Otto Klemperer – Flashes from the dark

Klemperer was a giant who towered, physically, over other prominent conductors in Germany in the 1920s and early 1930s. He is remembered particularly for championing new music, especially at the short-lived Kroll Opera in Berlin. His radicalism and his Jewishness made him a victim of the Nazis and, like so many others, his natural musical development and career were disrupted. He spent many years wandering the world in search of work. To this affliction was added ill-health. Klemperer suffered a number of crises and disfiguring accidents that would have laid low any lesser mortal. They happened, moreover, to a man who suffered from a condition once described as manic depression. This led to much erratic behaviour, and many odd and witty incidents. Unfortunately it also affected his music-making. On occasions everything would come together and his music would produce an overwhelming effect. On other occasions he would be over-driven or ponderous. His achievements as a Wagner conductor were dogged by ill health, ill temper, and ill fate. He created some brilliant performances, suffered a few disasters, and missed several opportunities.

Klemperer's record in Wagner calls for different treatment. Generally in this book, a brief biographical account of the conductor is followed by a consideration of a conductor's achievements in Wagner's late works. With Klemperer it is better to proceed chronologically, taking his life, his views, his conducting, his recordings, his ups and downs, as they come. So far as *Tristan*, the *Meistersinger*, the *Ring*, and *Parsifal* are concerned, there is not much from his mature years to go on. His spectacular successes were with the early works, the *Holländer*, *Tannhäuser* and *Lohengrin*. It is only fair to emphasise that his Wagner activities were but a small part of the overall man and musician. Some surveys of his life and work do not even mention his Wagner.[1] While this may say something about his contribution to the field, it also suggests that the fully-ripened fruits of his talent fell elsewhere.

[1] for example, Gdal Saleski, *Famous Musicians of Jewish Origin* (New York: Bloch Publishing Company, 1949), pp. 245-48; *Neue Deutsche Biographie*, Vol. 12 (Berlin: Duncker & Humblot, 1980), pp. 37-38; *Die Musik in Geschichte und Gegenwart – Personenteil*, vol. 10 (2003), pp. 260-263 (mentions only his *Holländer* at the Kroll Opera); William Steinberg, "Early Days with Klemperer," *Saturday Review*, 29 May 1965, pp. 47-48, 57 (mostly on the Cologne years 1917-1924, nothing on Wagner). For biographical details I have drawn principally on Peter Heyworth, *Otto Klemperer, his life and times*, 2 vols. (Cambridge University Press, 1983-1996).

The German years

He was born in Breslau on 14 May 1885. In early boyhood he showed promise as a musician through his piano-playing. When he was fifteen, a family friend and pianist, Max Mayer, was asked his opinion of the boy. After listening to him he said, "I cannot say that your son will be a Hans Richter, but I am sure he can become a good musician."[2] In 1901, at the age of sixteen, he was sent to the Hoch Conservatory in Frankfurt where he first heard the *Ring*. In later life, he said this "had made a lasting impression" on him.[3] In old age (1969) he was asked whether he had been a keen Wagnerian: "Immensely. In the first place I was enormously interested in the text. I took Wagner very seriously. I mean, I considered him Beethoven's successor. Heavens, I was sixteen. … I knew nothing."[4] After Frankfurt, Klemperer continued his piano studies in Berlin where he became drawn to Brahms. However, he attended the conducting classes of Hans Pfitzner. "One of the students played the piano, another conducted – and Pfitzner sang! We went through *Tristan* and *Götterdämmerung* in this way. It was very useful. I mean, I learnt the works…. He brought me back to Wagner to some extent."[5]

Klemperer had a number of encounters with Mahler which were to have a decisive influence on his career. One of his first assignments was to conduct an off-stage chorus in Mahler's *Symphony No. 2* in a performance in Berlin in 1905 conducted by Oscar Fried. Mahler was present and congratulated him, and the young man was understandably very proud. In 1907 he experienced Mahler rehearsing his *Symphony No. 3* and, although the work never impressed him, he was struck by Mahler's rehearsing technique. He heard Mahler conduct several times. "The first time was at the Vienna Opera in the second and third acts of *Die Walküre*, and then in concerts in Prague, where he conducted a number of things including the *Meistersinger* prelude … It was phenomenal. For me there was only one thought – to give up this profession, if one couldn't conduct like that."[6] Mahler was impressed with Klemperer's skill as a pianist and wondered why he should want to become a conductor. He was determined, so Mahler gave him a recommendation on the back of a visiting card saying he was "an outstanding musician" and "predestined for the career of a conductor."[7] With this document, which Klemperer treasured all his life, he was launched.

He first became an assistant to Artur Bodanzky, a conductor who had also worked briefly with Mahler, at the Lortzing Theatre in Berlin. After a short period, they both moved in 1907 to Prague, Bodanzky as first conductor of the German Theatre, and Klemperer as chorus-master. The two men became close friends and remained so until Bodanzky left for America in 1915. Klemperer described Bodanzky as "an excellent conductor from whom I learnt a great deal."[8] When Bodanzky left Prague suddenly in 1909, Klemperer was made second conductor and put in charge of a

[2] Peter Heyworth (ed.), *Conversations with Klemperer* (London, Gollancz, 1973), p. 25. All references will be to this first edition, unless a quotation in the revised edition (1985) differs.

[3] Otto Klemperer, *Minor recollections*, (trans.) J. Maxwell Brownjohn (London: Dennis Dobson, 1964), p. 77; he did not say who conducted it.

[4] Heyworth, *Conversations*, p. 26, and later: "What I find so offensive is when [Wagner] virtually describes himself as Beethoven's successor. That he really is not": p. 51.

[5] *ibid*, pp. 45, 23

[6] *ibid*, p. 31

[7] Heyworth, *Klemperer*, vol. 1, p. 28

[8] Heyworth, *Conversations*, p. 79

revival of *Lohengrin*. Whether this was successful is open to doubt according to his biographer, Peter Heyworth, who quoted differing critics. One, Felix Adler, a friend of Klemperer, wrote in *Bohemia*: "The evening provided Herr Kapellmeister with his first opportunity to prove himself as a Wagner conductor... An artist with absolutely his own intentions, he puts these into effect with burning enthusiasm, not, admittedly, without a certain excess of gesturing that a little self-control would easily remedy.... It is a long time since one has heard a *Lohengrin* played with so much warmth and life."[9] Klemperer did not last his full five years in Prague.

In 1910 he went to the Hamburg Theatre headed by Gustav Brecher who made a deep impression on him.[10] His debut as junior conductor was a performance of *Lohengrin*. The evening stands as one of the highest points in his career as a Wagner conductor. It was, Heyworth wrote, "an evening of triumph such as few young and unknown conductors have experienced."[11] Heinrich Chevalley described Klemperer in the *Hamburger Fremdenblatt* as "a musician of the utmost sensibility, of thrilling temperament and natural dramatic temperament...."[12] Ferdinand Pfohl wrote in the *Hamburger Nachrichten* of "a meteor fallen from heaven": "How shatteringly Klemperer built up to the great climaxes [of the prelude]... the brass theme was really overwhelming and came with all the majesty and brilliance of an opening in the heavens. At this point, as though carried away by an irresistible impulse, the conductor leapt to his feet and hurled cues at the brass with bold, uninhibited gestures."[13] Klemperer himself recalled: "In my life up to today [1969] I've never had such a success as I had then. It was unbelievable. The papers wrote of a meteor. I had a wonderful cast. The first of the first pages was Elisabeth Schumann, the second was Lotte Lehmann."[14] At a later performance, Klemperer asked Lehmann at short notice to sing Elsa for the first time:

> If I thought I knew the part, I realized my mistake after the first five minutes. Klemperer sat at the piano, like an evil spirit, thumping on it with long hands like tigers' claws, dragging my terrified voice into the fiery vortex of his fanatical will. Elsa's dreamy serenity became a rapturous ecstasy, her anxious pleading a challenging demand. For the first time I felt my nervous inhibitions fall from me, and I sank into the flame of inner experience... [Klemperer said:] "No idea of the part. We must work hard if you're to manage it."[15]

Manage it she did, for she believed she was "made" in Hamburg with the success of this performance, and with little help from Klemperer: "I forgot everything that the conductor and producer had pumped into me – I was just myself alone."[16]

Other Wagner works conducted by Klemperer in Hamburg never seem to have been on the same level. A performance of *Tannhäuser* in 1912 was found to be "over-

[9] 14 June 1909, quoted in Heyworth, *Klemperer*, vol. 1, p. 42; on 25 April 1910 Adler wrote a farewell tribute to Klemperer in *Bohemia*: "... the performances of *Lohengrin* and *Der fliegende Holländer*... he conducted with inspiration and idealism."

[10] *Minor Recollections*, p. 79; Lotte Lehmann came to the Hamburg Opera at the same time as Klemperer and recalls Brecher as "the quite exceptional first conductor of the Hamburg Theatre": Lotte Lehmann, *Wings of Song: an autobiography*, trans. Margaret Ludwig (London: Kegan Paul, Trench, Trubner, 1938), p. 92.

[11] Heyworth, *Klemperer*, vol. 1, p. 50

[12] 5 September 1910, quoted in Heyworth, *ibid*, p. 50

[13] 5 September 1910, *idem*

[14] Heyworth, *Conversations*, p. 40; Heyworth adds a footnote: "Schumann did not in fact sing in this performance."

[15] Lehmann, *Wings of Song*, p. 117

[16] *ibid*, p. 118

driven" and to have "express-train tempi"; and his tempi were considered erratic in his first *Ring* (Nikisch had conducted it in the previous two seasons).[17] If *Lohengrin* had been Klemperer's making in Hamburg, it was also his undoing. He was assaulted during a performance of *Lohengrin* by the offended husband of Elisabeth Schumann, with whom he had been having an affair. He had to leave Hamburg before his contract had run its course.[18]

He proceeded to Barmen in 1913 for two seasons. There he conducted almost all of Wagner's works and, in 1914, many performances of *Parsifal*.[19] He also gave a *Ring* cycle which appears to have been an improvement on Hamburg. Heyworth summarised: "From the enthusiastic comments of the local critics it is possible to deduce that Klemperer had started to achieve a restraint and authority that had eluded him in his earlier performances of Wagner."[20] Thence to Strasbourg in 1915 for two

Fig. 22.1. Otto Klemperer from his Strasbourg years, 1915-17

seasons under Hans Pfitzner where he conducted *Tannhäuser*, *Meistersinger*, and *Tristan* "within a matter of weeks. The performances were received with ovations such as Strasbourg had rarely experienced... [There was, however] some inner reservation which Altman [a local critic] may have sensed when he commented on 'a lack of rapture and elemental passion' in *Tristan*."[21] In 1916 he led revivals of *Meistersinger*, *Holländer*, and a new *Walküre*, and in 1917 a *Tannhäuser*. Heyworth noted that "at this

17 Heyworth, *Klemperer*, vol. 1, p. 72

18 Elisabeth Schwarzkopf, *On and Off the Record: A Memoir of Walter Legge* (New York: Scribner, 1982), p. 171

19 The Wagner works Klemperer conducted and the dates of the first performances were *Tristan* (8 October 1913), *Tannhäuser* (20 October 1913), *Lohengrin* (2 November 1913), *Meistersinger* (7 December 1913), *Parsifal* (4 January 1914), *Rheingold* (18 March 1914), *Walküre* (25 March 1914), *Siegfried* (1 April 1914), and *Götterdämmerung* (8 April 1914): information from the Stadtarchiv Wuppertal. The *New Grove Dictionary of Music and Musicians*, 2nd ed. (2001), Vol. 27, p. 591 (entry for "Wuppertal") states that Klemperer also conducted 25 performances of *Parsifal* at nearby Elberfeld, but this is an error: Hans Knappertsbusch was at Elberfeld at the time and is credited with having conducted the 25 performances there: *MGG – Personenteil*, Vol. 10 (2003), p. 330. Barmen and Elberfeld amalgamated in 1929 under the name of Wuppertal.

20 Heyworth, *Klemperer*, vol. 1, p. 86

21 *ibid*, p. 97

period of his life [Klemperer] came closer to Wagner than at any time before or after. Even so, he was never a Wagnerian in the full sense of the word."[22]

He went to Cologne in 1917 for seven years. Here and later we see the decline in his Wagner conducting, interspersed only with moments of fire. The critics frequently commented on "an uncharacteristic lack of commitment in his performances."[23] Klemperer commented in 1917: "When Wagner pleases me, I don't please myself."[24] "His approach to the *Ring*," Heyworth wrote, "was felt even by admirers to be 'too sharply analytical to be entirely authoritative.' ... Even in passages of great intensity he had a habit of highlighting detail to a point that threatened to undermine the balance and solidity of the music, a practice which, [Anton] Stehle claimed, derived from Mahler."[25]

Klemperer was a guest conductor in Barcelona in 1920 and 1921. A *Tristan* went well, but a *Tannhäuser* less so. He had not proposed to conduct Wagner, but that is what the public wanted. He gave a concert of Wagner excerpts: "Miserable, isn't it?" he wrote to his wife.[26] In November 1921 he gave three cycles of the *Ring* in Barcelona, in German for the first time in Spain. They did not go too well, with either singers or orchestra. He had divided *Rheingold* into two acts. He repeated the *Ring* on return to Cologne – his second last cycle – and *Siegfried* in Rome in December 1922. He was to farewell the *Ring* in Buenos Aires in 1931.

He spent two years in Wiesbaden, which included a new production of *Lohengrin* on 11 January 1925, and a triumphant *Meistersinger* on 15 May 1927. Heyworth wrote that "in later years he was to look back at his time in Wiesbaden as the happiest in his life." A critic and stage director who had been active in Mannheim and Wiesbaden under several conductors gave Klemperer this extraordinary accolade in 1947:

> Whether Bodanzky or Furtwängler or Klemperer was the greatest... is something I would not presume to decide.... But one thing I know and that with unshakeable certainty: Klemperer is the greatest of them all as a theatre conductor; scenically and musically, he is simply a master. In this field he has no rival, never has had one. Even Gustav Mahler, however much one may esteem his artistic personality, was only his forerunner as an operatic conductor. Mahler showed the path and the goal... it was Klemperer who first brought fulfilment.[27]

General statements such as these which are not tied to a particular performance, composer, or period should perhaps be read with circumspection. When we recall the impact Mahler had on the Vienna Opera, and the critical and public response to Klemperer up to this period, as documented by his biographer, there is nothing really comparable in their Wagner performances.

After his move to the Kroll Opera in Berlin in 1927 Klemperer made his first Wagner recordings, with the Berlin State Opera Orchestra, of the *Siegfried Idyll* and, for the first time by anyone on record, the prelude to *Tristan* with Wagner's own concert ending.[28] Record reviewers in the English-speaking world greeted these with pleasure. *Gramophone* was given only the second of the two *Tristan* records (a practice

[22] Heyworth, *Klemperer*, vol. 1, p. 97 [23] *ibid*, p. 127 [24] *idem*

[25] *Kölnische Volkzeitung*, 26 September 1918, quoted by Heyworth, *ibid*, p. 127

[26] Heyworth, *ibid*, p. 155

[27] Hagemann, *Bühne und Welt* (Wiesbaden: Der Greif, 1948), pp. 101-103, free translation by Heyworth, *ibid*, p. 247

[28] Other conductors soon followed: Karl Muck (1928) and Richard Strauss (1928).

not unheard of in those days) and judged the interpretation "remarkably strong and impassioned, and finely controlled"; indeed the reviewer concluded it was doubtful "if we could better it here. If the first record is as good, this must clearly be the standard performance for some time."[29] The *British Musician* wrote that Klemperer played the *Tristan* prelude "with a fire and passion and high musicianship that few of us have known at concerts, except when the conductor is Albert Coates or Bruno Walter."[30] The *Siegfried Idyll* was well received too, this time on the other side of the Atlantic, by the *Phonograph Monthly Review*: "the keynote of Klemperer's performance is a hushed and breathless tenderness which are profoundly moving… rarely, if ever, have I heard a phonographic performance in which a conductor has dared to be so delicate and restrained in his effects."[31] Reissued in 1988 with other recordings from the Kroll years, the more interesting excerpts now are those which display Klemperer's modern music-making, such as Kurt Weill's *Kleiner Dreigroschenmusik* whose first performance he gave in 1929.

The Holländer erupts at the Kroll

Much of Klemperer's fame, or notoriety, stems from his time at the Kroll Opera in Berlin (1927-1931), notably including the production of the *Holländer* in 1929. Produced by Jürgen Fehling with sets designed by Ewald Dülberg, it was a radical re-think destined to outrage the traditionalists. And it did. One critic wrote of Klemperer and Dülberg: "their ignorance of Wagner is a public disgrace."[32] In 1938 the production was cited by the Nazis as a prime example of degenerate music. Later still it was seen as a precursor to the New Bayreuth of the 1950s. Klemperer had decided, on the advice of Strauss, to present the original 1843 version in three acts, without the redemption motif and with the orchestration of the 1852 version softened. He said he regarded the original version as "a shattering manifestation of original power" and "far more effective."[33] And this is how it indeed seemed.

Alfred Einstein, writing in the *Berliner Tageblatt*, considered Klemperer had been correct to present the work in its original form. In spite of various things that disturbed "the harmony of the work and even constitute acts of violence," he concluded the presentation was "gripping and fascinating":

> because Wagner the primary dramatist, Wagner the essential musician, was in evidence and full force. Indeed, the dramatic essence of the action was more powerfully portrayed than I have ever seen it…. From a musical point of view, too, the *Dutchman* has seldom, if ever, been heard in a more harmonious presentation, thanks to its intrinsic musical strength, to Klemperer's good taste, and to a few clever play directions by Fehling. The "program opera" had almost disappeared. They should have taken the final step by doing away with the intermissions; then

29 January 1928, p. 334; the editor, Compton Mackenzie, subsequently wrote that it was "the best recording we have had of this immortal music": March 1928, p. 405; it was not clear whether by that stage *Gramophone* had both records. 30 February 1928, p. 310 31 April 1931, p. 211 (Robert H. S. Phillips)

32 unsourced newspaper clipping in the Otto Klemperer Archive, Library of Congress (Box 51, Folder 11), where other reviews cited below come from, unless noted otherwise. On this *Holländer* production generally, see Heyworth, *ibid*, pp. 278-83.

33 Klemperer interviewed in Buenos Aires, May 1931, and on Westdeutscher Rundfunk, 1962, in Martin Anderson (ed.), *Klemperer on music: shavings from a musician's workbench* (London: Toccata Press, 1986), pp. 42, 54

the tragic musical meaning of this "dramatized ballad" would have been thrust home with otal effectiveness.[34]

Wagner in "full force" through the medium of Klemperer's musicianship was what impressed many critics. "Klemperer throws himself at the work with all vigour, forcing everyone on stage and in the orchestra to give their very best," reported *Tempo*. "He doesn't permit a moment's relaxation, everything is filled to bursting with expression – with the right kind of expression. The low points feel like sinking, the climaxes like explosions.... In the great choral scene in the third act, Klemperer has the usually inaudible ghost choir sing from the orchestra, producing a dramatic effect of incomparable power."[35] Dühlberg and Fehling were under the compelling spell of Klemperer's "fiery, unbridled musical pulses," according to the *Berliner Morgenpost*. "These sweep across the music with hot dramatic breath of incredible power – and carry us along, up to extreme heights, and find their climax in the peerlessly arranged great choral scene between Daland and the Dutchman's men."[36] It was as if "electric shocks" emanated from the conductor's stand, reported *BZ am Mittag*. "Wonderful, this excitement, these eruptive crescendos and hammering rhythms! Klemperer is no friend of musical candyfloss – as is well known – so he is passionately devoted to this hard, cruel score. He even exaggerates it."[37] Bernard Diebold described Klemperer as a dramatic conductor, "because he was being Wagnerian," and marvelled at how, "with brilliant empathy and insight," he imbued the work with a simple spirituality. As for his tempi, "he sometimes accelerates beyond the familiar, but today I know: the familiar was wrong.... Klemperer is a magician by virtue of simplicity."[38]

The production created a political scandal. Klemperer and his collaborators were branded "a group of degenerates."[39] The *Allgemeine Musikzeitung* wrote: "What Klemperer and his helpmates offer... amounts to a total destruction of Wagner's work, a basic falsification of his creative intentions. That goes in almost equal degree for the musical performance, which coarsened the sound to an intolerable extent.... Tempi were ridiculously overdriven, finer dynamic shadings eliminated and all expression reduced to a minimum...."[40] In later life Klemperer remembered the production fondly: it "really was a great success."[41]

The Kroll years were soon to come to an end. In Leningrad in March 1929 he conducted concert excerpts from *Parsifal*, including the whole of the last act. It was not a work with which he had much sympathy. He never conducted excerpts from it again, not at least until his 1961 recording of the prelude. He went to Bayreuth in 1930 to hear Toscanini conduct *Tristan* and *Tannhäuser*. Toscanini silenced all comment, so

[34] *Berliner Tageblatt*, 16 January 1929, in Catherine Dower (ed.), *Alfred Einstein on Music: Selected Music Criticisms* (New York: Greenwood Press, 1991), pp. 89-91. Einstein also observed: "It is impossible to present Wagner in a more un-Wagnerian manner, or to more completely distort Wagner's ideas... [Wagner] was inflexible in the matter of scenery, insisting upon 'exact coordination of the scenic proceedings and the orchestra'... The revolutionary part of the performance was in the stage effects."

[35] 16 January 1929 (Viktor Zuckerkandl). The Holländer was sung by Fritz Krenn; Daland, Martin Abendroth; Senta, Moje Forbach; Erik, Eyvind Laholm; Mary, Marie Schultz-Dornburg; Steersman, Albert Peters; the chorus director was Hugo Rüdel.

[36] 16 January 1929 (Rudolf Kastner)

[37] 16 January 1929 (Dr. Erich Urban)

[38] unsourced newspaper clipping, possibly *Frankfurter Zeitung*, Otto Klemperer Archive

[39] *Signale für die musikalische Welt* (Max Chop) quoted in Heyworth, *Klemperer*, vol. 1, p. 282

[40] 25 January 1929 (Paul Schwers), *ibid*, p. 283

[41] Heyworth, *Conversations*, p. 62

far as Klemperer was concerned. As for Wagner, he wrote: "So much genius, and yet also dross (*Erdenreste*), such as one hardly finds... in any other genius."[42] Shortly before the Kroll Opera was folded into the Berlin State Opera in 1931, and Klemperer with it, there was a proposal for a *Tristan*, but the idea was abandoned. He was never to conduct the opera again.

In the brief period, as it turned out, that he was with the Staatsoper (1931-1933), there were two notable Wagner productions. One was a disastrous tour of the Staatsoper to Buenos Aires in 1931.

Götterdämmerung in South America

The first Wagner opera Klemperer conducted at the Teatro Colón was the *Meistersinger* in May 1931. It was a success.[43] What struck the German press was Klemperer's "fanatical enthusiasm" for his work, his "complete devotion," his "iron hand," his "rhythmic, relentlessly-suggestive signalling," and his apparent ability to

Fig. 22.2. Klemperer with Professor Max Hofmüller, Indendant of the Teatro Colón, and Magdelena de Sánchez Elia, President of the City Colón Committee. *Argentinisches Tageblatt*, 23 May 1931

[42] letter to Gerhard Meyer-Sichting dated 11 August 1930 quoted in Heyworth, *Klemperer*, vol. 1, p. 345

[43] Ludwig Hofmann sang Hans Sachs; Alexander Kipnis, Pogner; Erik Wirl, Beckmesser; Hans Wrana, Kothner; José Riavez, Walther; Maria Rajdl, Eva; Carla Raslag, Magdalena; and Karl Jöken, David. The chorus sang in Italian. The performance was cut, but the "cuts were generally imperceptible and skilfully executed; it was only in the meadow scene that severe cuts in Hans Sachs's lines became apparent." (*Argentinisches Tageblatt*, 23 May 1931, p. 4)

conduct the whole work "from memory alone."[44] The *Argentinisches Tageblatt* remarked that he never lost his eye for the whole: "despite a meticulous working-out of detail, all connections were retained, and he never lost sight of the great line."[45] His general approach, according to *Deutsche La Plata Zeitung*, was that *Meistersinger* was "not only musical comedy, not heavy-going drama, but a sparkling mirror of broad, great life." The Colón orchestra played the score "like intimate, magnificently festive chamber music, accompanying the singers without falling into meaningless passivity.... Tempi shed the stifling restrictions of tradition in favour of a freer flow of radiant vibrancy."[46] It was "on the whole," in the view of the *Buenos Aires Herald*, "a truly great performance from every point of view."[47]

When it came to the *Ring* in September, the press began to wonder whether the Staatsoper's Wagner would really take root "in the Latin soil of Buenos Aires."[48] The principal singers included Frida Leider and Lauritz Melchior. Melchior's biographer related how the singers had been looking forward to three *Ring* cycles and two *Tristans*, but because Klemperer had called for extra rehearsals, the management had to cancel six of the performances. "The public's original elation over the unprecedented number of German opera performances turned to rage. The artists, on the other hand, were most disturbed by the cancellation of their lucrative performances [as] payment for the cancelled performances was not forthcoming."[49] In the case of the orchestra, Klemperer quarrelled with them also. Heyworth vividly describes this occasion, "dogged with misfortune":

John Montés [critic of the *Argentinisches Tageblatt*], blamed Klemperer's relentless rehearsing for the weariness evident in *Das Rheingold* on 1 September. Five days later *Die Walküre* was given a gala performance in the presence of the new president. The audience was inattentive and to ensure that its patience should not be overtaxed severe cuts were made, even in the scene between Fricka and Wotan.[50] Klemperer's tempi were found fast and his interpretation lacking in inner commitment. *Siegfried* on 17 September fared little better and cuts were again so extensive that Wotan put only a single question to Mime and even his crucial encounter with Siegfried was curtailed. Not surprisingly, Klemperer seemed to Montés not to be "entirely gripped by his task". *Götterdämmerung* on 29 September was, however, considered by one critic to have far outstripped in dramatic intensity the performance given by Weingartner nine years earlier.[51] But Klemperer had by this time quarrelled with Melchior, whom he found artistically "inadequate" as Siegfried. Indeed, according to one recollection, relations with leading members of the cast were so tense that they refused to acknowledge applause in his company.[52] By this time the season was in any case running so far behind schedule that *Götterdämmerung* received no more than a single performance: no sooner had the curtain fallen than the principal

[44] *Argentinisches Tageblatt*, 23 May 1931, p. 4 (J. M.); *Deutsche La Plata Zeitung*, 23 May 1931, p. 9 (Fr.)

[45] 23 May 1931, p. 4 (J. M.) [46] 23 May 1931, p. 9 (Fr.) [47] 23 May 1931, p. 1 (B.W.)

[48] Heyworth, *Klemperer*, vol. 1, p. 380-82

[49] Shirlee Emmons, *Tristanissimo* (New York: Shirmer Books, 1990), p. 113; Frida Leider does not refer to Klemperer directly in her memoirs, but she refers to "dissensions," "several unpleasant incidents," and "minor vexations" that made her glad when the tour came to an end: Frida Leider, *Playing my part*, (trans.) Charles Osborne (London: Calder and Boyars, 1966), pp. 141-42.

[50] In an article in the Viennese musical periodical *Anbruch* (January 1933), Klemperer declared himself to be opposed to cuts: Anderson, *Klemperer on Music*, p. 188.

[51] Heyworth, citing *Deutsche La Plata Zeitung*, 7 October 1931; on 30 September 1931 that newspaper wrote: "even in 1922, no such unity and magnitude was achieved – not even remotely" (p. 8).

[52] Heyworth, citing information provided by John Montés

Fig. 22.3. Klemperer from his Hamburg years, 1910-1913

Fig. 22.4. Klemperer rehearsing Beethoven's *Ninth Symphony* in Berlin, 1929.
Photo by Felix H. Man

Fig. 22.5. Klemperer at the Kroll Opera, 1928 (top four), and 1931 (photo by Dr. Erich Salomon)

Fig. 22.6. Klemperer recording *Der fliegende Holländer*, London, 1968

singers, their bags already packed, made for the docks to embark that very night for Europe. Klemperer was never again to conduct the *Ring*.[53]

Opera had come to revolt him. After a Mozart production in Frankfurt in 1932 he wrote to his wife: "I don't want to see any more opera. I find the whole thing so disgusting."[54] Nevertheless, he went on to conduct more opera in Berlin that season. This was a period, Heyworth wrote, "when his operatic activities seemed to have reached a nadir."[55]

Triumph with Tannhäuser

His last Wagner opera at the Staatsoper Unter den Linden was *Tannhäuser* in February and March 1933, only days after the Nazis had installed themselves in power. It caused a scandal. Produced by Jürgen Fehling and designed by Oskar Strnad along the same lines as the Kroll *Holländer*, it was another original version that polarised the critics. The first performance was given on 13 February, the 50th anniversary of Wagner's death. The politically-charged audience greeted Klemperer with "a gale of whistling." Of the musical performance, there are varying, indeed quite opposing, accounts. For the scandalized *Deutsche Zeitung*, it was "a *Tannhäuser* parody," a "botched and lifeless" performance staged by those "who blithely ignored Wagner's instructions and almost half a century's worth of stage experience.... The ringleader of this renewed attack on Wagner is, of course, Otto Klemperer."[56] The *Allgemeine Musikzeitung* considered

[53] Heyworth, *Klemperer*, vol. 1, p. 382. Montés's account was broadly consistent with his contemporaneous reviews, but others in the German and English press were more impressed. Montés wrote in the *Argentinisches Tageblatt* of *Rheingold*: Klemperer's orchestra, "worn out by a multitude of rehearsals, sometimes sounded dull, and was not always able to follow the conductor's intentions"; *Walküre*: "some too hasty tempi betrayed an inner restlessness...; the *Ring* just doesn't seem to be as close to the heart of Klemperer, the master interpreter of the *Meistersinger*"; *Siegfried*: "the judgement made after the *Walküre*... is confirmed here"; *Götterdämmerung*: "one could feel the devotion, power and expressiveness of the orchestra, particularly from the Funeral March onwards, which was conducted with the highest intensity" (2, 8, 18 and 30 September 1931). *Deutsche La Plata Zeitung* wrote of *Rheingold*: "he recreates [it] without any personal additions"; *Siegfried*: "[it] suits him better than *Rheingold* and *Walküre*... the best *Siegfried* Buenos Aires has ever known... passionately smouldering, a piece of great inspiration"; *Götterdämmerung*: "[Klemperer] so painfully, so mercilessly took the work apart during rehearsals, and then managed to weld it together at the moment of recreation into dramatic life of the highest intensity! The climaxes were anything but urgent or nervous: there was no whipping up of any extraneous tongues of dramatic flame, but instead, contrasting effects of breath-taking suspense between tremendous pauses, resulting in a bold *al fresco* conception of the drama" (2, 18 and 30 September 1931, Fr.). The *New York Times* reported "an inspired and truly brilliant performance" of *Götterdämmerung* (15 November 1931, p. X10, I. G. LaBastille). The *Buenos Aires Herald* was impressed throughout, for example, after the *Walküre*: "As usual, Otto Klemperer was the great master dominating the entire proceedings, the orchestra being in their very best form throughout"; *Siegfried*: "the great genius of Klemperer was very much in evidence through the entire performance"; *Götterdämmerung*: "Klemperer conducted throughout as one inspired" (7, 18 and 30 September 1931, B. W.).

[54] letter (Brussels, 2 November 1932) quoted in Heyworth, *ibid*, p. 401

[55] *idem*. In light of this credible observation, Hagemann's view of Klemperer as a theatre conductor (above) seems to carry less weight.

[56] 13 February 1933 (Paul Zschorlich). This and other reviews of the performance are from the Otto Klemperer Archive in the Library of Congress. Tannhäuser was sung by Sigismund Pilinsky; Landgraf Hermann, Emanuel List; Wolfram, Herbert Janssen; Elisabeth, Franzi von Dobay (in place of Delia Reinhardt who was ill); Venus, Moje Forbach; Walter von der Vogelweide, Charles Kullmann; Biterolf, Eugen Fuchs. Klemperer's best soloist, according to the *Berliner Tageblatt*, was the chorus, directed by Hugo

Klemperer had built "an appalling memorial" to Wagner:

To begin at the beginning, he managed to prove that the *Tannhäuser* overture is a ghastly-sounding, exceedingly mediocre piece of music. Except for a few small passages, he also misunderstood the rest of the opera in a similar manner. Hard noise where you wanted intoxicating sound. A thin trickle where you would expect flourishing cantilenas. Jerky stammering when clear, broad accents are required. A disembodied shrinking of tonal representation where colourful lyrical beauty should be unfolding. Needless hurry next to dull distension. Strangulated expressions where strong sounds are what is needed. In a nutshell: Mr Klemperer has hardly managed to catch even a whiff of the character and meaning of the *Tannhäuser* music. The third act may have been a bit better overall, but there's no sense in judging small details when the overall impression was a crushing one. Enough of this![57]

These were only protests, however, from what the *Berliner Morgenpost* described as "dogmatic Wagnerians… enchanted by the Bayreuth tradition."[58] All critics acknowledged that Klemperer's interpretation was different, but not all were crushed by it. "One could not really expect to hear the usual traditional *Tannhäuser* from [Klemperer]," wrote the *Neue Zeit*. "Even the overture is hardly recognisable in many parts."[59] It sounded "completely unfamiliar" to the *Neue Berliner*. "One can hear beautifully guided middle voices which have usually been blurred in the past. Once again, everything has rhythmic precision and, above all, fascinating, intensifying dramatic power."[60] Klemperer seemed to have clarified, cleaned and toned down the score. "Nowhere in the orchestra was Wagnerian sonority apparent," reported the *Filmkurier*.[61] "Klemperer does not provide the utmost Wagnerian pathos," wrote the *Nachtausgabe*, but "he makes a sparklingly clean job of it – exact, energetic, and he gives it all he has got."[62] Likewise the *Berliner Volkszeitung*:

Everything focused on clear lines and utmost rhythmical precision. Many fine details of the instrumental fabric surfaced from the darkness. Even if they were only fine, inconspicuous accents in individual voices, they provided the overall sound picture with more lively colours and emphasized the dramatic nature of the action. The great restraint of tempos, recognisable at first in the overture, resulted in a growth of inner tension. Despite the clarity and transparency of the orchestra, which played magnificently, the warmth of its sound, its subtlety and passion, were never lost.[63]

On the question of tempi, it was "impossible for them to have been any different," declared the *Berliner Tageblatt*. "Everything is full of spirituality, without it being emphasized. None of the scenes, finales, acts aim for effect; they are all uniformly structured. This *Tannhäuser* is just the naïve, great, romantic opera Wagner had envisaged

Rüdel: *Abend-Ausgabe*, 13 February 1933, p. [2]; it was "magnificent": *Musical Times*, April 1933, p. 367 (Hugo Leichtentritt).

57 *Allgemeine Musikzeitung*, 17 February 1933. Of other critics, Ernst Schliepe in the *Deutsche Allgemeine Zeitung* of 14 February 1933 wrote: "the music was too sharply defined, at once fevered and cold": Heyworth, *ibid*, p. 410; Herbert Peyser in the *New York Times* condemned the performance – "the thin and ineffective old Dresden version" – as a "screaming libel on Wagner… how calculatingly its perpetrators have set out to ravage Wagner's conception and fly in the face of its every intent for the mere sake of being as 'different' and as subversive as possible;" he merely mentioned Klemperer as the conductor: 5 March 1933, p. X5.

58 14 February 1933 (Friedrich Deutsch)

59 14 February 1933 (Albert Hirte)

60 13 February 1933 (Dr. Hofer)

61 13 February 1933

62 13 February 1933 (Alfred Schattmann)

63 13 February 1933 (Lothar Band)

around 1845."[64] The unity of the musical performance struck *BZ am Mittag*: "Time and time again, the decisive component of [Klemperer's] performance was that he sees the whole, that he wants the whole. On the one hand, there is a harmony of music, action and scenes. On the other, there is a uniting of events, scenes and acts together into one great arc." One of the most striking moments, it concluded, was the final scene, "the completely unforgettable, solemnly stirring *piano* of the young pilgrims as they brought in the sprouting staff – they were not just singing *piano*, they were striding and moving in exactly the same manner – and then came the very sudden *forte* as the sinner's redemption was pronounced. It is all written in the score, but reading and reading are two different things."[65] "After such a wonderful performance," exclaimed the *Berliner Börsen-Courier*, "will there be anyone left daring to claim that Klemperer is no Wagner conductor?"[66]

Alas, "Klemperer's magnificent performance was not quite mirrored up on stage"[67] where his views on the need to adhere to Wagner's scenic rules – albeit with imagination and freedom – seem to have been taken too far.[68] He conducted two more performances, and then went on a short conducting tour to Italy and Hungary. When he returned, Heinz Tietjen had scrapped the production, and he found himself out of a job.[69] He fled to Switzerland. Carl Flesch was an important player in this period and an astute observer of musical performers in Germany. His view was that Klemperer "had not yet fully found himself" by 1933.[70]

The United States and Hungary

He was now doomed to wander the world in search of opportunities. For the next fourteen years (1933-1947) he would conduct no opera. In the eleven years of this time he was in the United States, he was never even asked to conduct opera. He missed it "very much. But the Met – didn't seem to want me. At any rate, the director, Johnson, never approached me. Then when I was asked, I was ill and couldn't accept."[71]

There were, however, two Wagnerian episodes of note during these years. He had been appointed music director of the Los Angeles Philharmonic Orchestra and conducted, among other things, *Ring* excerpts and the preludes to *Parsifal* and *Meistersinger*. A recording of the latter from 1 January 1934 is the only Wagner excerpt that has appeared on record from these concerts. Taken from a broadcast of a performance preceding a football game,[72] there are the usual problems of sound quality. Klemperer's tempi are erratic – one can hear moments of panic in the orchestra – and

64 *Berliner Tageblatt* (*Abend-Ausgabe*), 13 February 1933, p. [2] (Alfred Einstein)

65 13 February 1933 (Viktor Zuckerkandl)

66 13 February 1933 (Heinrich Strobel)

67 *Weser-Zeitung* (Bremen), 16 February 1933

68 *Vossiche Zeitung*, 13 February 1933 (Max Marschalk), which quoted from Klemperer's article in *Anbruch* (January 1933): "Render unto Wagner that which is Wagner's...You should observe his stage directions... a free, imaginative, courageous treatment of these instructions will always, it seems to me, be the most Wagnerian": Anderson, *Klemperer on Music*, p. 188.

69 Heyworth, *Conversations*, p. 69, where Klemperer also recalled: "The press reaction was awful – I don't know why... [It was] a severely stylised production."

70 Hans Keller (trans. and ed.), *The memoirs of Carl Flesch* (London: Rockliff, 1957), p. 344

71 Heyworth, *Conversations*, p. 78; he was to have conducted *Tristan* in December 1959.

72 *Los Angeles Times*, 2 January 1934, p. 1

it is an impulsive, improvisatory performance. For this reason, it is more interesting than his later versions. Kirsten Flagstad sang Wagnerian excerpts for him on some of these occasions, but she was not particularly enthusiastic about doing so. She suggested to him that her friend and conductor, Edwin McArthur, replace him. "There were reasons for frigidity on both sides. Several years before coming to America she had gone to Berlin to audition for him: he had not liked her then and had not engaged her."[73] Klemperer's old friend and former colleague, Artur Bodanzky, did not make that mistake when he auditioned her for the Metropolitan Opera.

In New York in 1941 Klemperer walked out of the New York Chamber Orchestra, a government-funded orchestra, over a dispute concerning the *Siegfried Idyll.* He said he refused to conduct it "because they wanted it with full orchestra. I told them it was a chamber work with single woodwind and strings. They wouldn't agree, so I said, 'Well you can do it without me. Goodbye.'"[74] He explained to the music editor of the *New York Times* that he wanted "to do it entirely with thirteen musicians, as it was originally written."[75] It is a pity Klemperer was so wedded to original versions. In this case, as Ernest Newman pointed out, as soon as Wagner had the money and the opportunity for a larger orchestra to play the *Siegfried Idyll* on a later occasion, he engaged one.[76] The result for Klemperer was that he was unemployed and "widely regarded as unemployable."[77]

He headed back to Europe only to run into more trouble in Paris. He withdrew from four performances of *Lohengrin* over what seems a petty dispute over the staging: whether *all* the women should fall to their knees when Lohengrin arrives in act one as Klemperer wanted, or merely *some* of them as the Paris Opera wanted. He did not get his way, and left. It was not until 5 February 1948, in Budapest, that he got to conduct *Lohengrin*, the first time since 1925. In April he revived *Tannhäuser*, without cuts, and the following year, *Meistersinger*, also without cuts, but after many weeks of rehearsal and many rows.[78]

A live recording of *Lohengrin*, sung in Hungarian, from 24 October 1948 survives. Whether this is a good thing is debatable, because it certainly does little credit to Klemperer. It includes the infamous breakdown towards the end of the opera, after Lohengrin's Narration, when Klemperer yelled at the audience for prolonging its applause and walked out. There is silence on the recording – or the uneasy shuffling, whistling and clapping of the audience – until he eventually returns and resumes, leading the opera to its conclusion. He wrote to the *Népszava* the next day: "I have conducted Wagner operas in Berlin and Vienna, in London and New York, and in Milan and Moscow, but my experience everywhere has been that audiences take care not to break into the continuity of Wagner's music. It would appear that some of the audiences on Sunday evening adhere to this bad custom."[79] Musically, the

[73] Edwin McArthur, *Flagstad: A Personal Memoir* (New York: Alfred A. Knopf, 1965), p. 80. According to Howard Vogt in *Flagstad: Singer of the Century* (London: Secker and Warburg, 1987), she *was* offered an engagement after the audition with Klemperer "but could not consider it then because she was under contract to the Stora Teatern in Göteborg": p. 74.

[74] Heyworth, *Conversations*, p. 84

[75] 2 February 1941, in Anderson, *Klemperer on Music*, p. 192

[76] Newman, *Life of Wagner*, vol. 4, p. 306

[77] Heyworth, *Klemperer*, vol. 2, p. 117

[78] *ibid*, pp. 182, 200

[79] Anderson, *Klemperer on Music*, p. 191; as Anderson points out, Klemperer had not in fact conducted Wagner operas in Vienna, New York, Milan, or Moscow.

performance displays some of the impetuosity, even impatience, that eventually manifested itself in Klemperer's outburst. One wonders why an opera containing some sublime music was not given more time to express itself. When excerpts were first issued by Hungaroton in 1982, one reviewer noted the difference between the volatile Klemperer on the records and the older conductor of the "often ponderous EMI recordings... For all I know, these extracts may well have come from what was, on stage, an exciting *Lohengrin*. But on repeated hearings, the scrappy ensemble would be difficult to take even were the performance more illuminating than it is."[80] After the complete recording came out in 1999, Andrew Farkas gave a detailed account of the production and the recording in *Opera Quarterly*. He commented on Klemperer:

> His conducting is characterized by dynamism, vitality, and a relentless forward thrust. Those familiar with his recordings made late in life in Knappertsbuschian languor will hear the galloping tempi of this *Lohengrin* with disbelief. Indubitably, he is in full control of the performance – moving, propelling, and occasionally driving the music with uncommon force.... Even if in spots the pit overtakes the stage ensemble for a moment, the effect is exhilarating. But there is no discernible reason to rush the chorus in act 2 (*Zum Streite säumet nicht*), just as the gathering of the army in the last scene is so compressed in time that it loses all shape, dignity, and in consequence, interpretation.[81]

The procession to the Minister (*Gesegnet soll sie schreiten*) is also rushed, and is not as solemn, stately and glorious as it can be. A spirited performance in passages where Ortrud and Frederick are plotting is quite in place; in other passages the melody needs time to breathe. But Klemperer was on this occasion heading for a crisis.

Excerpts from a Hungarian performance of *Meistersinger* on 11 April 1949 are even less satisfactory. The sound quality, the limitations of some of the singers, and the fragmentary nature of what does survive do not make it possible to get a reliable sense of the occasion.[82] Klemperer's pace is generally lively, sometimes excessively so. In act three, the quintet (*Selig wie die Sonne*) could have been taken more slowly to allow the summer-scented breeze to blow, and the arrival of the mastersingers could have been held back a little, to allow the broad chests of the burghers to swell with pride. Nevertheless, the pace does build into a wonderful, rousing finale.

Klemperer left Budapest after various disputes. A production of *Tristan* by Wieland Wagner at the Holland Festival in 1959 was started, but Klemperer had to withdraw after suffering third-degree burns in an accident in 1958. They also had plans for a *Meistersinger* at Bayreuth, but this too had to be abandoned,[83] along with a *Tristan* in New York. As the former director of the Metropolitan Opera, Rudolf Bing, put it: "we lost Klemperer, who had been signed to conduct *Tristan*, when he fell asleep with a lighted pipe in his mouth and awoke in a sheet of flame."[84]

80 *American Record Guide*, September 1983, p. 90 (Peter J. Rabinowitz)

81 Andrew Farkas, "Interrupted Melody: Otto Klemperer, *Lohengrin* and Budapest," *The Opera Quarterly*, vol. 18, no. 2 (2002), pp. 238-39

82 "The inspired interpretation... can be felt, albeit fitfully... it is hard to judge the true grandeur of Klemperer's reading": *Gramophone*, November 1981, p. 764 (Alan Blyth); "...not a recording to supplant any you might already have...": *Fanfare*, January/February 1982, p. 210 (Anthony D. Coggi).

83 Heyworth, *Conversations*, p. 84

84 Rudolf Bing, *5,000 nights at the opera* (London: Hamilton, 1972), p. 200; apparently "a 75% proof bottle of medicinal camphor" was to blame: Heyworth, *Klemperer*, vol. 2, pp. 273-274; Klemperer said of the proposed *Tristan*: "my health rebelled again. I couldn't do it and [Bing] never asked me again": Heyworth,

Arrival in England

The invitation to conduct a series of concerts in London in 1959 and 1960 brought Klemperer a degree of fame, and adoration, of a kind he had never enjoyed before. His concert performances were "uneven," but as Heyworth points out, as far as the public was concerned "he had inherited Toscanini's mantle as 'the great conductor' of the day. EMI were not slow to perceive the implications."[85] With Walter Legge as producer, and his own Philharmonia Orchestra at Klemperer's disposal, EMI sought to make as many recordings with him as possible. The first of a series of Wagner excerpts was released on Klemperer's 75th birthday, some of which according to Legge were "unfamiliar to the English-speaking world."[86] This was an over-blown claim: every excerpt was in the catalogue somewhere. In the context of a marketing strategy, however, its purpose is clear. Promotion was one of Legge's powerful skills, as he displayed in the following record-selling statement about Klemperer: "Unfortunately I never heard him conduct *Meistersinger* but his broad tempi and the weight as well as the clarity of the counterpoint in his recordings of the Overture, and the heavy-footed accents and the stolid lumpishness of his 'Dance of the Apprentices,' for me at least, came nearer to what must have been Wagner's own concept than any other performances I have heard. Wieland Wagner was of the same opinion."[87] How could anyone dissent? Of course, they may have been unaware of Wagner's wish, as noted by Felix Mottl in his diary, that the *Meistersinger* overture be taken at a "strong march tempo."[88] But Klemperer's heavy-going, slow performance as recorded by EMI (his live performances are a different matter) fulfilled Wagner's worst fears: his prelude was doomed to be taken too slowly. As for his Dance of the Apprentices, it was more of a dance of the giants. From a technical point of view, the excerpts were beautifully recorded. The rousing overture to *Rienzi* and the act three prelude to *Lohengrin* benefitted most in this regard.

When the excerpts were reviewed in *Gramophone*, the reviewer merely wrote that "Klemperer was a noted Wagner conductor earlier in his career... [and] we have to remember that in his Berlin years Klemperer's reputation was as a brilliant and stubborn champion of new music."[89] There were some perceptive comments about some of the excerpts, but nothing really quotable about Klemperer. Then, for a reason not entirely clear, the reviewer wrote about the very same records the following month, having listened to them this time on his own equipment. With a nod towards

Conversations, p. 84; Klemperer declined a proposed *Meistersinger* in West Berlin in the 1960s because his health would have made the long third act too risky: *idem*.

85 Heyworth, *Klemperer*, vol. 2, p. 286; orchestral players, as well as critics, had differing views about Klemperer. Gerald Jackson, who played in both the London Symphony Orchestra and the Royal Philharmonic Orchestra under Klemperer, remembers him terrorizing and insulting players; Jackson did not share in the "lavish encomiums" showered upon Klemperer: *First flute* (London: Dent, 1968), p. 77; Peter Beavan, on the other hand, wrote that Klemperer "still remains the most satisfying conductor for whom I have played. He made the music transcend notes and even sounds...": *Philharmonia days: a few brief memories of my early days with the Philharmonia Orchestra* (London: The Cook Robin Press, 1976), p. 6.

86 Walter Legge, "Otto Klemperer," *Gramophone*, May 1960, p. 567

87 Schwarzkopf, *A Memoir of Walter Legge*, p. 190

88 diary for 26 May 1876: "Wagner says that the *Meistersinger* prelude will without exception be taken too slowly. It should be a strong march tempo": Krienitz, "Felix Mottls Tagebuchaufzeichnungen," p. 196.

89 May 1960, pp. 568-69 (William Mann)

Legge's publicity, he found "Klemperer's reading [of the prelude to *Meistersinger*] unusually satisfying, though I wonder how soon I shall decide that his *ritenuti* are exaggerated"; but he reached the quotable conclusion: "it is plain from these four sides that Klemperer is a great Wagner conductor, probably the greatest in the world."[90] It was hyperbole such as this that made Klemperer into EMI's best-selling orchestral conductor.[91]

At a Philharmonia Orchestra concert in London on 10 February 1963, Klemperer included the prelude and Liebestod from *Tristan* in a programme that mainly consisted of Beethoven and Bruckner. The *Financial Times* critic was deeply impressed by the prelude (it overshadowed the Liebestod sung by Christa Ludwig, in his view): "I have never heard this music move on grander tides of rhythm, its form more continually implicit in its phrases, its phrases more nobly moulded, its orchestral polyphony more precisely articulated. Yet the passion of the music, so far from being monumentalised into petrifaction, was all the greater for being realised on a truly epic plane. The Wagnerian singing line was as faithfully transmitted as the Wagnerian vastness of scale."[92] This concert held promise for what was to be one of Klemperer's great performances of *Lohengrin*, at Covent Garden on 8 April 1963.

The London Lohengrin

With Klemperer conducting, the *Times Educational Supplement* wrote, "the result was one of the greatest Wagner performances that we have heard in this house since the war: every detail secure, the whole design massive but fluent, the textures luminous, the lyricism warmly expressive, the pageantry opulently ablaze. The orchestra played and the chorus sang with gigantic attack and verve. The total effect was sublime.... For once, the opera *sounded* so wonderful that one did not really mind how it looked."[93] It looked a "tame and conventional production," according to the *Sunday Times*, but Klemperer's conducting was "the strongest feature of the evening... A few passing flaws in the ensemble never impaired the general rightness of the whole."[94] Heyworth wrote in the *Observer*: "Klemperer exercises some rhythmic alchemy over these acres of four-in-a-bar. Even that famous bridal march acquires momentum, though only God and Klemperer know how. Shape and a sense of movement are miraculously imposed on great tracts of musical wasteland, climaxes mount up with an irresistible majesty (the choral singing is very fine) and are brought with unerring timing to a mighty culmination."[95] The *Financial Times* found Klemperer's reading "incontrovertibly great... The prelude, in fact, conjured up images of an ideal staging; they were more 'scenic' than what met the eye when the curtains parted.... As a total dramatic adventure, this *Lohengrin* was disappointing. As an evening of grand opera –

[90] *Gramophone*, June 1960, p. 22 (William Mann); several years later, Mann wrote of this recording: "it is generally reckoned *hors concours* for tonal splendour and tragic grandeur of expression.... it delves more deeply into Wagner's youthful masterpiece than any other: in Alan Blyth (ed.), *Opera on Record* (London, Hutchinson & Co., 1979), reprinted Harper Colophon, 1982, pp. 340-341.

[91] Heyworth, *Klemperer*, vol. 2, p. 39

[92] 12 February 1963, p. 22 (David Cairns); partially quoted in Heyworth, *Klemperer*, vol. 2, p. 303

[93] 3 May 1963, p. 915 ("a Special Correspondent"); partially quoted in Heyworth, *Klemperer*, vol. 2, p. 305; reviews quoted here were taken from clippings in the Royal Opera House Collections.

[94] 14 April 1963 (Desmond Shawe-Taylor)

[95] "Klemperer the Mighty," 14 April 1963, p. 20

and orchestrally, as a musical experience – it was splendid."[96] Some reviews suggested a heaviness in the tempi not welcome to all ears. The *Sunday Telegraph*, for example, wrote that Klemperer's "grave sense of pace is Wagnerian in a manner that plunges deep back into German tradition,"[97] and the *Evening Standard* found that Klemperer's "impact on the opera was rather diffuse because until he reached the Third Act his reading was spacious and drawn-out. From the Third Act onwards the climax built up dramatically."[98] By contrast, *Music & Musicians* wrote that "Klemperer's tempi tend to be on the fast side.... the only thing I missed being the last ounce of mysticism. Both the first act Prelude and Lohengrin's Narration could have been more other-worldly."[99] The BBC did not broadcast this "last great operatic achievement" of Klemperer.[100] In light of these reviews, it is unfortunate that it is the Budapest and not the London *Lohengrin* that has survived on record.

The spectre of the Holländer

What does survive is a recording – *two* recordings – of the *Holländer* from 1968, one an EMI recording from February and March, and the other from the culminating broadcast of the concert performance on 19 March. The version performed was the same as that used at the Kroll Opera in 1931, the original Dresden version. The singers stood behind the orchestra, "an arrangement that did not seem to flatter them,"[101] and the chorus too seemed to have suffered. Heyworth wrote of the concert in the *Observer*:

> This was Klemperer at his greatest. It was an interpretation before which all others I have heard pale into insignificance. Admittedly, it was far from unflawed. There is no point in politely evading that fact that Klemperer now controls a performance more by sheer act of presence than by anything that approximates a beat. How the New Philharmonia Orchestra and the BBC Chorus deduce from that fluttering baton precisely what is required is a miracle, and it was hardly surprising that there was some unpolished and even ragged detail on Tuesday. Though characteristically strong and forthright, the orchestral sound tended to be coarse, and the balance between it and the chorus was at moments virtually non-existent. Yet such imperfections faded before the heroic splendour of the performance as a whole....The BBC Chorus struggled bravely against the overwhelming orchestral tumult that Klemperer unleashed in the last act."[102]

The *Daily Telegraph* observed that the absence of a pit sometimes obscured the singers, and that Klemperer "permitted an occasional uncleanness of attack by the New Philharmonia Orchestra which he would not have tolerated in earlier days."[103]

The *Sunday Telegraph* wrote of "a feeling of slight anti-climax at the close of the first act.... it almost seemed as if everything had been said at the end of the overture," but a "sense of highly charged atmosphere" arrived in the second act.[104] The *Financial*

[96] *Financial Times*, 9 April 1963 (later editions) and 10 April 1963, p. 26 (Andrew Porter)

[97] 14 April 1963 (John Warrack) [98] 9 April 1963 (Sydney Edwards) [99] June 1963 (Michael Marcus)

[100] Heyworth, *Klemperer*, vol. 2, p. 305; in 1966 he was invited to conduct *Lohengrin* in Hamburg, but declined, fearing recollections of the scandal in 1912 when Elisabeth Schumann's husband assaulted him: *ibid*, p. 316.

[101] *Financial Times*, 20 March 1968, p. 28 (Andrew Porter)

[102] 24 March 1968, p. 30; Heyworth did not quote his own review in his biography.

[103] 20 March 1968, p. 17 (Gerald Abraham) [104] 24 March 1968, p. 14 (R. L. Henderson)

Times considered that "Klemperer's reading was on the whole powerful, massive, striking over the long spans rather than in particular points of delicacy. The cosy, domestic side of *Der fliegende Holländer* yielded to a grander view – but perhaps some of the simpler pleasures were lost."[105]

Fig. 22.7. Klemperer sketch by unknown artist

When Klemperer was asked whether he enjoyed making gramophone records, he said, "No, I hate it. I like to make a recording before a concert performance because then I have time to prepare a work properly. But I hate this business of constantly moving to the control room to hear what I have recorded."[106] He certainly had ample time to prepare the *Holländer* recording – fourteen days – yet the results caused EMI some hesitation on artistic and technical grounds, "so much so that EMI considered postponing its release until after the important pre-Christmas period."[107] Yet when it was released the producers could not have been happier. The *Gramophone* reviewer, Alec Robertson, wrote that he had first heard the *Holländer* at Covent Garden in 1910 under Richter – "my memory of the event is dim" – and that the performance given "on March 3rd of this year was greeted with universal praise by the critics… [The] performance… is as perfect as we have any right to demand."[108] The reviewer was mistaken on a number of points.[109] Most importantly, his reference to "universal praise" was, as we have read, not quite the case. A fellow reviewer pointed this out: "it was not received with such universal rapture as AR supposes. Perhaps I may quote a few sentences from my own *Sunday Times* review because I find they express

[105] 20 March 1968, p. 28 (Andrew Porter)

[106] Heyworth, *Conversations*, p. 94

[107] Heyworth, *Klemperer*, vol. 2, p. 338

[108] December 1968, pp. 881-882; when this recording was re-issued in 1990, Alan Blyth wrote that "there is throughout what Alec Robertson, back in 1968, called a 'blazing intensity' to the reading that brooks no denial"; he did detect, however "a want of propulsion" once or twice in the recording: *ibid*, February 1990, p. 1526; when it was re-issued by EMI as one of its "Great Recordings of the Century" he wrote that it "is anything but a staid performance": *ibid*, October 2000, p. 102.

[109] Richter did not conduct the opera at Covent Garden in 1910, and the performance in 1968 had been on 19 March.

very much what I now feel about the recording also: "[Klemperer] gave us more of the solid Norwegian timbre ["*timber*" in the original review] of this uneven, but delightful, opera than of its wild salt spray and bounding vigour...; [Klemperer gives a] masterly, but not very dashing, interpretation."[110] Distance in time as well as geography sometimes brings clarity to occasions such as these. When the recording was re-issued in the United States in 1995, the *American Record Guide* detected that the Klemperer of the 1960s appeared to have left the stage far behind him:

> As an exercise in exploring musical architecture, it's superb; you won't find such detail on any other recording of the opera.... To attain such balance and transparency, Klemperer sacrifices speed; and while it is interesting to hear the rapturous close of the Senta-Dutchman duet in Act 2 played with such unhurried deliberation, it's also impossible to discern the life-or-death passion in it. Daland's intrusions into the story take too long, Erik and the Steersman often sound like sluggish somnambulists, and there's no sizzle in the great final scene of Act 3. In a word, it's all much too slow... this is more a dissection of *Dutchman* than a dramatic presentation.[111]

Klemperer's view was that he " would prefer to record a performance than make a recording in a studio... A few mistakes don't matter."[112] In the case of the *Holländer* recordings, his preference was vindicated by the release of the concert in the 1990s: it marginally scores over the performance pieced together in the studio. There is a more homogeneous sound, possibly because fewer microphones were used than in the studio, and more of the work can be heard than was probably the case at the actual performance. And there are moments of drama unique to a live performance, like the frightening shriek from Senta when the Dutchman appears.

Wotan's goodbye

Lord Harewood recalled from his Covent Garden days that "in the late 1960s, there was something like a Klemperer-cult in London."[113] It is no wonder then that EMI was determined to squeeze still more out of the old Klemperer for its commercial ends. The company had him back in the recording studio (in fact All Saints Church, Tooting) in October 1969 for a complete *Walküre*. It was an optimistic idea. "As soon as sessions began on 21 October," wrote the historian of the Philharmonia Orchestra, "it was apparent that EMI would be lucky to complete Act I. The sessions went on and on: [other conductors] took the first half or so and then Klemperer would record for the remaining two hours."[114] Act one was finished within two weeks, but well behind schedule, and Klemperer was in no state to continue before the end of the year. By early 1970 he realised he would never complete the opera. A generous schedule for act two was put to him, "but he looked uninterested," the record producer recalled. "He said the first act of *Walküre* was complete in itself and a wonderfully constructed piece of music. As for the rest of it, he could not muster enough enthusiasm to commit

[110] *Gramophone*, January 1969, p. 985 (Desmond Shawe-Taylor); *Sunday Times*, 24 March 1968, p. 49

[111] November/December 1995, p. 229 (Ralph V. Lucano)

[112] Heyworth, *Conversations*, p. 95

[113] George Harewood, *The tongs and the bones: the memoirs of Lord Harewood* (London: Weidenfeld and Nicholson, 1981), p. 279

[114] Stephen J. Pettit, *Philharmonia Orchestra: A Record of Achievement 1945-1985* (London: Robert Hale, 1986), p. 153

himself to the hard work that would be involved. 'All those Walküre and their Ho-jo-to-hos can be very tiring at times…'. "[115] He only agreed to record Wotan's Farewell and the Magic Fire Music to fill up the final side of the planned two-record set. He conducted a concert performance of what he had just recorded, but it was not successful, as Heyworth summarised: "Several reviewers noted imprecisions in the orchestral playing; some expressed the hope that the recording might prove to be a more vivid experience than the concert. Andrew Porter, writing in the *Financial Times*, felt that the performance 'never quite took wing. Klemperer's reading was more "monumental" than picturesque or particularly dramatic…. Even on the concert platform the first act of *Die Walküre* should be more moving than this.'"[116]

When the recording was re-issued in 2000, the *American Record Guide* again came closest to the mark: "The only way to describe Klemperer's way with the tempestuous first act of *Walküre* is slow and dull. When Sieglinde sings *Du bist der Lenz*, there is no ecstasy, just another aria. When Siegmund declaims *Nothung*, there is no excitement, just notes. When brother and sister flee, there is no surging forward, just a clumpy close."[117] The recording was, the reviewer concluded, a "faded photograph."

In 1970 Klemperer made his very last Wagner recording – he died in Zurich on 6 July 1973 aged 88. It was Wotan's Farewell. The performance is so broad it suggests Wotan is stuck in purgatory, if not hell itself. This was a sad conclusion to Klemperer's association with Wagner, and could not have been one he would have wished. He had described his re-acquaintance with the *Walküre* at this time "as though I were encountering a woman I had loved forty years ago. And the strange thing was that she hadn't changed or grown older. I find the music thrilling. Thrilling! One can say this or that about Wagner, but no one else could have written that music. No one!"[118]

With this comment the old Klemperer returned to his youthful love of Wagner, at least for his music. But how sympathetic *was* he to Wagner's music? With Wagner's ideas, he was not at all sympathetic, as some of his comments above indicate. He did not like the way Wagner used "religious ritual to serve dramatic ends" in *Parsifal*, and "the heroic aspects of the *Ring* made little appeal."[119] Nietzsche, he said in late life, had showed him "that one shouldn't take Wagner's tragic pretensions all that seriously."[120] Wagner was no successor to Beethoven, and so on. As for his music, the best work was the earliest: "Young Wagner was already a great composer," he wrote to a friend, "With advancing years he developed backwards. *Der fliegende Holländer*, *Tannhäuser*, *Lohengrin* are surely more appealing than *Siegfried* or *Götterdämmerung*."[121] There may have been an element of mischief in this, but I doubt it. Klemperer "was never a whole-hearted Wagnerite," Adam Kurakin concluded in his notes to the recordings from the Kroll years, "he remained aloof from Wagner's work and philosophy."[122]

115 Suvi Raj Grubb, *Music makers on record* (London: Hamish Hamilton, 1986), p. 97

116 *Financial Times*, 30 October 1969, in Heyworth, *Klemperer*, vol. 2, p. 344

117 *American Record Guide*, July/August 2001, p. 221 (Lee Milazzo); to hear how thrilling the Act can be, the reviewer refers the reader to Toscanini or Böhm (the former only recorded the final scene)

118 Heyworth, *Conversations*, p. 51

119 Heyworth, *Klemperer*, vol. 1, p. 127

120 Heyworth, *Conversations*, p. 50; in the revised edition (1985) this became quite different: "[Nietzsche] showed that Wagner didn't take everything so tragically" (p. 56)

121 quoted in Heyworth, *Klemperer*, vol. 2, p. 334

122 Adam Kurakin (with assistance from Lotte Klemperer and Peter Heyworth), "Otto Klemperer – Die Kroll-Jahre," notes to Symposium CD 1042 (1988)

In a way it does not matter *what* Klemperer thought of Wagner or his works, *unless* it affected the way he performed his music. In his case, it probably did. Every conductor has struggles with theatre and orchestral managers, with singers and orchestral players, and Klemperer certainly had or created his share, yet in the end, we have to look at what is achieved. His record in this regard is, like the man, erratic. There were some good performances of the three early operas he spoke of. Unfortunately, the surviving recording of *Lohengrin* was not among them. There is the hint of promise in some of his recorded excerpts, but in the end, it was a promise unfulfilled.

23

Fritz Reiner – Keeping it clean

Reiner was an excellent musician. He worked hard, and knew his scores well. He was also a hard task-master, demanding high standards from his artists. He often insisted that the execution of music be "clean." He learned his craft in Budapest and Dresden, and was greatly inspired by Nikisch and Strauss, and later Toscanini. After his move to the United States in 1922, his predominant work was with symphony orchestras. He did, however, conduct some remarkable opera performances, including some landmark Wagner, in the mid 1930s and again between 1949 and 1955. Personally he was a cold and sometimes cruel man to work with. His relations with his family, his associates, and his employers seemed often to lead to dead ends or disasters. We are concerned here only with Reiner the musician, Reiner the Wagner conductor, to the extent that it is possible to separate man from musician.

The Wagnerian highlights

He was born in Budapest on 19 December 1888. His father loved music and could sing most of Schumann's songs from memory. His mother gave him his first piano lessons.[1] It was through piano transcriptions that Wagner made his first impression on the young boy:

I lived in a household which had a musical tradition of Rossini, Meyerbeer, the songs of Schubert and the piano music of Chopin. This family musical diet might have remained unchanged but for the visit of a friend, an amateur musician. It was he who, by playing the *Tannhäuser* Overture, introduced my family and me to the music of Richard Wagner – hardly a familiar name on the piano racks of the musical bourgeoisie of those days! The music made such a deep impression upon me that I promptly borrowed a piano score of *Die Walküre* from a distant relative and, at the age of ten, could play the entire first act from memory.[2]

[1] Gertrude Guthrie-Treadway, "Fritz Reiner, Symphony Conductor, Tells of His Early Experiences in Interview," *Cincinnati Enquirer*, 25 September 1927, sect. 3, p. 5. In a later interview he spoke of "the singing of Schubert's songs by Mama Reiner, a talented amateur": Cesar Saerchinger, "Fritz Reiner – Perpetual Prodigy," *Saturday Review of Literature*, 31 May 1958, p. 42. For biographical material, I have generally relied on Reiner's two biographies: the earlier, Philip Hart, *Fritz Reiner: A Biography* (Evanston: Northwestern University Press, 1994), gives more flavour of the man and the musician; the later, Kenneth Morgan, *Fritz Reiner, Maestro & Martinet* (Urbana and Chicago: University of Illinois Press, 2005), gives more facts about his career.

[2] Reiner in his foreword to Robert C. Bagar, *Wagner on records* (New York: Four Corners, 1942), p. [11]

At this age he was also going to the gallery of the opera as many times as he could afford. He took music lessons at the conservatory in Budapest while still at high school, where he had his first conducting experience, with the school orchestra. He never took his music studies very seriously, on his own account, though even as a boy he was favoured by visiting artists as an accompanist. The person who had the most influence on him as a musician was a slightly older boy, Leó Weiner, who became a coach at the comic opera, tried conducting, and failed. He recommended Reiner to replace him. Reiner was given the opportunity to conduct the chorus from behind the scenes, and immediately showed he could do it:

Leó Weiner was a very excellent musician in every way but one. He could not conduct. To conduct is a special ability. It cannot be learned. One must be born with the ability to conduct. I could tell you in half an hour all there is to tell about conducting, but I could not teach you in a lifetime to conduct unless you were born with the tendency which would make you a conductor.[3]

One night at the opera the conductor did not turn up and Reiner was directed to take his place. It was *Carmen*, it was a success, and his career path was determined.[4]

His first appointment as conductor was at Laibach (Ljubljana, Slovenia), as he recalled in one of his last interviews:

My first opera was *Tannhäuser* which I conducted with an orchestra of 28!... On the strength of *Bohème* I was engaged for the Budapest Volksoper and then on to Dresden. There I did a *Ring* cycle almost without rehearsal. I stayed up nights to study the scores. Then I'd work with singers during the day... It was in Budapest, incidentally, on New Year's Eve, 1914, that I gave the first performance of *Parsifal* allowed outside of Bayreuth. We started at midnight and ended at five in the morning. It was quite an occasion.[5]

In Budapest he also conducted *Lohengrin*, *Tannhäuser*, and *Meistersinger*. Then, after the death of the head of the Dresden Opera, Ernst von Schuch in 1913, and disagreement about a replacement,[6] Reiner was added to the conducting staff, though not as successor to Schuch as has often been claimed.[7] Indeed, with Schuch's death,

[3] Guthrie-Treadway, "Fritz Reiner," p. 5. Reiner taught conducting for several years at the Curtis Institute in Philadelphia. Leó Weiner (1885-1960) became a composer and teacher.

[4] Hart, *Reiner*, p. 6; Morgan, *Reiner*, pp. 29-30

[5] Jay S. Harrison, "Return of Reiner," *Musical America*, October 1963, p. 12. The performance was reported to have started "a few hours *after*" midnight by *Pester Lloyd* (*Morgenblatt*), 2 January 1914, p. 17.

[6] Eberhard Steindorf and Dieter Uhrig (eds.), *Staatskapelle Dresden* (Berlin: Henschelverlag Kunst und Gesellschaft, 1973), p. 28. Karl Muck was one of the possibilities the director refused to have. Another may have been Weingartner. Reiner claimed in an interview that both of these had been passed over in favour of his own appointment: Saerchinger, "Reiner," p. 42. He was confusing two different posts: see following note.

[7] For example, Reiner is listed as General Music Director, Dresden (1914-21) in David Wooldridge, *Conductor's World* (London: Barrie & Rockliff, 1970), p. 74. The matter was set right in 1994 by Reiner's first biographer (Hart, *Reiner*, p. 12), but the error seems to have crept back, e.g., Reiner was offered a contract "in succession to Ernst von Schuch" (Morgan, *Reiner*, p. 32), and Busch "succeeded Fritz Reiner as general music director of the Dresden State Opera": *Musical Quarterly*, vol. 85, no. 3 (Fall 2001), p. 457. Reiner did *not* succeed Schuch, nor did Busch "succeed" Reiner. There was no *Generalmusikdirektor* in Dresden between the death of Schuch in 1913 and the appointment of Busch in 1922. Reiner was appointed a *Kapellmeister* in 1914 (Hermann Kutzschbach was the senior *Königlicher Kapellmeister*); in 1915 Reiner was made a *Königlicher Kapellmeister*, with Kutzschbach still his senior; in 1918/19, following the revolution, all conductors reverted to *Kapellmeister*; in 1922 Busch was appointed *Generalmusikdirektor*: letter to the

the brilliance of the Dresden Opera seemed to disappear.[8] Reiner and his leading colleague Hermann Kutzschbach could not match Schuch.

Reiner had his share of repertory conducting during his seven years in Dresden, and this included a lot of Wagner – "I used to conduct *Parsifal* six days a week," he recalled – but the performances as reported are disappointing, though historians have not ruled out anti-Semitism as a factor.[9] In any case, Reiner did not establish a warm relationship with either the public or the orchestra. He began to show some characteristics that became familiar in later life: a tendency for the orchestra to be too driven and loud, and an objectionable manner in dealing with the orchestra. When he first went to Dresden he said he felt that he did not so much conduct the Wagner operas as the orchestra conducted *him*.[10] Perhaps it was from this orchestra that he imbibed Wagnerian traditions: "Even with my early enthusiasm for Wagner, I could hardly imagine that I would one day conduct in one of the great centers of Wagnerism – Dresden. It was here (1914-1922) that I occupied the post which 70 years before had been filled by the immortal Richard himself, and absorbed the style and tradition of the Wagnerian *Kunstwerk* first hand."[11] On one occasion he tried to correct this Dresden orchestra: "I expressed my disapproval of a passage dramatically, by holding my ears. A flute player in the orchestra stood up and said: 'Herr Hofkapellmeister, if you continue to express yourself in this manner, the orchestra will refuse to play for you.'"[12] On another occasion, during a performance of *Bohème*, the orchestra proceeded on its own way, playing the whole first act in a constant *mezzoforte*. When the infuriated conductor confronted the players during the interval, their spokesman responded: "Well, that is how you conduct it."[13] That may account for the description of a *Walküre* he conducted in 1918 in which the "rich orchestral sound" at times sounded "too sumptuous."[14]

During these years, Reiner conducted more opera, and more Wagner operas, than he would at any later stage of his life. A quarter of his operas were Wagner, and included eight *Ring* cycles.[15] Except for an abridged concert version of the *Ring* in New York in 1937, he would never perform the *Ring* again. He conducted a "highly acclaimed" revival of *Rienzi* in 1919,[16] but this too would remain a feature of his

author from the Sächsische Staatsoper Dresden dated 3 July 2008. The error stems not only from unclear statements emanating from Reiner and his press agents. As early as 1914 *Musical America* headed a report: "DRESDEN'S APPROVAL FOR NEW CONDUCTOR – Fritz Reiner Proving Worthy Successor to Von Schuch at Royal Opera." The correspondent wrote: "His temperament, individuality, true musicianship and serious artistic aims make him a conductor of the first rank, of whom great things may be expected": 12 December 1914, p. 21 (A. I.) after a performance of *Fidelio*.

8 Steindorf and Uhrig, *Staatskapelle Dresden*, p. 28

9 *ibid*, p. 28; Eberhard Steindorf, *Die Sächsische Staatskapelle Dresden* (Berlin: Henschel, 1997), pp. 79, 81; Gottfried Schmiedel, "Fritz Busch and the Dresden Opera," *Opera*, vol. 11, no. 3 (March 1960), p. 75, reprinted in Harold Rosenthal, ed., *The Opera bedside book* (London: Gollancz, 1965)

10 interview in the *New York Evening Post*, 6 August 1924, p. 8: "[Wagner] was my predecessor. I inherited his orchestra, and when we played the works of Richard Wagner I did not at first conduct the orchestra so much as the orchestra conducted me."

11 Bagar, *Wagner on records*, p. [12]

12 Reiner, "The Making of a Conductor," *Musical America*, 25 October 1941, p. 29

13 Hart, *Reiner*, p. 22

14 review quoted by Morgan, *Reiner*, p. 38. Other comments on this *Ring* are quoted below.

15 Morgan, *Reiner*, p. 35

16 Hart, *Reiner*, p. 15

Dresden years. It was a time, above all, of learning. He was impressed with what he saw of Nikisch and Strauss – "Ah! Nikisch was a miracle!"[17] – and adopted some of their conducting techniques.

Reiner became disillusioned with Dresden. He began guest appearances elsewhere – Berlin, Hamburg, Vienna, Rome, Barcelona, including Wagner performances[18] – and

Konzertdirektion Hermann Wolff und Jules Sachs.
Philharmonie.
Sonnabend, 2. Dez., 8 Uhr
Wagner-Abend
mit dem Philharmonischen Orchester.
Heinrich Knote
Kgl. bayr. Kammersänger
unter Mitwirk. von
Barbara Kemp
Königl. Hofopernsängerin
Dirigent: Fritz Reiner (Kgl. Hofoper, Dresden).
Lohengrin: „Vorspiel". Duett. — Siegfried: Idyll. — Vier Lieder.
Meistersinger: „Vorspiel". Preislied. — Walküre: Duett.
Karten 6, 5, 4, 3, 2, 1 Mk. b. Bote u. Bock, Wertheim und an der Abendkasse.

Fig. 23.1. Fritz Reiner's sole Wagner concert with the Berlin Philharmonic, 2 December 1916. *Vossische Zeitung*, 30 November 1916

then took up the offer of principal conductor of the Cincinnati Symphony Orchestra (1922-31).[19] His first concert in Cincinnati on 27 October 1922 included the *Meistersinger* overture and the prelude and Liebestod from *Tristan*. He continued guest appearances abroad, conducting *Walküre* and *Meistersinger* in Budapest and *Walküre*, *Tannhäuser*, *Meistersinger* and *Tristan* in Buenos Aires, all in 1926. By 1930 he had lost the confidence of the Cincinnati Symphony Orchestra board, and resigned. He conducted the *Meistersinger* overture at his final concert. He went to Philadelphia in 1931 to teach at the Curtis Institute and, among other things, to be principal conductor of the Philadelphia Grand Opera Company. It was with that company that he made his North American opera debut on 22 October 1931 in *Tannhäuser*. Later in the season he conducted *Lohengrin*. In 1932 the company collapsed.[20]

[17] as said to Sir Henry Wood in 1936: Wood, *My Life of Music* (London: Victor Gollancz, 1938), p. 160

[18] For example, *Meistersinger* in Rome in 1921-22, and *Lohengrin*, *Meistersinger*, *Walküre*, and *Tristan* in Barcelona in 1922. Reiner conducted an all-Wagner concert with the Berlin Philharmonic on 2 December 1916, his only Wagner with that orchestra: Peter Muck, *Einhundert Jahre Berliner Philharmonisches Orchester* (Tutzing: H. Schneider, 1982), Vol. 3, pp. 166, 175, 191, 192, 196. Heinrich Knote and Barbara Kemp were soloists, as Fig. 23.1 above shows: *Vossische Zeitung*, 30 November 1916, p. [15].

[19] Hart points out that there were openings of General Music Director in several German cities, including Cologne, Darmstadt, Mannheim and Frankfurt, but that Reiner received no invitations from them, not even to appear as a guest: *Reiner*, p. 22.

[20] Hart, *Reiner*, pp. 55-56, 69-71. He gave an all-Wagner concert with the Philadelphia Orchestra in 1931: "there were moments that approached dullness and some of the listeners might have felt that more of the 'dramatic' in Wagner's music might have been offered": *Evening Bulletin-Philadelphia*, 28 November 1931, p. 6; parts of the concert were recorded: see Discography.

He made a guest appearance in Budapest in 1933 with *Tannhäuser*, which made a brilliant impression.[21] On 19 October 1934 he conducted the "record-making, record-breaking" first uncut *Tristan* in the United States. It may have been a sign of devotion; it was certainly bold. It was "a staggering risk to run," wrote the *New York Herald Tribune*, but "the ultimate effect was curiously propulsive, exalting and restorative."[22] It was beyond the capacity of the audience, however, which "thinned out considerably" as the afternoon wore on.[23] A *Meistersinger* on 24 April 1935 was more successful.[24]

In spite of the financial woes of the Philadelphia performances, Reiner's artistic reputation was growing. When Knappertsbusch and Bodanzky were unavailable or too expensive for Covent Garden in 1936,[25] Reiner was engaged to conduct *Tristan* and *Parsifal*. After San Francisco had refused Bodanzky a full Wagnerian orchestra for another season in 1936,[26] Reiner was engaged to conduct *Tristan*, *Walküre*, and *Götterdämmerung*. These led to return visits – to Covent Garden in 1937 for *Holländer* and *Parsifal*, and to San Francisco in 1937 for *Tristan* and *Lohengrin*, and in 1938 for *Meistersinger*. He also conducted a concert version of the *Ring* at the Lewisohn Stadium in New York in July 1937.

After a period with the Pittsburgh Symphony Orchestra (1938-48), which included some Wagner concerts,[27] he became an opera conductor again with the Metropolitan Opera (1949-53). Of the 157 opera performances he conducted with the company, 40 were of Wagner works: *Meistersinger* (19), *Tristan* (10), *Holländer* (8), and *Parsifal* (3). The only Wagnerian highlight in his remaining years were two performances of *Meistersinger* in Vienna in 1955. He spent ten years with the Chicago Symphony Orchestra (1953-62) and then, while preparing *Götterdämmerung* for the Metropolitan Opera, caught pneumonia and died on 15 November 1963, aged 74.

[21] *Budapesti Hirlap*, 16 May 1933, p. 8

[22] 20 October 1934, p. 8 (Lawrence Gilman); the *New York Sun* (W. J. Henderson) wrote: "Fritz Reiner conducted and proved himself to be an operatic conductor of high distinction.... [In summary:] the chief value of the new venture was musical and was due principally to the great [Philadelphia] orchestra, authoritative conducting and the directing of all the elements toward a common purpose": 22 October 1934, p. 19.

[23] *Philadelphia Inquirer*, 20 October 1934, p. 5 (Linton Martin); cf. the *Evening Bulletin-Philadelphia*: "only a comparatively few members of the audience, evidently compelled to leave by the lateness of the hour [the matinee went from 1:30 to 6:25], were absent when the final curtain fell": 20 October 1934, p. 5. Later performances had to be cut: Morgan, *Reiner*, p. 91. Hans Grahl sang Tristan; Marga Dannenberg, Isolde; Emanuel List, King Marke; Julius Huehn, Kurwenal; Lyuba Senderowna, Brangäne.

[24] "Reiner brought out every charm and gallantry that fine musicianship, sensitive artistry and intimate authority could bring to a devoted reading": *Philadelphia Record*, 25 April 1935, p. 13 (Edwin H. Schloss); "there was the instrumental excellence of the Philadelphia Orchestra, under compelling command of Fritz Reiner...": *Philadelphia Inquirer*, 25 April 1935, p. 11 (Linton Martin)

[25] Hart, *Reiner*, pp. 90-91

[26] *New York Times*, 10 May 1936, p. N10

[27] For example, he conducted a concert on 27 and 29 February 1948 with Set Svanholm and Astrid Varnay as soloists: "If there was any question of Dr. Reiner's absolute mastery of the complexities of Wagnerian opera (and I doubt if any such exist anywhere in the world today) they were completely dispelled as the first act of *Die Walküre* and the final act of *Götterdämmerung* were unfolded before a highly enthusiastic audience at the Mosque. For the music of both operas, dramatic, intense, subjective rang out with conviction and authority...": *Pittsburgh Post-Gazette*, 28 February 1948, p. 9 (Donald Steinfirst); "Dr. Reiner finally achieved a performance which can go down in Pittsburgh music annals as the greatest playing which Pittsburgh has yet heard": *Pittsburgh Sun-Telegraph*, 28 February 1948, p. 4 (J. Fred Lissfelt); "Everyone felt the throb of the music under his command. The audience went wild...": *Pittsburgh Press*, 28 February 1948, p. 18 (Ralph Lewando). See also note to 1940 *Walküre* excerpt in Discography.

Reiner on Wagner

It is natural that someone who taught conducting wrote more about the technique of conducting than about music.[28] On the subject of Wagner, he did not have much to say. In the 1927 interview about his early experiences, which included the opera-intense years in Dresden, he did not mention Wagner.[29] He was, at least by experience, a man of the theatre. He knew that Wagner belonged in the opera house, not the concert hall. "Siegfried's Rhine Journey is a duet, not an orchestral piece. Only in the opera house does it sound at its best."[30] But he was also a symphonic conductor, and was naturally attracted to the sheer beauty of Wagner's music:

Strangely enough, the most glorious moments of his operas are those symphonic structures where boundaries of drama, philosophy and poetry are left behind and his music unfolds with hitherto undreamed-of instrumental color and emotional power. It is the orchestra which emphasizes the action and which recalls past happenings and reveals secrets. It is the symphonic element which becomes the spiritual projection of the drama. Verdi, Wagner's great Italian contemporary, said once that singing and melody are the two principal factors in opera. The singers have no franchise on singing and melody in the Wagnerian music drama. The orchestra has the very same priorities.[31]

Reiner was not inclined to be over-shadowed by the singers. On the eve of his outdoor concert performances of the *Ring* in 1937, he more or less threw down the gauntlet in a statement to the press entitled, somewhat enigmatically, "The Wagnerian Problem":

The human voice is not a subordinated factor in the *Gesammtkunstwerk* [*sic*], but there are many instances where Wagner treats the voices as he would an instrument in the orchestra to bring out a certain color. Wagner, as a *par excellence* man of the theatre, knew the importance of dramatic timing, underlining, and the power of his musical speech. Therefore it would be utterly foolish to believe that the musically dramatic highlights of his score should be used only like an "accompaniment of an aria" in the old Italian sense of the word, because the dynamic power of his orchestral writing surpasses in many moments anything that a voice could humanly express. His enormous seven-league-boot climaxes are conceived symphonically and lie in the orchestra. As a matter of fact, a great deal of this music, originally written for voices, has been transplanted to the symphonic repertory and stands on its own feet without voices....

Taking everything into consideration, the singers in a Wagnerian opera have to consider themselves as a co-ordinated part of the whole musical structure. Wagner has eliminated *Cadenzas* since the *Flying Dutchman*. Anybody therefore who expects the Wagnerian orchestra to be relegated to the role of so-called "accompanist" of the singers has misunderstood the meaning and purpose of the Wagnerian opera, and especially so in his later tragic works like *The Ring* and *Tristan*.

The orchestra of these two works is constantly underscoring, emphasizing and accentuating the tragic note of the scene. So the conductor faces a different problem from that offered, for instance by *Figaro*, *Barber of Seville* or *Carmen*.

[28] see Morgan, "Fritz Reiner and the Technique of Conducting," *Journal of the Conductors' Guild*, vol. 14, no. 2 (Summer/Fall 1993), pp. 91-100

[29] Guthrie-Treadway, "Fritz Reiner," *Cincinnati Enquirer*, 25 September 1927, sect. 3, p. 5

[30] Jay S. Harrison, "Return of Reiner," *Musical America*, October 1963, p. 12

[31] Reiner in his foreword to Bagar, *Wagner on records*, pp. [12-13]

Any conductor who attempts to underplay the Wagnerian orchestration and treat it as a pure accompaniment runs into the danger of destroying the drama and creating a luke-warm atmosphere, which ultimately, instead of helping the singers, would only let them down. Wagner, the master architect, doesn't build his monumental structures of tissue paper, but of blocks of granite and steel![32]

In other words: *Watch out for the orchestra!* His view seems somewhat at variance with Wagner's view of his orchestra as one of subordination and support to the sung drama through constant melodic flow.[33] Reiner, the symphonic conductor, was naturally more preoccupied with the orchestra. Whether his approach led at times to an undue prominence of the orchestra at the expense of the voices, we shall see from reviews.

Reiner believed a conductor could not "become accomplished under fifty."[34] He was thirty-eight when he went to Buenos Aires (1926) where some of his performances were very well received. He was almost fifty when he conducted Wagner at Covent Garden (1936-37) and in San Francisco (1936-38). At the Metropolitan Opera (1949-53) and in Vienna (1955) he was definitely in his mature years. We shall look at reviews of his performances of Wagner's late works from these years, including a few recordings, to gauge the measure of his accomplishments as a Wagner conductor.

Tristan und Isolde

Reiner's first *Tristan* at Dresden in 1916 was received enthusiastically by the public.[35] By the time he was at the Teatro Colón in Buenos Aires in 1926, the public was ecstatic. "Overall, it was one of the few times that this formidable love poem has resonated so intensely in this theatre," wrote *La Nación*. It described Reiner's direction as "intense, extraordinarily vigorous and poetic; it had a richness and variety of movement that lifted the work to its highest level of expression."[36] He displayed "a profound knowledge of the work," according to *La Razón*. "With precise movements, incisive accents and careful harmonies he achieved a performance that was full of life, and which alternated between heroic strength and piercing poetry, between exaltation and ecstasy. Maestro Reiner is most decidedly a great conductor...."[37] To *Deutsche La Plata Zeitung* it was a "truly extraordinary" performance, one that made the highly-strung, excitable nature of Tristan tangible, one that would "brightly illuminate [Reiner's] name in the history of German music in Buenos Aires":

The way he made the strings, particularly the cellos, sing, and the way he developed intoxicating tonal effects within an impeccable structural framework, again proved how exceptional he is.

[32] press release from Stadium Concerts, Inc. with the announcement of the program for the "Wagner Festival in Concert Form" (New York, 9-27 July 1937), from Reiner Archive, Music Library, Northwestern University, Evanston, Illinois

[33] see Wagner chapter, pp. 39-42

[34] Reiner, "The Technique of Conducting," *Etude*, October 1951, p. 17; Morgan, "Fritz Reiner and the Technique of Conducting," *Journal of the Conductors' Guild*, vol. 14, no. 2 (Summer/Fall 1993), p. 92

[35] *Musical America*, 28 October 1916, p. 15 (A. I.): report dated Dresden, 24 August

[36] 2 August 1926, p. 7. Rudolf Ritter sang Tristan; Alexander Kipnis, King Marke; Else Gentner-Fischer, Isolde; Friedrich Schorr, Kurwenal; Arnold Gabor, Melot; and Karin Branzell, Brangäne. He conducted two performances.

[37] 2 August 1926, p. 4

He is both a great musical temperament and a splendid educator of orchestras.... He particularly arranged the third act in a magnificent manner, echoing its hot-house, sultry mood, its feverish ecstasy and its elementary passion, with rich tonal colours. In the prelude, we experienced that assuredly escalating line, that natural surging and ebbing of sound waves which were so characteristic of Bülow's approach.[38]

There were calls, the newspaper reported, for Reiner to be appointed to a leading position in Buenos Aires.

Ten years later in London, when he had the most celebrated principal singers, Lauritz Melchior and Kirsten Flagstad, his reception was different. At the first performance at Covent Garden on 18 May 1936, "the evening started badly," the *Musical Times* reported, "with a performance of the Prelude which sounded like a parody, so much was its basic tempo ignored."[39] Ernest Newman in the *Sunday Times* also was not impressed: "I could not agree with Mr. Reiner in his general tempo for the prelude or in his accelerandi and ritardandi in it; but eccentricities of this kind became fewer as the performance proceeded, and the last act was the most convincing of the three."[40] The *Observer* too considered that in this last act the singers and conductor "neglected nothing that could help make an artistic success, dramatically and musically."[41] In act two Tristan's *Wohin nun Tristan scheidet* was "dragged almost out of recognition," according to the *Daily Telegraph*. "The conductor – an excellent conductor, whose intimate feeling for the music was beyond question – allowed the music to go to sleep here. He also might with advantage have kept a firmer hand on King Mark's address."[42] The *Musical Times* was more colourful on act two: "The many passages in the second Act where Isolde and Tristan are given similar music to sing simultaneously or consecutively reminded me of those cruel occasions at school when stewed fruit or treacle could only be acquired as an adjunct to suet."[43] The *Morning Post* noted there were some aspects of the singing that were unsatisfactory. "Nor was Fritz Reiner's direction of the orchestra remarkable; the playing was neither as incandescent nor as precise as it ought to have been, some of the unison passages in particular being the reverse of unanimous. And there was a tendency to drag at times."[44] *The Times*, on the other hand, was impressed, particularly with act two: Reiner "directed matters [so] that every detail of the singing came over the orchestra. The movement had urgency without hurry. The melody was never blurred by the physical excitement, so that the whole duet, from its softest moments to its fortissimo, was all of a piece, that is, a pure musical delight."[45]

The fourth performance, on 11 June 1936, was recorded in its entirety by the Gramophone Company. It does not sound as if he had improved from the first night. One listener to several recordings of *Tristan* in the 1930s found that "after a rather listless beginning, the Reiner performance picked up at Kurwenal's entrance, but never really pulled together; a competent piece of work, it never quite takes fire."[46] In

38 *Deutsche La Plata Zeitung*, 3 August 1926, p. 7 (Fr.)

39 Robert Lorenz, "Wagner at Covent Garden," *Musical Times*, June 1936, p. 552

40 24 May 1936, p. 7

41 24 May 1936, p. 18 (a review of acts one and three only)

42 19 May 1936, p. 12 (Richard Capell)

43 June 1936, p. 552

44 19 May 1936, p. 14

45 19 May 1936, p. 14

46 *Opera Quarterly*, vol. 9 no. 3 (September 1993), p. 165, David Hamilton, referring to his "*Tristan* in the Thirties: Part II," *Musical Newsletter*, vol. 7 no. 2 (Spring 1977), p. 18: "Reiner starts rather listlessly... much of the performance is rather staid, as if things hadn't really pulled together yet."

like spirit, the reviewer for *Fanfare* wrote: "his conducting is perfectly satisfactory, but I cannot join those who find him a great Wagner conductor. Beecham's conducting of the work, on a 1937 Covent Garden performance with a similar cast, has more warmth and life to it. And also greater precision: twice, near the beginning of act II, Reiner allows the complicated off-beat string rhythms to slip out of his control, and has to slow the tempo to bring them back."[47]

Later in 1936, Reiner took *Tristan* to San Francisco with the same principals. The performances satisfied some that he was "one of the great Wagner directors."[48] Yet there were echoes of the discontent in London. "Now and then the brass threatened to drown the voices in the climactic moments, but only for a moment," wrote the *San Francisco News*; "...this was a Wagnerian performance in which the singers sang and never resorted to shouting! The ensemble was a tonal orgy of glorious sound."[49] On the issue of volume, the *San Francisco Call-Bulletin* made a perceptive comparison: "the orchestra... sustained the mood without submerging the voices... [Reiner] did not minimize the importance of the orchestra so much as did Bodanzky last year in the Wagnerian operas, nor did he magnify it as does Alfred Hertz. The happy mean was quite acceptable."[50] The *San Francisco Examiner* acknowledged Reiner was "a first rate master of Wagner" and observed:

> To a degree he is not a rhapsodist in the ardent nineteenth century mode. He is a modern. He is brilliant and objective. Some of his tempos called attention to themselves by their unexpectedness. Where passages of symphonic melody were heart-felt, they sometimes cried out for additional affection in mood and phrasing. But as a unit Reiner's performance was glorious. It realized Wagner's power by its lightning alertness, clarity and strength.[51]

He returned to San Francisco in 1937, again with Melchior and Flagstad, and to warm praise. He also took the company to Los Angeles for one performance. The second act survives on record, but is such poor sound it tells us little of what it must have been like.[52] A concert version in New York in 1937, heavily cut but hugely popular, also tells us little of his style. It was the concluding work of a Wagner Festival at Lewisohn Stadium before an outdoor audience of 12,000.[53]

47 vol. 24 no. 4 (March/April 2001), p. 269 (William Youngren), reviewing the Naxos re-issue, which was also described in a much briefer review in the *Guardian*: "this is simply the greatest performance of Wagner's masterpiece to survive in sound": 15 December 2000, G2, p. 29 (Tim Ashley). Not surprisingly, this comment appears on Naxos's web site. In a review of excerpts from Reiner's *Holländer* at Covent Garden in 1937, Youngren wrote: "The great flaw lies with the orchestra and chorus. The playing and singing are often unpardonably sloppy, worthier of a student production than one from Covent Garden's 'Golden Age.'" He discussed recordings with the same orchestra under Beecham (*Tristan*, 1937) and Furtwängler (*Walküre*, 1937, and *Götterdämmerung*, 1938); in these the orchestra was "superb. So one must conclude that Reiner just didn't have it in him to get the best out of his forces": *Fanfare*, vol. 14 no. 3 (January/February 1991), p. 348. *The Times* made no comment on the conducting at the 7 June 1937 performance, some of which is on the recording discussed.

48 *San Francisco Chronicle*, 3 November 1936, p. 28 (Alfred Frankenstein)

49 3 November 1936, p. 11 (Marjory M. Fisher)

50 3 November 1936, p. 8 (Mary Hicks Davidson)

51 3 November 1936, p. 12 (Alexander Fried)

52 "At best the sound is atrocious, fading to indistinguishable at times as the singers moved about the stage": Philip Hart, "Underground Reiner," *ARSC Journal*, vol. 20 no. 2 (Fall 1989), p. 211; "the sound is terrible... As best as can be surmised, Reiner's work is theatrically vivid, but short on lyricism": *American Record Guide*, vol. 53 no. 1 (January/February 1990), pp. 104–105 (George W. Loomis)

53 The *New York Times* gives a sense of the cuts: in act two, "after a portion of the introduction, Isolde

Reiner conducted the work ten times with the Metropolitan Opera company in the 1950/51 season. Before the opening performance, he was given three full rehearsals on stage with orchestra – very unusual in those days for *Tristan* – and there had been many sessions with piano.[54] Yet the performance itself was "an uninspired production," according to the *World Telegram and Sun*:

> [It] had its moments of beauty, but as a whole it was considerably below Mr. Reiner's par – and almost everybody else's. For some reason the orchestra failed to light up, the way it usually does for Mr. Reiner. It seemed muffed in vapors at times. And too often it moved at a pace better suited to the solemnities of an oratorio than the rising fevers of Wagner's romantic music drama.[55]

It must have picked up, however. The *Post* described how Reiner "conducted the music with a passionate fervor and a sense of urgency which were rewarding."[56] But it appeared from the way he conducted it, that Reiner was not temperamentally suited to *Tristan*. The *Herald Tribune* wrote:

> Much of the success of any performance of this opera depends on the presence in the conductor's chair of a musician of incandescent temperament and poetic sensibilities; one who can convey convincingly the seething passion and tragic atmosphere of Wagner's matchless creation. Mr. Reiner's discourse of the orchestral score was not without its discerning moments; but for the most part it failed to unfold its contents compellingly. His pacing, especially of the first act, was unconscionably slow, so that its impassioned pages took on the static quality of an oratorio, with the result that the singers were often called upon to exercise almost superhuman efforts to encompass some of its more exacting measures. The orchestra frequently sounded coarse, as in the scene of Tristan's entrance in the second act and the essential sensuousness of sound was rarely forthcoming.[57]

After two performances in Boston and Cleveland, he never conducted the opera again.

Die Meistersinger von Nürnberg

A report of a "spirited performance" of the *Meistersinger* in 1916 indicated Reiner may have had a special affinity with the work. "As usual, Reiner excelled in splendid detail work and in a lucid, transparent adjustment of the accompanying orchestral parts to the soloists," wrote the correspondent for *Musical America*.[58] But in Buenos Aires in 1926, unlike his *Tristan*, he was unable to carry the day with *Meistersinger*, although he had the same players. "Disgracefully for the Colón," wrote *La Razón*, "the orchestra, a key element of the performance, was not up to the job. Even Maestro Reiner's authority was not enough to disguise the inferior nature of some of his subordinates, who only managed to get it right some of the time."[59] *Deutsche La Plata Zeitung*

rather hurriedly extinguished the torch, and after very little scarf-waving came Tristan and the love duet and Brangäne's warning. Tristan's tormenting visions were mercifully brief [etc.] … in face of the huge enjoyment of last night's listeners, discussion of the appositeness of the cuts dwindles to mere academic bickering": 28 July 1937, p. 15 (G. G.)

54 *New York Times*, 2 December 1950, p. 7 (Howard Taubman)

55 2 December 1950, p. 7 (Louis Biancolli)

56 3 December 1950, p. 17 (Harriett Johnson)

57 2 December 1950, p. 7 (Jerome D. Bohm)

58 28 October 1916, p. 15 (A. I.): review of the 13 August performance

59 7 August 1926, p. 7; "Reiner could not produce a worthy performance of this work last night": *La*

Fig. 23.2. Reiner from his Dresden years, 1914-1922

Fig. 23.3. Reiner in the pit at Dresden

Fig 23.4. Reiner rehearsing the Chicago Symphony Orchestra, October 1953

Fig. 23.5. Reiner rehearsing the Pittsburgh Symphony Orchestra, ca. 1946

Fig. 23.6. Reiner conducting the Metropolitan Opera Orchestra, 1950s

Fig. 23.7. Reiner conducting the Chicago Symphony Orchestra in Beethoven's *Seventh Symphony*, 8 April 1962 – from a film

was more forgiving: it could detect elements of Reiner's interpretation despite the orchestra's limitations. "His orchestra gradually found its way to Wagner.... He gives the prelude with meticulous clarity.... His tempi serve to create a clear structure.[60] He knows how to make the orchestral tone a warm and lively one, while at the same time retaining an exemplary, transparent outline.... Here we have a stylistically well-balanced *Meistersinger* interpretation."[61]

Twelve years later, with a *Meistersinger* at the Memorial Opera House in San Francisco, not all was well. "Chief point of carping criticism was the frequency with which the orchestra covered the singers," wrote the *San Francisco Chronicle* after the 14 October 1938 performance. Reiner had "seldom conducted more superbly, with greater spirit and understanding," but the "bad balance" which afflicted almost every opera conductor at the venue was not overcome.[62] Furthermore, "the orchestral work was of uneven merit," according to the *San Francisco News*. "Individual instrumentalists as well as singers occasionally made detours around the pitch and other things, but the masterly direction of Fritz Reiner always reunited the various factors and carried the performance to a more successful conclusion than seemed possible under the existing handicaps."[63] It was an augmented orchestra, and Reiner conducted it with "poetic feeling," according to the *San Francisco Call-Bulletin*.[64] Indeed, the "success of his conducting... owed much to his admirable body of musicians," wrote the *San Francisco Examiner*. "He led the orchestra with a fine discretion as well as with sweeping and rhythmic energy. Once or twice – as in the group finale of the first act – he held his performance to too deliberate a pace. In the main, he joined orchestra and voices into a pulsing rhapsodic ensemble."[65]

At the Metropolitan Opera in New York, *Meistersinger* was Reiner's most frequently-performed Wagner opera. Yet the opening night on 12 January 1950 failed to move Virgil Thomson, though he confessed he was "largely insensitive to the beauties of the work." He wrote that there was "little to say" about the performance except that "cast and performance were excellent. Fritz Reiner, conducting the work for the first time here, kept the orchestra out of the singers' way, made everything sound harmonious.... All the same, no magic casement opened...."[66] A complaint of another reviewer, who

Prensa, 7 August 1926, p. 15; "a lack of rehearsal and deficiencies in the orchestra did not allow for... a definitive judgement of the work as a whole, (Beckmesser's lute was replaced with a harp and the brass instruments were not always precise)": *La Nación*, 7 August 1926, p.15.

60 On this point, the *Argentinisches Tageblatt* described Reiner's tempi as "very broad": 8 August 1926, p. 9 (ke.). *Deutsche La Plata Zeitung* also described them as "broad," yet in 1931 it wrote: "in 1926, Fritz Reiner drove the *Meistersinger* to tempi which broke all sense of proportion and moderation": 30 September 1931, p. 8 (Fr.) (a review of Otto Klemperer's *Götterdämmerung*). Perhaps this was written of another of Reiner's 1926 performances.

61 *Deutsche La Plata Zeitung*, 7 August 1926, p. 7 (Fr.).

62 15 October 1938, p. 7 (Alfred Frankenstein)

63 15 October 1938, p. 3 The principal singers were: Friedrich Schorr, Sachs; Charles Kullman, Walther; Karl Laufkoetter, David; Irene Jessner, Eva; Kerstin Thorborg, Magdalena; and Arnold Gabor, Beckmesser.

64 15 October 1938, p. 4 (Marie Hicks Davidson)

65 15 October 1938, p. 7 (Alexander Fried). In his review of the season, Fried wrote that Reiner had been "at his best in *Elektra*," but generally, along with the other conductors, Merola and Papi, he "suffered from intermittent lapses into painful slowness. (In the pit, opera demands *élan*!)": undated newspaper clipping in the *San Francisco Opera Season 1938 Scrapbook*, San Francisco Public Library.

66 *New York Herald Tribune*, 13 January 1950, p. 14. The principal singers were: Ferdinand Frantz, Sachs; Set Svanholm, Walther; Peter Klein, David; Astrid Varnay, Eva; Margaret Harshaw, Magdalena; and Gerhard Fechner, Beckmesser.

had never seen the work before, was that "the volume of the orchestra was generally a trifle too loud and veiled parts of the singing."[67] Reiner's interpretation was "worthy of the finest traditions of the contemporary lyric theatre," according to the *Journal-American*.[68] The *New York Times*, which remarked upon the "long and painstaking preparation" the work had received, elaborated:

It had unity and cohesiveness. Whatever one may think of Mr. Reiner's conception as a whole, there was no gainsaying that it was his musical will that dominated. It was good to have a strong integrating hand in charge.

Mr. Reiner's conception is sound enough. His approach seems to be objective. He does not whip up the orchestra; he is content to let the poetic atmosphere emerge slowly and naturally. He does not overwhelm the singers. And he can – and does – capture the spirit of the grand, concerted pages. One feels that a little more flexibility and excitement would come in time as the production grows in repeated performances.[69]

Reports of later performances varied, as illustrated by the comment of *Musical America* in 1953: "Reiner obtained superb sonorities from the orchestra, although there was not much warmth or tenderness in his interpretation of the score."[70]

The re-opening of the Vienna State Opera in 1955 was to be a great occasion. Reiner was invited to conduct two performances of *Meistersinger* during the celebrations. The musical director in Vienna, Karl Böhm, had decreed that every conductor was to have as much time for rehearsal as he wished. Reiner was to have six orchestral rehearsals in June as a warm-up for intense rehearsals in November.[71] Yet the production "proved disappointing" according to the *New York Times*, "mainly because of Fritz Reiner's conducting."[72] He conducted "very skilfully and in a very superior and experienced manner," *Die Presse* acknowledged, "yet with little heart or sense of tonal colour. The orchestra played harshly, awkwardly, without any lustre. Over wide stretches, there was but a formal, standard tone. Yet in spite of all the instrumental subtleties of the score, the *Meistersinger* is not chamber music."[73] *Wiener Montag* wrote that it was only "the tried and tested ensemble" of singers that "safeguarded a careful performance."[74] According to *Das Kleine Volksblatt*, the singers were constrained by Reiner, for "his musical direction stopped them from fully developing their talents."[75] The *Neues Österreich* thought otherwise. It noted that Reiner's "tempos approached the early classical Bayreuth tempos… [yet] one could have wished for some passages to be more lively, buoyant, inspired. However, wherever the emphasis was on combining singers and orchestra in a tight union, making the singing voices victoriously shine above the polyphony of the iron-clad orchestra... Reiner was always the 'witness well chosen'."[76] The *Neuer Kurier* described Reiner's conducting and its impression:

[67] *Daily News*, 13 January 1950, p. 65 (Douglas Watt)

[68] 13 January 1950, p. 17 (Miles Kastendieck)

[69] 13 January 1950, p. 17 (Howard Taubman)

[70] 15 January 1953, p. 24 (R. S.)

[71] *New York Times*, 6 February 1955, p. X9

[72] 27 November 1955, p. 151 (Henry de La Grange). The performances were on 14 and 20 November 1955.

[73] 16 November 1955, p. 4 (Heinrich Kralik)

[74] 21 November 1955, p. 7 (Franz Hrastnik)

[75] 16 November 1955, p. 9 ("-ai-") "What the reasons were in favour of appointing this particular conductor to direct the *Meistersinger* performances within the framework of the opera festival, we don't know – his performance, however, hardly justified the appointment."

[76] *Neues Österreich*, 16 November 1955, p. 5 ("Y.")

He keeps a precise beat, giving exact cues, has properly studied the work, and provides it with several accents with his dynamic nuances and rhythmic profiling. Yet he doesn't get the best out of the orchestra and the excellently rehearsed choir. And that poetry, that magical mood developed by the Philharmonic members – it is not given because of, but in spite of his musical direction.... Although Reiner came out of his shell a bit more for the last scene, the overall impression remains pale. Rudolf Moralt... conducts a different, better *Meistersinger* performance.[77]

It was not only the critics who were displeased. "He did not go down at all well with the audience," wrote Vienna Opera historian, Marcel Prawy, "mainly because he kept his eyes glued to the score all the time."[78] It fell to an Englishman, Peter Heyworth, to give an extended description of the performance, in *Opera*:

This performance was without doubt the worst of the five productions I saw during my stay in Vienna... [the failure] must be laid fairly and squarely at the door of the conductor, Fritz Reiner.

It was not merely a performance clothed in what for this orchestra is shoddy sound. It was a fundamentally misconceived affair, lacking any of the humanity, warmth and tenderness that should irradiate the music. Not only was its mood destroyed, but its structure was at moments grotesquely out of shape. Notions about the basic tempo of the Prelude notoriously differ, but at all events it must remain a prelude and cannot be transformed, as Reiner tried to do, into a ponderous apotheosis. The wonderful modulation that is the musical accompaniment to Eva's cry of ecstasy as Walther enters in the third act was passed over without the slightest emphasis. Nor was this emotional deadness compensated by a dry, light-handed precision. Beckmesser's scene with Sachs in the third act, for instance, was leaden and humourless, notably because of Reiner's obsessive emphasis on the bass parts, so that the score became, as it were, bottom-heavy. His main preoccupation appeared to lie in revealing phrases whose importance is clearly subsidiary to the main musical effect. This tiresome habit of serving some passage on a platter with the air of "you haven't heard of *that* before" appeared at its most idiotic in the quintet, where, by underlining woodwind phrases that Wagner clearly marked *p dolcissimo*, he succeeded in disrupting Eva's vocal line. Nor was he more successful in communicating the symphonic urge of passages like the roll-call in the first act or the great riot in the second (here he entirely miscalculated his dynamics and failed to produce a real climax). Finally his reading lacked any sort of lucidity and was rhythmically cumbersome beyond belief.[79]

Reiner himself regarded his performances of *Meistersinger* in Vienna as "highlights of his long career."[80]

One can now hear the performance on disc, in far better sound than any of Reiner's live recordings from England or America. Though it is a crystal-clear recording in some respects, the chorus sometimes sounds distant, and the orchestra

77 15 November 1955, p. 4

78 Marcel Prawy, *The Vienna Opera* (Vienna-Munich-Zurich: Verlag Fritz Molden, 1969), p. 180, an observation confirmed by the *Neuer Kurier*, 15 November 1955, p. 4. As indicated above, there were questions as to why Reiner was conducting in Vienna at all. As Böhm had been engaged to conduct Reiner's Chicago Symphony Orchestra in February 1956, there was a deal of talk about an "exchange arrangement." Prawy noted: "surely there was no need for either Böhm or Reiner to stoop to such a practice in this context": p. 180.

79 vol. 7 no. 1 (January 1956), p. 28

80 Morgan, *Reiner*, p. 162; Morgan also refers to *Violins and Violinists* [Chicago], vol. 17 no. 1 (January-February 1956) which reported (incorrectly): "Critics of the Vienna papers were lavish in their praise of both the operatic performances and the concert": p. 17; cf. Hart, *Reiner*: "Reiner's *Meistersinger* received mixed reviews, more cordial from the Viennese press than from some foreign visitors": p. 176.

recessed or diffuse.[81] On the other hand, when solo instruments play they can be heard clearly, and they play beautifully as one would expect from the Vienna Philharmonic. Of the performance itself, enough may already have been said. The recording merely confirms a certain soullessness and smoothness extending over the whole, flattening disparate moods, making moments of joy and anxiety indistinguishable from one another. The orchestra is restrained to the point of dullness. The introduction to act three is played very slowly, as was Reiner's way at the Metropolitan Opera. It is in fact so drawn out, so stretched, that it loses its shape. If the intention was to portray the reflections of Hans Sachs, there is not a pang of anxiety in those reflections. The celebrations on the field swing between the laboured and the lukewarm. There is prolonged applause from the crowd or the audience, or both, when the mastersingers make their triumphant entry. The performance is of a kind that appeals to some,[82] but as for warmth and spirit, the "magic casement" remains shut.

Der Ring des Nibelungen

Apart from his youthful years in Dresden, where it is difficult to get the full measure of his interpretations,[83] Reiner never conducted a complete *Ring* cycle in the theatre. He conducted the *Walküre* in Buenos Aires in 1926 and in San Francisco in 1936, *Götterdämmerung* also in San Francisco in 1936, and a severely abridged *Ring* at an outdoor event in New York in 1937. These give us some idea of his style.

At the Teatro Colón in 1926, he had for his *Walküre* an "orchestra and instrumentalists of objectionable quality" in the words of *La Razón*. Nevertheless, he "capably dominated his subordinates while remaining vivacious and serene, passionate and contained."[84] His version was "not as good as last year," wrote *La Prensa*, "but was extremely musical and faithful, although not to everyone's taste because of tempo and the orchestra. The style, strength of accent and degree of expression and line were all to be admired."[85] The tempi were "brisk," according to the *Argentinisches Tageblatt*, though not without expressive effect.[86] *Deutsche La Plata Zeitung* considered that Reiner's interpretation more rooted in the romantic than the heroic. "He creates impulsively, his sense for sound is highly acute, he loves the natural vocal line in the orchestra, and he has the rare gift of being straightforward. His tempos are finely structured, his dramatic escalations breathe.... He lit up the last act beautifully, and knew how to endow it with great passion and warmth."[87] His triumph was "undeniable."[88]

[81] In his review of its first appearance on disc, Philip Hart considered "the superb Vienna Philharmonic [was] under-recorded by ORTF": *ARSC Journal*, vol. 28 no. 2 (Fall 1997), p. 252

[82] "[With two others], this set goes to the top of the list": *International Record Review*, February 2006, p.84 (Robert Levine); "Reiner's conducting... will not be to all tastes, prosaic in the overture, then given to marked *rallentandi* and some unusually slow speeds in Act 3... personally I like the flexibility and warmth of Reiner's conducting": *Gramophone*, May 2006, p. 102 (John Steane).

[83] For example, press comment of a *Ring* cycle he gave in 1918 reveals little. Reiner directed the *Rheingold* "in a spirited manner" according to the *Dresdner Volkszeitung*: 25 January 1918, p. 8; the *Walküre* was "a movingly magnificent evening": *ibid*, 28 January 1918, p. 7; in *Siegfried* "the orchestra sounded absolutely beautiful, particularly the horn:" *Dresdner Neueste Nachrichten* 30 January 1918, p.2; and the cycle "closed in a magnificent and solemn manner": *Dresdner Anzeiger* 3 February 1918, p.5, with "a lovely performance of *Götterdämmerung*. Reiner understood how to keep the orchestra's levels of sound within the appropriate limits": *ibid*, 3 February 1918, p.10. See also Morgan, *Reiner*, p. 38.

[84] 9 July 1926, p. 11

[85] 9 July 1926, p. 17

[86] 9 July 1926, p. 4

[87] 9 July 1926, p. 6 (Fr.)

[88] *La Razón*, 9 July 1926, p. 11

The San Francisco *Walküre* of 1936 was an extraordinary event. "It is trite to say," wrote the *San Francisco Chronicle*, "that no greater Wagnerian casts can be assembled, but it happens to be true." There was Lauritz Melchior, who understood "to the last degree the tragic implications of the character" of Siegmund. There was Lotte Lehmann as Sieglinde. "The purity, flexibility and poetic expressiveness of [her] soprano need no description. There is no Sieglinde like her, for no artist is more sensitive to the utmost implication of word and tone." There was Kirsten Flagstad as Brünnhilde. "She is like the Victory of Samothrace alive in action and song. Her voice has never been more brilliant than it was last night, never more surpassingly expressive of compassion and inspiration and deep, unnameable emotions that have their source in the heart of the music." And there was Fritz Reiner. He conducted with his "usual magic fire, although the orchestral response... was not altogether perfect."[89] The *San Francisco News* wrote of the orchestra:

> Tonal whisperings and thunderings were facilely accomplished in the orchestra pit. There were times, early in the evening, when the orchestral tone seemed unduly subdued. (But it was nice to know that it could be!) There were also times when it volleyed and thundered a bit too much to suit those sitting in the immediate vicinity of the drums and the brasses but not a bit too much for the ultimate dramatic effect. But there was one inexplicable episode wherein an organ joined in the thunderings and sounded, tonally, shockingly out of place. Whatever effect may have been intended through its use was obviously not achieved.[90]

To the *San Francisco Call-Bulletin*, "Reiner's dynamics were conducive to much of the unity and impressiveness. He moved it in majestic rhythm and permitted the orchestra to swell in full volume only when such fortissimo did not interfere with the voices."[91] Only a little lack of warmth was noted by the *San Francisco Examiner*. "Reiner conducted with a magnificent energy and decision. To his performances of Wagner's lyric passages, he could still add some further intimate warmth of feeling."[92]

Fortunately, the second act from this performance was broadcast and, such as it was, recorded. It is heavily cut, and missing the last forty-three bars, but all of Lotte Lehmann's lines are there. She sings Sieglinde with utter abandon. Her terror and delusion are *wholly* expressed. "She was not only Sieglinde, she was the *complete* Sieglinde," a French critic observed in 1933.[93] It is a performance of hair-raising and heart-breaking effect. Her appearance "fulfilled great expectations," wrote the *San Francisco Examiner*. "By temperament she is extraordinarily suited to Wagner's emotionalism. The poetry and passion of nineteenth century romanticism are alive in all her spirit.... Her voice in its rich upper range is worthy to vie with Mme. Flagstad's. If in her lower tones she abandons herself to guttural attacks, her purpose is only to give her character its due intense impulsiveness."[94] For Reiner too, this historic recording occupies a special position in his collaboration with the San Francisco Opera.[95]

[89] 14 November 1936, p. 7 (Alfred Frankenstein)

[90] 14 November 1936, p. 9 (Marjory M. Fisher)

[91] 14 November 1936, p. 4 (Marie Hicks Davidson)

[92] 14 November 1936, p. 14 (Alexander Fried)

[93] *Le Monde Musical*, 30 June 1933, p. 192 (Lazare-Lévy), on a performance at the Paris Opera under Furtwängler

[94] 14 November 1936, p. 14 (Alexander Fried)

[95] "Possibly San Francisco had never experienced conducting of quite this class": Arthur Bloomfield, *50 years of the San Francisco opera* (San Francisco: San Francisco Book Co., 1972), p. 67. The recording is described simply as "exciting" in Beaumont Glass, *Lotte Lehmann: A Life in Opera and Song* (Santa Barbara: Capra Press, 1988), p. 160.

Götterdämmerung preceded *Walküre* in San Francisco in 1936. Reiner's conducting of the first act was, according to the *San Francisco Chronicle*, "spirited, sonorous and full bodied to the verge of the boisterous. At times the balance between voices and orchestra was not as perfect as it should be."[96] His conducting "left nothing to be desired," wrote the *San Francisco Call-Bulletin*. "The Siegfried *Funeral March* was dramatically resonant, reaching a climax of tremendous concord."[97] For once, there was praise for warmth. His conducting was "brilliantly clear-patterned and decisive," remarked the *San Francisco Examiner*. "Often he was as subtle as he was at other times sweeping. And, happily, he discovered a warmer lyrical spirit for *Götterdämmerung* than he had recently for *Tristan*."[98] The orchestra "proved truly a co-star" to the *San Francisco News*. "Its weak moments were not conspicuous, and were quickly remedied by Mr. Reiner's extraordinarily explicit conductorial technique. But conspicuous indeed was the overwhelming magnificence of orchestral climaxes, and the thrilling performance of Siegfried's Funeral March and the orchestral score immediately preceding it."[99] There was a note of dissonance from the *News Letter and Wasp*. Although Reiner had lent proper support to the singers, "one was conscious of a heavier handling of volume than received from Bodansky [*sic*] last year. Too, the general tempo of the opera was considerably slowed down under Reiner's ministry, the result on the stage action being slightly harsh. For slow motion acting is all too noticeable in Wagner, and the retardation of tempo makes acting extremely difficult."[100]

Another festive occasion was the *Ring* cycle before an outdoor audience in New York in 1937. It was a concert version, and was heavily abridged. "The excisions, presumably Mr. Reiner's," the *New York Times* reported after *Rheingold*, "were judiciously contrived, creating no serious gaps in dramatic or musical continuity." The collaboration between Reiner and the orchestra on this introductory night was "technically – but for a few slips of the brass – of high proficiency, musically of revealing art."[101] *Walküre* was a little different. It was a "strangely chosen and incoherently assembled series of excerpts" and Reiner, the orchestra and the soloists "failed to create anything vital or impressive in mood or atmosphere throughout this garbled version of the masterpiece." Fragments from the first and third acts had been "hitched together without rhyme or reason." To anyone acquainted with the work, "it was more irritating than pleasurable."[102] Of *Siegfried*, there were but eighty minutes of music, but the *New York Times* considered it better to "set aside purist scruples and

[96] 8 November 1936, p. 9 (Alfred Frankenstein). The singers of the principal roles were: Siegfried, Lauritz Melchior; Brünnhilde, Kirsten Flagstad; Hagen, Emanuel List; Gunther, Friedrich Schorr; Waltraute, Kathryn Meisle; Gutrune, Dorothee Manski.

[97] 9 November 1936, p. 7 (Marie Hicks Davidson)

[98] 8 November 1936, p. 15 (Alexander Fried)

[99] 9 November 1936, p. 11 (Marjory M. Fisher). The newspaper's declaration that: "Fritz Reiner is unquestionably the finest operatic conductor who has ever directed the San Francisco Opera Company," was perhaps a barb aimed at Bodanzky, who had refused to return after the 1935 season because of the size of the orchestra. No other newspaper seems to have shared this view. In their reviews of the 1936 season, the *San Francisco Examiner* (Alexander Fried) wrote: "Fritz Reiner's Wagner conducting had first-rate clarity, individuality and power. Only in warmth of spirit is he not the equal of a Bodanzky or a Bruno Walter": 29 November 1936, Sect. E, p. 7; the *San Francisco Chronicle* had no substantive comment on Reiner: *San Francisco Opera Season 1936 Scrapbook*, San Francisco Public Library.

[100] vol. 80 no. 46 (14 November 1936), p. 31 (Harry Haswell)

[101] 13 July 1937, p. 22 (G. G.)

[102] *New York Times*, 15 July 1937, p. 17 (Noel Straus)

doubts concerning the advisability of certain cuts." Reiner and the orchestra made up for deficiencies. "There was unwonted verve and responsiveness from the ensemble, and frequently – as in the music of Siegfried's ascension, or Brünnhilde's awakening – a truly Wagnerian richness of tonal quality."[103] *Götterdämmerung* was the most popular evening – an estimated 7,000 persons were present – and it too was heavily truncated. The prologue and act one, comprising the first half of the evening, were compressed into forty-seven minutes. At the end of the prologue "Mr. Reiner passed without pause, by way of a convenient F sharp-major triad, to the third scene of the first act, presenting the whole of the Waltraute episode." Nevertheless, this first half of the evening, according to the *New York Times*, was "the finest work of the evening."[104] It is also preserved on record, though in very poor sound.[105] Despite what he had to say about Siegfried's Rhine Journey belonging in the opera house, he gave it a very atmospheric reading at this outdoor concert. The passage is, like the Rhine itself, susceptible to variable weather, and on this occasion there was a sharp, biting wind, and the spray from the Rhine blows in one's face. By contrast, the version he recorded with the Chicago Symphony Orchestra in 1959, portrays quite a dull day on the Rhine, rising only to relatively gentle breezes. What is confronting about the Stadium concert is the severity of the cuts. After the music of Siegfried passing through the fire to reach Brünnhilde on the rock, she cries out *Verrat! Wer drang zu mir?* ("Betrayed! Who comes to me?"). The answer is no one. There is no Siegfried. Only a hastily arranged orchestral ending. A real betrayal.

Parsifal

Apart from his youthful experiences in Budapest and Dresden, Reiner's *Parsifal* of his mature years were those at Covent Garden in 1936 and 1937, and at the Metropolitan Opera in 1949. The responses to the first of his two performances in London vary, but it seems a common thread of most reviews that he yielded to the singers, and that the orchestra was, if anything, understated. *The Times* had a "general impression for good, if not greatly inspired workmanship in the presentation of the music."[106] Likewise the *Morning Post* noted that "Reiner may not be remarkable for inspiration, but he is an uncommonly good, workmanlike conductor" who could give "a very steady and well-balanced performance from the orchestra."[107] It was an "equable" performance, according to the *Daily Telegraph*, equable "in its temper, in its respectfulness, and its ever-present suggestion of the swan-song. Mr. Reiner nurses his singers, and it was to them one listened principally. The rhythm of a good many orchestral phrases was made to yield to them."[108] Neville Cardus wrote:

> Like most continental conductors, he approached the score through the words, and saw to it that the singers were not distracted from a faithful treatment of the verbal accents by a purely

[103] *New York Times*, 21 July 1937, p. 18 (G. G.)
[104] 23 July 1937, p. 17 (Noel Straus)
[105] Indeed, the surface noise is sometimes so pervasive that it *is* the predominant sound. Waltraute's departure, for example, can barely be distinguished from the din.
[106] 30 April 1936, p. 12. Torsten Ralf sang Parsifal; Ludwig Weber, Gurnemanz; Herbert Janssen, Amfortas; Frida Leider, Kundry; Eduard Habich, Klingsor.
[107] 30 April 1939, p. 14
[108] 30 April 1936, p. 12 (Richard Capell)

symphonic performance from the orchestra. ...there was nothing strongly personal in [his] interpretation – it was all the better for that; the devotion and knowledge of a fine musician and conductor were to be felt always.[109]

The *Musical Courier* also noted the relation between the orchestra and the voices. "Instead of an orchestral performance with vocal obligatos..., we had a delicate, differentiated orchestral texture supporting the voices and permitting every nuance of expression to be heard."[110] The orchestral texture was commented upon too by Ernest Newman in the *Sunday Times*: Reiner "evidently had a complete understanding of the peculiar texture of the orchestral score, which was intended by Wagner to sound entirely different from any other of his scores – 'I want it to be like spun silk,' he said to Cosima; and the London Philharmonic played divinely."[111]

Not everyone remarked on the delicacy of the orchestral playing, however, or liked the freedom given to the singers. The *Observer* complained: "it must be possible to make the *Erlösungs-motif* sound less barbaric and more poignant, and we must hope that when the opera is repeated tomorrow Herr Reiner will have fitted his beat to the line of the soloists, or have got them to accept his line."[112] Then there was the question of warmth. Robert Lorenz wrote in the *Musical Times*:

I am repelled by the cold, calculated, impassive, and jerky methods of Mr. Fritz Reiner, despite implications of underlying power. ... The slow processional type of music in which *Parsifal* abounds suited Reiner well. While none of it is laboured – save in the second act which becomes steadily more tedious – one feels that great labour and the most scrupulous care went to the making of it. These are precisely the qualities in which Reiner excels. The concluding scene was largely spoiled by Reiner's inability to see the essential fitness of lingering over these last pages of Wagner's unique score as though he were loath to leave them. That, however, would imply a romantic strain in Herr Reiner which he palpably lacks.[113]

When Reiner returned to Covent Garden for three further performances in 1937, with the same principal singers,[114] most of the uncertainties seem to have been overcome. To *The Times*, the opening performance on 22 April was "on the whole one of the most satisfactory that has been given" at Covent Garden. "Clearness and mellowness of tone with steady movement were the salient characteristics of his reading."[115] The *Daily Telegraph* had high praise: it was "as good a *Parsifal* as we have ever had in London."[116] Ernest Newman in the *Sunday Times* went even further: "It was not only the best that Covent Garden has ever given us, but as good, on the whole, as anything we could hear in Europe today."[117] Reiner conducted "with the utmost sensitiveness," wrote the *Observer*, "and with that passionate interest in every detail of the score we have come to expect of him."[118] The only reservation was expressed by

[109] review dated 1 May 1936 in *Cardus on music: a centenary collection* (ed.) Donald Wright (London: H. Hamilton, 1988), p. 127

[110] 30 May 1936, p. 5 (Cesar Saerchinger)

[111] 3 May 1936, p. 7. "I cannot remember a better Parsifal, all in all, than that of Torsten Ralf," Newman wrote; and: "All in all, Covent Garden surpassed itself."

[112] 3 May 1936, p. 16

[113] June 1936, p. 551

[114] The new singers were Kersten Thorborg, as Kundry, and Adolf Vogel as Klingsor.

[115] 23 April 1937, p. 12. The *Musical Times* did not review the 1937 *Parsifal*.

[116] 23 April 1937, p. 12 (F. Bonovia)

[117] 25 April 1937, p. 7. Of Thorborg he wrote: "All in all I would rank her as the greatest Wagnerian actress of the present day."

[118] 25 April 1937, p. 16

the *Morning Post*: although "the conductor kept the orchestra within very reasonable bounds as to volume of tone," Gurnemanz's voice did not carry.[119]

Possibly it was on the strength of critical acclaim of the first performance of the season that the Gramophone Company arranged for test recordings to be made at the next two performances. Whatever the case, it is difficult to align the observations above with what is heard on the recordings. The direction seems to have a nervous energy that does not let the music breathe or flow. The Transformation music is too tightly held, and too fast. Sometimes the accompaniment to poor Amfortas is lacerating. There is no "spun silk" in the orchestral sound. These were test recordings afterall, and evidently someone considered they had not passed the test, for they were not released in their day.

Fig. 23.8. *Etwas reiner bitte* ("Somewhat cleaner please"). Reiner in Dresden. Drawing by Rudolf Scheffer, 1918. *Saturday Review of Literature*, 31 May 1958

The high-water mark of Covent Garden was not matched by his *Parsifal* at the Metropolitan Opera in 1949. The *New York Times* did not find it to be Reiner's opera. "Neither in tempi, in breadth or in point of that famous 'atmosphere' ... does he to us convey the inwardness of the score."[120] He conducted "fastidiously enough," according to the *Daily News*, "but with no special incandescence."[121] The *Post* noticed the "beautiful clarity and balance in the orchestral direction," but instead of "the unique sublimity of Wagner's inspiration," there was a "static quality."[122] Reiner had been greatly admired in *Salome* and *Falstaff*, the *Herald Tribune* wrote, but in *Parsifal* he was "not so wholly convincing":

[119] 23 April 1938, p. 15 (S.G.)

[120] 19 March 1949, p. 10 (Olin Downes). Charles Kullman sang Parsifal; Joel Berglund, Gurnemanz; Herbert Janssen, Amfortas; Rose Bampton, Kundry; Gerhard Pechner, Klingsor.

[121] 19 March 1949, p. 17 (Douglas Watt)

[122] 20 March 1949, sect. 2, p. 6 (Harriett Johnson)

It was not until the second scene of the second act that Mr. Reiner seemed able to identify himself fully with the score's implications. Then, however, his realization of the music's fusion of surging drama and sensuousness of sound was cogent in its impact. In the preceding Klingsor episode, the wild, demoniac character of the music emerged surprisingly tamed, and thin in texture.

In the first act, especially in the long scene in the Temple of the Grail, Mr. Reiner's conception was small in scale, and while much of the orchestral playing was transparent in quality the burning intensity and breadth of style demanded for a telling revelation of Wagner's ideas were not forthcoming and the work's inherent mysticism eluded him for the most part. There were no radical departures in pacing in general in evidence, although it was not always possible to agree with certain abrupt transitions in tempo resorted to.[123]

There was no "basic pulse" in the work, in the view of the *Sun*. Its reviewer was not present in the first act, and only intermittently in the second, "where the underplaying of the orchestra dulled the edge of Wagner's scoring." Even the Good Friday music "gave off but a dull glow, with little of the shading or highlighting implicit in its texture. Niceties of all sorts were there, constantly; but not with the kind of boldness, assurance or conviction that Reiner had led us to expect from his *Salome* or *Falstaff*."[124] The *New York World-Telegram* agreed: he had fallen short of the high standards he had set in Verdi and Strauss. "One suspected he preferred both composers over Wagner."[125]

Reinerdämmerung

Reiner was a master of technique, but that was not enough to make him a great Wagner conductor. Technique is a necessary but not sufficient skill. As the conductor himself said: "you have to forget technique to become an artist. Personality and the gift of interpretation are things which cannot be taught or acquired."[126] Reiner certainly had a strong personality, and it was in the expression of his personality, not technique, that he was his own worst enemy. The man in the musician cannot wholly be ignored. His way of coaching, of making music, and of dealing with people in ordinary life involved the humiliation of artists, deliberate cruelty and, at worst, the infliction and provocation of violence.[127] "Don't believe all the horrible stories you

[123] 19 March 1949, p. 9 (Jerome D. Bohm)

[124] 19 March 1949, p. 4 (Irving Kolodin)

[125] 19 March 1949, p. 5 (Louis Biancolli). *Falstaff* was his favourite opera: Reiner, "Favorite Opera," *The Chicago American Pictorial Living*, 31 March 1957, p. 2. He performed *Falstaff* three times at the Metropolitan Opera (February-March 1949). He and Lubja Welitsch made their celebrated debut at the Metropolitan with *Salome* on 4 February 1949. Altogether, he conducted *Salome* eighteen times with the Metropolitan Opera.

[126] Reiner, "The Making of a Conductor", *Musical America*, 25 October 1941, p. 29

[127] Astrid Varnay gave examples of his trickery, but she knew her work well and was not to be out-witted: Varnay, *Fifty-five years in five acts: my life in opera* (Boston: Northeastern University Press, 2000), p. 124. His second wife divorced him in 1930 after uncontested allegations of "mental and physical cruelty." His first biographer wrote: "On one occasion Reiner appeared at rehearsal with a bandaged head, a black eye, and his right arm in a sling. It was rumoured Berta had thrown him down the stairs": Hart, *Reiner*, p. 53. Instances of his sadism and deliberate cruelty were also given by his later biographer: Morgan, *Reiner*, pp. 47, 111. Morgan also related how, in one of Reiner's conducting classes, "a disturbed student actually brought a gun and bullets with the intention of shooting Reiner": "Fritz Reiner and the Technique of Conducting," *Journal of the Conductors' Guild*, vol. 14 no. 2 (Summer/Fall 1993), p. 97. The source of this story was Leonard Bernstein, another student in the class, who believed he too was a potential victim.

heard about Fritz Reiner," one musician confided, "He was actually a lot worse!"[128] It is no wonder observers detected an absence of warmth in his music-making, or to put it another way, that audiences cooled to him.[129] Technical perfection can only bring so much. There are other dimensions to music. "Conducting is the knowledge of what is behind the written music," he said. "The main thing is to know the music."[130] Some of Wagner's music he knew in the deepest sense. There were moments like Wotan's furious insistence that Brünnhilde obey his command in *Walküre*,[131] Beckmesser's anger and frustration in *Meistersinger* (*Verdammert Schuster!* – "Damned cobbler!"),[132] Kundry's rage as Parsifal spurns her,[133] and "the barbaric quality" of Hagen and his vassals in *Götterdämmerung*,[134] in which his conducting appears to have been wholly in sympathy with the drama. But these are only moments. There is a lot more to Wagner that Reiner did not reveal. *Tristan* appears not to have been his opera. Nor *Parsifal*. The *Ring* he never achieved in his mature years. His *Meistersinger* was clean, but cool. His recordings of orchestral excerpts are variable, and serve only as a dim testament. He was asked in the dusk of his years, when people were beginning to whisper that his planned *Götterdämmerung* would be the death of him – "*Reinerdämmerung*" –, whether he was a "Wagner fan," he responded: "It's hard to say. I've made so much music in my lifetime that I can't honestly answer that."[135] The magic casement remained closed.

[128] unidentified musician quoted in Kenneth H. Meltzer, "The Pittsburgh Symphony Orchestra – a centennial retrospective," in *The Carnegie Pittsburgh Symphony Orchestra: Sharing a Century of Glory – 100th anniversary* (2 March 1996) (Pittsburgh Symphony Society, 1996), n.p.

[129] Carl Flesch: "He is one of the best musicians… but he lacks, to some extent, that personal aura that creates sympathetic resonance in the audience and thus largely determines the effect an interpretation makes upon his listeners": *The memoirs of Carl Flesch,* Hans Keller (trans. and ed.), (London: Rockliff, 1957), p. 342

[130] Jay S. Harrison, "Return of Reiner," *Musical America*, October 1963, p. 13

[131] end of scene two, act two, 1936 recording

[132] scene one, act three, 1952 recording

[133] scene two, act two of *Parsifal*, 1949; see *New York Herald Tribune* comment on p. 592

[134] second act of *Götterdämmerung*: *New York Times*, 23 July 1937, p. 17 (Noel Straus)

[135] Harrison, "Return of Reiner," *ibid*, p. 12

Part X

Discographies

Introduction to the Discographies

The aim of the discographies has been to list every published Wagner recording of the conductors discussed in the book. While completeness might be a worthy aim, it continues to be frustrated by the welcome appearance of new recordings decades after the conductors last raised their bâton.

Finding the recordings has been a long process, and I am indebted to the compilers of catalogues, dealers' lists, encyclopaedias, discographies, libraries and archives for the leads that have made it possible. Much information and research has been found in disparate places, and has been helpful in making what is presented here as comprehensive as it is. I acknowledge this work in the first footnote of each discography, and thank those concerned.

The foremost source of information on opera recordings at the time of writing is Capon's List of Opera Recordings (CLOR), an online database compiled by Brian Capon.[1] This is an essential port of call for any opera collector. I have also found the several privately-published discographies of John Hunt invaluable. All are available in the British Library and at *John Hunt Discographies*.[2]

Compiling the discographies has been much more than consolidating the research of other people. What is presented here comes primarily from the recordings themselves, not from catalogues or lists. Errors have been corrected, including from my own *Parsifal on Record* (1992) and *Tristan und Isolde on Record* (2000), and doubtful issues are discussed in footnotes. There have been a few recordings, again mentioned in footnotes, which I have been unable to locate. These have been included because there is reliable evidence that they were once issued, however difficult it might now be to find them. There is also, on the other hand, a degree of unreliable information abroad about recordings which purportedly exist in private collections or archives. Unfortunately the owners of this material sleep, Fafner-like, on their hoard, and further information has been impossible to obtain. I have not included references to this information.

Having recordings in one's hands does not necessarily lead to certainty about them. The majority of recordings of complete performances listed below are live performances issued by "pirate" record companies or entrepreneurs: the original source material was probably unlawfully acquired, or published without the permission of those who were responsible for the recording, broadcast, or performance. In these circumstances, it has been impossible to verify the source of some recordings, and to be absolutely sure about what one is listening to. In the case of early recordings of this nature published by Edward J. Smith, the pioneering work of William Shaman

1 www.operadis-opera-discography.org.uk <accessed 1 May 2011>

2 www.vixenrecords.com/foxfox/johnhunt <accessed 1 May 2011>

and his colleagues[3] has been invaluable. In the case of some later recordings of unclear provenance, a number of opera houses and radio stations I have contacted have been unable to, or have refrained from, confirming that they are what they claim to be. These institutions are clearly in a delicate position. The Richard Wagner Museum in Bayreuth, for example, does not collect "pirate" recordings of performances from Bayreuth Festivals. The attention I have given to identifying Knappertsbusch's *Parsifal* at the 1951 and 1954 Bayreuth Festivals may serve to illustrate the difficulties of establishing absolutely reliable information. In the case of Hermann May's recordings from Vienna in the 1930s and 1940s, these were for the large part issued by Koch Schwann in their *Edition Wiener Staatsoper Live* series in the 1990s, but there are further putative recordings circulating which are impossible to verify. May's discs rest in the Österreichische Mediathek, where the link between the discs themselves and information as to what is on them (the labels themselves are not precise) has unfortunately been broken.

The discographies are set out in chronological order of recordings, not organised under titles of works. Generally, I have *included*:

- *published recordings*, ie, those that have been *commercially available* at some stage, whether from established record companies or otherwise;
- the *titles* of CD and LP sets where these differ from the name of the work recorded;
- the *dates* LP or CD sets were first issued;
- the *first issue* of a recording on 78, LP and CD as a minimum, and a *selection* of more recent or readily available CD issues;
- *foreign issues* of the Gramophone Company (HMV's) 78s, for example, EJ (Germany), ES (Austria), AW (Italy), W (France), AB (Spain), and Victor (United States);
- *matrix numbers* and, importantly, *take* numbers (ie, the actual recordings used from a recording session), in the case of recordings from the pre-LP era;
- *descriptions* of excerpts to show where they come in the opera, and to show exactly what music is included in the issued excerpt;
- *timings* of excerpts, including a section devoted to timings;
- *details of cuts* in abridged performances, mentioned in footnotes; and
- a *selection of broadcasts* which have not yet appeared on disc, but are more likely than others to do so, eg, Toscanini's NBC broadcasts, and broadcasts from the Bayreuth Festival and the Metropolitan Opera, in footnotes.

[3] William Shaman, William J. Collins, and Calvin M. Goodwin, *EJS, discography of the Edward J. Smith recordings: the golden age of opera, 1956-1971* (Westport: Greenwood Press, 1994), and their *More EJS: discography of the Edward J. Smith recordings : "Unique Opera Records Corporation" (1972-1977), "A.N.N.A. Record Company" (1978-1982), "special-label" issues (circa 1954-1981), and addendum to "The Golden age of opera" series* (Westport: Greenwood Press, 1999). These works are referred to in the discographies of Bodanzky, Böhm, Knappertsbusch and Toscanini below.

Generally I have *excluded*:

- in the case of pre-LP recordings, take numbers of *unpublished recordings*;
- *unpublished recordings generally*, whether in the archives of record companies or the collections of private individuals or otherwise;
- *single-side numbers*, as distinct from matrix and catalogue numbers;
- records and CDs containing *mere excerpts* of complete performances that are otherwise listed; and
- *every* issue or re-issue of a particular recording. Many re-issues have had a fleeting existence and are very difficult, if not impossible, to obtain. John Hunt's discographies include a large number of re-issues of the same recordings which may be of interest to the specialist collector.

I am indebted to a number of individuals and institutions for providing information and recordings I have otherwise been unable to acquire. These include: Andrew Burton, David E. Canfield, Edward F. Durbeck III, Christopher Dyment, Peter Fülöp, Leslie Gerber, Glen Gould, Stephen Hillyer, Silvia Kargl of the Historisches Archiv der Wiener Philharmoniker, Alan Kelly, Jon M. Samuels, Gert Schaefer, Al Schlachtmeyer, Marianne Seid of the Svenskt musikhistoriskt arkiv, Stockholm, Katja Mayer and Kristen Stencel of the Bayerische Staatsoper, Dr. Szomolányi Gy. István, and the staff of the Music Division of the Library of Congress, the Rodgers and Hammerstein Archives of Recorded Sound in the New York Public Library, Historical Sound Recordings at Yale University, the Sound Archive of the British Library, and the Deutsches Musikarchiv of the Deutsche Nationalbibliothek. I am especially grateful to William Shaman who provided much valuable advice as the discographies developed, and who read through and commented upon the final drafts.

1. Artur Bodanzky conducts Wagner[1]

Works recorded, including excerpts:

Tannhäuser: 1928, 1935, 1936
Lohengrin: 1927, 1934, 1935
Tristan und Isolde: 1933, 1934, 1935, 1937, 1938
Die Meistersinger von Nürnberg: 1927, 1936
Der Ring des Nibelungen:
Das Rheingold: 1937
Die Walküre: 1934, 1935, 1937
Siegfried: 1937, 1938
Götterdämmerung: 1936, 1939
Parsifal: 1938

1927

Lohengrin, Act 1 Prelude, Staatskapelle, Berlin, 9 September 1927[2]
(2-20333-1, 2-20334-2)

78: Parlophon P-9150;3 Odeon O-7738; Odeon 177005;4 Odéon 59089; Parlophone E106355

LP: *One Hundred Years of Great Artists at the Met - The Conductors 1883-1983*: MET 408 (1986)

CD: *Wagner Conductors on Record*: Pearl GEMS 0024 (1998)

1 Although there has been no discography of Bodanzky to speak of, partly because of his limited commercial recording activity, recordings of broadcasts from the Metropolitan Opera House in New York published by Edward J. Smith have been documented in detail by William Shaman et al. in *EJS* and *More EJS* (see introduction to discographies). Bodanzky's earliest broadcasts – the first was Act 3 of *Lohengrin* on 9 January 1932 - do not appear to have been recorded: see James R. Smart, *Radio Broadcasts in the Library of Congress 1924-1941: A Catalog of Recordings* (Washington D.C.: Library of Congress, 1982); details of performances broadcast are available from the online Metropolitan Opera Database maintained by the Metropolitan Opera Archives (www.metoperafamily.org). The earliest live recordings, at least until the *Tristan* of 9 March 1935, are fragmentary and in very poor sound.

2 The dates and matrix numbers for the first three of these excerpts are from Hansfried Sieben, *PARLOPHON, Band II, Die Matrizen-Nummern der elektrischen Aufnahmen 30 cm von 8860 bis 21833 (1926 bis 1933)* (Hansfried Sieben: Düsseldorf, 1990) and the same author's *ODEON - Die Matrizen-Nummern der Serie xxB (30 cm) von 6815-9598 (1923-1953)* (Hansfried Sieben: Düsseldorf, 1988). The date given with the MET LP is "June 14, 1928," and with the Pearl CD "9/9/1927." Both include transfers of P-9150. On these 1927-28 records, the German labels describe the orchestra as "Mitglieder der Staatskapelle, Berlin" whereas the English labels state "The Orchestra of the State Opera House, Berlin."

3 The matrix number on this pressing is 2-20333-2.

4 The matrix numbers on this Argentine pressing, not included in Sieben, are 2-20333-2 and 2-20334.

5 The matrix numbers of this English pressing are given as 2-20333-2 and 2-02334-2 in Frank Andrews, and Michael Smith, *The Parlophone 12 inch "E" series 1923-1959* (Wells-Next-The-Sea: City of London Phonograph and Gramophone Society, 2000)

Die Meistersinger, Act 1 Prelude, Staatskapelle, Berlin, 10 September 1927[6]
(2-20325-2, 2-20326-3, 2-20327-2 and xxB 7783-2, 7784-3, 7785-2)
78: Parlophone E10633/4; Odeon O-8320/21, O-6715/16; Decca 25555/6

Lohengrin, Act 3 Introduction, Staatskapelle, Berlin, 10 September 1927
(2-20328-2 and xxB 7786-2)
78: Parlophone E10634; Odeon O-8321; O-6716; O-7655; Decca 25556

1928

Tannhäuser, Overture, Staatskapelle, Berlin, 1 May 1928
(xxB 8073-1, 8074-1, 8075-1, 8076-1)
78: Odeon O-8348/49, O-6717/18

1933[7]

Tristan und Isolde, New York, live broadcasts, 3 and 11 March 1933, abridged[8], excerpts (ca. 89 mins)
3 March:
Act 1, Scenes 1 and 2: from *[Weh'! Ach] wehe, mein Kind!* (Sailor) to *Was wohl erwiedertest du?* (Tristan) (7' 39")
Act 1, Scene 3: from *Tod uns Beiden!* (Isolde) to *Wie magst du dich betören* (Brangäne) (0' 46")
Act 1, Scenes 3, 4 and 5: from *Kennst du der Mutter Künste nicht?* (Isolde) to *Ehr-Furcht hielt mich in Acht* (Tristan) (13' 35")
Act 2, Scene 1: from *Dem Freund zu lieb'*... (Isolde) to *die sie webt aus Lust [und Leid]* (Isolde) (3' 13")
11 March:
Act 1: fragment from the beginning of the Prelude (1' 01")
Act 1, Scene 1: from *Nimmermehr!* (Isolde) to *zerschlag'es, [dies trotzige Schiff]* (Isolde) (1' 18")
Act 1, Scene 2: from *Weh'! Ach wehe, mein Kind!* (Sailor) to *Was wohl erwiedertest du?* (Tristan) (7' 22")
Act 1, Scene 3: from *[Fluch dir, Ver]ruchter!* (Isolde) to *Welcher Wahn?* (Brangäne) (0' 58")
Act 1, Scene 4: from *Wähnst du die Alles Klug erwägt* (Brangäne) to the orchestral passage

[6] According to Sieben, *PARLOPHON*, there were two recording sessions for the *Meistersinger*, Act 1 Prelude, and the *Lohengrin*, Act 3 Introduction. The recordings from the first session, on 8 September 1927, were unpublished; those from the second, on 10 September 1927, were issued *both* on the British Parlophone label with Parlophone matrix numbers *and* on the German Odeon label with Odeon matrix numbers, as shown. Both the Parlophone and the Odeon records are the *same* performance/recording. Sieben, in *ODEON*, states that the Odeon recordings were "undertaken by Parlophon" and were assigned their Odeon matrix numbers on 5 October 1927. Andrews and Smith give the matrix number of part 2 (E 10633) as 2-20326-2; however, 20326-3 is printed both on the label and in the wax of the record.

[7] Not listed here is the finale from a 27 January 1933 broadcast of *Das Rheingold* which may have been used on EJS 452 (1968), but this has not been confirmed. Only a part of that performance was broadcast (3:15 - 5:00 pm). The same disc contains Erda's warning "alleged to be Feb. 26, 1932: Bodanzky" according to the label, but it is in fact Schumann-Heink's commercial recording from 1929 (Victor 7107) conducted by Rosario Bourdon: Shaman et al., *EJS*, pp. 443-8.

[8] The recorded excerpts show that at least Act 3 was abridged, as detailed above. The CD transfer by the Frida Leider Gesellschaft contains an appropriate warning about the sound quality of these recordings; however, it misspells both of Bodanzky's names, and contains only 79 minutes of the excerpts on EJS, omitting some of the poorer quality 3 March excerpts.

accompanying Tristan's entry, i.e., after Isoldes's *Herr Tristan trete nah* (12' 26")

Act 2, Scene 1: from *Dem Freund zu lieb'* (Isolde) to *Dein Werk? O thör'ge Magd!* (Isolde) (2' 23")

Act 2, Scene 2 (Liebesnacht): from *Soll der Tag noch Tristan wecken?* (Tristan) to *Hehr erhab'ne, Liebes-nacht!* (Tristan, Isolde) (1' 17")

Act 2, Scene 3: from a few bars before *Rette dich, Tristan!* (Kurwenal) to *Das sollst du, Herr, mir sagen, ob [ich ein recht verklagt?]* (Melot) (1' 15")

Act 2, Scene 3: from *[meiner Ehren Ende] erreiche?* to *Warum mir diese Schmach?* (King Marke) (1' 15")

Act 2, Scene 3: from *[Dein Blick, Isolde,] blendet' auch ihn* (Tristan) to the end of the Act, and applause (0' 41")

Act 3, Scene 1: from *Ich war - wo ich von je gewesen* (Tristan) to *noch dir, Isolden, scheint!* (Tristan) [then cut in the performance until] *Ach, Isolde! Süsse! Holde!* (Tristan) to *Noch ist kein Schiff zu seh'n* (Kurwenal) [then cut in the performance until] *Die alte Weise* (Tristan) to *vor Sehnsucht nicht zu sterben!* (Tristan) [then cut in the performance until] *Wie vom Herz zum Hirn* (Tristan) to *was je Minne sich gewinnt!* (Kurwenal) (12' 32")

Act 3, Scenes 1, 2 and 3: from *Und Kurwenal, wie?* (Tristan) to *Gebrochen der Blick!* (Isolde) [then cut in the performance until] *Tristan ha! horch' - er wacht! Geliebter* (Isolde), to *Todt denn Alles! Alles todt* (King Marke) [then cut in performance until] *Der Wahn häufte die Not!* (King Marke) to the end of the Act (21' 45")

Tristan, Lauritz Melchior; Isolde, Frida Leider; Kurwenal, Friedrich Schorr (3 March) and Gustav Schützendorf (11 March); Brangäne, Maria Olszewska; King Marke, Ludwig Hofmann; Melot, Arnold Gabor; Sailor's Voice, Hans Clemens; Shepherd, Hans Clemens; Metropolitan Opera Chorus and Orchestra

LP: The Golden Age of Opera EJS 499 (1970)

CD: Edition Frida Leider FLG 11031933 (2003)

1934

Tristan und Isolde, New York, live broadcast, 6 January 1934, abridged, excerpts (ca. 49 mins)

Act 1, Scene 2: from *Weh'! Ach wehe, mein Kind!* (Sailor) *Mir erkören, ...* (Isolde) to *... dem Eigenholde Furcht der Herrin sie, Isolde* (Brangäne) (7' 00")

Act 1, Scene 3: from *Fluch dir, Verruchter!* (Isolde) to *nicht hell zu sehen noch hören!* (Brangäne) (1' 20")

Act 1, Scenes 3 to 5: from *Kennst du der Mutter Künst nicht?* (Brangäne) to *Un-Sitte gegen sein eigen Gemahl?* (Isolde) (13' 30")

Act 2, Scenes 1 and 2: from *[Dem Freund zu lieb' erfand] diese List aus Mit-Leid* (Isolde) to *Endlich! Endlich! An meiner Brust!* (Tristan, Isolde) (6' 55")

Act 3, Scene 1: from *das kann ich dir nicht sagen* (Tristan) to *noch dir, Isolden, scheint!* (Tristan) [then cut in the performance until] *Ach, Isolde! Süsse! Holde!* (Tristan) to *Noch ist kein Schiff zu seh'n* (Kurwenal) [then cut in the performance until] *Die alte Weise* (Tristan) to *vor Sehnsucht nicht zu sterben!* (Tristan) [then cut in the performance until] *Wie vom Herz zum Hirn* (Tristan) to *was je Minne sich gewinnt* (Kurwenal) (13' 10")

Act 3, Scene 3: from *Hörst du uns nicht?* (Brangäne) ... *Mild und leise* ... to the end of the opera (Isolde) (6' 55")

Tristan, Lauritz Melchior; Isolde, Gertrude Kappel; Kurwenal, Friedrich Schorr; Brangäne, Doris Doe; Shepherd, Hans Clemens; Metropolitan Opera Chorus and Orchestra

LP: The Golden Age of Opera EJS 502 (1970)

Die Walküre, New York, live broadcast, 3 February 1934, abridged, excerpts (ca. 95 mins)

Act 1: from the beginning of the act to the end of scene 2: *hüte dich wohl!* (Hunding) (35' 45")

Act 2, scene 2: from *Schlimm, fürcht' ich* (Brünnhilde) [with a break in the recording at Wotan's *Den Ring, den er schuf*, resuming at *Die alles weiss*] [with a cut in the performance from *der der Liebe fluchte* to *trügend verraten, wer mir traut!* (Wotan)] to *den Freien erlang' ich mir nicht* (Wotan) (13' 13")

Act 2, scene 2: *So sah ich Siegvater nie... die Treue verlassen!* (Brünnhilde) (end of the scene) (3' 21")

Act 2, scene 4: from the orchestral passage introducing the *Todesverkundigung* to *Zu Walvater, der dich gewählt, führ' ich dich: nach Walhall [folgst du mir]* (Brünnhilde, with Siegmund) (7' 21")

Act 3, scenes 1 and 2: from *Schützt mich und helft in höchster Not!* (Brünnhilde, with the Valkyries) to *Wo ist Brünnhild', wo die Verbrecherin?* (Wotan) (8' 30")

Act 3, scenes 2 and 3: from the end of scene 2, *Wehe! Weh!* (Valkyries) to the end of the opera (26' 48")

Brünnhilde, Frida Leider; Siegmund, Paul Althouse; Sieglinde, Gertrude Kappel; Wotan, Ludwig Hofmann; Fricka, Karin Branzell; Hunding, Emanuel List; Gerhilde, Phradie Wells; Grimgerde, Philine Falco; Helmwige, Dorothee Manski; Ortlinde, Margaret Halstead; Roßweiße, Ina Bourskaya; Schwertleite, Irra Petina; Siegrune, Elda Vettori; Waltraute, Doris Doe; Metropolitan Opera Chorus and Orchestra

LP: The Golden Age of Opera EJS 501 (1970)

CD: Frida Leider Gesellschaft FLG 193434 (2005)[9]

Lohengrin, New York, live broadcast, 24 March 1934, abridged[10], excerpts (ca. 95 mins)

Act 1, scene 1: from *Hört! Grafen...* (Herald) to *Elsa, erscheine hier zur Stell'!* (Herald) (8' 30")

Act 1, scene 2: from *Einsam in trüben Tagen* (Elsa) to *dass er mir helf' in meiner Not!* (Elsa) (10' 40")

Act 1, scene 3: from *Nun sei bedankt, mein lieber Schwann!* (Lohengrin) *to durch Gottes Urteil werd' es dir bekannt!* (Lohengrin) (7' 45") with a break, at Elsa's *Mein Held! Mein Ritter!*

Act 1, scene 3: from the orchestral accompaniment to the battle between Lohengrin and Telramund to the end of the act (3' 10")

Act 2, scene 2 complete: from *Euch Lüften* (Elsa) to *der Räuber meiner Ehre soll vergehn!* Telramund) (19' 25")

Act 2, scene 4: from *Zurück, Elsa!* (Ortrud) to *wer seiner Sendung zweifeln kann!* (Elsa) (3' 50")

Act 2, scene 5: from *Heil! Heil! dem König!* (Men) to *Elsa! wie seh' ich er[beben!]* (Lohengrin) (7' 35")

Act 2, scene 5: from *[Mein Held! Entgegne kühn dem] Ungetreuen!* (King Heinrich) to the end of the act (5' 25")

Act 3, scene 2: from *Das süsse Lied verhallt* (Lohengrin), to *Rette dich! Dein Schwert, dein Schwert!* (Elsa) (15' 15")

Act 3, scene 3: from *In fernem Land* (Lohengrin) to the end of the opera (13' 45")

9 The Frida Leider Gesellschaft CDs omit the concluding orchestral passage, the *Feuerzauber*, on the basis that it is incorrectly attributed to this performance.

10 The cuts to the performance, as distinct from breaks in the recording, are not easily distinguishable: the sound on the LPs is very poor and faint, and the excerpts (one act per side) flow seamlessly one to another, without any bands or pauses; furthermore, in some of the excerpts listed above there is a break caused by a change in recording discs, with a consequential loss of a few bars. The cuts in the performance identified were: in Act 1, scene 1, from *die deutsches Land so oft aus Osten traf?* to *dass ohne Fürstin ihr in Zwietracht lebt!* (King Heinrich), in scene 3, from *Wie fasst uns selig süsses Grauen!* to *ein Wunder trug ans Land!* (Men and Women), and *Welch holde Wunder muss ich sehn?* to *shau' ich den wonnevollen Mann* (King, Men and Women); in Act 3, scene 2, from *Dein Lieben muss mir hoch entgelten* to *muss ich in deiner Lieb' ersehn!* (Lohengrin), and from *O Elsa! Was hast du mir angetan?* (Lohengrin) to *des Ostens Horden siegfreich nimmer ziehn!* (Lohengrin)

King Heinrich, Ludwig Hofmann; Lohengrin, Lauritz Melchior; Elsa, Elisabeth Rethberg; Telramund, Gustav Schützendorf; Ortrud, Maria Olszewska; Metropolitan Opera Chorus and Orchestra

LP: The Golden Age of Opera EJS 504 (2 LPs) (1970)

1935

Tannhäuser, New York, live broadcast, 12 January 1935, abridged[11], excerpts (ca. 37 mins)

Act 2, scene 3: from *Blick' ich umher* (Wolfram) to *auch, für ihn, auch für ihn* (Elsa) (13' 10")

Act 3, scene 1: from *[Wohl wusst' ich hier sie im Geb]et zu finden* to *O, würd' ihr Lindrung nur erteilt!* (Wolfram) (3' 00")

Act 3, scene 1: from *[Allmächt'ge Jungfrau, hör mein Flehen! Zu dir, Gepreisne,] rufe ich!* to *nur anzuflehn für seine Schuld* (Elisabeth) (4' 54")

Act 3, scene 2: from *Wie Todesahnung Dämmrung deckt die Lande… O du, mein holder Abendstern* to *ein sel'ger Engel dort zu werden!* (Wolfram) (4' 00")

Act 3, scene 3: from *Hör an, Wolfram, hör an! Inbrunst im Herzen* (Tannhäuser) to *Heil! [Heil! Der Gnade Wunder Heil!]* (Young Pilgrims) (12' 40")

Tannhäuser, Lauritz Melchior; Elisabeth, Maria Müller; Wolfram, Richard Bonelli; Venus, Dorothee Manski; Walther, Hans Clemens; Biterolf, Arnold Gabor; Reinmar, James Wolfe; Shepherd, Lillian Clark; Metropolitan Opera Chorus and Orchestra

LP: The Golden Age of Opera EJS 504 (2 LPs) (1970)

Die Walküre, New York, live broadcast, 2 February 1935, excerpts[12] (ca. 65 mins)

Act 1: complete (55')

Act 2, scene 3: from *Hinweg! Hinweg!* (Sieglinde) to *Was je Schande dir schuf, das büßt nun des Frev[lers Blut!]* (Siegmund) (3' 23")

Act 2, scene 3: from *[Horch! die Hörner,] hörst du den Ruf?* (Sieglinde) to *Schwester! Geliebte!* (Siegmund) and the orchestral passage introducing the *Todesverkundigung* (4' 45")

Act 2, scene 5: from *Kehrte der Vater nur heim!* (Sieglinde) to *sollen dich Hunde nicht halten!* (Hunding) (1' 25")

Siegmund, Paul Althouse; Sieglinde, Kirsten Flagstad; Hunding, Emanuel List; Metropolitan Opera Chorus and Orchestra

LP: The Golden Age of Opera EJS 200 (1960) (Act 1); EJS 444 (1968)[13] (Act 2 excerpts)

[11] As in the case of the *Lohengrin* excerpts on these LPs, the poor sound quality makes it difficult to distinguish between cuts to the performance and cuts in the recording or to the excerpts presented on the discs. Nevertheless, missing from the Act 2 excerpt are two passages: from *Den Bronnen, den uns Wolfram nannte* (Walter) to *ist wohlfeil, keines Streiches wert* (Biterolf), and from *Hinweg! Hinweg!* (Women) to *dem Himmelswort kann nicht ich widerstehn* (Men); and from the Act 3, scene 3 excerpt: from *Wie neben mir der schwerstbedrückte Pilger* to *um meines Engels Tränen zu versüssen!* (Tannhäuser). The four excerpts from Act 3 follow one another without any break.

[12] The excerpts on disc are not abridged.

[13] Bodanzky's name does not appear on the label; in addition to the Act 2 excerpts, *Winterstürme* from Act 1 has been added to an excerpt of Toscanini conducting the same scene in a 27 November 1932 New York Philharmonic Symphony Orchestra concert. Another Act 1 excerpt, *Ein Schwert verhiess mir der Vater*, appeared on EJS 501 (1970). From the excerpts on disc, it is not possible to determine whether other parts of the performance were abridged.

CD: Walhall WHL 21 (1995) and Archipel ARPCD 0039 (2001) (both sets also contain Act 1 and the Act 2 excerpts, as well as Acts 2 and 3 from the 18 December 1937 performance)

Tristan und Isolde, New York, live broadcast, 9 March 1935, abridged[14]
Tristan, Lauritz Melchior; King Marke, Ludwig Hofmann; Isolde, Kirsten Flagstad, Kurwenal, Friedrich Schorr; Melot, Arnold Garbor; Brangäne, Karin Branzell; Shepherd, Hans Clemens; [Steersman, James Wolfe][15]; Metropolitan Opera Chorus and Orchestra
LP: Die Goldene Aera Richard Wagners GAW 301 (1964)
CD: West Hill Radio Archives WHRA 6001 (2003)[16]

Lohengrin, New York, live broadcast, 21 December 1935, abridged[17]
Lohengrin, Lauritz Melchior; Elsa, Lotte Lehmann; Ortrud, Marjorie Lawrence; Telramund, Friedrich Schorr; King Heinrich, Emanuel List; Herald, Julius Huehn; Metropolitan Opera Chorus and Orchestra
CD: Melodram CDM 37049; Gebhardt JGCD 0023-3 (2000); Myto 00214 (2009)

1936

Götterdämmerung, New York, live broadcast, 11 January 1936, abridged[18]
Brünnhilde, Marjorie Lawrence; Siegfried, Lauritz Melchior; Gunther, Friedrich Schorr; Gutrune, Dorothee Manski; Hagen, Ludwig Hofmann; Waltraute, Kathryn

[14] The cuts in the performance were: in Act 2, Scene 2, from *Dem Tage! Dem Tage!* (Tristan) to *dass nachtsichtig mein Auge wahres zu sehen tauge* (Tristan), from *Tag und Tod* (Isolde) to *Tristan der Tod gegeben?* (Isolde), and in Scene 3 from *Wozu die Dienste ohne Zahl* to *Da liess e's denn so sein* (King Marke); in Act 3, Scene 1, from *Isolde noch im Reich der Sonne!* to *die selbst Nachts von ihr mich scheuchte?* (Tristan), from *Muss ich dich so versteh'n* to *Zu welchem Los?* (Tristan) [Melchior does not sing the few words after *Die alte Weise* and before *Nein! Ach nein!*], from *Die nie erstirbt* to *Der Trank! der furchtbare Trank!* (Tristan), in Scene 2, from *Gebrochen der Blick!* to *Nur einmal noch!* (Isolde), and in Scene 3, from *Mein Held! Mein Tristan!* to *Die Ernte mehrt' ich dem Tod* (King Marke).

[15] The Steersman's only lines in Act 3 are missing, together with Kurwenal's words *Stell' dich und hilf! So lang' ich lebe...* which follow; it appears to be an omission from the source recording, not the performance.

[16] The booklet inside the CD box contains the following information about the recording: "ticks, pops, distortion, crosstalk, pitch instability, surface noise, glips, cues are audible, crosstalk."

[17] The cuts in the performance were: in Act 1, scene 1, from *Soll ich euch erst der Drangsal Kunde sagen* (King Heinrich) to *Wohlauf! Mit Gott für deutschen Reiches Ehr'!* (Saxons), scene 3, from *zu siegen nimmer du vermagst!* to *Dein harret Unsieg, bittre Reu'!* (Nobles of Brabant); in Act 2, scene 1, from *Entsetzlich!* to *und meine Her' gewönn' ich neu?* (Telramund), in scene 3, *Nun hört, dem Lande will er uns entführen!* (Third Noble) to *der sei von mir des Gottestrugs beklagt!* (Telramund), in scene 5, from *Wie staub vor Gottes Hauch verwehe* to *dass sie ihm jetzt von mir gestellt* (Telramund), and from *Welch ein Geheimnis muss der Held bewahren?* (Men, Women, Nobles, King) to *Im Zweifel doch erbebt des Herzens Grund!* (Elsa); in Act 3, scene 2, from *Dein Lieben muss mir hoch entgelten* to *muss ich in deiner Lieb' ersehn!* (Lohengrin), from *Nie soll dein Reiz entschwinden* (Lohengrin) to *Wo fänd' ich dein' Gewähr?* (Elsa), in scene 3, from *Zum andern aber sollt ihr Klage hören* to *enthülle mein Geheimnis ich in Treuen* (Lohengrin), and from *O Elsa! Was hast du mir angetan?* to *des Ostens Horden siegreich nimmer ziehn!* (Lohengrin)

[18] The cuts in the performance were: in Act 1, scene 3, from *Als dem Gott entgegen* to *leucht' und lach' ich heut auf* (Brünnhilde); and in Act 3, scene 3, from *Kinder hört' ich greinen nach der Mutter* (Brünnhilde) to *die durch den Trank er vergaß!* (Gutrune)

Meisle; Alberich, Eduard Habich; First Norn, Doris Doe; Second Norn, Irra Petina; Third Norn, Dorothee Manski, Woglinde, Editha Fleischer; Wellgunde, Irra Petina, Flosshilde, Doris Doe; Vassals, Max Altglass, Arnold Gabor; Metropolitan Opera Chorus and Orchestra

LP: The Golden Age of Opera EJS 489 (1969)

CD: Walhall WHL 24 (1995); Naxos Historical 8.110041-43 (1999); Archipel ARPCD 0007-3 (2000); Naxos Historical 8.110228-30 (2002); *Der Ring des Nibelungen*: Naxos Historical 8.501106 (11 CDs) (2003) [*Die Walküre* in this set is conducted by Erich Leinsdorf, 1941]

Tannhäuser (Dresden version), New York, live broadcast, 18 January 1936, abridged[19]
Tannhäuser, Lauritz Melchior; Elisabeth, Kirsten Flagstad; Wolfram, Lawrence Tibbett; Venus, Margaret Halstead; Hermann, Emanuel List; Walther, Hans Clemens; Heinrich, Giordano Paltrinieri; Biterolf, Arnold Gabor; Reinmar, James Wolfe; Shepherd, Editha Fleischer; Metropolitan Opera Chorus and Orchestra

LP: The Golden Age of Opera EJS 109 (1956)

CD: Walhall WHL 30 (1996); Archipel ARPCD 0038 (2001); Cantus Classics CACD 5.00933 (2007) (audio in MP3 format)

Die Meistersinger, New York, live broadcast, 22 February 1936, abridged[20]
Hans Sachs, Friedrich Schorr; Eva, Elisabeth Rethberg; Walther von Stolzing, René Maison; Magdalene, Karin Branzell; David, Hans Clemens; Beckmesser, Eduard Habich; Pogner, Emanuel List; Kothner, Julius Huehn; Vogelgesang, Marek Windheim; Nachtigall. Louis D'Angelo; Ortel, Arnold Gabor; Zorn, Angelo Badà; Moser, Max Altglass; Eisslinger, Giordano Paltrinieri; Foltz, James Wolfe; Schwarz, Dudley Marwick; Night Watchman, Arnold Gabor; Metropolitan Opera Chorus and Orchestra

LP: The Golden Age of Opera EJS 492 (1970)

CD: Music & Arts CD-652; Guild Historical GHCD 2244/7 (2003)

[19] The cuts in the performance were: in Act 2, scene 4, from *Auch ihn darf mich so glücklich nennen* (Tannhäuser) to *Heil Wolfram! Preis sei deinem Liede!* (Chorus), and from *Dies Schwert wird dich erreichen* (Chorus) to *Ich nenn' es nicht mehr mein, nicht mehr mein* (Elizabeth); in Act 3, scene 3, from *Wir neben mir der schwerstbedrückte Pilger* to *um meines Engels Tränen zu versüssen!* (Tannhäuser)

[20] The cuts in the performance were: in Act 1, scene 2, from *Der Kurze, lang und überlang Ton* (David) to *…sing ich die eitel Brot- und Wasserweiss'* (David); in Act 2, scene 6, from *O Eva! Eva! Schlimmes Weib* (Sachs) to *O ha! Tralalei! Tralalei! O he!* (Sachs), from *O ha! Wollt mich beim Wahne fassen?* (Sachs) to *daß ich mich darnach richt* (Beckmesser), from *Oh, Ihr boshafte Geselle!* (Beckmesser) to *mit dem Hammer auf den Leisten halt ich Gericht* (Sachs); in Act 3, scene 2, from *Doch lehrt es wohl den Zauberspruch* (Sachs) to *Den Takt dazu hörtet Ihr auch!* (Sachs), from *Abendlich glühend* (Walther) to *des Traumes Deutung würd' er berichten* (Sachs); in scene 3, from *Und seht nur, wie mir's ergeht* to *mit dem besieg ich jed' Hindernis* (Beckmesser), from *Hans Sachs, mein Teurer* to *und brennt doch die Ferse* (Beckmesser); in scene 4, from *Nun schau, ob dazu mein Schuh geriet?* to *Wo Teufel er jetzt nur wieder steckt!* (Sachs); in scene 5, from *Herr Merker! Sagt, wie geht's?* (Sachs) to *doch hoff ich auf Eure Popularität* (Beckmesser), and from *Abendlich dämmernd* (Walther) to *Fahret fort, und schließt!* (Sachs).

1937

Tristan und Isolde, New York, live broadcast, 2 January 1937, abridged[21]
Tristan, Lauritz Melchior; Isolde, Kirsten Flagstad; Kurwenal, Julius Huehn; Brangäne, Kerstin Thorborg; King Marke, Ludwig Hofmann; Melot, Arnold Gabor; Sailor's Voice, Karl Laufkötter; Shepherd, Hans Clemens; Steersman, James Wolfe; Metropolitan Opera Chorus and Orchestra

LP: The Golden Age of Opera EJS 157 (1959) (Act 1 Prelude omitted)
CD: The 40s FT0 304.6 (1995);[22] Walhall WHL 22 (1995);[23] Walhall Eternity WLCD 0103 (2005)

Siegfried, New York, live broadcast, 30 January 1937, abridged[24]
Siegfried, Lauritz Melchior; Brünnhilde, Kirsten Flagstad; Wanderer, Friedrich Schorr; Erda, Kerstin Thorborg; Mime, Karl Laufkötter; Alberich, Eduard Habich; Fafner, Emanuel List; Forest Bird, Stella Andreva; Metropolitan Opera Chorus and Orchestra

LP: The Golden Age of Opera EJS 173 (1960)[25]; Bruno Walter Society IGI 373 (3 LPs)
CD: Music & Arts CD-696 (1991); Archipel ARPCD 0006-3 (2000); Naxos 8.110211-13 (2002); Guild Historical GHCD 2207/9 (2002)[26]; *Der Ring des Nibelungen*: Naxos Historical 8.501106 (11 CDs) (2003) [*Die Walküre* in this set is conducted by Erich Leinsdorf, 1941]

Das Rheingold, Boston, live broadcast, 3 April 1937, unabridged[27]
Wotan, Friedrich Schorr; Fricka, Karin Branzell; Alberich, Eduard Habich; Loge, René Maison; Erda, Doris Doe; Fasolt, Norman Cordon; Fafner, Emanuel List; Freia,

[21] The cuts in the performance were the same as those in the 1935 performance, except that all of King Marke's lines in Act 3 were retained.

[22] This CD set has "improved" the original recording on LP by substituting passages with the same singers from other performances recorded in better technical quality. There is no advice to the purchaser or listener that this has been done. The most obvious example is a sudden improvement in sound quality and corresponding drop in tension for a short passage in Act 1, scene 4, from *Herrn Tristan bringe meinen Gruss* (Isolde) to *nun harrt, wie er mich hört* (Kurwenal); the corresponding passage on the LPs has a minor defect; the substituted passage bears a striking resemblance to the recording of Erich Leinsdorf at the Metropolitan Opera on 23 March 1940 when Flagstad and Huehn were also singing Isolde and Kurwenal. I have not heard the other CD issues.

[23] This set includes prolonged applause at the end and commentary by Milton Cross.

24 The cuts in the performance were in the Wanderer/Siegfried scene in Act 3, scene 2, from *Ein Vöglein schwatzt wohl manches* (Wanderer) to *weh' ihm, holen sie's ein!* (Wanderer), and in the Brünnhilde/Siegfried scene (scene 3) from *birg' meinen Mut mir nicht mehr!* (Siegfried) to *O Weib, jetzt lösche den Brand!* (Siegfried). Acts 1 and 2 were uncut.

[25] The label gives the date as "January 22, 1937"; *Siegfried* was performed on that date, but it was the performance of 30 January that was broadcast. Excerpts were also issued on EJS 338 (1965) and UORC 159 (1973) (Act 3: Siegfried-Brünnhilde duet: *Heil dir Sonne!* to the end of the opera); and on UORC 158 (1973) (Act 1: *Nothung! Nothung!* to the end of the Act).

[26] The booklet accompanying the Guild set states: "A truly complete performance of a Wagner opera did not occur until Erich Leinsdorf took over Wagner production in 1940." This is incorrect: Bodanzky conducted several uncut performances of Wagner's works, as the MetOpera Database shows, and two such performances, *Das Rheingold* and *Die Walküre* from 1937, are listed above.

[27] *Das Rheingold* was performed in two sections, allowing an intermission before Wotan and Loge descend into Nibelheim. The Guild set recreates a single-act drama using parts of other recordings.

Dorothee Manski; Froh, Hans Clemens; Donner, Julius Huehn; Mime, Karl Laufkötter; Woglinde, Stella Andreva; Wellgunde, Irra Petina; Flosshilde, Doris Doe; Metropolitan Opera Chorus and Orchestra

LP: The Golden Age of Opera EJS 249 (1962)

CD: Walhall WHL 4 (1994); Naxos 8.110047-48 (1999); Guild Historical GHCD 2221/2 (2002)[28]; *Der Ring des Nibelungen*: Naxos Historical 8.501106 (11 CDs) (2003) [*Die Walküre* in this set is conducted by Erich Leinsdorf, 1941]

Die Walküre, New York, live broadcast, 18 December 1937, Acts 2 and 3, unabridged[29]
Brünnhilde, Marjorie Lawrence; Siegmund, Lauritz Melchior; Sieglinde, Kirsten Flagstad; Wotan, Friedrich Schorr; Fricka, Kerstin Thorborg; Hunding, Ludwig Hofmann; Gerhilde, Thelma Votipka; Grimgerde, Irra Petina; Helmwige, Dorothee Manski; Ortlinde, Irene Jessner; Roßweiße, Lucielle Browning; Schwertleite, Anna Kaskas; Siegrune, Helen Olheim; Waltraute, Doris Doe; Metropolitan Opera Orchestra

CD: Walhall WHL 21 (1995) and Archipel ARPCD 0039-3 (2001) (both sets also contain Act 1 and Act 2 excerpts from the 2 February 1935 performance)

1938

Tristan und Isolde, New York, live broadcast, 29 January 1938, excerpt, abridged[30]
Act 2, scene 2: from *O sink' hernieder* (Tristan, Isolde) to *Rette dich, Tristan!* (Kurwenal) (17' 34")
Tristan, Lauritz Melchior; Isolde, Kirsten Flagstad; Kurwenal, Julius Huehn; Brangäne, Gertrud Wettergren, Metropolitan Opera Orchestra

LP: *Kirsten Flagstad Memorial (1937 - 1949)*: The Golden Age of Opera EJS 258 (1963)

Parsifal, New York, live broadcast, 15 April 1938, Acts 1 and 3,[31] unabridged
Parsifal, Lauritz Melchior; Kundry, Kirsten Flagstad; Amfortas, Friedrich Schorr, Gurnemanz, Emanuel List; Klingsor, Arnold Gabor; Titurel, Norman Cordon; Voice, Doris Doe, First Esquire, Natalie Bodanya; Second Esquire, Helen Olheim; Third Esquire, Giordano Paltrinieri; Fourth Esquire, Karl Laufkötter; First Knight, George Cehanovsky, Second Knight, Louis D'Angelo; Metropolitan Opera Chorus and Orchestra

LP: The Golden Age of Opera EJS 484 (1969)

CD: Myto MCD 982.H013 (1998)

28 On this recording, the role of Erda is substituted by 1940 studio recordings of Kerstin Thorborg (Victor 17221).

29 Although the performance was unabridged, there were eleven short breaks in each act as the recording discs were changed, and therefore a loss of a few bars on each occasion.

30 The cut in the excerpt from the performance was from *Tag und Tod* (Isolde) to *Tristan der Tod gegeben?* (Isolde)

31 Erich Leinsdorf conducted Act 2

Siegfried, New York, live broadcast, 10 December 1938, excerpt, abridged[32]
Act 3, scene 3: *Heil dir Sonne!* to the end of the opera (26' 51")
Siegfried, Carl Hartmann; Brünnhilde, Kirsten Flagstad; Metropolitan Opera Orchestra
LP: The Golden Age of Opera EJS 550 (1971)

1939[33]

Götterdämmerung, New York, live broadcast, 12 May 1939, excerpt, unabridged
Prologue: *Zu neuen Taten* (Brünnhilde) to *Heil! Heil! Heil!* (Brünnhilde and Siegfried) (12' 11")
Brünnhilde, Kirsten Flagstad; Siegfried, Lauritz Melchior; Metropolitan Opera Orchestra
LP: The Golden Age of Opera EJS 167 (1959)

[32] The cut in the performance was from *birg' meinen Mut mir nicht mehr!* (Siegfried) to *O Weib, jetzt lösche den Brand!* (Siegfried).

[33] The Library of Congress holds a recording of the *Tristan und Isolde* broadcast from the Metropolitan Opera House on 8 April 1939 (Pelletier LWO 8944 and 8945). Act 3 is incomplete. The performance was abridged: two cuts in the Act 2 love duet and one in King Marke's monologue, and two cuts in Act 3 to Tristan's delirium.

2. Karl Böhm conducts Wagner[1]

Works recorded, including excerpts:

Rienzi: 1978-79

Der fliegende Holländer: 1939, 1963,1965, 1971, 1980

Tannhäuser: 1939, 1950, 1956, 1978-79

Lohengrin: 1939, 1965, 1967, 1975, 1980

Tristan und Isolde: 1949, 1960, 1962, 1966, 1968, 1969, 1970, 1973, 1980

Die Meistersinger von Nürnberg: 1935, 1936, 1938, 1939, 1940, 1943, 1944, 1959, 1964, 1965, 1968, 1975, 1977, 1978-79

Der Ring des Nibelungen: 1966-67

Das Rheingold:

Die Walküre: 1949, 1960, 1965, 1966

Siegfried:

Götterdämmerung:

Parsifal: 1978-79

1935

Die Meistersinger, live performance, 15 November 1935, excerpts

Act 1: Prelude (first 1' 37" only)

Act 3: Finale, from *Auf Meister Pogner!* (Meistersinger) (7' 18")

Hans Sachs, Wilhelm Rode; Walther von Stolzing, Eyvind Laholm; Veit Pogner, Wilhelm Schirp; Orchestra and Chorus of Deutsche Oper (formerly the Städtische Oper Berlin)

(German newsreel on the opening of the Deutsches Opernhaus)[2]

Video: *Great Conductors of the Third Reich*: Bel Canto Society BCS-0052 (VHS, 1997; DVD, 2005) (a film produced by Stefan Zucker); *Great Conductors*: Dreamlife DLVC 8092 (DVD, 2008)

[1] For early discographies, see F.F. Clough and G.J. Cuming, "A Karl Böhm Discography," *Audio and Record Review*, vol. 3, no. 9 (May 1964), 12-13; Robert Werba, "Karl-Böhm-Discographie," *Österreichische Musikzeitschrift*, vol. 24, no. 8 (1969), 489-493; Mike Ashman in *Records & Recording*, vol. 17 no. 12 (Sept 1974), p. 32, and vol. 18, no. 5 (Feb 1975), at p. 8; Franz Endler, *Karl Böhm: ein Dirigentenleben* (Hamburg: Hoffmann und Campe, 1981), at pp. 259-77; John Hunt, *Mid-Century Conductors* (London: John Hunt, 1992), at pp. 74-81; and John Hunt, *Wagner im Festspielhaus* (London: John Hunt, 2006). For this discography I confirmed Bayreuth Festival performance dates with the Richard Wagner Museum and, through them, broadcast dates with Bavarian Radio. I have added in footnotes performances broadcast from the Bayreuth and from the Metropolitan Opera House in New York which had not at the time of writing appeared on disc.

[2] Karl Böhm is not seen in the film, though his name is visible on a shot of the program. He replaced Wilhelm Furtwängler, who was ill. "One could not have found anyone better": *Berliner Morgenpost*, 17 November 1935, p. [37] (Josef Rufer).

1936

Die Meistersinger, Act 3, Prelude
Berlin Philharmonic Orchestra, 24 April 1936
(2RA 1109-2/1110-1)
78: Electrola EH962; HMV AF547 (Spain); HMV C2840 (England)
LP: *Berliner Philharmoniker100 Jahre*: EMI 1C 137-54 095/99 (RLS 768) (1982)
CD: *Berliner Philharmoniker Bruno Walter* [et al.]: Toshiba EMI SGR-7159 (2003)

1938

Die Meistersinger, Act 3, Staatsoper Dresden, August 1938
Hans Sachs, Hans Hermann Nissen; Veit Pogner, Sven Nilsson; Sixtus Beckmesser, Eugen Fuchs; Walther von Stolzing, Torsten Ralf; Eva, Margarete Teschemacher; Magdalene, Lene Jung; David, Martin Kremer, Chorus of the Dresden State Opera, the Saxon State Orchestra
(2RA 3054-3083)
78: Electrola DB 4562-76
LP: Electrola E 80983; *Böhm in Dresden - Volume IV - Oper - Sächsische Staatskapelle*: EMI Electrola 1C 137-53 514/19M (1979)
CD: Pearl GEMM CDS 9121 (1994) (gives recording date as 1939); Preiser 89236 (1999); Malibran CDRG 145 (1999); *Edition Staatskapelle Dresden Vol. 2*: Profil PH05038 (2005); *Karl Böhm conducts Richard Wagner: Edition Staatskapelle Dresden Vol. 22*: Profil PH07058 (2007) (Prelude to Act 3 and finale - *Verachtet mir die Meister nicht* - only)

1939

Lohengrin, Bridal Chorus
(ORA 3526/7-1), ca. January 1939
78: Electrola DA 4456

Die Meistersinger, Act 1, Prelude
(2RA 4042-2A, 4043-2A), July 1939
78: Electrola DB 4698

Tannhäuser, Overture
(2RA 4384-1, 4385-1, 4386-2, 4387-1), ca. August-September 1939
78: Electrola DB 5555/56

Der fliegende Holländer, Overture
(2RA 4388-2, 4389-1, 4390-1), ca. August-September 1939
78: Electrola DB 5553/54

Lohengrin, Act 3, Prelude
(2RA 4391-1), ca. August-September 1939
78: Electrola DB 5554

Lohengrin, Act 2, Procession to the Minster
(2RA 4392-2), ca. August-September 1939
78: Electrola DB 5551

Tannhäuser, Act 2, *Einzug der Gäste*
(2RA 4393-2), August-September 1939
78: Electrola DB 5551

Sächsische Staatskapelle, Chorus of Sächsische Staatsoper Dresden, Staatsoper Dresden
LP: *Böhm in Dresden - Volume IV - Oper - Sächsische Staatskapelle*: EMI Electrola 1C 137-53 514/19M (1979)
CD: *Karl Böhm conducts Richard Wagner: Edition Staatskapelle Dresden Vol. 22*: Profil PH07058 (2007)

1940

Die Meistersinger, Act 2, *Was duftet doch der Flieder*
Josef Herrmann (Hans Sachs), Sächsische Staatskapelle, Staatsoper Dresden
(2RA 4812-2, 4813-2), December 1940
78: Electrola DB 5623
LP: *Böhm in Dresden - Volume IV - Oper - Sächsische Staatskapelle*: EMI Electrola 1C 137-53 514/19M (1979)
CD: *Karl Böhm conducts Richard Wagner: Edition Staatskapelle Dresden Vol. 22*: Profil PH07058 (2007)

1943

Die Meistersinger, Vienna, live performance, 28 January 1943, excerpts (ca. 39 mins)
Act 2, scenes 3 and 4: from *Was duftet doch der Flieder* (Sachs) ... with the complete Eva-Sachs scene from *Gut'n Abend, Meister!* (Eva) to *Das dacht ich wohl! Nun heißt's: schaff rat!* (Sachs) (15' 13")
Act 2, scene 6: from *Drauf zu! Den Lung'rer mach' ich kalt* (Walther) (8' 20")... *Jerum! Jerum!* (Sachs) to *Die sind's gewöhnt: 's hört keiner drauf "O Eva! Eva!"* (Sachs) (8' 20")
Act 3, scene 4: from *Steh auf, Geselle* (Sachs)... with the complete quintet: *Selig wie die Sonne...auf den höchsten Preis* (Eva, with Sachs, Walther, David, Magdalene) (6' 18")
Act 3, scene 5: from *Morgenlich leuchtend in rosigem Schein* to *Parnaß und Paradies!* (Walther) (4' 24")
Act 3, scene 5: from *Verachtet mir die Meister nicht* to *die heil'ge deutsche Kunst!* (Sachs) (4' 21")
Hans Sachs, Josef Hermann; Sixtus Beckmesser, Erich Kunz; Walther von Stolzing, Max Lorenz; Eva, Maria Reining; Magdalene, Marta Rohs; David, Peter Klein, Chorus and Orchestra of the Vienna State Opera
CD: *Edition Wiener Staatsoper Live – Vol. 23*: Koch Schwann 3-1473-2 (1994)

Die Meistersinger, Vienna, live performance, 31 January 1943, excerpts (ca. 26 mins)
Act 1, scene 3: from *Am stillen Herd in Winterseit* (Walther) to *Ei nun, er wagt's!* (Vogelgesang) (with an interruption) (4' 25")
Act 1, scene 3: *Fanget an!* (Beckmesser) to *beleg ich erst noch vor der Meister Rat* (Beckmesser, with Walther and Pogner) (3' 54")
Act 3, scene 2: from *Abendlich glühend* (Walther) to *gelungen ist auch der zweite Bar* (Sachs) (2' 48")

Act 3, scene 3: from *"Weiten die Sterne…"* (Walther) to *Hat man mit dem Schuhwerk nicht seine Not!* (Sachs) (2' 46")

Act 3, scene 4: the complete quintet: *Selig wie die Sonne…auf den höchsten Preis* (Eva, with Sachs, Walther, David, Magdalene) (4' 31")

Act 3, scene 5: from *Wach auf, es nahet gen den Tag* to *Heil! Heil!* (Chorus) (3' 07")

Act 3, scene 5: from *Morgenlich leuchtend in rosigem Schein* to *Parnaß und Paradies!* (Walther) (4' 28")

Hans Sachs, Paul Schöffler; Veit Pogner, Kurt Böhme; Kunz Vogelgesang, Richard Sallaba; Konrad Nachtigall, Georg Monthy; Sixtus Beckmesser, Erich Kunz; Fritz Kothner, Fritz Krenn; Balthasar Zorn, Egyd Toriff; Ulrich Eißlinger, Hermann Gallos; Augustin Moser, William Wernigk; Hermann Ortel, Hans Schweiger; Hans Schwarz, Roland Neumann; Hans Foltz, Karl Ettl; Walther von Stolzing, Set Svanholm; Eva, Maria Reining; Magdalene, Martha Rohs; David, Peter Klein; Nightwatchman, Karl Ettl; Chorus and Orchestra of the Vienna State Opera

CD: *Edition Wiener Staatsoper Live – Vol. 19*: Koch Schwann 3-1469-2 (1994)

1944[3]

Die Meistersinger, Vienna, live performance, 19 January 1944, excerpts (ca. 84 mins)

Act 1, Prelude, to within a few bars of its end (with an interruption) (8' 18")

Act 1, scene 3: from *Am stillen Herd in Winterseit* (Walther) to *Entnahmt ihr was der Worte Schwall?* (Beckmesser) (4' 56")

Act 2, scenes 3 and 4: from *Was duftet doch der Flieder* (Sachs) …with the complete Eva-Sachs scene from *Gut'n Abend, Meister!* (Eva) to *brennt' er's lieber, da würd er doch warm!* (Eva) (with two interruptions) (13' 55")

Act 2, scene 6: from *Jerum! Jerum! Hallo hallohe!* (Sachs) to *"Den Tag seh ich erscheinen, der mir wohl gefall'n tut…"* (Beckmesser) (with two interruptions) (13' 41")

Act 2, scene 6: from *"Darf ich mich Meister nennen…"* (Beckmesser) into the riot scene and within a few bars of the end of the Act (4' 50")

Act 3, Prelude, complete (with an interruption) to *Gleich Meister! Hier!… Mir war's, als rieft Ihr mich eben?* (David) (8' 02")

Act 3, scene 1: from *Wahn! Wahn! Überall Wahn!* (Sachs) (the complete monologue, with an interruption)… *Grüß Gott, mein Junker* (Sachs) to *ich fürcht ihn mir vergehn zu sehn* (Walther) (8' 22")

Act 3, scene 3: from the orchestral passage preceding *Ein Werbelied! Von Sachs!* (Beckmesser) to *je besser bekommt's der Eh'!* (Sachs) (4' 41")

Act 3, scene 4: from *O Sachs! Mein Freund!* (Eva) …to *Ein Kind ward hier geboren… lud mich und die Pognerin zu Gewatter* (Sachs) (4' 53")

Act 3, scenes 4 and 5, after the end of the quintet: from *Jetzt all' am Fleck* (Sachs) to *Hungersnot! Hungersnot!* (bakers) (4' 46")

Act 3, scene 5: from *Seht, Meister Sachs! … Wach auf, es nahet gen den Tag* to *Heil! Heil!* (Chorus) (3' 30")

Act 3, scene 5: from *mit allem Hab' und Eigen* to *die Kunst und Ihre Meister ehrt* (Sachs) (1' 41")

Act 3, scene 5: from *Das Lied, fürwahr, ist nicht von mir* to *Der tret als Zeug in diesen Kreis!* (Sachs, with mastersingers and chorus) (2' 21")

Hans Sachs, Josef Herrmann; Veit Pogner, Kurt Böhme; Kunz Vogelgesang, Richard Sallaba; Konrad Nachtigall, Georg Monthy; Sixtus Beckmesser, Erich Kunz; Fritz Kothner, Fritz Krenn; Balthasar Zorn, Egyd Toriff; Ulrich Eißlinger, Hermann Gallos;

[3] see also Strauss discography below for an unverified recording by Böhm of the *Meistersinger* Prelude

Augustin Moser, William Wernigk; Hermann Ortel, Hans Schweiger; Hans Schwarz, Roland Neumann; Hans Foltz, Franz Worff; Walther von Stolzing, Torsten Ralf; David, Peter Klein; Eva, Maria Reining; Magdalene, Marta Rohs; Nightwatchman, Karl Ettl[4]; Chorus and Orchestra of the Vienna State Opera

CD: *Edition Wiener Staatsoper Live - Vol. 18*: Koch Schwann 3-1468-2 (1994)

Die Meistersinger, Vienna, live performances, 28-30 November, and 1, 4 & 5 December 1944

Hans Sachs, Paul Schöffler; Veit Pogner, Herbert Alsen; Kunz Vogelgesang, Anton Dermota; Konrad Nachtigall, Viktor Madin; Sixtus Beckmesser, Erich Kunz; Fritz Kothner, Fritz Krenn; Balthasar Zorn, Georg Maikl; Ulrich Eißlinger, Josef Witt; Augustin Moser, William Wernigk; Hermann Ortel, Alfred Muzzarelli; Hans Schwarz, Alfred Jerger; Hans Foltz, Marjan Rus; Walther von Stolzing, August Seider; Eva, Irmgard Seefried; Magdalene, Else Schürhoff; David, Peter Klein; Nightwatchman, Viktor Madin; Chorus and Orchestra of the Vienna State Opera

CD: Preiser 90234 (1995);[5] Arkadia 78061 (1995); Cantus Classics CACD 5.00143/44[6]

1949

Die Walküre, Act 2, scene 4, complete: *Siegmund, sieh' auf* (Brünnhilde, with Siegmund) (18' 00")

(2EA 13919-1, 13920-1B, 13921-2, and 13922-2)

78: DB 6962/63, 4 June 1949

Tristan und Isolde, Act 2, scene 2, *O sink' hernieder* to *höchste Liebes-Lust!* (23' 30")

(2EA 13923-2B, 13924-1C, 13927-1E, 13928-1E, 13925-2C, 13926-1C), 5 June 1949

78: DB 21112/14

Kirsten Flagstad, Set Svanholm, Constance Shacklock, Philharmonia Orchestra, Studio No. 1, Abbey Road, London

LP: Victor LM-1151 (1951); *Das Kirsten Flagstad-Album*: EMI 1C 147-01 491/92M (1973); *Kirsten Flagstad sings Wagner*: EMI EX 29 1227 3 (1987)

CD: *Kirsten Flagstad*: Testament SBT 1018 (1993)

[4] as given on the CD. The program lists Rouland Neumann as the Nightwatchman.

[5] Reviewing the Preiser set for *American Record Guide* (July/August 1995, p. 274), John P. McKelvey wrotes: "One of the 13 original reels of tape that held this performance was lost in the turbulent period at the end of WWII... The lost section, from the beginning of Act III up to the end of the Wahn monolog, consumes about 22 minutes (roughly 8%) of the total playing time. Preiser has solved the problem by splicing in the missing section from Abendroth's 1943 Bayreuth recording. This solution shows immediately why Böhm's performance excels both musically and sonically. It is as though a grey veil is lifted when Abendroth finishes, the bright sunlight breaking through on Böhm's return. Preiser's rationale for this solution is that Paul Schöffler sings Sachs in both recordings."

[6] This set has a short passage in Act 3, Scene 4 - *Mein Kind, von Tristan und Isolde...* to *Nehmet euren Stand!* (Sachs) (ca. 1' 33") missing between CDs 3 and 4, possibly the result of a production fault.

1950

Tannhäuser (Dresden version), Naples, live performance, 12 March 1950, abridged[7]
Landgraf Hermann, Boris Christoff; Tannhäuser, Hans Beirer; Wolfram, Carlo Tagliabue; Walther, Petre Munteanu; Biterolf, Augusto Romani; Heinrich, Gianni Avolanti; Reinmar, Igino Riccò; Elisabeth, Renata Tebaldi; Venus, Lyvia Pery; Young Shepherd, Gilda Martini Rossi; Orchestra and Chorus of the San Carlo Theatre, Naples
(sung in Italian with Beirer singing in German)

LP: The Golden Age of Opera EJS 424 (1968) (seven excerpts from Acts 1 and 3)[8]

CD: Hardy Classics HCA 6004-2 (1999); excerpts in *Tebaldi sings Wagner*: Legato Classics Standing Room Only SRO-834-1

1956

Tannhäuser (Dresden version), Naples, live performance, 17 March 1956, abridged[9]
Landgraf Hermann, Gottlob Frick; Tannhäuser, Rudolf Lustig; Wolfram, Marcel Cordes; Walther, Karl Terkal; Biterolf, Philip Curzon; Heinrich, Karl Gustav; Jehrlander, Reinmar, Ljubomir Pantscheff; Elisabeth, Leonie Rysanek; Venus, Birgit Nilsson; Young Shepherd, Patricia Brinton; Orchestra and Chorus of the San Carlo Theatre, Naples
(sung in German, except for the choruses of sirens and pilgrims, who sing in Italian)

CD: Melodram MEL 37073 (1990); I Grandi Della Classica 93.5137 (1993); Archipel ARPCD 0011 (2000); Walhall Eternity WLCD 0174 (2006); Andromeda ANDRCD 9065 (2010)

[7] There were several cuts (see note to 1956 performance), including in Act 1, scene 1, from *Dir töne Lob!... O Königin, Göttin! Lass mich ziehn!* (Tannhäuser) to *Geliebter, wessen klagest du mich an?* (sung in Italian) (Venus). Although the performance was recorded, it may not have been broadcast because of a prohibition by Böhm: he was concerned over the standard of the orchestra: Böhm, *A life remembered: memoirs,* trans John Kehoe (London: Boyars, 1992), p. 114. It is not listed for broadcast on either *Rete azzurra* or *Rete rossa* in *Il Tempi di Milano*, 12 March 1950, p. 4 (*RADIOTRASMISSIONI*). William Youngren commented on the recording: "he does what he can, pushing his inadequate band throught the music in his usual efficient, often exciting, fashion." *Fanfare*, September/October 1999, p. 376. Yet, for all that, "it was pretty much a sensational success." Böhm, *ibid*, p. 114

[8] Although Max Lorenz is listed as the singer of Tannhäuser in *Cronache del Teatro di S. Carlo 1948-1968* (Milan: Recordi, 1969), the singer is Hans Beirer. The notes to EJS 424 in William Shaman et al., *EJS*, state that "Hans Beirer sang, not Max Lorenz, who was forced to cancel because of ill health." The authors state that the complete performance was issued on HRE 201-3 (ca. 1976), which dates the performance as 1949 on its box. The recording is not listed in Hunt, *Mid-Century Conductors*.

[9] There were several small cuts. They were enumerated by William Youngren in his review in *Fanfare*, July/August 1990, p. 313, where he commented on the Melodram issue: "... you don't really need to bother with it. The mono sound is restricted and boxy; the orchestral playing is quite poor... Poor Böhm does what he can...." cf. Roland Graeme in *Opera Quarterly*, vol. 19 no. 1 (Winter 2003) on the Archipel issue: the "sound is decent... The orchestral playing is acceptable." (p. 90). The performance was not listed for broadcast on 17 March in *Corriere della Sera*, 17 March, p. 4 (*Radio transmissioni di oggi*).

1959

Die Meistersinger, New York, live broadcast, 7 March 1959, abridged[10]
Hans Sachs, Otto Edelmann; Veit Pogner, Giorgio Tozzi; Kunz Vogelgesang, Charles Anthony; Konrad Nachtigall, Calvin Marsh; Sixtus Beckmesser, Karl Dönch; Fritz Kothner, Marko Rothmüller; Balthasar Zorn, William Olvis; Ulrich Eißlinger, Robert Nagy; Augustin Moser, Gabor Carelli; Hermann Ortel, Osie Hawkins; Hans Schwarz, Ezio Flagello; Hans Foltz, Louis Sgarro; Walther von Stolzing, Sebastian Feiersinger; Eva, Aase Nordmo-Lövberg; Magdalene, Regina Resnik; David, Paul Franke; Nightwatchman, Clifford Harvuot; Metropolitan Opera Chorus and Orchestra
CD: Walhall Eternity WLCD 0303 (2010)

1960

Tristan und Isolde, New York, live broadcast, 9 January 1960, abridged[11]
Tristan, Ramon Vinay; Isolde, Birgit Nilsson; Kurwenal, Walter Cassel; Brangäne, Irene Dalis; King Marke, Jerome Hines; Melot, Calvin Marsh; Sailor's Voice, Charles Anthony; Shepherd, Paul Franke; Steersman, Louis Sgarro; Metropolitan Opera Chorus and Orchestra
CD: *Ramon Vinay*: Melodram MEL CDM 26519 (1990)[12] (Act 2 love scene only); Golden Melodram GM 1.0085 (2010);[13] Walhall Eternity WLCD 0307 (2011)

[10] The cuts in this performance were: in Act 1, scene 2, from *Der Kurze, lang und überlang Ton* (David) to *...sing ich die eitel Brot- und Wasserweiss'* (David), from *David!* (Apprentices) to *der wird als Meistersinger erkannt* (David); in scene 3, from *Was Euch zum Liede Richt und Schnur* to *des Lied erwerb sich Meisterpreis!* (Kothner); in Act 2, scene 6, from *O Eva! Eva! Schlimmes Weib* (Sachs) to *O ha! Tralalei! Tralalei! O he!* (Sachs), from *O ha! Wollt mich beim Wahne fassen?* (Sachs) to *daß ich mich darnach richt* (Beckmesser), from *Oh, Ihr boshafte Geselle!* (Beckmesser) to *mit dem Hammer auf den Leisten halt ich Gericht* (Sachs), from *Ich bin ja stumm!* (Sachs) to *"... um die Jungfrau zu frei'n"* (Beckmesser); in Act 3, scene 2, from *Mein Freund! Das grad ist Dichters Werk* (Sachs) to *Den Takt dazu hörtet Ihr auch!* (Sachs), from *Das nenn ich mir einen Abgesang* (Sachs) to *"...statt Frucht ein Sternenheer im Lorbeerbaum."* (Walther); scene 3, from *Und seht nur, wie mir's ergeht* to *mit dem besieg ich jed' Hindernis* (Beckmesser), from *Hans Sachs, mein Teurer* to *und brennt doch die Ferse* (Beckmesser); scene 5, from *Wenn ihr die Kunst so hoch schon ehrt* to *die Kunst und ihre Meister ehrt!* (Sachs), from *Herr Merker! Sagt, wie geht's?* (Sachs) to *doch hoff ich auf Eure Popularität* (Beckmesser), from *Wie er dazu kam, mag selbst er sagen* to *fänd er gerechte Richter* (Sachs, with Meistersinger and Volk), from *Abendlich dämmernd* (Walther) to *Fahret fort, und schließt!* (Sachs), and from *Drum, denkt mit Dank Ihr dran zurück* to *lebt's nicht in deutscher Meister Ehr* (Sachs).

[11] The cuts in this performance were: in Act 2, scene 2, from *Dem Tage! Dem Tage!* (Tristan) to *dass nachtsichtig mein Auge wahres zu sehen tauge* (Tristan, with Isolde); and in Act 3, Scene 1, from *Muss ich dich so versteh'n* to *Zu welchem Los?* (Tristan), and from *vor Sehnsucht nicht zu sterben!* to *Der Trank! Der Trank! der furchtbare Trank!* (Tristan).

[12] Incorrectly dated 16 January: there was no performance of *Tristan* on that date.

[13] WH Opera (New York, ca. 2005) issued what purported to be this performance under a catalogue number (WH 022) that had also been used for a broadcast performance of *Tristan* conducted by Georg Solti (Metropolitan Opera, 23 February 1963, same cast, except Karl Liebl sang Tristan and George Shirley the Sailor's voice). Whether or not this was a mistake, WH 022 and GM 1.0085 are clearly different performances. In the latter there are fewer cuts in the performance; there are recording drop-outs and gaps not present in WH022; and there is a radio announcement at the end that Tristan had been sung by Ramon Vinay.

Die Walküre, New York, live broadcast, 20 February 1960, Acts 2 and 3, abridged[14]
Brünnhilde, Birgit Nilsson; Siegmund, Jon Vickers; Sieglinde, Aase Nordmo-Lövberg; Wotan, Jerome Hines; Fricka, Irene Dalis; Hunding, Dezsö Ernster; Gerhilde, Carlotta Ordassy; Grimgerde, Martha Lipton; Helmwige, Heidi Krall; Ortlinde, Gloria Lind; Roßweiße, Margaret Roggero; Schwertleite, Belén Amparan; Siegrune, Helen Vanni; Waltraute, Mignon Dunn; Metropolitan Opera Chorus and Orchestra
CD: Treasure of the Earth TOE 2053 (2001)[15] (says "Wiener Staatsoper")

1962

Tristan und Isolde, Bayreuth, live broadcast, 24 July 1962
Tristan, Wolfgang Windgassen; Isolde, Birgit Nilsson; Brangäne, Kerstin Meyer; Kurwenal, Eberhard Wächter; King Marke, Josef Greindl; Melot, Niels Möller; Shepherd, Gerhard Stolze; Sailor, Georg Paskuda; Steersman, Hans Hanno Daum; Chorus and Orchestra of the Bayreuth Festival
LP: Melodram MEL 625 (1982)
CD: Golden Melodram GM 1.0073 (2005)

1963[16]

Der fliegende Holländer, New York, live broadcast, 16 February 1963
Holländer, George London; Senta, Leonie Rysanek; Erik, Sándor Kónya; Daland, Giorgio Tozzi; Mary, Lili Chookasian; Steersman, George Shirley, Metropolitan Opera Chorus and Orchestra
LP: excerpts on *Sándor Kónya*: Melodram MEL 658 (1984)
CD: GALA Classics GL 100.728 (2004)

1964[17]

Die Meistersinger, Bayreuth, live broadcast, 20 July 1964
Hans Sachs, Josef Greindl; Veit Pogner, Kurt Böhme; Kunz Vogelgesang, Ticho Parly; Konrad Nachtigall, Gerd Nienstedt; Sixtus Beckmesser, Carlos Alexander; Fritz Kothner, Gustav Neidlinger; Balthasar Zorn, Stefan Schwer; Ulrich Eißlinger, Günther Treptow; Augustin Moser, Hermann Winkler; Hermann Ortel, Zoltan Kelemen; Hans Schwarz, Fritz Linke; Hans Foltz, Ralph Telasko; Walther von Stolzing, Sándor Kónya; Eva, Anja Silja; Magdalene, Ruth Hesse; David, Erwin Wohlfahrt; Nightwatchman, Heinz Hagenau; Chorus and Orchestra of the Bayreuth Festival
CD: Golden Melodram GM 1.0074 (2005)

[14] The portions omitted from the performance were in Act 2, scene 2, from *der der Liebe fluchte* (Wotan) to *trügend verraten, wer mir traut!* (Wotan), in scene 4 from *Du sahst der Walküre sehrenden Blick* (Brünnhilde) to *Hella halte mich fest!* (Siegmund), and in Act 3, scene 3, from *Deinen leichten Sinn lass dich denn leiten* (Wotan) to *nicht kiesen kann ich es dir!* (Wotan, with Brünnhilde).

[15] Brünnhilde's lines at the end of Scene 2, *So sah ich Siegvater nie… Im [höchsten Leid muss dich treulos die Treue verlassen!]*, are missing from the recording.

[16] There was a live broadcast by Bavarian Radio on 26 July 1963 of Böhm's *Tristan* at Bayreuth.

[17] There was a live broadcast by Bavarian Radio on 18 July 1964 of Böhm's *Tristan* at Bayreuth.

1965[18]

Der fliegende Holländer, New York, live broadcast, 13 February 1965, (in three separate acts)
Dutchman, David Ward; Senta, Leonie Rysanek; Erik, Sándor Kónja; Daland, Giorgio Tozzi; Mary, Gladys Kriese; Steersman, George Shirley; Metropolitan Opera Chorus and Orchestra

CD: WH Opera WH 033

Lohengrin, Vienna, live performance, 16 May 1965
King Henry, Martti Talvela; Lohengrin, Jess Thomas; Elsa, Claire Watson; Telramund, Walter Berry; Ortrud, Christa Ludwig; Herald, Eberhard Wächter; Nobles, Kurt Equiluz, Fritz Sperlbauer, Herbert Lackner; Ljubomir Pantscheff; Chorus and Orchestra of the Vienna State Opera

LP: *Ouvertüren - Mozart, Beethoven, Wagner - Premieren der Wiener Staatsoper*: DG 2563 083[19] (Prelude to Act 1 and introduction to Act 3, scene 3)

CD: Golden Melodram GM 1.0045 (2000)[20]

Die Walküre, Bayreuth, live broadcast, 26 July 1965[21]
Siegmund, James King; Sieglinde, Leonie Rysanek; Wotan, Theo Adam; Brünnhilde, Birgit Nilsson; Hunding, Martti Talvela; Fricka, Ursula Boese; Gerhilde, Danica Mastilovic; Ortlinde, Isabella Doran; Waltraute, Gertraud Hopf; Schwertleite, Lili Chookasian; Helmwige, Liane Synek; Siegrune, Elisabeth Schärtel; Grimgerde, Ursula Boese; Roßweiße, Margarethe Bence; Orchestra of the Bayreuth Festival

CD: Premiere Opera 2234-3 (ca. 2005)[22]; excerpts on Legato Classics Standing Room Only SRO-833-2 (1992) (a performance of Strauss's *Elektra*)

[18] In addition to the recordings from the 1965 Bayreuth Festival of *Das Rheingold* and *Die Walküre* listed above (in the former case, in the footnote below), *Siegfried* and *Götterdämmerung* conducted by Böhm were broadcast on 28 and 30 July 1965 respectively. There was one cut in the *Ring* of 1965: "the Gutrune scene after the heroic dirge in Act III of *Götterdämmerung* was dropped and Hagen entered immediately, the hiatus being bridged by a drum roll." Wolfgang Wagner, *Acts: the autiobiography of Wolfgang Wagner*, trans. John Brownjohn (London: Weidenfeld & Nicolson, 1994), p. 136. John Culshaw, producer of the Solti *Ring* for Decca, characterised the cut somewhat differently: "in the 1965 production of *Götterdämmerung* at Bayreuth, Wieland Wagner cut the scene altogether, presumably with the connivance of the conductor, Karl Böhm, and proceeded directly from the end of the funeral march to the entry of Hagen in the final scene, thus saving two minutes and thirty-three seconds...." *Ring Resounding* (London: Secker & Warburg, 1967), p. 197.

[19] A record produced to support the Austrian Committee of the FAO-Freedom from Hunger Campaign.

[20] Although the Vienna State Opera has confirmed that a performance with this cast took place on 16 May 1965, the Preludes on DG (9' 56") and GM (8' 37") appear to be from different performances.

[21] Other Bavarian Radio broadcasts of the 1965 *Ring* were: *Das Rheingold* (25 July), *Siegfried* (28 July) and *Götterdämmerung* (30 July). Hunt does not list a complete recording of *Die Walküre* from 1965. He does, however, list a recording of *Das Rheingold* from 25 July on LP: Golden Treasury (USA) GTR 1 (*Wagner im Festspielhaus*, p. 120). No further information about this set or label has been forthcoming: they are not known to the dealers, collectors, discographers and libraries in the United States I have consulted. It may have been a private recording, as distinct from a "pirate" issue available commercially.

[22] A recording of the Bavarian Radio broadcast, with announcements, re-transmitted by the Broadcasting Foundation of America on WBAI (New York City) and WFMT (Chicago) in February 1966; the date on the discs is 14 August; however, Hunt dates the original Bavarian Radio broadcast as 26 July 1965 (*Wagner im Festspielhaus*, p. 120).

Die Walküre, Act 1, excerpts

Ein Schwert verhiess mir der Vater … lichtlose Glut! (Siegmund) (5' 26") [followed without a break by:]

Winterstürme wichen dem Wonnemond … Liebe und Lenz! (Siegmund) (2' 47")

Die Meistersinger, Act 1, Prelude (8' 51")

Jon Vickers, Toronto Symphony Orchestra, Massey Hall, Toronto, 10 October 1965, a CBC *Festival* concert telecast

DVD: *The Art of Karl Böhm*: VAI DVD 4233 (2003)

1966[23]

Tristan und Isolde, Bayreuth, 14-16 July (rehearsals), 4 and 16 August 1966 (live performances)

Tristan, Wolfgang Windgassen; Isolde, Birgit Nilsson; Brangäne, Christa Ludwig; Kurwenal, Eberhard Wächter; King Marke, Martti Talvela; Melot, Claude Heater; Shepherd, Erwin Wohlfahrt; Sailor, Peter Schreier; Steersman, Gerd Nienstedt; Chorus and Orchestra of the Bayreuth Festival

LP: Deutsche Grammophon LPM 39221-25 (1966); SLPM 139 221-25 (1966); 2713 001 (1966); 415 395-1 (side 10 is devoted to a rehearsal (29 mins) of the introduction and scene 1 from Act 3)

CD: Deutsche Grammophon 419 889-2 (1988); DG "Originals" 449 772-2 (1997); Philips 434 425-2 (1992); in *Wagner - The Great Operas from the Bayreuth Festival*: Decca 478 0279 (33 CDs) (2008)

Tristan und Isolde, Bayreuth, July 1966

Rehearsal of Act 3, Prelude and Scene 1 (29 mins)

LP: *Böhm in Bayreuth*: Philips 6833 195 (1 LP) (1976); *Karl Böhm bei den Bayreuther Festspielen*: Philips 6701 048 (2 LPs) (1976)

Tristan und Isolde, Bayreuth, live performance, 4 August 1966[24]

(same cast as for the July-August performances recorded by Deutsche Grammophon)

CD: Frequenz CML3 (1987)[25]

1966-67

Der Ring des Nibelungen, Bayreuth, live performances, July-August 1966-67

Das Rheingold, 26 July 1966

[23] The Bavarian Radio broadcasts of the 1966 *Ring* were: *Das Rheingold* (26 July), *Die Walküre* (27 July), *Siegfried* (29 July) and *Götterdämmerung* (31 July). The broadcasts of *Das Rheingold* and *Siegfried* were recorded and issued by Philips as part of the complete *Ring* cycle (see under **1966-67**).

[24] The 4 August performance was broadcast on 27 August.

[25] A production of Salvatore Caruselli; Hunt notes that the date 13 August on this disc and on other issues of this performance is incorrect. He lists the 4 August performance as having been broadcast (*Wagner im Festspielhaus*, p. 128). *Tristan* was conducted by Böhm at the 1966 Bayreuth Festival on 4, 16, and 20 August; it was broadcast by Bavarian Radio on 27 August.

Wotan, Theo Adam; Donner, Gerd Nienstedt; Froh, Hermin Esser; Loge, Wolfgang Windgassen; Alberich, Gustav Neidlinger; Mime, Erwin Wohlfahrt; Fasolt, Martti Talvela; Fafner, Kurt Böhme; Fricka, Annelies Burmeister; Freia, Anja Silja; Erda, Vera Soukupova; Woglinde, Dorothea Siebert; Wellgunde, Helga Dernesch; Floßhilde, Ruth Hesse

Die Walküre, July-August, 1967[26]
Siegmund, James King; Sieglinde, Leonie Rysanek; Wotan, Theo Adam; Brünnhilde, Birgit Nilsson; Hunding, Gerd Nienstedt; Fricka, Annelies Burmeister; Gerhilde, Danica Mastilovic; Ortlinde, Helga Dernesch; Waltraute, Gertraud Hopf; Schwertleite, Sieglinde Wagner; Helmwige, Liane Synek; Siegrune, Annelies Burmeister; Grimgerde, Elisabeth Schärtel; Roßweiße, Sona Cervená

Siegfried, 29 July 1966
Siegfried, Wolfgang Windgassen; Mime, Erwin Wohlfahrt; Brünnhilde, Birgit Nilsson; Wanderer, Theo Adam; Alberich, Gustav Neidlinger; Fafner, Kurt Böhme; Erda, Vera Soukupova; Waldvogel, Erika Köth

Götterdämmerung, 27 July and 14 August 1967[27]
Brünnhilde, Birgit Nilsson; Siegfried, Wolfgang Windgassen; Hagen, Josef Greindl; Alberich, Gustav Neidlinger; Gunther, Thomas Stewart; Gutrune, Ludmilla Dvoráková; Waltraute, Martha Mödl; Woglinde, Dorothea Siebert; Wellgunde, Helga Dernesch; Floßhilde, Sieglinde Wagner; Norns, Marga Höffgen, Annelies Burmeister, Anja Silja, Chorus and Orchestra of the Bayreuth Festival

LP: *Der Ring des Nibelungen*: Philips 6747 037 (16 LPs) (1973) and 420 325-1 (16 LPs)

CD: *Der Ring des Nibelungen*: Philips 420 325-2 (14 CDs) and 446 057-2 (14 CDs); in *Wagner - The Great Operas from the Bayreuth Festival*: Decca 478 0279 (33 CDs) (2008) (*Das Rheingold* and *Siegfried* are incorrectly dated 1971); Decca Collectors Edition 478 2367 (14 CDs) (2010)

1967

Lohengrin, New York, live broadcast, 21 January 1967, two excerpts

Act 1, scene 2: from *Einsam in trüben Tagen* (Elsa) to *Elsa, ich liebe dich!* (Lohengrin) (23' 30")

Act 3, scene 2: from *Das süsse Lied verhallt* (Lohengrin), with Elsa, to the end of the scene (21' 57")

Lohengrin, Sándor Kónya; Elsa, Ingrid Bjoner; [Ortrud, Christa Ludwig]; Telramund, Walter Berry; King Heinrich, John Macurdy; Herald, Sherrill Milnes; Noble, Dan Marek; Nobles, Robert Schmorr, Gene Boucher, and Ron Bottcher; Metropolitan Opera Chorus and Orchestra

CD: Gala GL 100.656 (2001)[28]

[26] Böhm conducted *Die Walküre* at the Bayreuth Festival on 23 July and 10 August 1967. The performances of *Das Rheingold*, *Die Walküre*, and *Siegfried* broadcast from the 1967 Festival were conducted by Otmar Suitner.

[27] The 27 July performance of *Götterdämmerung* was broadcast live by Bavarian Radio.

[28] The Gala set also includes excerpts from a Metropolitan Opera *Lohengrin* of 10 February 1968, purporting to be Karl Böhm conducting. However, Berislav Klobucar conducted *Lohengrin* on that occasion.

1968

Die Meistersinger, Bayreuth, live broadcast, 25 July 1968

Hans Sachs, Theo Adam; Veit Pogner, Karl Ridderbusch; Kunz Vogelgesang, Sebastian Feiersinger; Konrad Nachtigall, Dieter Slembeck; Sixtus Beckmesser, Thomas Helmsley; Fritz Kothner, Gerd Nienstedt; Balthasar Zorn, Günther Treptow; Ulrich Eißlinger, Erich Klaus; Augustin Moser, William Johns; Hermann Ortel, Heinz Feldhoff; Hans Schwarz, Fritz Linke; Hans Foltz, Hans Franzen; Walther von Stolzing, Waldemar Kmentt; Eva, Gwynwth Jones; Magdalene, Janis Martin; David, Hermin Esser; Nightwatchman, Kurt Moll; Chorus and Orchestra and the Bayreuth Festival

CD: Link 602-4 (ca. 1999); Golden Melodram GM 1.0038 (2000);[29] Orfeo d'Or C 753 084 L (2008)

Tristan und Isolde, Bayreuth, live broadcast, 28 July 1968

Tristan, Wolfgang Windgassen; Isolde, Birgit Nilsson; Brangäne, Grace Hoffman; Marke, Martti Talvela; Kurwenal, Gerd Feldhoff; Melot, Reid Bunger; Shepherd and Young Sailor, Hermin Esser; Steersman, Bengt Rundgren; Bayreuth Festival Chorus and Orchestra

CD: Live Opera Heaven LOH 1269 (ca. 2002)

1969

Tristan und Isolde, Bayreuth, live broadcast, 28 July 1969

Tristan, Wolfgang Windgassen; Isolde, Birgit Nilsson; Brangäne, Grace Hoffman; Marke, Martti Talvela; Kurwenal, Gerd Feldhoff; Melot, Reid Bunger; Shepherd, Hermin Esser; Steersman, Bengt Rundgren; Young Sailor, Hermin Esser, Bayreuth Festival Chorus and Orchestra

CD: OperaDepot.com OD 10143-3 (ca. 2008)[30]

1970[31]

Tristan und Isolde, Bayreuth, live broadcast, 24 July 1970

Tristan, Wolfgang Windgassen; Isolde, Birgit Nilsson; Brangäne, Grace Hoffman; Marke, Martti Talvela; Kurwenal, Gustav Neidlinger; Melot, Reid Bunger; Shepherd, Hermin Esser; Steersman, Bengt Rundgren; Young Sailor, Hermin Esser; Bayreuth Festival Chorus and Orchestra

CD: Link 611-4[32] (1999)

[29] Hunt states that this set is incorrectly dated 1969 (*Wagner im Festspielhaus*, p. 135); on the copy I have inspected, it is 1968.

[30] Included at the end of disc 3 are the multilingual announcements, including cast details, of Bavarian Radio.

[31] A performance of *Der fliegende Holländer*, conducted by Böhm, was broadcast from the Metropolitan Opera House on 31 January 1970. His last appearance in Wagner at the Metropolitan Opera was with this opera on 11 March 1970.

[32] This is the catalogue number as it appears on the CD set box and in the inset. The discs themselves bear the number "Link 611-2", and the markings "printed in U.S.A." and "(P) 1999 By Link Slovenian Made." Although not included in Hunt, he lists a recording of this performance as "private edition Vienna" (*Wagner im Festspielhaus*, p. 143). The performance is included in *Opera from Bayreuth*: [Michael Richter]

1971

Der fliegende Holländer, Bayreuth, live performances, August 1971[33]
Daland, Karl Ridderbusch; Senta, Gwyneth Jones; Erik, Hermin Esser; Mary, Sieglinde Wagner; Steersman, Harald Ek; Holländer, Thomas Stewart; Bayreuth Festival Chorus and Orchestra

LP: Deutsche Grammophon 2709 040; 2720 052; 2740 140; 413 291-1
CD: Deutsche Grammophon 437 710-2 (1993)

1973

Tristan und Isolde, Orange, live performance, abridged, 7 July 1973[34]
Tristan, Jon Vickers; Isolde, Birgit Nilsson; Brangäne, Ruth Hesse; Kurwenal, Walter Berry; King Marke, Bengt Rundgren; Melot, Stan Unruh; Shepherd, Sailor, and Steersman, Horst Laubenthal; Orchestre National de l'ORTF
LP: Historical Recording Enterprises HRE 359-4 (1982)
CD: Rodolphe RPC 32553.55 (1989); Opera d'Oro OPD-1297 (2001) (gives the date as 1971)

VHS Video: Dreamlife DMVB-18/19 (1993) (with Japanese subtitles)
LASER DISC: Dreamlife DMLB-18/19 (1993) (with Japanese subtitles)
DVD: Hardy Classic Video HCD 40009 (2003)

1975

Die Meistersinger, Act 1, Prelude, live performance, 19 March 1975
Vienna Philharmonic Orchestra, NHK Hall, Tokyo

LP: DG 415 164-1 in set 415 162-1 (4 LPs)
CD: *Die Aufnahme in der NHK Hall, Tokyo 1975*: DG POCG-3120 (1993); POCG-9406/12 (1993); POCG-90491/7 (1999)
DVD: *Karl Böhm Wiener Philharmoniker Live in Japan 1975*: NHK Classical NSDS-9483 (2 discs) (2006) (gives date as 18 March)

Die Meistersinger, Act 1, Prelude, live performance, 22 March 1975
Vienna Philharmonic Orchestra, NHK Hall, Tokyo

LP: DG 415 166-1 in set 415 162-1 (4 LPs)
CD: *Die Aufnahme in der NHK Hall, Tokyo 1975*: DG POCG-3121 (1993); POCG-9406/12 (1993); POCG-90491/7 (1999)

Audio Encyclopaedia AE203 (ca. 1999), a CD-ROM with thirteen Wagnerian operas in MP3 format.

[33] Böhm conducted *Der fliegende Holländer* on 1 and 10 August 1971. The performance of 1 August was broadcast by Bavarian Radio on 8 August.

[34] There was a cut in Act 2, Scene 2: from *Dem Tage! Dem Tage!* (Tristan) to *dass nachtsichtig mein Auge wahres zu sehen tauge* (Tristan). Böhm wrote in his memoirs that "sadly" he was rarely able to perform *Tristan* without cuts outside Bayreuth: *A Life Remembered*, p. 103. Of this particular performance he said, "you could have heard a pin drop as some 12,000 listeners followed the drama:" Robert Breuer, "Böhm Remembers," *Opera News*, August 1974, p. 15

Die Meistersinger, Act 1, Prelude, live performance, 25 March 1975
Vienna Philharmonic Orchestra, NHK Hall, Tokyo
LP: DG 410 891-1 in set 410 887-1 (4 LPs)
CD: *Die Aufnahme in der NHK Hall, Tokyo 1975*: DG POCG-3117 (1993); POCG-9406/12 (1993); POCG-90491/7 (1999)

Lohengrin, Act 3, Prelude, Vienna Philharmonic Orchestra, Musikvereinssaal, 2 June 1975
LP: *From the Heart - World Famous Artists Give Their Services for Cancer Research* [English title] *Stars im Zeichen eines guten Sterns* [German title]: Deutsche Grammophon 2563 555 (1975); 2531 288 (1981); 2543 211 (1981)
CD: Deutsche Grammophon 413 733-2

[1976][35]

1977

Die Meistersinger, Act 1, Prelude, dress rehearsal, 11 March 1977
Vienna Philharmonic Orchestra, Tokyo Bunka Kaikan
CD: TDK-OC005 (2001); JOYCD 9023/4

1978-79

Rienzi, Overture
Tannhäuser, Overture
Die Meistersinger, Act 1, Prelude
Parsifal, Act 1, Prelude (with concert ending)
Vienna Philharmonic Orchestra, Grosser Musikvereinsaal, Vienna, 20, 29 November 1978 and 12 March 1979
LP: Deutsche Grammophon 2531 214 (1979); 419 069-1 (1986) (all except *Rienzi*)
CD: Deutsche Grammophon 413 551-2 (ca. 1986)

1980

Der fliegende Holländer, Overture
Lohengrin, Prelude, Act 1
Tristan und Isolde, Prelude and Liebestod
Vienna Philharmonic Orchestra, Grosser Musikvereinsaal, Vienna, 19 March and 26 June 1980
LP: Deutsche Grammophon 2531 288 (1981); 2543 211 (1981); 419 069-1 (1986) (*Der fliegende Holländer* and *Lohengrin* only)
CD: Deutsche Grammophon 413 733-2 (1986); 419 069-2 (1986) (*Der fliegende Holländer* and *Lohengrin* only)

[35] There was a broadcast on 23 July 1976 of Böhm conducting the overture and festival meadow scene of *Die Meistersinger* as part of the Bayreuth Festival Centenary celebration, the last occasion on which he conducted there.

3. Hans von Bülow conducts Wagner

Hans von Bülow may have the distinction of being the first Wagner conductor on record.

At his farewell concert at the Metropolitan Opera House in New York on 2 May 1889, he conducted the Prelude to the *Meistersinger* among other works. The *Sun* reported:

During the entertainment the people on one side of the house observed with some curiosity a large funnel of varnished metal that was aimed from the opposite wing at the conductor's desk throughout the proceedings. The mysterious instrument was the receiver of a phonograph, the cylinders of which recorded faithfully every note of the programme.[1]

The recording is lost, or rather, has yet to be found.

[1] *Sun*, 3 May 1889, p. 2; also reported in the *Musical Courier*, 8 May 1889, p. 367, and *Musical Times*, 1 June 1889, pp. 363-4; John Bescoby-Chambers, *The archives of sound: including a selective catalogue of historical violin, piano, spoken, documentary, orchestral and composer's own recordings* (Lingfield: Oakwood Press, 1966), p. 95; Robert and Elia Dearling, *Guiness Book of Recorded Sound* (London: Guiness Books, 1984), p. 29; Alan Walker, *Hans von Bülow: A Life and Times* (Oxford University Press, 2010), pp. 412-13

4. Fritz Busch conducts Wagner[1]

Works recorded, including excerpts:

Der fliegende Holländer: 1936
Tannhäuser: 1932, 1946
Lohengrin: 1936, 1945, 1946, 1947
Tristan und Isolde: 1943, 1946, 1947
Die Meistersinger von Nürnberg: 1923, 1946
Der Ring des Nibelungen:
 Die Walküre: 1936
Parsifal: 1936, 1946

1923

Die Meistersinger, Act 3 Prelude
Dresden State Opera Orchestra, June 1923[2]
(matrix 212az)

78: Deutsche Grammophon/Polydor 69620 (B 20184) (1923); 65867 (B 20184) (1924); 65947 (B 20311) (1924)

CD: *Fritz Busch - Edition Staatskapelle Dresden, Vol. 30*: Profil PH07032 (3 CDs, 1 DVD) (2008)

[1] There is an online Busch discography by Gert Schäfer and Prof. Dr. Klaus Schöler, *Tonträgerverzeichnis (Diskografie) Fritz Busch (1890-1951)* (Karlsruhe-Durlach: Brüder Busch Archiv, 1 September 2010) at http://www1.karlsruhe.de/Kultur/Max-Reger-Institut/media/busch_diskografie.pdf (accessed 1 May 2011). Earlier discographies include John Hunt, *Sächsische Staatskapelle Dresden* (London: John Hunt, 2002); André Tubeuf, "Fritz Busch – cent ans après," *Diapason-Harmonie*, no. 357 (Feb 1990), pp. 30-36 (Wagner discography at p. 36); Jacques Dellalande (with Tully Potter), "The Busch Brothers – A Discography," *Recorded Sound*, no. 86 (July 1984), p. 29 (Wagner discography at pp. 78-80); and Jacques Delalande, *Hi Fi Stereophonie*, vol. 4, no. 2 (Feb 1965, vol 4., no. 3. (March 1965) p. 166, and vol. 4, no. 5 (May 1965), p. 291. Included in the footnotes that follow are broadcasts from the Metropolitan Opera House that have not, or not yet, appeared on disc.

[2] Schäfer and Schöler give June as the date based on entries in Busch's personal calendar - 8, 9, 11, 12, and 14 June - for his first series of recordings with the Dresden State Opera Orchestra. Deutsche Grammophon Aktiengesellschaft recordings, such as this one, also appeared for export on the Polydor label, amongst others. The recording (4' 54") is not the whole of the Prelude, but it was *not* continued on the other side of the record: 69620 and 65867 were coupled with Busch's recording of the Overture to the *Nutcracker Suite*, whereas 65947 was coupled with part 3 of the Prelude to *Tristan* with the Berlin State Opera Orchestra conducted by Walter Wohllebe. The whole of a Busch *Meistersinger* Act 3 Prelude (6' 06") survives from a 1946 concert with the Los Angeles Philharmonic (below).

1932

Tannhäuser, Overture
Dresden State Opera Orchestra
(*Das Weltkonzert VI* - a film by Comedia-Tonfilm GmbH, Berlin, 1932 or January/ February 1933; producer, Eberhard Frowein; artistic director, Franz Schreker)

LP: Friends of the Fritz Busch Society FB-101 (audio only, gives date as 1930)
CD: in *Tribute to the Staatskapelle of Dresden*: Tahra TAH 324-27 (1999) (see also DVD below)
VHS: *Great Conductors, Vol. 2*: Bel Canto Society 6003; *The Art of Conducting – Great Conductors of the Past*: Teldec 4509-95038-3 (1994) [gives date as 1932] (film from 38th bar only: 10' 45" of a total of 13' 08")
DVD: *The Art of Conducting – Great Conductors of the Past*: Teldec/Warner Music Vision 0927-42667-2 (2002); *Great Conductors*: Dreamlife DLVC 8092 (2008); *Fritz Busch - Edition Staatskapelle Dresden, Vol. 30*: Profil PH07032 (3 CDs, 1 DVD) (2008) (includes the film on DVD and the audio-only on CD)

1936

Lohengrin, Buenos Aires, live performance, 17 September 1936, abridged[3]
Lohengrin, René Maison; Elsa, Germaine Hoerner; Ortrud, Marjorie Lawrence; Telramund, Fred Destal; King Heinrich, Alexander Kipnis; Herald, Fritz Krenn; Teatro Colón Chorus [singing in Italian] and Orchestra

LP: Melodram MEL 310 (1985)
CD: Archipel ARPCD 0182-3 (2004)

Parsifal, Buenos Aires, live performance, 22 September 1936, abridged[4]
Amfortas, Martial Singher; Titurel, Fred Destal; Gurnemanz, Alexander Kipnis; Parsifal, René Maison; Klingsor, Fritz Krenn, Kundry, Marjorie Lawrence; Squires, Lucy Ritter, Irra Pettina, Hanns Fleischer, Luis Santoro; Flowermaidens, Edita Fleischer, Lucy Ritter, María Malberti, Irra Pettina, Emma Brizzio, Yolonda di Sábato; Knights, Hanns Fleischer, Jorge Andronoff; Teatro Cólon Chorus [singing in Italian] and Orchestra

CD: Marston 53003-2 (2002)

[3] The cuts in the performance were: in Act 2, scene 3, *Hoch der ersehnte Mann! … dem Schützer von Brabant!* (Men); scene 5, from *Welch ein Geheimnis muss der Held bewahren?* (Chorus with King) to *Im Zweifel doch erbebt des Herzens Grund!* (Elsa), and from *Wir stehn zu dir!* (Men) to *mein Nam' und Art auch nie genannt!* (Lohengrin); and in Act 3, scene 3: from *Zum andren aber sollt ihr Klage hören* to *vor König und vor Reich enthülle mein Geheimnis ich in Treuen* (Lohengrin, with the King and Chorus)

[4] This was the final of the five performances conducted by Busch in the season. The cuts in the performance were: in Act 1, scene 1: from *Hm! Schuf sie euch Schaden je?* to *dienet uns und hilft auch sich* (Gurnemanz and Squires), and from *Drum bleib es dem* to *den Gral auch wähnt er fest schon uns entwunden!* (Gurnemanz); in Act 2, scene 1: from *Da weckte dich ein And'rer?* to *hüt' ich mir selbst den Gral* (Klingsor, with Kundry); scene 2: from *Auf Ewigkeit* (Parsifal) to *nie heile mir die Wunde!* (Kundry); and in Act 3, scene 1: from *Du tolles Weib!* to *noch einmal ich dich entweckt?* (Gurnemanz), from *So kennst auch du mich noch?* to *O! Wunder! Heilig hehrstes Wunder!* (Gurnemanz, with Parsifal), and from *Ach, sie bedarf des Heiles* to *die mut - und führer - lose Ritterschaft* (Gurnemanz).

Die Walküre, Montevideo, live performance, 29 September 1936, abridged, excerpts[5] (ca. 69 mins)

Act 1: from the beginning of scene 2: *Müd' am Herd fand ich den Mann* (Sieglinde, with Hunding and Siegmund) to the end of the Act (41' 42")

Act 2: from the beginning to *Hojotoho!* (Wotan-Brünnhilde scene) (4' 22")

Act 2: from the beginning of scene 4, *Siegmund, Sieh auf mich!* (Brünnhilde, with Siegmund) to the end of the scene *Auf der Walstatt she ich dich wieder!* (Brünnhilde), with a cut in the performance from *Du sahest der Walküre sehrenden Blick* (Brünnhilde) to *Hella halte mich fest!* (Siegmund) (11' 22")

Act 3, scene 3: from *[War es so schmählich… die dunkle] Schuld* (Brünnhilde) to *dem freislichen Felsen zu nahn!* (Brünnhilde) (ie, immediately before Wotan's farewell), with two cuts in the performance, from *Als Fricka den eignen Sinn dir entfremdet* (Brünnhilde) to *Du wußtest es so und wagtest dennoch den Schutz?* (Wotan), and from *Du zeugtest ein edles Geschlecht* (Brünnhilde) to *nicht kiesen dann ich es dir!* (Wotan) (11' 30")

Siegmund, René Maison; Sieglinde, Germaine Boerner; Hunding, Alexander Kipnis; Brünnhilde, Marjorie Lawrence; Wotan, Fred Destal; Chorus and Orchestra of the Servicio Oficial de Difusión Radio y Espectáculos [SODRE]

LP: Unique Opera Records UORC 139 (1973)

Der fliegende Holländer, Buenos Aires, live performance, 19 September 1936

Holländer, Fred Destal; Senta, Marjorie Lawrence; Daland, Alexander Kipnis; Erik, René Maison; Mary, Irra Petina; Steersman, Hanns Fleischer; Teatro Cólon Chorus and Orchestra

CD:Pearl GEMM CDS 9910 (1992) (with a *Götterdämmerung* excerpt by Kleiber, 1948)

1943

Tristan und Isolde, Buenos Aires, live performance, 7 August 1943, abridged[6]

Tristan, Lauritz Melchior; Isolde, Helen Traubel; Kurwenal, Herbert Janssen; Brangäne, Lydia Kindermann; King Marke, Emanuel List; Melot, Renato Cesari; Sailor's Voice, Humberto di Toto; Shepherd, Rogelio Baldrich; Steersman, Angel Mattiello; Teatro Cólon Chorus and Orchestra

CD:Gebhardt JGCD 0039-3 (2002)

[5] There is a complete recording in the Brüder-Busch-Archiv at the Max Reger Institute: JS Editions Karlsruhe 08456-8 (3 CDs) (2008). Act 1 was unabridged. The cuts in Acts 1 and 2 were: Act 2, scene 1: from *als wüßtest fürwahr du nicht* (Fricka) to *dem Bund eines Zwillingspaars!* (Fricka, with Wotan), and from *Nichts lerntest du* (Wotan) to *die Göttin entweiht er nicht so!* (Fricka); scene 2, from *Als junger Liebe Lust mir verblich* to *der Welt weisestes Weib gebar mir, Brünnhilde, dich* (Wotan); from *Der der Liebe fluchte* (Wotan) to *trügend verraten wer mir traut!* (Wotan, with Brünnhilde); and from *Jetzt versteh ich den stummen Sinn* to *den Freien erlang ich mir nicht* (Wotan); scene 4, from *Du sahest der Walküre sehrenden Blick* (Brünnhilde) to *Hella halte mich fest!* (Siegmund); Act 3, scene 2, from *Weichet von ihr, der ewig Verworfnen* to *die mein Wunsch allein ihr schuf!* (Wotan, with Valkyries); scene 3, from *Als Fricka den eignen Sinn dir entfremdet* (Brünnhilde) to *Du wußtest es so und wagtest dennoch den Schutz?* (Wotan), and from *Du zeugtest ein edles Geschlecht* (Brünnhilde) to *nicht kiesen dann ich es dir!* (Wotan)

[6] This was the fourth performance conducted by Busch in the season. The cuts in the performance were: in Act 2, Scene 2, from *Dem Tage! Dem Tage!* (Tristan) to *dass nachtsichtig mein Auge wahres zu sehen tauge* (Tristan), and from *Tag und Tod* (Isolde) to *Tristan der Tod gegeben?* (Isolde); in Scene 3 from *Wozu die Dienste ohne Zahl* to *Da liess er's denn so sein* (King Marke); and in Act 3, Scene 1, from *Isolde noch im Reich der Sonne!* to *die selbst Nachts von ihr mich scheuchte?* (Tristan), from *Muss ich dich so versteh'n* to *Zu welchem Los?* (Tristan), and *Isolde ruft* to *darf ich dir sagen?* (Isolde).

1945

Lohengrin, New York, live broadcast, 26 November 1945, Act 1, abridged[7]
Lohengrin, Torsten Ralf; Elsa, Helen Traubel; Ortrud, Kerstin Thorborg; Telramund, Herbert Janssen; King Heinrich, Norman Cordon; Herald, Hugh Thompson; Metropolitan Opera Chorus and Orchestra

CD: *Great Conductors at the Metropolitan Opera*: Guild GHCD 2300/2 (2004)

1946[8]

Tristan und Isolde, Prelude and Liebestod
Die Meistersinger, Act 3 Prelude, Dance of the Apprentices and Entry of the Mastersingers
Los Angeles Philharmonic Orchestra, Alhambra High School Auditorium, Los Angeles, 10 March 1946, Standard Hour broadcast (NBC)

LP: Friends of the Fritz Busch Society E4-KP-1553 and FB-101 (*Tristan*); *The Art of Fritz Busch, Vol. 2*: Discocorp RR-397 (1976) (*Meistersinger*)
CD: Guild Historical GHCD 2366 (2010)

Parsifal, *Nur eine Waffe taugt*, XCO 36028, 28 March 1946 (71824-D/71829-D)
Lohengrin, *In fernem Land*, XCO 36029, 28 March 1946 (71826-D/71829-D)
Lohengrin, *Mein lieber Schwan!*, XCO 36030, 28 March 1946 (71826-D/71830-D)
Die Meistersinger, *Fanget an!*, XCO 36031, 28 March 1946 (71825-D/71827-D)
Die Meistersinger, *Morgenlich leuchtend*, XCO 36033,[9] 31 March 1946 (71825-D/71828-D)
Die Meistersinger, *Am stillen Herd*, XCO 36034, 31 March 1946 (71824-D/71830-D
Tannhäuser, *Inbrust im Herzen*, XCO 36035/6, 31 March 1946 (71823-D/71827/8-D)
Torsten Ralf, Metropolitan Opera Orchestra, Liederkranz Hall, New York

78: Columbia Set M-634/MM-634 (1947)
CD: *Torsten Ralf II*: Preiser 89152 (1997)

[7] The whole opera was broadcast, though only Act 1 has appeared commercially. The notes accompanying the Act 1 on Guild state: "the remainder of the broadcast located from a different source was in such bad sound that publication was out of the question." There is such a source in the Brüder-Busch-Archiv at the Max Reger Institute: JS Editions Karlsruhe 06576-578 (3 CDs) (2006). It is an almost complete recording (it lacks the Act 1 Prelude and lines lost when the recording discs were changed) and is in very poor sound, with frequent disc changes, track jumping (i.e. missed notes), track sticking (i.e. repeated notes), rhythmic fluctuations of speed, and abundant surface noise. None of the well-known passages from the opera is entirely intact. It is nevertheless possible to identify the cuts made in the performance: in Act 1, scene 1, from *Soll ich euch erst der Drangsal Kunde sagen* (King Heinrich) to *Wohlauf! Mit Gott für deutschen Reiches Ehr'!* (Saxons); in Act 2, scene 5, from *Welch ein Geheimnis muss der Held bewahren?* (Chorus) to *Im Zweifel doch erbebt des Herzens Grund!* (Elsa); in Act 3, scene 2, from *Nie soll dein Reiz entschwinden* (Lohengrin) to *wo fänd' ich dein' Gewähr?* (Elsa), in scene 3, from *Nun soll des Reiches Feind sich nahn* (King Heinrich) to *So sei des Reiches Kraft bewährt!* (Men), and from *O Elsa! Was hast du mir angetan?* to *des Ostens Horden siegreich nimmer ziehn!* (Lohengrin, with Elsa, King and Men). There was another performance of *Lohengrin* broadcast from the Metropolitan Opera House on 22 December 1945.

[8] There was a broadcast of Busch conducting *Tristan und Isolde* from the Metropolitan Opera House on 2 February 1946.

[9] It will be noted that XCO 36032 is not in the recordings listed above. The matrix number does not appear in the Columbia ledgers for 1946, so presumably was not used.

Tristan und Isolde, New York, live broadcast, 30 November 1946, abridged[10]
Tristan, Set Svanholm; Isolde, Helen Traubel; Kurwenal, Joel Berglund; Brangäne, Margaret Harshaw; King Marke, Dezsö Ernster; Melot, Emery Darcy; Sailor's Voice and Shepherd, John Garris; Steersman, Gerhard Pechner; Metropolitan Opera Chorus and Orchestra

CD: Myto 3 MCD 951.121 (1995); Myto 3CD 983.H020 (1998)

1947

Lohengrin, New York, live broadcast, 25 January 1947,[11] abridged[12]
Lohengrin, Lauritz Melchior; Elsa, Helen Traubel; Ortrud, Margaret Harshaw; elramund, Osie Hawkins; King Heinrich, Dezsö Ernster; Herald, Hugh Thompson; Metropolitan Opera Chorus and Orchestra

LP: Fonit Cetra LO 24 (1977); Accord 150031 (1982); Melodram MEL 310 (1985) (Act 3 *Prelude* and Liebesduett only, with the 1936 complete performance); *Hungarian Artists Wagner Recordings*: Hungaroton SLPX 12594-95 (1983) (King Heinrich's *Mein Herr und Gott* only)

CD: Grammofono 2000 AB 78747/49 (1997); Cantus Classics CACD 5.00505/06 (2004); Walhall Eternity WLCD 0205 (2007); GALA GL 100.640 (2008) (excerpts, as a "bonus" to a complete performance under Fritz Stiedry, 1953)

Tristan und Isolde, Act 2, Love Duet, 16 March 1947, abridged[13]
Tristan, Torsten Ralf; Isolde, Helen Traubel; Hertha Glaz, Brangäne, Metropolitan Opera Orchestra, Metropolitan Opera House, New York

[10] The cuts in the performance were: in Act 2, Scene 2, from *Dem Tage! Dem Tage!* (Tristan) to *dass nachtsichtig mein Auge wahres zu sehen tauge* (Tristan), from *Tag und Tod* (Isolde) to *Tristan der Tod gegeben?* (Isolde), in Scene 3 from *Wozu die Dienste ohne Zahl* to *Da liess er's denn so sein* (King Marke); in Act 3, Scene 1, from *Isolde noch im Reich der Sonne!* to *die selbst Nachts von ihr mich scheuchte?* (Tristan), from *Muss ich dich so versteh'n* to *zu welchem Los?* (Tristan), and in Scene 2, from *Gebrochen der Blick!* to *Nur einmal noch!* (Isolde).

[11] There are some reports (eg Delalande and on the LPs themselves) that the Fonit Cetra and Accord issues were of a performance on 16 or 26 November 1946. This is a mistake, however, for Busch conducted *Otello* at the Metropolitan Opera on 16 November, and nothing at all on 26 November.

[12] The cuts in the performance were: in Act 1, scene 1: from *Soll ich euch erst der Drangsal Kunde sagen* (King Heinrich) to *Wohlauf! Mit Gott für deutschen Reiches Ehr'!* (Saxons); [in Act 2, scene 1, a few bars – *er war in deiner Macht!* (Ortrud) *Entsetzlich!* (Friedrich) – are missing from the source tapes, not the performance]; in Act 2, scene 5: from *In wildem Brüten darf ich sie gewahren!* (Lohengrin) to *Im Zweifel doch erbebt des Herzens Grund!* (Elsa); Act 3, scene 2, from *Dein Lieben muß mir hoch entgelten* to *muß ich in deiner Lieb' ersehn* (Lohengrin), from *Nie soll dein Reiz entschwinden* (Lohengrin) to *wo fänd ich dein' Gewähr?* (Elsa), and from *[Allewiger,] erbarm dich mein* (Elsa) to the end of the scene; scene 3, from *Nun soll des Reiches Feind sich nahn* (King Heinrich) to *So sei des Reiches Kraft bewährt!* (Men), from *Zum andren aber sollt ihr Klage hören* to *enthülle mein Geheimnis ich in Treuen* (Lohengrin, with Chorus), and from *O Elsa! Was hast du mir angetan?* to *des Ostens Horden siegreich nimmer ziehn!* (Lohengrin, with Elsa, King and Men).

[13] The excerpt is from *O sink' hernieder* to *höschste Liebes-Lust!*, with Tristan's words *Stünd' er vor mir… die Liebe selbst zu erreichen* omitted. The second take of Part 3 (XCO 37482-2) has a few extra lines of Tristan, from *Stürb' ich nun ihr* to *Wie stürbe dann Tristan seiner Liebe?*, than has the first take of Part 3 (XCO 37482-1); the second take was issued on the Sony CD. In the other cases, the shorter first take was used. The longer, second take is described as "uncut" in Frederick P. Fellers, *The Metropolitan Opera on Record* (Westport: Greenwood Press, 1984), p. 53; this should not be understood, however, to mean that part three is continuous with part four: lines from the duet have been cut *whichever* take is used.

(XCO 37480, XCO 37481, XCO 37482-1 (3' 34"), XCO 37482-2 (4' 39"), XCO 37483)

78: Columbia 72246/7-D (Set-X 286) and 72248/9-D (Set-MX 286) (1948)

LP: Columbia ML-4055 (1949)

CD: *Helen Traubel*: MET 214 CD (1992); *Torsten Ralf II*: Preiser 89152 (1997); *Lauritz Melchior and Helen Traubel sing Wagner*: Sony Classical MK2K 60896 (1999)

[1948][14]

[14] There were broadcasts of *Tristan und Isolde* which Busch conducted at the Metropolitan Opera on 3 January and 11 December 1948. A recording purporting to be of the 3 January performance is in Brüder Busch Archiv at the Max Reger Institute (JS Editions Karlsruhe 08648-50, 3 CDs, 2008). On examination, however, this turned out to be the 30 November 1946 performance.

5. Albert Coates conducts Wagner[1]

Works recorded, including excerpts:

Die Feen: 1932
A Faust Overture: 1928
Rienzi: 1921
Tannhäuser: 1925-26, 1929
Lohengrin: 1923, 1924, 1925, 1929
Tristan und Isolde: 1923, 1926, 1927, 1929
Die Meistersinger von Nürnberg: 1921, 1922-23, 1925, 1926-27, 1930, 1932
Siegfried Idyll: 1921, 1922
Der Ring des Nibelungen: 1922-23, 1927-29, also -
Das Rheingold: 1926
Die Walküre: 1924, 1926, 1929
Götterdämmerung: 1924, 1926, 1929
Parsifal: 1925, 1927-28

1921

Siegfried Idyll
London Symphony Orchestra
(74268-2, 74269-2, 74270-2, 74271-2, Columbia Studios, London, 11 March 1921)
78: Columbia L1425-26, 65011-12 D

Die Meistersinger, Act 1 *Prelude*
Symphony Orchestra
(Cc 606-2,[2] Cc 607-2, Hayes, 28 October 1921)
78: HMV D590, AB25, S8110, W436, Victor 55171

[1] The standard, comprehensive Coates discography is by Christopher Dyment in *Recorded Sound*, nos. 57-58 (January-April 1975), pp. 382-405, and p. 464 (errata). There was also a Coates discography by Stephen M. Stroff in *Le Grand Baton* no. 45 (vol. 17 no. 1, March 1980), pp. 15-27, and comment by David Hamilton in no. 48 (December 1980), pp. 12-13. Philip Stuart's *LSO Discography* (August 2007 edition – online at lso.co.uk) has many details, including CD reissues, of Coates's recordings with the London Symphony Orchestra and the "Symphony Orchestra." Dyment's discography includes details of unpublished takes and the strength of the orchestral forces used in Coates's recordings. I have departed from a strict chronological listing. Where the Gramophone Company embarked on a project to record a set of excerpts, I have listed the excerpts in the order in which they appear in the drama, rather than the order in which they were recorded. Furthermore, for the sake of completeness, I have included in brackets those excerpts conducted by other conductors which were part of the sets. I have not described where many of the excerpts begin and end, and what was excised, leaving it instead to the titles of the excerpts on the records to tell the story.

[2] This part was re-recorded on 15 September 1923 as Cc 3310-2 and issued on later pressings.

Rienzi, *Overture*
Symphony Orchestra
(Cc 711-2, Cc 712-1, Hayes, 25 November 1921)
78: HMV D607, S8116, W450, AB18

1922

Siegfried Idyll
Symphony Orchestra
(Cc 1667-1, Cc 1668-2, Cc 1669-1, Cc 1670-2, Hayes, 17 July 1922)
78: HMV D649/650, AB31/32

1922-23

The Ring of the Nibelungs
excerpts sung in English, with Symphony Orchestra conducted by Albert Coates unless otherwise noted; recorded Hayes, London[3]

The Rhinegold

Alberich steals the gold; The Dawn over Valhalla
Alberich, Robert Radford; Rhinemaidens, Bessie Jones, Louise Trenton, Edith Furmidge
Cc 2243-3 18 December 1922 HMV D677, W536, Victor 55203

The descent to Nibelheim; Capture of Alberich
Robert Radford, Edith Furmidge
Cc 2244-2 18 December 1922 HMV D677, W536, Victor 55203

The Valkyrie

Act 1: *Prelude; Siegmund seeeks shelter from the storm* (orchestral arrangement)
Cc 1584-1 28 June 1922 HMV D678, W537, Victor 55204

[Act 1: *Siegmund sees the sword hilt in the tree*
Siegmund, Tudor Davies, Eugene Goossens
Cc 1840-1 18 September 1922 HMV D678, W537, Victor 55204]

[Act 1: *Siegmund greets the Spring night*
Siegmund, Tudor Davies, Eugene Goossens
Cc 1841-2 18 September 1922 HMV D679, W538, Victor 55205]

[Act 1: *Spring song*
Siegmund, Tudor Davies, Eugene Goossens
Cc 2438-2 25 January 1923 HMV D679, W538, Victor 55205]

[3] Of this set, D677-682 and DB439-441 were released in March 1923, D700-706 in June 1923. The set was also issued in France as W536/41 and 568/74, without separate catalogue numbers for the DB discs. The set has never been reissued on LP or CD but was included, with the exception of the DB numbers, in *From Which We Came – The first opera sets* [Michael Richter: Audio Encyclopaedia AE301 (1999)], a CD-ROM with audio in MP3 format.

Act 2: *Introduction; Brunnhilde's battle cry*
Brunnhilde, Florence Austral; Wotan, Robert Radford
Cc 2253-2 8 December 1922 HMV D680, W539, Victor 55206

[Act 2: *Wotan warns Brunnhilde not to disobey*
Brunnhilde, Florence Austral; Wotan, Robert Radford, Eugene Goossens
Cc 2254-2 11 December 1922 HMV D680, W539, Victor 55206]

Act 2: *Siegmund is told by Brunnhilde of his approaching death*
Brunnhilde, Florence Austral; Siegmund, Tudor Davies
Cc 2276-2 18 December 1922 HMV D681, W540, Victor 55207

Act 3: *Introduction; Ride of the Valkyries*
Cc 1666-2 17 July 1922 HMV D681, W540, Victor 55207

Act 3: *Brunnhilde gives Sieglinde the broken Sword*
Brunnhilde, Florence Austral; Sieglinde, Edith Furmedge; Wotan, Edward Halland
Cc 2250-2 8 December 1922 HMV D682, W541, Victor 55208

[Act 3: *Brunnhilde implores the protection of fire*
Brunnhilde, Florence Austral; Wotan, Robert Radford, Eugene Goossens
Cc 2255-2 11 December 1922 HMV D682, W541, Victor 55208]

Act 3: *Wotan bids farewell to Brunnhilde* (*Farewell, thou valiant*)
Wotan, Clarence Whitehill
Cc 1523-1 22 June 1922 HMV DB440, Victor 6435

Act 3: *Wotan kisses Brunnhilde into a deep slumber* (*Brightly gleams*)
Cc 1522-4 30 June 1922 HMV DB440, Victor 6435

Act 3: *The rock is surrounded by Fire* (*Fauerzauber*)
Wotan, Clarence Whitehill
Cc 1524-1 22 June 1922 HMV DB439[4], Victor 74857

Siegfried

Act 1: *Siegfried forges the broken sword*
Siegfried, Tudor Davies; Mime, Sydney Russell
Cc 1591-2 30 June 1922 HMV D700, W568, Victor 55209

[Act 2: *The Forest Bird warns Siegfried*
Siegfried, Tudor Davies; forest bird, Florence Austral; Mime, Sydney Russell; Eugene Goossens
Cc 2841-2 16 April 1923 HMV D700, W568, Victor 55209]

Act 2: *Siegfried follows the forest bird*
Siegfried, Tudor Davies; forest bird, Bessie Jones
Cc 2840-5 26 April 1923 HMV D701, W569, Victor 55210

[4] The reverse side of DB439 contains Clarence Whitehill's Amfortas' prayer from Act 3 of *Parsifal* (New York, 22 July 1914, matrix C-15076-1), accompanied by an orchestra and conductor not identified on the label.

Act 3: *Introduction; Wotan invokes Erda*
Wotan, Clarence Whitehill
Cc 1525-2 22 June 1922 HMV DB441, Victor 6436

Act 3: *Siegfried's ascent to the Valkyries' Rock*
Wotan, Clarence Whitehill; Siegfried, Tudor Davies
Cc 1592-2 30 June 1922 HMV DB441, Victor 6436

[Act 3: *Brunnhilde hails the radiant sun*
Brunnhilde, Florence Austral; Siegfried, Tudor Davies; Percy Pitt
Cc 2270-1 14 December 1922 HMV D701, W569, Victor 55210]

Act 3: *Brunnhilde recalls her Valkyrie days*
Brunnhilde, Florence Austral; Siegfried, Tudor Davies
Cc 2251-5 19 December 1922 HMV D702, W570, Victor 55211

Act 3: *The Goddess Maiden yields to Siegfried's pleading*
Brunnhilde, Florence Austral; Siegfried, Tudor Davies
Cc 2252-3 19 December 1922 HMV D702, W570, Victor 55211

The Twilight of the Gods

Prologue: *Brunnhilde bids farewell to Siegfried*
Brunnhilde, Florence Austral; Siegfried, Tudor Davies
Cc 2277-3, -78-3 19 December 1922 HMV D703, W571, Victor 55212

[Act 1: *Hagen meditates revenge*
Hagen, Robert Radford, Symphony Orchestra, Percy Pitt
Cc 1586-1 29 June 1922 HMV D704, W572, Victor 55213]

Act 1: *Gunther and Gutrune bid welcome to Siegfried*
Siegfried, Tudor Davies; Gunther, Robert Radford, Gutrune, Bessie Jones
Cc 2895-2 26 April 1923 HMV D704, W572, Victor 55213

[Act 3: *Rhinemaidens' scene*, orchestral arrangement, Eugene Goossens
Cc 2842-1 16 April 1923 HMV D705, W573, Victor 55214]

Act 3: *Brunnhilde kindles the funeral pyre* (Immolation scene, 3 parts)
Brunnhilde, Florence Austral; Hagen, unknown[5]
Cc 2303-2, Cc 2305-2, Cc 2306-2
22 December 1922 HMV D705/6, W573/4, Victor 55214/5

[5] Tudor Davies was the only male singer present in the recording studio on the day, to record other excerpts, according to the Gramophone Company's recording registers, but Hagen's few words (*Back from the Ring!*) do not sound like him. It may have been Coates himself.

The Mastersingers of Nuremberg, an abridged version sung in English[6]
Hans Sachs, Robert Radford; Eva, Florence Austral; Walther von Stolzing, Tudor Davies; Sixtus Beckmesser, William Michael, Magdalene, Doris Lemon and Nellie Walker; David, Tudor Davies; Veit Pogner, Robert Radford, Fritz Kothner, Edward Halland; Chorus, Bessie Jones, Edith Furmedge, Gladys Peel, Louise Trenton, Sydney Coltham, Walter Glynne, Leonard Hubbard, Edward Halland, Doris Lemon, Nellie Walker, Browning Mummery

Act 1: *Church scene*
Chorus: Jones, Furmedge, Peel, Trenton, Coltham, Glynne, Hubbard, Halland
Cc 2240-4 19 December 1922 HMV D745, W638

Act 1: *Meeting of Walther and Eva*
Lemon, Austral, Davies
Cc 3251-4 23 July 1923 HMV D745, W638

Act 1: *David and the apprentices*
Davies, chorus: Walker, Peel, Glynne, Mummery
Cc 3276-2 13 July 1923 HMV D746, W639

Act 1: *Entrance of the Mastersingers*
Davies, Michael, Radford, Lemon
Cc 3313-1 23 July 1923 HMV D746, W639

Act 1: *Pogner extols the love of singing- Then hear me*
Radford
Cc 3255-3 27 August 1923 HMV D747, W640

Act 1: *Walther confesses Nature his only teacher*
Davies, Radford, Michael
Cc 3279-2 16 July 1923 HMV D747, W640

Act 1: *Kothner announces the rules*
Davies, Michael, Halland
Cc 3363-2 27 August 1923 HMV D748, W641

Act 1: *Walther's song*
Davies, Michael, Radford
Cc 3252-3 18 July 1923 HMV D748, W641

Act 1: *Walther's Song displeases the Masters (Finale, Act 1)*
Davies, Radford, Michael, chorus: Walker, Peel, Glynne, Mummery, Hubbard, Halland
Cc 3270-1 13 July 1923 HMV D749, W642

[6] The abridgement skillfully presents all the "highlights" of the opera, some edited to fit onto the limited space of a single disc. There is approximately 48 minutes of Act 1, 27 minutes of Act 2, and 58 minutes of Act 3. The translation used was by Frederick Jameson (Mainz: B. Schott's Söhne, 1909). The recording of the excerpts began with the Prelude to Act 3 on 18 September 1922 under Eugene Goossens, but these takes were never issued. Perhaps they were an experimental recording session. Coates conducted all excerpts from that point, starting from the Church scene on 19 December 1922.

Act 2: *Apprentices celebrate Midsummer's Day* (Opening of Act)
Radford, chorus: Austral, Davies, Coltham
Cc 2952-2 8 May 1923 HMV D749, W642

Act 2: *The scent of the elder blossoms inspires Sachs*
Radford
Cc 3254-2 11 July 1923 HMV D750, W643

Act 2: *The Love of Sachs for Eva*
Austral, Radford, Lemon
Cc 3312-3 15 September 1923 HMV D750, W643

Act 2: *Walther tells Eva of the Masters' injustice*
Austral, Davies
Cc 3307-3 15 September 1923 HMV D751, W644

Act 2: *Sachs sings at his work*
Radford
Cc 2896-2 26 April 1923 HMV D751, W644

Act 2: *Beckmesser's serenade and finale*
Michael, Radford, chorus: Jones, Lemon, Brown, Walker, Davies, Glynne, Mummery, Halland, Hubbard
Cc 3269-2 13 July 1923 HMV D752, W645

Act 3: *Introduction*
Cc 1842-4[7] 27 April 1923 HMV D752, W645

Act 3: *Sachs laments the folly of mankind*
Radford
Cc 3285-1 18 July 1923 HMV D753, W646

Act 3: *Walther tells Sachs of the song he dreamt*
Davies, Radford
Cc 3305-4 27 August 1923 HMV D753, W646

Act 3: *Beckmesser limps into Sachs' workshop*
Davies, Michael
Cc 3277-2 16 July 1923 HMV D754, W647

Act 3: *Beckmesser obtains Walther's song*
Davies, Radford, Michael
Cc 3278-2 16 July 1923 HMV D754, W647

Act 3: *Sachs recognises Eva's love for Walther*
Austral, Davies, Radford
Cc 3306-3 15 September 1923 HMV D755, W648

[7] The first two takes were recorded on 18 September 1922. The orchestra was conducted by Eugene Goossens. They were never issued.

Act 3: *Sachs gives Eva and Walther his blessing*
Austral, Radford
Cc 3311-3 23 July 1923 HMV D755, W648

Act 3: *Quintet of Sachs and the lovers*
Austral, Walker, Davies, Mummery, Radford
Cc 3286-1 18 July 1923 HMV D756, W649

Act 3: *Procession of the Guilds*
Chorus: Davies, Mummery, Glynne, Hubbard, Halland
Cc3275-2 13 July 1923 HMV D756, W649

Act 3: *Dance of the apprentices*
Davies, chorus: Walker, Davies, Mummery
Cc 3304-1 20 July 1923 HMV D757, W650

Act 3: *The townspeople render praise*
Chorus: Jones, Furmedge, Peel, Trenton, Coltham, Glynne, Hubbard, Halland
Cc 2241-1 5 December 1922 HMV D757, W650

Act 3: *Walther's Prize song*
Davies, chorus: Jones, Walker, Glynne, Mummery, Hubbard, Halland
Cc 3274-2 13 July 1923 HMV D758, W651

Act 3: *Disdain not the Masters' ways*
Radford, chorus: Jones, Furmedge, Peel, Trenton, Coltham, Glynne, Hubbard, Halland
Cc 2242-4 18 December 1922 HMV D758, W651

78: HMV D745/58 (England); W638/651 (France)
CD: Aria Recordings 5001 (2001) (includes an Act 1 Prelude recorded on 26 October 1926)

1923

Lohengrin, Act 3, *Bridal procession*
Symphony Orchestra
(Cc 2898-3, Hayes, 27 April 1923)
78: HMV D937, AW4262

Tristan und Isolde, Act 2, scenes 1 and 2, abridged, sung in English[8]
Tristan, Tudor Davies; Isolde (and Brangäne), Florence Austral; Symphony Orchestra
(Cc 2955-6, Cc 2953-4, Cc 2954-3, Cc 2969-2, Hayes, 11 May 1923)
78: HMV D736/737
CD: in *Florence Austral*: Pearl GEMM CD9146 (1994) (gives the matrix numbers and takes as above, but dates them as 8 May, the day on which the artists recorded the first three parts of the love duet on unpublished takes); the last three parts were included in *The Mastersingers of Nuremberg*: Aria Recordings 5001 (2001)

[8] Without enumerating all the portions or cuts in this abridgement, it begins from the introduction to the act and ends with the exposure of the lovers, traversing a field, which lasts around 50 minutes in an uncut performance, in 17½ minutes.

1924

The Valkyrie, Act 3, *Wotan overtakes Brunnhilde*, sung in English
Wotan, Robert Radford; Brunnhilde, Gladys Ancrum; Valkyries: Louise Trenton, Mrs Valli, Beatrice Miranda, Nellie Walker, Gladys Peel, Symphony Orchestra, Hayes
Part 1: *Where is Brunnhilde, where the rebellious one* (Cc 4706-2, 2 July 1924)
Part 2: *Thou dost cast me off* (Wotan's Sentence) (Cc 4634-1, 25 May 1924)
78: HMV D929

Götterdämmerung, Act 2, scene 3, *Hagen summons the Vassals*, sung in English
Hagen, Robert Radford; Vassals, Tudor Davies, Browning Mummery, Edward Halland, William Michael, Symphony Orchestra
(Cc 4636-2 and Cc 4637-1, Hayes, 25 May 1924)
78: HMV D930

Tristan und Isolde, Act 1, *Isolde's narration and curse*, and *Finale*, sung in English[9]
Isolde, Florence Austral; Tristan, Tudor Davies; chorus, Louise Trenton, Browning Mummery, Edward Halland, Leonard Hubbard, Symphony Orchestra, Hayes, 6 June 1924
Isolde's narration (Cc 4703-1) and *Curse* (Cc 4704-1) HMV D911
They drink the love potion (Cc 4702-2) and *Finale* (Cc 4701-2) HMV D912
78: HMV D911/2

Lohengrin, Act 3 Prelude
Symphony Orchestra
(Cc 5271-2, Hayes, 22 October 1924)
78: HMV D937, AW4262

1925

Parsifal, excerpts, sung in English
Gurnemanz, Robert Radford; Parsifal, Walter Widdop; Titurel, George Baker; Amfortas, Percy Heming; Voice, Nellie Walker; Chorus: Misses Parry, Mitchell, Hallam, Rusel-Meyr, Walker, Graham, Bailey, Street, Sissons, Delma, Tweedy, E. Williams, Bember, M. Williams, Brath, Colls, Messrs Heaps, Young, Fenwick, Odell, Shacknoft (?), Quinn, De Vellen, Travers, Fort, Howell, Bibo, Wilde, Leer, Halland, Kitchen; Symphony Orchestra, Hayes, 28-31 July 1925

Act 1, *Prelude* (with concert ending)
Symphony Orchestra
(Cc 6418-1, 28 July; Cc 6419-2, Cc 6420-1, Hayes, 29 July 1925)
78: HMV D1025/26, W718/19, AB161/62, AW4156/57, ES13/14

[9] The narration and curse is complete from *Weh' Ach, wehe! dies zu dulden!* (Brangäne) to *Tod uns Beiden!* (Isolde), and the finale to Act 1 is from *Ho! he! ha! he!* (Sailors) to the end of the act, with the lines *Heil Tristan!* (Kurwenal) to *Welcher König?* (Tristan) omitted. It might be noted that Coates recorded a *Liebestod* with Florence Austral in English on 29 July 1925 (Cc 6423-1); it was assigned a catalogue number (4-0714) in August 1925, but was never in fact issued: information from EMI Archives, Hayes.

Act 1: *Gurnemanz reproaches Parsifal for slaying the swan*
(Cc 6432-1, 31 July 1925)
78: HMV D1026, W719, AB162, AW4158, ES14

Act 1: *Gurnemanz leads Parsifal to Montsalvat*
(Cc 6430-3, 31 July 1925)
78: HMV D1027, W720, AB163, AW4160, ES15

Act 1: *The Knights of the Grail assemble*
(Cc 6431-2, 31 July 1925)
78: HMV D1027, W720, AB163, AW4160, ES15

Act 1: *Amfortas' prayer and lament*
(Cc 6422-2, 29 July 1925)
78: HMV D1028, W721, AB164, AW4162, ES16

Act 1: *Grail scene* (3 parts) (abridged)
(Cc 6433-1, Cc 6434-1, 6435-2, 31 July 1925)
78: HMV D1028/29, W721/22, AB164/65, AW4162/64, ES16/17

Act 2: *Klingsor's Magic Garden and Flowermaidens' scene* (orchestral arrangement)
(Cc 6416-3, 6417-1, 28 July 1925)
78: HMV D1030, W723, AB166, AW4166, ES18

Act 3: *Good Friday Music* (orchestral arrangement)
(Cc 6414-3, Cc 6415-3, 28 July 1925)
78: HMV D1031, W724, AB167, AW4168, ES19

CD: all selections in *Albert Coates conducts excerpts from Wagner's* Die Meistersinger von Nürnberg *and* Parsifal: Claremont CDGSE 78-50-70/71 (1997) (includes the Kundry-Parsifal scene from Act 2 recorded in 1927-28 – see below)[10]

Die Meistersinger, *March of the Master Singers*, sung in English
Chorus, Symphony Orchestra, Hayes
(Cc 7079-2, 27 October 1925)
78: HMV AW4110; Victor 9017 (label says *Procession to the Cathedral* [*sic*])[11]

Lohengrin, excerpts, sung in English
Lohengrin, Walter Widdop; King, Edward Halland, with Bessie Jones, Nellie Walker, B. Molls, F. Odell; chorus, Symphony Orchestra, Hayes, 27 October - 3 November 1925

Act 1: *The appearance of the swan*
(Cc 7165-2, 3 November 1925)
78: HMV D1101, AB229, AW4112; Victor 9017 (label says *Swan Chorus*)

[10] In reviewing D1025-1031 in 1925, *Gramophone* included the *Herzeleide* scene from act two conducted by Eugene Goossens (DB862), implying it was part of the set: November 1925, p. 289 ("N. P.").

[11] This was only issued by HMV under the Italian AW catalogue number (there was no English D catalogue number or issue); because of the mis-description on the Victor label, it appeared as an excerpt from *Lohengrin* in the *Gramophone Shop Encyclopaedia* 1942, and was so described in Dyment's discography.

Act 1: *The King's Prayer* and *Quintet*
(Cc 7080-2, 27 October 1925)
78: HMV AW4110[12]

Act 3: *Prelude*
(Cc 7083-2, 27 October 1925)
78: HMV D1054, W935, AB172, AW4108, Victor 9005

Act 3: *Bridal Chorus*
(Cc 7081-2, 27 October 1925)
78: HMV D1054, W935, AB172, AW4108, Victor 9005

1925-26

Tannhäuser, excerpts, sung in English
Tannhäuser, Walter Widdop; Wolfram von Eschenbach, Edward Halland; Elisabeth and Shepherd Boy, Bessie Jones; British National Opera Chorus (sop: Williams, Mitchell, Parry, Rusel-Meyr, Tweedy, Hallam, Delma; con: Walker, Sissons, Colls, Street, Bailey, Hember), Symphony Orchestra, Hayes and Kingsway Hall, 29 July 1925 - 16 September 1926

Act 1: *Overture*
(CR 675-2A, CR 676-1, CR 677-1A, Kingsway Hall, 16 September 1926)
78: HMV D1138/39, AB199/200, AW4298/300, W796/7, Victor 9059/60, 36344/5
CD: *Great Conductors of the 20th Century: Albert Coates*: EMI 75486-2 (2002)

Act 1: *Venusberg (Bacchanale)*
(Cc 6428-1, Cc 6429-2, 30 July 1925; Cc 6421-2, Hayes, 29 July 1925)
78: HMV D1071/72, W843/44, AB186/87, AW4136/38, ES264/65, Victor 9027/28, 36345/6

Act 1: *Pilgrim's chorus*
(Cc 7163-2, Hayes, 3 November 1925)
78: HMV D1074, AB174, AW4144

Act 2: *March*
(Cc 7082-2, Hayes, 27 October 1925)
78: HMV D1101, AB229, AW4112, C 9128

Act 3: *Prelude*
(Cc 7035-5, Hayes, 27 October 1925)
78: HMV D1072, W844, AB187, AW4138, ES265, Victor 36345/6

Act 3: *Pilgrims' return*
(Cc 7164-1, Hayes, 3 November 1925)
78: HMV D1074, AW4144

[12] Dyment (*ibid.*) lists this as unissued, that is, he omits the Italian catalogue number. I am indebted to Alan Kelly's examination and transcription of the Gramophone Company's HMV registers for this detail. I have been unable to locate a copy of the recording.

CD: all selections in *Albert Coates conducts Wagner Tannhäuser, Weber Der Freischütz, Mendelssohn Elijah*: Claremont CDGSE 78-50-54 (1993) (includes two *Tannhäuser* excerpts recorded on 9 May 1930 with Friedrich Schorr and the New Symphony Orchestra conducted by Lawrance Collingwood, but mis-attributed to Coates)

1926

Der Ring des Nibelungen and ***Tristan und Isolde*,** orchestral excerpts
Symphony Orchestra, Queen's Hall, 25 January 1926

Das Rheingold, *Prelude*
(CR 142-1)
78: HMV D1088, AB182, AW4118, ES22, Victor 9163
CD: *Albert Coates, Leo Blech,* Die Walküre, Das Rheingold: Claremont CDGSE 78-50 35/36 (1990); *Der Ring des Nibelungen*: Pearl GEMM CDS9137 (1994) [date incorrectly given as 2 February 1926]

Das Rheingold, *Entry of the Gods*
(CR 138-1, 139-1)
78: HMV D1117, AB190, AW4076, Victor 9180/81
CD: *Albert Coates, Leo Blech,* Die Walküre, Das Rheingold: Claremont CDGSE 78-50 35/36 (1990); *Albert Coates conducts, Vol. 2*: Koch Historic 3-7704-2 (1992); *Great Conductors of the 20th Century: Albert Coates*: EMI 75486-2 (2002)

Die Walküre, Act 3, *Ride of the Valkyries*
(CR 143-1)
78: HMV D1088, AB182, AW4118, ES22, D1815, Victor 9163

Die Walküre, Act 3, *Magic Fire Music*
(CR 134-1, 135-2)
78: HMV D1079, AB177, AW4154, EJ32, ES262, Victor 9006
CD: *Albert Coates conducts, Vol. 2*: Koch Historic 3-7704-2 (1992); *Great Conductors of the 20th Century: Albert Coates*: EMI 75486-2 (2002)

Götterdämmerung, Prologue – *Siegfried's Rhine Journey*
(CR 136-3, CR 137-1)
78: HMV D1080, AB178, AW4078, EJ34, ES263, Victor 7113, 9007, 9180; also included in Victor's *Götterdämmerung* set M-60 (9459)/AM-60 (9584)/DM-60 (13472)[13]
CD: *Albert Coates – Leo Blech – Lawrance Collingwood: Götterdämmerung*: Claremont CDGSE 78-50-37/38 (1990); *Albert Coates conducts, Vol. 2*: Koch Historic 3-7704-2 (1992); *Great Conductors of the 20th Century: Albert Coates*: EMI 75486-2 (2002)

Götterdämmerung, Act 3, *Siegfried's Funeral Music*
(CR 217-2 [26 March], CR 141-3)

[13] HMV's *Götterdämmerung* set used Muck's *Rhine Journey* and *Funeral Music* (see 1927-29 below)

78: HMV D1092, AB193, AW4072, ES27, Victor 7114, 9049, 9102/03; also included in Victor's *Götterdämmerung* set M-60 (9469)/AM-60 (9588-9589), DM-60 (13471-13470)

CD: *Albert Coates – Leo Blech – Lawrance Collingwood: Götterdämmerung*: Claremont CDGSE 78-50-37/38 (1990); *Albert Coates conducts, Vol. 2*: Koch Historic 3-7704-2 (1992); *Der Ring des Nibelungen*: Pearl GEMM CDS9137 (1994)[14]

Tristan und Isolde, Act 1, *Prelude*
(CR 144-1, 145-1)
78: HMV D1107, AB183, AW4148, EJ40, ES32
CD: *Albert Coates, Dr Leo Blech, Lawrance Collingwood conduct* Tristan und Isolde: Claremont CDGSE 78-50-26 (1988)

1926-27

Die Meistersinger von Nürnberg
Symphony Orchestra, Kingsway Hall
Act 1: *Prelude*
(CR 663-3, CR 664-4, 26 October 1926)
78: HMV D1260, AB257, AW4062, ES229

Act 3: *Prelude*
London Symphony Orchestra, Kingsway Hall
(CR 912-1A, CR 913-1A, 6 January 1927)
78: HMV D1219, AB271, AW4064

Act 3: *Dance of the apprentices*
Symphony Orchestra, Kingsway Hall
(CR 814-2, 25 October 1926)
78: HMV D1139, AB200, AW4300, Victor 9060

CD: all selections in *Albert Coates conducts excerpts from Wagner's Die Meistersinger von Nürnberg and Parsifal*: Claremont CDGSE 78-50-70/71 (1997); the Act 1 Prelude is also in Aria Recordings 5001 (2001)

1927

Tristan und Isolde, excerpts from Act 3[15]
Tristan, Walter Widdop; Isolde, Göta Ljundberg; Kurwenal, Howard Fry (Charles Victor in *Isolde's ship appears*); Shepherd, Kennedy MacKenna; chorus; London Symphony Orchestra, Queen's Hall

14 incorrectly attributed to Lawrance Collingwood, and incorectly dated 26 January and 26 March 1926

15 Included here, in square brackets, are three excerpts conducted by Leo Blech and Lawrance Collingwood which were included in HMV's 10-side set of Act 3 (D1413/17), and which are in Claremont's CD re-issue. The recordings comprise basically three excerpts: (1) the Prelude, ending just before the shepherd's piping; (2) the scene between Kurwenal and Tristan beginning just after the conclusion of the shepherd's piping (*Kurwenal! He!*) and ending a few lines into Tristan's delirium (*das kann ich dir nicht sagen*); and (3) resuming after the delirium with Kurwenal's *Bist du nun tot?* and proceeding, without any cuts, to the end of the act.

Prelude
(CR 1537-1, 18 October 1927)
78: HMV D1413, AB394, Victor 9265, 9335

The shepherd's pipe awakens Tristan (*Kurwenal! He!*)
(CR 1557-1A, 24 October 1927)
78: HMV D1413, AB394, Victor 9265, 9336

Kurwenal tells Tristan how they came to Kareol
(CR 1556-2A, 24 October 1927)
78: HMV D1414, AB395, Victor 9266, 9337

Tristan awaits Isolde
(CR 1539-1A, 24 October 1927)
78: HMV D1414, AB395, Victor 9266, 9338

Isolde's ship appears
(CR 1538-1, 24 October 1927)
78: HMV D1415 AB396, Victor 9267, 9339

Tristan dies in Isolde's arms
(CR 1470-1, 24 August 1927)
78: HMV D1415, AB396, Victor 9267, 9339

Isolde weeps over the dead Tristan (*Isolde beweint Tristans*)
(CR 1471-1A, 24 August 1927)
78: HMV D1416, AB397, EJ265, Victor 9268, 9337

[*König Markes Ankunft* (*King Mark arrives*)
King Marke, Ivar Andrésen; Brangäne, Genia Guszalewicz; Melot, Marcel Noë; Shepherd [?], Kurwenal [?], Steersman, Eduard Habich; Staatskapelle, Leo Blech
(CWR 1327-2, 9 November 1927)
78: HMV D1416, AB397, EJ265, Victor 9268, 9337]

[*Tot denn alles, alles tot* (*King Mark grieves over the tragedy*)
King Marke, Ivar Andrésen; Brangäne, Genia Guszalewicz; Staatskapelle, Leo Blech
(CWR 1328-2, 9 November 1927)
78: HMV D1417, AB398, Victor 9269, 9338]

[*Isolde dies of grief for Tristan*
with orchestra conducted by Lawrance Collingwood
(CR 612-1, Kingsway Hall, 16 August 1926)
78: HMV D1417, AB398, Victor 9269, 9339]

78: [in addition to the above] Victor set M-41 (9265-9269), AM-41 (9335-9339)
CD: all selections in *Albert Coates, Dr Leo Blech, Lawrance Collingwood conduct Tristan und Isolde*: Claremont CDGSE 78-50-26 (1988); Naxos Historical 8.110200-2 (2003) (with *Tristan* (abridged), Bayreuth, 1928, Elmendorf)

1927-28

Parsifal, Act 2, *Parsifal-Kundry scene* (*Herzeleide*)
Göta Ljundberg, Kundry; Walter Widdop, Parsifal; London Symphony Orchestra

Part 1: *Ich sah das Kind*
(Cc 13706-1, Kingsway Hall, 11 October 1928)
78: HMV D1651, EJ459, ES573

Part 2: *Wehe! Wehe!*
(CR 1640-2, Kingsway Hall, 10 January 1928)
78: HMV D1651, EJ459, ES573

Part 3: *Seit Ewigkeiten harre ich deiner*
(CR 1469-2A, Queen's Hall, 24 August 1927)
78: HMV D1652, EJ460, ES574

Part 4: *Auf Ewigkeiten warst du verdammt mit mir*
(CR 1641-1, Kingsway Hall, 10 January 1928)
78: HMV D1652, EJ460, ES574

CD: all selections included with the 1925 excerpts in *Albert Coates conducts excerpts from Wagner's* Die Meistersinger von Nürnberg *and* Parsifal: Claremont CDGSE 78-50-70/71 (1997)

A Faust Overture
London Symphony Orchestra
(CR 1694-1A, CR 1695-1, Kingsway Hall, 16 February 1928)
78: HMV D1631, AB405, AW3994, EJ274, ES371, Victor 9734

1927-29

Der Ring des Nibelungen

Das Rheingold
Soloists: Walter Widdop, Arthur Fear, Nellie Walker, Elsie Suddaby, Louise Trenton, Howard Fry, Kennedy MacKenna, London Symphony Orchestra

Alberich steals the gold
Alberich, Fear; Rhinemaidens, Walker, Suddaby, Trenton
(CR 1540-3, Kingsway Hall, 5 January 1928)
78: HMV D1546, AB416, ES372

Wotan and Loge descend to Niebelheim
Loge, Widdop; Wotan, Fear; Fry, Walker, MacKenna
(CR 1541-2B, Queen's Hall, 18 October 1927)
78: HMV D1546, AB416, ES372

[*Einzug der Götter* (*Entry of the Gods*)
Friedrich Schorr, Waldemar Henke, Genia Guszalewicz
Staatskapelle Berlin, Leo Blech
(CDR 4700-2, 4701-3, 18 June 1927)
78: HMV AB303, D1319, EJ157, ES295
CD: *Friedrich Schorr sings Wagner*: Preiser 89214 (1994)]

CD: both Coates excerpts in *Albert Coates, Leo Blech, Die Walküre, Das Rheingold*: Claremont CDGSE 78-50 35/36 (1990); all are in *Der Ring des Nibelungen*: Pearl GEMM CDS9137 (1994), together with the 1926 Prelude to *Das Rheingold* HMV D1088, above)

Die Walküre

Siegmund, Walter Widdop; , Sieglinde, Göta Ljundberg and Louise Trenton; Hunding and Wotan, Howard Fry; Brünnhilde, Florence Austral, London Symphony Orchestra (except where otherwise indicated)

Act 1: *Siegmund seeks shelter* (Prelude, *Siegmund sucht Unterkunft*)
(CR 1485-1A, Queen's Hall, 26 August 1927)
78: HMV D1320, AB289, EJ202, ES403, Victor 9164

Act 1: *The sword hilt gleams* (*Der Schwertknauf glänzt*)
(CR 1467-1A, Queen's Hall, 23 August 1927)
78: HMV D1320, AB289, EJ202, ES296, ES403, Victor 9164

Act 1: *Sieglinde comes to Siegmund* (*Schlafet du Gast*)
(CR 1367-1A, Symphony Orchestra, Queen's Hall, 27 May 1927)
78: HMV D1321, AB290, EJ203, ES404, Victor 9165

Act 1: *Siegmund greets the spring night* (*Siegmund begrüsst des Lenzesnacht*)
(CR 1465-2, Queen's Hall, 23 August 1927)
78: HMV D1321, EJ203, AB290, ES404, Victor 9165

[Act 1: *Love duet*
Symphony Orchestra, Lawrance Collingwood
(CR 611-2A, 613-1, Queen's Hall, 16 August 1926)
78: HMV D1322, AB291, DB963, EJ204, ES405, Victor 9166]

Act 1: *Siegmund draws the sword* (*Siegmund zieht das Schwert aus dem Stamm*)
(CR 1466-2A, Queen's Hall, 23 August 1927)
78: HMV D1323, AB292, EJ205, ES406, Victor 9167

[Act 2: *Wotan-Bruünnhilde scene* (*Nun zäume dein Ross, reisige Maid*)
Friedrich Schorr, Frida Leider, Orchestra of the Berlin State Opera, Leo Blech
(CWR 1116-2, 1117-2, 1118-1, Berlin, 12 September 1927)
78: HMV D1323/24, AB292/93, EJ205/06, ES406/07, Victor 9167/68
CD: *Friedrich Schorr sings Wagner*: Preiser 89214 (1994)]

Act 2: *Siegmund and Sieglinde reach the mountain pass* (*Sieglinde und Siegmund erreichen die Bergeshöhe*)
(CR 1368-4, Queen's Hall, 10 January 1928)
78: HMV D1325, AB294, DB1056, EJ207, ES408, Victor 9169

Act 2: *Sieglinde is tormented with dread* (*Sieglindes Angsttraum*)
(CR 1369-1, Symphony Orchestra, Kingsway Hall, 27 May 1927)
78: HMV D1325, AB294, DB1056, EJ207, ES408, Victor 9169

Act 2: *Brunnhilde appears before Siegmund* (*Todesverkündigung*)
(CR 1462-1, Queen's Hall, 23 August 1927)
78: HMV D1326, AB295, EJ208, ES409, Victor 9170

Act 2: *Siegmund refuses to follow Brunnhilde* (*Todesverkündigung*)
(CR 1483-1A, Queen's Hall, 26 August 1927)
78: HMV D1326, AB295, EJ208, ES410, Victor 9170

Act 2: *Brunnhilde promises aid to Siegmund* (*Todesverkündigung*)
(CR 1484-1A, Queen's Hall, 26 August 1927)
78: HMV D1327, AB296, EJ211, ES410, Victor 9171

Act 2: *Siegmund challenges Hunding* (*Siegmund kampft mit Hunding*)
(CR 1463-3, Queen's Hall, 25 October 1927)
78: HMV D1328, AB297, EJ209, ES411, Victor 9171

Act 2: *Siegmund is slain* (*Siegmunds Tod*)
(CR 1464-1A, Queen's Hall, 23 August 1927)
78: HMV D1328, AB297, EJ210, ES411, Victor 9172

[Act 3 excerpts conducted by Leo Blech
Sieglinde, Göta Ljungberg; Brünnhilde, Frida Leider; Wotan, Friedrich Schorr; Valkyries, Göta Ljungberg, Elfriede Marherr, Genia Guszalewicz, Miss Alberti, Lydia Kindermann; Orchestra of the Berlin State Opera, recorded Berlin, June-November 1927
78: HMV D1327, 1329/33, Victor 9173-9177]

78: [in addition the above] Victor sets M-26/M-27
CD: *Albert Coates, Leo Blech, Die Walküre, Das Rheingold*: Claremont CDGSE 78-50 35/36 (1990); *Der Ring des Nibelungen*: Pearl GEMM CDS9137 (7 CDs) (1994)

Siegfried[16]
Siegfried, Lauritz Melchior; Mime, Albert Riess; Woodbird, Nora Grühn; Wanderer, Rudolph Bockelmann, Symphony Orchestra, Queen's Hall, London, 16-22 May 1929

[16] HMV's original 8-record set (1929) of selections from *Rheingold* and *Siegfried* comprised two discs of the *Rheingold* (D1546-1319) as listed above, and six *different* discs of *Siegfried* (D1530-35), with Rudolf Laubenthal, Siegfried; Frida Leider, Brünnhilde; Emil Schipper, Wotan; Maria Olszewska, Erda; with the Berlin State Opera Orchestra under Leo Blech, and the Vienna State Opera Orchestra under Karl Alwin. Electrola's 5-record set of *Siegfried* (EJ449-453), with Coates and others as detailed above, was issued in 1930.

Act 1: *Siegfried determines to learn fear* (*Fühltest du nie im finst'ren Wald*)
(CR 2197-3, 16 May 1929)
78: HMV D1690, AB506, EJ449, Victor 9805, 9815, 13251

Act 1: *Siegfried forges the sword*, part 1 (*Nothung! Nothung! neidliches Schwert!*)
(CR 2198-2B, 16 May 1929)
78: HMV D1690, AB506, DB1858, EJ449, IRX 125, Victor 9805, 9816, 13252

Act 1: *Siegfried forges the sword*, part 2 (*Hoho! hoho! hohei!*)
(CR 2199-1, 16 May 1929)
78: HMV D1691, AB507, EJ450, Victor 9806, 9817, 13253

Act 1: *Siegfried cleaves the anvil with his sword* (*Er schafft sich ein scharfes Schwert*)
(CR 2200-2, 17 May 1929)
78: HMV D1691, AB507, EJ450, Victor 9806, 9818, 13254

Act 2: *Siegfried meditates on his parentage* (*Dass der mein Vater nicht ist*)
(CR 2401-2, 17 May 1929)
78: HMV D1692, AB508, EJ451, Victor 9807, 9819, 13255

Act 2: *Siegfried tries to imitate the forest bird* (*Du holdes Vöglein!*)
(CR 2402-2A, 17 May 1929)
78: HMV D1692, AB508, EJ451, Victor 9807, 9820, 13256

Act 2: *Siegfried rests after slaying the dragon* (*Da lieg' auch du*)
(CR 2404-2B, 22 May 1929)
78: HMV D1693, AB509, EJ452, Victor 9808, 9821, 13257

Act 2: *The forest bird leads Siegfried to Brunnhilde's rock* (*Gönntest du mir wohl*)
(CR 2403-1, 17 May 1929)
78: HMV D1693, AB509, EJ452, Victor 9808, 9822, 13258

Act 3: *The Wanderer tries to bar Siegfried's path* (*Kenntest du mich kühner Spross*)
(CR 2405-3, 22 May 1929)
78: HMV D1694, AB510, DB7267, EJ453, Victor 9811, 9817, 13258

Act 3: *Siegfried passes on to the fire-girt rock* (*Zieh' hin! Ich kann dich nicht halten!*)
(CR 2406-2, 22 May 1929)
78: HMV D1694, AB510, DB7267, EJ453, Victor 9811, 9818, 13257

78: [in addition the above] HMV set 94; Victor set M-83 (9805-9814), AM-83 (9815-9824), DM-83 (13251-13261)
CD: in *Lauritz Melchior with Albert Coates in excerpts from Tannhäuser - Siegfried - Götterdämmerung*: Claremont CDGSE 78-50-33 (1989); *Der Ring des Nibelungen*: Pearl GEMM CDS9137 (1994); *Lauritz Melchior Anthology Vol. 5*: Danacord DACOCD319-321 (1998); *Siegfried (Excerpts)*: Naxos 8.110091-92 (2004)[17]

[17] The last three CD sets listed include other *Siegfried* excerpts conducted by Karl Alwin (D1533/34, 1928) and Robert Heger (D1836/37, May 1930; DB1578/83 and D1713, May 1931; and DB1710/13, May 1932).

Götterdämmerung

Siegfried, Walter Widdop; Brünnhilde, Florence Austral; Waltraute, Maartje Offers; Gunther, Arthur Fear; Hagen, Frederick Collier; Gutrune, Göta Ljungberg; Norns, Noel Edie, Evelyn Arden, Gladys Parker, London Symphony Orchestra (except where otherwise indicated)

Prologue: *Norn Scene*
(Cc 13724-2, 13725-1A, Kingsway Hall, 17 October 1928,
Cc 13726-5, 13727-5A, Kingsway Hall, 3 January 1929)
78: HMV D1572/3, AB511/2, ES537/8, Victor 9456-9457, 9578-9581, 13466-13469

Prologue: *The parting of Brunnhilde and Siegfried* (*Im Zeitmass*)
(Cc 13730-2, 13731-3, Kingsway Hall, 18 October 1928)
78: HMV D1574, AB513, ES539, Victor 9458, 9582-9583, 13470-13471

[Prologue: *Siegfried's Rhine Journey*
Berlin State Opera Orchestra, Karl Muck
(CWR 1418-2, Singakademie, Berlin, 10 December 1927)
78: HMV D1525, EJ224, ES344, ES540, Victor set M-37 (6859)/AM-37 (7016)/DM-37 (17266)

Act 1: *Gunther and Gutrune welcome Siegfried* (*Begrüsse froh, O Held*)
(Cc 13699-1, Kingsway Hall, 10 October 1928)
78: HMV D1575, AB514, EJ410, ES540, Victor 9459, 9585, 13473

[Act 1: *Hagen's watch*
Hagen, Ivar Andrésen; Berlin State Opera Orchestra, Fritz Zweig
(CLR 3883-1, Berlin, 17 February 1928)
78: HMV D1576, AB515, EH 227, EJ411, ES541, Victor 9460, 9586, 13474]

Act 1: *Seit er von dir geschieden* (Waltraute's narrative, part 1)
(CR 1460-3A, Kingsway Hall, 16 February 1928)
78: HMV D1576, AB515, DB4657, EJ411, ES541, Victor 9460, 9587, 13475

Act 1: *Seine Raben beide* (Waltraute's narrative, part 2)
(CR 1461-2, Queen's Hall, 23 August 1927)
78: HMV D1577, AB516, DB4657, EJ411, ES541, Victor 9461, 9588, 13476

Act 1: *Da sann ich nach* (Waltraute's narrative, part 3)
(CR 1473-3, Queen's Hall, 25 October 1927)
78 HMV D1577, AB516, DB4658, EJ412, ES542, Victor 9461, 9589, 13477

Act 1: *Brunnhilde refuses to give up the ring* (*Geh' heim*)
(CR 1474-3, Queen's Hall, 25 October 1927)
78: HMV D1578, AB517, DB4658, EJ413, ES543, Victor 9462, 9590, 13478

[Act 2: *Hoiho! Hoihohoho!* (*Hagens Ruf*')
Hagen, Ivar Andrésen; men's chorus of the Berlin State Opera; Staatskapelle, Leo Blech
(CDR 4708-2, 4709-1, Berlin, 21 June 1928)
78: HMV D1578/9, AB517/8, EJ150, EJ413/4, ES305, ES543/4, Victor 9462/3, 9591/2, 13479/80]

Act 2: *Siegfried's oath on Hagen's spear* (*Helle Wehr!*)
(Cc 13728-3A, chorus, Queen's Hall, 17 October 1927)
78: HMV D1579, AB518, DB4659, EJ414, ES544, Victor 9463, 9593, 13481

Act 2: *Hagen suggests revenge to Brunnhilde* (*Welches Unholds List*)
(Cc 13732-2A, Kingsway Hall, 18 October 1928)
78: HMV D1580, AB519, DB4659, ES545, Victor, 9464, 9578, 13481

Act 2: *Brunnhilde reveals Siegfried's vulnerability* (*O Undank*)
(Cc 13733-2, Kingsway Hall, 18 October 1928)
78: HMV D1580, AB519, DB4660, ES545, Victor 9464, 9579, 13480

Act 2: *The conspirators agree on Siegfried's death* (*Dich verriet er*)
(Cc 13734-1, Kingsway Hall, 18 October 1928)
78: HMV D1581, AB520, DB4660, ES546, Victor 9465, 9580, 13479

[Act 3: *Frau Sonne sendet lichte Strahlen*
Siegfried, Rudolf Laubenthal; Rhinemaidens, Tilly de Garmo, Lydia Kindermann, Elfriede Marherr; Berlin State Opera Orchestra, Leo Blech
(CLR 4488-1, 4489-1, 4490-2, 4491-2, Berlin, 10 September 1928)
78: HMV D1581/83, AB520/22, EJ416/18, ES546/48, Victor 9465/67, 9581/84, 13478/75]

[Act 3: *Mime hiess ein mürrischer Zwerg – In Lied zu dem Wipfel –Bünnhilde, heilige Braut*
Siegfried, Rudolf Laubenthal; Hagen, Emmanuel List; Gunther, Desider Zador; Berlin State Opera Orchestra, Leo Blech
(CLR 4483-2, 4484-1, 4482-1, Berlin, 7 September 1928)
78: HMV D1583/84, AB522/23, EJ418/19, ES548/49, Victor 9467/68, 9585/87, 13474/72]

[Act 3: *Siegfried's Funeral Music*
Berlin State Opera Orchestra, Karl Muck
(CWR 1419-3 and CWR 1420-2A, Singakademie, Berlin, 10 December 1927)
78: HMV D1585, EJ225, ES355, ES550, AW54, AB388, Victor M-37/AM-37/DM-37]

[Act 3: *Brunnhilde comes to grieve*
(CR 1472-3A, Lawrance Collingwood, Queen's Hall, 1 December 1927)
78: HMV D1586, AB525, Victor 9486, 9590, 13469]

Act 3: *Brunnhilde bids a funeral pyre be built*
(CR 1486-3, Queen's Hall, 25 October 1927)
78: HMV D1586, AB525, Victor 9486, 9591, 13468

Act 3: *Brunnhilde lights the pyre* (*Oh ihr, der Eide heilige Hüter!*)
(CR 1487-1, Queen's Hall, 26 August 1927)
78: HMV D1587, AB526, Victor 9487, 9592, 13467

Act 3: *Brunnhilde rides into the blazing pyre* (*Fliegt heim, ihr Raben*)
(CR 1475-2, Queen's Hall, 25 August 1927)
78: HMV D1587, AB526, Victor 9487, 9593, 13466

78: [in addition to the HMV discs listed above] EJ407/21 and 225, Victor sets M-60 (9456-9469/9486-9487), AM-60 (9578-9593), DM-60 (13466-13481)[18]
CD: *Albert Coates – Leo Blech – Lawrance Collingwood: Götterdämmerung*: Claremont CDGSE 78-50-37/38 (1990);[19] *Der Ring des Nibelungen*: Pearl GEMM CDS9137 (1994)

1929

Tannhäuser
Act 3: *Rome narration* (*Imbrunst im Herzen*)
Tannhäuser, Lauritz Melchior, Symphony Orchestra
(CR 2407-1, 2408-1, Queen's Hall, 22 May 1929)
78: HMV D1675, AB497, EJ433, ES454, Victor 9707
CD: in *Lauritz Melchior with Albert Coates in excerpts from* Tannhäuser - Siegfried - Götterdämmerung: Claremont CDGSE 78-50-33 (1989)

Tristan und Isolde, Act 2, scene 2, Love duet, abridged[20]
Tristan, Lauritz Melchior; Isolde, Frida Leider, (orchestras and dates as below)

Part 1: *Isolde! Tristan!*
(CLR 5612-1, Berlin State Opera Orchestra, Berlin, 13 September 1929)
78: HMV D1723, W1148, AW287, EJ482, ES605, Victor 7273

Part 2: *Doch es rächte sich*
(CLR 5613-1, Berlin State Opera Orchestra, Berlin, 13 September 1929)
78: HMV D1723, W1148, AW287, EJ482, ES605, Victor 7273

Part 3: *O sink hernieder, Nacht der Liebe*
(Cc 16620-2A, London Symphony Orchestra, Kingsway Hall, London, 6 May 1929)
78: HMV D1724, W1149, AW288, EJ483, ES606, Victor 7274

Part 4: *Soll ich lauschen*
(Cc 16621-1A, London Symphony Orchestra, Kingsway Hall, London, 6 May 1929)
78: HMV D1724, W1149, AW288, EJ483, ES606, Victor 7274

18 The Victor sets used Coates's recordings of the *Rhine Journey* and *Funeral Music* (see 1926 above).

19 The notes to this set do not have precise dates or matrix numbers; like the Pearl set, it has used Coates's 1926 recordings of *Siegfried's Rhine Journey* and *Funeral March*.

20 Omitted from the recording was the usual big cut in Act 2, from *Dem Tage! Dem Tage!* (Tristan) to *dass nachtsichtig mein Auge wahres zu sehen tauge* (Tristan), and all the lines from Brangänge's first warning *Einsam wachend… Bald entweicht die Nacht!* to her second *Habet Acht! Schon weicht dem Tag die Nacht!*, and a portion of the lovers' final passage, from *Nur banne das Bangen* to *von Erwachen's Not befreit.* The abridgement of a scene that, performed uncut, lasts around 30 minutes, lasts here 17 minutes.

LP: *Great Recordings of the Century: Frieda Leider, Lauritz Melchior*: HMV/Angel COLH 132 (1963); *Wagner on Record 1926 - 1942*: EMI RLS7711 (1983); *Les Introuvables du Chant Wagnérien*: EMI Pathé 2902123 (1984)

CD: *Albert Coates, Dr Leo Blech, Lawrance Collingwood conduct* Tristan und Isolde: Claremont CDGSE 78-50-26 (1988); *Les Introuvables du Chant Wagnérien - Wagner Singing on Record - Wagner-Gesang auf Schallplatte*: EMI CMS7 64008 2 (1991); *Great Conductors of the 20th Century - Albert Coates*: EMI 7243 5 75486 2 5 (2002)

Lohengrin, Act 3, Prelude
London Symphony Orchestra
(Cc 17832-1, Queen's Hall, 23 October 1929)
78: HMV D1815

Die Walküre and ***Götterdämmerung***, orchestral excerpts
London Symphony Orchestra, Queen's Hall, 29 October 1929

Die Walküre, Act 3: *Magic Fire Music*
(CR 2465-1A, CR 2466-2)
78: HMV D1797, W748, AB177, AB617, AW142, EJ32, ES262

Götterdämmerung, Prologue: *Siegfried's Rhine Journey*
(CR 2463-3, CR 2464-2A)
78: HMV D1777, W800, AB178, AB607, AW141, EJ34, EJ581, ES263, ES653

Götterdämmerung, Act 3: *Siegfried's Funeral Music*
(CR 2461-1, CR 2462-3B)
78: HMV D1810

1930[21]

Die Meistersinger, excerpts
Hans Sachs, Friedrich Schorr; Walther von Stolzing, Rudolf Laubenthal; London Symphony Orchestra (except where otherwise noted)

Act 1: *"Fanget an!"*
Laubenthal, New Symphony Orchestra
(Cc 18766-1, Kingsway Hall, 5 May 1930)
78: HMV DB1558 (32-1651)[22]

[21] In the notes accompanying *Friedrich Schorr sings Wagner* (Preiser 89214, 1994) there are two excerpts from *Tannhäuser* attributed to Coates (and incorrectly dated 10 May 1930). These were in fact conducted by Lawrance Collingwood: *Als du in kühnen Sange uns bestrittest* (BR 2492-3, 9 May 1930, HMV E 586, ER 343, EW87) and *Blick' ich umher in diesem edlen Kreise* (CR 2493-1, 9 May 1930, HMV D1866, EJ566, ES684).

[22] This record, coupled with the *Preislied*, is not in Dyment's discography. The record is listed without information as to conductor, orchestra, date, or matrix numbers in John R. Bennett and Eric Hughes, *Voices of the Past, Vol. 4: The International Red Label Catalogue of 'DB' & 'DA' His Master's Voice Recordings 1924-1956* (Oakwood Press, n. d.), p. 76. The details above come from the HMV registers transcribed by Alan Kelly. I have included, exceptionally, the single-side numbers after the catalogue number. I have been unable to locate a copy of the record itself.

Act 2: *Fliedermonolog* (*Was duftet doch der Flieder*)
(CR 2496-1, 2497-1, Queen's Hall, 10 May 1930)
78: HMV ES685, Victor 7425
CD: *Friedrich Schorr sings Wagner*: Preiser 89214 (1994)

Act 2: *Schusterlied* (*Jerum! Jerum!*)
(CR 2494-2, Queen's Hall, 10 May 1930)
78: HMV D1866, EJ566, ES684, Victor 7426
CD: *Friedrich Schorr*: Pearl GEMM CD9944 (1992); *Friedrich Schorr sings Wagner*: Preiser 89214 (1994)

Act 3: *Grüss Gott, mein Junker!*
(CR 2777-1, Kingsway Hall, 1 May 1930)
78: HMV D1990, EJ567, ES686, Victor 7427
CD: *Friedrich Schorr*: Pearl GEMM CD9944 (1992); *Friedrich Schorr sings Wagner*: Preiser 89214 (1994)

Act 3: *Mein Freund*
(CR 2778-1, Kingsway Hall, 1 May 1930)
78: HMV D1990, EJ567, ES686, Victor 7427
CD: *Friedrich Schorr*: Pearl GEMM CD9944 (1992); *Friedrich Schorr sings Wagner*: Preiser 89214 (1994)

Act 3: *Abendlich glühend*
(Cc 18760-2, Kingsway Hall, 1 May 1930)
78: HMV EJ568, ES687, Victor 7428
CD: *Friedrich Schorr*: Pearl GEMM CD9944 (1992)

Act 3: *Aha! Da streicht die Lene schon um's Haus*
(CR 2495-1, Queen's Hall, 10 May 1930)
78: HMV D2002, AB715, AW289, EJ568, EJ693, EJ696, ES687, ES761, Victor 7428
CD: *Friedrich Schorr*: Pearl GEMM CD9944 (1992); *Friedrich Schorr sings Wagner*: Preiser 89214 (1994)

Act 3: *Morgenlich leuchtend* (*Preislied*)
Laubenthal, New Symphony Orchestra
(Cc 18767-2, Kingsway Hall, 5 May 1930)
78: HMV DB1558 (32-1652)

CD: [in addition to those listed above] *Friedrich Schorr in* Die Meistersinger *and* Der Fliegende Hollander: Pearl GEMM 9944 (1992) (except the *Fliedermonolog*); *Friedrich Schorr sings Wagner*: Preiser 89214 (1994) (four excerpts as indicated above[23]); *Albert Coates conducts excerpts from Wagner's* Die Meistersinger von Nürnberg *and* Parsifal: Claremont CDGSE 78-50-70/71 (1997); *Die Meistersinger von Nürnberg - A Reconstruction of a Performance at the Staatsoper, Berlin, May 1928*: Symposium 1232 & 1233 (1998)

[23] The notes accompanying the Preiser set attribute one further excerpt to Coates which was in fact conducted by Robert Heger, namely: *Abendlich glühend*, Lauritz Melchior, Friedrich Schorr, London Symphony Orchestra (2B 530-1, 9 May 1931, HMV D2000, EJ700, Victor 7681).

1932

Die Feen, *Overture*
London Symphony Orchestra
(2B 2809-1, 2B 2810-1, Abbey Road, 19 February 1932)
78: HMV DB1679, Victor 36321

Die Meistersinger, Act 3: *Dance of the Apprentices*
London Symphony Orchestra
(2B 2824-1, Abbey Road, 25 February 1932)
78: HMV D1139

6. Wilhelm Furtwängler conducts Wagner[1]

Works recorded, including excerpts:

Der fliegende Holländer: 1949, 1952
Tannhäuser: 1935, 1936, 1949, 1951, 1952, 1954
Lohengrin: 1930, 1936, 1947, 1949, 1954
Tristan und Isolde: 1930, 1931, 1938, 1941, 1942, 1943, 1947, 1950, 1952, 1954
Die Meistersinger von Nürnberg: 1937, 1938, 1942, 1943, 1949, 1950, 1951
Siegfried Idyll: 1949, 1952
Der Ring des Nibelungen: 1950, 1953, also -
Die Walküre: 1936, 1937, 1938, 1949, 1952, 1954
Götterdämmerung: 1933, 1937, 1938, 1948, 1949, 1950, 1952, 1954
Parsifal: 1938, 1951

1930[2]

Lohengrin, Act 1, Prelude
Berlin Philharmonic Orchestra, Hochschule für Musik
(matrix 1085½BI, 1086¾BI, 1930)
78: Grammophon 95408;[3] Brunswick 90231; Decca CA 8089;[4] Fonit 91030

[1] There are three substantive discographies of Furtwängler, none comprehensive but each valuable in its own way. Henning Smidth Olsen's, *Wilhelm Furtwängler: a Discography*, 2nd Revised Edition (San Francisco: Mr L. Schipper & the North American Wilhelm Furtwängler Society, 1973) is indispensable for its detail on matrix numbers, dates, etc. despite its age. John Hunt's, *The Furtwängler Sound*, 6th edition (1999) has no matrix numbers but has extensive listings of re-issues, including those which misdescribe their contents, and is indispensable for the collector. René Trémine's, *Wilhelm Furtwängler: A Discography* (Paris: Tahra Productions, 1997) is, like Olsen's, chronologically arranged with fewer reissues listed, but has valuable appendices, including on the recordings of the *Ring* at La Scala (by Angelo Scottini), on pirate recordings, on fakes and dubious recordings, and on Furtwängler on film. An up-dated version of the discography, though limited to CDs, was issued as *Furtwängler: une CD-graphie*, FURT 1094, a CD-ROM accompanying *Wilhelm Furtwängler in Memoriam*: Tahra FURT 1090-1093 (2004). It was subsequently posted online at patangel.free.fr/furt/disco.htm (accessed 1 May 2011). While the discography in this book is indebted to all these sources, I have sought to add more detailed descriptions of certain excerpts, and to limit the vast number of LP and CD re-issues generally to the earliest and the more recent.

[2] According to Trémine, Furtwängler's 1930 recordings were made during three different sessions: 6 January, 7 February and 5 June.

[3] This was a recording of the Deutsche Grammophon Aktiengesellschaft (after the War called "Deutsche Grammophon Gesellschaft") whose export labels were "Polydor." This is the catalogue name used in some re-issues and discographies, including Olsen's, instead of Grammophon.

[4] Olsen lists a different matrix number for the Decca issue, namely 1086½ instead of 1086¾. However, 1086¾ appears on all copies of the Decca record inspected, including in the British Library.

Tristan und Isolde, Act 1, Prelude
Berlin Philharmonic Orchestra, Hochschule für Musik
(matrix 1087½BI, 1088½BI, 1089½BI, 1930)[5]

78: Grammophon 95438/39; Brunswick 90201/02; Decca CA 8039/CA 8156; Fonit 91028/29

Tristan und Isolde, Act 3, Liebestod
Berlin Philharmonic Orchestra, Hochschule für Musik
(matrix 1089½BI, 1090½BI, 1930)

78: Grammophon 95439; Brunswick 90202 Decca CA 8156; Fonit 91029

LP: Heliodor 88 012 (1969)

CD: *Wilhelm Furtwängler Early Recordings 1926-37*: Koch 3-7073-2 (1995); *Wilhelm Furtwängler enregistrements Polydor 1929/1937*: Société Wilhelm Furtwängler SWF 042/044 (2004); *Wilhelm Furtwängler The Complete Pre-War Studio Sessions*: Andromeda ANDRCD 5008 (2005)

1931

Tristan und Isolde, Bayreuth, live performance, 18 August 1931, Act 1 excerpts (ca. 11 mins)[6]
Isolde, Nanny Larsén-Todsen; Tristan, Gotthelf Pistor; Kurwenal, Rudolf Bockelmann; Brangäne, Anny Helm, Bayreuth Festival Chorus and Orchestra

Scene 3: Isolde's Narration - from *[darinnen krank ein] siecher Mann elend im Sterben lag* to *Das Schwert, ich liess es fallen* (Isolde) (3' 15")

Scenes 3 and 4: from *so reihte sie die Mutter* (Brangäne) to *an's Land ihn zu begleiten; nicht werd'*

[5] Both the end of the Prelude and the first part of the Liebestod occupy the third side (matrix 1089½BI) of the set. Both Decca CA 8039 and French Polydor 95439 mis-label their third side as Liebestod only. Olsen reports that takes 1089BI and 1089½BI were both issued on Polydor 95439 and that 1089BI was used exclusively for the American Brunswick and Italian Fonit sets. In the case of Brunswick 90202, all examined copies used 1089½BI. Fonit 91029 has not been checked. Re-issues on LP and CD are rarely sufficiently precise to know what original sources (matrices) were used. The SWF CD re-issue lists for the Prelude 1087½BI, 1088½BI, and 1089BI, and for the Liebestod, 1089½BI and 1090½BI. This implies (somewhat implausibly) that two different side 3s were available and used, one (1089BI) from which the last part of the Prelude was copied, and another (1089½BI) from which the first part of the Liebestod was copied.

[6] The very first broadcast from the Bayreuth Festival was on 18 August 1931, not 23 July as some writers have claimed. *The Times*, 18 August 1931, p. 8 gives details of the British and European stations that carried the broadcast; it was also relayed by short-wave to the United States. Only the second and third acts were broadcast in England, and these "were exceedingly well received:" *The Times*, 19 August 1931, p. 8. German newspapers also hailed 18 August as the first broadcast from Bayreuth: press clippings in the Richard-Wagner-Museum, Bayreuth. An Act 1 Prelude claiming to be from Bayreuth in 1931 was issued in *100 Years Bayreuth*: Acanta/BASF HB 22 863-0 (1976); *100 Jahre Bayreuther Festspiele - Ehrengabe der Stadt Bayreuth*: No. 2666 760 (1976); *Richard Wagner: Sein Werk in dokumentarischen Aufnahmen* Acanta 40.23 502 (1983); *Wilhelm Furtwängler dirigiert Wagner*: Acanta 43 121 (1987); and *Wilhelm Furtwängler dirigiert Wagner*: Pilz/Acanta 44 1055 (1992). However, it was in fact the 1938 studio recording (below). Olsen (p. 4) and Hunt (6th ed., p. 169) list a Prelude from Bayreuth, 18 August 1931 in German radio archives, unpublished and presumably lost. A Prelude bearing this date appeared on an LP issued by the Société Wilhelm Furtwängler (SWF 8207), but it was identical to the Acanta issues. Olsen and Hunt also list three excerpts from Acts 1 (Liebestrank) and Act 2 (Brangäne-Isolde scene and *O sink' hernieder*) from Bayreuth, 23 July 1931 in German radio archives, again unpublished and presumably lost.

[ich zur Seit' ihm gehen] (Isolde) (4' 29")
Scene 5: from *Müh't Euch die?* (Tristan) to *dass du nicht dir's [entfallen lässt!]* (Tristan) (3' 19")

LP: in *Great Singers in Copenhagen - Historical Live Recordings from The Archive of Danmarks Radio - Vol. 1 - 1931-1939*: Danacord 131-133 (1983) [gives date as 18 July]

CD: in *Wilhelm Furtwängler: The earliest Wagner recordings: Live recordings 1931 - 1936*: Istituto Discografico Italiano IDIS 330/31 (1999)

1933

Götterdämmerung, Act 3, Siegfried's Funeral March
Berlin Philharmonic Orchestra, Hochschule für Musik[7]
(matrix 733BE 1, 734½BE 1, 1933)

78: Grammophon 67054; Brunswick 90251; Decca CA 8173;[8] Fonit 91026

LP: Heliodor 88 012 (1969); *Great Conductors of the Bayreuth Festival 1928-1971*: DG 2721 113 (1976)

CD: *Wilhelm Furtwängler Early Recordings 1926-37*: Koch 3-7073-2 (1995); *Wilhelm Furtwängler The Complete Pre-War Studio Sessions*: Andromeda ANDRCD 5008 (2005)

1935

Tannhäuser, Vienna, live performances, 13, 15 and 18 October 1935,[9] excerpts (ca. 25 mins)

Tannhäuser, Gotthelf Pistor; Elisabeth, Anne Báthy; Hermann, Ludwig Hofmann; Wolfram, Sándor Svéd; Walter, Georg Maikl; Heinrich, William Wernigk; Biterolf, Franz Markhoff; Reinmar, Karl Ettl; Orchestra of the Vienna State Opera

a. Act 1, scene 4: *Als du in kühnen Sange… aufs neue leuchte uns ihr Stern!* (Wolfram) (2' 52")

b. Act 2, scene 1: *Dich, teure Halle… sei mir gegrüßt!* (applause) (Elisabeth) (3' 29")[10]

c. Act 2, scene 4: *Gar viel und schön* (Hermann)… *Du holden Kunst* (Knights and noble women) (4' 09")

d. Act 2, scene 4: *[Dir, hohe Lie]be, töne begeistert mein Gesang, die mir in Engels Schöne* (Wolfram)… *Dir, Göttin der Liebe…* (Tannhäuser)… *Hört es! Er war im Venusberg!* (chorus) (2' 21")

e. Act 2, scene 4: *[Vernehmt durch mich,] was Gottes Wille ist! Der Unglücksel'ge, den gefangen … reuvoll zur Buße lenke er den Schritt!* (Elisabeth) (3' 03")

f. Act 2, scene 4: *Ein Engel stieg aus lichtem Äther* (Hermann and chorus) …*Zum heil den Sündigen zu führen, die Gott-gesante nahte mir* (Tannhäuser) (2' 30")

g. Act 2, scene 4: *Erbarm' dich mein …* (Tannhäuser) …*Ich fleh' für ihn* (Elisabeth, with Hermann, chorus) (1' 18")

h. Act 3, scene 1: *Wohl wußt' ich hier sie im Gebet zu finden … O! Würd'ihr Lind'[rung nur ertheilt] Ihr Heil'gen, laßt erfüllt es sehen!* (Wolfram) (2' 56")[11]

[7] Olsen reported that DGG was unable to provide the recording dates for this item.

[8] Olsen lists a different matrix number for the Decca issue, namely 734BE 1 instead of 734½BE 1. However, 734½BE 1 appears on all copies of the Decca record inspected, including in the British Library.

[9] The dates of the individual excerpts are 13 October (b, c, d, e, f, g), 15 October (a), and 18 October (h, i).

[10] There is a longer orchestral introduction on Koch (22") than on UORC (10").

[11] The excerpt on TELDEC is slightly shorter (2' 32") than that on UORC (2' 56"), ending at *Ihr Heil'gen, laßt erfüllt es sehen!*, after which the sound quality deteriorates.

i. Act 3, scene 2: : *[O du mein holder Abendstern,] wohl grüsst' ich immer dich so gern… ein sel'ger Engel dort zu werden!* (Wolfram) (2' 09")[12]

LP: Unique Opera Records UORC 242 (1975) (all except c); *Wiener Staatsoper 1935*: Belvedere Teletheater: TELDEC 6.43333 AG (1985) (a, b, c, h, i)

CD: *Wilhelm Furtwängler dirigiert Wagner*: Pilz/Acanta 44 1055 (1992) (d); *Edition Wiener Staatsoper Live, Vol. 4*: Koch Schwann 3-1454-2 (1994) (a, f, i); *Edition Wiener Staatsoper Live, Vol. 10*: Koch Schwann 3-1460-2 (1994) (c); *Edition Wiener Staatsoper Live, Vol. 20*: Koch Schwann 3-1470-2 (1994) (b)

1936[13]

Tannhäuser, Vienna, live performance, 9 January 1936, excerpts (ca. 10 mins)
Tannhäuser, Max Lorenz; Elisabeth, Maria Müller
Orchestra of the Vienna State Opera

Act 1, scene 2: *[da ihr höchsten] Preis dir ward!* (Venus) … *Dir töne Lob!… O Königin, Göttin! Laß mich ziehn* (Tannhäuser) (2' 18")

Act 2, scene 1: *Dich, teure Halle… sei mir gegrüßt!* (applause) (Elisabeth) (3' 00")

Act 2, scene 2: *[O bleib und laß] zu deinen Füßen mich!* … *All mein Erinnern ist mir schnell geschwunden* (Tannhäuser, with Elisabeth) (1' 27")

Act 2, scene 4: *Seht mich, die Jungfrau… Ich fleh für ihn* (Elisabeth) … *Weh! Weh mir Unglück[sel'gem!]* (Tannhäuser) (2' 33")

Act 2, scene 4: *Zum Heil den Sündigen zu führen… Erbarm dich mein!* (Tannhäuser) (1' 19")

LP: *Wiener Staatsoper 1935* [*sic*]: Belvedere Teletheater: TELDEC 6.43333 AG (1985) (from *Dir töne Lob!* only - 1' 57")

CD: *Edition Wiener Staatsoper Live, Vol. 20*: Koch Schwann 3-1470-2 (1994)

Die Walküre, Vienna, live performances, 13 and 17 February 1936, excerpts (ca. 69 mins)
Siegmund, Franz Völker; Sieglinde, Maria Müller; Wotan, Walter Großmann; Brünnhilde, Anny Konetzni; Hunding, Alfred Jerger; Gerhilde, Eva Hadrabova; Ortlinde, Dora Komarek; Waltraute, Rosette Anday; Schwertleite, Enid Szantho; Helmwige, Luise Helletsgruber; Siegrune, Aenne Michalsky; Grimgerde, Bella Paalen; Roßweiße, Dora With; Orchestra of the Vienna State Opera

Act 1: Prelude to scene 1: *Wes Herd dies auch sei* (Siegmund) (3' 38")

Act 1, scene 1: *Labung biet' ich* (Sieglinde) …*Schmecktest du mir ihn zu?* (Siegmund) (4' 55")

Act 1, scene 2: *Weit her, traun!* (Hunding)… *der Eiche blühender Stamm* (Siegmund) (3' 47")

Act 1, scene 2: *auf den Leichen lag sie tot… warum ich Friedmund nicht heisse!* (Siegmund) (1' 08")

Act 1, scene 3: *Was gleisst dort hell…?* … *glimmt nur noch lichtlose Glut!* (Siegmund) (2' 53")

Act 1, scene 3: *Ich bin's: höre mich an!* (Sieglinde) … *der Lenz lacht in der Saal!* (Siegmund) (6' 44")

Act 1, scene 3: *Du bist der Lenz* (Sieglinde) … *Seligstes Weib!* (Siegmund) (2' 03")

Act 1, scene 3: *Ein Minnetraum… heraus aus der Scheide zu mir* (Siegmund, with Sieglinde) (5' 03")

Act 2: Prelude to scene 1: *Hojotoho! Heiaha!* (Brünnhilde, with Wotan) (4' 09")

Act 2, scene 3: *Verweile, süßestes Weib* (Siegmund)… *der ganz ihr Minne geweckt* (Sieglinde) (3' 55")

[12] The version on Koch (3' 00") appears to have added the opening words, *O du, mein holder Abendstern*, which are missing on UORC, from another performance; it also has a longer postlude (1' 05") than UORC (0' 29").

[13] There are excerpts from a 1936 *Götterdämmerung* purporting to be conducted by Furtwängler at Covent Garden in *Der Ring des Nibelungen Historical Recordings 1936-1958, Vol. 4*: Gala GL 100.671 (4 CDs) (2008). They were in fact conducted by Thomas Beecham at Covent Garden on 14 May 1936.

Act 2, scene 3: *Wo bist du, Siegmund? ... Kein Schwert frommt* (Sieglinde) (1' 07")
Act 2, scene 3: *Ich sehe die Not... Auf der Walstatt she' ich dich wieder!* (Brünnhilde, with Siegmund) (with a break) (8' 06")
Act 3, scene 1: Ride of the Valkyries ... *Wotan zu bringen die Wal* (Roßweiße) (4' 43")
Act 3, scenes 1 and 2: *Fort denn eile* (Brünnhilde) ... *wußte den Quell meines Willens!* (Wotan) (4' 53")
Act 3, scene 2: *[nicht] wählen darf er für dich... nicht kiesen kann ich es dir!* (Wotan, with Brünnhilde) (1' 52")
Act 3, scene 3: orchestral passage after *Der Augen leuchtendes Paar* in Wotan's farewell (2' 00")
Act 3, scene 3: orchestral passage (2' 51") to... *Loge, hör! ... Loge! Hieher!* (Wotan) (1' 05")
Act 3, scene 3: *Wer meines Speeres Spitze fürchtet* (Wotan) to end of the Act and applause (3' 00")
LP: The Golden Age of Opera EJS 451 (1968) (*Labung biet' ich* only)
CD: *Edition Wiener Staatsoper Live, Vol. 20*: Koch Schwann 3-1470-2 (1994)

Lohengrin, Bayreuth, live performance, 19 July 1936, Act 3 excerpts (ca. 30 mins)[14]
Lohengrin, Franz Völker; Elsa, Maria Müller; Ortrud, Margarete Klose; King Heinrich, Josef von Manowarda, Chorus and Orchestra of the Bayreuth Festival
Prelude (2' 55")... Scenes 1 and 2: ... *Treulich geführt* (Bridal chorus) (5' 10")... *Das süße Lied verhallt* (Lohengrin) ... *die nur Gott verleiht!* (Lohengrin and Elsa) (4' 20")
Scene 3: orchestral introduction (3' 41") ... *Heil, König Heinrich!* (Men of Brabant) (0' 18") ...*Habt Dank* (King Heinrich) ... *Was bringen die? Was tun sie kund?* (Chorus) (1' 52")
Scene 3: *In fernem Land ... bin Lohengrin genannt* (Lohengrin) ... *Hör ich so [seine höchste Art bewähren]* (King Heinrich , men and women) (4' 40")
Scene 3: *Mein lieber Schwan* (Lohengrin) to the end of the Act (8' 07")
LP: The Golden Age of Opera EJS 399 (1967); Fonit Cetra FE 25 (1981)
CD: *Wilhelm Furtwängler dirigiert Wagner*: Pilz/Acanta 44 1055 (1992); Archipel ARPCD 0284 (2004) (both EJS and Archipel contain the 30 sec. introductory broadcast announcements *Achtung!* etc.)

1937[15]

Die Walküre, London, Covent Garden, live performance, 26 May 1937, Act 3
Brünnhilde, Kirsten Flagstad; Sieglinde, Maria Müller; Wotan, Rudolf Bockelmann; Gerhilde, Mae Craven; Grimgerde, Gladys Garside; Helmwige, Elsa Stenning; Ortlinde,

[14] This *Lohengrin* was broadcast throughout Europe and beyond, though only the first two acts in England: *The Times*, 20 July 1936, p. 10.

[15] There are two fake recordings attributed to Furtwängler from 1937, both of which were partly exposed by David Hamilton in "Misremembering Bayreuth," *High Fidelity*, vol 32 no. 4 (April 1982), p. 58. First, in *Memories of Bayreuth – Wagner – Parsifal*: IGI-379 (1980) there is an excerpt from *Parsifal* purportedly conducted by Furtwängler at Bayreuth in 1937: from *Ja, Wehe!* (Herbert Janssen, Amfortas) to the end of Act 3. The excerpt is in fact an amalgam of two performances: Fritz Reiner conducting at Covent Garden on 3 May 1937 (from UORC 130), and Leopold Reichwein conducting at the Vienna State Opera on 4 April 1942 with Max Lorenz as Parsifal. (This has also been attributed to Richard Strauss: see his discography below.) Second, in *Memories of Bayreuth, Vol. II*: Educational Media Associates RR-540 (2 LPs) (1981) there are excerpts from *Götterdämmerung* purportedly conducted by Furtwängler at the Bayreuth Festival on 30 July and 17 August 1937. These are in fact a compilation of recordings from Covent Garden (1938), La Scala (1950), Berlin (1944) (*Brünnhilde! Heilige Braut!*, Max Lorenz, Orchestra of the Staatsoper Berlin, Robert Heger, radio recording), and Berlin (1928) (*Starke Scheite*, Frida Leider, Orchestra of the Staatsoper Berlin, Leo Blech: HMV D 2025/26), with an unidentified orchestral ending. The compilation was resissued in *Der Ring des Nibelungen Historical Recordings 1936-1958, Vol. 4*: Gala GL 100.671 (4 CDs) (2008) with the same false claim to be from Bayreuth in 1937.

Thelma Bardsley; Roßweiße, Evelyn Arden; Schwertleite, Gladys Ripley; Siegrune, Edith Coates; Waltraute, Linda Seymour; London Philharmonic Orchestra (Gramophone Company Technical Test Series 2EA 5238-5253)[16]

LP: The Golden Age of Opera EJS 450 (1968); Discocorp RR-417 (1978)

CD: *Wilhelm Furtwängler dirigiert Wagner*: Pilz/Acanta 44 1055 (1992); Music & Arts CD 1035 (1998); Myto 981.H003 (1998); Walhall Eternity WLCD 0045 (2004)

Götterdämmerung, London, Covent Garden, live performance, 1 June 1937, excerpts (ca. 102 mins)[17]

Prologue, scene 2: Dawn, *Zu neuen Taten* (Brünnhilde), Brünnhilde-Siegfried scene, Siegfried's Rhine Journey (beginning only) (12')

Act 1, scene 3: Waltraute arrives at Brünnhilde's rock, *Altgewohntes Geräusch* (Brünnhilde), Waltraute's narrat ive to the end of the Act (34')

Act 2, scene 4: *Heil dir, Gunther* (Vassals) to the end of the Act (33')

Act 3, scene 3: *Her den Ring!* (Hagen) to the end of the Act (22')

Brünnhilde, Kirsten Flagstad; Siegfried, Lauritz Melchior; Hagen, Ludwig Weber; Gunther, Herbert Janssen; Gutrune, Maria Nezadal; Waltraute, Kerstin Thorborg; London Philharmonic Orchestra (Gramophone Company Technical Test Series 2EA 5619-5645)

LP: The Golden Age of Opera EJS 431 (1968); [Educational Media Associates of America] RR-429 (1978)

CD: Eklipse EKR 62 (1997); Music & Arts CD 1035 (1998); Gebhardt JGCD 0003-2 (1999)[18]

Die Meistersinger, Vienna, live performance, 25 November 1937, excerpts (ca. 47 mins)

Act 1 Prelude (with break at 3' 45") to first line of the chorus *Da zu der Heiland kam* (5' 15")

Act 1, scene 3: *[Am stillen Herd im Winterszeit…] Wann dann die Flur vom Frost befreit… mir sinnend gab zu lauschen* (Walther, with Beckmesser, Vogelgesang, Kothner, Sachs) (2' 36")

Act 1, scene 3: *Fanget an!* (Beckmesser) … *"Fanget an!" So rief der Lenz in den Wald* … (Walther) *schweig ich schon ganz und gar* (Beckmesser) (4' 16")

Act 2, scene 6: *[Jerum! Jerum!] …Die Schuh' machen Euch große Sorgen* … (Sachs) … *Ja, besser Geduld* (Eva, with Walther and Beckmesser) (3' 57")

Act 2, scene 6: *Nun, gut denn! Fanget an!* (Sachs) *"Den Tag she' ich erscheinen"… Sachs! Seht!…* (Beckmesser) (4' 06")

Act 2, scene 6: *Zu Hilfe! Zu Hilfe!* (Magdalene) … riot scene ending just before the Nightwatchman's lines (2' 16")

16 Trémine reports that technical test recordings were made of *Das Rheingold* on 24 May 1937 (2EA 5201-5234) and *Siegfried* on 28 May 1937 (2EA 5609-5618). They have not been published.

17 Timings are approximate as they vary slightly from re-issue to re-issue. Moreover, the various issues of these excerpts contain more or less music than each other, mostly by a number of bars; the exception is the Music & Arts set which, although it is superior in sound, omits several minutes from scene 4 (*Heil dir, Gunther*), beginning at Brünnhilde's *Heil'ge Götter*: Gary Galo, *ARSC Journal*, vol. 30 no. 1 (Spring, 1999), p.60 (review of M&A CD 1035).

18 The original source discs suffer from scuffing during the last minute or so of the excerpts; Gebhardt avoided this problem by switching to another, quite different and unnamed, recording for the final two minutes; the effect on the integrity of the performance can readily be imagined.

Act 3 Prelude (part, with a break) (3' 37")
Act 3, scene 4: *Selig, wie die Sonne* (Eva, with Magdalene, Stolzing, David, Sachs) to the end of the quintet (4' 04")
Act 3, scenes 4 and 5: *Jetzt all' am Fleck!* (Sachs) ... transitional music into scene 5 ... *der viel Mut hatt' und Verstand* (Tailors) (4' 21")
Act 3, scene 5: *Silentium!* (Apprentices) ... "*Wach auf!...*" *Heil! Heil!* (Chorus) (3' 26")
Act 3, scene 5: *"Morgenlich leuchtend ... Parnaß und Paradies!"* (Walther, with the chorus, Mastersingers, Sachs) (4' 27")
Act 3, scene 5: *[Verachtet mir die Meister nicht...] ...im Drang der schlimmen Jahr'* (Sachs, with chorus) to the end of the opera (4' 24")

Hans Sachs, Karl Kamann; Veit Pogner, Herbert Alsen; Kunz Vogelgesang, Georg Maikl; Konrad Nachtigall, Georg Monthy; Sixtus Beckmesser, Hermann Wiedemann; Fritz Kothner, Fritz Krenn; Balthasar Zorn, Anton Arnold; Ulrich Eißlinger, Eduard Fritsch; Augustin Moser, Richard Tomek; Hermann Ortel, Walter Hellmich; Hans Schwarz, Hermann Reich; Hans Foltz, Karl Ettl; Walther von Stolzing, Max Lorenz; Eva, Maria Reining; Magdalene, Enid Szantho; David, Erich Zimmermann; Chorus and Orchestra of the Vienna State Opera

LP: *Wiener Staatsoper 1937*: Belvedere Teletheater:76.23596/7 (1987) (three excerpts only)
CD: *Edition Wiener Staatsoper Live, Vol. 20*: Koch Schwann 3-1470-2 (1994)

1938

Tristan und Isolde, Act 1, Prelude[19]
Berlin Philharmonic Orchestra, Beethovensaal, 11 February 1938
(matrix 2RA 2657-1, 2RA 2658-1, 2RA 2659-2)
78: HMV DB3419/20; RCA 14934/5 (set M 653); RCA 18033/4 (set DM 653)

Tristan und Isolde, Act 3, Liebestod[20]
Berlin Philharmonic Orchestra, Beethovensaal, 11 February 1938
(matrix 2RA 2659-2; 2RA 2660-2)
78: HMV DB3420; RCA 14935 (set M 653); RCA 18033/4 (set DM 653)

Parsifal, Act 1, Prelude, with concert ending[21]
Berlin Philharmonic Orchestra, Beethovensaal, 15 March 1938
(matrix 2RA 2741-2, 2RA 2742-2, 2RA 2743-2)
78: HMV DB3445/6; DB8494/6; RCA 15219/20 (set M 514); RCA 15222/4 (set AM 514)

19 This recording has appeared on a number of LPs and CDs purporting to be from Bayreuth 1931, eg, *Richard Wagner: Sein Werk in dokumentarischen Aufnahmen*: Acanta 40.23 502 (1983); *Furtwängler dirigiert Richard Wagner*: Pilz/Acanta 44 1055 (1992).

20 This recording was used by Andrea Catzel in 1993 as an accompaniment to her sung Liebestod in *Beautiful Cape Town - Fine Music - Voices*: Claremont GSE 1549 (1996).

21 This recording has appeared on a number of LPs and CDs purporting to be the "Staatskapelle Berlin, 1940", e.g. *Furtwängler dirigiert Richard Wagner*: Acanta 40.23520 FK (1983) and *Wilhelm Furtwängler dirigiert Wagner*: Pilz/Acanta 44 1055 (1992).

Parsifal, Act 3, Good Friday Music
Berlin Philharmonic Orchestra, Beethovensaal, 15 March 1938
(matrix 2RA 2744-1A, 2RA 2745-1A, 2RA 2746-1A)

78: HMV DB3446/7; DB8494/6; Victor Set M-514 (15220/15221)/AM 514(15222-15224)

LP: Pathé COLH 307 (1964); Seraphim IB-6024 (1968)
CD: *Furtwängler – Wagner – Operatic excerpts*: EMI 64935-2 (1993); *Furtwängler Wagner Vol. 1*: Dante LYS 115 (1996); *Wilhelm Furtwängler The Complete Pre-War Studio Sessions*: Andromeda ANDRCD 5008 (2005)

Die Walküre, London, Covent Garden, live performance, 1 June 1938, excerpt
Act 2, scene 1: *Hojotoho!* (Brünnhilde) … *des frech frevelnden Paars* (Fricka) (3' 35")
Brünnhilde, Frida Leider; Wotan, Karl Kamann; Fricka, Kerstin Thorborg; London Philharmonic Orchestra (private recording from broadcast)
LP: The Golden Age of Opera EJS 170 (1960); EJS 501 (1970) (*Hojotoho!* only)
CD: Frida-Leider-Gesellschaft: FLG 19361938 [2004]

Götterdämmerung, London, Covent Garden, live performance, 7 June 1938, excerpt
Act 2, scenes 4 and 5: *Heil dir, Gunther!* (Vassals) to the end of the Act (34')
Brünnhilde, Frida Leider; Siegfried, Lauritz Melchior; Gunther, Herbert Janssen; Hagen, Wilhelm Schirp; Gutrune, Anny von Stosch; London Philharmonic Orchestra (private recording from broadcast)
LP: The Golden Age of Opera EJS 242[22] (1965); Unique Opera Records UORC 234 (1975)
CD: Pearl GEMM CD 9331 (1989); Eklipse EKR 62 (1997); Gebhardt JGCD 0003-2 (1999); Frida-Leider-Gesellschaft: FLG 19361938 [2004]

Die Meistersinger, Nuremberg, live performance, 5 September 1938, excerpts (ca. 86 mins)[23]
Act 1: from a few bars into the Prelude to *seines Opfers wert zu sein* (Congregation) (10' 49")
Act 1, scene 3: *Halt! Meister! Nicht so geeilt!* (Sachs) … *brächt' er mir morgen die neuen Schuh'!* (Beckmesser, with Nachtigall, Kothner) (3' 03")
Act 2, scenes 3 and 4: the complete *Flieder* monologue *Was duftet doch der Flieder* (Sachs) and Eva-Sachs scene *Gut'n Abend, Meister…Zum Fenster gehst du für mich* (Eva, with Magdalene) (16' 11")
Act 2, scene 6: *Jerum! Jerum! Hallo hallohe!* (Sachs) …*O fort, laß uns fließen* (Eva, with Beckmesser, Walther) (5' 38")
Act 2, scene 6: Sachs-Beckmesser scene: *Oha! Wollt mich beim Wahne fassen* (Sachs) …*Schweigt ihr jetzt nicht auf der Stelle* (Beckmesser) (2' 05"); *So lang' als Beckmesser lebt* (Beckmesser) … *Dann ging't ihr morgen unbeschuht* (Sachs) (3' 16"); …*daß mit Vergunst – Ist das erlaubt, so spät zur Nacht?* (Beckmesser, with everyone) … fading in the riot scene (2' 52")

22 The bulletin accompanying this record (October 1965) referred to it as EJS 342. However, the number on the label and etched in the lacquer is EJS 242. This was apparently a mistake, as EJS 242 had already been issued, in May 1962, as quite a different recording, namely *Singers of the Past Volume I (1903-1908)*.

23 This timing is taken from the Koch CD. The timing given for UORC 242 in *More EJS* is "ca. 110". Although there are minor differences in the description of the excerpts on UORC and Koch, attributable mostly to the long fade-outs on some excerpts on Koch, the excerpts are basically the same. The "ca. 110" is a mistake.

Act 3 from a few bars into the Prelude (incomplete) (3' 11")
Act 3, scenes 1 and 2: complete *Wahn* monologue (with break) *Wahn! Wahn! Überall Wahn! ... Grüß Gott, mein Junker ... Was deutet Gut's! Erzählt mir den!* (Sachs, with Walther) (7' 57")
Act 3, scene 2: *Doch laßt dem Ruh'* (Sachs) ... *Mein Freund, in holder Jugendzeit ...von Lebensmüh' bedrängte Geister* (Sachs, with Walther) (3' 09")
Act 3, scene 4: *O Sachs, mein Freund* (Eva) ...*will ich nur gleich den Namen ihr geben* (Sachs) (6' 13") (with break during transitional music) *Selig, wie die Sonne* (Eva, with Magdalene, Stolzing, David, Sachs) to the end of the quintet and transitional music to scene 5 (6' 35")
Act 3, scene 5: "*Wach auf!...*" *Heil! Heil!* (Chorus) (2' 39")
Act 3, scene 5: *Sein Töchterlein, sein höchsten Preises Gut* (Sachs) ... *O Sachs! Mein Freund!* (Pogner)...*Das Lied! – bin's sicher – zwar niemand versteht* (Beckmesser) (3' 07")
Act 3, scene 5: *Das Lied, fürwahr, ist nicht von mir* (Sachs, with Mastersingers) ...*Mich dünkt, dem kann was Gut's erblüh'n* (Chorus) (3' 16")
Act 3, scene 5: *Verachtet mir die Meister nicht* (Sachs), with a break in Sachs's monologue, to the end of the opera (with chorus) (5' 40")

Hans Sachs, Rudolf Bockelmann; Veit Pogner, Josef von Manowarda; Kunz Vogelgesang, Julius Katona; Konrad Nachtigall, Erich Bürger; Sixtus Beckmesser, Eugen Fuchs; Fritz Kothner, Georg Hann; Balthasar Zorn, Georg Heckel; Ulrich Eißlinger, Karl Mikorey; Augustin Moser, Julius Brombacher; Hermann Ortel, Wolfgand Markgraf; Hans Schwarz, André von Diehl; Hans Foltz, Hans Krenn; Walther von Stolzing, Eyvind Laholm; Eva, Tiana Lemnitz; Magdalene, Rut Berglund; David, Erich Zimmermann; Chorus of the Nuremberg Opera House, Orchestra of the Vienna State Opera

LP: Unique Opera Records UORC 224 (1974)
CD: *Edition Wiener Staatsoper Live, Vol. 2*: Koch Schwann 3-1452-2 (1993); Walhall Eternity WLCD 0050 (2004) (with *Die Meistersinger*, Bayreuth 1943)

[1940][24]

1941[25]

Tristan und Isolde, Vienna, live performance, 25 December 1941, excerpts (ca. 28 mins)
Tristan, Max Lorenz; Isolde Anny Konetzni; Brangäne, Margarete Klose; Vienna State Opera Orchestra

a. Act 2, Scene 1: from *Hörst du sie nicht?* (Isolde) to *König Marke empfing* (Brangäne) (4' 17")

[24] In *Furtwängler dirigiert Wagner*: Acanta 40.2350 FK (1983) there are several recordings purporting to be Furtwängler conducting the Staatskapelle Berlin in 1940. They were in fact drawn from other recordings: a *Tannhäuser* overture (the 1952 HMV recording of the Vienna Philharmonic Orchestra), a *Parsifal* Act 1 Prelude (the 1938 HMV recording of the Berlin Philharmonic Orchestra), an orchestral passage from *Siegfried* (Siegfried breaking through the fire surrounding Brünnhilde, from the 1953 Rai *Ring* cycle), and Siegfried's Rhine Journey from *Götterdämmerung* (from the 1950 La Scala *Ring*). The recordings re-appeared in Discocorp 229 (1984), Acanta 43 121 (1987); Pilz/Acanta 44 1055 (1992); and *Furtwängler Wagner Vol. 1*: Dante LYS 115 (1996) (*Tannhäuser*, *Siegfried*, and Rhine Journey only).

[25] Trémine lists two unpublished excerpts (16 mins, in very poor sound) from *Die Walküre*, Vienna State Opera, 29 November 1939 – the end of Act 1 (Anny Konetzni, Hilde Konetzni, Max Lorenz) and the Ride of the Valkyries – in the Deutsche Rundfunkarchiv (DRA), Frankfurt (archive 1870705006). The excerpts do not appear in Olsen or Hunt. Olsen lists two unpublished excerpts with the Berlin Philharmonic Orchestra, 20 April 1940 – the *Tannhäuser* Bacchanale and the *Schmiedelieder* from *Siegfried* (Max Lorenz) – in a private archive in Vienna. The excerpts do not appear in Trémine or Hunt.

b. Act 2, Scene 1: from *Frau Minne kenntest du nicht?* (Isolde) to *sie zu löschen zag' ich nicht* (Isolde) (end of the scene) (3' 40")

c. Act 2, scene 2: *O sink' hernieder* to *bricht mein Blick sich wonn'* (Tristan, Isolde) (4' 11")

d. Act 2, scene 2: *Selbst dann bin ich die Welt... hold bewusster Wunsch* (Tristan, Isolde) ... *Einsam wachend* to *Bald entweicht die Nacht!* (Brangäne) (4' 10")

e. Act 2, scene 2: *So stürben wir* (Tristan) to *Seinen Trug ewig zu fliehn* (Isolde) (4' 30")

f. Act 2, Scene 3: from *Wohin nun Tristan scheidet* (Tristan) to the end of the Act (6' 57")

CD: *Edition Wiener Staatsoper Live, Vol. 6*: Koch Schwann 3-1456-2 (1994) (c, d and e); *Vol. 11*: Koch Schwann 3-1461-2 (1994) (a, b, and f)

1942

Die Meistersinger, Act 1 Prelude, AEG factory, Berlin, live performance, 26 February 1942
Berlin Philharmonic Orchestra (a *Zeit im Bild* documentary film of a *Kraft Durch Freude Konzert*)

LP: Société Wilhelm Furtwängler SWF 8803 (1988) (audio only)

CD: in *Wilhelm Furtwängler and the Berlin Philharmonic: Wartime Archives of the RRG (1942-1944)*: Tahra FURT 1034/39 (1998) (audio only)

VHS: in *Great Conductors of the Third Reich*: Bel Canto BCS-0052 (1997)

DVD: in *"The Reichsorchester" - The Berlin Philharmonic and the Third Reich*: Arthaus Musik 101 453 (2007)

Tristan und Isolde, Prelude and Liebestod, live performance, 8 - 10 November 1942
Berlin Philharmonic Orchestra, Philharmonie, Berlin
(Reichs-Rundfunk-Gesellschaft recording B 907 in the Sender Freies Berlin archive: 259617)

LP: Melodiya M10 45949 008 (1984)

CD: Seven Seas KICC 2118 (1990); Music & Arts CD-730 (1992); in *Wilhelm Furtwängler and the Berlin Philharmonic: Wartime Archives of the RRG (1942-1944)*: Tahra FURT 1034/39 (1998)

Tristan und Isolde, Prelude and Liebestod, Stockholm, live performance, 25 November 1942
Stockholm Philharmonic Orchestra, Konserthus
(Swedish Radio, Stockholm, archive LB 4567)

LP: Discocorp RR 505 (1976)

CD: Bis BIS-CD 424B in *Die Stockholmer Philharmonie und ihre Dirigenten - Jübiläumskonzert 75 Jahre*: BIS-CD 421 (1989); Seven Seas KICC 2110 (1990); *Wilhelm Furtwängler conducts Wagner from 1943-52 concerts*: Music & Arts CD 4794 (2002)

1943

Tristan und Isolde, Vienna, live performance, 2 January 1943, excerpts (ca. 115 mins)
Tristan, Max Lorenz; King Marke, Herbert Alsen; Isolde, Anny Konetzni; Kurwenal, Paul Schöffler; Melot, Georg Monthy; Brangäne, Margarete Klose; Shepherd, Hermann Gallos; Steersman, Karl Ettl; Sailor, Willy Franter; Vienna State Opera Chorus and Orchestra

Act 1, Scene 1: from *Westwärts schweift de Blick* (Sailor) to *...den lass' ich euch Winden zum Lohn!* (Isolde) (3' 48")
Act 1, Scene 2: from *...dass du zur Stell' ihr nahtest* (Brangäne) to *Den hab' ich wohl vernommen kein Wort das mir entging* (Isolde) (4' 24")
Act 1, Scene 5: from *Auf das Tau! Anker los!* (Sailors) to *Isolde! Herrin! Fassung nur heut'!* (Brangäne) (8' 37")
Act 2, Scene 2: from *Isolde! Geliebter!* (Tristan) (beginning of scene) to *Bald entweicht die Nacht!* (Brangäne) (23' 53")
Act 2, Scene 2: from *Lausch', Geliebter!* (Isolde) to *Rette dich, Tristan!* (Kurwenal) (end of the scene) (14' 22")
Act 3 complete, except for the first 50 bars: i.e., from shepherd's piping at the end of the Prelude (69' 45")
CD: *Edition Wiener Staatsoper Live, Vol. 11*: Koch Schwann 3-1461-2 (1994)

Die Meistersinger, Bayreuth, live performance, 15 July 1943,[26] almost complete[27]
Hans Sachs, Jaro Prohaska; Veit Pogner, Joseph Greindl; Kunz Vogelgesang, Benno Arnold; Konrad Nachtigall, Helmut Fehn; Sixtus Beckmesser, Eugen Fuchs; Fritz Kothner, Fritz Krenn; Balthasar Zorn, Gerhard Witting; Ulrich Eißlinger, Gustav Rödin; Augustin Moser, Karl Krollmann; Hermann Ortel, Herbert Gosebruch; Hans Schwarz, Franz Sauer; Hans Foltz, Alfred Dome; Walther von Stolzing, Max Lorenz; Eva, Maria Müller; Magdalene, Camilla Kallab; David, Erich Zimmermann; Ein Nachtwächter, Erich Pina; Chorus and Orchestra of the Bayreuth Festival
(Reichs-Rundfunk-Gesellschaft recording)
LP: Unique Opera Records UORC 266 (1975); EMI 1C 181 01797/801M (1976); Foyer FO 1043 (1983)
CD: Laudis LCD4.4008 (1987); Opera d'Oro OPD-1237 (2000); Opera Magic's OM24120 (2000); Walhall WLCD 0050 (2004); Music & Arts CD1153 (2004)

1947

Lohengrin, Act 1, Prelude, Lucerne, live performance, 30 August 1947
Lucerne Festival Orchestra, Kunsthaus
(matrices 2ZA 43-3 and 2ZA-43-3 [*sic*])[28]
78 and LP: not published

[26] Trémine and Hunt note that Furtwängler conducted four performances of *Die Meistersinger* at Bayreuth in 1943: 15, 18, 21 and 24 July. Trémine states: "Two recordings are extant: one labelled July 14 – 245' – and another one correctly labelled July 15 – 248' 34"." These performances are in fact the same one with the same cuts, especially the famous *Quintet* which is missing. A third recording, labelled July 15, has been discovered recently with a timing of 270' – RRG recording F 1600-1615." It appears this third recording was of the performance on 16 July 1943 conducted by Hermann Abendroth: Preiser 90174 (1993) - 262' 50". The Deutsche Rundfunkarchiv has advised the author that the copy of the 1943 *Meistersinger* it holds (archive no. 1941629) has the same two cuts (see following footnote) and times at 247' 51". Olsen lists an unpublished German radio *Meistersinger* from Bayreuth in 1944 where Furtwängler conducted it on 18 and 22 July. He notes: "According to Wolfgang Wagner, Bayreuth, this was recorded in stereo (sic!) by the German Reichsrundfunk Gesellschaft. The tapes, almost certainly, are stored in the Soviet Union." The recording has not emerged. It is not listed in Trémine or Hunt.

[27] The two missing portions (approximately 20 mins) are: in Act 1, scene 1, from the end of congregational singing, *Verweilt! Ein Wort* (Walther) to *Ratet mir gut!* (Walther), and in Act 3, scene 4, from *Ein Kind ward hier geboren* (Sachs) to the end of the Quintet *Selig, wie die Sonne* (Eva, with Sachs, Walther, David, Magdalene).

[28] These are the matrices given by Symposium; Testament gives "2ZA 42-43."

CD: *Wilhelm Furtwängler conducts Wagner*: Testament SBT 1141 (1998); in *Music in the Weimar Republic - Berlin, 1929*: Symposium 1340 (2003)

Tristan und Isolde, Act 2 abridged[29] and Act 3, Berlin, live performance, 3 October 1947
Tristan, Ludwig Suthaus; King Marke, Gottlob Frick; Isolde, Erna Schlüter; Kurwenal Jaro Prohaska; Melot, Kurt Rehm; Brangäne, Margarete Klose; Shepherd, Gerhard Witting; Steersman, Hasso Eschert; Sailor, Paul Schmidtmann; Staatsoperkapelle Berlin, Admiralspalast

LP: Société Wilhelm Furtwängler SWF 8205, 8206R, 8207 (1982); Fonit Cetra FE 43 (1984)[30]

CD: Fonit Cetra CDE 1046 (1987); Arkadia/Hunt WFE 358 (1990); Dante LYS 194/5 (1997); Société Wilhelm Furtwängler CD SWF 981-982 (1998); Archipel ARPCD 0029-2 (2001)

1948

Götterdämmerung, Act 3, scene 3, *Starke Scheite*, Abbey Road, London, 26 March 1948
Philharmonia Orchestra, Kirsten Flagstad (Brünnhilde)
(matrix 2EA 12850/4)

78: HMV DB6792/4

LP: Pathé FALP 119 (1951); Electrola 1C 147 01491-2M (1972)

CD: *Kirsten Flagstad, Wagner, Airs d'Opéras*: EMI Références CDH 7 63030 2 (1989); *Les Introuvables du Ring*: EMI CMS 5 65212 2 (1994); *Great Wagnerian Scenes*: Preiser 90676 (2005); *Wagner Overtures (Furtwängler: Commercial Recordings 1940-1950, Vol. 4)*: Naxos Historical 8.110997 (2006)

1949

Siegfried Idyll
Vienna Philharmonic Orchestra, Musikvereinsaal, Vienna, 16 - 17 February 1949
(matrix 2VH 7121-1, 7122-1, 7123-1, 7124-2)

78: HMV DB6916/17 (1949); Seraphim IB-6024 (1968)

LP: Pathé FALP 110; RCA Victor LHMV 1049 (1953)

CD: *Furtwängler dirigiert Wagner*: EMI CZS 25 2328 2 (1989); *Wilhelm Furtwängler conducts Wagner*: Testament SBT 1141 (1998)

Tannhäuser, Overture
Vienna Philharmonic Orchestra, Musikvereinsaal, Vienna, 17 and 22 February 1949
(matrix 2VH 7125-3, 7126-3, 7127-3)

78: not issued

[29] The cut in the performance is from the Love scene in Scene 2 of Act 2, from *Dem Tage! Dem Tage! Dem tükischen Tage* (Tristan) to *dass nachtsichtig mein Auge wahres zu sehen tauge* (Tristan). Trémine (p. 16 *bis*) gives the source of this recording as "Funkhaus-Berlin (archive StUM A/J 4619 – 148' 10") and DRA (archive 186047D02 – Act 2: 72' 04", Act 3: 75' 33") – Act 1 is lost."

[30] FE 43 omits part of the opening scene of Act 3, from *Kurwenal! He!* (Shepherd) to *du selig sollst gesunden* (Kurwenal); the omission has been replicated on some CD re-issues, e.g. Radio Years 103.04.

LP: Société Wilhelm Furtwängler SWF 8001 (1981)
CD: *Wilhelm Furtwängler conducts Wagner*: Testament SBT 1141 (1998)

Götterdammerung, Siegfried's Rhine journey
Vienna Philharmonic Orchestra, Musikvereinsaal, Vienna, 23 February 1949[31]
(matrix 2VH 7135-1, 7136-1, 7137-1)
78: HMV DB6949/50 (1949)
LP: Pathé FALP 110; RCA Victor LHMV 1049 (1953)
CD: *Wilhelm Furtwängler conducts Wagner*: Testament SBT 1141 (1998); *Wagner Overtures (Furtwängler: Commercial Recordings 1940-1950, Vol. 4)*: Naxos Historical 8.110997 (2006)

Der fliegende Holländer, Overture
Vienna Philharmonic Orchestra, Musikvereinsaal, Vienna, 30-31 March and 4 April 1949
(matrix 2VH 7128-4, 7129-1, 7130-1)
78: HMV DB6975/76 (1952), DB9727/28 (1952)
LP: Pathé FALP 289 (1954); Seraphim IB-6024 (1968)
CD: *Wagner – Operatic Excerpts – Furtwängler*: EMI Références CHS 7 64935 2 (1993); *Wilhelm Furtwängler – The Late Unforgettable Columbia Records*: Andromeda ANDRC 5034 (2005); *Wagner Overtures (Furtwängler: Commercial Recordings 1940-1950, Vol. 4)*: Naxos Historical 8.110997 (2006)

Die Walküre, Act 3, Ride of the Valkyries
Vienna Philharmonic Orchestra, Musikvereinsaal, Vienna, 31 March 1949
(matrix 2VH 7131-1)
78: HMV DB6950 (1949)
LP: RCA Victor LHMV 1049 (1953); Seraphim IB-6024 (1968)
CD: *Wagner – Operatic Excerpts – Furtwängler*: EMI Références CHS 7 64935 2 (1993); *Wagner Overtures (Furtwängler: Commercial Recordings 1940-1950, Vol. 4)*: Naxos Historical 8.110997 (2006)

Die Meistersinger, Act 1, Prelude
Vienna Philharmonic Orchestra, Musikvereinsaal, Vienna, 1 and 4 April 1949
(matrix 2VH 7163-1, 7169-2, 7161-1)
78: HMV DB6942/43 (1950)
LP: RCA Victor LHMV 1049 (1953); Seraphim IB-6024 (1968)
CD: *Furtwängler dirigiert Wagner*: EMI CZS 25 2328 2 (1989); *Wagner – Operatic Excerpts – Furtwängler*: EMI Références CHS 7 64935 2 (1993); *Wagner Overtures (Furtwängler: Commercial Recordings 1940-1950, Vol. 4)*: Naxos Historical 8.110997 (2006)

[31] A recording of Siegfried's Funeral March was also made at this session (matrix 2VH 7133-3 and 7134-3) but has never been issued.

Die Meistersinger, Act 3, Dance of the Apprentices
Vienna Philharmonic Orchestra, Musikvereinsaal, Vienna, 4 April 1949
(matrix 2VH 7171-2)
78: HMV DB6943 (1950)
LP: RCA Victor LHMV 1049 (1953)
CD: *Furtwängler dirigiert Wagner*: EMI CZS 25 2328 2 (1989); *Wagner – Operatic Excerpts – Furtwängler*: EMI Références CHS 7 64935 2 (1993); *Wagner Overtures (Furtwängler: Commercial Recordings 1940-1950, Vol. 4)*: Naxos Historical 8.110997 (2006)

Lohengrin, Act 1, Prelude
Lucerne Festival Orchestra, Lucerne, live performance, 29 August 1949[32]
(HMV test pressings matrix 2ZA 61, 2ZA 62)
LP: Société Wilhelm Furtwängler SWF 7801
CD: *Wilhelm Furtwängler at the Lucerne Festival – 1947-1953 Recordings & Broadcasts*: Music & Arts 1018 (1998)

Götterdämmerung, Act 3, Siegfried's Funeral March
Berlin Philharmonic Orchestra, Titania-Palast, Berlin, live performance, 19 December 1949
(RIAS, Berlin)
LP: DG 2535 826 (1979)
CD: DG 415 663-2 (1985); 427 406-2 (1989); *Wilhelm Furtwängler conducts Wagner from 1943-52 concerts*: Music & Arts CD 4794 (1 CD) (2002); *Wilhelm Furtwängler Live Recordings 1944-1953 (Original Masters)*: DG 474 030-2 (2002)

Die Meistersinger, Act 1, Prelude
Berlin Philharmonic Orchestra, Titania-Palast, Berlin, live performance, 19 December 1949
(RIAS, Berlin)
LP: *Grosse Dirigenten der Bayreuther Festpiele*: DG 2721 113 (1976); *Der Vermächtnis Wilhelm Furtwängler*: DG 2721 202 (1979); *100 Jahre Berliner Philharmoniker – Wilhelm Furtwängler*: DG 2740 260 (1982)
CD: DG 415 663 2 (1985); *Wilhelm Furtwängler Live Recordings 1944-1953 (Original Masters)*: DG 474 030-2 (2002)

1950

Götterdämmerung, Act 3, Siegfried's Funeral March
Vienna Philharmonic Orchestra, Musikvereinsaal, Vienna, 31 January 1950
(matrix 2VH 7133-4A, 7134-4A)
78: HMV DB6946 (1952)
LP: Pathé FALP 194 (1953); RCA Victor LHMV 1049 (1953)

[32] This recording is not listed in Olsen. Trémine gives 15 September 1949 as the date of recording, as provided by EMI; it is the date given on the Music & Arts CD. However, Hunt says the date is incorrect, and gives 29 August 1949 instead, which corresponds with the dates in his concert listing of Furtwängler's appearances at the Lucerne Festival: 24-28 August 1949. Research by Roger Smithson has confirmed 29 August as the correct date: *Newsletter 151* of the Wilhelm Furtwängler Society UK, August 1998, [p. 4].

CD: *Wilhelm Furtwängler conducts Wagner*: Testament SBT 1141 (1998);[33] *Wagner Overtures (Furtwängler: Commercial Recordings 1940-1950, Vol. 4)*: Naxos Historical 8.110997 (2006)

Die Meistersinger, Act 3, Prelude
Vienna Philharmonic Orchestra, Musikvereinsaal, Vienna, 1 February 1950
(matrix OVH 475 1A, 476 1B)
78: not issued
LP: *Furtwängler dirigiert Wagner*: EMI 1C 149-01197/99 M (1971); Unicorn WFS 2-3 (1971); Pathé 29 12343 (1987)
CD: *Wagner – Operatic Excerpts – Furtwängler*: EMI Références CHS 7 64935 2 (1993); *Wagner Overtures (Furtwängler: Commercial Recordings 1940-1950, Vol. 4)*: Naxos Historical 8.110997 (2006)

Der Ring des Nibelungen, La Scala, Milan, live performances,[34] 2 March - 6 April 1950, abridged[35]

Das Rheingold, 4 March 1950
Wotan, Ferdinand Frantz; Donner, Angelo Mattiello; Froh, Günther Treptow; Loge, Joachim Sattler; Alberich, Alois Pernerstorfer; Mime, Emil [Peter] Markwort; Fasolt, Ludwig Weber; Fafner, Albert Emmerich; Fricka, Elisabeth Höngen; Freia, Walburga

[33] The matrix numbers given in the Testament booklet "2VH 7133-44" are a printing error.

[34] The 1950 La Scala *Ring* cycle was performed three times: *Das Rheingold*, 2, 4 and 11 March; *Die Walküre*, 9, 13, and 16 March; *Siegfried*, 22, 24, and 26 March; *Götterdämmerung*, 2, 4 and 6 April. Angelo Scottini reports in "Furtwängler and the Recordings of the *Ring* at La Scala" (1997) (in Trémine, pp. 40-42) that Italian Radio broadcast the *Ring* twice: on 5, 12, 26 March and 2 April on *Rete Rosa* (the radio of northern Italy), and on 14, 21, 28 March and 4 April on *Rete Azzura* (the radio of central and southern Italy). As will be plain, these were not, or not all, direct broadcasts of live performances. The intention of Rai had been to record every performance "to allow us to offer our listeners the best possible version of the work": *Radiocorriere*, Nos. 10 and 11 (March 1950). This intention was not realised, however, because the broadcasts began before all performances had been completed. Rai recorded the performances simultaneously on two media: on tape and directly to disc. It was the tapes made on 4, 9, 22 March and 4 April, according to Rai Turin, that were used for all the LP and CD issues, supplemented in the case of Fonit Cetra by the disc recordings to fill up a number of "gaps". However, in 1995 Arkadia issued a *Götterdämmerung* purportedly from 2 April and the finale from *Siegfried* from 26 March (Arkadia WFE 364.4), recordings which, according to Scottini, had been prepared for *Rete Rossa* but which were previously unpublished. Hunt writes that these Arkadia discs were "incorrectly dated 2 April 1950"; he ascribes 4, 9, 22 March and 4 April as the dates for all versions of the *Ring* opera recordings. Olsen and Tremine do not ascribe a single date of recording for each opera. Gary Galo compared the Arkadia *Götterdämmerung* with earlier issues and concluded it was indeed a different performance: *ARSC Journal*, vol. 28 no. 2 (Fall 1997) p. 245. The authors of *EJS*, the discography of the labels on which the 1950 *Ring* first appeared, give dates of 2, ?9, 22 March and ?2 April for the individual *Ring* operas. Scottini concludes his article with the observation that the *Ring* may have been recorded complete on three separate occasions. His extensive researches in the Rai archives failed, however, to find them. The last three *Ring* operas were broadcast in England on 29 and 31 December 1950 and 2 January 1951.

[35] There were two cuts in the performance: in *Die Walküre*, Act 2, scene 2, from *Fahre denn hin, herrische Pracht* to *trügend verraten, wer mir traut!* (Wotan, with Brünnhilde), and in *Siegfried*, Act 3, scene 2, from *Ein Vöglein schwatzt wohl manches* to *weh' ihm, holen sie's ein!* (Wanderer, with Siegfried); cf. Elizabeth Furtwängler: "for the first time in Milan, the *Ring* was performed without any cuts:" *About Wilhelm Furtwängler*, (trans.) Hanni Raillard (Woodside, California: Wilhelm Furtwängler Society of America, 1993), p. 71. It is possible one or more of the performances *not* on disc were uncut.

Wegener; Erda, Margret Weth-Falke; Woglinde, Magda Gabory; Wellgunde, Margherita Kenney; Floßhilde, Sieglinde Wagner
LP: Unique Opera Records UORC 128 (1972)

Die Walküre, 9 March 1950
Siegmund, Günther Treptow; Sieglinde, Hilde Konetzni; Wotan, Ferdinand Frantz; Brünnhilde, Kirsten Flagstad; Hunding, Ludwig Weber; Fricka, Elisabeth Höngen; Gerhilde, Walburga Wegener; Ortlinde, Karen Marie Cerkall; Waltraute, Dagmar Schmedes; Schwertleite, Polly Batic; Helmwige, Ilona Steingruber; Siegrune, Margherita Kenney; Grimgerde, Sieglinde Wagner; Roßweiße, Margret Weth-Falke
LP: Golden Age of Opera EJS 534 (1971)

Siegfried, 22 March 1950
Siegfried, Set Svanholm; Mime, Emil [Peter] Markwort; Brünnhilde, Kirsten Flagstad; Wanderer, Josef Hermann; Alberich, Alois Pernerstorfer; Fafner, Ludwig Weber; Erda, Elisabeth Höngen; Waldvogel, Julia Moor
LP: Unique Opera Records UORC 123 (1972)

Götterdämmerung, 4 April 1950
Brünnhilde, Kirsten Flagstad; Siegfried, Max Lorenz; Hagen, Ludwig Weber; Alberich, Alois Pernerstorfer; Gunther, Josef Hermann; Gutrune, Hilde Konetzni; Waltraute, Elisabeth Höngen; Woglinde, Magda Gabory; Wellgunde, Margherita Kenney; Floßhilde, Sieglinde Wagner; Norns, Margret Weth-Falke, Margherita Kenney, Hilde Konetzni; Orchestra of La Scala
LP: Golden Age of Opera EJS 538 (1971)

Complete 1950 *Ring* cycle issued as:
LP: Discocorp RR-420 (1975); Murray Hill 940477 (1976); Fonit Cetra CFE 101 (1983)
CD: Arkadia/Hunt CD WFE 301 (1989); Fonit Cetra EDC 1000; Music & Arts CD 914 (1996); Opera d'Oro OPD-1154/57 (1998); Gebhardt JGCD 0018 (2000); Falcon Neue Medien fnm 35053 (2001); Archipel ARPCD 0413-16 (2009)

Tristan und Isolde, Prelude and Liebestod (with Kirsten Flagstad, Isolde)

Götterdämmerung, Prologue, Act 1: Dawn and Siegfried's Rhine Journey, and Act 3, final scene: *Starke Scheite* (with Kirsten Flagstad, Brünnhilde)

Philharmonia Orchestra, Royal Albert Hall, London, live performance,[36] 22 May 1950
CD: Testament SBT 1410 (2007)

[36] These recordings were not listed in Olsen, Trémine or Hunt, even as unissued. The *Meistersinger* Prelude and *Siegfried Idyll* were also performed at the 22 May 1950 concert.

1951[37]

Parsifal, Act 3, Good Friday Music
Berlin Philharmonic Orchestra, Alexandria, live performance, 25 April 1951
(Egyptian Radio, Cairo)

LP: DG 2535 826 (1979), 2721 202 (1979); *100 Jahre Berliner Philharmoniker – Wilhelm Furtwängler*: DG 2740 260 (1982)

CD: DG 415 663-2 (1985); 427 406-2 (1989); *Wilhelm Furtwängler conducts Wagner from 1943-52 concerts*: Music & Arts CD 4794 (2002); *Wilhelm Furtwängler Live Recordings 1944-1953 (Original Masters)*: DG 474 030-2 (2002)

Tannhäuser, Overture
Berlin Philharmonic Orchestra, Rome, live performance, 1 May 1951
(Rai, Rome)

LP: Discocorp RR 413 (1975); DG 2535 826 (1979); *100 Jahre Berliner Philharmoniker – Wilhelm Furtwängler*: DG 2740 260 (1982)

CD: DG 415 663-2 (1985); 427 406-2 (1989); *Wilhelm Furtwängler conducts Wagner from 1943-52 concerts*: Music & Arts CD 4794 (2002); *Wilhelm Furtwängler Live Recordings 1944-1953 (Original Masters)*: DG 474 030-2 (2002)

Die Meistersinger, Act 1, Prelude, live performance, December 1951, excerpts (ca. 5 mins)
Berlin Philharmonic Orchestra, Titania Palast, Berlin
(the opening 2' 42" and the final 1' 46" of the Prelude are in *Botschafter der Musik*, a film written and directed by Hermann Stöss, 1951)

LP: Period SPL 716 (1953) (contains the audio of the opening bars only)

LASER DISC: *Botschafter der Musik*: Dreamlife DMLB-20 (1992) (with Japanese sub-titles)

VHS: in *The Art of Conducting – Great Conductors of the Past*: TELDEC International Classics 4509-95038-3 (1994) (a film directed by Sue Knussen) (contains film of the opening 30 bars only, 1' 10") [38]

[37] There has been speculation that publication of a recording of *Parsifal* conducted by Furtwängler at La Scala, Milan on 24, 27, 29 March, 1 and 4 April 1951 was imminent. For example, Peter Pirie wrote: "There was a series of performances during March and April 1951 at La Scala of which a tape survives, not listed by Olsen, and Electrola have announced they will be issuing it": *Furtwängler and the Art of Conducting* (London: Duckworth, 1980), p. 100. This was unfortunately not the case: none of the performances was broadcast and no tape is otherwise known to have survived. Angelo Scottini has researched the issue in depth and has explained how the misunderstanding arose. There was a broadcast of *Parsifal* on Rai on 24 March 1951, but it was a re-transmission of the 20 November 1950 performance conducted by Vittorio Gui (with Maria Callas as Kundry), available on records since 1966. There had been plans to broadcast the Furtwängler *Parsifal* on 24 March 1951, but there was a strike, and the earlier recording was broadcast instead. He concluded it was improbable there was any recording: Scottini, *Furtwängler en Italie*, trans. Carlo Dionedi (Paris: Société Wilhelm Furtwängler, 1990), p. 25.

[38] The Teldec film and accompanying booklet date this excerpt as Berlin, Titania Palast, 1947. In Hunt's concert register for Furtwängler there is no performance of the *Meistersinger* overture listed for 1947. He dates the film excerpt as "Berlin, December 1951." Trémine also gives this date. Olsen ascribes no particular date in 1951, noting merely that: "The film [*Botschafter der Musik*] was produced by Start Film in 1951, and released in Germany in 1952." The only occasions Furtwängler conducted the work in Berlin between 1947 and 1951, according to Hunt's listing, were 18, 19, and 20 December 1949 at the Titania-Palast. The performance on 19 December was recorded (see below), but the DG CD appears to be different from the

DVD: in *The Art of Conducting – Great Conductors of the Past*: TELDEC International Classics 0927-42667-2 (2002) (as for VHS issue); *Botschafter der Musik*: Dreamlife DLVC 8093 (2008) (as for Laser Disc issue)

1952

Die Walküre, Act 1, Rome, live performance, 14 January 1952[39]
Sieglinde, Hilde Konetzni; Siegmund, Günther Treptow; Hunding, Otto von Rohr; Orchestra Sinfonica di Roma della Rai
LP: *Richard Wagner Brani scelti*: Fonit Cetra FE 47 (1985)
CD: Music & Arts CD 866; *Wilhelm Furtwängler – The Finest 1952 Rai Recordings*: Andromeda ANDRCD 5010 (2005)

Tristan und Isolde, Prelude and Liebestod, Turin, live performance, 11 March 1952
Orchestra Sinfonica di Torino della Rai, Audiorium di Torino della Rai
LP: Fonit Cetra FE 43 (1984) (with the *Tristan* excerpts from 1947 above)
CD: Fonit Cetra CDE 1012 (1987), CDE 1045 (1988), CDE 3007 (1994); CDAR 2032 (1995)

Götterdämmerung, Act 3, Rome, Rai, live performance, 31 May 1952
Brünnhilde, Kirsten Flagstad; Siegfried, Ludwig Suthaus; Hagen, Josef Greindl; Gunther, Josef Hermann; Gutrune, Hilde Konetzni; Woglinde, Julia Moor; Wellgunde, Elisabeth Lindenmeier; Floßhilde, Ruth Michaelis; Coro e Orchestra Sinfonica di Roma della Rai
LP: The Golden Age of Opera EJS 318 (1971); Fonit Cetra FE 20 (1982)
CD: Music & Arts CD 866; *Wilhelm Furtwängler – The Finest 1952 Rai Recordings*: Andromeda ANDRCD 5010 (2005); Myto MCD 00223 (2009)

Der fliegende Holländer, Overture
Siegfried Idyll
Götterdämmerung, Act 3, Siegfried's Funeral March
Orchestra Sinfonica di Torino della Rai, Turin, live performance, 6 June 1952
LP: *Richard Wagner Brani scelti*: Fonit Cetra FE 47 (1985)
CD: Fonit Cetra CDE 1012 (1987), CDAR 2032 (1995); Music & Arts CD-4712; *Wilhelm Furtwängler – The Finest 1952 Rai Recordings*: Andromeda ANDRCD 5010 (2005) (*Der fliegende Holländer* only)

Tristan und Isolde, complete, Kingsway Hall, London, 9-23 June 1952
Tristan, Ludwig Suthaus; Isolde, Kirsten Flagstad; Kurwenal, Dietrich Fischer-Dieskau; Brangäne, Blanche Thebom; King Marke, Josef Greindl; Melot, Edgar Evans; Sailor's Voice and Shepherd, Rudolf Schock; Steersman, Rhoderick Davis; Chorus of the Royal Opera House, Covent Garden; Philharmonia Orchestra

filmed excerpt on VHS (which may not have been transferred at the same pitch). The film was shown on PBS in the United States in 1995 as *Legendary Maestros: The Art of Conducting*.

[39] Hunt gives the date as 15 January 1952. Olsen does not list it. Trémine, and the LPs and CDs listed, give the date as 14 January 1952.

LP: HMV ALP 1030-5 (1953); Victor LM-6700 (1953); HMV HQM 1001-1005 (RLS 684) (1965);[40] Electrola 1C 147 00899-903M (1974)

CD: EMI CDS 747 322 8 (1986); Angel CDC 47321 (1986); EMI CDS5 56254-2 (1997); EMI Historical 5 85873-2 (2004); Naxos Historical 8.110321-24 (2004)

Götterdämmerung, Act 3, scene 3, *Starke Scheite*, Kingsway Hall, London, 23 June 1952
Philharmonia Orchestra, Kirsten Flagstad (Brünnhilde)

LP: HMV ALP 1016 (1954); RCA Victor LHMV 1072 (1954); Pathé FALP 30295 (1965); Angel M 60003 (1966); Electrola 1C 047 01149M (1971)

CD: *Wagner – Operatic excerpts – Furtwängler*: EMI Références CHS 7 64935 2 (1993); *Wilhelm Furtwängler – The Late Unforgettable Columbia Records*: Andromeda ANDRC 5034 (2005); *Furtwängler conducts Wagner*: Naxos Historical 8.111348 (2010)

Tannhäuser, Overture, Vienna, 2-3 December 1952
Vienna Philharmonic Orchestra

LP: Pathé FALP 289; HMV ALP 1220 (1955); Seraphim IB-6024 (1968) (incorrectly dated "February 1949")

CD: *Wagner – Operatic excerpts – Furtwängler*: EMI Références CHS 7 64935 2 (1993); *Wilhelm Furtwängler – The Late Unforgettable Columbia Records*: Andromeda ANDRC 5034 (2005) ; *Furtwängler conducts Wagner*: Naxos Historical 8.111348 (2010)

1953

Der Ring des Nibelungen
Auditorio del Foro Italico, Rome, live radio concerts, 26 October – 27 November 1953

Das Rheingold, 26 October 1953
Wotan, Ferdinand Frantz; Donner, Alfred Poell; Froh, Lorenz Fehenberger; Loge, Wolfgang Windgassen; Alberich, Gustav Neidlinger; Mime, Julius Patzak; Fasolt, Josef Greindl; Fafner, Gottlob Frick; Fricka, Ira Malaniuk; Freia, Elisabeth Grümmer; Erda, Ruth Siewert; Woglinde, Sena Jurinac; Wellgunde, Magda Gabory; Floßhilde, Hilde Rössl-Majdan; Orchestra Sinfonica di Roma della Rai

LP: EMI Italiano 3C 153-02275-77 (1972)

Die Walküre, 29 October (Act 1), 3 November (Act 2), 6 November 1953 (Act 3)
Siegmund, Wolfgang Windgassen; Sieglinde, Hilde Konetzni; Wotan, Ferdinand Frantz; Brünnhilde, Martha Mödl; Hunding, Gottlob Frick; Fricka, Elsa Cavelti; Gerhilde, Gerda Scheyrer; Ortlinde, Magda Gabory; Waltraute, Dagmar Schmedes; Schwertleite, Hilde Rössl-Majdan; Helmwige, Judith Hellwig; Siegrune, Olga Bennings; Grimgerde, Elsa Cavelti; Roßweiße, Ira Malaniuk; Orchestra Sinfonica di Roma della Rai

LP: EMI Italiano 3C 153-02278-82 (1972)

[40] EMI's producer of RLS 684, Suvi Raj Grubb, explained in his memoirs how he gave the orchestra greater prominence in the reissue than had been the case in the original recording: *Music makers on record* (London: Hamish Hamilton, 1986), pp. 112-113. In 2004 EMI took their re-issue from tapes whereas Naxos took theirs from LPs: *American Record Guide*, September/October 2004, p. 270 (John P. McKelvey).

Siegfried, 10 November (Act 1), 13 November (Act 2), 17 November 1953 (Act 3)
Siegfried, Ludwig Suthaus; Mime, Julius Patzak; Brünnhilde, Martha Mödl; Wanderer, Ferdinand Frantz; Alberich, Alois Pernerstorfer; Fafner, Josef Greindl; Erda, Margarete Klose; Waldvogel, Rita Streich; Orchestra Sinfonica di Roma della Rai

LP: EMI Italiano 3C 153-02283-87 (1972)

Götterdämmerung, 20 November (Act 1), 24 November (Act 2), 27 November 1953 (Act 3)
Brünnhilde, Martha Mödl; Siegfried, Ludwig Suthaus; Hagen, Josef Greindl; Alberich, Alois Pernerstorfer; Gunther, Alfred Poell; Gutrune, Sena Jurinac; Waltraute, Margarete Klose; Woglinde, Sena Jurinac; Wellgunde, Magda Gabory; Floßhilde, Hilde Rössl-Majdan; Norns, Margarete Klose, Hilde Rössl-Majdan, Sena Jurinac; Orchestra Sinfonica e Coro di Roma della Rai

LP: EMI Italiano 3C 153-02288-92 (1972)

Complete 1953 *Ring* cycle issued as:

LP: HMV RLS 702 (1972); Electrola 1C 147-02275-92 (1972); EMI EX 29 06703 (1986)

CD: EMI CZS 7 67123 2 (1990); 9 08161 2 (2011)

1954

Götterdämmerung, Act 3, Siegfried's Funeral March
Vienna Philharmonic Orchestra, Musikvereinsaal, 2 March 1954

LP: HMV ALP 1016 (1954); Pathé FALP 30295 (1965); Angel M 60003 (1966)

CD: *Wagner – Operatic excerpts – Furtwängler*: EMI Références CHS 7 64935 2 (1993); *Wilhelm Furtwängler – The Late Unforgettable Columbia Records*: Andromeda ANDRC 5034 (2005); *Furtwängler conducts Wagner*: Naxos Historical 8.111348 (2010)

Lohengrin, Act 1, Prelude
Vienna Philharmonic Orchestra, Musikvereinsaal, 4 March 1954

LP: HMV ALP 1220 (1955); Pathé FALP 362 (1956); Seraphim IB-6024 (1968)

CD: *Wagner – Operatic excerpts – Furtwängler*: EMI Références CHS 7 64935 2 (1993); *Wilhelm Furtwängler – The Late Unforgettable Columbia Records*: Andromeda ANDRC 5034 (2005); *Furtwängler conducts Wagner*: Naxos Historical 8.111348 (2010)

Götterdämmerung, Prologue and Act 1, Siegfried's Rhine Journey
Vienna Philharmonic Orchestra, Musikvereinsaal, 8 March 1954

LP: HMV ALP 1016 (1954); Pathé FALP 194; Electrola WALP 1016; Angel M 60003 (1966)

CD: *Wagner – Operatic excerpts – Furtwängler*: EMI Références CHS 7 64935 2 (1993); *Wilhelm Furtwängler – The Late Unforgettable Columbia Records*: Andromeda ANDRC 5034 (2005); *Furtwängler conducts Wagner*: Naxos Historical 8.111348 (2010)

Tannhäuser, Overture, Caracas, live performance, 21 March 1954
Venezuela Symphony Orchestra, Amfiteatro "José Angel Lamas"
LP : Tanaka AT 09/10 (1989)
CD: Wilhelm Furtwängler Society UK: FURT 102 (1987); *Furtwängler outside Europe*: WFS UK 2004 (2004); in *Bruckner Symphonies*: Andromeda ANDRCD 9008 (2006)

Tristan und Isolde, Prelude and Liebestod, Berlin, live performance, 27 April 1954
Berlin Philharmonic Orchestra, Titania Palast
LP: Fonit Cetra FE 25 (1981)
CD: DG 415 663 2 (1985); *Wilhelm Furtwängler Live Recordings 1944-1953 (Original Masters)*: DG 474 030-2 (2002)

Tristan und Isolde, Prelude and Liebestod, Turin, live performance, 14 May 1954
Berlin Philharmonic Orchestra, Rai Auditorium
LP: Japan AT 09/10 (1989)
CD: Disques Refrain DR 920031 (1992); *Furtwängler in Turin*: Tahra FURT 1041/42 (1999)

Die Walküre, Musikvereinsaal, Vienna, 28 September – 6 October 1954
Siegmund, Ludwig Suthaus; Sieglinde, Leonie Rysanek; Wotan, Ferdinand Frantz; Brünnhilde, Martha Mödl; Hunding, Gottlob Frick; Fricka, Margarete Klose; Gerhilde, Gerda Scheyrer; Ortlinde, Judith Hellwig; Waltraute, Dagmar Schmedes; Schwertleite, Ruth Siewert; Helmwige, Erika Köth; Siegrunc, Herta Töpper; Grimgerde, Johanna Blatter; Roßweiße, Dagmar Hermann; Vienna Philharmonic Orchestra
LP: HMV ALP 1257-61 (1955); RCA Victor LHMV 900 (1955)
CD: EMI Références CHS 7 630452 (1989); Naxos Historical 8.111056-58 (2006)

7. Erich Kleiber conducts Wagner[1]

Works recorded, including excerpts:

Der fliegende Holländer: 1926
Tannhäuser: 1927, 1946
Lohengrin: 1953
Tristan und Isolde: 1938, 1948, 1952
Die Meistersinger von Nürnberg: 1926, 1931
Der Ring des Nibelungen:
Das Rheingold: 1947
Die Walküre: 1940
Siegfried: 1938, 1946
Götterdämmerung: 1931, 1947, 1948
Parsifal: 1946

1926

Die Meistersinger, Act 1 Prelude
Berlin State Opera Orchestra
(2503 A, 2507 A, January 1926)
78: Vox 08034[2]

Der fliegende Holländer, Overture
Berlin State Opera Orchestra
(678 AA, 679 AA, 680 AA, 681 AA, November 1926)
78: Vox 08296-97

1927

Tannhäuser, Overture and Venusberg Music
Berlin State Opera Orchestra[3]
(1215-1AA, 1216-AA, 1217-1AA, 1216-1AA, April 1927)
78: Vox 08434E/35E; Kristall 1017/1018

[1] The standard Kleiber discography is by Cesar Dillon, *Erich Kleiber: A Discography* (Buenos Aires: Ediciones Tres Tiempos, 1990). John Hunt also included a discography of Kleiber in *More 20th Century Conductors* (London: John Hunt, 1993).

[2] The matrix number 2503 A is given by both Dillon and by Claude G. Arnold, *A discography of the orchestra, 1898-1925/26: an encyclopaedia of orchestral recordings made by the acoustical process* (Toronto: St. Michael's College, University of Toronto, 1983, p. 551, and appears on the copy of the record found by Dillon in Argentina. A different take, namely 2503½ A, is given by Rainer E. Lotz in his Online Discography of Vox records (www.lotz-verlag.de/Online-Disco-Vox.html), and appears on the copy of the record held by Historical Sound Recordings at Yale University. This was Kleiber's only acoustic recording of Wagner.

[3] This is according to Dillon; the label on the Vox records states: "Generalmusikdirektor Erich Kleiber mit grossem Symphonie-Orchester"; to this Lotz adds: "(Mitglieder des Philharmonischen Orchesters, Berlin)".

[1928][4]

1931

Götterdämmerung, Siegfried's Funeral March
Berlin Philharmonic Orchestra
(15172-2, 15173-2, 1931)
78: Ultraphon E 612; Telefunken E 612
LP: Ultraphon EP 254; Royale 545; King Record Company/Telefunken K17C 9402 (1984)

Die Meistersinger, Act 1 Prelude
Berlin Philharmonic Orchestra
(16183-2, 16184, 1931)
78: Kalliope A 4032[5]

1938

Tristan und Isolde, Buenos Aires, live performance, 18 September 1938, abridged[6]
Tristan, Max Lorenz; Isolde, Anny Konetzni; Brangäne, Karin Branzell; Kurwenal, Herbert Janssen; King Marke, Emanuel List; Melot, Herman Wiedermann; Shepherd, Erich Witte; Steersman, Victorio Bacciato; Young Sailor, Koloman von Pataky; Teatro Colón Chorus and Orchestra
CD: Archipel ARPCD 0167-3 (2004)[7]

[4] The Berlin State Opera playbill for the performance of *Die Meistersinger* on 22 May 1928, some of which was recorded by the Gramophone Company, lists Kleiber as the conductor (*Musikalische Leitung: Erich Kleiber*). However, the Gramophone Company's Weekly Return of recordings says "Dirigent Leo Blech." I am indebted to Alan Kelly's examination of the HMV registers for this information. The recordings have been reissued on Pearl GEMM CD 9340 (1989) and Symposium 1232 & 1233 (1998).

[5] Some 13 bars are missing from this recording of the Prelude, between the end of side 1 (3' 56"), which fades out, and the beginning of side 2 (3' 42"). Neither Dillon nor Hunt list the recording. A copy is held in the Deutsches Musikarchiv.

[6] This was the second performance of the season. The cuts in the performance were: in Act 2, Scene 2, from *Dem Tage! Dem Tage!* (Tristan) to *dass nachtsichtig mein Auge wahres zu sehen* (Tristan), from *Tag und Tod* (Isolde) to *Tristan der Tod gegeben?* (Isolde), and in Scene 3 from *Wozu die Dienste ohne Zahl* to *Da liess er's denn so sein* (King Marke); in Act 3, Scene 1, from *Isolde noch im Reich der Sonne!* to *die selbst Nachts von ihr mich scheuchte?* (Tristan), from *Der Trank! Der Trank!* (Tristan) to *je ich genossen* (Tristan); in Scene 2, from *Gebrochen der Blick!* to *Nur einmal noch!* (Isolde); and in Scene 3 from *Mein Held! Mein Tristan!* to *Die Ernte mehrt' ich dem Tod* (King Marke). Dillon lists a complete recording of this performance in a private archive.

[7] The CD box contains the warning: "The sound quality of this recording reflects the poor conditions under which the recording was made. Therefore purchase is advised only to collectors." The inset continues, noting that one track "contains some extremely damaged passages. But these defects derive from the master recording. No technical mistake on the compact disc," and that "some original acetate discs had been damaged, therefore some extreme cracks could not be eliminated. To preserve the recording complete we have not omitted those damaged passages." There are a few points where a very small passage is missing from the original recording, including the first bar and a half of the Prelude.

Siegfried, Buenos Aires, live performance, 4 October 1938, excerpts[8] (ca. 74 mins)
Siegfried, Max Lorenz; Mime, Erich Witte, Wanderer, Herbert Janssen, Fafner, Emanuel List; Orchestra of the Teatro Colón

Act 1: complete, with cuts[9] (59')

Act 2, scene 2: Forest Murmurs scene and the killing of the dragon: from *Fafner und Siegfried* (Mime) to *Dien Hirn brütete nicht, was du vollbracht* (Fafner, with Siegfried) (uncut) (15')

CD: Medici Arts 2056928-2 (2008) (with DVD *Max Lorenz – Wagner's Mastersinger – Hitler's Siegfried*: Medici Arts 2056928-1)

1940

Die Walküre, Buenos Aires, live performance, 23 August 1940, abridged[10]
Siegmund, René Maison; Sieglinde, Irene Jessner; Hunding, Emanuel List; Wotan, Herbert Janssen; Brünnhilde, Marjorie Lawrence; Fricka, Lydia Kindermann; Helmwige, Maria Malberti; Gerhilde, Judith Helwig; Ortlinde, Yolanda di Sabato; Waltraute, Maria Rubini; Siegrune, Clara Oyuela; Grimgerde, Emma Brizio; Schwertleite, Risë Stevens; Teatro Colón Orchestra

CD: Gebhardt JGCD 0028-3 (2000)

1946

Siegfried, Forest Murmurs
Parsifal, Act 1, Prelude
Parsifal, Act 3, Good Friday Music
Tannhäuser, Overture
NBC Symphony Orchestra, New York, broadcast performances, 10 March 1946

CD: Urania URN 22.116 (*Tannhäuser*); Urania URN 22.136 (2000) (*Siegfried* and *Parsifal*); *Erich Kleiber – The NBC Recordings*: Andromeda ANDRCD 5005 (2005) (all excerpts)

[8] This recording was listed in Dillon as unpublished, in a private archive, and also as including excerpts from Act 3. Elsewhere he refers (probably to this recording: he says 1937, yet dates it as 4 October 1938) to the loss of ten of the original recording discs, leaving some 135 minutes "in fairly accurate speed and tolerable surface noise."

[9] The cuts in Act 1 were: in scene 1, from *wie ich dich leiden könnt'* to *Ei, Mime* (Siegfried, with Mime), from *Mich dünkt, dess' gedachtest du schon!* (Siegfried) to *"... dein Lager schuf ich, dass leicht du schliefest"* (Mime); in scene 2, from *Gastlich ruht' ich bei Guten* (Wanderer) to *dir Weisem weis' ich den Weg!* (Mime), from *Gastlich nicht galt mir dein Gruss* to *mit der dritten Frage droh' ich nun!* (Wanderer, with Mime); in scene 3, from *Wirst du mir reden?* to *Ist's eine Kunst, was kenn' ich sie nicht?* (Siegfried, with Mime), and from *Er schafft sich ein scharfes Schwert* (Mime) to *heiaho! ho! ho! ho! ho! heiaho!* (Siegfried).

[10] The cuts in the performance were: in Act 2, scene 1, from *Eines höre! Not tut ein Held* (Wotan) to *daß nur deine List ihn lockte, wo er es fand'?* (Fricka), in scene 2, from *Als junge Liebe Lust mir verblich* to *gebar mir, Brünnhilde, dich* (Wotan), from *Der der Liebe fluchte* to *trügend verraten wer mir traut!* (Wotan, with Brünnhilde), from *Jetz versteh ich den stummen Sinn* to *den Freien erlang ich mir nicht* (Wotan); in scene 4, from *Du sahest der Walküre sehrenden Blick* (Brünnhilde) to *Hella halte mich fest!* (Siegmund); in Act 3, scene 2, from *So wißt denn, Winselnde* to *die mein Wunsch allein ihr schuf!* (Wotan); in scene 3, from *Als Fricka den eignen Sinn dir entfremdet* (Brünnhilde) to *Du wußtest es so und wagtest dennoch den Schutz?* (Wotan), and from *Du zeugest ein edles Geschlecht* (Brünnhilde) to *nicht kiesen dann ich es dir!* (Wotan).

Parsifal, Buenos Aires, live performances, September 1946, abridged,[11] excerpts (ca. 119 mins)

Act 1: complete, without the Prelude (81' 30")

Act 2: from the beginning of the Act to the end of the Flowermaidens' scene, *du – Tor!* (18' 06")

Act 3: from the opening scene from *Von dorther kam das Stöhnen* (Gurnemanz) to Parsifal's first word *Heil [mir]* (14' 48")

and from another performance:

Act 1: the opening scene from *He! Ho! Waldhüter ihr* (Gurnemanz) to *befahl er eifrig uns das Bad* (2nd Knight) (4' 24")

Act 1: the first part of Amfortas's lament from *Wehe! Wehe mir der Qual!* to *zu Ihm muss ich gelangen* (3' 57")

Act 1: the Grail scene from *Durch Mitleid wissend* to *"...um unsrer Liebe willen!"* (Boys' Chorus, with Titurel) (in Italian) (4' 36")

Parsifal, Torsten Ralf; Kundry, Rose Bampton; Amfortas, Herbert Janssen; Gurnemanz, Emanuel List; Klingsor, Victorio Bacciato; Titurel, Jorge Dantón; Voice, Lydia Kindermann; Knights, Humberto di Toto, Carlos Feller; Esquires, Consuelo Ramos, Tota de Irgazábal, Virgilio Tavini, Héctor Barbieri; Flowermaidens, Amanda Cetera, Nilda Hoffmann, María de Benedictus, Olga Chelavine, Mafalda Rinaldi, Zaira Negroni, Norma Palmieri; Teatro Colón Chorus and Orchestra

CD: Live Opera Heaven LOH 2669-2 (2006)

1947

Das Rheingold, Buenos Aires, live performance, 7 August 1947[12]

Wotan, Herbert Janssen; Donner, Angel Mattiello; Froh, Humberto di Toto; Loge, Set Svanholm; Fafner, Emanuel List; Fasolt, Jorge Dantón; Alberich, Fred Destal; Mime, Roberto Maggiolo; Freia, Nilda Hofmann, Fricka, Elsa Cavelti, Erda, Lydia Kindermann; Woglinde, Amanda Cetera; Wellgunde, Clara Oyuela; Flosshilde, Norma Palmieri; Gerhilde, María di Benedictus; Schwertleite, Zaira Negroni; Teatro Colón Chorus and Orchestra

CD: Gebhardt JGCD 0036-2 (2002)

[11] The source of this recording is unclear. Kleiber conducted *Parsifal* at the Teatro Colón in 1946 on 17, 20, 22, 25 and 28 September. All performances from the Colón were broadcast, according to Dillon (p. 61). The cuts in the performance as recorded were: in Act 1, from *Hm! Schuf sie euch Schaden je?* to *dienet uns und hilft auch sich* (Gurnemanz, with Squires), and from *Drum blieb es dem, nach dem ihr fragt* to *den Gral auch wähnt er fest schon uns entwunden* (Gurnemanz); and in Act 2 from *Da weckte dich ein And'rer? He?* (Klingsor) to *hüt' ich mir selbst den Gral* (Klingsor, with Kundry). There are on the CDs three further excerpts (ca. 13 minutes) from another performance of Act 1.

[12] This was the second performance conducted by Kleiber in the season.

Götterdämmerung, Buenos Aires, live performance, 2 September 1947, abridged[13]
Brünnhilde, Astrid Varnay; Siegfried, Set Svanholm; Gunther, Herbert Janssen; Hagen, Emanuel List; Alberich, Fred Destal; Gutrune, Rose Bampton; Waltraute, Lydia Kindermann; Norns, Lydia Kindermann, Tota de Irgazábal, Zaira Negroni, and Rose Bampton; Woglinde, Mafalda Rinaldi; Wellgunde, María de Benedictus; Flosshilde, Zaira Negroni; Men, Tullio Gagliardo and Héctor Barbieri; Teatro Colón Chorus and Orchestra

CD: Gebhardt JGCD 0046-3 (2002)[14]

1948

Tristan und Isolde, Buenos Aires, live broadcast, 20 August 1948, abridged[15]
Tristan, Set Svanholm; Isolde, Kirsten Flagstad; Brangäne, Viorica Ursuleac; Kurwenal, Hans Hotter; King Marke, Ludwig Weber; Melot, Angel Mattiello; Shepherd, Roberto Maggiola; Steersman, Tullio Gagliardo; Sailor, Humberto di Toto; Teatro Colón Chorus and Orchestra

LP: Rococo 5380 (Act 2 Love duet only)

CD: Melodram MEL 25007 (1989) (scenes only from Acts 1, 2 and 3); Myto 3 CD 993.HO31 (1999) (date given as 20.8.1948); Cantus Classics 5.00389/90 (2004); Walhall Eternity WLCD 0195 (2007)

Götterdämmerung, Buenos Aires, live performance, 3 September 1948, excerpts (ca. 65 mins)
Siegfried, Set Svanholm; Brünnhilde, Kirsten Flagstad; Hagen, Ludwig Weber; Waltraute, Lydia Kindermann; Woglinde, Mafalda Rinaldi; Wellgunde, Maria Cherry; Flosshilde, Zaira Negroni; Chorus [singing in Spanish] and Orchestra of the Teatro Colón

13 The cuts in the performance were: in Act 1, scene 1, from *Wo berg' ich mein Ross?* to *am Zaume ein Ross* (Siegfried, with Hagen), in scene 2, from *Als dem Gott entgegen* to *leucht' und lach' ich heut' auf!* (Brünnhilde), *Mit stummen Wink Walhalls Edle wies er zum Forst, die Weltesche zu fällen* (Waltraute) [these lines are missing between the end of CD1 and the beginning of CD2, and may not therefore be a performance cut], from *Mehr als Walhalls Wonne* to *Siegfried Liebe!* (Brünnhilde) [although these lines are missing, it may be the result of a tape change rather than a cut in the performance], and from *Dich werb' ich nun zum Weib* (Siegfried) to *Kommst du von Hellas nächtlichem Heer?* (Brünnhilde); in Act 2, scene 1, from *Hagen, mein Sohn* (Alberich) to *Zu seinem Verderben dient er mir schon* (Hagen). in scene 2, from *Sengte das Feuer ihn nicht?* (Gutrune) to *so nah – war Brünnhild' ihm fern* (Siegfried), and in scene 4, from *Achtest du so der eignen Ehre?* (Siegfried) to *Brach er die Treue?* (Women); there were no cuts in Act 3.

14 The faulty pitching of the Gebhardt CDs, and alternative sources of this recording, are discussed in *Opera Quarterly*, vol. 20 no. 1 (Winter 2004), p. 145 (Robert Baxter).

15 *Tristan* was performed at the Colón on 13, 15, 18, 20, and 28 August 1948. Dillon reports that "tapes or acetates from at least three broadcasts, partially or complete are known to exist." There is an unpublished tape of the 13 August performance which has Kurvenal's lines at the end of Act 1 included (*Heil! Tristan! Glücklicher Held!*): William Youngren, *Fanfare*, March/April 2000, p. 356; these lines are missing from the 20 August performance because, as Hotter explains in his memoirs, the paging system in the Colón broke down and he did not reach the stage in time to sing: *Memoirs*, (trans. and ed.) Donald Arthur (Boston: Northeastern University Press, 2006), p. 173. The cuts in the performance were: in Act 2, scene 2, from *Dem Tage! Dem Tage!* (Tristan) to *dass nachtsichtig mein Auge wahres zu sehen tauge* (Tristan); and in Act 3, scene 1, from *Isolde noch im Reich der Sonne!* to *die selbst Nachts von ihr mich scheuchte?* (Tristan), from *Muss ich dich so versteh'n* to *Zu welchem Los?* (Tristan), and from *Wie vom Herz zum Hirn* to *ich selbst, ich selbst* (Tristan).

Act 1: from the end of the Norns' scene … *Zu neuen Taten* (Brünnhilde)… to the end of Siegfried's Rhine Journey (10' 52")
Act 1: from the ending of Waltraute's narrative: *Sie – wahrt mir der Reif* (Brünnhilde) to the end of the act, with cuts: from *Dich werb ich nun zum Weib* (Siegfried) to *Kommst du von Hellas nächtligem Heer* (Brünnhilde), and from *Wotan! Ergrimmter, grausamer Gott!* to *nie – raubst du ihn mir!* (Brünnhilde, with Siegfried) (9' 43")
Act 2, scene 3: Vassals chorus, from *Gross Glück und heil* to *Willkommen* (Chorus with Hagen) (3' 15")
Act 3, scene 1: beginning orchestral passage … *Frau Sonne* (Rhinemaidens) to *Lasst und berraten* (Flosshilde) (6' 06")
Act 3, scene 2, death of Siegfried: from *In Leid zu dem Wipfel* (Siegfried) … to *Meineid rächt' ich!* (Hagen) [then a break, resuming at] *Brünnhilde, heilige Breit* (Siegfried) to the end of Siegfried's Funeral Music (17' 20")
Act 3, scene 3, Immolation scene: from *Starke Scheite* (Brünnhilde) to the end of the Act (18' 15")[16]

CD: Opera Depot OD 10382-1 [2008]; Pearl GEMM CDS 9910 (2 CDs) (1992) (*Der fliegende Holländer*, Busch, 19 September 1936; Immolation scene only);

[1949][17]

[1950][18]

1952

Tristan und Isolde, Munich, Prinzregententheater, live performance, 29 July 1952[19]
Tristan, Günther Treptow; King Marke, Ferdinand Frantz; Isolde, Helena Braun; Kurwenal, Rudolf Großmann; Brangäne, Margarete Klose; Melot, Albrecht Peter; Shepherd, Paul Kuen; Steersman, Rudolf Wünzer; Sailor, Richard Holm; Bavarian State Opera Chorus and Orchestra

LP: Melodram MEL 014 (1980)[20]

CD: Myto Historical MCD 032.H075 (2003); Cantus Classics 5.00496/97 (2004); Walhall Eternity WLCD 0044 (2004)

[16] The Immolation scene is cut on Opera Depot, or rather it is incomplete: approximately 3 minutes are missing, from *[er liebte] kein andrer* to *alles ward mir nun frei!*; the scene is complete on Pearl; different sources of the same performance appear to have been used in the CD issues.

[17] Dillon lists an unpublished recording of *Die Meistersinger* from the Teatro Colón in September 1949 in a private archive.

[18] Dillon lists an unpublished recording of the Prelude and Liebestod from *Tristan und Isolde* from Montevideo on 9 September 1950 in the SODRE Archive (B.91).

[19] There was a cut in the performance in Act 2, Scene 2, from *Dem Tage! Dem Tage!* (Tristan) to *dass nachtsichtig mein Auge wahres zu sehen tauge* (Tristan). All the LP and CD issues are incorrectly dated 20 July 1952; Kleiber conducted *Der Rosenkavalier* that evening. Dillon dates it correctly as 29 July 1952.

[20] At the end of the *Tristan* performance on side 8, there is a recording from a live performance of the Prelude to Act 3 of *Die Meistersinger*. There is no information on the label or box, or in the accompanying booklet, as to who is performing it, nor even mention that the excerpt is there at all.

1953

Lohengrin, Copenhagen, live performance, 22 February 1953, excerpts (sung in Danish)
Act 1, Prelude, and scenes 2 and 3 complete (40' 40")
Act 2, scenes 1 and 2 complete (34' 25")
Act 3, complete (57' 45")

Lohengrin, Erik Sjøberg; Elsa, Dorothy Larsen; Ortrud, Lilian Weber Hansen; Friedrich von Telramund, Holger Byrding; King Heinrich, Einar Nørby; Herald, Johannes Astrup; Pages, Lise Andersen, Anne Sophie Olsen, Bente Kirstein Christiansen, Grethe Lundberg
Chorus and Orchestra of the Kongelige Teater, Copenhagen
CD: Classico CLASSCD 5011-12 (2 CDs) [2005]

8. Otto Klemperer conducts Wagner[1]

Works recorded, including excerpts:

Rienzi: 1960
Der fliegende Holländer: 1960, 1968
Tannhäuser: 1960
Lohengrin: 1948, 1960
Tristan und Isolde: 1927, 1960, 1968
Wesendonck Lieder: 1962
Die Meistersinger von Nürnberg: 1934, 1949, 1956, 1960, 1968
Siegfried Idyll: 1927, 1961, 1968
Der Ring des Nibelungen:
  Das Rheingold: 1961
  Die Walküre: 1960, 1969, 1970
  Siegfried: 1961
  Götterdämmerung: 1960, 1961
Parsifal: 1961

1927

Siegfried Idyll
Berlin State Opera Orchestra, Singakademie, Berlin, 1927
(394bi-397bi)
78: Grammophon/Polydor 66604/5
CD: *Otto Klemperer – Die Kroll-Jahre*: Symposium 1042 (1988); *Great Conductors – Otto Klemperer – 1927-28 Recordings*: Naxos Historical 8.111274 (2008)

Tristan und Isolde, Act 1, Prelude, with Wagner's concert ending
Berlin State Opera Orchestra, Singakademie, Berlin, 23 June 1927
(BDR 4716-1, 4717-1, 4718-1, 4719-1)
78: Electrola E476/7, AV4223 and 4225, ER245/6, EW27/8
CD: *Wagner Conductors on Record*: Pearl GEMS 0024 (1998); *Great Conductors – Otto Klemperer – 1927-28 Recordings*: Naxos Historical 8.111274 (2008)

[1] The standard, comprehensive discography on Klemperer is Michael H. Gray's in Peter Heyworth's *Otto Klemperer, his life and times*, 2 vols. (Cambridge, 1983-1996) which contains details of the multiple re-issues of, and excerpts from, the recordings listed here.

1934

Die Meistersinger, Act 1, Prelude
Los Angeles Philarmonic Orchestra, live broadcast, 1 January 1934
CD: *Klemperer in Los Angeles*: Archipel ARPCD 0055 (2002)

1948

Lohengrin, Budapest, live performance, 24 October 1948 (sung in Hungarian)
Lohengrin, József Simándy; Elsa, Magda Rigó; Ortrud, Ella Némethy; Telramund, László Jámbor; King Heinrich, György Losonczy; Herald, Sándor Reményi; Nobles, Béla Hollay, Géza Lux, Gjozo Mally, Sándor Ilyés; Hungarian State Opera Chorus and Orchestra
LP: *Klemperer in Budapest - 4*: Hungaraton LPX 12436 (1982) (excerpts)
CD: Grammofono 2000 AB 78 886/88 (1999); Urania URN 22.147 (2000) (excerpts)

1949

Die Meistersinger, Budapest, live performance, 11 April 1949, excerpts (sung in Hungarian) (ca. 96 mins)
Act 1: Prelude (9' 10")
Act 1, Scene 3: *Das schöne Fest… Eva, mein einzig kind, zur Eh'* (Pogner) (3' 47")
Act 1, Scene 3: *Am stillen Herd* (Walter) to *Merkwürd'ger Fall!* (Nachtigall) (4' 14")
Act 1, Scene 3: *Fanget an!* (Walter) to the end of the Act (11' 31")
Act 2, Scene 2: *Laß sehn, on Meister Sachs zu Haus! … Das mag was Rechtes sein!* (Pogner) (4' 56")
Act 2, Scene 3: *Was duftet doch der Flieder to Hans Sachsen* (Sachs) (4' 50")
Act 2, Scene 6: *Den Tag seh' ich erscheinen… um die Jungfrau zu frei'n* (Beckmesser) (4' 58")
Act 3: Prelude (5' 43")
Act 3, Scene 1: *Am Jordan Sankt Johannes stand* (David) … *Wahn! Wahn!… und nie ohne ein'gen Wahngelingen* (Sachs) (9' 19")
Act 3, Scene 4: *Grüß Gott, mein Evchen!* (Sachs) … *Selig wie die Sonne* (Eva) to the end of the quintet (17' 15")
Act 3, Scene 5: *Sankt Krispin, lobet ihn!* (Shoemakers) (Procession of the Guilds, Dance of the Apprentices, Arrival of the Mastersingers) … *Heil! Heil!* (Chorus) (13' 18")
Act 3, Scene 5: *Morgenlich leuchtend im rosigen Schein* to the end of the opera (12' 12")
Hans Sachs, György Losonczy; Eva, Júlia Osváth; Walther von Stolzing, József Simándy; Magdalene, Mária Budanovits; David, János Sárdy; Beckmesser, Oszkár Maleczny; Pogner, Mihály Székely; Kothner, István Koszó; Vogelgesang, József Somló; Nachtigall, Lajos Katona; Ortel, Pál Rissay; Zorn, József Joviczky; Moser, Gyula Toronyi; Eisslinger, Lajos Somogyváry; Foltz, Ervin Galsay; Schwarz, Endre Várhelyi; Hungarian State Opera Chorus and Orchestra
LP: *Klemperer in Budapest - 2*: Hungaraton LPX 12430 (1981)
CD: Urania URN 22.118 (1999)

1956

Die Meistersinger, Act 1, Prelude
RAI Symphony Orchestra, Turin, live performance, 17 December 1956[2]
LP: Fonit Cetra LAR 37 (1983)
CD: Medici Masters MM030-2 (2008) (with Bruckner's *Symphony No. 7*)

1960

Tannhäuser, Overture, 23-24 February 1960
Der fliegende Holländer, Overture, 24-25 February 1960
Lohengrin, Act 1, Prelude, 25 February and 3 March 1960
Lohengrin, Act 3, Prelude, 27 February 1960
Götterdämmerung, Siegfried's Funeral Music, 27 February 1960
Die Meistersinger, Act 1, Prelude, 1-2 March 1960
Tristan und Isolde, Prelude and Liebestod, 1-3 March 1960
Rienzi, Overture, 2-3 March 1960
Tannhäuser, Act 3 Prelude, 3 March 1960
Die Meistersinger, Act 3, Dance of the Apprentices, and Entry of the Mastersingers, 8 March 1960
Die Walküre, Act 3, Ride of the Valkyries, 10 March 1960
Philharmonia Orchestra, Kingsway Hall, London
LP: Columbia 33CX1697/98 and 33CX1820 (*Tannhäuser* Act 3 and *Die Walküre*); Columbia SAXO-2347/48 (stereo) (Australia) (all except *Tannhäuser* Act 3 and *Die Walküre*); Angel 35875/76 (all except *Die Walküre* excerpt)[3]; HMV SLS 5075 (stereo) (all excerpts)
CD: EMI Masters 6 31827-2 (2010)

1961

Das Rheingold, Entry of the Gods into Valhalla, 24 October 1961
Siegfried, Forest Murmurs, 24 October – 13 November 1961
Siegfried Idyll, 25 October 1961
Parsifal, Act 1, Prelude, 14 November 1961
Götterdämmerung, Siegfried's Rhine Journey, 1961
Philharmonia Orchestra, Kingsway Hall, London
LP: Columbia 33CX1820; 33CX1808/9 (*Siegfried Idyll* only); HMV SLS 5075 (except *Siegfried Idyll*)
CD: EMI Masters 6 31827-2 (2010)

[2] broadcast 27 January 1957

[3] The booklet accompanying the Angel and Columbia sets contains an article by Klemperer "How I became a Conductor" which is different from the one of the same title in his *Minor Reflections* and reproduced in *Klemperer on music: shavings from a musician's workbench,* edited by Martin Anderson (London: Toccata Press, 1986).

1962

Wesendonck Lieder (orch. by Mottl), and ***Tristan und Isolde***, Liebestod
Christa Ludwig, Philharmonia Orchestra, Kingsway Hall, London, 22-23 March 1962
LP: Columbia 33CX1817; Angel S.35923
CD: EMI CDM 7 64074-2; *Christa Ludwig: Great Recordings of the Century*: EMI 61596-2 (2006)

1968

Der fliegende Holländer (1843 Dresden version)
Dutchman, Theo Adam; Daland, Martti Talvela; Senta, Anja Silja; Erik, Ernst Kozub; Mary, Annelies Burmeister; Steersman, Gerhard Unger; BBC Chorus, New Philharmonia Orchestra, Studio No. 1, Abbey Road, London, 17-19, 21-24, 28 February, 8-11, 13-14 March 1968
LP: Angel SAN 207/9; HMV SLS 934
CD: EMI CDMS 7 63344 2; CDS 5 55179 2; *Great Recordings of the Century*: 5 67408 2 (2000); 4 56470-2 (2010)

Der fliegende Holländer (1843 Dresden version)
London, Royal Festival Hall, live broadcast, 19 March 1968
Dutchman, Theo Adam; Daland, Martti Talvela; Senta, Anja Silja; Erik, James King; Mary, Annelies Burmeister; Steersman, Kenneth MacDonald; BBC Chorus, New Philharmonia Orchestra
CD: Hunt CD-561; Living Stage LS 347.06 (1999); Testament SBT2 1423 (2008)

Siegfried Idyll
Tristan und Isolde, Act 1, Prelude
Die Meistersinger, Act 1, Prelude
Vienna Philharmonic Orchestra, Musikvereinsaal, Vienna, live performance, 16 June 1968
CD: Hunt CD-708 (*Siegfried Idyll*); CD-578 (*Tristan und Isolde* and *Die Meistersinger*); Nuova Era 033.6709 (1988) (*Tristan und Isolde*); *Great German Conductors*: Memories HR 4587 (1995) (*Tristan und Isolde*); Living Stage LS 347.05 (1999) (*Siegfried Idyll*); Testament SBT8 1365 (2005) (all excerpts); Testament UCCN-1060 (Japan) [SBT 1399] (all excerpts)

1969

Die Walküre, Act 1
Siegmund, William Cochran; Sieglinde, Helga Dernesch; Hunding, Hans Sotin, New Philharmonia Orchestra, All Saints Church, Tooting, London, 22-24, 30-31 October and 3 November 1969
LP: Angel SAN 334/5; HMV SLS 968
CD: Testament 1205 (2000)

1970

Die Walküre, Act 3, Wotan's Farewell and Magic Fire Music
Wotan, Norman Bailey; New Philharmonia Orchestra, All Saints Church, Tooting, London, 24, 26-27 October 1970

LP: Angel SAN 334/5; HMV SLS 968

CD: EMI CDM 763835-2 (Wotan's Farewell only)

9. Hans Knappertsbusch conducts Wagner[1]

Works recorded, including excerpts:

Rienzi: 1940, 1947, 1950, 1962

Der fliegende Holländer: 1928, 1953, 1955, 1958, 1962

Tannhäuser: 1928, 1937, 1942, 1948, 1949, 1953, 1962

Lohengrin: 1928, 1936, 1947, 1956, 1962

Tristan und Isolde: 1942, 1947, 1950, 1959, 1962, 1963

Wesendonck Lieder: 1956

Die Meistersinger von Nürnberg: 1928, 1936, 1947, 1948, 1949, 1950, 1951, 1952, 1955, 1958, 1959, 1960, 1962, 1963

Siegfried Idyll: 1943, 1949, 1953, 1955, 1962, 1963

Der Ring des Nibelungen: 1937, 1956, 1957, 1958, also -

Die Walküre: 1928, 1936, 1938, 1941, 1943, 1953, 1956, 1957, 1958, 1963

Siegfried: 1936, 1937, 1941, 1943, 1950

Götterdämmerung: 1937, 1938, 1940, 1941, 1942, 1943, 1951, 1955, 1956, 1959, 1963

Parsifal: 1928, 1937, 1939, 1942, 1950, 1951, 1952, 1954, 1956, 1957, 1958, 1959, 1960, 1961, 1962, 1963, 1964

1928[2]

Die Meistersinger, Act 3, Prelude (735/4 bm) Grammophon 66780

Die Meistersinger, Act 1, Prelude (751/2 bm) Grammophon 66698

Tannhäuser, Entry of the guests (755 bm) Grammophon 66702

Die Meistersinger, Act 3, Dance of the apprentices (756 bm) Grammophon 66705

Lohengrin, Act 3, Prelude (762 bm) Grammophon 27185

Parsifal, Act 1, Transformation music (763/4 bm) Grammophon 66700

Die Walküre, Act 3, Ride of the Valkyries (765 bm) Grammophon 66705

[1] John Hunt's two discographies *Wagner im Festspielhaus – the Bayreuth Recordings* (2006) and *Kna – concert register and discography of Hans Knappertsbusch* (2007) are the standard, modern sources on Knappertsbusch's legacy on record. The latter expands on a chapter in his earlier work *Mid-Century Conductors* (1992). For this discography I have confirmed Bayreuth Festival performance dates with the Richard Wagner Museum and, through it, the broadcast dates with Bavarian Radio.

[2] There is some confusion over whether Knappertsbusch accompanied Theodor Scheidl in a recording of Amfortas' Lament (Grammophon 66671, 641 bm, 1928), not least because it appeared as such in the author's *Parsifal on Record* (1992) and then in John Hunt's discography *Kna* (2007). Most versions of this recording list no conductor. However, in *Grosse Stimmen in Bayreuth – Einst und Jetzt* (DG 2721 078, 3 LPs, n. d.) Knappertsbusch is named as conducting the Berlin Philharmonic Orchestra. In the later *Wagner Scenes and Arias 1925-1943* (DG 459 006-2, 1 CD, 1998) the conductor is given as Hermann Weigert with unidentified orchestra. It is believed this is correct. The precise dates of the Grammophon recordings are not known. Knappertsbusch recorded some Strauss waltzes with the Gramophone Company on 15 and 16 February 1928, the orchestra being described respectively as *Staatskapelle* and *Staatsorchester*.

Tannhäuser, Bacchanale (766/8 bm) Grammophon 66701/2
Der fliegende Holländer, Overture (769/70 bm) Grammophon 66699
Berlin Philharmonic Orchestra, 1928
78: Grammophon (catalogue numbers as above)
LP: Heliodor 88 031 (1966) (*Meistersinger, Parsifal, Walküre* excerpts and *Tannhäuser* Bacchanale only); *100 Jahre Berliner Philharmoniker – Frühe Aufnahmen 1913-1933*: DG 2740 259 (1982) (*Die Meistersinger, Tannhäuser* Bacchanale, *Die Walküre, Parsifal* only)
CD: *Hans Knappertsbusch dirigiert Richard Wagner*: Preiser 90286 (1996) (all excerpts)

1936

Siegfried, Vienna, live performance, 18 April 1936, excerpts (ca. 24 mins)
Act 1, scene 1: from the Prelude to *als schüf' ich Kindergeschmied!* (Mime) (5' 01")
Act 1, scene 3: from *Fühltest du nie im finstren Wald* (Mime) to *der fänd' wohl eher die Kunst* (Mime) (4' 48")
Act 3: scene 1: from the Prelude to *Wache, Wala! Wala! Erwach!* (Wanderer) (2' 03")
Act 3, scene 1: from *Stark ruft das Lied* (Erda) to *was fester Schlaf verschließt* (Wanderer) (1' 22")
Act 3, scene 1: from *Mein Schlaf ist Träumen* to *Was frägst du nicht die Nornen?* (Erda) (1' 15")
Act 3, scene 1: from *Männertaten umdämmern mir den Mut* (Erda) to *Die Walküre meinst du, Brünnhild', die Maid?* (Wanderer) (1' 45")
Act 3, scene 1: from *Wirr wird mir, seit ich erwacht* to *Schlaf verschließe mein Wissen!* (Erda) (2' 06")
Act 3, scene 1: from *Du bist nicht, was du dich nennst!* (Erda) to *Weißt du, was Wotan will?* (Wanderer) (0' 38")
Act 3: orchestral interlude from end of scene 2 *Jetzt lock' ich ein liebes Gesell!* (Siegfried) to the beginning of scene 3 [before *Selige Öde auf sonniger Höh'!* (Siegfried)] (5' 06")
Mime, Erich Zimmermann; Siegfried, Josef Kalenberg; Wanderer, Emil Schipper; Erda, Enid Szantho; Orchestra of the Vienna State Opera
CD: *Edition Wiener Staatsoper Live – Vol. 24*: Koch Schwann 3-1474-2 (1995)

Lohengrin, Vienna, live performance, 8 October 1936, excerpt
Act 1, scene 3: from *Du kündest nun dein wahr' Gericht* (Elsa, Lohengrin) to *an höchstem Lobe reich!* (Elsa) (4' 11")
Lohengrin, Torsten Ralf; Elsa, Luise Helletsgruber; King Heinrich, Ludwig Hofmann; Telramund, Emil Schipper; Ortrud, Anny Konetzni; Chorus and Orchestra of the Vienna State Opera
CD: *Edition Wiener Staatsoper Live – Vol. 1*: Koch Schwann 3-1451-2 (1994)

Die Walküre, Vienna, live performance, 13 October 1936, excerpts (ca. 63 mins)
Act 1: Prelude (3' 13")
Act 1, scene 1: *des Müden Last … Schmecktest du mir ihn zu?* (Siegmund, with Sieglinde) (3' 21")
Act 1, scene 2: *Fort aus dem Saal! … Dich, Wölfing, treffe ich morgen* (Hunding) (3' 25")
Act 1, scene 3: *Wälse! Wälse! Wo ist dein Schwert? … glimmt nur noch lichtlose Glut* (Siegmund) (3' 18")
Act 1, scene 3: *[Eine Waffe laß mich dir weisen:] O wenn du sie gewännst! … keinen Zoll entwich er dem Stamm* [then a break, resuming at] *süßeste Rache sühnte dann alles!* (Sieglinde) … *Winterstürme wichen … trennte von ihm* (Siegmund) (6' 55")
Act 1, scene 3: *O laß in Nähe zu dir mich neigen … O still! laß mich der Stimme Schall* (Sieglinde, with Siegmund) (3' 06")

Act 1, scene 3: *Siegmund heiß' ich, und Siegmund bin ich* (Siegmund, with Sieglinde) to fourteen bars before the end of the Act (3' 29")

Act 2, scene 1: *[Wann] ward es erlebt, daß leiblich Geschwister sich liebten? … in gehorsam der Herrin du gabst* (Fricka, with Wotan) (3' 16")

Act 2, scene 2: *Laß ich's verlauten … Als junge Liebe… und mit ihm maßlose Macht* (Wotan, with Brünnhilde) (3' 29")

Act 2, scene 3: *Ruhe nun aus, rede zu mir!* (Siegmund) … *Hinweg! Hinweg!… dir Herrlichem darf ich nimmer gehören* (Sieglinde) (4' 28")

Act 2, scene 4: *So jung und schön erschimmerst du mir* (Siegmund) …*Auf der Walstatt she ich dich wieder!* (Brünnhilde) and orchestral passage to the end of the scene (4'20")

Act 2, scene 5: *Drohst du mit Frauen, so ficht nun selber* (Siegmund, with Brünnhilde) …*Geh! Geh!* (Wotan) (3' 17")

Act 3, scene 1: *Lebe, O Weib, um der Liebe willen! … biete mich Wotan's rache* (Brünnhilde, with Valkyries) [then a break, resuming at] *Dorn und Gestein* (Brünnhilde) … *Dich segnet Sieglindes Weh!* (Sieglinde) (2' 55")

Act 3, scene 2: *der Mann dann fange die Maid …das künd' ich der Kühnen an!* (Wotan, with Valkyries) (2' 15")

Act 3, scene 3: … *der Gott! … Der Augen leuchtendes Paar … das oft im Sturm mir geglänzt* (Wotan) (3' 18")

Act 3, scene 3: *[so küßt er die Gottheit] von dir!* (Wotan) ... orchestral passage … *Loge, hör!* (Wotan) (2' 52")

Act 3, scene 3, concluding Magic Fire scene: *Wer meines Speeres Spitze fürchtet* (Wotan) to the end of the Act (2' 48")

Siegmund, Franz Völker; Sieglinde, Hilde Konetzni; Wotan, Ludwig Hofmann; Brünnhilde, Rose Merker; Hunding, Herbert Alsen; Gerhilde, Ella Flesch; Ortlinde, Margit Bokor; Waltraute, Dora With; Schwertleite, Elsa Weichert; Helmwige, Luise Helletsgruber; Siegrune, Aenne Michalsky; Grimgerde, Bella Paalen; Roßweiße, Frieda Stroinigg; Orchestra of the Vienna State Opera

CD: *Edition Wiener Staatsoper Live, Vol. 9*: Koch Schwann 3-1459-2 (1994) (excerpts incorrectly attributed to Bruno Walter)[3]

Die Meistersinger, Vienna, live performance, 19 October 1936, excerpts (ca. 7 mins)

Act 1, scene 3: from *Singt dem Herrn Merker zum Verdruß!* (Sachs) to the end of the Act (3' 00")

Act 3, scene 4: from *Selig wie die Sonne* (Eva) to *schnell auf die Füße!* (Sachs) (4' 10")

Hans Sachs, Ludwig Hofmann; Veit Pogner, Herbert Alsen; Kunz Vogelgesang, Georg Maikl; Konrad Nachtigall, Georg Monthy; Sixtus Beckmesser, Hermann Wiedermann; Fritz Kothner, Victor Madin; Balthasar Zorn, Anton Arnold; Ulrich Eißlinger, Eduard Fritsch; Augustin Moser, Richard Tomek; Hermann Ortel, Alfred Muzzarelli; Hans Schwarz, Hermann Reich; Hans Foltz, Karl Ettl; Walther von Stolzing, Josef Kalenberg; Eva, Vera Masinger; Magdalene, Kerstin Thorborg; David, Richard Sallaba; Chorus and Orchestra of the Vienna State Opera

CD: *Edition Wiener Staatsoper Live – Vol. 10*: Koch Schwann 3-1460-2 (1994)

Lohengrin, Vienna, live performance, 19 December 1936, excerpts (ca. 14 mins)

Act 1, scene 3: from *Heil, König Heinrich* (Lohengrin) to *Nun hört! Euch Volk und Edlen mach' ich kund* (Lohengrin) (with an interruption) (7' 01")

3 The Vienna Opera program lists Knappertsbusch as conductor, and a review of the performance in the *Neues Wiener Journal*, 14 October 1936, p. 11, discusses Knappertsbusch as the conductor.

Act 2, scene 2: from *Du Ärmste kannst wohl nie ermessen* to *es gibt ein Glück, das ohne Reu'* (Elsa, with Ortrud) (4' 31")

Act 2, scene 5: from *Was er verbirgt, wohl brächt' es ihm Gefahren* to *Im Zweifel doch erbebt des Herzens Grund!* (Elsa, with others) (2' 31")

Lohengrin, Paul Kötter; Elsa, Margarethe Teschemacher; King Heinrich, Herbert Alsen; Ortrud, Anny Konetzni; Chorus and Orchestra of the Vienna State Opera

CD: *Edition Wiener Staatsoper Live – Vol. 17*: Koch Schwann 3-1467-2 (1994)

1937

Götterdämmerung, Vienna, live performance, 24 January 1937, excerpts (ca. 23 mins)

Prologue: orchestral introduction (1' 39")

Prologue: from *Mehr gabst du, Wunderfrau* to *Brünnhildes zu gedenken* (Siegfried) (0' 59")

Prologue: from *Furch deine Tugend allein* (Siegfried) to *Heil! Heil!* (Siegfried, Brünnhilde) (2' 43")

Act 3, scene 1: from the beginning to *der Vaters Gold noch in ihr glänzte* (Rhinemaidens) (3' 20")

Act 3, scene 1: from *Siegfried! Siegfried! Siegfried! Schlimmes wissen wir dir* to *Im tiefen Rhein ihn zu bergen* (Rhinemaidens) (1' 58")

Act 3, scene 2: from *Hoiho!* (Hagen) to *Hier ist's frisch und kühl* (Siegfried) (1' 33")

Act 3, scene 2: from *Von des Wurmes Blut mir brannten die Finger* (Siegfried) to *Was nicht er geschmiedet, schmeckte doch Mime!* (Hagen) (2' 27")

Act 3, scene 2: from *In Leid zu dem Wipfel lauscht' ich hinauf* (Siegfried) to Siegfried's death *Meineid rächt' ich!* (Hagen) (4' 02")

Act 3, scene 2: from the end of the Immolation scene to the end of the act (4' 05")

Siegfried, Max Lorenz; Brünnhilde, Anny Konetzni; Woglinde, Luise Helletsgruber; Wellgunde, Aenne Michalsky; Floßhilde, Dora With; Chorus and Orchestra of the Vienna State Opera

CD: *Edition Wiener Staatsoper Live – Vol. 24*: Koch Schwann 3-1474-2 (1995)

Siegfried, Vienna, live performance, 18 April 1937,[4] excerpts from Act 3, scene 3 (ca. 15 mins)

from *Heil dir, Sonne! Heil dir, licht!* to *der mich erweckt* (Brünnhilde) (2' 36")

from *Heil euch, Götter! Heil dir, Welt!* (Brünnhilde) to *Seliger Held!* (Brünnhilde) (2' 10")

from *Du wonniges Kind!* (Brünnhilde) to *Siegfried erweckt* (Brünnhilde) (5' 03")

from *Ewig war ich, ewig bin ich* (Brünnhilde) to *mein sehnen schwänd' in der Flut!* (Siegfried) (4' 46")

Siegfried, Josef Kalenberg; Brünnhilde, Anny Konetzni; Orchestra of the Vienna State Opera

CD: *Edition Wiener Staatsoper Live – Vol. 6*: Koch Schwann 3-1456-2 (1994)

Der Ring des Nibelungen, Vienna, live performances, June 1937, excerpts -

Das Rheingold, Vienna, live performance, 10 June 1937, excerpt

Abendlich strahlt der Sonne Auge (Wotan) to *leg' es den Sinn dir dar!* (Wotan) (3' 29")

Wotan, Ludwig Hofmann; Fricka, Enid Szantho; Orchestra of the Vienna State Opera

CD: *Edition Wiener Staatsoper Live – Vol. 24*: Koch Schwann 3-1474-2 (1995)

4 This is the date appearing on the CD. However, *Die Zauberflöte* was performed at the Vienna Opera on that day, conducted by Josef Krips.

Die Walküre, Vienna, live performance, 12 June 1937, excerpt (3' 15")

Act 2, scene 1: from the beginning of the act to *Fricka naht, deine Frau* (Brünnhilde)

Wotan, Ludwig Hofmann; Anny Konetzni, Brünnhilde; Orchestra of the Vienna State Opera

CD: *Edition Wiener Staatsoper Live – Vol. 6*: Koch Schwann 3-1456-2 (1994)

Siegfried, Vienna, live performance, 16 June 1937, excerpts (ca. 28 mins)

Act 1, scene 2: from *'Wand'rer' heißt mich die Welt* (Wanderer) to *setze mein Haupt der Wissenswette zum Pfand* (Wanderer) (3' 32"), and from *Auf wolkigen Höh'n wohnen dir Götter* (Wanderer) to *Behalte mein Haupt ich frei?* (Wanderer) (3' 12")

Act 2, scene 2: from *[Dein Hirn brütete nicht,] was du vollbracht* (Fafner) to *Siegfried...!* (Fafner) (3' 25")*

Act 2, scene 2: from *Laß will ihn mir schon gewinnen* (Mime) to *Da war doch ein schlimmer Gesell?* (Mime) (3' 31")*

Act 2, scene 2: from *so recht ja rietest du schon* (Siegfried) to *Wie find' ich zum Felsen den Weg?* (Siegfried) (3' 22")*

Act 2, scene 3: from *Was ihr mir nützet, weiss ich nicht* (Siegfried)... *Hei! Siegfried gehört nun der Helm und der Ring!* (Forest Bird)... to *Er sinnt und erwägt der Beute Wert* (Mime) (1' 52")**

Act 2, scene 3: from *[Nun] sing! Ich lausche dem Gesang* (Siegfried) *Hei! Siegfried erschlug...* (Forest Bird) ... to *Wie find ich zum Felsen den Weg* (Siegfried) (3' 06")**

Act 3, scene 1: from *Der Weckrufer bin ich* (Wanderer) to *Männertaten umdämmern mir den Mut* (Erda) (3' 29"), and *Dir Unweisen ruf' ich ins Ohr* to *Urmütterfrucht!* (Wanderer) (3' 09")

Act 3, scene 2: from *Mein Vöglein schwebte mir fort!* (Siegfried) to *schuf ich das Schwert mir nicht neu* (Siegfried) (3' 11")

Wanderer, Ludwig Hofmann; Siegfried, Max Lorenz; Mime, William Wernigk; Erda, Enid Szantho; Fafner, Nikolaus Zec; Waldvogel, Elisabeth Schumann; Orchestra of the Vienna State Opera

LP: The Golden Age of Opera EJS 444 (1968) (excerpts marked **)[5]

CD: *Edition Wiener Staatsoper Live – Vol. 10*: Koch Schwann 3-1460-2 (1994) (except for excerpts marked * or **), and *Vol. 24*: Koch Schwann 3-1474-2 (1995) (excerpts marked *)

Götterdämmerung, Vienna, live performance, 19 June 1937, excerpts (ca. 5 mins)

Prologue: from *Dämmert der Tag?* (First Norn) to *Schwinget, Schwestern, das Seil!* (Third Norn) (3' 05")

Act 3, scene 3: from *Her den Ring!* (Hagen) to *der ewige Eide [er schwur]* (Brünnhilde) (2' 16")

First Norn, Edith Szantho; Second Norn, Rosette Anday; Third Norn, Wanda Achsel; Hagen, Alexander Kipnis; Brünnhilde, Anny Konetzni; Gutrune, Wanda Achsel; Orchestra of the Vienna State Opera

CD: *Edition Wiener Staatsoper Live – Vol. 24*: Koch Schwann 3-1474-2 (1995)

Parsifal, Vienna, live performance, 1 November 1937, excerpts (ca. 27 mins)

Act 1: Transformation scene: *Nun achte wohl...* (Gurnemanz) to *...die hehrste Gab empfan* (Knights) (4' 07")

Act 1: Grail scene: *Nehmet hin mein Blut* (Boys) to *O! heilige Wonne, wie hell grüsst uns heute Herr!* (Titurel) (3' 41")

Act 1: Grail scene: *Wein und Brot des letzten Mahles* (Boys) to *zu kämpfen mit seligem Mute!* (Knights) (4' 03")

Act 1: Grail scene: *Was stehst du noch da?* (Gurnemanz) to end of the Act (4' 04")

[5] contains another excerpt from *Siegfried* from 10 December 1943 (see below)

Act 3: Transformation music (3' 51")
Act 3: *Es birgt den Helden der Trauerschrein* (Knights) to *Ja/- Wehe! Wehe! Weh' über mich! So [ruf' ich willig mit euch]* (Amfortas) (3' 28")
Act 3: *Höschten Heiles Wunder!* (Boys, Knights) to end of the Act (4' 25")

Gurnemanz, Herbert Alsen; Amfortas, Fred Destal[6]; Titurel, Nikolaus Zec; a Voice, Helene Nikolaidi; Vienna State Opera Chorus and Orchestra

CD: *Edition Wiener Staatsoper Live - Vol. 13*: Koch Scwann 3-1463-2 (1994)

Tannhäuser, Vienna, live performance, 20 November 1937, excerpts (ca. 18 mins)
Act 1, scene 3: from *Zu ihr! Zu ihr!* (Tannhäuser) to the end of the act (2' 36)
Act 2, scene 1: from orchestral introduction to *Dich teurer Halle grüss' ich wieder* to *sei mir gegrüsst!* (Elisabeth) and applause (4' 25")
Act 2, scene 4: from *Ich fleh' für ihn* (Elisabeth) to *Weh! Weh mir Unglücksel'gem* (Tannhäuser) (1' 55")
Act 2, scene 4: from *Zum Heil den Sündigen zu führen* (Tannhäuser) to *Erlöser litt!* (Elisabeth, with chorus) (3' 25")
Act 2, scene 4: from *Versammelt sind aus meinen Landen* (Landgraf) to *der Gottes Urteil spricht* (Knights) (1' 42")
Act 3, scene 3: from *Von fern her tönten frohe Gnadenlieder* (Tannhäuser) to *nun sei der Hölle Lust erkoren!* (Tannhäuser) (4' 33")

Tannhäuser, Max Lorenz; Elisabeth, Maria Reining; Venus, Anny Konetzni; Landgraf, Herbert Alsen; Wolfram von Eschenbach, Arno Schellenberg; Walter von der Vogelweide, Georg Maikl; Biterolf, Viktor Madin; Heinrich der Schreiber, Hermann Gallos; Reinmar von Zweter, Karl Ettl; Chorus and Orchestra of the Vienna State Opera

CD: *Edition Wiener Staatsoper Live – Vol. 17*: Koch Schwann 3-1467-2 (1994)

1938

Die Walküre, Vienna, live performance, 19 September 1938, excerpts (ca. 11 mins)
Act 1, scene 3: from *Eine Waffe lass mich dir weisen* (Sieglinde) to *der Lenz lacht in der Saal!* (Siegmund) (6' 16") (with an interruption)
Act 2, scene 1: from *Hojotoho!* to *Heiaha!* (Brünnhilde) (0' 46")
Act 2, scene 2: from *Zu Wotans Willen sprichst du* to *wär' ich dein Wille nicht?* (0' 48")
Act 2, scene 4: from *Sieglinde lebe, und Siegmund lebe mit ihr* to *Auf der Walstatt she ich dich wieder* (Brünnhilde) (1' 09")
Act 3, scene 1: from *Fort denn eile* (Brünnhilde) to *Lebe wohl! Dich segnet Sieglindes Weh!* (Sieglinde) (2' 12")

Brünnhilde, Gertrude Rünger; Sieglinde, Hilde Konetzni; Siegmund, Julius Pölzer; Orchestra of the Vienna State Opera

CD: *Edition Wiener Staatsoper Live – Vol. 16*: Koch Schwann 3-1466-2 (1994), and *Vol. 19*: Koch Schwann 3-1469-2 (1994) (the Act 1 excerpt)

Götterdämmerung, Vienna, live performance, 25 September 1938, excerpts (ca. 8 mins)
Prologue: from *Es ragt die Burg* (Third Norn) to *da Loge einst entbrannt in lichter Brunst* (First Norn) (3' 07"), and from *bannte ihn Wotan* (Second Norn) to *Die Nacht weicht; nichts mehr gewahr' ich* (First Norn) (2' 03")
Prologue: from *Zu neuen Taten, teurer Helde* (Brünnhilde) to Brünnhildes zu gedenken! (Siegfried) (3' 15")

6 as given on the CD; the program lists Alfred Jerger as Amfortas

First Norn, Lela Bugarinovič; Second Norn, Dora With; Third Norn, Esther Réthy; Brünnhilde, Gertrude Rünger; Siegfried, Julius Pölzer; Orchestra of the Vienna State Opera

CD: *Edition Wiener Staatsoper Live – Vol. 10*: Koch Schwann 3-1460-2 (1994) (Norn excerpts), and *Vol. 16*: Koch Schwann 3-1466-2 (1994) (Brünnhilde- Siegfried excerpt)

1939

Parsifal, Vienna, live performance, 6 April 1939, excerpts (ca. 53 mins)

Act 1: Prelude (with two interruptions) (12' 10")
Act 1: *Nun achte wohl* (Gurnemanz) to *...die hehrste Gab empfahn* (Knights) (2' 56")
Act 2: Prelude to *Dein Meister ruft: herauf!* (Klingsor) (3' 55")
Act 2: *Wie lachen ihm die Rosen der Wangen* (Klingsor) to *...ja wehrten sie mir den Weg* (Parsifal) (3' 49")
Act 2: *Und willst Du uns nicht schelten* to *wir welken und sterben dahinnen* (Flowermaidens) (3' 50")
Act 2: *...sie beut dir heut' als Muttersegens letzten Gruss* (Kundry) to *Amfortas! Die Wunde! ... Das heil'ge Blut erglüht* (Parsifal) (4' 09")
Act 2: *Hilfe! Hilfe! Herbei!* (Kundry) to end of Act (3' 25")
Act 3: Prelude (3' 48")
Act 3: *Du siehst, das ist nicht so* to "... ihren Unschuldstag erwirbt" (Gurnemanz) (4' 09")
Act 3: *Ich sah sie welken...* (Parsifal) to *...dass dein Knecht dich geleite!* (Gurnemanz) and beginning of Transformation scene (3' 18")
Act 3: Transformation scene to *Gott selbst einst beschirmte?* (Knights) (3' 12")
Act 3: *Höchsten Heiles Wunder!* (Chorus) to end of the Act (4' 25")

Gurnemanz, Herbert Alsen; Kundry, Anny Konetzni; Klingsor, Hermann Wiedemann; Parsifal, Hans Grahl; Flowermaidens, Luise Helletsgruber, Elisabeth Rutgers, Maria Schober, Esther Réthy, Dora Komarek, Dora With; Chorus and Orchestra of the Vienna State Opera

CD: *Edition Wiener Staatsoper Live – Vol. 2*: Koch Schwann 3-1452-2 (1993)

1940

Rienzi, Overture
Vienna Philharmonic Orchestra
(2RA 4649/51-1, April 1940)
78: Electrola DB 5607/8
CD: *Hans Knappertsbusch dirigiert die Wiener Philharmoniker*: Preiser 90116 (1992)

Götterdämmerung, Siegfried's Rhine Journey
Vienna Philharmonic Orchestra, live performance, 12 May 1940
CD: *Hans Knappertsbusch: RRG Recordings 1940-1941*: Tahra TAH 309 (1998)

1941

Die Walküre, Vienna, live performance, 16 June 1941,[7] excerpts from Act 1, scene 3 (ca. 11 mins)

[7] This is the date on the CD. However, a closed performance of *Tosca* conducted by Josef Hietz was given for the Wehrmacht at the Vienna Opera on that date. Knappertsbusch conducted *Walküre* on 15 June 1941.

from *Ein Schwert verhieß mir der Vater* to *Ist es der Blick der blühenden Frau...?* (Siegmund) (3' 10")★★
from *Keiner ging, doch einer kam... Winterstürme* to *vereint sind Liebe und Lenz!* (Siegmund) (3' 49")
from *Siegmund bin ich und Siegmund Heiss ich* to the end of the act (3' 50")

Siegmund, Set Svanholm; Sieglinde, Hilde Konetzni; Orchestra of the Vienna State Opera
LP: The Golden Age of Opera EJS 451 (1968) (excerpt marked ★★)
CD: *Edition Wiener Staatsoper Live – Vol. 19*: Koch Schwann 3-1469-2 (1994) (the other two excerpts)

Siegfried, Vienna, live performance, 21 June 1941, excerpts (ca. 25 mins)
Act 2, scene 2: from *Daß der mein Vater nicht ist* to *Traurig wäre das, traun!* (Siegfried), and from *Heiß ward mir von der harten Last!* (Siegfried) to *Brünnhilde wäre dann sein!* (Waldvogel) (8' 37")
Act 3, scene 1: from *der Helden Wal hieß für sich er sie küren* (Erda) to *wehret dem Recht, herrscht durch Meineid?* (Erda) (4' 00")
Act 3, scene 1: from *Du bist nicht, was du dich wähnst!* to *Hinab! Hinab zu ew'gem Schlaf!* (Wanderer) (4' 16")
Act 3, scene 2: from *Mein Vöglein schwebte mir fort!* (Siegfried) to *sieh dich vor, sag' ich* (Siegfried) (3' 54")
Act 3, scene 2: from *Es floh dir zu seinem Heil!* (Wanderer) to *Jetzt lock' ich ein liebes Gesell!* (Siegfried) and the end of the scene (4' 27")

Siegfried, Set Svanholm; Wanderer, Paul Schöffler; Erda, Mela Bugarinovič; Waldvogel, Adele Kern; Orchestra of the Vienna State Opera
CD: *Edition Wiener Staatsoper Live – Vol. 24*: Koch Schwann 3-1474-2 (1995)

Götterdämmerung, Vienna, live performance, 27 June 1941, excerpts from Act 3 (ca. 15 mins)
Scene 1: from *Siegfried! Siegfried! Schlimmes wissen wir dir* (Rhinemaidens) to *Nothung zerhaut es den Nornen!* (Siegfried)
Scene 2: from *Hoiho! Hoiho!* (Hagen's men) to *Hier ist's frisch und kühl* (Siegfried) (0' 50")
Scene 2: from *Mime heiß ein mürrischer Zwerg* (Siegfried) to *Vergaltest du Mime?* (Hagen's men)
Scene 2: from *In Leid zu dem Wipfel* (Siegfried) to *Was hör ich!* (Gunther) (3' 21")
Scene 2: from *Brünnhilde, heilige Braut!* to *Brünnhild' bietet mir Gruß!* (Siegfried) (3' 56")

Siegfried, Set Svanholm; Hagen, Herbert Alsen; Gunther, Paul Schöffler; Wellgunde, Elisabeth Rutgers; Woglinde, Else Schürhoff; Flosshilde, Mela Bugarinovič; Chorus and Orchestra of the Vienna State Opera
CD: *Edition Wiener Staatsoper Live – Vol. 19*: Koch Schwann 3-1469-2 (1994)

Siegfried, Vienna, live performance, 12 October 1941, excerpts (ca. 34 mins)
Act 1, scene 2: from *Heil dir, weiser Schmied* (Wanderer) to *Hier sitz' ich am Herd und setze mein Haupt* (Wanderer) (4' 20")
Act 1, scene 2: from *Auf wolkigen Höh'n wohnen die Götter* (Wanderer) to *Kunde verbürgte mein Kopf* (Wanderer) (4' 17")
Act 1, scenes 2 and 3: from *Hahaha! Der witzigste bist du unter den Weisen* (Wanderer) to *was flimmert und schwirrt* (Mime) (4' 27")
Act 3, scene 1: from *Wache, Wala! Wale! Erwach!* (Wanderer) to *weck' ich dich aus dem Schlaf!* (Wanderer) 4' 22")
Act 3, scene 1: from *Die Walküre meinst du* (Wanderer) to *der Sorge Stachel in Wotans wagendes Herz: der Sorge...* (Wanderer) (4' 04")

Act 3, scene 1: from *Du bist nicht, was du dich wähnst!* to *Hinab den, Erda! Urmütter[furcht!]* (Wanderer) (4' 24")
Act 3, scene 2: from *Wer sagt' es dir, den Fels zu suchen* (Wanderer) to *Doch darunter fehlt dir ein Auge* (Siegfried) (4' 01")
Act 3, scene 2: from *Mit dem Auge, das als andres mir fehlt* (Wanderer) to *er vernichtete dich und mich!* (2' 35")
Act 3, scene 2: from *Fürchte des Felsens Hüter!* (Wanderer) to *so sperre mein Speer dir den Weg!* (Wanderer) (1' 35")

Wanderer, Hans Hotter; Siegfried, Joachim Sattler; Mime, William Wernigk; Erda, Mela Bugarinovič; Orchestra of the Vienna State Opera
CD: *Edition Wiener Staatsoper Live – Vol. 22*: Koch Schwann 3-1472-2 (1995)

1942

Tannhäuser, Rome narration, Max Lorenz, Tannhäuser (2RA 5382/3-1) Electrola DB 7602
Götterdämmerung, Siegfried's Rhine Journey (2RA 5384-2 and 5385-1) Electrola DB 5699
Götterdämmerung, Siegfried's Funeral Music (2RA 5386/7-1) Electrola: unissued
Vienna Philharmonic Orchestra, 31 January 1942
LP: *Das Max Lorenz Album*: EMI Electrola 1C 147-29 154/55M (1975) (*Tannhäuser* only)
CD: *Hans Knappertsbusch dirigiert die Wiener Philharmoniker*: Preiser 90116 (1992); *Max Lorenz – The complete Electrola recordings 1927-1942*: Preiser 89232 (1998) (*Tannhäuser* only)

Parsifal, Act 1, Prelude, and Act 3 complete, 31 March 1942
Ludwig Weber, Gurnemanz; Hans Reinmar, Amfortas; Elsa Larcen, Kundry; Carl Hartmann, Parsifal, German Opera House Orchestra
LP: Bellaphon/Acanta DE 23.036 (1977) (performance dated as 1943)
CD: Acanta AC 44 2100-2 (1993); Grammofono AB 78555 (1995); Preiser 90261; Music & Arts 1067; *Wagner - Knappertsbusch - The Legendary 1947/1956 London Recordings*: Archipel ARPCD 0347 (2006) (Prelude only)

Parsifal, Vienna, live performance, 10 November 1942, excerpts (ca. 42 mins)
Act 1: from *Nehmet hin mein Blut* (Knights) to *wie hell grüsst uns heute Herr!* (Titurel) (4' 00")
Act 1: from *Wehvolles Erbe, dem ich verfallen* to *fühl' ich sich gießen in mein Herz* (Amfortas) (4' 24")*
Act 1: from *[Von neuen] sprengt es dar Tor, daraus es nun strömt hervor* to *harre getrost* (Knights) (Amfortas) (4' 21")*
Act 2: from *Amfortas!* to *Erlöser, rette mich* (Parsifal) (4' 44")
Act 2: from *Erlöser! Heiland! Herr der Huld!* (Parsifal) to *Kenntest du den Fluch, der mich durch Schlaf und Wachen* (Kundry) (4' 27")
Act 2: from *Ich sah Ihn* to *nur eine Stunde mich dir vereinen* (Kundry) (4' 29")
Act 2: from *... nach dem ich jammernd schmachten sah* (Parsifal) to *und des Weges sollst du geleitet sein!* (Kundry) (4' 35")
Act 3: from *Ich sah sie welken* to *es lacht die Aue!* (Parsifal) (2' 10")[8]

[8] Part of this excerpt appeared on the LP Discocorp IGI-379 (1980) purporting to be Richard Strauss conducting.

Act 3: from *Mein Vater! Hochgesegneter der Helden!* to *Erlöser, gib meinem Sohne Ruh'!* (Amfortas) (4' 28")★
Act 3: from *Höchsten Heiles Wunder!* (Chorus) to the end of the act (4' 34")★
Gurnemanz, Sigmund Roth; Kundry, Helena Braun; Amfortas, Hans Hotter; Parsifal, Max Lorenz; Klingsor, Adolf Vogel[9]; Titurel, Franz Worff; Chorus and Orchestra of the Vienna State Opera
CD: *Edition Wiener Staatsoper Live – Vol. 6*: Koch Schwann 3-1456-2 (1994), and *Vol. 22*: Koch Schwann 3-1472-2 (1995) (excerpts marked ★)

Tristan und Isolde, Act 3, Prelude
Preußische Staatskapelle, Berlin, 1942
LP: [Bayerische Staatsoper München] ASTM 101 (1980)[10]

1943

Siegfried Idyll
Berlin Philharmonic Orchestra, Berlin
(2RA 5807-?/ 5808-?/5809-?/5810-?, 23 January 1943)
78: Electrola DB7659/60[11]

Götterdämmerung, Vienna, live performance, 30 June 1943, excerpts (ca. 24 mins)
Prologue: from the beginning to *weihlicher Äste Wald* (First Norn) (4' 04")
Prologue: from *Es ragt die Burg* (Third Norn) to *Brünnhildes Fels zu umbrenne* (Second Norn) (4' 27")
Prologue: from the orchestral interlude, and *Zu neuen Taten, teurer Helde* (Brünnhilde) to *Heil! Heil!* (Brünnhilde and Siegfried) and Siegfried's horn call at the beginning of the Rhine Journey (with two interruptions) (10' 17")
Act 2, scene 2: from *Hoiho, Hagen! Müder Mann!* (Siegfried) to *doch ich durchschritt es für ihn* (Siegfried) (4' 06")
First Norn, Elsa Schürhoff; Second Norn, Piroska Tutsek; Third Norn, Hilde Konetzni; Brünnhilde, Anny Konetzni; Siegfried, Set Svanholm; Hagen, Herbert Alsen; Gutrune, Daga Söderqvist; Orchestra of the Vienna State Opera
CD: *Edition Wiener Staatsoper Live – Vol. 17*: Koch Schwann 3-1467-2 (1994)

Die Walküre, Vienna, live performance, 1 December 1943, excerpts (ca. 42 mins)
Act 1, scene 1: from *[Wasser,] wie du gewollt!* (Sieglinde) to *die Sonne lacht mir nun neu* (Siegmund) (4' 09")
Act 1, scene 3: from *Nächtiges Dunkel deckte mein Aug'* to *Heil macht mich dein Nah'n!* (Siegmund, with Sieglinde) (2' 51")★★
Act 1: scene 3: from *Eine Waffe lass mich dir weisen* (Sieglinde) to *der Lenz lacht in den Saal!*

[9] as given on the CD; the program lists Hermann Wiedemann as Klingsor

[10] This is a seven-inch LP which accompanied the Bavarian State Opera Program for *Tristan und Isolde* on 27 July 1980; the source of the recording was "Ton Studio Grundheber, Munich." Hunt wrote of this recording that it "could not be verified" (*Kna*, p. 310).

[11] This recording is listed in Hunt (*Kna*, p. 304). It is Knappertsbusch's only early commercial recording not to have been issued on LP or CD. I am grateful to Michael H. Gray for the matrix numbers. I have been unable to locate a copy of the recording.

(Siegmund) (with one interruption) (6' 12")

Act 1: scene 3: from *Du bist der Lenz* (Sieglinde) to *dass hell ich schaue den hehren Schein* (Sieglinde) (2' 39")

Act 1: scene 3: from *was mich berückt, errat' ich nun leicht* (Siegmund) to *den Namen nehm ich von dir!* (Siegmund) (4' 17")

Act 1: scene 3: from *Siegmund, so nenn' ich dich* (Sieglinde) to the end of the act (3' 51")

Act 3, scene 1: from *Rette mich, Maid! Rette die Mutter!* (Sieglinde) to *Lebe wohl! Dich segnet Sieglindes Weh!* (Sieglinde) (3' 16")

Act 3, scene 2: from *Nicht straf' ich dich erst* (Wotan) to *der am Wege sie findet und weckt* (Wotan) (4' 34")

Act 3, scene 3: from *Leb wohl, du kühnes, herrliches Kind!* (Wotan) to the end of the act (12' 46") (with two interruptions)

Wotan, Hans Hotter; Brünnhilde, Helena Braun; Siegmund, Max Lorenz; Sieglinde, Hilde Konetzni; Helmwige, Daga Söderqvist; Gerhilde, Daniza Jlitsch; Ortlinde, Else Schulz; Waltraute, Dora With; Siegrune, Else Schürhoff; Roßweiße, Elena Nikolaidi; Grimberde, Olga Levko-Antosch; Schwertleite, Melanie Frutschnigg; Orchestra of the Vienna State Opera

LP: The Golden Age of Opera EJS 451 (1 LP) (1968) (the excerpt marked ★★, which is not on Koch, and the other excerpts from scene 3)

CD: *Edition Wiener Staatsoper Live – Vol. 24*: Koch Schwann 3-1474-2 (1995)

Siegfried, Vienna, live broadcast, 10 December 1943, excerpt (3' 58")

Act 1, scenes 2-3: from *wer wird aus den starken Stücken* (Wanderer) to *was schwebt dort und webt…?* (Mime)

Wanderer, Hans Hotter; Mime, William Wernigk; Orchestra of the Vienna State Opera

LP: The Golden Age of Opera EJS 444 (1968)[12]

1947

Tristan und Isolde, Stadttheatre, Zurich, live broadcast, 5 June 1947, excerpts (ca. 23 mins)

Kirsten Flagstad, Isolde; Max Lorenz, Tristan; Elsa Cavelti, Brangäne; Lubomir Vischegonov, Sailor; Tonhalle Orchestra, Zürich

Act 1, Scene 1: from *Entartet' Geschlecht, unwerth der Ahnen* (Isolde) to *Tod geweihtes Haupt!* (Isolde) (5' 06")

Act 1, Scene 5: from *[dass nicht dir's entfallen] lässt* (Tristan) *Wie sorgt' ich schlecht um deinen Herren* to the end of the Act, and applause (18' 10")

LP: A.N.N.A. Record Company ANNA 1025 (1979)

CD: *Kirsten Flagstad Volume 2: Live Performances 1935 – 1948*: SIMAX PSC 1822 (1995) (contains only a shorter excerpt, from Act 1, Scene 5: from *Wie sorgt' ich schlecht* (Isolde) to *Verräther, ich trink' sie dir!* (Isolde) (9' 40"))

[12] The excerpt from *Siegfried* on EJS 444 is a conflation of three excerpts conducted by Knappertsbusch (who is not mentioned on the label): this one is from 10 December 1943 (*Kna*, p. 310) and is followed by two from 16 June 1937 (above): the cast details and dates are from Shaman et al., *EJS*.

Lohengrin, Act 1, Prelude (SAR 168-1 and SAR 169-1)
Tonhalle Orchestra, Zürich, 18 June 1947
78: Decca K 1709

Die Meistersinger, Act 1, Prelude (SAR 245-1 and SAR 246-1)
l'Orchestre de la Suisse Romande, 1 July 1947
78: Decca K 1905

Rienzi, Overture (AR 11941-2, AR 11942-1, and AR 11943-1)
Lohengrin, Act 3, Prelude (AR 11944-1)
London Philharmonic Orchestra, 31 December 1947
78: Decca K. 1820/1
CD: *Hans Knappertsbusch in London and in Switzerland*: Preiser 90189 (1993); *Hans Knapperstbusch: Strauss, Wagner*: Testament SBT 1338 (2004) (*Rienzi* only); *Wagner - Knappertsbusch - The Legendary 1947/1956 London Recordings*: Archipel ARPCD 0347 (2006) (all except *Rienzi*)

Die Meistersinger, Act 2, scene 3: *Was duftet doch der Flieder*
Sachs, Paul Schöffler; Tonhalle Orchestra, Zürich, 18 June 1947[13]
(SAR 170/1-1)
78: Decca K. 1731
CD: *Paul Schöffler*: Preiser 90190 (1994), reissued as 89590 (2003)

1948

Die Meistersinger, Act 3, Prelude, Dance of the Apprentices, Arrival of the Mastersingers (AR 11945, AR 11946, AR 11947, AR 11948)
Tannhäuser, Overture and Bacchanale
(AR 11949, AR 11950, AR 11951, AR 11952, AR 11953, AR 11954)
London Philharmonic Orchestra, 31 December 1947 – 3 January 1948
78: Decca AK 2209/10 (*Meistersinger*); 2211/3 (*Tannhäuser*)
LP: London LPS 42 (1949) (*Tannhäuser* only)

1949

Tannhäuser, Act 2 *Dich, teure Halle*, and Act 3 *Allmächt'ge Jungfrau*
Elisabeth, Maria Reining; Tonhalle Orchestra, Zürich, 23 June 1949
(DRL.68, DRL.69)
78: Decca K 28165
LP: Decca LX 3021; London LPS 109; Preiser PR 9829
CD: *Maria Reining singt*: Preiser 90083 (1991)

[13] Hunt (*Kna*, p. 285) lists a further unpublished excerpt from *Die Meistersinger* from this session (*O Sachs mein freund!*).

Die Meistersinger, Act 2, scene 4: *Gut'n Abend Meister*[14]
Eva, Maria Reining; Sachs, Paul Schöffler; Tonhalle Orchestra, Zürich, 23 June 1949[15]
(SAR 397-1, SAR 398-1)
78: Decca X.312; K 28166
LP: Decca LX 3021; London LPS 109 (label incorrectly describes this as duet from Act 1); Preiser PR 9829
CD: *Maria Reining singt*: Preiser 90083 (1991); *Paul Schöffler*: Preiser 90190 (1994), reissued as 89590 (2003)

Siegfried Idyll
Vienna Philharmonic Orchestra, Salzburg, live performance, 30 August 1949
LP: Melodram MEL 711 (1982) (with Bruckner's *Symphony No. 7*)
CD: Serenade (Japan) SEDR-5006 (2003); Epitaphon RIPD-0002 (2009) (Japan)

1950

Parsifal, Act 1, Prelude
Vienna Philharmonic Orchestra, 14 June 1950
(DRL 525 – VAR 38/40)
LP: Decca LX 3036; London LLP 451; LPS 287
CD: King KICC 2107; Decca 440 062-2; *Hans Knapperstbusch: Strauss, Wagner*: Testament SBT 1338 (2004); *Hans Knappertsbusch – The Early Wagnerian Decca Records 1950-1953*: Archipel ARPCD 0332 (2005); *Hans Knappertsbusch conducts Richard Wagner*: Preiser 90699 (2005)

Siegfried, Forest Murmurs; Siegfried, Franz Lechleitner (DRL 532 – VAR 45/6)
Parsifal, Act 1, Transformation Scene (DRL 526 – VAR 47)
Rienzi, Overture (DRL 531/2)
Vienna Philharmonic Orchestra, 24 June 1950
LP: Decca LX 3034/36; LXT 2644 (*Siegfried* and *Parsifal*); Decca K 23052 (*Siegfried* only); London LLP 451; LLP 447 (*Siegfried* only); LPS 287 (*Parsifal* only)
CD: King KICC 2107 (all except *Siegfried*); Decca 440 062-2; *Hans Knapperstbusch: Strauss, Wagner*: Testament SBT 1338 (2004) (all except *Siegfried*); *Hans Knappertsbusch – The Early Wagnerian Decca Records 1950-1953*: Archipel ARPCD 0332 (2005) (all except *Parsifal*); *Hans Knappertsbusch conducts Richard Wagner*: Preiser 90699 (2005) (all except *Rienzi*)

Tristan und Isolde, Munich, Prinzregententheater, live performance, 23 July 1950
Tristan, Günther Treptow; King Marke, Ferdinand Frantz; Isolde, Helena Braun; Kurwenal, Paul Schöffler; Brangäne, Margarete Klose; Melot, Albrecht Peter; Shepherd,

[14] The *Music Review* wrote: "It is a great pity that Eva's lovely duet with Sachs is not allowed to finish on this record… we are left suspended on a dominant, waiting for the closing phrases that are not on the record and the illusion [that we are listening to an actual conversation] is destroyed:" vol. 11 (1950), p. 340 (John Boulton)

[15] This is the date given on Preiser 90190. Hunt (*Kna*, p. 285) dates the recording as 18 June 1947 (ie, with the other excerpts from *Die Meistersinger* above.

Paul Kuen; Sailor and Steersman, Fritz Richard Bender; Chorus and Orchestra of the Bavarian State Opera

LP: Educational Media Associates IGI-345 (1976); Movimento Musica 05.001 (1982)

CD: Laudis LCD4.4009 (1987); Gala GL 100.651 (1993); Orfeo d'Or C 355 943 D (1994); Arkadia 78075 (2004); Andromeda ANDRCD 9011 (2007)

Die Meistersinger von Nürnberg, Act 2, Vienna, Grosser Musikvereinsaal, 2-9 September 1950

Hans Sachs, Paul Schoeffler; Veit Pogner, Otto Edelmann; Kunz Vogelgesang, Hugo Meyer-Welfing; Konrad Nachtigall, Wilhelm Felden; Sixtus Beckmesser, Karl Dönch; Fritz Kothner, Alfred Poell; Balthasar Zorn, Erich Majkut; Ulrich Eißlinger, William Vernigk; Augustin Moser, Hermann Gallos; Hermann Ortel, Harald Pröglhöf; Hans Schwarz, Hans Bierbach; Hans Foltz, Ljubomir Pantscheff; Walther von Stolzing, Günther Treptow; Eva, Hilde Gueden; Magdalene, Elsa Schürhoff; David, Anton Dermota; Nightwatchman, Harald Pröglhöf; Chorus of the Vienna State Opera; Vienna Philharmonic Orchestra

LP: Decca LXT 2560-1 (1951)

CD: Decca 440 057-2 (1994); Naxos 8.111128-31 (2006)

Parsifal, Act 2, Flower Maidens Scene

Günther Treptow and Vienna State Opera Chorus, Vienna Philharmonic Orchestra, 11 September 1950

(DRL 526 – VAR 93/4)

LP: Decca LX 3036; LXT 2644; London LLP 447

CD: *Hans Knappertsbusch conducts Richard Wagner*: Preiser 90699 (2005); *Hans Knapperstbusch: Strauss, Wagner*: Testament SBT 1338 (2004)

1951

Parsifal, Bayreuth, live broadcast, 30 July 1951, excerpts (ca. 38 mins)

Act 1: Prelude (13' 57")

Act 3: from *Wie dünkt mich doch die Aue* to *nur trauern, ach! und weinen* (Parsifal, with Gurnemanz) (3' 30")

Act 3: from *da die entsündigte Natur* (Gurnemanz) to *du weinest, sich', es lacht die Aue!* (Parsifal) (3' 34")

Act 3: from *Mein Vater! Hochgesegneter der Helden!* (Amfortas) to the end of the Act (with the last seven bars omitted and replaced by one-and-a-half minutes of an unidentified performance of an orchestral arrangement of the Good Friday scene) (16' 45")

Amfortas, George London; Gurnemanz, Ludwig Weber; Parsifal, Wolfgang Windgassen; Orchestra of the Bayreuth Festival

LP: Allegro Elite 3095 (1953) (cast details given as Felix Meesen, Baritone; Herman Neumeyer, Tenor; Gerhard Ramms, Bass; Choir and Orchestra of the Dresden State Opera, conducted by Fritz Schreiber); Gramophone 2090 (1954) (cast details given simply as "National Opera Singers and Orchestra – recorded in Europe")[16]

[16] These two LPs are the same recording. On the copies I have inspected, Allegro 3095 has etched in the wax of side 1 "3095A" (or "2095A") scratched out and "2090A" beside it, and on side 2 "3095B";

Parsifal, Bayreuth, live performances, July-August 1951[17]
Amfortas, George London; Titurel, Arnold van Mill; Gurnemanz, Ludwig Weber; Parsifal, Wolfgang Windgassen; Klingsor, Hermann Uhde; Kundry, Martha Mödl; Knights, Walter Fritz, Werner Faulhaber; Squires, Hanna Ludwig, Elfriede Wild, Günther Baldauf, Gerhard Stolze; Flowermaidens, Erika Zimmermann, Hanna Ludwig, Paula Brivkalne, Maria Lacorne, Elfriede Wild, Ruth Siewert; Chorus and Orchestra of the Bayreuth Festival

LP: Decca LXT 2651-6 (1952)

CD: Decca 425 976-2 (1989); Teldec 9031 76047-2 (1993); Naxos Historical 8.110221-24 (2003); Membran Documents 223063-351 (2006)

Götterdämmerung, Bayreuth, live performance, 4 August 1951[18]
Brünnhilde, Astrid Varnay; Siegfried, Bernd Aldenhoff; Hagen, Ludwig Weber; Alberich, Heinrich Pflanzl; Gunther, Hermann Uhde; Gutrune, Martha Mödl; Waltraute, Elisabeth

Gramophone 2090 has on side 1 "~~3095~~A 2090A" and on side 2 "~~3095~~B 2090B". On the cover of the Allegro is "Copyright 1953 Record Corp. of America", and of the Gramophone "Copyright 1954 Record Corp. of America". The owner of the "Record Corporation of America" was Eli Oberstein who had occasion to produce records from broadcast tapes without authorization: see Ernst A. Lumpe, "Pseudonymous Performers on Early LP Records: Rumours, Facts and Finds", *ARSC Journal* vol. 21 no. 2 (Fall 1990), pp. 226-231, and "An Update", *ibid*, vol. 27 no. 1 (Spring 1996), pp. 15-40. The singers on the Allegro/Gramophone recording are clearly Windgassen, Weber and London. They sang the roles together at the 1951 and 1952 Bayreuth Festivals. *Parsifal* was broadcast in those years on 30 July 1951 and 1 August 1952: Hunt, *Wagner im Festspielhaus*. The 1952 broadcast has been issued in its entirety on Melodram and Archipel. The Decca recording was compiled from a number of rehearsals and performances at the 1951 Bayreuth Festival. The excerpts on the Allegro/Gramophone record are clearly different from the Melodram/Archipel and Decca performances, though they are very close in tempo and mood to the 1951 Festival performances as recorded by Decca. Because no complete recording of the 1951 broadcast has been published, and no tape survives in the archives of Bavarian Radio, it has not been possible to verify whether the Allegro/Gramophone excerpts come from this source, though it is highly probable they did. Hunt attributes them to the 1952 broadcast.

[17] The producer of the Decca recording, John Culshaw, said in 1962 that it had been compiled from "seven different performances and one or two general rehearsals." There were 149 cross-splices in Act 1 alone, he said. "The purpose of these splicings was to cut out terrible fits of coughing, noises of people dropping things, bad orchestral ensemble, wrong words (this happens a lot in the theatre), out-of-tune notes, out-of-time notes, ragged pizzicato entries on the double basses – and so on": "Kindling the Magic Spark," *High Fidelity Magazine*, vol. 12 (November 1962), pp. 44-47 and 142, at p. 46. Culshaw wrote later in his autobiography: "we taped the general rehearsal and two public performances…": *Putting the Record Straight:* (London: Secker & Warburg, 1981), p. 109.

[18] The performance of 4 August was broadcast by Bavarian Radio on 10 August. A recording of Act 3 purporting to be from 23 August 1951 appeared on Wing WCD 53, but Knappertsbusch did not conduct *Götterdämmerung* on that date. Hunt (*Kna*, p. 296) lists an unpublished *Rheingold* from 31 July 1951, (p. 311) a *Walküre* from 1 August 1951, and (p. 298) a *Siegfried* from 2 August 1951 from this cycle. These were the dates of the Bavarian Radio broadcasts. Testament gives the recording date as 4 August 1951. John Cushaw, the Decca record producer, wrote: "*Götterdämmerung*, of which we had one rehearsal and one performance, went excellently, and again I prepared a master version when I returned to London." *Putting the Record Straight: The Autobiography of John Culshaw* (London: Secker & Warburg, 1981), p. 109. The notes by Tony Locantro accompanying the Testament CDs give detailed background on the recording (and why it was not published earlier) and indicate it was Culshaw's edited master version that was used for the CDs. In this case, the recording cannot be solely from 4 August 1951. The notes explain how the recording engineer, Kenneth Wilkinson, used a number of microphones to record the performance: "a single English RK2 condenser microphone suspended high in the roof of the auditorium, the output of which was mixed with the sound from a number of German Neumann M49 microphones placed close to the orchestra and the singers." (p. 14). Hence, the CDs are not a reflection of the true "Bayreuth sound" – that is, what the audience actually heard in the auditorium – but an independently-mixed version manufactured by engineers.

Höngen; Woglinde, Elizabeth Schwarzkopf; Wellgunde, Hanna Ludwig; Floßhilde, Hertha Töpper; Norns, Ruth Siewert, Ira Malaniuk, Martha Mödl; a Voice, Ruth Siewert; Chorus and Orchestra of the Bayreuth Festival

CD: Testament SBT 4175 (1999)

Die Meistersinger von Nürnberg, Acts 1 and 3, Vienna, Grosser Musikvereinsaal, 11-20 September 1951

Hans Sachs, Paul Schoeffler; Veit Pogner, Otto Edelmann; Kunz Vogelgesang, Hugo Meyer-Welfing; Konrad Nachtigall, Wilhelm Felden; Sixtus Beckmesser, Karl Dönch; Fritz Kothner, Alfred Poell; Balthasar Zorn, Erich Majkut; Ulrich Eißlinger, William Vernigk; Augustin Moser, Hermann Gallos; Hermann Ortel, Harald Pröglhöf; Hans Schwarz, Hans Bierbach; Hans Foltz, Ljubomir Pantscheff; Walther von Stolzing, Günther Treptow; Eva, Hilde Gueden; Magdalene, Elsa Schürhoff; David, Anton Dermota; Nightwatchman, Harald Pröglhöf; Chorus of the Vienna State Opera; Vienna Philharmonic Orchestra

LP: Decca LXT 2646-7 (Act 1) and LXT 2648-50 (Act 3) (1952)

CD: Decca 440 057-2 (1994); Naxos 8.111128-31 (2006)

1952

Die Meistersinger von Nürnberg, Bayreuth, live broadcast, 3 August 1952

Hans Sachs, Otto Edelmann; Veit Pogner, Kurt Böhme; Kunz Vogelgesang, Karl Terkal; Konrad Nachtigall, Walter Stoll; Sixtus Beckmesser, Heinrich Pflanzl; Fritz Kothner, Werner Faulhaber; Balthasar Zorn, Josef Janko; Ulrich Eißlinger, Karl Mikorey; Augustin Moser, Gerhard Stolze; Hermann Ortel, Theo Adam; Hans Schwarz, Heinz Borst; Hans Foltz, Max Kohl; Walther von Stolzing, Hans Hopf; Eva, Lisa Della Casa; Magdalene, Ira Malaniuk; David, Gerhard Unger; Nightwatchman, Gustav Neidlinger; Chorus and Orchestra of the Bayreuth Festival

LP: Melodram MEL 522

CD: Golden Melodram GM 1.0003 (1998); Archipel 0111-4 (2003); Music & Arts CD-1014 (2008)

Parsifal, Bayreuth, live broadcast, 1 August 1952

Amfortas, George London; Titurel, Kurt Böhme; Gurnemanz, Ludwig Weber; Parsifal, Wolfgang Windgassen; Klingsor, Gustav Neidlinger; Kundry, Martha Mödl; Knights, Karl Terkal, Werner Faulhaber; Squires, Hertha Töpper, Hanna Ludwig, Gerhard Unger, Gerhard Stolze; Flowermaidens, Erika Zimmermann, Hanna Ludwig, Paula Brivkalne, Maria Lacorne, Hertha Töpper, Ruth Siewert; a Voice, Ruth Siewert; Chorus and Orchestra of the Bayreuth Festival

CD: Golden Melodram GM 1.0051 (2001); Archipel ARPCD 0112-4 (2003)

1953

Siegfried Idyll

Cologne Radio Symphony Orchestra, live performance, 7 May 1953

CD: *Knappertsbusch Wagner Concert*: Seven Seas KICC 2030 (1990); Music & Arts CD-1014 (with the 1952 Bayreuth *Meistersinger*); *Hans Knappertsbusch In*

Memoriam: Tahra TAH 606-609 (2007) (date given as 8 May when a repeat of the concert was given); Orfeo d'Or C 723 071 B (2007) (with Brahms *Symphony No. 4*); *Knappertsbusch conducts Wagner*: Dynamic IDIS 6569 (2009)

Tannhäuser, Overture and Bacchanale (ARL 1634 – VAR 347/52), 6 May 1953
Der fliegende Holländer, Overture (ARL 1635 – VAR 353/5), 7 May 1953
Die Walküre, Act 3, Ride of the Valkyries (ARL 1635 – VAR 356), 7 May 1953
Vienna Philharmonic Orchestra

LP: Decca LXT 2822; Decca Ace of Clubs ACL 22

CD: Decca 440 062-2; *Hans Knappertsbusch – The Early Wagnerian Decca Records 1950-1953*: Archipel ARPCD 0332 (2005); *Hans Knappertsbusch conducts Richard Wagner*: Preiser 90699 (2005)

1954

Parsifal, Bayreuth, live performance, 5 August 1954[19]
Amfortas, Hans Hotter; Titurel, Theo Adam; Gurnemanz, Josef Greindl; Parsifal, Wolfgang Windgassen; Klingsor, Gustav Neidlinger; Kundry, Martha Mödl; Knights, Gene Tobin, Theo Adam; Squires, Hetty Plümacher, Gisela Litz, Gerhard Stolze, Hugo Kratz; Flowermaidens, Ilse Hollweg, Friedle Pöltinger, Hetty Plümacher, Dorothea Siebert, Jutta Vulpius, Gisela Litz; a Voice, Hetty Plümacher; Chorus and Orchestra of the Bayreuth Festival

LP: excerpts (dated "Bayreuth 1956") in Melodram 583 (1981) (the 1958 Bayreuth *Parsifal*) and (dated "3.8.1954") in Melodram 643 (1984) (the 1964 Bayreuth *Parsifal*)

CD: Seven Seas KICC 2341/4 (1993) (dated "Bayreuth 1954"); Golden Melodram GM 1.0053 (2002) (dated "5.8.1954"); Archipel ARPCD 0283-4 (2005) (dated "Bayreuth 1954"); excerpts in *Hans Knappertsbusch In Memoriam*: Tahra TAH 606-609 (2007) (dated "5.VIII.1954")

[19] This is the date of the performance, not the broadcast. Hunt in *Wagner im Festspielhaus* (2006) and *Kna* (2007) gives the date of broadcast as 17 August 1954. Bayerischer Rundfunk advised the author in 1989 for his research for *Parsifal on Record* (1992) that "the broadcast performance" of *Parsifal* was 5 August 1954. Imprudently, this advice was not followed, notwithstanding its ambiguity. Instead the date of 3 August was used, as this appeared on the label and booklet accompanying Melodram 643 (not 5 August, as Hunt has it in *Wagner im Festspielhaus*). There was no performance of *Parsifal* in Bayreuth on 3 August 1954. Melodram had earlier, in any case, demonstrated its unreliability over dating by ascribing other 1954 excerpts to Bayreuth 1956. Bayerischer Rundfunk has since confirmed that it recorded *Parsifal* on 5 August for a broadcast which took place on 17 August 1954. In spite of the confusion of dates, all the recordings on LP and CD listed above are of the same performance. Different source tapes appear to have been used, however, and to have been transcribed at slightly differing speeds, which accounts for some differences in timing. The Archipel set is a clone of the earlier Melodram set, though there is a different distribution of tracks on CDs 2 to 4. As regards the Tahra set, the Prelude has been edited to dampen a crash heard clearly at 2:09-2:10 on the other recordings. Its booklet lists Ludwig Weber as the singer of Gurnemanz. Weber had been scheduled to sing Gurnemanz in all four performances of *Parsifal* in 1954, but he sang only on 17 and 21 August; he was ill on 29 July and 5 August and Josef Greindl stepped in. As Christian Merlin points out in his review in *Diapason* (février 2007, p. 115), the voice is clearly that of Josef Greindl, and the excerpts are from the 5 August performance already issued by Melodram.

1955[20]

Siegfried Idyll
Vienna Philharmonic Orchestra, 1 April 1955
LP: London LL 1586
CD: King KICC 2107; Decca 470 254-2 (with Brahms pieces); Testament SBT-1339 (2004) (with Bruckner's *Symphony No.3*)

Der fliegende Holländer, Bayeuth, live broadcast, 22 July 1955
Holländer, Hermann Uhde; Daland, Ludwig Weber; Senta, Astrid Varnay; Mary, Elisabeth Schärtel; Erik, Wolfgang Windgassen; Steersman, Josef Traxel; Chorus and Orchestra of the Bayreuth Festival
LP: Cetra LO 51; Melodram MEL 550; Discocorp RR 319
CD: Music & Arts CD-319 (1982), CD-876 (1987); Golden Melodram GM 1.0028 (2002); Arkadia MP451.4; Urania URN 22.271 (2004) (the latter two issues give the date incorrectly as 25 July 1955); Walhall Eternity WLCD 0161 (2006); Orfeo d'Or C 692 092 I (2009)

Götterdämmerung, Munich, live performance, 1 September 1955
Brünnhilde, Birgit Nilsson; Siegfried, Bernd Aldenhoff; Hagen, Gottlob Frick; Alberich, Otakar Kraus; Gunther, Hermann Uhde; Gutrune, Leonie Rysanek; Waltraute, Ira Malaniuk; Woglinde, Gerda Sommerschuh; Wellgunde, Elisabeth Lindermeier; Floßhilde, Ruth Michaelis; Norns, Imgarth Barth, Hertha Töpper, Marianne Schecht; Chorus and Orchestra of the Bavarian State Opera
LP: Melodran MEL 425 (1984)
CD: Orfeo d'Or C 356 944 L (1994)

Die Meistersinger von Nürnberg, Munich, live performance, 11 September 1955
Hans Sachs, Ferdinand Frantz; Veit Pogner, Gottlob Frick; Kunz Vogelgesang, Franz Klarwein; Konrad Nachtigall, Karl Hoppe; Sixtus Beckmesser, Heinrich Pflanzl; Fritz Kothner, Albrecht Peter; Balthasar Zorn, John Kuhn; Ulrich Eißlinger, Emil Graf; Augustin Moser, Karl Ostertag; Hermann Ortel, Adolf Keil; Hans Schwarz, Walter Bracht; Hans Foltz, Rudolf Wünzer; Walther von Stolzing, Hans Hopf; Eva, Lisa Della Casa; Magdalene, Hertha Töpper; David, Paul Kuen; Nightwatchman, Willi Schmitz; Chorus and Orchestra of the Bavarian State Opera
CD: Orfeo d'Or C 462 974 L (1997)

1956

Parsifal, Act 2, *Ich sah das Kind an seiner Mutter Brust*
Kundry, Kirsten Flagstad; Vienna Philharmonic Orchestra, 13-15 May 1956
LP: Decca LXT 5249; GRV 11
CD: Decca 414 625-2 (1986); *Wagner - Knappertsbusch - The Legendary 1947/1956 London Recordings*: Archipel ARPCD 0347 (2006); Urania URN 22.347 (2008)

[20] *Parsifal* was broadcast from Bayreuth on 16 August 1955; Bavarian Radio holds a tape of the broadcast in its archives; at the time of writing, the performance had not appeared on disc.

Götterdämmerung, Siegfried's Rhine Journey and Funeral Music
Vienna Philharmonic Orchestra, June 1956
LP: Decca SXL 2074; London LL 1586; Decca 6.42088 (1969)[21]
CD: Decca 414 625; 452 896; 448 581 (Rhine Journey only); *Wagner - Knappertsbusch - The Legendary 1947/1956 London Recordings*: Archipel ARPCD 0347 (2006)

Lohengrin, Act 1, *Einsam in trüben Tagen*
Wesendonck Lieder
Die Walküre, Act 1, *Der Männer Sippe*, and *Du bist der Lenz*
Kirsten Flagstad; Vienna Philharmonic Orchestra, 13-15 May 1956
LP: Decca LXT 5249; London OS 25101; AKKORD D-12702 (Russia); Decca GRV 11 (1982)
CD: Decca 421 877-2; *The Flagstad Edition*: Decca 440 490-2; Urania URN 22.347 (2008) (*Wesendonck Lieder* only)

Der Ring des Nibelungen, Bayreuth, live broadcasts, 1956

Das Rheingold, 13 August 1956
Wotan, Hans Hotter; Donner, Alfons Herwig; Froh, Josef Traxel; Loge, Ludwig Suthaus; Alberich, Gustav Neidlinger; Mime, Paul Küen; Fasolt, Josef Greindl; Fafner, Arnold van Mill; Fricka, Georgine von Milinkovic; Freia, Gré Brouwenstijn; Erda, Jean Madeira; Woglinde, Lore Wissmann; Wellgunde, Paula Lenchner; Floßhilde, Maria von Ilosvay

Die Walküre, 14 August 1956
Siegmund, Wolfgang Windgassen; Sieglinde, Gré Brouwenstijn; Wotan, Hans Hotter; Brünnhilde, Astrid Varnay; Hunding, Josef Greindl; Fricka, Georgine von Milinkovic; Gerhilde, Paula Lenchner; Ortlinde, Gerda Lammers; Waltraute, Elisabeth Schärtel; Schwertleite, Maria von Ilosvay; Helmwige, Hilde Scheppan; Siegrune, Luisecharlotte Kamps; Grimgerde, Georgine von Milinkovic; Roßweiße, Jean Madeira

Siegfried, 15 August 1956
Siegfried, Wolfgang Windgassen; Mime, Paul Küen; Brünnhilde, Astrid Varnay; Wanderer, Hans Hotter; Alberich, Gustav Neidlinger; Fafner, Arnold van Mill; Erda, Jean Madeira; Waldvogel, Ilse Hollweg

Götterdämmerung, 17 August 1956
Brünnhilde, Astrid Varnay; Siegfried, Wolfgang Windgassen; Hagen, Josef Greindl; Alberich, Gustav Neidlinger; Gunther, Hermann Uhde; Gutrune, Ludmilla Dvoráková; Waltraute, Jean Madeira; Woglinde, Lore Wissmann; Wellgunde, Paula Lenchner; Floßhilde, Maria von Ilosvay; Norns, Jean Madeira, Maria von Ilosvay, Astrid Varnay, Chorus and Orchestra of the Bayreuth Festival

LP: Melodram MEL 569 (*Götterdämmerung*)
CD: Golden Melodram GM 1.001; Music & Arts 4009; Orfeo d'Or C 660 513 Y (2005); Andromeda ANDRCD 9013-16 (2007)

[21] Decca 6.42088 is 4 seconds faster than London LL 1586.

Parsifal, Bayreuth, live broadcast, 19 August 1956
Amfortas, Dietrich Fischer-Dieskau; Titurel, Hans Hotter; Gurnemanz, Josef Greindl; Parsifal, Ramon Vinay; Klingsor, Toni Blankenheim; Kundry, Martha Mödl; Knights, Josef Traxal, Alfons Herwig; Squires, Paula Lenchner, Elisabeth Schärtel, Gerhard Stolze, Alfred Pfeifle; Flowermaidens, Ilse Hollweg, Friedle Pöltinger, Paula Lenchner, Dorothea Siebert, Jutta Vulpius, Elisabeth Schärtel; a Voice, Martha Mödl; Chorus and Orchestra of the Bayreuth Festival

LP: Cetra LO 79 (1979); Melodram MEL 563 (1982)

CD: Hunt LSMH 34035 (1990); Arkadia MP 434.4 (1995); Golden Melodram GM 1.0062 (2001); Walhall Eternity WLCD 0192 (2006)

1957

Parsifal, Bayreuth, live performance, 5 August 1957[22]
Amfortas, George London; Titurel, Arnold van Mill; Gurnemanz, Josef Greindl; Parsifal, Ramon Vinay; Klingsor, Toni Blankenheim; Kundry, Martha Mödl; Knights, Walter Geisler, Otto Wiener; Squires, Paula Lenchner, Elisabeth Schärtel, Hans Krotthammer, Gerhard Stolze; Flowermaidens, Ilse Hollweg, Friedle Pöltinger, Paula Lenchner, Dorothea Siebert, Lotte Rysanek, Elisabeth Schärtel; a Voice, Georgine von Milinkovic; Chorus and Orchestra of the Bayreuth Festival

CD: Walhall Eternity WLCD 0215 (2008)

Der Ring des Nibelungen, Bayreuth, live broadcasts, 1957

Das Rheingold, 14 August 1957
Wotan, Hans Hotter; Donner, Toni Blankenheim; Froh, Josef Traxel; Loge, Ludwig Suthaus; Alberich, Gustav Neidlinger; Mime, Paul Küen; Fasolt, Arnold van Mill; Fafner, Josef Greindl; Fricka, Georgine von Milinkovic; Freia, Elisabeth Grümmer; Erda, Maria von Ilosvay; Woglinde, Dorothea Siebert; Wellgunde, Paula Lenchner; Floßhilde, Elisabeth Schärtel

Die Walküre, 15 August 1957
Siegmund, Ramon Vinay; Sieglinde, Birgit Nilsson; Wotan, Hans Hotter; Brünnhilde, Astrid Varnay; Hunding, Josef Greindl; Fricka, Georgine von Milinkovic; Gerhilde, Paula Lenchner; Ortlinde, Gerda Lammers; Waltraute, Elisabeth Schärtel; Schwertleite, Maria von Ilosvay; Helmwige, Hilde Scheppan; Siegrune, Helena Bader; Grimgerde, Georgine von Milinkovic; Roßweiße, Hetty Plümacher

Siegfried, 16 August 1957
Siegfried, Berndt Aldenhoff; Mime, Paul Küen; Brünnhilde, Astrid Varnay; Wanderer, Hans Hotter; Alberich, Gustav Neidlinger; Fafner, Josef Greindl; Erda, Maria von Ilosvay; Waldvogel, Ilse Hollweg

Götterdämmerung, 18 August 1957
Brünnhilde, Astrid Varnay; Siegfried, Wolfgang Windgassen; Hagen, Josef Greindl; Alberich, Gustav Neidlinger; Gunther, Hermann Uhde; Gutrune, Elisabeth Grümmer;

22 broadcast on 13 August 1957

Waltraute, Maria von Ilosvay; Woglinde, Lore Wissmann; Wellgunde Paula Lenchner; Floßhilde, Maria von Ilosvay; Norns, Maria von Ilosvay, Elisabeth Schärtel, Birgit Nilsson Chorus and Orchestra of the Bayreuth Festival

CD: Golden Melodram GM 1.0048 (2002); Walhall Eternity WLCD 0216-19 (2008)

Die Walküre, Act 1
Kirsten Flagstad, Sieglinde; Set Svanholm, Siegmund; Arnold van Mill, Hunding; Vienna Philharmonic Orchestra, 28-30 October 1957
LP: Decca LXT 5429-5430, SLX 2074-5; GRV 26
CD: Decca/London 425 963-2

1958

Die Meistersinger, Act 2, Fliedermonolog (ZAL 4177), and Act 3, Wahnmonolog (ZAL 4178)
Der fliegende Holländer, Dutchman's monologue (ZAL 4177)
Die Walküre, Act 3, Wotan's farewell (ZAL 4178)
George London, Vienna Philharmonic Orchestra, 9-11 June 1958
LP: Decca SXL 2068
CD: Decca 425 787-2; 458 238-2; 467 904-2; Urania URN 22.347 (2008)

Parsifal, Bayreuth, live broadcast, 25 July 1958
Amfortas, Eberhard Wächter; Titurel, Josef Greindl; Gurnemanz, Jerome Hines; Parsifal, Hans Beirer; Klingsor, Toni Blankenheim; Kundry, Régine Crespin; Knights, Fritz Uhl, Donald Bell; Squires, Claudia Hellmann, Ursula Boese, Harald Neukirch, Gerhard Stolze; Flowermaidens, Lotte Schädle, Friedel Pöltinger, Hildegard Schünemann, Dorothea Siebert, Gertraud Prenzlow, Elisabeth Schärtel; a Voice, Maria von Hosvay; Chorus and Orchestra of the Bayreuth Festival
LP: Melodram 583 (1981)
CD: Golden Melodram GM 1.0058 (2001); Walhall Eternity WLCD 0256 (2009)

Der Ring des Nibelungen, Bayreuth, live broadcasts, 1958

Das Rheingold, 27 July 1958
Wotan, Hans Hotter; Donner, Erik Saeden; Froh, Sandor Konya; Loge, Fritz Uhl; Alberich, Frans Andersson; Mime, Gerhard Stoltze; Fasolt, Theo Adam; Fafner, Josef Greindl; Fricka, Rita Gorr; Freia, Elisabeth Grümmer; Erda, Maria von Ilosvay; Woglinde, Dorothea Siebert; Wellgunde, Claudia Hellmann; Floßhilde, Ursula Boese

Die Walküre, 28 July 1958
Siegmund, Jon Vickers; Sieglinde, Leonie Rysanek; Wotan, Hans Hotter; Brünnhilde, Astrid Varnay; Hunding, Josef Greindl; Fricka, Rita Gorr; Gerhilde, Marlies Siemeling; Ortlinde, Hilde Scheppan; Waltraute, Elisabeth Schärtel; Schwertleite, Maria von Ilosvay; Helmwige, Lotte Rysanek; Siegrune, Grace Hoffmann; Grimgerde, Rita Gorr; Roßweiße, Ursula Boese

Siegfried, 30 July 1958
Siegfried, Wolfgang Windgassen; Mime, Gerhard Stoltze; Brünnhilde, Astrid Varnay; Wanderer, Hans Hotter; Alberich, Frans Andersson; Fafner, Josef Greindl; Erda, Maria von Ilosvay; Waldvogel, Dorothea Siebert

Götterdämmerung, 1 August 1958
Brünnhilde, Astrid Varnay; Siegfried, Wolfgang Windgassen; Hagen, Josef Greindl; Alberich, Frans Andersson; Gunther, Otto Wiener; Gutrune, Elisabeth Grümmer; Waltraute, Jean Madeira; Woglinde, Dorothea Siebert; Wellgunde, Claudia Hellmann; Floßhilde, Ursula Boese; Norns, Jean Madeira, Ursula Boese, Rita Gorr
Chorus and Orchestra of the Bayreuth Festival

CD: Arkadia CDMP 441-444; Golden Melodram GM 1.0052 (2001); Walhall Eternity WLCD 0246/49 (2009)

1959

Parsifal, Bayreuth, live broadcast, 7 August 1959[23]
Amfortas, Eberhard Wächter; Titurel, Josef Greindl; Gurnemanz, Jerome Hines; Parsifal, Hans Beirer; Klingsor, Toni Blankenheim; Kundry, Martha Mödl; Knights, Georg Paskuda, Donald Bell; Squires, Claudia Hellmann, Ursula Boese, Harald Neukirch, Herold Kraus; Flowermaidens, Ruth-Margret Ptz, Rita Bartos, Gisela Schröter, Dorothea Siebert, Elisabeth Witzmann, Claudia Hellmann; a Voice, Ursula Boese; Chorus and Orchestra of the Bayreuth Festival

CD: Golden Melodram GM 1.0070 (2004); Walhall Eternity WLCD 0295 (2010)

Tristan und Isolde, Act 1, Prelude and Isolde's narration; Act 3, Liebestod
Vienna Philharmonic Orchestra; Birgit Nilsson, Isolde; Grace Hoffmann, Brangäne, Sofiensaal, Vienna, 22-25 September 1959
Act 1, Prelude and Scene 3 almost complete: from *Weh'! ah wehe! dies zu dulden…* (Brangäne) to *… der Trank ist's, der mir taugt!* (Isolde) (21' 30")

LP: Decca BR 3063 (1960); LXT 5559, SXL 2184 (1960); London 5537, OS 25138 (1960); Decca 6.42088 (1969) (Prelude only)

CD: Decca/London 414 625-2 (1986); in Decca 433 330-2 IMS (12 CDs); Decca/London 452 896-2 (1997); *Great Operas at the Met - Tristan und Isolde*: MET 506-CD (1989) (Act 1 extract only, ending after *Tod uns Beiden!* (Isolde))

Die Meistersinger, Act 1, Prelude
Tristan und Isolde, Prelude and Liebestod
Götterdämmerung, Siegfried's Rhine Journey and Funeral Music
Berlin State Opera Orchestra, live performance, 19 November 1959

LP: Discocorp RR-388 (1981) (*Meistersinger*, with Brahms *Symphony No. 2*); RR-

[23] There exists film of Knappertsbusch conducting part of the Act 1 Transformation Music, eg, in *Great Conductors, Vol. 2*: Bel Canto Society 6003 (VHS) (1 minute excerpt), which Japanese sub-titles claim is from the 1959 Bayreuth Festival, and *Great Conductors – The Golden Era of Germany and Austria*: Dreamlife DLVC 8094 (2008) (DVD) (20-second excerpt, no date given). The Richard Wagner Museum in Bayreuth has been unable to confirm the date of the filming.

535 (1981)[24] (*Tristan* and *Götterdämmerung*)

CD: *Knappertsbusch Wagner Concert*: Seven Seas KICC 2030 (1990) [gives date as 1951] (*Tristan* and *Götterdämmerung* only); Seven Seas KICC 2153 (*Götterdämmerung* only, with Bruckner's *Symphony No. 3*); *Knappertsbusch conducts Wagner*: Dynamic IDIS 6569 (2009) (all excerpts)

1960

Die Meistersinger, Bayreuth, live broadcast, 23 July 1960

Hans Sachs, Josef Greindl; Veit Pogner, Theo Adam; Kunz Vogelgesang, Wilfried Krug; Konrad Nachtigall, Egmont Koch; Sixtus Beckmesser, Karl Schmitt-Walter; Fritz Kothner, Ludwig Weber; Balthasar Zorn, Heinz-Günter Zimmermann; Ulrich Eißlinger, Harald Neukirch; Augustin Moser, Hermann Winkler; Hermann Ortel, Fritjof Sentpaul; Hans Schwarz, Hans-Günter Nöcker; Hans Foltz, Eugen Fuchs; Walther von Stolzing, Wolfgang Windgassen; Eva, Elisabeth Grümmer; Magdalene, Elisabeth Schärtel; David, Gerhard Stolze; Nightwatchman, Donald Bell; Chorus and Orchestra and the Bayreuth Festival

LP: Melodram 602 (1981)

CD: Melodram MEL 46013; Golden Melodram GM 1.0029 (1998); Myto MCD00274 (2011)

Parsifal, Bayreuth, live broadcast, 31 July 1960

Amfortas, Thomas Stewart; Titurel, David Ward; Gurnemanz, Josef Greindl; Parsifal, Hans Beirer; Klingsor, Gustav Neidlinger; Kundry, Régine Crespin; Knights, Wilfried Krug, Theo Adam; Squires, Claudia Hellmann, Ruth Hesse, Harald Neukirch, Herold Kraus; Flowermaidens, Ruth-Margre Pütz, Gundula Janowitz, Claudia Hellmann, Dorothea Siebert, Elisabeth Witzmann, Ruth Hesse; a Voice, Ruth Siewert; Chorus and Orchestra of the Bayreuth Festival

LP: Melodram 018 (1980); Melodram 603 (1980)

CD: Gala 100.655 (2000); Myto MCD00274 (2011)

1961

Parsifal, Bayreuth, live broadcast, 25 July 1961

Amfortas, George London; Titurel, Ludwig Weber; Gurnemanz, Hans Hotter; Parsifal, Jess Thomas; Klingsor, Gustav Neidlinger; Kundry, Irene Dalis; Knights, Niels Möller, David Ward; Squires, Ruth Hesse, Claudia Hellmann, Gerhard Stolze, Georg Paskuda; Flowermaidens, Gundula Janowitz, Claudia Hellmann, Dorothea Siebert, Rita Bartos, Elisabeth Schärtel; a Voice, Ursula Böese; Chorus and Orchestra of the Bayreuth Festival

CD: Golden Melodram GM 1.0049 (2000)

[24] The label of RR-535 states that Christa Ludwig is singing the Liebestod when in fact it is an orchestral arrangement. Henry Fogel in his review of the record commented that "there is clearly a splice right after the first climax of Siegfried's Rhine Journey, and a change at that splice to a different performance....The splice... calls into question the authenticity of *all* of the material on the disc, since clearly there cannot be a splice in a live performance." *ARSC Journal*, vol. 14 no. 2 (1982), p. 67.

1962

Siegfried Idyll
Munich Philharmonic Orchestra, live performance, 6 January 1962
CD: Living Stage LS 1008 (2002)

Tristan und Isolde, Prelude and Liebestod, live performance, 31 May 1962
Isolde, Birgit Nilsson; Vienna Philharmonic Orchestra, Theater an der Wien
CD: Disques Refrain DR 920026 (1994); Hosanna HOS-01 (1998)
Video: TDK TDBA0016 (2004); *Wiener Festwochens 1962-1963*: HX-0243 (Taiwan)

Parsifal, Bayreuth, live performances, 27 July – 21 August 1962[25]
Amfortas, George London; Titurel, Martti Talvela; Gurnemanz, Hans Hotter; Parsifal, Jess Thomas; Klingsor, Gustav Neidlinger; Kundry, Irene Dalis; Knights, Niels Möller, Gerd Nienstedt; Squires, Sona Červená, Ursula Böese, Gerhard Stolze, Georg Paskuda; Flowermaidens, Anja Silja, Else-Margrete Gardelli, Dorothea Siebert, Rita Bartos, Sona Červená; a Voice, Ursula Böese; Chorus and Orchestra of the Bayreuth Festival
LP: Philips 6729 002 (1964)
CD: Philips 416 390-2; PHCP 2409-2; 464 756; 475 7785 (2006)

Rienzi, Overture
Der fliegende Holländer, Overture
Siegfried Idyll
Lohengrin, Act 1, Prelude
Die Meistersinger, Act 1, Prelude
Tannhäuser, Overture
Tristan und Isolde, Prelude and Liebestod
Parsifal, Prelude[26]
Munich Philharmonic Orchestra, Bavaria Studio, Munich, November 1962
LP: Westminister MCA-1413; WST-717 (1966); WST- 17032; Electrola 1C 045-90 328 (1970)
CD: MCA Classics MCAD2-9811 (1988)

1963

Siegfried Idyll
Tristan und Isolde, Prelude and Liebestod, Christa Ludwig, Isolde
Die Meistersinger, Act 3, Prelude
Götterdämmerung, Brünnhilde's immolation, Christa Ludwig, Brünnhilde
Die Meistersinger, Act 1, Prelude
North German Radio Orchestra, Hamburg, Musikhalle, live performance, 24 March 1963

[25] There was a live broadcast of *Parsifal* on 5 August 1962. The other performances that year were on 27 July, 10 and 21 August.
[26] A rehearsal of the *Parsifal* Prelude with the Munich Philharmonic, undated, appears on Rare Moth RM 453-M.

LP: HGN 5055 (*Meistersinger*, Act 3 Prelude only) (7" LP accompanying the program for a new production of *Meistersinger* at the Bayerische Staatsoper in 1979); RR-535 (1981) (*Tristan* and *Götterdämmerung* only)

CD: Nuova Era 13.604 (1988); Arkadia/Hunt HN 730.1 (1989); Hunt 4 CDLSMH 34051 (1990) (with *Parsifal*, Bayreuth 1964); Arkadia CDMP 451.4 (1991); *L'Art de Knappertsbusch*: Tahra 132-135 (1995); Golden Melodram GM 40070 (2005)

Siegfried Idyll and ***Die Walküre***, Act 1, Vienna, live performance, 21 May 1963
Claire Watson, Sieglinde; Fritz Uhl, Siegmund; Josef Greindl, Hunding; Vienna Philharmonic Orchestra, ORF telecast[27]

CD: Hosanna HOS-01 (1998) (*Siegfried Idyll*); Living Stage LS 347.18 (*Die Walküre*)

DVD: TDK-376 (2003) (*Die Walküre* only)

Parsifal, Bayreuth, live broadcast, 24 July 1963
Amfortas, George London; Titurel, Kurt Böhme; Gurnemanz, Hans Hotter; Parsifal, Wolfgang Windgassen; Klingsor, Gustav Neidlinger; Kundry, Irene Dalis; Knights, Hermann Winkler, Gerd Nienstedt; Squires, Ruth Hesse, Margarethe Bence, Georg Paskuda, Erwin Wohlfahrt; Flowermaidens, Anja Silja, Sylvia Stahlmann, Dorothea Siebert, Rita Bartos, Sona Červená; a Voice, Ruth Hesse; Chorus and Orchestra of the Bayreuth Festival

CD: Golden Melodram GM 1.0034 (1999)

1964

Parsifal, Bayreuth, live performance, 13 August 1964[28]
Amfortas, Thomas Stewart; Titurel, Heinz Hagenau; Gurnemanz, Hans Hotter; Parsifal, Jon Vickers; Klingsor, Gustav Neidlinger; Kundry, Barbro Ericson; Knights, Hermann Winkler, Gerd Nienstedt; Squires, Ruth Hesse, Sylvia Stahlmann, Dieter Slembeck, Erwin Wohlfahrt; Flowermaidens, Anja Silja, Lieselotte Rebmann, Else-Margrete Gardelli, Dorothea Siebert, Rita Bartos, Sylvia Lindenstarnd; a Voice, Ruth Hesse; Chorus and Orchestra of the Bayreuth Festival

LP: Melodram MEL 643 (1984)

CD: Hunt 4 CDLSMH 34051 (1990); Arkadia CDMP 451.4 (1991); Golden Melodram 1.0004 (1998); Orfeo d'Or C 690 074 L (2007)

[27] The final eight minutes of the *Siegfried Idyll* appeared in a documentary film directed by Eva Hassencamp, *Hans Knappertsbusch zum hundersten Geburtstag* (Munich, 1988, 43 minutes).

[28] *Parsifal* was conducted by Knappertsbusch on 21, 29 July, 7 and 13 August 1964. The Schallarchiv of Bavarian Radio has informed the author that the performances were taped twice, on 21 July and 13 August. Some minor problems with the tape of 21 July made it unsuitable for broadcast, so Bavarian Radio decided to tape the performance of 13 August. This was broadcast on 14 April 1965. Bayerischer Rundfunk holds tapes of both performances. Hunt reports that the Golden Melodram edition, published in collaboration with the Hans-Knappertsbusch Gesellschaft: "...claims to be the actual final public performance by Knappertsbusch on 13 August 1964, of which Bayerischer Rundfunk also states it holds a tape in its archive." While this claim is correct, Hunt was mistaken to list the 21 July performance as having been broadcast (*Wagner im Festspielhaus*, p. 117). There was no broadcast in 1964, according to Bavarian Radio. Moreover, George London sang Amfortas on 21 July, whereas Thomas Stewart sang the role on 13 August and is clearly heard (and is listed by Hunt) on the recordings above.

10. Clemens Krauss conducts Wagner[1]

Works recorded, including excerpts:

Der fliegende Holländer: 1944, 1948
Tannhäuser: 1936
Tristan und Isolde: 1948, 1949
Wesendonck Lieder: 1948
Die Meistersinger von Nürnberg: 1933, 1934
Der Ring des Nibelungen: 1953, also -
Das Rheingold: 1933
Die Walküre: 1933, 1934
Götterdämmerung: 1933, 1934
Parsifal: 1933, 1949, 1953

1933

Die Meistersinger, Vienna, live performance, 20 January 1933, excerpts (ca. 17 mins)
Hans Sachs, Rudolf Bockelmann; Veit Pogner, Nikolaus Zec; Kunz Vogelgesang, Georg Maikl; Konrad Nachtigall, Hans Duhan; Sixtus Beckmesser, Hermann Wiedemann; Fritz Kothner, Viktor Madin; Balthasar Zorn, Anton Arnold; Ulrich Eisslinger, Herr Wolken; Augustin Moser, Richard Tomek; Hermann Ortel, Alfred Muzzarelli; Hans Schwarz, Hermann Reich; Hans Foltz, Karl Ettl; Walter von Stolzing, Josef Kalenberg; David, Erich Zimmermann; Eva, Viorica Ursuleac; Magdalene, Gertrude Rünger, Chorus and Orchestra of the Vienna State Opera

Act 1: Overture (with an interruption) to *Da zu dir der Heiland kam* (chorus) (7' 20")
Act 2, scene 6: *Zwar wenig Regel* to *drei Schlag ich jetzt pausieren kann* (Sachs, with Beckmesser, Walter, Eva) (4' 57")
Act 3, scene 5: from *[Das unsre Meister] sie gepflegt* (Sachs) to within a bar of the end of the act (Sachs, Die Meister, Walter, David, Eva, Magdalene, chorus) (4' 50")
CD: *Edition Wiener Staatsoper Live – Vol. 14*: Koch Schwann 3-1464-2 (1994)

Das Rheingold, Vienna, live performance, 28 February 1933, excerpts (ca. 13 mins)
Wotan, Josef von Manowarda; Fricka, Bella Paalen; Freia, Viorica Ursuleac; Froh, Gunnar Graarud; Donner, Viktor Madin; Loge, Josef Kalenberg; Mime, Erich

[1] Until the release of his live recordings (Vienna, 1933-34, Havana 1948, and Bayreuth 1953), Krauss's Wagner discography was not extensive: see, for example, the discographies by Götz Klaus Kende (*Phono*, Jan.-Feb. 1966, pp. 65-66) and Clemens Höslinger, (*Fono Forum*, April 1973, p. 327); among the non-commercial recordings in the archives of the West German Radio and the Clemens Krauss-Archiv, Vienna listed by Erik Maschat and Götz Klaus Kende (*Recorded Sound*, April-July 1971, p. 743-746), the only Wagner recording remaining unpublished is an Act 1 Prelude from *Die Meistersinger* with the Vienna Philharmonic Orchestra performed at Klagenfurt, Austria on 4 November 1952 (though this is not listed in the inventory of the Clemens Krauss-Archiv in the Austrian National Library).

Zimmermann; Alberich, Hermann Wiedermann; Fasolt, Franz Markhoff; Woglinde, Luise Helletsgruber; Wellgunde, Dora With; Flosshilde, Enid Szantho; Orchestra of the Vienna State Opera

Scene 1: from *Schaut, es lächelt in lichtem Schein* (Wellgunde, with Woglinde, Flosshilde, Alberich) to *nur wer der Liebe Lust verjagt* (Woglinde) (3' 40")

Scene 2: from *Der Wonne seligen Saal* (Wotan, with Fricka) to *hehrer, Herrlicher Bau!* (Wotan) (2' 17")

Scene 3: from *Nehmt euch in Acht! Alberich naht!* (Mime, with Wotan, Alberich, Loge) to *wenn Loge nie dir gelacht?* (Loge) (3' 31")

Scene 4: from *Sie kehrten zurück!* (Froh, with Donner, Fricka, Loge, Fasolt, Wotan) to *dass meinem Blick die Blühende ganz er verdeck'!* (Fasolt) (3' 25")

CD: *Edition Wiener Staatsoper Live – Vol. 14*: Koch Schwann 3-1464-2 (1994)

Die Walküre, Vienna, live performance, 1 March 1933, excerpts (ca. 30 mins)[2]
Siegmund, Franz Völker; Sieglinde, Viorica Ursuleac; Brünnhilde, Elisabeth Ohms; Wotan, Josef von Manowarda; Fricka, Rosette Anday; Hunding, Richard Mayr; Helmwige, Luise Helletsgruber; Ortlinde, Eva Hadrabová; Gerhilde, Maria Reining; Waltraute, Dora With; Siegrune, Fanny Salinger; Rossweise, Frieda Stroinigg; Grimgerde, Bella Paalen; Schwertleite, Enid Szantho; Orchestra of the Vienna State Opera

Act 1, scene 1: from *[Labung biet ich] dem lechzenden Gaumen* (Sieglinde) to *Gering sind sie, [der Rede nicht werth]* (Siegmund) (2' 46")

Act 1, scene 2: from *Heilig ist mein Herd… Der gliessend Wurm glänzt auch ihm aus dem Auge* (1' 19": Koch) to *wird sein Name nun [mir genannt]* (Hunding) (1' 58")

Act 1, scene 2: from *[eines Wolfes Fell nur] traf ich im Forst leer lag das vor mir* (Siegmund) to *dem fremd als Gast nahst* (Hunding) (2' 57")

Act 1, scene 3: from *Dich selige Frau* (Siegmund, with Sieglinde) to *nun lacht sie selig dem licht* (Siegmund) (3' 50") (on Koch only)

Act 1, scene 3: from *[Winterstürme…] Die Liebe lockte den Lenz* (Siegmund) … *Du bist der Lenz* (Sieglinde) to *Seligste Weib!* (Siegmund) (2' 45")

Act 1, scene 3: from *Heiligster Minne, höchste Not* (Siegmund) to *so blühe denn Wälsungenblut!* (Siegmund, with Sieglinde) [final 20 bars of orchestral music to end of the act not recorded] (2' 38")

Act 2, scene 1: from the beginning of the act to *Die armen Tiere ächzen vor Angst* (Brünnhilde, with Wotan) (2' 25")

Act 2, scene 1: from *Wo in Bergen du dich birgst* (Fricka) to *Heut – hast du's erlebt!* (Wotan) (3' 20")

Act 3, scene 2: from *Nicht send' ich dich mehr aus Walhall* to *Schreckt euch ihr Los?* (Wotan, with Brünnhilde and the Valkyries) (3' 17")

Act 3, scene 2: orchestral passage (Wotan puts Brünnhilde to sleep) to *Loge, [hör!]* (Wotan) (1' 27")

Act 3, scene 2: from *Wer meines Speeres Spitze* (Wotan) to a few bars before the end of the act (2' 29")

LP: Unique Opera Records Corporation UORC 347 (1977) (label gives date as "March 2, 1933") (all excerpts, except one, where noted)

CD: *Edition Wiener Staatsoper Live – Vol. 16*: Koch Schwann 3-1466-2 (1994) (two excerpts only, as noted)

Götterdämmerung, Vienna, live performance, 7 March 1933, excerpts (ca. 31 mins)
Siegfried, Josef Kalenberg; Brünnhilde, Henny Trundt; Waltraute, Rosette Anday; Hagen, Josef von Manowarda; Gunther, Emil Schipper; Norns, Enid Szantho, Rosette Anday, Eva Hadrabova; Orchestra of the Vienna State Opera

[2] The cast is as given on the CD. However, the program for the performance lists Enid Szantho as Fricka, Maria Reining as Ortlinde, and Eva Hadrabová as Gerhilde.

Prologue: from the beginning to *woran spannst du das Seil?* (Second Norn) (3' 19")
Prologue: from *Treu berat'ner Verträge Runen* (Second Norn) to *sehrend den glänzenden Saal* (Third Norn) (3' 28")
Prologue-Act 1: excerpt from Siegfried's Rhine Journey (3' 23")
Act 1, scene 1: from *So stelle Eide zum Schwur* (Gunther) to *So – trink' ich dir Treu'!* (Siegfried) (3' 21")
Act 1, scene 3: from *fühllose Maid!* (Brünnhilde) to *Blitzend Gewölk* (Brünnhilde) (3' 27")
Act 3, scene 2: from *Brünnhilde, heilige Braut* to *Brünnhildes [Lust!]* (Siegfried) (2' 44")
Act 3, scene 2: excerpt from Siegfried's Funeral March (2' 55")
Act 3, scene 3: from *Schweig eures Jammers jauchzenden Schwall* to *des hehrsten Helden wert* (Brünnhilde) (1' 29")
Act 3, scene 3: from *Starke Scheite, schichtet mir dort* to *treu dem Freunde* (Brünnhilde) (3' 02")
Act 3, scene 3: from *O ihr, der Eide ewige Hüter* to *Ruhe, ruhe, du Gott!* (Brünnhilde) (3' 34")
CD: *Edition Wiener Staatsoper Live – Vol. 14*: Koch Schwann 3-1464-2 (1994)

Parsifal, Vienna, live performance, 13 April 1933, excerpts (ca. 38 mins)
Parsifal, Gunnar Graarud; Gurnemanz, Richard Mayr;[3] Amfortas, Emil Schipper; Kundry, Gertrude Rünger; Klingsor, Hermann Wiedemann; Chorus and Orchestra of the Vienna State Opera

Act 1: from *Das ist ein And'res…* to *Ich stürm' herbei; von dannen Klingsor* (Gurnemanz) (2' 17")
Act 1: from *Du tatest das?* to *…siehst du den Blick?* (Gurnemanz, with squires) (3' 06")
Act 2: from *Wehe! Wehe! Was tat ich!* to *Nur dumpfe Torheit lebt in Mir!* (Parsifal, Kundry) (2' 57")
Act 2: from *Amfortas! Die Wunde!* to *'aus schuldbefleckten Händen!'* (Parsifal) (4' 23")
Act 2: from *Hilfe! Hilfe! Herbei!* to the end of the Act (Kundry, Klingsor, Parsifal) (3' 14")
Act 3: orchestral introduction (2' 15"), then from *Von dorther kam das Stöhnen* to *Mich dünkt, ich kenne diesen Klagenruf?* (Gurnemanz) (3' 08")
Act 3: from *Du wuschest mir die Füße* (Parsifal) to *Mitleidvoll Duldender* (Gurnemanz) (4' 16")
Act 3: from *Das dankt dann alle Kreatur* to *Knecht geleite!* (beginning of the Transformation music) (Gurnemanz, Parsifal) (4' 11")
Act 3: from *Enthüllet den Gral…* (Knights), *Nein, nicht mehr* (Amfortas) to *Grales Welle* (Parsifal) (Amfortas, Parsifal, chorus) (4' 54")
Act 3: from 1' 40" before *Höchsten Heiles Wunder* (Chorus) to the end of the Act (5' 23")
LP: The Golden Age of Opera EJS 460 (1969)[4] (Act 1 excerpts only, and some 6 bars (40") of the Act 3 excerpt: *Von dorther kam das Stöhnen* (Gurnemanz)); *Wiener Staatsoper 1933*: Teletheater 120747 (1984) (*Enthüllet den Gral…* only)
CD: *Edition Wiener Staatsoper Live – Vol. 14*: Koch Schwann 3-1464-2 (1994) (except the Act 1 excerpts)

Die Walküre, Vienna, live performance, 11 June 1933, excerpts (ca. 49 mins)
Wotan, Friedrich Schorr; Brünnhilde, Maria Jeritza; Sieglinde, Felice Hüni-Mihacsek; Siegmund, Franz Völker; Hunding, Richard Mayr; Helmwige, Luise Helletsgruber; Gerhilde, Eva Hadrabova; Ortlinde, Margit Bokor; Waltraute, Rosette Anday; Siegrune, Aenne Michalski; Roßweiße, Dora With; Grimgerde, Bella Paalen, Schwertleite, Enid Szantho; Orchestra of the Vienna State Opera[5]

3 *Edition Wiener Staatsoper Live* lists Josef von Manowarda as Gurnemanz; however, the Vienna Opera program for 13 April 1933 lists "Hr. Mayr, Ehrenmitglied" as the singer of Gurnemanz; Richard Mayr is also given on the Golden Age of Opera label.

4 The Golden Age of Opera label attributes its 1933 excerpts, without giving an exact date, to Weingartner, but he did not conduct *Parsifal* that year; Krauss did.

5 The program for this performances differs from the cast given on the CD in a number of cases, namely,

Act 1, scene 2: from *Feige nur fürchten den, der waffenlos einsam fährt* (Sieglinde, with Siegmund, Hunding) to *Den Nacht trunk rüste mir drin und harre mein zur Ruh* (Hunding) (5' 16")
Act 1, scene 3: from *Ein Schwert verhieß mir der Vater* to *tief in des Busens Berge glimmt nur noch lichtlose Glut.* (Siegmund) (4' 49")
Act 1, scene 3: from *Da wußt'ich, wer der war* (Sieglinde) to *vereint sind Liebe und Lenz!* (Siegmund) (5' 28")
Act 1, scene 3: from *Was in Busen ich barg, was bin ich* (Sieglinde) to *nun walt ich der hersten Wonnen!* (Siegmund) (5' 00")
Act 2, scene 1: from *Nun zäume dein Roß, reisige Maid* (Wotan), ...*Hojotoho!* (Brünnhilde) to *Doch stand muss ich hier halten!* (Wotan) (3' 36")
Act 2, scene 4: from *Der dir nun folgt, wohin führst du den Helden* (Siegmund, with Brünnhilde) to *grüss auch die holden Wünschesmädchen* (Siegmund) (5' 11")
Act 2, scene 4: from *Kennst du dies Schwert* (Siegmund) to *Sieglinde lebe und Siegmund lebe mit ihr! Beschlossen ist's* (Brünnhilde) (4' 35")
Act 3, scenes 1 to 2: from *Fort denn eile!* (Brünnhilde) to *Lass dich erweichen für sie, zähm deinen Zorn!* (Helmwige, Gerhilde, Ortlinde, Waltraute, Siegrune, Roßweiße, Grimgerde, Schwertleite) (3' 55")
Act 3, scene 3: from ... *gewahrte sein Auge, hörte sein Wort* (Brünnhilde) to *als mir göttlicher Not nagende Galle gemischt?* (Wotan) (5' 17")
Act 3, scene 3: from *Erwarte dein Los, wie sich's dir wirft* (Wotan) to *dem freislichen Felsen zu nahn!* (Brünnhilde), ending immediately before Wotan's *Leb wohl* (3' 35")
CD: *Edition Wiener Staatsoper Live – Vol. 14*: Koch Schwann 3-1464-2 (1994)

Götterdämmerung, Vienna, live performance, 15 June 1933, excerpts (ca. 42 mins)[6]
Norns, Gertrude Rünger, Bella Paalen, Enid Szantho; Brünnhilde, Gertrude Kappel; Waltraute, Gertrude Rünger; Gutrune, Wand Achsel; Hagen, Josef von Manowarda; Orchestra of the Vienna State Opera

Prologue: from the beginning *Welch Licht leuchtet dort?* (First Norn) to *schling' ich das Seil und singe* (Firt Norn, with Second and Third Norns) (4' 04")
Prologue: from *Weisst du, wie das wird?* (Second Norn) to *zuhauf geschichtete Scheite* (Third Norn) (5' 06")
Prologue-Act 1: Siegfried's Rhine Journey (5' 15") (on Koch only)
Act 1, scene 3: from *Mehr also Walhalls Wonne* (Brünnhilde, with Waltraute) to *zu mir nie steure mehr her!* (Brünnhilde) (4' 04")
Act 3, scenes 2 to 3: excerpt (3' 20") from Siegfried's Funeral March to *Ich fürchte Brünnhild'! Ist sie daheim?* (Gutrune) (4' 46") (on Koch only)
Act 3, scene 3: from *[Des Allen Erbe] fordert so sein Sohn* (Hagen, with Brünnhilde) to *das ihr den Gatten entrückt!* (Gutrune) (3' 18")
Act 3, scene 3: Immolation scene (with one interruption): from *Starke Schiete* (Brünnhilde) to the end of the act (no interruption to the orchestral ending) (16' 07")
LP: The Golden Age of Opera: EJS 460 (1969); Unique Opera Records Corporation UORC 347 (1977) (all excerpts except where otherwise noted)[7]
CD: *Edition Wiener Staatsoper Live – Vol. 9*: Koch Schwann 3-1459-2 (1994)

it lists Fr. Lehmann as Sieglinde, Fr. Achsel as Gerhilde, Fr. Reining as Ortlinde,

6 The program for this performance lists Robert Heger as the conductor, and Rosette Anday as Waltraute.

7 The labels of the EJS and UORC LPs and the booklet of Koch Schwann CDs give the conductor of this performance as Robert Heger; but Heger conducted only *Das Rheingold* (10 June) and *Siegfried* (13 June) for this *Ring* cycle; Krauss conducted *Die Walküre* (11 June) and *Götterdämmerung* (15 June).

1934

Die Meistersinger, Vienna, live performance, 13 April 1934, excerpts (ca. 14 mins)
Hans Sachs, Alfred Jerger; Eva, Viorica Ursuleac; Walter von Stolzing, Franz Völker; David, Erich Zimmermann; Magdalene, Enid Szantho; Beckmesser, Hermann Wiedemann; Chorus and Orchestra of the Vienna State Opera

Act 2, scene 6: from *[Jerum!] Jerum! Hallahallohe!* (Sachs) to *Freund Sachs! So hört doch nur ein Wort!* (Beckmesser) (with Walter and Eva) (4' 02")
Act 3, scene 2: from *Doch laß dem Ruh* (Sachs) to *wie wird er dem im Bild gewonnen* (Walter) (3' 50")
Act 3, scene 4: complete quintet, *Selig wir die Sonne* (Eva, Magdalene, Walter, David, Sachs) (3' 28")
Act 3, scene 5: final part of the Prize Song, from *Zeuge am Ort, fahret fort* (Sachs) ... *Abendlich dämmernd* (Walter) to *Reich ihm das Reis* (chorus) (3' 07")
CD: *Edition Wiener Staatsoper Live – Vol. 10*: Koch Schwann 3-1460-2 (1994)

Die Walküre, Vienna, live performance, 1 November 1934, excerpts (ca. 7 mins)[8]
Siegmund, Franz Völker; Sieglinde, Viorica Ursuleac; Orchestra of the Vienna State Opera

Act 1. scene 3: from *Wär Wälse dein Vater, und bist du ein Wälsung* (Sieglinde) to *so blühe denn Wälsungen-Blut!* (Siegmund) and almost the end of the Act (3' 43")
Act 2, scene 5: from *Zauberfest bezähmt ein Schlaf* to *Notung zahl ihm den Zoll!* (Siegmund) (3' 34")
CD: *Edition Wiener Staatsoper Live – Vol. 16*: Koch Schwann 3-1466-2 (1994)

Götterdämmerung, Vienna, live performance, 19 November 1934, excerpts (ca. 14 mins)
Hagen, Josef von Manowarda; Gunther, Emil Schipper; Norns, Enid Szantho, Rosette Anday, Gertrude Rünger, Chorus and Orchestra of the Vienna State Opera

Prologue: from *Durch des Speeres Zauber zähmte ihn Wotan* (Second Norn) to *Es riß!* (First Norn) (4' 15")
Act 1, scene 2: *Hier sitz' ich zur Wacht* to *des Niblungen Sohn* (Hagen) (3' 35")
Act 2, scene 3: *[Rüstig gezecht,] bis der Rausch euch zähmte* (Hagen) to *Heil! Willkommen!* (Men) (2' 58")
Act 2, scene 4: *Heil sei Gunther dir, und deiner Braut* (Men) to *der dich zum Weib gewann* (Gunther) (2' 59")
CD: *Edition Wiener Staatsoper Live – Vol. 16*: Koch Schwann 3-1466-2 (1994)

1936

Tannhäuser, excerpts
Heinrich Schlusnus, Orchester der Staatsoper [Berlin], 11 June 1936[9]

Act 1, scene 4: *Als du in kühnem Sange uns bestrittest* to *aufs neue leuchte uns ihr Stern!* (Wolfram) (matrix 2935 GN) (2' 38")
Act 2, scene 4: *O Himmel lass dich jetzt erflehen* to *wo ewig strahlt dein Stern* (Wolfram) (matrix 2934 GN) (1' 26")
78: Grammophon 30015; Polydor 561117
CD: *Heinrich Schlusnus - Arien und Szenen*: Preiser 89212 (2 CDs)

[8] This was an evening performance. In the morning, Toscanini conducted Verdi's *Requiem* in the opera house.
[9] date from the Deutsches Rundfunkarchiv (17 July 1992) in Clemens-Krauss-Archiv F59/155/3

1944

Der fliegende Holländer (in three acts)
Bavarian Radio broadcast, Deutsches Museum Kongresssaal, Munich, 13-15 March 1944[10]
Holländer, Hans Hotter; Daland, Georg Hann; Senta, Viorica Ursuleac; Mary, Luise Willer; Erik, Karl Ostertag; Steersman, Franz Klarwein; Chorus and Orchestra of the Bavarian State Opera
LP: Mercury MGL 2 (1950); Discocorp IGI-381 (1980); Acanta HA 23-135/7 (1980)
CD: Preiser 90250 (1995); Arkadia/The 78s 78048 (1998); Opera d'Oro OPD-1357 (2002); Membran Documents 221532-303 (2006)

1948

Der fliegende Holländer
Act 2, scene 1: Senta's ballad: *Johohoe!* (7' 12")

Tristan und Isolde
Act 2, scene 2: Love duet: *O sink' hernieder...* to *...hold bewusster Wunsch* (6' 40")
Act 3, scene 3: Liebestod: "Mild und leise" to "höchste Lust!" (6' 25")

Wesendonck Lieder
Engel, Stehe Still, Treibhaus, Schmerzen, Träume (18' 20")
Kirsten Flagstad, Set Svanholm, Havana Philharmonic, live performance, 24 October 1948
LP: *Kirsten Flagstad Tribute Concert Havana*: The Golden Age of Opera EJS 285 (1963)
CD: *Kirsten Flagstad in Concert 1948-1953*: Eklipse Records EKR CD 15 (1993); *Kirsten Flagstad singt Wagner*: Archipel ARPCD 0423 (2009)

1949

Tristan und Isolde
Act 1 Prelude and Act 3 Liebestod (AR13136-39)
Parsifal
Act 3: Good Friday Music (ARL 9-5BW)
London Philharmonic Orchestra, Kingsway Hall, London, 11 January 1949
78: Decca AK 2245/6 (*Tristan* excerpts)
LP: London LLP 14 (1949); Decca LPX 2527 (1950); Richmond B 19042 (1959)
CD: *Famous Conductors of the Past – Clemens Krauss*: Preiser 90499 (2005)

[10] The dates of recording are taken from Clemens Krauss's *Dirigier-Daten II. Band* (September 1938 – 31 December 1953), Clemens-Krauss-Archiv F59, 158/3

1953[11]

Parsifal, Bayreuth, live broadcast, 24 July 1953
Amfortas, George London; Titurel, Josef Greindl; Gurnemanz, Ludwig Weber; Parsifal, Ramón Vinay; Klingsor, Hermann Uhde; Kundry, Martha Mödl; Knights, Gene Tobin, Theo Adam; Squires, Hetty Plümacher, Gisela Litz, Hugo Kratz, Adele Stolte; Flowermaidens, Hetty Plümacher, Gisela Litz, Rita Streich, Erika Zimmermann, Anna Tassopolus, Gerda Wismar; a Voice, Maria von Ilosvay; Chorus and Orchestra of the Bayreuth Festival

LP: Rodolfe Productions RP 12378/81 (1982); Melodram MEL 533 (1983)
CD: Laudis LCD4 4006 (1988); Arlecchino ARLA 00018/21 (1998); Archipel ARPCD 0171 (2004); Andromeda ANDRCD 9060 (2010)

Der Ring des Nibelungen
Bayreuth, live broadcasts, 1953

Das Rheingold, 8 August 1953
Wotan, Hans Hotter; Donner, Hermann Uhde; Froh, Gerhardt Stolze; Loge, Erich Witte; Alberich, Gustav Neidlinger; Mime, Paul Küen; Fasolt, Ludwig Weber; Fafner, Josef Greindl; Fricka, Ira Malaniuk; Freia, Bruni Falcon; Erda, Maria von Ilosvay; Woglinde, Erika Zimmermann; Wellgunde, Hetty Plümacher; Floßhilde, Gisela Litz

Die Walküre, 9 August 1953
Siegmund, Ramón Vinay; Sieglinde, Regina Resnik; Wotan, Hans Hotter; Brünnhilde, Astrid Varnay; Hunding, Josef Greindl; Fricka, Ira Malaniuk; Gerhilde, Brünnhilde Friedland; Ortlinde, Bruni Falcon; Waltraute, Lisa Sorrell; Schwertleite, Maria von Ilosvay; Helmwige, Liselotte Thomamüller; Siegrune, Gisela Litz; Grimgerde, Sibylla Plate; Roßweiße, Erika Schubert

Siegfried, 10 August 1953
Siegfried, Wolfgang Windgassen; Mime, Paul Küen; Brünnhilde, Astrid Varnay; Wanderer, Hans Hotter; Alberich, Gustav Neidlinger; Fafner, Josef Greindl; Erda, Maria von Ilosvay; Waldvogel, Rita Streich

Götterdämmerung, 12 August 1953
Brünnhilde, Astrid Varnay; Siegfried, Wolfgang Windgassen; Hagen, Josef Greindl; Alberich, Gustav Neidlinger; Gunther, Hermann Uhde; Gutrune, Natalie Hinsch-Gröndahl; Waltraute, Ira Malaniuk; Woglinde, Erika Zimmermann; Wellgunde, Hetty Plümacher; Floßhilde, Gisela Litz; Norns, Maria von Ilosvay, Ira Malaniuk, Regina Resnik

LP: Foyer FO 1008-11 (1980)
CD: Archipel ARPCD 0250-13 (2004); Orfeo d'Or C 809 113 R (2010)

[11] There was a live BBC broadcast of *Die Meistersinger* conducted by Krauss at Covent Garden on 6 July 1953: *The Times*, 6 July 1953, p. 5. There were some cast changes to the first performance (noted in Krauss chapter above): Karl Kamann replaced Paul Schoeffler as Sachs, and Richard Holm replaced Murray Dickie as David.

11. Hermann Levi conducts Wagner

Hermann Levi died in 1900. He left no commercial recordings.

He last appeared at the Bayreuth Festival in 1894 to conduct *Parsifal.* The earliest recordings from Bayreuth were made in 1904: William Gaisberg visited with his recording equipment and piano accompanist Bruno Seidler-Winkler to make several recordings for the Gramophone & Typewriter Company. None of them was orchestral.[1]

The earliest known recording of Wagner's orchestral music, apart from the experimental Edison recording of Bülow conducting *Die Meistersinger* Prelude in 1889, was probably the *Lohengrin* selections played by the Hotel Victoria Orchestra in 1898 (Berliner 597).[2] These were made in the United States of America, where Levi never visited.

1 *100 Jahre Bayreuth auf Schallplatte*: Gebhardt JGCD 00062-12 (12 CDs) (2004)

2 listed in Claude G. Arnold, A *discography of the orchestra, 1898-1925/26: an encyclopaedia of orchestral recordings made by the acoustical process* (Toronto: St. Michael's College, University of Toronto, 1983), p. 544

12. Gustav Mahler conducts Wagner

Mahler made no recordings as a conductor.

The only evidence of Mahler as a performer are four pieces he recorded from his own works using the Welte-Mignon piano roll system in 1905.[1]

Listening to these, Mahler scholars have remarked on his "brisk tempos" and how, "within his basic tempos... [he] displays an unusual degree of freedom and flexibility, sometimes adopting sudden changes of tempo that are not called for in the score."[2] The Dutch composer and musicologist Marius Flothuis has noted "the liveliness of the tempos and the rigorous observance of the performance markings in the score, together with a number of slight rubati that do not affect the overall tempo."[3] Mahler's biographer Henry-Louis de La Grange has observed that "the sombre and imperious character of Mahler's interpretation, the sinewy rhythms, the sensitive phrasing, and the aptness of the tempo and its modifications all contribute to the sense that Mahler himself is actually playing – and this in spite of the limits inherent in the method of reproduction."[4]

Whether one can draw any inferences about Mahler's performance of Wagner from these documents is a matter for conjecture.

1 *Mahler plays Mahler*: [Pickwick] IMP Classics 790202 (1 CD) (1993)

2 Gilbert E. Kaplan and Hans W. Schmidt, "The Mahler Piano Rolls," *The Musical Times*, vol. 134, no. 1803 (May, 1993), pp. 252-53, at p. 253

3 in *Nachrichten zur Mahler-Forschung*, vol. 9 (September 1981), pp. 6ff, as summarised by Henry-Louis de La Grange, *Gustav Mahler, Vol. 4, A New Life Cut Short (1907-1911)* (Oxford University Press, 2008), p. 1631

4 *ibid*, p. 1632. La Grange devotes an appendix to the Welte-Mignon process: Appendix 2B: "Mahler as a Performer of his own Works (The piano rolls and their transfer to disc)," *ibid*, pp. 1619-35

13. Felix Mottl conducts Wagner[1]

There is only one recording of Mottl conducting, and that is Wagner:

Kaisermarsch, live performance, Metropolitan Opera House, excerpts (2' 25" and 1' 04") Metropolitan Opera Orchestra, New York, 17 January 1904 (?)[2]

LP: *The Mapleson Cylinders 1900-1904 Complete Edition*: [New York Public Library] R&H-100 (6 LPs) (1985)

CD: *Wagner at the MET 1903*: Truesound Transfers TT-1909 (1 CD); *100 Jahre Bayreuth auf Schallplatte - The Early Bayreuth Festival Singers 1876-1906*: Gebhardt JGCD 0062-12 (12 CDs) (2004)

On 2 June 1907, in Freiburg, Mottl recorded ten piano arrangements from Wagner using the Welte-Mignon process:

Lohengrin, Act 1 Prelude (Welte-Mignon catalogue No. 1345) (10' 15")
Parsifal, Act 1 Prelude (No. 1346) (12' 59")
Tristan und Isolde, Act 1 Prelude (No. 1347) (9' 58")
Lohengrin, Act 3, Bridal Chorus (No. 1348) (6' 03")
Lohengrin, Act 1, Elsa's dream (No. 1349) (7' 51")
Parsifal, Act 3, Good Friday Music (No. 1350) (10' 25")
Tristan und Isolde, Act 2, Love duet and Brangäne's warning (No. 1351) (9' 50")
Die Meistersinger, Act 1, *Am stillen Herd in Winterseit* (No. 1352) (5' 26")★★
Die Meistersinger, Act 3, Quintet (No. 1353) (4' 41")
Parsifal, Act 1, Transformation music and entry of the Knights of the Holy Grail (No. 1354) (10' 10")★★

CD: *The Welte-Mignon Mystery Vol. II Felix Mottl plays Wagner*: Tacet 135 (2 CDs) (2004) (with detailed notes and illustrations of the Welte-Mignon recording process)

★★These pieces also appeared in *Wagner mécanique – Instrumente im Münchner Stadtmuseum*: Oehms Classics OC 330 (1 CD) (2003) with quite different timings: *Die Meistersinger* 5' 04", and *Parsifal* 10' 21". (This is a disc with arrangements of Wagner for music box, fairground organ, etc., instruments which are more charming and atmospheric than reproduction pianos.)

[1] The select discography in Haas, *Felix Mottl*, pp. 413-415 includes recordings by others of Mottl's original works as well as his arrangements, but does not include the 1904 *Kaisermarsch* excerpts above.

[2] The R&H-100 notes to these two excerpts state in part: "The *Kaisermarsch* was performed at several Sunday-night concerts during the Mapleson years. On January 4 and again on March 8 in 1903, Alfred Herz conducted it, and the following year Felix Mottl played it on January 17. ...the ascription to Mottl seems more probable. This would appear to be his only recording (aside from the piano rolls)."

14. Karl Muck conducts Wagner[1]

Works recorded, including excerpts:

Der fliegende Holländer: 1928
Tannhäuser: 1928
Lohengrin: 1917, 1929
Tristan und Isolde: 1928
Die Meistersinger von Nürnberg: 1927
Siegfried Idyll: 1929
Der Ring des Nibelungen:
Götterdämmerung: 1927, 1930
Parsifal: 1927, 1928

1917

Lohengrin, Act 3, Prelude
(B 20818-2, 3 October 1917)
78:Victor 64744, 547
LP: RCA Victor LM 2651
CD: *The First Recordings of the Boston Symphony Orchestra*: BSO Classics 171002 (1995); *Wagner – Overtures and Preludes – Muck*: Naxos Historical 8.110858 (2002)

1927

Parsifal, excerpts from Acts 1 and 2, Bayreuth Festspielhaus, August 1927[2]
Flowermaidens, Ingeborg Holmgren, Anny Helm, Hilde Sinnek, Maria Nežádal, Charlotte Müller; Bayreuth Festival Chorus and Orchestra

Act 1: *Transformation scene* (Gurnemanz's and Parsifal's words omitted)
(WAX 3010-1, 3011-2)
78: Columbia L 2007; 67364-D (in set M-337)

Act 1: *Grail scene* (*Zum letzten Liebesmahle* - Titurel/Amfortas scene omitted)
(WAX 3012-1, 3013-2, 3014-2, 3015-1, 3016-1, 3017-1)
78: Columbia L 2008/10; 67365/67-D (in set M-337)

1 The standard, comprehensive discography on Karl Muck is by Jim Cartright and Christopher Dyment: *ARSC Journal*, vol. 9, no 1 (1977), pp. 69-77.

2 In an article accompanying his discography (*ibid.*, 66-68), Christopher Dyment discusses the difficulties, if not impossibility, of ascribing more precise dates to the Bayreuth recordings.

Act 2: *Flowermaidens' scene* (*Komm'! Komm'! Holder Knabe!*)
(WAX 3018-2, 3019-1)

78: Columbia L 2011; 67368-D (in set M-337)

LP: *Brani scelti da Parsifal*: Odeon 33QCX 10464 (1963)[3]; *Karl Muck conducts Wagner's 'Parsifal'*: OPAL 837/8 (1988)

CD: *Karl Muck conducts Wagner's 'Parsifal'*: OPAL CD9843 (1989); Naxos 8.110049-50 (1999) (with Alfred Hertz's 1913 *Parsifal* recordings); *100 Jahre Bayreuth auf Schallplatte - The Early Bayreuth Festival Singers 1876 - 1906*: Gebhardt JGCD0062-12 (12 CDs) (2004) (Transformation scene only)

Die Meistersinger, Act 1, Prelude
Berlin State Opera Orchestra
(CWR 1403-2, 1404-2A, Singakademie, Berlin, 8 December 1927)

78: Electrola E223/24, ES343/44, Victor 6858/59, 7013/15, 17263/65

Götterdämmerung, Prologue, *Siegfried's Rhine Journey*
Berlin State Opera Orchestra
(CWR 1418-2, Singakademie, Berlin, 10 December 1927)

78: HMV D1525, E224, ES344, ES540, Victor 6859, 7016, 17266

Götterdämmerung, Act 3, *Siegfried's Funeral Music*
Berlin State Opera Orchestra
(CWR 1419-3 and CWR 1420-2A, Singakademie, Berlin, 10 December 1927)

78: HMV D1585, E225, ES355, ES550, AW54, AB388, Victor 6860, 7017 & 7013, 17267

Parsifal, Act 1, Prelude
Berlin State Opera Orchestra
(CWR 1421-2, 1422-2, 1423-1A, 1424-1A, Singakademie, Berlin, 11 December 1927)

78: HMV 1400/01, E226/27, ES356/57, AB390/91, Victor 6861/62, 7014/17, 17266/63

CD: Naxos 8.110049-50 (1999)

1928

Tristan und Isolde, Act 1, Prelude
Berlin State Opera Orchestra
(CLR 4129-1, 4130-1A, 4131-1A, Singakademie, Berlin, 15 May 1928)

78: HMV D2028/29, E366/67, AW60/61, ES491/92, AB528/29

Der fliegende Holländer, Overture
Berlin State Opera Orchestra
(CLR 4132-1, 4133-2, 4134-1, Singakademie, Berlin, 16 May 1928)

78: HMV D2027/29, E367/68, ES492/93, AW61/62, AB529/30

Tannhäuser, Overture
Berlin State Opera Orchestra

[3] This includes the Act 3 *Prelude* and *Good Friday Scene* conducted by Siegfried Wagner, also recorded at Bayreuth in August 1927 (WAX 3023-2, 3024-1, 3020-1, 3021-2, 3022-1; Columbia L 2012/14).

(CLR 4135-1A, 4136-1A, 4137-2, 4138-1, Singakademie, Berlin, 17 May 1928)
78: Electrola E335/36, ES432/33

The above seven excerpts were in:
CD: Centaur CRC 2142 (1993) (except *Tannhäuser*); Preiser 90269 (1995); Appian APR 5521 (1996); *Wagner – Overtures and Preludes – Muck*: Naxos Historical 8.110858 (2002) (except *Rhine Journey* **and** *Parsifal*); Symposium 1345 (2005) (except *Parsifal*)

Parsifal, Act 3, abridged
Parsifal, Gotthelf Pistor; Gurnemanz, Cornelis Bronsgeest; Amfortas, Ludwig Hofmann; Berlin State Opera Chorus and Orchestra, Singakademie, Berlin, 10-14 October 1928
a. *Prelude*
(CLR 4609-2, 4610-2, 13 October 1928)
b. from the entry of Parsifal (*Heil mir, dass ich dich wieder finde!*) to the end of the Act
(CLR 4598-2, -99-2, 4600-2, -01-1, -02-2, -03-1, -04-2, -11-1, -12-1, -13-1, -14-1, -15-1, -16-1, -17-1, 10-14 October 1928)
78: HMV D1537/44; E373/80, ES561/68, Victor set M-67 (7160-7167)
LP: Preiser LV 100 (1970) (excluding the *Prelude*); *Karl Muck conducts Wagner's 'Parsifal'*: OPAL 837/8 (1988)
CD: OPAL CD9843 (1989); Centaur CRC 2142 (1993) (*Prelude* only); Naxos 8.110049-50 (2 CDs) (1999)

1929

Lohengrin , Act 3, Prelude
Berlin State Opera Orchestra
(CLR 5806-2A, Philharmonie, Berlin, 21 November 1929)
78: [assigned side number 32-1037] unpublished
CD: Appian APR 5521 (1996)

Siegfried Idyll
Berlin State Opera Orchestra
(CLR 5807-1A, 5808-2, 5809-1, 5810-2, Philharmonie, Berlin, 21 November 1929)
78: Electrola AN566/67, EH561/62, Victor 7381-7382
CD: Symposium 1345 (2005); *Wagner – Overtures and Preludes – Muck*: Naxos Historical 8.110858 (2002)

1930

Götterdämmerung, Act 3, *Siegfried's Funeral Music*[4]
Berlin Radio Orchestra, 1930
LP: *100 Jahre Bayreuth*: BASF HB 22 863-0 (4 LPs) (1976)

[4] Whether this recording is correctly attributed to Muck is doubtful. It is one of a small number of otherwise unpublished recordings purporting to be Muck conducting the "Berlin Funkorchester" in 1928 and 1930. Because the recordings were never located, only a list of them, the article about them foreshadowed in the Cartwright/Dyment discography (see note 1 above; p. 77) was never published.

15. Arthur Nikisch conducts Wagner

Nikisch conducted several orchestral recordings in 1913-1914 and 1920-1922, but there were no works of Wagner among them.[1]

However, in London on 1 July 1911, he accompanied Elena Gerhardt on the piano in a recording of *Schmerzen*, the fourth of Wagner's *Wesendonk Lieder*:

78: Gramophone 043204 (matrix 5118f)
LP: HMV HLM 1436031 (1983)
CD: *Elena Gerhardt*: Fono Enterprise 1102 (1995)

Reviewing the LP reissue of this song, J.B. Steane wrote that "for all the freedom of rubato and so forth, there are times when Gerhardt and Nikisch come closer than many modern artists to the letter of the score as well as its spirit. *Schmerzen*, from the *Wesendonk Lieder*, is an example: few modern performers observe the essential directions as faithfully."[2]

Gerhardt recorded the same work again in Berlin on 13 January 1914, this time with orchestra (HMV 043260, matrix 1310s), but the conductor was Bruno Seidler-Winkler.

In her memoirs, Elena Gerhardt recalled the time Nikisch first accompanied her at the Leipzig Conservatorium: "He was such a wonderful pianist, and so sensitive a musician that I felt as if I were carried through the song and lifted to another world."[3]

1 The complete orchestral recordings were re-issued on Symposium 1087 & 1088 (1991).
2 *Gramophone*, January 1984, p. 905
3 Elena Gerhardt, *Recital* (London: Methuen, 1953), p. 11

16. Fritz Reiner conducts Wagner[1]

Works recorded, including excerpts:

A Faust Overture: 1957
Rienzi: 1958
Der fliegende Holländer: 1937, 1950
Tannhäuser: 1941, 1950
Lohengrin: 1932, 1941, 1950, 1960
Tristan und Isolde: 1931, 1936, 1937, 1950, 1958
Die Meistersinger von Nürnberg: 1931, 1938, 1941, 1945, 1952, 1953, 1955, 1959
Siegfried Idyll: 1962
Der Ring des Nibelungen:
  Die Walküre: 1936, 1940
  Siegfried: 1941
  Götterdämmerung: 1937, 1959
Parsifal: 1931, 1937, 1938, 1958

1931

Die Meistersinger, Act 2, Watchman's solo (arrangement) (4' 22") and Act 3, Prelude (incomplete: 5' 08")
Tristan und Isolde, Act 3, Tristan's vision and death (arrangement) (8' 50")
Parsifal, Act 1, an arrangement which includes music from the Transformation scene (7' 37"); Act 2, Klingsor's magic garden (3' 00"); and Act 3, Good Friday music (11' 40")
Nightwatchman, unidentified;[2] Philadelphia Orchestra, live performance, Academy of Music, 27-28 November 1931
(Bell Laboratories experimental recordings)

[1] The most comprehensive discography of Reiner is Arthur J. Helmbrecht Jr.'s, *Fritz Reiner – The Comprehensive Discography of his Recordings* (Fritz Reiner Society, 1978). Helmbrecht was archivist of the Fritz Reiner Society and wrote in his 1976 introduction that "absolute completeness is impossible. There is simply no way to account for the myriad of privately taped recordings of Dr Reiner which are in private collections around the world." This remains the case. This discography excludes some items Helmbrecht listed as "unverified" or believed to be in the Library of Congress but which library staff could not locate in 2006, including some undated Armed Forces & Television Service recordings with the Detroit Symphony Orchestra (CX-13/14). They are, nevertheless, mentioned in footnotes. I have included recordings from the CD series *The Reiner Legacy: Concert and Broadcast Recordings from the Collection of Bruce Wellek*, copies of which are in the Reiner Archive at Northwestern University, Chicago, and the Library of Congress, Washington. Another recent discography is John Hunt's, *Hungarians in Exile: Reiner, Dorati, Szell* (London: John Hunt, 1997).

[2] The *Philadelphia Inquirer* noted the Nightwatchman had been sung "by an offstage and unnamed baritone" (28 November 1931, p. 12); the *Philadelphia Record* also noted that "the program did not disclose the owner of the hidden voice" (28 November 1931, p. 11). The concert, consisting of excerpts and arrangements from *Tristan*, *Parsifal* and the *Meistersinger*, was given on both 27 and 28 November 1931.

Tape: Fritz Reiner Society open-reel tape/cassette no. 11 (1988)
CD: Transformation music (7' 37") in *Volume 4: Guest Conductors of The Philadelphia Orchestra: The Centennial Collection – Historical Broadcasts and Recordings, 1917-1998* (12 CDs) (1998)

1932

Lohengrin, Philadelphia, Academy of Music, live performance, 18 February 1932 (ca. 30 mins of playable excerpts)[3]

Lohengrin, Paolo Marion; Elsa, Anne Roselle; Herald, Nelson Eddy; King Henry, Ivan Steschenko; Ortrud, Cyrena Van Gordon; Telramund, Chief Caupolican; Gottfried, Bernice Dollarton; Pages, Carol Deis, Agnes Davis, Virginia Kendrick, Ruth Carhart; Nobles, Daniel Healy, Albert Mahler, Conrad Thibault, John Cosby; Philadelphia Orchestra and Curtis Institute players

Disc 1: Act 1 Prelude (9' 26")
Disc 2: Act 1, Scenes 1 and 2: from *[Mein Gott für Reiches] Her'!* (Saxons), *Komm' ich zu euch nun, Männer von Brabant* (King Henry) to *Erkennst du mich als deinen Richter an?* (King Henry) (10' 20")
Disc 3: [unplayable]
Disc 4: Act 3, Scene 2: Lohengrin/Elsa duet, from shortly after *Das süsse Lied* (7' 30")
Disc 5: Act 3, Scene 3: from *Habt Dank, ihr Lieben von Brabant!* (King Henry) to *Welch' Unerhörtes muss ich nun erfahren* (King Henry and men), with *Wehe du! Elsa!* (Women) to *Geheimniss ich in Treuen* (Lohengrin) omitted from the performance (6' 20")
Disc 6: Act 3, Scene 3: from *an dem ist jedes Bösen trug* (Lohengrin, from his *In fernem Land*) to *Wonne zöhren* (Chorus) (3' 15"), then cut to Elsa and the chorus *Der Schwann! Der Schwann!* (0' 10")
LP: Library of Congress Series NCPB 02530-35 (6 discs) [Non Commercial Pressings Bell Laboratories]
Tape: Fritz Reiner Society open-reel tape/cassette no. 11 (1988) (Act 1 Prelude only - 9' 00"[4])

1936[5]

Tristan und Isolde, London, live performance, 11 June 1936, abridged[6]

Tristan, Lauritz Melchior; King Marke, Emanuel List; Isolde, Kirsten Flagstad; Kurwenal, Herbert Janssen; Melot, Frank Sale; Brangäne; Sabine Kalter; Steersman,

[3] I listened to these discs in the Library of Congress in August 2006, and report the details as much as I could hear them: only two auditions are allowed of archival material of this kind, and the discs were in very poor condition, particularly Disc 1 and Disc 3; the latter would not play through on either of the two occasions attempted by the audio engineer.

[4] As will be noted, the timing of the Fritz Reiner tape differs from the disc in the Library of Congress.

[5] Of the two *Parsifals* Reiner conducted at Covent Garden in 1936 - 29 April and 4 May - only Act 2 of the second performance was broadcast (Regional). Helmbrecht (pp. 28-29) lists unspecified excerpts from this performance among the radio transcription recordings in the Library of Congress.

[6] The cuts in the performance were: in Act 2, Scene 2, from *Dem Tage! Dem Tage!* (Tristan) to *dass nachtsichtig mein Auge wahres zu sehen tauge* (Tristan), and in Act 3, Scene 1, from *Isolde noch im Reich der Sonne!* to *die selbst Nachts von ihr mich scheuchte?* (Tristan). The three earlier performances conducted by Reiner were broadcast, in part, as follows: 18 May 1936 (Act 1) (Regional), 22 May 1936 (Act 2) (National), 2 June 1936 (Act 3) (Regional).

Leslie Horsman; Shepherd, Octave Dua; Sailor, Roy Devereux; Chorus of the Royal Opera House, Covent Garden, London Philharmonic Orchestra
(Gramophone Company Technical Test recording)

LP: The Golden Age of Opera EJS-465 (1969); Bruno Walter Society RR-471 (1978); Discoreale DR 10027-10030 (1981)

CD:[7] VAI Audio VAIA 1004-3 (1992) (shown as "May/June, 1936"); The Radio Years RY 39.41 (1995) (shown as recorded in New York); Dante LYS 162/64 (1997); Naxos 8.110068-70 (2000); Arkadia 78067 (2004)

Die Walküre, San Francisco, War Memorial Opera House, Act 2 abridged,[8] broadcast performance, 13 November 1936
Brünnhilde, Kirsten Flagstad; Siegmund, Lauritz Melchior; Sieglinde, Lotte Lehmann; Wotan, Friedrich Schorr; Fricka, Kathryn Meisle; Hunding, Emanuel List; San Francisco Opera Chorus and Orchestra

LP: The Golden Age of Opera EJS 234;[9] Discocorp RR-426;[10] Edizione Lirica EL 004;[11] Impresario Editions IE 5004

CD: Legato Classics LCD-133-1 (1989);[12] Grammofono 2000 AB-78545; Minerva MN A34; Music & Arts CD-1048 (1999);[13] Guild GHCD 2238/40; *Hojotoho!* in *Kirsten Flagstad*: SIMAX PSC 1822 (1995)

1937

Parsifal, London, live performances, excerpts from Act 1 (27 April 1937) and Act 3 (3 May 1937)

Act 1: *Vom Bade kehrt der König heim* (Gurnemanz) to *So ward es dir verhiessen* (Knights) (18' 00")[14]

[7] Parts of the Reiner recording (Act 1 and the second part of Act 3) were inadvertently issued by EMI purporting to be conducted by Thomas Beecham on CHS 7-64037-2 (3 CDs) (1991): for a full analysis, see David Hamilton's review of the EMI set in "Recordings", *Opera Quarterly*, vol. 9 no. 3 (Spring 1993), pp. 162-67.

[8] There were three cuts in the performance: in the Wotan/Fricka scene from *Nichts lerntest du* (Wotan) to *die Göttin entweiht er nicht so!* (Fricka); in Wotan's monologue from *Der der Liebe fluchte* to ... *wer mir traut*; and in the Brünnhilde/Siegmund scene from *Du sahst der Walküre* (Brünnhilde) to ... *sprich du wahrlich mir nicht!* (Siegmund). There were no cuts to Sieglinde's lines. The last 43 bars (ca. 1' 30") are missing because the broadcast was brought to an end prematurely. The timing of the music recorded is 71' 07" on EJS, 66' 57" on EL, and 68' 30" on Legato (with the closing bars added from another performance).

[9] Marcia Davenport's announcement at the end – see following footnote – is omitted.

[10] This record includes the announcement by Marcia Davenport (broadcast commentator, author and music critic) before the end of the Act, as Wotan despatches Hunding (*Geh hin, Knecht!*), "The curtain is now coming down very slowly, and I am sure there's nothing I can add to the emotion you must have as the consequence of this *most extraordinary* performance of *Die Walküre.*"

[11] This record includes the whole of the radio broadcast introduction (6' 23"), principally by Marcia Davenport, as well as her closing announcement – see preceding footnote; included in the set is Act 1, Scene 3 of *Die Walküre*, conducted by Toscanini in New York, 6 April 1947.

[12] Some of Marcia Davenport's introductory comments have been retained, but her announcement at the end has been cut, and a splice from another performance completes the Act.

[13] This CD retains the Marcia Davenport announcement at the end. The notes are by Arthur Bloomfield, author of *50 years of the San Francisco opera* (San Francisco: San Francisco Book Co., 1972).

[14] Some of the recording of this passage may have been lost: there is an abrupt change from the Transformation music to the Knights' Chorus. Part of the excerpt appeared in a concoction claiming to be Karl Muck conducting *Parsifal* at the 1931 Bayreuth Festival in *Historic Performances of Parsifal at Bayreuth*: Discocorp IGI-379 (1980).

Act 3: *Ich sah' sie welken* (Parsifal) to end of the Act (24' 35")

Gurnemanz, Ludwig Weber; Parsifal, Torsten Ralf; Amfortas, Herbert Janssen; Titurel, Robert Easton; Chorus of the Royal Opera House, Covent Garden, London Philharmonic Orchestra (Gramophone Company Technical Test Series)

LP: Unique Opera Records UORC 130 (1972)

CD: Dante LYS 159/160 (1996)

Der fliegende Holländer, London, live performances, 7 and 11 June 1937, excerpts (ca. 85 mins)

Dutchman, Herbert Janssen; Daland, Ludwig Weber; Senta, Kirsten Flagstad; Erik, Max Lorenz; Mary, Mary Jarred; Steersman, Ben Williams; Chorus of the Royal Opera House, Covent Garden, London Philharmonic Orchestra (Gramophone Company Technical Test Series)[15]

Act 1, scene 2: from *Die Frist ist um* (Dutchman) to *Ew'ge Vernichtung, nim mich uns auf!* (Dutchman's crew) (11' 02")

Act 1, scene 3: from *Weit komm' ich her* (Dutchman) to *Sogleich die Anker lichten wir* (Daland) (12' 45")

Act 2: from the beginning of the Act to the end of Senta's ballad *Hilf Himmel! Senta!* (Mary, Girls) (18' 23")

Act 2, scene 3: from *Mein Kind* (Daland) to the end of the Act (22' 28")

Act 3: from the beginning (orchestral interlude and Norwegian sailors' chorus) to *So nehmt! Der Nachbar hat's verschmäht* (Girls) (with *Habt ihr keine Brief'* (Sailors) to *Sie wollen nichts – was rufen wir?* (Girls) omitted) (8' 04")

Act 3, scene 2: from *Was muß ich hören, Gott, was muß ich sehn!* (Erik) to the end of the opera (11' 50")

LP: The Golden Age of Opera EJS 123 (ca. 1958) (excerpts from Acts 2 and 3 only); EJS 515 (1970) (as for EJS 123, with the Act 1 excerpts and the opening scene from Act 3); HRE-234; Discocorp RR-469; Rococco ROC-1008; *The Great Kirsten Flagstad*: Orpheum 8404 (1968) (Senta's ballad only)

CD: Standing Room Only SRO-808-1;[16] Italian Music Company CDI 205009 (1996); Dante LYS-159/160 (1996); Golden Melodram 1.0064 (2003);[17] *Kirsten Flagstad*: SIMAX PSC 1822 (1995) (Senta's ballad); *Kirsten Flagstad*: CDMOIR 403 (1990) (Senta's ballad and duet); *Ludwig Weber*: Myto 992. H029 (*Morgen du mein Kind*)

Götterdämmerung, New York, Lewisohn Stadium, live broadcast,[18] 22 July 1937 concert performance of a condensed Prologue, Dawn, *Zu neuen Taten*, Rhine Journey, and Waltraute's narrative (47' 21" in total)

Brünnhilde, Florence Easton; Siegfried, Paul Althouse; Waltraute, Kathryn Meisle; Chorus of the Grand Opera Choral Alliance; New York Philharmonic Symphony Orchestra

[15] Hunt gives matrix numbers 2EA 5600-5618. These are the standard transfer matrices from the original Technical Test Series recordings. Furthermore, he lists unspecified unpublished test pressings from a 16 June 1937 performance.

[16] This CD omits the first excerpt from Act 3 (the chorus).

[17] In his review of the Melodram set in *Fanfare* (January/February 2004, p. 229), William Youngren lists more cuts in the performance than I have listed above, which is taken from the IMC set.

[18] WABC broadcast between 8:00-9:00 pm. This was the only part of the 1937 Wagner Festival broadcast from the New York Stadium concerts. The other performances were *Rheingold* (12 July), *Walküre* (14 July), *Siegfried* (20 July), and *Tristan* (27 July).

LP: The Golden Age of Opera EJS 167 (Waltraute's narrative only - 23' 55'); IRCC LP-7022 (1963) (*Zu neuen Taten* only); A.N.N.A. Recording Company ANNA 1008 (1978) (label incorrectly states "London, 1936")

CD: *Symposium Opera Collection Vol. 8 - Florence Easton:* Symposium CD 1296 (2001) (*Willst du mir Minne schencken… heilig dir in der Brust!* (Brünnhilde) (1' 57"))

Tristan und Isolde, Los Angeles, Shrine Auditorium, Act 2, abridged,[19] live broadcast, 14 November 1937

Tristan, Lauritz Melchior; Isolde, Kirsten Flagstad; King Marke, Emanuel List; Brangäne, Katherine Meisle; Melot, George Cehanovsky; Kurwenal, Julius Huehn; San Francisco Opera Orchestra

CD: Legato LCD-145-1 (1989)

1938

Die Meistersinger, Act 1, Prelude[20] (CS 028843-1, 028844-1)

Parsifal, Prelude (CS 028845-1, 028846-1A, 028847-1, 028848-1)

New York Philharmonic Symphony Orchestra, Carnegie Hall, 22 November 1938

78: Victor 11580-D/M-549 (*Die Meistersinger*); World's Greatest Music [*New York Post*/RCA Victor] SR 11(*Die Meistersinger*)/12/13(*Parsifal*); Music Appreciation S 106-107 (*Parsifal*)

CD: *New York Philharmonic 150th anniversary*: Pearl GEMM CDS 9922 (*Parsifal* only); Dante LYS 083 (1996); Grammofono 2000 AB 78711/12

1940

Die Walküre, Act 3, Ride of the Valkyries (XCO 27048-1)

Pittsburgh Symphony Orchestra, Syria Mosque, Pittsburgh, 14 March 1940[21]

78: Columbia 11987-D, sets M/MM-549; 11644-D

LP: Columbia ML-4054

CD: Dante LYS 044/45; *Wagner conductors on record*: Pearl GEMS 0024 (1998)

[19] The two cuts in the performance are in Scene 2, from *Dem Tage! Dem Tage!* (Tristan) to *dass nachtsichtig mein Auge wahres zu sehen tauge* (Tristan), and in Scene 3, from *Wozu die Dienste ohne Zahl* to *Da liess er's denn so sein* (King Marke). The performance lasted 59' 23".

[20] Helmbrecht lists a *Die Meistersinger*, Act 1, Prelude, with the Curtis Symphony Orchestra, recorded 13 February 1939 among the radio transcription recordings in the Library of Congress (*ibid*, pp. 28-29).

[21] Helmbrecht (p. 43) lists further "unreleased" recordings from this session: *Tannhäuser,* Venusberg Music; *Lohengrin,* Act 3 Prelude; *Tristan und Isolde,* Prelude and Liebestod; *Die Meistersinger* Act 1 Prelude; and *Siegfried,* Forest Murmurs. Kenneth Morgan, *Fritz Reiner, Maestro & Martinet* (Urbana and Chicago: University of Illinois Press, 2005) reports that several Wagner pressings from this recording session (held in the Carnegie Music Hall, according to him) were either damaged or suffered "distortion and bad intonation" and were therefore not released (p. 180). On 23 February 1940 Reiner had conducted an all-Wagner program at the Syria Mosque which included the *Ride*, performed "with stupendous effect": *Pittsburgh Press*, 24 February 1940, p. 10 (Ralph Lewando); another account reported the *Ride* had been "unfortunately marred by some faulty trombone playing": *Pittsburgh Post-Gazette*, 24 February 1940, p. 4 (D. S. Steinfirst); it "escaped by a hair's breath [*sic*] a nasty upset, but Reiner's good beat held on to a successful finale": *Pittsburgh Sun-Telegraph*, 24 February 1940, p. 5 (J. Fred Lissfelt).

1941

Tannhäuser, Venusberg Music (Paris version) (XCO 29487/90)[22]
Siegfried, Forest Murmurs (XCO 29494/5)
Die Meistersinger, Act 1 Prelude (XCO 29491/2)
Lohengrin, Act 3 Prelude (XCO 29483-1)
Pittsburgh Symphony Orchestra, Syria Mosque, Pittsburgh, 9 January 1941
78: Columbia 11520/1; X/MX-193 (*Tannhäuser*); 11580-D and 11984-D (*Die Meistersinger*); 11644-D and 11987-D (*Lohengrin*); 11580-D; 11985-D (*Siegfried*); M/MM-549 (*Lohengrin*, *Siegfried* and *Die Meistersinger*)
LP: Columbia ML-4054 (*Lohengrin*, *Siegfried* and *Die Meistersinger*)
CD: PSO CD 1 (*Lohengrin*); Dante LYS 044/45 (all excerpts)

Die Meistersinger, Act 3 Prelude, Dance of the Apprentices, Procession of the Mastersingers (XCO 29491/2, XCO 31907/8)
Lohengrin, Act 1 Prelude (XCO 31905/6)
Pittsburgh Symphony Orchestra, Pittsburgh, 15 November 1941
78: Columbia 11739-D (*Prelude*); 11790-D (*Dance* and *Procession*); X/MX-218 (all three *Meistersinger* excerpts); 11772-D, 11986-D, M/MM-549 (*Lohengrin*)
LP: Columbia ML-4054 (*Lohengrin*)
CD: Dante LYS 044/45 (both excerpts)

1945

Die Meistersinger, Act 1 Prelude, Act 3 Prelude, Dance of the Apprentices, Finale (the four excerpts follow one another in an arrangement without a break) (13' 30")
Cleveland Orchestra, Severance Hall, live performance, 7 January 1945
CD: *The Reiner Legacy: Concert and Broadcast Recordings from the Collection of Bruce Wellek – Vol. 3* [2003]

[1946][23]

1950

Lohengrin, Act 3, Prelude
Tannhäuser, Festmarsch (Entry of the Guests)
RCA Victor Orchestra, Manhattan Center, New York City, 19 October 1950
45: RCA ERA-185
CD: RCA Victor/BMG 61792 2 (1994); Sony 88697690522 (2010)

[22] A review of this recording in the *Pittsburgh Sun-Telegraph* mentioned it had been made at Syria Mosque "with Goddard Lieberson in charge. The same portable recording unit was used that went to South America with Leopold Stokowski and the All-American Youth Orchestra. It comprised some 20 trunk-loads of equipment and requires two sound engineers to manipulate. The actual recording was supervised by Vincent Liebler, Columbia's director of recording operations." (23 March 1941, Sect. V, p. 6, Michael Shaw Jr.)

[23] Reiner conducted the NBC Symphony Orchestra in the Prelude to *Die Meistersinger* in a broadcast of 29 December 1946, the only Wagner he performed in his NBC broadcast appearances: Mortimer H. Frank, *Arturo Toscanini: The NBC Years* (Portland, Oregan: Amadeus Press, 2002), pp. 328, 334, 337-338, 340.

Tristan und Isolde, New York, live broadcast, 9 December 1950, abridged[24]
Tristan, Ramon Vinay; Isolde, Helen Traubel; Kurwenal, Paul Schoeffler; Brangäne, Blanche Thebom; King Marke, Sven Nilsson; Melot, Hugh Thompson; Sailor's Voice, Thomas Hayward; Shepherd, Leslie Chabay; Steersman, Lawrence Davidson; Metropolitan Opera Chorus and Orchestra
CD: Walhall Eternity WLCD 0175 (2006)

Der fliegende Holländer, New York, live broadcast, 30 December 1950
Dutchman, Hans Hotter; Senta, Astrid Varnay; Erik, Set Svanholm; Daland, Sven Nilsson; Mary, Hertha Glaz; Steersman, Thomas Hayward; Metropolitan Opera Chorus and Orchestra
LP: Unique Opera Records UORC 149 (1973); Raritas OPR-5[25] (missing final bars of Act 1 and second part of Senta's ballad); Melodram 41 (4 LPs) (1989) (a recording of *Der Rosenkavalier*, 28 February 1953; side 8 contains Senta's ballad and the duet with Erik)
CD: Arlecchino ARLA 35/36 (ca. 1996) (missing final bars of Act 1 and second part of Senta's ballad); Naxos 8.110189/90 (2002) (no missing parts)

[1951][26]

1952

Die Meistersinger, New York, live broadcast, 22 March 1952, abridged[27]
Hans Sachs, Paul Schöffler; Eva, Walburga Wegner; Walther von Stolzing, Hans Hopf; Magdalene, Hertha Glaz; David, Richard Holm; Beckmesser, Gerhard Pechner; Pogner, Alois Pernerstorfer; Kothner, Herbert Janssen; Vogelgesang, Thomas Hayward; Nachtigall,

[24] The cuts in the performance were: in Act 2, Scene 2, from *Dem Tage! Dem Tage!* (Tristan) to *dass nachtsichtig mein Auge wahres zu sehen tauge* (Tristan), and in Act 3, Scene 1, from *Isolde noch im Reich der Sonne!* to *die selbst Nachts von ihr mich scheuchte?* (Tristan), and from *Muss ich dich so versteh'n* to *Zu welchem Los?* (Tristan)

[25] Side 6 of this set contains (although the label says *Wagner: Flying Dutchman Varnay / Svanholm / Hotter / Nilsson / Cond.: Reiner / 1950*) the love scene from *Tristan und Isolde*: Tristan, Ramon Vinay; Isolde, Astrid Varnay; Brangäne, Herta Glaz; Chicago Symphony Orchestra, Fritz Reiner, 12 January 1953 according to the accompanying booklet. These details are, however, incorrect: in a letter to the author the Chicago Symphony Orchestra has said that Ramon Vinay and Herta Glaz never performed with the Orchestra, and Astrid Varnay only once, and that was not in Wagner. Nor did the three singers ever appear together in those roles at the Metropolitan Opera. Helmbrecht writes (p. 50) that it is "probably from 1950–51 Metropolitan Opera season rec. Jan. 12, 1953" [*sic*], but there was no performance on that date (or on Jan. 12, 1950, 1951, 1952). The recording is not included in Hunt's *Hungarians in Exile*. The claim that the recording is of Reiner is dubious.

[26] Helmbrecht lists a *Meistersinger* Prelude, NBC Symphony Orchestra, recorded on 12 August 1951 among the radio transcription tapes in the Library of Congress (pp. 28–29).

[27] The cuts in this performance were: in Act 2, scene 6: from *O ha! Wollt mich beim Wahne fassen?* (Sachs) to *daß ich mich darnach richt* (Beckmesser), from *Zwar wenig Regel…* (Sachs) to *mit dem Hammer auf den Leisten halt ich Gericht* (Sachs), from *Sachs! Seht* (Beckmesser) to *um die Jungfrau zu frei'n* (Beckmesser); in Act 3, scene 2 (Sachs/Walter), from *Mein Freund! Das grad ist Dichters Werk* (Sachs) to *wie faß ich da den Unterschied?* (Walter), from *Das nenn ich mir einen Abgesang!* (Sachs) to *ein Sternenheer im Lorbeersbaum* (Walter); in scene 3 (Sachs/Beckmesser), from *Und seht nur, wir mir's ergeht…* to *mit dem besieg ich jed' Hinderniss* (Beckmesser); in scene 4 (Sachs/Eva), from *Nun schau, ob dazu mein Schuh geriet?…* to *Wo Teufel er jetzt nur wieder steckt!* (Sachs); and in scene 5 (Preislied), from *Abendlich dämmernd* (Walter) to *Fahret fort, und schließt!* (Sachs).

Algerd Brazis; Ortel, Osie Hawkins; Zorn, Alessio De Paolis; Moser, Gabor Carelli; Eisslinger, Emery Darcy; Foltz, Lorenzo Alvary; Schwarz, Lawrence Davidson; Night Watchman, Clifford Harvuot; Metropolitan Opera Chorus and Orchestra

CD: *The Art of Fritz Reiner Vol. 6*: Arlecchino ARLA A40-A43 (ca. 1996); Archipel ARPCD 0063-4 (2002)

1953

Die Meistersinger, New York, live broadcast, 10 January 1953, abridged[28]
Hans Sachs, Paul Schöffler; Eva, Victoria de los Angeles; Walther von Stolzing, Hans Hopf; Magdalene, Hertha Glaz; David, Richard Holm; Beckmesser, Gerhard Pechner; Pogner, Josef Greindl; Kothner, Mack Harrell; Vogelgesang, Thomas Hayward; Nachtigall, Algerd Brazis; Ortel, Osie Hawkins; Zorn, Alessio De Paolis; Moser, Joseph Folmer; Eisslinger, Emery Darcy; Foltz, Lorenzo Alvary; Schwarz, Lawrence Davidson; Night Watchman, Clifford Harvuot; Metropolitan Opera Chorus and Orchestra
CD: Walhall Eternity WLCD 0273 (2009)

1955

Die Meistersinger, Vienna, live broadcast, 14 November 1955
Hans Sachs, Paul Schöffler; Eva, Irmgard Seefried; Walther von Stolzing, Hans Beirer; Magdalene, Rosette Anday; David, Murray Dickie; Beckmesser, Erich Kunz; Pogner, Gottlob Frick; Kothner, Hans Braun; Vogelsang, Karl Terkal; Nachtigall, Eberhard Wächter; Ortel, Harald Pröglhöf; Zorn, Erich Majkut; Moser, William Wernigk; Eisslinger, Fritz Sperlbauer; Foltz, Ljubomir Pantscheff; Schwarz, Adolf Vogel; Night Watchman, Frederick Guthrie; Vienna State Opera Chorus and Orchestra

CD: Melodram CDM 47083 (4 CDs) (1990); Orfeo C 667 054 L (4 CDs) (2005); Walhall Eternity WLCD 0163 (4 CDs) (2006)

1957

A Faust Overture
Chicago Symphony Orchestra, Orchestra Hall, broadcast performance, 31 October 1957

CD: *The Reiner Legacy: Concert and Broadcast Recordings from the Collection of Bruce Wellek – Vol. 31* [2003]

[28] The cuts in this performance were: in Act 1, scene 2, from *Der Kurze, lang und überlang Ton* (David) to *…sing ich die eitel Brot- und Wasserweiss'* (David); in Act 2, scene 6, from *O Eva! Eva! Schlimmes Weib* (Sachs) to *O ha! Tralalei! Tralalei! O he!* (Sachs), from *O ha! Wollt mich beim Wahne fassen?* (Sachs) to *daß ich mich darnach richt* (Beckmesser), from *Zwar wenig Regel…* (Sachs) to *mit dem Hammer auf den Leisten halt ich Gericht* (Sachs), from *Ich bin ja stumm!* (Sachs) to *" …um die Jungfrau zu frei'n"* (Beckmesser); in Act 3, scene 2, from *Mein Freund! Das grad ist Dichters Werk* (Sachs) to *ein Meisterlied: wie faß ich da den Unterschied* (Walther), and from *Das nenn ich mir einen Abgesang* (Sachs) to *"…statt Frucht ein Sternenheer im Lorbeerbaum."* (Walther); scene 3, from *Und seht nur, wie mir's ergeht* to *mit dem besieg ich jed' Hindernis* (Beckmesser); scene 4, from *Nun schau, ob dazu mein Schuh geriet?* to *Wo Teufel er jetzt nur wieder steckt!* (Sachs); scene 5, from *Wenn ihr die Kunst so hoch schon ehrt* to *die Kunst und ihre Meister ehrt!* (Sachs), from *Herr Merker! Sagt, wie geht's?* (Sachs) to *doch hoff ich auf Eure Popularität* (Beckmesser), from *Wie er dazu kam, mag selbst er sagen* to *fänd er gerechte Richter* (Sachs, with Meistersinger and Volk), from *Abendlich dämmernd* (Walther) to *Fahret fort, und schließt!* (Sachs), and from *Drum, denkt mit Dank Ihr dran zurück* to *lebt's nicht in deutscher Meister Ehr* (Sachs)

1958

Rienzi, Overture
Tristan und Isolde, Prelude and Liebestod
Parsifal, Act 3, Good Friday Music
Chicago Symphony Orchestra, Orchestra Hall, Chicago, 27 March 1958
(WBAI-FM tapes; the opening bars of the *Tristan* Prelude were missing)
LP: *Chicago Symphony Orchestra - From the Archives Volume III: Fritz Reiner*: CSO 873 (1988) (*Tristan* and *Parsifal*)
CD: *100th Birthday of Reiner*: CSO 88-2 (1988) (*Tristan* and *Parsifal*); CSO 96-2 (*Rienzi*); *The Art of Fritz Reiner - Volume 8*: Arlecchino ARLA 45 (ca. 1996) (all excerpts) (no missing opening bars from the *Tristan* Prelude)

1959

Die Meistersinger, Preludes to Acts 1 and 3, Dance of the Apprentices, and Procession of the Mastersingers
Götterdämmerung, Prologue, Siegfried's Rhine Journey and Funeral Music
Chicago Symphony Orchestra, Orchestra Hall, Chicago, 18 April 1959[29]
LP: RCA Victor LM/LSC-2441 (1960); ACL1-1278; LSC-5007 (*Meistersinger* Act 1 prelude only); *From Stock to Solti*: Limited Edition LP [Chicago Symphony Orchestra fund-raising marathon] DPL1-0213 (1976) (*Dance* and *Procession* only)
CD: RCA Victor/BMG 61792 2 (1994) and 63301; *Fritz Reiner: Great Conductors of the 20th Century*: EMI Classics 62866-2 (2004) (*Rhine Journey* only); Sony 88697690522 (2010)

1960

Lohengrin, Act 1 Prelude, live broadcast, 25 March 1960
Chicago Symphony Orchestra, Orchestra Hall, Voice of America transcription [WFMT production]
CD: CSO CD-96B/2; *The Reiner Legacy: Concert and Broadcast Recordings from the Collection of Bruce Wellek – Vol. 45* [2003]

1962

Siegfried Idyll
Chicago Symphony Orchestra, 31 January 1962 (WGN telecast 11 February 1962)
CD: *The Reiner Legacy: Concert and Broadcast Recordings from the Collection of Bruce Wellek – Vol. 24* (clipped version), *Vol. 28* (corrected version) [2003]

[29] Helmbrecht was unable to verify whether the *Ride of the Valkyries* was also recorded at this session.

17. Hans Richter conducts Wagner

When George Bernard Shaw attended a Richter concert in London in June 1891, he wrote that "there was a performance of the *Tannhäuser* overture which ought to have been phonographed as a model of correct and eloquent phrasing in the Pilgrim's March, and of consentaneous execution in the shakes and *tremolandos* of the Venusberg music. Such a model is badly wanted...."[1]

Unfortunately, neither then nor later, did anyone take the hint and record a performance of Richter, and "he never conducted a note of music for the growing gramophone industry."[2]

Richter had retired from England to Bayreuth shortly before the Gramophone Company made its first British orchestral recording of Wagner in London on 2 March 1912, *Die Meistersinger* Overture with Landon Ronald conducting the New Symphony Orchestra (6117ac and 6119ac, HMV 0817).

Another conductor, Percy Pitt, had worked with Richter to promote Wagner performances sung in English. After the conclusion of the 1908 *Ring* in English, both he and Richter came before the curtain to acknowledge the applause.[3] After the *Ring* had been repeated in January 1909, Pitt conducted an orchestra in recordings of two selections sung in English by Minnie Saltzmann-Stevens and Clarence Whitehill - *Seek not, O maiden* from *Die Walküre* (2812f, 12 February 1909, HMV 04041) and an excerpt from the Immolation scene from *Götterdämmerung* (2816f, 15 February 1909, HMV 03135).[4] He was later to assist Albert Coates in his recordings of the *Ring* in English in 1922.

[1] *World*, 24 June 1891, in *Shaw's music: the complete musical criticism in three volumes*, ed. Dan H. Laurence (New York: Dodd, Mead, 1981), vol. 2, p. 379

[2] Christopher Fifield, *True artist and true friend: a biography of Hans Richter* (Oxford: Clarendon Press, 1993), p. 324

[3] *The Star*, 4 February 1908, p. 1; *The Times*, 3 February 1908, p. 15

[4] re-issued in *Sänger auf dem grünen Hügel*: EMI 1C 181-30 669/78M (1976)

18. Anton Seidl conducts Wagner

Seidl made no recordings as a conductor or pianist.

It is a matter of speculation whether his style of conducting Wagner is reflected in the Wagner recordings made by his close associates, Victor Herbert (1859-1924) and Nahan Franko (1861-1930).

Victor Herbert was an Irish-born, German-trained, cellist who went to the United States in 1886 to join the Metropolitan Opera House Orchestra. He was principal cellist under Seidl in both opera and concerts. From 1889, he was Seidl's assistant conductor in the Brighton Beach concerts of the Seidl Society. He conducted various ensembles and bands. As conductor of the Pittsburgh Symphony from 1898 to 1904 he conducted many Wagner orchestral and vocal selections.[1] He made a few Wagner recordings for the Victor company in Camden between 1912 and 1919 with his own Victor Herbert Orchestra:

Lohengrin, Bridal March (C-12256-2) 28 June 1912 Victor 55048 (1st issue)
Träume (C-13340-1) 21 May 1913 Victor 55041 (both issues)
Tristan und Isolde, Liebestod (C-13360-3) 26 May 1913 Victor 55041 (1st issue)
Lohengrin, Bridal March[2] (C-19820-5) 21 May 1918 Victor 55048 (2nd issue)
Tristan und Isolde, Liebestod (C-13360-5) 29 April 1919 Victor 55041 (2nd issue)

Even making allowances for the dim sound in these early recordings, it is remarkable how the orchestra plays so sedately: the volume is subdued throughout. In the *Bridal March*, the music flows smoothly from note to note. There is nothing frantic or emphatic about the playing which sometimes afflicted orchestras trying to make an adequate impression in the acoustic recording process. The *Liebestod* is very sweetly played, and tender, with a *rallentando* before the climax. In *Träume*, a solo violin plays on a soft bed of pulsating accompaniment: a lovely dream that does not want to end. There just may be a trace of the subdued tone Seidl was noted for in his own accompaniments.

Nahan Franko was concertmaster of the Metropolitan Opera Orchestra from 1883. He first conducted at the Metropolitan Opera House at Seidl's Funeral Service on 31 March 1898 in a performance of Beethoven's *Dirge*. He made his opera debut when the Metropolitan Opera took *Lohengrin* to Houston, Texas on 4 November

[1] Joseph Horowitz, *Wagner Nights: An American History* (Berkeley, California: University of California Press, 1994), pp. 202-3n; Edward N. Waters, *Victor Herbert: A Life in Music* (New York: Macmillan Company, 1955), pp. 143, 595

[2] The label described this side (incorrectly) as the "Prelude to Act III."

1901. He conducted the work three times, all outside New York, and conducted no other Wagner opera. He did conduct occasional Wagner selections at concerts in the Opera House between 1899 and 1912, including the preludes to Acts 1 and 3 of *Die Meistersinger*, the overtures to *Rienzi* and *Tannhäuser*, the prelude to Act 1 of *Tristan*, the Entrance of the Gods into Valhalla from *Das Rheingold*, the Funeral March from *Götterdämmerung*, and accompanied a few vocal selections from these operas. In 1902 he made several Wagner recordings for Leeds & Catlin company with the Metropolitan Opera House String Orchestra.[3]

Die Meistersinger, Act 1, Prelude	8003
Rienzi, Overture	8004
Tristan und Isolde, Act 3, Liebestod	8006
Die Walküre, Magic Fire Music	8009
Der fliegende Holländer, Sailors' chorus	8010
Tannhäuser, Act 1, scene 4, "Hunting Horns"	8012
Lohengrin, Act 3, Introduction	8017

These were two-minute wax cylinders, so were necessarily abridged arrangements. They are also very rare, if they exist any longer at all.

[3] Claude G. Arnold, *A discography of the orchestra, 1898-1925/26: an encyclopaedia of orchestral recordings made by the acoustical process* (Toronto: St. Michael's College, University of Toronto, 1983), pp. 541-572 *passim* ("Wagner"); they are also listed in the appendix of Frederick P. Fellers, *The Metropolitan Opera on Record* (Westport: Greenwood Press, 1984), pp. 83-85, where the author comments: "We know of no one living who has heard any of them."

19. Richard Strauss conducts Wagner[1]

Works recorded, including excerpts:

Der fliegende Holländer: 1928
Tristan und Isolde: 1928

1928

Der fliegende Holländer, Overture
Berlin Philharmonic Orchestra
(1506 BM 1 and 1507 BM 1, 10 December 1928)[2]

78: Deutsche Grammophon/Polydor 66830; Brunswick 90120
LP: Heliodor 2548 736; *Great Conductors of the Bayreuth Festival 1928-1971*: DG 2721 113 (2 LPs) (1976); *Les grandes voix du Festival de Bayreuth – volume 1*: DG 410 854-1 (5 LPs) (1983) [gives date of recording as 1931]
CD: *Richard Strauss conducts*: Koch 3-7119-2 H1 (1991); *L'Heritage de Richard Strauss – Chef d'orchestre – Volume 4*: LYS 121 (1996); *Strauss conducts* Der Rosenkavalier: Dutton CDBP 9785 (2008)

Tristan und Isolde, Act 1, Prelude, with concert ending by Wagner
Berlin Philharmonic Orchestra
(1510 BM 1 and 1511 BM 1, 10 December 1928)

78: Deutsche Grammophon/Polydor 66832
LP: Heliodor 2548 736; [Bayerische Staatsoper München] ASTM 101 (7" LP) (1980)
CD: *Richard Strauss conducts*: Koch 3-7119-2 H1 (1991); *L'Heritage de Richard Strauss – Chef d'orchestre – Volume 4*: LYS 121 (1996); *100 Jahre Bayreuth auf Schallplatte – The Early Bayreuth Festival Singers 1876 - 1906*: Gebhardt JGCD 0062-12 (12 CDs) (2004); *Strauss conducts* Der Rosenkavalier: Dutton CDBP 9785 (2008)

[1] A complete Strauss discography by Peter Morse was published in *ARSC Journal*, vol. 9, no. 1 (1977), pp. 6-65, and vol. 9, nos. 2-3 (1979), pp. 210-15 (supplement)

[2] The date of the 1928 recordings is taken from Franz Trenner, *Richard Strauss: Chronik zu Leben und Werk* (Wien: Dr. Richard Strauss GmbH, 2003), p. 495 ("*11.00 Uhr Grammophon-Aufnahmen*"). 13 December appears in a number of other sources. However, Strauss was travelling to Magdeburg on this date (Trenner, *ibid*, p. 496). Strauss conducted a performance of *Tristan* in Berlin on 12 December 1928.

Inauthentic recordings

The following recordings have been *attributed* to Strauss by the producers of the respective records but are in fact not by him, as explained in the footnotes:

Parsifal, Act 3, Good Friday Scene, 1933
(from *Du salbtest mir die Füsse* to *es lacht die Aue!*)
Parsifal, Max Lorenz; Gurnemanz, Alexander Kipnis, Bayreuth Festival Orchestra

LP: *Historic Performances of* Parsifal *at Bayreuth*: Discocorp IGI-379 (1980);[3] *Richard Wagner: sein Werk in dokumentarischen Aufnahmen*: Acanta 40.23 502 (19 LPs) (1983) (includes only a shortened excerpt, from *Wie dünkt mich doch die Aue heut so schön*)

CD: *Max Lorenz Recital 1933-1957*: Myto MCD 934.88 (1994) (from *Wie dünkt mich doch die Aue heut so schön*) (no conductor is listed for the excerpt); *L'Heritage de Richard Strauss – Chef d'orchestre – Volume 4*: LYS 121 (1996)

Parsifal, Act 3, final scene: *Nur eine Waffe taugt*, 1933
Parsifal, Max Lorenz, Bayreuth Festival Orchestra

LP: *100 Jahre Bayreuth*: BASF HB 22 863-0 (4 LPs) (1976)[4]

Die Meistersinger, Act 1, Prelude, live performance,[5] 22 February 1944
Vienna Philharmonic Orchestra, Funkhaus, Grosser Sendesaal

CD: *Wiener Philharmoniker, Richard Strauss, 1944*: Deutsche Grammophon 435 333-2 (1991) (part of *150 Jahre Wiener Philharmoniker*: 435 321-2 (12 CDs) (1991)); *L'Heritage de Richard Strauss, Chef d'orchestre, Volume 4*: LYS 121 (1996)

[3] The Discocorp LP was reviewed by David Hamilton, "Misremembering Bayreuth," *High Fidelity*, vol 32 no. 4 (April 1982), p. 58; he identified Siegfried Wagner as the conductor, from his 1927 Bayreuth studio recording: Columbia L 2013/14, reissued in *Siegfried Wagner dirigiert Richard Wagner*: EMI 1C 147-30 647/48M (1976) and *Siegfried Wagner conducts Richard Wagner*: Trax TRXLP 112 (LP and CD) (1987-88). The excerpt on the Discocorp LP also includes Knappertsbusch conducting in Vienna on 10 November 1942, now on *Edition Wiener Staatsoper Live – Vol. 6*: Koch Schwann 3-1456-2 (1994).

[4] Hamilton (*ibid*) assumed this was Strauss conducting, but it was in fact Leopold Reichwein, at the Vienna State Opera on 4 April 1942, as became apparent when *Edition Wiener Staatsoper Live – Vol. 6*: Koch Schwann 3-1456-2 was published in 1994.

[5] This recording is not mentioned in Morse's discography. The Historical Archive of the Vienna Philharmonic initally confirmed to the author that the recording was by Strauss, but later conceded it could not be. Strauss conducted the *Meistersinger* Prelude only twice in Vienna: in 1895 with the Berlin Philharmonic, and in 1922 with the Vienna Philharmonic. He never conducted a performance of the complete *Meistersinger* in Vienna: Götz Klaus Kende, "Was Richard Strauss in Wien dirigierte," *Richard Strauss-Blätter*, New Series, no. 19 (June 1988), 29-41. Moreover, on 22 February 1944, the date given for the recording, Strauss was in Garmisch. At his 80th birthday concert in Vienna on 11 June 1944, a *Meistersinger* Prelude was conducted by Karl Böhm: Trenner, *ibid*, pp. 624, 626. Deutsche Grammophon has not replied to the author's correspondence on the issue. John Hunt in his discography of the Vienna Philharmonic, states that the recording was incorrectly described by DG as conducted by Strauss; he attributes it to Böhm at a concert otherwise conducted by Strauss on 17 February 1944 [*sic*, presumably a reference to the 11 June concert; there was none on 17 February according to Trenner, *ibid*, p. 624]: *Vienna Philharmonic Vol. 1* (London: John Hunt, 2000), p. 132. Raymond Holden includes a 1944 *Meistersinger* Prelude among Strauss's published recordings, but gives no precise date or label; he also lists a *Meistersinger* Prelude among a number of unpublished recordings Strauss made for Reichsender Wien between 12 and 15 June 1944: *Richard Strauss* (New Haven and London: Yale University Press, 2011), pp. 157, 230, 292 n111. Trenner does not list a *Meistersinger* Prelude at these sessions: *ibid.*, pp.626-7.

20. Arturo Toscanini conducts Wagner[1]

Works recorded, including excerpts:

A Faust Overture: 1935, 1938, 1941, 1946
Rienzi: 1938
Der fliegende Holländer: 1938, 1939, 1946
Tannhäuser: 1938, 1941, 1944, 1946, 1948, 1952, 1953, 1954
Lohengrin: 1936, 1938, 1941, 1946, 1948, 1951, 1953, 1954
Tristan und Isolde: 1932, 1934, 1938, 1941, 1942, 1944, 1951, 1952, 1953
Die Meistersinger von Nürnberg: 1936, 1937, 1946, 1951, 1952, 1953, 1954
Siegfried Idyll: 1936, 1946, 1952, 1953
Der Ring des Nibelungen:
  Die Walküre: 1932, 1938, 1941, 1944, 1946, 1947, 1948, 1951, 1952, 1953
  Siegfried: 1948, 1951, 1952, 1954
  Götterdämmerung: 1934, 1935, 1936, 1938, 1941, 1944, 1945, 1946, 1948, 1949, 1951, 1952, 1953, 1954
Parsifal: 1935, 1938, 1940, 1944, 1949, 1952

1932

Tristan und Isolde, fragments from a concert
Prelude (final 2' 05" only)
Liebestod (first 4' 20" only, ends after *soll ich atmen*, that is, just before the climax)

Die Walküre, Act 1, Scene 3, excerpt (13' 37")
from *Ein Schwert verhieß mir der Vater* to *glimmt nur noch lichtlose Glut* (Siegmund) (then a break, and continues at) *[Eine Waffe laß mich dir] weisen* (Sieglinde) to *siehe, der Lenz lacht in den Saal!* (Siegmund)

Elsa Alsen; Paul Althouse; Philharmonic-Symphony of New York, Metropolitan Opera House, live broadcast, 27 November 1933
LP: in *The Golden Age of Wagner*: The Golden Age of Opera EJS 444 (1968)[2]

[1] There is a large number of unpublished recordings of Toscanini extant, particularly from his later American years. "The Toscanini Legacy" in the New York Public Library, for example, includes 4,600 acetate discs of rehearsals and performances, broadcast or otherwise, 1,789 test pressings of released performances, 799 test pressings of unreleased performance, etc., etc.: see Don McCormick and Seth Winner, "The Toscanini Legacy", *ARSC Journal*, vol. 20, no. 2 (1989), pp. 182-190. Consistent with the practice followed elsewhere in this discography, only commercially released recordings are included here, whether "authorised" by the conductor, his recording company, or not. There are, in any case, no complete Wagner works among his known unpublished recordings, only further versions of the Wagner excerpts we already have on disc. I have included in footnotes references to broadcasts, mostly of NBC concerts, which have not yet appeared as commercially-available recordings. I have been assisted by John Hunt's, *3 Italian Conductors - 7 'Viennese' Sopranos - Discographies* (London: John Hunt, 1991) which includes many more issues of the recordings than listed here; Mortimer H. Frank's, *Arturo Toscanini: The NBC Years* (Portland: Amadeus, 2002); and Glen Gould's, *Toscanini Database* (www.laden-gould.com/toscanini/index.html, 2007).

[2] Toscanini's name does not appear on the label, and the recording is not listed in Hunt. The details

1934[3]

Götterdämmerung, Siegfried's Funeral Music
Vienna Philharmonic Orchestra, live performance, 26 August 1934[4]
LP: Arturo Toscanini Recordings Association ATRA 3008 (1979) (mislabelled "Siegfried's Rhine Journey"); Melodram 012 (5 LPs) (1980) (*Die Meistersinger*, Salzburg Festival, 1937)

Tristan und Isolde, Prelude and Liebestod[5]
Stockholm Philharmonic Orchestra, live performance, 2 December 1934
CD: *Royal Stockholm Philharmonic Orchestra: Great Recordings from the Archives*: IMG Artists RSPO 1000-2 (8 CDs) (2004)

1935

A Faust Overture, 3 and 5 June 1935
Parsifal, Prelude and Good Friday Music, 5 June 1935
Götterdämmerung, Siegfried's Death and Funeral Music, 5 June 1935
BBC Symphony Orchestra, Queen's Hall, London, live performances
LP: ATS 1008 (dated 5 June, but the same recording as EMI, without the applause)
CD: EMI CDH 7 63044 2 (1989)

1936[6]

Götterdämmerung, Dawn and Siegfried's Rhine Journey[7]
Philharmonic Symphony Orchestra of New York, Carnegie Hall, 8 February 1936
78: Victor 14007-B/14008; in set M-308; HMV DB 2860/61
LP: Camden CAL-375; RCA Victor AT 1074
CD: *Toscanini and the NYPSO 1926-36*: Pearl GEMM CDS 9373 (1989); *Toscanini Collection Vol. 66*: RCA 60318 (1992); Naxos 8.110843 (2001)

come from the record itself, and the notes to EJS 444 in Shaman et al., *EJS*.

3 There was also a broadcast in 1934 from Carnegie Hall (18 March) of Toscanini conducting the New York Philharmonic-Symphony Orchestra in the overture to *Der fliegende Holländer*.

4 There were no broadcasts, foreign or national, from Salzburg listed in *The Times* (London) on this date.

5 The sound quality of the original discs is very poor, so bad in fact that the Prelude is incomplete: the surface noise becomes so loud in the dying bars that the music becomes inaudible; the Liebestod rises unexpectedly, prematurely, from the hiss. There is 14' 34" of music in all.

6 In respect of his 1936 Victor records, Toscanini wrote at the time: "During the last few days, I let myself be persuaded to make a few records, after six years of refusing:" letter dated 11 April 1936 to Ada Mainardi in Harvey Sachs (ed. and trans.), *The Letters of Arturo Toscanini* (New York: Alfred A. Knopf, 2002), p. 198. He was not happy with the results: "I have heard Wagner records they are shameful for Victor[,] for musical experts who approved them [and] for me who should have trusted my own ears (stop) I am surprised they are already being sold I would like to warn the public not to buy them (stop) … I repeat once again Wagner records are shameful on any apparatus electrical or otherwise:" telegram to Bruno Zirato, early July, *ibid*, p. 206. Sachs suggests he may have heard them on inferior equipment. There was also in 1936 a broadcast from Carnegie Hall (29 April) of Toscanini conducting the Philharmonic Symphony Orchestra of New York in *Die Meistersinger*, Act 1 Prelude, *Siegfried Idyll*, *Tristan und Isolde*, Prelude and Liebestod, and *Die Walküre*, Ride of the Valkyries.

7 Toscanini performed his own arrangement of this piece.

Siegfried Idyll

Philharmonic Symphony Orchestra of New York, Carnegie Hall, 8 February 1936

78: Victor 14009/10, in set M-308; HMV DB 2920/21

LP: Camden CAL-309; RCA AT 1074

CD: *Toscanini and the NYPSO 1926-36*: Pearl GEMM CDS 9373 (1989); *Toscanini Collection Vol. 65*: RCA 60317 (1992); Naxos 8.110843 (2001)

Lohengrin, Act 3 Prelude

Philharmonic Symphony Orchestra of New York, Radio City, broadcast, 1 March 1936

LP: Toscanini Society ATS 1089

CD: *Toscanini: General Motors Concert*: Radio Years RY 46

Lohengrin, Act 1 Prelude, and Act 3 Prelude

Philharmonic Symphony Orchestra of New York, Carnegie Hall, 9 April 1936

78: Victor 14006 (Act 1) and 14007-A (Act 3); in set M-308; HMV DB 2920/21

LP: Camden CAL-375; RCA AT 1074

CD: *Toscanini and the NYPSO 1926-36*: Pearl GEMM CDS 9373 (1989); *Toscanini Collection Vol. 66*: RCA 60318 (1992); Naxos 8.110843 (2001)

Die Meistersinger, Salzburg, live broadcast,[8] 8 August 1936, excerpts

Act 1, almost complete (73' 30"), with three breaks and a loss of a few bars, until it fades out about 3 minutes before the end of the Act, at *Nicht weiter! Zum Schluss!* (Beckmesser)[9]

Act 3, scenes 1 to 3: from *Am Jordan Sankt Johannes stand* (David), the whole of Scene 2, and the orchestral beginning of Scene 3 (30' 59")

Act 3, scene 5: from *Das Lied, führwahr, ist nicht von mir* (Sachs) to the end of the opera (17' 27")

Hans Sachs, Hans Hermann Nissen; Veit Pogner, Herbert Alsen; Kunz Vogelgesang, Georg Maikl; Konrad Nachtigall, Rolf Telasko; Sixtus Beckmesser, Hermann Wiedemann; Fritz Kothner, Viktor Madin; Balthasar Zorn, Anton Dermota; Ulrich Eißinger, Eduard Fritsch; Augustin Moser, Hermann Gallos; Hermann Ortel, Alfred Muzzarelli; Hans Schwarz, Carl Bissuti; Hans Foltz, Karl Ettl; Walther von Stolzing, Charles Kullman; Eva, Lotte Lehmann; Magdalene, Kerstin Thorborg; David, Richard Sallaba; Nightwatchman, Carl Bissuti; Chorus of the Vienna State Opera; Vienna Philharmonic Orchestra

[8] *Die Meistersinger* was conducted by Toscanini at the 1936 Salzburg Festival on 8, 14, 18, and 22 August. The authors of the notes to UORC 257 (Shaman et al., *More EJS*, p. 178) write that only the portion of Act 1 appearing on UORC 257 was broadcast [in the United States, on 8 August]. They note further that, as only twenty-five minutes were broadcast, the producer, E. J. Smith, "obviously had access to the original European broadcast materials." Of broadcasts in Europe, the whole of the performance of 8 August was broadcast from Vienna (5-10.25 pm), and parts of it only from Radio-Paris (5-9 pm) and Oslo (5-7 pm). Act 2 on 14 August was broadcast from Warsaw (8.25-10.25 pm), and Act 3 on 22 August from London on BBC Regional (8.55-10.55 pm). The Rodgers & Hammerstein Archives of Recorded Sound in the New York Public Library holds a dub of the original source tape of the 8 August peformance, taken from Radio Hilversum in the Netherlands (*LT-10-7864), which contains excerpts from Act 3 only (55' 54", including applause). The Act 3 excerpts on Eklipse are dated 8 August. They appear to have had their origin in recordings given by Toscanini (or his son) to his editor and sound engineer at RCA, Richard Gardner, who in turn gave them to Richard Caniell, founder of the Immortal Performances Recorded Music Society, whence the tapes came for production on CD, without the Society's authorization.

[9] The *New York Times* reported that Act 1 lasted 77 minutes: 22 August 1936, p. 8. Of which performance this was is not clear.

LP: UORC 257 (1 LP) (1975) (Act 1 excerpts)
CD: Eklipse EKR 54 (1995) (Act 3 excerpts)

1937

Die Meistersinger, Salzburg Festival, live performances, August 1937[10]
Hans Sachs, Hans Hermann Nissen; Veit Pogner, Herbert Alsen; Kunz Vogelgesang, Georg Maikl; Konrad Nachtigall, Rolf Telasko; Sixtus Beckmesser, Hermann Wiedemann; Fritz Kothner, Viktor Madin; Balthasar Zorn, Anton Dermota; Ulrich Eißinger, Eduard Fritsch; Augustin Moser, Hermann Gallos; Hermann Ortel, Alfred Muzzarelli; Hans Schwarz, Carl Bissuti; Hans Foltz, Karl Ettl; Walther von Stolzing, Henk Noort; Eva, Maria Reining; Magdalene, Kerstin Thorborg; David, Richard Sallaba; Nightwatchman, Carl Bissuti; Chorus of the Vienna State Opera; Vienna Philharmonic Orchestra
LP: Melodram 012 (5 LPs) (1980)
CD: Melodram MEL 47041 (1989); Eklipse EKR 54 (1995); Andante AND 3040 (2003)

1938[11]

Der fliegende Holländer, Overture
NBC Symphony Orchestra, Studio 8H, New York, 26 February 1938, broadcast
LP: Toscanini Society ATS 116-7
CD: *Toscanini's Last Concert*: Hunt CDLSMH 34014 (1988) [a filler to the concert of 4 April 1954]; Arkadia MP 414

[10] The precise dates of recording are not entirely clear. *Die Meistersinger* was conducted by Toscanini at the 1937 Salzburg Festival on 5, 12 and 20 August. A recording of the complete performance of 5 August was made privately for Walter Toscanini on film using a Selenophone, a device invented by Dr. Oskar Czeija (see Donald McCormick, "The Toscanini Legacy," *ARSC Journal*, vol. 22, no.2 (1991)). The versions on Melodram and Eklipse both bear the date 5 August. Andante merely gives "August 1937". The reason for this is clear from the accompanying notes: the producer, Ward Marston, reports how he noticed when transferring the recording from film that an overlapping piece of music from Act 1 at the end of one reel and the beginning of another were of "definitely different performances." In addition to this recording on film, there were shortwave broadcasts in the United States on the NBC Red network on 5 August of portions of Act 1 (12.30-1.30 pm) and Act 2 (2.00-2.45 pm), and on the Blue network on 20 August of part of Act 3 (3.50-4.20 pm). Tapes of these broadcasts are in the Library of Congress, together with a complete recording on film without a precise date. The New York Public Library also holds a copy of the recording on film dated 5 August 1937. Of broadcasts in Europe, Act 2 (or part of it) of 5 August was broadcast from London on BBC National (7-8 pm); Acts 1 and 2 (or part of it) of 12 August were broadcast from Kalundborg (5-8 pm); and the complete performance of 20 August was broadcast from Vienna and Radio-Paris (5.05-10.30 pm). The complete performance also appeared on a number of "private" LPs not listed above, including [Roger W. Frank] MR-2993 and Private Edition-FWR 2003, [Mauro R. Fugette] MRF-16, Accord 150040, and Toscanini Society ATS 1062-6.

[11] There were also broadcasts in 1938 of Toscanini conducting the NBC Symphony Orchestra in *Die Meistersinger*, Act 1 Prelude (22 January), the *Siegfried Idyll* (12 February), *Parsifal*, Good Friday Music (12 November), *Die Meistersinger*, Act 3 Prelude (19 November), and the Lucerne Festival Orchestra in *Die Meistersinger*, Act 3 Prelude (25 August) and the *Siegfried Idyll* (25 August), and *Die Meistersinger*, Act 1 Prelude (27 August).

A Faust Overture
Lohengrin, Act 1 Prelude, and Act 3 Prelude
Tannhäuser, Overture (Dresden version)
Tristan und Isolde, Prelude and Liebestod
Parsifal, Act 1 Prelude
Götterdämmerung, Dawn and Siegfried's Rhine Journey
Die Walküre, Ride of the Valkyries
NBC Symphony Orchestra, Studio 8H, New York, broadcast, 5 March 1938
LP: Toscanini Society ATS 116-7

Rienzi, Overture
NBC Symphony Orchestra, Studio 8H, New York, broadcast,[12] 3 December 1938
LP: Music & Arts ATRA 3002
CD: Memories HR 4161/3; *Great Conductors of the Century: Arturo Toscanini*: EMI 6750724 (2004)

1939[13]

Der fliegende Holländer, Overture
NBC Symphony Orchestra, Studio 8H, New York, broadcast,[14] 25 February 1939
LP: Music & Arts ATRA 3002

1940

Parsifal, Symphonic synthesis (arranged by Toscanini) - Act 1 Prelude, Act 3 Good Friday Music, Act 2 Prelude, Act 3 Prelude, Act 2 Klingsor's Magic Garden, Act 3 Finale; NBC Symphony Orchestra, Studio 8H, New York, broadcast, 23 March 1940
LP: Music & Arts ATRA 3002
CD: Naxos 8.110838; Testament SBT 1382 (2006)

1941[15]

Lohengrin, Act 1 Prelude
Tannhäuser, Act 2, scene 1, *Dich teure Halle* (Elisabeth)
Die Walküre, Act 1, scene 3, *Ein Schwert verhiess mir der Vater* (Siegmund, Sieglinde)
Tristan und Isolde, Act 1 Prelude, with concert ending by Wagner
Götterdämmerung, Dawn music, Duet, Siegfried's Rhine Journey, Death and Funeral Music; Immolation scene

[12] Also broadcast from this concert were: *Siegfried*, Forest Murmurs, and *Götterdämmerung*, Siegfried's Funeral Music.

[13] There was also a broadcast in 1939 of Toscanini conducting the NBC Symphony Orchestra in *Die Meistersinger*, Act 1 Prelude on 7 January.

[14] Also broadcast from this concert were: *Tannhäuser*, Overture and Bacchanale and Act 3 Prelude, *Tristan und Isolde*, Prelude and Liebestod, *Die Walküre*, Ride of the Valkyries, and *Götterdämmerung*, Dawn and Siegfried's Rhine Journey.

[15] There were also broadcasts in 1941 of Toscanini conducting the NBC Symphony Orchestra in the *Parsifal* Prelude and Good Friday Music on 12 April, and the Good Friday Music on 6 December.

Elisabeth, Sieglinde, Brünnhilde, Helen Traubel; Siegmund, Siegfried, Lauritz Melchior
NBC Symphony Orchestra, Carnegie Hall, New York, broadcast, 22 February 1941
LP: RCA VIC 1369 (*Götterdämmerung* excerpts, except Immolation scene); Toscanini Society ATS 105 (Immolation scene)
CD: *Toscanini Collection Vol. 52*: RCA 60264 (1992) (*Die Walküre* only); Guild GHCD 2242/3 (2003) (whole concert); *Great Conductors of the Century: Arturo Toscanini*: EMI 6750724 (2004) (Immolation scene only)

Götterdämmerung, Act 3, Immolation scene
Brünnhilde, Helen Traubel; NBC Symphony Orchestra, Carnegie Hall, New York, 24 February 1941
78: RCA Victor M-978
LP: RCA VIC 1369
CD: *Toscanini Collection Vol. 53*: RCA 60304 (1992)

Götterdämmerung, Dawn music and Siegfried's Rhine Journey, Siegfried's Death and Funeral Music
NBC Symphony Orchestra, Carnegie Hall, New York, 17 March and 14 May 1941
78: RCA Victor set M-853; HMV DB 5994/96
LP: RCA AT 1082
CD: *Toscanini Collection Vol. 31*: RCA 60296 (1992) (Rhine Journey); *Toscanini Collection Vol. 53*: RCA 60304 (1992) (Death and Funeral Music)

Lohengrin, Act 1, Prelude
NBC Symphony Orchestra, Carnegie Hall, New York, 17 March and 6 May 1941
78: RCA Victor 11-88-7; set M-1074
LP: RCA AT 1082
CD: *Toscanini Collection Vol. 49*: RCA 60306 (1992)

A Faust Overture
NBC Symphony Orchestra, Studio 8H, New York, broadcast, 29 March 1941
CD: Naxos 8.110836/37 (2000)

Götterdämmerung, Siegfried's Death and Funeral Music
NBC Symphony Orchestra, Carnegie Hall, New York, 14 May 1941
78: RCA Victor M-853; HMV DB5994-6
LP: RCA AT 1082
CD: *Toscanini Collection Vol. 53*: RCA 60304 (1992); *Toscanini: Lauritz Melchior and Helen Traubel Sing Wagner*: Minerva MN A-32

1942[16]

[16] There was also a broadcast in 1942 (4 April) of Toscanini conducting the NBC Symphony Orchestra in the *Parsifal* Prelude and Good Friday Music.

Tristan und Isolde, Prelude and Liebestod
NBC Symphony Orchestra, Carnegie Hall, New York, 19 March 1942
CD: *Toscanini Collection Vol. 49*: RCA 60306 (1992) (Liebestod only); *Wagner Conductors on Record*: Pearl GEMS 0024 (1998)

[1943][17]

1944[18]

Parsifal, Prelude and Good Friday Music
NBC Symphony Orchestra, Studio 8H, New York, 9 April 1944, broadcast
CD: Naxos 8.110817 (with Mendelssohn, *Violin Concerto*, Heifetz)

Tannhäuser, Overture (Dresden version)
Götterdämmerung, Dawn and Siegfried's Rhine Journey
Tristan und Isolde, Prelude and Liebestod
Die Walküre, Ride of the Valkyries
NBC Symphony Orchestra and New York Philharmonic, Madison Square Garden, New York, broadcast, 25 May 1944
CD: Grammofono AB 78535/36 (1994)

1945[19]

Götterdämmerung, Siegfried's Death and Funeral Music
New York Philharmonic Orchestra, Carnegie Hall, New York, broadcast, 13 January 1945
LP: Toscanini Society ATS 1034/35
CD: AS Disc 600; LYS 547/48; Iron Needle IN 1335 (1996) ; Guild Historical GHCD 2368 (2010)

1946

Tannhäuser, Act 3 Prelude, original version
NBC Symphony Orchestra, Studio 8H, New York, broadcast,[20] 6 January 1946
LP: Toscanini Society ATS 1061; Music & Arts ATRA 3002

[17] In 1943 there were broadcasts of Toscanini conducting the NBC Symphony Orchestra in *Lohengrin* Act 3 Prelude, *Tristan und Isolde*, Prelude and Liebestod, *Die Meistersinger*, Act 1 Prelude (24 March), and *Die Meistersinger*, Act 3 Prelude, *Tannhäuser*, Overture and Baccanhale, *Tristan und Isolde*, Prelude and Liebestod, *Tannhäuser*, Overture and Baccanhale, and *Die Walküre*, Ride of the Valkyries (28 November).

[18] There was also a broadcast in 1944 of Toscanini conducting the NBC Symphony Orchestra in *Siegfried*, Forest Murmurs on 27 August.

[19] There was also a broadcast in 1945 of Toscanini conducting the NBC Symphony Orchestra in *Die Meistersinger*, Act 1 Prelude on 4 February.

[20] Also broadcast from this concert were: the *Siegfried Idyll*, *Die Meistersinger*, Act 1 Prelude, and *Götterdämmerung*, Dawn and Siegfried's Rhine Journey.

Die Meistersinger, Act 1 Prelude
Die Walküre, Ride of the Valkyries
Siegfried Idyll
NBC Symphony Orchestra, Carnegie Hall, New York, 11 March 1946
78: RCA Victor M-308 and HMV DB 6668-9 (*Siegfried Idyll*); RCA Victor 11-9385 (*Die Meistersinger*); RCA Victor M-1135 and HMV DB 6545-6 (*Die Walküre*)
LP: RCA Victor LCT 1116 (*Siegfried Idyll*); RCA Victor LM 6020 (*Die Meistersinger*); RCA AT 1082 (*Die Walküre*)
CD: *Toscanini Collection Vol. 31*: RCA 60296 (1992) (*Siegfried Idyll*); *Toscanini Collection Vol. 48*: RCA 60305 (1992) (*Die Meistersinger*); *Toscanini Collection Vol. 49*: RCA 60306 (1992) (*Die Walküre*)

Der fliegende Holländer, Overture
NBC Symphony Orchestra, Studio 8H, New York, broadcast, 31 March 1946
CD: Memories HR 4161/3; Testament SBT 1382 (2006)

Tannhäuser, Overture and Bacchanale (rehearsal) (7' 10")
La Scala Orchestra, Kunsthaus, Lucerne, July 1946
LP: *Toscanini in Luzern*: Relief 811/2

Die Meistersinger, Act 1 Prelude
Lohengrin, Act 1 Prelude, Act 3 Prelude
Tannhäuser, Overture and Bacchanale
La Scala Orchestra, Kunsthaus, Lucerne, broadcast,[21] 7 July 1946
LP: *Toscanini in Luzern*: Relief 811/2 (all except *Lohengrin*, Act 1 Prelude)
CD: Music & Arts CD-1027 (1998) (all except *Lohengrin*, Act 1 Prelude); APR 5538 (2000) (*Lohengrin* Preludes only)

A Faust Overture
NBC Symphony Orchestra, Studio 8H, New York, broadcast, 27 October 1946
LP: Toscanini Society ATS 1055-9 (1973)
CD: Memories HR 4161/3

A Faust Overture
NBC Symphony Orchestra, Carnegie Hall, New York, 11 November 1946
78: RCA Victor M 1135; HMV DB 6545-6
LP: RCA VIC 1247
CD: *Toscanini Collection Vol. 48*: RCA 60305 (1992)

Götterdämmerung, Dawn and Siegfried's Rhine Journey
NBC Symphony Orchestra, Studio 8H, New York, broadcast, 24 November 1946
CD: Naxos 8.110804 (with Beethoven, *Piano Concerto No. 3*, Myra Hess)[22]

[21] Toscanini also conducted La Scala Orchestra in a broadcast from the Venice Festival of *Die Meistersinger*, Act 1 Prelude on 3 September.
[22] Naxos give the date as 24 *December* 1946, and the place of recording as Rockefeller Center, New York.

1947

Die Walküre, Act 1, Scene 3 (*Ein Schwert verhieß mir der Vater* to end of the act)[23]
Sieglinde, Rose Bampton; Siegmund, Set Svanholm
NBC Symphony Orchestra, Carnegie Hall, New York, broadcast, 6 April 1947[24]
LP: Edizione Lirica EL 004 (2 LPs);[25] HRE 5004; Fonit Cetra ARK 12; *Svenska WAGNER – sångare*: SR Records SRLP 1406 (1983) (*Siegmund heiss ich* only)
CD: Guild GHCD 2242/43 (2003) (rehearsal excerpt only, ca. 20 mins)
Rehearsals for the above on 4, 5 and 6 April 1947:
LP: *Arturo Toscanini Pove con l'Orchestra NBC*: CLS ARPCL 22019 (1981) (ca. 24 mins)
CD: Myto MCD 90316 (2 CDs) and 053.H104 (2 CDs) (2005) (ca.153 mins)

1948

Lohengrin, Act 3 Prelude
Tannhäuser, Overture and Bacchanale
Siegfried, Forest Murmurs
Götterdämmerung, Dawn and Siegfried's Rhine Journey
Die Walküre, Ride of the Valkyries
NBC Symphony Orchestra, Studio 8H, New York, telecast, 20 March 1948
DVD: Testament SBDVD 1003 (2005)

Tannhäuser, Overture (Dresden version)
NBC Symphony Orchestra, Studio 8H, New York, telecast, 4 December 1948
LP: Toscanini Society ATS 1061
CD: Memories HR 4161/3
DVD: Testament SBDVD 1004 (2005)

1949[26]

Götterdämmerung, Dawn and Siegfried's Rhine Journey
Parsifal, Prelude and Good Friday Music
NBC Symphony Orchestra, Carnegie Hall, New York, 22 December 1949
78: RCA Victor DM 1376 and HMV DB 21270-2 (*Parsifal*)
LP: RCA Victor LM 6020

[23] There are four excisions from this scene, amounting to about 37 seconds, caused when the original transcription discs were changed; missing are (1) *traf mich abends ihr Schein* (Siegmund) (about 6 secs.); (2) *[was je] ich gelitten in grimmigem Leid, was je mich geschmerzt in Schande und Schmach* (Sieglinde) (about 11 secs.); (3) *deutlich und klar: als mein Auge dich sah, warst du mein [Eigen]* (Sieglinde) (about 8 secs); and (4) *[Doch] dem so stolz strahlte das Auge, wie, Herrliche, hehr dir es strahlt, der war – Wälse genannt* (Siegmund) (about 12 secs).

[24] Also broadcast from this concert was: *Parsifal*, Prelude and Good Friday Music.

[25] Coupled with the abridged Act 2 of *Die Walküre* conducted by Reiner in San Francisco, 13 November 1936.

[26] There were also broadcasts in 1949 of Toscanini conducting the NBC Symphony Orchestra in *Götterdämmerung*, Dawn and Siegfried's Rhine Journey (26 February); and *Götterdämmerung*, Dawn and Siegfried's Rhine Journey, Death and Funeral Music, *Die Walküre*, Ride of the Valkyries, and *Parsifal*, Prelude and Good Friday Music (17 December).

CD: *Toscanini Collection Vol. 48*: RCA 60305 (1992) (*Parsifal*); *Toscanini Collection Vol. 49*: RCA 60306 (1992) (*Götterdämmerung*)

[1950][27]

1951

Lohengrin, Act 1 Prelude, Act 3 Prelude
NBC Symphony Orchestra, Carnegie Hall, New York, 22 October 1951
LP: RCA Victor LM 6020
CD: *Toscanini Collection Vol. 48*: RCA 60305 (1992)

Siegfried, Forest Murmurs
NBC Symphony Orchestra, Carnegie Hall, New York, 29 October 1951
78: HMV DB 6546
LP: RCA Victor LRM 7029
CD: *Toscanini Collection Vol. 53*: RCA 60304 (1992)

Die Meistersinger, Act 3 Prelude
NBC Symphony Orchestra, Carnegie Hall, New York, broadcast, 24 November 1951[28]
CD: Memories HR 4161/3

Die Meistersinger, Act 3 Prelude
NBC Symphony Orchestra, Carnegie Hall, New York, 26 November 1951
78: HMV DB 21564
LP: RCA Victor LM 6020
CD: *Toscanini Collection Vol. 48*: RCA 60305 (1992)

Lohengrin, Act 1 Prelude
Siegfried, Forest Murmurs
Tristan und Isolde, Prelude and Liebestod
Götterdämmerung, Siegfried's Death and Funeral Music
Die Walküre, Ride of the Valkyries
NBC Symphony Orchestra, Carnegie Hall, New York, telecast, 29 December 1951
CD: Memories HR 4161/3 (*Siegfried*, *Lohengrin* only)
DVD: Testament SBDVD 1006 (2005) (all excerpts)

1952[29]

Götterdämmerung, Siegfried's Death and Funeral Music
Die Walküre, Ride of the Valkyries

[27] There was a broadcast on 18 March 1950 of Toscanini conducting the NBC Symphony Orchestra in *Die Meistersinger*, Act 1 Prelude.

[28] Also broadcast from this concert were: *Götterdämmerung*, Dawn and Siegfried's Rhine Journey.

[29] There was also in 1952 a broadcast of Toscanini conducting the NBC Symphony Orchestra in the *Siegfried Idyll* on 26 July.

NBC Symphony Orchestra, Carnegie Hall, New York, 3 January 1952
LP: RCA Victor LM 6020 (*Götterdämmerung*); LM 7032 (*Die Walküre*)
CD: *Toscanini Collection Vol. 49*: RCA 60306 (1992) (*Götterdämmerung*); *Toscanini Collection Vol. 52*: RCA 60264 (1992) (*Die Walküre*)

Tristan und Isolde, Prelude and Liebestod
NBC Symphony Orchestra, Carnegie Hall, New York, 7 January 1952
LP: RCA Victor LM 6020
CD: *Toscanini Collection Vol. 52*: RCA 60264 (1992)

Siegfried Idyll
NBC Symphony Orchestra, Carnegie Hall, New York, 29 July 1952
LP: RCA Victor LM 6020
CD: *Toscanini Collection Vol. 52*: RCA 60264 (1992)

Die Meistersinger, Act 1 Prelude
Siegfried, Forest Murmurs
Siegfried Idyll
Götterdämmerung, Dawn and Siegfried's Rhine Journey
Parsifal, Good Friday Music
Götterdämmerung, Siegfried's Death and Funeral Music
Tristan und Isolde, Prelude and Liebestod
Die Walküre, Ride of the Valkyries
La Scala Orchestra, Milan, broadcast, 19 September 1952
CD: *Arturo Toscanini: The Farewell Concert at La Scala*: Istituto Discografico Italiano: IDIS 6524/25 (2007)

Tannhäuser, Overture and Bacchanale
NBC Symphony Orchestra, Carnegie Hall, New York, 8 November 1952
LP: Fonit Cetra DOC 17 (1981)
CD: Music & Arts ATRA 601; Melodram 47041 (1989) (*Die Meistersinger*, Salzburg, 1937); *Toscanini Collection Vol. 49*: RCA 60306 (1992); *In Memoriam Arturo Toscanini*: Tahra TAH 624/625 (2007)

1953

Die Meistersinger, Act 1 Prelude
NBC Symphony Orchestra, Carnegie Hall, New York, broadcast, 7 February 1953
LP: Fonit Cetra DOC 17 (1981)
CD: Memories 4161/3

Lohengrin, Act 3 Prelude
Siegfried Idyll
Götterdämmerung, Siegfried's Death and Funeral Music
Tristan und Isolde, Prelude and Liebestod

Die Walküre, Ride of the Valkyries
NBC Symphony Orchestra, Carnegie Hall, New York, broadcast, 7 March 1953
LP: Fonit Cetra DOC 17 (1981)
CD: Hunt CD 539; Music & Arts ATRA 601; Memories HR 4161/3

Tannhäuser, Act 3 Prelude, original version
NBC Symphony Orchestra, Carnegie Hall, New York, broadcast, 29 November 1953
CD: Hunt CD 539; Memories HR 4161/3; Testament SBT 1382 (2006)

1954

Lohengrin, Act 1 Prelude
Siegfried, Forest Murmurs
Götterdämmerung, Dawn and Siegfried's Rhine Journey
Tannhäuser, Overture and Bacchanale
Die Meistersinger, Act 1 Prelude
NBC Symphony Orchestra, Carnegie Hall, New York, 4 April 1954
LP: Music & Arts ATRA 3008 (includes rehearsal of *Tannhäuser* Overture on 3 April)
CD: *Toscanini conducts Wagner: The Final Concert - in Stereo*: Music & Arts ATRA 3008 (1984); *Toscanini's Last Concert*: Hunt CDLSMH 34014 (1988); Istituto Discografico Italiano IDIS 6500/1 (2007); Guild Historical GHCD 2369/70 (2011)

21. Richard Wagner conducts Wagner

Wagner was never recorded. That has not prevented some, however, from suggesting otherwise.

In 1973 the Nippon Phonograph Co. Ltd. in Tokyo issued an LP entitled *Wagner conducts "Tristan und Isolde" and Great Wagner Singers*: SAMP-3. It contained a recording of the Love duet from *Tristan* purporting to be Amalie Materna, Albert Niemann, and Marianne Brandt, with Wagner conducting "Rec. C. 1880". In fact it was a cylinder recording made by Lionel Mapleson at the Metropolitan Opera on 9 February 1903, with Lillian Nordica (Isolde), Ernestine-Schumann-Heink (Brangäne), Georg Anthes (Tristan), and the Metropolitan Opera Orchestra conducted by Alfred Hertz. It had been re-issued (as a Mapleson cylinder) by the International Record Collectors' Club (Bridgeport, CT) on both 78 rpm (No. 167) and LP (L-7006 and L-7032) long before the Japanese LP had been issued. Subsequently it appeared on *The Mapleson Cylinders - Complete Edition 1900 - 1904* issued in 1985 by the Rodgers and Hammerstein Archives of Recorded Sound of the New York Public Library (R&H 100). This lavish and scholarly production did not deter perpetuation and elaboration of the fiction by Grammofono 2000 in a 1997 CD set *Wagner conducts Wagner* (AB 78753/54). They added the claim that Wagner was conducting the Bayreuth Festival Orchestra. Inside the accompanying booklet, and beyond the eyes of any prospective purchaser, was the following WARNING: "The piece recorded at the beginning of CD number 1 is the recording of a fragment of the Love Duet from *Tristan und Isolde.* The recording, made on a cylinder dating around the year 1880, is thought to have been conducted by Richard Wagner himself. We present it in two versions (original and restored) and offer it to musicologists as material for consideration and examination so that they may decide upon its authenticity."

It was not outside the bounds of possibility that Wagner could have made a recording. Thomas Edison had developed his tin-foil phonograph in 1878, and it made its way to Europe in that year. Its commercial development, however, did not take place for some years, well after Wagner's death in 1883.[1]

Wagner was nevertheless not outside the thoughts of Thomas Edison. After he had been experimenting with his invention in 1878 by playing a recorded song backwards, he wrote: "the song is still melodious in many cases, and some of the strains are sweet and novel, but altogether different from the song reproduced in the right way. Wagner hasn't the monopoly of the music of the future – I'm going into the machine composing business."[2]

1 Roland Gelatt, *The fabulous phonograph, from tin foil to high fidelity* (Philadelphia, Lippincott, 1955), p. 33, 79; Frank Lewis Dyer and Thomas Commerford Martin, *Edison, his life and inventions* (New York, London: Harper & Brothers, 1929), p. 233

2 letter to William Preece, 19 February 1878, in Reese V. Jenkins, (ed.), *The papers of Thomas A. Edison*, 5 vols. (Baltimore: Johns Hopkins University Press, 1989-1998), vol. 4, p. 94

22. Bruno Walter conducts Wagner[1]

Works recorded, including excerpts:

A Faust Overture: 1923, 1939
Rienzi: 1926
Der fliegende Holländer: 1926, 1934, 1936, 1959
Tannhäuser: 1926, 1961
Lohengrin: 1926, 1944, 1959
Tristan und Isolde: 1925, 1944, 1947, 1953
Wesendonck Lieder: 1952
Die Meistersinger von Nürnberg: 1925, 1930, 1932, 1946, 1959
Siegfried Idyll: 1924, 1926, 1930, 1935, 1939, 1947, 1949, 1953, 1955, 1957, 1959
Der Ring des Nibelungen:
Die Walküre: 1935
Götterdämmerung: 1924, 1927, 1931, 1932, 1947, 1952
Parsifal: 1925, 1927, 1949, 1952, 1954, 1959

1923

A Faust Overture
Berlin Philharmonic Orchestra,[2] Berlin
(1519as, 71az, 72az, 1923)
78: Grammophon/Polydor 65955/56 (B20298-300) (1924)[3]
CD: Classic Press CPCD-2005 (2002) (Japan)

1924

Siegfried Idyll
Royal Philharmonic Orchestra, Columbia Petty France Studios, London
(AX782-1/83-1, AX789-2/90-2, 3 and 5 December 1924[4])

[1] Of recent discographies of Walter the online discography *Recorded Performances of Bruno Walter*, compiled by James Altena, Steven Reveyoso, and Erik Ryding, a supplement to Ryding and Pechefsky's *Bruno Walter: A World Elsewhere*, at www.bwdiscography.net (4 June 2010 version, accessed 1 May 2011) is the most comprehensive. There is also a discography of Walter in John Hunt's *Gramophone stalwarts: 3 separate discographies* (London: John Hunt, 2001).

[2] Altena *et al.* record this as performed by the "Berlin Staatskapelle." However, the labels of DG 65955/56 in the British Library have "Berlin Philharmoniker." Furthermore, in the Polydor (export) catalogue of 1926/1927, Polydor 65955/56 appeared under "The Philharmonic-Orchestra, Berlin | conducted by: Bruno Walter". The precise date or dates of the recording are not known.

[3] The fourth side (B20301 - 1517as) was the Prelude to Act 3 of *Carmen*.

[4] Dates and matrix numbers of the early English Columbia recordings have been taken from Ronald Taylor, *Columbia Twelve-Inch Records in the United Kingdom 1906-1930: A Discography* (Symposium Records:

78: Columbia L 1653/54; 67099-D/67100-D (1925)
CD: EMI BCD-22 (Japan)

Götterdämmerung, Siegfried's Rhine Journey
Royal Philharmonic Orchestra, Columbia Petty France Studios, London
(AX798-2, AX799-2, 7 December 1924)
78: Columbia LX 1636; 67084-D (1925)
CD: EMI BCD-22 (Japan)

1925

Die Meistersinger, Act 3, Prelude
Royal Philharmonic Orchestra, Columbia Petty France Studios, London
(AX878-2, 11 February 1925)
78: Columbia L 1651; 67086-D (1925)
CD: EMI BCD-22 (Japan)

Tristan und Isolde, Act 3, Liebestod (orchestral arrangement)
Royal Philharmonic Orchestra, Columbia Petty France Studios, London
(AX879-1, AX880-2, 11 February 1925)
78: Columbia L 1652; 67163-D
CD: *Bruno Walter Early Wagner Recordings*: VAI Audio 1114 (1995); *Bruno Walter Vol. 5 1925-35 Wagner:* Dante LYS 441/43 (1999)[5]

Parsifal, Act 2, Klingsor's Magic Garden and Flower Maidens, orchestral arrangement
Royal Philharmonic Orchestra, Columbia Petty France Studios, London
(WAX 1156-2, 1157-1, 1158-1, 1159-2, 22 November 1925)
78: Columbia L 1746/47, 67190-D/91-D
CD: *Bruno Walter The Early Electrical Recordings 1925-1932*: VAI Audio 1059 (1995); Dante LYS 441/43 (1999); on CD accompanying Michele Selvini's *Bruno Walter - La porta dell'eternità 1876-1932* (1999)

Parsifal, Act 1, Prelude (with concert ending)
Royal Philharmonic Orchestra, London
(WAX 1167-2, 1168-2, 1169-2, 25 November 1925)
78: Columbia L 1744/45, 67572-D/73-D
CD: VAI Audio 1114 (1995); Dante LYS 441/43 (1999)

East Barnet, Hertfordshire, 1994), *Addenda/Errata* (dated 1996, published 1998), Michael Smith and Frank Andrews, *Columbia Gramophone Company... A Discography of 78 RPM Records* (Ashburton: City of London Phonograph and Gramophone Society, 2002), and Michael Smith et al., *Columbia Graphophone Company Limited... 1930-1959: A Discography* (Wells-next-the-Sea: City of London Phonograph and Gramophone Society, 2007).

[5] In some cases, the VAI and LYS re-issues give incomplete or incorrect information on dates or matrix numbers. I do not point this out in each case (see preceding footnote); nor do I repeat the full titles of VAIA 1114, VAIA 1059, and LYS 441/3 entries after their first occurrence.

Parsifal, Act 1, Transformation scene
Royal Philharmonic Orchestra, Columbia Petty France Studios, London
(WAX 1170-2, 25 November 1925)
78: Columbia L 1745; M 68
CD: Dante LYS 441/43 (1999)

1926

Tannhäuser, Venusberg scene
Royal Philharmonic Orchestra, Columbia Petty France Studios, London
(WAX 1607-1, 1608-1, 1609-1, 1610-3, 14 June 1926)
78: Columbia L 1982/83; 67315-D/16-D
CD: VAI Audio 1114 (1995); Dante LYS 441/43 (1999)

Rienzi, Overture
Royal Philharmonic Orchestra, Columbia Petty France Studios, London
(WAX 1613-1, 1614-1, 1615-1, 1616-1, 15 June 1926)
78: Columbia L 1820/21; 9063/64M
CD: VAI Audio 1114 (1995); Dante LYS 441/43 (1999)

Der fliegende Holländer, Overture
Royal Philharmonic Orchestra, Columbia Petty France Studios, London
(WAX 2165-2[6], 2166-2, 2166-2, 17 November 1926)
78: Columbia L 1961/62; M 68
CD: VAI Audio 1059 (1994); Dante LYS 441/43 (1999)

Siegfried Idyll
Royal Philharmonic Orchestra, Columbia Petty France Studios, London
(WAX 2180-1, 2181-2, 2182-1, 2183-2, 2184-2, 19 November 1926)
78: Columbia M 68[7]
CD: Dante LYS 441/43 (1999)

Lohengrin, Act 3, Prelude
Royal Philharmonic Orchestra, Columbia Petty France Studios, London
(WAX 2201-2, 22 November 1926)
78: Columbia L 1962; M 68[8]
CD: VAI Audio 1059 (1994); Dante LYS 441/43 (1999)

1927

Parsifal, Act 1, Prelude (with concert ending)
Royal Philharmonic Orchestra, Scala Theatre, London

6 Smith and Andrews (see note 2 above) state that take 1 was issued, Taylor states take 2.
7 This recording was not issued in England, but was assigned the catalogue numbers L 1653/54 (four parts).
8 Smith and Andrews list this recording as WAX 1929-1, 20 September 1926.

(WAX 2720-1, 2721-2, 2722-2, , 19 May 1927)
78: Columbia L 1744/45R, 67572-D/73-D (1927),[9] M 68
CD: VAI Audio 1114 (1995); Dante LYS 441/43 (1999); on CD accompanying Michele Selvini's *Bruno Walter - La porta dell'eternità 1876-1932* (1999)

Parsifal, Act 1, Transformation scene
Royal Philharmonic Orchestra, Scala Theatre, London
(WAX 2723-2, 19 May 1927)
78: Columbia L 1745R; 67573-D; M 68
CD: VAI Audio 1114 (1995); Dante LYS 441/43 (1999); on CD accompanying Michele Selvini's *Bruno Walter - La porta dell'eternità 1876-1932* (1999)

Götterdämmerung, Siegfried's Rhine Journey
Royal Philharmonic Orchestra, Scala Theatre, London
(WAX 2758-2, 2759-2, , 20 May 1927)
78: Columbia L 1636R; 67315-D/67316-D
CD: VAI Audio 1059 (1994); Dante LYS 441/43 (1999)

1930

Siegfried Idyll
Symphony Orchestra, Central Hall, Westminster, London
(WAX 5584-2, 5585-1, 5586-1, 5587-1, 16 May 1930)
78: Columbia LX 79/80; X 26; 68011-D/12-D
CD: Dante LYS 441/43 (1999)

Die Meistersinger, Act 1, Prelude
Symphony Orchestra, Central Hall, Westminster, London
(WAX 5588-2, 5589-2, , 16 May 1930)
78: Columbia DX 86
CD: VAI Audio 1114 (1995); Dante LYS 441/43 (1999); *Great Conductors of the 20th Century – Bruno Walter*: EMI CZS 5 75133 2 (2 CDs) (2002)

1931

Götterdämmerung, Siegfried's Funeral Music
British Symphony Orchestra, Central Hall, Westminster, London
(WAX 6108-2, 6109-1, 22 May 1931)
78: Columbia LX 156; 68044-D
CD: VAI Audio 1059 (1994); Dante LYS 441/43 (1999)

[9] Note that the 1925 and 1927 recordings of the *Parsifal* Prelude and Transformation scene were issued under the same catalogue numbers, a fact overlooked by the author in *Parsifal on Record* (1992).

1932

Götterdämmerung, Siegfried's Rhine Journey
British Symphony Orchestra, Central Hall, Westminster, London
(CAX 6385-2, 6386-2, 15 April 1932)
78: Columbia LX 191; 68101-D
CD: *Wagner Conductors on Record*: Pearl GEMS 0024 (1998); Dante LYS 441/43 (1999)

Die Meistersinger, Act 3, Prelude
British Symphony Orchestra, Central Hall, Westminster, London
(CAX 6383-1, 6384-1, 19 April 1932)
78: Columbia LX 180; CX 43
CD: VAI Audio 1114 (1995); Dante LYS 441/43 (1999)

Die Meistersinger, Act 3, Dance of the Apprentices
British Symphony Orchestra, Central Hall, Westminster, London
(CAX 6398-2, 19 April 1932)
78: Columbia LX 232; CX 43
CD: VAI Audio 1114 (1995); Dante LYS 441/43 (1999)

1934

Der fliegende Holländer, New York, live performance of excerpts, 23 December 1934[10]
Act 1, scene 2: *Die Frist ist um … Ew'ge Vernichtung, nimm mich auf* (Holländer) (complete monologue, followed by applause) (10' 17")
Act 2, from the end of scene 2: *Ach, möchtest du, bleicher Seemann, sie finden!* (Senta) to the end of the Act (24' 00")
Holländer, Friedrich Schorr; Daland, Emanuel List; Senta, Dorothee Manski; Philharmonic-Symphony Orchestra of New York, Carnegie Hall, WABC broadcast
LP: side 6 of The Golden Age of Opera: EJS 487 (3 LPs) (1969)

1935

Siegfried Idyll
Vienna Philharmonic Orchestra, Musikvereinsaal, Vienna
(2VH 90-2, 91-1, 92-2, 93-2, 19 June 1935)
78: HMV DB2634/35
LP: [EMI] World Records SH 193/194 (with Mahler's *Symphony No. 9*)
CD: Dante LYS 441/43 (1999)

[10] Altena lists further recordings from this concert in a private collection: two excerpts from *Die Walküre*: the Ride of the Valkyries, and Brünnhilde's Immolation scene leading to a concert abridgement of the Magic Fire Music.

Die Walküre, Vienna, 20-21 June, Act 1, and 26 June 1935, Act 2, scenes 3 and 5
Brünnhilde, Ella Flesch; Siegmund, Lauritz Melchior; Sieglinde, Lotte Lehmann; Wotan, Alfred Jerger; Hunding, Emanuel List; Vienna Philharmonic Orchestra, Musikvereinsaal
(Act 1: 2VH 94-1, 95-2, 96-2, 97-1, 98-3A, 99-2, 100-1, 101-1, 102-2, 103-2, 104-2A, 105-2, 106-1A, 107-1, 108-1, 109-1; Act 2, scene 3: 110-2, 111-1, 112-1; scene 5: 113-2A, 114-2)

78: HMV DB2636-2643 (1936) (Act 1), DB3719-3728 (1940) (Act 2)[11]

LP: *Great Recordings of the Century*: HMV/Angel COLH 133 (1962) (Act 1); *Les Introuvables du Chant Wagnérien*: EMI 2902123 (6 LPs) (1984) (Act 2)[12]

CD: EMI Références CDH 7 61020 2 (1988) (Act 1); CDH 7 64255 2 (1992) (Act 2);[13] Naxos Historical 8.110250-51 (2 CDs) (2003);[14] *Great Recordings of the Century*: EMI 3 45832 2 (1 CD) (2006)[15]

1936[16]

Der fliegende Holländer, live performance of excerpts, 15 March 1936

Overture (10' 00")

Act 1, scene 2: *Die Frist ist um* to *Um ew'ge Treu' auf Erden [ist's getan!]* (Holländer) (7' 36")

[11] Act 2 comprised scenes 3 and 5 conducted by Walter, with the cast listed above, and the remaining scenes conducted by Bruno Seidler-Winkler in Berlin in 1938, with the Berlin State Opera Orchestra, and Hans Hotter as Wotan, Marta Fuchs as Brünnhilde, and Margarete Klose as Fricka. The set was also issued in Germany and Italy on Columbia and in the United States on Victor, and on many LPs not shown here.

[12] In the CD set of the same name (EMI CMS 7 64008 2, 4 CDs, 1991), Act 2 was *not* included.

[13] This disc contains all the music conducted by Walter (scenes 3 and 5) and the remaining parts conducted by Seidler-Winkler. A note in the booklet explains: "To accommodate these recordings on 1 CD, it has been necessary to engineer a small cut in the orchestral music that links scenes 3 and 4. Cuts elsewhere in the performance conducted by Bruno Seidler-Winkler were made at the time of the recording."

[14] This set contains the complete Acts 1 and 2 as recorded, that is, Act 1, and Act 2, scene 3 and 5 conducted by Walter and the remaining parts conducted by Seidler-Winkler. A note by the producer, Mark Obert-Thorn, comments: "A recent, much-acclaimed restoration of Act 1 was pitched a semitone sharp and did not join several of the sides correctly, while EMI's transfer of Act II cut music from the original recording in order to squeeze it onto a single CD. For these transfers, I have taken care to pitch each side accurately (the Vienna sides were recorded at a notably lower speed than the Berlin sides), and Act II is presented complete as recorded, with the small cuts in Wotan's narrative and the *Todesverklärung* scene [neither of which were conducted by Walter] that were present on the original release." Walter said on the subject: "I am not in favor of the practice of 'cutting,' at any rate unless with the utmost discretion… the ruthless snipping away of pages can only be disastrous…:" *Musical America*, 24 February 1923, p. 3.

[15] This disc contains only those portions conducted by Walter, but not everything he recorded, as the booklet explains: "On this disc, Act 1 and Scene 5 of Act 2 are heard complete and exactly as they were recorded in 1935. However, to accommodate all these famous recordings on one CD, it was necessary to make two cuts in the orchestral music that precedes and follows the third scene of Act 2. The interlude between scenes 2 and 3 has been cut by 1' 19", and scene 3 starts at the moment in the score when Siegmund and Sieglinde, fleeing from Hunding, appear on the mountain-top, where Siegmund urges his sister to rest. The scene ends at the point where Sieglinde, terrified by thoughts of what Hunding's hounds might do to Siegmund, faints into the arms of her brother and sinks unconscious into his lap. Part of the postlude to this scene (47") and the whole of the prelude to scene 4 (2' 07") have been cut."

[16] Walter is incorrectly listed as the conductor of *Walküre* excerpts in Vienna on 13 October 1936 in *Edition Wiener Staatsoper Live, Vol. 9*: Koch Schwann 3-1459-2 (1994), and in Altena. The Vienna Opera program and a review of the performance in the *Neues Wiener Journal* (14 October 1936, p. 11) reveal that the conductor was in fact Knappertsbusch.

Holländer, Hans Hotter, Concertgebouw Orchestra, Concertgebouw, Amsterdam, Radio Netherlands broadcast[17]

LP: Bruno Walter Society BWS 1014 (Japan)

CD: Wing WCD 1-2 (Japan); *Anthology of the Royal Concertgebouw Orchestra, Volume 1: 1936-1950*: Q Disc 97017 (13 CDs) (2002) (Overture only)

[1938][18]

1939

A Faust Overture

Siegfried Idyll

NBC Symphony, New York, broadcast, 8 April 1939

CD: *Bruno Walter Rarities 14*: AS Disc AS 414 (1989) (*Faust Overture* only); Serenade SEDR-2007 (Japan) (*Siegfried Idyll* only); *Bruno Walter with the NBC Symphony Orchestra: The Complete Concert, 8 April 1939*: Music & Arts CD-1241 (2010)

[1943][19]

1944

Lohengrin, Preludes to Acts 1 and 3

Tristan und Isolde, Prelude and Liebestod (orchestral arrangement)

New York Philharmonic, Carnegie Hall, New York, broadcast, 14 May 1944

CD: *Bruno Walter Rarities 14*: AS Disc AS 414 (1989)

1946

Die Meistersinger, Act 1, Prelude

New York Philharmonic, Carnegie Hall, concert performance, 11 September 1946[20]

[17] These were the first two items of a Wagner-Festival concert broadcast by Radio Hilversham from 8.15 to 9.10: *Algemeen Handelsblad*, 16 March 1936, p. 11.

[18] Walter conducted the *Tannhäuser* Overture & Bacchanale and the *Tristan* Prelude and Liebestod at a Lucerne Music Festival concert at Villa Tribschen on 29 August 1938. The concert was broadcast over shortwave radio on the NBC Blue network from 15.40 to 16.35, a recording of which (in four parts) is held in the Library of Congress: RWA 2427 A1-4. Only the *Tristan* Prelude survives complete, not having been interrupted by the recording process. At the end of the concert, Walter comes to the microphone to send his greetings to America.

[19] Altena lists a broadcast recording of Siegfried's Funeral Music from *Götterdämmerung* (New York Philharmonic, Carnegie Hall, 7 February 1943) in a private collection.

[20] The date is taken from James H. North, *New York Philharmonic: the authorized recordings, 1917-2005: a discography* (Lanham, Md.: Scarecrow Press, 2006), p. 59. The recording was made for the film *Carnegie Hall* first released in the United States on 28 February 1947. In his filmography in Ryding and Pechefsky, *Bruno Walter*, Charles Barber noted: "The sound track was prerecorded. The visual track was filmed later, and synchronized to audio playback. Nearly all of this film was made at Carnegie Hall in the summer of 1946" (p. 417). After 58" of the Prelude, the music fades and becomes background music for a backstage scene which ends at 2' 34", at which point the scene returns to the auditorium and the music plays uninterrupted to the end of the Prelude.

VHS: *Carnegie Hall* (1947): Bel Canto Society BCS-791; *Great Conductors, Vol. 2*: Bel Canto Society 6003 (the final 2' 48" only)
DVD: *Carnegie Hall* (1947): Bel Canto Society BCS-D0791 (2005)

1947

Siegfried Idyll
Boston Symphony, Symphony Hall, Boston, broadcast, 18 March 1947
CD: Wing WCD 58 (Japan)

Tristan und Isolde, Act 3, Liebestod (*Mild und leise*)
Götterdämmerung, Act 3, Immolation scene (*Starke Scheite*)
Isolde and Brünnhilde, Helen Traubel, Hollywood Bowl Orchestra, Hollywood, broadcast,[21] 8 July 1947
CD: *Helen Traubel in Concert*: Eklipse EKR 56 (1996)

1949

Parsifal, Act 1, Prelude (with concert ending)
Siegfried Idyll
Los Angeles Standard Symphony Orchestra, broadcast, 19 June 1949
CD: *Bruno Walter conducts Wagner*: Music & Arts CD-838 (1994)

1952[22]

Wesendonck Lieder, with Bruno Walter on *piano*
Götterdämmerung, Act 3, Immolation scene (*Starke Scheite*)
Parsifal, Act 1, Prelude (with concert ending)
Kirsten Flagstad, New York Philharmonic, Carnegie Hall, New York, broadcast,[23] 23 March 1952
LP: The Golden Age of Opera: EJS 167 (1959) (*Götterdämmerung* only); *Great conductors as soloists with the New York Philharmonic*: New York Philharmonic/WQXR 1985 radiothon special edition NYP 851/2 (2 LPs) (1985) (*Wesendonck Lieder* only); Bruno Walter Society RR-531 (*Wesendonck Lieder* and *Götterdämmerung*)
CD: *Bruno Walter Rarities 21*: AS Disc AS 422 (1989) (*Wesendonck Lieder* and *Parsifal*); *Bruno Walter conducts Wagner*: Music & Arts CD-838 (1994) (*Wesendonck Lieder* and *Götterdämmerung*); Historical Performers HP 27 (1994) (*Wesendonck Lieder*

[21] Altena lists further recordings from this concert in a private collection, namely, the *Siegfried Idyll*, Siegfried's Funeral Music from *Götterdämmerung*, *Die Meistersinger* Act 1 Prelude, and the Overture and Venusberg Music from *Tannhäuser*.

[22] Walter conducted a New York Philharmonic concert at Carnegie Hall on 28 December 1952 that included the *Siegfried Idyll*, the Prelude to *Parsifal*, and the Prelude and Liebestod from *Tristan*. The concert was broadcast on WCBS radio from 2:30 to 4:00 pm.

[23] Altena also lists a recording in a private collection of the Venusberg Music from *Tannhäuser* from this concert.

and *Parsifal*); NYP Special Editions NYP-9707 in set NYP-9701 (10 CDs) (1997) (*Götterdämmerung* only)

1953

Siegfried Idyll
New York Philharmonic, 30th Street Studios, New York, 5 January 1953
LP: Columbia CB-5 (1955); ML 5338 (1959); Philips GBL 5504 (G 03508 L)

Siegfried Idyll
Tristan und Isolde, Prelude and Liebestod
Isolde, Margaret Harshaw, Los Angeles Philharmonic
KFAC broadcast, Hollywood Bowl, Los Angeles, 14 July 1953
CD: *Bruno Walter Rarities 21*: AS Disc AS 422 (1989)[24]; Historical Performers HP 27 (1994)[25]

1954

Parsifal, Act 1, Prelude (with concert ending)
San Francisco Symphony, San Francisco, broadcast, 18 April 1954
LP: *Bruno Walter dirige Wagner, Mozart, Haydn*: CLS RPCL 2031 (1981)[26]

1955

Siegfried Idyll
Orchestre National de la Radio Télévision Française, Théâtre des Champs-Élysées, Paris, broadcast performance, 5 May 1955
LP: *The Bruno Walter Legacy*: The Bruno Walter Society [Japan] BWS 0S-7021-6-BS (6 LPs) (1980)[27]
CD: *Bruno Walter à Paris*: Tahra TAH 587-589 (3 CDs) (2006)

1957

Siegfried Idyll
New York Philharmonic, Carnegie Hall, New York, WCBS broadcast, 10 February 1957
CD: Wing WCD 27 (Japan); Music & Arts CD-1212 (2008)

[24] Gives the date as 1950 and spells the name of the soprano "Marshaw".
[25] Gives the date as 1952.
[26] Hunt also lists the Good Friday Music on this record – its cover and label state *Preludio e Venerdì Santo* – but it is not in fact on the record.
[27] This set contains extensive interview excerpts with Walter, and the reminiscences of others, with transcripts in English and Japanese.

1959

Der fliegende Holländer, Overture, 20 February 1959
Parsifal, Act 1, Prelude (with concert ending), and Act 3, Good Friday Music, 25 February 1959
Siegfried Idyll (and 45' of a rehearsal), 27 February 1959
Lohengrin, Act 1, Prelude, 27 February 1959
Die Meistersinger, Act 1, Prelude, 4 December 1959
Columbia Symphony Orchestra, American Legion Hall, Hollywood

LP: Columbia ML 5482 (1960) and MS 6149 (1960) (*Holländer, Parsifal*, and *Meistersinger*); Philips SABL 114 (1961) (*Holländer, Parsifal*, and *Meistersinger*); Columbia MS 6507 (1963) (*Lohengrin*, and *Siegfried Idyll* without rehearsal segment); *Bruno Walter's Wagner*: Columbia M3S 743 (MS 6865-6866, BM 11) (1966) (all excerpts and rehearsal segment); CBS 78252 (1976) (all excerpts, but without rehearsal segment)

CD: CBS MPK 45701 (1989) (without rehearsal segment and *Parsifal*); *Bruno Walter - The Edition - Wagner*: Sony SM2K 64456 (1994); *Bruno Walter - The original jacket collection*: Sony BMG SX13K 92460 (13 CDs) (2004)

1961

Tannhäuser, Overture and Venusberg Music
Columbia Symphony Orchestra; Occidental College Concert Choir, American Legion Hall, Hollywood, 24 and 27 March 1961

LP: Columbia MS 6507 (1963); *Bruno Walter's Wagner*: Columbia M3S 743 (MS 6865-6866, BM 11) (1966); CBS 78252 (1976); CBS Coronet KLCS 2800/1 (with Bruckner's *Symphony No. 4*)

CD: CBS MPK 45701 (1989); *Bruno Walter - The Edition - Wagner*: Sony SM2K 64456 (1994); *Bruno Walter - The original jacket collection*: Sony BMG SX13K 92460 (13 CDs) (2004)

23. Felix Weingartner conducts Wagner[1]

Works recorded, including excerpts:

Rienzi: 1939
Der fliegende Holländer:
Tannhäuser: 1939
Tristan und Isolde: 1913, 1939
Die Meistersinger von Nürnberg: 1934, 1935
Siegfried Idyll: 1938
Der Ring des Nibelungen:
    Die Walküre: 1914
    Götterdämmerung: 1934, 1936, 1939
Parsifal: 1936

1913

Tristan und Isolde, Act 3, Liebestod (orchestral arrangement[2])
Columbia Symphony Orchestra, New York
(36611-1, 19 February 1913)
    78: Columbia A 5464; D 17711; L 1086
    LP: *Felix Weingartner Conducts Concert Favorites*: Past Masters PM 12 (1977)

1914

Die Walküre, Act 3, Magic Fire Music
Columbia Symphony Orchestra, New York
(36914-1, 23 March 1914)
    78: Columbia A 5594
    CD: *Legendary conductors: Strauss - Weingartner - Fried*: Arbiter 140 (2004)

[1] The standard, comprehensive discography on Weingartner is by Christopher Dyment in his *Felix Weingartner* (Triad Press, Rickmansworth, 1976). For the most part, the recordings from the Vienna State Opera in the 1930s which he lists as being in a private collection have been subsequently released in the *Edition Wiener Staatsoper Live* series (1994-95). (There may be other recordings of Weingartner during this period in Vienna, but it appears to be impossible to verify: see the introduction to these discographies.) Dyment includes two performances believed to have been recorded at Covent Garden in 1939, *Parsifal* and *Tannhäuser*. No substantive information was then available about these recordings, nor has anything been forthcoming since Dyment's study. A later Weingartner discography was included in John Hunt's, *More 20th Century Conductors* (London: John Hunt, 1993); the Wagner recordings are listed on pp. 146-47 and include some subsequent LP re-issues.

[2] Hunt suggests this is sung by Lucille Marcel. The discography in Simon Obert and Matthias Schmidt, eds, *Im Mass der Moderne: Felix Weingartner – Dirigent, Komponist, Autor, Reisender* (Basel: Schwabe Verlag, 2009) likewise lists Marcel as soprano (p. 440). The recording is in fact an arrangement for orchestra only.

1934[3]

Götterdämmerung, Vienna, live performance, 30 September 1934, excerpts (ca. 10 mins)[4]

Prelude: *Mehr gabst du, Wunderfrau* to *oft Brünnhildes Gruss!* (Siegfried, Brünnhilde) (4' 49")

Act 2: *Schweig ich die Klage* to *tu' es der Glückliche gleich!*, (Siegfried, Hagen, Brünnhilde, Vassals) (4' 45")

Siegfried, Lauritz Melchior; Brünnhilde, Anny Konetzni; Hagen, Josef von Manowarda, Chorus and Orchestra of the Vienna State Opera

LP: *Wiener Staatsoper 1934*: Teletheater 120841 (1985) – the Act 2 excerpt is shorter (2' 53") than on the CD, ending at the Vassals's *zu schweigen die wütende Schmach!*

CD: *Edition Wiener Staatsoper Live - Vol. 1*: Koch Schwann 3-1451-2 (1994) the first excerpt is shorter (3' 34") than on the LP, ending at Siegfried's *als Weihegruss meiner Treu'!*

Die Meistersinger von Nürnberg, Vienna, live performance, 30 December 1934, excerpt (7' 18")

Act 3, *Prelude*, Vienna State Opera Orchestra

CD: *Edition Wiener Staatsoper Live - Vol. 1*: Koch Schwann 3-1451-2 (1994)

1935

Die Meistersinger von Nürnberg, Vienna, live performances, 10 February and 20 September 1935, excerpts (ca. 14 mins)[5]

Act 1: *Prelude* (8' 36"), 10 February

Act 2: *Jerum! Jerum!* (Sachs, with Beckmesser, Eva, Walther) (1' 46"), 20 September

Act 3: *Selig wie die Sonne* (Eva, Magdalene, Walther, David, Sachs) (3' 27"), 20 September

Eva, Lotte Lehmann; Magdalena, Kerstin Thorborg; Walter von Stolzing, Eyvind Laholm; David, William Wernigk; Hans Sachs, Ludwig Hofmann; Beckmesser, Hermann Wiedemann, Vienna State Opera Orchestra

LP: *Wiener Staatsoper 1935*: Teletheater 6.43333 (1985)

CD: *Edition Wiener Staatsoper Live - Vol. 1*: Koch Schwann 3-1451-2 (1994) (Act 1 Prelude), and *Vol. 12*: Koch Schwann 3-1462-2 (1994) (the other excerpts)

1936

Parsifal, Vienna, live performance, 11 April 1936, excerpts (ca. 19 mins)

Act 1: Prelude - from bar 8 to bar 43 (2' 40")

Act 1: *Nun achte wohl* to *Zum letzten Liebesmahle gerüs[tet Tag für Tag]* (Gurnemanz-Knights of the Grail) (1' 38")

[3] Hunt notes that fragments from a live recording of *Lohengrin* in December 1934 have been preserved. In this and other cases below, there is no indication where these recordings are preserved. See introduction to the Discographies for a note on Hermann May's recordings.

[4] The *Rheingold* of this cycle was conducted by Josef Krips, and *Walküre* and *Siegfried* by Clemens Krauss.

[5] Hunt notes that a *Meistersinger* Act 3 Prelude from 1935 has also been preserved; perhaps this was the 1934 Prelude (above) which was issued after his discography had been published.

Act 1: Grail Scene: 12 bars before *Nehmet hin mein Blut, Nehmet hin meinem Leib auf dass ihr mein' gedenkt* to 11 bars thereafter (Boys' chorus) (2' 53")
Act 1: Grail Scene: 19 bars before, and to the conclusion of, *Was stehst du noch da? Weisst du, was du sahest? Du [bist doch eben nur ein Tor!]* (Gurnemanz) (1' 22")
Act 2: from *Den Waffen fern* to *wann sie suchend dann dich ereilt* (Kundry) (50")
Act 2: from *Pein und Lachen* to *in dir entsündigt sein und erlöst!* (Kundry) (4' 18")
Act 3: from beginning of the Transformation Scene to *er birgt die heilige Kraft, der Gott [einst selbst zur Pflege sich gab.]* (Knights of the Grail) (4' 55")

Gurnemanz, Alexander Kipnis; Kundry, Kerstin Thorborg; Chorus and Orchestra of the Vienna State Opera
LP: The Golden Age of Opera EJS 460 (1969) (there are no breaks between the excerpts)
CD: *Edition Wiener Staatsoper Live - Vol. 1*: Koch Schwann 3-1451-2 (1994) (second Kundry excerpt only)

Götterdämmerung, Vienna, live performance, 11 September 1936, excerpt
Act 3: Immolation Scene: *Starke Scheite* to *selig grüsst dich dein Weib!* (13' 26") [6]
Brünnhilde, Kirsten Flagstad; Vienna State Opera Orchestra
LP: *Wiener Staatsoper 1936*: Teletheater 76.23589 (1987)
CD: *Edition Wiener Staatsoper Live - Vol. 1*: Koch Schwann 3-1451-2 (1994) (the recording has one break)

1938

Siegfried Idyll
London Philharmonic Orchestra, No. 1 Studio, Abbey Road
(CAX 8349-1, 8361-1, 8362-1, 8363-1, 6 and 8 October 1938)
78: Columbia LX801/802
LP: Columbia ML 4680 (1953); Bruno Walter Society IGI 336 (ca. 1973)
CD: *Felix Weingartner Complete Edition, Vol. 22*: Shinseido/EMI SGR8542 (1999); *Great Conductors of the 20th Century - Felix Weingartner*: EMI 75965-2 (2003)

1939[7]

Tannhäuser, Act 3, Introduction
(CLX 2165-1/66-1, 12 May 1939)
78: Columbia LX 868

Tristan und Isolde, Act 3, Prelude
(CLX 2167-1/68-1, 12 May 1939)
78: Columbia LX 866

[6] Hunt notes that a *Siegfried's Rhine Journey* from September 1936 has also been preserved.

[7] Not included under this year are three unpublished recordings listed by Dyment (see note 1 above): an unissued Columbia recording of the Venusberg Music from *Tannhäuser* (18 February 1939), and performances of *Parsifal* (2 May 1939) and *Tannhäuser* (4 May 1939) from Covent Garden. Hunt notes that recordings of excerpts from these operas at Covent Garden in 1939 have been preserved, with no further information.

Rienzi, Overture
(CLX 2188, 2193-1/94-1, 21 July 1939)
78: Columbia LX 860/61

Götterdämmerung
Siegfried's Rhine Journey
(CLX 2185-1/86-1, 21 July 1939)
78: Columbia LX 925

Siegfried's Funeral Music
(CLX 2195-2/96-2, 22 July 1939)
78: Columbia 71385-D

Orchestre de la Société des Concerts du Conservatoire de Paris, Théâtre Pigalle; cor anglais solo in *Tristan* excerpt, Roger Lamorlette

LP: Columbia ML 4680 (1953) (except *Rienzi*); *Felix Weingartner Conducts Concert Favorites*: Past Masters PM 12 (1977) (Siegfried's Funeral Music); *The Art of Felix Weingartner*: HMV RLS 717 (3 LPs) (1975) (except *Götterdämmerung* excerpts)

CD: *L'Héritage de Felix Weingartner*, vol. 1: Dante LYS 080 (1996) (*Rienzi*); Arkadia HP 629.1 (1996) (except *Götterdämmerung* excerpts); *Felix Weingartner Complete Edition, Vol. 22*: Shinseido/EMI SGR8542 (1999); *Great Conductors of the 20th Century - Felix Weingartner*: EMI 75965-2 (2003) (*Rienzi*)

Timings

I always had quiet pity for those people witnessing the performances in the Festspielhaus with a stopwatch in their hands...

Karl Muck, Bayreuth, 13 April 1931

Timings tell us little more about a work than when it began and when it ended. They do not tell us about what happened in between, especially the supremely important modifications of tempo on which the effectiveness of the drama and the vitality of the music depend. Overall timings are nevertheless suggestive. At the more extreme limits they do allow us to infer something about the spirit in which a work was performed.

Listed here are the timings of recordings of the major operas performed by the conductors considered in the discographies. There is also a selection of performances *in italics* which are *not* on record, and whose details have been taken, unless otherwise indicated, from Egon Voss, *Die Dirigenten der Bayreuther Festspiele* (Regensburg: Gustav Bosse Verlag, 1976). I have included some of the Preludes and Overtures, as well as the *Siegfried Idyll* and two sung excerpts from *Götterdämmerung*: the first part of Waltraute's narrative and Brünnhilde's Immolation.

On occasions Voss's timings of Bayreuth performances differ from those on a recording from the relevant year. In these cases, I have given the timing of the recording. In the case of complete works, timings have been rounded to the nearest minute. In other cases, I have endeavoured to be more precise, but absolute precision can be elusive: some recordings (or re-issues) of the same performance have slightly different timings because they were transferred to disc at different speeds. The more egregious cases are noted in the footnotes. Furthermore, in some cases, the actual timing of a piece differs from the timing given on a disc, or in the digital information of a track which may include silences at the beginning and end. The timings given here are only the *actual music recorded.*

TABLE 1. *A Faust Overture*

9' 32"	Coates, London Symphony, 1928
11'	*Mahler, Brooklyn, New York, 1910*[1]
11' 13"	Toscanini, NBC Symphony, November 1946

[1] This timing appears on a programme drawn up in Mahler's own hand for a concert he conducted in Brooklyn, New York, on 13 February 1910: La Grange, *Mahler, Vol. 4*, p. 665, n. 157. Whether it was the timing of the actual or the projected performance is not clear.

11' 16"	Walter, NBC Symphony, 1939
11' 30"	*Richter, London, 1879 and 1880*[2]
11' 50"	Toscanini, NBC Symphony, October 1946
12' 02"	Toscanini, NBC Symphony, 1941
12' 11"	Walter, Berlin Philharmonic, 1923-24
12' 20"	Toscanini, BBC Symphony, 1935
12' 25"	Toscanini, NBC Symphony, 1938
13' 58"	Reiner, Chicago Symphony, 1957

TABLE 2. *Siegfried Idyll*

14' 30"	*Richter, London, 1880*[3]
15'	*Mahler, Brooklyn, New York, 1910*[4]
15' 38"	Weingartner, London Philharmonic, 1938
15' 50"	Toscanini, New York Philharmonic, 1936
15' 59"[5]	Coates, Symphony Orchestra, 1922
16' 01"	Coates, London Symphony Orchestra, 1921
16' 04"	Toscanini, NBC Symphony, 1946
16' 11"	Walter, Los Angeles Standard Symphony, 1949
16' 16"	Walter, New York Philharmonic, 1953
16' 24"	Toscanini, NBC Symphony, 1953
16' 24"	Walter, New York Philharmonic, 1957
16' 25"	Walter, Orchestre National de la Radio Télévision Française, 1955
16' 36"	Furtwängler, Vienna Philharmonic, 1949
16' 43"	Walter, NBC Symphony, 1939
16' 45"	Walter, Vienna Philharmonic, 1935
16' 46"	Walter, British Symphony, 1930
16' 47"	Toscanini, La Scala, 1952
16' 52"	Walter, Royal Philharmonic, 1926
16' 54"	Walter, Los Angeles Philharmonic, 1953
17' 23"[6]	Toscanini, NBC Symphony, 1952
17' 28"	Muck, Berlin State Opera, 1929
17' 46"	Furtwängler, Turin Radio Symphony, 1952
17' 48"	Klemperer, Philharmonia, 1961
17' 53"	Walter, Royal Philharmonic, 1924

[2] Herbert Thompson, later music critic of the *Yorkshire Post*, attended Richter's London concerts and noted this timing in his diaries: quoted in Fifield, *True Artist and True Friend*, pp. 143 and 150

[3] This was the timing at a Richter concert in London, 27 May 1880, attended by Herbert Thompson, later music critic of the *Yorkshire Post*, and noted in his diary: quoted in Fifield, *True Artist and True Friend*, p. 150. Hugo Wolf heard a performance in Vienna which seems to have conformed to this timing: "under Richter's 'winged' baton [it] took on the form of a gallopade. Whoever in the audience was hearing this heavenly work for the first time could not possibly have had any proper impression of the lovely magical mood that pervades this fragrant tone painting like May sunshine." *The Music Criticism of Hugo Wolf*, ed. and trans., Henry Pleasants (New York: Holmes and Meier Publishers, 1979), p. 272. Richter rehearsed the orchestra for the first performance conducted by Wagner on Christmas morning 1870, and played among the musicians. Presumably he had a good idea of Wagner's intended tempo.

[4] See note 1 above. Mahler too was criticised for his "sense of haste:" see Mahler chapter, p. 259.

[5] The timings of both the Coates recordings are the sum of the four parts recorded, which is fractionally more than the music in the score.

[6] This is the timing of RCA VIC-1247. The timing of the same piece on AT-400 is 17' 43". The labels of both LPs give the timing as "17:30".

18' 10"	Klemperer, Berlin State Opera, 1927
18' 12"	Walter, Columbia Symphony, 1959
18' 45"	Knappertsbusch, Munich Philharmonic, January 1962
18' 58"	Knappertsbusch, Vienna Philharmonic, 1955
19' 05"	Knappertsbusch, Munich Philharmonic, November 1962
19' 13"	Klemperer, Vienna Philharmonic, 1968
19' 23"	Knappertsbusch, Vienna Philharmonic, 1963
19' 58"	Reiner, Chicago Symphony, 1962
20' 07"	Knappertsbusch, Cologne Radio, 1953
20' 09"	Knappertsbusch, North German Radio, 1963
20' 36"	Knappertsbusch, Vienna Philharmonic, Salzburg, 1949

TABLE 3. *Der fliegende Holländer*[7]

Mottl, Bayreuth, 1901	*147'*
Busch, Buenos Aires, 1936 [in three acts]	123'
Krauss, Bavarian Radio, 1944 [in three acts]	143'
Reiner, New York, 1950 [in three acts]	133'
Knappertsbusch, Bayreuth, 1955	151'
Böhm, New York, 1963 [in three acts]	132'
Böhm, New York, 1965 [in three acts]	124'
Klemperer, London, 1968 [in three acts, live][8]	150'
Klemperer, London, 1968 [in three acts, studio]	152'
Böhm, Bayreuth, 1971	134'

TABLE 4. *Der fliegende Holländer* – Overture

9' 17"	Böhm, Metropolitan Opera, 1965
9' 18"	Busch, Teatro Colón, 1936
9' 30"	Strauss, Berlin Philharmonic, 1928[9]
9' 45"	Böhm, Sächsische Staatskapelle, 1939
9' 48"	Muck, Berlin State Opera, 1928
9' 55"	Toscanini, NBC Symphony, 1939
9' 57"	Walter, Royal Philharmonic, 1926
9' 57"	Böhm, Metropolitan Opera, 1963
10' 00"	Walter, Concertgebouw, 1936
10' 23"	Böhm, Bayreuth Festival, 1971
10' 26"	Krauss, Bavarian State Opera, 1944
10' 26"	Toscanini, NBC Symphony, 1946
10' 30"	Reiner, Metropolitan Opera, 1950
10' 41"	Toscanini, NBC Symphony, 1938
10' 42"	Klemperer, Philharmonia, 1960
11' 02"	Walter, Columbia Symphony, 1959
11' 20"	Furtwängler, Vienna Philharmonic, 1949
11' 22"	Furtwängler, RAI Turin, 1952
11' 25"	Klemperer, New Philharmonia, 1968 (studio)

[7] The timings of complete operas are rounded to the nearest minute. In the cases where *Der fliegende Holländer* was performed in three acts, the timings exclude the applause and intervals.

[8] Klemperer's performances listed here, and under Overture, were of the original Dresden version.

[9] This is the timing of the transfer on Koch and Lys; on Dutton it is 9' 21".

11' 31"	Knappertsbusch, Bayreuth Festival, 1955
11' 33"	Böhm, Vienna Philharmonic, 1980
11' 41"	Klemperer, New Philharmonia, 1968 (live)

TABLE 5. *Tannhäuser*[10]

	Act 1	Act 2	Act 3
Mottl, Bayreuth, 1891	*70'*	*67'*	*60'*
Strauss, Bayreuth, 1894	*74'*	*68'*	*61'*
Toscanini, Bayreuth, 1930	*71'*	*69'*	*60'*
Bodanzky, New York, 1936	68'	63' (cut)	49' (cut)
Böhm, Naples, 1950	52' (cut)	66'	52'
Böhm, Naples, 1956	53'	66'	51'

TABLE 6. *Tannhäuser* - Overture[11]

12'	*Wagner, Dresden*[12]
12'	*Mahler, Brooklyn, New York, 1910*[13]
12' 40"	Kleiber, New York, 1946
12' 52"	Bodanzky, Staatskapelle Berlin, 1928
12' 52"	Busch, Staatskapelle Dresden, 1932
12' 52"	Böhm, Naples, 1956
13' 00"	*Richter, London, 1880*[14]
13' 18"	Kleiber, Berlin, 1927
13' 30"	Furtwängler, Caracas, 1954
13' 40"	Toscanini, NBC Symphony, 1948
13' 43"	Toscanini, NBC Symphony & New York Philharmonic, 1944
13' 46"	Furtwängler, Vienna, 1949
13' 52"	Furtwängler, Vienna, 1952
13' 55"	Furtwängler, Rome, 1951
14' 03"	Böhm, Naples, 1950
14' 18"	Böhm, Sächsische Staatskapelle, 1939
14' 33"	Toscanini, NBC Symphony, 1938
14' 33"	Böhm, Vienna, 1978-79
14' 42"	Klemperer, Philharmonia, 1960 (original 1845 version)
14' 47"	Bodanzky, New York, 1936
15' 39"	Muck, Berlin State Opera, 1928

[10] The differences in timings are partly explained by the different versions of the score performed.

[11] Recordings of the Overture with Bacchanale are not included.

[12] Wagner wrote: "I have been informed that the overture to *Tannhäuser*, which, when I conducted it at Dresden, used to last twelve minutes, now lasts twenty": *On Conducting* (1869), p. 21. Leo Blech recorded it with the Berlin Staatsoper Orchestra on 7 March 1929 in 12' 20" (HMV EJ 521).

[13] See note 1 above.

[14] Herbert Thompson attended a Richter concert on 3 June 1880 and noted this timing in his diary: quoted in Fifield, *True Artist and True Friend*, p. 150.

TABLE 7. *Lohengrin*[15]

	Act 1	Act 2	Act 3
Wagner, Vienna, 1876[16]	*75'*	-	-
Mottl, Bayreuth, 1894	*70'*	*82'*	*69'*
Bodanzky, New York, 1935	61' (cut)	66' (cut)	52' (cut)
Busch, Buenos Aires, 1936	56'	66' (cut)	51' (cut)
Furtwängler, Bayreuth, 1936	*61'*	*79'*	*65'*
Busch, New York, 1945	58' (cut)	-	-
Busch, New York, 1947	56' (cut)	68' (cut)	47' (cut)
Klemperer, Budapest, 1948	55'	65'	49'[17]
Kleiber, Copenhagen, 1953	-	-	58'[18]
Böhm, Vienna, 1965	60'	76'[19]	56'

TABLE 8. *Lohengrin* - Act 1 Prelude

7' 31"	Toscanini, NBC Symphony, 29 December 1951
7' 44"	Reiner, Pittsburgh Symphony, 1941
7' 53"	Toscanini, NBC Symphony, 17 March and 6 May 1941
8' 04"	Bodanzky, Berlin State Opera Orchestra, 1927
8' 05"	Toscanini, NBC Symphony Orchestra, 1954
8' 14"	Walter, New York Philharmonic, 1944
8' 19"	Klemperer, Budapest, 1948
8' 30"	Walter, Columbia Symphony, 1959
8' 30"	Reiner, Chicago Symphony, 1960
8' 31"	Toscanini, NBC Symphony, 22 October 1951
8' 33"	Busch, Buenos Aires, 1936
8' 35"	Toscanini, New York Philharmonic, 1936
8' 36"	Busch, New York, 1945
8' 45"	Busch, New York, 1947
8' 50"	Toscanini, NBC Symphony, 22 February 1941
9' 01"	Furtwängler, Lucerne, 1949
9' 05"	Toscanini, NBC Symphony, 1938
9' 05"	Furtwängler, Lucerne, 1947
9' 24"	Toscanini, La Scala Orchestra, 1946
9' 26"	Reiner, Philadelphia Orchestra, 1932[20]
9' 35"	Furtwängler, Berlin, 1930

15 After Liszt had conducted the first performance of *Lohengrin* in Weimar in 1850, Wagner responded to reports that it had lasted almost five hours: Act 1 should be "not much more than an hour", Act 2 "1¼ hours" and Act 3 "a little over an hour" [ie. ca. 3½ hours]: letter to Liszt from Zurich, 8 September 1850, in Wagner, *Selected Letters*, p. 214. Hans von Bülow conducted *Lohengrin* in Hannover on 21 September 1879 in 4¼ hours: Fischer, *Hans von Bülow in Hannover*, p. 49. Closer to the mark were Anton Seidl and Wilhelm Furtwängler. "Under Mr Anton Seidl's bâton, a performance of *Lohengrin* lasts only three hours and twenty minutes, excluding intermissions": Finck, *Wagner and His Works*, vol. 1, p. 250n. Furtwängler's 1936 performance in Bayreuth (above) amounted to three hours and twenty-five minutes. See also next note.

16 *fünf Viertelstunden* according to the *Wiener Abendpost*, 3 March 1876, p. 2; the newspaper did not report the timings of the other Acts.

17 This excludes the 2½ minute break when Klemperer walked out.

18 Only excerpts survived from Act 1 (scenes 2 and 3) and Act 2 (scenes 1 and 2).

19 This excludes 1' 15" of applause at the end of Ortrud's invocation (Christa Ludwig sang Ortrud).

20 There was some groove-jumping when this experimental disc was played in the Library of Congress.

9' 45"	Kleiber, Copenhagen, 1953
9' 45"	Böhm, Vienna, 1980
9' 48"	Furtwängler, Vienna, 1954
9' 52"	Klemperer, Philharmonia, 1960
9' 56"	Böhm, Vienna, 1965[21]
10' 02"	Bodanzky, New York, 1935
10' 15"	Mottl, Freiburg, 1907, piano roll[22]

TABLE 9. *Das Rheingold*

Richter, Munich, 1868 (rehearsal)[23]	*150'*
Richter, Bayreuth, 1876	*151'*
Mottl, Bayreuth, 1896[24]	*152'*
Mottl, London, 1900[25]	*150'*
Richter, London, 1907[26]	*140'*
Bodanzky, New York, 1930[27]	*135'*
Busch, Buenos Aires, 1935[28]	*133'*
Furtwängler, Bayreuth, 1936	*156'*
Bodanzky, Boston, 1937 (cut)[29]	131'
Kleiber, Buenos Aires, 1947	155'
Furtwängler, Milan, 1950	146'
Knappertsbusch, Bayreuth, 1951	*162'*
Furtwängler, Rome, 1953	155'
Krauss, Bayreuth, 1953	144'

21 The timing (9' 56") is taken from DG 2563 083 which has a recording date of 16.5.1965. The Prelude from the complete performance of the same date on Golden Melodram GM 1.0045 is 8' 37".

22 At a performance of the complete *Lohengrin* in London in May 1900, Mottl put "all the chronometer-critics into a flutter by taking ninety-four seconds longer – that, I am told, is the exact figure – over the *Lohengrin* Prelude than any other conductor has ever done in London:" *World*, 23 May 1900, p. 31 (Alfred Kalisch).

23 Wagner wrote of *Das Rheingold*: "the music, (it was reported) lasted exactly two hours and a half at rehearsals under a conductor whom I had personally instructed": *On Conducting* (1869), p. 21.

24 Nicolai Malko recalled: "Mottl's *Rheingold* took two hours, twenty-one minutes and some seconds [141']. Compared to the performance of Hans Richter, the difference was a matter of only several seconds:" Malko, *A Certain Art* (New York, 1966), p. 133. Malko studied with Mottl in Munich. It is not clear to which performances he was referring.

25 reported by the *Illustrated Sporting and Dramatic News*, 9 June 1900, p. 577

26 This is according to diary entries by Adrian Boult, 8 and 22 May 1907, who attended this London *Ring*: as appears in Fifield, *True Artist and True Friend*, p. 398.

27 There are conflicting reports of the length of this uncut *Rheingold* on 21 February 1930. The *New York Times* wrote: "The audience, or the prompt part of it, assembled at the hour of 2:30 and retired from the theatre at 4:45" [135'] (22 February 1930, p. 18, Olin Downes), whereas the *New York Journal* wrote of "two hours and thirty-five minutes of uninterrupted music" [155'] (22 February 1930, K. W.). Another uncut performance on 9 February 1937 was "round two hours and twenty minutes" [140'], according to the *New York Times*, 10 February 1937, p. 19 (Olin Downes).

28 Fritz Busch wrote to his brother from Buenos Aires on 19 August 1935: "It has amused me to note that each of my performances of *Das Rheingold*, played through without pauses, takes exactly 2 hours and 13 minutes. This seems to me proof of a sure sense of tempo and pace." Irene Busch Serkin, *Adolf Busch: Letters - Pictures – Memories*, trans. Russell Stockman (Walpole, New Haven: Arts & Letters Press, 1991), Vol. 2, p. 336. One newspaper reported after the first performance of "a two-and-a-quarter-hour piece:" *La Nación*, 17 August 1935, p. 13.

29 This timing is taken from the Guild CD set which recreated a single-act drama using parts of other recordings. The broadcast performance from Boston on 3 April 1937 had an intermission before Wotan and Loge descended into Nibelheim.

Knappertsbusch, Bayreuth, 1956	157’
Knappertsbusch, Bayreuth, 1957	154’
Knappertsbusch, Bayreuth, 1958	158’
Böhm, Bayreuth, 1965	*140’*
Böhm, Bayreuth, 1967	137’

TABLE 10. *Die Walküre*

	Act 1	Act 2	Act 3
Richter, Bayreuth, 1876	*62’*	*87’*	*70’*
Mottl, Bayreuth, 1896	*66’*	*92’*	*70’*
Richter, London, 1907[30]	*65’*	*80’ (cut?)*	*65’*
Bodanzky, New York, 1935	55’	-	-
Walter, Vienna, 1935	62’	-	-
Busch, Montevideo, 1936	55’	62’ (cut)	50’ (cut)
Furtwängler, Bayreuth, 1936	*65’*	*86’*	*67’*
Bodanzky, New York, 1937	-	77’[31]	58’[32]
Furtwängler, London, 1937	-	-	62’
Reiner, San Francisco, 1936	-	67’ (cut)	-
Kleiber, Buenos Aires, 1940	61’	67’ (cut)	54’ (cut)
Furtwängler, Milan, 1950	62’	80’ (cut)	65’
Knappertsbusch, Bayreuth, 1951	*65’*	*96’*	*72’*
Furtwängler, Rome, 1952	69’	-	-
Krauss, Bayreuth, 1953	62’	85’	65’
Furtwängler, Rome, 1953	68’	95’	71’
Furtwängler, Vienna, 1954	67’	93’	70’
Knappertsbusch, Bayreuth, 1956	64’	93’	72’
Knappertsbusch, Vienna, 1957	63’	-	-
Knappertsbusch, Bayreuth, 1957	65’	93’	73’
Knappertsbusch, Bayreuth, 1958	67’	94’	73’
Böhm, New York, 1960	62’	72’ (cut)	56’ (cut)
Knappertsbusch, Vienna, 1963	65’	-	-
Böhm, Bayreuth, 1965	61’	84’	65’
Böhm, Bayreuth, 1967	62’	84’	64’

TABLE 11. *Siegfried*

	Act 1	Act 2	Act 3
Richter, Bayreuth, 1876	*83’*	*77’*	*80’*
Mottl, Bayreuth, 1896	*81’*	*74’*	*81’*
Richter, London, 1907[33]	*85’*	*75’*	*70’ (cut?)*
Furtwängler, Bayreuth, 1936	*83’*	*72’*	*83’*
Bodanzky, New York, 1937	71’[34]	69’	63’ (cut)
Kleiber, Buenos Aires, 1938	59’ (cut)	-	-
Furtwängler, Milan, 1950	80’	74’	71’ (cut)
Knappertsbusch, Bayreuth, 1951	*84’*	*76’*	*85’*

30 See the footnote to Richter’s 1907 *Rheingold* above; presumably Act 2 was cut.

31 This is the length of the recorded music. Although there were no cuts in the performance, there were eleven short breaks as the recording discs were changed, and therefore a loss of a few bars on each occasion.

32 Likewise, there were eleven short breaks in Act 3 with a loss of a few bars on each occasion.

33 See the footnote to Richter’s 1907 *Rheingold* above.

34 *sic*: Acts 1 and 2 were uncut.

Krauss, Bayreuth, 1953	83'	75'	79'
Furtwängler, Rome, 1953	88'	88'	84'
Knappertsbusch, Bayreuth, 1956	87'	78'	85'
Knappertsbusch, Bayreuth, 1957	85'	76'	81'
Knappertsbusch, Bayreuth, 1958	89'	79'	85'
Böhm, Bayreuth, 1967	79'	69'	76'

TABLE 12. *Götterdämmerung*

	Prologue & Act 1	Act 2	Act 3
Richter, Bayreuth, 1876	*117'*	*64'*	*78'*
Mottl, Bayreuth, 1896	*116'*	*62'*	*76'*
Richter, London, 1907[35]	*110'*	*65'*	*75'*
Knappertsbusch, Munich, 1932[36]	*135'*	-	-
Bodanzky, New York 1936	96' (cut)	59'	63' (cut)
Kleiber, Buenos Aires, 1947	100' (cut)	50' (cut)	69'
Furtwängler, Milan, 1950	113'	60'	73'
Knappertsbusch, Bayreuth, 1951	128'	69'	82'
Furtwängler, Rome, 1952	–	–	82'
Krauss, Bayreuth, 1953	115'	67'	78'
Furtwängler, Rome, 1953	116'	68'	82'
Knappertsbusch, Munich, 1955	117'	67'	77'
Knappertsbusch, Bayreuth, 1956	122'	70'	80'
Knappertsbusch, Bayreuth, 1957	121'	70'	77'
Knappertsbusch, Bayreuth, 1958	123'	70'	81'
Böhm, Bayreuth, 1967	113'	61'	74'

TABLE 13. *Waltraute's narrative* (first part)
(Act 1, Scene 2: from *Seit er von dir geschieden* to *Ende der Ewigen Qual!*)

8' 09"	Kathryn Meisle, Bodanzky, Metropolitan Opera, 1936
8' 18"	Maartje Offers, Coates, London, 1927
8' 48"	Ira Malaniuk, Krauss, Bayreuth, 1953
9' 10'	Kerstin Thorborg, Furtwängler, Covent Garden, 1937
9' 13"	Kathryn Meisle, Reiner, New York Philharmonic, 1937
9' 30"	Margarete Klose, Furtwängler, Rome, 1953
9' 32"	Ira Malaniuk, Knappertsbusch, Munich, 1955
9' 43"	Elisabeth Höngen, Furtwängler, Milan, 1950
9' 43"	Jean Madeira, Knappertsbusch, Bayreuth, 1956
9' 50"	Maria von Ilosvay, Knappertsbusch, Bayreuth, 1957
9' 54"	Martha Mödl, Böhm, Bayreuth, 1967
10' 05'	Jean Madeira, Knappertsbusch, Bayreuth, 1958
11' 00"	Elisabeth Höngen, Knappertsbusch, Bayreuth, 1951

35 See the footnote to Richter's 1907 *Rheingold* above.

36 as reported in the *New York Times*, 28 August 1932, p. X4; no information on the other two acts

TABLE 14. *Brünnhilde's Immolation*
(Act 3, final scene: from *Starke Scheite* to *selig grüsst dich dein Weib!*)[37]

[10' 40'	Blech, Berlin, 1928 (Frida Leider)]
11' 14"	Bodanzky, New York 1936 (Marjorie Lawrence)
12' 06"	Walter, New York Philharmonic-Symphony, 1952 (Kirsten Flagstad)
12' 38"	Böhm, Bayreuth, 1967 (Birgit Nilsson)
12' 43"	Walter, Hollywood Bowl, 1947 (Helen Traubel)
13' 07"	Kleiber, Buenos Aires, 1947 (Astrid Varnay)
13' 14"	Weingartner, Vienna, 1936 (Kirsten Flagstad)
13' 35"	Furtwängler, Covent Garden, 1937 (Kirsten Flagstad)
13' 35"	Furtwängler, Milan, 1950 (Kirsten Flagstad)
13' 45"	Kleiber, Buenos Aires, 1948 (Kirsten Flagstad)
13' 45"	Knappertsbusch, Munich, 1955 (Birgit Nilsson)
13' 59"	Krauss, Bayreuth, 1953 (Astrid Varnay)
14' 15"	Furtwängler, London, 1950 (Kirsten Flagstad)
14' 16"	Toscanini, New York, 1941 (live) (Helen Traubel)
14' 20"	Furtwängler, London, 1948 (Kirsten Flagstad)
14' 26"	Knappertsbusch, Bayreuth, 1957 (Astrid Varnay)
14' 34"	Knappertsbusch, Bayreuth, 1956 (Astrid Varnay)
14' 40"	Furtwängler, Rome, 1953 (Martha Mödl)
14' 45"	Knappertsbusch, Bayreuth, 1958 (Astrid Varnay)
14' 56"	Furtwängler, London 1952 (Kirsten Flagstad)
14' 58"	Furtwängler, Rome, 1952 (Kirsten Flagstad)
15' 02"	Toscanini, New York, 1941 (studio) (Helen Traubel)
15' 13"	Knappertsbusch, Bayreuth, 1951 (Astrid Varnay)
16' 13"	Knappertsbusch, North German Radio, 1963 (Christa Ludwig)

TABLE 15. ***Tristan und Isolde***

	Act 1	Act 2	Act 3
Mottl, Bayreuth, 1886	*80'*	*75'*	*75'*
Richter, London, 1908[38]	*75'*	*65' (cut?)*	*70'*
Toscanini, Bayreuth, 1930	*90'*	*81'*	*80'*
Furtwängler, Bayreuth, 1931	*83'*	*75'*	*77'*
Bodanzky, New York, 1935[39]	77'	60' (cut)	60' (cut)
Reiner, London, 1936[40]	78'	64' (cut)	67' (cut)
Reiner, Los Angeles, 1937	-	59' (cut)	-
Bodanzky, New York, 1937	74'	57' (cut)	58' (cut)
Kleiber, Buenos Aires, 1938	77'	62' (cut)	64' (cut)
Busch, Buenos Aires, 1943	74'	57' (cut)	62' (cut)
Busch, New York, 1946	77'	57' (cut)	63' (cut)
Furtwängler, Berlin, 1947	-	73' (cut)	77'
Kleiber, Buenos Aires, 1948	78'	68' (cut)	66' (cut)

[37] The 1927 recording of Albert Coates and Florence Austral has not been included because it is incomplete (Lawrance Collingwood conducted the first 50") and is abridged.

[38] This is according to diary entries by Adrian Boult quoted in Fifield, *True Artist and True Friend*, p. 398; although Fifield cites the entries for 8 and 22 May 1907, presumably he had access to later entries.

[39] These timings are taken from the CDs; each of the Acts on LP is about one minute longer.

[40] These timings are taken from the EJS LPs which, in total (208:38), differ slightly from the transfers on VAI (211:13) and Naxos (210:14).

Knappertsbusch, Munich, 1950	80'	75'	70'
Reiner, New York, 1950	74'	58' (cut)	61' (cut)
Furtwängler, London, 1952	85'	87'	83'
Kleiber, Munich, 1952	82'	72' (cut)	75'
Böhm, New York, 1960	74'	62' (cut)	62' (cut)
Böhm, Bayreuth, 1962	77'	77'	73'
Böhm, Bayreuth, 13 August 1966	74'	71'	70'
Böhm, Bayreuth, 1966 [DGG]	75'	72'	71'
Böhm, Bayreuth, 1968	78'	75'	73'
Böhm, Bayreuth, 1969	76'	72'	70'
Böhm, Bayreuth, 1970	80'	77'	73'
Böhm, Orange, 1973	73'	64' (cut)	70'

TABLE 16. *Tristan und Isolde* - Prelude[41]

8' 56"	Coates, London, 1926
9' 28"	Böhm, Orange, 1973
9' 53"	Klemperer, Philharmonia, 1960
9' 54"	Knappertsbusch, Munich, 1950
9' 58"	Mottl, Freiburg, 1907, piano roll
10' 00"	Busch, New York, 1946
10' 10"	Walter, New York Philharmonic, 1944
10' 10"	Busch, Los Angeles, 1946
10' 11"	Toscanini, NBC Symphony, 1944
10' 13"	Toscanini, NBC Symphony, 1942
10' 15"	Toscanini, NBC Symphony, 1951
10' 19"	Toscanini, NBC Symphony, 1953
10' 22"	Krauss, London Symphony, 1949
10' 20"	Furtwängler, Berlin, 1930
10' 20"	Böhm, New York, 1960
10' 23"	Busch, Buenos Aires, 1943
10' 25"	Knappertsbusch, North German Radio, 1963
10' 25"	Böhm, Bayreuth, 13 August 1966
10' 32"	Walter, Los Angeles Philharmonic, 1953
10' 33"	Böhm, Bayreuth, 1966 [DGG]
10' 47"	Reiner, New York, 1950
10' 48"	Furtwängler, Stockholm, 1942
10' 52"	Furtwängler, Turin, 1952
10' 57"	Toscanini, La Scala, 1952
10' 57"	Furtwängler, Berlin, 1954
10' 57"	Böhm, Bayreuth, 1969
11' 01"	Furtwängler, London, 1952
11' 02"	Böhm, Bayreuth, 1962
11' 06"	Kleiber, Buenos Aires, 1948
11' 07"	Furtwängler, Berlin, 1938[42]

[41] Preludes recorded with the concert ending, by Klemperer (1927), Muck (1928), Strauss (1928), and Toscanini (1941), are not included.

[42] This recording has been reissued on a number of labels purporting to be Furtwängler in Bayreuth in 1931, but in those cases was transferred at a slightly faster speed, which accounts for different timings (ca. 10' 40") from the EMI transfer on CD (11' 07").

11' 09"	Böhm, Bayreuth, 1968
11' 13"	Bodanzky, New York, 1937
11' 13"	Böhm, Bayreuth, 1970
11' 15"	Toscanini, New York, 1938
11' 21"	Reiner, London, 1936
11' 22"	Bodanzky, New York, 1935
11' 23"	Furtwängler, London, 1950
11' 23"	Toscanini, NBC Symphony, 1952
11' 25"	Furtwängler, Turin, 1954
11' 27"	Kleiber, Munich, 1952
11' 47"	Böhm, Vienna, 1980
11' 51"	Furtwängler, Berlin, 1942
12' 10"	Klemperer, Vienna Philharmonic, 1968
12' 40"	Kleiber, Buenos Aires, 1938[43]

TABLE 17. *Die Meistersinger von Nürnberg*

	Act 1	Act 2	Act 3
Bülow, Munich, 1868	*77'*[44]	*?*	*?*
Richter, Bayreuth, 1888	*83'*	*61'*	*120'*
Mottl, Bayreuth, 1892	*82'*	*59'*	*115'*
Richter, London, 1907[45]	*75'*	*120'*[46]	*110'*
Busch, Bayreuth, 1924	*81'*	*60'*	*114'*
Muck, Bayreuth, 1925	*80'*	*59'*	*120'*
Bodanzky, New York, 1936	69' (cut)	49' (cut)	103' (cut)
Toscanini, Salzburg, 1936	*77'*[47]		
Toscanini, Salzburg, 1937	78'	57'	115'
Böhm, Dresden, 1939	-	-	111'[48]
Furtwängler, Bayreuth, 1943[49]	-	61'	-
Böhm, Vienna, 1944	81'	60'	125'
Knappertsbusch, Vienna, 1950	85'	60'	120'
Reiner, New York, 1952	85'	53' (cut)	98' (cut)
Knappertsbusch, Bayreuth, 1952	87'	65'	122'
Reiner, New York, 1953	75" (cut)	49' (cut)	97' (cut)
Knappertsbusch, Munich, 1955	82'	64'	118'
Reiner, Vienna, 1955	80'	58'	118'
Böhm, New York, 1959	67' (cut)	49' (cut)	97' (cut)
Knappertsbusch, Bayreuth, 1960	87'	67'	123'
Böhm, Bayreuth, 1964	77'	59'	117'
Böhm, Bayreuth, 1968	78'	59'	111'

[43] The first bar and a half are missing from the recording.

[44] The *New York Times* reported that Act 1 of Toscanini's *Meistersinger* at the 1936 Salzburg Festival had lasted 77 minutes, "exactly the time taken by von Bülow at the first performance in Munich and several minutes less than the average German performance." (22 August 1936, p. 8).

[45] See the footnote to Richter's 1907 *Rheingold* above.

[46] *sic*, as it appears in Fifield, *True Artist and True Friend*, p. 398, but presumably an error in the transcription from Boult's diary.

[47] Only 73' 30' of Act 1 survives on record. *The New York Times* reported that Act 1 lasted 77 minutes: see the note under von Bülow's performance above.

[48] Only Act 3 was recorded. The timing is taken from the Profil CDs; the timing of the Pearl CDs is 113'.

[49] The timings for the recorded Act 1 (70') and Act 3 (111') are not included because the complete recorded performance does not survive. Voss gives 79' for Act 1 and 120' for Act 3.

TABLE 18. ***Die Meistersinger von Nürnberg***
Act 1 *Prelude* [timing to point of entry of chorus, ie, excluding concert endings]

8'	*Wagner, Mannheim, 1871*[50]
8' 06"	Coates, London, 1921
8' 16"	Reiner, Pittsburgh, 1941
8' 20"	Muck, Berlin State Opera, 1927
8' 28"	Böhm. New York, 1959
8' 30"	Knappertsbusch, Munich, 1955
8' 34"	Furtwängler, Berlin, 1942[51]
8' 31"	Coates, London, 1926
8' 36"	Weingartner, Vienna, 1935
8' 41"	Toscanini, NBC Symphony, 1946
8' 42"	Reiner, New York, 1938
8' 42"	Walter, New York, 1946[52]
8' 43"	Bodanzky, New York, 1936
8' 45"	Böhm, Toronto Symphony, 1965
8' 47"	Böhm, Sächsische Staatskapelle, 1939
8' 50"	Walter, Symphony Orchestra, 1930
8' 53"	Bodanzky, Berlin State Opera Orchestra, 10 September 1927
8' 53"	Knappertsbusch, Vienna, 1950
8' 54"	Toscanini, NBC Symphony, 1954
8' 54"	Böhm, Bayreuth, 1964
8' 55"	Toscanini, Salzburg, 1936
8' 58"	Toscanini, La Scala, 1952
9'	*Richter, London, 1879*[53]
9'	*Mahler, Brooklyn, New York, 1910*[54]
9' 01"	Toscanini, Salzburg, 1937
9' 02"	Furtwängler, Bayreuth, 1943
9' 03"	Toscanini, NBC Symphony, 1953

[50] Wagner took "a few seconds over eight minutes" at a concert in Mannheim on 20 December 1871 according to Richard Pohl who was present: *Richard Wagner: Studien und Kritiken: Gesammelte Schriften über Musik und Musiker: Band 1* (Leipzig: Schlicke, 1883), p. 199. Felix Mottl, who was in Bayreuth to assist in the 1876 Festival rehearsals, wrote in his diary for 26 May: "Wagner says that the *Meistersinger* prelude will without exception be taken too slowly. It should be a strong march tempo": Krienitz, "Felix Mottls Tagebuchaufzeichnungen", *Neue Wagner-Forschungen*, I, (1943), p. 196. Leo Blech's two recordings of the Prelude with the Berlin State Opera Orchestra were 7' 58" (1926 studio recording EJ 43, in Symposium 1232 & 1233 - 1998) and 7' 34" (1932 filmed performance, in *Great Conductors*: Dreamlife DLVC 8092, 2008). Albert Coates is closest to Wagner's timing.

[51] The timing (8' 34") is taken from the filmed version on *"The Reichsorchester" - The Berlin Philharmonic and the Third Reich*: Arthaus Musik 101 453 (DVD); the timing of the same film on *Great Conductors of the Third Reich:* Bel Canto Society VHS BCS-0052 is 9' 04"; the audio transfer on *Wilhelm Furtwängler and the Berlin Philharmonic: Wartime Archives of the RRG (1942-1944)*: Tahra FURT 1034/39 is 9' 10".

[52] This is the timing of the soundrack of Bruno Walter conducting in the 1947 film *Carnegie Hall*; during part of the Prelude (namely, for 1' 40"), the music becomes background music to a scene enacted backstage; for some of this period the music is so faint that it is not possible to tell whether the Prelude is continuous or interrupted.

[53] This timing was noted in the diary of Herbert Thompson, later music critic of the *Yorkshire Post*, who attended a Richter concert on 12 May 1879: quoted in Fifield, *True Artist and True Friend*, p. 143. Presumably the timing included an additional couple of seconds for the concert ending.

[54] See note 1 above.

9' 03"	Böhm, Bayreuth, 1968
9' 04"	Furtwängler, Berlin, 1949
9' 09"	Klemperer, Los Angeles Philharmonic, 1934
9' 10"	Klemperer, Budapest, 1949
9' 12"	Kleiber, Berlin, 1926
9' 18"	Reiner, New York, 1953
9' 20"	Böhm, Vienna, 1944
9' 20"	Reiner, Vienna, 1955
9' 25"	Toscanini, La Scala, 1946
9' 30"	*Richter, London, 1880*[55]
9' 30"	Furtwängler, Vienna, 1949
9' 36"	Knappertsbusch, Bayreuth, 1952
9' 42"	Böhm, Tokyo, 1977 (dress rehearsal)
9' 45"	Reiner, Chicago, 1959
9' 45"	Knappertsbusch, Bayreuth, 1960
9' 46"	Knappertsbusch, Berlin, 1959
9' 47"	Böhm, Tokyo, 19 March 1975
9' 47"	Böhm, Vienna, 1978-79
9' 51"	Klemperer, Turin, 1956
10' 00"	*Levi, Karlsruhe*[56]
10' 00"	Reiner, New York, 1952
10' 03"	Walter, Columbia Symphony, 1959
10' 43"	Knappertsbusch, Munich, 1962
10' 45"	Klemperer, Philharmonia, 1960
10' 55"	Klemperer, Vienna Philharmonic, 1968
11' 53"	Knappertsbusch, North German Radio, 1963

TABLE 19. *Parsifal*

	Act 1	Act 2	Act 3
Levi, Bayreuth, 1882	*107'*	*62'*	*75'*
Mottl, Bayreuth, 1888	*106'*	*67'*	*82'*
Seidl, Bayreuth, 1897	*108'*	*64'*	*87'*
Muck, Bayreuth, 1901	*116'*	*67'*	*83'*
Toscanini, Bayreuth, 1931	*126'*	*72'*	*90'*
Strauss, Bayreuth, 1933	*106'*	*64'*	*78'*
Furtwängler, Bayreuth, 1936	*112'*	*63'*	*77'*
Busch, Buenos Aires, 1936	97' (cut)	52' (cut)	61' (cut)
Bodanzky, New York, 1938[57]	102'	-	67'
Knappertsbusch, Berlin, 1943	-	-	76'
Furtwängler, Milan, 1951[58]	*101'*	*65'*	*72'*
Knappertsbusch, Bayreuth, 1951	118'	73'	82'
Knappertsbusch, Bayreuth, 1952	113'	71'	79'
Krauss, Bayreuth, 1953	103'	59'	70'
Knappertsbusch, Bayreuth, 1954	116'	71'	81'

55 Fifield, *ibid*, p. 150 (concert of 10 May 1880)

56 Pohl, *Richard Wagner*, 1883, p. 199. No date given, but presumably 6 February 1869 when Pohl attended Levi's performance of the complete work (*ibid*, pp. 154-158).

57 Add to the timings for this performance approximately two minutes for Act 1 and one minute for Act 3 for music lost in the recording process (see note 64). Both acts were unabridged. Bodanzky yielded the baton to Erich Leinsdorf for the second act due to fatigue.

58 timings reported in the *Corriere d'informazione*, 24-25 March 1951, p. 2

Knappertsbusch, Bayreuth, 1956	111'	68'	78'
Knappertsbusch, Bayreuth, 1957	111'	66'	77'
Knappertsbusch, Bayreuth, 1958	108'	69'	73'
Knappertsbusch, Bayreuth, 1959	106'	68'	74'
Knappertsbusch, Bayreuth, 1960	107'	67'	72'
Knappertsbusch, Bayreuth, 1961	110'	70'	74``
Knappertsbusch, Bayreuth, 1962	107'	69'	73'
Knappertsbusch, Bayreuth, 1963	109'	71'	75'
Knappertsbusch, Bayreuth, 1964[59]	107'	71'	72'

TABLE 20. *Parsifal* - Act 1 Prelude[60]

11' 50"	Knappertsbusch, Bayreuth, 1958
11' 56"	Knappertsbusch, Bayreuth, 1963
11' 57"	Knappertsbusch, Bayreuth, 1962
12' 07"	Krauss, Bayreuth, 1953
12' 08"	Knappertsbusch, Bayreuth, 1959
12' 03"	Knappertsbusch, Bayreuth, 1964
12' 15"	Knappertsbusch, Bayreuth, 1960
12' 31"	Knappertsbusch, Bayreuth, 1961
12' 32"	Knappertsbusch, Bayreuth, 1956
12' 47"	Knappertsbusch, Bayreuth, 1957
12' 59"	Mottl, Freiburg, 1907, piano roll
13'	*Wagner, Bayreuth, 25 December 1878*[61]
13' 03"	Klemperer, Philharmonia, 1960
13' 06"	Toscanini, NBC Symphony, 1940
13' 15"	Knappertsbusch, Bayreuth, 1952
13' 29"	Knappertsbusch, Bayreuth, 1954[62]
13' 53"	Knappertsbusch, Berlin, 1943
13' 57"	Knappertsbusch, Bayreuth, 31 July 1951
13' 59"	Busch, Buenos Aires, 1936
14' 03"	Furtwängler, Berlin, 1938
14' 13"	Knappertsbusch, Bayreuth, July-August 1951
14' 18"	Reiner, New York, 1938
14' 30"	*Wagner, Munich, 12 November 1880*[63]
15' 06"	Toscanini, London, 1935
15' 30"	Bodanzky, New York, 1938[64]
15' 53"	Muck, Berlin, 1927
16' 38"	Kleiber, New York, 1946

59 The timings are taken from the Orfeo CDs which differ from the Hunt CDs to a very minor extent, probably due to the condition of the differing tape sources.

60 Preludes with concert endings, as performed by Böhm (1978-79), Coates (1925), Furtwängler (1938), Toscanini (1938, 1944, 1949), and Walter (1925, 1927, 1949, 1952, 1954, 1959), are not included.

61 Voss, *Die Dirigenten der Bayreuther Festspiele*, p. 100.

62 The timing (13' 29") is from the complete performance on Melodram and Archipel. As an indication of the variability of transciption speeds, the same performance is 13' 15" on Seven Seas and 13' 35" on Tahra.

63 Voss (*ibid*) and Ludwig Strecker, *Richard Wagner als Verlagsgefährte* (Mainz: B. Schotts Söhne, 1951), p. 299; Wagner conducted the Prelude twice on this occasion (a private performance for King Ludwig); Strecker says the timing was the same for each.

64 Add to this approximately 20 seconds for music lost in two breaks: the person recording the performance changed discs about every seven minutes.

Selected Bibliography

This is a list of of works which most illuminate what conductors thought of or did in relation to Wagner's music – if one had to choose but one for each conductor. Wagner calls for more. A few especially perceptive books by others which comment on several conductors have been included. Further bibliographical references are in the footnotes to each chapter.

Betz, Rudolf, and Walter Panofsky. *Knappertsbusch*. Ingolstadt: Donau Kurier, (1958).

Bodanzky, Artur. "Fourteen Years at the Metropolitan Opera House." With Donald Marshall. *Saturday Evening Post*. 29 October 1929, pp.10-11, 89-90, 92; and 9 November 1929, pp. 22-23, 63, 65-66.

Böhm, Karl. *A Life Remembered: Memoirs*. Translated by John Kehoe. London: Marion Boyars, 1992.

Bülow, Hans von. *Über Richard Wagner's Faust-Ouverture*. Leipzig: C.F. Kahnt, 1860.

Busch, Fritz. *Pages from a Musician's Life*. Translated by Marjorie Strachey. London: Hogarth Press, 1953.

Fifield, Christopher. *True artist and true friend: A Biography of Hans Richter*. Oxford: Clarendon Press, 1993.

Flesch, Carl. *The Memoirs of Carl Flesch*. Translated and edited by Hans Keller. London: Rockliff, 1957.

Furtwängler, Wilhelm. *Notebooks 1924-1954*. Edited by Michael Tanner. Translated by Shaun Whiteside. London: Quartet Books, 1989.

Gross, Felix. "Albert Coates." *Spotlight* (Cape Town). 17 October 1947, pp. 41 and 54-55.

Haas, Frithjof. *Der Magier am Dirigentenpult: Felix Mottl*. Karlsruhe: Info-Verlag, 2006.

———. *Zwischen Brahms und Wagner: Der Dirigent Hermann Levi*. Zurich: Atlantis Musikbuch, 1995.

Hart, Philip. *Fritz Reiner: A Biography*. Evanston: Northwestern University Press, 1994.

Heinel, Norbert. *Richard Wagner als Dirigent*. Vienna: Praesens, 2006.

Heyworth, Peter. *Otto Klemperer: His Life and Times*. 2 vols. Cambridge: Cambridge University Press, 1983-1996.

Hotter, Hans. *Memoirs*. Edited and translated by Donald Arthur. Boston: Northeastern University Press, 2006.

Kalisch, Alfred. "Arthur Nikisch." *Musical Times* 63, no. 649 (1 March 1922), pp. 172-74

La Grange, Henry-Louis de. *Gustav Mahler*. 4 vols. London: Gollancz; and Oxford University Press, 1974-2008.

Maschat, Erik. "Clemens Krauss." Translated by Peter Hutchison. *Recorded Sound*, nos. 42-43 (April-July 1971), pp. 740-46

Muck, Peter. 2003. *Karl Muck: Ein Dirigentenleben in Briefen und Dokumenten*. Tutzing: Hans Schneider, 2003.

Newman, Ernest. *The Life of Richard Wagner*. 4 vols. London: Cassell, 1933-1947.

Russell, John. *Erich Kleiber: A Memoir*. London: André Deutsch, 1957.

Sachs, Harvey. *Toscanini*. Philadelphia: Lippincott, 1978.

Schuh, Willi, ed. *Richard Strauss: Recollections and Reflections*. Translated by L. J. Lawrence. London: Boosey & Hawkes, 1953.

Seidl, Anton, "On Conducting," in *The Music of the Modern World*. vol. 1. Edited by Anton Seidl. New York: Appleton, 1895. Reprinted in Henry T. Finck, ed., *Anton Seidl: A Memorial By His Friends*. New York: Scribner's, 1899; Da Capo Press, 1983.

Shaw, Bernard. *Shaw's Music: The Complete Musical Criticism in Three Volumes*. Edited by Dan H. Laurence. New York: Dodd, Mead, 1981.

Voss, Egon. *Die Dirigenten der Bayreuther Festspiele*. Regensburg: Gustav Bosse, 1976.

Wagner, Richard. *On Conducting*. 1869. Translated by Edward Dannreuther. London: William Reeves, 1887, and New York: Dover, 1989.

Walter, Bruno. *Of Music and Music-making*. Translated by Paul Hamburger. London: Faber and Faber. 1961.

Weingartner, Felix. *On Conducting*. 1901. Translated by Ernest Newman. London: Breitkopf & Härtel, 1906. Reprinted in *Weingartner on Music & Conducting; Three Essays*. New York: Dover, 1969.

Sources of illustrations

Austrian National Library, Vienna: fig. 10.5, 10.8, 19.1, 19.2

Austrian Theatre Museum, Vienna: fig. 11.4, 11.6, 18.3

Bayreuth Festival: fig. 18.6, 18.7, 19.3

Bibliothèque nationale de France: fig. 18.4

Boston Symphony Orchestra Archives: fig. 7.2, 7.5, 8.4

Bildagentur für Kunst, Kultur und Geschichte (bpk), Berlin: fig. 5.5, 11.3, 12.5, 22.4

Chicago Symphony Orchestra, Rosenthal Archives: fig. 23.7

Collection Mediathèque Musicale Mahler, Paris: fig. 10.3

Corbis Images: fig. 5.2

Darmstadt Theatre Collection, Technical University, Darmstadt: fig. 11.7, 17.1, 17.6, 20.1

Deutsche Fotothek/Sächsische Landes- Staats- und Universitätsbibliothek Dresden (SLUB): fig. 3.9, 16.1, 16.2, 16.5, 19.5

EMI Records: fig. 9.2, 9.3, 15.4, 15.6

Free Library of Philadelphia, The Print and Picture Collection: fig. 13.4, 23.4

Harvard Theatre Collection, Houghton Library, Harvard University: fig. 1.13, 8.1, 8.2

Hungarian National Library: fig. 8.6

J. C. Senckenberg University Library, Frankfurt am Main: fig. 21.2

Karlsruhe Regional Archive: fig. 6.1

Library of Congress: fig. 22.3, 22.5, 22.6

Los Angeles Public Library: fig. 14.5, 23.5

The Metropolitan Opera Archives: fig. 14.3, 14.6, 23.6

Munich City Archive: fig. 2.7, 5.1, 6.3, 6.6, 10.4, 18.1, 21.1

Music Division, The New York Public Library for the Performing Arts, Astor, Lenox and Tilden Foundations: fig. 3.7, 4.1, 4.2, 10.1, 10.2, 12.1, 12.3, 12.6, 13.1, 13.3, 13.6, 14.4, 16.3, 20.5, 21.5

Reiss-Engelhorn-Museen Mannheim, Theater- und Musikgeschichtliche Sammlungen: fig. 1.3 (photo by Jean Christen of original drawing), 15.1, 11.1

Richard Wagner Museum/National Archives of the Richard Wagner Foundation, Bayreuth: fig. 1.5, 1.6, 1.11 (bottom right), 2.2, 3.3, 3.8, 5.3, 5.4, 6.2, 7.3, 13.2, 18.2

Richard Wagner Museum, Lucerne, Switzerland: fig. 1.7, 17.8

Sächsische Staatsoper Dresden Archives: fig. 20.2, 23.2, 23.3

Städtische Galerie Dresden – Kunstsammlung, Museen der Stadt Dresden: drawings photographed by Franz Zadnicek: fig. 1.8-10

Theatre Collection, University of Cologne: fig. 3.4, 6.7, 8.3, 11.2, 12.2, 17.2, 17.3, 19.4, 20.3, 20.6, 21.4, 22.7

Ullstein Bild: fig. 17.4

Reprinted from –

Herbert Barth, Dietrich Mack, and Egon Voss, *Wagner: a documentary study* (1975), by permission of Thames & Hudson, London: fig. 1.4

Oscar Bie, *Im Konzert* (1920): fig. 12.7

Otto Böhler, *Dr. Otto Böhler's Schattenbilder* (1914): fig. 1.17, 2.9

Robert Bory, *Richard Wagner: sein Leben und sein Werk in Bildern* (1938): fig. 2.1

Heinrich Chevalley, *Arthur Nikisch: Leben und Wirken* (1922): fig. 8.8

Erich W. Engel, *Richard Wagners Leben und Werke im Bilde* (1913): fig. 1.16

Henry T. Finck, *Anton Seidl: A Memorial By His Friends* (1899): fig. 4.3, 4.4, 4.5

John Grand-Carteret, *Richard Wagner en caricatures* (1891): fig. 3.2

Herman Klein, *Musicians and mummers* (1925): fig. 3.1

Heinrich Kralik, *Die Wiener Philharmoniker* (1938): fig. 6.5

Ernst Kreowski and Eduard Fuchs, *Richard Wagner in der Karikatur* (1907): fig. 1.2

Ib Melchior, *Lauritz Melchior: The Golden Years of Bayreuth* (2003), by permission of Baskerville Publishers, Inc.: fig. 16.6

Alfred Roller, *Die Bildnisse von Gustav Mahler* (1922): fig. 10.6

Hans Schliessmann, *Schliessmann-Album* (1920): fig. 2.8

———. *Wiener Schattenbilder* (1892): fig. 3.11, 6.9

Theo Zasche, *Lachendes Wien* (1923): fig. 8.7, 11.8, 21.6

Author's collection: fig. 2.3, 2.4, 2.5, 3.10, 6.4, 6.8, 7.1, 8.8, 9.1, 9.5, 9.6, 9.7, 12.8, 13.5, 14.1, 14.8, 17.7, 18.8, 18.9, 19.6, 19.7, 20.7, 20.8, 22.1, 23.8

Stills from historical films –

Don Giovanni (1954): DG/Unitel 073 019-9 (DVD, 2001): fig. 15.5

Great Conductors: Dreamlife DLVC 8092 (DVD, Japan, ca. 2008): fig. 12.4, 16.4

Great Conductors: The Golden Era of Germany and Austria: Dreamlife DLVC 8094 (DVD, Japan, ca. 2008): fig. 17.5, 18.5, 20.4

The Art of Conducting: Great Conductors of the Past: Teldec 4509-95038-3 (VHS, 1994): fig. 11.5, 23.7

Two Girls and a Sailor (1944): Warner Archive Collection (DVD, 2009): fig. 9.4

Author's collection: fig. 8.5, 21.3

List of operas and major excerpts covered in the Discographies

Der fliegende Holländer

1936 Busch, 1937 Reiner (excerpts), 1944 Krauss, 1950 Reiner, 1955 Knappertsbusch, 1963 and 1965 Böhm, 1968 Klemperer (studio and live), 1971 Böhm

Tannhäuser

1925-26 Coates (excerpts), 1935 (excerpts) and 1936 Bodanzky, 1950 and 1956 Böhm

Lohengrin

1934 (excerpts) and 1935 Bodanzky, 1936 Furtwängler (excerpts), 1936 Busch, 1945 (excerpts) and 1947 Busch, 1948 Klemperer, 1953 Kleiber (excerpts), 1965 and 1967 Böhm (excerpts)

Tristan und Isolde

1927 Coates (excerpts), 1933-34 (excerpts) and 1935 Bodanzky, 1936 Reiner, 1937 Bodanzky, 1937 Reiner (Act 2), 1938 Kleiber, 1941-43 Furtwängler (excerpts), 1943 and 1946 Busch, 1947 Furtwängler (Acts 2 and 3), 1948 Kleiber, 1950 Knappertsbusch, 1950 Reiner, 1952 Furtwängler, 1952 Kleiber, 1960, 1962, 1966, 1968, 1969, 1970, and 1973 Böhm

Die Meistersinger von Nürnberg

1922-23 and 1930 Coates (excerpts), 1936 Toscanini (excerpts), 1937 Bodanzky, 1937 Toscanini, 1938 Böhm (Act 3), 1943 Furtwängler, 1944 Böhm, 1949 Klemperer (excerpts), 1950-51 and 1952 Knappertsbusch, 1952, 1953 and 1955 Reiner, 1955 and 1960 Knappertsbusch, 1959, 1964 and 1968 Böhm

The Ring

1922-23 and 1927-29 Coates (excerpts), 1950 Furtwängler, 1953 Krauss, 1953 Furtwängler, 1956, 1957 and 1958 Knappertsbusch, 1966-67 Böhm

Das Rheingold

1937 Bodanzky, 1947 Kleiber

Die Walküre

1935 Walter (excerpts), 1934 and 1935 Bodanzky (excerpts), 1936 Reiner (Act 2), 1936 Busch, 1937 Furtwängler (Act 3), 1937 Bodanzky (excerpts), 1940 Kleiber, 1952 Furtwängler (Act 1), 1954 Furtwängler, 1957 Knappertsbusch (Act 1), 1960 Böhm, 1963 Knappertsbusch (Act 1), 1965 Böhm, 1969 Klemperer (Act 1)

Siegfried

1937 Bodanzky, 1938 Kleiber (excerpts)

Götterdämmerung

1936 Bodanzky, 1937 Furtwängler (Act 3 excerpts), 1947 Kleiber, 1951 Knappertsbusch, 1952 Furtwängler (Act 3), 1955 Knappertsbusch

Parsifal

1925 Coates (excerpts), 1927-28 Muck (excerpts) and Coates (excerpts), 1936 Weingartner (excerpts), 1936 Busch, 1937 Reiner (excerpts), 1937 Knappertsbusch (excerpts), 1938 Bodanzky, 1942 (excerpts), 1951 and 1952 Knappertsbusch, 1953 Krauss, 1954, 1956, 1957, 1958, 1959, 1960, 1961, 1962, 1963, and 1964 Knappertsbusch

Index

The titles of Wagner's works appear alphabetically. Comments on how they were performed are to be found under the respective headings in each chapter; there are only occasional references in the index. References to a conductor within his own chapter are not indexed. Wagner is an exception. The names of cities and music critics are not generally included. Singers mentioned in the text are included, but not from cast lists in the footnotes or discographies.